CRITICAL STRATEGIES FOR

Academic Thinking and Writing

A Text with Readings

THIRD EDITION

CRITICAL STRATEGIES FOR

Academic Thinking and Writing

A Text with Readings

Mike Rose
UNIVERSITY OF CALIFORNIA, LOS ANGELES

Malcolm Kiniry
RUTGERS UNIVERSITY—NEWARK

BEDFORD BOOKS BOSTON

For Bedford Books
President and Publisher: Charles H. Christensen
General Manager and Associate Publisher: Joan E. Feinberg
Managing Editor: Elizabeth M. Schaaf
Developmental Editor: Beth Castrodale
Editorial Assistant: Maura E. Shea
Production Editor: Sherri Frank
Production Assistant: Deborah Baker
Copyeditor: Mary Day McCoy
Text Design: Claire Seng-Niemoeller
Cover Design: Hannus Design Associates
Composition: Stratford Publishing Services, Inc.
Printing and Binding: Haddon Craftsmen, Inc.

Library of Congress Catalog Card Number: 97–74962

Manufactured in the United States of America.

2 1 0 9 8 7
f e d c b a

For information, write: Bedford Books, 75 Arlington Street, Boston, MA 02116
(617–426–7440)

ISBN: 0–312–11561–X

Acknowledgments

George D. Abell. "The Big Bang Theory." Excerpt from *Exploration of the Universe,* Third Edition, by George D. Abell. Copyright © 1975 by Saunders College Publishing, reprinted by permission of the publisher.

Acknowledgments and copyrights are continued at the back of the book on pages 716–723, which constitute an extension of the copyright page.

PREFACE FOR INSTRUCTORS

The Rationale for the Book

The labels vary — critical thinking, academic discourse, higher-order cognition — but the fundamental issue seems to be the same. A high percentage of college students — from those entering community college to those enrolled in upper-division university courses — have trouble when they must generate concise definitions or summarize a scholarly discussion, when they need to detail a laboratory procedure, explain a method, or evaluate a taxonomy, when they're asked to compare two theories, analyze a text, or argue a position. Though some educators label such activities "the new basics," these are, in fact, very sophisticated cognitive-rhetorical activities — that is, activities that involve the complex interplay of thinking and writing. We forget, sometimes, how hard it is to learn how to do them. They require immersion in certain kinds of language use — ongoing practice and successive approximation in settings where teachers have the training, time, and reasonable class load to comment and advise. We see the freshman composition course as a central place to focus on these thinking-writing activities, which we're calling here critical strategies. Such a course provides an opportunity for students not only to improve their ability to summarize, explain, and analyze but to step outside of such procedures and consider their nature and purpose. *Critical Strategies for Academic Thinking and Writing* is our attempt to provide an approach and a set of materials that can contribute to such a process.

To affirm the need for a curriculum focused on critical strategies is not to deny that students define and classify and analyze continually in their day-to-day lives.

These are basic human activities. But many students have not had extended opportunity to engage in the kinds of defining and classifying and analyzing that occur in academic contexts, have not done so with academic materials in ways that are complex and exploratory rather than formulaic, have not had multiple opportunities to reflect on the intellectual activities in which they're engaged, have not been encouraged to complicate thinking and writing. This lack of experience will significantly limit them, of course, because the kinds of strategies they must command are not straightforward, mechanical routines but heuristic, generative, and flexible — they resist easy procedure.

Unfortunately, the most familiar embodiments of such critical strategies are the formulaic approaches and static models students find in traditional English textbooks. The dynamic act of comparing, for example, is reduced to two or three compare/contrast essay patterns or is represented in a fixed way through models to imitate, where the messy, interactive *work* of comparing is long since past and students have before them the closed and polished comparison essay. While we rely on familiar chapter headings — that is, comparing, analyzing[1] — our book does not function traditionally. What we try to do is create conditions that encourage students to employ critical strategies flexibly and in combination, inviting them to engage problematic materials and seize interpretive opportunities, experimenting with and reevaluating the thinking and writing they do. Our goal is the development of a performative competence, a sense of how to take on certain kinds of intellectual work rather than merely to search for the correct form, the right answer.

The Context of the Book

Our curriculum began a number of years ago in a preparatory course for adults entering college, and it was influenced during development by insights and procedures gained from two movements: English for specific (or academic) purposes — work emerging primarily from the fields of applied linguistics and ESL instruction — and writing across the curriculum. One exceptionally useful byproduct of the English for academic purposes research was the attempt to determine the kinds of writing tasks actually required of college students. An early survey conducted by one of us was influenced by this research, and it revealed — as have other such surveys — that students are commonly called on to define, sum-

[1]To avoid a confusion of static modes with dynamic processes, we tried to come up with a different labeling system for the strategies. We thought about following Mina Shaughnessy's lead and labeling by functional descriptions: For example, "This Is What Happened" instead of "Serializing" or "This Is Like (or Unlike) This" instead of "Comparing." But the functional descriptions got cumbersome as we got into increasingly complex activities ("Analyzing" became "This Is How Phenomena Change in Meaning as One Shifts Perspectives"). We thought, as well, about creating a new set of terms that would stress the heuristic nature of the strategies. But this resulted in a foreign terminology that created more problems than it solved. We decided, then, to stay with more familiar terms but to make them participles to indicate action, to modify and explain their varied nature in the introductions and assignments, and to use them in ways that illustrate their critical purpose and their strategic flexibility.

marize, compare, and analyze. And as the courses we taught and the programs we managed took us increasingly across disciplinary boundaries, we had opportunity to examine the contexts of written language use in the academy, and what we found meshed with the writing-across-the-curriculum discussions emerging at our conferences and in our journals.

The tremendous value of these movements has been to increase teachers' awareness of the specialized reading and writing demands of various disciplines and, more theoretically, to move them to examine communities of discourse within the academy. One potential liability of these movements has been their tendency to represent writing instruction in a fairly service-oriented, product-directed way, that is, to assist students in learning the forms and conventions of sociology, biology, literature, and so on. Such instruction is valuable and sorely needed, and at places in this book we try to provide it. But our sense is that, at least in some settings, it is not adequately critical and self-examining. It teaches, say, how to summarize material for a literature review but doesn't create the conditions for students to consider the act of summarizing. So while we see our book as oriented toward cross-curricular needs, we try not to imprison writers within those needs. We want to develop a curriculum that equips students to write well in college but is not narrowly functional in its orientation — a book that encourages critical reflection, that is intellectually unpredictable and vital.

Part of that vitality, we hope, also comes from trying to bridge some of the divides that have characterized discussions of academic writing. Whenever possible, we rely on informal classroom talk, exploratory writing, and expressive discourse as pathways to formal, transactional exposition. We try, as well, to present multiple opportunities to test academic claims and theories against personal experience.

New and Strengthened Features

It is very hard, perhaps impossible, to teach complex intellectual processes through static print alone. What we have tried to do through various editions of *Critical Strategies for Academic Thinking and Writing* is to create a kind of sourcebook of discussions, examples, readings, and assignments that can help establish the conditions to foster academic thinking and writing.

Though reviewers' comments about the second edition were rich and varied, they expressed, in different ways, a desire for a book with a more coherent, accessible structure and more guidance for students. Our revision, then, attempts to make *Critical Strategies for Academic Thinking and Writing* more user-friendly and engaging without sacrificing its intellectual edge. The following new and strengthened features all work to those ends.

A clearer organization, with a cross-curricular theme linked to each chapter. We eliminated the two-part structure of the second edition — with the strategies covered in part one and with readings for applying the strategies in part two — and, instead, with each of the six strategies we integrated readings on a cross-curricular theme.

Essentially, each chapter of the book now has a two-part movement. The first part of each chapter (Defining Across the Curriculum, Summarizing Across the Curriculum, and so on) provides a series of activities and readings that help students become familiar with the strategy at hand. An "Opening Problem" engages students in the strategy right from the start, encouraging them to use it to work through the problem presented and to think critically about the strategy's possibilities and limitations. After the Opening Problem comes a more general set of introductory comments, offering an overview of the nature and purpose of the strategy as used in academic reading and writing. This overview is followed by Working Examples (formerly "Cases"), showing how students might use the strategy to address some typical assignments. Next is a Professional Application, a new feature that shows how a professional writer used the strategy for a particular purpose. Then comes a set of assignments (formerly "Options") based on representative academic readings from a variety of academic fields.

The second part of each chapter includes readings from across the curriculum on an engaging theme: "Reconsidering Intelligence" for Defining (Chapter 1); "The Dimensions of Child Poverty" for Summarizing (Chapter 2); "Crime Stories: Constructing Guilt and Innocence" for Serializing (Chapter 3); "U.S. Immigration Patterns" for Classifying (Chapter 4); "Methods of Inquiry in Primate Research" for Comparing (Chapter 5); and "Caribbean Literature and Cultural Politics" for Analyzing (Chapter 6). In addition to unifying the readings at the end of each chapter, these themes are picked up at three other points in the chapter: in the Opening Problem, in the Professional Application, and in at least one writing assignment. By including the new thematically linked readings and replacing other selections, we've added 52 new readings to the book (half of the total).

We chose the themes we did for a number of reasons. First of all, we wanted to select themes that would lend themselves to the particular strategy at hand. It is hard to discuss *intelligence,* for example, without considering how one *defines* intelligence; thus, we paired these two issues in Chapter 1. In considering the ways we tell stories about crime, or the ways a lawyer constructs a case, or the ways we record a criminal or legal event in print, it's essential to pay attention to the way we *sequence events.* And so Chapter 3 invites students to focus on the order of events in the telling of crime stories.

We also wanted to find themes that were broad enough for students to engage in a number of ways. The theme of intelligence, for example, can be addressed as a concept in psychology and education, or it can be considered in its social and cultural contexts, or it can be written about from a more personal perspective: Every reader of this book has encountered various measures of intelligence through school, and talk about intelligence surrounds us. The theme of Caribbean literature and cultural politics, in Chapter 6, opens itself to literary analysis, to questions about the history, economics, and culture of a region, to discussions of colonialism, "post-colonialism," and tourism, and to considerations of family organization and gender roles.

We also wanted to select themes that would represent a range of disciplines: psychology, literature, sociology, biology, political science, history, and so on. As well, we wanted the themes to reflect topics of current interest: the changing conceptualization of intelligence; child poverty in the United States, immigration; crime and the law; primate research and what it reveals about language, cognition, and social organization; and the relation between literature and the history, culture, and politics of the place and people that produce that literature. And finally, we wanted to select themes that had a solid academic core to them, but that had wide social implications which students would find interesting and relevant. We hope we've been successful.

A streamlined approach. In addition to getting rid of the two-part structure from the second edition, we further simplified the third edition by trimming and focusing those assignments from previous editions that our reviewers found to be most useful. (And the old "First Passes" and "Options" are now simply called "Assignments.") Clearer headings and a new design reflect the book's simplified approach.

Substantially revised and expanded apparatus. In an effort to keep assignments fresh — and make them both more interesting and representative of a wide range of disciplines — we replaced all of the Opening Problems that start each chapter and revised or replaced 40 percent of the writing assignments. In addition, we've tried to provide more guidance with assignments wherever possible.

Before each of the end-of-chapter readings, we provide a headnote that highlights important details and points out, where appropriate, notable features of the writing. Following each reading are "Considerations" questions which get students to examine the reading on its own terms, but also in relation to the strategy under discussion, and to at least one other reading in the chapter. We've also added new sets of "Further Assignments" at the end of each chapter, intended to get students to examine and apply strategies across readings and to do some research on their own.[2]

Substantially revised field research assignments, now in an appendix. These projects, which get students to apply the strategies in their own field research, increase in complexity, beginning by asking students to use personal observation to

[2]To underscore the importance of documenting sources in academic work, we've made another, smaller improvement: We've preserved any bibliographic footnotes and endnotes that originally appeared with the professional examples and with the end-of-chapter readings. (For the sake of consistency, these notes have been edited to conform to MLA style.) We did not include bibliographic notes with readings in the Opening Problems and in other assignments, where we thought such documentation would be cumbersome.

examine greeting behavior on campus and ending with "Exploring the Discourse of Your Major," which requires them to choose an area of study of interest to them and investigate how it functions. This final project also includes a range of optional readings about academic language, issues, and controversies, and encourages students to consider how new technology such as the Internet and e-mail affect academic discourse.

A thoroughly revised instructor's manual. *Resources for Teaching Critical Strategies for Academic Thinking and Writing,* written by Barbara Gross along with the authors of *Critical Strategies,* contains a revised introduction for new teachers, a feature that first- and second-year graduate students, especially, have found useful in working with the book's nontraditional material and approaches. The manual also includes advice for working with individual readings, facilitating class discussion, and reflecting on the strategies.

Though we've tried to make the third edition more coherent in its structure and movement, we should also stress that *Critical Strategies for Academic Thinking and Writing* is not intended to lock you into a linear progression of activities and readings. In the introductions, assignments, and, particularly in the instructor's manual, interrelations are drawn, and teachers are encouraged to make this book their own, drawing connections and creating assignments that fit the needs of their particular classes and institutions.

The Writing Students Will Do

The varied writing opportunities in each chapter will help students build expertise as they encounter similar intellectual problems in shifting academic contexts. Let us illustrate by looking at a sequence of *defining* assignments from Chapter 1. The Opening Problem introduces the strategy of defining by asking students to consider psychologist Howard Gardner's critical examination of what we typically regard as "intelligent" behavior. Moving on to the Assignments, students can consider the way that a familiar word — for example, *mechanism* — takes on a different meaning in a passage by biologist Stephen Jay Gould. Then they are asked to consider — by writing about the etymology of the word *intelligence,* for one thing — how words shift in meaning over time. Later in the Assignments section, students might write about how the word *eugenics* gets defined by its historical context. Or they might write about the politics of defining as illustrated in the piece by Alston Chase about the U.S. national park system: Who gets to define the meanings of such terms as *protection, restoration,* and *management*?

The amounts and kinds of writing students are asked to do build both in length and complexity as a chapter proceeds. The writing in a chapter like "Defining" can vary from the few sentences required to write about the word *mechanism* in the passage by Gould to the essay needed to write about the issues of defining raised by Chase. The materials and their sequences in the first part of each chapter in *Critical Strategies,* then, are intended to contribute to a dynamic classroom in which students are continually reading, discussing, drafting, encountering new data, revising, and presenting what they have written.

The readings in the second part of each chapter give students more opportunities to investigate and apply the strategies, and to complicate and enrich the work they've done earlier in the chapter. The readings at the end of Chapter 1 — for instance, Douglas Harper's observations about the "working" intelligence of a mechanic — open more possibilities for students as they consider how intelligence is, and can be, defined. The Considerations questions after each reading and the Further Assignments concluding each chapter further encourage students to take a critical approach as they write about such issues.

Acknowledgments

The materials at the heart of this project have had a long and varied life, and we would like to thank the many people who have been involved with them — the students who used these materials while in development, particularly those in the Veterans Special Educational Program and the Freshman Preparatory Program, and our colleagues at UCLA and at Rutgers who taught with us and helped us critique and develop assignments. Barbara Gross, in addition to her remarkable work in producing the third edition's instructor's manual, has been a steady source of thoughtful advice throughout this project.

While preparing the third edition of *Critical Strategies for Academic Thinking and Writing,* we benefited from the insights and suggestions of perceptive reviewers: Richard Batteiger, Richard Bullock, Johnson Cheu, John Connor, Ellen Cushman, Melvin Donalson, Cheryl Glenn, Claudia Ingram, Rita Malenczyk, Peter Marx, Keith Miller, Carmel Myers, Lisa J. McClure, Martin McKoski, Shirley Rose, Rosa Valdes, and John Warnock. We appreciate, too, the comments we received from instructors who responded to a questionnaire for the second edition: Janet Bacon, Kevin Bezner, Gail S. Corso, Barbara Estermann, Hartmut Heep, Douglas Hesse, Marybeth Holleman, J. Roger Kurz, Patricia Linton, Grace McLaughlin, Gregory T. McManus, John Mitchell, Kate Mohler, Walt Nott, Charlotte Pressler, John D. Schaeffer, Daniel Steven Shiffman, Robert A. Stein, Jacqueline S. Thursby, and Sandra Urban.

We were also fortunate to have the research assistance of Quentin Miller, an enthusiastic user of the book who helped us find just the right materials for many chapters and even contributed an assignment of his own. Some sections of the book would not have taken shape without Quentin, and we are grateful for his resourcefulness and constant willingness to help out.

At Bedford Books, several people deserve thanks for the time they gave us — and for their remarkable competence, patience, and careful attention to detail. We thank Chuck Christensen, who has helped us to envision, and to re-envision, this project. Joan Feinberg encouraged us throughout the book's history — keenly, warmly, tactfully, persistently.

Through the first, second, and third editions, we have been fortunate to have exceptionally skilled people in charge of production. For the third edition, we'd like to thank Elizabeth Schaaf, Sherri Frank, Deborah Baker, and our designer, Claire Seng-Niemoeller. Sherri deserves special thanks for making the production process run so smoothly, for her many helpful suggestions, and for staying on top of a multitude of details. We'd also like to express our appreciation to Mary Day McCoy for her thoughtful copyediting and to Carolyn Woznick for clearing permissions with remarkable expertise and professionalism.

Joanne Diaz provided valuable research assistance early in the revision process, finding many important readings, and Maura Shea diligently researched biographical footnotes, helped with permissions, and attended to a variety of editorial details with competence and enthusiasm. Joanne and Maura deserve special thanks.

As our development editor for the first edition, Ellen Darion shaped the book day by day, helped us work out text and assignments, and continued to make helpful suggestions even after the book was published. Jane Betz, editor of the second edition, showed a keen sense of what teachers and students need, a remarkable editorial touch, and a resourceful mix of tenacity and good humor. Jane's close involvement has continued through the third edition. This edition's editor, Beth Castrodale, has, as well, provided unfailing good sense and immense energy. She, like her two predecessors, is a gifted writer and editor. Beth took pen in hand at many points in the development of this book, drafting material and revising our textual blunders. From the outset of her involvement, she has understood both the premises and the nuances of the project, and she has encouraged us in broadening and clarifying our material. This edition would not have been completed without her.

BRIEF CONTENTS

CONTENTS

CRITICAL STRATEGIES FOR

Academic Thinking and Writing

A Text with Readings

INTRODUCTION FOR STUDENTS

Critical Strategies for Academic Situations

The Movement of this Book

Our aim in *Critical Strategies* is to help you, as a writer, to think and write responsively and flexibly in academic situations. By writing responsively, we mean in thoughtfully close relation to what you've been asked to read or hear or observe. By writing flexibly, we mean with confident awareness of the many choices open to you. By academic situations, we mean the many opportunities you'll have in college to reconstruct what you've learned and to articulate what you think about it.

Each of the six chapters in the book is built around a versatile set of strategies — defining, summarizing, serializing, classifying, comparing, and analyzing — that are central to academic thinking and writing. The first part of each chapter includes an Opening Problem that calls for a short piece of writing involving the strategy under discussion. This problem quickly immerses you in a representative academic situation and encourages you to reflect upon the choices you find yourself making as a writer. The Opening Problem is followed by some introductory discussion and Working Examples, showing how you might use the strategy to meet the requirements of some typical college assignments. Next is a Professional Application, an example of how a writer has used the strategy for a particular purpose. Then comes a set of optional assignments based on representative academic readings from a variety of academic fields.

Each chapter is also tied to a particular theme. The themes range from reconsidering assumptions about intelligence for Chapter 1 (Defining) to investigating the literature and cultural politics of the Caribbean for Chapter 6 (Analyzing), and each theme lends itself especially well to the application and investigation of its chapter's guiding strategy. Readings relating to the theme appear in the Opening Problem, in the Professional Application, and in at least one of the cross-disciplinary assignments. If the topic woven through the first part of the chapter interests you and you want to spend more time with it, you may also want to work with the second part of the chapter: a set of readings that deals entirely with the theme. Concluding each chapter are Further Assignments that include opportunities to examine and apply the strategy broadly across the chapter's readings and to do some research of your own.

Critical Strategies also includes an appendix of assignments that invite you to conduct field research into such issues as the kinds of literacy used in various settings or examples of the comic. In these assignments, the strategies drive your investigation and help you to write about the results. The final and most involved project, "Exploring the Discourse of Your Major," asks you to choose a major area of study on your campus and investigate how it functions. It also includes a set of optional readings about academic language, conventions, and controversies, readings that can enrich your fieldwork. Accompanying the readings and assignments in "Exploring the Discourse of Your Major" are questions that ask you to reconsider — and make fresh use of — what you have found.

Critical Strategies

The six strategies that provide the structure for this book — defining, summarizing, serializing, classifying, comparing, and analyzing — are mental operations you perform all the time. You may not feel comfortable with these terms, but you have had plenty of experience with the operations themselves. They are strategies we all use to make sense of our lives. Let us illustrate with an example.

Imagine getting a late-night phone call. You've been asleep; at first you're disoriented and don't recognize the voice. Then you realize it's a friend you've lost track of — you wonder uneasily what he wants. Gradually, as the conversation goes on, your anxiety eases — he's been talking to a mutual friend who passed along your number: He just thought he'd call for old times' sake. You've made a few calls like that yourself: You know what they are like. You've started to *define* the experience: It's a friendly catch-up phone call, nothing more. But later, after the long, rambling, and one-sided conversation has ended, you're not so sure. You're troubled, so you try to *summarize* what has happened: The caller began with reminiscences but turned eventually to an assortment of complaints about his job, his family, even the friend who gave him your number; he also said several times that he might want to come visit you "to see what college is like." Puzzled, you try to reconstruct the sequence of events he mentioned that led to your friend's phone call, *serializing* those events chronologically, looking for connections and trying to see what led to what: He took a job, his friends went away, his job lost appeal, he sought out someone he used to know well, your friend disappointed him, he called you.

Thinking about the call the next morning, you find yourself remembering other one-sided conversations you have had, or, better yet, one-sided conversations in which you've felt something was being left unsaid. You are *classifying* the latest experience by placing it first in a general, then a more specific category. Then you remember one conversation in particular: a long talk you had with a cousin who had moved to another state. It had that same kind of friendly opening and troubled undertone to it — but there are important differences too. You try to *compare* the two calls in detail, remembering what you felt at the time, what the outcome was. You decide you think you know what has happened: Your friend's anxiety about deciding not to go to college has made him reach out, but also lash out, toward others around him. You go back over the phone call, remembering details that fit that interpretation. You are *analyzing* the experience. If you were to then call your mutual friend, trying to persuade that person to share your interpretation of what has gone wrong, you also would be arguing, and you would make use of whichever previous insights seemed helpful as evidence to persuade that friend to share your view.

You may have noticed or felt, as we flashed them by just now, that these strategies seem to prompt one another; some even seem to merge, making it hard to say, for example, where classifying leaves off and comparing begins. That's often how the strategies work in academic situations too. Summarizing a problem will help you to better define it; classifying items enables you to compare them; as you serialize an event, you start to analyze that event. A single strategy may be at the heart of your approach to an assignment, but seldom will you rely upon that strategy alone to carry you from your first thoughts to a completed piece of writing. Although some college writing situations call for a single strategy (for example, a lab report that requires you to describe a step-by-step procedure or an exam question that asks you to summarize a reading), in most writing situations, including those offered in this book, you will have the opportunity to bring these strategies into helpful interplay.

Nevertheless there are great benefits in working with and thinking about these strategies one at a time. If they are to become real resources for you as a writer, you will need to put them to work in various contexts, testing their power and their usefulness. For although the general strategies themselves are familiar, they are not always easy to call upon in academic situations, particularly in the face of demanding college readings. And they can be especially difficult to use in active, critical ways. By *critical* we mean the willingness to probe, to judge, to weigh evidence, to look for explanations, to trade a weak explanation for a stronger one — even to turn a strategy back on itself, looking at its limitations.

In the example of the phone call, it is not so hard to think critically: You are the expert on events in your own life; there is no one else to do the interpreting for you, at least no one better qualified. In college, though, you are surrounded not only by unfamiliar material but by authorities who seem to be telling you what to think about it. You will feel an urge merely to absorb, rather than reshape, what you are given. Yet it's in the reshaping that you find your stance as a thinker and a writer.

As you move through this book, you will need to think critically not only about the readings but about the strategies themselves. When, in Chapter 2, you are asked to summarize an interview with a labor organizer, you are also asked to think about how your summary reshapes his story. When you are asked, in Chapter 4, to use an anthropologist's observations about "little communities" to classify various communities, you'll want to reflect upon what is both powerful and potentially misleading in such a scheme. In Chapter 6, as you analyze the experiences of the scientific researcher Anna Brito from the perspective suggested by the historian of science Evelyn Fox Keller, you will need to evaluate whether Keller's perspective does explain Brito's experience or whether that possible explanation obscures some better way of understanding. In this way, as you try them out in shifting contexts, the strategies become both the vehicles and the objects of your critical thinking.

The Writing You Will Do

Let us say a little more about the kinds of writing you will be doing as you work with *Critical Strategies*. The materials you will write about may seem unusual, but what you are asked to do with them may sometimes seem unusual as well. Much of the writing you do will be rough, and some of it won't be graded. You might be asked to take five or ten minutes in class and write a short summary or reaction to a reading. Or you might be given a half hour to begin developing a comparison between two texts — then be asked to stop and, together with a small group of classmates, read aloud what you've written or talk about your progress. You might be asked to draft at home an essay that becomes raw material for revising during the next class. Sometimes you may be asked to start something that you're not asked to finish. Such assignments are rehearsals, first efforts meant to prepare you for longer, more formal assignments. Their value is in the competence, and the confidence, they help you to develop.

You may also be asked to write reflective, exploratory pieces about the very thinking processes in which you're engaged. You will be asked to take stock of what you are doing. As an example, take a moment to look at the Art Assignment in Chapter 4, Classifying. This assignment provides you with fifteen paintings and sketches of the human form and asks you to create a category system to classify them. Creating such a system will enable you to make some powerful intellectual moves: Instead of detailing fifteen separate images, you will be able to generalize more efficiently, noticing trends or tendencies in how artists represented human forms, at least during the 1920s. The assignment asks you to write an essay that explains and illustrates your system; but you are also asked to write, as a postscript, a paragraph or two in which you reflect both on what your system enables you to do and what it hinders you from doing. Any of the strategies in this book — defining, comparing, and the others — can be both a window and a cage, enabling you to perceive some things but preventing you from moving in other directions.

If your teacher asks you to collaborate with classmates on some assignments, that experience may also be an unfamiliar one for you. In fact, some students report that in earlier school years they were discouraged from sharing work as writers. Yet a good deal of the writing that gets done in science and industry, in journalism and the arts, and in business and the professions is collaborative (the introduction you are reading now is one example). Many college writing situations, you will find, are also social situations.

Of course you will also be asked to write a more familiar kind of paper: an essay that you draft, revise, and proofread on your own and submit to your teacher for a formal evaluation. But you are apt to find even this familiar process getting more complex. Let us illustrate by describing the composing methods of one of our students, Marie Lewis. See if it rings true for you. Over the years Marie developed a successful method of writing her compositions for English classes. She would find a quiet place at home and think for a few minutes about her topic, making a brief outline or taking a few notes. Her early papers required her to express an opinion or to recount an event in her life. Later, she was asked to write responses to pieces of literature — a short story or novel, a poem or a play. She got good at doing these assignments, for she usually had opinions or feelings about the motives of characters or about a theme she thought an author was trying to convey. So after gathering her thoughts, and perhaps after a false start or two, she would simply write out her essay in a single effort. She could do most of her assignments, she said, in forty-five minutes or an hour. Once she finished drafting her essay, she would recopy it, making it neater, checking for spelling, and getting it ready to turn in. Does this match your own experience of writing for school? Before going on, take a few minutes to see if you can describe your typical method.

If your composing process has been similar to Marie's, a number of assignments in *Critical Strategies* may push you to rethink the way you write. You will have to take some papers through a number of revisions — beginning, for example, with a rough, unfinished draft in class that you revise at home as a second draft before receiving feedback from your teacher or classmates and then revising again in response to their comments. You will find that some papers do not lend themselves to a neat composing process of plan–write–edit. For instance, in writing about the benefits and limitations of a strategy you've been employing, you may find that you haven't yet articulated what you think — sometimes you will discover something you really can say only after failing to say it at all the first time. You will find, too, that many assignments ask you to work with readings that make little contact with your own experience: What you write may feel uncertain, disconnected, or awkward. Sometimes you may feel less in control of your writing than you used to feel.

As unsettling as all this may be, it is also a sign that you are growing as a writer, that you are moving into less familiar territory. As you challenge some of your basic assumptions, you may come to see your writing involve more work but yield richer intellectual payoffs. Even if you are someone who needs the pressure of a deadline and sits down to write papers the night before they are due, you will find that the process of writing will spread out over time. Some of your work will take place in class as you engage in critical discussion of material you are writing about; some will take place in your car or on the bus, or when you get up in the morning. In a sense you will be writing as you speak, in response to their comments, with your teacher or classmates. What might once have been a predictable and neatly confined process will occur in phases, will require more reading, will raise doubts and frustrations, will prompt you to seek the reactions of others. Your internal sense of how writing gets done may gradually change, and the change will help you engage more effectively in critical writing.

The Reading You Will Do

The critical strategies you will be using are as much strategies of reading as of writing. They have as much to do with the perceptions formed through critical interaction with texts as with the forming of sentences, paragraphs, and essays. So let us say a little more about the sorts of reading we will be asking of you.

As you start each chapter, we ask you to become a reader who quickly adjusts to new surroundings. You will step in and out of very different academic situations as you read an astrophysicist's speculation about the end of the universe, a poet's reflection on adolescence, two scholars' analyses of the way legal arguments are crafted. Your best attitude is to maintain your curiosity about the world you have momentarily entered. Who are these people? What is important to them, and how can we tell? How do they speak to us? How do we start to make sense of what they say for ourselves?

You will also want to be a reader who is willing to work through texts that, at first, seem remote or boring. We hope that you'll find most of the readings you encounter interesting in one way or another. But you may find some very tough going — and apparently not worth the effort. You may sometimes find yourself in the presence of jargon — specialized language that seems more designed for readers already in the writer's field than for students who are trying to understand basic concepts. Even in readings where the language seems accessible, you may find the subject abstract, very general, and distant from your own experience. You may sometimes find yourself, understandably, only going through the motions as a reader and writer. You may even want to say so: "This piece is boring; I don't care about it." But be careful of this reaction — or at least be willing to examine its source. Sometimes boredom is a response to feeling out of one's league, or uncomfortable, or even intimidated. One advantage in developing a repertoire of critical strategies is that you will be more able to define, or summarize, or analyze what it is about the reading that bothers you and engage that reading critically. As you work critically with the reading, that effort itself creates interest — if not in the reading itself, at least in the work of articulating your own response to it.

Another good way to respond as a reader is to seek a personal connection to the material. Sometimes such connections are hard to find, but they are seldom impossible. You might not feel much personal connection, for example, to a textbook discussion of rites of passage in various societies. But the anthropologist who wrote the textbook probably expected readers to consider rites of passage that they're familiar with as a way of understanding his observations. If you've experienced, say, a bar mitzvah or a club initiation, you may use memories of these experiences to reflect upon — and evaluate — the textbook discussion, and to take a point of view on it. Do you agree or disagree with the anthropologist? Do your own examples seem to support, or contradict, what he is saying? Suddenly, you've invested an abstract, potentially lifeless topic with a personal and critical interest. This may not be the kind of personal writing you've done in other English classes, where you may have been encouraged to write essays that were entirely autobiographical. But you will find in college that there are always ways to draw on your own experience and knowledge in responding to what others have said and written.

Academic Voices and Your Own

This discussion of personal responses to academic reading and writing brings us to the tricky issue of voice. You already may have spent some time getting comfortable with your voice as a writer — the words you choose, the order you give them, the overtones you ask them to carry. You may have developed a personal style which, though quite different from your speaking voice, has come to feel fairly natural and unstrained.

By contrast, the voices that you encounter as an academic reader may sound alien and artificial, as though you've been set down in a part of the country where a different idiom is spoken. In general, you recognize the language, but the words, phrasings, sentence patterns, and tones of voice aren't yours. When asked to write in response to such language, you are likely to feel contradictory pressures. You may think that you ought to be imitating these voices, assuming, "This is what college writing is like." Yet you might also feel that such writing is beyond you. Simultaneously you may feel resistant to the idea of taking on new language: "This writing sounds phony; I'll stick to my own words."

Good college writing often negotiates among such pressures. Maintaining a voice of your own is important, and borrowing someone else's entire way of speaking is bound to sound forced and inauthentic. Besides, it is almost impossible to control a terminology that you are trying to use for the first time — the words often have unsuspected overtones that interfere with what you mean to say. Yet it would also be a mistake to ignore altogether the language of the writers and speakers you have been asked to write about. You can seldom deal fairly with what people have said apart from how they have said it. In academic writing, it is often as though you are joining an ongoing conversation. What you say, if it's to be well heard, needs to take into account the language of others.

One way to let others have their voices while maintaining your own is through the thoughtful use of quotations. Selective quotations can help you strike to the heart of a discussion. Quotations enable you to let people speak for themselves while keeping a space for your own voice to comment, evaluate, and make new points. When dealing with more than one reading, your own voice may recede to the background, almost as if you were serving as a moderator for a panel of energetic speakers. But in good academic writing your own voice comes to the forefront at appropriate times to take control of the proceedings. (The Working Examples near the start of each chapter may give you ideas about how to draw on academic discussions while maintaining your own voice.)

As you enter into these academic conversations, you may notice your writing voice beginning to change. If you make choices of wording unthinkingly, your voice can change for the worse — falling, for example, into unexamined jargon, using pretentiously inflated words where simple ones would do. But it can also change for the better, growing more supple and finding more range. You'll want to evaluate the new language to which you're exposed, trying out the words and phrases that seem to earn their keep and discarding those that don't.

As your academic experience broadens, you'll also start to notice — perhaps you've started already — how much the voices vary as you move from one field of study to another. Some academic language remains the same across the university, but each discipline also has its specialized vocabulary and emphases — a different variety of language for representing its own angle on the world. As you become familiar with the ways that people within a particular academic discipline communicate, you will pick up much of that language for yourself. Of course, there's no way we can do more than offer glimpses of such differences in a textbook like this one — though the book's final assignment on exploring the discourse of your major does offer an opportunity to examine more closely the language of academic and disciplinary work. If you work with that assignment, see what you learn about the field you choose by listening closely to the voices of its speakers and writers. But whether or not you engage that project, you will want to pay close attention to the varieties of language you encounter as you move among the readings in this book.

1

DEFINING

Negotiating Meanings

DEFINING Across the Curriculum

The first part of this chapter includes a range of readings — most accompanied by assignments — that will get you to think critically about the ways in which defining is used across the curriculum: in psychology, political science, literature, biology, and other fields. In addition to covering various disciplines, we offer various types of writing: dictionary entries, personal reflection, descriptions of places and processes, and presentations of research, both for academic and more general audiences. We begin with an Opening Problem that immediately involves you with using — and thinking about — defining. We then present examples of writers drafting papers on academic topics that involve the strategy (Working Examples, p. 13), followed by a piece showing how a professional writer uses defining to serve a particular purpose (A Professional Application, p. 20). Next comes a series of cross-curricular assignments intended to deepen and enrich your investigation of the strategy's possibilities and limitations (p. 21).

Woven throughout the first part of this chapter (in the Opening Problem; in the Professional Application; and in the Psychology Assignment, p. 38) are readings about intelligence, a topic that lends itself especially well to the application and investigation of defining. If this topic interests you and you want to spend more time with it, consider working with Readings: Reconsidering Intelligence in the second part of this chapter.

Opening Problem: Defining Intelligence

Here is a reading that will involve you in the process of defining. In the passage, psychologist Howard Gardner describes a situation that will be familiar to a good many of you — the taking of an intelligence quotient (IQ) test — and then proceeds to raise some critical questions about it. What concerns does he raise about traditional IQ testing and the definition of intelligence that supports such testing and is reinforced by it? Write a brief essay (it can be rough and speculative) explaining these concerns and offer a best guess at the kind of definition of intelligence Gardner would find more satisfactory. If you like, you can add a section to your essay — a concluding paragraph or a postscript — in which you consider your own intelligence in light of Gardner's discussion.

A young girl spends an hour with an examiner. She is asked a number of questions that probe her store of information (Who discovered America? What does the stomach do?), her vocabulary (What does *nonsense* mean? What does *belfry* mean?), her arithmetic skills (At eight cents each, how much will three candy bars cost?), her ability to remember a series of numbers (5, 1, 7, 4, 2, 3, 8), her capacity to grasp the similarity between two elements (elbow and knee, mountain and lake). She may also be asked to carry out certain other tasks — for example, solving a maze or arranging a group of pictures in such a way that they relate a complete story. Some time afterward, the examiner scores the responses and comes up with a single number — the girl's intelligence quotient, or IQ. This number (which the little girl may actually be told) is likely to exert appreciable effect upon her future, influencing the way in which her teachers think of her and determining her eligibility for certain privileges. The importance attached to the number is not entirely inappropriate: After all, the score on an intelligence test does predict one's ability to handle school subjects, though it foretells little of success in later life.

The preceding scenario is repeated thousands of times every day, all over the world; and, typically, a good deal of significance is attached to the single score. Of course, different versions of the test are used for various ages and in diverse cultural settings. At times, the test is administered with paper and pencil rather than as an interchange with an examiner. But the broad outlines — an hour's worth of questions yielding one round number — are pretty much the way of intelligence testing the world around.

Many observers are not happy with this state of affairs. There must be more to intelligence than short answers to short questions — answers that predict academic success; and yet, in the absence of a better way of thinking about intelligence, and of better ways to assess an individual's capabilities, this scenario is destined to be repeated universally for the foreseeable future.

But what if one were to let one's imagination wander freely, to consider the wider range of performances that are in fact valued throughout the world? Consider, for example, the twelve-year-old male Puluwat in the Caroline Islands, who has been selected by his elders to learn how to become a master sailor. Under the tutelage of master navigators, he will learn to combine knowledge of sailing, stars, and geography so as to find his way around hundreds of islands. Consider the fifteen-year-old

Iranian youth who has committed to heart the entire Koran and mastered the Arabic language. Now he is being sent to a holy city, to work closely for the next several years with an ayatollah, who will prepare him to be a teacher and religious leader. Or, consider the fourteen-year-old adolescent in Paris, who has learned how to program a computer and is beginning to compose works of music with the aid of a synthesizer.

A moment's reflection reveals that each of these individuals is attaining a high level of competence in a challenging field and should, by any reasonable definition of the term, be viewed as exhibiting intelligent behavior. Yet it should be equally clear that current methods of assessing the intellect are not sufficiently well honed to allow assessment of an individual's potentials or achievements in navigating by the stars, mastering a foreign tongue, or composing with a computer. The problem lies less in the technology of testing than in the ways in which we customarily think about the intellect and in our ingrained views of intelligence. Only if we expand and reformulate our view of what counts as human intellect will we be able to devise more appropriate ways of assessing it and more effective ways of educating it.

— Howard Gardner, *Frames of Mind: The Theory of Multiple Intelligences*

Thinking about Thinking

- Gardner writes that "the score on an intelligence test does predict one's ability to handle school subjects, though it foretells little of success in later life." How could this be?
- Gardner further writes that "[t]he problem lies less in the technology of testing than in the ways in which we customarily think about the intellect and in our ingrained views of intelligence." Look at the description of testing he offers in his first paragraph. What are the elements of intelligence that the questions are trying to probe? Gardner suggests that they provide an inadequate "view of intelligence." Do you agree?
- Speculate about the kinds of things you'd have to do — tests you'd need to give, people or situations you'd have to study, what you'd need to know more about — to try to define intelligence more comprehensively than the way provided by the traditional IQ test.
- Consider this formula sometimes used in examinations: "What is the definition of ______?" Based on what you've read about "intelligence," what misimpression does this formula convey about the process of defining?

As Howard Gardner suggests, just about anyone who moves through the educational system in the United States will encounter intelligence tests. And, as he suggests, these tests, and the assumptions behind them, have a significant influence on the way we define intelligence in our society. But there are other definitions as well, other ways of thinking about intelligence, both among the populace and, increasingly, among scholars who study intelligence, or, more broadly, the way we think — cognition. In several of the assignments in this chapter and in the cluster of readings that come at the end, we ask you to think about intelligence and to consider a variety of perspectives on this topic, which emerges continually in school, in the workplace, on the street, in casual talk.

Clearly, if you've been thinking of definition as a passive or mechanical act — copying words you've looked up in a dictionary or giving memorized answers from textbooks — you'll need to revise your thinking. Defining is a continuous process, crucial to receptive reading and persuasive writing, and it is fundamental to the critical thinking encouraged in all college courses.

To define something is to look at it more clearly. We speak of something as well defined when we can perceive its boundaries against a background. Biology students, for example, quickly learn to define the nucleus of a cell by its central location, its distinct coloration, and the membrane that separates it from the rest of the cell's cytoplasm. In an American history course, you begin to define the office of secretary of state as you learn what the secretary's powers and responsibilities are and how those powers and responsibilities are limited by the structure of the government as a whole. If you go further, you will probably see that your general understanding of what the secretary of state does needs to be modified to account for how the job has changed over time. Further still, you might conclude that no two secretaries of state handled the office in exactly the same way: Henry Kissinger defined his role in the Nixon administration much differently than Warren Christopher did in the Clinton administration. Defining is seldom a matter of understanding an idea in isolation — it calls for seeing and understanding relationships.

As pieces of writing, too, definitions seldom occur in isolation. They are used in coordination with other strategies. Asked on a biology exam to describe the stages of photosynthesis, you might decide to begin with an overview definition before going on to describe the process sequentially. For a political science term paper, "The Influence of Interest Groups in U.S. Politics," you might decide to organize your essay as a classification of the various types of U.S. interest groups and introduce that classification with a definition establishing what all the types have in common. In an essay comparing the thought of two social philosophers, you might arrive at a pivotal point where a definition helps you to make a distinction crucial to your comparison: "For Marx, then, unlike Weber, the concept of 'surplus value' is central to understanding the operation of modern economies. Marx sees surplus value as. . . ." In an interpretive essay for a literature class, you might produce a summary of a novel's key events and follow with a definition that refocuses attention on an aspect of the novel that the rest of your paper will go on to analyze. Asked in an education class to write a position paper for or against bilingual programs in elementary schools, you might find yourself defining a number of terms along the way as they become necessary for your argumentative purpose.

Definitions are flexible. They can expand, contract, or shift in emphasis, all according to the uses to which they are put. They are also powerful. When we look at complex problems such as the nature of *intelligence* (above), definitions help to shape what we see and don't see. Or consider a term like *adolescence.* Take a moment and write out your definition of the word. Then compare your definition with someone else's. How might you expect your definition or a classmate's to be different from a parent's or a teacher's? How do you think a biologist's definition might differ from a psychologist's? How might the uses various people make of this term help account for their different emphases in defining it?

Working Examples

A Working Example Using the Word model

As readers, we do most of our defining on the run. As we encounter new words, or familiar words used in new ways, we struggle with them as best we can, forming hesitant, even semiconscious, conclusions about what they mean. If we're attentive, we notice that some of these words are more important than others and that some recur as we move from one subject to another. Paying attention to such terms can help develop a useful vocabulary for thinking and writing critically.

We can illustrate this process by trying to build a definition of an academic term you're likely to encounter frequently, the word *model.* Most of us start with some familiar sense of the word, and then at some point in our reading we realize that our definition needs revising. For instance, we think of a model as a person whose job is displaying clothes. Or we might think of a model as a small-scale replica, like a model airplane. We may feel puzzled, when we think about it, by the apparent disparity between these two uses of the word. But neither use prepares us to make sense of a passage like this one:

> Why does the market model still attract academic economists, Galbraith asks, in the radically different conditions of today? First, because the intellectual framework with which a profession is familiar exerts a powerful hold over the minds of its members, even when changing conditions make it less applicable. It provides them with familiar concepts and assumptions to bring to bear on contemporary issues. Second, in the age of technology and technique, the simplifying assumptions of the market model provide a base from which mathematical models can be constructed and refined; the form of the model is nicely adapted to the style of thought preferred by social scientists.
>
> — Michael H. Best and William E. Connolly,
> *The Politicized Economy*

Evidently, in the way economists use the term, a model isn't as tangible as a person or a replica. It's something that can be "applied," something involving an "intellectual framework," and something that, for some people at least, involves mathematics. Do you feel at sea? Try writing a definition that makes some connection between this new use of the term and the earlier ones.

If you feel bewildered by the model in the economics passage, you'll probably feel a little relieved by the following passage, which describes a science writer's visit to the lab of a famous chemist.

> On the tables were models. They were surprisingly large, and at first difficult to take in; they were responsible for the room's impression of clutter. We went over to one. It was built, like the others, within a cubical frame of steel straps that defined the edges, about four feet long. The floor of the cube was thick, unpainted plywood. From that, within the cube, a jungle sprang up of thin metal rods. Looping through these like creepers were several lengths of flexible, plastic-coated cable, red or white. The rods only provided support. The trick was to ignore them totally, though they obscured almost everything else, and concentrate on where the colored cables led.
>
> This model before us, Perutz said, was a single molecule of hemoglobin of horse in its oxygen-carrying state. The living hemoglobin molecule, human or horse, was made of 574 amino acids, in four chains, ten thousand atoms strong, and totaling 64,500 times the weight of a single hydrogen atom, or about 4,000 times the weight of a single atom of oxygen. That was all required to transport just four molecules of oxygen each made of two atoms. At those ratios, the breath of life requires about 280 million hemoglobin molecules in each red blood cell, and there are about 160 trillion red blood cells in a pint of blood.
>
> Perutz picked up a pointer to trace the twisting, swooping paths of the four chains in the model — two identical chains termed "alpha," another identical pair called "beta." These were constructed out of thousands of short, straight bits of brass wire socketed together at angles, each bit precisely in scale with the length of a chemical bond, and the sockets where the wires intersected showing the positions of principal atoms. The tracery was clamped at hundreds of places to the supporting rods. The red cords and white ones, Perutz said, were not the real structure but only aids to the eye, Ariadne threads tracing beta and alpha chains.
>
> — Horace Freeland Judson, *The Eighth Day of Creation: Makers of the Revolution in Biology*

Here we have a model that we think we recognize. It's not so different from the model airplane. Of course, we'd have to modify our notion that a model is a "small-scale replica," since Perutz's hemoglobin model is vastly larger than a hemoglobin molecule. We might be tempted to reduce our definition to a synonym — a model is a replica — but when we look back at the passage we may suddenly feel reluctant to say even that. For notice that Perutz's model is *not* a replica if by replica we mean an exact, proportionate image of how something looks. His model is dominated by metal rods that have no equivalent in the structure of the actual hemoglobin molecule and by red and white cables that represent alpha and beta chains not as they are but only as "aids to the eye." Perutz's model is not so much a replica of how the hemoglobin molecule "looks" as a sort of visualized description of how its parts must be related. When understood, it can help to tell something about how hemoglobin carries oxygen in the bloodstream.

What does this latest recognition do to our effort to join the hemoglobin and the airplane in a single definition? The new emphasis might lead us to this reformulation:

```
A model is a simplified image of how something looks or works.
```

We've said "looks or works" to cover ourselves. One word fits the airplane, the other the molecule. It may not be the best definition, but it's one we can live with, at least until we have to think about the word again. But what if we're reminded of the economics passage we left behind? Or what if a new piece of reading, like the following excerpt from a sociology text, reminds us of our earlier difficulty?

> The *concentric zone model* . . . presents the city as a set of circles, each one ringing the smaller one within it. At the center is the business district, where property values favor the income-earning uses of land. The only residents there are transients living in rundown hotels. The next zone, ringing the center, is the home of wholesale businesses and light industry. Third is a zone in transition. Formerly containing decent housing, it has been blighted by the encroachment of the business center. As its residential desirability declines and as housing is neglected by owners who anticipate selling their property to business or factory interests, this area becomes the home of the poor and minorities. Next is a zone of middle-class homes. These in turn are encircled by an outer ring of upper-class homes.
>
> — Peter I. Rose, Myron Glazer, and Penina Migdal Glazer, *Sociology: Inquiring into Society*

Here again we find the emphasis on a model as something imaginary, something theoretical, something that some experts favor and others criticize. When we think of the definition we've built around the airplane and the hemoglobin molecule, we find to our surprise that that definition is still useful. The emphasis on "how it works" — in this case how a city develops — leads us toward an even fuller and clearer definition. Instead of simply settling for a one-sentence statement, we can go on to explain and illustrate what we mean:

```
     A model is a simplified image of how something looks or
works or develops. Chemists construct models to describe the
structures of molecules, economists to describe how an economy
functions, and sociologists to describe the patterns in which
cities have developed. Models are not necessarily replicas of
what exists; they are educated guesses about how things are, how
they have come to be, or how they will behave.
```

What we have been doing with the word *model* is similar, in a way, to what dictionary makers do. You may have the impression that a dictionary is essentially a grammar book — that it authoritatively tells you the permissible meanings of words. Actually, dictionaries are compilations of what words have meant and are likely still to mean. But a dictionary's authority comes only from its accuracy in categorizing and describing how particular words have been used. Its descriptions are always incomplete because the meanings of words keep shifting as they are used in new situations or as some meanings of words come into new or sharper prominence. Look back at the definition we've constructed for the word *model.* Now look at the following entry in the *Random House College Dictionary:*

> **mod•el** (mod'^{ə}l), *n., adj., v.,* **-eled, -el•ing** or (*esp. Brit.*) **-elled, -el•ling.** —*n.* **1.** a standard or example for imitation or comparison. **2.** a representation, generally in miniature, to show the structure or serve as a copy of something. **3.** an image in clay, wax, or the like, to be reproduced in more durable material. **4.** a person or thing that serves as a subject for an artist, sculptor, writer, etc. **5.** a person, esp. an attractive young woman, whose profession is posing with, wearing, using, or demonstrating a product for purposes of display or advertising. **6.** a pattern or mode of structure or formation. **7.** a typical form or style. —*adj.* **8.** serving as a model: *a model apartment.* **9.** worthy of serving as a model; exemplary: *a model student.*

Do any of these definitions much resemble ours? Perhaps the sixth entry comes closest; "a pattern or mode of structure or formation" is so general that it probably includes our definition. But what emphasis is missing? Would any of the definitions you see here help you to decipher the word we met in the economics or sociology texts?

Our point is not that dictionaries can't be trusted. They are useful tools for helping us work out meanings; and they can be particularly helpful in showing how the meanings of a word may vary and how those meanings may change over time (some of the assignments in this chapter ask you to think about words historically). But the real burden of defining will fall on you — on your powers of inference as a reader and your powers of management as a writer.

Working Examples from Political Science

One useful defining strategy begins with an act of classification. When we say that *acculturation* refers to "social interaction" or that *Brown v. Board of Education* is "a Supreme Court decision," we've begun to define those terms by placing them in categories. Having established a meaningful general category, we offer particulars:

```
Acculturation is a social interaction in which a subordinate
group adjusts its behavior to conform to that of a dominant
group.

Brown v. Board of Education is the Supreme Court decision that
in 1954 made segregated public school systems illegal.
```

This two-part strategy of discovering a category and then filling in distinguishing details, sometimes called "formal definition," is useful not only in presenting definitions but in thinking them through. It offers a flexible way to alter our wording as our thinking changes. We can play with the general category, sharpening or broadening it; or we can experiment with the particulars, adding, deleting, or substituting features. Imagine, for example, that you keep running up against the term *refugee* in a course on contemporary political issues. You try writing out a definition:

`A refugee is a person who has come to the United States from another country.`

Once you've written out a rough definition like this one, you can start to rethink it, looking for ways to make it more accurate or more helpful. Here the general category "person" seems too general to be helpful, and the particular phrase "has come to the United States" seems imprecise and misleading (don't other countries have refugees?). You might improve the last part of the definition with more careful phrasing, but you might also realize that there is a single word — *immigrant* — that you can substitute for the category "person," thus making the last part of the definition unnecessary:

`A refugee is an immigrant. . . .`

Are all refugees immigrants? Yes, you think so. Are all immigrants refugees? If you don't think so, you can try to construct a definition that gets more specific:

`A refugee is an immigrant who . . .`

In looking back over your reading, you might notice that refugees seem to be people who are not merely leaving their countries but anxiously fleeing from them. As you think about that, you might notice that the word *refugee* contains the word *refuge,* a place of safety. You fill in the definition a little more:

`A refugee is an immigrant who flees from one country, seeking safety in another.`

This definition is more satisfying and might hold up well. But you might try quarreling with it a bit. See if you can find ways to tighten it. If you think there's something missing, try to pinpoint what it is. In this case, you might object that the definition fits smugglers and tax dodgers. Further, you might notice that *refugee* usually seems to connote fear. You modify your definition to read:

`Refugees are immigrants fleeing the political conditions in one country and seeking safety in another.`

This revised definition seems stronger and clearer still, and it would probably serve you well if you ever had to define the term in a general way. But in the context of a course about contemporary politics — and, in fact, in the context of any political discussion — a pointed and probing set of questions might push you a little further: "What's at stake in this definition?" "To whom does it matter?" "How would this definition be used?" If you return to your reading with such questions in mind, you may find yourself alert to important disagreements. In the case of *refugee,* the problem of definition can be crucial, for those people defined by the U.S. government as refugees are often allowed to stay in this country while other immigrants face much tighter restrictions. Are people fleeing from Cuba defined as refugees? From Bosnia? From Mexico? How might the official definition of what a refugee is differ in practice from the one we've worked out in theory? What social and political factors will affect the definition? Pursuing the implications of this effort at definition might lead you beyond your two-part definition to a more extended essay about the problem of defining what a refugee is.

We have been demonstrating another defining strategy — using examples. The general statement "A model is a simplified image" seems vague until you illustrate it with the hemoglobin molecule or with an example of an economic prediction. Well-chosen examples invariably clarify and solidify definitions that otherwise would be lifelessly abstract. However, one problem in using an example to tie down a definition is that a specific example is often so powerful that it colors the entire definition, becoming in effect more than just an example. If we were given only the hemoglobin molecule as an example, what misimpression about models might we come away with?

Sometimes a single example will do the job well; at other times you'll find it helpful to use several. In all cases, you'll want to make sure that your specific examples effectively illustrate your general statements.

Besides helping you to present definitions clearly and vividly, examples help you to think through definitions as you try to reformulate them. As we constructed our definition of *refugee,* it helped us at one stage to ask whether smugglers fit our definition, and at a later stage to wonder whether — and why — the United States would be more apt to define as refugees immigrants from Cuba than immigrants from El Salvador. By calling up specific examples in this way, you can keep probing and readjusting your general definitions.

A related defining strategy is the use of comparisons. With a comparison we can show one thing against another, sometimes highlighting resemblances and sometimes differences. Definitions sharpen as such comparisons become explicit. And discovering good comparisons can make definitions convincing.

Sometimes comparisons are of opposites. We can define and explain *autocracy* by opposing it to *democracy.* At other times comparisons are of complements — we need one term to define the meaning of another. In Marxist political theory, for example, it would be difficult to define *bourgeoisie* without defining *proletariat.* But the most frequent use of comparison is to distinguish between terms that otherwise might be confused or thought identical. An effective definition leaves us with a better sense of both terms. For most of us, for instance, the term *cruise missile* means little more than the term *ballistic missile* or the term *missile* alone. The term gains definition when we are told, "Unlike ballistic missiles, which are designed to climb at a high trajectory over great distances and plunge steeply toward their targets, cruise missiles are designed to fly much more horizontally, close to the earth and over a smaller range."

Let us illustrate how comparison can be used in developing a more extended definition. Suppose that you are asked on a political science examination to discuss the *coup d'état* as a political action. Comparisons can help you to think through the definition as well as to shape it. You might begin with the observation that a *coup* is "the takeover of a national government." A quick comparison of other "takeovers" convinces you that you haven't produced an effective definition yet — this one could apply equally to a revolution, an occupation by a foreign nation, a civil war, and even perhaps to the change of administration after a presidential election. Once you've narrowed the definition more effectively — "A *coup* is a violent takeover of a nation's government by a portion of that nation's military" — you can put comparisons to further use in clarifying and developing the essay itself.

> A coup d'état is an armed takeover of a nation's government by a portion of that nation's military. Unlike a more broad-based revolt or insurrection, a coup is usually the result of a rapid action by a few highly placed soldiers. Unlike a civil war, which involves all segments of a society over some length of time, a coup d'état, if successful, is completed almost instantaneously. Like some political assassinations, a coup usually aims to topple only the head of state, leaving the rest of the country's administrative structure intact. While a genuine revolution depends on the widespread dissatisfaction and participation of the populace, a coup depends only on public indifference.

To clarify and extend some of your comparative points, you would probably want to interweave some illustrative examples, which themselves might be compared. Which better fits the definition of a *coup,* for example, the removal of Ferdinand Marcos as president of the Philippines in 1986 or the ousting of Romanian dictator Nicolae Ceauşescu in 1989?

Sometimes comparisons define by pointing to underlying similarities, and sometimes they define by moving beyond apparent similarities to make finer distinctions. A comparison that proceeds at some length often becomes an analogy. Analogies are extended comparisons that lay out a whole set of correspondences between the things being compared. As a defining strategy, developing an analogy can help you to think freshly and to write persuasively. But because analogies are almost always comparisons of two complex systems that are dissimilar in some fundamental way, you also need to regard analogies skeptically. Even when they have proved useful, most analogies can be criticized.

As an exercise in building and unbuilding analogies, think back to what you know about *coups d'état.* Try developing, then criticizing, these two analogies: (1) a *coup d'état* is like surgery; (2) a *coup d'état* is like a corporate takeover. Which works better? What are the limitations of each analogy?

Whatever defining strategy you use, it's important to consider the limitations of a commonsense understanding of a word. Reconsider the concept of *intelligence:* In what ways are our immediate definitions of this word problematic? How — in light of other perspectives, like Howard Gardner's — might we be forced to revise our early definitions? How does our use of a word in a particular context lead us to reshape our understanding of its meaning?

A Professional Application

In the following excerpt from his best-selling book, *Emotional Intelligence,* psychologist Daniel Goleman uses a story and a brief summary of some research on IQ to develop a definition of what he calls "emotional intelligence." Earlier in this chapter, we wrote that constructing a definition often goes beyond the offering up of a dictionary listing — and that the process of defining can involve critical thinking and persuasion. This passage is a good example. Notice how Goleman tells the opening story in a way that makes us question traditional definitions of intelligence ("How could someone of such obvious intelligence do something so irrational?") and sets the stage for him to question the usefulness of a common measure of intelligence — the IQ test — in predicting success. As he goes about the business of defining, he is also trying to persuade us. In the last paragraph he poses an explicit definition. Do you find it convincing? Why or why not?

When Smart Is Dumb

From *Emotional Intelligence*

DANIEL GOLEMAN

Exactly why David Pologruto, a high-school physics teacher, was stabbed with a kitchen knife by one of his star students is still debatable. But the facts as widely reported are these:

Jason H., a sophomore and straight-A student at a Coral Springs, Florida, high school, was fixated on getting into medical school. Not just any medical school — he dreamt of Harvard. But Pologruto, his physics teacher, had given Jason an 80 on a quiz. Believing the grade — a mere B — put his dream in jeopardy, Jason took a butcher knife to school and, in a confrontation with Pologruto in the physics lab, stabbed his teacher in the collarbone before being subdued in a struggle.

A judge found Jason innocent, temporarily insane during the incident — a panel of four psychologists and psychiatrists swore he was psychotic during the fight. Jason claimed he had been planning to commit suicide because of the test score, and had gone to Pologruto to tell him he was killing himself because of the bad grade. Pologruto told a different story: "I think he tried to completely do me in with the knife" because he was infuriated over the bad grade.

A psychologist and behavioral and brain science writer for the *New York Times,* DANIEL GOLEMAN (b. 1946) has authored and co-authored many books, including *Vital Lies, Simple Truths* (1985), *The Meditative Mind* (1988), and *Emotional Intelligence* (1995), from which this excerpt is taken.

After transferring to a private school, Jason graduated two years later at the top of his class. A perfect grade in regular classes would have given him a straight-A, 4.0 average, but Jason had taken enough advanced courses to raise his grade-point average to 4.614 — way beyond A+. Even as Jason graduated with highest honors, his old physics teacher, David Pologruto, complained that Jason had never apologized or even taken responsibility for the attack.

The question is, how could someone of such obvious intelligence do something so irrational — so downright dumb? The answer: Academic intelligence has little to do with emotional life. The brightest among us can founder on the shoals of unbridled passions and unruly impulses; people with high IQs can be stunningly poor pilots of their private lives.

One of psychology's open secrets is the relative inability of grades, IQ, or SAT scores, despite their popular mystique, to predict unerringly who will succeed in life. To be sure, there is a relationship between IQ and life circumstances for large groups as a whole: Many people with very low IQs end up in menial jobs, and those with high IQs tend to become well-paid — but by no means always.

There are widespread exceptions to the rule that IQ predicts success — many (or more) exceptions than cases that fit the rule. At best, IQ contributes about 20 percent to the factors that determine life success, which leaves 80 percent to other forces. As one observer notes, "The vast majority of one's ultimate niche in society is determined by non-IQ factors, ranging from social class to luck."

Even Richard Herrnstein and Charles Murray, whose book *The Bell Curve* imputes a primary importance to IQ, acknowledge this; as they point out, "Perhaps a freshman with an SAT math score of 500 had better not have his heart set on being a mathematician, but if instead he wants to run his own business, become a U.S. Senator, or make a million dollars, he should not put aside his dreams. . . . The link between test scores and those achievements is dwarfed by the totality of other characteristics that he brings to life."

My concern is with a key set of these "other characteristics," *emotional intelligence:* abilities such as being able to motivate oneself and persist in the face of frustrations; to control impulse and delay gratification; to regulate one's moods and keep distress from swamping the ability to think; to empathize and to hope. Unlike IQ, with its nearly one-hundred-year history of research with hundreds of thousands of people, emotional intelligence is a new concept. No one can yet say exactly how much of the variability from person to person in life's course it accounts for. But what data exist suggest it can be as powerful, and at times more powerful, than IQ.

Assignments

A Language Assignment

In academic reading, we often encounter words we don't know and simply need to learn. But other words often trick us with their familiarity. A word we commonly use or easily recognize may be used by a writer in a special sense. If we don't register and begin to think about the difference in meaning, we're apt to read imprecisely, never getting a good grip on what we're reading.

Each of the following passages makes specialized use of a word you probably know already. Before reading each passage, write out your general sense of what the word means. Then after you have read the passage, write a few sentences explaining why that usual meaning doesn't seem to apply in this context.

Here are some suggestions and some questions to consider:

- As you move from paragraph to paragraph, take some brief notes on the difficulties you encounter. When you've considered all three paragraphs, you might reflect on which word was most difficult to redefine, and why.
- After wrestling with the paragraphs a bit, you might want to consult a dictionary. If you decide to do this, comment on whether or not you find it helpful. Is the dictionary you looked at equally helpful — or unhelpful — for all three terms?
- What did these particular uses of the three words lead you to think about the ways the definitions of words might change or expand?

1. What does the word *environment* usually mean? What does it seem to mean in the following passage?

> To facilitate our analysis of writing, we have divided the writer's world into three major parts: the task environment, the writer's long-term memory, and the writing process.
>
> The task environment includes everything outside the writer's skin that influences the performance of the task. It includes the writing assignment, that is, a description of the topic and the intended audience, and it may include information relevant to the writer's motivation. For example, the teacher's stern expression when he presents an assignment may tell the writer that the assignment must be taken very seriously. Once writing has begun, the task environment also includes the text which the writer has produced so far. This text is a very important part of the task environment because the writer refers to it repeatedly during the process of composition.
>
> — John R. Hayes and Linda S. Flower, *Identifying the Organization of Writing Processes*

2. What does the word *mechanism* usually mean? What does it seem to mean in the following passage?

> Darwin begins his orchid book with an important evolutionary premise: Continued self-fertilization is a poor strategy for long-term survival, since offspring carry only the genes of their single parent, and populations do not maintain enough variation for evolutionary flexibility in the face of environmental change. Thus, plants bearing flowers with both male and female parts usually evolve mechanisms to ensure cross-pollination. Orchids have formed an alliance with insects. They have evolved an astonishing variety of "contrivances" to attract insects, guarantee that sticky pollen adheres to their visitor, and ensure that the attached pollen comes in contact with female parts of the next orchid visited by the insect.
>
> — Stephen Jay Gould, *The Panda's Thumb*

3. What does the word *grammar* usually mean? What does it seem to mean in the following passage?

> The basic grammar of schooling, like the shape of classrooms, has remained remarkably stable over the decades. Little has changed in the ways that schools divide time and space, classify students and allocate them to classrooms, splinter knowledge into "subjects," and award grades and "credits" as evidence of learning. In 1902 John Dewey warned against dismissing the way schools are organized "as something comparatively external and indifferent to educational purposes and ideals." In fact, he declared, "the manner in which the machinery of instruction bears upon the child . . . really controls the whole system." . . . Continuity in the grammar of instruction has puzzled and frustrated generations of reformers who have sought to change these standardized organizational forms.
>
> — David Tyack and Larry Cuban, *Tinkering Toward Utopia: A Century of Public School Reform*

A Word History Assignment

The meanings of words don't remain stable but change over time as people adapt them for new situations and purposes. The *Oxford English Dictionary (O.E.D.)* can be a helpful research tool because it contains rich information about the histories of English words. It also provides examples of past usages. By consulting the *O.E.D.*, we can learn about the paths by which words have arrived at their current meanings and about the overtones or connotations they sometimes still carry. By way of example consider the *O.E.D.* entry for the word *career.*

Career (kăɪɪ̄ᵊ·ɹɹ), *sb.* Forms: 6–7 **carriere, careere,** (6 **carire, -eire, carrire**), 6–8 **carier(e, carrier, -eer,** 7 **carrere, carere, (carrear, -eere, -eir, careir),** 6– **career.** [a. F. *carrière* race-course; also career, in various senses;= It., Pr. *carriera,* Sp. *carrera* road, career: — late L. *carrāria* (*via*) carriage-road, road, f. *carr-us* wagon.

The normal Central Fr. repr. of late L. *carraria is* OF. charriere, still usual in the dialects; it is not clear whether *carrière* is northern, or influenced by It. or Pr.]

† *1.* The ground on which a race is run, a race-course; also, the space within the barrier at a tournament. **b.** *transf.* The course over which any person or thing passes; road, path way. *Obs.*

1580 SIDNEY *Arcadia* (1622) 286 It was fit for him to go to the other end of the Career. **1642** HOWELL *For. Trav.* (Arb.) 46 In the carrere to Her mines. a *1649* DRUMM. OF HAWTH. *Poems* Wks. (1711) 6 Rowse Memmon's mother . . . That she thy [Phœbus'] career may with roses spread. **1651** HOWELL *Venice* 39 Since the Portuguais found out the carreer to the East Indies by the Cape of Good Hope. **1751** CHAMBERS *Cycl., Career,* or *Carier,* in the manage, a place inclosed with a barrier, wherein they run the ring.

† **2.** Of a horse: A short gallop at full speed (often in phr. *to pass a career*). Also a charge, encounter (at a tournament or in battle). *Obs.*

1571 HAMMER *Chron. Irel.* (1633) 139 Seven tall men . . . made sundry Carreers and brave Turnaments. **1591** HARINGTON *Orl. Fur.* xxxviii. 35 (N.) To stop, to start, to pass carier. **1598** BARRET *Theor. Warres* v. ii. 142 The Lanciers . . . ought to know how to manage well a horse, run a good carrier, etc. **1617** MARKHAM *Caval.* II. 203 To passe a Cariere, is but to runne with strength and courage such a conuenient course as is meete for his ability. **1667** MILTON *P. L.* I. 766 Mortal combat or career with Lance. **1751** CHAMBERS *Cycl., Career* . . . is also used for the race, or course of the horse itself, provided it do not exceed two hundred paces. **1764** HARMER *Observ.* XXVII, vi, 284 Horses . . walking in state and running in full career.

3. By extension: A running, course (usually implying swift motion); formerly [like Fr. *carrière*] applied *spec.* to the course of the sun or a star through the heavens. Also *abstr.* Full speed, impetus: chiefly in phrases like *in full career,* † *to take, give* (*oneself or some thing*) *career,* etc., which were originally terms of horsemanship (see 2).

c **1534** tr. *Pol. Verg. Eng. Hist.* (1846) I. 55 Theie . . tooke privilie there carier abowte, and violentlie assailed the tents of there adversaries. **1591** SPENSER *Ruins Time* xvi, As ye see fell Boreas . . To stop his wearie cáriere suddenly. **1606** T. H. *Canissin's Holy Crt.* 31 Dolphins . . leape and bound with full carrere in the tumultuous waues. **1667** MILTON *P. L.* IV. 353 The Sun . . was hasting now with prone carreer To th' Ocean Iles. *a* **1677** BARROW *Serm.* Wks. 1716 III. 35 Sooner may we . . stop the Sun in his carriere.

b. *Hawking.* (See quot.)

1727–51 CHAMBERS *Cycl., Career,* in falconry, is a flight or tour of the bird, about one hundred and twenty yards.

4. *fig.* (from 2 and 3) Rapid and continuous 'course of action, uninterrupted procedure' (J.; formerly also, The height, 'full swing' of a person's activity.

(continued)

1599 SHAKS. *Much Ado* II. iii. 250 Shall quips and sentences.. awe a man from the careere of his humour? **1611** —*Wint. T.* II. 286 Stopping the Cariere Of Laughter, with a sigh. *1603* FLORIO *Montaigne* I. ix. (1632) 15 He takes a hundred times more cariere and libertie unto himselfe, than hee did for others. **1643** W. BURTON *Beloved City* 57 Antichrist, in the full course and carrére of his happynes. **1663** CROWLEY *Verses Ess.* (1669) 35 Swift as light Thoughts their empty Carriere run. **1675** TRAHERNE *Chr. Ethics* XXV. 389 Quickly stopt in his careir of vertue. **1722** WOLLASTON *Relig. Nat.* ix. 174 Not to permit the reins to our passions, or give them their full carreer. **1767** FORDYCE *Serm. Yug. Women* II. viii. 29 A.. beauty.. in the career of her conquests. **1848** MACAULAY *Hist. Eng.* II. 599 In the full career of success.

5. A person's course or progress through life (or a distinct portion of life), *esp.* when publicly conspicuous, or abounding in remarkable incidents; similarly with reference to a nation, a political party, etc. **b.** In mod. language (after Fr. *carrière)* freq. used for: A course of professional life or employment, which affords opportunity for progress or advancement in the world.

1803 WELLINGTON in Gurw. *Disp.* II. 424 A more difficult negotiation than you have ever had in your diplomatic career. **1815** *Scribbleomania* 200 That great statesman's public career. **1860** MOTLEY *Netherl.* 1868 I. i. 7 A history.. which records the career of France, Prussia, etc. **1868** GEO. ELIOT *F. Holt* 20 Harold must go and make a career for himself. **1884** *Contemp. Rev.* XLVI. 99 An artist, even in the humblest rank, had a career before him.

At first an *O.E.D.* entry may look impenetrable, full of mysterious abbreviations, foreign word forms, and references to obscure people and books. But once you've skimmed an entry and begun to use the dictionary's table of abbreviations (see below), you'll be able to draw some conclusions. We learn that *career* came from the French *carrière,* meaning racecourse, and that the word's early uses in English, now obsolete, concern horses in motion. The term was almost immediately used in a figurative sense too, to mean a strong, "uninterrupted" course, like the movement of the sun through the sky or even, for Shakespeare, a "cariere of laughter" (a laughing fit?). Today's sense of the word — "a person's course or progress through life" — didn't become prominent until the nineteenth century and then referred mainly to "publicly conspicuous" lives, as in diplomatic careers. The latest *O.E.D.* entry for the word defines career as "afford[ing] opportunity for progress or advancement in the world." We can gather that the word's meaning has broadened to something like "field of employment" though *career* is not yet synonymous with *job.* Today's word doesn't retain the *O.E.D.*'s sense of a life "abounding in remarkable incidents," does it? We might even wonder if some of the older sense of the word is sneaking back into it, carrying something of the frenzied circularity of a horse race.

See what conclusions you can draw from the following *O.E.D.* entry for the word *technology.* Use the table of abbreviations (p. 26) as needed.

technology (tɛk'nɒlədʒi). [ad. Gr. τεχνολογία systematic treatment (of grammar, etc.), f. τέχνη art, craft: see -LOGY. So F. *technologie* (1812 in Hatz.-Darm.).]

1. a. A discourse or treatise on an art or arts; the scientific study of the practical or industrial arts.

1615 BUCK *Third Univ. Eng.* xlviii, An apt close of this general Technologie. **1628** VENNER *Baths of Bathe* 9 Heere I cannot but lay open Baths Technologie. **1706** PHILLIPS (ed. Kersey), *Technology,* a Description of Arts, especially the Mechanical. **1802–12** BENTHAM *Ration. Judic. Evid.* (1827) I. 19 Questions in technology in all its branches. **1881** P. GEDDES in *Nature* 29 Sept. 524/2 Of economic physics, geology, botany, and zoology, of technology and the fine arts. **1882** *Mechanical World* 4 Mar. 130/1 The Department of Applied Science and Technology.

b. *transf.* Practical arts collectively.

1859 R. F. BURTON *Centr. Afr.* in *Jrnl. Geog. Soc.* XXIX. 437 Little valued in European technology it [the chakazi, or 'jackass' copal] is exported to Bombay, where it is converted into an inferior varnish. **1864** — *Dahome* II. 202 His technology consists of weaving, cutting canoes, making rude weapons, and in some places practising a rude metallurgy. **1949** in W. A. Visser t'Hooft *First Assembly World Council of Churches* 75 There is no inescapable necessity for society to succumb to undirected developments of technology. **1958** J. K. GALBRAITH *Affluent Society* ix. 99 Improvements in technology.. are the result of investment in highly organized scientific and engineering knowledge and skills. **1971** *Daily Tel.* (Colour Suppl.) 10 Dec. 18/2 In the production of millions of children a year, it is not surprising that occasionally nature's complex technology should break down to produce an imbalance of hormones with masculinisation of the female foetus or feminisation of the male. **1975** *Ecologist* V. 120/1 Guiding technological development effectively is not a matter of being for or against technology, which is the form the discussion usually assumes.

c. With *a* and *pl.* A particular practical or industrial art.

1957 *Technology* Apr. 56/1 It [*sc.* Chemical Engineering] is now recognized as one of the four primary technologies, alongside civil, mechanical, and electrical engineering. **1960** *Electronic Engin.* Mar. 148/1 Electronic data-processing for business is a young technology. **1979** *Computers in Shell* (Shell Internat. Petroleum Co.) 2 Highly complex problems involving the many technologies needed within the energy and associated industries.

d. high technology applied *attrib.* to a firm, industry, etc., that produces or utilizes highly advanced and specialized technology, or to the products of such a firm. Also (unhyphened) as *sb. phr.* Similarly **low-technology.** Cf. *high tech* s.v. TECH[3] 1.

1964 S. M. MILLER in I. L. Horowitz *New Sociology* 292 The youthful poor possess limited or outmoded skills and inadequate credentials in a high-technology, certificate-demanding economy. **1970** *Physics Bull.* Apr. 146/1 'High technology' industries demand huge capital and R and D investments. **1973** *Newsweek* 18 June 92/2 As their old, low-technology industries wilt under the pressure of mounting labor costs.

2. The terminology of a particular art or subject; technical nomenclature.

1658 SIR T. BROWNE *Gard. Cyrus* v. 70 The mother of Life and Fountain of souls in Cabalisticall Technology is called Binah. **1793** W. TAYLOR in *Monthly Rev.* XI. 563 The port-customs, the technology, and the maritime laws, all wear marks of this original character. **1802–12** BENTHAM *Ration. Judic. Evid.* (1827) IV. 252 An engine, called, in the technology of that day, *fork.* **1862** *Morn. Star* 21 May, Aluminium, and its alloy with copper—which the manufacturers, with a slight laxity of technology, denominate bronze.

4. Special Combs.: **technology assessment,** the assessment of the effects on society of new technology; **technology transfer,** the transfer of new technology or advanced technological information from the developed to the less developed countries of the world.

1966 *Inquiries, Legislation, Policy Stud. Subcomm. Sci., Res., & Devel.* (U.S. Congress: House: Comm. Sci. & Astronaut.) 27 We must be cognizant of what technology is doing to us—the bad as well as the good. Toward this end we would consider the exploration of legislation to establish a Technology Assessment Board—with the somewhat appropriate acronym TAB, since this would be its function. **1979** *Bull. Amer. Acad. Arts & Sci.* Mar. 21 Unanswered questions are threatening to leave technology assessment a mere intellectual pastime. **1969** *Listener* 24 July 106/3 This seems to show that Africa can use western techniques to her advantage, but only so long as the different cultural, intellectual and material contexts are kept firmly in mind when the technology-transfer is being planned. **1978** *Internat. Relations Dict.* (U.S. Dept. State Library) 40/2 *Technology transfer* has been defined as 'the transfer of knowledge generated and developed in one place to another, where it is used to achieve some practical end.'

Here are some suggestions for working with this entry and for thinking about word histories in general.

- Lists of abbreviations, even short ones, can look formidable. But you'll find the one on page 26 easy to use if you work systematically, reading a dictionary entry, and looking up each abbreviation as you go.
- Note that the cited examples for each definition follow the format: date, author, and an abbreviated title of the source in which the example appears. Do you find any of the examples of particular interest?
- Try distinguishing several key phases in the history of the word. Passing over some of the information and focusing upon a few key points will help you to arrive at an overview.
- What are some of the ways words diverge from their original meanings? Speculate about why they do so.

List of abbreviations, signs, etc.

a. (in Etymol.)	adoption of, adopted from	G., Ger.	German
a., adj., adj.	adjective	Gr.	Greek
ad. (in Etymol.)	adaptation of	*Gram.*	in Grammar
adv., adv.	adverb	It.	Italian
attrib.	attributive, -ly	L.	Latin
Cf., cf.	*confer,* compare	*Obs., obs.,* obs.	obsolete
Dict.	Dictionary	OF., OFr.	Old French
esp., esp.	especially	orig.	original, -ly
etym.	etymology	*phr.*	phrase
f. (in Etymol.)	formed on	pl., *pl.*	plural
f. (in subordinate entries)	form of	Pr.	Provençal
		pref.	prefix
		sb., *sb.*	substantive
fig.	figurative, -ly	Sp.	Spanish
F., Fr.	French	*transf.*	transferred sense
freq.	frequently		

Before a word or sense

† = obsolete
‖ = not naturalized
* = In the quotations, sometimes points out the word illustrated

In the list of forms

1 = before 1100
2 = 12th c. (1100 to 1200)
3 = 13th c. (1200 to 1300)
5–7 = 15th to 17th century

In the etymologies
* indicates a word or form not actually found, but of which the existence is inferred
:— = extant representative, or regular phonetic descendant of

The printing of a word in SMALL CAPS indicates that further information will be found under the word so referred to.

. . indicates an omitted part of a quotation.

Dictionary definitions can help you understand the scope of a word and all of its potential uses. By carefully examining a more extensive entry, you can get a better handle on the sense, or connotation, of a word like *intelligence.*

intelligence (ɪnˈtɛlɪdʒəns), *sb.* Also 5–6 **-ens.** [a. F. *intelligence* (12th c. in Hatz.-Darm.), ad. L. *intelleg-, intelligentia* understanding, from *intellegent-em* INTELLIGENT: see -ENCE.]

1. The faculty of understanding; intellect. ... **1664** POWER *Exp. Philos.* III. 158 To say, this Polary direction proceeds from itself, is to put a Soul, or Intelligence, at least, into the Stone. **1802** PALEY *Nat. Theol.* iv. §3 (1819) 49 There being no difference, as far as argument is concerned, between an intelligence which is not exerted, and an intelligence which does not exist. **1830** HERSCHEL *Stud. Nat. Phil.* 4 He is led to the conception of a Power and an Intelligence superior to his own.

2. Understanding as a quality of admitting of degree; *spec.* superior understanding; quickness of mental apprehension, sagacity. (Said also in reference to animals.) ... **1568** GRAFTON *Chron.* I. Ep., That some learned Englisheman of good intelligence would ... confute such errors. **1780** BURKE *Sp. Econ. Ref.* Wks. 1842 I. 232 We can proceed with confidence, because we can proceed with intelligence. **1837** *Penny Cycl.* IX. 350/1 Baron Cuvier.. observes [of elephants] that.. he never found their intelligence surpass that of a dog nor of many other carnivorous animals. ... **1872** YEATS *Techn. Hist. Comm.* 428 It is clear that intelligence has ever proved itself superior to ignorance.

3. a. The action or fact of mentally apprehending something; understanding, knowledge, cognizance, comprehension (*of* something). Now *rare* or *Obs.* ... **1620** T. GRANGER *Div. Logike* 2 God doth not reason.. but with one simple apprehension, or intelligence he knowes all things. **1790** HAN. MORE *Relig. Fash. World* (1791) 75 A disposition to enjoy them, arising from an intelligence of their nature, and a reverence for their value. **1819** SHELLEY *Peter Bell* v. xi, Of lakes he had intelligence; He knew something of heath and fell. ... **4. a.** An impersonation of intelligence; an intelligent or rational being; esp. applied to one that is or may be incorporeal; a spirit. ... The diuine intelligences or good Angels. **1667** MILTON *P.L.* VIII. 181 How fully hast thou satisfi'd mee, pure Intelligence of Heav'n, Angel serene! **1685**

BOYLE *Enq. Notion Nat.* 53 The School Philosophers.. teach, the Cœlestial Orbs to be moved or guided by Intelligences, or Angels. **1756** NUGENT *Montesquieu's Spir. Laws* (1758) I. I. I. The intelligences superior to man have their laws. ... **b.** An embodiment of intelligence; a person of superior intellect. *rare.*

1824 MISS MITTFORD *Village Ser.* I. (1863) 177 'Really', said Charles Grover, our intelligence—a fine old steady judge..'they are no better than so many old women'.

5. a. Interchange of knowledge, information, or sentiment; mutual conveyance of information; communication, intercourse. Now *rare* or *Obs.* ...

1560 BIBLE (Genev.) *Dan.* xi. 30 He shal euen returne, & haue intelligence with them that forsake the holie couenant. **1614** RALEIGH *Hist. World* I. (1634) 120 That they might repayre to each other and keepe intelligence by River. **1664** BUTLER *Hud.* II.iii. 848 [Constellations] as they came from hence, With us many hold Intelligence. **1717** LADY M. W. MONTAGU *Let. to Pope* 12 Feb., They took it into their heads.. that he was of intelligence with the enemy. ... †**b.** esp. applied to the communication of spies, secret or private agents, etc. *Obs.*

1587 FLEMING *Contn. Holinshed* III. 1372/1 Diuerse aduertisements thereof sent.. by other good meanes and intelligences from hir ambassadors and seruants residing in other countries. **1695** TEMPLE *Hist. Eng.* 565 He practis'd private Intelligences in the Danish Court. ... †**6.** A relation or footing of intercourse between persons or parties; a good (or other) understanding *between* or *with. Obs.*

1597–8 BACON *Ess., Followers* (Arb.) 32 That ill intelligence that we many times see between great personages. ... **1696** PHILLIPS (ed. 5), *Intelligence,.. the Union and Amity between two or more Persons that rightly understand one another.* **1734** tr. *Rollin's Anc. Hist.* (1827) VII. XVI. §6. 43 He sent an embassy.. to renew the good intelligence between them. **1827** SCOTT *Napoleon* VIII. 405 Having made the truce with Joachim.. it was to last no longer than his good intelligence with her ally. ... **7. a.** Knowledge as to events, communicated by or obtained from another; information, news, tidings; *spec.* information of military value.

c **1450** *Cov. Myst.* xiii. (Shaks. Soc.) 125 The aungel Gabryel apperyd hym to, That hese wyff xulde conseyve he ȝaff hym intelligence. ... **1695** TEMPLE *Hist. Eng.* (1699) 5 These were the Men from whom Cæsar drew his best Intelligence concerning the Country. ... **1799** G. HARRIS *Diary* 4 Apr. in Wellington *Disp.* (1837) I. 24 If our intelligence is true, his [*sc.* Tippoo Sultaun's] whole army are in a complete state of terror. **1818** JAS. MILL *Brit. India* II. v. v. 485 Intelligence poured in from all quarters, that one place after another was assailed. **1880** MCCARTHY *Own Times* IV. xlix. 29 The most accurate source of intelligence in all matters of public interest. **1899** *McClure's Mag.* Mar. 473/2 The swift single cruisers, the purveyors of intelligence. **1925** FRASER & GIBBONS *Soldier & Sailor Words* 125 'Intelligence', *i.e.* information of military value. The use of the word as a military technical term dates from the 16th Century, but in the War of 1914–18 it was used to denote specially the department of the General Staff dealing with information. ... †**b.** *pl.* A piece of information or news. *Obs.*

1592 T. HENAGE *Let.* in *Sir H. Unton's Corr.* (Roxb.) 268 The business of procuringe the intelligences of the world. ... **1750** [R. PALTOCK] *Life P. Wilkins* xl. (1883) 114/2, I sent for Nasgig to obtain some intelligences I wanted to be informed of.

c. The obtaining of information; the agency for obtaining secret information; the staff of persons so employed, secret service. Cf. INTELLIGENCER.

1602 MARSTON *Antonio's Rev.* IV. i. Wks. 1856 I. 117 When will the Duke holde feed Intelligence, Keepe warie observation in large pay? **1617** MORYSON *Itin.* II. 240 We have here the worst intelligence, of any Instruments that any Prince in Christendome doth imploy in so waighty a businesse. ... **1697** DAMPIER *Voy.* I. 133 To land some Men purposely to get Prisoners for intelligence. **1915** KIPLING *France at War* 21 The Intelligence with its stupefying photo-plans of the enemy's trenches. ... **1974** *Listener* 31 Jan. 142/1 Tizard has managed to get it through that someone should be seconded to British Intelligence for a while.

d. *Comb.* (sense 7c) ***intelligence agency, corps, officer, operator, service; intelligence department,*** a department of a state organization or of a military or naval service whose object is to obtain information (esp. by means of secret service officers or a system of spies); **Intelligence Office** (*U.S.*), 'an office or place where information may be obtained, particularly respecting servants' (Webster, 1864).

1951 *Intelligence Agency [see *C.I.A.* s.v. C III. ... The American intelligence agencies monitor as many as five million words daily from foreign radio broadcasts alone. ... **1888** *Times* (weekly ed.) 3 Feb. 9/1 An intelligence department—that is, a department which gathers information of every class and character to enable the administration in that department to use their Services if called upon. ... **8.** *attrib.* and *Comb.*, as **intelligence quotient** [ad. G. *intelligenz-quotient* (W. L. Stern, 1912)], a number arrived at by means of intelligence tests and intended to express the degree of intelligence of an individual in relation to the average for the age-group, which is fixed at 100; abbrev. *I.Q.* (I. III); so **intelligence test, tester, testing.**

1921 C. BURT *Mental & Scholastic Tests* 151 If a child's mental age be divided by his chronological age, the quotient will state what fraction of ability the child actually possesses... This fraction may be termed.. the child's '*intelligence quotient'. **1922** R. S. WOODWORTH *Psychol.* xii. 274 Brightness or dullness can also be measured by the intelligence quotient. **1944** H. READ *Educ. Free Men* iii. 13 Truth, we say, is not found exclusively in the possession of those with a high 'intelligence quotient' ... **1971** *Nature* 2 Apr. 306/1 The worship of the Intelligence Quotient, mercifully a-dying, is still not entirely dead. **1972** KAGAN & HAVEMANN *Psychol.* (ed. 2) xiv. 473 The intelligence quotient, or I.Q., is simply the relationship of mental age to chronological age; it is obtained by the formula I.Q. = MA/Chronological age × 100... This is the general principle for computing the I.Q. on the Stanford-Binet. In actual practice.. the I.Q. is usually determined from tables that make it possible to compare the child's raw score with the scores made by other children of the same age. This latter method is also the one used with all other intelligence tests... This statistical method of computing the I.Q. is valuable because the concept of mental age.. is not meaningful for adults. **1914** *Eugenics Rev.* Apr. 42 General ability, estimated by *intelligence tests, is largely hereditary. **1957** *Technology* Mar. 10/1 The trade school, however, is well equipped to sort wheat from chaff—each candidate is given the latest types of intelligence and aptitude tests. **1927** A. HUXLEY *Proper Stud.* 65 The *intelligence-testers would isolate.. the sum of the activities of the whole mind. **1962** H. J. EYSENCK *Know your own I.Q.* 31 From the point of view of the intelligence tester it is very undesirable to have mixed groups to deal with. **1972** J. L. DILLARD *Black English* i. 28 Some intelligence testers.. have suffered from lack of valid information about Black English in standard sources on American dialects. **1919** *Elem. School Jrnl.* Sept. 26 (*title*)
*Intelligence testing as an aid to supervision. **1958** [see *child welfare* (CHILD *sb.* 22)]. **1972** J. L. DILLARD *Black English* i. 28 An intelligence-testing procedure which is completely invalid because of its cultural and linguistic bias.

Here are some further suggestions for working with entries like these:

- Consider the various terms, phrases, and examples used to define the word. What does each of them suggest? How do they work together to give you a complete sense of the word? Do you find any of the descriptive terms surprising?
- Consider the word's various synonyms; for example, *understanding, apprehension,* and *sagacity.* Look up one of these words in an unabridged dictionary and compare it with the definition offered here for *intelligence.* How do the definitions overlap? How do they vary?

Write a brief esssay on what your study of the word *intelligence* helps you understand about the way the concept of intelligence is used in our society, its various meanings, and its connotations.

If you are interested in the subject of intelligence, you may want to do this assignment in coordination with the related material in the Opening Problem (p. 10), the Professional Application (p. 20), the Psychology Assignment (p. 38), and in Readings: Reconsidering Intelligence (p. 54).

A Personal Essay Assignment

In the essay "On Being a Cripple," defining and redefining take on a highly personal meaning for author Nancy Mairs. Draft a brief essay in which, by using Mairs's essay as a central example, you consider the powers and limits of self-defining.

Suggestions and questions:

- Why does Mairs object to various alternatives to the word *cripple*? Why does she prefer this term?
- To what extent does Mairs feel that her multiple sclerosis (MS) has defined who she is?
- Mairs says, "Some realities do not obey the dictates of language." Does Mairs imply, then, that many realities *do* obey the dictates of language? What does that mean? After reading Mairs's essay, can you illustrate this idea, drawing upon either her experience or your own?
- Notice that although Mairs provides straightforward definitions — as when she tells us what MS is — she also uses anecdotes, personal impressions, and other subtler, more wide-ranging techniques to create a definition of disability. What else do you notice about the techniques she uses to define her experiences?

On Being a Cripple

NANCY MAIRS

The other day I was thinking of writing an essay on being a cripple. I was thinking hard in one of the stalls of the women's room in my office building, as I was shoving my shirt into my jeans and tugging up my zipper. Preoccupied, I flushed, picked up my book bag, took my cane down from the hook, and unlatched the door. So many movements unbalanced me, and as I pulled the door open I fell over backward, landing fully clothed on the toilet seat with my legs splayed in front of me: the old beetle-on-its-back routine. Saturday afternoon, the building deserted, I was free to laugh aloud as I wriggled back to my feet, my voice bouncing off the yellowish tiles from all directions. Had anyone been there with me, I'd have been still and faint and hot with chagrin. I decided that it was high time to write the essay.

First, the matter of semantics. I am a cripple. I choose this word to name me. I choose from among several possibilities, the most common of which are "handicapped" and "disabled." I made the choice a number of years ago, without thinking, unaware of my motives for doing so. Even now, I'm not sure what those motives are, but I recognize that they are complex and not entirely flattering. People — crippled or not — wince at the word "cripple," as they do not at "handicapped" or "disabled." Perhaps I want them to wince. I want them to see me as a tough customer, one to whom the fates/gods/viruses have not been kind, but who can face the brutal truth of her existence squarely. As a cripple, I swagger.

But, to be fair to myself, a certain amount of honesty underlies my choice. "Cripple" seems to me a clean word, straightforward and precise. It has an honorable history, having made its first appearance in the Lindisfarne Gospel in the tenth century. As a lover of words, I like the accuracy with which it describes my condition: I have lost the full use of my limbs. "Disabled," by contrast, suggests any incapacity, physical or mental. And I certainly don't like "handicapped," which implies that I have deliberately been put at a disadvantage, by whom I can't imagine (my God is not a Handicapper General), in order to equalize chances in the great race of life. These words seem to me to be moving away from my condition, to be widening the gap between word and reality. Most remote is the recently coined euphemism "differently abled," which partakes of the same semantic hopefulness that transformed countries from "undeveloped" to "underdeveloped," then to "less developed," and finally to "developing" nations. People have continued to starve in those countries during the shift. Some realities do not obey the dictates of language.

Mine is one of them. Whatever you call me, I remain crippled. But I don't care what you call me, so long as it isn't "differently abled," which strikes me as pure verbal garbage designed, by its ability to describe anyone, to describe no one. I subscribe to George Orwell's thesis that "the slovenliness of our language makes it easier for us to have foolish thoughts." And I refuse to participate in the degeneration of the language to the extent that I deny that I have lost anything in the course of this calamitous disease;

NANCY MAIRS (b. 1943) is a freelance writer living in Tucson, Arizona. In addition to authoring numerous magazine and newspaper articles, she wrote *Remembering the Bonehouse* (1989), *Carnal Acts (1990)*, *Ordinary Time* (1993), *Voice Lessons* (1994), and *Waist-High in the World* (1997). "On Being a Cripple" appears in her 1986 essay collection, *Plain Text*.

I refuse to pretend that the only differences between you and me are the various ordinary ones that distinguish any one person from another. But call me "disabled" or "handicapped" if you like. I have long since grown accustomed to them; and if they are vague, at least they hint at the truth. Moreover, I use them myself. Society is no readier to accept crippledness than to accept death, war, sex, sweat, or wrinkles. I would never refer to another person as a cripple. It is the word I use to name only myself.

I haven't always been crippled, a fact for which I am soundly grateful. To be whole of limb is, I know from experience, infinitely more pleasant and useful than to be crippled; and if that knowledge leaves me open to bitterness at my loss, the physical soundness I once enjoyed (though I did not enjoy it half enough) is well worth the occasional stab of regret. Though never any good at sports, I was a normally active child and young adult. I climbed trees, played hopscotch, jumped rope, skated, swam, rode my bicycle, sailed. I despised team sports, spending some of the wretchedest afternoons of my life, sweaty and humiliated, behind a field-hockey stick and under a basketball hoop. I tramped alone for miles along the bridle paths that webbed the woods behind the house I grew up in. I swayed through countless dim hours in the arms of one man or another under the scattered shot of light from mirrored balls, and gyrated through countless more as Tab Hunter and Johnny Mathis gave way to the Rolling Stones, Creedence Clearwater Revival, Cream. I walked down the aisle. I pushed baby carriages, changed tires in the rain, marched for peace.

When I was twenty-eight I started to trip and drop things. What at first seemed my natural clumsiness soon became too pronounced to shrug off. I consulted a neurologist, who told me that I had a brain tumor. A battery of tests, increasingly disagreeable, revealed no tumor. About a year and a half later I developed a blurred spot in one eye. I had, at last, the episodes "disseminated in space and time" requisite for a diagnosis: multiple sclerosis. I have never been sorry for the doctor's initial misdiagnosis, however. For almost a week, until the negative results of the tests were in, I thought that I was going to die right away. Every day for the past nearly ten years, then, has been a kind of gift. I accept all gifts.

Multiple sclerosis is a chronic degenerative disease of the central nervous system, in which the myelin that sheathes the nerves is somehow eaten away and scar tissue forms in its place, interrupting the nerves' signals. During its course, which is unpredictable and uncontrollable, one may lose vision, hearing, speech, the ability to walk, control of bladder and/or bowels, strength in any or all extremities, sensitivity to touch, vibration, and/or pain, potency, coordination of movements — the list of possibilities is lengthy and, yes, horrifying. One may also lose one's sense of humor. That's the easiest to lose and the hardest to survive without.

In the past ten years, I have sustained some of these losses. Characteristic of MS are sudden attacks, called exacerbations, followed by remissions, and these I have not had. Instead, my disease has been slowly progressive. My left leg is now so weak that I walk with the aid of a brace and a cane; and for distances I use an Amigo, a variation on the electric wheelchair that looks rather like an electrified kiddie car. I no longer have much use of my left hand. Now my right side is weakening as well. I still have the blurred spot in my right eye. Overall, though, I've been lucky so far. My world has, of necessity, been circumscribed by my losses, but the terrain left me has been ample enough for me to continue many of the activities that absorb me: writing, teaching, raising children and cats and plants and snakes, reading, speaking publicly about MS and depression, even playing bridge with people patient and honorable enough to let me scatter cards every which way without sneaking a peek.

Lest I begin to sound like Pollyanna, however, let me say that I don't like having MS. I hate it. My life holds realities — harsh ones, some of them — that no right-minded human being ought to accept without grumbling. One of them is fatigue. I know of no one with MS who does not complain of bone-weariness; in a disease that presents an astonishing variety of symptoms, fatigue seems to be a common factor. I wake up in the morning feeling the way most people do at the end of a bad day, and I take it from there. As a result, I spend a lot of time *in extremis*[1] and, impatient with limitation, I tend to ignore my fatigue until my body breaks down in some way and forces rest. Then I miss picnics, dinner parties, poetry readings, the brief visits of old friends from out of town. The offspring of a puritanical tradition of exceptional venerability, I cannot view these lapses without shame. My life often seems a series of small failures to do as I ought.

I lead, on the whole, an ordinary life, probably rather like the one I would have led had I not had MS. I am lucky that my predilections were already solitary, sedentary, and bookish — unlike the world-famous French cellist I have read about, or the young woman I talked with one long afternoon who wanted only to be a jockey. I had just begun graduate school when I found out something was wrong with me, and I have remained, interminably, a graduate student. Perhaps I would not have if I'd thought I had the stamina to return to a full-time job as a technical editor; but I've enjoyed my studies.

In addition to studying, I teach writing courses. I also teach medical students how to give neurological examinations. I pick up freelance editing jobs here and there. I have raised a foster son and sent him into the world, where he has made me two grandbabies, and I am still escorting my daughter and son through adolescence. I go to Mass every Saturday. I am a superb, if messy, cook. I am also an enthusiastic laundress, capable of sorting a hamper full of clothes into five subtly differentiated piles, but a terrible housekeeper. I can do italic writing and, in an emergency, bathe an oil-soaked cat. I play a fiendish game of Scrabble. When I have the time and the money, I like to sit on my front steps with my husband, drinking Amaretto and smoking a cigar, as we imagine our counterparts in Leningrad and make sure that the sun gets down once more behind the sharp childish scrawl of the Tucson Mountains.

This lively plenty has its bleak complement, of course, in all the things I can no longer do. I will never run again, except in dreams, and one day I may have to write that I will never walk again. I like to go camping, but I can't follow George and the children along the trails that wander out of a campsite through the desert or into the mountains. In fact, even on the level I've learned never to check the weather or try to hold a coherent conversation: I need all my attention for my wayward feet. Of late, I have begun to catch myself wondering how people can propel themselves without canes. With only one usable hand, I have to select my clothing with care not so much for style as for ease of ingress and egress, and even so, dressing can be laborious. I can no longer do fine stitchery, pick up babies, play the piano, braid my hair. I am immobilized by acute attacks of depression, which may or may not be physiologically related to MS but are certainly its logical concomitant.

These two elements, the plenty and the privation, are never pure, nor are the delight and wretchedness that accompany them. Almost every pickle that I get into as a result of my weakness and clumsiness — and I get into plenty — is funny as well as maddening and sometimes painful. I recall one May afternoon when a friend and I were go-

[1]***in extremis:*** In extreme circumstances; near death (Latin) [Eds.].

ing out for a drink after finishing up at school. As we were climbing into opposite sides of my car, chatting, I tripped and fell, flat and hard, onto the asphalt parking lot, my abrupt departure interrupting him in mid-sentence. "Where'd you go?" he called as he came around the back of the car to find me hauling myself up by the door frame. "Are you all right?" Yes, I told him, I was fine, just a bit rattly, and we drove off to find a shady patio and some beer. When I got home an hour or so later, my daughter greeted me with "What have you done to yourself?" I looked down. One elbow of my white turtle-neck with the green froggies, one knee of my white trousers, one white kneesock were blood-soaked. We peeled off the clothes and inspected the damage, which was nasty enough but not alarming. That part wasn't funny: The abrasions took a long time to heal, and one got a little infected. Even so, when I think of my friend talking earnestly, suddenly, to the hot thin air while I dropped from his view as though through a trap door, I find the image as silly as something from a Marx Brothers movie.

I may find it easier than other cripples to amuse myself because I live propped by the acceptance and the assistance and, sometimes, the amusement of those around me. Grocery clerks tear my checks out of my checkbook for me, and sales clerks find chairs to put into dressing rooms when I want to try on clothes. The people I work with make sure I teach at times when I am least likely to be fatigued, in places I can get to, with the materials I need. My students, with one anonymous exception (in an end-of-the-semester evaluation), have been unperturbed by my disability. Some even like it. One was immensely cheered by the information that I paint my own fingernails; she decided, she told me, that if I could go to such trouble over fine details, she could keep on writing essays. I suppose I became some sort of bright-fingered muse. She wrote good essays, too.

The most important struts in the framework of my existence, of course, are my husband and children. Dismayingly few marriages survive the MS test, and why should they? Most twenty-two- and nineteen-year-olds, like George and me, can vow in clear conscience, after a childhood of chicken pox and summer colds, to keep one another in sickness and in health so long as they both shall live. Not many are equipped for catastrophe: the dismay, the depression, the extra work, the boredom that a degenerative disease can insinuate into a relationship. And our society, with its emphasis on fun and its association of fun with physical performance, offers little encouragement for a whole spouse to stay with a crippled partner. Children experience similar stresses when faced with a crippled parent, and they are more helpless, since parents and children can't usually get divorced. They hate, of course, to be different from their peers, and the child whose mother is tacking down the aisle of a school auditorium packed with proud parents like a Cape Cod dinghy in a stiff breeze jolly well stands out in a crowd. Deprived of legal divorce, the child can at least deny the mother's disability, even her existence, forgetting to tell her about recitals and PTA meetings, refusing to accompany her to stores or church or the movies, never inviting friends to the house. Many do.

But I've been limping along for ten years now, and so far George and the children are still at my left elbow, holding tight. Anne and Matthew vacuum floors and dust furniture and haul trash and rake up dog droppings and button my cuffs and bake lasagna and Toll House cookies with just enough grumbling so I know that they don't have brain fever. And far from hiding me, they're forever dragging me by racks of fancy clothes or through teeming school corridors, or welcoming gaggles of friends while I'm wandering through the house in Anne's filmy pink babydoll pajamas. George generally calls before he brings someone home, but he does just as many dumb thankless chores as the children. And they all yell at me, laugh at some of my jokes, write me funny letters when we're apart — in short, treat me as an ordinary human being for whom they have some use. I think they like me. Unless they're faking. . . .

Faking. There's the rub. Tugging at the fringes of my consciousness always is the terror that people are kind to me only because I'm a cripple. My mother almost shattered me once, with that instinct mothers have — blind, I think, in this case, but unerring nonetheless — for striking blows along the faultlines of their children's hearts, by telling me, in an attack on my selfishness, "We all have to make allowances for you, of course, because of the way you are." From the distance of a couple of years, I have to admit that I haven't any idea just what she meant, and I'm not sure that she knew either. She was awfully angry. But at the time, as the words thudded home, I felt my worst fear, suddenly realized. I could bear being called selfish: I am. But I couldn't bear the corroboration that those around me were doing in fact what I'd always suspected them of doing, professing fondness while silently putting up with me because of the way I am. A cripple. I've been a little cracked ever since.

Along with this fear that people are secretly accepting shoddy goods comes a relentless pressure to please — to prove myself worth the burdens I impose, I guess, or to build a substantial account of goodwill against which I may write drafts in times of need. Part of the pressure arises from social expectations. In our society, anyone who deviates from the norm had better find some way to compensate. Like fat people, who are expected to be jolly, cripples must bear their lot meekly and cheerfully. A grumpy cripple isn't playing by the rules. And much of the pressure is self-generated. Early on I vowed that, if I had to have MS, by God I was going to do it well. This is a class act, ladies and gentlemen. No tears, no recriminations, no faint-heartedness.

One way and another, then, I wind up feeling like Tiny Tim, peering over the edge of the table at the Christmas goose, waving my crutch, piping down God's blessing on us all. Only sometimes I don't want to play Tiny Tim. I'd rather be Caliban, a most scurvy monster. Fortunately, at home no one much cares whether I'm a good cripple or a bad cripple as long as I make vichyssoise with fair regularity. One evening several years ago, Anne was reading at the dining-room table while I cooked dinner. As I opened a can of tomatoes, the can slipped in my left hand and juice spattered me and the counter with bloody spots. Fatigued and infuriated, I bellowed, "I'm so sick of being crippled!" Anne glanced at me over the top of her book. "There now," she said, "do you feel better?" "Yes," I said, "yes, I do." She went back to her reading. I felt better. That's about all the attention my scurviness ever gets.

Because I hate being crippled, I sometimes hate myself for being a cripple. Over the years I have come to expect — even accept — attacks of violent self-loathing. Luckily, in general our society no longer connects deformity and disease directly with evil (though a charismatic once told me that I have MS because a devil is in me) and so I'm allowed to move largely at will, even among small children. But I'm not sure that this revision of attitude has been particularly helpful. Physical imperfection, even freed of moral disapprobation, still defies and violates the ideal, especially for women, whose confinement in their bodies as objects of desire is far from over. Each age, of course, has its ideal, and I doubt that ours is any better or worse than any other. Today's ideal woman, who lives on the glossy pages of dozens of magazines, seems to be between the ages of eighteen and twenty-five; her hair has body; her teeth flash white, her breath smells minty, her underarms are dry; she has a career but is still a fabulous cook, especially of meals that take less than twenty minutes to prepare; she does not ordinarily appear to have a husband or children; she is trim and deeply tanned; she jogs, swims, plays tennis, rides a bicycle, sails, but does not bowl; she travels widely, even to out-of-the-way places like Finland and Samoa, always in the company of the ideal man, who possesses a nearly identical set of characteristics. There are a few exceptions. Though usually white and often blonde, she may be black, Hispanic, Asian, or Native American, so long as she is unusually sleek. She may be old, provided she is selling a laxative or is Lauren Bacall. If she is selling a detergent, she may be married and have a flock of strikingly messy children. But she is never a cripple.

Like many women I know, I have always had an uneasy relationship with my body. I was not a popular child, largely, I think now, because I was peculiar: intelligent, intense, moody, shy, given to unexpected actions and inexplicable notions and emotions. But as I entered adolescence, I believed myself unpopular because I was homely: my breasts too flat, my mouth too wide, my hips too narrow, my clothing never quite right in fit or style. I was not, in fact, particularly ugly, old photographs inform me, though I was well off the ideal; but I carried this sense of self-alienation with me into adulthood, where it regenerated in response to the depredations of MS. Even with my brace I walk with a limp so pronounced that, seeing myself on the videotape of a television program on the disabled, I couldn't believe that anything but an inchworm could make progress humping along like that. My shoulders droop and my pelvis thrusts forward as I try to balance myself upright, throwing my frame into a bony "S." As a result of contractures, one shoulder is higher than the other and I carry one arm bent in front of me, the fingers curled into a claw. My left arm and leg have wasted into pipe stems, and I try always to keep them covered. When I think about how my body must look to others, especially to men, to whom I have been trained to display myself, I feel ludicrous, even loathsome.

At my age, however, I don't spend much time thinking about my appearance. The burning egocentricity of adolescence, which assures one that all the world is looking all the time, has passed, thank God, and I'm generally too caught up in what I'm doing to step back, as I used to, and watch myself as though upon a stage. I'm also too old to believe in the accuracy of self-image. I know that I'm not a hideous crone, that in fact, when I'm rested, well dressed, and well made up, I look fine. The self-loathing I feel is neither physically nor intellectually substantial. What I hate is not me but a disease.

I am not a disease.

And a disease is not — at least not singlehandedly — going to determine who I am, though at first it seemed to be going to. Adjusting to a chronic incurable illness, I have moved through a process similar to that outlined by Elizabeth Kübler-Ross in *On Death and Dying.* The major difference — and it is far more significant than most people recognize — is that I can't be sure of the outcome, as the terminally ill cancer patient can. Research studies indicate that, with proper medical care, I may achieve a "normal" life span. And in our society, with its vision of death as the ultimate evil, worse even than decrepitude, the response to such news is, "Oh well, at least you're not going to *die.*" Are there worse things than dying? I think that there may be.

I think of two women I know, both with MS, both enough older than I to have served me as models. One took to her bed several years ago and has been there ever since. Although she can sit in a high-backed wheelchair, because she is incontinent she refuses to go out at all, even though incontinence pants, which are readily available at any pharmacy, could protect her from embarrassment. Instead, she stays at home and insists that her husband, a small quiet man, a retired civil servant, stay there with her except for a quick weekly foray to the supermarket. The other woman, whose illness was diagnosed when she was eighteen, a nursing student engaged to a young doctor, finished her training, married her doctor, accompanied him to Germany when he was in the service, bore three sons and a daughter, now grown and gone. When she can, she travels with her husband; she plays bridge, embroiders, swims regularly; she works, like me, as a symptomatic-patient instructor of medical students in neurology. Guess which woman I hope to be.

At the beginning, I thought about having MS almost incessantly. And because of the unpredictable course of the disease, my thoughts were always terrified. Each night I'd get into bed wondering whether I'd get out again the next morning, whether I'd be able to see, to speak, to hold a pen between my fingers. Knowing that the day might come when I'd be physically incapable of killing myself, I thought perhaps I ought to do so right away, while I still had the strength. Gradually I came to understand that the Nancy who might one day lie inert under a bedsheet, arms and legs paralyzed, unable to feed or bathe herself, unable to reach out for a gun, a bottle of pills, was not the Nancy I was at present, and that I could not presume to make decisions for that future Nancy, who might well not want in the least to die. Now the only provision I've made for the future Nancy is that when the time comes — and it is likely to come in the form of pneumonia, friend to the weak and the old — I am not to be treated with machines and medications. If she is unable to communicate by then, I hope she will be satisfied with these terms.

Thinking all the time about having MS grew tiresome and intrusive, especially in the large and tragic mode in which I was accustomed to considering my plight. Months and even years went by without catastrophe (at least without one related to MS), and really I was awfully busy, what with George and children and snakes and students and poems, and I hadn't the time, let alone the inclination, to devote myself to being a disease. Too, the richer my life became, the funnier it seemed, as though there were some connection between largesse and laughter, and so my tragic stance began to waver until, even with the aid of a brace and a cane, I couldn't hold it for very long at a time.

After several years I was satisfied with my adjustment. I had suffered my grief and fury and terror, I thought, but now I was at ease with my lot. Then one summer day I set out with George and the children across the desert for a vacation in California. Part way to Yuma I became aware that my right leg felt funny. "I think I've had an exacerbation," I told George. "What shall we do?" he asked. "I think we'd better get the hell to California," I said, "because I don't know whether I'll ever make it again." So we went on to San Diego and then to Orange, up the Pacific Coast Highway to Santa Cruz, across to Yosemite, down to Sequoia and Joshua Tree, and so back over the desert to home. It was a fine two-week trip, filled with friends and fair weather, and I wouldn't have missed it for the world, though I did in fact make it back to California two years later. Nor would there have been any point in missing it, since in MS, once the symptoms have appeared, the neurological damage has been done, and there's no way to predict or prevent that damage.

The incident spoiled my self-satisfaction, however. It renewed my grief and fury and terror, and I learned that one never finishes adjusting to MS. I don't know now why I thought one would. One does not, after all, finish adjusting to life, and MS is simply a fact of my life — not my favorite fact, of course — but as ordinary as my nose and my tropical fish and my yellow Mazda station wagon. It may at any time get worse, but no amount of worry or anticipation can prepare me for a new loss. My life is a lesson in losses. I learn one at a time.

And I had best be patient in the learning, since I'll have to do it like it or not. As any rock fan knows, you can't always get what you want. Particularly when you have MS. You can't, for example, get cured. In recent years researchers and the organizations that fund research have started to pay MS some attention even though it isn't fatal; perhaps they have begun to see that life is something other than a quantitative phenomenon, that one may be very much alive for a very long time in a life that isn't worth living. The researchers have made some progress toward understanding the mechanism of the disease: It may well be an autoimmune reaction triggered by a slow-acting virus. But they are nowhere near its prevention, control, or cure. And most of us want to be cured. Some, unable to accept incurability, grasp at one treatment after another, no matter how bizarre: megavitamin therapy, gluten-free diet, injections of cobra venom, hypothermal suits, lymphocytopharesis, hyperbaric chambers. Many treatments are probably harmless enough, but none are curative.

The absence of a cure often makes MS patients bitter toward their doctors. Doctors are, after all, the priests of modern society, the new shamans, whose business is to heal, and many an MS patient roves from one to another, searching for the "good" doctor who will make him well. Doctors too think of themselves as healers, and for this reason many have trouble dealing with MS patients, whose disease in its intransigence defeats their aims and mocks their skills. Too few doctors, it is true, treat their patients as whole human beings, but the reverse is also true. I have always tried to be gentle with my doctors, who often have more at stake in terms of ego than I do. I may be frustrated, maddened, depressed by the incurability of my disease, but I am not diminished by it, and they are. When I push myself up from my seat in the waiting room and stumble toward them, I incarnate the limitation of their powers. The least I can do is refuse to press on their tenderest spots.

This gentleness is part of the reason that I'm not sorry to be a cripple. I didn't have it before. Perhaps I'd have developed it anyway — how could I know such a thing? — and I wish I had more of it, but I'm glad of what I have. It has opened and enriched my life enormously, this sense that my frailty and need must be mirrored in others, that in searching for and shaping a stable core in a life wrenched by change and loss, change and loss, I must recognize the same process, under individual conditions, in the lives around me. I do not deprecate such knowledge, however I've come by it.

All the same, if a cure were found, would I take it? In a minute. I may be a cripple, but I'm only occasionally a loony and never a saint. Anyway, in my brand of theology God doesn't give bonus points for a limp. I'd take a cure; I just don't need one. A friend who also has MS startled me once by asking, "Do you ever say to yourself, 'Why me, Lord?'" "No, Michael, I don't," I told him, "because whenever I try, the only response I can think of is 'Why not?'" If I could make a cosmic deal, who would I put in my place? What in my life would I give up in exchange for sound limbs and a thrilling rush of energy? No one. Nothing. I might as well do the job myself. Now that I'm getting the hang of it.

A Biology Assignment

Defining in the life sciences is seldom simply a matter of assigning terms to static categories: "*Hypertension* is the disease of high blood pressure" or "*Thirst* is the desire for liquids." To begin to understand a biological term is to see it in terms of ongoing processes. One definition leads to another; defining becomes a matter of understanding interrelationships. Any single feature, as we learn to define it better, becomes linked with others. And in some of the most accurate biological definitions we also arrive at statements about limitations — admissions of what remains imperfectly understood.

Read the passage below, "What Sodium Does," by Jane Brody. Then write an essay that defines both *thirst* and *hypertension* in terms of the functions and misfunctions of sodium in the human body.

What Sodium Does

JANE E. BRODY

Of course, sodium is a vital constituent of the human body. Our tissues swim in a salty sea — a vestige, perhaps, of our aquatic evolution. The more salt in that sea, the more water is needed to dilute it to maintain the proper concentration of sodium. Sodium and its equally essential companion chloride (the combining form of chlorine) are the principal regulators of the balance of water and dissolved substances outside cells. [Balancing water and dissolved substances] is the job potassium does within cells. These three minerals — called electrolytes — also regulate the balance of acids and bases in body fluids and cells. If the balance of water and electrolytes or acids and bases is disturbed, normal metabolic functions may grind to a near halt.

Eating something salty makes you thirsty because when salt is added to the body, extra water is needed to dilute it. Bartenders cash in on this fact of human physiology by offering salty nuts and pretzels gratis to patrons. It's good for business. And if you lose water through sweating, the increased concentration of salt in your blood also stimulates thirst. The "purpose" of thirst is to keep the body functioning properly by maintaining the concentration of salt within a certain narrow range.

The body's machinery for keeping a normal level of sodium in its fluids is the *kidneys.* When the body has too much sodium, the kidneys dump it out into the urine and excrete it. When the body needs sodium, the kidneys reabsorb it from urine and pump it back into the blood. Unfortunately, in a significant percentage of people, perhaps as a result of having to dump excess sodium for years, this machinery fails to operate properly and the kidneys don't get rid of enough sodium. The retained sodium holds water, and the volume of blood rises. The blood vessels become water-logged and more sensitive to nerve stimulation that causes them to contract. Since more blood now has to pass through the same ever-narrower channels, the blood pressure increases. The heart rate also increases because the heart has more blood to pump around the body. This in turn sets up a vicious cycle in which the blood vessels contract to reduce the blood flow. The pressure then rises even further until you have hypertension.

While this is a vast oversimplification of a mechanism that is still incompletely un-

---

Science and health writer JANE E. BRODY (b. 1941) has written a number of books on nutrition, including *Jane Brody's Nutrition Book* (1981), excerpted here, *The New York Times Guide to Personal Health* (1982), *Jane Brody's Good Food Book* (1985), and *Jane Brody's Cold and Flu Fighter* (1995). Her column "Personal Health" is published in several newspapers nationwide.

derstood, it gives you some idea of how excess consumption of sodium can cause high blood pressure in susceptible persons. Stress adds further to the problem by stimulating the release of an adrenal-gland hormone, aldosterone, which signals the kidneys to hold on to sodium and water. But even in the absence of stress, too much sodium can do serious damage.

A Psychology Assignment

Take a few minutes to jot down a definition of intelligence. What does the term typically mean, in your experience? If you worked on the Opening Problem (p. 10), you can use the definition you generated there. You might also want to consult the varied definitions of intelligence provided in the entry from the *Oxford English Dictionary* (p. 26).

Now read the two brief discussions of intelligence in a cross-cultural perspective that follow. One is by psychiatrist Barry Nurcombe, the other by psychologist David Matsumoto. Building on the writing you've done, try to expand your definition of intelligence so that it is more culturally inclusive — or you might want to comment on the difficulty of generating a definition of intelligence that applies to a wide range of cultures. If you have knowledge of a culture in which intelligence might be defined in ways different from mainstream Western definitions, feel free to incorporate that knowledge.

If you are interested in the subject of intelligence, you may want to do this assignment in coordination with other related readings in this chapter. Besides the Opening Problem and the *Oxford English Dictionary* entry mentioned above, see the Professional Application (p. 20) and Readings: Reconsidering Intelligence (p. 54).

From *Children of the Dispossessed*

BARRY NURCOMBE

All cultures have words that denote "intelligent." It is a matter of common observation that in any community there are individuals who stand out in wisdom, accuracy of prediction, ability to solve problems, craftiness, or in their accumulation of traditional knowledge and technical skills. Most people are not outstanding in competence. A few are so markedly backward that they may be called "dull." "Intelligent" connotes goodness, power, activity. In Western societies "dullness" connotes badness, impotence, passivity. Take these synonyms from *Roget's Thesaurus* (1965):

Australian BARRY NURCOMBE (b. 1933) is professor of psychiatry and director of child and adolescent psychiatry at the University of Queensland in Australia. The passage here is from his work *Children of the Dispossessed* (1976). His other published works include *An Outline of Child Psychiatry* (1972; 2nd edition 1975) and *Child Mental Health & the Law* (1994), co-authored with David Partlett.

Adj. *intelligent,* quick of apprehension, keen, acute, alive, brainy, awake, bright, quick, sharp; quick-, keen-, clear-, sharp-, -eyed, -sighted, -witted; wide awake; canny, shrewd, astute; clear-headed; far-sighted; discerning, perspicacious, penetrating, piercing, nimble-witted; sharp as a needle; alive to; clever; arch.

Wise, sage, sapient, sagacious, reasonable, rational . . .

Adj. *un-intelligent,* -intellectual, -reasoning; brainless; having no-head; not-bright; in-apprehensible.

addle-, blunder-, muddle-, pig-headed.

weak-, feeble-minded; shallow-, rattle-, lack-brained; half-, nit-, short-, dull-, blunt-witted; shallow-, addle-pated; dim-, short-sighted; thick-skulled; weak in the upper story.

Shallow, weak, wanting, soft; dull; stupid . . .

And so on.

Despite the ubiquity of the concept "intelligent," the particular astute behaviors that are most valued vary from culture to culture. . . . In Rhodesian Shona society an individual's esteem rests upon the degree of cohesion his actions foster in his kin group. Intelligent behavior tends to incorporate a keen awareness of interpersonal relations. Force and life are imputed to words and natural objects, and the ancestral spirits of kinfolk are regarded as involved in personal transactions. The Shona equivalent for "act intelligently" is *ngware,* a word that connotes caution, prudence, and diplomacy. This is markedly different from — if not antithetical to — the Western ideal of independent, individual, competitive achievement. One culture values the judicious choice and application of traditional forms; the other, the creation of new forms of problem-solving. One stresses the group and its continuity with ancestral spirits and the world of nature; the other promotes the individual who masters nature and stands out from others.

Cultural Differences in the Meaning and Concept of Intelligence

DAVID MATSUMOTO

Many languages have no word that corresponds to our idea of intelligence. Definitions of intelligence often reflect cultural values. The closest Mandarin equivalent, for instance, is a Chinese character that means good brain and talented. Chinese people often associate this with traits such as imitation, effort, and social responsibility. Such traits do not constitute important elements of intelligence for most mainstream Americans.

The Baganda of East Africa use the word *obugezi* to refer to a combination of mental and social skills that make a person steady, cautious, and friendly. The Djerma-Sonhai in West Africa use a term that has an even broader meaning, *lakkal,* which is a combination of intelligence, know-how, and social skills. Still another society, the Baoule, uses the term *n'glouele,* which describes children who are not only mentally alert but also willing to volunteer their services without being asked.

DAVID MATSUMOTO (b. 1959) is professor of psychology and director of the Intercultural and Emotion Research Laboratory at San Francisco State University. He is the author of more than ninety works on culture and emotion, including *Culture and Modern Life* (1997) and *People: Psychology from a Cultural Perspective* (1994), excerpted here.

Because of such enormous differences in the ways in which cultures define intelligence, it is difficult to make valid comparisons of this notion of intelligence from one society to another. People in different cultures not only disagree about the very nature of what intelligence is, but they also have very different attitudes about the proper way to demonstrate one's abilities. In some cultures such as the mainstream U.S. society, individuals are typically rewarded for displaying knowledge and skills. This same behavior may be considered improper, arrogant, or rude in societies that stress personal relationships, cooperation, and modesty.

These points are important to cross-cultural studies of intelligence because successful performance on a task of intelligence may require behavior that is considered immodest and arrogant in culture A (and therefore only reluctantly displayed by members of culture A) but desirable in culture B (and therefore readily displayed by members of culture B). Clearly, such different attitudes toward the same behavior can result in inaccurate conclusions about differences in intelligence between culture A and culture B.

It is also difficult to compare intelligence cross-culturally for another reason. Namely, because tests of intelligence often rely on knowledge that is particular to a culture, investigators who are based in another culture may not know what to test for. A test designed for one culture is often not suitable for another, even when the test is carefully translated into a second language. For example, one U.S. intelligence test includes the following question: "How does a violin resemble a piano?" Clearly, this question assumes prior knowledge about violins and pianos, which is a reasonable expectation of middle-class Americans, but not of cultures that use other musical instruments.

A Genetics Assignment

French geneticist Albert Jacquard, in the opening chapter of his book *In Praise of Difference,* calls into question one of our most routine biological terms: *sexual reproduction.* Its continued use, he suggests, is owing more to theories of the past than to present knowledge. After reading this passage, write an essay explaining why in Jacquard's view the term *sexual reproduction* is tied to a misleading view of biological inheritance. You might want to consider some of the social implications of this view.

Sexual Reproduction

ALBERT JACQUARD

Any discourse pertaining to genetics has as its basic reference point the obvious fact that there is a certain similarity between children and parents. Throughout the living world, the transmission of particular traits is part of the transmission of life itself. What is the mechanism that governs this transmission? The answer to this question seems to defy

ALBERT JACQUARD (b. 1925) lives in France and works as a demographer and population geneticist at Institut National D'Etudes Demographiques. His many works include *In Praise of Difference* (1984), the first chapter of which is excerpted here.

common sense. A rereading of some classical texts illustrates the difficulty of finding a reasonable solution to this problem, even when it is posed in simple terms.

SOME PRE-MENDELIAN NOTIONS

Some authors confined themselves to observation and description, without suggesting an explanation. For instance, Ambroise Paré wrote, at the end of the seventeenth century:

> Children resemble their father and mother not only physically (in size, in weight, in posture, and in build) and in their manner of speaking and walking: They are also subject to the same diseases as those to which their father and mother are subject, called hereditary diseases. This is seen to be true of people afflicted with leprosy, gout, epilepsy, kidney stone, melancholia, and asthma. Thus, when one of these people engenders a child, it is likely to be afflicted with the same disease. However, experience shows that this does not always happen. It is prevented by the good quality of the woman's seed and the favorable conditions in her womb which correct the imbalance in the male seed just as the man's seed can correct the woman's.

Similarly, Montaigne[1] expressed dismay at being afflicted with kidney stones at the same age as his father. How, he wondered, had the latter transmitted this disorder to him?

> How did this slight bit of his substance, with which he made me, bear so great an impression of it for its share? And moreover, how did it remain so concealed that I began to feel it forty-five years later, the only one to this hour out of so many brothers and sisters, and all of the same mother? If anyone will enlighten me about this process, I will believe him about as many other miracles as he wants; provided he does not palm off on me some explanation much more difficult and fantastic than the thing itself.[2]

What an apt warning to pedants whose explanations are more complex and mysterious than the question asked!

Others dreamed up theories which seem very strange to us and, indeed, it is difficult to understand how they could ever have been proposed as rigorous scientific theories. For example, Buffon[3] thought that the male and female "seminal fluids" contained particles emanating from all parts of the body, which fell miraculously into place to constitute a child.

> I therefore believe that the male seminal fluid, which is spread on the vagina, and the corresponding female fluid which is spread in the uterus are both equally active substances and equally loaded with organic molecules, endowed with engendering properties.
>
> I think that, when the two seminal fluids mix, the activity of the organic molecules in each of the fluids is, in some manner, stabilized by the counterbalancing action of the other, in such a way that each organic molecule becomes immobile at an appropriate location, this being none other than that which it occupied previously in the body. Thus,

[1]**Montaigne:** French essayist Michel de Montaigne (1533–1592) [Eds.].

[2]Donald M. Frame, tr., *Montaigne's Essays and Selected Writings: A Bilingual Edition* (New York: St. Martin's Press, 1963).

[3]**Buffon:** French naturalist Georges-Louis Leclerc de Buffon (1707–1788) [Eds.].

all the molecules which came originally from the spinal cord will be relocated in a comparable way, in relation both to the structure and to the position of the vertebrae.

Darwin's attempt at explaining the transmission of traits was scarcely more convincing than Buffon's. He proposed that the various characteristics and functions of each cell in an organism are dependent on one or more very small particles called gemmules. Gemmules from both father and mother meet in each of the embryo's cells, which are thus endowed with characteristics that are intermediate between those of the corresponding maternal and paternal cells.

Let us forget what we may have learned and try to imagine how one individual might be generated from two others. This everyday event seems so inexplicable that one's first thought is to suggest that only one of the two parents plays a real part. Such was the point of view adopted by the "spermatists," according to whom each sperm contains a fully formed baby who merely grows bigger in the mother's womb.

This theory was developed soon after the first observations of sperm through a microscope; these had revealed the presence of tiny living particles, called "homunculi." It was readily accepted because it gave an easy answer to certain problems, for instance, that of original sin. Some Christians were unwilling to accept responsibility for a sin that they had not committed. The spermatists' theory appealed to them because it included the notion of "boxes within boxes": The baby in the sperm has itself testicles inside which are sperm each containing a baby which itself. . . . All generations, past and future, are thus nested in each other, like a series of Russian dolls, from Adam down to the end of the world. We were therefore present in Adam's body when he rebelled against God; it is right that we are punished! Thus, a biological theory develops and is generally accepted only to the extent that it corresponds to the preoccupations of the time. It therefore runs the risk of being deflected from its real goal and of being used as a justification for arguments outside of it; we will see some contemporary examples of this later on.

The "spermatists" were challenged by the "ovists." These claimed that, on the contrary, the baby is prefabricated in the mother's egg and that the sperm merely triggers the developmental process, without contributing anything essential.

The problem with both of these theories is that the offspring receives its biological heritage from only one of the two parents and, therefore, has no reason to resemble the other; this prediction is clearly contradicted by the evidence.

Buffon's fluids theory and Darwin's gemmules theory, which was fairly universally accepted at the end of the nineteenth century, both admit that the two parents participate equally in the production of their child. However, this idea also leads to an insurmountable paradox. It suggests that each of the child's traits represents the average between those of its parents. Within a population taken as a whole, the variability of traits among individuals should therefore diminish with each new generation; rapidly, all individuals should become, if not identical, at least, very similar. Again, this does not correspond to our observations.

This "variance paradox" could not be overcome until the discovery of entirely new concepts. The "model" allowing us to understand the mechanism of sexual reproduction was first proposed by Gregor Mendel, a monk in a monastery in Brno, Czechoslovakia. As early as 1865, he had published a new explanation for the transmission of traits. However, on account of their very novelty, his ideas were ignored. Not until 1900, in a more receptive intellectual environment, could this model which has since become the foundation of the science of genetics finally be understood, accepted, and developed.

MENDEL'S CONTRIBUTION

Mendel's extraordinary genius lies in not having sidestepped the essential difficulty encountered during his hybridization experiments: the disappearance and subsequent reappearance of various traits from one generation to the next.

Let us imagine the following "experiment." We populate an island with women chosen from a population where everyone, for numerous generations, has been of the Rhesus positive blood group, and with men from a population where everyone belongs to the Rhesus negative group. One notices that their children all belong to the positive group; the negative trait has disappeared completely from this first generation. In the next generation, however, this trait reappears and is manifested by about a quarter of the grandchildren.

This remarkable result is observed every time we repeat the experiment, each time with the same frequency of one quarter.

Since it reappears, the Rhesus negative trait must have been present in some of the children of the first generation; but under what form? Why did it not manifest itself?

Mendel, observing generations of peas rather than of people (which made the experiments simpler without in the least altering their basic significance), had noted precisely the same phenomenon as that which has just been described. His ingenious idea was to suggest that each trait under study (in our imaginary example, the Rhesus system; in his own experiments, the green versus yellow color of the cotyledons and the round versus wrinkled surface of the seeds) is governed not by *one* hereditary factor, but by *two* factors, one of which comes from the father, the other from the mother. These two factors function in concert; the trait under observation results from the activity of both; but they remain unchanged throughout the entire life of the individual. They coexist, but they do not modify each other. When an individual procreates, he transmits one of these factors, chosen at random, to the child.

In Mendel's case, this could be no more than a hypothesis or, as we say today, a model. The progress achieved in our knowledge of cells, their nuclei and their chromosomes, has shown that this theory corresponds to reality in every respect. The "factors" mentioned by Mendel are what we now call "genes," and are series of chemical molecules situated at specific locations on the chromosomes. Their mode of action and of transmission from parents to offspring is consistent with Mendel's theory.

Each cell belonging to a hypothetical human individual, X (and his body is made up of hundreds of billions of them), has a nucleus containing 23 pairs of filaments called chromosomes. These 46 filaments represent an exact copy of the 23 chromosomes supplied by the paternal sperm and of the 23 chromosomes supplied by the maternal egg. The various processes necessary for the development and functioning of the organism are defined and regulated by information inscribed in coded form (the famous genetic code) on the chromosomes. Each of X's cells, whether belonging to his liver or to his brain, knows the amazing secret which allows for the construction of X in his entirety, starting from a single cell. Besides being a liver or nerve cell with a set of specific functions, it "knows" that it belongs to X and is recognized as such by its neighboring cells.

The sex cells, however, are exceptions: The sperm made by X (if a man), the eggs (if a woman), contain a series of only 23 chromosomes, one of each pair. They therefore contain only half of the genetic information that X received at conception. The process of generating eggs and sperm is such that this half is drawn equally from material contributed by X's father and X's mother. It is clear that this biological mechanism affects the transmission of traits in a manner that coincides exactly with the Mendelian model.

Such a vision of the hereditary process profoundly changes our spontaneous "commonsense" ideas on the subject, but it is far from easy for this change to become part of our consciousness. This is shown by the contradiction that often exists between the usual connotations of the words that we use to describe heredity and the precise meaning that must now be ascribed to them.

WORDS AND THEIR MEANINGS

Each word has a precise meaning, ascribed specifically to it and to no other. At the same time, it connotes a particular world view, which is revealed partly by its etymology. It is remarkable that the statements we make about procreation often harbor a contradiction between their precise meaning and this world view. For example, the statement "an individual reproduces himself" is doubly contradictory.

The word *individual* suggests *indivisibility.* An individual cannot be reduced to his constituent parts without being destroyed. In other words, he cannot be divided. However, in the course of reproduction, such a division must, of necessity, take place. More precisely, each sperm or each egg receives a copy of half the information that had initially been transmitted to this individual by his parents at conception, and based on which he was gradually constructed.

It is necessary to understand thoroughly that this mechanism is the very opposite to that accepted prior to Mendel, for instance by Darwin. The latter suggested that each parent transmits all his biological information to the child, in accordance with the concept of indivisibility; the two stores of information, one from the father and one from the mother, mix together to form an average, just as white and red liquids mix and become pink. Mendel suggested, on the contrary, that each parent contributes only half of the information which he carries; in the child, these two halves are juxtaposed, without being mixed, to constitute a complete whole. Moreover, this whole, which is really a collection of different pieces of information, is entirely new, differing as much from one parent as from the other.

"Reproduction" does not, therefore, take place. This word implies the making of an image as close as possible to the original. Such is indeed the case with bacteria, which are capable of self-duplication by producing an exact copy of themselves, and with nonsexual species in general. However, the invention of sexuality, that is of a mechanism necessitating the collaboration of two beings for the making of a third, eliminated this capacity for reproduction. A sexual being cannot reproduce itself. Since the child is not a reproduction of anyone, it is a definitively unique creation. This uniqueness is a result of the amazing number of different children that could be produced by any one couple. Let us imagine that, for a given trait, for example, the Rhesus blood group, the father and mother each carry two different genes, *a* and *b;* their children can receive either two *a* genes or two *b* genes, or an *a* gene and a *b* gene. For each trait, three combinations are therefore possible; for two traits together, $3^2 = 9$ combinations; for *n* traits, 3^n combinations. This last number becomes astronomical as soon as *n* is larger than 30 or so. Thus, for a total of 200 traits, the number becomes 3^{200}, which is practically infinite since it

gives rise to a 94-digit number, billions of times greater than the total number of atoms in our universe, including the farthest galaxies.

This possibility for diversity is the specific contribution of sexual reproduction. There may be but a single realized event, but the possibilities are infinitely great.

A History Assignment

Some ideas can best be defined by describing the uses to which they have been put, their social history. In the following passage, notice how Ted Howard and Jeremy Rifkin, without offering a one-sentence definition, clarify the concept of *eugenics* by summarizing its history. Also notice that they offer this historical account from their own strong point of view as critics of those who favor genetic engineering. After reading their account several times, try sketching a summary of their summary. Then write an essay that defines eugenics from the historical point of view of Howard and Rifkin.

As an alternative assignment, after reading the passage, write a speculative essay defining *genetic engineering.* What are the overtones of this phrase? Why do you think that Howard and Rifkin seem eager to connect this term with *eugenics*? Does a dictionary give you any help with either term? Do you think that experimental scientists in the field of genetics use this term to define their work?

Eugenics in America

TED HOWARD AND JEREMY RIFKIN

Eugenics is not a new idea. Writing in *The Republic,* Plato asserted that "the best of both sexes ought to be brought together as often as possible and the worst as seldom as possible and that the former unions ought to be reared and that of the latter abandoned, if the flock is to attain to first-rate excellence."

Caesar was so interested in improving the stock of Rome's best family lines that he offered a thousand sesterces to every "Roman" mother for each child. Augustus later offered two thousand, but to no avail. The birthrate among the rich continued to decline.

The recognized father of modern-day eugenics was Sir Francis Galton. A cousin of Charles Darwin's, Galton was very much influenced by the publication of *Origin of Species.* Galton believed that Darwin's theory of evolution and the survival of the fittest also applied to the human species, so he set out to construct a theory which interpreted human social actions and behavior on the basis of his biological origins. In his book *Hereditary Genius,* Galton laid down much of the theory that was to be later used by so-called Social Darwinists to rationalize the worst abuses of unrestrained capitalism and racism in America. Galton's initial interest in this whole matter of eugenics (a term which he originated) stemmed from his desire to better understand why his family tree was decorated with so

---

TED HOWARD was a minister and writer. Author and activist JEREMY RIFKIN (b. 1945) is president of the Foundation on Economic Trends in Washington, D.C. This passage is from their 1977 book *Who Should Play God?*

many outstanding personages. Galton was a fascinating character, one of those rare breed of English gentlemen who could honestly claim the title of true Renaissance Man. According to his biographers, Galton could read at age two and a half. During his lifetime he contributed to fields ranging from photography to meteorology. He is especially well regarded by Scotland Yard,[1] because he invented the fingerprint as a means of identifying criminals. It's no wonder then that he strongly believed in what are called "natural talents." What's more, according to his peers, he was as well endowed physically as he was mentally. Beatrice Webb, the noted Fabian socialist,[2] described Galton's appearance this way: "That tall figure with the attitude of perfect physical and mental poise, the clean shaven face, the thin compressed mouth with its enigmatic smile, the long upper lip and firm chin and as if presiding over the whole personality of the man the prominent dark eye brows from beneath which gleamed with penetrating humor, contemplative eyes. Fascinating to me was Francis Galton's all-embracing, but apparently impersonal beneficence."

With attributes like those, it's not hard to understand why Galton might come to believe in the superiority of certain biological types.

In *Hereditary Genius* Galton concludes that the modern European (of which he considered himself the best of the lot) possesses much greater natural ability than do those of "lower" races. He then speculates as to the potential of a eugenics program. "There is nothing either in the history of domestic animals or in that of evolution to make us doubt that a race of sane men may be formed, who shall be as much superior mentally and morally to the modern Europeans, as the modern European is to the lowest of the Negro races." Galton sums up his hopes for humankind's future by asserting that just as it is easy "to obtain by careful selection a permanent breed of dogs or horses gifted with peculiar powers . . . so it would be quite practical to produce a highly gifted race of men" by similar means.

One man who read Galton's thesis, and decided it was time to put the theory into practice, was utopian socialist John Humphrey Noyes, the founder of the Oneida Colony in New York State. "Every race horse, every straight backed bull, every premium pig," said Noyes, "tells us what we can do and what we must do for man." In 1869, Noyes had fifty-three women and thirty-eight men sign a pledge to participate in an experiment to breed healthy perfectionists by "matching those most advanced in health and perfection." The women pledged that they would "become martyrs to science," and with that the first American experiments in eugenics began.

From his theory of eugenics, Galton concocted a new view of charity, one that would be later taken up by American eugenics reformers in their campaign to purify the racial stock of the nation. Charity, said Galton, should "help the strong rather than the weak, and the man of tomorrow rather than the man of today; let knowledge and foresight control the blind emotions and impetuous instincts." So convinced was Galton of the wisdom of applying his theory to human beings that he regretted that "there exists a sentiment for the most part quite unreasonable against the gradual extinction of an inferior race."

Just a few short years after Galton constructed his theories, new discoveries in genetics provided just enough meager evidence (later proven erroneous) to construct the thinnest "scientific" rationales for a eugenics movement. And that was all that many people needed to hop on board the eugenics bandwagon in America.

[1]**Scotland Yard:** Headquarters of the London Metropolitan Police.

[2]**Fabian socialist:** A member of the Fabian society of socialists, founded in London in 1883.

First, in 1900, geneticists rediscovered the laws of Gregor Mendel, an Austrian monk who discovered the theory behind transmission and distribution of traits by simple genes in certain plants. Applying Mendel's laws, geneticists "could make predictions about the number and type of offspring to be expected from different types of matings." Mendel's laws were quickly taken up in plant and animal breeding, and geneticists came to believe that they could be soundly applied to humans as well.

Second, geneticists became convinced that most if not all traits are determined by single genes acting independently. (Like Mendel's law, this was later proven incorrect as it applied to humans.) This gave scientists confidence in their ability to breed better human stock.

Finally, the distinguished German scientist August Weisman "produced experimental evidence that characteristics acquired by an organism from environmental pressures could not be inherited by its descendants." This was used by eugenicists as proof that environmental reforms would have absolutely no effect on improving the human condition. In the question of better environment versus heredity, the hereditarians now claimed the scientific ammunition they needed to promote a full-scale eugenics effort for the country. All that was necessary to ensure a ready and accepting audience was the enthusiastic support of major American scientists. The nation was not to be disappointed.

Between 1900 and 1915, leading American geneticists were largely responsible for spearheading the early eugenics movement. According to Kenneth Ludmerer in his seminal work, *Genetics and American Society,* nearly half the geneticists in the country became involved in the eugenics movement in one way or another. The reason, which is more than apparent in their own speeches and writings, was their "alarm by what they considered to be a decline in the heredity quality of the American people." Scientists became active in leadership roles in the eugenics cause in the hope "that they could help reverse the trend." With almost religious vengeance, these scientists jumped right up onto the center stage of American politics and demonstrated for all that their crusading fervor was at least on a par with their scientific accomplishments.

Without so much as flinching a muscle, Michael F. Guyer of the University of Wisconsin boldly proclaimed that "all available data indicate that the fate of our civilization hangs on the issue." The famed geneticist Edward G. Conklin dispassionately observed "that although our human stock includes some of the most intelligent, moral, and progressive people in the world, it includes a disproportionately large number of the worst human types."

Not to be outdone, Professor H. S. Jenings of Johns Hopkins informed the American public that:

> The troubles of the world and the remedy of these troubles lie fundamentally in the diverse constitutions of human beings. Laws, customs, education, material surroundings are the creations of men and reflect their fundamental nature. To attempt to correct these things is merely to treat specific symptoms. To go to the root of the troubles, a better breed of men must be produced, one that shall not contain the inferior types. When a better breed has taken over the business of the world, laws, customs, education, material conditions will take care of themselves.

In 1906 the American Breeders Association set up the first functioning Committee on Eugenics. Its stated purpose was to investigate and report on heredity in the human race and to emphasize the value of superior blood and the menace to society of inferior blood.

The Committee's membership included such famous people as Luther Burbank, David Starr Jordan, and Charles Davenport.[3]

Four years later, Davenport convinced Mrs. E. H. Harriman (wife of the famous industrialist) to purchase a tract of land at Cold Spring Harbor, New York, where he established the Eugenics Record Office. Davenport, who was director, and Harry H. Laughlin, the superintendent, were soon to become the dominant voices in the eugenics drive during this period. By the way, according to Davenport, Mrs. Harriman's enthusiasm for the program was due to "the fact that she was brought up among well-bred race horses [which] helped her to appreciate the importance of a project to study heredity and good breeding in Man."

After 1910 eugenics societies sprang up in cities all over the country. Among the most influential were the Galton Society of New York and the Eugenic Education Societies of Chicago, St. Louis, Madison, Minnesota, Utah, San Francisco, and Battle Creek, Michigan. In 1913 the Eugenics Association began, and in 1922 the Eugenics Committee of the United States (later the American Eugenics Society) was formed.

By World War I eugenics was a favorite topic not only in the schools and on political forums, but at women's clubs, church meetings, professional gatherings, and in popular magazines of the day.

The urgency of eugenicists' appeals often bordered on near hysteria, as when the president of the University of Arizona warned that it is "an optimist indeed who can see in our trend toward race degeneracy . . . anything other than a plight in which the race must find its final destiny in trained imbecility."

Some even began to call for a basic change in our form of government to accommodate a eugenics ideology. One was William McDougall, chairman of the psychology department of Harvard University. McDougall so feared that democracy would eventually result in the "lower breeds" outnumbering the "best stock" and overtaking the machinery of the state that he openly advocated a caste system for America, based on biological differences, in which political rights would depend on one's caste.

Academics were so convinced of the wisdom and virtue of applied eugenics that many of them threw all scholarly caution to the wind. "We know enough about eugenics," said Charles R. Van Hise, president of the University of Wisconsin, "so that if the knowledge were applied, the defective classes would disappear within a generation."

By 1915, most of the leading educators already agreed with Irving Fisher, the well-known Yale economist, that "eugenics is incomparably the greatest concern of the human race." It's not surprising, then, that by 1928 over three fourths of all the colleges and universities in America were teaching eugenics courses. Their teachers were men like Earnest A. Hooton of Harvard, who preached that "crime is the resultant of the impact of environment upon low grade human organisms." "The solution to the crime problem," he told Harvard undergraduates, is the "extirpation of the physically, mentally, and morally unfit or (if that seems too harsh) their complete segregation in a socially aseptic environment."

The eugenics creed also found willing adherents within the media. The *New York Times* helped fan the eugenics hysteria with statements like "labor disturbances are brought about by foreigners" and "demonstrations are always mobs composed of for-

[3]**Luther Burbank . . . Davenport:** American turn-of-the-century scientists. Burbank (1849–1926) was a horticulturalist; Jordan (1851–1931), a biologist; and Davenport (1866–1944), a zoologist [Eds.].

eign scum, beer smelling Germans, ignorant Bohemians, uncouth Poles, and wild-eyed Russians."

It might interest today's subscribers to the prestigious left-liberal magazines the *Nation* and *The New Republic* that the founders of both publications were crusaders for eugenics reform. Edwin Laurence Godkin, founder of the *Nation,* believed that only those of superior biological stock should run the affairs of the country, and Herbert David Croly of *The New Republic* was convinced that blacks "were a race possessed of moral and intellectual qualities inferior to those of the white man."

Imagine, if you will, a president of the U.S. writing in *Good Housekeeping* (a favorite forum of presidents) that "there are racial considerations too grave to be brushed aside for any sentimental reasons." According to President Coolidge, biological laws tell us that certain divergent people will not mix or blend. Coolidge concludes that the Nordics propagate themselves successfully, "while with other races, the outcome shows deterioration on both sides."

Even some of America's great heroes succumbed to the eugenics fever. Alexander Graham Bell was one of them. Speaking before the American Breeders Association in Washington in 1908, Bell remarked: "We have learned to apply the laws of heredity so as to modify and improve our breeds of domestic animals. Can the knowledge and experience so gained be available to man, so as to enable him to improve the species to which he himself belongs?" Bell believed that "students of genetics possess the knowledge . . . to improve the race" and that education of the public was necessary to gain acceptance for eugenics policies.

Many modern-day feminists will be chagrined to learn that Margaret Sanger, a leader in the fight for birth-control programs, was a true believer in the biological superiority and inferiority of different groups. In some of the toughest-sounding words to ever come out of the eugenics movement, Sanger remarked that "it is a curious but neglected fact that the very types which in all kindness should be obliterated from the human stock, have been permitted to reproduce themselves and to perpetuate their group, succored by the policy of indiscriminate charity of warm hearts uncontrolled by cool heads." Sanger had her own solution to the problem of human biological contamination of society and better breeding: "There is only one reply to a request for a higher birth rate among the intelligent and that is to ask the government to first take the burden of the insane and feebleminded from your back. . . . Sterilization," said Sanger, "is the solution."

The eugenics ideology became so pervasive between 1900 and 1930 that some historians even attempted to rewrite world history from a eugenics perspective. Thus, David Starr Jordan, president of Stanford University, claimed that Rome's decline resulted from its frequent military conquests, in which its best blood was sent out to battle and scattered throughout the empire. This left Rome to the stable boys, slaves, and camp followers, whose poor biological stock multiplied and populated the city with an inferior genetic species. Ironically, this kind of eugenics analysis of history led many like Jordan to become pacifists, on the grounds that war would take away and destroy the best blood of the nation.

It was this obsessive concern with the blood of the nation that so animated the eugenicists. Jordan best summed up the attitude of the supporters of eugenics when he declared that "the blood of the nation determines its history . . . the history of a nation determines its blood." To Jordan and his cohorts, "the survival of the fittest in the struggle for existence is the primal cause of race progress and race changes." Just a few years later, a house painter from Munich was to echo that exact same sentiment from his jail cell in Germany as he put the final touches on a work which he entitled *Mein Kampf.*

Even the success of the fledgling Boy Scout movement in America was attributable to some degree to the interest in eugenics. As a matter of fact, David Starr Jordan served as the vice-president of the Boy Scouts of America in those early days. Jordan and his colleagues believed that the Scout program could help rear the "eugenic new man."

One of the most bizarre twists in the eugenics movement was Fitter Family Contests, run by the American Eugenics Society. Blue ribbons were presented at county and state fairs all over the Midwest to those families that could produce the best family pedigrees. Families were judged on their physical and mental qualities, right alongside pigs and cows.

The acceptance of eugenics by much of the general public as a scientifically sound theory was due in large part to the early and enthusiastic support of eugenics by some of America's most prominent scientists. The scientists legitimized the theory of eugenics in the public mind, although in the end they largely refused to accept any responsibility for the consequences that flowed from its application. The story of its ruthless application represents one of the darkest pages in American history.

An Ecology Assignment

The following passage by Alston Chase is part of an article that appeared in *The Atlantic* in July 1987. After thinking about the article, write an essay that discusses how environmental issues become matters of political definition. Among the concepts you might consider are *National Park, National Park Service, protection, management, restoration,* and *ecosystem.* In what ways might the definitions of such terms vary? Who tries to do the defining? What determines which definitions prevail?

Here are two suggestions. The terms *ecology* and *restoration ecology* are central to Chase's discussion, so before you start, be sure you have a sense of the meaning of these terms. And when you reach the bottom of the sixth paragraph, stop and see if you can articulate the distinction between *preservation* and *restoration.* Ask yourself why Chase favors the one over the other.

How to Save Our National Parks

ALSTON CHASE

What our national parks need, more than protection, is restoration. If the parks are to be preserved, they must first be restored to a semblance of ecological balance. Restoration of the land, moreover, is not a utopian ideal but a developing science. The task of restoration ecology is like searching for and then assembling parts of a puzzle to make a

---

ALSTON CHASE (b. 1935) is a former contributing editor to *Traveler* magazine and to *Outside* magazine and has a nationally syndicated column on environmental issues. An adjunct professor of philosophy at Montana State University, Chase is the author of *Playing God in Yellowstone* (1986) and *In a Dark Wood: The Fight over Forests and the New Tyranny of Ecology* (1995). "How to Save Our National Parks" is part of an article that appeared in *The Atlantic in* 1987.

picture. Ecologists find isolated communities of native genetic types and carefully transplant representative individuals of these species to preserves that are reconstructed to replicate their original habitat.

Many promising examples of ecological restoration are visible today. Throughout the Midwest and the West wetlands and grasslands prairies have been nursed back to life. The University of Wisconsin Arboretum, for example, was founded in 1934 for this specific purpose. "Our idea," wrote its first director, Aldo Leopold, "is to reconstruct . . . a sample of original Wisconsin — a sample of what Dane County looked like when our ancestors arrived here during the 1840s." Today the arboretum has been reasonably successful in restoring about a third of its 1,280 acres of wetlands, forest, and prairie.

Reclamation, however, can never be complete. We cannot suppose that even after a relatively successful restoration parks could be left alone. We cannot bring extinct species back to life, nor can we reproduce all the conditions that prevailed before the coming of the white man. Animals that evolved in ecosystems the size of half a continent cannot be expected to survive unaided in the relatively tiny areas we call national parks, any more than Indians can be expected to live as hunter-gatherers on the postage-stamp-sized reservations to which they are now consigned.

The habitat of scavengers like condors and grizzly bears, for example, cannot be completely reclaimed. In pre-Columbian times these species depended heavily on natural deaths in abundant and widespread animal species such as bison and spawning salmon, and also on carrion left by Indians and predators. Yet the animal world will never be as fecund or widely dispersed as it once was, nor will Indians and predators be playing their ecological role to the extent they once did. So if we wish to preserve scavengers, we may have to find substitutes for the food sources on which they once depended.

Restoration therefore leads to a kind of management we might call sustenance ecology. In national parks this process would go forward in four steps. First would come the collection of what scientists call baseline data — information gathered by historians, anthropologists, archaeologists, and biologists which would tell us what the parks were like in pre-Columbian times. Second would be an inventory of changes in the park's wildlife population, noting what species had been lost and what exotic species had been introduced. Third would be the removal of exotic species and the reintroduction of native plants and animals now missing. And fourth, ecologists would make and implement strategies to compensate for conditions that prevailed in pre-Columbian times but cannot be recovered. Such strategies might include, for example, providing carrion for scavengers, culling game herds, and burning forests and grasslands to replace lost Indian hunting and fire practices.

Protectionism in its ordinary form neither allows for any human use of wilderness nor offers any plan for reversing the changes in the wilderness that our civilization has already introduced. Sustenance ecology does both. It is a philosophy specifically for parks, dedicated to re-establishing and sustaining ecological equilibrium in lands that receive a reasonable amount of public use.

Restoring and sustaining our national parks is not a new idea. As early as the 1930s thoughtful wildlife ecologists and rangers were aware of the limitations of protectionism. Yet the policies of protection were still prevailing when, in 1962, President John F. Kennedy's Secretary of the Interior, Stewart Udall, created a committee known as the Advisory Board on Wildlife Management and directed the committee to address wildlife problems then afflicting the national park system. The conclusions of this committee — which was chaired by A. Starker Leopold, a professor of zoology at the University of California, and the son of Aldo — were far-reaching, containing both the outline of a philosophy of wildlife management and a statement of purpose for national-parks preservation.

"As a primary goal [of park management]," the committee stated, "we would recommend that the biotic associations within each park be maintained, or where necessary recreated, as nearly as possible in the condition that prevailed when the area was first visited by the white man. A national park should represent a vignette of primitive America."

Yet most of the parks, the Leopold committee noted, had changed dramatically since the white man first came on the scene.

> Many of our national parks — in fact most of them — went through periods of indiscriminate logging, burning, livestock grazing, hunting, and predator control. Then they entered the park system and shifted abruptly to a regime of equally unnatural protection from lightning fires, from insect outbreaks, absence of natural controls of ungulates, and in some areas elimination of normal fluctuations in water levels. Exotic vertebrates, insects, plants, and plant diseases have inadvertently been introduced. And of course lastly there is the factor of human use — of roads and trampling and camp grounds and pack stock. The resultant biotic associations in many of our parks are artifacts, pure and simple. They represent a complex ecologic history but they do not necessarily represent primitive America.
>
> Restoring the primitive scene is not done easily nor can it be done completely. . . . Yet if the goal cannot be fully achieved it can be approached. A reasonable illusion of primitive America could be recreated, using the utmost in skill, judgment, and ecologic sensitivity. This, in our opinion, should be the objective of every national park and monument.

The Leopold report was made official Park Service policy by the Department of the Interior in 1963. In 1968 the Park Service published policies for management of natural areas (in a publication known as the Green Book) that it claimed incorporated the recommendations of the Leopold report. These policies, in slightly revised form, are still in force.

Yet, surprisingly, little restoration was attempted following publication of the Green Book. Few baseline studies were ever undertaken; almost no historical, archaeological, or anthropological research was done in parks classified as natural zones; native-species restoration — of wolves, in particular — was stalled, and proliferating exotic species, rather than being removed, were for many years ignored.

In truth, the Park Service was unable to implement the Leopold report. When Udall accepted the committee's recommendations, the National Park Service research program was almost nonexistent. A study of Park Service science done that year by the National Academy of Sciences reported that "for the year 1962 the research staff (including the Chief Naturalist and field men in natural history) was limited to 10 people and . . . the Service budget for natural history research was $28,000 — about the cost of one campground comfort station."

Unfortunately, attempts to strengthen Park Service resource management and research met with considerable resistance from the ranger corps, which saw development of a professional cadre of scientists and resource managers as a threat to its control of the Service. The only way reformers could increase the science budget was to put research and resource management under the supervision of the rangers, which is what they did.

Government research in the national parks, the Service decided, would be "mission-oriented." That was interpreted to mean that the role of scientists was to provide "service to the superintendents." Scientists in the major national parks reported to the superintendents, were graded by the superintendents, could do only research approved by the superintendents, and had every incentive to publish only those findings that pleased the superintendents. Similarly, resource managers reported to the chief rangers, whose primary function was visitor protection.

Funding for research by university scientists was increased substantially, but such work remained under the control of the rangers. Funds were awarded by contract between the National Park Service or its contracting agencies and the individual researcher or his institution. Decisions regarding who was to receive a contract were either delegated to the field level — that is, to the superintendent or his supervisor of research — or made by university-based "cooperative park-study units," on which park administrators or district headquarters often had considerable influence.

Further, each of the Park Service regional headquarters (their number has grown from six in 1968 to ten today) was given control of research and resource management in its region. The major parks were to a large degree autonomous. In these ways superintendents and regional directors acquired nearly total control over scientific activity. Being untrained in ecology, they had little appreciation for the kind of baseline research that was needed to accomplish restoration.

Through the delegation of such powers to the regions and superintendents, the Service was decentralized, preventing any coordinated scientific undertaking. Park studies tended to be short-term and politically directed. Both the flow of information and the chain of accountability between the parks and Washington were broken. Results of research that might reflect badly on a park administration could be — and often were — prevented by the superintendent from leaving the park.

The balkanization of the Park Service was further encouraged by the national park system reorganization of 1964, which divided the parks into three categories: natural, historical, and recreational. The emphasis built into this functional separation effectively discouraged the kind of sustained interdisciplinary research that true restoration ecology required.

While mission-oriented biological research continued in natural zones like Yellowstone, historical research — which the Leopold report had said was "the first step" in restoration — was almost never undertaken.

Through this evolution the Park Service, while spending more and more money on research, was making little of the effort necessary to save the park system. To make matters worse, the retrograde nature of this trend was obscured by describing park policy in a new and attractive way: its goal, the Park Service decided, should be to "perpetuate the natural ecosystems."

Ecosystems management was supposedly the translation into policy of the Leopold report. Yet the committee explicitly declared that parks are *not* ecosystems: "Few of the world's parks," the report stated, quoting a 1962 report from the First World Conference on National Parks, "are large enough to be in fact self-regulatory ecological units." Nevertheless, by 1968 the Park Service was calling our parks "natural, comparatively self-contained ecosystems." What the Leopold report in 1963 regarded as a challenge — the creation of vignettes of primitive America — the Park Service in 1968 took as a given, though it had done no restoration work at all. By defining intact ecosystems into existence, the Park Service created a rationale for continuing its policy of protection. If parks were intact ecosystems, then restoration was unnecessary. Nature could be left to take its course. Nor was scientific research required. Parks could be run by people trained as policemen. That this is a kind of voodoo ecology is not lost on professional biologists. Bruce A. Wilcox, the director of the Center of Conservation Biology, at Stanford University, explained last year, "A laissez-faire approach to management is simply not tenable any longer."

READINGS: RECONSIDERING INTELLIGENCE

The readings in this section offer opportunities to think further about defining by working once again with the topic that is woven throughout this chapter. If you would like to look back at the earlier readings about intelligence, see the excerpt from *Frames of Mind* by Howard Gardner (Opening Problem, p. 10), the excerpt from *Emotional Intelligence* by Daniel Goleman (A Professional Application, p. 20), the definition of intelligence in the Word History Assignment (p. 26), and the Psychology Assignment (p. 38).

The following readings prompt us to think critically about what we regard as intelligence and why. Even in combination, however, these readings are not intended to address more than a few strands of this complex topic. In order to contribute to — and to challenge — your work with defining, we have chosen a range of pieces: an analysis of a mechanic doing his work, a description of a classroom, theoretical essays about the nature of intelligence. These readings, either directly or implicitly, offer a number of ways to think about intelligence, some of which may be familiar to you, while others may push you to think of — and define — intelligence in new ways.

Sociologist Douglas Harper, in an excerpt from his book *Working Knowledge,* introduces us to a mechanic whose experience with the properties of metals provides a basis for subtle on-the-job judgments. In her profile of biologists Mimi Koehl and Sharon Emerson, Deborah Franklin challenges stereotypes about scientific research by connecting Koehl and Emerson's research accomplishments as much with play and improvisation as with experimentation and data gathering. In an excerpt from *Possible Lives* by Mike Rose, high school teachers Ed Murphy and Larry Stone preside over a video production class in which students distinguish themselves as editors and producers. Next, in the article "Social Organization of Distributed Cognition," Edwin Hutchins makes the argument that groups may develop a form of collective intelligence that differs significantly from the intelligence of individuals. Finally, in an argument that challenges some of our basic presumptions about human minds and "artificial intelligence," John Haugeland redefines the question of whether computers can be designed to think: "The real issue is whether . . . we are computers ourselves."

At the end of each reading, you will find Considerations questions intended to help you think about the reading mostly on its own terms but also in relation to the defining strategies stressed in this chapter. At the end of the section, you will also find suggestions for writing about these readings in relation to one another and for pursuing the topic of intelligence through research.

Willie, the subject of the following excerpt, is a mechanic who lives in rural northern New York. In Working Knowledge, *sociologist Douglas Harper combines observation with extensive interviews with Willie to analyze the kinds of knowledge and skills involved in the work Willie does. In this excerpt, Harper discusses that aspect of Willie's "working knowledge" that deals with his understanding of the properties of materials. By the way, notice how Willie uses definitions and examples to describe the work he does.*

From *Working Knowledge: Skill and Community in a Small Shop*

DOUGLAS HARPER

The basis of Willie's working knowledge is his deep understanding of many materials. It is knowing how metal, wood, plastic, or even paper and cardboard respond to attempts to alter their shape, density, or pliability. The knowledge is so detailed it leads to engineering: forming materials into machines or correcting design problems in the process of repair. Fixing and making are often very close together on the continuum of Willie's working knowledge, both grounded in a basic knowledge of the materials.

Willie learned about metal in his father's blacksmith shop. At the forge a person comes to understand metal in a fine and detailed way, through heavy handwork, altering metal with heat and then reforming it with the hammer and the cold of water or ice. Willie explains:

> "In a manner of speaking the blacksmith was a machinist. Everything was molded and drilled. When it came to farm machinery, when you had a broken part — usually it was steel — very little cast [iron] used at that time — you'd use what they call a 'blacksmith's weld' to weld them back. You'd get your metals to a certain temperature and then put the two pieces together and hammer them. You'd hammer them right back into one piece. If you wanted to weld two pieces together, you would heat one piece and work it out longer. You can stretch metal by working it. And do the same for the other piece, but do it the opposite way. You make each piece so it overlaps the other one. Then they had a — some of them used it and some of them didn't — they had a flux[1] that they dipped

[1]**flux:** In soldering, a substance used to help metals fuse together [Eds.].

DOUGLAS HARPER (b. 1948) is professor of sociology at Duquesne University in Pittsburgh and the founding editor of *Visual Sociology.* He is the author of *Good Company* (1982) and *Working Knowledge: Skill and Community in a Small Shop* (1987), from which this excerpt is taken. His current research is on the culture of the dairy farmer and the sociology of jazz.

> them into. They'd put them in the forge and get them to almost melting hot, they'd dip it in the flux, slap it together and start hammering. A forge could be as big as this table-top — it would have a three-, four-foot top. But you had a small pot in the center where it heated. Take the two pieces and band them together when they're almost melting hot. You judge that by color. You had to know your temperatures and you had to know your metals to do a blacksmith's weld. You've got to know the same things for gas welding — which metals will weld together and which ones won't. Each type of metal has its own heat range. Well, you had to do the same thing with your forge — you had to use a different heat range for different metals. You altered the amount of time you left it in the forge. If you get to white hot — the next step is melting. If you go too far you start all over again! You had to have an eye for it."

Tempering metal, adjusting its hardness or pliability with heat and cold, was a procedure similar to welding. Like welding, it depended on the eye as well as the hand. Willie explains:

> "When you were tempering something you get it to what they call a cherry red. One piece of steel you might need to get to a cherry red, maybe another one a little redder. You cool it in certain ways as you go along. It draws the temper into the steel. Makes it harder. But if you cool it too quickly it gets tempered so hard it's just like glass — you can break it.
>
> They have what they call flame temper, an oil temper, or a water temper. Like if you sharpen a pick — you hammer the point out on a pick and then you want to temper it so it won't burr over when you hit a stone — that's a cherry temper. But if you temper it *too* hard and you hit a stone, it'll pop the end right off. You dip it in the water slow. And it'll turn a bluish color as the temper works out into it. And your coal temper — a temper out of a coal forge — is a lot better than your gas temper. See, they use gas forges now. Or I can temper with a torch, but you've got to be very careful with it. When you're using gas you're only heating one side at a time. When you're using coal you're poking the metal right into the hot ashes. It heats it more evenly, all the way through and around. Where with your gas you don't get that. And you only heat one side with the torch, and it's not as good."

Learning about metal through the blacksmith's techniques became, for the first generation of welders, the basis for gas welding. These welders, like Willie, could understand welding because they understood metal in a deeper and more fundamental way than welders who learn first with the torch. The progress at the forge was slow, the changes in the metal relatively gradual, all controlled by hand. The blacksmith's weld is an extension of forming, bending, and adapting metal. Gas welding, which evolved from the blacksmith's techniques, is a more efficient method of cutting and binding metal that, for basic work, requires less knowledge. The gas welder is a tool that can change metal relatively easily and very quickly. The operator of a gas welder, to do crude work, need know only the basics of how to use the tool. On the other hand, a modern welder who learned his or her trade as a blacksmith summons a detailed and many-sided knowledge that refines the use of the technique.

Traditional bodywork — straightening bent metal on automobiles, for example, depended upon techniques similar to those of the blacksmith. The traditional "body man" reformed metal rather than filling in dents with body fill, an epoxy compound that is applied to metal and then sanded to shape. Filling in dents with epoxy is relatively simple, but if the area being filled is large the repair may not be permanent. Traditional body men like Willie use epoxy compound for final, surface corrections after the large bends and dents in the metal have been reformed. Willie explains the connection between the two:

> "The things I learned working with my dad in the blacksmith's shop, about how metal acts when it's heated up and cooled off — that's part of body and fender work. You can move metal any way you want to with bodywork. You can use heat to shrink metal, or you can use heat to expand metal. Ice, water . . . you've seen me use ice. I don't think you've seen me use heat. I've got a hammer up there they call a 'shrinking hammer.' It's knurled.[2] One end of it is square and it's full of knurls. And it makes those knurls right into the metal. The other end is round with the same type of knurls in it. I don't use it very often. It actually draws the metal together. . . . They don't do that kind of bodywork any more — they use body fill."

The traditional method of bodywork involved not only different hand techniques, but a view of the mass of metal as an interconnected, interdependent entity:

> "[To work metal this way] you do one thing at a time, but you're always thinking of the project as a whole and how it's being affected by what you're doing. You might have a dent on the top of the fender, but you don't work on it there — you work on it on the bottom, to draw it out. Most people don't see that you're working on it if you're not pounding right on it where you can see the dent. You never start bringing out the big bump first. You bring it out the way it went in. And it will come out 100 percent better. If you start pushing the big bump out first — on a fender, or a quarter panel, or something like that — you'll be leaving all this little crinkly stuff around that will be harder to work out later on. Where if you start working it out the way it came in it goes better."

These skills make the work of fixing and fashioning part of the same basic technique:

> "A blacksmith could take a sheet of metal and do anything with it he wants to," Willie says. "If he's a *blacksmith.* We used to take a sheet of metal and make fenders — during World War II, when you couldn't get parts. We made Cadillac fenders, Chevrolet fenders; front ones, back ones — it didn't matter. We'd just take a sheet of metal; mold it. Heat and the hammer. All you had for a mold was the look of the one fender that was sitting there. You shaped it to that."

Material is pushed and bent, heated and cooled, pounded and twisted. Knowledge of the materials allows Willie to redefine the fixability of objects. It also lets him adopt the perspective of the engineer who designed the machine, to redesign as a part of repair.

[2]**knurled:** Having a series of small beads or ridges, as along the edge of a coin [Eds.].

Considerations

1. Select several of Willie's examples of working with materials and try to specify the thinking processes involved in each example.
2. See whether you can think of an example from your own life — or from someone you know — of knowledge of the properties of materials. Describe these properties precisely, and, as best as you can, explain the intellectual processes involved in working with them.

3. Willie offers definitions (for example, of *temper* and *cherry temper*) in the course of describing the work he does. Why is it so important, in the context of Willie's work, to have a clear understanding of such terms? What do these terms and definitions have in common?

4. Using Willie as an example, or any other example from your own experience, speculate as to how knowledge becomes *working* knowledge, that is, knowledge that becomes a part of craft or performance. (If you have read, or plan to read, the next selection, "The Shape of Life," you may also want to speculate on how working knowledge develops in those doing research in the sciences and other fields.)

Mimi Koehl and Sharon Emerson are biologists interested in biomechanics and evolution, that is, in the application of the principles of mechanics to the structure of living organisms — and the adaptive function these structures might serve. In the following passage, science writer Deborah Franklin describes some of the experiments Koehl and Emerson conduct and elaborates the questions that drive those experiments.

The Shape of Life

DEBORAH FRANKLIN

One October day three years ago, in California's Berkeley hills, Mimi Koehl walked to the edge of her redwood deck and hurled pink plastic frogs into the clear autumn sky. Seventeen feet below, evolutionary biologist Sharon Emerson stood squinting in the afternoon sun, carefully noting each frog's trajectory.

"Pitch," Emerson yelled when a frog tumbled head over heels; "roll," when it tumbled arm over outstretched arm.

"The neighbors thought we were crazy," Koehl remembers. "But that happened to be the perfect place to get the information we needed."

That information was key to understanding how flying frogs really fly. And what Koehl and Emerson discovered on that day enabled them to start rewriting the book on amphibian aerodynamics.

At forty-three, Koehl is a rising star in the field of comparative biomechanics — this past year she received what's commonly known as a MacArthur genius award — and she makes her living asking some of biology's biggest questions: How do an organism's size

---

DEBORAH FRANKLIN (b. 1957) is a senior staff writer for *Health Magazine.* She has contributed articles to numerous magazines and newspapers, including *Science 86, Science News,* the *New York Times,* and the *Washington Post.* The passage reprinted here is from her article "The Shape of Life," which appeared in *Discover* magazine in December 1991.

and shape affect how it lives and moves? How do the laws of physics influence whether a creature eats or is eaten? Her reputation rides on her innovative ways of getting answers, ways that often manage to combine serious science with great, goofy fun. When live organisms don't cooperate — either because they are too small or too fast to be easily studied or, more problematically, because they're extinct — Koehl builds models of them, using a treasury of unlikely materials: carpet scraps, dental plastic, even raspberry Jell-O. Mundane they may be, but her menagerie of models has led to a wealth of insights into how frogs came to fly and why insects first developed wings — the sorts of questions that have long charmed storytellers and bedeviled biologists.

Perhaps because she was born to an artist mother and a physicist father, Koehl has always seen science and art as two sides of her quest. "What I'm really interested in is natural form," she says. . . . "You can look at natural form and express it through art, or you can try to understand how it works through science. To me the science has always been more satisfying, because I'm curious about how things work." And she found bioengineering more satisfying than straight biology because it adds an extra measure of precision to the answers. "Instead of saying something fuzzy, like 'this is stronger than that,' you can actually get numbers."

The desire to get beyond fuzziness is what led her to measure the trajectories of frogs flying off her deck in Berkeley. This project got its start a year earlier and thousands of miles away, in the forests of the Southeast Asian island of Borneo. There Emerson, who has joint appointments at the University of Utah and the Field Museum of Natural History in Chicago, had been doing fieldwork on the evolutionary origins of "flight" among frogs that leap forty feet from tree to tree as they work their way from the jungle canopy down to the ground. She had spent weeks watching and analyzing the frogs' behavior, but her research had hit a snag.

"You can answer some interesting questions from the field," Emerson says. "For example: Why do they fly? To get to the ground without being eaten by snakes and other predators that hang out on the tree trunks. And why do they need to get to the ground? To breed. There aren't enough large, long-lasting puddles in the canopies to sustain tadpoles." But watching the animals couldn't provide answers to the "how" questions that Emerson needed to ask: How do the frogs do what they do in the air, and how did they get that ability?

Flying frogs are a specialized subset that evolved from a more general group of tree-dwelling frogs. Two major developments have gone into making the fliers different from their nonflying brethren: The fliers have an array of unusual features — enlarged hands and feet, full webbing on their fingers and toes, and rubbery skin flaps sticking out from their upper arms and thighs. And they strike distinctive poses when leaping. Instead of sticking their legs straight out as most frogs do to jump long distances, the fliers fling themselves through the air in a Charleston-like[1] posture, arms and legs akimbo.

Textbooks had it that funny poses developed first because they enabled the frogs to fly farther and the specialized physical features evolved later to enhance this effect. The idea is part of a more general notion that changes in behavior are followed by changes

[1]**Charleston:** A dance, popular in the 1920s, in which dancers bend their arms and legs and make twisting, pivoting steps [Eds.].

in anatomy that go in the same evolutionary direction. But nobody had ever tested the theory on these frogs and Emerson wasn't seeing anything that either proved or disproved it. So on her return to the United States she sought out Koehl.

"I knew little about frogs," Koehl says, "but we spent a lot of time teaching each other. I'd say, 'Okay, tell me what they look like when they jump. Do they bank in the wind?' Then she'd tell me about the animals' behavior and natural history, and I'd try to figure out what we needed to do to mimic the forces that affect them."

Catching Koehl's experimental spirit, Emerson asked her dentist to make the limbs and torsos of the model frogs out of a plastic gel usually used for making molds of gums for denture fittings. This time the gel was poured into molds taken from real frogs brought back from Borneo. Koehl and Emerson then stuck stiff wires through the plastic arms and legs so the models could easily be posed in flier or nonflier postures. To make two interchangeable sets of hands and feet — some with the minimal webbing of nonfliers, the others fully webbed — the researchers strung thread over five wire toes, then dipped each fake foot in a gel commonly sold in hobby shops for making plastic flowers. The models looked almost as much like flying dentures as flying frogs. But their aerodynamics were very close to the real thing.

Koehl and Emerson next needed a way to simulate a frog's leap from a tree. What they did, in essence, was turn the tree on its side. They attached a foot-long metal rod to the back of each fake frog and hung it in front of an eight-foot-long wind tunnel, a large cardboard tube with a fan on one end. The air blowing past a stationary frog was the lab equivalent of the frog moving through the jungle air.

Then Koehl set about measuring the two forces that largely determine a leaping frog's travel ability. The first is lift, or the upward thrust of the air against the frog's outstretched body, which increases forward flight distance. The second force is drag, which pushes back against the frog's forward-facing surfaces and thus limits its forward motion. The greater the ratio of lift to drag, the farther a frog goes.

In their experimental world Koehl and Emerson were able to separate and measure the lift and drag experienced by each frog body type using electrical monitors that transmitted a different strength signal depending on how the frog was deflected by the wind. Koehl was able to plug this information into a series of equations that described not only flying distance but other aspects of aerial behavior that Emerson had observed in the jungle, such as turning ability and overall time in the air.

Then Koehl and Emerson systematically interchanged the various body parts, giving models with the pose of a nonflying frog the webbed feet of a flier, for example, or posing a flier in the legs-outstretched posture of a nonflier. By running each variously cobbled model through the same wind-tunnel simulations, the researchers were able to see how each physical or behavioral adaptation helped or hindered frog flight.

Much to their surprise, the two researchers found that bent-legged flying posture and special anatomy, taken individually, not only failed to improve flying distance but actually made it worse. Putting the two together made up some of the lost ground, but not all of it. For long-distance leaps a frog was still better off with straight legs and unwebbed toes. Contrary to the textbook supposition, there was no evidence that the physical changes evolved because they improved the flight characteristics of the flying posture, since the posture didn't help the frogs at all. What the frogs did gain from these features, Koehl and Emerson found, was the ability to turn sharply. Bending the legs caused a slight improvement in a standard frog's turning ability. Fully webbed feet on a straight-legged frog, however, caused a greater improvement. Combined, the two features let frogs make the sharpest turns of all.

The combined changes also made the frogs much better at parachuting. Other experiments done outside the wind tunnel — the tests done off Koehl's deck, in fact — indicated that webbing slowed frogs' descent considerably, even if their legs stayed straight. Bent legs alone made the frogs drop faster. But bent legs did add one important element to web-footed parachuting: they kept the frog from landing upside down.

In short, flying frogs aren't built for flying at all. They're built for falling. "Flying frogs act quite a bit like parachutists," Koehl says. "They're lousy gliders, but they're good at steering." And that makes a lot of sense, she points out, if you consider where the frogs live. They make their homes in multilevel forests, not open plains, and being able to maneuver around branches and land softly is probably more important to their survival than being able to glide long distances.

Considerations

1. What has been the traditional explanation for why flying frogs are structured as they are and why they function as they do in the air? What have Koehl and Emerson's experiments led the two biologists to understand?
2. The author says that Mimi Koehl "has always seen science and art as two sides of her quest." List some of the ways that the work Koehl and Emerson do involves the kind of intelligence we'd usually call scientific, and list the ways that work involves intelligence we'd typically call artistic. As you make your lists, do you see any problems with this way of categorizing intelligence, or does it seem to hold true?
3. Speculate as to where the "intelligence" of Koehl and Emerson's work is to be found: In their collaboration? In their modeling of the frogs? In the experiments? This is an odd question, we realize, but let your mind play over it.
4. As already noted, Koehl's scientific work reflects, in certain ways, an artistic sensibility. If you've read the previous piece about Willie the mechanic, can you see ways in which Willie's work incorporates creativity? If so, how? Can you make any other connections between the "working knowledge" of Koehl and Emerson and of Willie?

Ed Murphy teaches a class in video production in Bell, California, a predominantly working-class community southeast of Los Angeles. In the following account, Mike Rose describes Murphy's classroom, some of the work the students do, and the way that work builds on the work of others. Notice the way details and quotations help convey a concrete sense of the students' thinking and achievement.

From *Possible Lives: The Promise of Public Education in America*

Mike Rose

Directly east of Watts, about four miles, across turf boundaries kids from Watts rarely used to cross, lies Bell, a city of 34,000, another of the blue-collar communities that had grown with the development of LA's once robust industry. I came the long way, driving south out of downtown, picking up the Long Beach Freeway, passing over expansive freight yards, dark factories, storage tanks, and tract houses. Huge power grids ran alongside the freeway; graffiti were on the railroad bridges and the exit signs; and, to the west, the dry LA River. I took the off ramp at Florence Avenue, headed west, passing over the river, and in a few minutes saw a small brick wall displaying the raised metal outline of a bell. WELCOME TO BELL. The smog was thick, the air still and hot. Bell High School sits in the middle of the southern residential edge of the city. I found a parking space under the full trees on Flora Avenue between two customized Toyotas — lowered, miniature mag wheels, many layers of maroon, lustrous. LA car culture. A tricked-out VW Beetle drove by, tinted windows, boom box throbbing, and took a sharp turn into a gated driveway. A kid ran from within the school yard and scrambled, hand over hand, up the chain links, half rolling, half vaulting over the top, leaping down to the pavement. He got into the VW, and it sped off.

Not too far inside that gate Ed Murphy and Larry Stone were teaching their classes in video production, using the old drama room that Ed, over the years, had converted into a studio. Both men were English teachers who have developed their expertise by trial and error. Ed started twenty-two years ago with Super-8 technology and, through donations, grants, and personal expense, has built a classy video production facility; Larry joined in about five years ago as the student demand for the courses continued to grow. Now the students' one-minute public service announcements (about smoking, drugs, rape, gangs) and their video essays (usually three- to four-minute arrangements of images set to popular or original music) regularly win local and state contests. Students enroll in the classes now because they hear so much about them in the school yard. Herbert Aparicio, a senior who has contributed original music to a number of videos, said this: "I started seeing these big changes in my friends. They were starting to

---

MIKE ROSE (b. 1944) is a professor in the Graduate School of Education and Information Studies at the University of California, Los Angeles. Among his books are *Lives on the Boundary: The Struggles and Achievements of America's Underprepared* (1989), and *Possible Lives: The Promise of Public Education in America* (1995), from which this passage is taken.

get more responsible. These guys! A big change — real quick. I thought, 'What's the big deal here?' So I went to Mr. Murphy and said, 'Do you need help with music?' And he said, 'Yeah, sure.' And I said, 'Well, I'd love to try.'"

Central to Ed's success, and to Larry Stone's, is the fact that they have fostered a culture of achievement, one that includes both college-bound students and students who are sleepwalking through the rest of the curriculum. Ed begins each term with technical instruction — how to use the camera, basic shots, fundamentals of script writing — and uses as illustration videos from his growing library of student work. He then divides the class into groups and turns them loose to develop and execute their projects. From that point until the end of the term, most of his instruction takes place through individual and small group conferences. So, on any given day, you would find Ed up at his desk going over a script with a student while other students were coming in and out with video equipment, or working on scripts at the computer terminals, or surveying the video encyclopedia for just the right images, or whirring through footage at the editing machines. There would be a constant but shifting blend of voices — English, Spanish, street talk, laughter — the beeps and tones of electronic equipment, scuffles behind the stage where scripts were being rehearsed, and music — Metallica, Doctor Dre, Chicano rapper Kid Frost — as students tried to synchronize images with a lyric and a beat.

Driving it all is a demand for quality and originality — generated by the collective student work, both past and present. So student projects get shown in "premieres" and are celebrated continually. During the first of my visits, Ed premiered two recently completed videos. In the first, a sixty-second instructional video, a soft-spoken, bespectacled boy named Frank had dubbed a lesson on amphibians onto a clip from a Teenage Mutant Ninja Turtles cartoon. To match the new dialogue with the cavorting turtles, Frank had worked and reworked his script, finding different ways to phrase things, running the tape over and over again — more than twenty times, Mr. Murphy said — to create the right fit between word and image. So when Raphael turns to Donatello, nose to nose, he asks "Did you know there are many kinds of amphibians?" And when the four muscle-bound mutants dive into water, they are asked by a fifth character if they found amphibians there. Finally, as the cartoon closes, the turtles turn to the screen and in farewell say, "So remember, dudes, when you think amphibious, think land and water."

The second video, a video essay, done by two girls in Larry Stone's class was entitled "Civil Wars" (after the Guns 'n' Roses song "Civil War"), and it took Melanie Alvarenga and Leonor Martinez two months to produce. A visitor from a public television station said it was one of the most professional pieces of student work he had ever seen. The video opened with the scene from *Cool Hand Luke* where Strother Martin knocks Paul Newman into a ditch and, looking down at him, says, "What we have here is failure to communicate." Then "Civil War" fades in and the screen delivers a series of images of battlefields, candlelight vigils, cross burnings, hooded Klansmen, mourners, demagogic speeches, the Vietnam War Memorial, hospital corridors lined with bodies, an autopsy — all paced to the urgent rhythm of the song, the images moving in slow motion or staccato or real time, their shift each to the other enhanced by computer graphics: wipes and fades and a frame folding into a box and tumbling out of sight. The words BOSNIA, EL SALVADOR, KUWAIT, VIETNAM flash in red across the screen; at the end we freeze on IF THIS WAS OUR PAST, LET'S NOT MAKE IT OUR FUTURE.

"It's really powerful," Helen Salcedo said as she walked over to an editing machine. "We don't get a chance in other classes to show our work like this. I like watching other people's stuff. You can make comparisons with what you're doing, and you can learn that way."

Leticia Lopez sat at another editing machine trying to tighten her video essay on rape. "I learned a lot about rape doing this," she explained. "Other students have done videos on rape, but I wanted to do one from a woman's perspective. I wanted it to be different. I didn't want to do a video that was violent; I think that's tasteless. I wanted to get my message across in a different way, so I have the camera follow this young lady through her day — there are no explicit scenes — and at the end the camera zooms in on a pamphlet about rape that's sitting on her coffee table. Would you like to see it?"

Ed had gone across the room to check on Jesse Barrios, who was leaning over a table, looking at a script, tapping his pencil, running his free hand through his orange hair; he wore a nose ring and an oversized jean jacket that smelled of tobacco. He was stuck. Using footage shot by another student, he was trying to create a documentary on a local artist. As he viewed the film, and then viewed it again, he became interested in the painter's involvement with her Mexican heritage. He wanted to do more with that, and was trying to figure out how he could use his film in this new thematic context. And how he could make it interesting. "I don't want it to be just a talking head. Maybe background music — something Latin — maybe fresh angles, maybe computer graphics . . . I don't know. I might have to go back and shoot again, but I'd like to see if I can do something with what I have." As one of seven children, Ed would later tell me, Jesse had to work just about full-time, so he often had to do a lot with a little. "He never liked school," Ed explained, "never thought of himself as someone who could do much. But now he's beginning to see he has potential, and he's tying some hopes to this work."

After Jesse, I spent time with Juan Jauregui and Frank Santos.

Juan was the most prolific of Ed's students, producing eight public service announcements. He had a distinctive style, and his topics were disturbing: AIDS from shared needles, gang violence, death from smoking, alcohol, and drugs. And his images came at you quickly, sharply, but rhythmic, skillfully timed: gangsters, guns, cocaine; hooded chess players, fingers splayed, caressing a rook, a bishop; car grills and tires, chain link and concrete; graveyards; lost, anguished faces. Harsh, but flowing somehow through eerie music or driving guitar or rap.

Frank's style, on the other hand, was playful, celebratory. He came to the United States four years ago from Mexico, took courses in English as a second language, and moved into the standard curriculum as an LEP (limited English proficiency) student. He still spoke an unsure English, but, Ed said, was "probably the most technically adept student" he had ever had. "He learned it all so quickly, and now he virtually lives here; morning, lunch, he's just here." I saw two of Frank's projects. In the first, young and old Mexicans dance in a local club to Banda Machos's "Casimira": cowboy hats, bandannas, women in jeans and ruffled dresses, the images up close, receding, modulated to the catchy syncopation and back beat of this music, called *banda.* In his manipulation of the images, Frank conveyed the joy of the dance that accompanies *banda, la quebradita* or "the little break": elbows pumping, shoulders dipping, a young woman, chin up, lips pursed, flashing her eyes at the camera, while around the dance a multicolored frame shimmers — *¡Orale!* (all right!), *¡Arre!* (giddy-up!) — with bright encouragement. The second was a brief animated French lesson, in which a boy lies on his bed while his mother berates him for not doing his homework. "If you do not do your homework (*Si tu ne fais ton devoir*)," she says, "you are not going to find a job (*tu ne vas pas trouvé de job*)." The boy remains immobile, grumpy: *"Je ne désire pas trouvé de job!"* — I don't want to find a job! The futile exchange continues — you won't be able to get married (so what?), have a family (so?) — until Mom adds the clincher: then you must not fall in love and can't kiss the girls. *Ooh la la,* the cartoon boy says, springing from bed and doing a half-dance to his desk. "I can't talk to you anymore, because I have homework to do!"

And at the end of the day, I got a chance to sit and talk with Melanie and Leonor, who made "Civil Wars." Melanie was from El Salvador, Leonor from Colombia, both seniors who had met in tenth-grade geometry and who had collaborated on two other videos. They had spent two months on "Civil Wars," trying to get it right, despairing, coming back again. They were good friends, close, effective partners, and they occasionally completed each other's sentences:

> There were times when we felt like quitting. And it wasn't until Mr. Stone pushed us — he said, "Girls, you have to do this." And we were procrastinating. We got so tired looking for the *right* shots. I mean, *shots* — we had plenty of them. But looking for the right one, well . . . then Mr. Stone would say, "It'll work out, I believe in you." We don't like to do simple work. We like to get into what we're doing. Quality work is what we like — that's what we're all about.

Melanie had applied to college, wanting to major in film. Leonor was a single mother who had to stay close to home and make an immediate, practical choice: She would most likely go to nearby East Los Angeles Community College and train to be a physician's assistant. A number of Ed and Larry's students lived with limits. (Seventy-five percent of the students at Bell were from families categorized as "low income.") Some of these young people had had their sights set on college for a while, but a number were not in the college track at all — weren't oriented that way, weren't interested, had, in all kinds of ways, been scared or barred from it. The video classes provided one of the few opportunities for such a range of students to work together and see what each could do. And it was often the student who was less successful by traditional standards who excelled. Some visitors might find a class like Ed Murphy's too unstructured, too loud; might worry, too, about the focus of so much student work on drugs, gangs, violence. And Ed has tried to get his students to reflect critically on this focus — does it inadvertently feed stereotypes about communities like Bell? — but with little result. What seemed undeniable, though, was that the students were engaged, had a sense of importance, worked within a tradition of recognized student achievement, and gave expression to deeply held concerns. Melanie lost her father in the Salvadoran civil war and saw people killed in front of her house. And as a secondary result of the work, some students who had never imagined themselves in college began to see possibilities. It was not uncommon for Ed and Larry's students to gear themselves up for the local community college or for California State University at Los Angeles, just back up the Long Beach Freeway, four miles northeast.

Considerations

1. How did teacher Ed Murphy (and his colleague Larry Stone) arrive at the current structure and curriculum of the video production class? How would you characterize the kinds of intelligence they display?
2. From what you can tell, what are some of the kinds of intelligence that seem to go into the production of the videos described here? What do the students need to know

about? What do they need to know how to do? What kinds of problems do they need to know how to solve?

3. It is common in Western culture to speak of intelligence as an individual characteristic, as a quality each of us possesses in our own particular way that can be assessed through measures of what each of us knows and can do. But in what ways might we talk of the intelligence of this *classroom;* that is, not of the students' work individually, but of all of them collectively?

We tend to think of cognition or thinking (or, for that matter, intelligence) in individual terms, but in the following passage, Edwin Hutchins encourages us to think of the ways that cognition is often distributed among the members of a group or society — and the various accomplishments that result from such distribution. Hutchins is trying to articulate a theory about intelligence here, but notice how he relies on examples — hydraulic farming and information retrieval among Native American tribes — to build the theory. As you read, make sure you understand what he's describing in those examples.

From "The Social Organization of Distributed Cognition"

EDWIN HUTCHINS

In the history of anthropology, there is scarcely a more important concept than the division of labor. In terms of the energy budget of a human group and the efficiency with which a group exploits its physical environment, social organizational factors often produce group properties that differ considerably from the properties of individuals. For example, Wittfogel (1957; cited in Roberts, 1964), writing about the advent of hydraulic farming and oriental despotism, says

> A large quantity of water can be channeled and kept within bounds only by the use of mass labor; and this mass labor must be coordinated, disciplined, and led. Thus a number of farmers eager to conquer arid lowlands and plains are forced to invoke the organizational devices which — on the basis of premachine technology — offer the one chance of success; they must work in cooperation with their fellows and subordinate themselves to a directing authority (pp. 17–18).

Thus, a particular kind of social organization permits the efforts of individuals to combine in ways that produce results — in this case, a technological system called *hydraulic farming* — that could not be produced by any individual farmer working alone. This kind of effect is ubiquitous in modern life, but it is largely invisible to us. The skeptical reader may wish to look around right now and see whether there is anything in the current environment that was not either produced or delivered to its present location by

---

EDWIN HUTCHINS (b. 1948) is a professor in the Department of Cognitive Science at the University of California, San Diego. This excerpt is from an edited volume entitled *Perspectives on Socially Shared Cognition* (1991).

the cooperative efforts of humans working in socially organized groups. The only thing I can find in my environment that meets this test is a striped pebble that I found at the beach and carried home to decorate my desk. Every other thing I can see from my chair is not only the product of coordinated group rather than individual activities but is also *necessarily* the product of group rather than individual activity.

All divisions of labor require some distributed cognition in order to coordinate the activities of the participants. Even a simple system of two men driving a spike with hammers requires some cognition on the part of each to coordinate his own activities with those of the other. When the labor that is distributed is cognitive labor, the system involves the distribution of two kinds of cognitive labor: the cognition that is the task, and the cognition that governs the coordination of the elements of the task. In such a case, the group performing the cognitive task may have cognitive properties that differ from the cognitive properties of any individual.

Given the importance of social organization and the division of labor as transformers of human capacities, it is something of a surprise that the *division of cognitive labor* has played a very minor role in cognitive anthropology. There have been few analogous investigations of the many ways in which the cognitive properties of human groups may depend on the social organization of individual cognitive capabilities. In recent years there has been increasing interest in intracultural variability, the question of the distribution of knowledge in a society (Romney, Weller, and Batchelder, 1986; Boster, 1985). For the most part, this work has addressed the question of the reliability and representativeness of individual anthropological informants and is not oriented toward the question of the properties of the group that result from one or another distribution of knowledge among its members.

The notion that a culture or society, as a group, might have some cognitive properties differing from those of the individual members of the culture has been around since the turn of the century, most conspicuously in the writings of the French sociologist Emile Durkheim (1893/1949; 1915/1965) and his followers, and largely in the form of programmatic assertions that it is true. This is an interesting general assertion, but can it be demonstrated that any particular sort of cognitive property could be manifested differently at the individual and group levels? Making a move in that direction, Roberts (1964) suggested that a cultural group can be seen as a kind of widely distributed memory. Such a memory is clearly more robust than the memory of any individual and undoubtedly has a much greater capacity than any individual memory has. Roberts even speculated on how retrieval from the cultural memory might be different from individual memory retrieval and how changing social organizational devices might be required to continue to support memory retrieval functions in increasingly complex cultures. Roberts explored these issues in a comparison of four American Indian tribes. Information retrieval (scanning) at the tribal level among the Mandan was held to be more efficient than among the Chiricahua because "The small geographical area occupied by the tribe, the concentrated settlement pattern, the frequent visiting, the ceremonial linkages, made even informal mechanisms [of retrieval] more efficient" (1964, p. 448).

Roberts noted that the tribal level information retrieval processes of the Cheyenne had properties different from those of the Mandan or Chiricahua, and linked the properties to particular features of social organization.

> If the membership of a council represents kin and other interest groups in the tribe, each member makes available to the council as a whole the informational resources of the

groups he represents. . . . Councils have usually been viewed as decision-making bodies without proper emphasis on their function as information retrieval units. (Roberts, 1964, p. 449)

In the sentences just cited, Roberts attributes the differences in retrieval efficiency at the group level to variables such as group size, the pattern of interactions among individuals, the distribution of knowledge, and the time course of interaction. How could we demonstrate the effects of variables such as these? Even this small number of variables defines a very large parameter space. To investigate that space experimentally and tease out the effects of each of these variables and their possible interactions with each other is a very expensive proposition.

Still, it seems important to come to an understanding of the ways that the cognitive properties of groups may differ from those of individuals. In the comparison of the physical accomplishments of pre- and post-hydraulic agriculture societies, it is obvious that the differences in physical accomplishment are due to differences in the social organization of physical labor rather than to differences in the physical strength of the members of the two societies. Similarly, if groups can have cognitive properties that are significantly different from those of the individuals in the group, then differences in the cognitive accomplishments of any two groups might depend entirely on differences in the social organization of distributed cognition and not at all on differences in the cognitive properties of individuals in the two groups.

WORKS CITED

Boster, J. S. "Requiem for the Omniscient Informant: There's Life in the Old Girl Yet." *Directions in Cognitive Anthropology.* Ed. J. Doughert. Urbana: University of Illinois Press, 1985. 177–97.

Durkheim, E. *The Division of Labor in Society.* Trans. G. Simpson. Glencoe, IL: Free Press, 1949. Original work published 1893.

———. *The Elementary Forms of the Religious Life.* Trans. J. W. Swain. New York: Free Press, 1965. Original work published 1915.

Roberts, J. "The Self-Management of Cultures." *Explorations in Cultural Anthropology: Essays in Honor of George Peter Murdock.* Ed. W. Goodenough. New York: McGraw-Hill, 1964. 433–54.

Romney, A. K., S. C. Weller, and W. H. Batchelder. "Culture as Consensus: A Theory of Culture and Informant Accuracy." *American Anthropologist* 88(2)(1986): 313–38.

Considerations

1. Hutchins, following Roberts, writes that "a cultural group can be seen as a kind of widely distributed memory." What does he mean by that? Hutchins goes on to summarize research on "retrieval [of information] from the cultural memory" of various Native American tribes. What are some of the characteristics of a cultural group that might help or hinder such information retrieval?
2. Try to apply Hutchins's theory about distributed cognition to your own environment — home, school, work, or recreation — and see whether you can find tasks or events in which "the group performing the cognitive task may have cognitive properties that differ from the cognitive properties of the individual." Pick one such task or event and specify as best you can the ways that the group's cognitive properties differ from the cognitive properties of any individual.

3. One way to explain Hutchins's theory is that it calls on us to shift our attention from the particular intelligence of particular individuals to the intelligence that emerges when those individuals come together in a group. What do you think about this shift in focus? If we as a society thought about intelligence more in this way, what might be some implications for education or for work?
4. If you've read the previous selection about the subculture of the video production class, try applying Hutchins's generalizations about "distributed cognition" to the culture of that classroom.

Who or what can claim intelligence? Humans only? Animals? In the following passage, cognitive scientist John Haugeland argues for the intelligence of computers. As he does so, he makes some interesting claims about human intelligence as well. Notice how Haugeland draws on examples from the history of artificial intelligence to make new arguments about computer science and about intelligence itself.

From *Artificial Intelligence: The Very Idea*

JOHN HAUGELAND

MINDS: ARTIFICIAL AND NATURAL

What are minds? What is thinking? What sets people apart, in all the known universe? Such questions have tantalized philosophers for millennia, but (by scientific standards anyway) scant progress could be claimed . . . until recently. For the current generation has seen a sudden and brilliant flowering in the philosophy/science of the mind; by now not only psychology but also a host of related disciplines are in the throes of a great intellectual revolution. And the epitome of the entire drama is *Artificial Intelligence,* the exciting new effort to make computers think. The fundamental goal of this research is not merely to mimic intelligence or produce some clever fake. Not at all. "AI" wants only the genuine article: *machines with minds,* in the full and literal sense.[1] This is not science fiction, but real science, based on a theoretical conception as deep as it is daring: Namely, we are, at root, *computers ourselves. . . .*

We've all chuckled nervously over the cartoon computer typing out "I think, there-

[1]Perhaps Artificial Intelligence should be called "Synthetic Intelligence" to accord better with commercial parlance. Thus artificial diamonds are fake imitations, whereas synthetic diamonds are genuine diamonds, only manufactured instead of dug up (compare also artificial maple flavoring versus, say, synthetic insulin). Despite the name, AI clearly aims at genuine intelligence, not a fake imitation.

Professor of philosophy at the University of Pittsburgh, JOHN HAUGELAND (b. 1945) has written numerous articles and books, including *Mind Design* (1981), *Artificial Intelligence: The Very Idea* (1985), excerpted here, *Mind Design II* (1997), and *Having Thought* (1997).

fore I am" or some comparable profundity. But when it comes to taking Artificial Intelligence seriously, people tend to split into "scoffers" and "boosters." Scoffers find the whole idea quite preposterous — not just false, but ridiculous — like imagining that your car (really) hates you or insisting that a murderous bullet should go to jail. Boosters, on the other hand, are equally certain that it's only a matter of time; computers with minds, they say, are as inevitable as interplanetary travel and two-way pocket TV. The remarkable thing is how utterly confident each side is: "It's so obvious," they both say (while thumping the table), "only a *fanatic* could disagree." Well, here we shall not be fanatics in either direction, no matter who disagrees. Artificial Intelligence is neither preposterous nor inevitable. Rather, it is based on a powerful idea, which very well might be right (or right in some respects) and just as well might not. . . .

FICTION, TECHNOLOGY, AND THEORY

The concept of Artificial Intelligence did not, of course, spring up from nowhere, nor did it originate with computers. . . . We can distinguish two familiar and well-developed themes on intelligent artifacts in science fiction. One is the "creature feature" genre, starring monsters or androids — basically like natural animals except for being man-made (and thus somehow peculiar, superior, or horribly flawed). Included are the mythical creations of Hephaestus and Dr. Frankenstein as well as miscellaneous anthropoid slaves, indistinguishable from ordinary people save for serial numbers, emotional oddities, and the like. The other genre is populated by various mechanical "robots": typically blinking, clanking contraptions, with springs and pulleys in lieu of flesh, wires for nerves, and maybe wheels instead of legs — plus emotional limitations even more serious than the androids'. . . .

While the monster theme often invokes mystery and black magic, robots tend to be extrapolations of industry's latest high-tech marvel. Early designs were based on the intricate gear and ratchet mechanisms that so enchanted Europe when clockworks were new; and, through the years, steam engines, automatic looms, hydraulic controls, and telephone switchboards have all fueled fantastic projections. Contemporary Artificial Intelligence, needless to say, is rooted in fancy programmable electronics; in particular, no current work is based on chemical wizardry or bioengineering. . . . AI, therefore, is direct heir to the contraption line. But there's one crucial difference: Whereas few respectable scientists ever tried to build intelligent clockworks or switchboards (let alone androids), research on intelligent computers is big time. Why?

The real issue has nothing to do with advanced technologies . . . but with deep theoretical assumptions. According to a central tradition in Western philosophy, thinking (intellection) essentially *is* rational manipulation of mental symbols (viz., ideas). Clocks and switchboards, however, don't do anything at all like rational symbol manipulation. Computers, on the other hand, can manipulate arbitrary "tokens" in any specifiable manner whatever; so apparently we need only arrange for those tokens to be symbols, and the manipulations to be specified as rational, to get a machine that *thinks.* In other words, AI is new and different because computers actually do something very like what minds are supposed to do. Indeed, if that traditional theory is correct, then our imagined computer ought to have "a mind of its own": a (genuine) *artificial mind.*

To call something a symbol or a manipulation is to characterize it quite abstractly. That doesn't mean the characterization is vague, formless, or even hard to understand, but rather that inessential details are omitted. Consider, for instance, two ways of specifying the motor for an appliance. One engineer might describe it in great detail, giving the precise shape of each little part, what it's made of, how it's attached, and so on. (That would be a "concrete" characterization, the opposite of abstract.) Another engineer, however, might stipulate only the minimum horsepower required, the space into which it has to fit, and how quietly it must run — leaving the details up to the motor designer. The resulting motor could be made of metal or plastic, be round or square, be based on one physical principle or another, and still satisfy the abstract specifications exactly.

According to the symbol manipulation theory, intelligence depends only on a system's organization and functioning as a symbol manipulator — which is even more abstracted from concrete details than are horsepower and noise level. Hence low-level specifics, such as what the symbols are made of or their precise shapes, are irrelevant to whether the system might be intelligent; the symbols need only satisfy some higher-level, abstract specifications. In other words, various "details," like whether the underlying structure is electronic or physiological (or hydraulic or fiber optical or whatever), are entirely beside the point. By the same token, contemporary computer technology is relevant only for economic reasons: Electronic circuits just happen to be (at the moment) the cheapest way to build flexible symbol manipulating systems.

But the lesson goes deeper: If Artificial Intelligence really has little to do with computer technology and much more to do with abstract principles of mental organization, then the distinctions among AI, psychology, and even philosophy of mind seem to melt away. One can study those basic principles using tools and techniques from computer science, or with the methods of experimental psychology, or in traditional philosophical terms — but it's the same subject in each case. Thus a grand interdisciplinary marriage seems imminent; indeed, a number of enthusiasts have already taken the vows. For their new "unified" field, they have coined the name *cognitive science.* If you believe the advertisements, Artificial Intelligence and psychology, as well as parts of philosophy, linguistics, and anthropology, are now just "subspecialties" within one coherent study of cognition, intelligence, and mind — that is, of symbol manipulation.

Artificial Intelligence in this sense (as a branch of cognitive science) is the only kind we will discuss. For instance, we will pay no attention to commercial ventures (so-called "expert systems," etc.) that make no pretense of developing or applying psychological principles. We also won't consider whether computers might have some alien or inhuman kind of intellect (like Martians or squids?). My own hunch, in fact, is that anthropomorphic prejudice, "human chauvinism," is built into our very concept of intelligence. This concept, of course, could still apply to all manner of creatures; the point is merely that it's the only concept we have — if we escaped our "prejudice," we wouldn't know what we were talking about.

Be that as it may, the only *theoretical* reason to take contemporary Artificial Intelligence more seriously than clockwork fiction is the powerful suggestion that our own minds work on computational principles. In other words, we're really interested in AI as part of the theory that *people* are computers — and we're all interested in people.

WHAT IS INTELLIGENCE?

How shall we define intelligence? Doesn't everything turn on this? Surprisingly, perhaps, very little seems to turn on it. For practical purposes, a criterion proposed by Alan Turing satisfies nearly everyone. Turing was annoyed by fruitless disputes over word meanings; he thought you could never find out anything interesting about what machines could do by armchair philosophizing about what we mean by "think" and "intelligent." So he suggested that we ignore the verbal issue and adopt a simple test which he devised; then we could concentrate on building and observing the machines themselves. He predicted that by the year 2000 computer systems would be passing a modest version of his test and that contrary "definitions" would eventually just look silly (and quietly fade away).

Turing's test is based on a game, called the "imitation game," played by three mutual strangers. Two of them are "witnesses," and they are of opposite sex; the third player, the "interrogator," tries to guess which witness is which, purely on the basis of how they answer questions. The trick is that one witness (say the man) is trying to fool the interrogator (by systematically pretending to be the woman), while the other (the woman) is doing all she can to help the interrogator. If the interrogator guesses correctly, the woman wins, otherwise the man does. In order to avoid any extraneous clues, like tone of voice, all questions and answers are transmitted via teletype. So far no computers are involved. Turing's idea, however, was to substitute a computer for the male witness and see whether, against average women opponents, it can fool the average (human) interrogator as often as the average man can. If it can, it "passes" the test.[2]

But why would such a peculiar game be a test for general (human-like) intelligence? Actually, the bit about teletypes, fooling the interrogator, and so on, is just window dressing, to make it all properly "experimental." The crux of the test is *talk:* Does the machine talk like a person? Of course this doesn't mean sounding like a person, but rather saying the sorts of things that people say in similar situations. But again, why should that be a sign of general intelligence? What's so special about talking? Turing says: "The question and answer method seems to be suitable for introducing almost any one of the fields of human endeavor that we wish to include." That is, we can talk about pretty much anything.

Further, and more important, to converse beyond the most superficial level, you have to know what you're talking about. That is, understanding the words alone is not enough; you have to understand the topic as well. Turing points out (1950, p. 446) how similar his imitation game is to an oral quiz and gives us a sample:

> *Interrogator:* In the first line of your sonnet which reads "Shall I compare thee to a summer's day,"[3] would not "a spring day" do as well or better?
>
> *Witness:* It wouldn't scan.[4]
>
> *Interrogator:* How about "a winter's day"? That would scan all right.
>
> *Witness:* Yes, but nobody wants to be compared to a winter's day.
>
> *Interrogator:* Would you say Mr. Pickwick reminded you of Christmas?
>
> *Witness:* In a way.

[2]Turing doesn't mention whether the interrogator is told that a computer has been substituted for the man; and that would surely make a difference to the questioning. But, as the next paragraph shows, the essence of the test is much simpler, and the ambiguity doesn't really matter.

[3]"Shall I compare thee to a summer's day" is actually the first line of a sonnet by William Shakespeare [Eds.].

[4]"It wouldn't scan," that is, it couldn't be computed by the witness [Eds.].

Interrogator: Yet Christmas is a winter's day, and I do not think Mr. Pickwick would mind the comparison.

Witness: I don't think you're serious. By a winter's day one means a typical winter's day, rather than a special one like Christmas.

This student has displayed not only competence with the English language, but also a passable understanding of poetry, the seasons, people's feelings, and so on — all just by talking. The same could be done for politics, fine wines, electrical engineering, philosophy . . . you name it. What if a machine could pass all those examinations? That's why the Turing test is so powerful and compelling.

It's also quite convenient in practice; typing and reading at a terminal, after all, are the standard means of interacting with a computer. Since there's no physical barrier to having a friendly conversation with a machine, AI research is free to attack the underlying theoretical issues. By accepting the Turing test (in spirit, if not the letter), scientists can concentrate almost entirely on the "cognitive" aspects of the problem: What internal structure and operations would enable a system to say the right thing at the right time? In other words, they can dispense with messy incidentals and get on with computational psychology.

"THEY CAN ONLY . . ."

Many people are especially doubtful about "automating" creativity, freedom, and the like. No computer, they suppose, could ever be truly inventive, artistic, or responsible, because "it can only do what it's programmed to do." Everything depends, however, on just what this alleged limitation means. In one technical and boring sense, of course, it's perfectly true that computers always follow their programs, since a program is nothing but a careful specification of all the relevant processes inside the machine. That, however, doesn't prove anything because a similar point might be made about us. Thus, assuming there were a "careful specification" of all the relevant processes in our brains (laws of neuropsychology, or something like that), it would be equally easy to say: "We — or rather our brain parts — always act only as specified."[5] But, obviously, no such fact could show that we are never creative or free — and the corresponding claim about computers is no more telling.

The underlying problem with the argument is that it ignores distinctions of *organizational level.* A stereo, for instance, can be described as a device for reproducing recorded music, as a complicated tangle of electronic components, or as a giant cloud of subatomic particles. What you can say about it depends on the level of description you adopt. Thus, none of the components (let alone the particles) could properly be termed "high fidelity"; that characteristic makes sense only at the level of music reproduction. Likewise, none of our individual brain functions, and none of the individual operations in a computer, could properly be termed "creative" or "free"; such descriptions

[5]One might reject this comparison on the grounds that *our* thoughts take place in *immaterial* (perhaps immortal) souls and have at most incidental relations to our brains. Such a position, however, would rule out Artificial Intelligence from the start. Hence, for purposes of discussion, [I] must and will assume that human intelligence is (or at least could be) realized in matter — such as brains.

belong at a completely different level — a level at which one speaks of the system or person as a whole.[6]

Unfortunately, confusions remain because the notion "is-programmed-to" is ambiguous. Instead of the above sense, in which programming refers to a detailed specification of internal processes, one can use the term more broadly, to describe a system's overall design or intended capacities. For example, I might say "this computer is programmed to keep the payroll accounts" or "that computer is programmed to find the best flight path in bad weather." These descriptions apply to the system as a whole; yet even at this level it seems that the systems "can only do what they're programmed to do" — as long, anyway, as they don't malfunction. Here the underlying problem is quite different: namely, it's simply not clear that being "programmed" (in this sense) is incompatible with being creative or free. After all, why not just program the system to be creative, free, or whatever? Then it would have those characteristics by design.

You might think that being "programmed for creativity" is a contradiction in terms. But it can't be, as we can see by again considering ourselves. In some sense, surely, we are elaborate integrated systems with an overall design — the result of evolution, perhaps. Thus when we're healthy (not malfunctioning), we "only do what we're designed to do." But then, assuming that creativity and freedom are not (always) unhealthy, we must be "designed for creativity," etc. This is no contradiction because the relevant sense of "design" relates only to overall capacities and characteristics; but that's also the very sense of "programming" in question.

Still, there's one last argument: It's only a metaphor to say that we were "designed" by evolution; evolution is not an actual designer, but only a mindless natural process. Computers, on the other hand, are quite literally *programmed* by actual (human) programmers. So when we're creative, it's all our own; but when a computer printout contains something artistic, that's really the programmer's artistry, not the machine's. But wait: How does that follow? Why should an entity's potential for inventiveness be determined by its ancestry (like some hereditary title) and not by its own manifest competence? What if, for instance, the very same computer system had resulted from an incredible laboratory accident; could *that* make any difference to whether the resulting system was creative? Or, turning the tables, what if you or I had been concocted out of petroleum by-products at Exxon; would that mean that all our later inventions and artworks automatically belonged to a team of chemists? I certainly hope not.

Of course, if those inventions had actually been dreamt up in advance by the relevant programmers or chemists and merely stored in the machine or us for later "playback," then the credit would be theirs. But that's not at all the way AI works, even today. What gets programmed directly is just a bunch of general information and principles, not unlike what teachers instill in their pupils. What happens after that, what the system does with all this input, is not predictable by the designer (or teacher or anybody else). The most striking current examples are chess machines that outplay their programmers, coming up with brilliant moves that the latter would never have found. Many people are amazed by this fact; but if you reflect that invention is often just a rearrangement (more or less dramatic) of previously available materials, then it shouldn't seem so surprising.

[6]Philosopher Dan Dennett has been particularly assiduous in making this point in a variety of contexts.

None of this proves that computer systems *can* be truly creative, free, or artistic. All it shows is that our initial intuitions to the contrary are not trustworthy, no matter how compelling they seem at first. If you're sitting there muttering: "Yes, yes, but I *know* they can't; they just couldn't," then you've missed the point. Nobody knows. Like all fundamental questions in cognitive science, this one awaits the outcome of a great deal more hard research. Remember, the real issue is whether, in the appropriate abstract sense, we are computers ourselves.

Considerations

1. As specifically as you can, state why Haugeland makes the claim that "we are, at root, computers ourselves." What do you think of that claim? What does Haugeland gain by trying to redefine the issue this way?
2. In a footnote, Haugeland suggests discomfort with the term "artificial intelligence." Why? Would using his alternative term "synthetic intelligence" change the way we think about the issues?
3. What is the Turing test?
4. This first chapter of *Critical Strategies* concerns itself with definition. Relying on the Turing test, Haugeland states that *defining* intelligence might not be so important a task. He suggests that *talk* may be a better indicator of intelligence than an abstract definition. What do you think of that claim? Imagine some scenarios in which *talk* might be a powerful indicator of intelligence and scenarios in which talk would be a very poor indicator.

FURTHER ASSIGNMENTS

1. Using whatever materials in this chapter you need, write an essay defining intelligence.

2. Think of another quality that, like intelligence, is subject to a broad range of interpretations and, at the same time, has important consequences for those considered to lack or possess it. (Here are some concepts to get you thinking: *beauty, patriotism, courage, creativity.*) What are some of the various ways in which this trait might be defined? (You might want to jot some notes about different definitions before undertaking your essay. If it's helpful, ask friends and family for their own definitions, or consult a good dictionary.) In a brief essay, describe the various definitions you came up with and explain the extent to which they are useful or limiting. Who tends to define the trait in our society? Who benefits from these definitions? Who is harmed by them?

3. As a student, you will come across many definitions as you work through the courses in your major. Identify a term that comes up over and over again in a textbook for another course (e.g., *norms* or *normative* in a sociology textbook). Then, reading the word carefully in various contexts, sketch out its shades of meaning. After making some notes, come up with your own unified definition of the word and compare it to the one in the dictionary. In an essay, discuss the ways in which the dictionary definition enhances or complicates your working understanding of the word. Some questions to get you started:

- In what ways does the dictionary definition make you rethink your own definition?
- What, if any, nuances that you have uncovered in the word do not appear in the dictionary definition? Why, do you suppose, does the dictionary not include them?

4. As mentioned earlier in this chapter, definitions are often developed through examples and comparisons. In an essay drawing on examples from the readings in this chapter — and from your own observations and experiences — compare different views of intelligence and argue for the definition you think is best.

5. Looking ahead to Chapter 2, we see that summaries are usually condensed presentations of material appearing elsewhere in fuller forms. Often, summarizing is used in conjunction with other strategies to set up an argument or to illustrate a point. (For a more detailed description of summarizing, see p. 81.) Using summaries of readings in this chapter to back you up, write an essay that does one or more of the following:

- lays out different views of intelligence
- describes your own intelligence
- argues for a new or revised view of intelligence.

6. The period of the early development of the IQ test in America was a troubling one, politically and socially. French educator Alfred Binet originally developed the test in 1905 to identify students who might benefit from remedial education. After Binet's death in 1911, some educators in the United States planned to use the test for the purposes of social engineering. Test proponent Lewis Terman, for example, wanted to "bring tens of thousands of these high-grade defectives under the surveillance and protection of society. This will ultimately result in curtailing the reproduction of feeble-mindedness and in the elimination of an enormous amount of crime, pauperism, and industrial inefficiency." Terman published the American version of Binet's test — the "Stanford-Binet" test — in 1916. In a research paper, trace the history of the influence of the test in the United States, perhaps making connections to the history of the eugenics movement (see the History Assignment, p. 45). What were the early arguments in favor of the tests? What, over

time, have been the consequences of these tests, socially and politically? How are they viewed and used today?

7. Willie the mechanic (p. 55), the researchers Mimi Koehl and Sharon Emerson (p. 58), and the students in Ed Murphy's class (p. 61) show what might be described as "working intelligence." Collect examples of the ways in which the business world talks about and defines the roles of workers. You might refer to help-wanted ads, articles, and advice columns about work from newspapers and popular magazines and any other employment literature. Analyze the language of these materials, picking out particular words and phrases used to describe the ideal worker (e.g., "self-starter," "team player," "problem solver"). In a paper drawing on examples from employment literature, take up one or more of the following questions:

- In what ways does the literature encompass, or fail to acknowledge, your understanding of "working intelligence"? (You might want to draw on insights you've gained from some of the readings in this chapter.)
- Do certain fields seem to value particular types of intelligence over other types? Why do you suppose this is so?
- Based on your analysis, would you argue for new types of descriptions in employment literature? If so, what types and why?
- To what extent does "working intelligence," as opposed to other traits, appear to have economic value?

2

SUMMARIZING

Synthesis and Judgment

SUMMARIZING Across the Curriculum

The first part of this chapter includes a range of readings and other materials — most accompanied by assignments — that will get you to think critically about the ways in which summarizing is used across the curriculum: in anthropology, biology, economics, history, and other fields. In addition to covering various disciplines, we offer various types of material: an interview, an essay, short stories, charts and graphs, and presentations of research, both for academic and more general audiences. We begin with an Opening Problem that immediately involves you with using — and thinking about — summarizing. We then present examples of writers drafting papers on academic topics that involve the strategy (Working Examples, p. 82), followed by a piece showing how a professional writer uses summarizing to serve a particular purpose (A Professional Application, p. 94). Next comes a series of cross-curricular assignments intended to deepen and enrich your investigation of the strategy's possibilities and limitations (p. 99).

Woven throughout the first part of this chapter (in the Opening Problem; in the Professional Application; in the Oral History Assignment, p. 103; and in the Economics Assignment, p. 113) are readings about the dimensions of poverty — in particular, child poverty — in the United States, a topic that lends itself especially well to the application and investigation of summarizing. If this topic interests you and you want to spend more time with it, consider working with Readings: The Dimensions of Child Poverty in the second part of this chapter. All of those readings invite you to synthesize some of the causes and effects of child poverty and contribute to a more comprehensive understanding of the problem.

Opening Problem: Summarizing Trends in Child Poverty

Here is a reading that will involve you in the process of summarizing. It is a newspaper article that summarizes a large comparative study of child poverty in the United States and seventeen other countries. Although brief, it contains a chart, statistical findings, and policy implications. Write a one-paragraph summary of the article, trying, as best you can, to reflect both findings and implications. If you'd like, you can add a postscript on your reaction to this report and what was relatively easy or difficult in trying to summarize it.

The United States is proud to be No. 1 in a lot of things, including the size of its economy. Ironically, it also has the highest child poverty rate of any industrial country.

If, as many experts predict, the latest welfare reform bill signed into law by President Clinton pushes another 1.1 million children into poverty, America's lead over the rest of the developed world will only grow.

More than 21 percent of American children were poor in 1991, according to University of Syracuse researchers Timothy Smeeding and Lee Rainwater, who head an international research project called the Luxembourg Income Study.

The next closest country, Australia, had a child poverty rate of 14 percent. France's rate was only 6.5 percent, less than a third of America's. And in Sweden, a mere 2.7 percent of children counted as poor, using a consistent definition the scholars developed.

In nearly every one of the seventeen foreign countries they examined, children in the poorest 20 percent of households had higher family incomes than their counterparts in the United States, even though the foreign countries aren't as rich as the United States.

In Sweden and Switzerland, the bottom 20 percent of children have family incomes 72 percent higher than those in the United States. Even in Italy, the poorest fifth of children have incomes 15 percent higher than here.

People at the bottom of the income ladder in most other developed countries do better than here because the spread between rich and poor is much narrower. (By the same token, people at the top of the income ladder do far better in the United States.)

As Smeeding shows in an article in the latest issue of *Challenge* magazine, the affluent in the United States (those at the 90th percentile) earn 5.7 times more than the poor (those at the 10th percentile). That ratio is under 3 in West Germany, the Netherlands, Belgium, and Scandinavia.

Economists don't fully understand the causes of great inequality in the United States. One reason is that the U.S. labor market has fewer constraints such as high minimum wages and strong unions, which keep wages of low-skilled workers from falling in Europe.

In addition, most other developed countries have much more generous safety nets — including family or child allowances, subsidized child care, and national health care — that make it easier for single women to hold jobs.

Finally, there are demographic differences: 23 percent of all families in the United States were headed by a single parent in 1990, compared to rates of 13 percent to 15 percent in Canada and much of Western Europe. Single-parent families are also far more likely to be poor here than in other countries that have more generous social programs.

What, if anything, the United States should do about its extremes of child poverty is a matter of values more than pure economics. In the current political climate, welfare reformers have paid more attention to changing the behavior of nonworking parents than giving more resources to needy kids.

Smeeding and Rainwater propose replacing the federal personal income tax deduction for children, which disproportionately helps affluent families in high tax brackets, with a $750-per-child tax credit for all children, regardless of parents' income level. Even families who owe no taxes would be eligible.

They also favor a government-guaranteed minimum level of child support to protect single parents whose divorced or absent partners cannot or will not pay.

Such support would let the single parent "go out and find a job, keep a job, pay

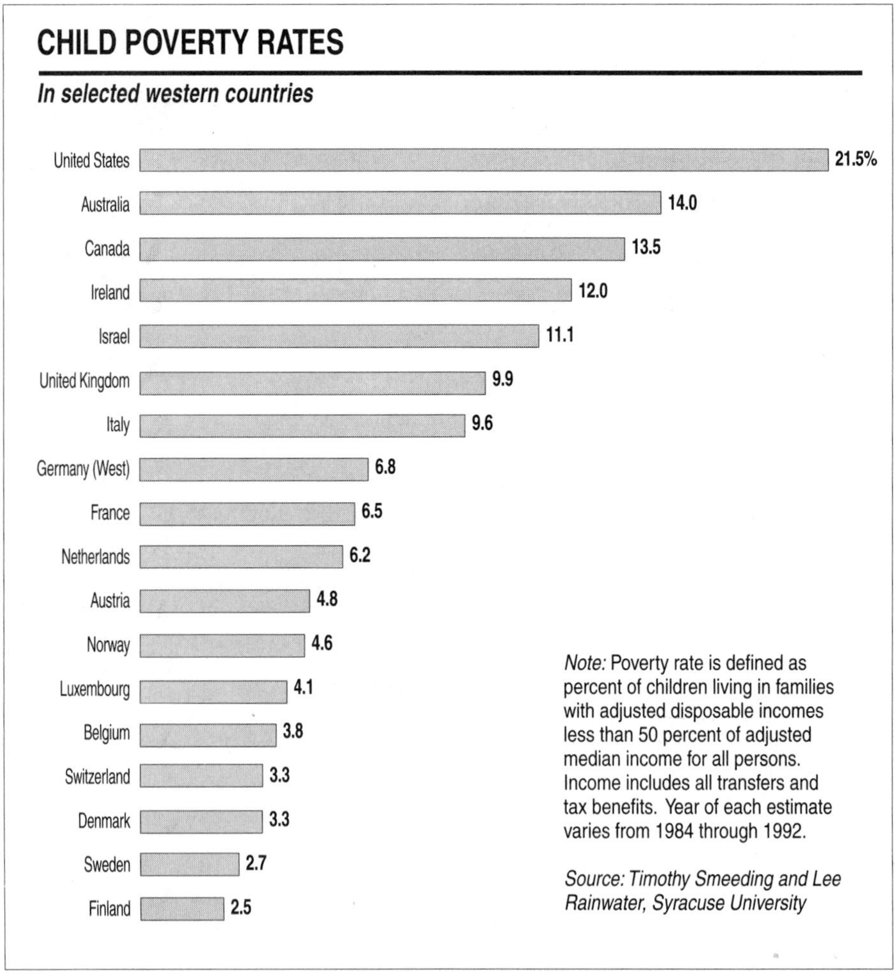

for some portion of subsidized child care, and otherwise substitute for the lack of a partner who can share work and child rearing responsibilities," Smeeding and Rainwater observe.

— Jonathan Marshall, "Child Poverty Is Abundant"

Thinking about Thinking

- In the process of writing a summary, you have to make a number of decisions about what to include from the original text and what to leave out. What influenced you to include the things you included? What were some things you left out? Why?
- Try to further summarize your one-paragraph summary in a single sentence. What were some of the decisions you made?
- Jonathan Marshall's article is a summary of a larger report by researchers Timothy Smeeding and Lee Rainwater, so Marshall had to make some of the kinds of choices you made in writing your summary: what to include, what to leave out. As you read Marshall's article, were there places where you wanted to know more than he offers? Did you find places where he provides too much information? Look again at your own summary in light of your reaction to Marshall's. Are there places where you should expand or trim back?
- What is lost in producing summaries like the ones you and Marshall have written? Is anything gained?

Academic experience is full of summarizing. Open a social science textbook. Chances are that each of its chapters begins or ends with a summary of the chapter's contents. Locate a scientific article. Probably it is prefaced with an especially careful form of summary, an abstract. Look up a book review. More than likely it contains a short summary of the book under discussion. Most college lectures are summaries — they aim to condense and simplify complex information into something readily grasped by listeners. Even many textbooks can be seen as summaries: Each statement in a biology textbook, for example, is a generalization founded on the published research of scientists.

Summaries are condensed presentations of material appearing elsewhere in fuller forms. As a student you will be exposed to summaries again and again. Sometimes you also will be asked to write summaries, as when you must provide an abstract for an experiment performed in chemistry lab or when an instruction on an American history exam says, "Summarize Frederick Jackson Turner's thesis about the American frontier." At other times you may be expected to summarize without explicitly being told to do so. Deceptively wide-open exam questions such as "What were the causes of World War I?" or "How do dominant cultures typically treat religious minorities?" can be thinly disguised requests to condense and present long stretches of information from a textbook or lecture notes.

Assignments like these last ones contribute to the misimpression that summarizing is essentially a passive undertaking calling for accuracy perhaps, but little more. But, as you saw when working with the Marshall article, the act of summarizing often calls for careful and critical attention. Like the rest of the strategies we present in this book, summarizing can be an instrument of active, creative thinking and writing. Used well, summaries can engage our judgment, our critical thinking, and our interpretive intelligence.

The assignments in this chapter ask for focused summaries of specific texts. But you'll want to keep in mind that summaries most often work in coordination with other strategies. An essay defining what anthropologists mean by "participant observation" might summarize one anthropologist's account of her experience to illustrate the concept. In a history essay about the Napoleonic Wars, you might follow a sequential account of important battles with a summary paragraph clarifying the pattern of Napoleon's rise and fall. A psychology paper classifying personality types might be subdivided into summaries of several psychologists' descriptions of particular types. A comparison for an economics class of the role of the national banking system before and after the Great Depression might interweave one scholar's description of the earlier system with another's description of the later one. An analysis of a novel for an English literature course might contain in its early paragraphs a brief summary of the crucial events of the novel. An argumentative essay for an ethics class might first summarize opposing arguments before making a case for stronger gun-control laws.

Working Examples

A Working Example from Psychology

Writing summaries depends on being able to recognize, connect, and represent generalizations — abstractions. We offer as an example a short passage and a summary constructed from it. The passage, about alcoholism, is taken from a psychology textbook.

> Despite public concern over the increasing use of marijuana and hard drugs, alcohol is still the most widely used and abused drug in this country. It is estimated that some 9 million people in the United States are alcoholics or problem drinkers, and alcohol consumption appears to be steadily increasing. The cost in terms of lost productivity and medical care for alcohol-related illnesses is staggering. Other social consequences include increased crime (homicides and child abuse are both related to alcohol use), family discord, deaths and injuries on the highway, and suicide.
>
> The stereotype of an alcoholic — the skid-row drunk — constitutes only a small proportion of the individuals who have serious drinking problems. The depressed housewife who takes a few drinks to get through the day and a few more to gear up for a social evening, the businessman who needs a three-martini lunch to make it through the afternoon, the overworked physician who keeps a bottle in her desk drawer, and the high-school student who drinks more and more to gain acceptance from peers are all on their way to becoming alcoholics. There are various definitions

of alcoholism, but almost all of them include the *inability to abstain* (the feeling that you cannot get through the day without a drink) and/or a *lack of control* (an inability to stop after one or two drinks). . . .

An individual can progress from social drinking to alcoholism in many ways. One survey of alcoholics describes the following four stages.

1. *Prealcoholic stage.* Individual drinks socially and on occasion heavily to relieve tension and forget about problems. Heavy drinking becomes more frequent, and in times of crisis, the person resorts more and more to the bolstering effects of alcohol.
2. *Prodromal stage.* Drinking becomes furtive and may be accompanied by "blackouts," during which the person remains conscious and relatively coherent but later cannot recall events. The individual becomes preoccupied with drinking and feels guilty about it but worries about when and where she or he will have the next drink.
3. *Crucial stage.* All control is lost; once the person starts drinking, he or she continues until sick or stuporous. Social adjustment deteriorates, and the drinking becomes evident to family, friends, and employers. The person starts drinking in the morning, neglects his or her diet, and may go on the first "bender"— several days of continuous drinking. Abstinence is still possible (the individual may go for several weeks or even months without drinking), but once he or she takes a drink, the whole pattern begins again. This is called the "crucial" stage because unless the individual seeks help, she or he is in danger of becoming a chronic alcoholic.
4. *Chronic stage.* Drinking is continual; the individual lives only to drink. The body has become so accustomed to alcohol that the person may suffer withdrawal symptoms without it. Malnutrition and alcohol have produced numerous physiological disorders. The person has lost all concern for physical appearance, self-esteem, family, friends, and social status. This is the stage of the skid-row drunk.

Not all elements of these stages have been corroborated. Some alcoholics seldom get drunk but consume enough alcohol each day to maintain a certain level of relaxation, and some never experience blackouts. Nevertheless, the general progression from stage to stage is typical of many alcoholics.

— Rita L. Atkinson, Richard C. Atkinson, and Ernest R. Hilgard,
Introduction to Psychology, 8th ed.

In attempting to represent this passage in a summary, we notice immediately that the bulk of the passage is given over to describing the four stages of alcoholism. It is likely that we can let the four stages that structure the reading structure our summary too:

```
prealcoholic stage

prodromal stage

crucial stage

chronic stage
```

We might even attempt to capture the structure in a single sentence:

> According to Atkinson, Atkinson, and Hilgard in Introduction to Psychology, alcoholism can be described in four stages: the prealcoholic stage, during which a person drinks to relieve tension; the prodromal stage, during which the person becomes preoccupied with drinking; the crucial stage, during which the person loses control but is still capable of abstaining; and the chronic stage, during which the person lives only to drink.

We composed this summary sentence by working up a lead-in phrase to identify the book and authors, establishing the topic, and then filling in the four stages, describing each in a few words. Along the way, we made a few adjustments in wording, and we had to settle on a phrasing strategy for keeping the four entries parallel.

Notice that as a summary is constructed, the material becomes more abstract. In this instance, details about each stage of alcoholism drop from sight. A summary can expand or contract to suit a writer's purpose. Any piece can be summarized in a single sentence; the question is always how much detail we are willing to do without. Here a less abstract summary would force us to choose which other points are important enough to include. Should we say that most definitions of alcoholism include something about the lack of control? Should we work in the statistic about nine million Americans? Should we acknowledge the authors' qualifying statement that "not all elements of these stages have been corroborated"? As you look back over the summary we offered as an example, reevaluate it: Do you see any ways in which, without sacrificing much conciseness, the summary can be strengthened?

A Working Example from Sociology

Summarizing calls for the ability to see connections between general, more abstract points and the specific points supporting and complicating them. It also means seeing how those generalizations are related. The more readily we can see a pattern in the general sentences of a piece, the easier it is to summarize and the more confident we feel in our accuracy.

All summaries involve some interpretive decisions. We can illustrate this a little better by looking at another example. Once again, we've chosen a very structured piece (this one organized as a classification), a passage written by a sociologist about the purposes of imprisonment.

> Lying somewhere between total annihilation of the offender on the one hand and warning or forgiveness on the other, imprisonment is generally viewed as the appropriate consequence of most serious crimes. The issue is put more bluntly by prisoners themselves in their aphorism "If you can't pull the time, don't pull the crime," but the thought is much the same.

Yet why is imprisonment appropriate? On what grounds is imprisonment justified? It is a cliche of modern penology that placing the offender in prison is for the purposes of punishment, deterrence, and reform. There is a beguiling neatness and simplicity about this three-pronged aim, but it requires examination. . . .

The idea of punishment as the purpose of imprisonment is plain enough — the person who has committed a wrong or hurt must suffer in return. The State, through its agent the prison, is entitled if not morally obligated to hurt the individual who has broken the criminal law, since a crime is by definition a wrong committed against the State. Imprisonment should be punishment, not only by depriving the individual of his liberty, but also by imposing painful conditions under which the prisoner must live within the walls.

Now it is true that there are few persons directly concerned with handling the offender who will advance this view of the prison's purpose as baldly as we have stated it here. Penologists, prison psychiatrists, prison administrators, judges — all are far more apt to claim that we do not place the criminal in prison to secure retribution but to accomplish better things. Yet there is some reason to doubt that this denial of punishment as a legitimate aim of imprisonment accurately reflects the opinions of the general public. However harsh an insistence on retribution may appear to be, it cannot be ignored as a social force shaping the nature of the penal institution, whether in the form of community reactions to accusations of "coddling" prisoners or the construction of budgets by the state legislators.

The idea of deterrence as the aim of imprisonment is somewhat more complicated, for the argument contains three parts which need to be treated separately. First, it is claimed that for those who have been imprisoned the experience is (or should be) sufficiently distasteful to convince them that crime had best be avoided in the future. This decision to forgo crime is not expected to come from a change in the attitudes and values concerning the wrongness of crime. Rather, it supposedly flows from a sharpened awareness of the penalties attached to wrongdoing. Second, it is argued that imprisonment is important as a deterrent not for the individual who has committed a crime and who has been placed in prison but for the great mass of citizens who totter on the edge. The image of the prison is supposed to check errant impulses, and again it is fear rather than morality which is expected to guide the individual in his action. Third, there is the assertion that the deterrent effect of imprisonment is largely a matter of keeping known criminals temporarily out of circulation and the major aim of imprisonment is to keep offenders within the walls where they cannot prey on the free community, at least for the moment.

Like those who argue for imprisonment as retribution, the adherents of imprisonment as deterrence tend to support those policies which would make life in prison painful, with the possible exception of those who argue for simple custody alone. They are faced with a moral dilemma when it comes to justifying punishment for the criminal in order to deter the noncriminal, for as Morris Cohen has pointed out, we feel uneasiness in hurting Peter to keep Paul honest. A more serious problem, however, is presented by the fact that the view of imprisonment as deterrence is based on a hypothetical, complicated cause-and-effect relationship. Does the prison experience actually induce the criminal to refrain from wrongdoing through fear of another period in custody? Does the image of the prison, for those who have never been within its walls, really check the potential criminal in mid-act? Affirmative answers to these questions must be secured before the use of imprisonment for the purpose of deterrence is rationally justified, and this has proven to be no easy task. The usual procedure has been to make the commonsense assumption that men are rarely so good by either nature or training that they will always conform to the law without the threat of the pains of imprisonment in the background. For those who are too humanitarian to claim vengeance as the goal of confinement and too cynical, perhaps, to hope for real reform in the majority of cases, the objective of deterrence offers a comfortable compromise.

When we turn to the idea of imprisonment as reform, it is clear that there are few who will quarrel with such a desirable goal — the disputes center on how it can be accomplished, if at all. In seeking to use imprisonment for the rehabilitation of the offender, the aim is to eradicate those causes of crime which lie within the individual, and imprisonment is commonly regarded as a device to hold the patient still long enough so that this can be achieved.

Unfortunately, the advocates of confinement as a method of achieving rehabilitation of the criminal have often found themselves in the position of calling for an operation where the target of the scalpel remains unknown. In recent years, with the rise of sociological and psychological interpretations of human behavior, the search for causal factors underlying criminality has grown more sophisticated but the answer remains almost as elusive as before. Yet in spite of the confusion in this area, there are many students of the problem who believe that the reformation of the offender requires a profound change in the individual's personality and that this change can be won only by surrounding the prisoner with a "permissive" or "supportive" social atmosphere. For those devoted to a psychiatric view of criminal behavior, psychotherapy in individual or group sessions is often advanced as the most hopeful procedure; for those with a more sociological bent, self-government, meaningful work, and education are frequently claimed as minimal steps in the direction of reformation. Both factions — divergent though they may be in their theoretical arguments — are apt to agree that the punishing features of imprisonment should be reduced or eliminated if efforts at rehabilitation are to be effective.

— Gresham M. Sykes, *The Society of Captives: A Study of a Maximum Security Prison*

Recognizing how a piece of writing is organized helps us summarize it. In the case of this sociological essay, that means seeing the categories (punishment, deterrence, reform) that organize the passage from the end of the second paragraph to the end of the excerpt. Another key is to find some comfortable way of mapping out the main points so that we can see their relationships. The more complex the text we are trying to summarize, the more we may need to construct a rough text of our own as go-between, a set of notes from which we can work more easily than from the text itself. One such intermediary text is an outline. Outlines aren't always useful in writing summaries, but they can be very helpful when the text seems subdivided into balancing parts.

When we see in the essay about imprisonment that paragraphs 3 and 4 are about punishment, 5 and 6 about deterrence, and 7 and 8 about reform, a tentative outline begins to form (even if we're not sure what to do about paragraphs 1 and 2):

```
Purposes of Imprisonment

A.   Punishment

B.   Deterrence

C.   Reform
```

As we look more closely, having noticed that there are two paragraphs for each purpose, we suspect that each set works in a similar way. We can say at least that in each pairing the first paragraph establishes one of the purposes while the second goes on to do something else. What that something else is we're not sure. But we can play with some possibilities. Does each of the follow-up paragraphs raise objections? Or is each second paragraph about how the motive of punishment, deterrence, or reform has helped to shape prison policy? Or perhaps the relations between paragraphs are not so parallel after all (maybe the follow-up paragraphs simply add miscellaneous comments — our expectations of order aren't always fulfilled). After some further hesitation, we decide that each of the follow-up paragraphs says something about who favors a particular purpose — and why. Tentatively, as we begin to find some of the phrasing we will use in our summary, we can map our interpretation of how the piece is held together:

```
Purposes of Imprisonment

A.   Punishment
     1.   Justification: State is entitled to harm those who
          break its laws by harming others.
     2.   Favored by parts of the general public who insist on
          retribution.
B.   Deterrence
     1.   Justification
          a.   Imprisonment keeps offender from repeating if
               penalty is strong enough.
          b.   Threat of imprisonment prevents "the great mass
               of citizens who totter on the edge" from falling
               into crime.
```

```
            c.   Imprisonment at least keeps current inmates off
                 the streets and so prevents the crimes they might
                 commit if they were free.
       2.   Favored by those "who are too humanitarian to claim
            vengeance" and "too cynical" to hope for real reform.
  C.   Reform
       1.   Justification: Imprisonment provides the opportunity
            "to eradicate those causes of crime which lie within
            the individual."
       2.   Favored by most people, but there is no agreement on
            how to reform criminals, except that most profes-
            sionals believe prisoners will change only in a sup-
            portive atmosphere.
            a.   Psychiatrists stress group therapy.
            b.   Sociologists stress "self-government," meaningful
                 work, education.
```

Such outlines aren't ends in themselves; the test of their value is how well they help you to summarize a text succinctly and accurately. Before attempting to write a summary from an outline, you'll probably want to check back to the text itself, reevaluating how well the outline represents the original. Notice that while conforming to general principles of balance, the outline we've constructed has also opened up subdivisions where points grow more complicated. Even so, at a last run-through we may discover important emphases that we've neglected. For example, we might feel that the outline doesn't reflect Sykes's objections about deterrence. Rather than finding some new slot in our outline for these objections, we can just jot ourselves a reminder in the margin: "Include something about the lack of evidence that deterrence works." Notice that we are preparing for the actual sentences we'll be using in the summary by paraphrasing and by quoting distinctive phrases.

One further consideration before trying to convert the outline to a summary: We need to ask ourselves how we want to begin. Remember that we passed over the opening paragraph in constructing the outline. It's possible that we pass over it again, moving right to the heart of the matter: "According to Gresham M. Sykes, three purposes are served by sending criminal offenders to prison." But do you see any difficulties in starting this way? In the first place, we've made Sykes sound enthusiastic about sending people to prison, but his own presentation sounds more neutral than that. Second, we're missing the opportunity to come closer to the way Sykes himself frames his material: How is imprisonment justified? So a better sentence might read, "In *The Society of Captives,* Gresham M. Sykes asks how we justify placing criminals in prison." Another alternative is to try framing our own version of the question before introducing Sykes at all: "We usually assume that people convicted of crimes should be imprisoned. But why? In *The Society of Captives,* Gresham M. Sykes reviews the traditional answers."

Here, after some collapsing and editing of the sort we practiced earlier, is one draft of a summary constructed from our outline:

> We usually assume that people convicted of crimes should be imprisoned. But why? In The Society of Captives, Gresham M. Sykes reviews the three traditional answers to this question. First, we imprison people to punish them. We feel that those who hurt others should be hurt in return. Punishment is favored by most of the general public. Second, some feel that imprisonment deters further crime. It can do so in three ways: by discouraging released criminals from repeating crimes, by preventing citizens "who totter on the edge" from falling into crime, and by keeping potential repeaters off the streets. Sykes says that evidence is lacking to show a cause and effect relation between punishment and deterrence, but he says that people "too humanitarian to claim vengeance" and "too cynical to hope for real reform" see deterrence as a "comfortable compromise." Third, we imprison people in hopes of reforming them. Imprisonment provides the opportunity "to eradicate those causes of crime which lie within the individual." Most people agree that this is a good aim, but there is no general agreement about how to accomplish it. Psychiatrists stress group therapy, while sociologists stress "self-government, meaningful work, and education."

This is an effective summary. It preserves most of the main emphases of the original, and it holds together coherently in its own right, thanks partly to the clear signposts provided by "First . . . Second . . . Third." But if you still feel a little dissatisfied, as we do, try putting your finger on the difficulty.

So far we have been treating the excerpt as though our job were simply to report on the contents of the passage. In most academic situations, however, our summary would have some other purpose. Perhaps we've been asked to examine several writers' views on the functions of prisons; perhaps we've been asked to analyze and criticize Sykes's views; perhaps we're writing an essay on the role of psychologists and sociologists in prisons. In any case, our purpose will very much affect our summary. If, for example, we were writing about the function of prison psychiatry, we might be using our summary of Sykes's writing to show that psychiatrists' efforts to help inmates must compete with prison's other functions, and perhaps even with other professionals' strategies for helping prisoners. Summarizing Sykes's work might get us started on an essay about the resistance met by psychiatrists in prisons.

Let's assume, in following through just a little further with this example, that we are writing an essay on the topic "What Do We Want Our Prisons to Do and How Well Can They Do It?" In such a context, our use of Sykes's work might change significantly to fit our purposes without distorting his. Note some of the changes in this version:

> In The Society of Captives, Gresham M. Sykes maintains that our prison system pursues three purposes: punishment, reform, and deterrence. Most of the general public believes in imprisonment as punishment or retribution; prisons are meant to hurt those who have hurt others. Many people also believe that prisons are a place of reform; individuals get the opportunity to "eradicate" the causes of crime in themselves. Some people also believe that the thought of prison deters crime: by discouraging those convicted from repeating their crimes, by frightening potential criminals, or by keeping proven criminals out of circulation.
>
> Taken together, these three purposes may seem a strong argument for our present prison system. Yet when we look more closely, we see that the first two aims, punishment and reform, are conflicting; it's hard to reform someone whom you're also punishing. Perhaps it's this contradiction that makes sensitive people reach for the theory of deterrence, which Sykes sees as a "comfortable compromise" for those who cannot believe wholeheartedly in either punishment or reform. But Sykes, writing in 1958, could point to no solid evidence that deterrence actually works. Do we know any more today?

What adjustments have been made in arrangement or emphasis? What purpose is the summary of Sykes now being asked to serve?

A Working Example from Folklore

Let's consider one last example of the problems and strategies of summary writing, this time working with a piece that does not lend itself to outlining. The following fairy tale, "The Singing Bone," taken from the collection of the Brothers Grimm, is the sort you might be asked to analyze in a folklore class.

> There was once in a country great trouble about a wild boar, who attacked the peasants in the fields, and had killed and torn to pieces several men with his tusks. The king of the country promised a large reward to anyone who would free the land from this plague. But the animal was so large and strong that no man would even venture near the forest where he lived.
>
> At last, the king made a proclamation that he would give his only daughter in marriage to any man who would bring the wild boar to him dead or alive.
>
> There lived two brothers in that country, the sons of a poor man, who gave notice of their readiness to enter on this perilous undertaking. The eldest, who was clever and crafty, was influenced by pride; the youngest, who was innocent and simple, offered himself from kindness of heart.
>
> Thereupon the king advised that, as the best and safest way would be to take opposite directions in the wood, the eldest was to go in the evening, and the youngest in the morning.
>
> The youngest had not gone far when a little fairy stepped up to him. He held in his hand a black spear, and said, "I will give you this spear because your heart is innocent and good. With this you can go out and discover the wild boar, and he shall not be able to harm you."
>
> He thanked the little man, took the spear, placed it on his shoulder, and, without delay, went farther into the forest. It was not long before he espied the animal coming towards him, and fiercely making ready to spring. But the youth stood still, and held the spear firmly in front of him. In wild rage the fierce beast ran violently towards him, and was met by the spear, on the point of which he threw himself, and, as it pierced him to the heart, he fell dead.
>
> Then the youngster took the dead monster on his shoulder, and went to find his brother. As he approached the other side of the wood, where stood a large hall, he heard music, and found a number of people dancing, drinking wine, and making merry. His eldest brother was amongst them, for he thought the wild boar would not run far away, and he wished to get up his courage for the evening by cheerful company and wine.
>
> When he caught sight of his youngest brother coming out of the forest laden with his booty, the most restless jealousy and malice rose in his heart. But he disguised his bitter feelings and spoke kindly to his brother, and said:
>
> "Come in, and stay with us, dear brother, and rest awhile, and get up your strength by a cup of wine."
>
> So the youth, not suspecting anything wrong, carried the dead boar into his brother's house, and told him of the little man he had met in the wood, who had given him the spear, and how he had killed the wild animal.
>
> The elder brother persuaded him to stay and rest till the evening, and then they went out together in the twilight, and walked by the river till it became quite dark.

A little bridge lay across the river, over which they had to pass, and the eldest brother let the young one go before him. When they arrived at the middle of the stream, the wicked man gave his youngest brother a blow from behind, and he fell down dead instantly.

But, fearing he might not be quite dead, he threw the body over the bridge into the river, and through the clear waters saw it sink into the sand. After this wicked deed he ran home quickly, took the dead wild boar on his shoulders, and carried it to the king, with the pretense that he had killed the animal, and that therefore he could claim the princess as his wife, according to the king's promise.

But these dark deeds are not often concealed, for something happens to bring them to light. Not many years after a herdsman, passing over the bridge with his flock, saw beneath him in the sand a little bone as white as snow, and thought that it would make a very nice mouthpiece for his horn.

As soon as they had passed over the bridge, he waded into the middle of the stream, for the water was very shallow, took up the bone, and carried it home to make a mouthpiece for his horn.

But the first time he blew the horn after the bone was in, it filled the herdsman with wonder and amazement; for it began to sing of itself, and these were the words it sang:

Ah! dear shepherd, you are blowing your horn
With one of my bones, which night and morn
Lie still unburied, beneath the wave
Where I was thrown in a sandy grave.
I killed the wild boar, and my brother slew me,
And gained the princess by pretending 'twas he.

"What a wonderful horn," said the shepherd, "that can sing of itself! I must take it to my lord the king."

As soon as the horn was brought before the king and blown by the shepherd, it at once began to sing the same song and the same words.

The king was at first surprised, but his suspicion being aroused, he ordered that the sand under the bridge should be examined immediately, and then the entire skeleton of the murdered man was discovered, and the whole wicked deed came to light.

The wicked brother could not deny the deed; he was therefore ordered to be tied in a sack and drowned, while the remains of his murdered brother were carefully carried to the churchyard, and laid to rest in a beautiful grave.

—"The Singing Bone" from *The Complete Brothers Grimm Fairy Tales*

As with other narratives, this one doesn't lend itself to outlining because there is no quick way to perceive a hierarchy of points: One event simply follows another. Our choices about which parts to emphasize are hard to make, and many of the choices we do make will seem arbitrary. But if outlining is not likely to help, some other form of note taking might. One possibility is to construct a "scratch" outline, simply listing in notation form (or even in sentences) the points that seem important enough to choose among later. Here's an example of a scratch outline made from "The Singing Bone":

"The Singing Bone"

Boar terrorizing a kingdom.

King promises reward.

King ups the ante by offering daughter.

Two brothers, oldest proud, younger kind, undertake the mission.

Young brother encounters fairy who gives him a spear.

He encounters the boar and kills it.

Goes to tell older brother the good news; older brother reacts as if pleased but feels malice.

At his first opportunity older brother kills younger brother and tosses him into a stream.

He takes the boar and claims the princess.

Some years later a herdsman finds a bone in the stream.

He uses the bone to make a mouthpiece for his horn.

The horn plays itself and tells the story of the murdered young man.

The herdsman takes the horn to the king who makes the right deductions, discovers the body of the young brother.

The older brother is drowned, and the younger buried.

By combining some entries, passing over others, and retrieving a point or two that we decide we need after all, we might produce a summary like this one:

In the fairy story "The Singing Bone," a king offers his daughter to any man who can kill the wild boar that has been ravaging his kingdom. Two brothers undertake the mission. While the older brother waits at an inn, the younger brother enters the forest, where he meets a fairy who gives him a magic spear. With the spear, the young man soon kills the boar and returns to tell his brother the good news. The older brother pretends to be pleased, but at the first opportunity he kills his brother, tosses the body into a river, and takes the boar to the king. Some years later a herdsman finds a bone in the river and makes it into a mouthpiece for his horn. The horn is capable of playing itself and tells the story of the murdered man. The herdsman takes his horn to the king, who deduces what has happened and orders his son-in-law drowned.

Note that even a straightforward summary like this is the product of dozens, if not hundreds, of very particular decisions about what to include, exclude, combine, and connect. For example, we decided not to characterize the two brothers as "innocent" and "proud," preferring to let those characteristics remain implied. We decided to ignore the slight upbeat of the ending emphasizing the younger brother's peaceful grave. We characterized the spear as "magic," even though there's no absolute evidence that it's anything more than a good spear. By omitting the king's stipulation that the two brothers hunt separately and at different times, we've made the older brother seem not only arrogant but slothful. Are these serious omissions and distortions of the original? It's hard to tell without knowing what purpose our summary is supposed to serve. Imagine how the retelling of this story might shift to accommodate the following perspectives: a student of folklore looking at a variety of tales that offer princesses as rewards, a child psychologist examining how fairy tales deal with sibling rivalries, or a literature student thinking about the conventional ways stories are opened and closed.

Let us risk a short summary of our comments on summarizing. In academic contexts, you'll be exposed to summaries as abstracts, as introductions and conclusions to textbook chapters, as reviews, as lectures, and as textbooks themselves. But the most common form of summary occurs when one writer summarizes the work of another, whether to understand it, to pass it on, to build on it, or to criticize it. Writing an effective summary calls on your ability to see relations between general points, to express those relations in a coherent way, to take advantage of parallels, to make use of apt quotations, and to edit for compression. Summaries can vary in length according to your purposes, gaining or losing detail at each level of abstraction. A summary will always attempt to represent the original fairly — in structure, in emphasis, in tone. But any summary involves numerous decisions and invariably becomes an interpretation of the original. Above all, you'll want any summary that you write to help express some purpose of your own.

A Professional Application

In the following excerpt from her study of women factory workers, *Bitter Choices: Blue-Collar Women In and Out of Work,* sociologist Ellen Israel Rosen summarizes research on the new global economy and its consequences for American labor. Notice how, in constructing her summary, she incorporates statistical data (e.g., wages, numbers of jobs lost), quotations from other researchers, specific examples of cities and trades, and mini-summaries of other books and articles (e.g., the stories from the *New York Times* and the *Wall Street Journal* on unemployed steel and auto workers). Notice, too, how she shapes her summary of the new global economy toward the topic of her book: women blue-collar workers in the United States. (She explicitly does this in paragraph 9 on p. 96). And notice how, in line with the topic of her discussion, she is able to acknowledge the broad effects of global economic restructuring, while maintaining her focus on women workers — a good example is found in the first two sentences of paragraph 19 on page 98.

The New International Division of Labor

ELLEN ISRAEL ROSEN

What many now call "the global economy" or "the new international division of labor" has been discussed extensively in a large, and still growing, body of research which explores the growth of multinational corporations in the past forty years or so. Much of this work theoretically and empirically examines not only the structure and patterns of the new global industrial shifts, but the consequences of these patterns for employment — both domestically and abroad.

In brief, it is argued that the past forty years have witnessed the growth of vast, often American-dominated, multinational corporations which have achieved new levels of centralization and control over a worldwide network of productive enterprises. The growth of multinational corporations since World War II has generated a massive restructuring of worldwide industrial production. The existence of American industrial hegemony after World War II initiated this growth, which was also made possible by the development of technological breakthroughs in transport and communication and by supportive federal tax and trade policies which favored capital integration. The reemergence of European and Japanese capital, with a greater investment in new, labor-saving technologies, has, however, begun to challenge American hegemony as the leader of international capitalism.

At the forefront of new technological breakthroughs in steel, automaking, and microelectronics, European and Japanese firms have become, in the past twenty years or so, serious rivals to America's industrial hegemony in world markets. One of the most serious consequences of these changes has been the loss of high-wage, unionized, manufacturing jobs. These losses have fallen mostly on male workers who are employed in the steel, auto, machine tool, and other "heavy" industries. The inability of American manufacturing to continue to compete with the higher productivity and typically lower wages of foreign manufacturing has mobilized public attention and has generated serious policy discussions about a new industrial policy for America.

Cities like Youngstown, Ohio, Pittsburgh, and Detroit continue to provide graphic examples of the toll in human suffering wrought by "deindustrialization." Barry Bluestone and Bennett Harrison estimate that there has been a loss of fifteen million jobs in

---

ELLEN ISRAEL ROSEN (b. 1945) is an associate professor of sociology in the Department of Social Services at Nichols College in Massachusetts. She has contributed articles to several journals, including *Economic Development Quarterly* and *Descent,* and she is currently writing about the apparel industry. Her book *Bitter Choices: Blue-Collar Women In and Out of Work* was published in 1987.

this country between 1968 and 1976 as a result of industrial contractions and plant closures. In addition to large-scale unemployment, these changes have created severe problems for a labor movement weakened by the waning number of jobs. The past fifteen years or so has witnessed new onslaughts of union busting and intensified demands for concessions.

Another important thrust of research concerned with the effects of the new international division of labor has focused on the changed economic relations between developed and Third World countries. These scholars point out that until recently many Third World countries were primarily sources of cheap raw materials which were transported to industrialized countries to be used in domestic manufacturing. Today, instead of exporting raw materials, these underdeveloped countries are exporting their labor. Multinational corporations, in search of cheaper labor, have set up new, deskilled manufacturing operations abroad. Or, indigenous manufacturing operations have "run away" to "export processing zones" where they benefit from low taxes and most importantly, low wages. June Nash and Patricia Fernandez-Kelly write,

> According to the United Nations Industrial Development Organization, there are at present almost 120 export-processing zones in areas as far distant from one another as the Orient, Latin America, Africa, Western Europe, and the United States. Almost two million people are currently employed in EPZs throughout the world and many more are directly or indirectly affected by their existence.

Wages in these zones are far below what comparable workers in the United States would be paid. The average wage in Hong Kong is $1.18 per hour, Taiwan offers $.57, South Korea $.63. In the Peoples Republic of China wages are $.16 an hour.

Grossman and Ehrenreich have documented some of the effects of what they call "the global assembly line." They point out that most of the manufacturing to be found in the new export processing zones provides few jobs for skilled workers. Instead, recent technological changes have made it possible to deskill production processes, enabling the multinationals to hire large numbers of young, peasant women who are "first generation immigrants" to industrial society. Grossman estimates that there are more than two million, mostly young, unmarried women, employed in places like Malaysia, Taiwan, and in Mexican border towns, making garments, textiles, toys, footwear, pharmaceuticals, appliances, and computer components.

Many anthropologists who have studied the effects of this development have concluded that it is not only destructive to the texture and fabric of traditional ways of life, but it is extremely exploitative of young women. Unfettered by protective labor legislation or regulation of any kind, these enterprises have recreated industrial conditions similar to, perhaps worse than, those found in the workshops of Europe and America more than a hundred years ago. The women work long hours, often in dangerous settings, where many are exposed to a variety of health hazards. Ehrenreich describes "wages on a par with what an eleven-year-old boy could earn on a paper route, and living conditions resembling what Engels found in Manchester." Further, management has found ways of manipulating the subservience of traditional women in order to keep the "factory girls" in line and avoid protest or rebellion.

The employment dislocations wrought by the new international division of labor, however, are not limited to Third World women and American men. Though few observers have noticed their plight, women in domestic manufacturing have also suffered from the effects of these international economic transformations. Unable to compete with women in South Korea who earn $.63 an hour, they have been losing their jobs in record numbers for the past twenty years. As I have already pointed out, in the past twenty years 800,000 jobs have been lost in the clothing, apparel, and textile industries, industries which employ women extensively.

Both the *New York Times* and the *Wall Street Journal* ran a series of front-page stories describing the personal and family effects of mass unemployment during the 1981–82 shakeout in the steel and auto industries. The men who lost their jobs were some of the most highly paid workers in the country, backed by powerful labor unions. Most were heads of families who had wives, children, and mortgages to support. Yet the quiet desperation of countless numbers of displaced women workers in garment shops and light manufacturing plants all over the country has been publicly ignored.

As Sol Chaikin, President of the International Ladies' Garment Workers' Union, has pointed out in testimony before the Subcommittee on Economic Stabilization of the House Committee on Banking, Finance and Urban Affairs,

> In the process of assessing the growing decline of capital intensive industries, the equally, and in a sense, more severe problems confronting labor intensive manufacture are being overlooked. Perhaps this occurs because labor intensive manufacture is, by and large, conducted on a small scale with the average firm employing fewer than fifty workers. For example, when an apparel factory, employing an average of fifty workers, mainly women, closes, it attracts little media attention. Even if 200 such shops around the nation close at one time — as is the case — the same lack of attention prevails. When a steel or auto plant closes down, on the other hand, the unhappy event usually results in front-page stories and extensive television coverage.

Perhaps there is no TV coverage when garment shops close because the displaced workers are "only women."

The failure to notice the impact of unemployment on women results from erroneously accepting the conventional wisdom. First, many believe that women don't need jobs to support themselves and their children. Second, it is assumed that losing a "woman's" blue-collar job does not represent much of a problem. Presumably, if garment workers are unable to compete with women in South Korea who earn $.63 an hour they can simply get other low-wage jobs which are in plentiful supply; they can become secretaries and waitresses. As we will show in this volume, both of these assumptions are frequently belied by the evidence.

But the problems of today's women factory workers are not limited to job displacement and unemployment. The new international division of labor has also contributed to the reversal of a historical trend in which women had begun to considerably improve their situation in manufacturing employment. In the 1960s changes began to occur in women's production jobs just at the point that paid employment became increasingly important to millions of working women, married women with children. The effects of a deteriorating work situation are felt unevenly across industries and between regions. However, many blue-collar women who continue to work in manufacturing are experiencing significant wage declines and an overall deterioration in their working conditions.

There are new case studies of women employed in a variety of domestic manufacturing jobs which give us a glimpse of the exploitation that is currently being experienced by women in production jobs. Researchers and journalists have recently documented the existence of small shops in which recent immigrants, both legal and illegal, work in sweatshops for less than the minimum wage. New forms of industrial homework are emerging in the assembly of electronic equipment.

Competition with women employed on Third World global assembly lines is not only creating unemployment for domestic women production workers. It is also creating downward pressure on the wages of women who continue to be employed in our nation's mills and factories. In 1971 women who worked full-time and year-round as "operatives" in manufacturing earned 107 percent of the wages of comparably employed saleswomen. By 1981, their earnings had dropped to 91 percent of the earnings of full-time women salesworkers. In 1971 women operatives earned 115 percent of the wages of women in service jobs. Ten years later they earned only 103 percent of what women service workers made. Their earnings compared to women in craft jobs had dropped as well. In 1971 they earned 88 percent of craft workers' salaries. By 1981 the proportion had dropped to 78 percent.

The wage declines experienced by America's blue-collar women have been exacerbated by massive regional shifts of employment from the Frost Belt to the Sun Belt. Inevitably, these changes have meant the deunionization of America's women factory workers. For ultimately it was unionization which created the wage advantage experienced by blue-collar women in the postwar period. A comparison of statewide employment data from the 1970 and 1980 census shows that the greatest increases in women's blue-collar jobs were in Texas, Florida, and California, while the greatest declines were in New York, New Jersey, and Pennsylvania.

As firms in the older, mill-based industries have closed their doors in the heavily unionized industrial areas, blue-collar women have inevitably left the union rolls. While it is difficult to get complete data on union membership we do know that between 1956 and 1976 blue-collar unions lost roughly 100,000 women members. The apparel and textile unions lost the greatest number of women members; but the Bakery Workers, the Electrical Workers (IUE), the Meatcutters and the Auto Workers also lost women union members during this period.

The deunionization of America's women production workers, and indeed, all workers, has been exacerbated by the new forms of union busting we have begun to see during the past decade. In a brilliant article in the *University of California Law Review,* Jules Bernstein has described some of the more sophisticated strategies management consultants have begun to use against union organizing efforts.

Union busting efforts are certainly not limited to women or to workers in manufacturing jobs. But blue-collar women may become increasingly vulnerable to the efforts of employers to prevent them from organizing, primarily because management can now more easily threaten to relocate jobs overseas. Firms can threaten to move production sites not only from region to region domestically, but to the new export processing zones outside the country in order to head off union drives. A variety of untenable working conditions may become more acceptable if the alternative is to be without any work at all.

Women employed in other types of work have not yet become as vulnerable to deunionization as their blue-collar counterparts. During the same period that blue-collar unions lost 100,000 women members, a total of 1.1 million working women joined labor unions. They accounted for about half the growth in total union membership in the twenty-year period. While union membership rose only 13 percent during this period, the numbers of women in unions rose by 34 percent. The greatest increases in women's union membership between 1956 and 1976 were among teachers, government workers, and not surprisingly, among service employees and retail clerks. Growing numbers of blue-collar women then will probably continue to be susceptible to both lower wages and the risk of displacement in coming years. It is hardly surprising that black women, immigrants, and other minorities are increasing their numbers in these jobs as they become less desirable to hold.

Assignments

An Anthropology Assignment

This selection comes from an introductory anthropology text. Some of it is straightforward, but at times it gets fairly technical. A suggestion: Don't get bogged down in the technical language. Keep asking yourself what the main focus of the passage is — and try to come up with personal examples to ground the discussion in familiar experience.

As a warm-up, write a brief summary of Kottak's discussion of rites of passage. Then refocus your summary to help you write an essay about the rites of passage you find most typical of your culture. Come up with several examples, and discuss at least one of those examples in some detail.

Rites of Passage

CONRAD PHILLIP KOTTAK

Early in this century Arnold van Gennep, a Belgian anthropologist, studied rites of passage in a variety of societies. Passage rites, found throughout the world, are exemplified by such phenomena as vision quests of certain Native American populations in North America. As boys moved from boyhood to socially recognized manhood, they temporarily separated themselves from their communities to journey alone to the wilderness. After a period of isolation, often accompanied by fasting and drug consumption, the young men would see a vision, which would become their personal guardian spirit. On return to their communities they would be reintegrated as adults. In contemporary societies, rites of passage include confirmations, baptisms, bar mitzvahs, and fraternity hazing. Passage rites do not refer only to such changes in social status as from boyhood to manhood, or from nonmember to fraternity brother, but apply more generally to any change in place, condition, social position, or age.

Examining data from a variety of societies, van Gennep generalized that all rites of

---

CONRAD PHILLIP KOTTAK (b. 1942) is a professor of anthropology and chair of the anthropology department at the University of Michigan, where he has taught since 1968. He has published several books, contributed many articles to academic journals, and written for popular magazines like *Natural History* and *Psychology Today.* The passage reprinted here comes from his college textbook, *Cultural Anthropology* (3rd Edition, 1982).

passage have three phases: separation, margin, and aggregation. Separation is exemplified by the initial detachment of individuals from the group or their initial movement from one place to another; aggregation, by their reentry into society after completion of the rite. More recently, anthropologist Victor Turner has focused on the marginal period or condition, the position between states, the limbo during which individuals have left one place or state but have not yet entered or joined the next. Van Gennep used the Latin term *limen* (threshold) to refer to this in-between period, and Turner's designation of it as the *liminal* phase of a passage rite will be used here.

On the basis of data from several societies, Turner identified generalized attributes of liminality. Liminal individuals occupy ambiguous social positions. They exist apart from ordinary status distinctions and expectations, living in a time out of time. They are cut off from normal social intercourse. Turner points out that liminal periods are ritually demarcated by a variety of contrasts with regular social life. For example, among the Ndembu of Zambia, whom Turner studied, a newly chosen chief had to undergo a passage rite before taking office. During the liminal period, his past and future positions in society were ignored, even reversed, and he was subjected to a variety of insults, harangues, instructions, and humiliations.

In contrast to the vision quest and the initiation of the Ndembu chief, which are individualistic, passage rites are often collective. A group of people — boys undergoing circumcision, fraternity initiates, men attending military boot camps, football players at summer training camps, women becoming nuns — pass through the rites together. Turner lists contrasts or oppositions between liminality and normal social life. Most notable is a social aspect of collective liminality that he calls "communitas." People who experience liminality together characteristically form an egalitarian community; whatever social distinctions have existed before, or will exist afterwards, are temporarily forgotten. Liminal individuals experience the same treatment and conditions and are expected to act alike. Liminality may be marked ritually and symbolically by reversals of ordinary behavior. Sexual taboos may be intensified or, conversely, sexual excess may be encouraged.

Turner also points out that not only is liminality always a temporary part of any passage rite, it may, in certain social contexts, become a permanent attribute of particular groups. This will occur, Turner suggests, in the most socially diverse societies, presumably state-organized societies and particularly modern nations. Religious sects often use liminal characteristics to set themselves off from the rest of the society. Such requirements as humility, poverty, equality, obedience, sexual abstinence, and silence may be conditions of sect membership. The ritual aspect of persons, settings, and events may also be communicated through liminal attributes that set them off as extraordinary — outside normal social space and regular time. Thus . . . Turner focuses on the social functions of rituals, in this case of passage rites. Their role in creating temporary or permanent social solidarity is his main interest.

A Biology Assignment

The following passage by virologist Stephen S. Morse presents the beginnings of an argument about the role human alterations of the environment play in the spread of life-threatening viruses. In one paragraph summarize the gist of Morse's argument, using whatever illustrations you need to support your explanation.

Here are some suggestions to help you organize your summary.

- As a scientist who wants to reach a popular audience, Morse builds up to his argument through dramatic vignettes and historical cases; he doesn't present his argument right away. Thus you'll probably need to read the passage several times to understand his claim. When you reread it, mark those sections that serve as illustrations and those in which he explicitly lays out his argument.
- Although the passage reads in a straightforward way, to highlight Morse's argument you may not want to summarize it paragraph by paragraph. You may need to change the order of Morse's observations or deemphasize some parts in favor of others. Why?

Once you have finished your paragraph, jot down a few sentences (they don't have to be perfectly crafted) in response to the following questions: What about the original made writing your summary easy or difficult? What did you have to omit, deemphasize, or play up?

Stirring Up Trouble

STEPHEN S. MORSE

The fever came on without warning, the kind every traveler fears: temperature of 103 degrees Fahrenheit, bloodshot eyes, flushed face. The victim, a young Australian man, had spent an idyllic summer hitchhiking through southern Africa with a companion before he fell ill and was rushed to a hospital. Suspecting a bacterial infection, perhaps typhoid fever, physicians administered antibiotics; yet the following day the patient's symptoms were even more serious and included copious and bloody vomiting and diarrhea as well as a rash covering most of his body. Within two more days the bleeding became uncontrollable, and the young man died abruptly of cardiorespiratory arrest. Two days later his companion checked into the hospital with similar symptoms but managed to recover after several painful weeks, as did the young nurse who had tended both patients.

Laboratory tests later confirmed the illness as Marburg disease, a mysterious virus that first made headlines in 1967, when twenty-five laboratory workers in Marburg, West Germany, and Belgrade, Yugoslavia, contracted it after handling infected monkeys; seven of them eventually died of the disease. The Marburg virus was not seen again until the two Australian travelers were stricken eight years later. Even now epidemiologists are not sure how the two came to be exposed to it.

Marburg disease is only one of many examples of what might be called emerging

---

Virologist STEPHEN S. MORSE (b. 1951) is a project manager at the Defense Advanced Research Project Agency of the Defense Sciences Office (DARPA/DSO) in Virginia. A Fellow at Rockefeller University in New York, he is also the editor of two books on viruses: *Emerging Viruses* (1992) and *Evolutionary Biology of Viruses* (1993). This article appeared in *The Sciences* magazine (September/October 1990).

viruses: viral infections that strike seemingly out of nowhere. They are often exotic and can be as lethal as they are infectious. Ebola virus, which is closely related to Marburg, made its first appearance in 1976, causing two epidemics in which death rates ranged from 50 percent in Sudan to nearly 90 percent in Zaire. In the past decade more than half a million people around the world have been stricken by acquired immune deficiency syndrome, or AIDS. The causative agent is the human immunodeficiency virus, or HIV. It is estimated that more than six million people carry the virus, which may lie dormant in the body for months or years, but whose work is often tragically swift and has so far proved unstoppable. A full list of the viruses that have emerged in recent years ranges from the familiar, such as influenza, to the decidedly foreign: dengue fever, Rift Valley fever, Argentine hemorrhagic fever, and Japanese encephalitis, to name just a few.

In the attempt to address this threat, scientists have had to reexamine how it is that infectious diseases arise. Common wisdom held that an emerging virus sprang forth so suddenly because it had evolved de novo.[1] The view made sense because of the great array of viruses and the speed with which they accumulate genetic mutations. If this picture were the norm, the evolution of new viruses such as Marburg or Ebola would be difficult, if not impossible, to predict. In addition, most viruses cannot be fought with the antibiotics that have brought so many bacterial diseases under control. As a result, grappling with the problem of emerging viruses has frequently seemed as hopeless as fighting off the Andromeda strain, the rugged, otherworldly viral protagonist of Michael Crichton's 1969 best-seller that inflicts a gruesome death on everyone who encounters it.

The emphasis on the multiformity of emerging viruses, however, has diverted attention from the features many of them share. As it happens, the great majority of "new" viruses are not really new at all but are by-products of a phenomenon I call viral traffic: the transfer to humans of diseases that exist within some animal population. Recent cases of Marburg disease, for instance, have been linked to the same region in Uganda that supplied the green monkeys handled by laboratory workers in 1967, which gave rise to speculation that the viral carrier is simian. Even a virus as frightening as HIV may not be as novel as it first seemed to be. In recent years investigators have found numerous relatives of HIV in other animal species, including close relatives among monkey populations in western Africa. In the end the novelty of AIDS may have reflected only our imperfect knowledge of the natural world, not a radical new trend in viral evolution.

The question remains: What directs the flow of viral traffic? The catalyst, it turns out, is human activity — in particular, the growing impact of that activity on the environment. The changes wrought by war, migration, agriculture, deforestation, and population growth have expedited the movement of viruses from isolated animal reservoirs to the larger, human community. Consequently, the emergence of viruses such as Marburg and HIV serves as a reminder that infectious diseases are not a vestige of our premodern past but the price we all pay for living in an organic world. Yet one need not become resigned to the next viral catastrophe. People bear enormous responsibility for bringing about the emergence of viruses; but that very capacity for effecting change implies that people's collective ability to prevent the appearance of viruses is greater than most have ever imagined.

[1]**de novo:** Anew, afresh [Eds.].

Throughout the history of civilization almost every infectious disease — even nonviral diseases — entered the human population by way of animals. One of the most notorious instances was the black death, a scourge of bubonic plague that may have killed as much as two-thirds of the population of Europe and Asia during two decades in the middle of the fourteenth century. The bacillus that causes plague is harbored by rats — a species long adapted to human settlements — and is transmitted by the fleas they carry. In medieval times, and again in the nineteenth century when a wave of plague swept across China, shipboard rats spread the disease throughout continents and across oceans, leaving social and political turmoil in their wake. A similar disease mechanism, associated with rats, lice, and fleas, generated devastating outbreaks of typhus on European battlegrounds from the sixteenth century through the 1940s.

Malaria, a persistent tropical killer, also appears to be a by-product of human-induced traffic with animals. The disease, caused by a parasitic protozoan, evidently gained a foothold long ago in western Africa, when slash-and-burn agriculture began to cut into the rainforest. The new clearings offered prime breeding grounds for a species of mosquito, *Anopheles gambiae,* whose preferred bill of fare is human blood. As tropical agriculture spread and clearings became more numerous, *A. gambiae* supplanted mosquito species that were unable to adapt to the new surroundings. In essence, by disrupting the established ecological order, people inadvertently encouraged the adaptation of a "weed" species that more often than not brought them fever and misery.

The spread of an equally terrifying tropical disease, yellow fever, was aided by an even more peculiar adaptation. *Aedes aegypti,* the mosquito that carries the yellow fever virus, is highly domesticated: It breeds better in manufactured containers such as cisterns and water casks than in natural bodies of water. This odd affinity allowed *A. aegypti* to stow away aboard seagoing vessels and cross into the New World with the slave trade. By the middle of the seventeenth century Yellow Jack came to be dreaded among sailors of the tropical Caribbean seas. Because the mosquito that carries yellow fever can survive a voyage of weeks or months, a ship's crew could be ravaged by a chain of on-board epidemics whose cause no one understood. In spite of modern attempts to control the insect, yellow fever remains a major health problem in tropical nations and is still a required immunization for anyone traveling in those regions.

If history teaches one lesson, then, it is that infectious diseases do not arise in a vacuum. Disease-carrying pests have been highly successful at taking advantage of the novel ecological niches — trash heaps, forest clearings, stagnant water sources — opened up by human habitation. Exploration and development too have brought people into contact with isolated reservoirs of illness: Ornithosis, or parrot fever, killed three dozen Americans in 1929 and 1930 when infected tropical birds were imported into the United States. More than any single carrier, it is human encroachment that ultimately precipitates the emergence of killer viruses.

An Oral History Assignment

The following is from a collection of interviews with people about the work they do. Roberto Acuña, the young man being interviewed, speaks about his development and eventual involvement in a labor union. Summarize Acuña's story in one to two paragraphs, focusing on the central idea you think he's trying to convey. What seems to be the main reason he tells us what he tells us? Some questions to help you get started:

- What events in his life does Acuña consider the most influential?
- What events or ideas does he mention more than once?

Once you have planned and begun writing your paper, consider the aspects of Acuña's story you're choosing to *exclude* from your summary. What criteria are you using to make these decisions? What are you gaining or losing? You can write a brief postscript addressing these questions.

Acuña's story touches on the problem of child poverty. If this subject interests you, you may want to do this assignment in coordination with the material in the Opening Problem (p. 79), the Professional Application (p. 94), the Economics Assignment (p. 113), and Readings: The Dimensions of Child Poverty (p. 144).

Roberto Acuña

STUDS TERKEL

I walked out of the fields two years ago. I saw the need to change the California feudal system, to change the lives of farm workers, to make these huge corporations feel they're not above anybody. I am thirty-four years old and I try to organize for the United Farm Workers of America.[1]

His hands are calloused and each of his thumbnails is singularly cut. "If you're picking lettuce, the thumbnails fall off 'cause they're banged on the box. Your hands get swollen. You can't slow down because the foreman sees you're so many boxes behind and you'd better get on. But people would help each other. If you're feeling bad that day, somebody who's feeling pretty good would help. Any people that are suffering have to stick together, whether they like it or not, whether they be black, brown, or pink."

According to Mom, I was born on a cotton sack out in the fields, 'cause she had no money to go to the hospital. When I was a child, we used to migrate from California to

[1]**United Farm Workers of America:** The union that labor leader Cesar Chávez organized among agricultural workers in California, many of whom were Mexican-American like himself [Eds.].

STUDS TERKEL (b. 1912) is a radio and television broadcaster and journalist living in Chicago. He is the host of the interview show "Wax Museum" on radio station WFMT, Chicago, and the author of *Coming of Age* (1995) as well as the Pulitzer Prize–winning *The Good War* (1985). Robert Acuña's story appears in Terkel's book *Working* (1974), a collection of first-person accounts of "people talk[ing] about what they do all day and how they feel about what they do." *Working* was adapted as a musical that was produced on Broadway in 1978.

Arizona and back and forth. The things I saw shaped my life. I remember when we used to go out and pick carrots and onions, the whole family. We tried to scratch a livin' out of the ground. I saw my parents cry out in despair, even though we had the whole family working. At the time, they were paying 62½ cents an hour. The average income must have been $1,500, maybe $2,000.[2]

This was supplemented by child labor. During those years, the growers used to have a Pick-Your-Harvest Week. They would get all the migrant kids out of school and have 'em out there pickin' the crops at peak harvest time. A child was off that week and when he went back to school, he got a little gold star. They would make it seem like something civic to do.

We'd pick everything: lettuce, carrots, onions, cucumbers, cauliflower, broccoli, tomatoes — all the salads you could make out of vegetables, we picked 'em. Citrus fruits, watermelons — you name it. We'd be in Salinas about four months. From there we'd go down into the Imperial Valley. From there we'd go to picking citrus. It was like a cycle. We'd follow the seasons.

After my dad died, my mom would come home and she'd go into her tent and I would go into ours. We'd roughhouse and everything and then we'd go into the tent where Mom was sleeping and I'd see her crying. When I asked her why she was crying she never gave me an answer. All she said was things would get better. She retired a beaten old lady with a lot of dignity. That day she thought would be better never came for her.

"One time, my mom was in bad need of money, so she got a part-time evening job in a restaurant. I'd be helping her. All the growers would come in and they'd be laughing, making nasty remarks, and make passes at her. I used to go out there and kick 'em and my mom told me to leave 'em alone, she could handle 'em. But they would embarrass her and she would cry.

"My mom was a very proud woman. She brought us up without any help from nobody. She kept the family strong. They say that a family that prays together stays together. I say that a family that works together stays together — because of the suffering. My mom couldn't speak English too good. Or much Spanish, for that matter. She wasn't educated. But she knew some prayers and she used to make us say them. That's another thing: When I see the many things in this world and this country, I could tear the churches apart. I never saw a priest out in the fields trying to help people. Maybe in these later years they're doing it. But its always the church taking *from the people.*

"We were once asked by the church to bring vegetables to make it a successful bazaar. After we got the stuff there, the only people havin' a good time were the rich people because they were the only ones that were buyin' the stuff. . . ."

I'd go barefoot to school. The bad thing was they used to laugh at us, the Anglo kids. They would laugh because we'd bring tortillas and frijoles to lunch. They would have their nice little compact lunch boxes with cold milk in their thermos and they'd laugh at us because all we had was dried tortillas. Not only would they laugh at us, but the kids would pick fights. My older brother used to do most of the fighting for us and he'd come home with black eyes all the time.

[2]"Today [i.e., the early 1970s — Eds.], because of our struggles, the pay is up to $2.00 an hour. Yet we know that is not enough."

What really hurt is when we had to go on welfare. Nobody knows the erosion of man's dignity. They used to have a label on canned goods that said, "U.S. Commodities. Not to be sold or exchanged." Nobody knows how proud it is to feel when you bought canned goods with your own money.

"I wanted to be accepted. It must have been in sixth grade. It was just before the Fourth of July. They were trying out students for this patriotic play. I wanted to do Abe Lincoln, so I learned the Gettysburg Address inside and out. I'd be out in the fields pickin' the crops and I'd be memorizin'. I was the only one who didn't have to read the part, 'cause I learned it. The part was given to a girl who was a grower's daughter. She had to read it out of a book, but they said she had better diction. I was very disappointed. I quit about eighth grade.

"Any time anybody'd talk to me about politics, about civil rights, I would ignore it. It's a very degrading thing because you can't express yourself. They wanted us to speak English in the school classes. We'd put out a real effort. I would get into a lot of fights because I spoke Spanish and they couldn't understand it. I was punished. I was kept after school for not speaking English."

We used to have our own tents on the truck. Most migrants would live in the tents that were already there in the fields, put up by the company. We got one for ourselves, secondhand, but it was ours. Anglos used to laugh at us. "Here comes the carnival," they'd say. We couldn't keep our clothes clean, we couldn't keep nothing clean, because we'd go by the dirt roads and the dust. We'd stay outside the town.

I never did want to go to town because it was a very bad thing for me. We used to go to the small stores, even though we got clipped more. If we went to the other stores, they would laugh at us. They would always point at us with a finger. We'd go to town maybe every two weeks to get what we needed. Everybody would walk in a bunch. We were afraid. (Laughs.) We sang to keep our spirits up. We joked about our poverty. This one guy would say, "When I get to be rich, I'm gonna marry an Anglo woman, so I can be accepted into society." The other guy would say, "When I get rich I'm gonna marry a Mexican woman, so I can go to that Anglo society of yours and see them hang you for marrying an Anglo." Our world was around the fields.

I started picking crops when I was eight. I couldn't do much, but every little bit counts. Every time I would get behind on my chores, I would get a carrot thrown at me by my parents. I would daydream: If I were a millionaire, I would buy all these ranches and give them back to the people. I would picture my mom living in one area all the time and being admired by all the people in the community. All of a sudden I'd be rudely awaken by a broken carrot in my back. That would bust your whole dream apart and you'd work for a while and come back to daydreaming.

We used to work early, about four o'clock in the morning. We'd pick the harvest until about six. Then we'd run home and get into our supposedly clean clothes and run all the way to school because we'd be late. By the time we got to school, we'd be all tuckered out. Around maybe eleven o'clock, we'd be dozing off. Our teachers would send notes to the house telling Mom that we were inattentive. The only thing I'd make fairly good grades on was spelling. I couldn't do anything else. Many times we never did our homework, because we were out in the fields. The teachers couldn't understand that. I would get whacked there also.

School would end maybe four o'clock. We'd rush home again, change clothes, go back to work until seven, seven thirty at night. That's not counting the weekends. On Saturday and Sunday, we'd be there from four thirty in the morning until about seven thirty in the evening. This is where we made the money, those two days. We all worked.

I would carry boxes for my mom to pack the carrots in. I would pull the carrots out and she would sort them into different sizes. I would get water for her to drink. When you're picking tomatoes, the boxes are heavy. They weigh about thirty pounds. They're dropped very hard on the trucks so they have to be sturdy.

The hardest work would be thinning and hoeing with a short-handled hoe. The fields would be about a half a mile long. You would be bending and stooping all day. Sometimes you would have hard ground and by the time you got home, your hands would be full of calluses. And you'd have a backache. Sometimes I wouldn't have dinner or anything. I'd just go home and fall asleep and wake up just in time to go out to the fields again.

I remember when we just got into California from Arizona to pick up the carrot harvest. It was very cold and very windy out in the fields. We just had a little old blanket for the four of us kids in the tent. We were freezin' our tail off. So I stole two brand-new blankets that belonged to a grower. When we got under those blankets it was nice and comfortable. Somebody saw me. The next morning the grower told my mom he'd turn us in unless we gave him back his blankets — sterilized. So my mom and I and my kid brother went to the river and cut some wood and made a fire and boiled the water and she scrubbed the blankets. She hung them out to dry, ironed them, and sent them back to the grower. We got a spanking for that.

I remember this labor camp that was run by the city. It was a POW camp for German soldiers. They put families in there and it would have barbed wire all around it. If you were out after ten o'clock at night, you couldn't get back in until the next day at four in the morning. We didn't know the rules. Nobody told us. We went to visit some relatives. We got back at about ten thirty and they wouldn't let us in. So we slept in the pickup outside the gate. In the morning, they let us in, we had a fast breakfast and went back to work in the fields.[3]

The grower would keep the families apart, hoping they'd fight against each other. He'd have three or four camps and he'd have the people over here pitted against the people over there. For jobs. He'd give the best crops to the people he thought were the fastest workers. This way he kept us going harder and harder, competing.

When I was sixteen, I had my first taste as a foreman. Handling braceros, aliens, that came from Mexico to work. They'd bring these people to work over here and then send them back to Mexico after the season was over. My job was to make sure they did a good job and pushin' 'em even harder. I was a company man, yes. My parents needed money and I wanted to make sure they were proud of me. A foreman is recognized. I was very naive. Even though I was pushing the workers, I knew their problems. They didn't know how to write, so I would write letters home for them. I would take 'em to town, buy their clothes, outside of the company stores. They had paid me $1.10 an hour. The farm workers' wage was raised to 82½ cents. But even the braceros were making more money than me, because they were working piecework. I asked for more

[3]"Since we started organizing, this camp has been destroyed. They started building housing on it."

money. The manager said, "If you don't like it you can quit." I quit and joined the Marine Corps.

"I joined the Marine Corps at seventeen. I was very mixed up. I wanted to become a first-class citizen. I wanted to be accepted and I was very proud of my uniform. My mom didn't want to sign the papers, but she knew I had to better myself and maybe I'd get an education in the services.

"I did many jobs. I took a civil service exam and was very proud when I passed. Most of the others were college kids. There were only three Chicanos in the group of sixty. I got a job as a correctional officer in a state prison. I quit after eight months because I couldn't take the misery I saw. They wanted me to use a rubber hose on some of the prisoners — mostly Chicanos and blacks. I couldn't do it. They called me chicken-livered because I didn't want to hit nobody. They constantly harassed me after that. I didn't quit because I was afraid of them but because they were trying to make me into a mean man. I couldn't see it. This was Soledad State Prison."

I began to see how everything was so wrong. When growers can have an intricate watering system to irrigate their crops but they can't have running water inside the houses of workers. Veterinarians tend to the needs of domestic animals but they can't have medical care for the workers. They can have land subsidies for the growers but they can't have adequate unemployment compensation for the workers. They treat him like a farm implement. In fact, they treat their implements better and their domestic animals better. They have heat and insulated barns for the animals but the workers live in beat-up shacks with no heat at all.

Illness in the fields is 120 percent higher than the average rate for industry. It's mostly back trouble, rheumatism and arthritis, because of the damp weather and the cold. Stoop labor is very hard on a person. Tuberculosis is high. And now because of the pesticides, we have many respiratory diseases.

The University of California at Davis has government experiments with pesticides and chemicals. To get a bigger crop each year. They haven't any regard as to what safety precautions are needed. In 1964 or '65, an airplane was spraying these chemicals on the fields. Spraying rigs they're called. Flying low, the wheels got tangled on the fence wire. The pilot got up, dusted himself off, and got a drink of water. He died of convulsions. The ambulance attendants got violently sick because of the pesticides he had on his person. A little girl was playing around a sprayer. She stuck her tongue on it. She died instantly.

These pesticides affect the farm worker through the lungs. He breathes it in. He gets no compensation. All they do is say he's sick. They don't investigate the cause.

There were times when I felt I couldn't take it any more. It was 105 in the shade and I'd see endless rows of lettuce and I felt my back hurting . . . I felt the frustration of not being able to get out of the fields. I was getting ready to jump any foreman who looked at me cross-eyed. But until two years ago, my world was still very small.

I would read all these things in the papers about Cesar Chavez and I would denounce him because I still had that thing about becoming a first-class patriotic citizen. In Mexicali they would pass out leaflets and I would throw 'em away. I never participated. The grape boycott didn't affect me much because I was in lettuce. It wasn't until Chavez came to Salinas, where I was working in the fields, that I saw what a beautiful man he was. I went to this rally, I still intended to stay with the company. But something — I don't know — I was close to the workers. They couldn't speak English and wanted me to be their spokesman in favor of going on strike. I don't know — I just got caught up with it all, the beautiful feeling of solidarity.

You'd see the people on the picket lines at four in the morning, at the camp fires, heating up beans and coffee and tortillas. It gave me a sense of belonging. These were my own people and they wanted change. I knew this is what I was looking for. I just didn't know it before.

My mom had always wanted me to better myself. I wanted to better myself because of her. Now when the strikes started, I told her I was going to join the union and the whole movement. I told her I was going to work without pay. She said she was proud of me. (His eyes glisten. A long, long pause.) See, I told her I wanted to be with my people. If I were a company man, nobody would like me any more. I had to belong to somebody and this was it right here. She said, "I pushed you in your early years to try to better yourself and get a social position. But I see that's not the answer. I know I'll be proud of you."

All kinds of people are farm workers, not just Chicanos. Filipinos started the strike. We have Puerto Ricans and Appalachians too, Arabs, some Japanese, some Chinese. At one time they used us against each other. But now they can't and they're scared, the growers. They can organize conglomerates. Yet when we try organization to better our lives, they are afraid. Suffering people never dreamed it could be different. Cesar Chavez tells them this and they grasp the idea — and this is what scares the growers.

Now the machines are coming in. It takes skill to operate them. But anybody can be taught. We feel migrant workers should be given the chance. They got one for grapes. They got one for lettuce. They have cotton machines that took jobs away from thousands of farm workers. The people wind up in the ghettos of the city, their culture, their families, their unity destroyed.

We're trying to stipulate it in our contract that the company will not use any machinery without the consent of the farm workers. So we can make sure the people being replaced by the machines will know how to operate the machines.

Working in the fields is not in itself a degrading job. It's hard, but if you're given regular hours, better pay, decent housing, unemployment and medical compensation, pension plans — we have a very relaxed way of living. But the growers don't recognize us as persons. That's the worst thing, the way they treat you. Like we have no brains. Now we see they have no brains. They have only a wallet in their head. The more you squeeze it, the more they cry out.

If we had proper compensation we wouldn't have to be working seventeen hours a day and following the crops. We could stay in one area and it would give us roots. Being a migrant, it tears the family apart. You get in debt. You leave the area penniless. The children are the ones hurt the most. They go to school three months in one place and then on to another. No sooner do they make friends, they are uprooted again. Right here, your childhood is taken away. So when they grow up, they're looking for this childhood they have lost.

If people could see — in the winter, ice on the fields. We'd be on our knees all day long. We'd build fires and warm up real fast and go back onto the ice. We'd be picking watermelons in 105 degrees all day long. When people have melons or cucumber or carrots or lettuce, they don't know how they got on their table and the consequences to the people who picked it. If I had enough money, I would take busloads of people out to the fields and into the labor camps. Then they'd know how that fine salad got on their table.

An Anthropology Assignment

This selection is from a historical study of the deaf population on a small island off the coast of Massachusetts. Groce begins with a vignette about touring the island with a longtime resident, then shifts to an analysis that involves population genetics, anthropology, and deaf studies. Write a summary of Groce's account that explains the setting for her analysis and gives the reader a sense of the issues she raises about society, disability, and difference.

From *Everyone Here Spoke Sign Language: Hereditary Deafness on Martha's Vineyard*

NORA ELLEN GROCE

One of Gale Huntington's favorite activities is driving his guests around the island of Martha's Vineyard, Massachusetts, at speeds never exceeding thirty-five miles an hour, and pointing out spots of historical interest. Gale's memory of the region goes back over eighty years, when coasting vessels crowded Vineyard Haven harbor and whale ships were still seen in New Bedford. He knows as much about the Island as anyone alive today. In the course of one of these jaunts "up-Island," in late October 1978, Gale pointed out Jedidiah's house to me. "He was a good neighbor," said Gale, "He used to fish and farm some. He was one of the best dory men on the Island, and that was pretty good, considering he had only one hand."

"What happened to the other one?" I asked.

"Lost it in a mowing machine accident when he was a teenager." As an afterthought, he added, "He was deaf and dumb too."

"Because of the accident?" I asked.

"Oh no," said Gale, "he was born that way."

On the way back to Vineyard Haven, as we puttered down a sandy ridge overlooking a wide expanse of Vineyard Sound, Gale glanced at a weatherbeaten clapboard house on the left and said, "Jedidiah's brother lived there." Nathaniel had owned a large dairy farm. "And," said Gale, putting his foot on the brakes by way of emphasis, "he was considered a very wealthy man — at least by Chilmark standards. Come to think of it, he was deaf and dumb too."

I wondered aloud why both brothers had been born deaf. Gale said no one had ever known why; perhaps the deafness was inherited. I suggested that it might have been

---

NORA ELLEN GROCE (b. 1952) is a cultural and medical anthropologist and a professor in the Department of Public Health at the Yale School of Medicine. Her work *Everyone Here Spoke Sign Language: Hereditary Deafness on Martha's Vineyard,* from which this excerpt was taken, was published in 1985.

caused by disease. But Gale didn't think so, because there were so many deaf people up-Island, and they were all related. There had been deaf Vineyarders as long as anyone could remember. The last one died in the early 1950s.

"How many deaf people were there?" I asked.

"Oh," said Gale, "I can remember six right offhand, no, seven."

"How many people lived in town here then?"

"Maybe two hundred," Gale replied, "maybe two hundred fifty. Not more than that."

I remarked that that seemed to be a very large number of deaf people in such a small community. Gale seemed surprised but added that he too had occasionally been struck by the fact that there were so many deaf people. No one else in town had treated this as unusual, however, so he had thought little more about it.

One rainy afternoon on my next trip to Martha's Vineyard, I sat down with Gale and tried to figure out the genealogies of the deaf Islanders whom he remembered. I thought that the deafness up-Island might have been the result of an inherited trait for deafness, and I wanted to do some research on the topic.

Gale's knowledge of Island history and genealogy was extensive. He sat in his living room smoking a few of those cigarettes expressly forbidden by his doctor and taking more than a few sips of his favorite New England rum as he reminisced about times long past and friends who had been dead half a century or more. As we talked, he recalled from his childhood three or four additional deaf people. When he was a boy in the early 1900s, ten deaf people lived in the town of Chilmark alone.

I had already spent a good part of the afternoon copying down various genealogies before I thought to ask Gale what the hearing people in town had thought of the deaf people.

"Oh," he said, "they didn't think anything about them, they were just like everyone else."

"But how did people communicate with them — by writing everything down?"

"No," said Gale, surprised that I should ask such an obvious question. "You see, everyone here spoke sign language."

"You mean the deaf people's families and such?" I inquired.

"Sure," Gale replied, as he wandered into the kitchen to refill his glass and find some more matches, "and everybody else in town too — I used to speak it, my mother did, everybody."

ANTHROPOLOGY AND THE DISABLED

Hereditary disorders in relatively isolated communities have long been known, and geneticists and physical anthropologists have studied a number of examples of recessive deafness in small communities. Martha's Vineyard is one more such case. For over two and a half centuries the population of this island had a strikingly high incidence of hereditary deafness. In the nineteenth century, and presumably earlier, one American in every 5,728 was born deaf, but on the Vineyard the figure was one in every 155. In all, I have identified at least seventy-two deaf persons born to Island families over the course of three centuries. At least a dozen more were born to descendants of Vineyarders who had moved off-Island. . . .

I concentrate on the history of this genetic trait and on the history of the people who carried it, for the two are inseparable. A genetic disorder does not occur in a vacuum, somehow removed from the lives of the human beings affected by it. How do the affected people function within their society, and how do they perceive their own role in the community?

Traditionally, disabilities have been analyzed primarily in medical terms or, by social scientists, in terms of deviance. In the social science literature, deviance is defined as an attribute that sets the individual apart from the majority of the population, who are assumed to be normal. Deafness is considered one of the most severe and widespread of the major disabilities. In the United States alone, 14.2 million people have some hearing impairment that is severe enough to interfere with their ability to communicate; of these, 2 million are considered deaf (National Center for Health Statistics 1982).

A deaf person's greatest problem is not simply that he or she cannot hear but that the lack of hearing is socially isolating. The deaf person's knowledge and awareness of the larger society are limited because hearing people find it difficult or impossible to communicate with him or her. Even if the deaf person knows sign language, only a very small percentage of the hearing population can speak it and can communicate easily with deaf people. The difficulty in communicating, along with the ignorance and misinformation about deafness that is pervasive in most of the hearing world, combine to cause difficulties in all aspects of life for deaf individuals — in education, employment, community involvement, and civil rights.

On the Vineyard, however, the hearing people were bilingual in English and the Island sign language. This adaptation had more than linguistic significance, for it eliminated the wall that separates most deaf people from the rest of society. How well can deaf people integrate themselves into the community if no communication barriers exist and if everyone is familiar and comfortable with deafness? The evidence from the Island indicates that they are extremely successful at this.

One of the strongest indications that the deaf were completely integrated into all aspects of society is that in all the interviews I conducted, deaf Islanders were never thought of or referred to as a group or as "the deaf." Every one of the deaf people who is remembered today is thought of as a unique individual. When I inquired about "the deaf" or asked informants to list all the deaf people they had known, most could remember only one or two, although many of them had known more than that. I was able to elicit comments about specific individuals only by reading informants a list of all the deaf people known to have lived on the Island. My notes show a good example of this when, in an interview with a woman who is now in her early nineties, I asked, "Do you know anything similar about Isaiah and David?"

"Oh yes!" she replied. "They both were very good fishermen, very good indeed."

"Weren't they both deaf?" I prodded.

"Yes, come to think of it, I guess they both were," she replied. "I'd forgotten about that."

On the mainland profound deafness is regarded as a true handicap, but I suggest that a handicap is defined by the community in which it appears. Although we can categorize the deaf Vineyarders as disabled, they certainly were not considered to be handicapped. They participated freely in all aspects of life in this Yankee community. They grew up, married, raised their families, and earned their livings in just the same manner as did their hearing relatives, friends, and neighbors. As one older man on the Island remarked, "I didn't think about the deaf any more than you'd think about anybody with a different voice."

Perhaps the best description of the status of deaf individuals on the Vineyard was given to me by an island woman in her eighties, when I asked about those who were handicapped by deafness when she was a girl. "Oh," she said emphatically, "those people weren't handicapped. They were just deaf."

An Economics Assignment

Often, doing library research requires gathering information from different sources and then integrating the varied materials into a coherent whole. This assignment calls on you to combine statistics from a chart and a table with observations, examples, and statistics from brief textual sources, of the kind you might have copied during your research.

Table 1, compiled by the Congressional Budget Office, illustrates changes in family income from 1977 to 1988. Figure 1, a graph provided by the U.S. Census Bureau, illustrates the increase of mean (or average) family income from 1954 to 1986. Take a moment to study the table and the graph, making a few notes on general trends. You'll notice that the table and graph cover different time frames but that they overlap. You'll also notice that the table measures income in deciles, or tenths of the population. The graph divides the population into quintiles (fifths) and singles out the upper 5 percent as a category of special interest within the upper quintile. Summarize the story that you think is told by these two sets of statistics.

Next, read the brief selections by political analyst Kevin Phillips. Then write a summary that blends the statistical information you gain from the table and the graph with the discussion and statistics presented by Phillips. The table and graph will provide general trends while Phillips will provide some specific quotations, anecdotes, and descriptions as well as some further, more precise statistics. Your

TABLE 1. Income Gains and Losses, 1977–1988 (Changes in Average Family Income, 1987 Dollars)

	Average Family Income		Percentage Change	Change in Average Family Income
Income Decile	1977	1988[1]	1977–88	1977–88
First	$ 4,113	$ 3,504	–14.8%	$ –609
Second	8,334	7,669	–8.0	–665
Third	13,140	12,327	–6.2	–813
Fourth	18,436	17,220	–6.6	–1,216
Fifth	23,896	22,389	–6.3	–1,507
Sixth	29,824	28,205	–5.4	–1,619
Seventh	36,405	34,828	–4.3	–1,577
Eighth	44,305	43,507	–1.8	–798
Ninth	55,487	56,064	1.0	577
Tenth	102,722	119,635	16.5	16,913
Top 5%	134,543	166,016	23.4	31,473
Top 1%	270,053	404,566	49.8	134,513
All families	33,527	34,274	2.2	747

[1]CBO projection of 1988 incomes.

Source: Challenge to Leadership, Urban Institute.

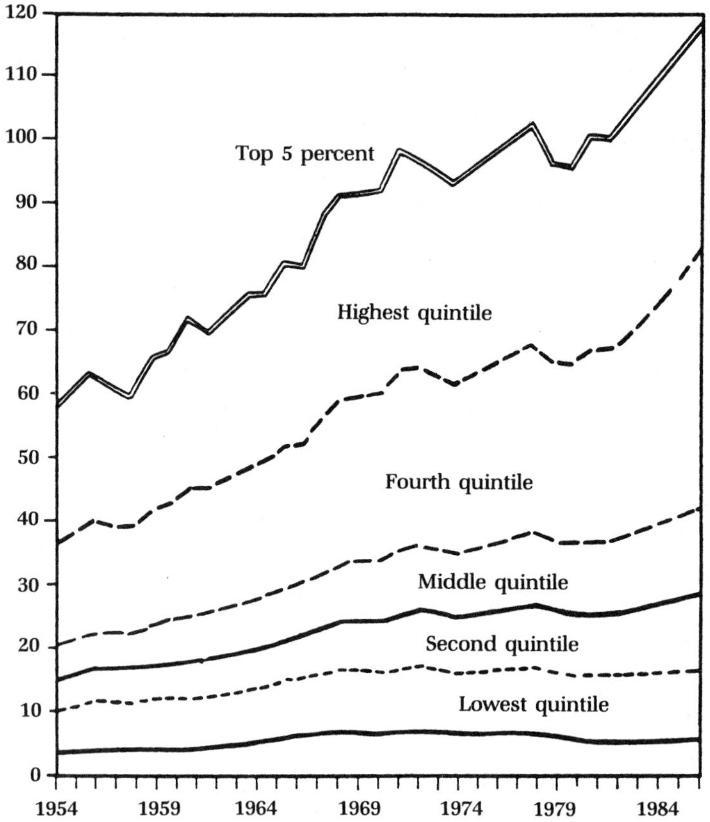

FIGURE 1. Mean Incomes of Population Quintiles, 1954–1986 (Thousands of 1986 Dollars).

summary should be structured to emphasize general trends about income distribution in our time, to make sense of them, add flesh to them, and provide context for them with help from Phillips.

The charts, and Phillips' observations, underscore the financial strains on low- and middle-income families. If you are interested in this subject — and, particularly, in the topic of child poverty — you may want to do this assignment in coordination with the related material in the Opening Problem (p. 79), the Professional Application (p. 94), the Oral History Assignment (p. 103), and Readings: The Dimensions of Child Poverty (p. 144).

The Downside of the American Dream

Kevin Phillips

By 1988 anecdotal proof abounded that the imperiled "American dream" had become an emerging battleground of national politics. The average manufacturing wage seemed to buy less. Low-income households were in trouble, especially female-headed ones. Here and there, off the main roads, large patches of small-town America were dying. Big-city poverty was on the rise. Young married couples, needing two incomes to meet bills, postponed having children and gave up buying their own homes. And in blue-collar factory towns, where a job on the production line at Ford or Bethlehem Steel had helped two generations of workers climb into the middle class, the next generation saw no such opportunity.

But if hearsay evidence was everywhere, a precise statistical portrait was a lot harder to come by — in part because there was such a confusion of numbers. Different data series gave different — and often contradictory — pictures. Take national per capita income. As figured in constant 1987 dollars, it had expanded almost automatically during the decade as a growing percentage of Americans (women especially) went to work, rising from $10,740 in 1980 to $11,301 in 1984, and $12,287 in 1987. But critics called this a deceptive measurement and pointed instead to inflation-adjusted weekly *per worker* income, which went down during the same period, dropping from $366 in 1972 to $318 in 1980 and $312 in 1987. Others preferred to cite the weakness in inflation-adjusted U.S. family median incomes. . . .

By 1988 quibbling and ambiguity were everywhere. Too much could be made of any single broad yardstick of family, per capita, or household income. As each index measured something slightly different, virtually every pundit or politician might find some statistics to document a particular case. And critics overplayed their thesis of a whole economy in decline. The Congressional Budget Office, looking for a moderate middle ground, calculated in 1987 that family income went up 11 percent from 1973 to 1986, with a meaningful percentage increase between 1981 and 1986. In many ways, though, the larger story — and the worrisome symptom — was not the slight *overall* growth in median family income. It was the comparative advances or regressions of families in different brackets. "If you look at subgroups you can see that inequality is rising more than it seems to be if you just look at the aggregate numbers," said Sheldon Danziger, a sociologist at the University of Michigan. "There's a lot more going on in the pieces than in the larger picture."

Politically the economic viability of U.S. families had started to become an important issue. Academicians and politicians might be able to play ping-pong with statistics seeking to define *overall* family trends, but there was no way to argue with the official government portrait of a shift of income between 1980 and 1988 away from the bottom 80 percent of the U.S. population toward the most affluent fifth. . . .

Political analyst Kevin Phillips (b. 1940) is a newspaper columnist and radio commentator as well as president of the American Political Research Corporation. He has written several books on politics, including *Arrogant Capital* (1994), *Boiling Point* (1993), and the *Politics of Rich and Poor* (1990), from which we appropriated both statistics and text.

White males serving as their family's only breadwinner were, as a category, particularly conspicuous. By one calculation, their median inflation-adjusted income fell 22 percent between 1976 and 1984. After the 1983 recovery, many squeezed or depressed households discovered that their economic problems weren't simply recession hangovers. As domestic and global economic restructuring continued, well-paid manufacturing jobs and the purchasing power of manufacturing paychecks shrank. For *all* workers, white-collar as well as blue-collar, their real average weekly wage — calculated in constant 1977 dollars — fell from $191.41 a week in 1972 to $171.07 in 1986.

But even that decline disguised the larger negative impact on men partly offset by a slight overall rise for women. Well-paid male blue-collar union members suffered the greatest loss, especially younger men and those with no more than a high school diploma. According to Marvin Kosters, a conservative economist at the Washington-based American Enterprise Institute, the median real earnings of men between the ages of twenty-five to thirty-four, measured in constant 1985 dollars, were $10.17 an hour in 1973, $9.70 an hour in 1980, and $8.85 in 1987. For men of all ages with nothing more than high school diplomas the figures were $9.90 in 1973, $9.37 in 1980, and $8.62 in 1987. Frank Levy observed that "back in the early 1970s, the average guy with a high school diploma was making $24,000 in today's dollars. Today a similar guy is making about $18,000."

The high-paying jobs lost in Hibbing or River Rouge had been more than just employment; they had been cultural and economic ladders to middle-class status for millions of families all across industrial America. Newspaper writers from Appalachia to the Iron Range wrote more or less the same story: "Once blue-collar sons could follow their fathers into the plants and make $13, $14 an hour. That meant the middle class, a car, maybe a little cabin on a lake, a chance for kids to go to college. Once, but not anymore." Caste and class restraints that had eased after World War II began to reemerge. . . .

Moreover, many people were not in the work force at all: members of the underclass, for example, or those no longer looking for a job. The 5.3 percent unemployment rate was misleading because definitions of the work force excluded a growing number of Americans. By the summer of 1988, 45.3 percent of New York City residents over the age of sixteen could not be counted as labor force participants because of poverty, lack of skills, drug use, apathy, or other problems. Similar circumstances were reported in Detroit and Baltimore, while the ratio of uncountables for the nation as a whole was 34.5 percent. Thus the paradox: *Millions of jobs might be going begging, but huge numbers of Americans remained either unemployed or unemployable.* Circumstances like this resulted in the destitution and homelessness that perturbed cities and suburbs everywhere as economic polarization intensified.

Many women had also been losers. Families were not just shrinking; they were breaking down. Households headed by females ranked well down the income scale — especially those with children. In the spring and summer of 1988 polls showed that half of all men characterized the U.S. economy as "excellent" or "good," but only one third of the women did so. Women preferred the Democrats largely for economic reasons, not only because of broken homes, but, as we have seen, because of the pressure on family life when wives and mothers take marginal jobs. Families were sacrificing psychic income for dollar income, a trade-off that the Census Bureau chose not to quantify, but which was probably considerable. One survey found that Americans' leisure time declined by 37 percent between 1973 and 1987 — from 26.2 hours a week to 16.6 hours.

By the mid-1980s a new two-tier wage system had arisen in troubled industries as senior employees kept their previous pay scales but *new* hires — from airline pilots to supermarket checkout clerks — came in at lower rates. At the same time, more people could find only part-time jobs as employers spread work and costs more carefully. This "contingent work force" — part-timers and temporaries — had doubled between 1980 and 1987, expanding to include roughly one quarter of the total work force, while the percentage of the working poor with short periods of unemployment rose. Not surprisingly, given these pressures, the uncertainty and unreliability of employment also grew as an issue; a 1988 poll found "job security" reemerging as employees' number one concern. Emphasis on the low official unemployment rate was deceptive to the extent that it ignored these offsets.

Corporate chairmen and presidents as a class feasted in the 1980s, but the number of midlevel management jobs lost during those years was estimated to be as high as 1.5 million. In 1987 one survey found 41 percent of respondents acknowledging job-loss fears premised on corporate restructuring or foreign competition. Blue-collar America had paid a larger price, but suburbia, where fathers rushed to catch the 8:10 train to the city, was quietly counting its casualties, too. In September 1988, Peter Drucker observed that "the cynicism out there is frightening. Middle managers have become insecure, and they feel unbelievably hurt. They feel like slaves on an auction block."

Thus "downward mobility" emerged as a real fear within the U.S. work force, white-collar and blue-collar alike. The *Los Angeles Times* reported in 1988 that "not in half a century has the United States seen so many 'givebacks' affecting so many people. But from musicians with the Honolulu Symphony Orchestra to lumbermen in the Pacific Northwest, from steelworkers in West Virginia to Greyhound bus drivers in Montana, thousands of Americans with years of experience are experiencing the vicissitudes of MAAD — middle-aged and downward. . . .

Many families found themselves emptying savings accounts and going in debt, often to meet the soaring price of homeownership or to put a child through college. For a family with 1985 earnings equal to the median national income, keeping a child in a four-year private college or university would have taken 40 percent of that income, up from 30 percent in 1970. Buying a house was even tougher. Homeownership had reached a record 65 percent of U.S. households in 1980, after climbing steadily from 1940, when 43.6 percent of households owned their own residences. After 1980, however, the homeownership rate would drop year by year, falling to 63.8 percent in 1986 and leveling off. Young people, in particular, found that home buying was next to impossible.

A Literature Assignment

Select one of the following two short stories and write an essay summarizing it. On one level, each of the stories could be summarized fairly simply, for each has a relatively straightforward plot. "English as a Second Language" is the story of an English teacher trying, not too successfully, to settle into a new job. And "The Kind of Light That Shines on Texas" is the story of a developing confrontation between two young men in a Texas high school. But to summarize these stories along those lines alone would miss much that makes the stories interesting; the most effective summaries of works of fiction do more than simply retell the plot.

If, for example, you choose "English as a Second Language," take note of the many kinds of language explored in this story: the developing, although insightfully used, English of the foreign student; Spanish, and its use to bring the two men together physically; the language of poetry; and the language of fashion design. Considered another way, the story offers a language of loneliness and connection and a language of teaching and learning.

If you choose "The Kind of Light That Shines on Texas," note the way McKnight manages the story's dramatic action — that is, the way he uses a series of charged events to develop the story. Note, too, the central character's growing awareness: of race, of power, of what else? And note McKnight's use of light and color imagery.

English as a Second Language

BERNARD COOPER

"You may be wondering," said Mr. Rowlands, "why I am wearing this hat." I, for one, was wondering. Except for a conical party hat with crepe paper fringe, Mr. Rowlands was the picture of officiousness — starched white shirt, drab navy tie, shoes shined to a high gloss. He paced among tables of attentive faculty, some of us new to The Institute of Fashion, others veterans. "I intend to show you," Mr. Rowlands continued, "that appearing foolish is not only easy . . ." dramatic pause, his party hat askew, "but is also necessary for successful teaching. After all, what is it that a teacher does?" Silence from the assembly. "A teacher, my friends, goes out on a limb." He drew a tree limb on the blackboard behind him, slashed an X at the furthermost end. "A teacher takes risks, introduces new ideas to a room brimming with formative minds. As one philosopher put it, 'A teacher affects eternity.'" I glanced at my watch. "I tip my hat to you all," he said. The hat flew back with a snap of elastic.

Mr. Rowlands was not a regular member of the Institute. He was a Group Spirit Facilitator, offering his services to schools and corporations wishing to extract a sense of goodwill from their reticent employees. He'd breezed onto "campus" — the sixth and seventh floors of the Barker Brothers furniture outlet in downtown Los Angeles — in order to lead forty teachers through the Get-To-Know-Your-Fellow-Faculty game, a round-robin during which we were asked to announce our names, areas of expertise, pet peeves, and favorite colors.

Writer BERNARD COOPER (b. 1951) is the author of *Truth Serum* (1996) and *Maps to Anywhere* (1990), and his work is represented in *Best American Essays* (1988). "English as a Second Language" appeared in the anthology *Men on Men 3* (1990), edited by George Stambolian.

"Red," chirped the cheerful Miss Bartlett, instructor of Color Theory I, II, and III, dressed in red from head to toe. "And human pyramids," she said, crimson lips curled in disdain, "I hate them. All those people piled up. What's the point?"

"Excellent," crooned Mr. Rowlands.

Miss Bartlett blushed and took her seat.

"And you," he said, pointing at me, "up, up, up."

I stood, heart heaving beneath my wrinkled shirt. "I'm Richard Cole. I'll be teaching English. I like gray . . ."

"Gray is not a color," murmured Miss Bartlett.

". . . and I can't stand cold spaghetti." It was delicate; I wanted to participate in the game, to charm these strangers, and yet I hoped my ambivalence would show, would send out a signal to potential allies who found the proceedings as absurd as I did.

It took more than a half hour for everyone to introduce themselves. Mr. Rowlands seemed pleased by each response, liberal with his grin. The atmosphere had, I must admit, turned genial, and sensing that his mission was accomplished, Mr. Rowlands gave us over to the president of the Institute, Barbara Bundy.

Large Barbara Bundy strode to the podium, clutched the neck of the microphone and wrenched it into position. Her black hairdo was sliced in two by a streak of gray. "First," she said, after mild applause, "let me share some exciting news with you. The Mayor visited our facilities just last week. He was terribly impressed by our new architectural carpeting. You know, I told him, this will be the first opportunity for many of our minority students to function in a carpeted public area."

I left the room to get a drink of water, to breathe and stretch, to reassess my livelihood. I was followed out the door by a tall black woman, Janet, who shook my hand and told me she worked in the Research Center. "Call it the library," she said. "That'll drive Bundy crazy." Lit by yards of track lighting, we faced one another in the corridor. Suddenly, Janet gazed at the carpet and drawled, "Whut is dat, Porgy? Some kinda fungus?"

The Sunday before school began, I sprawled on an old foam chair — it sagged beneath me in a sorry heap — rereading the poems I'd use for my class, Introduction to Literature. I'd stop between stanzas, convinced I had nothing insightful to say. At least not these days; after teaching literature for five years at various schools, I'd never grown accustomed to the harsh remarks that greeted my favorite works. "Spray him with Raid," was one young man's reaction to Gregor Samsa's metamorphosis. After what I thought was an aptly impassioned lecture on the deprivation and death of Akaky Akakyavitch in Gogol's "The Overcoat," the daughter of Hollywood celebrities looked at me in wonderment and said, "Like, get a grip. It's only a coat." Not a titter had hailed the humor of Dorothy Parker or James Thurber. And — when I'd made the mistake of reading surrealist verse — if eyes could make noise, their rolling would have been heard for miles.

I put down my book and drifted out to the porch. The neighborhood children had gathered on Sunland Avenue, and above the distant mariachi music and the clatter of cars grinding up the hill, I could hear them argue.

"I bet there's a ton of blood in a body," said one boy rocking on his rickety bike.

"Don't be stupid," shouted the girl next to him. "That would mean you'd weigh a ton."

"Ton of blood, ton of blood," sang a set of twins.

The bungalows of my apartment complex — pitched roofs, clapboard walls —

glowed with the last of autumn light. On the stoop next door, Ricardo was combing his cat, Titanic, and laughing at bits of the escalating argument. Titanic tried to dart from his arms.

"I guess," said Ricardo, snatching at cat hairs drifting through the air, "we're all nothing but big bags of blood."

"A pleasant thought," I said. Titanic finally freed herself, raced to the nearest patch of dirt where she writhed and raised a cloud of dust. Ricardo and I sat on our steps. We craned our faces into the sunlight, continued to talk with our eyes closed.

"I'm horny," said Ricardo. "Or maybe I'm lonely. Do you ever get to the point where you can't tell the difference?"

"There must be a word for that."

"Desperation?"

"An even better word."

"You're the word man," he said. "You suggest something."

The sun felt good on my skin. Optical dots flashed under my eyelids. I didn't want to think about loneliness, my own or anyone else's.

"Do you think Trent ever gets lonely?" Ricardo asked after a long silence. Trent lived across the street. Every evening he walked to his mailbox dressed in a pair of skimpy shorts. Trent was a one-man geometry lesson, his physique a marvel of volumes and planes.

"Ricardo," I said, "I can't even look at Trent — he wants me to look, wants everyone to look."

"Those thighs, those biceps," said Ricardo. "Forget fondling. I'd be happy just to measure them. Tell the truth. Wouldn't you?"

My eyes were still closed, but I pictured Ricardo seated on his stoop — brown skin, black hair. Since he'd moved next door in October, I'd welcomed his endless, ingenuous questions, and never felt obliged to answer.

On the first day of the Fall semester, I found Janet in the faculty lounge, guzzling cups of coffee and tugging at the shoulder pads imbedded in her sweater. "Are they even?" she asked me.

"Perfect," I replied. "Are you trying out for quarterback?"

Miss Bartlett, dressed in a red jumpsuit and squinting at color swatches in the corner, said "Those are called Pagoda Shoulders. They're absolutely darling."

"They weigh a ton," said Janet. "I think these pagodas are made of cement. I'll never shrug again." She poured more coffee into a Styrofoam cup and looked me up and down. "Honey," she said, "a word of advice: Bundy hates it when her teachers wear jeans."

"Unless," Miss Bartlett broke in, "they're clean and ironed with a neat crease."

"Betty," said Janet, turning to Miss Bartlett, "no one *wants* a crease in their jeans."

"I think a crease in denim is quite chic," said a woman wearing the most elaborate earrings I'd ever seen. They were like Calder mobiles, tinkling and turning and catching the light. "I have a wire insert you just slip into wet jeans for an even crease. So convenient."

"Isn't Valenti coming out with precreased jeans?" someone asked.

Janet grabbed my hand and dragged me to a sofa in an empty section of the lounge. "Look," she said, "there are two rules for survival in this place. One: Talk only with people whose names don't rhyme."

My eyebrows bunched.

"Haven't you noticed that everyone here in a position of power has a rhyming name? Barbara Bundy. Frank Fox. You're an English teacher; isn't there a word for that?"

"Alliteration."

"Right. William Pope, Dorothy Layton; *they* can be trusted. And two," she said, batting at her shoulder pads, "dress the part. That's all that counts." Janet gave my knee a squeeze, rose and dashed for the door.

Before the door could close, Barbara Bundy swept into the room. "Attention everyone. The Student Finance Association has created bumper stickers to be given to those children delinquent on their loans." She held up a strip of paper that read, *If you're late with your loan, you won't have anything to stick this on.* "Aren't they just . . . what's the word I'm looking for?" She turned to me.

"Adorable?" I offered.

I got lost on the way to my classroom. The halls of the Institute were long and spotless, each named after a famous designer. The Edith Head Hall contained large blowups of Miss Head's sketches, women in voluminous skirts, some as fluffy as cumulus clouds. The Bill Blass hall was painted dark green, and hung along its walls were party dresses in metallic fabrics, pressed under glass like giant flowers. When I finally found room 702 (I'd confused the Calvin with the Anne Klein hallway), my students — twenty girls and one boy — were quietly waiting.

I fished the roll sheet from my briefcase. As the readout unraveled, I noticed the boy had raised his hand.

"Yes?"

"Can I go?" he asked.

"Go?"

"Yeah. Can I leave?"

"Aren't you enrolled in this class?"

"Yeah. But it's going to rain." I gave a sidelong glance out the window. Ominous clouds slid over the city.

"I'm afraid I don't understand."

The boy lifted the lapel of his jacket. "It's suede," he said. "If I leave right now, it won't get wet."

"I'm sorry," I said, "but I think W. H. Auden, the writer whose work we'll examine today, is every bit as important as your jacket." I imagined a giant silver scale: On one side sat Auden, legs crossed, nursing a cigarette; on the other lay a crumpled jacket. The scale seesawed up and down.

After everyone was accounted for, I passed out Xerox copies of Auden's poem *Musée des Beaux Arts.*

"Isn't this an English class?" grumbled a girl in the front row.

"Of course," I said through thirty-two teeth. "I'll translate the title in a moment. But first let me give you some biographical information."

When I turned to the blackboard, I distinctly heard her snap, "Thank you, daddy." I wrote down the dates of birth and death. I filled in Auden's early history — doctor father, Oxford pranks — then walked around the room with a photograph of Auden, wrinkled and wry, at the age of fifty.

"Assuming that a person's history shows on his face, what kind of life do you think Auden led?"

"Not enough moisture," guessed a dewy, fair-haired girl.

"You're probably right. Auden drank a great deal and smoked four packs of unfiltered Camels a day." But my statement was lost in a flurry of talk erupting in the corner.

"Excuse me," I shouted. My glasses slid down my nose. "Is that conversation pertinent to Auden?"

"No," a small voice volunteered.

"Well, stop," I said, adding, "please."

"The point I'm trying to make is that, like many of us, Auden's sensibility consisted of two distinct aspects. On one hand, he had tremendously formal ideas about what poetry should and should not be. He considered poetry, as he put it, 'a game of the intellect.' He disliked poetry that was theatrical. He once went so far as to say that a poem should be like a person in a parlor — well-groomed, and well behaved. On the other hand, he was adventurous, lusty . . ." random giggles ". . . he lived by his wits. He was an ambulance driver in the Spanish Civil War. He was openly homosexual . . ." collective intake of breath ". . . and he wrote some of the most important poems in the twentieth century. His face is the record of a rich and complex life. Any questions before we read?"

"Awdeng?" said Sun Ha. "Please to spell."

After class, Sun Ha explained in halting phrases that she'd been mistakenly placed in my class instead of English as a Second Language. She promised, with a slightly fearful conviction, to work very hard if I let her stay. I told her I would, suggesting books that might be of help. She wrote down the titles and authors of each with great concentration. To seal our agreement, Sun Ha reached into her Institute of Fashion canvas carryall — every student was required to buy one — and dug out a package of Hostess Twinkies. "Sir," she asked, head cocked, "you like a Twinkie?"

"Great. I'm starved. Also," I called as she left the room, "you don't have to call me sir."

The cake was spongy, so sweet it stung. I sat on the edge of my desk, gazing out the window. Clouds obscured the afternoon sky, their dark bottoms sagging toward the skyline. There was an instant, before the first drops, when the streets beneath me gleamed gold, and the glass facades of nearby buildings burned with an otherworldly light. Then the hiss of hard rain, like whispers in a foreign language.

"How would you paraphrase," I'd asked my class, "what Auden means when he says that suffering 'takes place/While someone else is eating or opening a window or just walking dully along'?" Their answer was this: a few stifled yawns; furtive glances at the clock; a sketch of eyes in the margin of a Xerox. And then Sun Ha had raised her hand. "He mean," she ventured in a shaking voice, "pain of one not felt by other?"

"Yes," I'd said, wiping my forehead. "Thank you. Yes."

During the drive home — the traffic was wet and treacherous — I wondered if there was any difference between me and Mr. Rowlands. I pictured myself in a party hat, teetering on the limb of a tree. After a day of extracting answers, I found that what I wanted, second to an aspirin, was to hear Ricardo asking questions.

The rainfall was mild by the time I reached my street. Searching for a parking spot, I drove by Trent at his mailbox, shirtless despite the weather. His shoulders and chest were slick with rain. He shifted his weight from foot to foot and his mammoth anatomy seemed to shimmer. Trent's head was bent toward the mail, but I saw him watch me from the corner of his eye; he shuffled through the envelopes so his triceps could bulge to their best advantage.

To avoid walking by him, I sat in my car and stared at raindrops streaking the windshield. Soon my breath was fogging the glass, my own breath, blooming before me. I thought of writing something with my finger, but couldn't think what to say. I dragged my palm across the haze and saw that Trent had gone.

The neighborhood children were gathered on the street. They bickered again. Their raincoats glistened.

"If there *are* Martians living on earth, why," asked the girl, "would they look like us?"

The boy on the bike said, "So they can go to the supermarket and become president and . . ."

"No way," said one twin.

"Is so," said the other.

The children eyed me with suspicion as I passed.

I went straight to Ricardo's. Titanic was curled in the corner of the porch, deep in a feline dream. I pressed the bell and a buzzer rumbled. *"Quien es?"* he said, and then, "Who is it?"

"It's Trent," I said in my deepest voice.

I heard water gush through the pipes, footsteps on the wooden floor, the rustle of tidying up. When Ricardo finally opened the door, his shoulders were squared, eyes expectant, hair coated with fragrant tonic. He saw it was me and bellowed, "Weasel!"

"Jesus," I said, "I didn't think you'd actually believe me."

He loomed in the doorway, disappointed. His black hair and dark eyes absorbed the evening light.

"When you recover, can I come in?" He spun on his heels and I followed him inside, closing the door behind me. Ricardo crumpled onto the couch. He shook his fist in my direction, and with his free hand patted the cushion. I sat beside him with my briefcase on my lap. Second by second, his features softened, released from the tension of wishing for Trent. The room was ripe with the scent of his tonic. We faced the dining room table, a slab of plywood lit from above. Scattered atop it were parts of the models Ricardo built for an architect: balsa wood windows, cardboard walls, rolls of paper shingles and brick. Ricardo had often asked me over to see the completed models; he'd remove the roof with care, talk about what the architect intended, his finger hovering over the rooms like the finger of a giant.

"Do you think I'm a jerk?" he asked. "Wouldn't you like a visit from Trent? Knock knock. Richard, it's Trent. I have something to show you."

My impersonation, I told him, was better.

"Richard," he said. "Why can't you just admit to lust once in a while? Why can't you just ogle someone and enjoy it?"

"Like the wolf in cartoons? Eyeballs popping out on springs?"

"You're so . . . intellectual."

"Oh, goodness no," I mocked. "Not that. Isn't this the part where you take off my glasses and unpin my hair to reveal the sexpot seething beneath the prim exterior?"

He thought a moment and pounced at my glasses. I tried to grab them back. My briefcase fell to the floor.

"Why, Miss Cole," he said in a Southern accent, dangling my glasses out of reach, "you're lovely as a magnolia blossom."

The room was a blur. I sat back and asked for an aspirin. Ricardo brought me two, and a glass of wine to wash them down.

"How about a toast?" he said, reclining on the rug.

"To what?" I mumbled with the tablets on my tongue.

"Al placer."

I looked at him, puzzled.

He asked, "Don't you know any Spanish?"

"Margarita. Tacquito."

"We'll take care of that," he said, draining his glass in a single gulp.

It must have been the wine. Later that night, after a shower, I posed before my bathroom mirror — head-on and profile, bemused and seductive and nonchalant — imagining how I looked to Ricardo. The task, I thought, was impossible. I'd seen my face for thirty years: straight hair, green eyes — straight, green, from every angle. How, I wondered, could Trent muster such self-regard.

The doorbell put an end to my reverie. I went to get dressed before I answered, but Ricardo had let himself in. He whistled as I ran by the bedroom door. "I didn't know you had hair on your chest," he called from the living room. I pulled on my pants in a dark corner. "I love that," he added. "It makes my *dedos del pia* curl."

"Your what?" I yelled as I slipped on a shirt.

"Toes," he said when I entered the room. "You look nice, by the way."

"What's this?" I asked, squinting at a stack of cardboard he held in his hand.

"This," he said, "is lesson one." He fanned out the cards; on each he'd printed a Spanish word in red ink. While I threaded my belt through the loops of my jeans, Ricardo rushed around the room, taping nouns to appropriate objects. *Silla, mesa, lampara, ventena, libro, reloj, cortina, puerta.* I watched muscles stretch his shirt as he ripped pieces of tape from the roll. Thunder sputtered far away. Rain drummed the metal awnings. The radiator rasped. *"Perfecto,"* he said when the last card was in place. We stood side by side and surveyed the room. "I'll come back tomorrow night and test you." Ricardo was about to turn toward the door when I caught his arm and drew him toward me. I could feel the heat within his sleeve. His broad chin was shadowed with stubble. His pulse stammered at his temple and throat.

"Can I ask you something?" he whispered as he reached for the light.

"Now?" I asked as the light went out.

"How many times does someone have to tell you they're lonely before you get the message?"

In the dark, all around me, hung unfamiliar words. "I guess," I said, "I'm a slow learner."

The following day at school, I was trying to define onomatopoeia, but all I could think about was the V of Ricardo's stomach, slowly bared as I undid his zipper. I would have pictured the folds of his pants parting over and over — a moment so sharp with anticipation, the rain had seemed to stop in abeyance — if I hadn't been interrupted by a question.

"Like, *sizzle* and *boom* and stuff," said the boy, "I get that. But couldn't any word be oma . . ."

"Onomatopoetic."

". . . yeah, if you said it the right way?"

"Could you be more specific?"

"Well, like the word *tree.* Couldn't that be onomato — whatever if you said it to sound like a tree?"

I walked around my desk, faced the class. I bent my arms like the branches of an oak. I intoned the word tree, but drew out the e-e-e-e for as long as I could and made the sound waver like leaves in a wind. "Like so?" I said. And laughed. Alone.

"Excuse me, Mr. Cole." Barbara Bundy was standing at the door. I felt like an acorn had caught in my throat. "You look very busy and I hate to disturb you, but we have a problem."

"I was attempting to illustrate . . ."

"There have been," she continued, "several complaints . . ."

". . . oma . . ."

". . . about the window display in the Calvin Klein hall."

"Oh," I exhaled. "How may I help you?"

"I'm afraid the only access to the window is through your room." She pointed to a narrow door. Everyone turned. "Have you seen the window in question, Mr. Cole?"

I'd seen the window on the way to class. Against a bright yellow backdrop, a mannequin swung a tennis racket and beamed a wicked grin. She was dressed in typical tennis clothes except for a jacket with a map of Vietnam embroidered on the back. A sign read, Tennis Anyone?

"Frankly, Miss Bundy, I thought the effect was very offensive."

"How could one not?" She thrust a hand on her ample hip. "The yellow backdrop and black jacket — they clash something awful. I'll see to it," she said, "this instant," and disappeared through the narrow door.

"Don't worry," said Janet, laughing. "If Bundy saw this" — she yanked my tie — "she probably didn't notice the oak. You look like a real professor in that suit."

"I feel like a public accountant," I said. We had to shout; the lunchroom teemed with rowdy students parading their outfits up and down the aisles.

Janet eyed the crowd and said, "I've finally figured out the school's admissions policy: You're in if you can button your clothes."

Across from our table, a video monitor flickered with a fashion show from Europe. A few students stood before it, reverent transfixed. "My in-floo-ence," the designer was saying in an undiscernible accent, "Iz microbiology." Women wearing flaccid hats and drooping skirts spun on the runway. "Ezpecially amoebas."

"Hey," said Janet, "look at that." She pointed to Miss Bartlett who was shoving coins in a vending machine. "Notice anything different?" Miss Bartlett was dressed in navy blue. "I've never seen her in anything but red." Janet sighed and sipped her coffee. "Kind of shakes my faith in the status quo."

"I know," I said, "I know." The weather, my clothes, my romantic life had all been altered without any warning, and Miss Bartlett — prim in blue, wrestling with a candy wrapper — seemed a harbinger of sudden change.

I said goodbye to Janet and went to collect the essays waiting in my box. The halls were noisy, jammed with people. I passed by a group of prospective students who were touring the Edith Head hall. "This is Edith Head's actual signature," said the Institute's public relations man, tapping a framed piece of paper. An *oooh* rose from the cluster of girls, but I saw they were looking into his eyes, a moist, Rasputin blue.

In the faculty lounge, two teachers were grading patterns for men's pajamas. I slid the essays out of my box and pictured Ricardo inside his apartment, seated at a slab of wood, holding the walls of a house together, waiting for the glue to dry. I willed myself to remember his scent, his compact body beneath my sheets. The night before, he'd burrowed his head into the pillow and cast an arm across my chest, incanting Spanish words in his sleep.

I was about to put the papers in my briefcase when Sun Ha's handwriting caught my eye.

Here is poem I chose by W. C. Williams:

THIS IS JUST TO SAY

I have eaten
the plums
that were in
the ice box

and which
you were probably
saving
for breakfast

Forgive me
they were delicious
so sweet
and so cold

I like the poem. In Korea where I come from, my mother sometime put note on ice box. He have ice box. Maybe he write poem to put on ice box. He saying with really deep feeling he can't help to eat sweet plums. He had to. Sorry. No more I can say.

I looked up and the lounge was empty. A pot of coffee brewed on a burner. From the window overlooking Figueroa, I saw the tangled afternoon traffic, headlights and brakelights doubled in puddles. As I loaded my briefcase and buttoned my coat "... sweet plums . . . had to ..." resounded like an echo.

The Kind of Light That Shines on Texas

REGINALD MCKNIGHT

I never liked Marvin Pruitt. Never liked him, never knew him, even though there were only three of us in the class. Three black kids. In our school there were fourteen classrooms of thirty-odd white kids (in '66, they considered Chicanos provisionally white) and

---

REGINALD MCKNIGHT (b. 1956) is professor of English at the University of Maryland, College Park. This story, which was originally published in *The Kenyon Review* in 1989, appears in his 1992 collection *The Kind of Light That Shines on Texas.* McKnight's other works include a short story collection titled *Moustapha's Eclipse* (1988) and the novel *I Get on the Bus* (1990).

three or four black kids. Primary school in primary colors. Neat division. Alphabetized. They didn't stick us in the back, or arrange us by degrees of hue, apartheidlike. This was real integration, a ten-to-one ratio as tidy as upper-class landscaping. If it all worked, you could have ten white kids all to yourself. They could talk to you, get the feel of you, scrutinize you bone deep if they wanted to. They seldom wanted to, and that was fine with me for two reasons. The first was that their scrutiny was irritating. How do you comb your hair — why do you comb your hair — may I please touch your hair — were the kinds of questions they asked. This is no way to feel at home. The second reason was Marvin. He embarrassed me. He smelled bad, was at least two grades behind, was hostile, dark skinned, homely, close-mouthed. I feared him for his size, pitied him for his dress, watched him all the time. Marveled at him, mystified, astonished, uneasy.

He had the habit of spitting on his right arm, juicing it down till it would glisten. He would start in immediately after taking his seat when we'd finished with the Pledge of Allegiance, "The Yellow Rose of Texas," "The Eyes of Texas Are upon You," and "Mistress Shady." Marvin would rub his spit-flecked arm with his left hand, rub and roll as if polishing an ebony pool cue. Then he would rest his head in the crook of his arm, sniffing, huffing deep like black-jacket boys huff bagsful of acrylics. After ten minutes or so, his eyes would close, heavy. He would sleep till recess. Mrs. Wickham would let him.

There was one other black kid in our class, a girl they called Ah-so. I never learned what she did to earn this name. There was nothing Asian about this big-shouldered girl. She was the tallest, heaviest kid in school. She was quiet, but I don't think any one of us was subtle or sophisticated enough to nickname our classmates according to any but physical attributes. Fat kids were called Porky or Butterball; skinny ones were called Stick or Ichabod. Ah-so was big, thick, and African. She would impassively sit, sullen, silent as Marvin. She wore the same dark blue pleated skirt every day, the same ruffled white blouse every day. Her skin always shone as if worked by Marvin's palms and fingers. I never spoke one word to her, nor she to me.

Of the three of us, Mrs. Wickham called only on Ah-so and me. Ah-so never answered one question, correctly or incorrectly, so far as I can recall. She wasn't stupid. When asked to read aloud she read well, seldom stumbling over long words, reading with humor and expression. But when Wickham asked her about Farmer Brown and how many cows, or the capital of Vermont, or the date of this war or that, Ah-so never spoke. Not one word. But you always felt she could have answered those questions if she'd wanted to. I sensed no tension, embarrassment, or anger in Ah-so's reticence. She simply refused to speak. There was something unshakable about her, some core so impenetrably solid, you got the feeling that if you stood too close to her she could eat your thoughts like a black star eats light. I didn't despise Ah-so as I despised Marvin. There was nothing malevolent about her. She sat like a great icon in the back of the classroom, tranquil, guarded, sealed up, watchful. She was close to sixteen, and it was my guess she'd given up on school. Perhaps she was just obliging the wishes of her family, sticking it out till the law could no longer reach her.

There were at least half a dozen older kids in our class. Besides Marvin and Ah-so there was Oakley, who sat behind me, whispering threats into my ear; Varna Willard with the large breasts; Eddie Limon, who played bass for a high school rock band; and Lawrence Ridderbeck, whom everyone said had a kid and a wife. You couldn't expect me to know anything about Texan educational practices of the 1960s, so I never knew why there were so many older kids in my sixth grade class. After all, I was just a boy and had transferred into the school around midyear. My father, an air force sergeant, had been sent to Viet Nam. The air force sent my mother, my sister Claire, and me to Connolly Air Force Base, which during the war housed "unaccompanied wives." I'd been to so many different schools in my short life that I ceased wondering about their differences. All I knew about the Texas schools is that they weren't afraid to flunk you.

Yet though I was only twelve then, I had a good idea why Wickham never once called on Marvin, why she let him snooze in the crook of his polished arm. I knew why she would press her lips together, and narrow her eyes at me whenever I correctly answered a question, rare as that was. I knew why she badgered Ah-so with questions everyone knew Ah-so would never even consider answering. Wickham didn't like us. She wasn't gross about it, but it was clear she didn't want us around. She would prove her dislike day after day with little stories and jokes. "I just want to share with you all," she would say, "a little riddle my daughter told me at the supper table th'other day. Now, where do you go when you injure your knee?" Then one, two, or all three of her pets would say for the rest of us, "We don't know, Miz Wickham," in that skin-chilling way suckasses speak, "where?" "Why, to Africa," Wickham would say, "where the knee grows."

The thirty-odd white kids would laugh, and I would look across the room at Marvin. He'd be asleep. I would glance back at Ah-so. She'd be sitting still as a projected image, staring down at her desk. I, myself, would smile at Wickham's stupid jokes, sometimes fake a laugh. I tried to show her that at least one of us was alive and alert, even though her jokes hurt. I sucked ass, too, I suppose. But I wanted her to understand more than anything that I was not like her other nigra children, that I was worthy of more than the nonattention and the negative attention she paid Marvin and Ah-so. I hated her, but never showed it. No one could safely contradict that woman. She knew all kinds of tricks to demean, control, and punish you. And she could swing her two-foot paddle as fluidly as a big league slugger swings a bat. You didn't speak in Wickham's class unless she spoke to you first. You didn't chew gum, or wear "hood" hair. You didn't drag your feet, curse, pass notes, hold hands with the opposite sex. Most especially, you didn't say anything bad about the Aggies, Governor Connolly, LBJ, Sam Houston, or Waco. You did the forbidden and she would get you. It was that simple.

She never got me, though. Never gave her reason to. But she could have invented reasons. She did a lot of that. I can't be sure, but I used to think she pitied me because my father was in Viet Nam and my uncle A.J. had recently died there. Whenever she would tell one of her racist jokes, she would always glance at me, preface the joke with, "Now don't you nigra children take offense. This is all in fun, you know. I just want to share with you all something Coach Gilchrest told me th'other day." She would tell her joke, and glance at me again. I'd giggle, feeling a little queasy. "I'm half Irish," she would chuckle, "and you should hear some of those Irish jokes." She never told any, and I never really expected her to. I just did my Tom-thing. I kept my shoes shined, my desk neat, answered her questions as best I could, never brought gum to school, never cursed, never slept in class. I wanted to show her we were not all the same.

I tried to show them all, all thirty-odd, that I was different. It worked to some degree, but not very well. When some article was stolen from someone's locker or desk, Marvin, not I, was the first accused. I'd be second. Neither Marvin, nor Ah-so nor I were ever chosen for certain classroom honors — "Pledge leader," "flag holder," "noise monitor," "paper passer outer," but Mrs. Wickham once let me be "eraser duster." I was proud. I didn't even care about the cracks my fellow students made about my finally having turned the right color. I had done something that Marvin, in the deeps of his never-ending sleep, couldn't even dream of doing. Jack Preston, a kid who sat in front of me, asked me one day at recess whether I was embarrassed about Marvin. "Can you believe that guy?" I said. "He's like a pig or something. Makes me sick."

"Does it make you ashamed to be colored?"

"No," I said, but I meant yes. Yes, if you insist on thinking us all the same. Yes, if his faults are mine, his weaknesses inherent in me.

"I'd be," said Jack.

I made no reply. I was ashamed. Ashamed for not defending Marvin and ashamed that Marvin even existed. But if it had occurred to me, I would have asked Jack whether he was ashamed of being white because of Oakley. Oakley, "Oak Tree," Kelvin "Oak Tree" Oakley. He was sixteen and proud of it. He made it clear to everyone, including Wickham, that his life's ambition was to stay in school one more year, till he'd be old enough to enlist in the army. "Them slopes got my brother," he would say. "I'mna sign up and git me a few slopes. Gonna kill them bastards deader'n shit." Oakley, so far as anyone knew, was and always had been the oldest kid in his family. But no one contradicted him. He would, as anyone would tell you, "snap yer neck jest as soon as look at you." Not a boy in class, excepting Marvin and myself, had been able to avoid Oakley's pink bellies, Texas titty twisters, moon pie punches, or worse. He didn't bother Marvin, I suppose, because Marvin was closer to his size and age, and because Marvin spent five-sixths of the school day asleep. Marvin probably never crossed Oakley's mind. And to say that Oakley hadn't bothered me is not to say he had no intention of ever doing so. In fact, this haphazard sketch of hairy fingers, slash of eyebrow, explosion of acne, elbows, and crooked teeth, swore almost daily that he'd like to kill me.

Naturally, I feared him. Though we were about the same height, he outweighed me by no less than forty pounds. He talked, stood, smoked, and swore like a man. No one, except for Mrs. Wickham, the principal, and the coach, ever laid a finger on him. And even Wickham knew that the hot lines she laid on him merely amused him. He would smile out at the classroom, goofy and bashful, as she laid down the two, five, or maximum ten strokes on him. Often he would wink, or surreptitiously flash us the thumb as Wickham worked on him. When she was finished, Oakley would walk so cool back to his seat you'd think he was on wheels. He'd slide into his chair, sniff the air, and say, "Somethin's burnin. Do y'all smell smoke? I swanee, I smell smoke and fahr back here." If he had made these cracks and never threatened me, I might have grown to admire Oakley, even liked him a little. But he hated me, and took every opportunity during the six-hour school day to make me aware of this. "Some Sambo's gittin his ass broke open one of these days," he'd mumble. "I wanna fight somebody. Need to keep in shape till I git to Nam."

I never said anything to him for the longest time. I pretended not to hear him, pretended not to notice his sour breath on my neck and ear. "Yep," he'd whisper. "Coonies keep ya in good shape for slope killin." Day in, day out, that's the kind of thing I'd pretend not to hear. But one day when the rain dropped down like lead balls, and the cold air made your skin look plucked, Oakley whispered to me, "My brother tells me it rains like this in Nam. Maybe I oughta go out at recess and break your ass open today. Nice and cool so you don't sweat. Nice and wet to clean up the blood." I said nothing for at least half a minute, then I turned half right and said, "Thought you said your brother was dead." Oakley, silent himself, for a time, poked me in the back with his pencil and hissed, "*Yer* dead." Wickham cut her eyes our way, and it was over.

It was hardest avoiding him in gym class. Especially when we played murderball. Oakley always aimed his throws at me. He threw with unblinking intensity, his teeth gritting, his neck veining, his face flushing, his black hair sweeping over one eye. He could throw hard, but the balls were squishy and harmless. In fact, I found his misses more intimidating than his hits. The balls would whizz by, thunder against the folded bleachers. They rattled as though a locomotive were passing through them. I would duck, dodge, leap as if he were throwing grenades. But he always hit me, sooner or later. And after a while I noticed that the other boys would avoid throwing at me, as if I belonged to Oakley.

One day, however, I was surprised to see that Oakley was throwing at everyone else but me. He was uncommonly accurate, too; kids were falling like tin cans. Since no one was throwing at me, I spent most of the game watching Oakley cut this one and that one down. Finally, he and I were the only ones left on the court. Try as he would, he couldn't hit me, nor I him. Coach Gilchrest blew his whistle and told Oakley and me to bring the red rubber balls to the equipment locker. I was relieved I'd escaped Oakley's stinging throws for once. I was feeling triumphant, full of myself. As Oakley and I approached Gilchrest, I thought about saying something friendly to Oakley: Good game, Oak Tree, I would say. Before I could speak, though, Gilchrest said, "All right boys, there's five minutes left in the period. Y'all are so good, looks like, you're gonna have to play like men. No boundaries, no catch outs, and you gotta hit your opponent three times in order to win. Got me?"

We nodded.

"And you're gonna use these," said Gilchrest, pointing to three volleyballs at his feet. "And you better believe they're pumped full. Oates, you start at that end of the court. Oak Tree, you're at th'other end. Just like usual, I'll set the balls at mid-court, and when I blow my whistle I want y'all to haul your cheeks to the middle and th'ow for all you're worth. Got me?" Gilchrest nodded at our nods, then added, "Remember, no boundaries, right?"

I at my end, Oakley at his, Gilchrest blew his whistle. I was faster than Oakley and scooped up a ball before he'd covered three quarters of his side. I aimed, threw, and popped him right on the knee. "One-zip!" I heard Gilchrest shout. The ball bounced off his knee and shot right back into my hands. I hurried my throw and missed. Oakley bent down, clutched the two remaining balls. I remember being amazed that he could palm each ball, run full out and throw left-handed or right-handed without a shade of awkwardness. I spun, ran, but one of Oakley's throws glanced off the back of my head. "One-one!" hollered Gilchrest. I fell and spun on my ass as the other ball came sailing at me. I caught it. "He's out!" I yelled. Gilchrest's voice boomed, "No catch outs. Three hits. Three hits." I leapt to my feet as Oakley scrambled across the floor for another ball. I chased him down, leapt, and heaved the ball hard as he drew himself erect. The ball hit him dead in the face, and he went down flat. He rolled around, cupping his hands over his nose. Gilchrest sped to his side, helped him to his feet, asked him whether he was OK. Blood flowed from Oakley's nose, dripped in startlingly bright spots on the floor, his shoes, Gilchrest's shirt. The coach removed Oakley's T-shirt and pressed it against the big kid's nose to stanch the bleeding. As they walked past me toward the office I mumbled an apology to Oakley, but couldn't catch his reply. "You watch your filthy mouth, boy," said Gilchrest to Oakley.

The locker room was unnaturally quiet as I stepped into its steamy atmosphere. Eyes clicked in my direction, looked away. After I was out of my shorts, had my towel wrapped around me, my shower kit in hand, Jack Preston and Brian Nailor approached me. Preston's hair was combed slick and plastic looking. Nailor's stood up like frozen flames. Nailor smiled at me with his big teeth and pale eyes. He poked my arm with a finger. "You fucked up," he said.

"I tried to apologize."

"Won't do you no good," said Preston.

"I swanee," said Nailor.

"It's part of the game," I said. "It was an accident. Wasn't my idea to use volleyballs."

"Don't matter," Preston said. "He's jest lookin for an excuse to fight you."

"I never done nothing to him."

"Don't matter," said Nailor. "He don't like you."

"Brian's right, Clint. He'd jest as soon kill you as look at you."

"I never done nothing to him."

"Look," said Preston, "I know him pretty good. And jest between you and me, it's cause you're a city boy —"

"Whadda you mean? I've never —"

"He don't like your clothes —"

"And he don't like the fancy way you talk in class."

"What fancy —"

"I'm tellin him, if you don't mind, Brian."

"Tell him then."

"He don't like the way you say 'tennis shoes' instead of sneakers. He don't like coloreds. A whole bunch a things, really."

"I never done nothing to him. He's got no reason —"

"*And,*" said Nailor, grinning, "*and,* he says you're a stuck-up rich kid." Nailor's eyes had crow's-feet, bags beneath them. They were a man's eyes.

"My dad's a sergeant," I said.

"You chicken to fight him?" said Nailor.

"Yeah, Clint, don't be chicken. Jest go on and git it over with. He's whupped pert near ever'body else in the class. It ain't so bad."

"Might as well, Oates."

"Yeah, yer pretty skinny, but yer jest about his height. Jest git im in a headlock and don't let go."

"Goddamn," I said, "he's got no reason to —"

Their eyes shot right and I looked over my shoulder. Oakley stood at his locker, turning its tumblers. From where I stood I could see that a piece of cotton was wedged up one of his nostrils, and he already had the makings of a good shiner. His acne burned red like a fresh abrasion. He snapped the locker open and kicked his shoes off without sitting. Then he pulled off his shorts, revealing two paddle stripes on his ass. They were fresh red bars speckled with white, the white speckles being the reverse impression of the paddle's suction holes. He must not have watched his filthy mouth while in Gilchrest's presence. Behind me, I heard Preston and Nailor pad to their lockers.

Oakley spoke without turning around. "Somebody's gonna git his skinny black ass kicked, right today, right after school." He said it softly. He slipped his jock off, turned around. I looked away. Out the corner of my eye I saw him stride off, his hairy nakedness a weapon clearing the younger boys from his path. Just before he rounded the corner of the shower stalls, I threw my toilet kit to the floor and stammered, "I — I never did nothing to you, Oakley." He stopped, turned, stepped closer to me, wrapping his towel around himself. Sweat streamed down my rib cage. It felt like ice water. "You wanna go at it right now, boy?"

"I never did nothing to you." I felt tears in my eyes. I couldn't stop them even though I was blinking like mad. "Never."

He laughed. "You busted my nose, asshole."

"What about before? What'd I ever do to you?"

"See you after school, Coonie." Then he turned away, flashing his acne-spotted back like a semaphore. "Why?" I shouted. "Why you wanna fight me?" Oakley stopped and turned, folded his arms, leaned against a toilet stall. "Why you wanna fight *me,* Oakley?" I stepped over the bench. "What'd I do? Why me?" And then unconsciously, as if scratching, as if breathing, I walked toward Marvin, who stood a few feet from Oakley, combing his hair at the mirror. "Why not him?" I said. "How come you're after *me* and not *him*?" The room froze. Froze for a moment that was both evanescent and eternal, somewhere between an eye blink and a week in hell. No one moved, nothing happened; there was no sound at all. And then it was as if all of us at the same moment looked at Marvin. He just stood there, combing away, the only body in motion, I think. He combed his hair and combed it, as if seeing only his image, hearing only his comb scraping his scalp. I knew he'd heard me. There's no way he could not have heard me. But all he did was slide the comb into his pocket and walk out the door.

"I got no quarrel with Marvin," I heard Oakley say. I turned toward his voice, but he was already in the shower.

I was able to avoid Oakley at the end of the school day. I made my escape by asking Mrs. Wickham if I could go to the restroom.

"'Restroom,'" Oakley mumbled. "It's a damn toilet, sissy."

"Clinton," said Mrs. Wickham. "Can you *not* wait till the bell rings? It's almost three o'clock."

"No ma'am," I said. "I won't make it."

"Well, I should make you wait just to teach you to be more mindful about . . . hygiene . . . uh things." She sucked in her cheeks, squinted. "But I'm feeling charitable today. You may go." I immediately left the building, and got on the bus. "Ain't you a little early?" said the bus driver, swinging the door shut. "Just left the office," I said. The driver nodded, apparently not giving me a second thought. I had no idea why I'd told her I'd come from the office, or why she found it a satisfactory answer. Two minutes later the bus filled, rolled and shook its way to Connolly Air Base.

When I got home, my mother was sitting in the living room, smoking her Slims, watching her soap opera. She absently asked me how my day had gone and I told her fine. "Hear from Dad?" I said.

"No, but I'm sure he's fine." She always said that when we hadn't heard from him in a while. I suppose she thought I was worried about him, or that I felt vulnerable without him. It was neither. I just wanted to discuss something with my mother that we both cared about. If I spoke with her about things that happened at school, or on my weekends, she'd listen with half an ear, say something like, "Is that so?" or "You don't say?" I couldn't stand that sort of thing. But when I mentioned my father, she treated me a bit more like an adult, or at least someone who was worth listening to. I didn't want to feel like a boy that afternoon. As I turned from my mother and walked down the hall I thought about the day my father left for Viet Nam. Sharp in his uniform, sure behind his aviator specs, he slipped a cigar from his pocket and stuck it in mine. "Not till I get back," he said. "We'll have us one when we go fishing. Just you and me, out on the lake all day, smoking and casting and sitting. Don't let Mamma see it. Put it in y' back pocket." He hugged me, shook my hand, and told me I was the man of the house now. He told me he was depending on me to take good care of my mother and sister. "Don't you let me down, now, hear?" And he tapped his thick finger on my chest. "You almost as big as me. Boy, you something else." I believed him when he told me those things. My heart swelled big enough to swallow my father, my mother, Claire. I loved, feared, and respected myself, my manhood. That day I could have put all of Waco, Texas, in my heart. And it wasn't till about three months later that I discovered I really wasn't the man of the house, that my mother and sister, as they always had, were taking care of me.

For a brief moment I considered telling my mother about what had happened at school that day, but for one thing, she was deep down in the halls of "General Hospital," and never paid you much mind till it was over. For another thing, I just wasn't the kind of person — I'm still not, really — to discuss my problems with anyone. Like my father I kept things to myself, talked about my problems only in retrospect. Since my father wasn't around, I consciously wanted to be like him, doubly like him, I could say. I wanted to be the man of the house in some respect, even if it had to be in an inward way. I went to my room, changed my clothes, and laid out my homework. I couldn't focus on it. I thought about Marvin, what I'd said about him or done to him — I couldn't tell which. I'd done something to him, said something about him; said something about and done something to myself. *How come you're after* me *and not* him? I kept trying to tell myself I hadn't meant it that way. *That* way. I thought about approaching Marvin, telling him what I really meant was that he was more Oakley's age and weight than I. I would tell him I meant I was no match for Oakley. *See, Marvin, what I meant was that he wants to fight a colored guy, but is afraid to fight you cause you could beat him.* But try as I did, I couldn't for a moment convince myself that Marvin would believe me. I meant it *that* way and no other. Everybody heard. Everybody knew. That afternoon I forced myself to confront the notion that tomorrow I would probably have to fight both Oakley and Marvin. I'd have to be two men.

I rose from my desk and walked to the window. The light made my skin look orange, and I started thinking about what Wickham had told us once about light. She said that oranges and apples, leaves and flowers, the whole multicolored world, was not what it appeared to be. The colors we see, she said, look like they do only because of the light or ray that shines on them. "The color of the thing isn't what you see, but the light that's reflected off it." Then she shut out the lights and shone a white light lamp on a prism. We watched the pale splay of colors on the projector screen; some people ooohed and aaahed. Suddenly, she switched on a black light and the color of everything changed. The prism colors vanished, Wickham's arms were purple, the buttons of her dress were as orange as hot coals, rather than the blue they had been only seconds before. We were all very quiet. "Nothing," she said after a while, "is really what it appears to be." I didn't really understand then. But as I stood at the window, gazing at my orange skin, I wondered what kind of light I could shine on Marvin, Oakley, and me that would reveal us as the same.

I sat down and stared at my arms. They were dark brown again. I worked up a bit of saliva under my tongue and spat on my left arm. I spat again, then rubbed the spittle into it, polishing, working till my arm grew warm. As I spat, and rubbed, I wondered why Marvin did this weird, nasty thing to himself, day after day. Was he trying to rub away the black, or deepen it, doll it up? And if he did this weird nasty thing for a hundred years, would he spit-shine himself invisible, rolling away the eggplant skin, revealing the scarlet muscle, blue vein, pink and yellow tendon, white bone? Then disappear? Seen through, all colors, no colors. Spitting and rubbing. Is this the way you do it? I leaned forward, sniffed the arm. It smelled vaguely of mayonnaise. After an hour or so, I fell asleep.

I saw Oakley the second I stepped off the bus the next morning. He stood outside the gym in his usual black penny loafers, white socks, high water jeans, T-shirt and black jacket. Nailor stood with him, his big teeth spread across his bottom lip like playing cards. If there was anyone I felt like fighting, that day, it was Nailor. But I wanted to put off fighting for as long as I could. I stepped toward the gymnasium, thinking that I shouldn't run, but if I hurried I could beat Oakley to the door and secure myself near Gilchrest's office. But the moment I stepped into the gym, I felt Oakley's broad palm clap down on my shoulder. "Might as well stay out here, Coonie," he said. "I need me a little target practice." I turned to face him and he slapped me, one-two, with the back, then the palm of his hand, as I'd seen Bogart do to Peter Lorre in "The Maltese Falcon." My heart went wild. I could scarcely breathe. I couldn't swallow.

"Call me a nigger," I said. I have no idea what made me say this. All I know is that it kept me from crying. "Call me a nigger, Oakley."

"Fuck you, ya black ass slope." He slapped me again, scratching my eye. "I don't do what coonies tell me."

"Call me a nigger."

"Outside, Coonie."

"Call me one. Go ahead."

He lifted his hand to slap me again, but before his arm could swing my way, Marvin Pruitt came from behind me and calmly pushed me aside. "Git out my way, boy," he said. And he slugged Oakley on the side of his head. Oakley stumbled back, stiff-legged. His eyes were big. Marvin hit him twice more, once again to the side of the head, once to the nose. Oakley went down and stayed down. Though blood was drawn, whistles blowing, fingers pointing, kids hollering, Marvin just stood there, staring at me with cool eyes. He spat on the ground, licked his lips, and just stared at me, till Coach Gilchrest and Mr. Calderon tackled him and violently carried him away. He never struggled, never took his eyes off me.

Nailor and Mrs. Wickham helped Oakley to his feet. His already fattened nose bled and swelled so that I had to look away. He looked around, bemused, wall-eyed, maybe scared. It was apparent he had no idea how bad he was hurt. He didn't even touch his nose. He didn't look like he knew much of anything. He looked at me, looked me dead in the eye in fact, but didn't seem to recognize me.

That morning, like all other mornings, we said the Pledge of Allegiance, sang "The Yellow Rose of Texas," "The Eyes of Texas Are upon You," and "Mistress Shady." The room stood strangely empty without Oakley, and without Marvin, but at the same time you could feel their presence more intensely somehow. I felt like I did when I'd walk into my mother's room and could smell my father's cigars, or cologne. He was more palpable, in certain respects, than when there in actual flesh. For some reason, I turned to look at Ah-so, and just this once I let my eyes linger on her face. She had a very gentle-looking face, really. That surprised me. She must have felt my eyes on her because she glanced up at me for a second and smiled, white teeth, downcast eyes. Such a pretty smile. That surprised me too. She held it for a few seconds, then let it fade. She looked down at her desk, and sat still as a photograph.

A Composition Assignment

As is the case with many articles in academic journals, the following article by composition researcher Nancy Sommers begins with a review of the literature — that is, a review of other research that is related to hers and an explanation of how her research will confirm or challenge the other work. Then comes a discussion of the methods Sommers used in conducting her research. Finally, Sommers presents her results and the implications of those results for her discipline, in this case the teaching of writing.

Experiment with different kinds of summaries that could be used for different purposes. You might try a single-sentence summary, of the kind you would include in a literature review like Sommers's. You might also try writing a brief paragraph, an abstract of Sommers's article for a paper you are writing on research on the composing process of college writers. Or you might try shifting your audience and writing an essay for other student writers your age, reporting to them the results of Sommers's research and its implications for them. Though Sommers's article lends itself to a neat four-part summary (review-methods-results-implications), you also might want to consider the benefits (and liabilities) of organizing your summary in other ways.

Revision Strategies of Student Writers and Experienced Adult Writers

NANCY SOMMERS

Although various aspects of the writing process have been studied extensively of late, research on revision has been notably absent. The reason for this, I suspect, is that current models of the writing process have directed attention away from revision. With few exceptions, these models are linear; they separate the writing process into discrete stages. Two representative models are Gordon Rohman's suggestion that the composing process moves from prewriting to writing to rewriting and James Britton's model of the writing process as a series of stages described in metaphors of linear growth, conception–incubation–production.[1] What is striking about these theories of writing is that they

[1]D. Gordon Rohman and Albert O. Wlecke, "Pre-writing: The Construction and Application of Models for Concept Formation in Writing," Cooperative Research Project No. 2174, U.S. Office of Education, Department of Health, Education, and Welfare; James Britton, Anthony Burgess, Nancy Martin, Alex McLeod, Harold Rosen, *The Development of Writing Abilities* (11–18) (London: Macmillan Education, 1975).

NANCY SOMMERS (b. 1951) is the Sosland Director of the Expository Writing Program at Harvard University, where she has launched a longitudinal study of one hundred students to understand the role of writing in undergraduate education. This article appeared in the professional journal *College Composition and Communication* in December 1980.

model themselves on speech: Rohman defines the writer in a way that cannot distinguish him from a speaker ("A writer is a man who . . . puts [his] experience into words in his own mind" . . .); and Britton bases his theory of writing on what he calls (following Jakobson) the "expressiveness" of speech.[2] Moreover, Britton's study itself follows the "linear model" of the relation of thought and language in speech proposed by Vygotsky, a relationship embodied in the linear movement "from the motive which engenders a thought to the shaping of the thought, *first* in inner speech, *then* in meanings of words, and *finally* in words." . . . What this movement fails to take into account in its linear structure — "first . . . then . . . finally"— is the recursive shaping of thought by language; what it fails to take into account is *revision.* In these linear conceptions of the writing process revision is understood as a separate stage at the end of the process — a stage that comes after the completion of a first or second draft and one that is temporally distinct from the prewriting and writing stages of the process.[3]

The linear model bases itself on speech in two specific ways. First of all, it is based on traditional rhetorical models, models that were created to serve the spoken art of oratory. In whatever ways the parts of classical rhetoric are described, they offer "stages" of composition that are repeated in contemporary models of the writing process. Edward Corbett, for instance, describes the "five parts of a discourse" — *inventio, dispositio, elocutio, memoria, pronuntiatio* — and, disregarding the last two parts since "after rhetoric came to be concerned mainly with written discourse, there was no further need to deal with them,"[4] he produces a model very close to Britton's conception [*inventio*], incubation [*dispositio*], production [*elocutio*]. Other rhetorics also follow this procedure, and they do so not simply because of historical accident. Rather, the process represented in the linear model is based on the irreversibility of speech. Speech, Roland Barthes says, "is irreversible":

> A word cannot be retracted, except precisely by saying that one retracts it. To cross out here is to add: If I want to erase what I have just said, I cannot do it without showing the eraser itself (I must say *"or rather . . ." "I expressed myself badly . . ."*); paradoxically, it is ephemeral speech which is indelible, not monumental writing. All that one can do in the case of a spoken utterance is to tack on another utterance.[5]

What is impossible in speech is *revision:* Like the example Barthes gives, revision in speech is an afterthought. In the same way, each stage of the linear model must be exclusive (distinct from the other stages) or else it becomes trivial and counterproductive to refer to these junctures as "stages."

By staging revision after enunciation, the linear models reduce revision in writing, as in speech, to no more than an afterthought. In this way such models make the study of revision impossible. Revision, in Rohman's model, is simply the repetition of writing; or to pursue Britton's organic metaphor, revision is simply the further growth of what is al-

[2]Britton is following Roman Jakobson, "Linguistics and Poetics," in T. A. Sebeok, *Style in Language* (Cambridge, Mass.: MIT Press, 1960).

[3]For an extended discussion of this issue see Nancy Sommers, "The Need for Theory in Composition Research," *College Composition and Communication,* 30 (February 1979), 46–49.

[4]*Classical Rhetoric for the Modern Student* (New York: Oxford University Press, 1965), p. 27.

[5]Roland Barthes, "Writers, Intellectuals, Teachers," in *Image-Music-Text,* trans. Stephen Heath (New York: Hill and Wang, 1977), pp. 190–191.

ready there, the "preconceived" product. The absence of research on revision, then, is a function of a theory of writing which makes revision both superfluous and redundant, a theory which does not distinguish between writing and speech.

What the linear models do produce is a parody of writing. Isolating revision and then disregarding it plays havoc with the experiences composition teachers have of the actual writing and rewriting of experienced writers. Why should the linear model be preferred? Why should revision be forgotten, superfluous? Why do teachers offer the linear model and students accept it? One reason, Barthes suggests, is that "there is a fundamental tie between teaching and speech," while "writing begins at the point where speech becomes *impossible*."[6] The spoken word cannot be revised. The possibility of revision distinguishes the written text from speech. In fact, according to Barthes, this is the essential difference between writing and speaking. When we must revise, when the very idea is subject to recursive shaping by language, then speech becomes inadequate. This is a matter to which I will return, but first we should examine, theoretically, a detailed exploration of what student writers as distinguished from experienced adult writers *do* when they write and rewrite their work. Dissatisfied with both the linear model of writing and the lack of attention to the process of revision, I conducted a series of studies over the past three years which examined the revision processes of student writers and experienced writers to see what role revision played in their writing processes. In the course of my work the revision process was redefined as *a sequence of changes in a composition — changes which are initiated by cues and occur continually throughout the writing of a work.*

METHODOLOGY

I used a case study approach. The student writers were twenty freshmen at Boston University and the University of Oklahoma with SAT verbal scores ranging from 450 to 600 in their first semester of composition. The twenty experienced adult writers from Boston and Oklahoma City included journalists, editors, and academics. To refer to the two groups, I use the terms *student writers* and *experienced writers* because the principal difference between these two groups is the amount of experience they have had in writing.

Each writer wrote three essays, expressive, explanatory, and persuasive, and rewrote each essay twice, producing nine written products in draft and final form. Each writer was interviewed three times after the final revision of each essay. And each writer suggested revisions for a composition written by an anonymous author. Thus extensive written and spoken documents were obtained from each writer.

The essays were analyzed by counting and categorizing the changes made. Four revision operations were identified: deletion, substitution, addition, and reordering. And four levels of changes were identified: word, phrase, sentence, theme (the extended statement of one idea). A coding system was developed for identifying the frequency of revision by level and operation. In addition, transcripts of the interviews in which the writers interpreted their revisions were used to develop what was called a *scale of concerns* for each writer. This scale enabled me to codify what were the writer's primary concerns, secondary concerns, tertiary concerns, and whether the writers used the same scale of concerns when revising the second or third drafts as they used in revising the first draft.

[6]"Writers, Intellectuals, Teachers," p. 190.

REVISION STRATEGIES OF STUDENT WRITERS

Most of the students I studied did not use the terms *revision* or *rewriting.* In fact, they did not seem comfortable using the word *revision* and explained that revision was not a word they used, but the word their teachers used. Instead, most of the students had developed various functional terms to describe the type of changes they made. The following are samples of these definitions:

> *Scratch Out and Do Over Again:* "I say scratch out and do over, and that means what it says. Scratching out and cutting out. I read what I have written and I cross out a word and put another word in; a more decent word or a better word. Then if there is somewhere to use a sentence that I have crossed out, I will put it there."
>
> *Reviewing:* "Reviewing means just using better words and eliminating words that are not needed. I go over and change words around."
>
> *Reviewing:* "I just review every word and make sure that everything is worded right. I see if I am rambling; I see if I can put a better word in or leave one out. Usually when I read what I have written, I say to myself, 'that word is so bland or so trite,' and then I go and get my thesaurus."
>
> *Redoing:* "Redoing means cleaning up the paper and crossing out. It is looking at something and saying, no that has to go, or no, that is not right."
>
> *Marking Out:* "I don't use the word rewriting because I only write one draft and the changes that I make are made on top of the draft. The changes that I make are usually just marking out words and putting different ones in."
>
> *Slashing and Throwing Out:* "I throw things out and say they are not good. I like to write like Fitzgerald did by inspiration, and if I feel inspired then I don't need to slash and throw much out."

The predominant concern in these definitions is vocabulary. The students understand the revision process as a rewording activity. They do so because they perceive words as the unit of written discourse. That is, they concentrate on particular words apart from their role in the text. Thus one student quoted above thinks in terms of dictionaries, and, following the eighteenth-century theory of words parodied in *Gulliver's Travels,* he imagines a load of things carried about to be exchanged. Lexical changes are the major revision activities of the students because economy is their goal. They are governed, like the linear model itself, by the Law of Occam's razor that prohibits logically needless repetition: redundancy and superfluity. Nothing governs speech more than such superfluities; speech constantly repeats itself precisely because spoken words, as Barthes writes, are expendable in the cause of communication. The aim of revision according to the students' own description is therefore to clean up speech; the redundancy of speech is unnecessary in writing, their logic suggests, because writing, unlike speech, can be reread. Thus one student said, "Redoing means cleaning up the paper and crossing out." The remarkable contradiction of cleaning by marking might, indeed, stand for student revision as I have encountered it.

The students place a symbolic importance on their selection and rejection of words as the determiners of success or failure for their compositions. When revising, they primarily ask themselves: Can I find a better word or phrase? A more impressive, not so clichéd, or less hum-drum word? Am I repeating the same word or phrase too often? They approach the revision process with what could be labeled as a "thesaurus philosophy of writing"; the students consider the thesaurus a harvest of lexical substitutions and believe that most problems in their essays can be solved by rewording. What is revealed in the students' use of the thesaurus is a governing attitude toward their writing: that the meaning to be communicated is already there, already finished, already produced, ready to be communicated, and all that is necessary is a better word "rightly worded." One student defined revision as "redoing"; "redoing" meant "just using better words and eliminating words that are not needed." For the students, writing is translating: the thought to the page, the language of speech to the more formal language of prose, the word to its synonym. Whatever is translated, an original text already exists for students, one which need not be discovered or acted upon, but simply communicated.[7]

The students list repetition as one of the elements they most worry about. This cue signals to them that they need to eliminate the repetition either by substituting or deleting words or phrases. Repetition occurs, in large part, because student writing imitates — transcribes — speech: Attention to repetitious words is a manner of cleaning speech. Without a sense of the developmental possibilities of revision (and writing in general) students seek, on the authority of many textbooks, simply to clean up their language and prepare to type. What is curious, however, is that students are aware of lexical repetition, but not conceptual repetition. They only notice the repetition if they can "hear" it; they do not diagnose lexical repetition as symptomatic of problems on a deeper level. By rewording their sentences to avoid the lexical repetition, the students solve the immediate problem, but blind themselves to problems on a textual level; although they are using different words, they are sometimes merely restating the same idea with different words. Such blindness, as I discovered with student writers, is the inability to "see" revision as a process; the inability to "re-view" their work again, as it were, with different eyes, and to start over.

The revision strategies described above are consistent with the students' understanding of the revision process as requiring lexical changes but not semantic changes. For the students, the extent to which they revise is a function of their level of inspiration. In fact, they use the word *inspiration* to describe the ease or difficulty with which their essay is written, and the extent to which the essay needs to be revised. If students feel inspired, if the writing comes easily, and if they don't get stuck on individual words or phrases, then they say that they cannot see any reason to revise. Because students do not see revision as an activity in which they modify and develop perspectives and ideas, they feel that if they know what they want to say, then there is little reason for making revisions.

The only modification of ideas in the students' essays occurred when they tried out two or three introductory paragraphs. This results, in part, because the students have been taught in another version of the linear model of composing to use a thesis statement as a controlling device in their introductory paragraphs. Since they write their introductions and their thesis statements even before they have really discovered what they want to say, their early close attention to the thesis statement, and more generally the linear model, function to restrict and circumscribe not only the development of their ideas, but also their ability to change the direction of these ideas.

Too often as composition teachers we conclude that students do not willingly revise.

[7]Nancy Sommers and Ronald Schleifer, "Means and Ends: Some Assumptions of Student Writers," *Composition and Teaching,* II.

The evidence from my research suggests that it is not that students are unwilling to revise, but rather that they do what they have been taught to do in a consistently narrow and predictable way. On every occasion when I asked students why they hadn't made any more changes, they essentially replied, "I knew something larger was wrong, but I didn't think it would help to move words around." The students have strategies for handling words and phrases and their strategies helped them on a word or sentence level. What they lack, however, is a set of strategies to help them identify the "something larger" that they sensed was wrong and work from there. The students do not have strategies for handling the whole essay. They lack procedures or heuristics to help them reorder lines of reasoning or ask questions about their purposes and readers. The students view their compositions in a linear way as a series of parts. Even such potentially useful concepts as "unity" or "form" are reduced to the rule that a composition, if it is to have form, must have an introduction, a body, and a conclusion, or the sum total of the necessary parts.

The students decide to stop revising when they decide that they have not violated any of the rules for revising. These rules, such as "Never begin a sentence with a conjunction" or "Never end a sentence with a preposition," are lexically cued and rigidly applied. In general, students will subordinate the demands of the specific problems of their text to the demands of the rules. Changes are made in compliance with abstract rules about the product, rules that quite often do not apply to the specific problems in the text. These revision strategies are teacher-based, directed toward a teacher-reader who expects compliance with rules — with preexisting "conceptions" — and who will only examine parts of the composition (writing comments about those parts in the margins of their essays) and will cite any violations of rules in those parts. At best the students see their writing altogether passively through the eyes of former teachers or their surrogates, the textbooks, and are bound to the rules which they have been taught.

REVISION STRATEGIES OF EXPERIENCED WRITERS

One aim of my research has been to contrast how student writers define revision with how a group of experienced writers define their revision processes. Here is a sampling of the definitions from the experienced writers:

> *Rewriting:* "It is a matter of looking at the kernel of what I have written, the content, and then thinking about it, responding to it, making decisions, and actually restructuring it."
>
> *Rewriting:* "I rewrite as I write. It is hard to tell what is a first draft because it is not determined by time. In one draft, I might cross out three pages, write two, cross out a fourth, rewrite it, and call it a draft. I am constantly writing and rewriting. I can only conceptualize so much in my first draft — only so much information can be held in my head at one time; my rewriting efforts are a reflection of how much information I can encompass at one time. There are levels and agenda which I have to attend to in each draft."
>
> *Rewriting:* "Rewriting means on one level, finding the argument, and on another level, language changes to make the argument more effective. Most of the time I feel as if I can go on rewriting forever. There is always one part of a piece that I could keep working on. It is always difficult to know at what point to abandon a piece of writing. I like this idea that a piece of writing is never finished, just abandoned."
>
> *Rewriting:* "My first draft is usually very scattered. In rewriting, I find the line of argument. After the argument is resolved, I am much more interested in word choice and phrasing."

> *Revising:* "My cardinal rule in revising is never to fall in love with what I have written in a first or second draft. An idea, sentence, or even a phrase that looks catchy, I don't trust. Part of this idea is to wait a while. I am much more in love with something after I have written it than I am a day or two later. It is much easier to change anything with time."
>
> *Revising:* "It means taking apart what I have written and putting it back together again. I ask major theoretical questions of my ideas, respond to those questions, and think of proportion and structure, and try to find a controlling metaphor. I find out which ideas can be developed and which should be dropped. I am constantly chiseling and changing as I revise."

The experienced writers describe their primary objective when revising as finding the form or shape of their argument. Although the metaphors vary, the experienced writers often use structural expressions such as "finding a framework," "a pattern," or "a design" for their argument. When questioned about this emphasis, the experienced writers responded that since their first drafts are usually scattered attempts to define their territory, their objective in the second draft is to begin observing general patterns of development and deciding what should be included and what excluded. One writer explained, "I have learned from experience that I need to keep writing a first draft until I figure out what I want to say. Then in a second draft, I begin to see the structure of an argument and how all the various subarguments which are buried beneath the surface of all those sentences are related." What is described here is a process in which the writer is both agent and vehicle. "Writing," says Barthes, unlike speech, "develops like a seed, not a line,"[8] and like a seed it confuses beginning and end, conception and production. Thus, the experienced writers say their drafts are "not determined by time," that rewriting is a "constant process," that they feel as if (they) "can go on forever." Revising confuses the beginning and end, the agent and vehicle; it confuses, *in order to find,* the line of argument.

After a concern for form, the experienced writers have a second objective: a concern for their readership. In this way, "production" precedes "conception." The experienced writers imagine a reader (reading their product) whose existence and whose expectations influence their revision process. They have abstracted the standards of a reader and this reader seems to be partially a reflection of themselves and functions as a critical and productive collaborator — a collaborator who has yet to love their work. The anticipation of a reader's judgment causes a feeling of dissonance when the writer recognizes incongruities between intention and execution, and requires these writers to make revisions on all levels. Such a reader gives them just what the students lacked: new eyes to "re-view" their work. The experienced writers believe that they have learned the causes and conditions, the product, which will influence their reader, and their revision strategies are geared toward creating these causes and conditions. They demonstrate a complex understanding of which examples, sentences, or phrases should be included or excluded. For example, one experienced writer decided to delete public examples and add private examples when writing about the energy crisis because "private examples would be less controversial and thus more persuasive." Another writer revised his transitional sentences because "some kinds of transitions are more easily recognized as transitions than others."

[8]*Writing Degree Zero* in *Writing Degree Zero and Elements of Semiology,* trans. Annette Lavers and Colin Smith (New York: Hill and Wang, 1968), p. 20.

These examples represent the type of strategic attempts these experienced writers use to manipulate the conventions of discourse in order to communicate to their readers.

But these revision strategies are a process of more than communication; they are part of the process of *discovering meaning* altogether. Here we can see the importance of dissonance; at the heart of revision is the process by which writers recognize and resolve the dissonance they sense in their writing. Ferdinand de Saussure has argued that meaning is differential or "diacritical," based on differences between terms rather than "essential" or inherent qualities of terms. "Phonemes," he said, "are characterized not, as one might think, by their own positive quality but simply by the fact that they are distinct."[9] In fact, Saussure bases his entire *Course in General Linguistics* on these differences, and such differences are dissonant; like musical dissonances which gain their significance from their relationship to the "key" of the composition which itself is determined by the whole language, specific language (*parole*) gains its meaning from the system of language (*langue*) of which it is a manifestation and part. The musical composition — a "composition" of parts — creates its "key" as in an overall structure which determines the value (meaning) of its parts. The analogy with music is readily seen in the compositions of experienced writers: Both sorts of composition are based precisely on those structures experienced writers seek in their writing. It is this complicated relationship between the parts and the whole in the work of experienced writers which destroys the linear model; writing cannot develop "like a line" because each addition or deletion is a reordering of the whole. Explicating Saussure, Jonathan Culler asserts that "meaning depends on difference of meaning."[10] But student writers constantly struggle to bring their essays into congruence with a predefined meaning. The experienced writers do the opposite: They seek to discover (to create) meaning in the engagement with their writing, in revision. They seek to emphasize and exploit the lack of clarity, the differences of meaning, the dissonance, that writing as opposed to speech allows in the possibility of revision. Writing has spatial and temporal features not apparent in speech — words are recorded in space and fixed in time — which is why writing is susceptible to reordering and later addition. Such features make possible the dissonance that both provokes revision and promises, from itself, new meaning.

For the experienced writers the heaviest concentration of changes is on the sentence level, and the changes are predominantly by addition and deletion. But, unlike the students, experienced writers make changes on all levels and use all revision operations. Moreover, the operations the students fail to use — reordering and addition — seem to require a theory of the revision process as a totality — a theory which, in fact, encompasses the *whole* of the composition. Unlike the students, the experienced writers possess a nonlinear theory in which a sense of the whole writing both precedes and grows out of an examination of the parts. As we saw, one writer said he needed "a first draft to figure out what to say," and "a second draft to see the structure of an argument buried beneath the surface." Such a "theory" is both theoretical and strategical; once again, strategy and theory are conflated in ways that are literally impossible for the linear model. Writing appears to be more like a seed than a line.

[9]*Course in General Linguistics,* trans. Wade Baskin (New York, 1966), p. 119.

[10]Jonathan Culler, *Saussure* (Penguin Modern Masters Series; London: Penguin Books, 1976), p. 70.

Two elements of the experienced writers' theory of the revision process are the adoption of a holistic perspective and the perception that revision is a recursive process. The writers ask: What does my essay as a *whole* need for form, balance, rhythm, or communication? Details are added, dropped, substituted, or reordered according to their sense of what the essay needs for emphasis and proportion. This sense, however, is constantly in flux as ideas are developed and modified; it is constantly "re-viewed" in relation to the parts. As their ideas change, revision becomes an attempt to make their writing consonant with that changing vision.

The experienced writers see their revision process as a recursive process — a process with significant recurring activities — with different levels of attention and different agenda for each cycle. During the first revision cycle their attention is primarily directed toward narrowing the topic and delimiting their ideas. At this point, they are not as concerned as they are later about vocabulary and style. The experienced writers explained that they get closer to their meaning by not limiting themselves too early to lexical concerns. As one writer commented to explain her revision process, a comment inspired by the summer 1977 New York power failure: "I feel like Con Edison cutting off certain states to keep the generators going. In first and second drafts, I try to cut off as much as I can of my editing generator, and in a third draft, I try to cut off some of my idea generators, so I can make sure that I will actually finish the essay." Although the experienced writers describe their revision process as a series of different levels or cycles, it is inaccurate to assume that they have only one objective for each cycle and that each cycle can be defined by a different objective. The same objectives and sub-processes are present in each cycle, but in different proportions. Even though these experienced writers place the predominant weight upon finding the form of their argument during the first cycle, other concerns exist as well. Conversely, during the later cycles, when the experienced writers' primary attention is focused upon stylistic concerns, they are still attuned, although in a reduced way, to the form of the argument. Since writers are limited in what they can attend to during each cycle (understandings are temporal), revision strategies help balance competing demands on attention. Thus, writers can concentrate on more than one objective at a time by developing strategies to sort out and organize their different concerns in successive cycles of revision.

It is a sense of writing as discovery — a repeated process of beginning over again, starting out new — that the students failed to have. I have used the notion of dissonance because such dissonance, the incongruities between intention and execution, governs both writing and meaning. Students do not see the incongruities. They need to rely on their own internalized sense of good writing and to see their writing with their "own" eyes. Seeing in revision — seeing beyond hearing — is at the root of the word *revision* and the process itself; current dicta on revising blind our students to what is actually involved in revision. In fact, they blind them to what constitutes good writing altogether. Good writing disturbs: It creates dissonance. Students need to seek the dissonance of discovery, utilizing in their writing, as the experienced writers do, the very difference between writing and speech — the possibility of revision.

Acknowledgment: The author wishes to express her gratitude to Professor William Smith, University of Pittsburgh, for his vital assistance with the research reported in this article and to Patrick Hays, her husband, for extensive discussions and critical editorial help.

Readings: The Dimensions of Child Poverty

The readings in this section offer opportunities to think further about summarizing by working once again with the topic that is woven through the chapter — child poverty. If you would like to look back at the earlier readings about child poverty and related topics, see the reading on low-income children (Opening Problem, p. 79), the excerpt from Ellen Israel Rosen's *Bitter Choices: Blue-Collar Women In and Out of Work* (A Professional Application, p. 94), Studs Terkel's interview with Roberto Acuña (Oral History Assignment, p. 103), and the tables and text from Kevin Phillips's the *Politics of Rich and Poor* (Economics Assignment, p. 113).

The following readings bring into focus some dimension of child poverty in the United States. You may read them singly or in combination. Even in combination, however, these readings are not intended to cover thoroughly the issues of child poverty but only to introduce a few strands of that complex topic. In order to contribute to — and to challenge — your work with summarizing, we have chosen a range of writing about child poverty: writing shaped by the discipline of history, writing that is personal and reflective, writing of the kind produced by policy analysts, and the spare, diagrammatic writing of a chart.

The first reading, an excerpt from *Wasting America's Future: The Children's Defense Fund Report of the Costs of Child Poverty,* calls into consideration our definition of poverty and, with the aid of a chart, portrays the depth, extent, and effects of child poverty in the United States. In an excerpt from *The Welfare of Children,* Duncan Lindsey uses historical and economic perspectives to raise questions about our child welfare system. Next, Michael B. Katz provides a brief history of the changes in the way work was organized in nineteenth-century America and the effects those changes had on poverty. Then Melanie Scheller offers a reflection on the personal and psychological toll of growing up poor. And, finally, in an excerpt from *Within Our Reach: Breaking the Cycle of Disadvantage,* Lisbeth B. Schorr presents a summary of the qualities of programs that are successful in moving families out of poverty.

At the end of each reading, you will find Considerations questions intended to help you think about the reading mostly on its own terms but also in relation to summarizing strategies stressed in this chapter. At the end of the section, you will also find suggestions for writing about these readings in relation to one another and for pursuing the topic of child poverty through research.

The Children's Defense Fund is a nonprofit national organization that distributes information about and lobbies for children's causes. This report begins with an analysis of the means by which we define poverty in the United States and goes on to sketch the depth and extent of child poverty in our country. The report also provides a chart (see p. 149) tracing the many effects of poverty on families and on children's health, nutrition, safety, education, and opportunity. As you read, notice how the author uses illustrations and statistics to make a compelling argument.

From *Wasting America's Future: The Children's Defense Fund Report on the Costs of Child Poverty*

ARLOC SHERMAN

Imagine that you support yourself and two children on a yearly income of $12,000. Each month you pay $541 for rent and utilities — an amount that was fairly typical for a modest two-bedroom apartment in the United States in 1992[1] — and you spend $340 on food,[2] or about $1.24 per family member per meal. After paying for these necessities you have $119 left. To keep your job, you also must spend $175 each month on child care and $40 per month for bus fare.[3] If you get food stamps, they save you about $150 on food, leaving you a total of $54 per month for everything else. This $54 must cover all clothes, repairs for broken appliances, cleaning supplies, medical checkups, braces, prescription medicines, school supplies and school fees, a children's toy or book, entertainment, furniture, and even the newspaper and telephone you need to look for a better job. Every time you pay a bill, you think about something important your family must do without. Every day you face impossible choices about cutting back on food, housing quality, and your children's other needs.

What is remarkable about your all-too-common situation is that by government

[1]$541 equals the federal government's 1992 nationwide Fair Market Rent for a modest two-bedroom apartment. Unpublished calculations, Economic and Market Analysis Division, Office of Policy Development and Research, U.S. Department of Housing and Urban Development, February 1994. The nationwide Fair Market Rent represents the cost of a private, unsubsidized apartment or housing unit ranked somewhat below the middle of the price range (calculated for a weighted average of housing markets in the United States).

[2]Human Nutrition Information Service, "Cost of Food at Home for Food Plans at Four Cost Levels, July 1992, U.S. Average" (Hyattsville, MD: U.S. Department of Agriculture, 1992). Data are for a mother age 35 and two children, ages 7 and 10. Calculations by the Children's Defense Fund.

CDF chose the Agriculture Department's Low-Cost Food Plan rather than the even-lower-cost Thrifty Food Plan for this comparison because the Agriculture Department has long warned that: "If the standard [for food costs in public assistance programs] is to be a reasonable measure of basic needs for a good diet, it should be as high as the cost of the low-cost plan. Of families spending at even this level, many will have poor diets. The agency that sets its food cost standard as low as the cost of the economy plan should recognize that almost one-half of the families that spend this amount for food are likely to have diets that fall far short of nutrient needs." Betty B. Peterkin, "USDA Food Plans and Costs — Tools for Deriving Food Cost Standards for Use in Public Assistance," *Family Economics Review* (March 1965): 19–23, p. 21. See also note 13.

[3]The average parent with children ages 5 to 14 in paid child care spent $40.40 per week on child care in Fall 1991, or about $175 per month. Parents below the official poverty line tend to pay less for child care on average, but only very slightly (5 percent) less, according to figures for all ages of children. U.S. Census Bureau [Lynne M. Casper and others], *Who's Minding the Kids? Child Care Arrangements: Fall 1991,* Current Population Reports P70-36 (Washington, D.C.: U.S. Government Printing Office, 1994), p. 37, table 10.

Bus fare expenses of $40 per month represent a round-trip fare of $1.00 each way for five days per week for four weeks.

ARLOC SHERMAN (b. 1965) is senior program associate in the Family Income Division of the Children's Defense Fund, where he has spent the last seven years writing and speaking about poverty, employment, marital status, welfare reform, and the status of children in rural communities. His most recent publication is *Wasting America's Future: The Children's Defense Fund Report on the Costs of Child Poverty* (1994), from which this excerpt is taken.

standards your yearly income is *several hundred dollars above* the 1992 poverty line; you are not, in the eyes of the federal government, officially poor.

The government has an official definition of poverty, which the Census Bureau uses for tallying the number of poor Americans every year. These poverty thresholds take into account total family income, family size, and an adjustment each year for inflation in consumer prices. According to the latest poverty thresholds, families with less than the following amounts of annual cash income in 1992[4] were considered poor:

One person (not in a family)	$ 7,143
Family of two people	9,137
Family of three people	11,186
Family of four people	14,335
Family of five people	16,952

Poor families' incomes are usually far below these thresholds — an average of $6,289 below it in 1992. For example, only one in six among poor children's families had incomes within even $2,000 of the poverty line. More than half of all poor families with children have incomes that are at least $5,700 below the poverty line. Given how meager these annual incomes are, the many consequences of child poverty described in this book become even easier to understand.

The official poverty definition is low by almost anyone's standard. When the Gallup polling organization asked Americans where they would draw the poverty line for a family of four, the average response was 24 percent higher than the government's poverty line — meaning that Americans believe a family of four would have needed more than an additional $3,000 (in 1992 dollars) in order not to be poor. In Idaho, a special commission established by state officials tallied up a minimal budget item by item. The commission found the bare minimum needed to get by, even in low-cost Idaho, was 17 percent higher than the federal poverty line.[5] A similar commission in New Hampshire concluded in 1991 that a four-person family needed $17,940 a year to get by — 29 percent more than the 1991 poverty line.[6]

Even by the government's low official standard, however, the number of American children whose families have such inadequate incomes is staggering.

More Than 14 Million Children Are Living in Poverty. In 1992 more than one out of every five American children younger than 18 (21.9 percent) lived in a family whose income

[4]In addition to the poverty thresholds used by the Census Bureau, there is another set of federal poverty lines called poverty guidelines. These guidelines are a simplification of the poverty thresholds, and are published every February in the *Federal Register* by the U.S. Department of Health and Human Services to help determine eligibility for a variety of federal programs. By contrast the Census Bureau's poverty thresholds are used primarily for statistical purposes and are published in the Census Bureau's annual poverty report.

[5]Charles L. Skoro and David A. Johnson, "Establishing an Updated Standard of Need for AFDC Recipients," *Social Work Research and Abstracts* 27, no. 3 (September 1991):22–7, p. 26.

[6]Lawrence Neil Bailis and Lynn Burbridge, *Report on Costs of Living and AFDC Need and Payment Standard Options: Executive Summary* (Concord, NH: State of New Hampshire, Committee for SB 153, 1991). The commission's list of expenses did not even count child care or other work expenses.

was below the poverty line.[7] Among children younger than six, one in four (25.7 percent) lived in poverty, according to the latest Census Bureau figures.[8] These rates are nearly double those for adults ages 18 to 64 (11.7 percent in 1992). The number of poor children younger than 18 has increased by 5 million (from 9.6 million to 14.6 million since 1973), while the poverty rate of children has increased by one-half (from 14.4 to 21.9 percent).

Nearly one out of every three American children (32 percent) experiences at least one year of official poverty before turning 16.[9]

Children Are Falling Deeper and Deeper into Poverty. There are disturbing signs that poor children are falling even further below the poverty line than before. Nearly one in two poor children (46 percent) lives in extreme poverty, in families with incomes below one-half of the poverty line. This proportion has risen steadily — from 31 percent in 1975 (the first year for which data on extreme poverty are available) to its present record-high level.

Poor Children Do Not Fit Stereotypes. Although past and continuing racial discrimination in employment, housing, and education contribute to making Black and Latino children more likely to be poor than non-Latino White children — Black and Latino child poverty rates are about three times those of non-Latino White children — the *number* of poor non-Latino White children (6.0 million) is still considerably larger than the *number* of poor Black children (4.9 million) or poor Latino children (3.1 million).

Contrary to stereotypes, more poor children live outside cities — in suburban areas and nonmetropolitan smaller cities and rural areas — than in cities. Also, not all poor families are on welfare or out of work. Poor children's families receive about twice as much income from work as from welfare, and about two out of three poor families with children work at least part-time or part-year. Families in poverty no longer tend to be large families; the average poor family with children contains an average of only 2.2 children (only slightly larger than the average of 1.9 children in all families).

Reasons for the Rise in Child Poverty. One major reason for the rise in child poverty in recent years is the failure of hourly wages to keep pace with inflation, particularly for young workers and those with less than a college education. A second major reason is the rising number of families headed by a single parent, usually the mother; mother-only families are at high risk of poverty due to the absence of a second adult earner, the historically lower earning power of women, and the failure of absent parents to provide financial support or of state child support enforcement agencies to ensure that payments are made. (However, the poverty caused by marital changes appears to be more than

[7]U.S. Census Bureau, *Poverty in the United States: 1992,* Current Population Reports Series P60-185 (Washington, D.C.: U.S. Government Printing Office, 1993), p. 4, table 3. Unless otherwise mentioned, all poverty data in this chapter are from the U.S. Census Bureau.

[8]U.S. Census Bureau, unpublished tables from the Current Population Survey. Calculations by the Children's Defense Fund.

[9]Karl Ashworth and others, "Economic Disadvantage During Childhood," Leicestershire, England: Centre for Research in Social Policy, Loughborhough University of Technology, 1992). Information about this study is available from its coauthor, Martha S. Hill, Institute for Social Research, University of Michigan, Ann Arbor.

balanced by other changes in family characteristics that reduced poverty. These include a substantial decline in women's fertility and a large increase in the number of mothers who have completed a high school education.) A third reason for high and rising child poverty rates, and in particular for the greater depth of children's poverty, is a decline in the value of government assistance for poor families with children. The inflation-adjusted value of Aid to Families with Dependent Children (AFDC) plus food stamps declined by 26 percent between 1972 and 1992.[10] By comparison with other nations, the United States lifts a far smaller proportion of low-income families with children out of poverty. The relative importance of these three causes of rising child poverty has been described in other research reports.[11]

Why is the poverty line so low? One problem is that the poverty line originally was designed around the cost of a minimal diet (called the Economy Food Plan) that was unrealistically low from the start. The poverty line was set at three times the cost of the Economy Food Plan, to ensure that nonpoor families had enough income to purchase food and other items. Although families that bought the foods listed in the Economy Food Plan were supposed to get adequate amounts of most nutrients, even the U.S. Department of Agriculture (USDA), which designed the plan, warned at the time that it was meant only for "temporary or emergency use when funds are low."[12] (Later, USDA stressed that "the cost of this plan is not a reasonable measure of basic money needs for a good diet," and suggested that states designing assistance programs for families consider a food plan that cost "about 25 percent more than the Economy Plan."[13])

[10]U.S. House of Representatives, Committee on Ways and Means, *Overview of Entitlement Programs: 1993 Green Book* (Washington, D.C.: U.S. Government Printing Office, 1993), p. 665. This decline represents a weighted average of states' AFDC and food stamp benefits for a family of three persons with no other income.

[11]For a comparison of how much economic conditions and marital and other family changes contributed to poverty trends for White and Black children, see Peter Gottschalk and Sheldon Danziger, "Family Structure, Family Size, and Family Income: Accounting for Changes in the Economic Well-Being of Children, 1968–1986," in Sheldon Danziger and Peter Gottschalk eds., *Uneven Tides: Rising Inequality in America* (New York, NY: Russell Sage, 1993). For a discussion of how many conventional analyses (including that of Danziger and Gottschalk, above) may overstate the impact of single parent families on child poverty, see Donald J. Hernandez, *America's Children: Resources from Family, Government, and the Economy* (New York, NY: Russell Sage, 1993), especially pp. 308–13. For data on earnings, family structure, and government benefits, and a detailed discussion of child poverty and family income in America's families headed by someone younger than 30, see Clifford M. Johnson and others, *Vanishing Dreams: The Economic Plight of America's Young Families* (Washington, D.C.: Children's Defense Fund, 1992). For a discussion of the falling value of wages as a contributor to poverty for all age groups, see Rebecca M. Blank, "Why Were Poverty Rates So High in the 1980s?" in Dimitri B. Papadimitriou and Edward N. Wolff, eds., *Poverty and Prosperity in the USA in the Late Twentieth Century* (New York, NY: St. Martin's Press, 1993). For cross-national comparisons of levels and trends in income assistance, see Timothy M. Smeeding, "Cross-National Perspectives on Income Security Programs," testimony for the Congress of the United States, Joint Economic Committee, September 25, 1991.

[12]Betty Peterkin, "Family Food Plans, Revised 1964," *Family Economics Review* (October 1964), p. 12.

[13]45 *Federal Register* 22001 (1980). Federal studies confirmed that most families whose food expenditures were equal to the dollar amount of this food plan were falling substantially short of the recommended allowance of one or more major nutrients. Betty B. Peterkin and Richard L. Kerr, "Food Stamp Allotment and Diets of U.S. Households," *Family Economics Review* (Winter, 1982), pp. 23–6.

To better reflect families' true nutritional needs, the government economist who designed the present official poverty line also proposed an alternative poverty line that was 25 percent higher. For many years the Census Bureau published much of its poverty data using both definitions.

A second problem is that the poverty definition is based on outdated family spending and homemaking patterns from 1955. The Thrifty Food Plan (the successor to the Economy Food Plan) still assumes families will bake daily and cook all their food from scratch, never buy fast food or eat out, use dried beans and no canned food, be experts in nutrition, and have a working refrigerator, freezer, and stove, and ample shelf space free from rodents and roaches. More importantly, no adjustments have been made for changes since 1955 in spending patterns for nonfood items — including the increase in such costly new necessities as child care for working mothers and heightened expectations that employees and job applicants should own an extensive store-bought wardrobe,

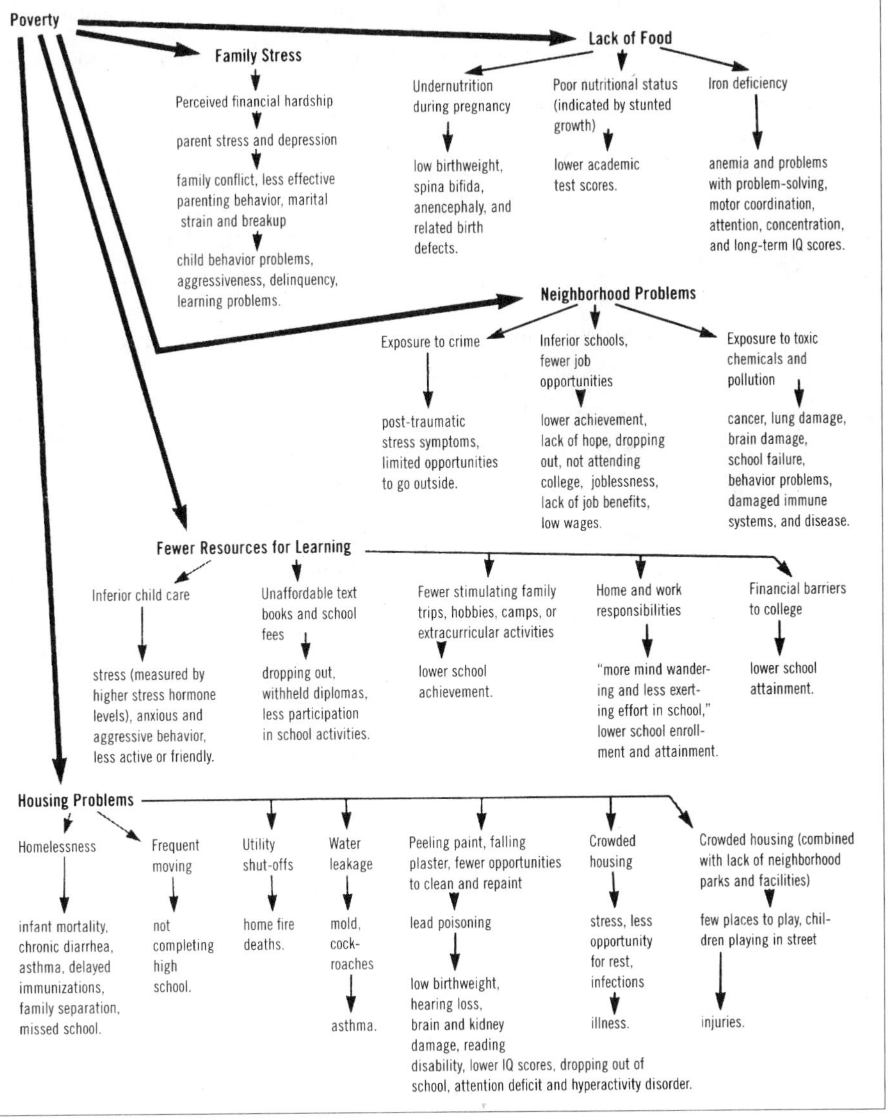

Examples of "pathways" from poverty to adverse child outcomes

have a car, and be reachable by telephone. All of these changes increase the amount of money families need to "get by." Updating the official poverty line with more up-to-date spending patterns would raise the poverty line by as much as two-thirds (to 1.68 times the value of the current official line).[14] Updating the poverty line would be consistent with the views of its original users, who stated that it should be revised periodically to account for changes in specific spending patterns and general standard of living.[15]

[14]Patricia Ruggles, *Drawing the Line: Alternative Poverty Measures and Their Implications for Public Policy* (Washington, D.C.: Urban Institute Press, 1990), p. 53, table 3.4. Ruggles calculated the updated poverty line the same way the original poverty line was calculated but substituting the assumption that families spend about one out of every 5.6 dollars on food (or 17.7 percent of their budgets) rather than one out of every three dollars (33.5 percent) as was the original assumption. She therefore multiplied the cost of the Thrifty Food Plan by about 5.6 instead of by three.

[15]Ida C. Merriam, who supervised the work of the Social Security Administration economist who invented the poverty line (Mollie Orshansky), wrote in 1967 that "obviously today's measure, even if corrected year by year for changes in the price level — the purchasing power of money — should not be acceptable twenty, ten, or perhaps even five years hence. . . . What changes over time is the kinds of goods and services actually available and the perception of the relevant groups in society as to what constitute necessities . . . ready-made dresses becoming standard, for example." I. C. Merriam, "The Meaning of Poverty-Effectiveness," interdepartmental memorandum, draft, January 4, 1967.

Considerations

1. What is the current official definition of poverty, what are its origins, and what does the Children's Defense Fund report claim is wrong with it?
2. What are the current statistics on and trends for childhood poverty in the United States? What are some explanations for these trends and statistics?
3. What are some of the stereotypes about childhood poverty? What are the facts?
4. How does the information in the chart (p. 149) differ from the summary in the text preceding it? Write a few sentences reflecting on the benefits and liabilities of each form of summary.
5. If you read "Child Poverty Is Abundant," which opens this chapter (see the Opening Problem, p. 79), you are familiar with research indicating that America's poor children generally are worse off than their counterparts in other nations. Attempt a single summary of "Child Poverty Is Abundant" and the excerpt from the Children's Defense Fund report that explains the problem of child poverty in the United States and puts it in a global perspective.

In these excerpts from his book The Welfare of Children, *Duncan Lindsey criticizes our child welfare system and goes on to place child poverty in broader social and economic contexts. As he does this, he raises questions about the adequacy of our traditional definitions of child abuse. Notice how Lindsey begins by summarizing the problem of child poverty as a way of setting up an argument against current policies.*

From *The Welfare of Children*

DUNCAN LINDSEY

When we examine how a society cares for its children we are peering directly into the heart of a nation. Today, the United States, the wealthiest country in the world, has more children living in poverty than any other industrialized nation. Millions of children wake up to dangerous neighborhoods, dilapidated and violent schools, impoverished and stressful homes, and futures devoid of opportunity. While poverty has essentially been eliminated for groups such as the elderly, it continues to blight the lives of millions of children. Further, the country that pioneered strategies to prevent child abuse and now spends more money fighting it than do all other industrialized countries has the highest rate of child abuse. In fact, more children are reported for child abuse and neglect in the United States than all the other industrialized nations combined.

In our society we assign primary responsibility for the care and nurturing of children to the family, which is understood as a haven in an often uncaring and impersonal world. Collective responsibility for children has been restricted to reclaiming children from situations where the family has been unable to meet its obligation. This approach was adequate during a period when most families were able to meet the needs of their children. However, in North America major social change during the last several decades has left large numbers of families unable to meet those needs. Although the TV family of the 1950s where the father goes off to work while the mother stays home with the children still dominates our imagination, the lone-mother struggling to support her children is today quite literally the more common family structure. For the millions of children living in such families, poverty is the prevailing condition.

Impoverished families who are unable to meet the needs of their children are, in overwhelming numbers, relying on the child welfare system for help. Yet the child welfare system has been transformed and is no longer able to cope with the problems of child poverty. From its inception the child welfare system has focused on the children left out. In the early years orphanages and foster families cared for abandoned and neglected children. As long as the problems could be confined to a limited, "residual" group of children, services could be developed to meet their needs. In recent decades, the economic hardship and social changes experienced by so many families has unraveled that system. As a consequence, the residual approach within which child welfare operates no longer makes sense. The avalanche of child abuse and neglect reports in the last decade has transformed the child welfare system into a child protection system directed toward investigating child abuse reports and occasionally removing children from families and placing them in foster care. Child welfare social workers spend most of their time investigating reports of child abuse, trying to rescue children from crises, when they should be working in a framework that will effectively prevent those crises.

What should be done? Should we stress "family values" and hope that everything will work out? Should we continue to blame parents? We do that already but to no avail.

DUNCAN LINDSEY (b. 1947) is a professor at the School of Public Policy and Social Research at the University of California, Los Angeles. Editor-in-chief of *Children and Youth Services Review,* his most recent book is *The Welfare of Children* (1994), excerpted here. He also manages a Web site on child welfare (www.childwelfare.com).

Perhaps, as many would like to think, the child welfare professionals are the real culprits. If only they could . . . well, do their job more effectively. But social workers are not miracle workers, and it is hard to imagine how they could do more, given their crushing caseloads and shrinking resources. Daily struggling to aid multitudes of children caught in a web of social disintegration, poverty, substance abuse, and despair, most are doing all that is humanly possible. Increasingly, child abuse regulations are placing them in a position where they can do little more than conduct criminal abuse investigations — something for which most have neither the training nor aptitude.

The problem is, in fact, with the perspective that guides current understanding of what can be accomplished. The residual approach to child welfare demands that aid should be invoked only after the family is in crisis and other immediate support groups (kin, neighborhood) fail to meet a child's minimal needs. From this perspective the child welfare agency becomes the site of triage, a battlefront hospital where casualties are sorted and only the most seriously wounded receive attention. But because the damage to children is so great by the time they enter the system, the number who survive and benefit is minimal. A growing proportion of children are being left to fend for themselves in an increasingly competitive high-technology market economy.

By every standard this residual perspective and the system it has spawned has failed to make progress for children. While the system has seen periods of progress, overall it has not adapted to the major demographic and structural changes that have occurred. In critical ways, the system lacks the instruments to effectively solve the problems confronting children today. While the residual approach may stave off the most brutal and horrific instances of abuse and poverty, it cannot return the millions of children who live in poverty into the economic and social mainstream. Approaches that may have been appropriate one hundred, fifty, or even thirty years ago are no longer effective today.

It is significant to note that the situation children face is not tolerated in other areas of our society. For example, government policies and programs ensure collective action to provide the technology, infrastructure, and resources that businesses require to compete in the global economy. Entrepreneurs and investors routinely look to government to provide a suitable environment for their economic enterprises. Likewise, senior citizens have been able, through Social Security, to see poverty ended among their ranks. . . .

Despite our fabulous wealth, poverty has gotten worse, poverty among families, especially lone-parent families, among people of color, and of particular concern, among children (Bush, 1987; Sarri and Finn, 1992a, b).

In examining this poverty, it is useful to pull back and review the economic circumstances of the United States and Canada as examples of how free enterprise market economies create income and wealth. My interest is to examine how well modern economies have provided and continue to provide for children. A nation's collective economic and social future is shaped by the manner in which it provides for its children. We behold our future in the faces of our children, not only as a species, but as a nation and society. If many of our children are despairing, suffering from poverty and disease, especially in the midst of plenty, not only are we as guardians called to question, a warning is sounded for our society as well.

Examined within a broader sociological and economic prism, society is seen as an organization that allows for the production and distribution of resources among its members. The social order established plays a major role in determining what kind of opportunities children have and the type of life they will be able to achieve for themselves. If there is a system in place that allows every child to have an equal or at least a fair start, then opportunity will be assured. However, if there is substantial inequality and no measures are taken to ensure a fair start for all children, then the life prospects of many children will be significantly diminished. A society concerned with equity, fairness, and opportunity for all children pursues strategies and policies to ensure all children, regardless of the socioeconomic status they were born into, a fair start and real opportunity.

The problem with the residual view of child welfare is that it assumes that child abuse is something that can only happen within the family — that it is centered around the parent/child relationship. This may be true of severe cases of child abuse that involve the brutal and horrible assault of children. But child abuse and neglect can also happen at a broader societal level (Gil, 1970). Children living in poverty in a nation of great material abundance suffer from abuse. It may be a less acute form of abuse; rather, it is a form of chronic abuse. Yet, it is the corrosive and indifferent character of this chronic abuse which makes it so difficult to endure. The brutality of severe physical abuse and the horror and betrayal of sexual assault of children are easily recognized, but too often we acquiesce to the inequity and unfairness of a situation where children, because of the life of poverty they were born into, are denied the basic economic resources for a decent life and as a result have little chance for achieving personal success in a market economy. As David Archard (1993, pp. 156–157) points out, "More children suffer significantly reduced life opportunities as a result of their socioeconomic circumstances than are injured as a result of parental behavior . . . there is a general political unwillingness to see that the elimination of child abuse requires a major egalitarian programme of social and economic reform." Yet, it is the broad and extensive child poverty that is the fundamental problem which confronts child welfare. To understand child poverty requires viewing it within a broader economic perspective.

WORKS CITED

Archard, D. *Children: Rights and Childhood.* London: Routledge, 1993.

Bush, M. *Families in Distress.* Los Angeles and Berkeley: University of California Press, 1987.

Gil, D. *Violence Against Children.* Cambridge, MA: Harvard University Press, 1970.

Sarri, R., and J. Finn. "Child Welfare Policy and Practice: Rethinking the History of Our Certainties." *Children and Youth Services Review* 14 (1992a): 219–36.

———. "Introduction to Special Issue on Child Welfare Policy and Practice: Rethinking the History of our Certainties." *Children and Youth Services Review* 14 (1992b): 213–16.

Considerations

1. According to Lindsey, what is the current condition of child poverty in the United States? How does that condition compare to the state of child poverty in other industrialized countries?

2. Why was the child welfare system developed? What does Lindsey mean when he writes that in our time the child welfare system has "transformed . . . into a child protection system"? What are some of the reasons for that transformation?

3. Lindsey writes that "[m]y interest is to examine how well modern economies have provided and continue to provide for children." What does he say about the relation of modern economies and child poverty?
4. What, according to Lindsey, are the limits of defining child abuse as "something that can only happen within the family"? How would he redefine child abuse?
5. If you have also read the previous piece by Arloc Sherman for the Children's Defense Fund, try bringing these two readings into a common focus by briefly summarizing each. How does your effort to link them influence your summarizing of each?

The following excerpt from Michael B. Katz's In the Shadow of the Poorhouse: A Social History of Welfare in America *provides an overview of poverty in nineteenth-century America. The root cause of the considerable and growing poverty in the nation, Katz asserts, was a transformation of the way work was organized: the growth of industry, the disappearance of older home and craft manufacturing and the economic and social relations surrounding it, mechanization, and so on. As you read this history, ask yourself to what degree the conditions Katz describes have persisted or changed. Ask yourself, as well, how these conditions would affect children, then and now.*

By the way, notice how Katz — in writing his summary of nineteenth-century American poverty — supports his discussion of general trends with statistics and other numerical data, particular historical events, and quotations from historical figures and from other contemporary scholars.

Poverty

MICHAEL B. KATZ

Myths of abundance in early American history notwithstanding, poverty was a serious and growing problem. Indeed, no clear line separated ordinary working people from those in need of help, because periodic destitution was one structural result of the great social and economic transformations in American life. The reasons for this prevalence of poverty vary, although most of them may be traced in one way or another to the organization of work.

Increasingly, throughout the early nineteenth century, most people worked for someone else during their entire adult lives. "Nothing more clearly distinguishes the years in which the factory system was built from the modern age, inured to its ranks of wage and salary earners," writes Daniel Rodgers, "than that the simple fact of employ-

---

Social historian MICHAEL B. KATZ (b. 1939) is Sheldon and Lucy Hackney Professor of History at the University of Pennsylvania. In addition to *In the Shadow of the Poorhouse: A Social History of Welfare in America* (1986, revised 1996), excerpted here, Katz is author of *The Undeserving Poor: From the War on Poverty to the War on Welfare* (1989) and *Improving Poor People: The Welfare State, the "Underclass," and Urban Schools as History* (1995).

ment should have deeply disturbed so many Americans." This spread of wage labor can be traced in various ways: through an analysis of the proportion of workers simply called "laborers" on the New York City assessment rolls between 1750 and 1850 (the proportion rose from 6 percent to 27 percent); through manuscript censuses and city directories (which show the numerical domination of most trades by wage laborers at a ratio of ten or eleven employees for each proprietor by at least the middle of the century); or by the spread of trade unions, labor newspapers, and working-class militancy as early as the 1830s. (In Philadelphia, the General Trades Union, a loose organization of unskilled and skilled workers, staged successful collective actions in the 1830s until they were decimated by the severe depression of 1837.)[1]

The uneven character of economic development complicates attempts to generalize about the relations between the history of work and poverty. Throughout the first half of the nineteenth century, handcrafts coexisted with manufactured goods; goods were produced in homes as well as in factories. Some large workplaces were collections of hand workers; in some the work was subdivided into its component parts; a few introduced steam-driven machinery. Even within the same trades, widely different work settings and manufacturing processes coexisted. Nonetheless, everywhere, a reorganization of economic life eroded the position of independent journeymen artisans. For whatever their work setting, almost all of them became wage laborers, employees rather than independent craftsmen owning their raw materials and tools and selling their products directly. As wage workers, they lost the flexibility that had marked artisan manufacture. Most also lost their skill monopoly as the logic of production subdivided work into smaller components that required less skill and less time to learn.[2]

As young men entered trades with increased ease, apprenticeships shortened or disappeared, and a glutted labor market led to lower wages. In fact, to keep their wages as low as possible, employers often fired apprentices as soon as their term expired so that they could avoid paying them adult journeyman wages.[3] Two factors intensified the problems of apprentices and adult artisans thrown out of work. One was the absence of any cushion against unemployment. Very few workers could save enough to tide them over a prolonged period of unemployment, and, without aid from their families, their alternatives were to seek relief or to travel in search of work. Here the ecology of home and workplace — the second factor — came into play. Until very late in the nineteenth century, most working people had to live within walking distance of their jobs. Few could

[1]David M. Gordon, Richard Edwards, Michael Reich, *Segmented Work, Divided Workers: The Historical Transformation of Labor in the United States* (New York: Cambridge University Press, 1982), pp. 48–99; Maurice Dobb, *Studies in the Development of Capitalism,* rev. ed. (New York: International Publishers, 1967), chs. 1–2; Charles Tilly, *As Sociology Meets History* (New York: Academic Press, 1981), ch. 7; Daniel Rodgers, *The Work Ethic in Industrial America, 1850–1920* (Chicago: University of Chicago Press, 1978), p. 30; Kaestle, *Evolution of an Urban School System, New York City, 1750–1850* (Cambridge: Harvard University Press, 1973) p. 102; Katz, Doucet, and Stern, *Social Organization of Early Industrial Capitalism* (Cambridge: Harvard University Press, 1982), chap. 1; David Montgomery, "The Shuttle and the Cross: Weavers and Artisans in the Kensington Riots of 1844," *Journal of Social History* (Summer, 1972), pp. 411–46.

[2]Richard A. McLeod, "The Philadelphia Artisans 1828–1850," Ph.D. diss. Univ. of Missouri, 1971, pp. 35 and 54–74, is good on these points. See also Bruce Laurie and Mark Schmitz, "Manufacture and Productivity: The Making of an Industrial Base: Philadelphia, 1850–1880," in Theodore Hershberg, ed., *Philadelphia: Work, Space, Family, and Group Experience in the Nineteenth Century* (New York: Oxford University Press, 1981), ch. 2.

[3]McLeod, "Philadelphia Artisan," p. 61.

afford the early forms of public transportation such as the horse-drawn street railways introduced in many cities in the 1860s. Because most workplaces were relatively small, most workers found only a limited number of jobs within walking distance of their homes, and, as a consequence, losing a job often meant traveling to find new work. This is one reason historians have found extraordinary population mobility everywhere in nineteenth century America. (Recent studies rarely have discovered more than a third of households remaining in the same town or city for at least a decade around the middle of the nineteenth century.) People on the road looking for work usually had almost no money. Often hungry and desperate, they sometimes sought relief in poorhouses or from public officials. In this way, transiency helped swell the roles of public relief.[4]

Sometimes, mechanization also drove people to relief. Consider the example of threshing machines in New York, where in 1853 an observer wrote:

> It is not very long since all the grain raised in this State was threshed out with flails. It requires no intellect whatever to perform this labor; any one, not a perfect idiot, can stand and pound upon the floor of a barn. This employment was usually relied on by laborers for their winter's employment. Now there is scarcely a farmer to be found who threshes with a flail. Threshing machines are everywhere used, and have completely cut off this source of winter employment.

The replacement of hand threshing by machines underlines the existence of rural, as well as urban, poverty. Nearly every county, rural or urban, had its poorhouse. One source of rural poverty was the mechanization of agriculture, which reflected the increased influence of market forces during the first half of the nineteenth century. In the Genesee Valley, observes Hannon, after 1925, commercial wheat production "was accompanied by rapid population growth, increased average farm size, a decline in self-sufficient household production, a shortening of the average tenant contract to one year, a decline in the tenancy rate, and increased use of seasonal labor." In 1857, the editor of a local newspaper explained that "after employment for a few weeks or months," farm laborers "were left to beg, steal, or go the poorhouse. . . . This has been the situation of farm laborers in western New York for the past ten or twenty years." As the manufacture of domestic goods — clothes, small home furnishings, and so on — began to move out of homes and into shops and factories, farm women lost an important source of supplementary income. In fact, Hannon found the decline of home manufacture, far more than either industrialization or urbanization, associated with rising rates of pauperism in antebellum New York. Another source of rural poverty was the pressure of population on land, especially in long-settled areas of the East where the productivity of land had declined and farmers had run out of land to subdivide for their children. Rural poverty arose, too, from periodic crop failures caused by bad weather or insects, as in the Kansas "Grasshopper Scourge" (1874–75) that left many families destitute, or the droughts and crop failures in the same state between 1885 and 1895.[5]

[4]There are many studies of population mobility in nineteenth-century America. The first book to call attention to the phenomenon was Stephan Thernstrom, *Poverty and Progress: Social Mobility in a Nineteenth-Century City* (Cambridge: Harvard University Press, 1964).

[5]"Letters to the Secretary of State on the Subject of Pauperism," first published in the *Columbia Republican,* in the fall of 1853, in New York Secretary of State Annual Report on Statistics of the Poor, 1855, New York Senate Documents, No. 72, 1855, p. 79; Nancy Cott, *The Bonds of Womanhood: "Women's Sphere" in New England, 1780–1835* (New Haven: Yale University Press, 1977), pp. 23–46; Joan Underhill Hannon, "Poverty in the Antebellum Northeast: The View from New York

Everywhere, the seasonality of work menaced working-class security, and poorhouse populations swelled during winter months. Much unskilled labor took place outdoors: unloading ships, digging canals, building railways. In cold climates where lakes and canals froze, all this employment ended in the winter. So did most construction work, another major source of employment.[6]

For most people work remained unsteady as well as seasonal. Because the availability of work varied with demand, few manufacturers employed a consistent number of workers throughout the year, and very few people found steady work. As much as low wages, this irregular employment — in the urban South as well as in the North — often dropped families into poverty. The great periodic depressions had the same effect. During each depression, thousands of workers, their jobs lost, were left without resources, dependent on relatives, friends, or charity. At times, even the well-to-do were plunged into poverty, and many workers fled cities. Others stayed and suffered. During one depression in antebellum Philadelphia, laborers worked for fifty cents a day; the wages of handloom weavers were slashed; the demand for domestic servants and seamstresses declined; and everywhere, disease, hunger, and destitution stalked the streets.[7]

The availability of work for every ablebodied person who really wants a job is one of the enduring myths of American history. In fact, work was no more universally available in the early and mid-nineteenth century than it is today, as unskilled and semiskilled workers overstocked urban labor markets. In 1822, Josiah Quincy, addressing the Grand Jury of Suffolk County, Massachusetts, pointed to the 700 men "for whom work cannot be obtained" on the books of Boston's Employment Society. "These men long for work; they anxiously beg for it; yet it is not to be found." In 1828, Matthew Carey, attacking the proposed abolition of outdoor relief in Philadelphia, observed:

> Many citizens entertain an idea that in the present state of society in this city, every person able and willing to work may procure employment; that all those who are thus employed, may earn a decent and comfortable support; and that if not the whole, at least the chief part of the distresses of the poor, arises from idleness, dissipation, and worthlessness.

Nothing could be further from the truth, wrote Carey. Even in the "most prosperous times," he pointed out, "some trades and occupations" always were "depressed," and a "deficiency of employment" consumed the modest savings of the most "frugal and industrious."[8]

State's Poor Relief Rolls," *Journal of Economic History,* XIV, No. 4 (December, 1984), pp. 1,028–1,031 (quote p. 1,030; newspaper quote pp. 1,030–1,031); Grace A. Browning, *The Development of Poor Relief Legislation in Kansas* (Chicago: University of Chicago Press, 1935), pp. 76–84.

[6]Benjamin Joseph Klebaner, "Public Poor Relief, America 1790–1860," Ph.D. diss., Columbia University, 1952, pp. 74–75.

[7]Priscilla F. Clement, "The Response to Need: Welfare and Poverty in Philadelphia. 1800–1850," Ph.D. diss., University of Pennsylvania, 1977, pp. 267–270; Barbara Lawrence Bellows, "Tempering the Wind: The Southern Response to Urban Poverty, 1850–1865," Ph.D. diss., University of South Carolina, 1983, pp. 199–201.

[8]Matthew Carey, "Essays on the Public Charities of Philadelphia," (1828), p. 171, reprinted in David J. Rothman, ed., *The Jacksonians on the Poor: Collected Pamphlets* (New York: Arno Press and the *New York Times,* 1971).

Carey highlighted another great source of poverty: the low wages paid women. Some philanthropic societies had attempted to help women — especially widows — by starting workshops where they could earn money sewing. Other women earned a little money sewing for individual masters. Carey showed that even the philanthropists did not pay women enough to survive. Even so, work was so scarce that every time contracts for making clothes for soldiers were announced, "the applications" were "too numerous to be supplied." Women in the urban South faced similar problems, as the editor of the Richmond *Daily Dispatch* pointed out in 1857. Women compelled "to make their living by their industry," he observed, were paid far less than men: 50 or 60 cents a day was considered enough to make a woman "entirely independent," and some with children to support, were "actually making up shirts and drawers for 6¼ cents each."[9]

Carey also traced the relation among the wretched wages paid male workers, their working conditions, and the growth of poverty. Thousands of laborers, he pointed out, "travel hundreds of miles in quest of employment on canals" at less than a dollar a day, paying "a dollar and a half or two dollars per week for their board, leaving families behind, depending on them for support." Often, they worked "in marshy grounds, where they" breathed "pestiferous miasmata" that destroyed "their health, often irrecoverably." They returned "to their poor families, broken hearted, and with ruined constitutions, with a sorry pittance, most laboriously earned" and took to their beds "sick and unable to work." Still, their places filled quickly with other men desperate for any work. Hundreds were "most laboriously employed on turnpikes, working from morning till night, at from half a dollar to three quarters per day, exposed to the broiling sun in summer, and all the inclemency of our severe winters." Always there was "a redundance of wood pilers in our cities, whose wages are so low, that their utmost efforts do not enable them to earn more than from 35 to 50 cents per day." Even the "painful situation of a watchman" was an "object of desire." There never was "a want of scavengers"; nor was there any work "whatever, how disagreeable, or loathsome, or dangerous, or deleterious soever it may be, or however reduced the wages," that did not "find some persons willing to follow it, rather than beg or steal."[10]

Usually low to begin with, wages frequently were reduced. For instance, in one Philadelphia cotton mill, handloom weavers making cotton ticking earned one dollar per cut in 1820, 70 cents in 1833, and 60 cents in 1840. When wages were reduced, Walter Channing pointed out in 1843, the effect was not only to lessen "the amount paid to each" but also to discharge "from regular employment a certain number of operatives." The net effect left large numbers of people suddenly "without the means of subsistence for themselves, and for their families. These last, after no very long time, must become dependent on foreign aid for support. They are made paupers."[11]

With figures from the Board of Canal Commissioners, Carey calculated an annual income for a laborer consisting of ten months' work at $12 per month, two months' work at $5 per month, and a wife's annual income of $13. The total, which implied the avail-

[9]Carey, "Essays," pp. 167, 172; Bellows, "Tempering the Wind," p. 204.

[10]Carey, "Essays," p. 173.

[11]McLeod, "Philadelphia Artisan," p. 151; Walter Channing, "An Address on the Prevention of Pauperism," p. 35, in Rothman, ed., *Jacksonians.*

ability of work throughout the year, was $143. As he stressed, this total income did not allow *"for one day's want of employment of the husband, or one day's sickness of him or his wife!"* Against the income he set a modest budget, 50 cents a week for rent, a total of $65.20 for food, $24 for clothes for the couple and $16 for their two children. With fuel and a few other expenses this bare bones budget totaled $145.74, more than they could expect to earn. Without "allowance of one day or one dollar for sickness, or want of employment," both of which were common, with no provision for unemployment, Carey's hypothetical family still could not quite match income and expenses. Their plight would have been worse, Carey pointed out, had he increased the number of their children, which would not have been unreasonable. The same results, he said, would emerge from calculating the income and expenses of the laborers on the railroad. Nor was the plight of weavers any better.[12]

Carey was right to stress the role of sickness, because illness was a major cause of destitution. A great many almshouse inmates were sick, and in histories of families on relief, illness almost always stands out as a major theme. The reasons are not hard to find. Work was dangerous and unhealthy; diets were inadequate; sanitary conditions in cities were dreadful; medical care was poor. When men took sick and died, they usually left no life insurance and few assets, and their widows had almost no way short of prostitution to support their families. Some widows with young children combined help from family, friends, and charity with sweated work sewing or washing. But when they took sick — and not surprisingly they often did — they had no alternatives to private charity, relief, or the poorhouse. Families often survived by putting all possible members to work. Even young children were expected to help by taking care of their younger brothers and sisters, collecting bits of fuel from the streets, wharves, and woods, or by begging. Those families in which at least one person remained well enough to work survived best.[13]

Landlords and grocers often helped by giving credit that enabled poor people to weather periods of unemployment or sickness. (Indeed, the role of credit as a form of relief never has received the attention it deserves from students of poverty.) Yet, often no one could earn any money. Fathers were dead or sick; mothers were consumed with the care of very young children or ill; children were too young to work, sick themselves, or had left home. To be sure, kin were expected to help each other, and charity workers almost always tried to find relatives who could assist a family before they gave it very much relief. But most poor families only had very poor relatives with no surplus to share. In other cases, kin lived too far away from each other to be of any help.[14]

Problems intensified in old age. Men did not retire. They worked until they were fired or could continue no longer. Women, who usually outlived their husbands, inherited almost nothing. A few men had small life insurance policies, and a fortunate

[12]Carey, "Essays," p. 11.

[13]As an example of the problem of widows, see the case history in Michael B. Katz, *Poverty and Policy in American History* (New York: Academic Press, 1983), pp. 18–54.

[14]The best way to get a sense of how families survived and of the awesome pressures under which they lived is to read the case histories compiled by agents and visitors for various voluntary societies, such as charity organization societies.

minority of working-class people had bought and paid for a home. Otherwise, elderly people usually lived with their children. With no savings, no pension, no social security, or if they lacked children willing or able to care for them, old people often found themselves completely destitute.[15]

Immigration also intensified the problem of poverty. Between 1820 and 1860 more than five million immigrants entered the United States. Although it seems unlikely that foreign countries, as protesters claimed at the time, were dumping their paupers on American shores, the massive antebellum immigration — especially because of the Irish famine in the 1840s and early 1850s — did exacerbate the problem of poverty and poor relief. Many immigrants had used up all their money simply to get to America; some arrived sick from the trip; others could not find work; many, contemporaries said, "had been accustomed to receiving relief in their old homes, and so were not abashed to ask for it when they came to the New World." And, of course, immigrants helped overstock the labor market for unskilled work. (However, it is crucial to remember that without massive immigration America would have lacked an adequate labor supply to build its infrastructure of canals, railroads, and turnpikes. American homes would have lacked domestic servants, and American factories would have lacked enough hands.)[16]

Even this cursory overview shows why poverty was a major problem in early and mid-nineteenth century America. The great transformation of social and economic structure disrupted social relations and created a class of highly mobile wage laborers subject to irregular, seasonal, dangerous, unhealthy, often badly paid work. Even in the urban South, "the incidence of poverty increased throughout the antebellum period." Public policy made no provision for the periodic unemployment endemic to the emerging system, no provision for the women left widows, or for the elderly without families. Those in need of relief were young men thrown out of apprenticeships or looking for work, unemployed household heads with families, widows without working children, and those sick and elderly people without kin who could care for them. Crises were woven into the very fabric of working-class experience, and periods of dependence were normal. They were integral to the structure of social and economic life. With luck, some people pulled themselves out. They got well or found work. Others were not so fortunate. Working-class experience was a continuum; no clear line separated the respectable poor from paupers. This is why all attempts to divide the poor into classes and all policies based on those divisions ultimately failed.

[15]On life insurance, see Viviana A. Zelizer, *Morals and Markets: The Development of Life Insurance in the United States* (New York: Columbia University Press, 1979). In most medium-sized cities around the middle of the nineteenth century, about one-quarter to one-third of families owned their own homes. In big cities the proportion was smaller, about 11 percent in Philadelphia and probably less than half that in New York. For an estimation of the proportion of elderly who lived with their children, see Steven Ruggles, "Prolonged Connections: Demographic Change and the Rise of the Extended Family in Nineteenth Century England and America," Ph.D. diss., University of Pennsylvania, 1984.

[16]Klebaner, "Public Poor Relief," pp. 612–13.

Considerations

1. "The availability of work for every ablebodied person who really wants a job," writes Katz, "is one of the enduring myths of American history." Why does he call this belief a myth? How does his overview challenge it?
2. Are any of the conditions and trends Katz discusses still in evidence today? In the same regions, or new ones? Affecting the same groups of people, or new ones? If things are different, what are some reasons for the difference? If they are more or less the same, in what way and for whom?
3. Child poverty is obviously linked to the poverty of families, to un- and underemployment, to the absence of work-related benefits and protections, to the availability of welfare. What does Katz's overview help you understand about the existence of child poverty in the United States, in the last century and in our time?
4. Consider Katz as a summarizer. What are some of the sources he summarizes, and does he seem to be doing more than summarizing them? When does he summarize his own presentation and what does he accomplish by doing this?
5. If you have read either of the preceding pieces by Arloc Sherman (for the Children's Defense Fund), page 145, or Duncan Lindsey, page 151, consider how this piece by Katz could be used to support or complicate their arguments. Write a paragraph using summary to connect this piece with either, or both, of the other readings.

Author and journalist Melanie Scheller begins her essay on poverty with a vivid recollection of a patient she encountered during her volunteer work in a psychiatric hospital, then shifts to a painful reminiscence about growing up poor in the rural South. If the previous readings in this section provide a sense of the economics, sociology, and history of child poverty in America, Melanie Scheller's essay provides a sense of the way being poor exacts a psychological toll on children.

On the Meaning of Plumbing and Poverty

MELANIE SCHELLER

Several years ago I spent some time as a volunteer on the geriatric ward of a psychiatric hospital. I was fascinated by the behavior of one of the patients, an elderly woman who shuffled at regular intervals to the bathroom, where she methodically flushed the toilet.

MELANIE SCHELLER (b. 1953) has been writing about health and medicine since 1984. Her work has appeared in *Medical Self-Care, American Baby,* and *Women's World.* She is also the author of the highly praised book for children *My Grandfather's Hat.* "On the Meaning of Plumbing and Poverty" first appeared in the *North Carolina Independent Weekly* on January 4, 1990, and was reprinted in the March/April 1991 issue of the *Utne Reader.*

Again and again she carried out her sacred mission as if summoned by some supernatural force, until the flush of the toilet became a rhythmic counterpoint for the ward's activity. If someone blocked her path or if, God forbid, the bathroom was in use when she reached it, she became agitated and confused.

Obviously, that elderly patient was a sick woman. And yet I felt a certain kinship with her, for I too have suffered from an obsession with toilets. I spent much of my childhood living in houses without indoor plumbing and, while I don't feel compelled to flush a toilet at regular intervals, I sometimes feel that toilets, or the lack thereof, have shaped my identity in ways that are painful to admit.

I'm not a child of the Depression, but I grew up in an area of the South that had changed little since the days of the New Deal. My mother was a widow with six children to support, not an easy task under any circumstances, but especially difficult in rural North Carolina during the 1960s. To her credit, we were never seriously in danger of going hungry. Our vegetable garden kept us stocked with tomatoes and string beans. We kept a few chickens and sometimes a cow. Blackberries were free for the picking in the fields nearby. Neighbors did their good Christian duty by bringing us donations of fresh fruit and candy at Christmastime. But a roof over our heads — that wasn't so easily improvised.

Like rural Southern gypsies, we moved from one dilapidated Southern farmhouse to another in a constant search for a decent place to live. Sometimes we moved when the rent increased beyond the $30 or $40 my mother could afford. Or the house burned down, not an unusual occurrence in substandard housing. One year, when we were gathered together for Thanksgiving dinner, a stranger walked in without knocking and announced that we were being evicted. The house had been sold without our knowledge and the new owner wanted to start remodeling immediately. We tried to finish our meal with an attitude of thanksgiving while he worked around us with his tape measure.

Usually, we rented from farm families who'd moved from the old home place to one of the brick boxes that are now the standard in rural Southern architecture. The old farmhouse wasn't worth fixing up with a septic tank and flush toilet, but it was good enough to rent for a few dollars a month to families like mine. The idea of tenants' rights hadn't trickled down yet from the far reaches of the liberal North. It never occurred to us to demand improvements in the facilities. The ethic of the land said we should take what we could get and be grateful for it.

Without indoor plumbing, getting clean is a tiring and time-consuming ritual. At one point, I lived in a five-room house with six or more people, all of whom congregated in the one heated room to eat, do homework, watch television, dress and undress, argue, wash dishes. During cold weather we dragged mattresses from the unheated rooms and slept huddled together on the floor by the woodstove. For my bathing routine, I first pinned a sheet to a piece of twine strung across the kitchen. That gave me some degree of privacy from the six other people in the room. At that time, our house had an indoor cold-water faucet, from which I filled a pot of water to heat on the kitchen stove. It took several pots of hot water to fill the metal washtub we used.

Since I was a teenager and prone to sulkiness if I didn't get special treatment, I got to take the first bath while the water was still clean. The others used the water I left behind, freshened up with hot water from the pot on the stove. Then the tub had to be dragged to the door and the bath water dumped outside. I longed to be like the woman in the Calgon bath oil commercials, luxuriating in a marble tub full of scented water with bubbles piled high and stacks of thick, clean towels nearby.

People raised in the land of the bath-and-a-half may wonder why I make such a fuss about plumbing. Maybe they spent a year in the Peace Corps, or they backpacked across India, or they worked at a summer camp and, gosh, using a latrine isn't all that bad. And of course it's *not* that bad. Not when you can catch the next plane out of the country, or pick up your duffel bag and head for home, or call mom and dad to come and get you when things get too tedious. A sojourn in a Third World country, where everyone shares the same primitive facilities may cause some temporary discomfort, but the experience is soon converted into amusing anecdotes for cocktail-party conversation. It doesn't corrode your self-esteem with a sense of shame the way a childhood spent in chronic, unrelenting poverty can.

In the South of my childhood, not having indoor plumbing was the indelible mark of poor white trash. The phrase "so poor they didn't have a pot to piss in" said it all. Poor white trash were viciously stereotyped, and never more viciously than on the playground. White-trash children had cooties — everybody knew that. They had ringworm and pinkeye — don't get near them or you might catch it. They picked their noses. They messed in their pants. If a white-trash child made the mistake of catching a softball during recess, the other children made an elaborate show of wiping it clean before they would touch it.

Once a story circulated at school about a family whose infant daughter had fallen into the "slop jar" and drowned. When I saw the smirks and heard the laughter with which the story was told, I felt sick and afraid in the pit of my stomach. A little girl had died, but people were laughing. What had she done to deserve that laughter? I could only assume that using a chamber pot was something so disgusting, so shameful, that it made a person less than human.

My family was visibly and undeniably poor. My clothes were obviously hand-me-downs. I got free lunches at school. I went to the health department for immunizations. Surely it was equally obvious that we didn't have a flush toilet. But, like an alcoholic who believes no one will know he has a problem as long as he doesn't drink in public, I convinced myself that no one knew my family's little secret. It was a form of denial that would color my relationships with the outside world for years to come.

Having a friend from school spend the night at my house was out of the question. Better to be friendless than to have my classmates know my shameful secret. Home visits from teachers or ministers left me in a dither of anticipatory anxiety. As they chattered on and on with Southern small talk about tomato plants and relish recipes, I sat on the edge of my seat, tensed against the dreaded words, "May I use your bathroom, please?" When I began dating in high school, I'd lie in wait behind the front door, ready to dash out as soon as my date pulled in the driveway, never giving him a chance to hear the call of nature while on our property.

With the help of a scholarship I was able to go away to college, where I could choose from dozens of dormitory toilets and take as many hot showers as I wanted, but I could never openly express my joy in using the facilities. My roommates, each a pampered only child from a well-to-do family, whined and complained about having to share a bathroom. I knew that if I expressed delight in simply having a bathroom, I would immediately be labeled as a hick. The need to conceal my real self by stifling my emotions created a barrier around me and I spent my college years in a vacuum of isolation.

Almost twenty years have passed since I first tried to leave my family's chamber pot behind. For many of those years, it followed behind me — the ghost of chamber pots past — clanging and banging and threatening to spill its humiliating contents at any moment. I was convinced that everyone could see it, could smell it even. No college degree or job title seemed capable of banishing it.

If finances had permitted, I might have become an Elvis Presley or a Tammy Faye Bakker, easing the pain of remembered poverty with gold-plated bathtub fixtures and leopard-skinned toilet seats. I feel blessed that gradually, ever so gradually, the shame of poverty has begun to fade. The pleasures of the present now take priority over where a long-ago bowel movement did or did not take place. But, for many Southerners, chamber pots and outhouses are more than just memories.

In North Carolina alone, 200,000 people still live without indoor plumbing. People who haul their drinking water home from a neighbor's house or catch rainwater in barrels. People who can't wash their hands before handling food, the way restaurant employees are required by state law to do. People who sneak into public restrooms every day to wash, shave, and brush their teeth before going to work or to school. People who sacrifice their dignity and self-respect when forced to choose between going homeless and going to an outhouse. People whose children think they deserve the conditions in which they live and hold their heads low to hide the shame. But they're not the ones who should feel ashamed. No, they're not the ones who should feel ashamed.

Considerations

1. Scheller concludes her essay by repeating "they're not the ones who should feel ashamed." Given both the economic statistics and the memories of particular events she provides us, whom do you think Scheller believes should feel shame?
2. "If finances had permitted," Scheller writes, "I might have become an Elvis Presley or a Tammy Faye Bakker, easing the pain of remembered poverty with gold-plated bathtub fixtures and leopard-skinned toilet seats." What does she suggest about the way some adults try to compensate for the psychological effects of child poverty?
3. Scheller uses indoor plumbing in general and the flush toilet in particular as a means to discuss the shame attached to poverty. Can you think of an object, convenience, procedure — something that represents for you a painful recognition about your past or your place in society?

"Many Americans," writes policy analyst Lisbeth B. Schorr, "have soured on 'throwing money' at human problems that seem only to get worse. They are not hard-hearted, but don't want to be soft-headed either. Even when their compassion is aroused by moving stories of desperate families or neglected children, they feel helpless and are convinced that nothing can be done." What Schorr does in her book Within Our Reach: Breaking the Cycle of Disadvantage *is to survey a wide range of programs for poor people that* are *successful, that do get something done. At the end of her survey — the section reprinted here — she offers a summary of the characteristics of these programs. Note that, as she proceeds, she implies comparison with less successful "prevailing services."*

The Lessons of Successful Programs

LISBETH B. SCHORR

At every stage of a child's development, interventions exist that can improve the odds for a favorable long-term outcome. But the programs that have succeeded in changing outcomes for high-risk children are different, in fundamental ways, from prevailing services, and we cannot build on these programs unless we understand the differences.

ATTRIBUTES OF INTERVENTIONS THAT WORK

Programs that are successful in reaching and helping the most disadvantaged children and families typically offer a *broad spectrum of services.* They recognize that social and emotional support and concrete help (with food, housing, income, employment — or anything else that seems to the family to be an insurmountable obstacle) may have to be provided before a family can make use of other interventions, from antibiotics to advice on parenting. A Washington, D.C., agency seeking to provide a high-risk population with prenatal care, for example, reports that unless it responds to the needs that the pregnant women themselves consider more immediate — like housing — then "you just can't get them to pay attention to prenatal care."[1]

Dr. David Rogers, as president of the Robert Wood Johnson Foundation, came to a similar conclusion. The foundation's accumulating experience, he wrote, made him aware that "human misery is generally the result of, or accompanied by, a great untidy basketful of intertwined and interconnected circumstances and happenings" that often all need attention if a problem is to be overcome.[2] Successful programs recognize that they cannot respond to these "untidy basketfuls" of needs without regularly *crossing traditional professional and bureaucratic boundaries.*

Most successful programs find that interventions cannot be routinized or applied uniformly. Staff members and program structures are fundamentally *flexible.* Professionals are able to exercise discretion about meeting individual needs (which new mother needs three home visits every week and which needs only one during the first month), and families are able to decide what services to utilize (whether and when to enroll their child in the available day care program) and how they want to participate (whether to work in their child's school as a library volunteer, a paid aide, or a member of the parent advisory body).

Successful programs *see the child in the context of family and the family in the context of its surroundings.* The successful school mobilizes parents in a collaborative effort to impart a love of reading, and of every other kind of academic learning. The clinician treating an infant for recurrent diarrhea or a child with anemia sees beyond the patient on the

[1]Personal communication from Joan Maxwell, President, The Better Babies Project, Washington, D.C., 1985.

[2]Robert Wood Johnson Foundation, *Annual Report, 1984.*

Child and family policy analyst LISBETH B. SCHORR (b. 1931) teaches social medicine at Harvard University Medical School. Schorr's most recent publication is *Common Purpose: Strengthening Families and Communities to Rebuild Urban America* (1997). Written in collaboration with her husband, Daniel Schorr, senior news analyst for National Public Radio, *Within Our Reach: Breaking the Cycle of Disadvantage* was published in 1988.

examining table to whether a public health nurse or social worker needs to find out what kind of nonmedical help the family may require (qualifying for food stamps or the WIC[3] nutrition program, help with homemaking), or whether something must be done about a contaminated water supply. Successful programs are able to offer services and support to parents who need help with their lives as adults before they can make good use of services for their children.

Successful programs describe their staffs as skilled and highly committed. Often staff become models to parents of effective ways of caring for and teaching children, and models to children of roles they could aspire to. The programs emphasize that their staffs have the training, support, and time to establish solid personal relationships. Professionals in these programs are perceived by those they serve as *people who care about them and respect them, people they can trust.* It is hard to know to what extent these relationships are the product of acquired skills informed by the insights of psychiatry and human development, of the unusual personal attributes of a gifted staff, of the availability of sufficient time — or of some combination of these. But their importance is clear.

Successful programs with a large number of multiproblem families see to it that *services are coherent and easy to use.* Most are convinced that relying too readily on referrals to other agencies interferes with the development of a good working relationship with client or patient and with getting needed services to the individual or family. These programs take special pains to maintain continuity in relationships, especially with high-risk populations and at critical life junctures. They ensure that a nurse who has gotten close to a teenage mother during her pregnancy can continue to see her during the early months of parenthood. The *continuity* does not necessarily have to be provided by a single individual, but often is maintained by a small, committed team.[4]

In these programs someone takes responsibility for assuring that child and family needs are in fact met, regardless of bureaucratic or professional compartments. No one says, "this may be what you need, but helping you get it is not part of my job or outside our jurisdiction." What is perhaps most striking about programs that work for the children and families in the shadows is that all of them find ways to *adapt or circumvent traditional professional and bureaucratic limitations when necessary to meet the needs of those they serve.*

Professionals venture outside their own familiar surroundings to provide services in nontraditional settings, including homes, and often at nontraditional hours. The program does not ask that families surmount formidable barriers unassisted before they can get what they need. It makes sure that payment arrangements and eligibility determinations do not pose insuperable obstacles. It does not set preconditions — such as keeping a series of fixed appointments in faraway places or displaying adequate "motivation" — that may screen out those most in need. On the contrary, successful programs try to re-

[3]**WIC:** Women, Infants, and Children [Eds.].

[4]The importance of continuity of supportive relationships from the time of the mother's pregnancy into the early months of parenting has emerged as a major factor from the experience and research of K. Barnard, et al., "Caring for High-Risk Infants and Their Families," in *The Psychosocial Aspects of the Family,* 1985; V. Seitz, N. H. Apfel, and L. K. Rosenbaum, "Schoolaged Mothers: Infant Development and Maternal Educational Outcomes," Paper delivered at the Biennial Meeting of the Society for Research in Child Development, Detroit, 21 Apr. 1983; J. Hardy, "A Comprehensive Approach to Adolescent Pregnancy," in *Teenage Parents and Their Offspring,* 1981.

duce the barriers — of money, time, fragmentation, geographic, and psychological remoteness — that make heavy demands on those with limited energy and organizational skills. Rather than wait passively to serve only those who make it through the daunting maze, these programs persevere to reach the perplexed, discouraged, and ambivalent, the hardest to reach, who are often the ones who would benefit most.

In successful programs, *professionals are able to redefine their roles* to respond to severe, but often unarticulated, needs. [For example,] the Tacoma Homebuilders' therapist who helps the mother to clean house, the neonatologist in Watts who helps run a magnet high school, the pediatrician in Baltimore who founded a Head Start program to work with lead-poisoned children and their mothers, and the child psychiatrist in New Haven who has spent most of several years working in the local school system with teachers, parents, principals, and administrators. These professionals have found a way to escape the constraints of a professional value system that confers highest status on those who deal with issues from which all human complexity has been removed.[5]

In short, the programs that succeed in helping the children and families in the shadows are intensive, comprehensive, and flexible. They also share an extra dimension, more difficult to capture: Their climate is created by skilled, committed professionals who establish respectful and trusting relationships and respond to the individual needs of those they serve. The nature of their services, the terms on which they are offered, the relationships with families, the essence of the programs themselves — all take their shape from the needs of those they serve rather than from the precepts, demands, and boundaries set by professionalism and bureaucracies.

This suggests a fundamental contradiction between the needs of vulnerable children and families and the traditional requirements of professionalism and bureaucracy — a contradiction that future attempts to build on the programs that have been successful in the past must carefully take into account. This contradiction helps to explain why programs that work for populations at risk are so rare, while less effective programs are so much more common.

[5]A. Abbott, "Status and Status Strain in the Professions," *American Journal of Sociology,* 1981.

Considerations

1. Given what you've read about child (and family) poverty, why do you think the programs Schorr describes work so well?
2. After summarizing the qualities of effective programs, Schorr notes "a fundamental contradiction between the needs of vulnerable children and families and traditional requirements of professionalism and bureaucracy." Although she doesn't specify them in the passage we provide, what do you suppose — given what she does say — some of the traditional requirements of professionalism and bureaucracy are? And what, do you think, is the "fundamental contradiction" she refers to?
3. Each of the programs Schorr studied makes a difference in the lives of particular families and children. But place her discussion next to Michael B. Katz's discussion of

American poverty (p. 154). Although Katz is writing about poverty in nineteenth-century America, his discussion implies a point of view about our economic system and poverty. Given that point of view, what do you think Katz would say is needed to significantly reduce poverty among our nation's children?

FURTHER ASSIGNMENTS

1. Using a range of the readings and assignments in this chapter (e.g., those by Kevin Phillips, Ellen Israel Rosen, Duncan Lindsey, Michael B. Katz, etc.), write an essay summarizing what we know about the causes of child poverty in the United States.

2. Melanie Scheller's description of growing up in poverty (p. 161) supplies a concrete, extended example of the effects of poverty described and addressed in the articles in this chapter and in the Children's Defense Fund chart on page 149. Using a summary of Scheller's story as a departure point, write an essay that draws on the other readings in this chapter to:

- show how her experience fits in with typical patterns or circumstances involving the poor, and/or
- show how her situation might be addressed by public policy.

3. Four of the articles in this chapter (those by Jonathan Marshall, p. 79; Arloc Sherman for the Children's Defense Fund, p. 145; Duncan Lindsey, p. 151; and Lisbeth B. Schorr, p. 165) describe problems with current policies toward the poor and, to varying degrees, recommend solutions. Write an essay that summarizes the recommendations by these writers, perhaps drawing on some further research into policies toward the poor. You can bring a critical perspective to your summary by considering the following questions:

- As summaries themselves, what do the articles and policy recommendations fail to address? Do you see any ways in which the recommendations seem unrealistic? Too simple?
- Do you see any particular obstacles to implementing the types of policies recommended by the authors?

4. Both Duncan Lindsey (p. 151) and Lisbeth B. Schorr (p. 165) identify problems with current policy on poverty. In a brief essay, compare their views of the problems and their proposed solutions. As you formulate your essay, consider how one author's views enrich or complicate the other's.

5. Inadequate definitions of poverty are at the heart of Arloc Sherman's article for the Children's Defense Fund (p. 145). Sketch out the official definitions of poverty as presented in this article. Then summarize the author's response to these definitions. As a further step, you might attempt to draft a new definition of poverty — one that would address some of the concerns that the Children's Defense Fund article raises.

6. Given what you've read and your own experience and understanding, what does it mean to be poor?

7. In his article, Michael B. Katz (p. 154) picks up several threads when he discusses poverty from a historical perspective: the erosion of the journeymans' position in favor of mass employment in industry, the rise of a transient work force, the low wages of women, and the effects of immigration. Choose one of these threads and investigate it further. For instance, you might want to research the plight of a particular set of workers (e.g., women producing needlework out of their homes) with the rise of mechanized production and the division of labor. Write a research essay that summarizes the information you've gathered and, further, draws on conclusions about the causes and effects of poverty in the situation that you have chosen to investigate. To further hone your investigation, you might want to focus on the effects of poverty on the children of the group you are studying.

8. In 1996, President Clinton signed legislation that will end federal welfare "as we know it." This legislation, among other things, is intended to limit federal assistance to low-income families and to turn much of the responsibility for administering aid to the poor over to states. Investigate the current — and anticipated — effects of this policy change on your state, city, or town by researching newspapers and other sources at the library (or on the Internet) and, perhaps, by interviewing public policy experts on your campus or those who administer local programs for the poor. Then write an essay in which you summarize the local effects of the legislation. You might want to use your summary to argue for certain measures, policies, or programs to help your local government — and poor families in your area — cope with changes in federal policy.

3

SERIALIZING

Establishing Sequence

SERIALIZING Across the Curriculum

The first part of this chapter includes a range of readings — most accompanied by assignments — that will get you to think critically about the ways in which serializing is used across the curriculum: in criminology and legal studies, journalism, biology, geography, and other fields. In addition to covering various disciplines, we offer various types of writing: narratives, chronologies, poetry, accounts of investigations, and presentations of research, both for academic and more general audiences. We begin with an Opening Problem that immediately involves you with using — and thinking about — serializing. We then present examples of writers drafting papers on academic topics that involve the strategy (Working Examples, p. 178), followed by a piece showing how a professional writer uses serializing to serve a particular purpose (A Professional Application, p. 186). Next comes a series of cross-curricular assignments intended to deepen and enrich your investigation of the strategy's possibilities and limitations (p. 189).

Woven throughout the first part of this chapter (in the Opening Problem; in the Professional Application; in the Criminal Studies Assignment, p. 191; and in the History Assignment, p. 201) are readings that invite you to think about the way we sequence events to determine guilt or innocence in a legal context, a topic that lends itself especially well to the application and investigation of serializing. If this topic interests you and you want to spend more time with it, consider working with the end-of-chapter pieces in Readings: Crime Stories: Constructing Guilt and Innocence.

Opening Problem: Constructing a Serial Account

Here is a problem that will involve you in the process of serializing. Serializing refers to expository writing ordered sequentially. This sequencing can be explicitly marked ("First . . . Next . . . Then . . . Finally . . ."), or it can be developed in less direct ways, as in a story. Writers serialize when they need to pay close attention to the steps in a process or procedure, to a sequence of events, or to the relationships between effects and their possible causes.

Consider the following excerpt from criminal justice professor Jim Fisher's account of the kidnapping of the infant son of Colonel Charles A. Lindbergh — the first person to fly solo across the Atlantic — and Anne Morrow Lindbergh, the daughter of the U.S. ambassador to Mexico. In this passage, Fisher provides a detailed description of the Lindbergh estate and the sequence of events leading to and surrounding the discovery of the infant's disappearance.

As with many "true crime" accounts, the author writes the passage in a way that places us directly at the scene of the crime. We're going to ask you to do several things with this passage, the first of which is to make note of your own reactions as you move through the passage: What questions come to your mind? What do you want to know? What do you feel as you move through the house? What do you think the author wants you to feel?

> The new house, over seventy feet long and forty feet wide, was constructed of natural fieldstone. Covering the twenty-eight-inch thick boulders were several coats of sparkling whitewash. In addition to the living room, dining room, kitchen, four bathrooms, and five bedrooms, the house included two servants' bedrooms and a servants' sitting room. There was also a spacious pantry, a den, and a three-car garage. The front yard included a fifty-five-acre landing strip. Behind the house, beyond the area that had been cleared, were dense woods.
>
> The fourteen- by twelve-foot nursery, situated at the southeast corner of the house directly above Colonel Lindbergh's den, had three shuttered windows. Two of the baby's windows faced south and the other east.
>
> Except for landscaping and a few other odds and ends, the Lindbergh home was completed in 1931. . . .
>
> In January and February of 1932, the Lindberghs and their baby began spending weekends at their newly built home. At this time they were served by three domestic employees. Residing at the Lindbergh estate were Oliver and Elsie Whately, a middle-aged English couple who functioned as butler and cook. The Whatelys had been with the Lindberghs for two years. Oliver Whately, called Ollie, was forty-seven years old, stocky and bald. He had come to America in March 1929. In England, Whately had worked as a jeweler, munitions worker, and machinist. His wife, Elsie, also forty-seven and a rather handsome woman, had arrived in America a year later. The Lindberghs had hired the Whatelys through an employment service. . . . They had moved into the new Lindbergh home in December 1931.
>
> The other servant, twenty-eight-year-old Betty Gow, the child's nursemaid, was from Glasgow, Scotland. She had been serving the Lindberghs since February 25,

1931. She had been hired on the recommendation of Mary Beattie, a lady's maid employed by Mrs. Morrow [Anne Morrow Lindbergh's mother]. Miss Gow had come to America in May 1929. Slender, dark-haired, and very pretty, Betty Gow was not in the habit of accompanying the Lindberghs and the baby on their weekend excursions to the estate at Hopewell.[1]

Colonel Lindbergh had built his new home in this rugged, remote area of New Jersey to get away from reporters, autograph hunters, and ordinary people who flocked to him at every chance. He was also hounded by cranks and mental cases. The Lindberghs felt endangered by these people and took every measure to avoid them.

There wasn't a major road to the Lindbergh estate. The only direct access to the house was a dirt lane. So it was here, in the Sourland Hills of New Jersey, that Lindbergh hoped to find peace and solitude.

On Monday, February 29, the Lindberghs decided not to follow their regular schedule of returning to Englewood on Monday morning. It was chilly, windy, and rainy, and the baby was still getting over a cold he had picked up on Saturday. On Sunday, Mrs. Lindbergh had kept the baby in his room all day. She had been giving him milk of magnesia and putting drops in his nose. At 11:00 Tuesday morning, Colonel Lindbergh telephoned the Morrow home and arranged to have Mrs. Morrow's chauffeur, Henry Ellison, drive the baby's nursemaid to Hopewell.

Mrs. Lindbergh, suffering from a cold herself, had periodically checked on the baby all night Sunday and Monday. After two nights of broken sleep, she was exhausted. Colonel Lindbergh thought his wife could use a little help in caring for the child.

Betty Gow arrived at the Lindbergh home at 1:30 on Tuesday. After eating her lunch, she went to the nursery, where she played with the baby while Mrs. Lindbergh, three months pregnant with her second child, strolled about the estate.

Outside the nursery the raw winds were damp and biting. At 3:30 Mrs. Lindbergh paused beneath the two nursery windows on the east side of the house. She picked up a handful of pebbles and tossed them, one by one, at the windows until a few of them bounced off the glass. Betty Gow appeared at the window with the baby in her arms. The pudgy, golden-haired child caught sight of his mother and smiled. The nursemaid helped him wave. Mrs. Lindbergh waved back, then continued her stroll.

At 6:00 the nursemaid carried the child to the nursery for his supper. While he was eating, Mrs. Lindbergh came into the room to help prepare him for bed.

Before tucking him into his crib, Betty gave the baby some milk of magnesia. He resisted the medicine and some of it spilled on his nightclothes. When the nurse undressed him for a change of clothes, she decided to make him a little flannel shirt to wear next to his skin for protection against the cold. Betty asked Mrs. Lindbergh to watch the baby while she went for scissors and thread. When she returned she cut out a sleeveless shirt from a piece of flannel cloth. Betty rubbed Vicks Vaporub on

[1]The Lindberghs had been living with Mrs. Lindbergh's parents in Englewood, NJ, about seventy-five miles from this new home in Hopewell; then, once their home was completed, they began spending weekends there [Eds.].

the baby's chest, then pulled the homemade garment onto his body. She placed a second shirt, a store-bought one, over the one she had made. The baby now wore two shirts and a pair of diapers enclosed in a rubber covering. Next came the one-piece sleeping suit with enclosed feet and buttons in the back. It also had a flap in the seat. Betty hooked on the two metal guards that kept the baby from sucking his thumbs. She tied the strings securely around his wrists and over the sleeves of the sleeping suit. Lowering the crib rail, she laid him on the mattress. She covered him with a blanket and pulled it snugly across his shoulders, then hooked it to the mattress with two large safety pins.

After putting the baby to bed, Mrs. Lindbergh closed the window shutters. The ones to the French windows on the south wall and the window on the north side of the east wall were tightly closed and latched. But the shutters on the southeast window were warped and couldn't be brought together tight enough to be locked.

Mrs. Lindbergh walked out of the nursery and returned to the first floor. Betty sat in the little room until 8:00, then reported to Mrs. Lindbergh that the baby was sleeping peacefully. The nursemaid went to the sitting room and had supper with Mrs. Whately. Oliver Whately was working in the pantry.

At about 8:30, Mrs. Lindbergh heard Colonel Lindbergh's car pull into the garage at the west end of the house. He had been in New York City, where he was scheduled to attend a dinner at New York University. He had gotten his dates mixed up and instead of appearing at the dinner had driven home. The rain that had been falling all day had just stopped and it was turning cold. The Colonel climbed out of his Franklin sedan and entered the house through the kitchen. He greeted the servants, then joined Mrs. Lindbergh for dinner.

After supper, the Lindberghs walked into the living room and sat down on the sofa. It was 9:00. While sitting there, the Colonel heard a noise that made him think that slats of an orange crate had fallen off a chair in the kitchen. A few minutes later the Lindberghs retired to the bedroom. After a bath, the Colonel walked downstairs to his den, directly below the nursery. Mrs. Lindbergh remained upstairs and drew herself a bath.

At 10:00, Betty Gow decided that it was time for her to check on the baby. The only light in the nursery came from a small lamp in the hallway. She plugged in a small electric heater to take the chill out of the air, then placed her hand on the rail of the crib and peered into the bed. She couldn't see much because her eyes hadn't adjusted to the darkness. But she didn't hear the baby breathing. Startled, she ran her hands frantically over the bedclothes. He wasn't in his crib! The nursemaid rushed out of the nursery and into Mrs. Lindbergh's room.

"Mrs. Lindbergh, do you have the baby?"

"No," the mother replied. She had a startled look on her face. "I don't have him."

"Where is the Colonel?" Betty asked. "He may have him. Where is he?" she blurted, trying not to panic.

"He's downstairs in the den," Mrs. Lindbergh said. There was fear in her voice.

Betty ran to Colonel Lindbergh's den. He was still at his desk reading. "Colonel, do you have the baby? Please don't fool me," she cried.

"No," he said. "Isn't he in his crib?" The Colonel stood up.

"No!"

Lindbergh shot out of the room with Betty behind him. He climbed the stairs two at a time.

In the nursery, the side rail to the crib was up. The blanket was still pinned to the mattress. There was a pocket between the cover and the bed where the baby had been. It was clear to Colonel Lindbergh that the child had not gotten out of the crib by himself.

"Anne!" Lindbergh cried out, "They've stolen our baby!"

Colonel Lindbergh surveyed the nursery and saw that the right-hand shutter on the southeast window was standing open — and the window down. He felt the night air that had seeped into the room. The Colonel's eyes fell upon a small, white envelope on top of the radiator case that formed the window's sill. He assumed it contained the ransom demand and didn't pick it up for fear of ruining any fingerprints. The side of the envelope that he could see bore no writing.

Mrs. Lindbergh rushed into the room. She looked into the crib, then opened the baby's closet. The child was not under his bed or anywhere else in the room — he was gone! She ran back into her bedroom and threw open the windows. She leaned out over the sill. There was nothing to see, but she thought she heard something. It sounded like a cry, coming from the direction of the woodpile. Elsie Whately came up behind her. "That was the wind," she said.

Colonel Lindbergh said he was going outside, but before he left, he warned everybody not to touch the white envelope. With his rifle in hand, Lindbergh made his way a hundred feet or so along the road in front of the mansion before realizing his search was futile. He turned and walked back to the house, which now was ablaze with lights.

The first police to show up were Hopewell officers Harry Wolfe and Charles E. Williamson. They got there at 10:40 and were met at the door by Lindbergh, who took them directly to the nursery. Following a quick look into the baby's room where they noticed clumps of soil on the baby's leather suitcase beneath the southeast window, Lindbergh and the officers went outside. Beneath this window, the officers found two indentations in the mud, impressions made by a ladder. With the aid of a flashlight, they followed a set of footprints that led them from the house in a southeasterly direction. The footprints led them to a homemade ladder. The ladder was in two sections and lay about seventy-five feet from the house. It was the ladder the kidnapper had used to get up to the nursery window. Approximately ten feet away they found the wooden ladder's third, or top, section. The men returned to the house, where they waited for the New Jersey State Police. They left the ladder as they had found it.

— Jim Fisher, *The Lindbergh Case*

Thinking About Thinking

- First, in your own words provide a serial account of the events at the Lindbergh house on Monday, February 29, 1932. You can sketch out charts or diagrams in addition to your writing. Note how you connect these events, that is, how you indicate to the reader that they're in a sequence.

- Reflecting back on your reading of this passage — and using the notes you took during your reading — write a brief essay in which you take us through the account of the kidnapping, describing what you thought and felt as the events unfolded. That is, what effect did the presentation of events, the sequence of them, have on you, the reader?
- Consider this: The author, Jim Fisher, was born in 1939, seven years after the events he writes about. He was not at the scene, and most of those who were there or were closely involved in the case had died by the time of his writing. Yet notice the immediacy of Fisher's writing, the way he seems to be in all rooms of the house at all times and the way he seems to know what people were thinking and feeling. This, of course, is a common technique, a dramatic recreation of events, and it has a powerful effect on readers: We think we're *there,* seeing the truth. How does Fisher do this? What techniques does he use? Write a brief essay taking us through the passage serially, explaining how Fisher achieves this sense of reality, the sense of truth, of what really happened.

As you saw in working with the passage on the Lindbergh kidnapping, when we read a serial presentation we are guided partly by how well the writer controls our sense of passing time. Notice how important the ordering of events becomes. In writing a lab report, a description of a physical or biological process, or an account of an event, your control of time and sequence is critical. For different reasons, lawyers, journalists, and historians have to craft their renderings of events so that they are logical, believable.

Many college assignments call directly for serializing, but others, without specifying so, will also lend themselves to serial approaches. Learning to recognize these opportunities can help you become more flexible as a thinker and expand your repertoire as a writer.

Examination questions often require you to order material sequentially. Consider the following assortment:

Describe how sand dunes are formed. (From a geology class)

Illustrate the principle of linguistic diffusion. (From a linguistics class)

Explain the process of amending the U.S. Constitution. (From a political science class)

How are etchings produced? (From an art history class)

Such questions call for the recollection of course information, usually in the same form you have read or listened to it. They reward accuracy, clarity, and careful attention to the transitions from one step to another. But they do not require much critical thinking. Similarly, a paper topic that calls for a serial presentation sometimes seems simply to be requesting a rehash of course material:

> Trace the history of antitrust legislation from the turn of the century through the Truman administration.

But sometimes a question such as this one is designed to make you rethink the course material, with an eye for seeing new patterns and making new connections. You may know something about individual antitrust acts, but looking at them as a series may put you in a position to make informed generalizations.

The questions we've quoted so far demand serializing. But there are other questions — many questions actually — where you can discover the opportunity to serialize. Look over this imposing set of paper topics, for example:

1. What made *Brown v. Board of Education* a landmark decision of the Supreme Court?
2. In Plato's *Republic,* how does Socrates answer Thrasymachos's argument that injustice is more profitable than justice?
3. In *Huckleberry Finn,* why does Huck decide "All right, then, I'll go to hell"?

Questions like these can sometimes leave a writer floundering, without a strong sense of how to proceed or with only a few sentences' worth to say. It helps to see that the "What," "How," and "Why" are disguising opportunities to proceed sequentially. One way to take on the question about the Supreme Court case is to see *Brown v. Board of Education* as the climax in a sequence of legal actions. An essay on the topic might be structured like this:

> The decision in Brown v. Board of Education did not appear out of thin air. It was the climax of years of tugging back and forth between branches of the state and federal governments. . . .
>
> After the Civil War, the 13th, 14th, and 15th Amendments extended the full protection of the law to all citizens regardless of race. These provisions, however, applied only in theory. In practice. . . .
>
> With the passage of Jim Crow laws in the following decades, state governments were further able to restrict the gains. . . .
>
> Then in Plessy v. Ferguson (1896), the policy of "separate but equal" was firmly established. . . .
>
> In the years that followed, the Supreme Court began to move away from Plessy v. Ferguson in a series of decisions that questioned whether equal facilities were maintained. . . .
>
> Finally, in 1954, the Court ruled in Brown v. Board of Education that separate facilities were "inherently unequal.". . .

Similarly, the question about Plato's *Republic* lends itself to a stage-by-stage approach:

> In responding to Thrasymachos, Socrates first argues that a tyrant is the least happy of men because he is driven by excess. . . .
>
> He develops a second argument about the superiority of seeking wisdom. . . .
>
> Socrates' third argument. . . .
>
> Finally Socrates turns to the question of whether justice is something valuable in and of itself. . . .

And a similar sequential strategy could be used in answering the question about *Huckleberry Finn:*

> At the outset of the novel Huck is presented as a clever but unreflective boy. With Tom Sawyer he plays happily at the game of robbers, content to follow the lead of his friend. . . .
>
> Huck soon finds himself having to make difficult choices. When life with Pap becomes unbearable, he plans to escape. . . .
>
> Then finding himself on the river with Jim the runaway slave, he takes on more responsibility. . . .
>
> At the Phelps place, he faces his strongest crisis of conscience. Local "morality" tells him he should turn Jim in. But his own conscience, of which he has only recently become aware, tells him the opposite. . . .

Serial presentations like these are vehicles for independent thinking. They force you to make interpretive judgments, decisions about how items, events, or stages relate to one another, about their relative importance and their position in an overall sequence. Thus serializing, like defining, is more than a mechanical operation or a pat form for giving back information. Serializing, like defining and the other strategies we present in this book, can work not only as the overarching strategy for organizing a piece of writing (as in the preceding example) but also in coordination with other strategies. You might use serializing to illustrate a definition: The best way to support a definition of the term *etymology* (an account of the historical development of a word), for instance, might be to illustrate the shifting meanings of a particular word as it has changed over time. You might use a serial presentation in service of comparison: In a political science essay about flexibility and inflexibility in U.S. government you might compare how relatively easy it is to pass a bill through Congress and how difficult it is to amend the Constitution. You might use serializing in support of classification: For a marketing class you might write a term paper classifying small businesses on the basis of how they respond to first opportunities for expansion. Or you might use a serial account as a component of an argument: A persuasive essay on tighter controls over food processing might include a serial account of the production of hot dogs.

Working Examples

A Working Example from Biology

Most lab reports in science classes include a methods section that describes the procedures used in an experiment or field observation. Sometimes, particularly when the procedures are merely those outlined in a lab manual, writing up a methods section involves little more than translating instructional language ("Take two samples and expose them to two hours of direct sunlight") into report language ("The two samples were then exposed to two hours of direct sunlight"). But usually you need to do much more. When you hold some responsibility for choosing and describing your own procedures, your decisions about serializing can make a great difference.

Consider the following example, a Methods and Materials section from a biology lab report. Biology reports consist of four main parts: an Introduction, which acquaints readers with the general problem being investigated and the specific hypothesis being tested; a Methods and Materials section, which describes how the experiment was conducted; a Results section, which reports the data obtained; and a Discussion section, which interprets the results. The particular experiment we consider here investigated whether differing levels of salinity affected the fertilization abilities of sea urchin sperm (the term *gametes* in the report refers to both sperm and eggs). This Methods and Materials section is fairly technical, but read it through once, trying to get a general idea and ignoring terms that are foreign to you. Then, with the general idea in mind, read it once more, doing your best to understand the technical language in context.

> METHODS AND MATERIALS
>
> Gametes of *Strongylocentrotus purpuratus* were obtained by injecting 2 ml of 0.5M KCl into the perivisceral cavities of male and female urchins. This muscle stimulant forced the release of gametes through the gonopores of the animal at the aboral surface. Sperm were collected undiluted by inverting the male over a petri dish. A beaker was filled with 40 ml of chilled seawater, and the eggs were collected by inverting the female over the beaker.
>
> Five concentrations of seawater — 60%, 80%, 100%, 120%, and 140% — were prepared, either by the dilution of natural seawater with tap water or the addition of concentrated Instant Ocean (Aquarium Systems, Mentor, Ohio). Slides were prepared by applying Vaseline jelly to the slide in a circular pattern to raise the cover slip, thus protecting the gametes and forming a seal to prevent evaporation and

desiccation. Ten-ml quantities of the five concentrations were prepared and placed in separate test tubes and set in an ice bath. One drop of the concentrated sperm was placed in each test tube. The solution was mixed thoroughly and allowed to sit for five minutes. One drop of the egg solution was placed by pipette onto each of the five slides. Then one drop of the sperm solution from the 60% salinity seawater was added to the egg solution. After a minute, when all the fertilization that could be expected to occur would have occurred, each solution was examined through a microscope at 100× magnification. Percent fertilization was determined by comparing the total number of eggs in a central area of the slide to the total number of eggs that had formed fertilization membranes.

This procedure was repeated for each salinity. Then at five-minute intervals the entire procedure was repeated to see whether the influence of the various salinities increased over time. Seven trials were conducted over a total period of forty minutes.

We find this description hard to follow. Some of the difficulty may be caused by the technical features of the experiment, but the problem also lies in the writing itself. Try rereading the passage once more to see if you can get a clearer idea of what went on in the experiment. Could the writer have done more to help us? Can you locate trouble spots where readers are apt to get confused? Mark them.

The following is a second version of the Methods and Materials section, revised with readers more in mind. Go through the two versions with an eye to the way each organizes material and offers guides to the reader; pinpoint places in the second version that seem clearer than corresponding places in the first. What do you think were the writer's key decisions in reshaping this material? Do you find the second version a clear improvement, or are there some features you prefer about the first?

METHODS AND MATERIALS

To test the fertilization success of sea urchin sperm at varying concentrations of salinity, five solutions of seawater were prepared — at 60%, 80%, 100%, 120%, and 140% salinity. The 60% and 80% solutions were obtained by diluting seawater with tap water, and the 120% and 140% solutions were obtained by adding a saline concentrate (Instant Ocean from Aquarium Systems, Mentor, Ohio). Ten ml of the five salinities were then poured into separate test tubes and set in an ice bath, ready for the addition of sperm. Next, to receive the eggs, seven sets of slides were prepared — five slides per set — by forming circular receptacles of Vaseline on each slide.

Gametes of *Strongylocentrotus purpuratus* were obtained by injecting 2 ml of 0.5 KCl, a muscle stimulant, into the perivisceral cavities of male and female urchins. The eggs were collected by inverting a female over a beaker containing 40 ml of chilled seawater. Sperm were collected undiluted by inverting a male over a petri dish. Then a drop of sperm was added to each of the five test tubes containing the seawater and allowed to mix in solution for five minutes. In the meantime a drop of egg solution was placed with a pipette into the Vaseline circle on each of the first five slides. To each drop of egg solution a drop of sperm solution was added from one of the five concentrations.

When a minute had elapsed (enough time for maximum fertilization) each slide was examined at 100× magnification, and percentages of fertilization were calculated by comparing the total number of eggs in a sector to the number that had formed a fertilization membrane. To test whether the salinity level affected the sperm's fertilization success over time, the sperm and egg solutions were mixed again, and percentages calculated, at five-minute intervals over a period of forty minutes.

Working Examples from Literature

Serializing is always an option in writing about literature. Your experience of reading a literary work over time can be used to help structure what you find to say about it: "As the novel opens . . . Then a new issue arises. . . . The turning point comes when . . .". The risk of this approach is that you will simply retell what happens rather than interpreting what happens. But subordinated to some central question or concern, serializing can help you both in structuring essays and in working out ideas.

We've suggested here and in the *Huckleberry Finn* example how you might employ serializing to begin thinking critically about a piece of fiction. Plays too are well approached sequentially. Since plays are written to be performed in consecutive scenes, serial accounts of how scenes build on one another can be an effective way of thinking about and writing about drama. One useful interpretive device is to look at a sequence of scenes and examine how they work in coordination. Another strategy is to try grasping an entire play, like a piece of music, in terms of a few basic movements. What do the first scenes accomplish? How does our interest get heightened? How is the action resolved? Are there strong turning points? How are we left at the end? A few questions like these can often lead to a simple but persuasive overview of a play's rhythm or pattern, a set of actions developing in several phases. Here's how one student got herself off to a good start in an essay about Shakespeare's *Hamlet.*

Editors divide Hamlet into five acts. But when we imagine the play acted, this five-part structure disappears. We're aware only of the passage of scenes, some happening quickly and others more slowly. I see the action of Hamlet consisting of three movements. During the first, we observe the rising outrage of Hamlet as he learns of his father's murder and watches his mother with Claudius. This movement climaxes with the rapid events in the confrontation scene between Hamlet and his mother. The second group of scenes, the middle movement of the play, occurs after Hamlet has left for England. Much happens during

```
this phase of the play: Fortinbras appears, Ophelia runs mad and
drowns herself, Laertes returns home to find his father and
sister dead, Horatio receives a letter from Hamlet. But these
scenes do not seem to build in power like the earlier ones. It's
hard to grasp where events are heading or where to invest our
feelings. With Hamlet's arrival back on stage, the play's third
and final movement begins, and from the graveyard scene on, the
action intensifies toward its bloody conclusion.
    In this essay I'd like to look more closely at the portion
of the play I've called the second movement. In these scenes is
Shakespeare simply taking care of plot details, or is he doing
something more? . . .
```

This looks like the start of a very good essay. Perhaps the writer will go on to consider the middle scenes in the sequence they occur. In the meantime, look how she has put serializing to use in the opening paragraph by boldly dividing the play into three phases. This interpretive decision could be challenged by her English teacher, but by asking us to consider the play this way, she is able to seize a problem worth investigating. She'll need to find something persuasive or interesting to say about the scenes she has decided to focus on, but she's got us set up for her delivery.

You'll also find that serializing can work well in writing about poetry. Most critical writing about poetry serializes to some extent, but serializing is particularly prevalent in writing about short poems. In fact, one variety of poetry interpretation — explication — consists entirely of line-by-line commentary meant to guide a reader carefully through a poem. But you can also treat a poem sequentially without committing yourself to interpreting every line. One helpful strategy is to view a poem, like the student viewed *Hamlet,* as something experienced in stages. The stages can be temporal or geographical — the speaker moving from one time or place to another — or the stages can be psychological, different degrees or levels of awareness that develop in the speaker or in the reader. Consider the poem "And Your Soul Shall Dance" by the contemporary American poet Garrett Kaoru Hongo.

for Wakako Yamauchi

Walking to school beside fields
of tomatoes and summer squash,
alone and humming a Japanese love song,
you've concealed a copy of *Photoplay*
between your algebra and English texts.
Your knee socks, saddle shoes, plaid dress,
and blouse, long-sleeved and white
with ruffles down the front,

come from a Sears catalogue
and neatly complement your new Toni curls.
All of this sets you apart from the landscape:
flat valley grooved with irrigation ditches,
a tractor grinding through alkaline earth,
the short stands of windbreak eucalyptus
shuttering the desert wind
from a small cluster of wooden shacks
where your mother hangs the wash.
You want to go somewhere.
Somewhere far away from all the dust
and sorting machines and acres of lettuce.
Someplace where you might be kissed
by someone with smooth, artistic hands.
When you turn into the schoolyard,
the flagpole gleams like a knife blade in the sun,
and classmates scatter like chickens,
shooed by the storm brooding on your horizon.

— Garrett Hongo, "And Your Soul Shall Dance"

One way of taking on "And Your Soul Shall Dance," which seems to address a Japanese-American schoolgirl, is to discuss the adjustments in mood and understanding you find yourself making as you move through the poem. After thinking about those adjustments, come up with a thesis that describes or characterizes those adjustments and then use your serial response to the poem to support your claim. If you like, you can try using the following transitional signposts to help you to map out an interpretation.

```
     The first five lines of Garrett Hongo's "And Your Soul
Shall Dance" focus on a Japanese-American schoolgirl. . . .
     Lines 6 through 10 further develop . . .
     With lines 11 through 17, the focus widens. . . .
     Then, suddenly with line 18 the readers are given ac-
cess . . .
     Finally, as the girl enters the schoolyard in the last four
lines, there's the ominous recognition . . .
```

Working Examples from History

Most historical accounts employ serializing. In fact, looked at superficially, some historical accounts seem simply to be the serial retelling of events. But the "simply" in the previous sentence is deceptive. The first question is, What constitutes an event? And in sequencing several events into a single account, other troubling questions arise: what to include, what to omit, and how to shape what is included. To consider the problems you may encounter in trying to construct meaningful sequences of events, look at the following chronology pertaining to the Iran–U.S. crisis of 1979–1981. Then as an exercise, write a short serial account based on the list.

1. The shah leaves Iran (Jan. 16, 1979).
2. Khomeini returns from exile as head of revolutionary government (Jan. 31, 1979).
3. American hostages are seized at the U.S. embassy in Teheran (Nov. 4, 1979).
4. President Carter suspends Iranian oil imports to the United States (Nov. 12, 1979).
5. The shah dies of cancer in Egypt (July 27, 1980).
6. Iran's conflicts with Iraq escalate to open war when Iraq attacks Iranian airfields and oil refineries (Sept. 22 and 23, 1980).
7. The American hostages are released (Jan. 20, 1981), the same day that Ronald Reagan is inaugurated as president of the United States.

Here is one writer's attempt at a narrative of these events:

> Two weeks after the shah left Iran in early 1979, Khomeini returned as head of a revolutionary government. On November 4, American hostages were seized at the U.S. embassy in Teheran. A week later President Carter suspended Iranian oil imports. In July 1980 the shah died of cancer in Egypt. In September Iraq attacked Iranian airfields and oil refineries, escalating their border conflict to outright war. The following January the hostages were released on the day that Ronald Reagan was inaugurated as U.S. president.

Why do we find this account unsatisfying? Why the mention of the shah's cancer? For that matter, why stress the U.S. suspension of oil imports? Do the events make any pattern? The writer has made few decisions about what to include and what to leave out, and the paragraph as a whole reads disjointedly.

Notice how hard the writer has tried to stay with all the facts as presented in the list, as though determined not to fall from objectivity into interpretation. Part of the problem may be the sketchiness of the information available. Events like Khomeini's return and the Iraqi attack are themselves outcomes of complex processes, events we risk oversimplifying unless we know more. But notice, too, that interpretations are impossible to avoid. Sometimes the mere positioning of sentences implies an interpretation, in this case a relationship of cause and effect. Look at the first two sentences. Taken together, they imply that the hostages were seized with the cooperation of the Iranian government — an interpretation. Now look at the last two sentences. What do they imply about the release of the hostages?

Since interpretations are unavoidable, it is better to take charge of them. Viewed a little more selectively, the Iranian events, for example, could be presented in a more coherent sequence:

> Two weeks after the departure of the shah in January 1979, the Khomeini government assumed control of Iran. That government had been in power less than a year when the American hostages were seized in November. With government approval, the hostages remained captives for the next fourteen months, despite U.S. economic reprisals and long after the death of the shah. The hostages were finally released on January 20, 1981, only after a war with Iraq had begun to preoccupy Iran.

If we had more information to work with, our interpretation might get even bolder. Any of these sentences, for example, might serve as the opening for an effective serial interpretation:

> The hostage-taking in Iran played an important part in stabilizing the new government. . . .
>
> The U.S. role in the hostage crisis was a futile one. . . .
>
> The resolution of the hostage crisis, like its beginning, had more to do with conflicts within the Mideast than with U.S. foreign policy. . . .
>
> The taking and the releasing of the hostages resulted in political gains both for the Khomeini government and the Reagan administration. . . .

We offer another example of the interpretive pressure placed on historical accounts. Imagine that you are asked to write a short essay explaining the data in Table 1 (from *Sociology: Inquiring into Society* by Peter I. Rose, Myron Glazer, and Penina Migdal Glazer). If you took the most cautious serial approach to this information, you would have to settle for something like this:

> From 1890 to 1979, the number of women in the civilian labor force increased from 3.7 million to 43.5 million. From 1890 to 1900 the number climbed by 1.3 million. In the period from 1900 to 1920, it grew another 3.2 million to a total of 8.2 million. . . .

TABLE 1. Women in Civilian Labor Force, 1890–1979

Year	Number (millions)
1890	3.7
1900	5.0
1920	8.2
1930	10.4
1940	13.8
1945	19.2
1947	16.7
1950	18.4
1955	20.6
1960	23.2
1965	26.2
1970	31.5
1975	37.1
1979	43.5

Source: United States Department of Labor, Bureau of Labor Statistics.

But an essay like this does little more than translate lines from the table into sentences. An instructor would have had more in mind in asking for your commentary. You might try getting speculative, using your general knowledge to help you follow the sequence of the data, highlighting the features that seem most significant to you. One student, for example, decided to use something he knew about World War II — that sending troops overseas depleted the labor force at home:

> The big shift in women's working patterns began during the years of World War II. Until then the number of women in the civilian labor force had been rising, but only at the rate of about 210,000 jobs per year. Then in the five-year period from 1940 to 1945, when many men left their jobs to go to war, another 5.4 million women joined the labor force, their numbers reaching a peak of 19.2 million in 1945. Women's employment fell off a little when men returned to their civilian jobs after the war, but many women by then had become a permanent part of the workforce. There followed another period of steady growth as young working women were joined by mothers of the baby boom era. . . .

An instructor will almost always prefer an interpretive response like this one to a flat restatement of undifferentiated facts — so long as your inferences make sense. If you feel yourself speculating on something you know too little about, look for ways of qualifying or restricting your interpretations as you make them. Here, for example, after a short serial treatment of the data, the writer turns back to look critically at its limitations:

> This table shows a steady growth in the number of women workers throughout this century. Two periods stand out. The first is the years of World War II, when women joined the civilian workforce in large numbers, compensating for the absence of male workers who had gone to war. The second is the 1970s, when the total number of working women increased at the rate of 1.3 million per year, more than double the number during the 1950s and 1960s. How do we explain this dramatic increase in the 1970s, and what does it tell us about changes in our society?
>
> To answer these questions convincingly, we would need to know more. Does the rise in women's employment simply correspond to the rising number of total jobs, or do women fill an increasing percentage of the total labor market? Do the figures include part-time jobs? And what kinds of jobs? . . .

Serial strategies, then, are helpful whenever you want to convey a process or set of procedures, the flow of events, or the development of awareness over time. They serve not only to convey information but to raise questions. Some assignments call for serializing; others gain by it. In some essays, serial presentations can be embedded within larger structures. In others, they can provide the larger structures, serving as containers for the rest of what you find to say. In all cases writing serially should engage your interpretive intelligence.

A Professional Application

The following passage comes from law professor Patricia J. Williams's book *The Alchemy of Race and Rights,* a reflection on the role race, gender, and class play in the theory and practice of law. The passage begins with an account of the killing of a woman named Eleanor Bumpurs by a New York City police officer and takes the reader through the officer's subsequent trials and appeals. Then Williams begins to place the event and its aftermath in broader social and racial contexts.

Notice how Williams moves the reader through the chronology of events by using words and phrases that establish a time line:

On October 29, 1984, . . .

During the course . . .

At some point, . . .

. . . pumped his gun, and shot again . . .

The case . . . was not brought to trial until January 1987 . . .

Initially . . .

. . . but in 1986 . . .

In the two-and-a-half-year interval . . .

And so on. As you can see, Williams walks us through time, pausing occasionally to backtrack ("Initially . . . but . . ."), to provide detail, or to reflect on the meaning of the sequence of events she's providing us. Notice, too, how she uses the sequence to introduce a broader issue she wants to raise about race and the law.

From *The Alchemy of Race and Rights*

PATRICIA J. WILLIAMS

On October 29, 1984, Eleanor Bumpurs, a 270-pound, arthritic sixty-seven-year-old woman, was shot to death while resisting eviction from her apartment in the Bronx. She was $96.85, or one month, behind in her rent. Mayor Ed Koch and Police Commissioner Benjamin Ward described the struggle that preceded her demise as involving two officers with large plastic shields, one with a restraining hook, one with a shotgun, and at least one other who was supervising. All of these officers also carried service revolvers. During the course of the attempted eviction, Mrs. Bumpurs wielded a knife that Commissioner Ward says was "bent" on one of the plastic shields and escaped the constraint of the restraining hook twice. At some point, Stephen Sullivan, the officer positioned farthest away from her and the one with the shotgun, took aim and fired at her. He missed (mostly — it is alleged that this blast removed half of the hand that held the knife and, according to the Bronx district attorney's office, "it was anatomically impossible for her to hold the knife"), pumped his gun, and shot again, making his mark the second time around.

What has not been made clear in discussion relating to this case is that Mrs. Bumpurs was evicted on a default judgment of possession and warrant of eviction issued without any hearing of any kind. She was never personally served because, allegedly, she was not at home on the two occasions the process server says he called. Since Mrs. Bumpurs did not appear in court to answer the petition for her eviction, the default judgment for possession and warrant for her eviction were signed by the Civil Court judge solely on the papers submitted. From what we know now . . . there is serious doubt about the validity of those papers.

PATRICIA J. WILLIAMS (b. 1951) is a lawyer and a professor of law at Columbia University. Her works include *The Rooster's Egg: On the Persistence of Prejudice* (1995) and *The Alchemy of Race and Rights* (1991), excerpted here.

> Only last year, in announcing the indictments of five process servers, the Attorney General and the New York City Departments of Consumer Affairs and Investigation issued a report on service of process in Civil Court, finding that at least one-third of all default judgments were based on perjurious affidavits.[1]

The case against Officer Sullivan was not brought to trial until January 1987. Initially a grand jury indicted him for reckless manslaughter. Two lower courts rejected the indictment, but in 1986 the New York Court of Appeals reversed and ordered a trial regarding the second shot.

In the two-and-a-half-year interval between the incident and the trial, controversy billowed and swirled around the poles of whether Mrs. Bumpurs ought to have brandished a knife or whether the officer ought to have used his gun. In February 1987 a New York Supreme Court justice found Officer Sullivan innocent of manslaughter charges. The case centered on a very narrow use of language pitted against circumstance. District Attorney Mario Merola described the case as follows: "*Obviously* [emphasis added], one shot would have been justified. But if that shot took off part of her hand and rendered her defenseless, whether there was any need for a second shot, which killed her, that's the whole issue of whether you have reasonable force or excessive force." My intention in this chapter is to analyze the task facing judges and lawyers in undoing institutional descriptions of what is "obvious" and what is not; and in resisting the general predigestion of evidence for jury consumption.

Shortly after Merola's statement, Sullivan's attorney expressed eagerness to get the case before a jury. Then, after the heavily publicized attack in Howard Beach,[2] the same attorney decided that a nonjury trial might be better after all. "'I think a judge will be much more likely than a jury to understand the defense that the shooting was justified,' said Officer Sullivan's lawyer, Bruce A. Smiry, when asked why he had requested a nonjury trial. 'The average lay person might find it difficult to understand why the police were there in the first place, and why a shotgun was employed . . . Because of the climate now in the city, I don't want people perceiving this as a racial case.'"

Since 1984 Mayor Koch, Commissioner Ward, and a host of other city officials have repeatedly termed the shooting of Eleanor Bumpurs as completely legal. At the same time, Ward admitted publicly that Mrs. Bumpurs should not have died. Koch admitted that her death had been the result of "a chain of mistakes and circumstances that came together in the worst possible way, with the worst possible consequences." The officers could have waited until she calmed down, or they could have used tear gas or Mace, Ward said. But, according to Ward, all that is hindsight (prompting one to wonder how often this term is used as a euphemism for short-circuited foresight). As to whether this white officer's shooting of a black woman had racial overtones, Ward said he had "no evidence of racism." (Against this, it is interesting to note that in New York City, where blacks and Latinos account for close to half the population, "86.8% of police officers are white; 8.6% are black; 4.5% Latino; and 0.1% Asian or American Indian.") The commissioner pointed out that he is sworn to uphold the law, which is "inconsistent with treating blacks differently," and that the shooting was legal because it was "within the

[1]This excerpt is from a *New York Times* article on the Bumpurs case [Eds.].

[2]**Howard Beach:** A 1986 incident in which a gang of white teens in Howard Beach, New York, were accused of forcing a black man to walk out in traffic to his death and of attacking two of his friends [Eds.].

code of police ethics." Finally, city officials resisted criticism of the police department's handling of the incident by accusing "outsiders" of not knowing all the facts and not understanding the pressure under which officers labor.

Assignments

A Geography Assignment

In the following passage from a physical geography textbook, William M. Marsh and Jeff Dozier describe the hydrologic cycle, the water exchange among land, air, and ocean. Or, rather, they describe the traditional, idealized model of that cycle and how that model developed historically. Take a few moments to read the passage and study the figure. Then write a brief essay in which you describe in your own words the traditional model for the interaction of land, air, and ocean, explaining as you do some of the historical forces and events that helped shape this model.

Here are some suggestions:

- When producing or critically examining a serial presentation, don't hesitate to sketch steps, stages, or possible connections — an illustration can help you to think through as well as question a particular serial strategy.
- When producing or critically examining a serial presentation, pay attention to the use of transitional words. Do they suggest, for example, that steps or events simply follow each other or that there is some important, or even necessary, connection between them?
- Marsh and Dozier call the hydrologic cycle an *idealized* model of the "flow of water from atmosphere to land, land to atmosphere, and land to oceans" and suggest that, because this model is so cyclical and regular, it is limited. What do you think it means to say that a scientific model is "idealized," and what does that idealization suggest about the possible limits of such models? You may want to conclude your essay by reflecting on this question.

The Hydrologic Cycle

WILLIAM M. MARSH AND JEFF DOZIER

We begin our discussions of water by introducing the "hydrologic cycle." This is an idealized model of the land-ocean-atmosphere water exchange, or cycle, which includes evaporation from the sea, movement of water vapor over the land, condensation, precipitation, surface runoff, subsurface runoff, and so on. In reality, the flow of water from atmosphere to land, land to atmosphere, and land to oceans is complex and irregular

WILLIAM M. MARSH (b. 1942) is a professor of physical geography at the University of Michigan, Flint. JEFF DOZIER (b. 1944) is dean of the School of Environmental Science and Management at the University of California, Santa Barbara. This excerpt is from their work *Landscape: An Introduction to Physical Geography* (1981).

over time and geographical space. This fact is not widely appreciated, however, because of the acceptance of a "standard" hydrologic cycle which has become more or less a norm of modern academic thought. Since this hydrologic cycle is a fundamental concept in natural science today, it is appropriate here to outline briefly its origins so that we may better understand its meaning and scientific utility. . . .

Humans have long puzzled over the origins of rainfall, rivers, streams, springs, and their interrelations, but our understanding of the true nature of the hydrologic cycle is comparatively recent. Prior to the sixteenth century, it was generally believed that water discharged by springs and streams could not be derived from the rain, for two reasons:

1. Rainfall was thought to be inadequate in quantity;
2. The earth was thought to be too impervious to permit penetration of water very far below the surface.

The ancients did, however, recognize that the oceans did not fill up and that rivers continued to flow. They recognized then that somehow the water got from the sea into the rivers and in the process lost its salt content. The Bible says:

> All the rivers run into the sea, yet the sea is not full; unto the place from whence the rivers come thither they return again. (Ecclesiastes 1:7)

Generally the removal of salt was attributed to various processes of either filtration or distillation. The elevation of the water above sea level was ascribed to vaporization; subsequent underground condensation, to rock pressure, to suction of the wind, to a vacuum produced by the flow of springs, and other processes.

The recognition of the role of infiltration in supplying water to springs and rivers began in the sixteenth century. Leonardo da Vinci, an exceptional genius who was in charge of canals in the Milan area, is generally credited with one of the earliest accurate descriptions of the hydrologic cycle:

> Whence we may conclude that the water goes from the rivers to the sea and from the sea to the rivers, thus constantly circulating and returning, and that all the sea and rivers have passed through the mouth of the Nile an infinite number of times. . . . The conclusion is that the saltness of the sea must proceed from the many springs of water which, as they penetrate the earth, find mines of salt, and these they dissolve in part and carry with them to the ocean and other seas, whence the clouds, the begetters of rivers, never carry it up. (John P. Richter, *Literary Works of Leonardo da Vinci*)

In the seventeenth century the French scientist Pierre Perrault measured rainfall for three years in the drainage basin of the Seine River above a point in the province of Burgundy. He computed that the total volume of the rainfall was six times the river flow. Although his measurements were crude, he was able to disprove the fallacy that the rain was inadequate to supply the flow in rivers. Edmund Halley, the English scientist after whom Halley's comet was named, made estimates of evaporation from the Mediterranean Sea and demonstrated that it was as great as the flow of all rivers into the Mediterranean.

This was a period in history of energetic dialogue between Christian theologians and natural scientists, and new ideas about nature were carefully scrutinized by the Church. Although the theory of the hydrologic cycle was initially rejected by theolo-

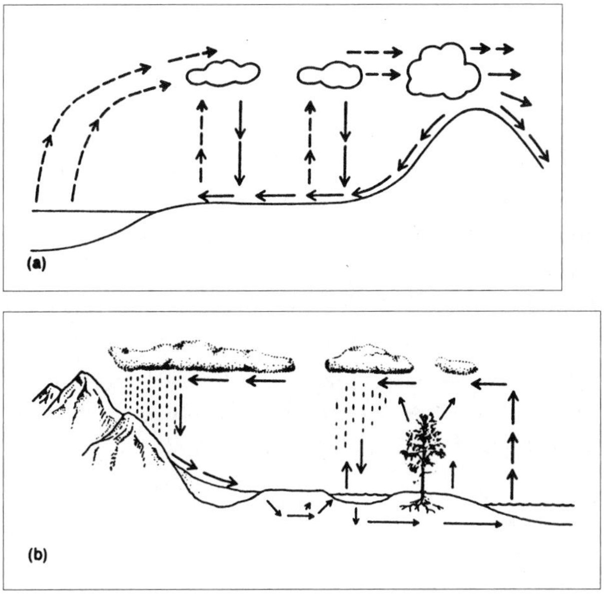

FIGURE 1. Conceptions of the hydrologic cycle: (a) in the style of that presented in the seventeenth century by natural theologian John Ray; (b) as fashioned in a modern earth science textbook in which the authors admit to oversimplification, but nonetheless present a cycle little changed from that of John Ray.

gians, the modern geographer Yi-Fu Tuan tells us that the theory gained favor when it became clear that it could be used to support the doctrine of the Divine plan of nature. This doctrine held that the earth was created by God expressly as the home of humans and that all of its processes were parts of a great ordered scheme with humans at its center. In early versions of the hydrologic cycle, natural theologians saw verification by science of a portion of the Divine plan of nature. Eventually they adopted and idealized the model, and over the course of the past several centuries a more or less standard hydrologic cycle evolved. This model appears in academic texts today in a form little changed from that, for example, presented by theologians such as John Ray in the seventeenth century. Figure 1 shows presentations of the hydrologic cycle in seventeenth- and twentieth-century publications.

A Criminal Studies Assignment

We're all at least *slightly* familiar with the way trial lawyers in criminal cases use evidence to construct "their side of the story." Legal persuasion depends less on the facts than on the way in which lawyers put the facts together. This process involves arranging the evidence in a strategic way and communicating a pattern that a jury can understand. In many cases, lawyers must work to control the sense of passing time.

Imagine that you are a lawyer in the following case:

Simon Fletcher is charged with murdering his brother-in-law, Norton McCarthy. McCarthy's wife discovered him, murdered, in his apartment on the night of November

30th at approximately 9:15 PM. The county coroner officially pronounced him dead at 10:30 PM; the cause of death was listed as "excessive bleeding from thirteen separate knife wounds and trauma from being beaten over the head with a blunt instrument."

On the basis of the following evidence and testimony, construct a serial account of Simon Fletcher's activities on November 30th. Whether you are arguing that he is innocent or guilty, remember that your job is to put a series of events into a logical sequence, not to argue the entire case. Take into account what you know as well as what you don't know.

If you are interested in the subject of how serial strategies are used to construct guilt and innocence, you may want to do this assignment in coordination with the related material in the Opening Problem (p. 171), the Professional Application (p. 186), the History Assignment (p. 201), and in the set of readings concluding the chapter (Crime Stories: Constructing Guilt and Innocence, p. 231).

Reconstructing a Crime

QUENTIN MILLER

1. Norton McCarthy's wife, Sarah, last saw him alive at approximately 11:35 AM on November 30th, just before she left for work.
2. Simon Fletcher was watching the nightly news with his wife, Mary, and their three-year-old daughter at approximately 11:15 PM when Sarah McCarthy called to tell him of her husband's murder.
3. Fletcher and McCarthy had a violent argument on Thanksgiving Day, two days before the murder, about hunting rights. Fletcher's parents say that their son claimed "Everyone has the right to bear arms in this country." They say that their son-in-law claimed that "Hunting should be outlawed until wildlife develops the ability to shoot back." Sarah McCarthy agreed that the argument went "pretty much like that," and she added that both her brother and her husband "used foul language."
4. Fletcher returned from work at 5:50 PM ("just in time to fix his plate before the nightly news") on November 30th and did not leave the house all night, according to Mary Fletcher.
5. McCarthy worked as a freelance writer for a living. No witnesses saw him on the day of his murder, but his publisher received a brief phone call from him at "lunchtime, around 12:30" on that day.
6. It takes Simon Fletcher approximately twenty minutes to drive home from work "on a good day, without any traffic." He finishes at 5:00 PM, but there is no time clock at

---

QUENTIN MILLER (b. 1967) recently received a doctorate in English from the University of Connecticut and is now an assistant professor of English at Gustavus Adolphus College in Minnesota. Miller, who is currently at work on a novel, wrote this assignment specifically for the third edition of *Critical Strategies.*

Rinaldi Enterprises. His boss, Gary Miller, claims that "Most of the guys leave at 5:00, give or take fifteen minutes. I don't pay attention to everyone. They're honest guys."

7. Simon Fletcher's lunch break lasts one hour, from noon until 1:00 PM.
8. Norton McCarthy's house is a twenty-minute drive from Rinaldi Enterprises, where Simon Fletcher works.
9. Simon Fletcher was arrested on May 13 [of the same year as the murder] for fighting in a bar. No charges were filed.
10. No knives were missing from either the Fletcher or the McCarthy household, according to Mary Fletcher and Sarah McCarthy.
11. Simon Fletcher brought home a gallon of milk and a lottery ticket on the evening of November 30th when he returned from work. The convenience store where he purchased it is on the route home from work.
12. Simon Fletcher's coworker William Parnell last saw Fletcher at his desk at "approximately 4:35." Parnell claims that Fletcher "was busy" and that he "didn't look like he was about to leave anytime soon."
13. Fletcher ate lunch alone on November 30th, "at Burger King." Burger King garbage was discovered in his car.
14. A call was made from Fletcher's phone at work at 12:03 PM on November 30th to a client who verified that he talked with Fletcher about an account.
15. Sarah McCarthy called home from work at 7:30 PM to tell her husband that she was going out for a drink after work ended at 8:00 PM. He did not answer; she left a message on their answering machine.
16. Erin and Stan Johnson, McCarthy's neighbors, claim that they saw a car drive into McCarthy's driveway at approximately 5:00 PM on November 30th. When asked to describe the car, they were unable to do so. When asked if the car was "big or small, dark or light," they declined to speculate. When asked if it could have been a "red Ford Escort with rust spots," Stan Johnson replied, "could have been. Actually, that sort of rings a bell." Simon Fletcher drives a red Ford Escort with rust spots.
17. It takes fifteen minutes to drive from the McCarthy household to the Fletcher household.
18. Fletcher attended a mandatory staff meeting on November 30th that began at 1:00 PM and lasted until 3:00 PM.

A Literature Assignment

The following poem "Digger Goes on Vacation" was written by Jim Daniels and is taken from a collection of poems about working-class life. Write an interpretation of this poem by guiding a reader serially through it. (If you haven't yet, you might want to look at the discussion of Garrett Hongo's poem "And Your Soul Shall Dance" on p. 181.)

Here are some questions to consider while doing this assignment.

- As Digger moves through the events in the poem, does he come to any greater understanding of his situation? Do we?

- There is frequent direct or indirect reference to weight in the poem. Does the meaning of "weight" change as we move through the poem?
- In what ways can you use Digger's physical journey to structure your discussion of the meaning of this poem?
- We often think of poetry as being written in a formal, even elevated language. What kind of language does Daniels use? How might it connect to the theme of the poem? To its structure?

Digger Goes on Vacation

JIM DANIELS

The maps from AAA, the tourbooks,
you are well-prepared:
Florida here we come.
For the first time
your son will not go with you.
He has a legitimate excuse:
a job at the corner store.
It is only you and the girls.
You think of your wife
as a girl.
You think
that you have given her nothing.
At the first Stuckey's on the road
you buy her a box of peanut brittle
and smile weakly
as she kisses your cheek.
Then you think of the plant
she is kissing you good-bye
in the morning.
You feel a chill
maybe wind on your neck.
You have two weeks.
Your body shakes
as you pull back on the road:
you have fifteen more years.

First night
you stop at a motel
off of I-75 in Kentucky.

JIM DANIELS (b. 1956) teaches writing at Carnegie Mellon University. He has published four collections of poems: *Blessing the House* (1997), *M-80* (1993), *Punching Out* (1990), and *Places/Everyone* (1985), in which "Digger Goes on Vacation" appears.

At a diner
you eat a late dinner
the girls nodding off to sleep
in their hamburgers.

You look at your wife.
If somehow she could lose some weight.
Then you look at your belly
hanging over your belt:
but mine's hard, you tell yourself,
muscle.

You punch your gut:
if we could just lose
all this weight.

"Digger?"
"Oh . . . yeah."
You pay the bill
and walk across the street
to the motel
squeezing your wife's hand
like a snowball
you want to melt.

You lie in the sand
the sun crisp on your back.
You will get burned.
You always do.
You try to read a book
in the bright glare —
the same book you brought
on vacation last year:
The Godfather.
At a cabin in Northern Michigan
you read 150 pages
and killed mosquitoes.
She packed it to keep me busy,
keep my eyes off the women.

You look over at your wife
wearing a floppy sun hat and bulging out
from her bathing suit.
You throw sand on her belly:
"hey Loretta, gimme a beer."
She hands you one
from the cooler by her side.

She really does
care about me,
you think, and suddenly
you are happy and smile.
You put the cold beer
against her neck
and she jumps up screaming.
"Hey baby, I love you."
"What?"
She takes off her sunglasses
and smiles, hugging you.
"You haven't said that since . . .
last year's vacation!"

You stare out at the sea of skin
and wonder when
you'll say it again.

At the beach
your foot in the sand
outlines the part
you weld onto axles.
"What's that, Daddy?"
You kick sand
over the drawing,
"Nothin'."
But no matter how many times
you kick the sand
it still looks like
something.

In a motel in Tennessee
you peel off your skin
to gross your daughters out.
"Oh Daddy, that's sick!"
You laugh
and rub your vacation beard:
"when all this skin is gone
I'll be a new person."
"Who will you be then, Daddy?"
"I'll be an astronaut.
So I could get lost in space."
"You're already lost in space,"
your wife shouts from the bathroom.

That night after dinner
you drink alone

at a local bar.
Your hands hold up your head
like obedient stilts.
This is how you always
become a new person.
You talk to the bartender:
"I used to be an astronaut."
And he believes you.

A Biology Assignment

In this excerpt, biologist Jeannette Thomas describes some of her research on the sounds made by Antarctic seals. The article, written for the magazine *Natural History,* is not a formal scientific report but a brief overview of Thomas's own research experience against the backdrop of what is generally known about seal behavior. Her article is particularly interesting for what it shows about how a scientist sometimes learns both to sharpen her research techniques and to shift her focus of study.

After you've read the following excerpt, write a brief essay that illustrates the sequence through which Thomas has moved in refining her bioacoustic research on the Weddell species of seal.

Here are some questions to guide you.

- What does Thomas see as the high point, or climax, of her seal research? In writing about her work, how will you make this clear?
- In what ways was Thomas's research shaped by prior research, or new technology, or newly available research methods?
- What did Thomas learn — or hypothesize — about how the sounds of seals themselves change over time? What factors may account for those changes?

In a postscript that can be rough and experimental, consider how you have shaped and defined the record of Thomas's research by serializing it. What impression of how knowledge is gained — gradually or by sudden insight — does your serial account convey? Does your serial account imply something about a project's relation to earlier research? Are there any assumptions about intellectual development embedded in a serial account? Is later research presumably better research?

The Sounds of Seal Society

Jeanette A. Thomas

Throughout the history of antarctic exploration, investigators have commented on the intriguing underwater sounds made by seals. In 1820, James Weddell, a British sealer who made the first detailed maps of the sea region of Antarctica later named for him, discovered a "mermaid . . . making a musical noise." This seal species now bears Weddell's name as part of its own, *Leptonychotes weddelli.* In 1905, surgeon, artist, and zoologist Edward Wilson, who accompanied Robert Falcon Scott on his first attempt to reach the South Pole, heard Weddell seals "produce a variety of musical noises, both laryngeal and œsophageal." The sounds were striking to the explorers because they broke the overwhelming silence that surrounds the frozen sea. Often the only other sounds heard by explorers were the creaking noises of the moving ice. This eerie accompaniment to the seal sounds may have contributed to the image of an antarctic mermaid.

There are four species of antarctic seals: Weddell, crabeater, leopard, and Ross. When researchers drop a hydrophone into the water to eavesdrop, they often are hit with a cacophony that has been described as everything from jungle noises to sirens. The sounds may represent many seals of one species calling at the same time, as well as more than one species. These seals use overlapping areas of antarctic waters: some inhabiting solid shorefast ice; and some, floating chunks of pack ice. The number of vocalizations in the seals' repertoires, the types and quality of the sounds they produce, and the context of their calls vary among the four species. Each also has a different social system, position on the food chain, breeding habit, and preferred ice habitat. One of my long-term research objectives has been to understand the ecology of these seals and to evaluate the adaptive significance of their various vocalizations.

From 1976 to 1981, I had the opportunity to spend most austral springs (October through December) studying the vocal behavior of antarctic seals. I worked in conjunction with Donald Siniff and his associates from the University of Minnesota, who were conducting long-term population studies, and with researchers from Hubbs Marine Research Institute at Sea World in San Diego. I collected recordings near two U.S. research stations in the Antarctic: McMurdo, which lies south of New Zealand, and Palmer, which is located south of Tierra del Fuego.

Studies near Palmer Peninsula were conducted from a sailing ship working its way through pack ice. Lying in my bunk at night, I could often hear the underwater vocalizations of leopard seals through the wooden hull. With his years of antarctic experience, our captain, Peiter Lenie, could maneuver the ship through floating ice and deposit scientists and equipment on floes without even waking nearby sleeping seals. While my shipmates tagged, weighed, and put radio transmitters on seals, I dropped a hydrophone over the edge of the ice floe and made tape recordings of underwater sounds. But there was one major problem: Ship noise masked my recordings. For one brief mo-

---

Jeanette A. Thomas (b. 1952) is professor of biology at Western Illinois University, Moline. Currently, she is studying the hearing and echolocation abilities of the Pacific white-sided dolphin, ultrasonic sounds in mice and shrews, and vocalizations in Weddell seals. Thomas is the first editor of *Sensory Abilities of Cetaceans* (1990) and *Marine Mammal Sensory Systems* (1992) and co-editor of several publications. This article appeared in the March 1991 issue of *Natural History.*

ment, I considered asking the captain if he could turn off the ship's engines, refrigerators, and generators so I could make quiet recordings. The only realistic alternative was for the ship to deposit me on an ice floe and then move far enough away so that my hydrophone could no longer detect the ship's noise.

This technique did provide quiet recordings of crabeater seals, leopard seals, and killer whales, but the experience was often harrowing. The best recordings were made when the ship was out of sight and when leopard seals and killer whales were swimming nearby. On more than one occasion, I was stalked by leopard seals. These twelve-foot-long predators think nothing of jumping onto ice floes to seize penguins; then, with a shake of the head, they skin their prey, toss the feathered pelt into the water, and devour the carcass. They also eat newly weaned crabeater seal pups, as well as fish, seabirds, and krill. Knowing the leopard seal's hunting methods, I was very disconcerted to see one circling the floe I was on, periodically lifting its massive head out of the water to see if I was worth the effort of hauling out to catch. Pods of killer whales also patrolled the pack ice. After that first season, I decided that if I wanted to write my thesis, I had to find a better way to record.

There was a better way, a much better way, called sonobuoys. These electronic devices typically are dropped from military aircraft onto the ocean surface to listen for ships or submarines and then telemeter underwater sounds back to a plane or ship. Safely aboard ship, I dropped sonobuoys in the water, and as the ship moved away from the site, I could listen to seals as I sipped coffee on the ship's bridge and record during all times of the day and night. It was wonderful.

On the other side of Antarctica, at McMurdo Sound, I conducted a series of concentrated studies on the most vocal of antarctic pinnipeds, Weddell seals. Field logistics at McMurdo were very different from those around Palmer Peninsula because these seals lived near shorefast ice. We lived in a ten-by-twenty-foot wooden hut about one hundred feet from one colony and traveled back and forth among seven others. Each austral spring, Weddell seals return to traditional fast-ice sites in the sound to give birth to pups and to mate. They congregate in groups of up to one hundred seals in sites next to long cracks in the ice. Females haul out on the ice to give birth, nurse their pups intensely, and fast for about two months. During this time, male Weddell seals establish underwater territories along cracks, caused by tidal rise and fall, running through the colony. When pups are weaned, mothers go into the water and mate in the underwater territories below the pupping colony. As the fast ice breaks up, Weddell seals leave to feed at sea, mostly on fish and invertebrates.

The various social interactions going on in the colony during this time (mother/pup, male/male, female/male) require an elaborate vocal repertoire. Mothers and their pups "bawl" and "cry," usually on the ice, to locate one another and minimize aggressive interactions with other mothers and pups. During dives, Weddell seals' lungs are collapsed and their mouths are closed, yet somehow the animals still vocalize. Thirty-four types of underwater calls are associated with territorial defense, aggression, submission, and some as yet unknown functions.

Some underwater vocalizations of Weddell seals are as loud as jet engines. And since sound travels farther in the ocean than in air and propagates especially well under polar fast ice (the thick ice cover dampens water movement, which could attenuate sound travel), seals can be heard underwater when none are visible for miles around. Making loud sounds that travel for miles may enable seals in different breeding colonies to communicate. In addition, a loud voice is undoubtedly useful when the seals are hauled out on the ice, for Antarctica is a windy place, with wind speeds sometimes in excess of sixty knots, effectively drowning out all but the loudest of sounds.

Words alone cannot adequately describe the underwater sounds of the Weddell seal, but I will try. Males have eleven types of frequency-modulated, descending "trills," which can last up to seventy-three seconds. These trills are used by dominant males in advertising and defending their territories. Both sexes produce aggressive sounds in a series that sometimes slows down,

> "Chug Chug   Chug   Chug   Chug,"

or speeds up in repetition rate,

> "Chug   Chug   Chug   Chug Chug!"

"Chirps" also occur in accelerating and retarding series, but their context seems to be submissive. Underwater fights are accompanied by aggressive chugs and responding chirps. The function of the "knock," a common call that sounds like someone rapping on the door five times in a row, is unknown. Other calls of unknown role are a seventy-five second "mew" and a cheeplike sound that descends in frequency in a steplike manner:

> "Seitz, Seitz, Seitz
>   Seitz, Seitz, Seitz,
>   Seitz, Seitz, Seitz."

One of the most interesting characteristics of the Weddell seal's repertoire is the use of short sounds as punctuation. For example, an especially loud, long trill may be preceded by a short, ascending whistle, seemingly to warn the listener to pay attention to an upcoming threat. A series of accelerated, aggressive chugs most often winds up with a "grr-gulp" sound that emphasizes the message. A threatening, guttural "glug" is preceded by a warning whistle and ends with two exclamations: "pop" and "crack."

For three breeding seasons, I systematically sampled underwater vocalizations by setting up an automated cassette recorder programmed to turn on for two minutes every hour, night and day. As I had expected, with the approach of mating time and heightened territorial defense, the Weddell seals vocalized more and more often, up to seventy-five times per minute. Conversely, after the pups were weaned and mating was accomplished, the number of sounds decreased.

I didn't expect, however, what happened on December 10, 1976. On that day, my automated equipment suddenly stopped detecting any Weddell seal sounds. Fearing that my first year of thesis data would be incomplete, I thoroughly checked all the electronic equipment but could find no problems. The silence lasted for a couple of anxious days. Then the recorder system started picking up sounds again, but different ones this time. I recognized these new vocalizations as coming from leopard seals. Also about this time, we saw and made recordings of killer whales near the edge of the fast ice. Sometimes they came close enough that I could feel the spray of their blows on my face. The new arrivals had come, I believe, in hopes of getting something to eat, for just about this time — as pups are being weaned and their mothers are returning to the water — the fast ice often breaks up, giving the predators easier access to the seals. I saw the same pattern in 1977 and 1979, when almost to the day, Weddell seals again dramatically reduced their underwater vocalizations and leopard seals and killer whales were sighted in the area. My observations convinced me that the sudden silence of these highly vocal seals was aimed at avoiding detection.

Since my 1976 to 1979 recordings of Weddell seals in McMurdo Sound, Ian Stirling and I have examined recordings made in other locations around Antarctica: Palmer Peninsula, Davis Station, and Cape Hallett. There were some basic similarities, in that all had trills, chugs, and chirps, but each site had calls heard only at that location. We wondered how this geographical variation comes about.

At weaning, pups stop their "bawling" puppy cries and begin to practice adult vocalizations. We don't know how much of the adult repertoire is innate rather than learned, but some learning certainly appears to go on. One day, I watched as a near-weaning male pup comically tried to make the trill of an adult male. The pup could not control the frequency or duration of the sound. Instead of a smooth, descending sweep, the best he could do was a warbling, intermittent sound that occasionally "cracked" like the voice of an adolescent boy. I believe that as pups lie on the ice in a colony and listen to the sounds produced by territorial males in the water below, they learn the appropriate adult repertoire. This learning presents a mechanism for geographical isolation and change in the repertoire. Suppose an adult male developed a new sound that was somehow more attractive to females or that helped him defend a territory. The pups would then be exposed to this new sound (since only successful territorial males hang around the colony) and could incorporate it into their developing repertoire. Each year, I would hear a few isolated sounds that did not fit into the colony's existing call categories, which suggests that Weddell seals do "experiment" vocally.

A History Assignment

The following essay by Len Cooper reveals a largely hidden history of black peonage in the twentieth century South — peonage is a system by which debtors are held captive to work for their creditors — and renders, as well, a deeply personal journey to uncover that history.

As you read "The Damned," pay attention to the stages of the various interlocking stories told by Cooper. There's the original story of his grandfather's boyhood experience. Then there's the larger historical, political, and legal story — Cooper's overview of the peonage system as he eventually came to understand it. There's also Cooper's personal story, the intensification of his own research as he proceeds from question to question and from source to source. Write a serial essay that describes Cooper's journey, making sure that your account reflects the intellectual and emotional dimensions of that journey.

If you are interested in the subject of how serial strategies are used to construct guilt and innocence, you may want to do this assignment in coordination with the related material in the Opening Problem (p. 171), the Professional Application (p. 186), the Criminal Studies Assignment (p. 191), and Readings: Crime Stories: Constructing Guilt and Innocence (p. 231) in the second part of this chapter.

The Damned

LEN COOPER

I was hot, I was tuckered, I was angry. I was a little boy, picking cotton for my grandfather on his 360-acre farm in Alabama, and I was feeling like a slave. Lincoln freed the slaves a hundred years ago, I informed my grandfather sourly.

"Mister Lincoln ain't freed no slaves," he said. Slavery lasted well into the twentieth century, he said, to his personal knowledge.

My brothers and I were on break, sitting in the shade of towering oaks, stupid with exhaustion, sipping sweet lemonade from dented tin cups. Daddy-Yo, which is what we called our grandfather, had us transfixed and terrified as he sat and stroked his old gold pocket watch and told us how white folks stole black children off the streets of Alabama and took them to plantations as far away as the Mississippi Delta. How this was done entire generations after the Emancipation Proclamation. How black people were held in bondage. Daddy-Yo had seen it happen, he told us.

I wondered if those white men might someday come for me. I was ten.

By and by I grew bigger and stronger, and Daddy-Yo grew smaller and feebler, but the tale he told never got less vivid or more benign. As a bent old man, he wept with each word as if ghosts had returned from the past to feast on his soul.

Those summers on his farm were the cruelest and the kindest of my life. The spiny points on the cotton buds ripped our cuticles, making our fingers bleed. Once the skin toughened, the pain would leave, replaced by something dark and gnarled and protective.

The scars on my hands have faded. The demons of the past revisit me as they did my father and grandfather. Daddy-Yo is dead and his gold pocket watch belongs to me now. Today I find myself stroking it, and telling my own children my grandfather's story, pretty much the way he told it:

It was 1918, and he was near seven years old. Daddy-Yo and his friend Cleveland and two other boys were playing along a dirt road in Sumter County. They were big kids, and strong looking. Suddenly, up pulled a brand-new automobile. Lot of dust hanging behind. Two fancy-dressed white men settin' in the front.

Hey y'all nigra boys, have y'all ever seen the likens of such a beautiful machine?

"I can't reckon we have, suh," my grandfather replied, removing his cap and lowering his eyes. It was considered a sign of disrespect for Negroes to meet the stare of a white person. In some parts, Negroes were thrown in jail and fined $25 for "reckless eyeballing," which meant they made eye contact with a white woman.

LEN COOPER (b. 1953) is a freelance journalist who writes regularly for several major newspapers and television networks nationwide. "The Damned" first appeared in the *Washington Post* on June 16, 1996.

I'll tell you boys what. How about hoppin' in for a ride down to York? We'll be back before you know it.

Poor Negro boys riding in such elegance was unheard of. They were more accustomed to traveling on splintery cross boards on the back of mule-drawn wagons. My grandfather was wary:

"We sho' do appreciate it, suh', but I reckon we'd better be headed on back to the house now," he said. "We're much obliged, though."

Suddenly the driver jumped from the car, cursing and swearing.

The four boys broke toward the wooded area along the roadside. My grandfather didn't stop running until he was on the front porch of his house. He waited for a few minutes, praying the others would soon join him. They never did.

My grandfather told his father what had happened. Within minutes, a dozen men on mules and wobbly old field wagons were on the roads, searching for the three stolen Negro children. But the boys were gone. Authorities were notified. Authorities said nothing could be done, if anything at all had happened. Negro boys sometimes get ideas into their heads, and just plumb run away.

The story didn't end there. It ended twenty years later. My grandfather was sitting on his front porch, when he saw a family of derelicts emerging from the back of a delivery truck.

He blinked and stared, then slowly rose to his feet. The oldest derelict, with the grizzled face and the watery eyes, was his old friend Cleveland, who had been by his side that day twenty years before but not as fast on his feet.

"When Cleveland saw us, it took more than an hour to settle him down," said Daddy-Yo. "We had to try to get him pacified from that. There were two or three children standing out there not far from him. When he learned his father had passed on, Cleveland cried."

Cleveland told Daddy-Yo he had been taken to the Mississippi delta, sold into slavery and held for twenty years on a plantation surrounded by two rivers and protected by armed guards, barbed wire, and dogs. He said he eventually escaped with the help of a white laborer, who drove him off with the woman who had become Cleveland's wife on the plantation. There were other plantations, all over the South, Cleveland said. Men kept under lock and key. Men whipped for insubordination, men killed on a whim.

Anyway, that was Daddy-Yo's story.

Story like that stays in your head.

In high school during Negro History Week, I took issue with students and instructors who considered President Lincoln the ultimate emancipator of the Negro people. I objected when slavery was presented as an atrocity lost in the distant past. When challenged for an explanation, I stammered that my grandpa knew, and my grandpa wouldn't lie.

This would result in an indulgent silence.

BACK TO SUMTER

What I remember of rural Alabama are lush fields of swaying emerald-green corn and endless rows of linen-white cotton. What I am looking at right now are overgrown mud fields. Loggers are at work, stripping the remaining timberland for pulp wood.

I've come back, carrying my grandfather's tales in my head, to see what I can find.

Sumter County is nestled in the flatland of west-central Alabama; its lushness has been ruined, but its people have not. Civility abounds. White children show great respect to black elders and racial tension seems to be an aberration of the past.

The past, it was very different.

At Livingston University, social science professor Louis Smith tells me that after the Civil War and well into the twentieth century, more black people were lynched in Sumter County than anywhere else in the state of Alabama, more than most anywhere in the South. Smith says that when blacks returned here from World War I, some were hauled from the trains and hanged in their military uniforms; it was payback for what black soldiers had been known to do in France. This is what they had been known to do in France: talk to French women.

But what about modern-day slavery?

Smith doesn't know. He says there were some egregious cases of what he called "debt labor," blacks working in plantation-like conditions to pay off debts. And there was, of course, sharecropping, in which blacks toiled endlessly in other men's fields in the usually futile hope of one day owning land of their own. Smith urges me to seek historical records under slavery at Ole Miss, at various local historical libraries and at the county probate court. I do. The records are riveting but irrelevant; there are ancient property conveyances, births and deaths, and there are chilling oral histories, the testimony of former slaves. Black men in Alabama were chained and whipped and many were worked to death. But these are stories from the 1830s through the early 1860s. After that, nothing.

Kate Nicholson is a splendidly ornery woman who lives with her blind husband in a small house on a rural road outside of York. She is my great-aunt. She is eighty-three. Sews quilts in her living room and raises chickens in her back yard, sells them both for profit, takes guff from no man. I ask her about slaves during her lifetime, and she says she doesn't know what I am talking about. I tell her what my grandfather — her brother — told me, and she says she heard the same story from him, but she doesn't remember it herself, and can't speak to its truth. She is so dismissive I do not pursue it.

I returned to Washington, wondering whether my grandfather's story was nothing but talk, a campfire tale embellished by bitterness and marinated in superstition, a myth that became real over time and retelling. I began to visit the Library of Congress manuscript division, asking for files on servitude in America after the Civil War. I spent weeks in the stacks inspecting records on black economic privation, on sharecropping, on the decades of economic inequality that went unchallenged until the civil rights movement of the 1950s. Sad stuff, but nothing I hadn't known. Finally, a librarian brought me another cart of yellowed documents. It was labeled "peonage." I hadn't seen that word before.

The first sheet was unlike the others I had been reading. There was nothing official about it. It wasn't typed. It had no letterhead. It was in laborious longhand, so unschooled as to be nearly unintelligible. Beneath it was a pile of twenty more just like it.

Beneath that were a dozen more piles.

Hours passed. Twice, the librarian returned to ask me if I was okay.

I suspect the Library of Congress research room doesn't get many large black men who sit there, crying.

Omaha, Neb., Oct. 8, 1923

Gentlemen as I can not read or write I got a friend to write this I never in school in my life. I worked on this man's farm all my life I didn't get a cent for my labor until I run away.

I am thirty-five years old, all we Negroes got to eat was corn bread and bacon and few clothes and forced to ten–twelve lived in rooms. His over seers carried sticks and whip and gun. They whipped children and women and men. They would make men and women strip their clothes down and get on their knees and some time tie them to place and whip them from twenty-five to one hundred lashes at time. You dare not to ask for money or any thing else . . . The over seers suduced any young girls they wanted and parents could not help them. I would send my name but I don't want to go back to this farm. I did never commit a crime.

Coffee, Ga., Aug. 10, 1919

. . . I am in slavery. What I want to do now is leave this place. I am here at this place and my husband are working turpentine and the poor men here are only getting something to eat, and not very much of that, and when a man gets ready to leave he are not allowed to go. We got to show what these wicked men and women do, but the boss man will not allow no officer to come in here. I saw with my own eyes this past week a colored woman packed her clothes and sold her chickens to get money to pay a man to let her go home and when she got to the depot the boss man taken her luggage and brought it back to the quarters and she had to stay.

Danville, Va., June 12, 1933

God knows there are some out in West Va. now that needs help they have been writing such pittiful letters to theire wives and mothers. . . . A man came here over two weeks ago and said he wanted men to work in a mine at a place called Oiminar but he took them on to a place called Shirrat West Va. where they found to thire horror and dismay they were surround by guards and forced to go in the new mine they are opening up and some have been out there two months and have not been paid one cent. Most of them never saw a mine before and that they have to brace up the mine and they are being killed five and six at the time and they have to stay in there all the time the white man that owns the place is named Jones and he told them men out there were making three four and eight dollars a day and he just lied to them and I am afraid they will all be killed before they can get away. . . . They are 580 miles from home and some refused to go in that death trap and they had them put in jail and then they are going to force them back in again . . .

A NATIONAL SHAME

Mississippi. Nebraska. Tennessee. Arkansas. Virginia. Georgia. Florida. South Carolina. West Virginia. The letters were from everywhere, written furtively, smuggled out of cotton plantations and turpentine farms and coal mines. Some were addressed to the U.S. Justice Department, but most were sent in desperation to the New York headquarters of the National Association for the Advancement of Colored People.

The NAACP did what it could, investigated where it could, issued indignant press releases, demanded justice. But the fact is, these files are not filled with follow-up. Mostly, they contain heartbreaking one-way correspondence, in fat folders marked "peonage," held for posterity. Peonage meant holding people against their will to pay off an alleged debt. It was against federal law, but it was only fitfully prosecuted.

The letters are too scattered, and too painfully naive, to be a conspiracy of propaganda. They are what they are: a case-by-case chronicle of incomprehensible inhumanity lasting from the Civil War up to World War II.

For days in the Library of Congress I sifted through the testimony of the damned, men and women of my grandfather's generation who never knew life as free people.

Slowly, the broader story took shape, not from any scholarly overview or detailed congressional study — peonage never really became a hot-button social issue — but from the slow accretion of detail, one sickening tragedy at a time.

> Darien, Ga., March 10, 1922
>
> I a poor widow woman will tell you my trouble and if the Good Lord be willing I am asking you to help me if you can. My name is Nona Harris. I worked for a man in Forest Glen, Ga. a white man, farming on his place. . . . I married in January and left the farm in September and came to Darien and that was 1919, now today my poor boy who worked with this man two years after I had left and made two crops for him and he never got anything from him but food and lodging and one pair of shoes and $10. Now in January my son was here with me in Darien and this white man sent the sheriff for him and they carry my son back to Forest Glen and make him work for this same man til a debt of $329.50 is paid and he say he will send back and get the whole family of us and put us all on the chain gang or back on his farm if I don't pay him the money to him by the first of April.

Fear ruled the South in the years after the Civil War. Blacks feared the wrath of whites, whites feared financial ruin from the sudden dearth of free labor. Blacks were technically emancipated, but they were benumbed by ignorance and cowed by generations of servitude. In this caldron of desperation, the unscrupulous could thrive. By manipulating the ledgers, some swindled the sharecropper into debt so permanent he could never work himself out of it.

But for other Southern whites, creative accountancy was hardly necessary. Protected by sympathetic local law enforcement, many farmers kept their plantations operating much as they had before Lincoln — with armed overseers, "whipping bosses" for discipline, and stockades to place the insubordinate worker. Sometimes people were born and died on these plantations, never knowing they were legally free. These brutal places seemed to thrive everywhere in the agricultural belt from Florida to Nebraska.

How did these places get their slaves? Any way they could. In Southern city courtrooms, plantation owners were known to place what was called a "watcher," someone who kept an eye out for black men against whom fines were levied for minor crimes. The watcher paid the fine, allegedly in return for the accused working off the debt on his plantation. It was a common ruse: The man arrived and found himself a prisoner. Others were recruited in bus stations and train depots and other public places to which the indigent gravitate. Coerced by the promise of work, they were then given a sandwich on their way to the plantation. Upon arriving, they were billed for the food — a bill they would never seem to repay. For years, they tried to work that sandwich off.

The public, by and large, was ignorant of these farms. The files contain the occasional bemused newspaper story about someone arrested for vagrancy in one Northern town or another, who claimed to have escaped from slavery.

From an affidavit by an escaped slave, obtained by the NAACP in Philadelphia, concerning a farm outside Vicksburg, Mississippi:

> . . . I remained on this farm for a period of about thirty days when I approach Mr. A. F. Hamilton with reference to payment of my wages. At that time Hamilton was sitting on a box on the porch of the comissary. He state that he would give me my pay in a few moments. He was talking to some of the colored foremen at the time and I continued to stand and wait in expectation of receiving my money. Hamilton then ordered four of

> these colored guards to seize me, which they did, and stripped me of my outer clothing and gave me a severe beating. When they had finished, he stated this was my pay . . .

One undated newspaper clipping reports the curious case of a Georgia farmer named Pascell who wrote to the governor of Honolulu asking for 300 slaves. "If there is no danger of the savages eating me up over here," Pascell wrote, "I will come and pick my choice from the drove you have on the market and pay you good money . . ."

The governor answered indignantly, saying that although Hawaii was only a territory it was a civilized place, and dryly noted that Honolulu does not lynch people the way Georgia does. There is no indication that any authorities ever investigated what use the good farmer Pascell had for slaves.

"This peonage system was the dying gasp of that reign of terror called slavery and the people didn't want to let go of it," Elizabeth Clark-Lewis, professor of history at Howard University, told me. "Southerners were committed to the subjugation of the African American," she said. "The social reformers in Washington and throughout the country weren't necessarily writing and keeping records on African Americans in the peonage system. Who cared about African Americans?"

In fact, some people of conscience did, and eventually, they would help bring this system down. The files at the Library of Congress contain the occasional letter from free people, white and black, appalled at what was going on in the countryside.

> Peace, Ark., Feb. 6, 1922
>
> Gentlemen:
>
> I live in the county of Cleveland. We have no law to protect us. The system of debt slavery rules in this county. If a Negro is arrested he is taken to jail, kept there a while then he is taken to a big man's farm and put to work with out any trial whatever. When ever a white man kills a Negro he is taken and (the Negro) buried and that is all there is to it. . . . I am writing what I know, not what I think.
>
> I am willing to testify to these things any where if it cost my life for I know the miserable conditions of my people here.
>
> Yours truly, Rev. W. H. Booker

And this, from a white woman to the NAACP:

> On last Thursday, June 21, 1923, I was on my way to Harwell, Ga. I had to wait over about three and one half hours in order to make the proper connection, at a very small place called Calhoun Falls, S.C. While sitting there an old grandmother came up to me and she was terribly distressed. She had a daughter in New York who had sent for her but she had two very dear grandchildren that she was so anxious to see before leaving the place.
>
> The mother of the children is dead and they are kept as slaves under a man by the name of John McCollie (White). He is located ten miles from the little town, running a big farm. He has an over seer by the name of Peach Alexander with one eye, who is indeed cruel. There are more than one hundred Negroes in absolute slavery. They are half clothed, half fed, and have no money. . . . If they show at any time the least resentment, they are whipped severely, very often shot and at times killed and thrown into the river. They are well guarded at all times so that no one will know of their whereabouts. . . .
>
> When ever the mother and father of a family become too old to work, the children have to be given over and they remain there until they become too old. They are perfectly ignorant.
>
> There was a girl quite young and unmarried who became a mother. When the baby was between four and five months old, she was forced to go to the field at the dawn of

a day and work till night with her baby in a box. She was so far from the baby at one time that it fell out of the box and the ants ate little holes in the sides of its nostrils, gnawed its ears and around its mouth . . . This is only one case. . . .

What can be done? Please see after this matter at once and if it is investigated, be very careful on entering the place for it is well guarded at all times.

These are true facts.

OFFICIAL INACTION

During the early part of the century, the Justice Department aggressively prosecuted a number of cases of debt peonage, but its prosecutions soon flagged. In some of the worst cases, where the allegations were of simple slavery — where debt was not an issue, and federal peonage law did not apply — the federal government often referred the case back to the states, where wealthy landowners were protected by corrupt or coerced law enforcement officers.

From time to time, largely through lobbying efforts of the NAACP, charges of slavery were filed. Often they went nowhere. In Southern towns, it was next to impossible to convict a white man solely on the testimony of blacks, particularly poor blacks.

If there was one case that summarized the pervasive horror of peonage and slavery, it was the one that came to light in Jasper County, Ga., in 1921. Federal agents entered the farm owned by respected local landowner John S. Williams and began questioning him about the allegedly inhumane conditions of the workers there. The agents informed Williams that it was illegal to "work a nigger against his will."

Williams was dumbfounded. If that is the case, he told the agents, "I and most all of the farmers in this county must be guilty of peonage."

The extent of Williams's brutality became evident in the next year, when he was tried for running a "Murder Farm." The newspapers called him Simon Legree.

Williams's overseer, a twenty-seven-year-old black man named Clyde Manning, expressionlessly testified to having killed as many as eleven black workers on Williams's orders, shortly after the visit of the federal agents. He said he had drowned several, after binding their hands, weighing them down with rocks and dropping them off a bridge into the Alcovy River as they begged for their lives. Others Manning beat to death with an ax. The motive: self-protection. Williams was concerned that if he had been tried for peonage, those men might testify against him.

Indeed, some of the slaves from the plantation testified that they spent their adult lives on the Williams farm, never having left even for a day, not knowing the name or the location of the nearest store, five miles away.

Williams was convicted and sentenced to a long prison term.

It was the start of a series of public trials that began to get significant attention in the press.

Peonage Farm "Didn't Use Force," Merely Whipped Negroes.

June 10, 1922

New York, June 10: Although Dr. W. R. King, proprietor of an alleged peonage farm in Oglethorpe County, Ga., admitted he struck and whipped Negroes, he denied having used force to keep them on his plantation and was acquitted of the peonage charge by a federal court jury in Athens, Ga. . . .

Flogged to Work, Negroes Testify

Pensacola, Fla., 1925

DeWitt Stoner admitted that he was forced at the point of revolvers in the hands of the defendants to beat Henry Sanders, Galvester Jackson and George Diamond with large, rough oak sticks or "black jacks" after the Negroes had been intercepted in the attempt to leave the county.

He testified the white men looked on as he whipped the three other Negroes, one at a time, after they had been stripped of their clothing and made to lie on their stomachs in the road.

The two accused white turpentine farm operators were convicted. Things were moving forward, but at a glacial pace. This was, after all, the American South in 1925. For the crime of having ordered the flogging of workers who had dared to try to escape their farm, the two men received sentences of sixty and ninety days in prison, respectively.

THE SHADOW OF SLAVERY

After three weeks, I walked out of the Library of Congress, and left the peonage files for the next man. I had not read them all, but I had read enough.

Mine were not the first set of eyes on these documents. They had been pored through a quarter century ago, by a young Tennessee professor named Pete Daniel, working on his doctoral dissertation. Daniel's research resulted in a powerful, elegant, heart-wrenching book, *The Shadow of Slavery: Peonage in the South, 1901–1969* published by the University of Illinois Press. I found it shortly before finishing this article.

It is all in there, all the Library of Congress and Justice Department files, dispassionately analyzed in all their bleakness. In his introduction, Daniel calls his book "the record of an American failure." He is talking about a system of institutional apathy, and casual racism, that permitted peonage to exist unchecked for so long.

According to the publisher, over the past twenty-five years Pete Daniel's book has sold 8,200 copies. That is about what Danielle Steel moves on a slow Thursday.

Pete Daniel is now the curator of the Smithsonian's National Museum of American History. I phoned him, asked how he felt when he first read those letters.

"Outraged," he said. "It was amazing material. Day after day I read these things, many of which were not followed up on. I was outraged that this could have happened in the twentieth century. A lot of people didn't believe me when I told them about it. At an interview once for a teaching job, a prospective employer, an academic, told me this *couldn't* have happened. He called everything I had fraudulent." Daniel laughed. "I didn't get the job."

BACK TO SUMTER

I had one more question, and it involved something a haunted old man had told me a long time ago.

The story my grandfather had told me now rang true. It must have been true. But what I could not understand was how it could have been forgotten. How could children have been stolen off the road of Sumter County, Ala., and no one remembered? Or did no one want to remember?

I went back to visit my feisty great-aunt Kate, and I told her what I had learned from my research. She listened intently, sat back in her chair and smiled sadly. I don't know if she suddenly recalled something, or if she suddenly decided that, through my labors, I had earned her trust. Daddy-Yo and his sister Kate always did have a fierce work ethic.

Ever hear of the Dial family? she asked me.

I guess I had. They are a prominent family in the area, to this day. They are neighbors.

Well, the Dials had been slave owners, Kate said. Right up to the 1950s. In the little sleepy Sumter County town of Boyd. They whupped black people.

I raced to the local library. It was there, in old newspaper clips.

Two Guilty of Slavery

> Birmingham, Ala. — Two prosperous Alabama brothers were found guilty tonight of holding Negroes in slavery. Fred N. Dial, 25 years old, and Oscar Edwin Dial, 34, were . . . convicted of conspiracy to hold Coy Lee Tanksly, 25, of Klindike, Miss., and Hubert Thompson, in voluntary servitude by acts of violence.
>
> Fred Dial also was convicted on a peonage count involving Mr. Thompson. The jury held that Dial forced him to work in payment of an alleged debt.
>
> The government charged that Mr. Thompson died three days after he was beaten when he attempted to escape from the brothers' farm in West Alabama last year.
>
> . . . Witnesses said Thompson was tied by the neck, feet and waist with ropes to a bale of hay and beaten by eight men with ropes.

The date was May 14, 1954. It was one of the last slavery convictions in the United States. The brothers Dial, of Sumter Co., Ala., received prison sentences. Eighteen months apiece.

One of the most prominent families in town. Still respected.

I began to understand something about the silence of my great-aunt Kate, the silence of Sumter County, the specter of slavery. I am writing this on a day in 1996 when yet another black Southern church was burned to the ground.

Daddy-Yo's old friend Cleveland is still alive, still living in rural Alabama. I spoke to an old friend of his, Booker T. Larkin, who told me that in the years he has known him, Cleveland never talked about his time in the Delta. Never said a word. Never confirmed its truth. Larkin explained that old black people in those parts still have a fear of the plantation, and it mutes them.

Sure enough, when I phoned Cleveland and told him what I wanted to talk about, he hung up on me.

Then his wife took the phone, and said he would have nothing to say about this. Nothing. Ever.

I wanted to pursue it, to go to his door, to explain what I was doing, to urge him to say how he had suffered so we could all understand and benefit. To *demand* that he tell his story. That is what I wanted to do, as a writer.

But as a black man, I decided to let him be.

An Astronomy Assignment

This speculative essay by physicist James S. Trefil was written for *Smithsonian* magazine as the second of two parts. In Part 1, Trefil sketched and discussed theories about the origins of the universe. Here he turns to theories about its end. After reading the article, answer one of the following questions.

- What are the possible fates of the universe, according to Trefil? Briefly describe these possibilities in separate serial paragraphs.
- Trefil's subject is vast and hard to connect to our lives. But he helps us to envision cosmic events by creating useful metaphors. Write an essay that takes a reader through the article, treating each major metaphor as a separate stage of Trefil's presentation and discussing how each metaphor adds to the reader's understanding of the way(s) the universe will end.
- On the whole, do you think Trefil feels that the universe will end "in fire" or "in ice"? Defend your position by presenting serially the cases for the closed and open universes.

Trefil does a good job of making complex astrophysical processes accessible; still, following his speculations takes some concentration. You might find it helpful, therefore, to sketch out — with a list of phrases or a diagram or maybe even a flow chart — the events or stages that could lead to each of the several possible ends of the universe.

If you had trouble following Trefil, you might want to add to your paper a brief postscript speculating on the limitations of print in presenting actual or imagined physical processes. What writing techniques does Trefil use to help us understand such processes? Did they work for you?

How the Universe Will End

JAMES S. TREFIL

In most lines of work, it is far easier to know the past than to predict the future: Ask any Monday-morning quarterback. But when it comes to talking about the ultimate fate of the Universe, the rule does not hold. Looking backward in time to the Big Bang, as we did last month in Part One of this series, involves the development of complex new theories about the behavior of matter in very unusual environments. Tracing the future of the Universe from the present onward is not nearly so hard; we do not need any new

---

JAMES S. TREFIL (b. 1938) is Clarence J. Robinson Professor of Physics at George Mason University. He co-wrote (with E. D. Hirsch and Joseph Kett) *Cultural Literacy: What Every American Needs to Know* (1988, revised 1993). His recent work includes *Are We Unique: A Scientist Explores the Complexity of the Human Brain* (1997) and *The Edge of the Unknown* (1996). "How the Universe Will End" appeared in *Smithsonian* magazine in 1983.

way of looking at the world. All that we really need to plot out our future are a few good measurements.

This does not mean that we can sit down today and outline the future course of the Universe with anything like certainty. There are still too many things we do not know about the way the Universe is put together. But we do know exactly what information we need to fill in our knowledge, and we have a pretty good idea of how to go about getting it.

Perhaps the best way to think of our present situation is to imagine a train coming into a switchyard. All of the switches are set before the train arrives, so that its path is completely determined. Some switches we can see, others we cannot. There is no ambiguity if we can see the setting of the switch: We can say with confidence that some possible futures will not materialize and others will. At the unseen switches, however, there is no such certainty. We know the train will take one of the tracks leading out, but we have no idea which one. The unseen switches are true decision points in the future, and what happens when we arrive at them determines the entire subsequent course of events.

When we think about the future of the Universe, we can see our "track" many billions of years into the future, but after that there are decision points to be dealt with and possible fates to consider. The goal of science is to reduce the ambiguity at the decision points and find the true road that will be followed.

Just as we have no trouble predicting the path of the train as it enters the switchyard, we have a pretty good idea about the short-term fate of the Universe. We expect that the galaxies will continue to separate and stars will continue to form and evolve for many billions of years. The Universe is now about 15 billion years old, and the Earth and sun a little less than 5. In another 5 billion years the sun will have used up all the hydrogen it can. The sun will then swell monstrously into what astronomers call a "red giant," and the Earth will be swallowed up.

Ten billion years is a typical lifetime for a star the size of the sun; smaller stars, of which there are more, live longer. Depending chiefly on the mass of the star, the end product can be a white dwarf, a very dense star about the size of a planet (this will be the fate of the sun); a neutron star, an extremely dense object only a few miles across; or a black hole, an object with a gravitational field so strong that no light can escape. It might also self-destruct completely, returning its material to the galaxy. But whatever the end product of stellar evolution, each star uses up a certain amount of raw material. In 40 or 50 billion years, then, we expect that star formation will have slowed down considerably from what we see now. Stars will continue to go out: first the bright ones (which burn up their fuel most profligately, and therefore can die within a few million years), then more sedate stars like the sun. By this point in the future, our own galaxy may be a rather dull place, made up primarily of unspectacular stars much smaller than the sun.

Of course, when we talk of the future of the Universe, the fate of any single galaxy is not terribly important. Conversely, because other galaxies form a completely insignificant part of the spectacle of the night sky, what happens to distant galaxies will have little effect on what is observed from the Earth. Nevertheless, we do know that other galaxies are receding from us because of the Universe's expansion, and we believe that this expansion has been going on for roughly 15 billion years. It will surely continue to go on for comparable times into the future. The question that must be asked is whether the expansion will someday slow down and reverse itself, or whether it will continue forever. This question is the first (and most important) decision point we must face.

If a ball is thrown upward from the surface of the Earth, we know that eventually it will slow down, stop, and reverse its direction because of the gravitational attraction of the Earth. If the ball were thrown fast enough (more than about seven miles a second), however, we know that it would not fall back, but would sail off into space instead. Whether the ball will fall back to the ground, then, depends on two things: how fast it is moving and how hard the Earth is pulling on it. The force of gravity exerted by the Earth, in turn, depends on how much matter it contains.

We can think of the present expansion of the Universe in the same way. A given galaxy is now receding from us at a particular velocity, a velocity which we can measure. Whether it will ever stop and start falling back toward us depends on how much of a gravitational attraction the rest of the Universe exerts on it. If there is enough matter to exert a strong enough force, we can expect that the outward-rushing Universe will someday start to contract. If there is not enough matter, then the expansion may slow down, but it will never stop.

In the terminology of the cosmologists, a universe with enough matter to reverse the expansion is "closed," while a universe which has less than this critical amount is "open." (A universe with exactly the critical amount is also considered to be open and will end pretty much the same way.) The first decision point, then, is marked by the fundamental question: "Is the Universe open or closed?"

At first glance it might seem strange that we do not know enough to answer this fundamental question. After all, our telescopes are capable of detecting galaxies 10 billion light years away (one light year is approximately 6 trillion miles). Why can't we just add up all the matter we see and have our answer?

It turns out that if we took all the stars and galaxies and spread their matter out uniformly through space, we would find about one hydrogen atom in a volume that could be carried by a dump truck. (This may seem like a very thin distribution of matter, but remember that there is a lot of just plain emptiness out there.) If we wanted to close the Universe, we would need a lot more than this: at least one to three atoms per cubic yard. If we count only the luminous matter we can see we have only a few percent of the amount needed to close the Universe. We seem forced to conclude that the Universe is open.

But this statement is premature, for it depends on the assumption that we can see all the matter there is. We know this is not always true. For example, someone looking at the solar system from another star would see the sun because it is luminous, but he probably would not see any of the other bodies we know are here: planets, asteroids, comets, and so on. In the case of the solar system this is probably not too important, because all of these bodies add up to only a tiny fraction of the mass of the sun. But in looking at galaxies the situation may very well be different. It may be that a large percentage of the matter in a galaxy is not visible to someone looking at it through a telescope. If the matter we see does not close the Universe, then perhaps the matter we do not see will be enough to do the job.

UNSEEN MATTER IN THE GALAXIES?

At least two lines of evidence suggest that there might be a lot of matter, the existence of which we can deduce from its effects on other bodies. One line comes from studies of galaxies themselves, the other from studies of clusters of galaxies. Galaxies like the Milky Way and our neighbor Andromeda are shaped like spirals and rotate around their centers. The sun, for example, makes a grand circuit around the Milky Way every 200 million years or so. This rotation is complex, with different parts of the galaxy going around at different speeds. We are sure, however, that we understand the way matter should behave when it is at the outermost edges of the system. Just as the outer planets like Jupiter and Saturn move more slowly in their orbits than the Earth, so too should matter in the outer fringe of a galaxy exhibit gradual slowing down as the distance from the center increases. We say that the rotation should become Keplerian (named for Johannes Kepler, who discovered the true nature of planetary motion).

When we speak of the "outer fringes" of a galaxy in this context, we are talking about tenuous material, mostly hydrogen atoms, that does not emit light and is not visible to the naked eye or an optical telescope. It does, however, emit radio waves which allow us to detect its presence and determine its speed of rotation. Radio maps reveal that in most galaxies, this hydrogen gas is rotating faster than would be expected unless there were still more matter involved.

The only way this puzzling fact can be explained is to assume that there *is* still more matter (and therefore mass) in addition to the hydrogen that we can detect with our radio telescopes. Many galaxies, then, have an extensive halo of "invisible" matter . . . , a halo which could very well contain even more material than the stars themselves.

What the galactic halos teach us is that we should not be too hasty in declaring the Universe to be open. Even though we can directly see only a small percentage of the matter required to reverse the Universal expansion, we believe there is a great deal of matter in the Universe that we cannot see. If we assume that most galaxies have halos, then we should multiply the amount of visible matter by a number between two and ten to get a rough idea of how much mass is really out there. Of course, doing so does not get us to the critical amount of mass by a long shot, but this episode does make us wonder whether there are not other unseen masses waiting to be discovered.

Another candidate for unseen matter arises from studies of clusters of galaxies — concentrations that can contain a thousand or more galaxies. A few of these clusters seem to be in a kind of equilibrium. Think of adding hot water to a partially full bathtub. For a while the area where you add the water will be hotter than the rest of the tub, but eventually everything will even out and you will be left with a uniform temperature throughout. At this point we say that the water has reached what is known as thermal equilibrium.

Now if you put your hand into a tub of water and found that the temperature was pretty evenly distributed, you would be justified in assuming that the water had been in the tub long enough for any initial unevenness in the temperature to be smoothed out. When astronomers look at clusters of galaxies, they see strong evidence that a different type of equilibrium has been established, leading them to conclude that the system has been together long enough for this to occur.

In a few spots in the Universe, such as the Coma cluster, we have the paradoxical situation that a cluster is in equilibrium even though it does not seem to contain enough visible mass to hold everything together. Adding mass for galactic halos and diffuse background light does not solve this problem (although it makes the discrepancy less acute). Conclusion: There is additional unseen mass in that cluster of galaxies. In Coma, for example, the actual mass of the system must be ten or twenty times that of the matter we observe in the galaxies. Adding this extra intergalactic mass to clusters still will not give us enough to close the Universe, but it brings us nearer.

A similar conclusion can be reached by looking at the Universe as it existed three minutes after the Big Bang, the time when nuclei were formed. By measuring abundances of light nuclei *now,* we can deduce the density of nuclear matter *then.* The result: If we count only nuclei, the Universe is open.

Such is the current state of our knowledge about the first decision point in the future of the Universe. The amount of luminous matter that we know about is not the amount needed to reverse the expansion, but we already have two sources of unseen additional matter that were hitherto unexpected. Whether we will keep adding new unseen matter in bits and pieces until we achieve the critical amount or whether we now know about most of the matter in the Universe is an open question.

A few years ago, for example, it appeared that the neutrino, a particle presumed since its theoretical prediction and then its actual discovery to have no mass, might have a small mass after all. Cosmologists have speculated that if such were the case, there might be enough invisible mass in the form of neutrinos to close the Universe. When experiments in the United States and the Soviet Union seemed to indicate that the neutrino did indeed have mass, the excitement spilled over into the news media. After all, we have reason to believe that there are as many neutrinos in the Universe as there are photons (the particles that are light and other radiation), and so if neutrinos had mass, there are so many of them that they might indeed add up to enough to close the Universe. Unfortunately, a new generation of experiments has weakened the evidence, and the question of what, if anything, will provide the unseen mass remains unanswered.

This sort of on-again, off-again sequence is typical of the history of this problem, so it probably makes sense to agree that while at present it looks as if the Universe is open, there is enough uncertainty to leave the closed future a strong possibility. The fact that the question is yet to be answered, however, does not mean that it is unanswerable. We could acquire the knowledge necessary to determine whether the Universe is open or closed in many ways, from measuring the deceleration of distant galaxies to developing a better understanding of the problem of unseen mass. At the moment, however, neither our observational nor theoretical capabilities are up to the job.

EXPLORING ALL THE POSSIBILITIES

We have no choice, then, but to follow each possible outcome of the first decision point and see where it leads. Let us begin by assuming that nature has chosen to hide 90 percent or so of the mass and that the Universe is actually closed. In this case we are in for a spectacular future. For another 40 or 50 billion years the Universe will continue to expand, but ever more slowly. Then, like the ball falling back to Earth, the expansion will reverse at some point — 50 billion years is a reasonable guess — and a great contraction will begin. Instead of a universe where light from distant galaxies is shifted toward the red (indicating that the source is receding from us), we will find such light is blue-shifted.

Eighty or a hundred billion years from now the Earth and the sun will be long dead. The galaxies will be decidedly less luminous than they are now, with populations of white dwarfs, neutron stars, and other faint objects. As the contraction progresses, galaxies move closer together and the cosmic background radiation begins to shift toward the visible part of the spectrum. . . . The sky will eventually blaze with light. By this time, the Universe will have contracted to a thousandth or less of its present size. The stars and planets themselves will dissolve into a Universal sea of hot material, and atoms and molecules will dissociate into their constituent nuclei and electrons. From this point on, the stages of the Big Bang that we described last month will simply play backward — nuclei dissociating into quarks . . . and so on — until we are back to the original state in which it is thought the Big Bang occurred.

This scenario leads inevitably to the most fascinating question of all. Will the Universal contraction (which cosmologists half-jokingly call the "Big Crunch") be followed by another expansion (the "Big Bounce")? In other words, will the Universe arise phoenixlike from its ashes and repeat the entire cycle? The picture of a universe which is reborn every hundred billion years or so is very attractive to some people. The main advantage of an eternally oscillating universe is that the questions "Why did it all start? Where did it all come from?" simply do not have to be asked. The Universe always *was* and always *will be.* A hundred billion years from now the Universe may again consist of a large collection of separating galaxies. And perhaps there will be another version of you reading another version of this magazine.

It is a fascinating thought, but before we go too far into speculation, I should warn you that there are some serious problems with this picture. At least a few theorists argue that unless some of the basic laws of physics change during part of the cycle, the average disorder of the Universe might have to increase during each bounce, so that eventually the system would have to run down. And, of course, the whole idea of oscillations depends on the presence of enough mass to close the Universe and initiate the Big Crunch. Our present information seems to favor a quite different future.

So let us go back to our first decision point and look at the other option, the case in which there simply is not enough matter around to stop the expansion.

Scientists used to think that the universal tendency of every system to run down would eventually result in a universe in which everything had come into equilibrium at the same low temperature. This was called the "heat death" of the Universe. But this cannot happen in an eternally expanding system, because the components become too isolated to interact, so some thought has to be given to what will actually take place. Freeman J. Dyson, one of the most inventive minds in the fraternity of theoretical physicists, has explored the possible future course of the Universe. He did so not only because of the intrinsic interest of the problem, but also to examine a much deeper question: Could life survive in an open universe? Besides, a closed universe gives him a feeling of claustrophobia.

Because the expected lifetime of an open universe is infinite, we will have to think about very long times indeed if we are to follow the twists and turns of this possible future. Scientists like to write large numbers in what is called exponential notation. For example, the number 10^3 should be interpreted as a one followed by three zeros, or 1,000. The Universe is now roughly 10 billion years old, a number with ten zeros that we would render as 10^{10} years. The life cycle of a closed universe is often taken to be around a hundred billion, or 10^{11}, years. Each time the power of ten is increased by one unit, the number being represented increases tenfold.

When we talk about looking into the future, it is tempting to imagine watching a film being run at a uniform speed. Another way to think about it — one that will give a better feeling for the immense time scales involved — is to imagine that the film speed is multiplied by ten when the power of ten goes up one digit. Thus, if we imagine that we are watching such a film being run at the rate of 10 billion years every minute, then right now we are a little less than two minutes into the story following the Big Bang. Eight minutes from now we will be seeing the Universe when it is 100 billion (or 10^{11}) years old. The power of ten has gone up one digit, so at that point the film speed increases by ten. The next ten minutes will take us to a trillion (10^{12}) years, at which point the speed again increases by ten, so that time is going by at the rate of a trillion years a minute, and so on. Adopting this way of looking at things is the only way we can even begin to imagine the immense time scales involved in working out the death of the Universe.

THE OPENING STAGES OF AN OPEN UNIVERSE

If the Universe is open, the only change in the expansion will be a slowing down. The process of star formation may be winding down in the next 100 billion years or so, as we have already seen. The burning-out process would go on for a long time. Small, slow-burning stars could last as long as 10^{14} years, giving a pale illumination to the sky. As these stars cool off, other kinds of dissipation begin to become important. Some stars will evaporate from the outer regions of the galaxy in a time scale of 10^{19} years, while the densely packed stars in the galactic center may collapse together into a large black hole. When the Universe is a billion times older than it is now, corresponding to nine changes in film speed, we will see an ever thinner sea of background radiation in which an occasional black hole is embedded. Scattered around among these landmarks in nothingness will be the solid remains of the evaporated stars and such debris as has escaped capture up to this point. The Universe will keep this aspect through twelve more increases in film speed until the next point, which occurs at about 10^{31} years.

At this point we have to ask about the fate of the remnant solid matter. According to current theories, the protons that make up all matter are unstable, and have a lifetime of roughly 10^{31} years. If the proton is indeed unstable on this very long scale, then by the time the film gets near to this point matter will be disintegrating fast enough to be visibly disappearing in our cosmic version of time-lapse photography.

If, on the other hand, matter is stable, nothing of this sort will have happened by 10^{31} years. The Universe will go on expanding and cooling off. Occasionally some of the miscellaneous solid material will fall into a black hole, producing radiation as it does so. A hypothetical astronomer observing the Universe would be getting very bored, because this state of affairs would persist until 10^{65} years had passed.

With the film now running at about 10^{65} years per minute, an important process is starting to take place among the black holes the size of, say, our sun. We think of black holes as bodies so dense that nothing can ever escape their gravitational pull, yet on long time scales it turns out that this is not quite accurate. Black holes will lose appreciable energy through thermal radiation. In a sense, the black hole is like the ember of a fire, giving off radiation to its surroundings. When the film is running at 10^{65} years per minute, a black hole will start radiating substantial energy, getting brighter and brighter as it does so. In one minute of film time, the black hole will brighten the sky and then disappear, its only monument an addition to the expanding sea of radiation. As the film runs on, speeding up every ten minutes, larger and larger black holes will undergo the same process and evaporate themselves away. For the next thirty-five changes in film speed, this is what we would see, an expanding universe with occasional fireworks as a black hole dies. This process goes on until all black holes are gone, and by the time it is over the film will be running at the speed of 10^{100} years per minute.

If the protons have decayed, this is the end of our story, because there is nothing left in the Universe to produce any real change. If the proton does not decay, however, the disappearance of the black holes still leaves us with some solid matter to watch. The film now runs for ten days, until each minute corresponds to 10^{1500} years. Just writing the zeros in this number would require a full typewritten page! On this time scale matter turns to iron, the most stable nucleus. As we watch the film, then, we will see whatever solid material is left transform itself into iron. On still longer time scales — scales so long that we might have to watch our film for longer than the lifetime of the Earth — these iron spheres would transform into black holes, which would eventually evaporate.

This means that at some distant time in the future, the Universe will probably be a cold, thin sea of radiation, with perhaps a few forlorn particles. Undaunted by this bleak prospect, Freeman Dyson argues that life could evolve away from flesh and blood — possibly into clouds of electrically charged particles — and outlast the stars and galaxies themselves while the Universe cools.

The great debate over whether the Universe is open or closed comes down to the question of whether it will all end in fire or in ice, whether everything will fall back in on itself only to repeat the cycle, or whether the last bits of matter and radiation will disappear into a darkness that expands forever.

This is, in a sense, the last, the ultimate, question of science. The cosmic switch has already been thrown; the answer, though unknown, is already ordained, and Man cannot influence the outcome. But simply to discover it would be a triumph of the human intellect.

A Geology Assignment

The following discussion of earthquakes is excerpted from an introductory geology textbook, and it is typical in style and detail of textbook descriptions of physical and biological processes. The authors define "earthquake" and explain the conditions that create it, the processes of earthquake activity, and the results. Their discussion is rich with examples of particular earthquakes, with figures to illustrate the various geophysical processes, and with metaphors or comparisons to help the reader understand these processes.

Earthquakes hold a fascination for most of us, but a technical understanding of them takes some work. To read this excerpt most effectively, pause occasionally to see whether you can explain a particular process in your own words and whether you can visualize it. Draw pictures or charts. The authors provide a number of illustrations and metaphors (such as the movement of springs and ropes on p. 224 to illustrate seismic waves). Spend a little time with those, recalling, for example, your own experiences pulling on a spring or snapping a rope. The authors also recommend simple experiments; do these when possible. If you do not have a technical background, talk to someone who does; form discussion groups in and out of class. The problem many students have reading science textbooks is that the material remains abstract, inert on the page. The techniques we suggest here should help you better understand and be able to use the information in this text on earthquakes — and help you read other physical and life sciences textbooks more effectively.

Once you've read "Earthquakes," write an essay in which you first describe the various conditions that make earthquakes possible. Then describe the process by which a quake occurs. When variation in conditions can lead to earthquakes occurring in different ways, explain the differences and the different processes that can result. Finally, describe the possible effects of an earthquake and the various factors that can enhance or impede those effects. If you use technical terms, define them as best you can in your own language, although you should feel free to use the metaphors provided by the authors. Use serial strategies to help you.

Earthquakes

FREDERICK K. LUTGENS AND EDWARD J. TARBUCK

On October 17, 1989, at 5:04 PM Pacific Daylight Time, strong tremors shook the San Francisco Bay area. Millions of Americans and others around the world were just getting ready to watch the third game of the World Series but instead saw their television sets go black as the shock hit Candlestick Park. Although the Loma Prieta earthquake was centered in a remote section of the Santa Cruz Mountains, about 16 kilometers north of the city of Santa Cruz, major damage occurred in the Marina District of San Francisco 100 kilometers to the north. . . . Here, as many as sixty row houses were so badly damaged that they had to be demolished. Although wood frame structures often survive earthquakes with little or no structural damage, many of these homes were built over garages that were supported only by thin wooden columns. Simply, there were no walls on the lower levels to resist the horizontal stresses.

The most tragic result of the violent shaking was the collapse of some double-decked sections of Interstate 880, also known as the Nimitz Freeway. . . . The ground motions caused the upper deck to sway, shattering the concrete support columns along a mile-long section of the freeway. The upper deck then collapsed onto the lower roadway, flattening cars as if they were aluminum beverage cans. Other roadways that were damaged during this earthquake included a fifty-foot section of the upper deck of the Bay Bridge, which is a major artery connecting the cities of Oakland and San Francisco. The vibration caused cars on the bridge to bounce up and down vigorously. A motorcyclist on the upper deck described how the roadway bulged and rippled toward him, "It was like bumper cars — only you could die . . . !" Fortunately, only one motorist on the bridge was killed.

The Loma Prieta earthquake lasted just fifteen seconds and occurred along the northern segment of the San Andreas fault. This active fault zone and associated faults, including the Hayward fault, which runs through Oakland, and the San Jacinto fault near San Bernadino, extend northward from southern California for over 1,000 kilometers. It

---

FREDERICK K. LUTGENS (b. 1945) is professor of earth sciences at Illinois Central College. EDWARD J. TARBUCK (b. 1940) is chair of the Math, Science, and Engineering Department at Illinois Central College. Lutgens and Tarbuck have co-authored several college texts, including *Earth Science* (5th ed., 1997), *Earth: An Introduction to Physical Geology* (5th ed., 1996), and *Essentials of Geology* (4th ed., 1995), from which this excerpt is taken.

is along this fault system that two great sections of the earth, the North American plate and the Pacific plate, grind past each other at the rate of a few centimeters per year. Along much of this fault zone the rocks on either side tend to remain locked, resisting the overall motion. In time the stress builds to a point where the strength of the rocks is exceeded and the plates slide past each other, releasing the stored energy in short bursts. The result is an earthquake. . . .

It is estimated that over 30,000 earthquakes that are strong enough to be felt occur worldwide annually. Fortunately most of these are minor tremors and do very little damage. Generally only about seventy-five significant earthquakes take place each year, and many of these occur in remote regions. However, occasionally a large earthquake occurs near a large population center. When such an event takes place, it is among the most destructive natural forces on earth. The shaking of the ground coupled with the liquefaction of some soils wreak havoc on buildings and other structures. In addition, when a quake occurs in a populated area, power and gas lines are often ruptured, causing numerous fires. In the 1906 San Francisco earthquake, much of the damage was caused by fires which ran unchecked when broken water mains left firefighters with only trickles of water.

WHAT IS AN EARTHQUAKE?

An earthquake is the vibration of the earth produced by the rapid release of energy. This energy radiates in all directions from its source, the focus, in the form of waves analogous to those produced when a stone is dropped into a calm pond (Figure 1). Just as the impact of the stone sets water waves in motion, an earthquake generates seismic waves that radiate throughout the earth. Even though the energy dissipates rapidly with increasing distance from the focus, instruments located throughout the world record the event. . . .

What mechanism does produce a destructive earthquake? Ample evidence exists that the earth is not a static planet. Numerous ancient wave-cut benches can be found many meters above the level of the highest tides, which indicates crustal uplifting of comparable magnitude. Other regions exhibit evidence of extensive subsidence. In ad-

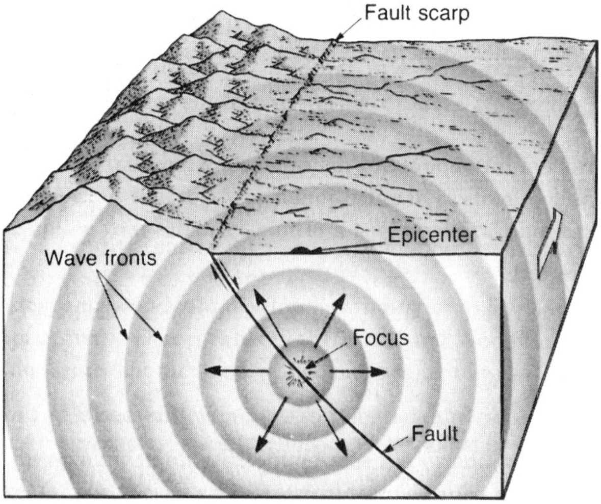

FIGURE 1. The focus of every earthquake is located at depth. The surface location directly above it is called the epicenter.

dition to these vertical displacements, offsets in fence lines, roads, and other structures indicate that horizontal movement is also prevalent. These movements are frequently associated with large fractures in the earth called faults. Most of the motion along faults can be satisfactorily explained by the plate tectonics theory. This theory proposes that large slabs of the earth are continually in motion. These mobile plates interact with neighboring plates, straining and deforming the rocks at their edges. It is along these plate boundaries that most earthquakes occur.

The actual mechanism of earthquake generation eluded geologists until H. F. Reid conducted a study following the great 1906 San Francisco earthquake. The earthquake was accompanied by displacements of several meters along the northern portion of the San Andreas fault, a 1,000-kilometer (600-mile) fracture which runs northward through southern California. Using land surveys conducted several years apart, Reid discovered that during the fifty years prior to the 1906 earthquake the land at distant points on both sides of the San Andreas fault showed a relative displacement of slightly more than 3 meters (10 feet). The mechanism for earthquake formation which Reid deduced from this information is illustrated in Figure 2. Tectonic forces ever so slowly deform the crustal rocks on both sides of the fault as illustrated by the bent features. Under these conditions, rocks are bending and storing elastic energy, much like a wooden stick would if bent. Eventually, the frictional resistance holding the rocks together is overcome. As slippage occurs at the weakest point (the focus), displacement will exert stress farther along the fault where additional slippage will occur until most of the built-up strain is released. This slippage allows the deformed rock to "snap back." The vibrations we know as an earthquake occur as the rock elastically returns to its original shape. The "springing back" of the rock was termed elastic rebound by Reid, since the rock behaves elastically, much like a stretched rubber band does when it is released.

The intense vibrations of the 1906 San Francisco earthquake lasted about forty seconds. Although most of the displacement along the fracture occurred in this rather short period, additional movements and adjustments in the rocks occurred for several days following the main quake. The adjustments that follow a major earthquake often generate smaller earthquakes called *aftershocks.* Although these aftershocks are usually much weaker than the main earthquake, they can sometimes cause significant destruction to already badly weakened structures. This occurred, for example, during the 1988 Armenian earthquake, when a large aftershock of magnitude 5.8 collapsed many structures that had been weakened by the main tremor. In addition, small earthquakes called *foreshocks* often precede a major earthquake by days or in some cases by as much as several years. Monitoring of these foreshocks has been used as a means of predicting forthcoming major earthquakes. . . .

The tectonic forces responsible for the strain that was eventually released during the 1906 San Francisco earthquake are still active. Currently laser beams[1] are used to establish the relative motion between the opposite sides of this fault. These measurements have revealed a displacement of 2 centimeters per year. Although this rate of movement seems slow, it is fast enough to produce substantial movement over millions of years of geologic time. In 30 million years such a rate of displacement is sufficient to slide the western portion of California northward so that Los Angeles would be adjacent to San

[1]Laser beams are used in very precise surveying instruments because of their incredibly accurate straight-line qualities.

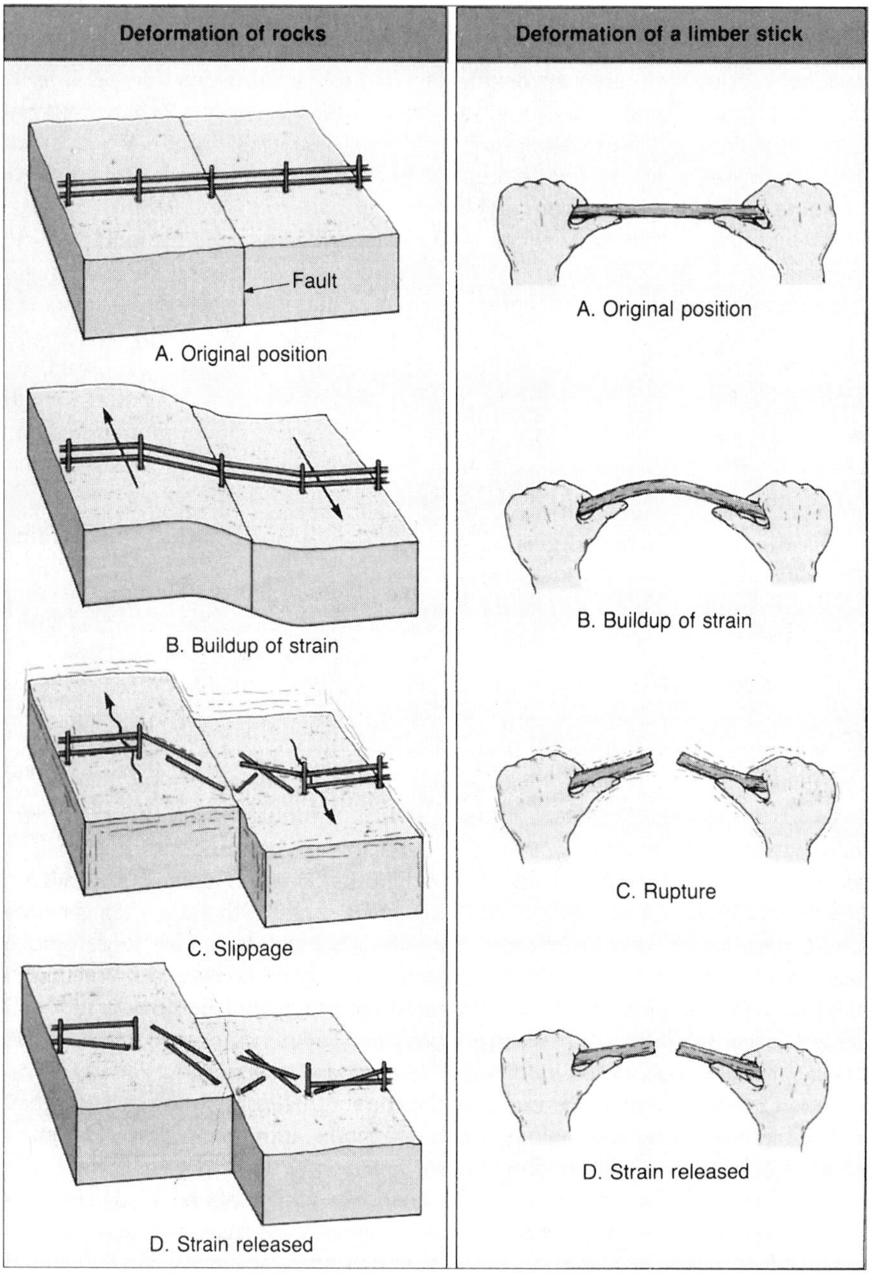

FIGURE 2. Elastic rebound. As rock is deformed it bends, storing elastic energy. Once the rock is strained beyond its breaking point it ruptures, releasing the stored-up energy in the form of earthquake waves.

Francisco. Thus, the processes that generate earthquakes are repetitive. That is, as soon as one earthquake is over, the continuing motion of the plates begins to add strain to the rocks until they fail again. It is estimated that great earthquakes occur about every 50 to 200 years along plate boundaries such as the San Andreas fault. This repetitive process is often described as *stick-slip motion,* since elastic energy is stored over a period of time and then released through slippage.

Not all motion along the San Andreas fault is of the stick-slip type. Along certain portions of this fault the motion is a slow *creep.* Thus, while some sections of the fault are continuously creeping, other "locked" segments are building up strain that could result in a major earthquake.

In addition, not all movement along faults is horizontal. Vertical displacement along faults, in which one side is lifted higher than the other, is also common. . . . In the same manner, the 1964 Good Friday earthquake in Alaska produced a 15-meter vertical offset at one location. Further, many earthquakes occur at such great depths that no displacement is evident at the surface.

EARTHQUAKE WAVES

The study of earthquake waves, seismology, dates back to attempts by the Chinese almost 2,000 years ago to determine the direction to the source of each earthquake. The principle used in modern seismographs, instruments which record earthquake waves, is rather simple. A weight is freely suspended from a support that is attached to bedrock. . . . When waves from a distant earthquake reach the instrument, the inertia[2] of the weight keeps it stationary, while the earth and the support vibrate. The movement of the earth in relation to the stationary weight is recorded on a rotating drum.

Modern seismographs amplify and record ground motion, producing a trace as shown in Figure 3. These records, called seismograms, provide a great deal of information about the behavior of seismic waves. Simply stated, seismic waves are elastic energy which radiates outward in all directions from the focus. The propagation (transmission) of this energy can be compared to the shaking of gelatin in a bowl which results as some is spooned out. Whereas the gelatin will have one mode of vibration, seismograms reveal that two main groups of seismic waves are generated by the slippage of a rock mass. One of these wave types travels along the outer layer of the earth. These are called *surface waves.* Others travel through the earth's interior and are called *body waves.* Body waves are further divided into two types called *primary,* or *P, waves* and *secondary,* or *S, waves.*

Body waves are divided on the basis of their mode of propagation through intervening materials. P waves push (compress) and pull (dilate) rocks in the direction the wave is traveling (Figure 4A). This wave motion is analogous to that generated by human vocal cords as they move air to create sound. Solids, liquids, and gases resist a change in volume when compressed and will elastically spring back once the force is removed. Therefore, P waves, which are compressional waves, can travel through all these

[2]Simply stated, inertia refers to the fact that objects at rest tend to stay at rest and objects in motion tend to remain in motion unless acted upon by an outside force. You probably have experienced this phenomenon when you tried to quickly stop your automobile and your body continued to move forward.

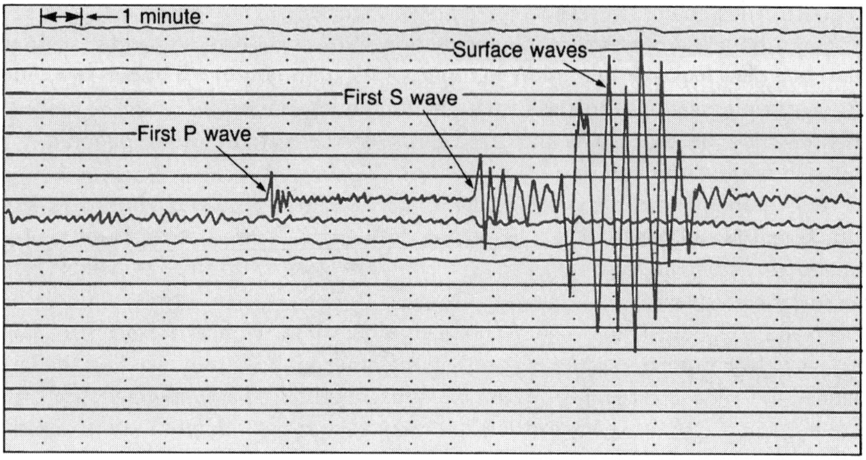

FIGURE 3.

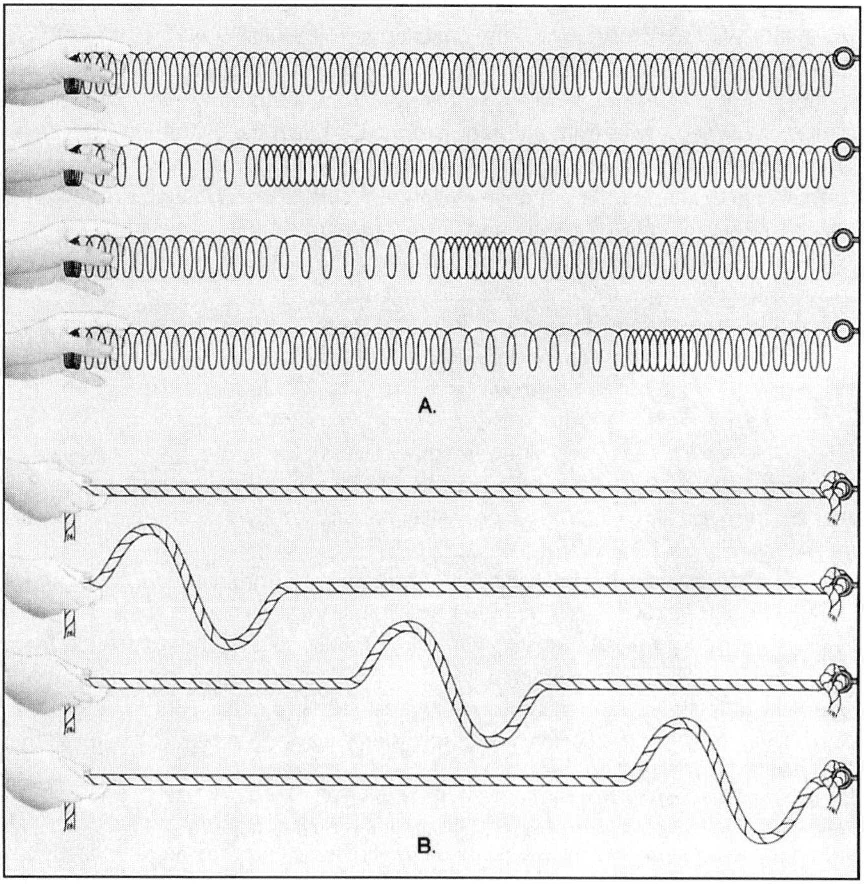

FIGURE 4.

materials. S waves, on the other hand, "shake" the particles at right angles to their direction of travel. This can be illustrated by tying one end of a rope to a post and shaking the other end as shown in Figure 4B. Unlike P waves, which change the volume of the intervening material, S waves change only the shape of the material that transmits them. Since fluids (gases and liquids) do not resist changes in shape, they will not transmit S waves.

The motion of surface waves is somewhat more complex. As surface waves travel along the ground, they cause the ground and anything resting upon it to move, much like ocean swells toss a ship. In addition to their up-and-down motion, surface waves have a side-to-side motion similar to an S wave oriented in a horizontal plane. This latter motion causes most of the structural damage to buildings and their foundations.

By observing a "typical" seismic record, as shown in Figure 3, one of the differences between these seismic waves becomes apparent: P waves arrive at the recording station before S waves, which themselves arrive before the surface waves. This is a consequence of their relative velocities. For purposes of illustration, the velocity of P waves through granite within the crust is about 6 kilometers per second, whereas S waves under the same conditions travel at 3.5 kilometers per second. Differences in density and elastic properties of the transmitting material greatly influence the velocities of these waves. However, in any solid material, P waves travel about 1.7 times faster than S waves, and surface waves can be expected to travel at 90 percent of the velocity of the S waves.

As we shall see, seismic waves allow us to determine the location and magnitude of earthquakes. In addition, seismic waves provide us with a tool for probing the earth's interior. . . .

EARTHQUAKE INTENSITY AND MAGNITUDE

Early attempts to establish the size or strength of earthquakes relied heavily on subjective descriptions. There was an obvious problem with this method — people's accounts varied widely, making an accurate classification of the quake's intensity difficult. Then in 1902 a fairly reliable intensity scale based on the amount of damage caused to various types of structures was developed by Giuseppe Mercalli. . . .

By definition, earthquake intensity is a measure of the effects of a quake at a particular locale. It is important to note that earthquake intensity depends not only on the strength of the earthquake, but on other factors as well. These include the distance from the epicenter, the nature of the surface materials, and building design. Recall that the modest 6.9-Richter-magnitude Armenian earthquake of 1988 was very destructive mainly because of inferior construction practices. Moreover, the nature of the surface materials contributed significantly to the destruction in central Mexico City during the 1985 quake. Thus, the destruction wrought by earthquakes is not always an adequate means for comparing their relative size. Furthermore, many earthquakes occur in

---

FIGURE 3. Typical seismic record. Note the time interval between the arrival of the first P wave and the arrival of the first S wave.

FIGURE 4. Types of seismic waves and their characteristic motion. (A) P waves cause the particles in the material to vibrate back and forth in the same direction as the waves move. (B) S waves cause particles to oscillate at right angles to the direction of wave motion.

oceanic areas or at great focal depths and either are not felt or their intensities do not reflect their true strength.

In 1935, Charles Richter of the California Institute of Technology introduced the concept of earthquake magnitude when attempting to rank earthquakes of southern California. Today a refined *Richter scale* is used worldwide to describe earthquake magnitude. Using Richter's scale, the magnitude is determined by measuring the amplitude of the largest wave recorded on the seismogram (see Figure 3). Although seismographs greatly magnify the ground motion, large-magnitude earthquakes will cause the recording pen to be displaced farther than small-magnitude earthquakes. In order for seismic stations worldwide to obtain the same magnitude for a given earthquake, adjustments must be made for the weakening of seismic waves as they move from the focus and for the sensitivity of the recording instrument.

The largest earthquakes ever recorded have Richter magnitudes near 8.6. These great shocks released energy roughly equivalent to the detonation of one billion tons of TNT. Conversely, earthquakes with a Richter magnitude of less than 2.5 are usually not felt by humans. Table 1 shows how earthquake magnitudes and their effects are related.

As we have seen, earthquakes vary enormously in strength. Furthermore, great earthquakes produce traces having wave amplitudes that are thousands of times larger than those generated by weak tremors. To accommodate this wide variation, Richter used a logarithmic scale to express magnitude. On this scale a tenfold increase in recorded wave amplitude corresponds to an increase of one on the magnitude scale. Thus, the amplitude of the largest surface wave for a 5-magnitude earthquake is ten times greater than the wave amplitude produced by an earthquake having a magnitude of 4. More importantly, each unit of magnitude increase on the Richter scale equates to roughly a thirtyfold increase in the energy released. Thus, an earthquake with a magnitude of 6.5 releases thirty times more energy than one with a magnitude of 5.5 and roughly 900 times (30×30) more energy than a 4.5-magnitude quake. A major earthquake with a magnitude of 8.5 releases millions of times more energy than the smallest earthquakes felt by humans. This dispels the notion that a moderate earthquake decreases the chances for the occurrence of a major quake in the same region. Thousands of moderate tremors would be needed to release the amount of energy released by one "great" earthquake. . . .

TABLE 1. Earthquake Magnitudes and Expected World Incidence

Richter Magnitudes	Earthquake Effects	Estimated Number per Year
<2.0	Generally not felt, but recorded.	600,000
2.0–2.9	Potentially perceptible.	300,000
3.0–3.9	Felt by some.	49,000
4.0–4.9	Felt by most.	6,200
5.0–5.9	Damaging shocks.	800
6.0–6.9	Destructive in populous regions.	266
7.0–7.9	Major earthquakes. Inflict serious damage.	18
≥8.0	Great earthquakes. Produce total destruction to communities near epicenter.	1.4

Source: Earthquake Information Bulletin and others.

EARTHQUAKE DESTRUCTION

The most violent earthquake to jar North America this century — the Good Friday Alaskan Earthquake — occurred at 5:36 PM on March 27, 1964. Felt throughout that state, the earthquake had a magnitude of 8.3–8.4 on the Richter scale and reportedly lasted three to four minutes. This brief event left 131 persons dead, thousands homeless, and the economy of the state badly disrupted. Had the schools and business districts been open, the toll surely would have been higher. Within twenty-four hours of the initial shock, twenty-eight aftershocks were recorded, ten of which exceeded a magnitude of 6 on the Richter scale.

Many factors determine the amount of destruction that accompanies an earthquake. The most obvious of these are the magnitude of the earthquake and the proximity of the quake to a populated area. Fortunately, most earthquakes are small and occur in remote regions of the earth. However, about twenty major earthquakes are reported annually, one or two of which are catastrophic.

Destruction Caused by Seismic Vibrations. The 1964 Alaskan earthquake provided geologists with new insights into the role of ground shaking as a destructive force. As the energy released by an earthquake travels along the earth's surface, it causes the ground to vibrate in a complex manner by moving up and down as well as from side to side. The amount of structural damage attributable to the vibrations depends on several factors, including (1) the intensity and duration of the vibrations; (2) the nature of the material upon which the structure rests; and (3) the design of the structure.

All of the multistory structures in Anchorage were damaged by the vibrations; the more flexible wood-frame residential buildings fared best. However, many homes were destroyed when the ground failed. . . .

Poor construction practices were blamed for the deaths of an estimated 25,000 persons in the 1988 earthquake that jolted Soviet Armenia. To quote a seismologist who was asked about this destructive event, "Earthquakes don't kill people, buildings do." Many of the taller structures in the region were made of precast concrete slabs that were held together by metal hooks. A San Francisco structural engineer studying the destruction stated, "There was very little reinforcing to tie these buildings together. The buildings basically came apart the way they were put together." In addition, many of the village homes had thick roofs made of mud and rock, which were deadly when they collapsed. Nearly the entire town of Spitak, which was located adjacent to the fault break, was leveled. Not far away, in northwestern Iran, poor building construction was also responsible for a large share of the approximately 50,000 deaths that resulted from an earthquake in June 1990. The earthquake had a Richter magnitude of at least 7.3. When it struck, thousands of mud, brick, and concrete buildings were reduced to rubble. In addition to the large death toll, an estimated one-half million people were left homeless.

Most of the large structures in Anchorage were damaged even though they were built to conform to the earthquake provisions of the Uniform Building Code of California. Perhaps some of that destruction can be attributed to the unusually long duration of this earthquake, which was estimated at three to four minutes. Most earthquakes consist of tremors that last less than one minute. For example, the San Francisco earthquake of 1906 was felt for about forty seconds, whereas the strong vibrations of the 1989 Loma Prieta earthquake lasted less than fifteen seconds.

Although the region within 20 to 50 kilometers of an epicenter will experience about the same degree of ground shaking, the destruction will vary considerably within this area. This difference is mainly attributable to the nature of the ground on which the structures are built. Soft sediments, for example, generally amplify the vibration more than solid bedrock. Thus, the buildings in Anchorage, which were situated on unconsolidated sediments, experienced heavy structural damage. By contrast, most of the town of Whittier, although located much nearer to the epicenter than Anchorage, rests on a firm foundation of granite and hence suffered much less damage from the seismic vibrations. However, Whittier was damaged by a seismic sea wave.

The 1985 Mexican earthquake gave seismologists and engineers a vivid reminder of what had been learned following the 1964 Alaskan earthquake. The Pacific coast of Mexico, where the earthquake was centered, experienced unusually mild tremors despite the strength of the quake. As expected, the seismic waves became progressively weaker with increasing distance from the epicenter. However, in the central section of Mexico City, nearly 400 kilometers (250 miles) from the source, the vibrations intensified to five times that experienced in outlying districts. Much of this amplified ground motion can be attributed to soft sediments, remnants of an ancient lake bed, that underlie portions of the city.

To understand what happened in Mexico City, recall that as seismic waves pass through the earth they cause the intervening material to vibrate much as a tuning fork vibrates when struck. Although most objects can be forced to vibrate over a wide range of frequencies, each has a natural period of vibration that is preferred. Various earth materials, like different-length tuning forks, also have different natural periods of vibration.[3]

Ground motion is amplified when the natural period of ground vibration matches that of the seismic waves. A common example of this phenomenon occurs when a parent pushes a child on a swing. As the parent periodically pushes the child in rhythm with the frequency of the swing, the child moves back and forth in a greater and greater arc. By chance, the column of sediment beneath Mexico City had a natural period of vibration of about two seconds, matching that of the strongest seismic waves. Thus, when the seismic waves began shaking the soft sediments, a resonance developed which greatly increased the amplitude of the vibrations. This amplified motion began throwing the ground back and forth about 40 centimeters (16 inches) every two seconds for a period of nearly two minutes. Such shaking was too intense for many of the poorly designed buildings in the city. In addition, buildings of intermediate height (five to fifteen stories) swayed back and forth within a period of about two seconds. Thus, resonance also developed between these buildings and the ground, and most of the building failures were in this height range. . . .

In areas where unconsolidated materials are saturated with water, earthquakes can generate a phenomenon known as liquefaction. Under these conditions, what had been a stable soil turns into a fluid that is not capable of supporting buildings or other structures. . . . As a result, underground objects such as storage tanks and sewer lines may literally float toward the surface, while buildings and other structures may settle and col-

[3]To demonstrate the natural period of vibration of an object, hold a ruler over the edge of a desk so that most of it is not supported by the desk. Start it vibrating and notice the sound it makes. By changing the length of the unsupported portion of the ruler, the natural period of vibration will change accordingly, as reflected by the change in sound.

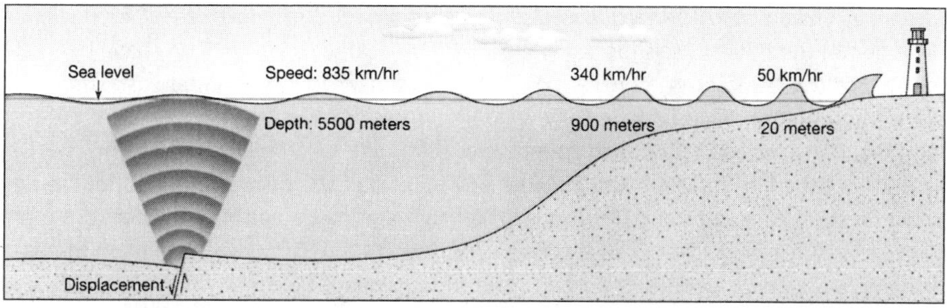

FIGURE 5. Schematic drawing of a tsunami generated by displacement of the ocean floor. The speed of a wave column correlates with ocean depth. As shown, waves moving in deep water advance at speeds in excess of 800 kilometers per hour. Speed gradually slows to 50 kilometers per hour at depths of 20 meters. Decreasing depth slows the movement of the wave column. As waves slow in shallow water, they grow in height until they topple and rush onto shore with tremendous force. The size and spacing of these swells are not to scale.

lapse. In San Francisco's Marina District, foundations failed and geysers of sand and water shot from the ground, indicating that liquefaction occurred during the Loma Prieta earthquake of 1989.

Tsunami. Most deaths associated with the 1964 Alaskan quake were caused by seismic sea waves, or tsunamis.[4] These destructive waves have popularly been called "tidal waves." However, this name is not accurate since these waves are not generated by the tidal effect of the moon or sun.

Most tsunamis result from vertical displacement of the ocean floor during an earthquake as illustrated in Figure 5. Once formed, a tsunami resembles the ripples formed when a pebble is dropped into a pond. In contrast to ripples, tsunamis advance at speeds between 500 and 950 kilometers (300 and 600 miles) per hour. Despite this striking characteristic, a tsunami in the open ocean can pass undetected because its height is usually less than one meter and the distance between wave crests ranges from 100 to 700 kilometers. However, upon entering shallower coastal waters, these destructive waves are slowed and the water begins to pile up to heights that occasionally exceed 30 meters (100 feet). As the crest of a tsunami approaches shore, it appears as a rapid rise in sea level with a turbulent and chaotic surface.

Usually the first warning of an approaching tsunami is a rather rapid withdrawal of water from beaches. Residents of coastal areas have learned to heed this warning and move to higher ground. About five to thirty minutes later the retreat of water is followed by a surge capable of extending hundreds of meters inland. In a successive fashion, each surge is followed by rapid oceanward retreat of the water. These waves, separated by intervals of between ten and sixty minutes, are able to traverse large stretches of the ocean before their energy is totally dissipated.

The tsunami generated in the 1964 Alaskan earthquake inflicted heavy damage to communities in the vicinity of the Gulf of Alaska, completely destroying the town of

[4]Seismic sea waves were given the name *tsunami* by the Japanese, who have suffered a great deal from them. The term *tsunami* is now used worldwide.

Chenega. The town of Seward was also heavily damaged as most of its port facilities were demolished by this seismic sea wave . . . . The deaths of 107 persons have been attributed to this tsunami. By contrast, only nine persons died in Anchorage as a direct result of the vibrations. Tsunami damage following the Alaskan earthquake extended along much of the west coast of North America, and in spite of a one-hour warning, twelve persons perished in Crescent City, California, where all of the deaths and most of the destruction were caused by the fifth wave. The first wave crested about 4 meters (13 feet) above low tide and was followed by three progressively smaller waves. Believing that the tsunami had ceased, people returned to the shore, only to be met by the fifth and most devastating wave, which, superimposed upon high tide, crested about 6 meters higher than the level of low tide.

Fire. Fire caused only minor damage during the 1989 Loma Prieta earthquake, but often it is the most destructive force. The 1906 earthquake centered near the city of San Francisco reminds us of the formidable threat of fire. The central city contained mostly large, older wooden structures and brick buildings. Although many of the unreinforced brick buildings were extensively damaged, the greatest destruction was caused by fires which started when gas and electrical lines were severed. The fires raged out of control for three days and devastated over 500 blocks of the city. . . . The problem was compounded by the initial ground shaking which broke the city's water lines into hundreds of unconnected pieces.

The fire was finally contained when buildings were dynamited along a wide boulevard to provide a fire break. Although only a few deaths were attributed to the fires, that is not always the case. An earthquake which rocked Japan in 1923 triggered an estimated 250 fires, which devastated the city of Yokohama and destroyed more than half the homes in Tokyo. Over 100,000 deaths were attributed to the fires, which were driven by unusually high winds.

Landslides and Ground Subsidence. In the 1964 Alaskan earthquake, it was not ground vibrations directly, but landslides and ground subsidence triggered by the vibrations that caused the greatest damage to structures. At Valdez and Seward the violent shaking caused deltaic materials to liquefy; the subsequent slumping carried both waterfronts away. Because of the threat of recurrence, the entire town of Valdez was relocated about 7 kilometers away in a region of stable ground. The destruction at Valdez was compounded by the tragic loss of thirty-one lives. While waiting for an incoming vessel, the thirty-one persons died when the dock slid into the sea.

Most of the damage in Anchorage was attributed to landslides caused by the shaking and lurching ground. Many homes were destroyed in Turnagain Heights when a layer of clay lost its strength and over 200 acres of land slid toward the ocean. A portion of this landslide was left in its natural condition as a reminder of this destructive event. The site was named "Earthquake Park." Downtown Anchorage was also disrupted as sections of the main business district dropped by as much as 3 meters (10 feet).

Landslides were also a significant factor in the June 1990 Iranian earthquake. Although building failures were responsible for the loss of many lives, rockslides and rock avalanches also caused much death and destruction. Entire hillside villages in this mountainous region slid downslope or were buried. Equally significant were the transportation difficulties that resulted because roads were blocked by landslide debris. Many who might have been helped did not survive because rescue teams and equipment could not reach isolated villages.

Readings: Crime Stories: Constructing Guilt and Innocence

The readings in this section offer opportunities to think further about serializing in the context of issues of crime and the law, the topic woven through this chapter. If you would like to look back at some of the chapter's earlier readings and assignments touching upon this topic, see Jim Fisher's account of the Lindbergh kidnapping (Opening Problem, p. 171), the excerpt from Patricia J. Williams's *The Alchemy of Race and Rights* (A Professional Application, p. 186), the Criminal Studies Assignment (p. 191), and the History Assignment (p. 201).

The following readings examine cases in which serializing plays a role in constructing versions of guilt or innocence. You may read them singly or in combination. Even as a group, however, the readings are not intended to cover thoroughly the legal issues examined but only to introduce a few areas in a complex social territory. To contribute to — and to challenge — your work with serializing, we have chosen a range of readings in which a central concern is the sequencing of events, or attempts to establish one sequence rather than another, or the very act of sequencing itself: analyses of particular trials, a firsthand account of the famous Watergate investigation, an illustration of the complexities of environmental law, a scholarly discussion of the role of storytelling in the courtroom.

In a profile of filmmaker Errol Morris, journalist Mark Singer describes the contested events in a Texas murder case that became the basis of the film *The Thin Blue Line.* Next comes an excerpt from *All the President's Men,* the account by reporters Carl Bernstein and Bob Woodward of the unfolding of the Watergate burglary and cover-up by the Nixon administration. In "Woburn, Science, and the Law," Renee Loth introduces some of the complexities of environmental litigation by which lawyers must attempt to link, or refute the linkage, of several cases of childhood leukemia. Next, journalism professor Helen Benedict analyzes dramatic differences in the coverage of a much-publicized rape trial in an excerpt from her book *Virgin or Vamp: How the Press Covers Sex Crimes.* Finally, in an excerpt from *Reconstructing Reality in the Courtroom: Justice and Judgment in American Culture,* legal scholars W. Lance Bennett and Martha S. Feldman offer an assessment of the crucial role played in complex trials by serial narratives.

At the end of each reading, you will find Considerations questions intended to help you think about the reading mostly on its own terms but also in relation to the serializing strategies stressed in this chapter. At the end of the section you will also find suggestions for writing about these readings in relation to one another and for pursuing through further research the topic of serial constructions and the law.

The following is taken from a profile of filmmaker Errol Morris, whose research for his film The Thin Blue Line *played a significant role in the retrial and acquittal of a man unjustly convicted of murder. Morris (who also directed* A Brief History of Time, Dark Wind, *and* Vernon, Florida*) was in the early stages of researching another project connected with capital crime in the state of Texas when he began interviewing death-row inmates. Although it was not uncommon for the men he interviewed to profess their innocence, one man, thirty-six-year-old Randall Dale Adams, caught Morris's attention. The excerpt begins there and provides an account of the crime Adams was accused of committing — the murder of a Dallas policeman — the subsequent trial and conviction of Adams, and the events leading to Adams's appeal and eventual acquittal. Notice how Singer carefully builds his story of the murder case, leading up to his final, compressed presentation of the judge's findings during Adams's appeal.*

Profile of Filmmaker Errol Morris

Mark Singer

A thirty-six-year-old . . . Randall Dale Adams . . . was an inmate of the Eastham Unit, a maximum-security prison in southeast Texas. In the spring of 1977, Adams had been convicted of and sentenced to die for the murder, the previous fall, of Robert Wood, a Dallas police officer. Wood had been shot five times by the driver of a car that he and his partner, Teresa Turko, had stopped in west Dallas for a minor traffic violation. Nearly a month elapsed between the murder of Wood and Adams's arrest. Adams told [Errol] Morris that he had been framed, and that the actual killer was David Harris — "the kid," he kept calling him during that first conversation — who had been the principal prosecution witness at Adams's trial. . . . [Morris] didn't really believe the story Adams told him, because he had no particular reason to believe it. Nevertheless, he went to Austin three weeks later and read the transcripts of several trials. A number of passages in the Adams transcript aroused the possibility that Adams was telling the truth. After Morris met David Harris, two weeks later, in a bar outside Beaumont, his doubts about Adams's guilt and his curiosity about the case deepened. . . .

As a "director-detective" — a phrase Morris used to describe himself when he was promoting *The Thin Blue Line* — not the least of his accomplishments was cultivating Henry Wade, for thirty-six years the District Attorney of Dallas County. Instead of handling the Adams prosecution himself, Wade assigned it to Douglas Mulder, one of

---

A staff writer for *The New Yorker,* Mark Singer (b. 1950) is also the author of *Funny Money* (1985) and *Mr. Personality* (1989) and co-author, with Gary Fisketjon and Sonny Mehta, of *Citizen K: The Deeply Weird American Journey of Brett Kimberlin* (1996). This excerpt from his profile of filmmaker Errol Morris appeared in *The New Yorker* on February 6, 1989.

his most experienced assistants. After gaining access to the files in Wade's office, Morris became convinced that Mulder had seriously tampered with the truth and that Adams had received anything but a fair trial.

Randall Adams and David Harris met by chance the morning before Officer Wood was killed. Adams had run out of gas and was walking along a road in west Dallas when Harris, a sixteen-year-old with an extensive criminal record, driving a car that he had stolen in his home town of Vidor, Texas, pulled over and offered to help him refill the tank. They spent the rest of the day, a Saturday, together — bumming around a shopping mall, drinking beer, visiting pawnshops, shooting pool, smoking marijuana. That evening, they ended up at a drive-in theatre that featured two soft-core porn movies. Officer Wood was shot at 12:30 Sunday morning — almost three hours after Harris, according to Adams's testimony, had dropped him off at the motel where he was living. That became Adams's alibi: He was home asleep when the crime was committed.

Teresa Turko proved to be a poor eyewitness to the slaying of her patrol partner, and gave an inaccurate description of the car that the killer had been driving. The first break in the case came because David Harris, back in Vidor, told several friends that he had killed a policeman in Dallas. After being arrested and leading the Vidor police to the murder weapon, a .22-caliber handgun that belonged to his father, Harris was turned over to the Dallas police. At this point, he changed his story and said that he had only been bragging — that the real killer was a hitchhiker he had picked up and spent the day with. Which is how Adams, who had no prior criminal record, came to be charged with murder.

Initially, Adams was represented by Edith James, a lawyer whose criminal-trial experience included no homicide-defense work. She brought in as co-counsel a general practitioner named Dennis White. In one of White's previous head-to-heads with Doug Mulder, things had ended badly for his clients — two brothers named Ransonette who had made the mistake of kidnapping the daughter-in-law of a Dallas newspaper publisher. At the sentencing hearing in that case, White argued that the victim had not been harmed by her captors, and suggested a lenient prison term of five years. The prosecution mentioned a term of 5,000 years. The jury, aspiring to Solomonic wisdom, said, in effect, "Okay. Let's compromise," and sentenced each defendant to 5,005 years. Dennis White was simply no match for Doug Mulder, who is said to have once boasted, "Anybody can convict a guilty man. It takes talent to convict an innocent man."

Testifying during Adams's trial, David Harris offered a chronology of the events surrounding the murder that varied from Adams's version by approximately two and a half hours. Adams and Harris agreed that they had left the drive-in theatre during a movie called *Swinging Cheerleaders.* Mulder elicited from Harris testimony that their departure had occurred shortly after midnight; Adams said they left around 9:30. In the D.A.'s files, Morris discovered a memorandum from Mulder's own chief investigator stating that there had been no late showing of *Swinging Cheerleaders* that night and that the final feature had ended shortly after 10:00.

This was the sort of serious defect in Harris's version of the facts that Mulder apparently had no intention of allowing to interfere with his prosecution of Adams — who, at twenty-eight, was eligible for capital punishment, whereas Harris, at sixteen, was not. It was also, unfortunately, the sort of discrepancy that Adams's attorneys failed to make clear to the jury. Nor were Edith James and Dennis White prepared when Mulder produced three mysterious witnesses, all of whom testified that they had driven past the scene of the crime moments before Officer Wood was murdered and that Randall Adams was in the driver's seat — the position from which the shots were fired. The three witnesses, Emily Miller, Robert Miller, and Michael Randell, all of whom were aware of a five-figure reward for information leading to the conviction of the killer, appeared in court on a Friday and impressed the jury. White, outmaneuvered by Mulder's strategy of presenting his "eyewitnesses" during the rebuttal phase rather than as part of his case-in-chief, conducted an ineffectual cross-examination. That weekend, White received a call from a woman named Elba Carr, who knew Emily and Robert Miller and expressed the opinion that "Emily Miller had never told the truth in her life." When, back in court the following Monday, White asked to question the Millers and Michael Randell further, Mulder told the judge that all three had left town or were otherwise unreachable. Actually, all three witnesses were still in Dallas. The Millers, in fact, were ensconced in the Alamo Plaza Motel as guests of Dallas County. Not until nine years later, when Morris came along and found in the District Attorney's files bills for phone calls that the Millers had made from the Alamo Plaza, did Mulder's role in this apparent deception become evident.

Toward the end of *The Thin Blue Line,* Errol Morris asks David Harris, "Would you say that Adams is a pretty unlucky fellow?" and Harris responds, "Definitely — if it wasn't for bad luck, he wouldn't have had none." Ironically, of course, Harris's reply is accurate only up to the moment when Morris met Adams. Not only did Morris discover important evidence in the prosecution's file; he discovered the absence of some important documents — specifically, the official record of a police lineup at which, according to Emily Miller's trial testimony, she had positively identified Randall Adams. Most significantly, Morris tracked down the three rebuttal witnesses themselves and persuaded them to appear on film. Emily Miller, a bleached blonde, whose childhood ambition was to be a detective or the wife of a detective, told Morris that she had failed to identify Adams in the lineup but that a policeman had told her the correct suspect, "so that I wouldn't make that mistake again." Robert Miller told him, "I really didn't see anything." Michael Randell, who had testified in 1977 that he was on his way home from playing basketball when he drove past the murder scene, told Morris that in fact he had spent that evening in an adulterous endeavor and that he was drunk "out of my mind." Each of the state's rebuttal witnesses, it therefore appeared, had committed damaging perjury. Putting David Harris on film posed a significant challenge. The first interview appointment, Morris says, Harris missed "because he was off killing somebody" — Mark Walter Mays, a Beaumont citizen, whose apartment Harris had broken into, and whose girlfriend he had abducted. Another interview had to be postponed when Harris tried to use Morris in an escape attempt from the jail where he was awaiting trial for these crimes. The climactic interview finally took place in the Lou Sterret Jail, in Dallas, by which time Harris had been convicted and sentenced to death for the Mays murder, and it included this exchange:

> *Morris:* Is he [Adams] innocent?
>
> *Harris:* Did you ask him?
>
> *Morris:* Well, he's always said he's been innocent.
>
> *Harris:* There you go. Didn't believe him, huh? Criminals always lie.
>
> *Morris:* Well, what do you think about whether or not he's innocent?
>
> *Harris:* I'm sure he is.
>
> *Morris:* How can you be sure?
>
> *Harris:* Because I'm the one that knows. . . .

Officer Robert Wood was murdered Thanksgiving weekend in 1976. Twelve years later almost to the day, Adams and his attorneys returned to the room where he had been convicted of the murder and handed a death sentence — Criminal District Court No. 2, on the fourth floor of the Dallas County Courthouse. By Texas statute, the judge who presides at a trial — in this instance, District Judge Don Metcalfe, whose evidentiary rulings against Adams formed part of the basis for the writ — also presides at any subsequent appellate-writ hearing. Adams's bad luck, while consistent, was not absolute, however, and Metcalfe had since left the bench. In 1984, he was succeeded by Larry W. Baraka, a respected former prosecutor and defense attorney, whose special distinction is that he is the only member of the Texas judiciary who is black, a Muslim, and a Republican. . . .

Testifying for three hours [at the writ hearing], Harris said that he had been alone in a stolen car and in possession of a stolen gun when Wood pulled him over. In a videotaped interview that was introduced as evidence, he said that he had had his finger on the trigger as Wood approached him. Judge Baraka, no quibbler, announced, "As far as the court is concerned, he's in fact telling me he did it." [Adams's appellate lawyer] Randy Schaffer read aloud a letter from Harris to his mother, written in September 1988 — just two months earlier — that said, "It seems like my whole life is surrounded by 'wrongs' of some kind and it seems like I've never done the right thing when I could and should have. Absolving Randall Dale Adams of any guilt is a difficult thing for me to do, but I must try to do so because he is innocent. That is the truth."

Next, Schaffer called Teresa Turko, Robert Wood's patrol partner, as a witness. He wanted to make plain to the judge that Turko's initial description of the killer, recorded immediately after the shooting, differed measurably from the one she had offered at Adams's trial. Dennis White had not cross-examined Turko about the first statement, because, in violation of a cardinal principle of criminal-trial procedure, Mulder had not given him a copy. Nor would the document have come to light, of course, if Morris had not insinuated himself into the Dallas District Attorney's good graces and scrutinized Mulder's old files. . . .

The drama of Harris's confession notwithstanding, it did not, in a technical sense, really help Adams. In Texas, evidence of innocence is insufficient to win a new trial. What Schaffer had to prove was that Adams's original trial had been "unfair" on constitutional grounds. Even if Baraka were to grant Adams's writ, his ruling would have the effect only of a recommendation to the Texas Court of Criminal Appeals, a nine-judge panel, which in 1977 had unanimously upheld Adams's conviction. Harris's testimony was useful, however, in bolstering some of the other claims in the writ — most significantly, that Harris and Mulder had an understanding in 1977 whereby in exchange for testimony against Adams unresolved criminal charges against Harris in another county would be dropped. (Under cross-examination at the original trial, Harris had insisted that no quid pro quo existed — an avowal that Mulder has always maintained. Further harm to Adams was done when Judge Metcalfe refused even to allow into evidence the fact that Harris had such charges pending.) . . .

The first witness on Day Two was Emily Miller. Randy Schaffer expected to score several points while she was on the stand: her failure to identify Adams in a lineup; the intervention of the Dallas policeman, who then pointed out to her the "right" suspect; her subsequent perjury regarding her performance at the lineup; and evidence that, like David Harris, she had struck an implicit deal with Mulder — specifically, her testimony against Adams in exchange for the dismissal of an outstanding robbery charge against her daughter.

A week after the murder of Robert Wood, at which time a $20,000 reward was being offered for information leading to the arrest and conviction of the killer, Emily Miller had given a formal statement to the Dallas police. According to what she saw while driving past the crime scene moments before the shooting, the suspect was "either a Mexican or a very light-skinned black man." That this description would divert suspicion from Adams, an auburn-haired Caucasian, perhaps explains why Mulder never showed the statement to Adams's attorneys. By the time of Adams's trial, Emily Miller's description of the killer had metamorphosed so that it matched the defendant. In Judge Baraka's courtroom, when Schaffer presented Emily Miller with a copy of her original statement she said that she had left her eyeglasses at home and couldn't read it. When Schaffer then read it to her and proceeded through a barbed interrogation, she said, "I don't remember nothing that happened back then. Specifics, I don't remember who asked me what or who said what or who did what. That was twelve years ago."

As far as the officer who had coached her at the police lineup was concerned, she said, "I didn't base nothing I said on anything anybody told me. It was what I seen. And I'm sorry I ever seen it."

"You're not the only one, I'm sure," Schaffer replied. . . .

The next morning, Doug Mulder gave a poised and self-assured courtroom performance. As Leslie McFarlane[1] lobbed him across-the-letters questions, Mulder, a handsome man in his late forties with a squarish face, not much of a neck, and a stocky, athletic build, effortlessly swatted them out of the ballpark.

McFarlane: "Everything that you discovered and everything that you reviewed in preparation for this case indicates Adams's guilt, is that correct? . . . Did you find anything inconsistent with that?"

Mulder: "Nothing that comes to mind, no."

Schaffer, when his turn arrived, proved somewhat less ingratiating. His gambit, for instance, went "Well, I guess today you've returned to the scene of one of your greatest triumphs." Leslie McFarlane objected to the argumentative tone, and the judge agreed with her, telling Schaffer, "That's not the way to start." From there on, Schaffer and Mulder duelled for more than an hour — until it was apparent that the judge had had enough and that Mulder was not going to throw up his hands and declare, "Okay, ya got me, my legal career's a shambles, I'm finished in this town." The judge's impatience with Schaffer belied the fact that he had already made up his mind on the basic question. After a masterly summation by Schaffer — sufficient in its eloquence for McFarlane, when her turn came, to apologize, accurately, that her closing argument would be notably devoid of eloquence — Baraka said he was ready with his decision.

Of the thirteen grounds for relief cited in Adams's writ, Baraka agreed on six: that Metcalfe, the original trial judge, had erroneously denied the admissibility of David Harris's prior criminal record; that Teresa Turko's initial statement describing the killer

[1]**Leslie McFarlane:** The appellate lawyer assigned to represent the Dallas County District Attorney [Eds.].

had been illegally suppressed; that, similarly, Emily Miller's initial statement describing the killer had been illegally suppressed; that evidence of Emily Miller's failure to identify Adams in the police lineup and subsequent coaching by a police officer had been suppressed; that Emily Miller had later committed perjury regarding her performance at the lineup; and that Adams had been denied effective assistance of counsel.

It seemed that, because Baraka had rejected seven of the contentions cited in the writ, a final observation he made was designed to eliminate any remaining ambiguity: "I think over all, when we look at this trial, all the nuances that are involved, I think there's no question that the defendant did not get a fair opportunity to a trial. I would not go so far as to say that the defendant is innocent of this. I would go so far as to say that if the defendant were to be retried, considering all the testimony elicited and what would be presented to the jury or a court, that more likely than not the defendant would be found not guilty."

Considerations

1. Write a serial account of the State of Texas's version of the events leading to the crime and the crime itself. Then critique that account with other information presented in the article and provide a more accurate account of the events.
2. If you attempted to write a serial account of the events surrounding the hypothetical murder case in the Criminal Studies Assignment (p. 191), compare your experiences constructing that account with your efforts to serialize Singer's story.
3. Errol Morris said, "Almost everything I do now in my work is about epistemic concerns: How do we come by certain kinds of knowledge." (*Epistemic* means having to do with knowledge or the act or ways of knowing.) Given what you now know about the Adams case, explain why it would interest Morris.
4. *The Thin Blue Line* was released in 1988 and can be found in many video stores. Now that you know about the background of the Adams case, view this film and consider the way Errol Morris uses the material he gathered. How, for example, does he use a serial strategy in the film? How does he get us to think about the time line of events in the case — who was where and what happened when?

The following excerpt comes from Washington Post *reporters Carl Bernstein and Bob Woodward's account of the Watergate burglary and its aftermath,* All the President's Men. *(Although Bernstein and Woodward are telling their own story, they write about themselves in the third person.) On June 17, 1972, during the presidential primary campaigns, five men were arrested for breaking into the offices of the Democratic National Committee. They were carrying photographic equipment and bugging devices. The break-in sparked a long and wide-ranging series of investigations — legal, legislative, and journalistic — that revealed a broad program of political spying and sabotage, resulting, finally, in the resignation of the President of the United States, Richard M. Nixon. The excerpt comes about one third of the way through* All the President's Men, *at the point at which the scope and seriousness of the Watergate burglary are widening and deepening. As we pick up the case, the Federal Bureau of Investigation (FBI) and the Justice Department have begun investigations, a grand jury has been impaneled, and reporters from various newspapers are also pursuing leads.*

As you read, consider the way the story unfolds — the sequence of events, encounters, and conversations — and your own reactions as you move through the narrative.

A number of politicians, political staffers, lawyers, and journalists are mentioned in this passage. Some are identified in context, and some are not that important to the story. We will identify the more important of them for you in footnotes.

From *All the President's Men*

CARL BERNSTEIN AND BOB WOODWARD

The night of September 28. . . .

The caller introduced himself as a government lawyer who had nothing to do with the Watergate investigation. He said he might have some information that might or might not have something to do with the things Bernstein and Woodward had been writing about.

Such calls were becoming more frequent, though most of the "tips" the reporters received were requests that the *Post* pursue theories about the deaths of John Kennedy, Mary Jo Kopechne,[1] Martin Luther King, and others.

As for tips related to Watergate, they had checked out dozens which had proven to be either inconsequential or without foundation.

The lawyer on the phone now said he had a friend who "had been approached . . . to go to work for the Nixon campaign in a very unusual way."

Bernstein put a sheet of paper in the typewriter and began taking it down.

The caller said his friend was named Alex Shipley, an assistant attorney general of the state of Tennessee, living in Nashville. In the summer of 1971, Shipley had been asked by an old Army buddy to join the Nixon campaign.

"Essentially, the proposal was that there was to be a crew of people whose job it

[1]**Mary Jo Kopechne** died in an automobile accident involving Senator Edward Kennedy in the summer of 1969. The event, known as "Chappaquiddick" because it took place on a bridge to Chappaquiddick Island off Martha's Vineyard, haunted Kennedy's political career because of an alleged cover-up over Kopechne's death and Kennedy's actions on the night of the accident [Eds.].

Journalist and former ABC news correspondent CARL BERNSTEIN (b. 1944) is currently a visiting professor at New York University. Author BOB WOODWARD (b. 1943) is the assistant managing editor of the *Washington Post. All the President's Men* was published in 1974.

would be to disrupt the Democratic campaign during the primaries. This guy told Shipley there was virtually unlimited money available."

The caller didn't know the name of the man who had approached Shipley. "This guy was a lawyer. The idea was to travel around, there would be some going to towns and waiting for things to happen. For instance, some guy would be waiting to see if the Democratic candidates were renting a hall to have a rally. Then his job would be to call up the owner of the hall and say the event had been rescheduled, to fuck up the logistics."

Shipley had told the story "during a drunken conversation at a picnic" and the caller did not remember many other details. At the time Shipley was approached, he was still in the Army, stationed in Washington. He had talked to people who had worked for former Senator Albert Gore[2] of Tennessee. "They advised him to lead this guy along while trying to figure out what was going on." The caller didn't know what had happened after that.

Reluctantly, he gave Bernstein his name and telephone number, on the condition that he never be disclosed as the source of the information. Bernstein thanked him and asked him to stay in touch.

Bernstein got Alex Shipley's number from Nashville information, but there was no answer.

The next day, Bernstein showed Howard Simons[3] his notes and said he was convinced the information — admittedly very sketchy — was important. By itself, the Watergate bugging made little sense, particularly since it had occurred when the Nixon campaign was at its strongest. But if it had been part of something much broader, it might make some sense, Bernstein said. And there was evidence of a broader scheme, though the information was disparate. . . . Perhaps the White House had been in the political intelligence business in a much bigger way and for much longer than most people figured. Watergate could have been scheduled before the President's re-election chances looked so good and perhaps someone had neglected to pull the plug.

Simons was interested and urged Bernstein to get to Shipley fast. The managing editor shared Bernstein's fondness for doping things out on the basis of sketchy information. At the same time, he was cautious about what eventually went into print. On more than one occasion, he told Bernstein and Woodward to consider delaying a story or, if necessary, to pull it at the last minute if they had any doubts. "I don't care if it's a word, a phrase, a sentence, a paragraph, a whole story or an entire series of stories," he said. "When in doubt, leave it out." . . .

Bernstein tried to stir Woodward's interest in Shipley's story, but Woodward was skeptical.

That night, Bernstein reached Shipley at home. He sounded pleasant and was surprised that a reporter would be so interested in the approach that had been made to him.

"The deal I was offered was slick," Shipley said. "We'd say we were working for So-and-so in the Democrats and really we'd be working for Nixon. Say, for instance, my

[2]**Albert Gore** was a powerful Democratic senator for Tennessee (1953–1971) and father of current vice president Al Gore [Eds.].

[3]**Howard Simons** was managing editor of the *Washington Post* at the time of the Watergate affair [Eds.].

job would be to go to a Kennedy[4] rally. I'd say to one of Kennedy's people: 'I'm also with you people. We want you to go get a job in the Muskie[5] office. And when you find out anything, you let me know and we'll get it back to Kennedy.'"

Somewhere, Bernstein had been told that the CIA [Central Intelligence Agency] did that kind of thing abroad. He had heard it called Mindfuck, but the agency called it Black Operation.

Shipley continued, "There would be as much money as needed. I was promised the pie in the sky by and by. Expenses plus salary. I'd be working for him." Shipley did not want to give the man's name until he decided to tell the whole story.

"I've been thinking about talking to somebody. About six months ago, I made a memo to myself and it's up at the office — I've got dates. And I'll give you the best of my memory."

First, however, he wanted to obtain permission from his boss before talking to the press. He thought his boss would approve. The attorney general of Tennessee was a Democrat, and so was Shipley. That was perhaps the strangest aspect of the approach in Shipley's mind.

"This guy came to me. I said, 'I'm a man with a picture of Franklin Roosevelt on the wall since I've been a child. Why me?' He said, 'It could be for purely selfish reasons — we can do a lot for you.' Liking the Democrats more, I didn't follow it up."

Beyond the man's word, Shipley had no proof that the offer was made on behalf of Richard Nixon's re-election campaign. He had known the man in the Army. "My impression was that he would not be very effective at spy stuff. But he said he was working for Nixon."

Bernstein did not want to press for the recruiter's name — yet.

He called Shipley the next evening. The Democratic attorney general of Tennessee told Shipley to do what he thought right, and Shipley had gotten his notes together. The man who had approached him was named Donald Segretti.

"The first time he called would have been 26 June, 1971. He had called and told me he would be in Washington, and he came to a dinner party at my apartment on 26 June. Nothing was said that night. On 27 June, I met him for breakfast. That's when he first mentioned the deal. He asked would I be interested, because I was getting out of the Army? Both of us were getting out shortly. We were all captains in the Judge Advocate General Corps. None of us had anything lined up. He told me he had come to Washington for an interview at the Treasury Department." . . .

Shipley had picked Segretti up at the Georgetown Inn the morning of June 27, 1971 and driven him to Dulles Airport. "On the way to Dulles, he said, 'How would you like to work in an operation doing a little political espionage?' I said, 'What are you talking about?' He said, 'For instance, we go to a Kennedy rally and find an ardent Kennedy worker. Then you say that you're a Kennedy man too but you're working behind the scenes; you get them to help you. You send them to work for Muskie, stuffing envelopes

[4]**Edward "Ted" Kennedy,** Democratic senator from Massachusetts, was a potential presidential candidate in 1972. He ultimately did not seek candidacy largely because of the controversy over the Chappaquiddick incident [Eds.].

[5]**Edwin Muskie,** a Democratic senator from Maine, was a presidential candidate in 1972. He withdrew his candidacy on April 27, 1972 [Eds.].

or whatever, and you get them to pass you the information. They'll think that they are helping Kennedy against Muskie. But actually you're using the information for something else.' It was very strange. About three quarters of the way to the airport, I said, 'Well, who would we be working for?' He said Nixon. I was really taken aback, because all the actions he had talked about would have taken place in the Democratic primaries.

"The main purpose was that the Democrats not have the ability to get back together after a knock-down drag-out campaign, he said. 'What we want to do is cause enough havoc so they can't.' I said, 'Well, it sounds interesting, let me think about it.'"

The following week, Segretti had called Shipley from Fort Ord, California, to renew the offer.

"On Thursday, 1 July," Shipley continued, "I went and had an interview with a friend who had worked for Senator Albert Gore's administrative assistant and asked him what I should do. I told him I wasn't interested, but was wondering if it might help the Democrats if I played along. Or whether I should drop it immediately. He said, 'Don't stick your neck out, but don't say no; see what you can find out.'

"On the 19th of July, Segretti called and asked that I think of five names of people that I might contact [to join the operation]. I don't recall if I told him any or not. On Sunday morning, the 25th of July, he called me from Chicago and . . . said he had made a similar proposal to another Army captain there — Roger Lee Nixt, who was stationed at an Army post in Chicago, Fifth Army headquarters, I think. He said he wanted to fly to Washington to talk to me. . . . The gist of that conversation was 'Are you with me or not?'

"I asked him what he wanted me to do. He said 'Enlist people — be imaginative.'

"One thing he did stress was asking people who were fairly free to travel, and he was asking lawyers because he stressed he didn't want to do anything illegal. It wasn't represented as strictly a strong-arm operation. He stressed what fun we could have. . . .

"He said that when a rally was scheduled for 7:00 PM at a local coliseum 'you would call up and represent that you were the field manager for the candidate and you had information that some rowdies, hippies, and what-have-you were going to cause trouble. So you ask him to postpone the rally from 7:00, when it was actually scheduled, to 9:00, thereby insuring that the coliseum manager had the place padlocked when the candidate showed up.'"

Then again on July 28, Segretti had called Shipley and had asked him to fly to Atlanta to help enlist another former Army captain, Kenneth Griffiths. Shipley didn't go.

The last time Shipley heard from Segretti was on October 23, 1971: "He called from California and asked me to check into Muskie's operation in Tennessee. . . . All these times he would give me these proposals, I would say, 'Sure,' but I just never did anything about it."

Did Shipley know where to get in touch with Segretti, where he lived?

"About two weeks ago, I tried to get a phone number in Los Angeles for him, but there was no listing. He told me he was going to be in a law firm by the name of Young and Segretti — he said it was a cover, that he would be doing only political work."

Shipley had finished going through his notes. Bernstein asked him to try to recall his conversations with Segretti in more detail.

"At one time, Segretti said it might be good to get a false ID to travel under, that it would be harder for anyone to catch up with us. He mentioned he might use the pseudonym Bill Mooney for himself. Just in passing, he said, 'Why don't you think up a good one and get an ID card?' I said, 'I'm not particularly good at that kind of thing.' He also told me we would be taken care of after Nixon's re-election. I would get a good job in the government. I said, 'How in hell are we going to be taken care of if no one knows what we're doing?' And Segretti said, 'Nixon knows that something is being done. It's a typical deal. Don't-tell-me-anything-and-I-won't-know.'"

How sure was Shipley that Segretti was working for the Nixon campaign?

"I don't know if he ever worked for Nixon," he said, "I don't have any proof. He could have been working for Kennedy, Muskie or Sam Yorty,[6] for all I know." But Segretti had told Shipley that if he stayed with the operation, it would lead to a permanent job in the administration.

Bernstein asked whether Shipley knew of others Segretti had approached.

Peter Dixon, an attorney in San Francisco.

"All the people whose names I listed were in Vietnam together as Army captains in JAG in '68 and '69. Nixt is working for a law firm in Denison, Iowa, I think. Griffiths is still in Atlanta."

What other details could he remember?

"Well, Segretti said that the people who contacted him about the operation were Los Angeles people. They could have been law-school people, old friends of the family, I have no idea. He never told me any names. He said that's the way we'll operate. I was not to tell him the names of any operatives working for me. . . . He said he wanted to cover the country. Frankly, I don't think he could do it because he's not that kind of guy, he doesn't have the right personality. He's a small guy with a big smile on his face all the time — naïve."

Bernstein asked for a physical description of Segretti.

"Short, baby-faced, less than five foot, maybe 150 pounds."

Shipley didn't know much about Segretti's politics. "I always assumed he was fairly liberal. I don't think we ever had a political discussion."

Segretti had said that he "would more or less be the head coordinator of the operation for the whole country," but a lot of the things he proposed to do didn't seem that damaging: "He said we could get a post-office box in Massachusetts in the name of the Massachusetts Safe Driving Committee and award a medal to Teddy Kennedy.

"One thing that struck me was that he seemed to be well financed. He was always flying across the country. He said that money was no problem, that the people we would be working for wanted results for the cash that would be spent."

Shipley had pressed him on the financing, but Segretti had said, "'Don't ask me any names because I'm not going to tell you any.' I had the feeling it was some big spender, but not a government man."

Bernstein asked Shipley not to discuss the information with anyone else, and called Woodward at home. They were on the way, Bernstein said. It would take a few days, but the story was in sight. This time, Woodward was intrigued.

Kenneth Griffiths, Roger Lee Nixt, and Peter Dixon all had listed phone numbers.

Nixt didn't want to talk about it. "I had just one conversation about it with Don. He's a friend and I'm just not going to discuss it, out of consideration for him. . . . I didn't

[6]**Sam Yorty**, a conservative Democratic mayor of Los Angeles in the early 1970s, entered the presidential race in 1972 without any real expectation of winning [Eds.].

do anything. . . . Yes, he proposed some undercover work for the Nixon campaign, but I'm not going to talk about it."

At Griffiths's home in Atlanta, there was no reply. That left Dixon in San Francisco. His secretary said he was on a camping trip, but was expected to arrive that afternoon in Reno, Nevada, at the home of a friend, Paul Bible.

The Senator's son? asked Bernstein.

Yes.

That was great. Senator Alan Bible of Nevada and his family had lived next door to the Bernstein family in Silver Spring, Maryland, for more than a dozen years. Paul was a few years older than Bernstein, but they knew each other, had played street football together. He remembered when Paul had gotten his '58 Chevy Impala. It was jet black, lowered, and had dual exhausts and spinners. Bernstein had been envious.

He called Bible in Reno and told him what he was working on. He was sure Paul would help.

Bible was flabbergasted. Segretti? He couldn't imagine it. Bible, too, had served in the Army with Segretti, and Don wasn't the type of guy to get into this kind of mess. He would have Dixon call back and meanwhile gave Bernstein the names of other officers who had served in Segretti's outfit.

Dixon called from Bible's house: "Don called and asked if I'd be interested in doing some work for the re-election of the President. I said, 'Gee, Don, I'm not interested in political matters, I'm not a Republican anyway.' He didn't go into it any further."

Two acknowledgments. Bernstein reached Griffiths after two more tries. He didn't want to talk about his dealings with Segretti. They had lunched together, had talked about the campaign. Segretti had tried to recruit him to do something for the President; the word "undercover" or "underground" had come up — he didn't remember which. "I said that, much as I'd like to do something for the President, I didn't have time to do more than send him a contribution.". . .

Bernstein and Woodward tried to figure out what to do next. One of them, or another reporter, should get on Segretti's tail right away. They called Sussman[7] at home. He suggested using the *Post*'s West Coast correspondent or a "stringer" recommended by the national desk. Robert Meyers, a twenty-nine-year-old former *Newsweek* stringer — the term for a reporter hired by a newspaper for special assignments on a story-by-story basis — would track down Segretti. Meyers projected an image more professional than reporter-like — pipe-smoking, a wispy goatee, rimless eyeglasses. When Bernstein reached him at home, he was soaking in the bathtub. He had followed the *Post*'s Watergate coverage closely, and Bernstein brought him up to date on Segretti. . . .

Bernstein renewed a contact made in June when he had been retracing the movements of the five men arrested inside the Watergate. He had called an employee of a credit-card company who, if promised anonymity, said he could obtain selected records.

A credit card leaves a trail of hotel and restaurant charges and airplane tickets giving dates, times, places, costs, transactions. The FBI usually goes to those records first, gobbling them up with subpoenas.

Segretti, whose last name means "secrets" in Italian, had crisscrossed the country

[7]**Barry Sussman,** the District of Columbia editor of the *Washington Post* during Watergate [Eds.].

more than ten times during the last half of 1971, according to his credit-card records, usually staying in a city for no longer than a night or two. The stops had included Miami; Houston; Manchester, New Hampshire; Knoxville; Los Angeles; Chicago; Portland; San Francisco; New York; Fresno; Tucson; Albuquerque and — repeatedly — Washington. Many of the cities were in key political states for the 1972 presidential campaign, mostly primary states. In New Hampshire, Florida, Illinois and, particularly, California, Segretti had moved from city to city, leaving his trail in territories where the Democratic primaries would be fought hardest. The travel records supported Shipley's account.

Bernstein passed the reporters' information about Segretti on to Meyers, who was staking out Segretti's apartment and talking to his neighbors. Marina del Rey, where Segretti lived, was on the water and, if you believed the ads, represented the ultimate in swinging-singles living. Lots of sailing, saunas, mixed-doubles tennis, pools, parties, candlelight, long-stemmed glasses, Caesar salads, tanned bodies, mixed double-triple-multiple kinkiness in scented sandalwood splendor.

Meyers climbed up to Segretti's balcony and looked inside. There were dirty dishes on a counter. The apartment looked comfortable — thick white wall-to-wall carpeting, a gas-jet fireplace with fake logs, a battery of stereo equipment, books, magazines, and records stacked on tables. Meyers could see a ten-speed bicycle in a hallway that appeared to lead to the bedroom.

Two of Segretti's neighbors said he had left in a hurry in his white Mercedes sports coupé on Saturday afternoon and had mentioned that he might not be back for a few days. They didn't know about his work, except that he was a lawyer and traveled a lot. He didn't talk about politics much.

The garage under Segretti's building resembled something between a sports-car showroom and a racetrack pit stop. Somebody seemed to be working on a car at almost any hour of the day or night. Meyers spent a lot of time in the garage, checking there for Segretti's 280-SL, inspecting the vacant parking space for oil drippings in case he had missed a quick return. But the floor remained dry; the mail in Segretti's mailbox accumulated.

On Thursday morning, a matchstick Meyers had wedged into the interface of Segretti's front door had dropped to the floor. But there was no answer when Meyers knocked, and Segretti's car was not in the garage. Meyers waited. Segretti was back that afternoon and answered the door. Meyers introduced himself as a reporter for the *Post.* The *Post* had information about certain work Segretti had done in behalf of Teddy Kennedy, or possibly Hubert Humphrey,[8] he said. Could they talk?

Segretti remained silent in the doorway. He looked younger than his thirty-one years, more as if he were in his early or mid-twenties. He had a friendly face, though it was unsmiling.

Meyers asked if he had any connection with Kennedy or Humphrey.

No.

Meyers wanted to get inside. The *Post* had extensive information on Segretti, he said, about his work in the Democratic primaries. Segretti let him inside.

Did he know Alex Shipley?

[8]**Hubert Humphrey** was a U.S. senator (1949–1965 and 1971–1978) and a Democratic presidential candidate in 1968 [Eds.].

"Why?"

Because the *Post* had information connecting Segretti with an attempt to recruit Shipley for undercover political work.

"I don't believe it," Segretti said.

In fact, hadn't Segretti attempted to recruit Shipley during a drive to Dulles Airport on June 27, 1971, to do work concerning the primary campaign of Humphrey or Muskie?

"I don't remember."

Did he know Alex Shipley?

"No comment."

Hadn't he called Shipley from Chicago and told him he wanted to talk to him about a job?

"I don't remember."

And later, hadn't he called Shipley and asked him to fly to Atlanta to recruit Kenneth Griffiths?

"I don't remember."

He did know Shipley, correct?

"No comment."

Had he called Shipley from California on October 23, asking him to check on Muskie's operation in Tennessee?

Segretti's demeanor remained mild, even affable. "This is ridiculous," he told Meyers. "I don't know anything about this. This all sounds like James Bond fiction."

Meyers asked him about Dixon, Nixt, and whether the Treasury Department had picked up any of his tabs; about his law practice, and about his travels, and again about Shipley.

Segretti remained impassive, a faint smile on his face. What about the name Bill Mooney, a false ID that Segretti said he might use? Did that ring a bell?

"Ridiculous."

Segretti moved toward the door. Reaching for a 35-millimeter camera under the back of his jacket, Meyers said he wanted to take a picture before he left, and started clicking. Segretti ran outside into the hallway, yelling "No pictures!" A moment later, he came back and Meyers pointed the lens at his head. Just one more, Meyers said, aiming the camera again. Segretti tried to grab it and missed, then seized Meyers's left arm and pushed him toward the open door, the camera still clicking.

Meyers rushed to a pay phone. Bernstein was talking to Sussman in the city editor's office. Things were breaking. During a routine telephone check with a Justice Department official that morning, Bernstein had asked if the official had ever heard of Donald Segretti. It had been a throwaway question.

"I can't answer your question because that's part of the investigation," the Justice official replied.

Bernstein was startled. Woodward and he had thought they were alone in pursuing Segretti.

There could be no discussion of Segretti because he was part of the Watergate investigation, right?

That was correct, but the official would not listen to any more questions about Segretti. Bernstein went down his list of checks, crossing out each item, writing "no" or "nothing" in the margin.

Herbert W. Kalmbach?[9]

"That's part of the investigation, too, so I can't talk about it," the official said.

Sloan[10] had refused to say if Kalmbach was among those who could give out money from Maurice Stans'[11] safe. But since the fund was intended for "intelligence-gathering," Segretti might have been bankrolled that way. Shipley had the impression that Segretti had got money from a "big spender" who was not in government. That would fit Kalmbach, President Nixon's personal attorney.

Was there a connection between Segretti and Kalmbach?

The official would say nothing more.

Sussman and Bernstein were discussing all this when a copy aide rushed into the city editor's office to say Meyers was waiting on the phone, sounding all out of breath.

"Jesus, I nearly got my ass beaten trying to take pictures,"[12] he told Bernstein. Then he got his breath back and put the scene into better focus.

Bernstein told Meyers that the Feds knew about Segretti. Sussman came over to talk to Meyers. All agreed he should go back and contact anyone who might know Segretti, find out if his acquaintances had been contacted by the FBI, what questions had been asked, everything they might know about him. The University of Southern California and Boalt Hall law school at Berkeley, where Segretti had studied, seemed the best places. The next day, Meyers called to say that, as a USC undergraduate, Segretti had been close to several persons who were to become part of the Nixon White House. Among the USC graduates at the White House were Ron Ziegler, the President's press secretary; Dwight Chapin, the presidential appointments secretary; Bart Porter, a former White House advance man and CRP scheduling director who had received money from the fund; Tim Elbourne, who had served as a Ziegler press assistant; Mike Guhin, a member of Henry Kissinger's[13] National Security Council staff; and Gordon Strachan, Haldeman's[14] political aide and the White House liaison to CRP.

Bernstein and Woodward sent feelers out through the *Post* newsroom, looking for anyone who had more than superficial contact with members of the White House staff. Their expectations weren't very high, given the relationship between the Nixon administration and the *Washington Post.* That heady era of good feeling, in which reporters had rubbed elbows and shoulders with President Kennedy's men in touch football and candlelit backyards in Georgetown and Cleveland Park, was a thing of the past.

But Karlyn Barker, a former UPI reporter who had joined the city staff on the same day as Woodward, said a friend of hers had gone to USC with the White House boys and stayed in close touch with them. Within a few hours, Barker had given Bernstein a memo headed "Notes on USC Crowd."

Her friend had known Segretti, Chapin, and Tim Elbourne since college. He referred

[9]**Herbert W. Kalmbach** was the deputy finance chairman of the Committee for the Re-election of the President (CRP) and a personal attorney to Nixon [Eds.].

[10]**Sloan:** Hugh W. Sloan Jr., treasurer of the CRP [Eds.].

[11]**Maurice Stans** was the finance chairman of the CRP and the secretary of commerce from 1969 to 1972 [Eds.].

[12]None of them came out. His camera had been incorrectly loaded.

[13]**Henry Kissinger** was the assistant to the president for national security affairs from 1969 to 1973 and secretary of state under Gerald Ford (1973–1977) [Eds.].

[14]**H. R. Haldeman** was an assistant to Nixon and the White House chief of staff from 1969 to 1973 [Eds.].

to the "USC Mafia" in the White House and said Segretti and Elbourne had been called by their schoolmates Dwight Chapin and Ron Ziegler to help in the Nixon election business.

All belonged to a campus political party called Trojans for Representative Government. The Trojans called their brand of electioneering "ratfucking." Ballot boxes were stuffed, spies were planted in the opposition camp, and bogus campaign literature abounded. Ziegler and Chapin had hooked onto Richard Nixon's 1962 campaign for governor of California — managed by Bob Haldeman. After graduation, Ziegler and Chapin and Elbourne had joined the J. Walter Thompson advertising agency in Los Angeles, where Haldeman was a vice president. Segretti had been summoned to Washington and trained to work in a presidential election, according to Karlyn Barker's friend.

Bernstein called the Justice Department official who had originally told him that Segretti was part of the Watergate investigation. It was Saturday, October 7.

"No, I can't talk about him," the official said once more. "That's right, even though he's not directly linked to Watergate, to the break-in. . . . Obviously, I came across him through the investigation. . . . Yes, political sabotage is associated with Segretti. I've heard a term for it, 'ratfucking.' There is some very powerful information, especially if it comes out before November 7," the day of the election.

Could that powerful information involve Dwight Chapin? Had he hired Segretti? Or had Ziegler? Or . . .

"I won't say anything on either Ziegler or Chapin."

Bernstein guessed Chapin. The official said he certainly didn't want to discourage anything the *Post* might be pursuing.

In the rough code they had evolved, Bernstein interpreted the remark as confirming that there was a connection between Segretti and Chapin.

Did Segretti have anything to do with the Canuck Letter?[15]

The official said he couldn't talk about that letter either; it was also part of the investigation.

• • •

[15]The so-called Canuck Letter had been the beginning of the end of the Muskie campaign, as far as some of the Senator's campaign aides were concerned. On February 24, two days before Muskie was scheduled to campaign in Manchester, New Hampshire, William Loeb's right-wing newspaper, the *Manchester Union Leader,* had published an anti-Muskie editorial on its front page. Titled "Senator Muskie Insults Franco-Americans," it accused Muskie of hypocrisy for supporting blacks while condoning the term "Canucks" — a derogatory name for Americans of French-Canadian ancestry, tens of thousands of whom were New Hampshire voters.

The "evidence" was a semi-literate letter ostensibly mailed to Loeb from Deerfield Beach, Florida, and published in the *Union Leader* the same day as the editorial. The signer claimed that a Muskie campaign aide at a Fort Lauderdale meeting had said that "we don't have blacks but we have Cannocks" (sic), and the Senator reportedly concurred laughingly, saying, "Come to New England and see." The Muskie campaign had contended that the letter was a fake, and had undertaken an investigation but failed to find the author.

On February 25, Loeb had reprinted a two-month-old *Newsweek* item about the Senator's wife. Titled "Big Daddy's Jane," it reported she sneak-smoked, drank, and used off-color language on the press plane.

The next morning, standing in a near-blizzard on the back of a flatbed truck, Muskie had abandoned his prepared text and attacked Loeb as a "gutless coward." Then, while defending his wife, he broke down and cried. There was no dispute among Muskie's backers, his opponents, and the press that the incident had a disastrous effect on his campaign. It shattered the calm, cool, reasoned image that was basic to Muskie's voter appeal, and focused the last-minute attention of New Hampshire voters on the alleged slur against the French-Canadians who would be a formidable minority of voters in the Democratic primary.

Bernstein groped through the paper effluvia on his desk and retrieved a manila file marked "Phones." In June he had begun jotting down phone numbers of persons contacted on the story, logging them on a sheet of copy paper. He started going through the pages, looking for people who might know about Donald Segretti, ratfucking, Dwight Chapin, the USC Mafia, the Canuck Letter.

Bernstein had been reading the clippings on the primaries for any examples of malicious dirty tricks.

Finally he hit with one call.

"Ratfucking?" The word struck a raw nerve with a Justice Department attorney. "You can go right to the top on that one. I was shocked when I learned about it. I couldn't believe it. These are public servants? God. It's nauseating. You're talking about fellows who come from the best schools in the country. Men who run the government!"

Bernstein wondered what "right to the top" meant. But he wasn't given time to ask. The attorney had worked himself into a rage.

"If the Justice Department could find a law against it, a jury of laymen would convict them on that. It's absolutely despicable. Segretti? He's indescribable. It would be useful for you to write an article about this type of conduct. I was so shocked. I didn't understand it. It's completely immoral. All these people, unbelievable. Look at Hunt.[16] I don't think he's involved in the ratfucking. But he's capable of anything. And he had access to the White House.

"The press hasn't brought that home. You're dealing with people who act like this was Dodge City, not the capital of the United States.". . .

Bernstein was impressed. He had never known the man to be so outraged.

The Chapin-Segretti connection?

"Look at it more to see if your facts are straight," the attorney advised.

The secret fund — had it financed the ratfucking?

"That's a fruitful area." He was calm for a moment, then became angry again. "Why else would they have all that money lying around? It's a scandal. But it will all come out at the trial. . . ."

The Canuck Letter?

"The Muskie letter is part of it."

Kalmbach?

"I won't discuss names. There are so many things that nothing would surprise me. It'll come out at the trial, which is the best context of all because the people will know it is the truth. The prosecutors have the truth. They want an opportunity to show it. The people who did this are going to take the stand."

John Mitchell?[17]

"Mitchell? They won't call him. But it will be there. He can't say he didn't know about it, because it was strategy — basic strategy that goes all the way to the top. Higher than him, even."

The attorney realized he had gone too far. *Higher than Mitchell*? Dwight Chapin was

[16]**E. Howard Hunt Jr.** was a consultant to the White House and a longtime CIA clandestine officer [Eds.].

[17]**John N. Mitchell** was campaign director of the CRP and the former attorney general of the United States (1969–1972) [Eds.].

a functionary, an advance man and glorified valet, servant to Richard Nixon and H. R. Haldeman. At most, there were three persons who went *higher than John Mitchell:* John Ehrlichman[18] (maybe), Haldeman, and Richard M. Nixon.

Basic strategy that goes all the way to the top. The phrase unnerved Bernstein. For the first time, he considered the possibility that the President of the United States was the head ratfucker.

"When I am the candidate, I run the campaign." Richard Nixon had said that after his aides had botched the management of the 1970 mid-term elections. Sitting at his desk, Bernstein remembered the quote and wished Woodward were there, but Woodward had gone to New York for the weekend. After almost four months of working together, a kind of spiritual affinity had developed between Woodward and Bernstein. People at the paper would occasionally kid them that they were out to get the President. What if they really had to confront such a situation — not *getting the President,* but obtaining persuasive evidence that he was involved?

Bernstein tried thinking as Woodward would. What did he have: Three attorneys said they had been approached by Segretti. There was no evidence, beyond a Justice Department lawyer's angry reactions. There were the travel records — circumstantial. There was no evidence that a law had been broken.

What they had was ephemeral, but there were enough pieces to try writing *something.* The rule was: Lay it out piece by piece, write what you know is solid; the big picture can wait.

Bernstein tried a lead:

> Three attorneys have told the *Washington Post* that they were asked to conduct political espionage and sabotage on behalf of President Nixon's re-election campaign by a man who is under FBI investigation in connection with the Watergate bugging incident.

The words "espionage" and "sabotage" could not be lightly chosen. They were war terms. Bernstein and Woodward had talked about that, about the fact that the White House and CRP regarded the President's re-election campaign as a holy war.

Bernstein wrote late into the night, came in early on Sunday morning, called Sussman at home. A draft would be ready by midday for Sussman to look at. He arrived about 2:00, read the draft, then read it over the phone to Woodward in New York.

Sussman and Bernstein wanted to run the story. Woodward argued that not enough details about the sabotage operations were known, and that their scope and purposes were unclear. Moreover, the implications should not be hinted at until there was more solid information.

Woodward prevailed. He would catch the next plane to Washington and contact Deep Throat.[19]

[18]**John D. Ehrlichman** was the assistant to the president for domestic affairs from 1969 to 1973 [Eds.].

[19]**Deep Throat** was the nickname given by *Washington Post* editor Howard Simons to Bob Woodward's anonymous source for information about the Watergate affair. Deep Throat had access to both the CRP and the White House. Deep Throat's identity was (and still is) unknown to everyone except Woodward, who would meet his informant secretly, taking extreme caution to avoid telephone conversations and to keep all meetings strictly clandestine [Eds.].

He left New York on the last Eastern shuttle and, from a telephone booth at National Airport, called Deep Throat at home.

They had recently arranged a method by which Woodward could call to request a garage meeting without identifying himself. Woodward put his suitcase in a locker and got a hamburger. He took a cab to a downtown hotel, waited ten minutes, took another, walked the final stretch and arrived at the garage at 1:30 AM.

Deep Throat was already there, smoking a cigarette. He was glad to see Woodward, shook his hand. Woodward told him that he and Bernstein needed help, really needed help on this one. His friendship with Deep Throat was genuine, not cultivated. Long before Watergate, they had spent many evenings talking about Washington, the government, power.

On evenings such as those, Deep Throat had talked about how politics had infiltrated every corner of government — a strong-arm takeover of the agencies by the Nixon White House. Junior White House aides were giving orders on the highest levels of the bureaucracy. He had once called it the "switchblade mentality" — and had referred to the willingness of the President's men to fight dirty and for keeps, regardless of what effect the slashing might have on the government and the nation. There was little bitterness on his part. Woodward sensed the resignation of a man whose fight had been worn out in too many battles. Deep Throat never tried to inflate his knowledge or show off his importance. He always told rather less than he knew. Woodward considered him a wise teacher. He was dispassionate and seemed committed to the best version of the obtainable truth.

The Nixon White House worried him. "They are all underhanded and unknowable," he had said numerous times. He also distrusted the press. "I don't like newspapers," he had said flatly. He detested inexactitude and shallowness. . . .

Of late, he had expressed fear for the future of the Executive Branch, which he was in a unique position to observe. Watergate had taken its toll. Even in the shadows of the garage, Woodward saw that he was thinner and, when he drew on his cigarette, that his eyes were bloodshot.

That night, Deep Throat seemed more talkative than usual. "There is a way to untie the Watergate knot," he began. "I can't and won't give you any new names, but everything points in the direction of what was called 'Offensive Security.'. . . But please be balanced and send out people to check everything, because a lot of the [CRP] intelligence-gathering was routine. They are not brilliant guys, and it got out of hand," Deep Throat said. "That is the key phrase, the feeling that it all got out of hand. . . . Much of the intelligence-gathering was on their own campaign contributors, and some to check on the Democratic contributors — to check people out and sort of semi-blackmail them if something was found . . . a very heavy-handed operation."

Deep Throat had access to information from the White House, Justice, the FBI, and CRP. What he knew represented an aggregate of hard information flowing in and out of many stations. Reluctantly, after prodding, he agreed that Woodward and Bernstein were correct about the involvement of higher-ups in the Watergate break-in and other illegal activities as well.

Mitchell?

"Mitchell was involved."

To what extent?

"Only the President and Mitchell know," he said.

"Mitchell conducted his own — he called it an investigation — for about ten days after June 17. And he was going crazy. He found all sorts of new things which astounded even him. . . .

Woodward asked if the Watergate bugging and spying were isolated, or if they were parts of the same operation as other activities Deep Throat referred to.

"Check every lead," Deep Throat advised. "It goes all over the map, and that is important. You could write stories from now until Christmas or well beyond that. . . . Not one of the games [his term for undercover operations] was free-lance. This is important. Every one was tied in."

But he would not talk specifically about Segretti's operation. Woodward could not understand why.

"Just remember what I'm saying. Everything was part of it — nothing was free-lance. I know what I'm talking about."

Ratfucking?

He had heard the term; it meant double-cross and, as used by the Nixon forces, it referred to infiltration of the Democrats. . . .

Deep Throat had said there were "games" going on all over the map. For instance?

"I know of intelligence-gathering and games in Illinois, New York, New Hampshire, Massachusetts, California, Texas, Florida, and the District of Columbia." The President's forces had been out to wreck the campaigns both of the Democrats and of Nixon's challengers within his own party — Representative Paul McCloskey of California and Representative John Ashbrook of Ohio. . . .

Deep Throat confirmed what the reporters' other sources had hinted. The FBI's and the grand jury's investigations had been limited to the Watergate operation — and had ignored other espionage and sabotage. "None of the outside games were checked," he said. "If it wasn't limited to Watergate proper, they would never have finished, believe me. There was also non-corroborative testimony before the grand jury, driving everyone wild, certain perjury.". . .

It was 3:00 AM. There was more general discussion about the White House, its mood, the war atmosphere. Woodward and Deep Throat sat down on the garage floor. Neither wanted to end the conversation. Their heads and backs rested against the garage wall. Exhaustion loosened them up. Woodward said that he and Bernstein couldn't go much further, what they had was too vague. Watergate would not expose what the White House had done — not without more *specific* information.

Deep Throat again told Woodward to concentrate on the other games — not the break-in at Democratic headquarters.

Still, they needed help, Woodward said. Could they say for certain that the games were White House sponsored?

"Of course, of course, don't you get my message?" Deep Throat was exasperated. He stood up.

What games? Woodward asked. One couldn't publish stories based on vague references to higher-ups, on information that might or might not have been leaked to the press. . . .

"There's nothing more I can say," Deep Throat replied, and began to walk off.

Woodward said that he and Bernstein needed more — something that went beyond generalities. What about the Canuck Letter?

Deep Throat stopped and turned around. "It was a White House operation — done inside the gates surrounding the White House and the Executive Office Building. Is that enough?"

It was not. They needed to know the scope of the intelligence-gathering, of the games. Were most of them carried out, or merely planned? Woodward grabbed Deep Throat's arm. The time had come to press to the limit. Woodward found himself angry. He told Deep Throat that both of them were playing a chickenshit game — Deep Throat for pretending to himself that he never fed Woodward primary information, and Woodward for chewing up tidbits like a rat under a picnic table that didn't have the guts to go after the main dish.

Deep Throat was angry, too, but not at Woodward.

"Okay," he said softly. "This is very serious. You can safely say that fifty people worked for the White House and CRP to play games and spy and sabotage and gather intelligence. Some of it is beyond belief, kicking at the opposition in every imaginable way. You already know some of it."

Deep Throat nodded confirmation as Woodward ran down items on a list of tactics that he and Bernstein had heard were used against the political opposition: bugging, following people, false press leaks, fake letters, canceling campaign rallies, investigating campaign workers' private lives, planting spies, stealing documents, planting provocateurs in political demonstrations.

"It's all in the files," Deep Throat said. "Justice and the Bureau know about it, even though it wasn't followed up."

Woodward was stunned. Fifty people directed by the White House and CRP to destroy the opposition, no holds barred?

Deep Throat nodded.

The White House had been willing to subvert — was that the right word? — the whole electoral process? Had actually gone ahead and tried to do it?

Another nod. Deep Throat looked queasy.

And hired fifty agents to do it?

"You can safely say more than fifty," Deep Throat said. Then he turned, walked up the ramp and out. It was nearly 6:00 AM.

Considerations

1. Write your own serial account of the trail that leads Bernstein and Woodward to Donald Segretti, and then explain why this trail to a very minor figure in electoral politics is important. In other words, place your serial account in a larger political and legal context.

2. Consider the way that Bernstein and Woodward develop their narrative to give a sense of the growing importance of Segretti. That is, what do Bernstein and Woodward do in their writing to enhance our sense that they, and we, are on to something?

3. Why do you think Bernstein and Woodward wrote this story in the third person?

4. How do the journalists in this account seem to determine whether or not something counts as legitimate evidence? Granted this is an exceptional story pursued by two ex-

ceptional reporters, but can you speculate as to what criteria investigative journalists might use to determine valid evidence?

Woburn, Massachusetts, an industrial city of 35,000 located about twelve miles north of Boston, has been the site of a series of environmental lawsuits and negotiations that, in 1991, led to the largest settlement of its kind in New England, with four companies agreeing to pay $69 million for hazardous waste cleanup. Several books and a number of articles have been written about Woburn. Renee Loth's piece from the Boston Globe Magazine *(written just before one of the major civil trials in 1986) is a typical — although particularly well-done — example of the attempts to bring the complex case before the public. We present it here because, although accessible, it has woven through it difficult scientific and legal issues: for example, questions about causality versus association or correlation. (Do events co-occur in time but not connect to each other causally, or does one event or series of events cause another to occur?) There are historical events described in the article that may or may not be linked to disease. There is the possibility of biological/epidemiological causal connections. Whether or not these events can be sequenced into a causal chain becomes part of a legal argument (and counterargument) about culpability. Think about these issues of association versus causality as you read the article.*

Woburn, Science, and the Law

RENEE LOTH

In Woburn, Massachusetts, eight families believe the cost [of industrial pollution] has been the lives of children stricken with cancers and birth defects that could only have been caused by the mutative properties of toxic chemicals. They have sued two industrial companies . . . for polluting the well water serving their homes, and thus for denying them, according to their court complaint, "the quiet enjoyment of their property," and for causing them to suffer "direct adverse physical effect and an increased risk of . . . illness and disease." And, the families allege, the chemicals from the companies caused five of their children, Jimmy Anderson, age twelve, and his neighbors Jarrod, three, Michael, eight, Carl, nine, and Patrick, eleven, to "consciously suffer pain and mental anguish" — and death.

Journalist and political commentator RENEE LOTH (b. 1952) is deputy editor of the *Boston Globe*'s editorial page. "Woburn, Science, and the Law" appeared in the *Boston Globe Magazine* on February 9, 1996, when Loth was a staff writer.

The case of *Anderson et al. v. Cryovac et al.* (Cryovac is a Woburn-based division of W. R. Grace & Co., an international conglomerate headquartered in New York) . . . is a case dense with implications, not just for the eight families involved, but for science, business, politics, and the law. . . .

THE VICTIMS

The issue of toxic waste insinuated its way into the national consciousness in 1978, when a deadly soup of chemicals was discovered beneath the homes of families in Love Canal, New York. Since that time, official response has varied from state to state. . . .

Unlike car crashes or other accidents, it is exceedingly difficult to pinpoint the cause — and therefore, in a legal sense at least, the "responsible party" — of a toxic injury. The effects of chemical exposure sometimes take years to develop, most chemicals metabolize quickly and leave no traces in the body, and very few people recall with any precision their living habits from years past. Epidemiology (the study of the causes and control of epidemics) is "a very inexact science," says Dr. John Cutler, who was assigned to the Woburn case from the national Centers for Disease Control in Atlanta. "We're all exposed to many chemicals, so it's difficult to isolate one probable cause." This is particularly true in a heavily industrialized city like Woburn.

The Grace company, which has been accused in the suit of dumping toxic solvents behind its Cryovac manufacturing plant on Washington Street in Woburn, hopes to use these empirical uncertainties to its advantage. The plaintiffs charge that Grace's solvents contributed to an excess of childhood leukemia and other diseases in Woburn, but according to documents filed in United States District Court, Grace is staking its defense in part on convincing the jury that "there is no scientific basis for concluding that the alleged exposure of the plaintiffs [to the chemicals] caused any harm.". . .

THE EVIDENCE

The poisoning of Woburn was a documented fact more than a century ago. The 1876 annual report of the state Board of Health noted that in Woburn, "the little mill pond was full of dead fish, some floating, some sunken." The report continued, stating that "the industry which thus poisons this valuable stream is the washing of hair scraped from hides . . . also the manufacture of glue from the refuse of the slaughterhouses." Woburn, now a city of 35,000 located twelve miles northwest of Boston, has long been an industrial center, producing leather hides, pesticides, even carnations. Woburn State Representative Nicholas Paleologos, whose grandfather emigrated from Greece and worked in a Woburn tannery, says, "It's ironic, but the very industry that nourished the grandparents may now be poisoning the children."

Almost exactly a century after the Board of Health report, construction workers grading the old site of the tannery to develop an industrial park unearthed ancient pits of dried arsenic and chromium (chemicals used in the tanning process that are now known to be carcinogens) and open lagoons of arsenic and lead. The EPA [Environmental Protection Agency] has placed the complex, called Industri-plex, on its national priority list, giving it a hazard rating of 72.4 (out of a possible 100), which makes it the most dangerous site in New England and the fifth-highest priority nationwide.

As threatening to the public health as the Industri-plex site appeared, another discovery would soon redirect attention to two municipal wells that had been providing drinking water to different sections of Woburn. Eventually, residents would accuse two manufacturing companies unrelated to Industri-plex with poisoning the wells. In the spring of 1979, workers at the MBTA [Massachusetts Bay Transit Authority] commuter rail station in Woburn came upon 184 metal barrels mysteriously dumped beside the tracks. They asked the state's Department of Environmental Quality Engineering to investigate. DEQE tested the contents of the barrels and found that they contained polyurethane. Because the barrels had been dumped near the Aberjona River, which was believed to feed into municipal wells G and H, the DEQE quickly began testing these wells. It found no traces of polyurethane in the well water, but it did find a terrible concoction of even more sickening chemicals, including trichloroethylene (TCE), a chemical solvent. TCE is known to cause cancer in laboratory animals, and it can also cause liver damage, cell mutations, and neurological disorders. It was found in concentrations five times the level recommended by the EPA to guard against chronic illness. The wells were ordered closed immediately.

For Anne Anderson, a mother of three who had been living on nearby Orange Street in Woburn for fourteen years, the two discoveries gave palpable weight to her deepest fears. Her ten-year-old son Jimmy had been suffering from leukemia since 1972, when he was three years old. (He died of the leukemia in 1981.) But there was an even more frightening coincidence: She had started to notice women whose children were being treated at the same hospital unit as Jimmy around her neighborhood — at the supermarket, in the bank. One mother's house was visible across Walker Pond from her own home. That same year, Jimmy's physician, Dr. John Truman of Massachusetts General Hospital, reported to the Centers for Disease Control that he had treated six cases of childhood leukemia in one six-block area of Woburn, near Walker Pond, during the previous five years.

What Anne Anderson was seeing in Woburn was in fact an epidemic. From the Greek words meaning "on top of the people," an epidemic is any medical condition increasing at a rate of 5 percent or more a year. And these leukemia cases were located in a "cluster" in a relatively small geographic area. In 1980, CDC's Cutler began an investigation of the Woburn leukemia cluster. Working with the Massachusetts Department of Public Health, Cutler conducted a "case-controlled" study, comparing the habits of twelve families with leukemia victims with twenty-four healthy families. The study confirmed a significantly higher number of leukemia cases in Woburn than would normally be expected for a town of its size — the number was seven times greater in East Woburn, where Anne Anderson lives.

The study also confirmed that wells G and H were pumping water to the affected households during the mid to late 1960s, which the study noted was probably the "critical exposure period" for the leukemia cases. But because the wells weren't tested until 1979, Cutler and his associates couldn't know whether the drinking water had been contaminated during that critical exposure period, so they couldn't establish a scientific association between the disease and the wells. Ultimately, the study results were frustratingly inconclusive. "We can't rule anything in or out," says Cutler.

A second study conducted in 1982 by the Harvard School of Public Health did show an association between the wells and disease — and not just leukemia, but lung and kidney disorders and birth defects such as cleft palate as well. With the help of volunteers from the Woburn citizens' group FACE (For a Cleaner Environment), the Harvard researchers interviewed 3,200 Woburn families about their medical histories and living habits and related the responses to the locations of Woburn's municipal wells and water system in general.

The study carried some weight, since it was directed by two outstanding researchers, Dr. Marvin Zelen, chairman of the epidemiology department at the Sidney Farber Cancer Institute, and Dr. Stephen Lagakos, a professor at Harvard's School of Public Health. But the Harvard study was attacked by other researchers because it used untrained volunteers to conduct the interviews, and because it relied too heavily on individual memories. Rev. Bruce Young of Woburn's Trinity Church, who with Anne Anderson founded FACE, believes the Harvard study could be the families' best evidence in the courtroom, as close as their side can come to convincing the jury that the wells were responsible for the leukemia. "If we have to show the smoking gun we will not be able to find it," Young says. He predicts that when the trial begins, "there will be a great effort to discredit the Harvard study."

It wasn't until 1982, after exhaustive groundwater engineering studies by EPA and DEQE, that residents felt they had sufficient evidence to accuse Grace and the John J. Riley tannery (a division of Chicago-based Beatrice Foods that is unrelated to the nineteenth-century tannery on the Industri-plex site) with poisoning the wells. The studies traced the path of Woburn's groundwater past Grace's Cryovac plant and the Beatrice-owned tannery, where residents believe it was polluted with a variety of contaminants that eventually seeped into wells G and H. On the strength of this evidence, residents filed suit against Grace and Beatrice. (A third company, Unifirst, settled out of court for an undisclosed amount late last year [1985].) Although the Industri-plex site is not mentioned in the Woburn suit, lawyers for Grace and Beatrice may use Industri-plex in their defense, arguing that the earth around wells G and H is so saturated with chemicals from so many businesses that it is impossible to know where the groundwater picked up the contaminants.

Further complications in the evidence arose last year, when newly collected data revealed that childhood leukemia rates were still higher than average in Woburn, even though wells G and H had been shut down for five years. According to Richard Clapp at the state Department of Public Health's cancer registry, there were two newly reported cases of childhood leukemia in 1982, three in 1983, and one in 1985. Some experts think the new cancers undermine the argument that the drinking water in wells G and H caused the initial leukemias. Zena Stein, professor of epidemiology at Columbia University, headed a specially commissioned advisory panel that made long-term recommendations to the Department of Public Health last June. In her report, Stein advised continued monitoring of new leukemia cases to test the theory of the wells. "In the event that the excess of cases of childhood leukemia continues," she wrote, "the hypothesis would be weakened."

Mark Stoler, assistant counsel for W. R. Grace, stresses that the issue to be put before the jury in the Anderson case will not be merely whether the wells were contaminated, but whether they were sufficiently contaminated to have caused the particular leukemias alleged in the complaint, and — equally as important — whether the activities of Grace and Beatrice caused the damaging contamination. "The EPA laws are public health laws," says Stoler. "They take the most conservative look at safety standards. Their question is, 'At what [contamination] level can we guarantee there will be no harm?' That's not the issue in this case. The question here is, did those exposures cause these particular illnesses?"

Epidemiology is an old science, but it has only recently been applied to chronic (long-term) diseases, and it has not yet succeeded in proving that childhood leukemia can be caused by poisons in the groundwater. Between the mysterious pathways taken by the chemicals through the earth to create contaminated drinking water and the mysterious pathways taken by the contamination through the body to create disease, what the law calls "the train of evidence" is not very clear at all.

"The scientific community has been very limited in its ability to handle the Woburn situation," says Ken Geiser, professor of environmental policy at Tufts University. "There is a certain arrogance to science that it has all the answers. It is bound by its discipline to proof. These citizens don't want proof, they want justice."

THE LAW

Some actions are illegal, others are not. Though it may seem a black-and-white discipline, the law is actually an organic, even creative art that can be manipulated to respond to society's needs. In civil cases, litigation is situational; it deals not with proof but with probability. Case by case over the last several years, the law has been shaped to recognize new complications arising out of toxic-waste suits. Massachusetts courts are particularly liberal in their interpretation of some fine points of the law, which could help the eight families prove their case. "Massachusetts has a more enlightened view of latent-disease cases than other jurisdictions," says Neil Leifer, an associate with Thornton & Early, a law firm that deals primarily with toxic-tort litigation, mostly for people exposed to asbestos.

For example, in most civil cases in Massachusetts, the statute of limitations (the window of time in which a claim remains "alive") doesn't start running until a plaintiff has discovered he has been injured. In New York, the statute starts running from the moment of exposure, which can be years before a victim discovers he has been harmed. At Love Canal, fifty-two cases against the Hooker Chemical Company were thrown out of court because the statute of limitations had expired.

Ultimately, the defendants in the Woburn case are still innocent until proven guilty, and the burden is on the eight families to prove an association between their suffering and the actions of the two companies. Unlike a criminal case, however, where one must prove guilt "beyond a reasonable doubt," there is a different standard of proof for civil complaints like *Anderson v. Cryovac.* In a civil case, the plaintiffs must only prove, through a preponderance of the evidence, that "it is more likely than not" that the association exists. In other words, though a criminal defendant must be proved 100 percent guilty without even 1 percent of reasonable doubt, a civil defendant can be held liable as soon as the scales tip into the realm of "more likely than not," which is at roughly 51 percent.

In this case, the eight families are seeking compensatory damages for their actual health-care costs and other financial losses, and also general damages for pain and suffering. They have charged Grace and Beatrice with the "wrongful death" of the five children and with causing the diseases of two others. And the families are also seeking protection against future harm that could come to them from having drunk the contaminated well water; they want to be compensated for their increased risk of developing cancer or other diseases later on in life. Finally, the eight families are claiming that they have suffered particular mental anguish over their *fear* of getting sick at some later time, and they want to be compensated for that as well.

As unorthodox as they might appear, those last two claims do have precedents. In 1983 in Jackson Township, New Jersey, a court awarded $17 million to ninety-seven families that had been exposed to toxic chemicals, and it set aside half of that to pay for an elaborate system of annual health screenings as a protection against future medical conditions. In 1982 a Massachusetts case known as *Payton v. Abbott Labs,* involving women exposed to the pregnancy drug DES [diethylstilbestrol], determined that if a plaintiff shows a demonstrable symptom that could form a "reasonable basis" for fear, the plaintiff could be compensated for that anticipatory distress.

But the defendants have had their victories as well. Last month, federal district court judge Walter J. Skinner ruled that the family of Carl Robbins, who died from his leukemia in August 1981, could not be included among the Woburn plaintiffs because the last possible day of his exposure to the chemicals (the day the wells were closed in May 1979) was more than two years before his death, and so the two-year statute of limitation for wrongful-death claims had expired. The judge also ruled that the plaintiffs couldn't seek damages for the emotional distress they suffered as a result of seeing their children become sick, only for the distress inflicted by their own illnesses. . . .

Most companies vulnerable to charges of product liability or malpractice rely upon insurance for protection in case of a suit. Malpractice insurance has become such a growing burden to the casualty industry, however, that many companies are trying to get out of that business. Beginning last June and culminating at the end of the year, member companies in the Alliance of American Insurers refused to write any new policies for pollution coverage. In Massachusetts, the boycott precipitated a crisis, since transporters and other handlers of hazardous wastes are required to carry insurance here in order to be licensed. "The insurance industry is not in a position to assume the liabilities that will arise [out of toxic tort suits]," says Liberty Mutual's John Purkis. "The potential for growth is tremendous, and the individual cost structures [for each suit] are great."

The insurance companies want to reform the whole body of tort law in an attempt to reduce the number of suits against their clients. Particularly egregious to the Alliance is a legal standard known as strict liability, which eliminates the old notion that a defendant must be found negligent in order to be held liable. Also troubling is the area of punitive damages, which compensates victims above their actual costs and are intended both to punish and deter the guilty parties. "Punitive damages provide windfalls to plaintiffs and their attorneys," reads an Alliance report on recommended reforms in the civil justice system.

But advocates for toxic-waste victims think the insurance industry's complaint should be with companies that handle chemicals irresponsibly, not with the laws. Jan Schlictmann, the lawyer representing the eight Woburn families, is voluble on the subject. "They're asking for a fundamental change in our system of justice," he says. "It's very much a well-planned — I don't want to say conspiracy — but a plan by the insurance industry to induce selected crises in the hopes that society . . . will say, 'We have to bring down the cost of insurance, so let's give up our rights.' The genius of our system of civil justice is that we have accountability. You have to give the corporations an incentive not to engage in this kind of [irresponsible] activity."

Considerations

1. Look up in a dictionary or in a statistics or research methods textbook the definitions of *correlation, association,* and *causality.* Try to articulate in your own words what these terms mean and what the differences are among them.
2. Using historical, biological/epidemiological, and legal information from the article, think through, or with diagrams sketch out, or write in an essay a serial account that enables you to argue that the plaintiffs or the defendants have a case. (Although the companies in Woburn agreed to pay $69 million for cleanup, they came to this agreement out of court, so the key issue about the connection between toxic waste and disease was never formally addressed in a court of law.)
3. What would you want to know to make tighter your claims about causality or the lack of it?
4. The Woburn case did not involve a recent misdeed — some of the key events described by Loth occurred decades before — nor did the case involve an act of direct physical violence or a "crime of passion." Do you think that makes any difference in how the Woburn case and other cases involving environmental contamination are or should be viewed by the press, the public, and the legal profession? Why?

The following excerpt is from journalism professor, and former reporter, Helen Benedict's book Virgin or Vamp: How the Press Covers Sex Crimes, *a study of the assumptions and myths that influence the way the press reports on rape or on sex-related assault or murder. As Benedict examines press coverage, she also examines the broader "public attitudes toward women, sex, and violence," particularly as they play out in court.*

The case discussed here is the Greta and John Rideout marital rape case, which took place in Salem, Oregon, from 1978 to 1979. Oregon was one of the first states to make marital rape illegal, and the Rideout case was the first tried in Oregon under the new law. The excerpt begins with early press reports on the case. Notice, by the way, how Benedict effectively weaves such reports, and interviews, into her writing to fashion her argument about press attitudes toward sex crimes.

From *Virgin or Vamp: How the Press Covers Sex Crimes*

Helen Benedict

THE FIRST STORIES: A QUIET RESPONSE

The Rideout story initially belonged to local reporter Janet Evenson, who stumbled across it during a routine check of indictments at the district attorney's office. She wrote a short, plain story that was published inside the paper under a small headline:

Wife Accuses Husband of Rape

> A Salem man was charged Wednesday with raping his wife.
>
> His indictment by Marion County Grand Jury is believed to be the first such charge in Oregon — and possibly in the nation.
>
> (*Statesman Journal,* 10/14/78.)

Evenson, who was then thirty-four and had been covering courts for the *Statesman Journal* for ten years, said she had to argue with her editors in favor of naming Greta because the paper had a "staunch policy" not to use victims' names in rape stories. She won the argument. "I strongly advocated using the name because it was the first case like this," she told me. "The victim was over twenty-one — not a minor. She knew her attacker, obviously. It was generally felt that she probably knew what she was getting into when she brought the charge. We had no idea that the publicity was going to go the way it did . . . I guess to be really dramatic about it, the publicity never would have happened had we not identified her in the first place." The decision to use Greta Rideout's name was followed by all the other papers without a word of debate.

On the same day as Evenson's first story, *The Oregonian,* a larger paper based in Portland, also ran a small story about the case and it was not long before the story went out on the wires, but there was no hint of the attention to come. For the first month of the case, Evenson was still the only reporter to cover the early details of the case, the defense attorney's pretrial moves.

Husband Charged with Rape Disputes Law

> A man charged with raping his wife challenged Friday the constitutionality of Oregon's recently revised rape law.
>
> He maintains the law attempts to invade a fundamental right retained by the people — private marital relations.
>
> (*Statesman Journal,* 11/4/78.)

In Evenson's follow-up front-page story, she quoted the judge as saying, "I don't think there's a contractual consent to forceful intercourse just because a person's married."

Author Helen Benedict (b. 1952) is associate professor at Columbia University's Graduate School of Journalism. She is well known for her writings on rape and sex crimes, and her published works include a novel, *Bad Angel* (1996) as well as *Recovery: How to Survive Sexual Assault* (1994), *Portraits in Print* (1991), and *Virgin or Vamp: How the Press Covers Sex Crimes* (1992), from which this excerpt is taken.

The story later quoted the prosecutor, D.A. Gary Gortmaker: "It is absurd to claim that the victim of this crime, by her unfortunate marriage to this defendant, has irrevocably subjected herself to brutal sexual attack by her husband" (*Statesman Journal*, 11/30/78).

These first stories reflected the fundamentally feminist nature of the case and why the nation became so fascinated by it: It dealt with a man's sexual rights over a woman, with the rights of women over their own bodies, and with the place of the law in domestic relations.

The AP and UPI were running stories in regional newspapers all along the west coast by the end of the first month of coverage, but national attention was still lacking. The first stories were only what Timothy Kenny, the UPI reporter, called "curtain raisers," explaining the new law and how this case would relate to it. Only one reporter paid any attention to Greta herself during this early stage of the case; Betty Liddick of the *L.A. Times*.

Liddick was then a thirty-seven-year-old feature writer who had been reporting for the *L.A. Times* for six years. "I had a particular interest during those years in women's issues and I wanted to do [that story] very badly," she told me. Liddick flew to Salem and conducted a remarkably candid interview with Greta, which ran two weeks before the start of the trial. In contrast to the plain and unemotional language of the other reporters, Liddick used some New Journalism[1] techniques to set a scene, create a mood, and to draw a sympathetic picture of Greta as a long-suffering, lonely, and poor single mother — a victim:

> Early winter snow came during the night, covering the tall forest high in the mountains . . .
>
> Greta Rideout watched the soft snow shower from an open window and suddenly felt a chill beyond the weather. A panic. She had begun to realize only in the past few weeks the importance of a phone call she had made — one that women's rights advocates predict may have a national impact on their fight for legal rights.
>
> That cold afternoon, Oct. 10, she had given no thought to political consequences. She reacted out of personal terror, Ms. Rideout said. She called Salem police to report she had been raped and beaten.
>
> (*L.A. Times*, 12/3/78.)

The story, Liddick said, was based on preliminary research, two days of reporting, and detailed questioning of Greta. "I wanted to write those details, not just the cold facts of the case," she said. She also tried to interview John to get his side, but his attorney had advised him not to speak to reporters. Instead, Liddick interviewed his mother.

> She walked through the yard filled with dogs, chickens, and haystacks the other afternoon, explaining that bad weather had forced the plowing under of the barley crop, the well had gone dry, and now she faced the stress of her son's legal troubles.
>
> "We're starving to death," Mrs. Fennimore said, tears welling in her eyes. She could talk no more about the case except to add, "It's a nightmare."

In spite of this touching moment with John's mother, the piece sounded unmistakably pro-Greta. I asked Liddick what her impression of Greta had been. "I felt that she was

[1]A journalistic style — popularized by such writers as Tom Wolfe, Truman Capote, and Hunter S. Thompson — in which nonfiction writers use the techniques of fiction (e.g., portraying people's thoughts and setting scenes) to "bring stories alive" for readers [Eds.].

somebody who was pretty unsophisticated and without skills who somehow had the courage to say, 'I'm not going to take anymore of this kind of life,'" Liddick replied. "And I felt admiration for her."

Liddick's story illustrates the freedom reporters have to interpret a case before the attorneys take possession of it during a trial. Liddick not only helped the reader picture Greta alone and thoughtful in her apartment — she even had us feel Greta's chill — she reconstructed Greta's day, checked on the weather as a backdrop, and wrote the story as if she had access to Greta's intimate thoughts.

> She turned off the light and lay on the floor pallet in her near-empty apartment and, for the first time in a long while, feeling the pressures of the past weeks slip away, slept as peacefully as the snow falling outside her window.

Most significantly, Liddick was one of the only reporters during the entire case to think of putting Greta's troubles in the context of battered women:

> At the women's Crisis Service Center here, where Greta Rideout has been provided counselors and advocates . . . staff counselor Norma Joyce predicted, "Perhaps more women now will realize they are not property in a marriage."
>
> Said board director Nancy Burch: "The value of the case is that as it becomes more publicized, women will react — speak out — against the violence they receive from men."

In the same story, Liddick also gave a colorful example of the conflicts the case unearthed:

> Testifying at a committee hearing on the bill, Lawrence Smith of the state public defender's office said, "This (bill) puts a policeman in every marital bedroom. If the wife says, 'Not tonight, John,' or if she is slightly intoxicated after a party and the couple has intercourse, the husband could be convicted of rape."

I asked Evenson why she did not write a story like Liddick's — following up Greta, filling in background, describing her and her life. "Oh God," she said, laughing, "that's not quite my style of writing. I'm real straightforward. I don't get into a lot of the personal things. I guess that could be a defect in some people's eyes."

Sandra McDonough, who covered the case for *The Oregonian,* said much the same thing. "I was really green at the time. I felt under pressure to beef up my leads, but I was not a flashy kind of reporter."

The difference between Liddick's reporting and that of her local colleagues revealed not so much a defect as a different approach to reporting. Evenson, McDonough, Kenny of UPI, and Kramer of the AP were writing for editors of the old school, who demanded balanced, impersonal, terse reporting. These reporters saw their job as an obligation to record the facts of the case and its legal repercussions, not to examine its subtler and more slippery implications. Liddick, on the other hand, who was writing in the school of New Journalism, went after the color, the psychology, and the emotion. Also, as Kramer pointed out, Evenson and the other local reporters were swamped by the daily details of the case, whereas Liddick was able to sweep in with some perspective and write just one feature.

In spite of Liddick's revealing story, which was carried to other newspapers through the *L.A. Times–Washington Post* news service, local reporters still dominated the coverage. As a result, at this early stage of the trial, their careful but unexciting style set the tone for the coverage — a tone that the majority of national reporters tended to reflect once they descended upon the town. . . .

THE TRIAL: A SPECTACLE

On the day the trial started, December 19, 1978, the national and world media crammed into the hitherto peaceful and unassuming Salem courthouse in such untoward numbers that, according to Evenson, who still works at the *Statesman Journal,* Salem judges have refused to allow television crews into courtrooms ever since. The effect of this barrage was . . . to carry the Rideout case all over the country. . . .

"By the time the case got to trial, Greta and John weren't really the center of the story," commented McDonough. "The story was the fact that it was a trial about a man accused of raping his wife. . . . It was more the sensationalism of the trial than them. They became pawns in an important test case."

McDonough and Kenny described the way they saw the circuslike atmosphere in the courtroom: The jury, eight women and four men, were packed in by the public and the press. Television cameras, lights, and wires were everywhere. Reporters from all the major networks, from local television and radio stations, from the wire services, and from newspapers and broadcast stations in Canada and elsewhere were crammed into every crevice. And there in the middle sat skinny John, nervous in his unaccustomed suit, next to his attorney, the frail but charismatic Charles Burt. (Greta was not allowed in the courtroom except to give testimony.)

Evenson described John: "John was a kind of product of his attorney's imagination. The first time I saw him in court, he was greasy-haired, lots of pimples, a sloppy dresser — nobody that I'd want to have around, frankly. And Charlie Burt, I guess, gave him some kind of hormone shots and whisked him off right away to clean him up, which is typical. Attorneys do that with their clients. But John came off looking far more the home-grown boy than the first time I saw him."

Even the attorneys were flamboyant. Gary Gortmaker, the prosecutor, was a heavy-set man of about six feet, four inches, who basked in the spotlight and played up to his audience with dramatic gestures and statements. In Dickensian contrast, Charles Burt, the defense attorney and one of the most important lawyers in the state, was small and hunchbacked, and manipulated the jury with quiet, mesmerizing skill. Through it all, the lights glared and the crowds shifted. As UPI's Kenny said, "It was real entertainment!"

McDonough wrote a column about the amount of attention attracted by the case. . . . "I've always wondered how much the fact that the trial became a spectacle affected the jury. Even though they weren't reading the newspapers, they were in the room and there were so many reporters there and this was Salem, Oregon — we don't see that kind of thing! It was a spectacle. That's what it was all about, the spectacle, and I probably as much as anybody else got caught up in that."

Kenny said he thought the media attention certainly affected D.A. Gortmaker. "This was the most important case he had prosecuted as a lawyer, I'm sure, and I saw him become enamored of the attention. He had that kind of personality anyway — the kind of guy who enjoyed attention. I saw him become sort of impressed with himself as the trial went on."

The story of the trial's opening ran in the national press from one coast to the other. "Salem hits the big time," as Evenson said. With this attention, she and other local reporters suddenly found themselves in demand. McDonough sold stories to the Los

Angeles *Herald Examiner* and to the briefly revived *Look* magazine. Evenson sold stories to the *Washington Star* and the *Chicago Tribune.* Her *Tribune* story ran at the top of the front page, under the headline, "Landmark rape case: man vs. wife." (Note the semantics of this familiar phrase: While John was allowed the dignity of his gender, Greta was only defined in her relation to him. Similarly, elsewhere, John was called Rideout and Greta only Mrs. Rideout. In the context of marital rape, this tradition of defining women in relation to men was particularly ironic. Furthermore, legally speaking the case was not man versus wife, but John Rideout versus The People — in rape cases, the state is the accuser, the victim is only a witness.) On either side of the story, which was set off in a box, were pictures of Greta and John looking inappropriately happy — pictures that were to run in almost every paper all week. Evenson's text, however, emphasized the feminist and legal interest in the case.

> Tuesday, in a county courthouse in Salem, Ore., one of those fixed ideas in the law will begin to change.
>
> John Joseph Rideout is going on trial on a charge of rape — specifically, for raping his wife.
>
> The mere fact of the charge goes against legal tradition. Although the law has few absolutes, one, certainly, has been that forced sexual relations between a married couple was no crime. . . .
>
> As women's rights advocates see it, a couple's interest in privacy is not so great that violence can occur in the sex life without any criminal charge resulting. No theories of privacy prevent prosecution for other types of violence within the family, feminists note.
>
> On the other side, those who oppose "spousal rape" laws argue that no aspect of marriage is more entitled to be shielded from government interference than sexual relations.
>
> (*Chicago Tribune,* 12/19/78, p. 1.)

The era of this story is reflected by the fact that it mentions women's rights advocates and feminists in respectful, unremarkable tones. There is not the implication seen so often today that the word *feminist* denotes man-hating extremism. Nor is there evidence of the even more recent shunning of the term *feminist* altogether.[2]

The Defense: Serious Sexual Problems. Once both attorneys had made their opening statements on the first day of the trial, the press had a new job: It had to reflect the arguments of the attorneys instead of explaining the legal implications of the case, as Evenson had done in her *Tribune* story. This meant reporters were now more subject to manipulation by attorneys and less free to interpret the case themselves. How they fared under this pressure can be seen by their choice of leads in the very first trial stories.

> **Defense in Spouse-Rape Trial**
> **Claims Wife Had Sexual Problems**
>
> Salem, Ore. Dec. 21 (UPI) — The attorney for a man accused of raping his wife has told jurors he intends to prove the witness "has severe sexual problems," and that the publicity from the case is a "source of gratification" to her . . .

[2]In my interviews with reporters and editors who worked on the 1989–1990 Central Park Jogger case, I discovered they were unwilling to even speak the words *feminist* or *sexist* aloud and instead tended to stumble in the search for a euphemism.

> Defense attorney Charles Burt told jurors in opening remarks Wednesday the couple's marriage was unstable, with a history of "quarrel, make up, have sex; quarrel, make up, have sex." In addition, said Burt, Mrs. Rideout once told her husband she was raped by another man, later denying the story.
>
> She also told Rideout that "she had a lesbian sexual relationship," Burt said. "She told John that she later abandoned it."
>
> (by Timothy Kenny, the *Washington Post,* 12/22/78, p. A10.)

Kenny's decision to make the defense's attack on Greta his lead turned out to be typical of the press that day. McDonough made the same choice for *The Oregonian* and Evenson for the *Statesman Journal* and *Washington Star.* The neglect of the prosecution's side was blatant — Kenny devoted only his last paragraph to it, without even mentioning the alleged rape.

> District Attorney Gary Gortmaker told the jury in the Marion County Circuit Court case the couple quarreled the afternoon of the alleged incident, with Rideout chasing his wife outside.

The only exception to this bias against Greta's side was Kramer's first AP story of the day (she switched to the prosecution's side in a second story):

> Greta Rideout will testify that her husband repeatedly struck her on the face and then raped her as their 2½-year-old daughter watched and cried, "Mommy, Mommy," the prosecution said in opening statements Wednesday.

I asked Kenny why he chose to emphasize the defense's arguments over the prosecution's in his story. He replied: "I don't recall having one bias or another, or not one that I was aware of. It must have been the thing I thought was the most interesting or sexiest part of the story. . . . Linda's [Kramer] was better. She had a lot more experience as a wire service reporter at that point."

Kenny added that he may have filed that story by telephone after hearing Burt's opening remarks and before returning to the courtroom to hear Gortmaker's. The contrast between his story and Kramer's, however, points to a difficulty every reporter has when covering a trial: Which side do you put in the lead, and how do you avoid sounding biased?

One answer to that question was provided by *The Washington Star,* the only paper to make a real attempt at a balanced account of the trial's opening. The *Star* used Evenson's story from the *Statesman Journal,* but although it opened with the "serious sexual problems" lead, the editors balanced the story with a careful, if unexciting headline, a bold typeface layout, and an introductory paragraph:

> **Rape Jury Hears 2 Versions of Events**
>
> Salem, Ore. — A woman who has charged her husband with rape has "a very serious sexual problem" that neither she nor her husband "could understand or solve," a defense attorney contends. . . .
>
> During the opening statements, Burt and District Attorney Gary Gortmaker gave differing accounts of what they believe happened at the apartment.
>
> Gortmaker said Greta Rideout's testimony will show that John Rideout woke up from a nap around 2:30 or 3:00 PM that day and indicated he wanted to have sexual intercourse.

> She resisted and left the apartment, running to a neighbor's house, Gortmaker said. . . .
>
> The defendant found her, "grabbed her by the arm," and took her back to the apartment, he said. There she resisted him again, she screamed, he struck her on the left side of her face, put his hand over her mouth and applied pressure to a vein on her neck, Gortmaker said.
>
> Soon after, they had sexual intercourse as "he kept one hand on her throat," he said.
>
> Burt told the jurors his client did not force his wife to have intercourse. "He honestly believed that if you are married to a woman, you have a right to sex," Burt said.
>
> The attorney said the Rideouts did have an argument that day. "She had kneed him in the groin . . . he slapped her on the face."
>
> The couple later made up and had intercourse, he said.
>
> (12/22/78, p. 2.)

Thanks to the attention reporters had given to Burt's accusations against Greta, the defense's case was looking strong by the end of the second day of the trial: Newspaper readers had now been told that Greta had sexual problems (never defined), that her sexual behavior was corrupt (her alleged lesbian and extramarital affairs, including one with her husband's half brother, were mentioned later in every story, even though these allegations were based on statements by John that Greta was never allowed to refute), and that she often lied (she retracted her accusation that this brother-in-law had raped her). All the reader knew about John, however, was that his wife had accused him of "slapping" and raping her.

Later, posttrial stories revealed more: John had also had extramarital affairs and admitted as much in court — a story that did not make it into most papers. In an interview with *In These Times,* Greta said she was indeed raped by her brother-in-law but had retracted her story when he threatened to hurt her. In another interview, she explained that she had told John about lesbian fantasies, which she made up, because she was worried he had homosexual leanings and wanted to encourage him to talk about them.[3] We cannot know if these last two statements are true, but the slant against Greta in the printed stories early in the trial was so unmistakable that when McDonough read her stories from the perspective of ten years later, she was shocked: "Boy, these stories here certainly aren't very sympathetic to Greta!" she exclaimed. "I was just covering what Charlie Burt said!"

Several of the reporters I interviewed echoed McDonough's reaction and admitted that they had allowed themselves to be manipulated by the charismatic Burt. Their gullibility was probably exacerbated by their inexperience. McDonough was only twenty-four and this was her first trial. Kramer was twenty-eight and had five years' experience with AP, but this was the first trial she had covered on a day-to-day basis. Kenny, although thirty with about five years' experience as a reporter and editor, was new at his job as a wire service reporter and overwhelmed at having to cover the case alone. "It was too difficult," he said. "I never had the sense that I was on top of things. I was kind of scrambling around. Everybody else had other people helping them. It was just too tough to keep up with."

[3]"Rideout still uncertain of wife's relationships," by Janet Evenson, *Oregon Statesman Journal,* Dec. 27, 1978.

Burt's control of the reporters and the courtroom was so complete that when he declared in his opening statements that Greta had "serious sexual problems," neither Gortmaker nor the reporters challenged him to define what he meant. Without anyone forcing him to clarify the phrase, he managed to leave the impression that Greta's sexual problems consisted partly of frigidity, and that John, therefore, was driven to aggressive sex (the "rapist is motivated by lust" myth) — or, as Burt might have had it, to exercising his husbandly rights — an impression the press helped to promote. I asked Kenny and the others why no one challenged Burt to define the vague and damaging phrase, "serious sexual problems."

"I'm surprised that nobody did," Kenny said. "It certainly would have been possible." But, he added, because the phrase was part of Burt's opening remarks, and because Burt was not holding press conferences, it was hard to find a chance to ask him any direct questions. Also, Kenny said, the crowded courtroom made interviewing all the principals in the case difficult: "I didn't do a very good job, frankly," Kenny said. "I did the best I could, but in retrospect I can see the sort of job I could do now with more experience. There were definitely holes, and I think that was true of all the reporting, partly because it was the first marital rape case. People didn't know the kinds of things to ask, so we were led pretty much around by the lawyers on both sides."

Kramer said it would have been possible to challenge Burt to define the phrase in the halls during trial recesses or outside the courtroom but that there was no guarantee he would have answered. "But the stories still could have included a line about he was asked and didn't answer," she added.

Pursuing the matter of Burt's manipulations, I asked the reporters if they had formed opinions during the trial about whether John Rideout was guilty: If they were all secretly on Burt's side, that might explain his sway over them. That is not, however, what I discovered.

"I had no question about [his guilt] all the way through," McDonough said. "It was pretty obvious."

"I thought the evidence was clear that he was guilty," said Evenson.

Kenny said, "I guess my inclination was that he was guilty and that it was his fault and that she was the victim. I came to sort of understand what his predicament was. He was a kid who was largely uneducated, he was in his early twenties and didn't really know what the heck was going on. Not to excuse his behavior, but he was raised in an environment where it was, I suspect, almost acceptable to treat women this way."

Kramer was the only one who said she does not even recall whether she believed John was guilty. She was trying to be objective, she said, and she was mostly interested in whether marital rape would be recognized as a crime in general.

On one hand, these reporters deserve credit for showing their opinions so little in their reporting. "I tried not to let my reactions affect what I was writing," said Kenny, and he succeeded. On the other hand, the reporters must be criticized for leaning so far in the opposite direction, perhaps in their eagerness not to appear biased, that they allowed the side they did not agree with, the defense, to dominate.

Burt's charisma and ability to produce quotable phrases — it was generally acknowledged that he was the more effective of the two lawyers — may well have been why he so successfully won over the reporters, but there was another reason his argument attracted, as well. Burt was relying on three well-worn rape myths to appeal to his audience: "Rapists are motivated by lust," "only bad women are raped," and "women cry rape for revenge," concepts easily understood by everyone. Gortmaker, on the other hand, had to tread the controversial, sordid, and untried ground of rape within the sanctity of marriage. Given the inexperience of the reporters, the newness of the subject, the competition of the packed newsroom, and the tendency of the press to fall into clichés in the rush of deadline, it is not surprising that they fell into Burt's mythmaking like wasps into honey.

Midtrial: Greta as Feminists' Pawn. Over the next two days, December 22 and 23, the prosecution called twenty-seven witnesses to the stand: neighbors who had heard the couple fight, friends and strangers who had seen Greta's bruises, the crisis center volunteers who had taken Greta's call for help, and the police who had arrested John.

The defense called only four witnesses, but they were effective. One said Greta had nothing but a "slight black eye" after the fight with John, another said John was a nice boy, and a third testified that Greta had boasted about the money she would make selling her story to the movies. One of the defense witnesses was John's half brother, the very man Greta had said had raped her, and another was his wife. They both called her story of the two rapes lies.

> Rideout's sister-in-law, Nancy Hinkle . . . described Rideout as a "gentle person." She also testified she never had seen him get mad or physical in the seven years she has known him.
>
> (*Statesman Journal,* 12/22/78.)

The jury also heard a friend of Greta's say that Greta had claimed to have had a lesbian affair with her but that the claim was a lie. In addition, several papers quoted the same witness saying that Greta was an honest person but tended to lie about sex. (Greta's refutations of these statements were never allowed in court — her rebuttal was confined to posttrial interviews.)

Perhaps the most damaging evidence against Greta, however, was Burt's wily suggestion that she had become a pawn in the hands of feminists. Burt planted this idea by mentioning that, when Greta had visited the local rape crisis center, she had seen a sign on the wall that read, "When a woman says no, it's rape." That, he hinted, along with the urging of the rape crisis center advocates, had given Greta the idea of charging her husband with rape. (Burt was ignoring the glaring question of what Greta was doing in the rape crisis center in the first place. She had gone, she later told reporters, to seek help as a battered woman.) She had even threatened John with the charge just before the alleged incident, witnesses said.[4] (Greta denied this, but again went unheard.) Burt used these pieces of evidence to suggest that Greta was looking for a chance to accuse John of rape as a way of wielding power over him — the old "women cry rape for revenge" myth. A quote at the bottom of the story from a friendly witness revealed the view of women that Burt was relying on to bolster his antifeminist argument:

[4]"Wife-rape trial/Threat to husband reported." "The day before Greta Mary Rideout allegedly was raped by her husband, she threatened to use Oregon's revised rape law against him, a witness at John Rideout's trial indicated Thursday." Evenson, *Statesman Journal,* 12/22/78.

> [The witness] added that she never has known Mrs. Rideout to be dominant nor vindictive. "I like Greta," she said.[5]

By the time the trial adjourned for Christmas, the jury and the public were left with an overwhelmingly negative impression of Greta. They had heard utterly convincing evidence that she had been beaten by John badly enough to give her a black eye and a noticeably bruised face, and that she had been afraid enough to call the crisis center and the police, but that was irrelevant because the charges of battery had been dropped. They had also heard a good deal about how much she lied, about her unconventional sexuality, and about how excited she supposedly was over the money she might get for selling her story. (John also sold his story rights to the movies, but nothing was ever made of that.) Above all, they had heard the idea that Greta was incited by feminists to cry rape for revenge, an idea that, in this marital rape case, plugged into the old myth with a new twist: the "rape lie" as a weapon with which to subordinate that foundation of society, the institution of marriage.

The trial, and the press, took a break over Christmas and reconvened on December 27.

The Final Testimony. After two days of wrap-up stories, quoting fresh witnesses and reiterating what had gone before, the long-awaited moment arrived: John and Greta themselves were to take the stand. As with the opening statements, the press was left to choose which testimony to put first — hers or his — and which to give the most space. This time, the choice was more varied.

> Greta and John Rideout told their separate and different versions Tuesday of what happened in their Salem apartment the day Mrs. Rideout claims her husband raped and beat her.
>
> (McDonough, *The Oregonian,* 12/27/78.)

Michael Seiler, who had been covering the case for the *L.A. Times* after Liddick's solitary story, emphasized Greta's side:

> Greta Rideout, who has accused her husband of rape, testified in court here Tuesday that her enraged husband chased her around their apartment, caught up with her in an adjacent public park and threatened to beat and rape her there if she did not return home with him.
>
> (*L.A. Times,* 12/27/78.)

Kramer switched away from her usual allegiance to Greta:

> John Rideout testified Thursday he slapped his wife after she kneed him in the groin, but that he did not force her to have sex.

Evenson wrote four huge stories on the case that day, giving both sides, but her main wrap-up story attempted balance:

> Greta Rideout said Tuesday her husband "beat me into submission" Oct. 10.
>
> John Rideout later testified his wife voluntarily had intercourse with him that day.
>
> (*Statesman Journal,* 12/27/78.)

[5]Ibid.

These stories allowed Greta's side to come across as more convincing than it had earlier. Several papers quoted her testimony at length (one paper said it was twenty-seven minutes long, another said almost two hours), for it was dramatic and moving. McDonough said: "When I think about it now, I don't think I could go through what Greta went through. It was pretty grueling for her. The story she told about John storming through the house while she ran to a neighbor's house and hid under the table — it was a pretty horrible thing to have to be recounting to a crowded, standing-room only courtroom, with people in line to get in." The reporters were sympathetic toward Greta, and they said there was a feeling in the courtroom that she had won over a lot of the public. It therefore came as a shock when, the next day, right after the public had read Greta's detailed account of John's brutality, the jury announced his acquittal.

The Acquittal. The announcement of the acquittal came on Thursday, December 28, the same day the court heard the attorneys' closing statements. The news stories, therefore, had to include both reactions to the verdict and an account of the closing statements.

Most of the acquittal stories took the same form: The fact that John was acquitted, a reiteration of the charge and its historical significance, the make-up of the jury, quotes from jury members saying they were neither sure of his innocence nor sure enough of his guilt to convict him, quotes from John saying he was not certain of how he felt, quotes from Greta saying she was disappointed and hoped the verdict would not discourage other women in her position from pressing charges, and a summary of the attorneys' arguments. The slant of the stories, however, was affected by how much of the final testimony the reporters decided to include, and by whether they emphasized John's story or Greta's.

Many of the stories, such as Seiler's for the *L.A. Times,* reiterated the defense's stand, once again running over Greta's alleged "sexual problems" and affairs and even mentioning her supposed abortions. Seiler's story, which stood out as among the most slanted against Greta, ran on the front page under the head "Husband Innocent of Rape." After including only a three-line mention of the defense's case, it concluded with two paragraphs about Greta's lies and promiscuity — reinforcing the oft-remarked fact that in rape cases it is the victim who is put on trial, not the accused — and brought up further besmirching and unsubstantiated details about her life by quoting Burt at length.

> Burt also reminded the jury of Mrs. Rideout's two abortions, at least one of which was the result of a relationship with another man while she was married to John, according to the attorney.
>
> (*L.A. Times,* 12/28/78.)

The acquittal stories by the news magazines and the *New York Times* were more balanced than the local stories, but they shared one flaw: They gave the impression that the jury had nothing to judge by but Greta's word against John's, neglecting any mention of the testimony by the twenty-seven prosecution and four defense witnesses, or of the photographs of Greta's battered face. Jerrold K. Footlick's story in *Newsweek* serves as an example:

> In the end, the case turned into what lawyers call a swearing contest. "I was crying . . . he was pulling my pants down," Greta Rideout said on the witness stand. "I didn't force her in any way," said John Rideout under oath.
>
> (1/8/79.)

I asked McDonough if the out-of-town press ignored the witnesses because their evidence was so contradictory as to be of no help to the jury. "No, I remember thinking that the witnesses were very strong," she replied, "especially the neighbors, who recounted the violence that was going on in that house. It made an impression on me that's lasted till this day. When you mentioned the trial, my first thought was that he was guilty."

The press's neglect of the witnesses, which either came about because of sloppy reporting or overediting, resulted in an unintentional bias, for it played into the hands of the marital rape law critics by reinforcing the notion that the new law should be dropped because rape cases never amount to more than the accuser's word against the accused's, and so can never be proved. The argument that marital rape laws are no good because you cannot prove rape became increasingly heard in the debate about the case, as will be seen shortly.

The acquittal stories that stood out as the most unusual and colorful, although also by far the most unrepentantly sympathetic to Greta, were two stories by Cynthia Gorney for the *Washington Post.* The balance of her information was markedly different from Seiler's and the local reporters' and included a revealing quote from John that was not seen anywhere else.

In the first story she wrote,

> The jury's unanimous verdict was met with a burst of applause in the courtroom. John Rideout . . . got up slowly, looking too stunned to smile, and shook his attorney's hand . . .
>
> John Rideout was asked when it was over how he felt, and he stood in front of the television cameras in the courthouse hallway, speaking slowly, looking scared. He said he was pleased, of course. "I don't believe this has happened to me, to start with," Rideout said. "You have a lot of mixed-up confused ideas in your head. I'm only 21 years old and I have a long way to go."
>
> (*Washington Post,* 12/28/78, p. A2.)

Even though it could be argued that Gorney's article was infused with personal opinion — her description of John looking stunned does make him sound a bit guilty — she brought up a point that few others had: the Rideouts' youth. The theme came up again in Gorney's second, bigger story the next day, under the head "The Rideouts: Case Closed, Issue Open." Here, she conveyed a sense of John and Greta as people and how they had been affected by this gruelling case.

> No, Greta Rideout said afterward, over and over, she did not feel like a martyr. She would be all right. She was stunned and disappointed and she thought the jury did wrong in acquitting her husband . . .
>
> "Justice was not done," she kept saying — but she would be all right. She would probably go back home to Spring Park, Minn. . . . and be close to her family for a while. Her father had seen her on television, seen the face of his skinny 23-year-old daughter while reporters spoke about her sexual history and this violent rape she had described, and he wept. He broke down crying on the telephone. Greta said, "I've never seen my father cry, never."
>
> (*Washington Post,* 12/29/78, p. D1.)

Gorney also quoted John saying something so revealing that his lawyer ordered him to stop talking to the press shortly afterward:

> John Rideout said he figured he'd take a day off from work, thank you, and then go back to cooking at the Silverton Sambo's. "I think the jury — wasn't looking — at the moral side of it," he said slowly, his voice cracking once or twice. "I think they looked at the evidence. I don't know why I say it, but that's what I truly believe."

McDonough and Evenson both said they took this statement by John as tantamount to a confession. "In one of the stories he admitted that he thought the law was right and good and all that stuff," Evenson said. "He almost as much as admitted what he did was wrong." Kramer also put another quote from John in a January 11 story that revealed a hint of his guilt.

> "I said a few things to the press this morning to get rid of them, but my attorney said I'd better shut up," Rideout said. "We've been through a traumatic experience and I don't want to end up in jail . . . I don't understand it, but it has to do with the testimony at the trial."
>
> Rideout was asked: "Do you mean that something you might say now could conflict with your testimony at the trial?"
>
> "Something like that," Rideout replied, refusing to elaborate.

Gorney went on to give perhaps the frankest description of the Rideouts that had yet reached print:

> They seemed so much smaller than the questions they had unleashed — one thin blond woman with the face of a determined teenager, gazing at the jury with her hands clasped on her knees; and one thin dark-haired man, the traces of acne still on his cheeks, staring up at her with wide brown eyes that rarely blinked . . . A man in the courtroom watched the two of them and said softly, "I think they're both a couple of losers, personally."

The most remarkable achievement of Gorney's stories, even if their somewhat melodramatic language was not to everyone's taste, was that she managed to get across the view of the Rideouts that everyone, including the reporters, seems to have held at the time: That Greta and John were young, inexperienced, unimpressive people — as the man in the courtroom said, losers.

"The way I saw it at the time was two really young people who emotionally weren't ready for this marriage," said McDonough. "My impression of Greta was, well I don't think I would have called her particularly brilliant. I thought she was really sad. When I think of Greta I think of her on the stand, crying, describing the rape and getting beaten up by the lawyers. I had the sense that she had a sad life and was going to have a sad life."

Evenson had the same impression: "They were pretty ding-y, really."

Kenny felt sorry for them. "They were young, unsophisticated people. The attention from the media and from the general public had put them in the spotlight, and they weren't able to handle that."

Kramer saw them as rather pathetic. "Real people have blemishes," she said, "and Greta and John had blemishes, both of them."

The reporters' perception of Greta and John as unsophisticated losers was significant. "Reading some of the stuff I wrote now," McDonough said, "I'm wondering if I took it seriously. My newspaper didn't take that story very seriously. Just look at how we covered it! We were more interested in the spectacle of the trial than in the story of what was really going on."

If John and Greta had been rich, glamorous, or merely upper class, the press probably would have taken their story more seriously; it certainly would have paid much more attention to the two of them as individuals. . . .

THE EARLY OPINIONS

While local reporters were filing day-by-day accounts of the trial, the issues raised by the case were being busily discussed at dinner tables, in barrooms, in letters to the editor, and in opinion columns: The rights of husbands over wives, and whether the law should be allowed into the privacy of the marital bedroom.[6]

On one side were columnists such as Richard Cohen, Carl R. Rowan, Ellen Goodman, and Colman McCarthy, who stood up for the protection of women against rape in or out of marriage. They argued that the law was already used to intervene in families for the protection of children, and so should be allowed to do so for women. On the other side were columnists such as George Will and Mike Royko, who were worried about women using the rape law for revenge and about the law interfering with marital privacy.

At the start of the trial, Richard Cohen published a long column in the *Washington Post* under the title, "Lack of Law Bolsters Male Fantasy, Myth." He began by mocking the myth that women like rape by depicting himself as a teenage boy watching the movie, *Gone With the Wind:*

> She squirmed and fought, but in the morning she awoke with a smile. She was happy at last. Her husband had finally raped her.
>
> Oh boy! In the balcony we understood. . . . What she needed was a good you-know-what and her husband, as was his right, had given it to her. Women were like that — fighting, but then giving in. Sometimes you had to be a little rough. In the balcony we knew that. We knew that in this sense, at least, a man could do what he wanted with his wife.
>
> It turns out we were right. This is almost beyond comprehension because we were right on almost nothing else. . . . But on the marital rape business we were right. You can do it. The law, it turns out, is still in the balcony.
>
> (*Washington Post,* 12/21/78.)

Cohen went on to explain the Rideout case and its legal pros and cons, but he came down clearly in favor of the new law:

> In the end, the marital status of the victim should not matter.

Syndicated columnist George F. Will took a different view:

> The idea that marriage implies or requires perpetual consent, under all circumstances, to sex is grotesque. And a partner in a marriage must have recourse to the law when the other partner resorts to violence. But it is a grave business when the law empowers one partner to charge the other with a felony punishable by twenty years in prison.
>
> (*Washington Post,* 12/28/78.)

After the acquittal, columnists and editorial writers fiercely debated whether the jury was right, the case worth it, and the law sound. The day after the acquittal was

[6]Several of the local reporters said the case was a major topic of conversation in Salem.

announced, one of the few syndicated female columnists of the time, Judy Mann, lamented the verdict and charged that the jury had avoided the larger, constitutional questions the case raised. Like Will, she also pointed out how hard rape cases are to prove in general and suggested that other types of charges might work better.

> "Quite frankly, I was shocked at the verdict because that particular case had more corroborating evidence of rape than most rape cases ever have," says Mary Ann Largen of the Health, Education and Welfare Department's rape task force.
>
> If the Rideout case proves anything, it is that spousal rape cases are going to be the hardest rape cases to prosecute. And it raises the question of whether violence in marriage, which takes the form of rape, should be prosecuted as assault — a crime that "traditionally" has carried life and death penalties.
>
> (*Washington Post,* 12/19/78.)

Even though Mann, like other national reporters, neglected to take into account either the evidence from the witnesses at the Rideout trial or the mores of the traditionalist, rural jury,[7] she did go on to make a point that had been sorely missing in the discussion of the case so far — that marital rape is a form of domestic violence. She also turned out to be right in predicting how reluctant women would be to press rape charges against their husbands. In spite of the dire warnings by the new law's opponents that women would now be crying rape whenever they wanted, in Oregon, at least, at the time of this writing, there have been no marital rape cases since the Rideouts', according to Evenson. Instead, Evenson said, prosecutors are relying on the more easily proved charge of assault and battery — the very solution Mann suggested.

The Oregonian ran both columns and letters about the case, many of which concerned fundamental questions of male–female relations and women's rights. One woman wrote:

> "It was hard to assess the truth in the Rideout case, but Greta Rideout appears to have, to some extent, attempted to provoke her husband into abusing her so that she might accuse him."
>
> (1/6/79, p. A19)

Another woman wrote an attack on "radical women" and "libbers."

> "Surely, neither spouse must be beaten or subjected to cruelty; but the case Ms. Rideout lost will be only one of a series of attacks on that which is a bugaboo to the 'libbers' — marriage."
>
> (1/7/79, p. C2)

A man from Lake Oswego mocked the new law:

> "Now that the Oregon Legislature has made marital rape a crime, it would seem the next logical step would be the crime of theft. If either of the spouses were to remove money from the other's possession without that spouse's approval, then that spouse could be cited for theft."
>
> (1/23/79, p. B6)

[7]Kenny and other local reporters characterized the jury as traditional, rural people not sophisticated enough to be able to accept the concept of rape within marriage.

Ellen Goodman, the only other female columnist besides Judy Mann to write about the case, came out for the marital rape law. Like Mann, she made the essential point that rape, "in or out of marriage" is "a crime of violence rather than . . . a crime of sex."[8] That only three columnists, two of them women, made this point, even though the majority of columnists supported the marital rape law, was revealing. (Colman McCarthy was the sole man.) Without an understanding that rape is an act of violence, there could be little understanding of what Greta was doing in court and, indeed, of why there was a law against marital rape at all. . . .

[8]"Redefining 'Rape'," by Ellen Goodman. Syndicated column, 1/2/79.

Considerations

1. *Virgin or Vamp* is primarily about the way assumptions and myths about women and sexuality influence the reporting of sex crimes, but there are other assumptions and biases that seem to emerge in this case as well. List all the assumptions, biases, and beliefs that you see emerging in the trial itself, in the press accounts, and in the public's reaction to the Rideout case.
2. Write your own serial account of the press's coverage of the case over time. Indicate key points in the history of that reporting and the various ways John Rideout and Greta Rideout were defined and redefined in the process.
3. We often hear complaints about the bias of the press — for example, many conservative politicians complain of the press's liberal bias. Given what Helen Benedict enables us to understand about journalism through her interviews with reporters, do you think they have a liberal or a conservative bias? Or do they try to be objective, to present both sides of the story? If there are biases with reporting, how would you characterize them, using the Rideout case and Benedict's follow-up interviews as an example?
4. What do you think of Helen Benedict's attempt to tell the story of the stories of the Rideout case?
5. The Rideout case and some other cases described in this chapter (see, for instance, that of Eleanor Bumpurs as described by Patricia J. Williams, p. 187, and that of Randall Dale Adams as described by Mark Singer, p. 232) suggest that the race, class, and gender of central figures in criminal trials have serious consequences for the way their cases are handled in the courts and by the press. What are these consequences?

Having done extensive research on criminal trials, legal scholars W. Lance Bennett and Martha S. Feldman argue that a central method by which judgment is reached during a trial is through the creation of stories — the stories attorneys tell as they present evidence to a jury, the stories jurors form as they attempt to make sense of an array of complex and sometimes contradictory information. In this excerpt, drawn from two chapters in Bennett and Feldman's book Reconstructing Reality in the Courtroom, *the authors begin with a general discussion of the nature of story and its function in a criminal trial. They then provide an example of the way the elements of a story and the sequencing of events in a story — its "time frame" — play such an important role in, as they put it, "reconstructing reality in the courtroom" and affecting jurors' judgments of guilt or innocence. Notice how the authors effectively repeat and explain the term "story" as a legal concept. Also, note how they use a hypothetical murder case — and a diagram illustrating events in the case — to support their discussion of storytelling and the law.*

From *Reconstructing Reality in the Courtroom: Justice and Judgment in American Culture*

W. Lance Bennett and Martha S. Feldman

The question to be explored in these pages is a deceptively simple one: How is justice done by ordinary people in criminal trials? Formal justice processes like the criminal trial require the participation of average citizens who have no formal legal training. As witnesses who introduce evidence, as jurors who evaluate evidence and interpret it within the law, as defendants who must understand the case against them if they are to contribute to their own defense — even as spectators who follow cases and draw conclusions about the fairness of the justice system — these untrained citizens all play a part in the trial process.

If trials make sense to untrained participants, there must be some implicit framework of social judgment that people bring into the courtroom from everyday life. Such a framework would have to be shared by citizen participants and legal professionals alike. Even lawyers and judges who receive formal legal training must rely on some commonsense means of presenting legal issues and cases in ways that make sense to jurors, witnesses, defendants, and spectators.

Our search for the underlying basis of justice and judgment in American criminal trials has produced an interesting conclusion: The criminal trial is organized around storytelling. . . .

The story is an everyday form of communication that enables a diverse cast of courtroom characters to follow the development of a case and reason about the issues in it. Despite the maze of legal jargon, lawyers' mysterious tactics, and obscure court procedures, any criminal case can be reduced to the simple form of a story. Through the use of broadly shared techniques of telling and interpreting stories, the actors in a trial present, organize, and analyze the evidence that bears on the alleged illegal activity.

W. Lance Bennett (b. 1948) is professor of political science at the University of Washington, Seattle. His work on communication and politics focuses on public opinion, the cultural bases of political rhetoric, the press and politics, and language in the courtroom. Martha S. Feldman (b. 1953) is associate professor of political science and public policy at the University of Michigan, Ann Arbor. Her research interests involve how people construct their social reality. Bennett and Feldman's *Reconstructing Reality in the Courtroom: Justice and Judgment in American Culture* was published in 1981.

The significance of stories in the trial justice process can be summarized as follows: In order to understand, take part in, and communicate about criminal trials, people transform the evidence introduced in trials into stories about the alleged criminal activities. The structural features of stories make it possible to perform various tests and comparisons that correspond to the official legal criteria for evaluating evidence (objectivity, reasonable doubt, and so on). The resulting interpretation of the action in a story can be judged according to the law that applies to the case.

If the importance of storytelling in the justice process can be demonstrated, several of the mysteries surrounding criminal trials can be cleared up. First and most obviously, the storytelling perspective answers the question of how jurors actually organize and analyze the vast amounts of information involved in making a legal judgment. Stories are systematic means of storing, bringing up to date, rearranging, comparing, testing, and interpreting available information about social behavior. As witnesses deliver testimony bearing on alleged illegal behavior, a juror operates much like someone reading a detective novel or watching a mystery movie replete with multiple points of view, subplots, time lapses, missing information, and ambiguous clues.

Stories also illuminate the methods and strategies of case construction in trials. If the impact of evidence is understood according to the way it fits into a developing story, it becomes much easier to explain the significance of lawyers' behavior and to distinguish between the important and irrelevant aspects of cases.

In addition to its implications for legal judgment and the principles of case construction, the storytelling perspective provides a systematic way of thinking about the connections among diverse elements of trials. . . .

Moreover, the interpretation of stories requires that teller and listener share a set of norms, assumptions, and experiences. If witnesses and jurors differ in their understanding of society and social action, stories that make sense to one actor in a trial may be rejected by another. The biases that result from storytelling in trials are more subtle and more difficult to combat than the sort of bias that is based on straightforward social prejudice. . . .

In everyday social situations people use stories as a means of conveying selective interpretations of social behavior to others. Stories, by starting at a particular point in time and culminating at a crucial moment or climax, also provide an understanding of an action's development. By emphasizing a particular action in a particular developmental context, stories have the capacity to create clear interpretations for social behavior — interpretations that might not have been obvious outside the story context. For example, if an individual goes on a vacation, and recounts the vacation to a friend, the account of the vacation will probably not consist of the flat documentary record of all events presented in minute descriptive detail. Rather, the account will probably emerge as a set of stories, possibly told in serial fashion following the chronology of the trip, or perhaps related in nonserial fashion and organized according to the most interesting, relevant, or similar activities. Each story will take an activity out of the historical record of the trip and provide it with an interpretive context that makes the event meaningful for both the teller and the listener, and for the relationship they share to the story subject. In this fashion, any strip of experience may be reconstructed in numerous ways, to make numerous points, relevant for different audiences.

The interpretive powers of stories take on special significance in the courtroom. The overriding judgmental tasks in a trial involve constructing an interpretation for the defendant's alleged activities and determining how that interpretation fits into the set of legal criteria that must be applied to the defendant's behavior. This judgment process is a demanding one that must take into account large amounts of information and process that information in special ways that conform to the norms of justice and the legal requirements of cases. There are several characteristics of stories that make them suitable frameworks of legal judgment.

First, stories solve the problems of information load in trials by making it possible for individuals continuously to organize and reorganize large amounts of constantly changing information. New pieces of evidence can be fit within the structural categories in an incident. Evidence gains coherence through categorical connections to story elements such as the time frames, the characters, the motives, the settings, and the means. Evidence that cannot be organized within a developing story structure can be held up immediately as a possible sign of lawyers' or witnesses' deceptions, or as an indication that the emerging story is not adequate.

Not only do stories make it possible to organize large amounts of information in coherent fashion, they are ideally suited to organizing information in the way in which it is presented in trials. Once the basic plot outline of a story begins to emerge it is possible to integrate information that is presented in the form of subplots, time disjunctures, or multiple perspectives on the same scene. Readers of novels and viewers of movies are familiar with literary devices such as flashbacks, flash-forwards, subplots, and multiple points of view. As long as a plot outline can be constructed at some point, it is possible to assimilate such disjointed information into a coherent framework. In trials cases often unfold in a more complex and disjointed fashion than do plots in novels or movies. The juror or spectator in a trial may be confronted with conflicting testimony, disorienting time lapses, the piecemeal reconstruction of a scene from the perspectives of many witnesses and experts, and a confusing array of subplots. Without the aid of an analytical device such as the story, the disjointed presentations of information in trials would be difficult, if not impossible, to assimilate. . . .

Stories organize information in ways that help the listener to perform three interpretive operations. First, the interpreter must be able to locate the central action in a story. This is the key behavior around which the point of the story is drawn. Second, the interpreter must construct inferences about the relationships among the surrounding elements in the story that impinge on the central action. The connections among this cast of supportive symbols create the interpretive context for the action or behavior at the center of the story. Finally, the network of symbolic connections drawn around the central action in a story must be tested for internal consistency and descriptive adequacy or completeness. This simply means that the interpreter must determine that the various inferences that make up a general interpretation for a story are both mutually compatible (in light of what is known about similar episodes in the real world) and sufficiently specified to yield an unequivocal interpretation. These three cognitive operations constitute the explanation of legal judgment developed in this [text]. . . . [I]t may be useful to work through a hypothetical example of how these operations enter into the judgments of average persons serving as jurors.

Suppose that you have been selected to serve as a juror on a murder trial. The state opens its case by announcing that a woman has been killed. The police found her body in bed. They had been called that morning by her husband who, according to his story, became alarmed when his efforts to awaken his sleeping wife had failed. The coroner's autopsy determined that the cause of death was poisoning. The poison had been administered the evening before. There was no evidence of any third party in the home that evening, nor was there any known motive that would account for the involvement of an outside party in the incident. There was, however, a motive for the husband. He had been named as the beneficiary in a large insurance policy taken out shortly before the woman's death. The prosecutor concludes his statement by telling you that the state will prove that the defendant killed his wife in order to receive the insurance money. Even though the central action in the incident has not been specified as yet, we know already how to recognize it. We know that the central action will be some behavior that could have caused the death (e.g., the wife might have taken an overdose of sleeping pills or the husband might have poisoned her bedtime cocoa). It is this behavior that must be interpreted in order to determine whether the death was suicide, accident, or homicide. Somehow from the sketchy story presented in the opening remarks of the prosecutor we have developed criteria for separating the central action out of all the other actions described in the forthcoming testimony. This is the first cognitive operation facilitated by stories.

The state then produces three witnesses who offer accounts that fit into the general story told by the prosecutor. First, the detective assigned to the case testifies that he questioned a man at the scene of the death who identified himself as the husband of the deceased. The man said he had been the only person with the woman during the past twenty-four hours. That man is in the courtroom today. He is the defendant. The detective goes on to say that when he asked the man about the existence of any insurance policies on the deceased, the man became visibly nervous. The defense lawyer objects to this speculation about his client's nervousness, and the judge orders it stricken from the record. The next prosecution witness is the coroner. He testifies that he performed an autopsy and determined the cause of death to be a massive dose of strychnine. Finally, an insurance agent takes the stand and describes an incident that occurred a week prior to the death. The defendant came to his office and made arrangements to purchase a large policy on his wife. The woman did not accompany her husband to the office. The man took the policy with him and returned several days later with her signature. The policy named the defendant as beneficiary.

At this point the state rests its case. Suppose that the defense does not put on a case, but simply argues that the state has failed to prove that the defendant had anything to do with the woman's death. The defense lawyer tells you that the prosecution case is based on the flimsiest of circumstantial evidence. He also tells you that the prosecutor has not even shown how the woman was killed, let alone whether the defendant was involved in any way. What would you do?

It is true that the central action has not been defined formally, but you probably have made some connections among isolated elements that surround the as yet unspecified central action in the prosecutor's story. For example, from all possible categorizations that could be made to establish relationships between the two actors in the story, you have probably selected "marriage" and "insurance." You connect the actors in the story with categories like "husband-wife" and "beneficiary-insured." The connection "husband-wife" gives us access to general empirical knowledge about that sort of relationship. We may use that knowledge to establish other connections. For example, we may see significance in the connection between the fact that the actors are husband and wife and the fact that they were at home alone on the evening in question. We might even infer from these connections that the sort of intimacy characterized by this relationship could have provided many opportunities for such a crime to be committed while they were alone in each other's presence. The connection between "insured" and "beneficiary" might take us along another generalized path to the act in question. For example, we know that beneficiaries collect money from policies upon the death of the insured. The policy in this case was large. The beneficiary would stand to gain great wealth from the woman's death. The beneficiary was the husband. Perhaps he had a motive. . . . These inferences represent the second type of cognitive operation facilitated by story structure.

The inferences established thus far among the elements surrounding the central action in the story do have a certain appeal. However, the defense response to this case is credible also. None of the actions contained in the prosecution story really qualifies as a good central action. We simply do not have a description of an action committed by the husband that could be called "murderous" in the context of the inferences already established. We know that there are still too many gaps in the story to establish a tight causal sequence leading necessarily to a murderous act. How do we know that the inferences drawn thus far, while internally consistent, are incomplete from the standpoint of establishing a clear interpretation for the incident? We can know these things only if the story structure is parallel to some general cognitive model of the systematic relations among analogous elements in real-world situations. The third type of cognitive operation associated with stories allows us to know whether the inferences drawn from a story are consistent with other familiar situations. It also helps us determine if the inferences are complete or systematic enough to yield a clear interpretation for the story. Finally, if the story is judged incomplete, this cognitive operation provides us with knowledge about what is missing.

In this case, it is obvious what is missing. Either we need information about the action that directly induced the poison into the victim's body, or we need to establish a sequence of actions that would leave no doubt about the description of that action. Imagine that the prosecution had called another witness. This person, a neighbor of the defendant, testifies that he was watching television the night of the death. He went to the kitchen during a commercial and as he passed a window noticed a light in the garage next door. Thinking that something might be amiss, he went to the window that provided a better view of the garage. He saw the defendant emerge from the garage carrying a box of rat poison. The defendant then went into the house. The prosecutor now recalls the detective to the stand. The detective testifies that the police crime lab analyzed a sample of ashes from the fireplace of the house and found abnormal amounts of strychnine along with other elements commonly found in rat poison. The coroner then resumes the stand to testify that the woman ingested some hot chocolate shortly before retiring. Such a drink would disguise the flavor of the poison.

These additional elements would allow most of us to infer that the husband poisoned the wife's bedtime drink and then destroyed the evidence in the fireplace. These connections between the husband and the probable means of death tighten our infer-

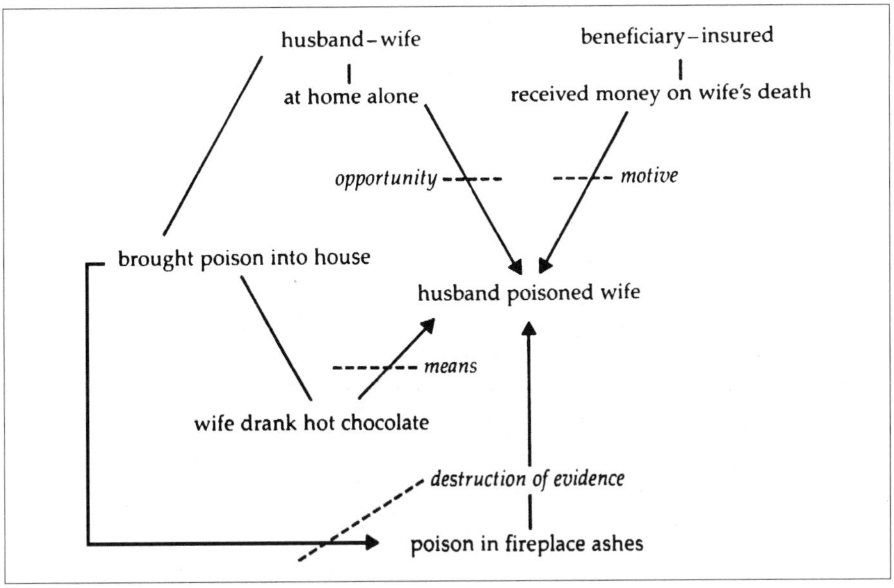

FIGURE 1. Completed inferences about a murder case based on the storytelling model.

ence that the death was probably not attributable to accident, suicide, or some outside party. It also strengthens the conclusion that the husband was responsible for the act that killed his wife, and the circumstances indicate that he probably intended to kill her. We now have a more adequate explanation for the incident — an explanation that offers a clear interpretation for the central action in question in the trial. This explanation was formed by working back and forth between isolated connections among story symbols and the way these symbols fit into our generalized notions of social life.

Although the interpretation diagrammed in Figure 1 may not satisfy everyone "beyond a reasonable doubt," it will come much closer to doing so than the first version of the story. The point that emerges from this exercise is that we know implicitly how to connect relevant symbols in a story and how to systematize and interpret their bearing on the action that lies at the center of the story. We can, then, compare this interpretation with our understanding of social reality. Through this procedure we distinguish the central action in the story from other, peripheral actions, and we either assign a clear interpretation to it or determine that the information presented in the story is not sufficient to warrant a confident judgment.

Considerations

1. In your own words, explain the basic claims being made by Bennett and Feldman. What do you think of those claims?
2. Explain the "three interpretive operations" that stories aid people in performing. This discussion is on page 278.
3. Think about the role stories play in your own life, in your family, among your friends.

Why do you and those you know tell stories? What functions do they serve? What do you and others achieve with them? Compare your responses to Bennett and Feldman's discussion about the use of stories in the courtroom. What are the differences? The similarities?

4. What do you think Bennett and Feldman would say "truth" is in a court of law? How is it determined?

5. Apply Bennett and Feldman's "storytelling model" to one of the legal cases discussed in this chapter (see, for instance, the discussion of the Randall Dale Adams case in Mark Singer's profile of Errol Morris, p. 232, or the portrayal of the Rideout marital rape case, p. 260). How were the "interpretive operations" of stories applied by journalists, lawyers, jurors, and so on? (For example, how were central events determined?) Do you see any limitations to the "storytelling model" in understanding the case you are examining?

Further Assignments

1. The title of W. Lance Bennett and Martha S. Feldman's book on the use of stories in criminal trials is *Reconstructing Reality in the Courtroom: Justice and Judgment in American Culture.* We'd like you to adapt their ideas about the reconstruction of reality to a discussion of written texts. Select one or more of the following: the excerpt from *The Lindbergh Case* (p. 171), "The Damned" (p. 202), or the excerpt from *All the President's Men* (p. 238). Write an essay discussing the ways reality gets "reconstructed" in these accounts, and be sure to consider the role of serializing in the reconstruction.

2. Over the last few years, a number of criminal trials have captured national attention — the Menendez brothers' trial, for example, and even more so, the trial of O. J. Simpson. Select one of these trials — or, if you'd like, a less famous and perhaps local trial — and consider it in terms of Bennett and Feldman's *Reconstructing Reality in the Courtroom* (p. 276). What was what they would call the "central event" of the case? What were the "inferences" and "connections" surrounding this event? What various stories did lawyers, witnesses, and other key players put forth? What, as best you can tell, made one story more convincing than the others?

3. Mark Singer's profile of Errol Morris (p. 232) involves a film, *The Thin Blue Line,* and *All the President's Men* (p. 238) was made into a movie in 1976. Both films are available in most video stores. Watch one or both and write an essay on the filmmaker's use of the serial strategy. How is it used to develop the story, to provide narrative coherence to information that may be complex or contradictory, to create suspense, to raise questions about what we know and how we know it? If writing that uses a serial strategy relies on transition words and other linguistic means to indicate sequence, what techniques do filmmakers have at their disposal? What are the similarities and differences between serializing in written text and in film?

4. We began this chapter by defining serializing as "expository writing ordered sequentially" and then noted that writers serialize "when they need to pay close attention to the steps of a process or procedure, or a sequence of events, or the relationships between effects and their possible causes." We go on to provide assignments from a range of disciplines: from physical and life sciences to history, literature, journalism, and legal studies. If you worked on assignments in more than one discipline, write a brief essay in which you consider the similarities or differences of the use of serializing in these different disciplinary contexts. Do there seem to be differences by discipline or not?

5. In a way, this chapter has been about time. The assignments and readings and your writing related to them have dealt in some fashion with the passing of time, with chronology, with a time line of events. We have considered the phases of a physical process, the development of scientific understanding, the awareness and interpretation that emerges from literary texts, the sequencing of events, and the creation of a coherent narrative in history, journalism, and the law. We want to pose a hard question, so your answer can be rough and experimental. If you worked on assignments in this chapter that involved two or more disciplines, write a paper in which you try to define *time* in these different contexts: the passage of time in literature or film; psychological time; the time elapsed in physical processes (is it, for example, measurable in ways that psychological time is not?); legal time frames, the construction of time in a court of law. Do you see differences? Or, as you reflect on our question, do you think that time is not really so different, discipline by discipline?

6. In movies and news stories about legal cases — and in informal discussions with friends and family — we often hear that "the system" — the legal system, that is — doesn't work; it doesn't deliver justice fairly or equitably. But what do we really mean by "the system," and what realistic alternatives to it do we have? As best you can, define "the system," perhaps listing all of the people it consists of. (It may be helpful for you to think of specific cases in this chapter — such as the Bumpurs case described by Patricia J. Williams, p. 187, or the Rideout case described by Helen Benedict, p. 260 — as you develop your definition. You can go beyond the courtroom, if you think this is appropriate.) Then identify perceived problems with "the system," based on your own experience and on insights from friends, family, the media, and perhaps the cases in this chapter. Finally, write an essay in which you pose your definition of "the system" and build a carefully supported argument that (1) it is the best — although perhaps imperfect — way of delivering justice or (2) that it needs serious reform.

7. A murder or kidnapping, or any violent crime, tears at the basic fabric of our lives and is a horrible violation. It is anything but sensible, rational. We always ask "Why?"

In a court of law or in a presentation of such cases in writing, the events leading up to a crime and the moment-by-moment details of the crime itself are discussed, debated, and, to the degree possible, established. The legal purpose, of course, is to determine responsibility. But there may be other social and cultural effects as well.

Write an essay in which you speculate about the ways a sequencing of events, the placing of them in a temporal pattern, may provide a sense of order in the face of a most basic violation of order.

8. In the excerpt we provide from her book, *The Alchemy of Race and Rights* (p. 187), Patricia J. Williams raises the issue of race and the law. The excerpt (and her book) reflects a new area of legal scholarship called critical legal theory or critical legal studies, the purpose of which is to examine the law through the lenses of race, gender, and class. Although not critical legal theorists, W. Lance Bennett and Martha S. Feldman raise a related issue on page 276 of the excerpt we provide from their book *Reconstructing Reality in the Courtroom.* "If witnesses and jurors differ in their understanding of society and social action," they write, "stories that make sense to one actor in a trial may be rejected by another." Our background, our position in society, and a host of sociocultural variables may influence significantly the way we construct and interpret legal stories.

We'd like to pose several options: You could do some library research on critical legal theory and write an essay explaining its key assumptions, the basic questions it raises, the way it affects our understanding of the workings of the law. You could, if you like, go a step further and reflect on the way critical legal theory, as you've explained it, could affect our understanding of how legal stories, as Bennett and Feldman define them, are constructed and interpreted. Might class standing, gender, race, or ethnicity influence a person's perception of the "central event" of a case, as discussed by Bennett and Feldman, or the "inferences" and "connections" surrounding it? A further option would be to research a case — a current or historical one, a nationally visible or local one — and consider its "central event," "inferences," and "connections" through the lens of critical legal theory.

9. At the library or on the Internet, find interviews with or articles about famous trial lawyers, such as F. Lee Bailey, Vincent T. Bugliosi, Johnnie L. Cochran Jr., Marcia Clark, and Gerry Spence. How do they build their cases? How do they construct a version of the "truth"? Summarize your findings in a brief, researched essay that, possibly, considers the lawyers' success in terms of the "storytelling model" put forth by Bennett and Feldman (p. 276).

4

CLASSIFYING

Creating and Evaluating Categories

CLASSIFYING Across the Curriculum

The first part of this chapter includes a range of readings and other materials — most accompanied by assignments — that will get you to think critically about the ways in which classifying is used across the curriculum: in composition studies, art, psychology, sociology, and other fields. In addition to covering various disciplines, we offer various types of materials: tables and charts, drawings and works of art, essays, nonfiction passages, and presentations of research, both for academic and more general audiences. We begin with an Opening Problem that immediately involves you with using — and thinking about — classifying. We then present examples of writers drafting papers on academic topics that involve the strategy (Working Examples, p. 294), followed by a piece showing how a professional writer uses classifying to serve a particular purpose (A Professional Application, p. 308). Next comes a series of cross-curricular assignments intended to deepen and enrich your investigation of the strategy's possibilities and limitations (p. 311).

Woven throughout the first part of this chapter (in the Opening Problem; in the Professional Application; and in the Sociology Assignment, p. 331) are readings that invite you to explore the history and patterns of immigration to the United States, a topic that lends itself especially well to the application and investigation of classifying. If this topic interests you and you want to spend more time with it, consider working with Readings: U.S. Immigration Patterns in the second part of this chapter. All of those readings can contribute to a richer understanding of immigration to the United States.

Opening Problem: Classifying Characteristics of Immigration to the United States

Following are tables and charts on various characteristics of immigration to the United States. They depict:

- the numbers of immigrants and the percentage of the nation's population comprised of immigrants;
- the land of origin of immigrants;
- the occupation of immigrants;
- the gender of immigrants;
- the percentage of immigrants who stay or return home.

Using these charts and tables, sketch out a simple classification scheme (a main heading and set of categories) that will display some of the characteristics of immigration to the United States. Your scheme could be headed "Characteristics of U.S. Immigration Over Time," and it could include categories that you take from the charts and tables ("Countries of Origin," "Occupations," and so on). Then write a brief essay explaining your classification scheme (you might write separate paragraphs for each of your categories). Use your essay to help a reader understand something that you think is important about the nature of immigration to the United States.

Table 1 provides the rate of immigration to the United States by decade. Note that the numbers in the second column are by thousands (152, then, equals 152,000). The third column indicates the rate of immigration per one thousand

TABLE 1. Immigrants Admitted and Immigration Rate per 1,000 Residents per Decade, 1820–1988.

	Immigrants (1,000)	Rate
1821–30	152	1.2
1831–40	599	3.9
1841–50	1,713	8.4
1851–60	2,598	9.3
1861–70	2,315	6.4
1871–80	2,812	6.2
1881–90	5,247	9.1
1891–1900	3,688	5.3
1901–10	8,795	10.4
1911–20	5,736	5.7
1921–30	4,107	3.5
1931–40	528	.4
1941–50	1,035	.7
1951–60	2,515	1.6
1961–70	3,322	1.7
1971–80	4,493	2.1
1981–88	4,711	2.5
Total	54,367	3.3

Source: U.S. Bureau of the Census 1990, 9.

U.S. residents per decade. So between 1821 and 1830, 152,000 immigrants were admitted to America, and 1.2 people per thousand U.S. residents were new immigrants. *Note:* Often, rates are expressed as percentages. In this table, however, the rate is a *per mil,* or per thousand, rate.

Figure 1 depicts the percentage of immigrants admitted to the United States between 1820 and 1900 who worked in domestic service/general labor jobs and agricultural jobs. (Note that each bar represents a twenty-year increment.) Thus, between 1881 and 1900, about 33 percent of immigrants admitted to the United States worked in domestic service/general labor. In this same period, about 7 percent of immigrants worked in agriculture.

Figure 2 gives a visual representation of the occupations in which recent immigrants have been employed. For example, of all of the immigrants admitted to the United States between 1976 and 1990, 23 percent held professional, technical, executive, administrative, and managerial jobs, 20 percent held service jobs, etc.

Figure 3 gives a visual sense of the proportions of immigrants arriving in and departing from the United States between 1900 and 1979. For example, of the approximately 650,000 immigrants who arrived in the United States between 1900 and 1904, about 235,000 eventually departed, leaving a net addition of 400,000 immigrants.

Table 2 gives a decade-by-decade breakdown, through 1970, of where immigrants came from. Note that the numbers are in thousands. The last line (labeled "All Countries") lists total immigration per decade.

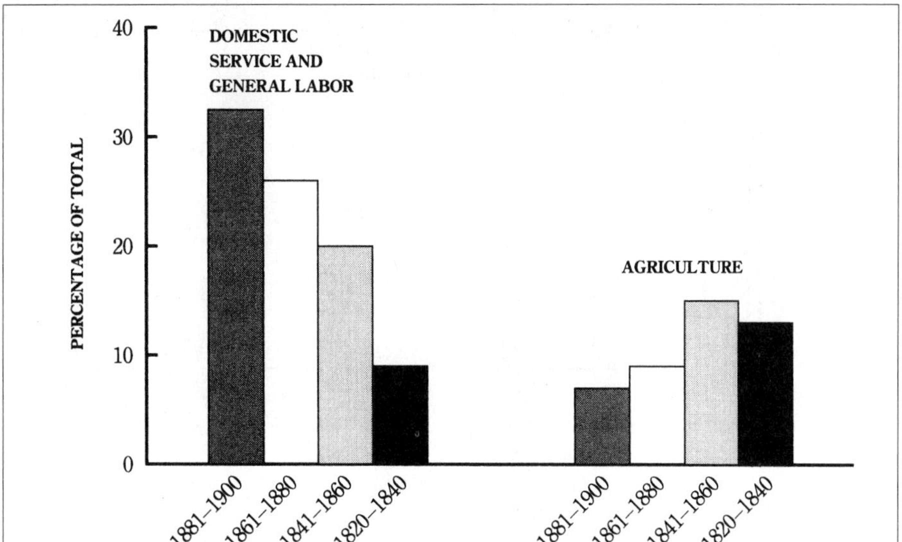

FIGURE 1. Immigrants Admitted to the United States by Occupational Group, 1820–1900. As the industrial revolution took hold in the mid-1800s, immigrants in industrial labor and service jobs outnumbered those in agriculture.

Source: 1990 Statistical Yearbook of the Immigration and Naturalization Service (Washington, D.C.: U.S. Government Printing Office, 1991), p. 20.

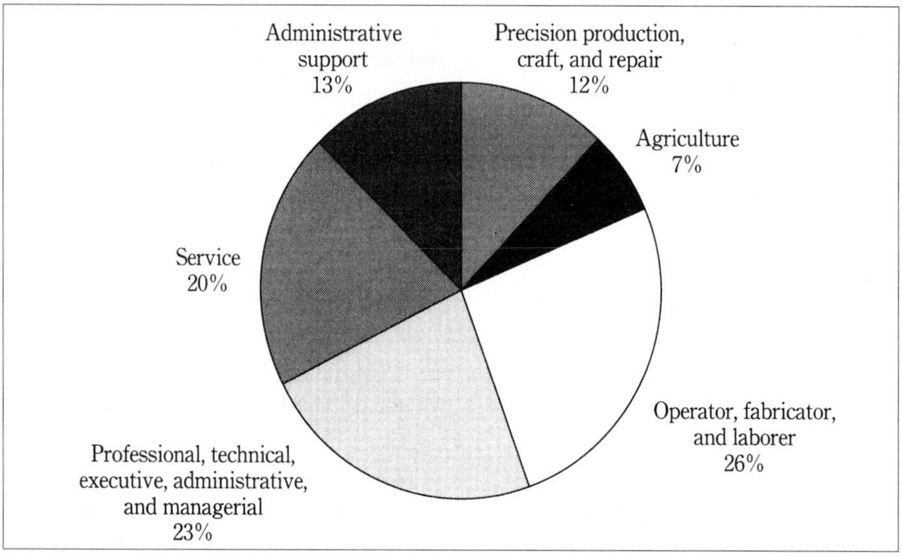

FIGURE 2. Immigrants Admitted to the United States by Occupational Group, 1976–1990. While the immigrants before the Great Depression were almost uniformly working class, a large fraction of recent immigrants have been professional and white-collar workers.

Source: 1990 Statistical Yearbook of the Immigration and Naturalization Service (Washington, D.C.: U.S. Government Printing Office, 1991), p. 32.

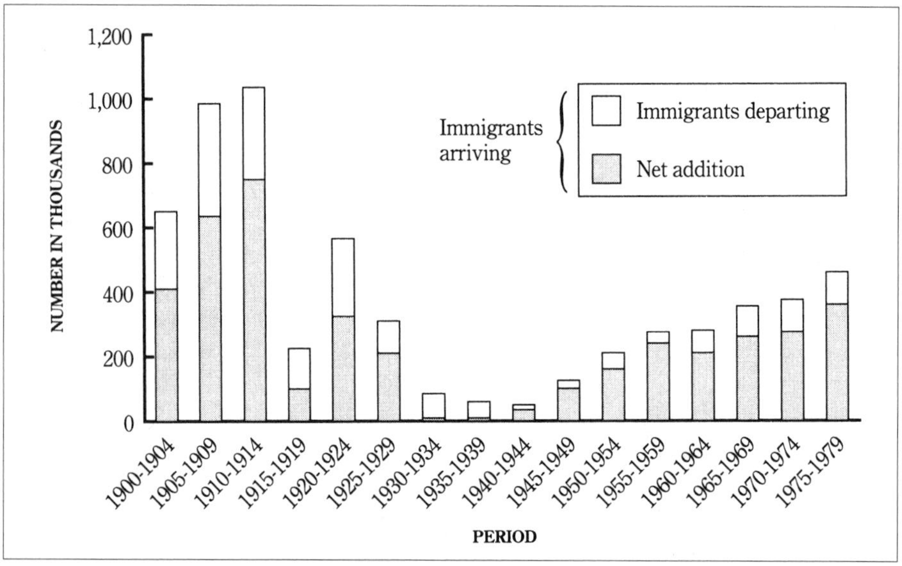

FIGURE 3. Annual Average Number of U.S. Immigrants Admitted and Departing, by Period, 1900–1979. In the early years of the twentieth century, many immigrants to the United States returned home after earning money to bring back to their families. After World War II, a greater proportion of immigrants remained permanently, but since the 1960s the rate of return migration has been rising again.

Source: Robert Warren and Ellen Percy Kraly, *The Elusive Exodus: Emigration from the United States* (Washington, D.C.: Population Reference Bureau, 1985), p. 4.

TABLE 2. Immigration to the United States. Number of immigrants by country: 1831–1970 (in thousands).

Country	1831–1840	1841–1850	1851–1860	1861–1870	1871–1880	1881–1890	1891–1900	1901–1910	1911–1920	1921–1930	1931–1940	1941–1950	1951–1960	1961–1970
Great Britain	76	267	424	607	548	807	272	526	341	330	29	132	195	210
Ireland	207	781	914	436	437	655	388	339	146	221	13	27	57	37
Scandinavia	2	14	25	126	243	656	372	505	203	198	11	26	56	42
Other Northwestern Europe[1]	47	91	92	52	96	124	76	163	139	92	25	67	123	86
Germany	152	435	952	787	718	1,453	505	341	144	412	114	227	478	191
Poland	—	—	1	2	13	52	97	—	5	228	17	8	10	54
Other Central Europe[2]	5	5	25	31	101	436	624	2,180	923	195	31	47	122	48
Soviet Union	—	—	—	3	39	213	505	1,597	921	62	1	—	—	2
Other Eastern Europe[3]	—	—	—	—	—	6	13	92	38	136	19	7	15	29
Italy	2	2	9	12	56	307	652	2,046	1,110	455	68	58	185	214
Other Southern Europe[4]	3	3	10	9	20	24	52	265	343	110	16	19	75	207
Asia	—	—	42	65	124	70	75	324	247	112	16	32	150	427
Canada and Newfoundland	14	42	59	154	384	393	3	179	742	925	109	172	378	413
Mexico	7	3	3	2	5	2	1	50	219	459	22	61	300	454
Other American	13	17	12	11	15	32	35	133	182	133	29	122	319	849
Africa	—	—	—	—	—	1	—	7	8	6	2	7	14	29
Australia and New Zealand	—	—	—	—	10	7	3	12	12	8	2	14	12	20
All Countries	599	1,713	2,598	2,315	2,812	5,247	3,688	8,795	5,736	4,107	528	1,035	2,515	3,322

[1]Includes Belgium, France, the Netherlands, and, after 1930, Luxembourg.
[2]Includes Austria, Hungary, Switzerland, and, after 1910, Czechoslovakia.
[3]Includes Bulgaria and Romania; after 1910, Finland and Yugoslavia; and, after 1930, Albania, Estonia, Latvia, and Lithuania.
[4]Includes Greece, Portugal, and Spain.

Derived from *1971 Annual Report, Immigration and Naturalization Service* (Washington, 1971).

Table 3 shows the percentages of employed immigrants holding various jobs in the decades between 1901 and 1989. For example, between 1901 and 1910, 1.4 percent of all employed immigrants held professional jobs.

Table 4 gives a breakdown of immigration by gender. For example, between 1831 and 1835, 65.6 percent of all immigrants were male; 34.4 percent were female.

TABLE 3. Employed Immigrants, by Occupation, 1901–1989 (percentage).

	1901–1910	1911–1920	1921–1930	1931–1940	1941–1945	1946–1950
Professional	1.4	2.7	4.5	17.3	24.2	16.2
Proprietors, managers	2.7	2.7	3.5	15.3	15.2	7.1
Clerical, sales	1.5	[a]	7.0	10.6	16.7	17.5
Skilled crafts, supervisors	17.8	22.4	23.7	19.3	21.9	30.7
Farmers, farm managers	1.6	2.2	4.9	4.2	2.3	9.1
Farm laborers	24.5	27.2	8.5	2.9	1.1	1.6
Laborers	35.1	25.7	24.7	8.6	5.2	5.3
Domestics	14.1	16.8	17.2	15.0	7.8	7.5
Service workers	1.3	0.4	6.0	6.7	5.6	4.9

	1951–1960	1961–1970	1971–1979[f]	1982–1985	1986–1989
Professional	15.6	23.0	25.0	19.4	13.9
Managers	4.5	4.5	7.3	9.5	7.4
Sales	[b]	[b]	2.1	4.3	4.4
Clerical	16.7	16.7	9.7	9.2	8.4
Skilled crafts	16.6	14.1	12.2	11.5	11.5
Operatives (nontransport)	14.3	11.1	13.8	22.7	26.0
Transport operatives	[c]	[c]	0.2	[c]	[c]
Laborers	11.3	8.8	9.0	[c]	[c]
Farmers, farm managers	4.2	1.8	1.0	5.0	5.3
Farm laborers	3.7	3.9	4.4	[d]	[d]
Service workers	5.9	7.4	9.4	18.3	23.0
Household workers	8.0	8.7	5.2	[e]	[e]

[a]Combined with proprietors and managers.
[b]Sales workers included with clerical.
[c]Transport operatives or laborers included with operatives.
[d]Farm laborers included with farmers and farm managers.
[e]Household workers included with service workers.
[f]No data available for 1980–1981.

Sources: Conrad Taeuber and Irene Taeuber, *Changing Population of the United States* (New York: John Wiley, 1958), p. 70; *Statistical Abstract of the United States, 1984,* p. 93; Commissioner-General of Immigration, *Annual Reports, 1927,* Tables 96, 97. Compiled from *Statistical Yearbook of the Immigration and Naturalization Service, 1985–1989.*

TABLE 4. Distribution of Immigrants by Sex, 1831–1989 (percentage).

Years	Males	Females
1831–1835	65.6	34.4
1836–1840	63.3	36.7
1841–1845	58.3	41.7
1846–1850	59.8	40.2
1851–1855	57.8	42.2
1856–1860	58.1	41.9
1861–1865	59.5	40.5
1866–1870	61.0	39.0
1871–1875	60.4	39.6
1876–1880	62.8	37.2
1881–1885	60.5	39.5
1886–1890	61.6	38.4
1891–1895	61.2	38.8
1896–1900	61.6	38.4
1901–1905	69.8	30.2
1906–1910	69.7	30.3
1911–1915	65.0	35.0
1916–1920	58.3	41.7
1921–1924	56.5	43.5
1925–1929	60.0	40.0
1930–1934	45.2	54.8
1935–1939	44.0	56.0
1936–1940	45.2	54.8
1941–1945	41.0	59.0
1946–1950	40.3	59.7
1951–1960	45.9	54.1
1961–1970	44.8	55.2
1971–1979	46.9	53.1
1982–1985	50.4	49.6
1986–1989	50.2	48.8

Sources: Imre Ferenzci and Walter F. Willcox, *International Migrations* (New York: National Bureau of Economic Research, 1929), vol. 1, p. 211; U.S. Bureau of the Census. *Statistical Abstract of the United States, 1942,* p. 123; *Statistical Abstract of the United States, 1954,* p. 106; *Statistical Abstract of the United States, 1984,* p. 93; compiled from *Statistical Yearbook of the Immigration and Naturalization Service, 1985,* p. 46; *Statistical Yearbook, 1989,* p. 24.

Thinking about Thinking

- What were some of the assumptions you had about immigration before you began working with the charts and tables? Did your work confirm or qualify those assumptions?
- How did the process of developing a classification scheme affect your understanding of immigration? Was it in any way a hindrance?
- As you worked with the data in the charts and tables what questions came to you that your classification scheme couldn't answer? What kind of information do you think you'd need to answer those questions?

To classify is to sort into categories. "Is it animal, vegetable, or mineral?" goes one of our most comprehensive — though not often useful — classification systems. Classifying occurs all the time: when we call one person a friend and another an acquaintance, when we describe one movie as realistic and another as fantasy, when we refer to our hometowns as rural, suburban, or urban. In a sense, all words are categories, grouping particular experiences or ideas in general terms that we can differentiate from other general terms.

In academic situations we are constantly exposed to categories. Only recently you may have found yourself categorized as a freshman, a high school graduate, a commuter, a math major, or a minority student. The English class for which you are reading this paragraph is itself part of a system of categories: There are broad categories of subject areas (humanities, for instance), of disciplines (sociology), of specializations (chemical engineering). Particular courses are regarded as categories ("The Eighteenth Century"), and often they organize their material in further categories (poetry, fiction, drama). Textbooks, too, are often organized as classifications, and so are the chapters within textbooks. And you'll find many college lectures organized by category — they are the ones for which it's possible to take neatly outlined notes.

Thinking critically in academic situations means being willing to evaluate other people's categories, use them (as you did in the Opening Problem), or even resist them. Sometimes it also means formulating categories of your own. To be honest, you could probably go through an entire collegiate career without seriously reexamining or challenging the categories imposed upon you. The question to ask yourself is, why would you want to be so passive? As a student you will frequently find yourself on the receiving end of other people's categories, and it's crucial to recognize that these categories are not statements of fact but acts of interpretation. (For example, the occupational groups presented in Figure 2 of the Opening Problem were the result of a decision — or perhaps several decisions — about how to categorize jobs.)

It's important to learn to think critically about categories. That implies being able to look at categories not as natural parts of the world but as human constructions, groupings and divisions created by some people to shape and influence the thinking of others. Sometimes, particularly when encountering a subject for the first time, you will seem to have little choice but to accept material according to the categories in which you receive it. You have no critical distance, no awareness of other possible ways to organize the information. But you needn't stay in this helpless state for long. Almost immediately, you can begin to examine the role played by categories in shaping such material. Let us offer a few strategies for probing classifications you encounter. First, you can ask on what basis the categories are being differentiated. Effective categories have some unifying principle to make the system coherent. In the tables and figures that open this chapter, the fact that all the statistics relate to immigration provides a common ground from which to proceed.

Another question to help you think critically is to ask whether the categories are meant to be absolute or only approximate. Are they meant neatly and definitively to divide all possibilities into specific categories, or is there deliberately some overlap, imprecision, or flexibility in the system? (How would you describe the category system you devised for the immigration statistics?) Many classifications, particularly those of the either/or type, are meant to be absolute: living or nonliving, moving or at rest, accepted or rejected, under budget or over budget. Similarly, just as playing cards are absolutely either spades, clubs, hearts, or diamonds, votes in an American presidential election can be categorized absolutely as Democrat, Republican, or other. Sometimes, however, even the most clear-cut system does not work as absolutely as we might think. Neither living nor nonliving, for example, quite fits the viruses, which some biologists think of as alive and others as not. Many classification systems are not intended to provide absolute categories. Differences among categories are matters of emphasis and degree. Understanding how rigid or flexible a system of categories is meant to be can put us in a good position to judge how well it works.

Another question to ask is whether the classification system is meant to be all-inclusive. Is it meant to include all possible instances? (Again, how would you describe the category system you developed? What statistics did you have to eliminate in the course of refining your classification of immigration patterns?) It's important to remember that many classifications do not attempt inclusiveness. A chapter of a biology textbook beginning with the sentence,"There are three major types of plant hormones that have been discovered thus far," admits with the words *major* and *thus far* that other categories may exist. So too when a lecturer in a political science course begins, "Let's look today at several types of parliamentary government," she implies that there are other types the class won't be hearing about. Some classifications, by contrast, are meant to be inclusive. For example, literature anthologies are sometimes organized into the categories poetry, drama, fiction, and nonfiction prose. This system covers all the literary possibilities, partly because nonfiction prose is a catch-all category that can include essays, letters, newspaper articles, diaries, and so on. A classification presented as inclusive makes a stronger claim than one presented as merely helpful or interesting. It's a good mental habit to test classification systems that make strong claims by inventing examples of your own. Does the system really work as a method of dividing up the territory? See if you can come up with problem cases, examples that the existing categories are unable to handle.

Perhaps the most helpful critical question of all is this one: Of what use is the classification? What does it enable us to do or see? What is gained by using it? Of what use, for example, might be the work you've done above with the immigration statistics? If you noticed, say, different patterns in eighteenth- and nineteenth-century immigration, what else did an awareness of these patterns lead you to discover?

Besides being useful in its own terms, classification complements most of the other academic strategies we present in this book. As we stressed in Chapter 1, classifying is one of the means by which we can arrive at definitions. When we can begin to classify abstract terms such as *political authority, epics,* or *phosphates* into more specific kinds of political authority, epics, and phosphates, we begin to grasp a surer sense of the larger terms themselves. Classification can also be useful in summarizing. By noticing that a particular article is organized into clear subdivisions, for example, we can make effective decisions about how to summarize it — perhaps by giving each section a roughly equivalent emphasis or perhaps by summarizing each section in a parallel sentence. Classification also aids analysis, often by suggesting an appropriate framework from which to begin analyzing. Asked to analyze an essay by the political columnist George Will, we might begin by recognizing that Will writes from a conservative point of view. The "conservative" category alerts us to features of his essay that we might not have noticed otherwise (but it also might close our eyes to other features — we need to be provisional and flexible in trying out analytical categories). Classifying can also aid argument. Categorizing an opposing point of view, for example, is often a good way to stress its limitations.

Above all, classification enables comparison. Sometimes the comparisons are across categories. Having established that China's economic system is communist and Japan's capitalist, a writer can go on to look at how the two economic systems control the way the two countries conduct international trade. At other times the comparisons are within categories. Having decided that both cacti and fir trees are temperature-adapted, a naturalist can go on to compare how adaptations to extreme heat in the cactus compare with adaptations to extreme cold in the fir tree. Having categorized both Edgar Allan Poe and Stephen King as horror writers, a student could go on to compare the qualities of horror in the two writers' work.

The assignments in this chapter are of two types. One type asks you to take someone else's classification system and thoughtfully apply it. The other asks you to generate a classification system of your own. In your undergraduate courses, you'll find the first type of assignment much more frequent than the second. You'll also find that applying someone else's categories isn't difficult when the system itself is easy to grasp. But when the system is complex, such assignments put pressure on your abilities to read, interpret, and explain. The second type of assignment, creating categories, gives you a chance to assert your intellectual independence. In many courses, such assignments never appear. The construction of categories seldom is required of you; rather, it's an opportunity to be seized. In the two following cases, we offer an example of each type of assignment.

Working Examples

A Working Example from Sociology

Imagine that for a sociology course you are asked to read an article by Talcott Parsons titled "Social Systems." In one section of the article Parsons offers a classification of social organizations. Later in the term you are asked to write a short essay demonstrating your understanding of Parsons's system of categories.

Taken out of its full context, here is the most relevant portion of Parsons's article, the section in which he offers his classification of social organizations. Don't be intimidated by these paragraphs. They are tough going, and you'll need to read them several times; but you needn't understand them completely to start working with Parsons's ideas.

CLASSIFICATION OF TYPES OF ORGANIZATION

Organizations are of course always part of a larger social structure of the society in which they occur. There is necessarily a certain variability among organizations which is a function of this wider societal matrix; an American organization is never quite like a British one even though they are nearly cognate in function. Discounting this type of variability, however, organizations may in the first instance be classified in terms of the *type of goal or function* about which they are organized. . . .

Seen in these terms the principal broad types of organization are:

1. *Organizations oriented to economic production.* The type case in this category is the business firm. Production should be understood in the full economic sense as "adding value"; it is by no means confined to physical production, e.g., manufacturing. It has been emphasized several times that every organization contributes in some way to every primary function (if it is well integrated in the society); hence we can speak only of economic *primacy*, never of an organization as being exclusively economic. This applies also to the other categories.

2. *Organizations oriented to political goals,* that is, to the attainment of valued goals and to the generation and allocation of power in the society. This category includes most organs of government, but in a society like ours, various other organizations are involved. The allocation of purchasing power through credit creation is an exercise of power in this sense; hence a good part of the banking system should be treated as residing in primarily political organizations. More generally, it seems legitimate to speak of incorporation as an allocation of power in a political sense; hence the corporate aspect of formal organizations generally is a political aspect.

3. *Integrative organizations.* These are organizations which on the societal level contribute primarily to efficiency, not effectiveness. They concern the adjustment of conflicts and the direction of motivation to the fulfillment of institutionalized expectations. A substantial part of the functions of the courts and of the legal profession should be classed here. Political parties, whose function is the mobilization of support for those responsible for government operations, belong in this category, and, to a certain extent, "interest groups" belong here, too. Finally, those organizations that are primarily mechanisms of social control in the narrower sense, for example hospitals, are mainly integrative.

4. *Pattern-maintenance organizations.* The principal cases centering here are those with primarily "cultural," "educational," and "expressive" functions. Perhaps the most clear-cut organizational examples are churches and schools. (Pattern maintenance is not here conceived to preclude creativity; hence research is included.) The arts so far as they give rise to organization also belong here. Kinship groups are ordinarily not primarily organizations in our technical sense, but in a society so highly differentiated as our own the nuclear family approaches more closely the characteristics of an organi-

zation than in other societies. As such it clearly belongs in the pattern-maintenance category.

— Talcott Parsons, "Social Systems," *Structure and Process in Modern Societies*

Here is the sociology assignment based on the reading: Explain Talcott Parsons's classification of social organizations and show how he would apply it to the following organizations.

the Republican Party
the Postal Service
a labor union
a professional athletic team
a college athletic team
a public high school
a private high school
a poker club
a street gang
a police department
the John Birch Society
an alumni organization
the American Medical Association (AMA)
the Federal Reserve Bank
the Environmental Protection Agency (EPA)
a mental institution
an insurance company
a health maintenance organization (HMO)

This assignment stretches a student's ability to make sense of Parsons, a notoriously difficult writer. A sociology teacher would probably reward you simply for demonstrating that you have done the reading thoughtfully, whether or not you sorted out the organizations exactly as Parsons would.

With a difficult piece of reading like this one, it's often a good idea to try putting into your own words what you think you understand, while also admitting, at least to yourself, what you don't. The act of writing out both sets of ideas may help you clarify them. Let's follow an imaginary student trying this strategy. As he wrestles his way through paraphrasing the categories, he makes points and raises questions, some of which will find their way into his eventual essay.

`Organizations oriented to economic production`. No problem with this one. Parsons is talking about businesses. Not just businesses that "add value" by producing things, but businesses that provide services too. The emphasis is on organizations that add something of value to the economy.

Organizations oriented to political goals. This one sounds straightforward, but I have trouble with it. I think I understand what Parsons means by "the generation and allocation of power," but I don't see what he means by saying these organizations are oriented toward "the attainment of valued goals." How is that different from the economic category? I'm also surprised by his bank example. I think of banks as businesses, but he thinks of them as political. But maybe I see what he means. Banks decide who gets how much and when. They allocate. They pull the strings that determine who gets what.

Integrative organizations. These seem to be organizations that help other organizations, and society as a whole, function smoothly. I don't get what he means by saying they're "efficient, but not effective" though. To integrate means to put together in a well-coordinated way, so integrative organizations coordinate things, perhaps without adding any value besides coordination. The example of lawyers and the legal system bothered me at first, until I thought of lawyers as go-betweens. Lawyers are always between opposing interests. By determining outcomes of these conflicts, lawyers help the system as a whole to operate.

Pattern-maintenance organizations. These are organizations with educational and cultural purposes. I think these look distinct enough. Except that I don't understand the label itself. Why "pattern maintenance"? I guess the emphasis is on how these organizations preserve a society's status quo through education and culture. People in the PTA tend to perpetuate the school system as it is. People in an Italian-American Society tend to build solidarity that can be passed down among Italian-Americans. I see how churches are a particularly clear example, preserving particular religious values from generation to generation.

Having worked through the categories in this way, our student is better prepared to use the categories to think about the organizations in the assignment question. Let's follow this student through the next stage of his thinking as he tries to figure out how to group the examples themselves. In his notes he probes — developing details, raising questions, trying out more than one category per organization. Here's a sampling of his notes.

Republican Party. Integrative. Parsons says so. Strange, though. Why aren't political parties "political"? Maybe because they simply serve as pipelines for politicians. It's only the elected officials who exercise power; the parties only provide the "raw material" in a fairly efficient way.

Postal Service. Integrative. It helps keep other organizations running, especially businesses, but also the government. Lately it has become privately operated, a sort of corporation, but I still don't think it fits the business category.

Professional athletic team. Pattern maintenance? I think of teams as part of culture. But pro sports are also businesses, maybe mainly businesses. I see the next category is "college athletic teams." I suppose I'm expected to place them in different categories. Well, the more I think about it, the stronger the business angle seems. Pro teams certainly add value--consumers pay plenty.

A public high school. There's another pairing here, with private high school. I suppose it depends on which high schools we have in mind. My high school did a good job. I suppose Parsons sees it as pattern maintenance, but I see that it could be called integrative too. It starts the sorting out process for people's professional roles, their jobs. "Efficiently"? That might be going too far. I'm pretty sure that Parsons would say that the main function of schools is to pass on cultural values, to keep those patterns in place.

Federal Reserve Bank. Clearly political. The biggest bank of all. It controls how much goes where and when.

Environmental Protection Agency. Another big branch of government. It's supposed to protect the environment for us all and so could be called pattern maintenance. But I think Parsons would call it political. From what I've heard of it lately, it hasn't done all that much protecting anyway. The question of how much gets protected and which polluters get leaned on is very political.

Mental institution. Definitely pattern maintenance. It takes troublesome people off the streets--though with all the homeless that may also be a political question. Helps keep the rest of us in line, fulfilling our social functions. Wait a minute, maybe that makes it "integrative." I'm starting to lose my grip on these categories again.

Insurance company. I wish I knew more about how these work. They're businesses and in some sense "add value," but they're also like banks in their power to throw money around. They could also be seen as integrative like the lawyers. Maybe I'll have to give over a section of my essay to the organizations that do not seem to fall within a single function.

HMO. These are like hospitals, which Parsons calls integrative. This will give me a chance to contrast the AMA. I think I'm starting to see what Parsons means by efficient rather than effective. HMOs seem a good way of getting people medical help quickly and adequately. But they're not necessarily the most effective or satisfying way.

This sort of note taking might have gone on mentally, without the writing. But writing out these ideas gives the writer more opportunity to retain and evaluate them. Notice that this student sometimes changes his mind or makes a discovery in the act of writing a note. He also composes some sentences and phrases that will find their way into the essay he ultimately writes.

As a next step, the student uses lists to sort the examples into Parsons's categories.

ECONOMIC	POLITICAL	INTEGRATIVE	PATTERN MAINTENANCE
Professional team	Labor union?	Rep. Party	College team
	AMA	Postal Service	Public school
	Federal Reserve	Labor union?	Private school?
	EPA	Private school?	Street gang?
		Police dept.	John Birch Soc.
		Mental instit.?	Alumni org.
Insurance co.?	Insurance co.?	Insurance co.?	Mental instit.?
		HMO	

Notice that in sorting the organizations into lists, the writer has made liberal use of question marks to indicate placements he is unsure about. His classifications are still provisional as he approaches the job of actually writing the essay. Although it's an advantage to know where an essay is going, there are also advantages in leaving room for more decisions and rethinking.

Looking over the number of uncertain placements and thinking about his uncertain interpretation of the categories themselves, this student faces a hard decision. Should he simply go for it, making the calls as best he sees them and leaving it at that? Or should he write the essay in a way that admits his hesitations about the placements? Before going further, he decides to ask himself some of the critical questions about classification schemes: Is this system meant to be absolute? Of what use is it? He quickly sees that Parsons doesn't mean it to be absolute. He decides that one of its uses is to help us become aware of the social organizations we take for granted and the various ways in which they influence our lives. Parsons also wants to suggest that some institutions are deceptive: They don't necessarily do what we think they do. The student decides that Parsons's system is deliberately an imprecise one and that Parsons intends the overlap between categories. He decides to stress a sentence in Parsons's entry on economic organizations: "Every organization contributes in some way to every primary function." That statement gives the student some leeway. He needs only to establish a "primary" function, and where he cannot see one, maybe he can say so. This decision enables the student to put his many hesitations to work for him.

The following is one of the later drafts of the student's essay in response to the assignment on page 296. What do you think of it?

According to Talcott Parsons, our most important social organizations can be classified into four types. These types he calls "organizations oriented to economic production," "organizations oriented to political goals," "integrative organizations," and "pattern-maintenance organizations." By the economic type he means businesses, organizations that exist because they "add value," economic value, to the social system as a whole. By the political type he means organizations that exert power and determine who benefits from that power. By integrative organizations he seems to mean organizations that are concerned primarily neither with economics nor with political power but with helping the society as a whole, including the other organizations, function smoothly. Finally, pattern-maintenance organizations have to do with preserving culture. They function mainly to keep new members of society behaving in the same general ways as the established members. Parsons doesn't see his categories as mutually exclusive. Most complex organizations fulfill several functions, but he thinks it's worth seeing which goals are most important to which organizations. Although I'm not sure I can follow every turn in Parsons's argument, I do think his system is a useful one for examining the institutions that influence our lives, sometimes in ways we don't realize.

Among the organizations I have been asked to classify, Parsons would find few that are oriented primarily for economic production. The insurance company is one possibility, but I think it could as easily belong to one of the other categories, and I'll discuss it later. The purest example of an economic organization, oddly enough, is a professional sports team. An economic function is to add value, not necessarily goods, and a professional athletic team does that by providing something for which people are willing to pay. We could argue that professional teams are also pattern-maintaining. Families pass down their Green Bay Packer tickets from generation to generation, and people in Chicago are always asking, "Do the Cubs have a chance this year?" But I think that as organizations their cultural function is dominated by their economic one.

Quite a few of the organizations on the list are political in Parsons's terms, but not as many as we might at first think. The Federal Reserve Bank is a strong political force. When it makes credit easier or harder to come by, its influence is felt by people all over the country. Here we can see the difference between what Parsons calls political and what he calls economic. The Federal Reserve, like other banks, doesn't add value, it distributes value by "allocating" it. That's power. Other governmental departments, including the Environmental Protection Agency, have the same role. Even if in theory that agency's role is to protect the entire public, in practice it protects some more than others. During most of the 1980s that agency, in a sense, allocated more power to businesses by not enforcing much environmental legislation. Again, that's politics. I'd include the American Medical Association and the bigger labor unions on this list of power allocators, though someone else might argue that they do not directly exert power but only seek to influence those who do. That's one of the main differences between Parsons's second and third categories. Political institutions allocate power directly, whereas integrative organizations make it possible for power to be distributed efficiently.

Most of the organizations on the list can be seen as mainly integrative or pattern-maintaining. The integrative ones include organizations like the Postal Service and the police department, which help keep various other segments of society either running smoothly or in check. An HMO is another good example of an integrative organization, and it illustrates what Parsons means in saying that integrative organizations are efficient but not necessarily effective. People insist on health care, and HMOs have developed as the most efficient way to get it to them, though that is not to say that the medical care they offer is the best care.

The Republican Party, it's interesting to notice, would also be classified by Parsons as integrative, even though they think of themselves as political. By calling political parties integrative, he seems to mean that political parties themselves don't distribute power, just juggle various of their members into position to get it if elected. This seems to me a somewhat shaky point though. Aren't those preparing for power also participating in power, and don't the elected politicians function also as party members?

Among the pattern-maintenance organizations Talcott

Parsons would also place public and private schools, alumni organizations, college athletic teams, and (probably) mental institutions. All of these are primarily involved in preserving the status quo, that is, in keeping cultural arrangements essentially the way they are from one year or one generation to the next. This category is quite flexible, though, and most of the organizations we place in it tend to tilt toward one of the other functions. Thus college sports are also businesses; public high schools have a major integrative function (sorting students toward their eventual social positions and roles); and mental institutions, besides maintaining cultural patterns, are also integrative and, in some way, businesses. Certainly for families that send troublesome members to them, they "add value," and the families pay highly for it.

The greatest value of Parsons's system is that it helps us to see that an organization fulfills several functions and that sometimes its apparent functions are not its most important. His classification, I want to point out, works primarily for large, important institutions, ones that affect us all. Thus I don't think the John Birch Society, which is primarily a cultural nuisance, or poker clubs, which are mainly a way of circulating money among the same men week after week, are major organizations in any of the four senses. On the other hand, something like an insurance company seems so hard for me to understand that I suspect it fulfills all the functions. It's a business because it adds a value that people are willing to pay for. But it's also political, in that where and how an insurance company distributes its funds can make other things happen or not happen. And insurance companies are integrative in the same way that the legal profession is--they manage conflict between other groups. And the insurance business does a lot to maintain at least the impression of continuity, as the images of umbrellas and fire hats seem to tell us. "You're in good hands with Allstate." Some organizations' functions seem so mixed that even Parsons might not want to try untangling them.

A Working Example from Public Health

As the previous example has demonstrated, applying someone else's classification system can demand interpretation, judgment, and decision making. These same abilities are called on when you develop categories on your own, but more pressure is placed on inventing than receiving.

As an example of this second sort of classifying, imagine yourself in a public health class that has stressed issues of public responsibility in national health care. As a final assignment at the end of the course, you are asked to classify the diseases on the following list. Some of the diseases you have read about in the course; others you only vaguely know as names. Rather than launching into lengthy research on the various diseases, you decide that your first step is to look them all up in a scientific dictionary, hoping that an effective way of grouping and dividing the diseases will occur to you. Do you see any possible drawbacks to this strategy?

Here is the assignment, followed by a compilation of the diseases with short definitions taken from a scientific dictionary:

> In light of the public health issues discussed in this course, develop a meaningful classification for the following diseases.

African sleeping sickness [MED] A disease of man confined to tropical Africa, caused by the protozoans *Trypanosoma gambiense* or *T. rhodesiense;* symptoms include local reaction at the site of the bite, fever, enlargement of adjacent lymph nodes, skin rash, edema, and during the late phase, somnolence and emaciation. Also known as African trypanosomiasis; maladie du sommeil; sleeping sickness.

Alzheimer's disease [MED] A type of presenile dementia associated with sclerosis of the cerebral cortex.

arteriosclerosis [MED] Thickening of the lining of arterioles, usually due to hyalinization or fibromuscular hyperplasia.

cancer [MED] Any malignant neoplasm, including carcinoma and sarcoma.

cirrhosis [MED] A progressive, inflammatory disease of the liver characterized by a real or apparent increase in the proportion of hepatic connective tissue.

cystic fibrosis [MED] A hereditary disease of the pancreas transmitted as an autosomal recessive; involves obstructive lesions, atrophy, and fibrosis of the pancreas and lungs, and the production of mucus of high viscosity. Also known as mucoviscidosis.

diabetes [MED] Any of various abnormal conditions characterized by excessive urinary output, thirst, and hunger; usually refers to diabetes mellitus.

elephantiasis [MED] A parasitic disease of man caused by the filarial nematode *Wuchereria bancrofti;* characterized by cutaneous and subcutaneous tissue enlargement due to lymphatic obstruction.

gonorrhea [MED] A bacterial infection of man caused by the gonococcus (*Neisseria gonorrhoeae*) which invades the mucous membrane of the urogenital tract.

kwashiorkor [MED] A nutritional deficiency disease in infants and young children, mainly in the tropics, caused primarily by a diet low in proteins and rich in carbohydrates. Also known as nutritional dystrophy.

leukemia [MED] Any of several diseases of the hemopoietic system characterized by uncontrolled leukocyte proliferation. Also known as leukocythemia.

malaria [MED] A group of human febrile diseases with a chronic relapsing course caused by hemosporidian blood parasites of the genus *Plasmodium,* transmitted by the bite of the *Anopheles* mosquito.

multiple sclerosis [MED] A degenerative disease of the nervous system of unknown cause in which there is demyelination followed by gliosis.

parkinsonism [MED] A clinical state characterized by tremor at a rate of three to eight tremors per second, with "pill-rolling" movements of the thumb common, muscular rigidity, dyskinesia, hypokinesia, and reduction in number of spontaneous and autonomic movements; produces a masked facies, disturbances of posture, gait, balance, speech, swallowing, and muscular strength. Also known as paralysis agitans; Parkinson's disease.

pertussis [MED] An infectious inflammatory bacterial disease of the air passages, caused by *Hemophilus pertussis* and characterized by explosive coughing ending in a whooping inspiration. Also known as whooping cough.

plague [MED] An infectious bacterial disease of rodents and humans caused by *Pasteurella pestis,* transmitted to humans by the bite of an infected flea (*Xenopsylla cheopis*) or by inhalation. Also known as black death; bubonic plague.

poliomyelitis [MED] An acute infectious viral disease which in its most serious form involves the central nervous system and, by destruction of motor neurons in the spinal cord, produces flaccid paralysis. Also known as Heine-Medin disease; infantile paralysis.

rickets [MED] A disorder of calcium and phosphorus metabolism affecting bony structures, due to vitamin D deficiency.

rubella [MED] An infectious virus disease of humans characterized by coldlike symptoms, fever, and transient, generalized pale-pink rash; its occurrence in early pregnancy is associated with congenital abnormalities. Also known as epidemic roseola; French measles; German measles; röteln.

scarlet fever [MED] An acute, contagious bacterial disease caused by *Streptococcus hemolyticus;* characterized by a papular, or rough, bright-red rash over the body, with fever, sore throat, headache, and vomiting occurring 2–3 days after contact with a carrier.

sickle-cell anemia [MED] A chronic, hereditary hemolytic and thrombotic disorder in which hypoxia causes the erythrocyte to assume a sickle shape; occurs in individuals homozygous for sickle-cell hemoglobin trait.

smallpox [MED] An acute, infectious, viral disease characterized by severe systemic involvement and a single crop of skin lesions which proceeds through macular, papular, vesicular, and pustular stages. Also known as variola.

syphilis [MED] An infectious disease caused by the spirochete *Treponema pallidum,* transmitted principally by sexual intercourse.

trichinosis [MED] Infection by the nematode *Trichinella spiralis* following ingestion of encysted larvae in raw or partially cooked pork; characterized by eosinophilia, nausea, fever, diarrhea, stiffness and painful swelling of muscles, and facial edema.

tuberculosis [MED] A chronic infectious disease of humans and animals primarily involving the lungs caused by the tubercle bacillus, *Mycobacterium tuberculosis,* or by *M. bovis.* Also known as consumption; phthisis.

— *McGraw-Hill Dictionary of Scientific and Technical Terms*

How might you try to classify these diseases? Try brainstorming a list of possible ideas on which you might base a classification. Write out your list.

One of the first ideas to occur to most people is to classify the diseases on the basis of their *causes.* Here's a sketch of categories you might establish after a quick run through the list.

PROTOZOA	NEMATODES	BACTERIA	PARASITES	VIRUSES	HEREDITY
African sleeping sickness	elephantiasis	gonorrhea	malaria	poliomyelitis	cystic fibrosis
		plague		rubella	sickle-cell anemia
		scarlet fever		smallpox	
		syphilis			
		tuberculosis			
		pertussis			

DIETARY DEFICIENCIES	DETERIORATION	INFLAMMATION	OTHER	UNKNOWN
kwashiorkor	Alzheimer's disease	cirrhosis	diabetes	cancer
rickets	arteriosclerosis			leukemia
	parkinsonism			
	multiple sclerosis			

This scheme helps a little; it gives some order to the list. But the categories seem unwieldy, don't they? Some seem imprecise; more important, there are simply too many categories. Because not enough diseases are combined, the categories do not seem to lend themselves well to generalizations. One strategy is to try to merge some of the causes in more general terms. A revised set of categories might look like this:

Diseases Caused by

Microorganisms

Others

Heredity

Dietary Deficiencies

Unknown

Or perhaps a two-way scheme like this one could handle various subcategories:

Infectious Diseases

Noninfectious Diseases

Do either of these possibilities seem more promising to you? Do you see other sorts of simpler groupings on the basis of cause?

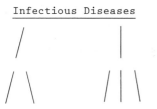

Using some system like those we just devised, we can imagine beginning the essay:

> Human diseases can be classified into three [or two, or four] main types. . . .

Before launching into such an essay, however, we should probably step back and reevaluate where we are heading. Notice how the classification of diseases has become an end in itself, divorced from the question and the issues of the public health class. We might want to reexamine our earlier decisions: for example, our silent assumption to regard all of these diseases as equals. Similarly, we might start to question our early decision to base our classification on our list of medical definitions. (Where did that decision lead us?) Look back at your own list of possible bases for classification. Do any of them seem more promising? Or any from the following list?

Possible Bases for Classifying Diseases

Causes
Treatments
Prevalence (which affect the most people?)
Severity
Organs & systems affected
Recurring or acute
Contagiousness
Future threat
Distribution
Expense
Research opportunities
Curability

To use one of these possible bases effectively, you would need to draw on whatever you had learned about the importance of the diseases in the public health course — and that is probably the intent of the question. With these considerations in mind, you might reshuffle your categories this way:

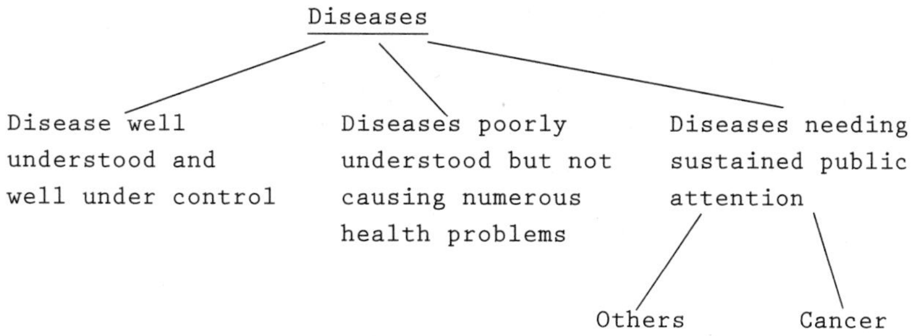

In what ways, given the question and the course, does this last classification seem to have advantages over the earlier ones? What might the opening paragraph of this student's essay look like? Without making yourself into a public health expert, but simply drawing on your general knowledge and a few of the facts from the definitions, try drafting that opening paragraph.

A readiness to think critically about classifying can enrich your academic writing. In most situations we are neither completely dependent on nor completely free of categories constructed by other people. In learning to recognize, apply, and modify the categories of other writers, we learn to participate in their ways of thinking. And in learning to develop categories of our own we begin to find ways to affect the thinking of others.

A Professional Application

In the following essay, law professor David Cole, writing for the current affairs weekly *The Nation,* uses a classifying scheme to analyze and debunk various myths that fuel opposition to immigration. Notice how Cole — a descendant of Irish immigrants — puts current opposition in historical context to show that arguments against immigration have always existed and, he contends, always proved unwarranted. As Cole takes up each myth, he uses statistical information, evidence from history and current policy, and other specific details to make his counterclaims. Cole's essay shows how classification can be used effectively in the service of arguments, helping the writer take apart, and then take up, opposing views.

Five Myths about Immigration

David Cole

For a brief period in the mid-nineteenth century, a new political movement captured the passions of the American public. Fittingly labeled the "Know-Nothings," their unifying theme was nativism. They liked to call themselves "Native Americans," although they had no sympathy for people we call Native Americans today. And they pinned every problem in American society on immigrants. As one Know-Nothing wrote in 1856: "Four-fifths of the beggary and three-fifths of the crime spring from our foreign population; more than half the public charities, more than half the prisons and almshouses, more than half the police and the cost of administering criminal justice are for foreigners."

At the time, the greatest influx of immigrants was from Ireland, where the potato famine had struck, and Germany, which was in political and economic turmoil. Anti-alien and anti-Catholic sentiments were the order of the day, especially in New York and Massachusetts, which received the brunt of the wave of immigrants, many of whom were dirt-poor and uneducated. Politicians were quick to exploit the sentiment: There's nothing like a scapegoat to forge an alliance.

DAVID COLE (b. 1958) is a professor of law at Georgetown University Law Center. He contributes regularly to several periodicals, including *The Nation* and *Legal Times.* "Five Myths about Immigration" first appeared in *The Nation* on October 17, 1994.

I am especially sensitive to this history: My forebears were among those dirt-poor Irish Catholics who arrived in the 1860s. Fortunately for them, and me, the Know-Nothing movement fizzled within fifteen years. But its pilot light kept burning, and is turned up whenever the American public begins to feel vulnerable and in need of an enemy.

Although they go by different names today, the Know-Nothings have returned. As in the 1850s, the movement is strongest where immigrants are most concentrated: California and Florida. The objects of prejudice are of course no longer Irish Catholics and Germans; 140 years later, "they" have become "us." The new "they" — because it seems "we" must always have a "they" — are Latin Americans (most recently, Cubans), Haitians and Arab-Americans, among others.

But just as in the 1850s, passion, misinformation and shortsighted fear often substitute for reason, fairness and human dignity in today's immigration debates. In the interest of advancing beyond know-nothingism, let's look at five current myths that distort public debate and government policy relating to immigrants.

1. *America is being overrun with immigrants.* In one sense, of course, this is true, but in that sense it has been true since Christopher Columbus arrived. Except for the real Native Americans, we are a nation of immigrants.

It is not true, however, that the first-generation immigrant share of our population is growing. As of 1990, foreign-born people made up only 8 percent of the population, as compared with a figure of about 15 percent from 1870 to 1920. Between 70 and 80 percent of those who immigrate every year are refugees or immediate relatives of U.S. citizens.

Much of the anti-immigrant fervor is directed against the undocumented, but they make up only 13 percent of all immigrants residing in the United States, and only 1 percent of the American population. Contrary to popular belief, most such aliens do not cross the border illegally but enter legally and remain after their student or visitor visa expires. Thus, building a wall at the border, no matter how high, will not solve the problem.

2. *Immigrants take jobs from U.S. citizens.* There is virtually no evidence to support this view, probably the most widespread misunderstanding about immigrants. As documented by a 1994 A.C.L.U. Immigrants' Rights Project report, numerous studies have found that immigrants actually *create* more jobs than they fill. The jobs immigrants take are of course easier to see, but immigrants are often highly productive, run their own businesses, and employ both immigrants and citizens. One study found that Mexican immigration to Los Angeles County between 1970 and 1980 was responsible for 78,000 new jobs. Governor Mario Cuomo reports that immigrants own more than 40,000 companies in New York, which provide thousands of jobs and $3.5 billion to the state's economy every year.

3. *Immigrants are a drain on society's resources.* This claim fuels many of the recent efforts to cut off government benefits to immigrants. However, most studies have found that immigrants are a net benefit to the economy because, as a 1994 Urban Institute report concludes, "immigrants generate significantly more in taxes paid than they cost in services received." The Council of Economic Advisers similarly found in 1986 that "immigrants have a favorable effect on the overall standard of living."

Anti-immigrant advocates often cite studies purportedly showing the contrary, but these generally focus only on taxes and services at the local or state level. What they fail to explain is that because most taxes go to the federal government, such studies would also show a net loss when applied to U.S. citizens. At most, such figures suggest that some redistribution of federal and state monies may be appropriate; they say nothing unique about the costs of immigrants.

Some subgroups of immigrants plainly impose a net cost in the short run, principally those who have most recently arrived and have not yet "made it." California, for example, bears substantial costs for its disproportionately large undocumented population, largely because it has on average the poorest and least educated immigrants. But that has been true of every wave of immigrants that has ever reached our shores; it was as true of the Irish in the 1850s, for example, as it is of Salvadorans today. From a long-term perspective, the economic advantages of immigration are undeniable.

Some have suggested that we might save money and diminish incentives to immigrate illegally if we denied undocumented aliens public services. In fact, undocumented immigrants are already ineligible for most social programs, with the exception of education for schoolchildren, which is constitutionally required, and benefits directly related to health and safety, such as emergency medical care and nutritional assistance to poor women, infants and children. To deny such basic care to people in need, apart from being inhumanly callous, would probably cost us more in the long run by exacerbating health problems that we would eventually have to address.

4. *Aliens refuse to assimilate, and are depriving us of our cultural and political unity.* This claim has been made about every new group of immigrants to arrive on U.S. shores. Supreme Court Justice Stephen Field wrote in 1884 that the Chinese "have remained among us a separate people, retaining their original peculiarities of dress, manners, habits, and modes of living, which are as marked as their complexion and language." Five years later, he upheld the racially based exclusion of Chinese immigrants. Similar claims have been made over different periods of our history about Catholics, Jews, Italians, Eastern Europeans and Latin Americans.

In most instances, such claims are simply not true; "American culture" has been created, defined and revised by persons who for the most part are descended from immigrants once seen as anti-assimilationist. Descendants of the Irish Catholics, for example, a group once decried as separatist and alien, have become Presidents, senators and representatives (and all of these in one family, in the case of the Kennedys). Our society exerts tremendous pressure to conform, and cultural separatism rarely survives a generation. But more important, even if this claim were true, is this a legitimate rationale for limiting immigration in a society built on the values of pluralism and tolerance?

5. *Noncitizen immigrants are not entitled to constitutional rights.* Our government has long declined to treat immigrants as full human beings, and nowhere is that more clear than in the realm of constitutional rights. Although the Constitution literally extends the fundamental protections in the Bill of Rights to all people, limiting to citizens only the right to vote and run for federal office, the federal government acts as if this were not the case.

In 1893 the executive branch successfully defended a statute that required Chinese laborers to establish their prior residence here by the testimony of "at least one credible white witness." The Supreme Court ruled that this law was constitutional because it was reasonable for Congress to presume that nonwhite witnesses could not be trusted.

The federal government is not much more enlightened today. In a pending case I'm handling in the Court of Appeals for the Ninth Circuit, the Clinton Administration has argued that permanent resident aliens lawfully living here should be extended no more

First Amendment rights than aliens applying for first-time admission from abroad — that is, none. Under this view, students at a public university who are citizens may express themselves freely, but students who are not citizens can be deported for saying exactly what their classmates are constitutionally entitled to say.

Growing up, I was always taught that we will be judged by how we treat others. If we are collectively judged by how we have treated immigrants — those who appear to-day to be "other" but will in a generation be "us" — we are not in very good shape.

Assignments

A Psychology Assignment

Here are a number of scribbles made by young children. (They appear in Rhoda Kellogg's *Analyzing Children's Art.*)

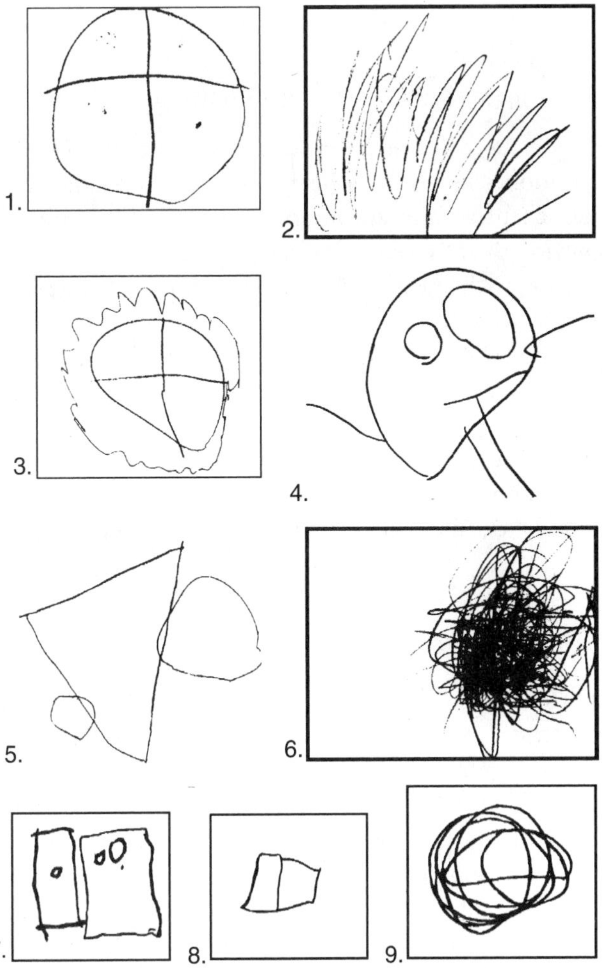

Selected Children's Scribbles.

And here's a discussion of developmental patterns in children's scribbles, adapted from psychologist Howard Gardner's discussion of *Analyzing Children's Art.*

> Somewhere between the ages of two and two-and-a-half, a child's scribbles begin to assume recognizable shapes: roughly, ovals and circles, rectangles, triangles, and crosses. Circular scribbles begin to look more like circles or they become more angular and take the shape of rectangles or triangles. Early squares become more "square-like" as the lines of the square even up and their angles become sharper. And so on. Around the age of three, the child begins to superimpose the forms on one another. Kellogg calls these superimposed or embedded patterns "combines." Examples would be a circle filled with lines, or a triangle inside a circle, or a square embedded in a triangle. When these forms are placed close together, Kellogg calls them "aggregates."

There are several possible classification schemes you could adapt from the above discussion: classifying the scribbles by age or, in one of several ways, by form. Try applying at least two of these schemes, trying one, then trying another to see what each enables you to do. Write up the results of each in two brief paragraphs that can be rough and experimental.

Here are some suggestions and some questions.

- Be playful and expect that you'll make changes in both the way you represent your classification scheme and where you place individual scribbles. Though classification schemes are meant to bring order to objects and events, developing and applying them is a complex, messy process.
- Once you adapt a scheme and apply it, ask yourself: Is there any way to simplify things further — either in the categories you created or in the way you placed the scribbles? Ask yourself the opposite question as well: Does any category seem unduly cluttered, do you need to break things out even more?
- Which of the classification schemes you used seemed more satisfying to you, was neater, led you to see something that perhaps you didn't see before you classified the scribbles?
- Did applying the classification schemes limit what you could see or say about the scribbles?

A Composition Assignment

Writing researcher Barbara Tomlinson has studied the comparisons (usually metaphors) professional writers use when they talk about their writing. The following statements appear in her book *The Buried Life of the Mind: Writers' Metaphors for Their Writing Processes.* Read them closely and develop a classification scheme to identify the different ways these writers talk about the act of writing, the different kinds of comparisons they make. Then write a short essay presenting your scheme. At the end of your presentation, you might want to consider whether any of these kinds of comparisons reflect your own writing process. Think of how you would describe your own writing process as a metaphor and consider your metaphor in relation to the scheme you just developed.

Here are some cues.

- Look for something very specific in each of the statements — this will usually be central to the comparison the writer is making.
- If you're feeling a little overwhelmed by the number of comparisons you have to work with, start small. Find two statements that share the same basic comparison, then find another, different, pair, and so on. These can form the beginning of your classification scheme.
- You might not be able to develop a scheme that works for all eighteen statements. Reality seldom conforms to our attempts to classify it. You may need to use a category labeled Miscellaneous.
- Realize that you may have to revise your scheme as you develop it. And maybe revise it again. Many classification schemes are fluid and evolving.

From *The Buried Life of the Mind: Writers' Metaphors for Their Writing Processes*

BARBARA TOMLINSON

1. It must be like chiseling a sculpture; if the sculptor does too fine a work too soon on what's big, heavy, gross work, then it's out of balance somewhere.

   — William Goyen

2. While I'm finishing a book it's a bit like tying a lot of knots that keep slipping and you're just impatient to get it done.

   — Nelson Algren

3. Finally, when I got within twenty pages of the end, I realized that I still hadn't delivered this [section]. I had a lot of threads, and I'd overlooked this one. . . . Putting in [that section] was like setting in a sleeve.

   — Joan Didion

4. "Consumer's Report" [the title of a poem] . . . was a breech-birth. The first thing to protrude was its bottom stanza. Then I had to urge forth the rest of it.

   — X. J. Kennedy

5. I always felt as if I were not writing the book myself, but rather as if I were serving as a subject for some intelligence which had decided to use me to write the book.

   — Norman Mailer

BARBARA TOMLINSON (b. 1946) is an associate professor of literature and director of the Muir Writing Program at the University of California, San Diego. Her current research focuses on the rhetoric of academic discourse. These statements appear in her unpublished work *The Buried Life of the Mind: Writers' Metaphors for Their Writing Processes.*

6. It wasn't a matter of rewriting but simply of tightening up all the bolts.

— Marguerite Yourcenar

7. Barnacles growing on a wreck or rock. . . . Things attach themselves to wrecks. Strange fish find your wreck or rock to be a good feeding place; after a while you've got a situation with possibilities.

— Donald Barthelme

8. Someone takes over and you just copy out what is being said.

— Henry Miller

9. Each book is worked over several times. I like to compare my method with that of painters centuries ago, proceeding, as it were, from layer to layer.

— Albert Moravia

10. Details, ideas: like so many free-floating metal shavings in want of a magnet.

— James Baker Hall

11. I'm more an oil painter now. More deliberate. A good deal less certain.

— Gore Vidal

12. I literally give birth to the ideas which wiggle in me wanting to come out.

— Abelardo Delgado

13. You work at it long enough, and it becomes so impersonal and so much an object that you're working on . . . it's like a car you've been trying to get to run, an old Hupmobile.

— Fred Chappell

14. The construction gave me some trouble, and I let in a hemstitch here, a gusset there.

— Lawrence Durrell

15. It just takes a little — a tiny seed. Then it takes root, and it grows.

— Katherine Anne Porter

16. I like to do first drafts at night, when I'm tired, and then do the surgical work in the morning when I'm sharp.

— Alex Haley

17. I type draft after draft almost obsessively until that first soft clay shapes itself into the poem it has to become.

— Laura Chester

18. All I know is that at a very early stage in the novel's development I get this urge to collect bits of straw and fluff, and to eat pebbles.

— Vladimir Nabokov

An Anthropology Assignment

In his study *The Little Community*, anthropologist Robert Redfield employs a kind of category system composed of four "defining qualities" to explain what he means by a "little community." The following passage appears in his opening chapter.

Read it once, then reread it, making sure you understand what he means by each of his "defining qualities." In fact, it would be a good idea to jot down, in your own words, a brief definition of each.

Then proceed on to the descriptions of five different societies, ones we have constructed from studies done by other anthropologists and sociologists. Once you have read the descriptions, select three and write an essay classifying the societies on the basis of Redfield's category system. How well does Redfield's system apply to each of them? Which societies seem to fit the best? Least well?

What does that fit or lack of fit help you understand about the societies? About Redfield's scheme? In the conclusion to your paper, try to respond to these last two questions.

Little Communities

ROBERT REDFIELD

The small community has been the very predominant form of human living throughout the history of mankind. The city is a few thousand years old, and while isolated homesteads appeared in early times, it was probably not until the settlement of the New World that they made their "first appearance on a large scale." To Tocqueville, the village or township was "the only association . . . so perfectly natural that wherever a number of men are collected it seems to constitute itself." One estimate is that today three-quarters of the human race still live in villages. . . .

In the development of systematic investigation of human life the small community has come to provide a commonly recognized unit of subject matter. Anthropologists have done most of their field work in little communities, and no small part of empirical sociology derives from the investigation of villages, small towns, and urban neighborhoods. . . .

What, then, do we mean more particularly by a little community? I put forward, first, the quality of distinctiveness: Where the community begins and where it ends is apparent. The distinctiveness is apparent to the outside observer and is expressed in the group-consciousness of the people of the community.

Second, the community we are here concerned with is small, so small that either it itself is the unit of personal observation or else, being somewhat larger and yet homogeneous, it provides in some part of it a unit of personal observation fully representative of the whole. A compact community of four thousand people in Indian Latin-America can be studied by making direct personal acquaintance with one section of it.

Third, the community to which we are to look in these chapters is homogeneous. Activities and states of mind are much alike for all persons in corresponding sex and age

---

Anthropologist and sociologist ROBERT REDFIELD (1897–1958) studied primitive villages in Mexico and Guatemala. He was considered an authority on Middle American folk culture. His books include *Tepoztlan, A Mexican Village* (1930), *A Village That Chose Progress* (1950), *Peasant Society and Culture* (1956), and *The Little Community* (1955), from which this passage is taken.

positions; and the career of one generation repeats that of the preceding. So understood, homogeneous is equivalent to "slow-changing."

As a fourth defining quality it may be said that the community we have here in mind is self-sufficient and provides for all or most of the activities and needs of the people in it. The little community is a cradle-to-the-grave arrangement. A club, a clique, even a family, is sectional or segmental contrasted with the integral little community.

These qualities — distinctiveness, smallness, homogeneity, and all-providing self-sufficiency — define a type of human community that is realized in high degree in the particular bands and villages to be mentioned in these chapters.

Summaries of Studies on Community

HUALCAN, PERU, 1952

Hualcan is a mountain village in Peru. It has been described by anthropologist William Stein, who visited it in the 1950s and wrote about it in his book *Life in the Highlands of Peru.*

In 1952 Hualcan had 740 residents, all Indians and all dependent on farming. Although most families had small plots of their own, many residents relied on farm work at nearby estates. They were seldom paid in wages, but in crops or grazing rights. According to Stein, two-thirds of the parents of children born in Hualcan during 1951 were born there themselves.

The main economic units in Hualcan are extended families. Few families consist only of husband, wife, and children. A newly married couple lives with the parents of one of them; or sometimes the families of brothers and sisters live together as a single household. Each household pools its resources under the leadership of a senior male, who assumes responsibility for all of that household's economic decisions — from purchases and labor contracts to fines, bribes, and community contributions.

A large portion of the community's time and resources go into religious festivals. There are six major festivals and numerous minor ones. Each festival is run by a *mayordomo* (steward). It is considered a great honor to be chosen *mayordomo* for one of the festivals, but in return the *mayordomo* must convert a sizable portion of his family's wealth to the expenses of the festival. It's an honor no one can refuse, one that only the older senior men have the resources to meet. The most prestigious role is that of *mayordomo* of the festivity of St. Ursula, saint of the harvest.

After having been *mayordomo,* a villager can be appointed to the commission of *varyok,* six men who are in effect the ruling political body of the town. They decide on public projects, collect taxes, and listen to disputes. Technically, the highest-ranking official in Hualcan is an officer stationed there by the Peruvian government, which does not officially recognize the *varyok.* But this official must yield to the real power of the *varyok.*

Although families seem to function independently economically, the system of religious festivals subordinates individual wealth to community purposes. And tying political power to these same religious celebrations ensures a gradual rise to political power of men committed to community traditions.

SPRINGDALE, NEW YORK, 1958

In *Small Town and Mass Society,* Arthur J. Vidich and Joseph Bensman describe the town of Springdale as it existed in 1958. A small town in upstate New York, Springdale is within a short drive of several small cities and within relatively easy reach of New York City and Washington, D.C. In 1958 it had about 2,500 residents. Many of those residents were farmers, and many of its businesses were farm-related. The town's largest single business was a sawmill owned and operated by two local families.

The stream that runs through the center of town originally split the community into two distinct neighborhoods, with separate shopping centers and even separate fire companies. But by 1958 there were few signs of the social tensions once felt between the two areas. Though no longer important as a boundary, the stream itself remained important enough to the community that a few years earlier the townspeople collectively contributed to reconstructing its dam.

The social life of the community revolved around churches, schools, and private homes. Local organizations included the Masons, the American Legion, the Grange, the local fire brigades, weekly book clubs, a community club, 4-H, and booster groups. Residents of Springdale spoke of themselves as "just plain folks" and saw their town as a place where "everybody knows everybody" and "where you can say hello to anybody." People passing on the street would regularly stop to exchange greetings; in fact, people not stopping would be regarded as snobs. Springdalers were very aware of the nearby cities and seemed very proud to think of themselves as rural people.

Much of the town's economy revolved around farming. Many of the town's small businesses depended on the trade of farmers, and many of the farmers, in turn, relied on stable grain prices. Small fluctuations in milk prices could be felt throughout the community. When fixed agricultural costs rose, the town's general economy suffered.

Next to farming, the closest thing to a major enterprise in Springdale, according to Vidich and Bensman, was the community school, employing about sixty people. Located in the center of town, it was also viewed as the social and moral hub of the community, and its tax support was seen by most residents as an investment in the town's future.

According to Vidich and Bensman, one-fourth of the adults living in Springdale in 1958 were born there. Some of them had not lived in Springdale continuously, however. One-third of the town's population arrived during the years between 1940 and 1952.

THE VICE LORDS, CHICAGO, 1967

R. Lincoln Keiser closely studied the Vice Lords, a group of street gangs inhabiting Chicago's major black ghettos (*The Vice Lords: Warriors of the Streets*). Keiser characterized the Vice Lords' social organization as a "federation," each branch "with its own name, set of officers, and territory." Most groups also had female auxiliaries. The number of branches kept shifting as old groups dissolved and new ones came into being. Keiser estimated that the size of the Vice Lords in the late 1960s varied between 600 and 3,000.

In his study, Keiser described the oldest branch of the Vice Lords, the City Lords. The City Lords were formed in 1958 at the Illinois State Training School for Boys in St. Charles, Illinois. It had a seven-man group of officers, including not only president, vice-president, and secretary-treasurer, but "supreme war counselor, war counselor, gun keeper, and sergeant-at-arms." The center of the City Lords' territory became 16th and Lawndale. The precise boundaries of that territory were hard to define. As Keiser puts it, a Vice Lord's territory "is that part of Chicago in which there is little chance that a Vice Lord will be attacked by an enemy group but a significantly larger chance that a member of an enemy club will be attacked by a group of Vice Lords."

Violent exchanges with other street gangs are frequent. Sometimes they occur by chance, while at other times they occur when Vice Lords deliberately enter enemy territory or when they perceive an invasion into their own. Despite the constant violence, membership in the group is also perceived as a defense against violence. Young boys often see membership in the group as a way to prevent being harassed by older boys. The Vice Lords replenish their numbers by recruiting such boys. A young boy entering the brotherhood usually must go through a trial period, during which time an older member is assigned to watch out for him. Bonds usually form quickly, and there is a strong sense of group unity.

Despite the group's solidarity, membership is also very fluid among the older members. Keiser estimates the 1967 membership of the City Lords to be about 150, though he admits that an accurate number was hard to estimate, even for the City Lords themselves:

> A person may get a job, start supporting a family, and cease to take part in most Vice Lord activities. Occasionally, however, he may come out on the corner, drink wine, and shoot craps with other Vice Lords. While he is on the corner he acts like and is treated by others as a Vice Lord. . . . Further, an individual himself may claim to be a part of the group in one instance but deny he is a member at other times.

THE IKS, UGANDA, 1967

The Iks are a small tribe of hunter-gatherers described by Colin Turnbull in his book *The Mountain People.* Turnbull visited the tribe between 1964 and 1967, soon after the once nomadic tribe had been restricted by the Ugandan government to a mountainous region near the Kenyan border.

The Iks observed by Turnbull lived clustered in isolated villages. They foraged for food, but without the ability to move from place to place, they had to undergo great scarcities during some times of the year. When food was available, they consumed it immediately. The Iks made no attempt to share food with one another. Even little children had to compete for food, with the weaker children often dying.

Turnbull observed little social cooperation among the Iks. Husbands often beat their wives and discarded them casually whenever they wished. Most young women became prostitutes as a way of feeding themselves. Both men and women seemed to age very quickly, and old people were not tolerated for very long. When no longer self-sufficient they often were turned out of their homes to die. The Iks acknowledged few family bonds.

An Ik village consisted of a cluster of thatched huts, surrounded and interpenetrated by a dense maze of brush. The largest village visited by Turnbull, "village Number Five," comprised thirty such huts. The village was without any central clearing or meeting place. Moving from hut to hut through the tangle of surrounding brush was very difficult, but each hut had a narrow crawl space leading to an outer edge of the compound. According to Turnbull, no villager had any need to see fellow villagers, and whole days passed without human interaction. Most villagers were distrustful of one another and particularly antagonistic toward their closest neighbors. Turnbull quotes a characteristic greeting and reply: "Brinji Ngag.". . ."Bera Ngag" ("Give me food.". . ."There is no food").

The Iks practiced no agriculture, and they were no longer successful hunters — though in the past they had flourished by hunting cooperatively. The Iks did have some income: They let Ugandan cattle thieves hide cattle within their thickets. Indirectly cattle raids became their major economic activity, something quite irritating to the young and struggling Ugandan government, a government otherwise indifferent toward them.

THE HUTTERITES, JASPER, CANADA, 1967

The Hutterites are a religious sect that colonized Jasper, Saskatchewan, emigrating from South Dakota during the 1950s and early 1960s. By the mid-1960s six separate Hutterite colonies existed in the Jasper region, representing about 8 percent of Jasper's total population. This account of their life-style is drawn from *Hutterite Brethren* by John W. Bennett.

The Hutterites are Anabaptists and can point to a 500-year tradition of religious harassment. Their religious beliefs and practices are not unlike those of other Protestant groups; what makes them different is their commitment to communal living and their rejection of the society around them.

The Hutterites colonize by buying up farmland. A settlement stops growing and divides when it reaches a size of about 150 people. According to Bennett, a colony any larger than this "becomes difficult to manage by means of the intimate forms of social control used by the Hutterites, and difficult to support on the amount of land usually available." When a new colony starts up, it is located far enough away from established colonies to appease fears among other Jasper residents that the Hutterites are trying to buy up the entire district. The various colonies, though self-sustaining, do maintain social and economic contact with one another.

The Hutterites live by agriculture. Because of their thorough commitment to rural life, their culture seems to have a peasant quality. They have a deep respect for traditional craftmanship and for conservative education. Yet they are not entirely resistant to modern developments, showing themselves quite willing, for example, to take advantage of advances in farm machinery.

The Hutterites antagonize other residents of Jasper by having little or nothing to do with them. Their only contact with the town is their use of it for delivering, shipping, and receiving mail. Although the Hutterites do some buying and selling with the outside world, their economy does not seem to rely on such trade. When shortages occur, the Hutterites manage to get by on their reserves.

The Hutterites preach self-help and avoidance of worldly corruption. They practice adult baptism. They associate only with other Hutterites, and they regard all those who do not practice communal living as fallen Christians. And they consider all who are not Christians heathen.

An Art Assignment

Develop a system for classifying the human images that follow, all works of art produced in and around the 1920s. Explain your classification system in an essay. We realize that not everyone has a rich vocabulary for talking about art, but describe what you see as well as you can. You can get started by asking yourself what methods the artists seem to be using to depict their figures. What do the figures look like? What features do you notice? How are they arranged against the background? What do you feel when you look at them?

As a postscript to your essay, write an additional paragraph or two, reflecting on how this effort of classifying has affected how you look at these works of art. Is something lost as well as gained?

Selected Images of the Human Form

FIGURE 1. George Grosz. *Republican Automatons.* 1920. Watercolor on paper, 23⅝″ × 18⅝″ (60 × 47.3 cm). Collection, The Museum of Modern Art, New York. Advisory Committee Fund. Photograph: © 1997 The Museum of Modern Art, New York.

FIGURE 2 (above). Glenn O. Coleman. *Minetta Lane.* 1928. Lithograph, printed in black, 11¼″ × 11″ (28.5 × 27.9 cm). Collection, The Museum of Modern Art, New York. Gift of Abby Aldrich Rockefeller. Photograph: © 1997 The Museum of Modern Art, New York.

FIGURE 3 (left). Marc Chagall. *Before the Easel,* plate 18 from *Mein Leben,* by Marc Chagall. Berlin, Paul Casirer, 1923. Etching and drypoint, printed in black, 9¾″ × 7½″ (24.8 × 19 cm). Collection, The Museum of Modern Art, New York. The Louis E. Stern Collection. Photograph: © 1997 The Museum of Modern Art, New York.

FIGURE 4 (above left). Pablo Picasso. *Four Dancers.* 1925. Pen and ink on paper, $13\frac{7}{8}'' \times 10''$ (35.2 × 25.4 cm). Collection, The Museum of Modern Art, New York. Copyright © 1997 Estate of Pablo Picasso/Artists Rights Society (ARS), New York. Reprinted with permission of ARS. Photograph: © 1997 The Museum of Modern Art, New York.

FIGURE 5 (above right). Henri Matisse. *La Persanne — Odalisque with Veil.* 1929. Lithograph. Sheet: 635 × 447 mm ($25'' \times 17\frac{1}{2}''$); image: 480 × 300 mm ($19'' \times 11\frac{3}{4}''$). Bequest of W. G. Russell Allen. Courtesy, Museum of Fine Arts, Boston.

FIGURE 6 (below). George Scholz. *Daily Paper.* 1922. Lithograph, printed in black, $7\frac{7}{8}'' \times 8\frac{5}{8}''$ (20 × 22 cm). Collection, The Museum of Modern Art, New York. Purchase. Photograph: © 1997 The Museum of Modern Art, New York.

FIGURE 7 (above). Dod Proctor. *Morning.* 1926. Tate Gallery, London/Art Resource, New York.

FIGURE 8 (below left). Alfred Henry Maurer. *Standing Female Nude.* c. 1927–1928. Casein on gesso on composition board, 21 13/16″ × 18¼″. Collection, Frederick R. Weisman Art Museum, University of Minnesota, Minneapolis. Gift of Ione and Hudson Walker. Photograph: © 1997 Frederick R. Weisman Art Museum, University of Minnesota, Minneapolis.

FIGURE 9 (below right). Erich Heckel. *Self-Portrait (Portrait of a Man).* 1919. Woodcut, printed in color, 18 3/16″ × 12¾″ (46.2 × 32.5 cm). Collection, The Museum of Modern Art, New York. Purchase. Photograph: © 1997 The Museum of Modern Art, New York.

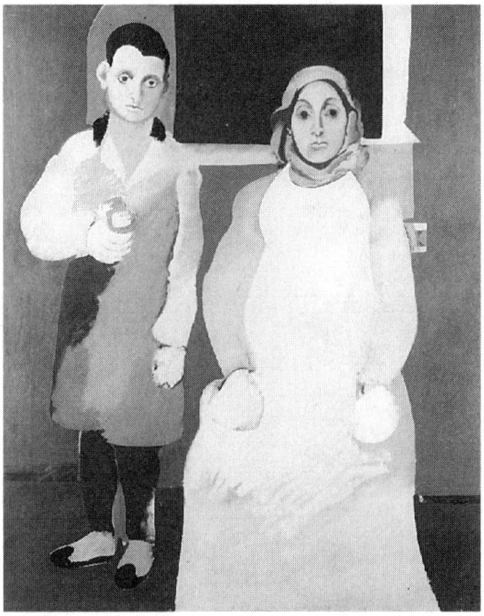

FIGURE 10 (top). Edward Hopper. *Night Shadows.* 1921. Etching, printed in black, $6\frac{15}{16}''\times 8\frac{3}{16}''$ (17.6 × 20.7 cm). The Museum of Modern Art, New York. Gift of Abby Aldrich Rockefeller. Photograph: © 1997 The Museum of Modern Art, New York.

FIGURE 11 (bottom left). Max Beckmann. *Group Portrait, Eden Bar.* 1923. Woodcut, printed in black, $19\frac{1}{2}''\times 19\frac{5}{8}''$ (49.5 x 49.8 cm). Collection, The Museum of Modern Art, New York, Abby Aldrich Rockefeller Fund. Photograph: © 1997 The Museum of Modern Art, New York.

FIGURE 12 (bottom right). Arshile Gorky. *The Artist and His Mother.* c. 1926–1936. Oil on canvas, 60″ × 50″ (152.4 × 127 cm). Collection of the Whitney Museum of American Art. Gift of Julien Levy for Maro and Natasha Gorky in memory of their father. Photograph: © 1997 Whitney Museum of American Art.

Figure 13 (left). Edvard Munch. *Three Girls on the Bridge.* 1918. Woodcut, printed in color, 19 3/4″ × 17 1/16″ (50.2 × 43.3 cm) (irreg.). Collection, The Museum of Modern Art, New York. Purchase. Photograph: © 1997 The Museum of Modern Art, New York.

Figure 14 (bottom left). Fernand Léger. *Skating Rink.* Costume design for the ballet produced by Ballet Suédois, Paris. 1922. Watercolor and pencil on paper, 12 3/8″ × 9 1/2″ (31.4 × 24.1 cm). Collection, The Museum of Modern Art, New York. W. Alton Jones Foundation Fund. Photograph: © 1997 The Museum of Modern Art, New York.

Figure 15 (bottom right). Georges Rouault. Trial proof for *And of the Lost Life of the Prostitute Who Gave Herself for a Bone to Gnaw,* rejected plate from *Miserere.* (Commissioned, but unpublished by Vollard.) Print executed c. 1922–1927. Lift ground aquatint and etching with roulette over photogravure, printed in black, 24 1/16″ × 17 5/16″ (61.2 × 44 cm). Collection, The Museum of Modern Art, New York. Abby Aldrich Rockefeller Fund. Photograph: © 1997 The Museum of Modern Art, New York.

A Biology Assignment

The following passage from Michael L. McKinney's textbook *Evolution of Life: Processes, Patterns, and Prospects* relies on classifying both conceptually and in the way it's organized. Write a brief essay in which you discuss the relation of classifying to evolutionary theory. (You can use both McKinney's text and illustrations.) Include in your essay some discussion of the strengths and limitations of the use of classifying in evolutionary theory.

As a postscript, you might want to comment on the effectiveness of McKinney's use of the classifying strategy in his writing and the effectiveness of the way he incorporates illustrations into written text.

From *Evolution of Life: Processes, Patterns, and Prospects*

MICHAEL L. MCKINNEY

Evidence for evolution by selection of variation is shown by indications that life has changed through descent with modification (to use Darwin's phrase for evolution). . . . If descent with modification has occurred, then we would expect that, going back in time, all life ultimately originated with a single ancestor whose descendants have since progressively diversified and branched off. Even though life has become highly varied through branching, we would still expect some very basic similarities that unite all life on earth, as an imprint from that common origin. Since life begins with chemical evolution, we would expect these most basic similarities to be chemical in nature. In addition, we can expect similarities in anatomy and embryological development. Indeed, this is what we find.

BIOCHEMICAL SIMILARITIES

All life on earth today, from bacteria to whales to plants, shows two kinds of biochemical similarities. One, in the chemistry of heredity, the same DNA code is used by all organisms. Thus, a gene in a rose can, for example, "read" that from a human. Two, in the chemistry of physiology, many molecules of cellular function are the same, using the same biochemical pathways to respire, use energy, and so on. For instance, adenosine triphosphate (ATP)[1] and cytochrome proteins[2] are involved in respiration in every organism. Furthermore, biochemical traits are more similar in groups that have a more recent common ancestry. For example, blood proteins are similar in all mammals, but those of humans are more similar to the blood proteins of other primates than to those of dogs.

[1]**adenosine triphosphate:** An energy source in metabolic reactions [Eds.].
[2]**cytochrome proteins:** Proteins important in cell metabolism [Eds.].

MICHAEL L. MCKINNEY (b. 1953) is associate professor of geology at the University of Tennessee, Knoxville. His published work includes *Environmental Science: Systems and Solutions* (1996) and *Evolution of Life: Processes, Patterns, and Prospects* (1993), excerpted here.

ANATOMICAL SIMILARITIES

Similarity of organs also reveals patterns of common ancestry. For instance, as shown in Figure 1, the forelimbs of humans, whales, dogs, and birds are all composed of the same bones. This is in spite of the forelimb's vastly different functions in each animal: flight in the bird, swimming (steering) in the whale, running in the dog, and grasping in the human. This indicates that all of these four creatures shared a common ancestor with a forelimb that was modified in different ways. Selection has variously "tinkered" with the ancestral forelimb as the groups separated and took up different ways of life. These are called *homologous* organs because they are derived from the same ancestral organ. As you might expect, homologous organs often differ most between groups that separated in the more distant past, especially where they have taken up very different ways of life. Thus, the bird forelimb is more different from the human forelimb than the dog's is (Figure 1). This is because, in addition to a flying lifestyle, the birds separated from the line leading to dogs and humans over 100 million years ago, whereas dogs and the human lineage separated many millions of years after that.

An interesting kind of homologous organ is the *vestigial organ.* Such organs are no longer useful, but have not yet been fully eliminated by natural selection. For instance, horse evolution involved the reduction of all digits ("toes"), except for the middle (third) one on which horses now run . . . . However, the remnants of the digits next to this middle toe are still present, being called "splint bones." These splint bones are homologous to the second and fourth toes on humans, modified from a common mammalian ancestor with five-digit limbs. Another example is the python snake, which has small, useless hind limbs, retained from its lizard ancestor. The human appendix is yet another of many possible examples, being the remnant of a once useful digestive organ. . . .

DEVELOPMENTAL SIMILARITIES

You may be wondering how we can recognize organs as being homologous, when they differ between two groups (such as the bird's wing and the human limb). The answer is that each bone and organ can be traced as it originates and develops during the growth

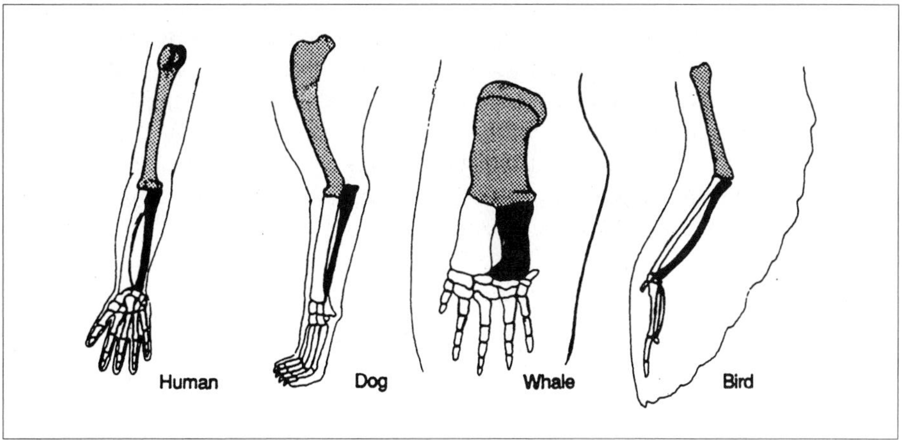

FIGURE 1. Homologous organs can serve different functions. For example, the forelimbs of humans, dogs, whales, and birds are different in function, but are composed of the same elements and have similar embryological origins. From R. Wicander and S. Monroe, *Historical Geology* (St. Paul, MN: West Publishing, 1989), p. 138.

of the embryo. Homologous organs come from the *same embryonic precursors.* This is a very crucial point because it shows that evolution occurs by modifying development. People usually visualize evolutionary change by noting species' differences among adults. But in reality, the only way to create different adults is to *alter how they develop* (are "assembled") into adults.

In general, only the later part of development is modified — early changes tend to alter too many later events. For instance, if a small group of cells in an embryo eventually forms the entire digestive system, even a slight change of those few cells could interfere with the development of the entire system. An entire organ could be lost if the few precursor cells that multiply into that organ are removed. On the other hand, a change in a few cells after the digestive system has formed (and grown to consist of billions of cells) would hardly be noticed. Thus, most evolution has occurred by altering only the later parts of development. Mutations that alter earlier parts are much more likely to be fatal and not passed on. Therefore, when we compare the entire developmental sequence of various groups, we see many developmental similarities among them. For example, a comparison of development in the major vertebrate groups, shown in Figure 2, reveals the most similarity at earlier stages. At eight weeks old, humans have gill structures, a primitive tail, a circulatory pattern, and the general shape of a fish. As shown in the fossil record, this is because humans are descended from certain fish that became the first land vertebrates. This is true of all the other vertebrates, from amphibians to birds, which also have these fish as ancestors. As humans (and other vertebrates) evolved, the newer traits (such as lungs, body hair, arms, larger brain, and so on) tended to be added on at the end of development.

This process of evolution through modification later in development leads to the following two basic observations. One, more closely related groups will tend to have more similar developmental sequences, usually not diverging until near the end of development. Compare, for instance, the human versus mammal and human versus salamander sequences (Figure 2). Human and mammal development diverge later than that of human and salamander. Two, in a very general way, the developmental sequence will repeat the evolutionary changes of the past. Because modifications are made at the end of the sequence, old evolutionary stages are retained. For instance, the human retention of gill structure and a tail give evidence that fish are ancestors of humans. When this was first observed by embryologists, this led to the *theory of recapitulation,* which said that developmental sequences always "recapitulated" (in other words, "repeated") the organism's evolutionary past. However, we now know that this is an oversimplification. . . . Nevertheless, the basic pattern of evolutionary modification can often be seen in the developing embryo, even though development does not exactly repeat each evolutionary change of the species' ancestry.

SIMILARITIES AND THE CLASSIFICATION OF LIFE

The chemical, anatomical, and developmental similarities discussed above are inevitably going to affect how we perceive and organize living things. It is obvious that some groups, such as snakes and lizards, are more closely related than others, such as snakes and dogs. Generally speaking, descent with modification means that *more similar groups have more recently become separated.* Conversely, the longer that groups have been sep-

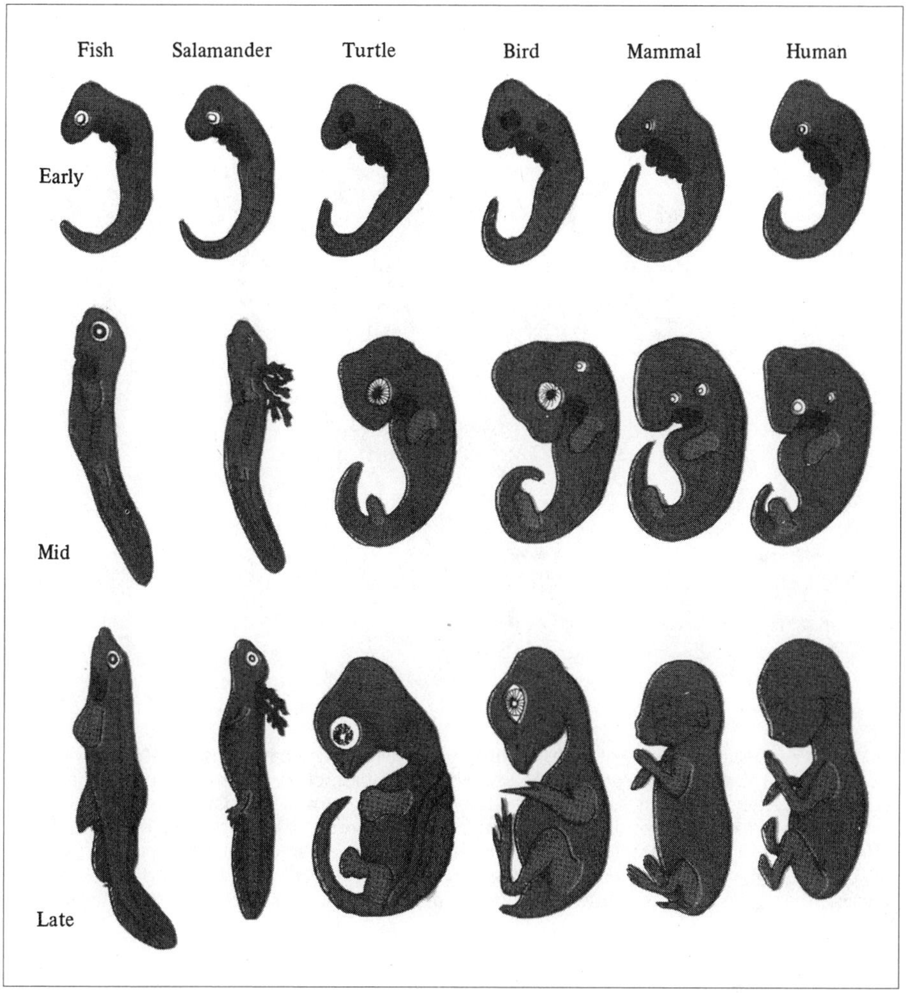

FIGURE 2. A comparison of development in major vertebrate groups. Similarities in appearance tend to occur in the earliest stages. From J. Barrett et al., *Biology,* p. 755.

arated, the more they anatomically (and behaviorally) diverge, as they continue to be modified in different ways. . . . This progressive separation, much like a family tree, inevitably leads to a hierarchical classification, or nesting, whereby groups can be classified into more closely related subgroups and less closely related supergroups. In short, descent with modification causes a hierarchical pattern of similarity.

Such a pattern is shown in Figure 3, the formal biological system of classification, using the coyote as an example. So apparent is the hierarchy of life that this formal scheme — species, genus, and so on — was proposed by Carolus Linnaeus in the 1700s, well before evolution through natural selection was even heard of. Similar genera are grouped into families, which are grouped into orders, which are grouped into classes. The process of classifying organisms into this scheme is called *taxonomy.* In the case of the coyote (Figure 3), it is a mammal (specified by the class) and a member of the order

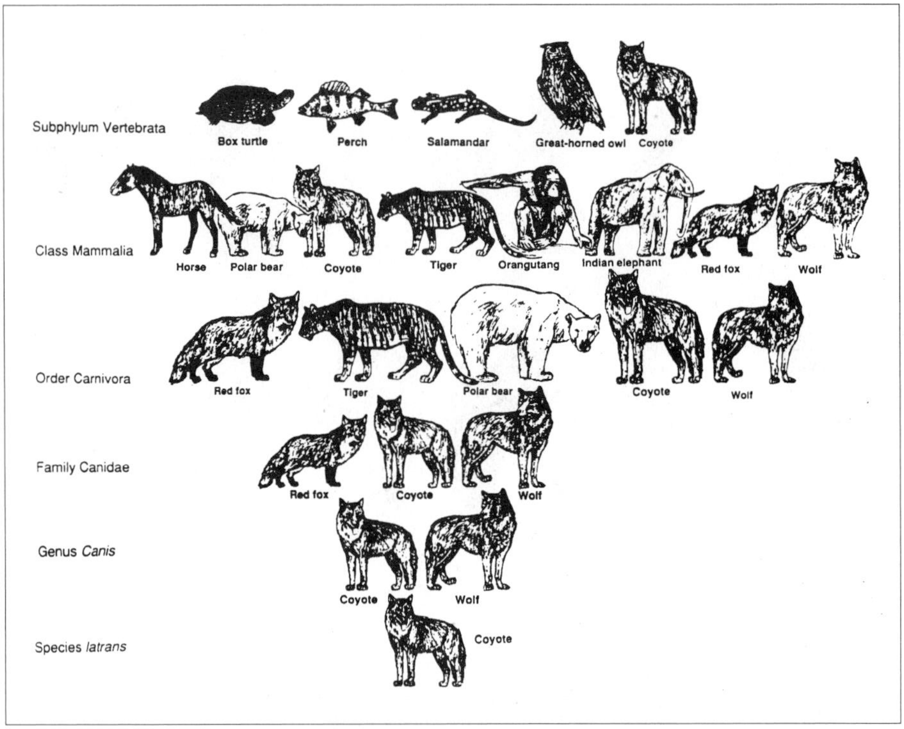

FIGURE 3. A classification of organisms according to their shared characteristics. Members of the subphylum *Vertebrata,* including fish, amphibians, reptiles, birds, and mammals, have a segmented vertebral column. Among these, however, only warm-blooded animals with hair or fur and mammary glands are considered mammals. Eighteen orders of mammals are recognized, including the order Carnivora, which is distinguished by specialized teeth necessary for an all-meat diet. The family Canidae and genus *Canis* include only doglike carnivores and closely related species. From R. Wicander and S. Monroe, *Historical Geology* (St. Paul, MN: West Publishing, 1989), p. 137.

Carnivora (meat-eaters). Within this order, it belongs to the subset that includes only dog relatives, the family Canidae. (Thus, cats fall within a different family, the Felidae, although they are also in the order Carnivora.)

Taxonomy may seem straightforward enough, but there are many practical problems in classifying life forms. For instance, "similarity" is a very subjective perception — to some taxonomists, two groups may seem much more closely related than to other taxonomists. The main problem is deciding which traits are most important as criteria for classifying. *Cladistics* is one of the new methods that attempts to objectively classify traits. For example, *primitive traits* are those that are shared by many organisms (such as hair in mammals). In contrast, *derived traits* are traits that are more recently evolved, usually being therefore limited to fewer organisms (such as grasping hands in primate mammals).

The problems of classification are greatly magnified in fossils, where most traits and many species are not preserved. Yet since over 99 percent of all life is now extinct, taxonomic classification of fossils must be attempted if we are to understand evolutionary relationships. Also, the sheer number of species makes that job very difficult. Even ignoring the fossil record, over a million living species have been described and classified; yet there may be thirty times that number undescribed (many of these are insects).

A Sociology Assignment

Culture shock is a general term for describing the problems that people experience in making the transition from a familiar to an unfamiliar setting. The first reading is an excerpt from a book written for nurses by nursing professors Pamela J. Brink and Judith Saunders. The authors define four distinct phases of culture shock. Each of the phases of culture shock becomes a kind of category of experience, a way to classify patterns of feelings and behaviors — and Brink and Saunders theorize that these phases come in a particular order.

Brink and Saunders's piece is followed by readings portraying the experiences of five people adjusting to life in the United States: Wood Chuen Kwong came to San Francisco from Canton, China, as an adult in 1979; Amitar Ray, who received a medical degree in his native India, immigrated to the United States, where there was a shortage of physicians, in 1972; Negi, a young girl whose story is told in Esmeralda Santiago's memoir, *When I Was Puerto Rican,* moved with her mother, sister, and brother to her grandmother's home in Brooklyn, where she had to adjust to a new school and a new way of life; Alex Bushinsky, a Russian Jew, immigrated to New York for work in 1976 and faced many economic and cultural challenges; finally, Haroutioun Yeretzian, an Armenian from Lebanon, also arrived in America in 1976 and eventually opened an Armenian bookstore in Hollywood.

As you read each passage, ask yourself two things: Do the feelings and behaviors of the central character or characters fit those feelings and behaviors described in any of the phases described by Brink and Saunders? If they do, do they come in the order suggested by the theory? Then write an essay using specific details from the readings to discuss the legitimacy of Brink and Saunders's portrayal of culture shock.

In a separate, brief paper — one that can be rough and experimental — reflect on the act of trying to apply a classification scheme and a theoretical model to particular cases: the ways this process helped you understand people's experience and the ways it narrowed or misrepresented their experience.

For those of you who immigrated to the United States or have spent a significant amount of time in another culture, we offer a further option: Write an essay discussing your own experience of crossing cultures using Brink and Saunders's model, specifically considering the ways the model fits and illuminates your experience and the ways it doesn't.

If you are interested in the subject of immigration, you may want to do this assignment in coordination with the related material in the Opening Problem (p. 286), A Professional Application (p. 308), and Readings: U.S. Immigration Patterns (p. 356).

The Phases of Culture Shock

Pamela J. Brink and Judith Saunders

[The researcher] Oberg's original paper isolated and described four phases of culture shock and named the first phase the "Honeymoon Phase.". . . The other three phases were described but not named. The following discussion is an attempt to name and extend Oberg's discussion.

Phase one. "The Honeymoon Phase" is marked by excitement. The desire to learn about the people and their customs is great; sightseeing is anticipated with pleasure; and getting to work and accomplishing all the goals envisioned at home provide the basis for this phase. Travelers, visiting dignitaries, and other temporary functionaries may never experience any other phase but this one.

Phase two. "The Disenchantment Phase" generally does not begin until the individual has established residence, i.e., when he begins to become aware of the setting as his area of residence. This sense of awareness often is associated with the realization that one is "stuck here" and cannot get out of the situation. What was "quaint" may become aggravating. Simple tasks of living are time consuming because they must be done in a different way. This beginning awareness often results in frustration — either frustration because the indigenous population is too stubborn to see things your way or frustration because you can't see things their way and are constantly making social errors. Embarrassment coupled with feelings of ineptness attack self-image or self-concept.

Particular, individual styles of behavior are developed over the years through the principles of inertia and economy. Usually the individual is unaware of the operation of these principles and their effect on him. They form part of ethnocentrism: "The way I do things is the right way (and perhaps for some the only way) to do things." The disenchantment phase directly threatens ethnocentrism because the host country believes exactly the same way about its customs and sees no reason to change its ways. Phase two includes a reexamination of one's self from the vantage point of another set of values. In this phase failure often outweighs success.

To this, add loneliness. No one knows you well enough to reaffirm your sense of self-worth. The distance from home is magnified. Home itself assumes the aura of Mecca — distant, unattainable, beautiful. This form of nostalgia for the past and the familiar seems to have two effects. Mail and visitors from home assume immense importance as a contact with people who believe in you and think you are important. To protect yourself from these feelings of loneliness and lack of self-esteem, you attack the presumed cause of these feelings — the host country. Feelings of anxiety and inadequacy are often expressed through depression, withdrawal, or eruptions of anger at frustration; or by seeking out fellow countrymen to the exclusion of the indigenous population. This period in

---

Nurse-anthropologist Pamela J. Brink is a professor of nursing and anthropology at the University of Alberta in Edmonton. Judith Saunders, a nurse-thanatologist, is assistant professor in the Department of Nursing at the University of Southern California, Los Angeles. This article originally appeared in the anthology *Transcultural Nursing: A Book of Readings* (1976), which Brink edited.

the culture shock syndrome is the most difficult to live through and this is the period where people "give up and go home."

Phase three. "The Beginning Resolution Phase." Oberg described this phase . . . as the individual seeking to learn new patterns of behavior appropriate to the setting, attempting to make friends in the indigenous population, and becoming as much of a participant-observer as possible in the ceremonies, festivals, and daily activities of the new setting.

This phase seems to be characterized by the reestablishment of a sense of humor. Social errors no longer are devastating to the ego. The host culture no longer is considered all bad and home all wonderful. This phase seems to be facilitated greatly by the arrival of fellow countrymen who are "worse off" and need help. You can show off what you have learned, you are important because you are sought for advice, you feel needed by the newcomer.

At this point also, the individual becomes aware that things seem easier; friendships are being developed; home is still distant, but less relevant. Letters from home somehow seem peripheral to current interests and concerns. Letters to home become more superficial; explanation of what is becoming familiar would take up too much time. Current friendships have the same frame of reference for conversation, a frame of reference that is unknown at home.

Without really becoming aware of the process one slowly adapts to the new situation. Each small discovery, each small victory in learning the new rules is satisfying, and helps to restore one's sore and damaged ego.

Phase four. "The Effective Function Phase." This means being just as comfortable in the new setting as in the old. Having achieved this phase, the individual will probably experience reverse culture shock when he returns home. Or, the individual may decide only to go home for visits, but make the new culture his own.

From *New Immigrants: Portraits in Passage*

THOMAS BENTZ

WOOD CHUEN KWONG

"I wouldn't leave Chinatown, even if I were offered a job somewhere else," said Wood Chuen Kwong from his apartment in the heart of the world's largest Chinese community outside of Asia. This city is wonderfully textured with the Chinese sensibility. Graceful calligraphy blinks brilliantly from neon signs on banks, fish markets, and boutiques. The Chinese language is spoken at every turn and other aspects of Chinese culture are seen everywhere. Chinatown is like a haven between hemispheres, an oasis of the Orient firmly planted on our western shore.

THOMAS BENTZ (b. 1943) is a writer and editor, and a minister of the United Church of Christ. In addition to *New Immigrants: Portraits in Passage* (1981), where Wood Chuen Kwong's story appears, he has written a book of poems, *The Power of One* (1977).

"I wanted to stay in San Francisco for a year or two, to get acquainted, to get to know the people here. It is such a beautiful city and the weather is wonderful. But it is very difficult to find a job." For now, Wood and his son, Ching Yu, work as dishwashers and busboys, but they hope this is only temporary. Wood is a mechanical engineer and has an extensive background in electronics.

"In Canton, I was a radio repairman for thirty-two years in my spare time. The locally made radios and parts were easy to come by in China, and we always saved any extra parts. In America I see people who are so wasteful. They will throw out a radio if a single part breaks down. All these electric gadgets you have here are luxuries you don't need. We had to cook in China on a messy coal stove. It would be very helpful to have what you have here, the Japanese-made electric frying pans, rice cookers, and toasters. But there the people couldn't afford them even if they were available. Here you have useless electric razors and toothbrushes too.

"In Canton our whole family was allowed only 10 kilowatts of electricity each month. One 40-watt lightbulb and one 60-watt fan were all we could afford. All our work and reading had to be done by that one bulb. We also had one 3-watt fluorescent lamp we could put in the socket for dim and minimal lighting. There was, of course, no air-conditioning in our apartment, or anywhere else in Canton, even though the heat hit 90 degrees in the autumn and 100 degrees in the summer.

"Living in China, you have to learn how to fix almost anything and everything in your household. For others to fix what you have would take too long and cost too much. So I learned carpentry and began to make tables and chairs. If a leg on something broke, or our bed broke down, I had to fix it. Soon I had repaired a whole house. So did all the other workers that I knew who got about $40 a month for their normal labors.

"All the people were willing to help. If you needed to move something or paint a wall, you could just call on your friends and they would all come and give you a hand to do anything or go anywhere. And they didn't need to be paid." It is just this sort of cooperation between people that Wood finds to be lacking in the United States. Even though he and his wife, Foong Ying Dang, and their son, Ching Yu, and daughter, Ming Yu, feel relatively secure within the cultural haven of Chinatown, they know that they are now living in more threatening surroundings. Rival Chinese street gangs have been trying to assert their dominance, and their presence breeds fear in the new and old residents alike.

"I would not come home late at night, or go out of Chinatown," admitted Wood. "I have never had any trouble, but I don't feel safe. In China I knew everybody who lived on our block, but here, even people in the same building don't say hello. There may not be enough freedom in China but there is too much here. They have far less crime, very little theft or murder, because the offender in China is handled much more thoroughly and properly. Picking someone's pocket there would get you twenty days to three months in jail. Burglary draws at least two years, armed robbery is ten to twenty years. Murder is for life, with no probation. When the rule and punishment are straight and strong, then you can have restraint. There is no gambling in China because the people don't have the greed that makes them want to take what doesn't belong to them instead of earning it themselves."

Wood takes pride in being able to earn what his family needs though he has known disappointment along these lines and understands that fairness and justice are not always available to everyone. "For about eight years in the 1950s I took part in a Chinese government-promoted plan to provide housing, employment, and services. We put our money in the bank, and with the interest the government built homes and left the principal in the bank for future investment. No one person in China could build or afford to buy a house. So the money made some housing available. And each new year we drew lots and several people won the houses. The Cultural Revolution wiped this out before I could win my house. But you know, if the savings and loans in San Francisco would follow that scheme, there would be lots of investors and we could both build houses and provide employment for people in the process."

Wood can see that there is good and bad in both countries. He knows that China could certainly use some American technology and suspects that the U.S. would do well to have more of the will and spirit that the Chinese worker has. "Opening trade has been and will continue to be beneficial to both the U.S. and China. If China doesn't look to the U.S. for technical progress it will never catch up to the new and better ways that the world can work. And if the U.S. doesn't meet the real spirit of the Chinese people, it will never get out of its old red-devil fear. We are different, but each of us has good points and weaknesses. If we come together we can learn to complement each other."

"I just finished a manpower training program in the Chinatown Resources Development Center and I have already had several interviews for jobs. I've just applied and taken a written examination in English for a government position that I have high hopes for. It is a civil service mechanical technician at $800 a month."

In Canton he made much less money, $113 a month, but his expenses were much less too. His food cost about $10 a month and his rent, for a three-bedroom apartment, was $13.49 a month. He was not dissatisfied with his life there and though he applied for a visa to come here for six years, he only wanted to visit and to see his parents. However the Chinese government refused his requests. Finally his father's influence made the difference.

"My father had studied at Ohio State University before spending his life teaching, first in Canton and then from 1946 to 1968 in Hong Kong. In 1952 one of my sisters and her husband came to the United States. In 1968, my parents followed after my sister's petition for reunification was accepted. None of the rest of us seven children could come out of China with them then.

"In 1979 my father petitioned for me to come out because of the special case of his illness. He was also a commissioner on the housing authority in San Francisco, so through his connections, my case was expedited. I was able to come and be with him before he died. It had been so difficult to get out of China just for a visit that I decided that once I came here I would want to stay. I am now a permanent resident alien. I think I'll decide after five years whether I want to become a U.S. citizen."

Meanwhile one of his sisters has no such choice. She is now a permanent resident alien in a country she doesn't want to be in. She came out of China to Hong Kong at the same time that Wood flew to San Francisco to be with his father. "Father also petitioned for Kin. But when she came out of China in June of 1979, a lot of other people were going to Hong Kong to be processed for America. So the U.S. consulate just listed people in the order of the requests for immigration. She was put way back on the list. When our father died, so did his petition for Kin. The case was closed. Now she cannot come to America nor can she go back to China.

"Kin was a doctor in China, but she can't get recognized in Hong Kong, so she works as an aide in a school for the blind. Her husband was an X-ray specialist in China, but he can't find a job in Hong Kong. They have a very difficult life now. I don't know who is to blame. I often write to her and send money to help. I don't know what else to do."

Amitar Ray

From *Immigrant America: A Portrait*

ALEJANDRO PORTES AND RUBÉN G. RUMBAUT

After finishing medical school, Amitar Ray confronted the prospect of working *ad honorem* in one of the few well-equipped hospitals in Bombay or moving to a job in the countryside and to quick obsolescence in his career. He opted instead for preparing and taking the Educational Council for Foreign Medical Graduates (ECFMG) examination, administered at the local branch of the Indo-American Cultural Institute. He passed it on his second attempt. In 1972, there was a shortage of doctors in the United States, and U.S. consulates were directed to facilitate the emigration of qualified physicians from abroad.

Amitar and his wife, also a doctor, had little difficulty obtaining permanent residents' visas under the third preference of the U.S. immigration law, reserved for professionals of exceptional ability. He went on to specialize in anesthesiology and completed his residence at a public hospital in Brooklyn. After four years, nostalgia and the hope that things had improved at home moved the Rays to go back to India with their young daughter, Rita. The trip strengthened their professional and family ties, but it also dispelled any doubts as to where their future was. Medical vacancies were rare and paid a fraction of what he earned as a resident in Brooklyn. More important, there were few opportunities to grow professionally because he would have had to combine several part-time jobs to earn a livelihood, leaving little time for study.

At fifty-one, Amitar is now associate professor of anesthesiology at a midwestern medical school; his wife has a local practice as an internist. Their combined income is in the six figures, affording them a very comfortable lifestyle. Their daughter is a senior at Bryn Mawr, and she plans to pursue a graduate degree in international relations. There are few Indian immigrants in the mid-sized city where the Rays live; thus, they have had to learn local ways in order to gain entry into American social circles. Their color is sometimes a barrier to close contact with white middle-class families, but they have cultivated many friendships among the local faculty and medical community.

Ties to India persist and are strengthened through periodic trips and the professional help the Rays are able to provide to colleagues back home. They have already sponsored the immigration of two bright young physicians from their native city. More

---

Sociologist and educator ALEJANDRO PORTES (b. 1944) is a consultant on United States immigration policy. He teaches at Johns Hopkins University. RUBÉN G. RUMBAUT (b. 1948) is a professor of sociology at Michigan State University and a senior research fellow at Michigan State University's Institute for Public Policy and Social Research. This excerpt is from their work *Immigrant America: A Portrait* (1990, revised edition 1996).

important, they make sure that information on new medical developments is relayed to a few selected specialists back home. However, there is little chance that they will return, even after retirement. Work and new local ties play a role in this, but the decisive factor is a thoroughly Americanized daughter whose present life and future have very little to do with India. Rita does not plan to marry soon; she is interested in Latin American politics, and her current goal is a career in the foreign service.

Negi

From *When I Was Puerto Rican*

ESMERALDA SANTIAGO

Uniformed women with lacquered hair, high heels, and fitted skirts looked down on us, signalled that we should fasten our safety belts, place parcels under the seat in front of us, and sit up.

"Stewardesses," Mami said, admiring their sleek uniforms, pressed white blouses, stiff navy ribbons tied into perfect bows in their hair. None of them spoke Spanish. Their tight smiles were not convincing, did not welcome us. In our best clothes, with hair combed, faces scrubbed, the dirt under our nails gouged out by Mami's stiff brush, I still felt unclean next to the highly groomed, perfumed, unwrinkled women who waited on us.

"Someday," Mami mused, "you might like to be a stewardess. Then you can travel all over the world for free.". . .

The sky darkened, but we floated in a milky whiteness that seemed to hold the plane suspended above Puerto Rico. I couldn't believe we were moving; I imagined that the plane sat still in the clouds while the earth flew below us. The drone of the propellers was hypnotic and lulled us to sleep in the stiff seats with their square white doilies on the back. . . .

I dozed, startled awake, panicked when I didn't know where I was, remembered where we were going, then dozed off again, to repeat the whole cycle, in and out of sleep, between earth and sky, somewhere between Puerto Rico and New York.

It was raining in Brooklyn. Mist hung over the airport so that all I saw as we landed were fuzzy white and blue lights on the runway and at the terminal. We thudded to earth as if the pilot had miscalculated just how close we were to the ground. A startled silence was followed by frightened cries and *aleluyas*[1] and the rustle of everyone rushing to get up from their seats and out of the plane as soon as possible.

Mami's voice mixed and became confused with the voices of other mothers telling their children to pick up their things, stay together, to walk quickly toward the door and not to hold up the line. Edna, Raymond, and I each had bundles to carry, as did Mami,

[1]***aleluyas:*** Hallelujahs (Spanish) [Eds.].

Writer, independent filmmaker, and battered women's advocate ESMERALDA SANTIAGO (b. 1948) was born and raised in Puerto Rico and now lives in Westchester County, New York. She is the author of the novel *America's Dream* (1996) and a memoir, *When I Was Puerto Rican* (1993), from which this excerpt was taken.

who was loaded with two huge bags filled with produce and spices *del país.*[2] "You can't find these in New York," she'd explained.

We filed down a long, drafty tunnel, at the end of which many people waited, smiling, their hands waving and reaching, their voices mingling into a roar of *hello*'s and *how are you*'s and *oh, my god, it's been so long*'s.

"Over there," Mami said, shoving us. On the fringes of the crowd a tall woman with short cropped hair, a black lace dress, and black open-toed shoes leaned against a beam that had been painted yellow. I didn't recognize her, but she looked at me as if she knew who I was and then loped toward us, arms outstretched. It was my mother's mother, Tata. Raymond let go of Mami's hand and ran into Tata's arms. Mami hugged and kissed her. Edna and I hung back, waiting.

"This is Edna," Mami said, pushing her forward for a hug and kiss.

"And this must be Negi," Tata said, pulling me into her embrace. I pressed against her and felt the sharp prongs of the rhinestone brooch on her left shoulder against my face. She held me longer than I expected, wrapped me in the scratchy softness of her black lace dress, the warmth of her powdered skin, the sting of her bittersweet breath, pungent of beer and cigarettes.

Behind her loomed a man shorter than she, but as imposing. He was squarely built, with narrow eyes under heavy eyebrows, a broad nose, and full lips fuzzed with a pencil mustache. No one would have ever called him handsome, but there was about him a gentleness, a sweetness that made me wish he were a relative. He was, in a manner of speaking. Mami introduced him as "Don Julio, Tata's friend." We shook hands, his broad, fleshy palm seeming to swallow mine.

"Let's get our things," Mami said, pulling us into a knot near her. "You kids, don't let go of each others' hands. It's crazy here tonight."

We joined the stream of people claiming their baggage. Boxes filled with fruit and vegetables had torn, and their contents had spilled and broken into slippery messes on the floor. Overstuffed suitcases tied with ropes or hastily taped together had given way, and people's underwear, baby diapers, and ratty shoes pushed through the stressed seams where everyone could see them. People pointed, laughed, and looked to see who would claim these sorry belongings, who could have thought the faded, torn clothes and stained shoes were still good enough for their new life in Brooklyn.

"That's why I left everything behind," Mami sniffed. "Who wants to carry that kind of junk around?"

We had a couple of new suitcases and three or four boxes carefully packed, taped at the seams, tied with rope, and labelled with our name and an address in New York that was all numbers. We had brought only our "good" things: Mami's work clothes and shoes, a few changes of playclothes for me, Edna, and Raymond, some of them made by Mami herself, others bought just before we left. She brought her towels, sheets, and pillowcases, not new, but still "decent looking."

"I'll see if I can find a taxi," Don Julio said. "You wait here."

We huddled in front of the terminal while Don Julio negotiated with drivers. The first one looked at us, counted the number of packages we carried, asked Don Julio where we were going, then shook his head and drove along the curb toward a man in a business

[2]***del país:*** Literally, "from the country" (Spanish) [Eds.].

suit with a briefcase who stood there calmly, his right hand in the air as if he were saluting, his fingers wiggling every so often. The second driver gave us a hateful look and said some words that I didn't understand, but I knew what he meant just the same. Before he drove off, Mami mumbled through her teeth *"Charamanbiche."* Don Julio said it was illegal for a driver to refuse a fare, but that didn't stop them from doing it.

Finally, a swarthy man with thick black hair and a flat cap on his head stopped, got out of his taxi, and helped us load our stuff. He didn't speak Spanish, none of us spoke English, and, it appeared, neither did he. But he gave us a toothy, happy smile, lifted Raymond into Mami's lap, made sure our fingers and toes were inside the taxi before he closed the doors, then got in with a great deal of huffing and puffing, as his belly didn't fit between the seat and the steering wheel. Tata and Don Julio sat in the front seat with the driver, who kept asking questions no one understood.

"He wants to know where we're from," Mami figured out, and we told him.

"Ah, Porto Reeco, yes, ees hot," he said. "San Juan?"

"Yes," Mami said, the first time I'd ever heard her speak English.

The driver launched into a long speech peppered with familiar words like America and President Kennedy. Mami, Tata, and Don Julio nodded every once in a while, uh-huhed, and laughed whenever the taxi driver did. I wasn't sure whether he had no idea that we didn't understand him, or whether he didn't care.

Rain had slicked the streets into shiny, reflective tunnels lined with skyscrapers whose tops disappeared into the mist. Lampposts shed uneven silver circles of light whose edges faded to gray. An empty trash can chained to a parking meter banged and rolled from side to side, and its lid, also chained, flipped and flapped in the wind like a kite on a short string. The taxi stopped at a red light under an overpass. A train roared by above us, its tiny square windows full of shapes.

"Look at her," Tata laughed from the front seat, "Negi's eyes are popping out of her head."

"That's because the streets are not paved with gold, like she thought," Mami teased.

The taxi driver grinned. I pressed my face to the window, which was fogged all around except on the spot I'd rubbed so that I could look out.

It was late. Few windows on the tall buildings flanking us were lit. The stores were shuttered, blocked with crisscrossed grates knotted with chains and enormous padlocks. Empty buses glowed from within with eerie gray light, chugging slowly from one stop to the next, their drivers sleepy and bored.

Mami was wrong. I didn't expect the streets of New York to be paved with gold, but I did expect them to be bright and cheerful, clean, lively. Instead, they were dark and forbidding, empty, hard. . . .

[We pick up after Negi, her mother, brother, and sister have arrived at Tata's house.]

There were angels on the ceiling. Four fat naked cherubs danced in a circle, their hands holding ivy garlands, their round buttocks half covered by a cloth swirling around their legs. Next to me, Mami snored softly. At the foot of the bed, Edna and Raymond slept curled away from each other, their backs against my legs. The bedroom had very high ceilings with braided molding all the way around, ending in a circle surrounded by more braid above the huge window across from the bed. The shade was down, but bright sunlight streaked in at the edges. The cherubs looked down on us, smiling mysteriously, and I wondered how many people they had seen come in and out of this room. Slowly I crawled over Mami, out of bed.

"Where are you going?" she mumbled, half asleep.

"To the bathroom," I whispered.

The bed was pressed into the corner against the wall across from the window, next to a wide doorway that led into the next room. A long dresser stretched from the doorway to the window wall, leaving an aisle just wide enough to open the drawers halfway out.

It was six in the morning of my first day in Brooklyn. Our apartment, on the second floor, was the fanciest place I'd ever lived in. The stairs coming up from Tata's room on the first floor were marble, with a landing in between, and a colored glass window with bunches of grapes and twirling vines. The door to our apartment was carved with more bunches of grapes and leaves. From the two windows in the main room we could look out on the courtyard we had come through the night before. A tree with broad brown leaves grew from the middle of what looked like a well, circled with the same stones that lined the ground. Scraggly grass poked out between the cracks and in the brown dirt around the tree. The building across from ours was three stories high, crisscrossed by iron stairs with narrow landings on which people grew tomatoes and geraniums in clay pots. Our building was only two stories high, although it was almost as tall as the one across the courtyard. We, too, had an iron balcony with a straight ladder suspended halfway to the ground. It made me a little dizzy to look down. . . .

The first day of school Mami walked me to a stone building that loomed over Graham Avenue, its concrete yard enclosed by an iron fence with spikes at the top. The front steps were wide but shallow and led up to a set of heavy double doors that slammed shut behind us as we walked down the shiny corridor. I clutched my eighth-grade report card filled with A's and B's, and Mami had my birth certificate. At the front office we were met by Mr. Grant, a droopy gentleman with thick glasses and a kind smile who spoke no Spanish. He gave Mami a form to fill out. I knew most of the words in the squares we were to fill in: NAME, ADDRESS (CITY, STATE), and OCCUPATION. We gave it to Mr. Grant, who reviewed it, looked at my birth certificate, studied my report card, then wrote on the top of the form "7–18."

Don Julio had told me that if students didn't speak English, the schools in Brooklyn would keep them back one grade until they learned it.

"Seven gray?" I asked Mr. Grant, pointing at his big numbers, and he nodded.

"I no guan seven gray. I eight gray. I teeneyer."

"You don't speak English," he said. "You have to go to seventh grade while you're learning."

"I have A's in school Puerto Rico. I lern good. I no seven gray girl."

Mami stared at me, not understanding but knowing I was being rude to an adult.

"What's going on?" she asked me in Spanish. I told her they wanted to send me back one grade and I would not have it. This was probably the first rebellious act she had seen from me outside my usual mouthiness within the family.

"Negi, leave it alone. Those are the rules," she said, a warning in her voice.

"I don't care what their rules say," I answered. "I'm not going back to seventh grade. I can do the work. I'm not stupid."

Mami looked at Mr. Grant, who stared at her as if expecting her to do something about me. She smiled and shrugged her shoulders.

"Meester Grant," I said, seizing the moment, "I go eight gray six mons. Eef I no lern inglish, I go seven gray. Okay?"

"That's not the way we do things here," he said, hesitating.

"I good studen. I lern queek. You see notes." I pointed to the A's in my report card. "I pass seven gray."

So we made a deal.

"You have until Christmas," he said. "I'll be checking on your progress." He scratched out "7–18" and wrote in "8–23." He wrote something on a piece of paper, sealed it inside an envelope, and gave it to me. "Your teacher is Miss Brown. Take this note upstairs to her. Your mother can go," he said and disappeared into his office.

"Wow!" Mami said, "you can speak English!"

I was so proud of myself, I almost burst. In Puerto Rico if I'd been that pushy, I would have been called *mal educada*[3] by the Mr. Grant equivalent and sent home with a note to my mother. But here it was my teacher who was getting the note, I got what I wanted, and my mother was sent home.

"I can find my way after school," I said to Mami. "You don't have to come get me."

"Are you sure?"

"Don't worry," I said. "I'll be all right."

I walked down the black-tiled hallway, past many doors that were half glass, each one labelled with a room number in neat black lettering. Other students stared at me, tried to get my attention, or pointedly ignored me. I kept walking as if I knew where I was going, heading for the sign that said STAIRS with an arrow pointing up. When I reached the end of the hall and looked back, Mami was still standing at the front door watching me, a worried expression on her face. I waved, and she waved back. I started up the stairs, my stomach churning into tight knots. All of a sudden, I was afraid that I was about to make a fool of myself and end up in seventh grade in the middle of the school year. Having to fall back would be worse than just accepting my fate now and hopping forward if I proved to be as good a student as I had convinced Mr. Grant I was. "What have I done?" I kicked myself with the back of my right shoe, much to the surprise of the fellow walking behind me, who laughed uproariously, as if I had meant it as a joke.

Miss Brown's was the learning disabled class, where the administration sent kids with all sorts of problems, none of which, from what I could see, had anything to do with their ability to learn but more with their willingness to do so. They were an unruly group. Those who came to class, anyway. Half of them never showed up, or, when they did, they slept through the lesson or nodded off in the middle of Miss Brown's carefully parsed sentences.

We were outcasts in a school where the smartest eighth graders were in the 8-1 homeroom, each subsequent drop in number indicating one notch less smarts. If your class was in the low double digits (8-10 for instance), you were smart, but not a pinhead. Once you got into the teens, your intelligence was in question, especially as the numbers

[3]***mal educada:*** Rude or bad-mannered (Spanish); usually written as one word [Eds.].

rose to the high teens. And then there were the twenties. I was in 8-23, where the dumbest, most undesirable people were placed. My class was, in some ways, the equivalent of seventh grade, perhaps even sixth or fifth.

Miss Brown, the homeroom teacher, who also taught English composition, was a young black woman who wore sweat pads under her arms. The strings holding them in place sometimes slipped outside the short sleeves of her well-pressed white shirts, and she had to turn her back to us in order to adjust them. She was very pretty, with almond eyes and a hairdo that was flat and straight at the top of her head then dipped into tight curls at the ends. Her fingers were well manicured, the nails painted pale pink with white tips. She taught English composition as if everyone cared about it, which I found appealing.

After the first week she moved me from the back of the room to the front seat by her desk, and after that, it felt as if she were teaching me alone. We never spoke, except when I went up to the blackboard.

"Esmeralda," she called in a musical voice, "would you please come up and mark the prepositional phrase?"

In her class, I learned to recognize the structure of the English language, and to draft the parts of a sentence by the position of words relative to pronouns and prepositions without knowing exactly what the whole thing meant.

The school was huge and noisy. There was a social order that, at first, I didn't understand but kept bumping into. Girls and boys who wore matching cardigans walked down the halls hand in hand, sometimes stopping behind lockers to kiss and fondle each other. They were *Americanos* and belonged in the homerooms in the low numbers.

Another group of girls wore heavy makeup, hitched their skirts above their knees, opened one extra button on their blouses, and teased their hair into enormous bouffants held solid with spray. In the morning, they took over the girls' bathroom, where they dragged on cigarettes as they did their hair until the air was unbreathable, thick with smoke and hair spray. The one time I entered the bathroom before classes they chased me out with insults and rough shoves.

Those bold girls with hair and makeup and short skirts, I soon found out, were Italian. The Italians all sat together on one side of the cafeteria, the blacks on another. The two groups hated each other more than they hated Puerto Ricans. At least once a week there was a fight between an Italian and a *moreno,*[4] either in the bathroom, in the school yard, or in an abandoned lot near the school, a no-man's-land that divided their neighborhoods and kept them apart on weekends.

The black girls had their own style. Not for them the big, pouffy hair of the Italians. Their hair was straightened, curled at the tips like Miss Brown's, or pulled up into a twist at the back with wispy curls and straw straight bangs over Cleopatra eyes. Their skirts were also short, except it didn't look like they hitched them up when their mothers weren't looking. They came that way. They had strong, shapely legs and wore knee socks with heavy lace-up shoes that became lethal weapons in fights.

It was rumored that the Italians carried knives, even the girls, and that the *morenos* had brass knuckles in their pockets and steel toes in their heavy shoes. I stayed away from both groups, afraid that if I befriended an Italian, I'd get beat up by a *morena,* or vice versa.

[4]***moreno:*** Literally, a brown person. Often used to refer to black people. (Spanish) [Eds.].

There were two kinds of Puerto Ricans in school: the newly arrived, like myself, and the ones born in Brooklyn of Puerto Rican parents. The two types didn't mix. The Brooklyn Puerto Ricans spoke English, and often no Spanish at all. To them, Puerto Rico was the place where their grandparents lived, a place they visited on school and summer vacations, a place which they complained was backward and mosquito-ridden. Those of us for whom Puerto Rico was still a recent memory were also split into two groups: the ones who longed for the island and the ones who wanted to forget it as soon as possible.

I felt disloyal for wanting to learn English, for liking pizza, for studying the girls with big hair and trying out their styles at home, locked in the bathroom where no one could watch. I practiced walking with the peculiar little hop of the *morenas,* but felt as if I were limping.

I didn't feel comfortable with the newly arrived Puerto Ricans who stuck together in suspicious little groups, criticizing everyone, afraid of everything. And I was not accepted by the Brooklyn Puerto Ricans, who held the secret of coolness. They walked the halls between the Italians and the *morenos,* neither one nor the other, but looking and acting like a combination of both, depending on the texture of their hair, the shade of their skin, their makeup, and the way they walked down the hall.

Alex Bushinsky

From *Today's Immigrants, Their Stories*

Thomas Kessner and Betty Boyd Caroli

"I always thought of going to the States. The American Jews I met (mainly at the Moscow Synagogue) impressed me. They were so smart, so businesslike, so warm, educated, polite. I loved them. But in the end I went to Israel. Officially that is the only place to which you can emigrate but it is possible to come to America. Still, I felt if you claim you are Jewish you go to your country, join your own people, speak your own language. I was a moderate Zionist. And America was more distant. It was scary to think of getting a job without perfect English. My parents told me that competition was so high that I would not succeed. We thought of America as a prosperous country, but where a Russian would be a second-class citizen.

"Israel has to be a disappointment. You expect so much. All the happiness you did not have. I got a terrific job in computer programming. But when things began to change in the organization and it seemed that I might lose this job, I started to lose my good feeling for the country. I realized that my good feeling toward Israel was because I was happy in general. I had a good job, good status, a nice environment, and friends. When this was threatened my attitude changed. Later, in the United States, I was once on a plane with a woman from San Diego. I asked her if she liked San Diego. She said she hated it. Why? She started to tell me, 'Well you know I got divorced and. . . .' and I realized that she hated it because that's where she became unhappy.

Thomas Kessner (b. 1946) is professor of history at the Graduate Center of the City University of New York. Betty Boyd Caroli (b. 1938) taught women's history and immigration history at Kingsborough Community College of CUNY until 1994. This excerpt is taken from their co-authored work *Today's Immigrants, Their Stories* (1981).

"I learned about Judaism in Israel. I met a fine, very good man. He was Russian and he managed even in Russia to be religious. He was so righteous. He devoted so much time to teach me from the beginning. Of course this was not for money. Now I had a religion.

"Then I was invited by an American company to the States to try a job with the company. In Russia I was sometimes a technical translator and I came into contact with Americans. I kept up the friendships and now they got me an invitation to try out for a job and the company would pay my expenses for two months. I did not really expect to stay. I did not close the idea that I might stay, but I didn't think I would be so attracted to the States.

"I was delayed for half a year in Israel because of the incredible bureaucracy there. So I arrived here late. The same day I arrived they told me, 'Listen we waited too long so we cannot give you the job now. It is not available anymore.' They didn't feel sorry. They made $30,000 or $40,000 — when I wrote to them that I made $500 a month, they wrote back you probably mean $500 a week. They felt I had money, that I could get a job just like that.

"I had only $300 with me. I was scared. I spoke to the lawyer for the company. I told him I don't have money. He told me, 'If you want money why don't you just go to work?' I had no choice, I had to go to work. I bought a *New York Times.* I saw an ad with all my skills listed. I went there. It was an agency. The secretary asked for my résumé and in a few minutes an agent came out and said, 'Hi, my name is so and so, I have arranged several interviews for you already, and I am expecting some more calls.' He gave me a list of nine companies — Irving Trust Company, Chemical Bank, Automated Concept, Sperry Univac, Salomon Bros., Royal Globe Insurance, and some others. I got a job. Three days after coming to America I had a job. I was fascinated by working for an American company.

"My first exposure to New York impressed me. It turned out to be clean somehow. Later I learned it's not clean, but when I came it was clean. I expected huge piles of garbage but it wasn't that bad. I liked the tall buildings. They were gleaming from the sun. In the first two days I hated the city. I lost a job. I had no money. Definitely I hated it. I felt insecure, terrible. But in five days when I saw I could get a job just like that, I started to work and half a month later I realized my prospects were much better here than in Israel. Within a month I got a second job teaching a class in data processing at a university.

"This was a new world for me. There were so many things I did not have: language, American education; I was an American immigrant, a Russian, and still I got a job. I decided to remain here (I usually like to say until things get worse,) because of the tremendous opportunities and the freedom.

"I was lucky. The Russians had copied all of the computer software from the States and I knew the necessary languages. Today I have a position as systems analyst. It is very satisfying. I have confidence in my career and I am satisfied with my salary. I have every right that you have except the right to vote and at the moment that does not concern me too much. I feel so comfortable, completely at home. I could not go anywhere after the States.

"I knew I wouldn't get a break in Russia because I was a Jew. It would be hard to get a good job, an apartment. Here, I got a job in a few days. It needed furniture. I got it in a week. Later, I wanted a vacation, so I went for twenty-four days. I took my paycheck and a little money out of the bank and I went across the United States, and saw the nice things. Terrific. It didn't take a year's salary. I appreciate it. I really do. In Russia you make peanuts, usually your parents help support you even after you are married. I was lucky. My father used to be a director of a factory and when I wanted to take a vacation he gave me money. Here I took fourteen different trips by plane. I changed reservations daily. Still I failed to confuse the American airlines. I even got a letter saying because of round-trip fares I am entitled to a $12 refund. In Russia I would not change anything (or I would lose my trip). I would never, never get money back. It could happen that you wait ten years to have a telephone installed in Russia, really, ten years.

"I don't mind all the different types of people and the mixed cultures. The greatest thing in New York is that it is the capital of immigrants. An immigrant feels at home. In the first place he sees a lot of immigrants around. In the second place he realizes Americans have a good stereotype of foreigners, that they are professionals, and that they work hard and that they are smart. They don't care about your English. You are equal. You feel it. A foreigner and still equal.

"This is New York's asset. You can find any society. In my office you have Japanese, Chinese, Greek, Spanish, and Italian. More immigrants than Americans. Tens of different accents. They are all managers and you speak better English than they do. Of course you feel at home.

"There are a few Russian communities in New York, especially in Brighton Beach, Brooklyn. I did not live in that area of mostly Odessa Jews. I am not married and have no relatives here so I do not have a very strong connection with the Russian community. It's not really a community. People from Moscow, Leningrad, and Odessa do not mix in the States. It's not just a city. It's a type. In Israel there are circles by the year you come. The 1972 circle. The 1973 circle. Psychologically it is easy to understand. In the beginning it is difficult to adjust, to form your credo, your point of view. It is painful to have to go over this stage again with somebody just arriving. It is new for him and he needs to discuss his problems. You have been through it already. It is hard to go through the beginning again. . . .

"People ask if it is difficult to come from a Marxist Communist State and adapt to American capitalism. I would say Russians are more materialist than Americans. Could you believe that? For example, I still cannot understand that people voluntarily go to demonstrate or vote. In Russia we do not do anything voluntarily, we don't believe we can affect the destiny of the country. When you see thousands of people waving flags at Brezhnev at an airport welcoming him, they were transported there by State buses, from work. They were even given the flags. Here and in Washington I marched in some demonstrations for Soviet Jewry and the fact that people keep coming voluntarily amazes me. In Russia you do not do anything voluntarily or they think you are crazy. In this capitalist country you have volunteer work and charity.

"I was amazed that Americans do not work hard except where they are building a career. The office empties at five o'clock. We are paid overtime, a lot of money, and still almost no one works. It looks like they do not need the money. When there was a big snow I was the only one to come to work. Many lived nearby — they could take the subway, the underground subway — like I did. Yet they lived in Manhattan and they did not come. In Russia you come. The weather could be even worse, you still come. Even if you are sick you come in and say you are sick and they send you home.

"There are problems in New York: crime, the race problem, and the weather, but my basic needs are satisfied. When I went to California I found nice clean communities and the climate is just perfect. Life looks much easier. It looks like this. I'm not sure it's exactly like this. I know someone who left New York and went to live there and came back in three months. She said people were too easy going there, not serious enough, and they are very materialistic. After three days in San Francisco I could not stand the idea of New York's dirt, climate, and crowds. But I came back.

"The biggest problem in New York I think is fear of crime. People pay for a 'good' neighborhood. They live in ugly homes, in less attractive areas, and make many other compromises but the area is 'exclusive.' People are afraid and nervous. Perhaps many people do not even experience it, but they cannot escape an awareness of it from television, radio, the newspapers and this keeps them from doing things. There may be more crime here than in Russia (there is plenty of crime and street violence there too) but this shows me a level of freedom and civilization somehow. Really. But yes, it does make me tense. I have to be careful. That is the way New York is.

"It is overcrowded, dirty, and the climate — I hate the climate. It is also very competitive, very tense. The city has a high standard of living. It creates new desires for things you never thought you needed before. It offers museums, theaters, everything.

"I am here now. I feel very far away from Russia. I have a very good job, a good salary. I am Jewish, I know *Yiddishkeit.* I am not afraid that this will keep me back. I am in America, in New York, and it is good, it is good for the important things.

Haroutioun Yeretzian

From *The New Americans: Immigrant Life in Southern California*

ULLI STELTZER

The main immigration of Armenians into this country took place over 100 years ago, at the time of the massacres.[1] Most of these immigrants were poor people. They came here to help their families back in Armenia. Their children were unable to fight the American culture, they became assimilated. All they kept was the Armenian church and Armenian food. We call them the shish kebab generation. The election of (George) Deukmejian as governor of California was instrumental in bringing the older Armenians back to their roots. But it is the influx of Armenians from the Middle East during the last ten years that has brought the culture back on a big scale. Now we are publishing in Los Angeles maybe more than twelve newspapers — dailies, weeklies, monthlies — in the Armenian language.

I started out with a monthly magazine when I first came here in 1976. Then I started a small printing shop to print that magazine. During that period of time people kept

[1]For years, Armenians struggled under Turkish (and Russian) domination, sometimes culminating in violence, as in the 1894–1896 massacre of Armenians under Sultan Abdul. The worst single massacre of Armenians, however, came during deportation by the Turks between 1915 and 1918 [Eds.].

Photographer and writer ULLI STELTZER (b. 1923) was born in Germany and lives in Vancouver. Her published works, all with original photographs, include *Coast of Many Faces* (1979), *Inuit: The North in Transition* (1985), *Building an Igloo* (1995), and *The New Americans: Immigrant Life in Southern California* (1988), excerpted here.

coming by asking about books. That gave me the idea that there is an interest. This is the first Armenian commercial bookstore in Hollywood. Of course it is more a community service than a business. People don't buy books every day, but they know where to go. They know I am here.

Many Armenian kids can't afford the Armenian private schools. In Hollywood, Pasadena, and Glendale, where most of the Armenian community is living, the public schools have special Armenian instructors teaching the language, history, and culture to the Armenian students. I know that, because all these schools come to buy books from me.

My son goes to an Armenian school. When he comes home from school he immediately turns on the TV. We fight with him every day; learn your Armenian lessons! He studies his English, his math, his social science, everything, but not the Armenian language, because it is very difficult. There is a difference between learning what you want to know, as grown-ups do, and being forced to learn something you did not choose for yourself. How the kids feel, having to make that extra effort, we don't know. But we know how important it is to keep our language, our culture, alive so that one day the Armenian people will be able to go back to their homeland.

A Literature Assignment

Each of the following paragraphs is the opening of a nonfiction book or essay. Read them, making notes on differences in style, person, tone, or any other characteristic that interests you. Then, as a way to consider the various strategies writers can use to open their work, experiment with different ways to classify these paragraphs.

If you get stuck, start small, finding two or three paragraphs that seem clearly similar — and ask yourself what it is that makes them similar. That characteristic can become your first category; then move on to other clusters of paragraphs. Another way to begin is to ask yourself what each of the authors seems to be trying to do to the reader: Why does he or she begin in this way? The answers to this question could provide the beginnings of a category system.

After you have decided on a category system that makes sense to you, write an essay explaining and illustrating your system.

As a postscript, you might indicate which type(s) of opening you tend to use in your own writing and which type(s) you'd like to try.

Selected Opening Paragraphs from Works of Nonfiction

1. This is a book about the ways in which the developing child perceives the world around him, and about his growing ability to make sense of what he perceives.

— T. G. R. Bower, *The Perceptual World of the Child*

2. In the center of Belten High School there is a courtyard: an attractive space with grass, trees, and shrubs, protected from the wind, but not from the Michigan cold, by the hallways and classrooms that surround it. Between classes and during lunch hour,

the courtyard comes to life. There are boys wearing flared or bell-bottomed jeans, running shoes, rock concert T-shirts, parkas, jeans jackets. A few have chains attaching their wallets to a belt loop; a few wear black jackets with DETROIT on the back. Many of them have long hair, and stand slightly stooped, leaning somewhat confidentially toward their companions. Many hold cigarettes in their mouths, or cupped in hands held slightly behind their thighs. There are girls with virtually the same clothes, a number with long straight hair, darkly made-up eyes. Many of them stand slightly stoop-shouldered, toes pointed inward, holding cigarettes before them between extended fingers.

— Penelope Eckert, *Jocks and Burnouts: Social Categories and Identity in the High School*

3. Our interest here is community organization. It has also variously been termed community planning, community relations, planned change, and community work. Others have preferred terms such as neighborhood work, social action, intergroup work, and community practice. Under whatever label, we will be dealing with intervention at the community level oriented toward improving or changing community institutions and solving community problems. This activity is performed by professionals from many disciplines — social work, public health, adult education, public administration, city planning, and community mental health — as well as by citizen volunteers in civic associations and social action groups.

— Fred M. Cox, John L. Erlich, Jack Rothman, and John E. Tropman (Eds.), *Strategies of Community Organization*

4. Eddie Mason opened his eyes. The long window was a ghost of gray winter light. He reached for his cigarettes. Through the first puff of smoke he stared at the cold dawn and tried to remember why today was supposed to be so special. He said out loud, "Damn!"

— Ben H. Bagdikian, *Caged: Eight Prisoners and Their Keepers*

5. Cognition is the activity of knowing: the acquisition, organization, and use of knowledge. It is something that organisms do and in particular something that people do. For this reason the study of cognition is a part of psychology, and theories of cognition are psychological theories.

— Ulrich Neisser, *Cognition and Reality*

6. I undertook the writing of this book in a mood of anxiety and with a sense of urgency. Affirmative-action programs, adopted in the face of adverse public opinion, seemed to operate in a conspiracy of silence on the part of public officials, whose behavior defied their responsibility to defend their actions publicly. The field of public discourse had been left largely to opponents of affirmative action, who, in their arguments, had preempted the appeal to the ideals of justice and equality. Moreover, when the argument against affirmative action was not met with silence, it was often countered by evasion. Were the weightiest arguments really on that side of the issue?

— John C. Livingston, *Fair Game? Inequality and Affirmative Action*

7. In 1600, Elizabethan England had good reason to sing the praises of the art of arithmetic. The century just brought to a close had been characterized by continual expansion. Marked population growth, monetary inflation, and overseas discoveries stretched the boundaries of thought and custom in ways that called to mind size, number, and measure. Certainly it was an indulgence in hyperbole for the author of the

paean to arithmetic, Thomas Hill, to single out counting as the essence of humanity, the skill that distinguished man from the beasts. But the exaggeration served to emphasize the paramount importance of arithmetic in a country rapidly becoming a center of commercial capitalism.

— Patricia Cline Cohen, *A Calculating People: The Spread of Numeracy in Early America*

8. In the spring of 1975 I traveled the Dakotas with a band of UCLA students and my four-year-old daughter. The university let me teach an on-the-road seminar with a base at Jamestown College in Jamestown, North Dakota. We lived roughly equidistant from five reservations in North Dakota, between rural mid-America and the open plains, small towns and Indian tribal grounds. We talked with Native Americans, primarily Sioux, Chippewa, Mandan, Arikara, and Hidatsa, and with white farmers, ranchers, and merchants who lived near them. *The Good Red Road* is an ethnographic narrative taken from this field experience and from subsequent visits. The number of people present at gatherings and their names have been altered to tell the story.

— Kenneth Lincoln with Al Logan Slagle, *The Good Red Road: Passages into Native America*

9. A quiet early morning fog shrouds rolling hills blanketed by pine-green stands of timber, patched with fields of red clay. As the sun rises and burns off the fog, the blue sky is feathered with smoke let go from chimney stacks of textile mills: This is the Piedmont of the Carolinas.

— Shirley Brice Heath, *Ways with Words*

10. This book is about the look of cities, and whether this look is of any importance, and whether it can be changed. The urban landscape, among its many roles, is also something to be seen, to be remembered, and to delight in. Giving visual form to the city is a special kind of design problem, and a rather new one at that.

— Kevin Lynch, *The Image of the City*

11. Writing groups, the partner method, helping circles, collaborative writing, response groups, team writing, writing laboratories, teacherless writing classes, group inquiry technique, the round table, class criticism, editing sessions, writing teams, workshops, peer tutoring, the socialized method, mutual improvement sessions, intensive peer review — the phenomenon has nearly as many names as people who employ it. The name, of course, matters less than what it describes, which is writers responding to one another's work. Writing groups, as I choose to call them, operate both within and outside schools. Specifics, like the names, vary. Groups range in size from three to more than forty. When writing groups meet in classrooms, some instructors structure tasks and provide explicit direction, while others avoid interfering with student commentary. Some groups exchange written drafts and receive verbal or written comments, while some read aloud and receive oral response. Some shift the procedure to suit the material (reading long essays or poems and listening to shorter prose selections, for example). Groups observe differing codes for response. Some intervene directly in members' writing — helping generate ideas or telling the writer what to do next — while others restrict responses to what has already been written.

— Anne Ruggles Gere, *Writing Groups: History, Theory, and Implications*

12. "Where are our intellectuals?" In his 1921 book, *America and the Young Intellectual,* Harold Stearns (1891–1943), a chronicler of his generation, asked this question. He found them fleeing to Europe, an act he supported and soon followed, joining what became the most celebrated of American intellectual groupings, the lost generation.

— Russell Jacoby, *The Last Intellectuals: American Culture in the Age of Academe*

13. After nearly two decades of benign neglect, schools are once more the subject of an intense national debate. In the recent past, discussion has centered on three issues: whether schools can be the central institution for achieving racial and sexual equality; in higher education, whether the traditional liberal arts curricula are still "relevant" to a changing labor market; and whether the authoritarian classroom stifles the creativity of young children or, conversely, how permissiveness has resulted in a general lowering of educational achievement. All of these issues are still with us, but they have been subsumed under a much larger question: how to make schools adequate to a changing economic, political, and ideological environment.

— Stanley Aronowitz and Henry A. Giroux, *Education under Siege: The Conservative, Liberal and Radical Debate over Schooling*

14. Intending to have Cheerios for breakfast, Mary goes to the cupboard. But she can't find any Cheerios. She decides that Elizabeth must have finished off the Cheerios the day before. So, she settles for Rice Krispies. In the process, Mary has modified her original intentions and beliefs.

— Gilbert Harman, *Change in View: Principles of Reasoning*

15. As we reach the end of this century, and with it the end of this millennium, there remain fewer and fewer musicians like those described in this book. A handful can be found who were born in the age of the horse and buggy before telephones, electric appliances, air travel, and computers accelerated the speed of life around us. The archaic sounds of Dennis McGee and Sady Courville, Bois-sec Ardoin and Canray Fontenot, Lula Landry and Inez Catalon come from a time before high speed and high tech had taken over. You can hear it in their voices and in their instrumental renditions. Younger musicians from city and country learn from them; some slavishly imitate their intonation, ornamentation, idiosyncratic stylish ways, and maybe in time those younger people will capture what their role models have — a rock-solid quality of being centered, personally and esthetically. But we do not know that they will.

— Barry Jean Ancelet, *The Makers of Cajun Music*

16. Philosophers usually write their books for other philosophers, and express parenthetical hopes that the book will prove useful to students and lay readers as well. Such hopes are usually vain. In hopeful contrast, I have written this book primarily and explicitly for people who are not professionals in philosophy, or in artificial intelligence, or in the neurosciences. It is the imagination of the general reader, and of the student, that I am here aiming to capture. I do indeed have subsidiary hopes that this compact volume will prove useful, as a comprehensive summary and source book, to my professional colleagues and to advanced graduate students. But I did not write this book for them. I have written it for newcomers to the philosophy of mind.

— Paul M. Churchland, *Matter and Consciousness*

17. The not-for-profit are different from you and me. Tennis courts, a swimming pool, a baseball diamond, a croquet lawn, a private hotel, 400 acres of woods and rolling hills, cavorting deer, a resident flock of Canada geese — I'm loving every minute here at the Educational Testing Service, the great untaxed, unregulated, unblinking eye of the American meritocracy.

— David Owen, *None of the Above: Behind the Myth of Scholastic Aptitude*

18. "Elite Babies: The Weapon of the Future." So said the *London Times* headline to a 1981 article describing a forty-three nation conference held in Montreal the previous week. The topic of the conference: how to identify and educate an elite. "Our final hope is to develop the brain as a natural resource," said Venezuela's Dr. Luis Alberto Machado, minister for the development of intelligence. "Any country which develops its intelligence will become the most powerful in the world. Human intelligence will be the weapon of the future."

— James Crouse and Dale Trusheim, *The Case against the SAT*

19. The study of human beings using language is notoriously suspect because it must be conducted by human beings using language. The field of discourse is thus bedeviled by circularities and loopholes, the dangers of which can be avoided only by taking stock, from the outset, of guiding principles and theoretical foundations. It will not be enough to produce or stipulate a "workable" definition of rhetoric and then to proceed from these, thus using rhetoric to study rhetoric. Our first task is to discover and articulate larger frameworks which will provide bases for adequate definition.

— Walter H. Beale, *A Pragmatic Theory of Rhetoric*

20. When I was small, my mother often told me that animals, insects, and plants are to be treated with the kind of respect one customarily accords to high-status adults. "Life is a circle, and everything has its place in it," she would say. That's how I met the sacred hoop, which has been an integral part of my life, though I didn't know to call it that until the early 1970s when I read John G. Neihardt's rendering of the life story of Oglala Lakota Holy Man Black Elk in *Black Elk Speaks.*

— Paula Gunn Allen, *The Sacred Hoop: Recovering the Feminine in American Indian Traditions*

21. This is a book about college students and their lives on campus. It attempts to describe the variety of ways that undergraduates have defined themselves, viewed their professors and fellow collegians, formed associations, and created systems of meaning and codes of behavior. Although my story begins at the end of the eighteenth century, my real concern is the present. The primary question that I am asking is: How did we get where we are now? Because I have a historian's cast of mind, the answer to the question lies in the evolution of the past into the present.

— Helen Lefkowitz Horowitz, *Campus Life*

22. Between 1948 and 1952, tens of thousands of mutilating brain operations were performed on mentally ill men and women in countries around the world, from Portugal, where prefrontal leucotomy was introduced in 1935, to the United States, where under the name of "lobotomy" the procedure was widely used on patients from all walks of life. From our present perspective, these operations — referred to collectively as "psy-

chosurgery" — seem unbelievably primitive and crude. After drilling two or more holes in a patient's skull, a surgeon inserted into the brain any of various instruments — some resembling an apple corer, a butter spreader, or an ice pick — and, often without being able to see what he was cutting, destroyed parts of the brain. In spite of the huge amount of psychosurgery done during the peak of its popularity, by 1960 this practice was drastically curtailed. Not only had chlorpromazine and other psychoactive drugs provided a simple and inexpensive alternative, but it had also been discovered that these operations were leaving in their wake many seriously brain-damaged people. Today lobotomy has largely fallen into disrepute and is now considered an evolutionary throwback, akin more to the early practice of trepanning the skull to allow the demons to escape than to modern medicine.

— Elliot S. Valenstein, *Great and Desperate Cures: The Rise and Decline of Psychosurgery and Other Radical Treatments for Mental Illness*

23. The purpose of this book is to draw attention to the mbira, a uniquely African contribution to the world of music. Although it is one of the most well-established and popular melodic instruments in black Africa, the mbira has rarely received the attention in the West that it deserves. Many Westerners have the limited view that African music consists entirely of drumming. They are unaware that the melodic traditions of African music are rich and varied, having as important a history and as profound a meaning in certain cultures as the magnificent drumming ensembles have in others.

— Paul F. Berliner, *The Soul of Mbira*

24. The decade of the 1970s was a critical period for ethnic minorities and women in the United States. The intellectual and political atmosphere of this period made these groups more introspective, leading them to examine critically their own history and culture. The result was an outpouring of writing, both creative and analytical, which offered a new way of seeing what had always been there. For the first time in the history of people of Mexican descent in the United States, a significant body of written literature emerged. To be sure, Spanish-speaking people in the United States had written and published before the mid-1960s. In the contemporary period, however, a literary expression has emerged from working-class Mexican-Chicano communities. Since the 1960s such writings have been designated as Chicano literature, including works by a modern generation of Chicano authors in various classifications: poetry, novel, dramatic play, essay, and short story. Although continuous with the literary expression, usually transmitted orally, which previously existed in Mexican-Chicano communities, these contemporary writings have had a different perspective: The modern generation of Chicano authors has exhibited a political, social, and cultural self-consciousness.

— Marta Ester Sanchez, *Contemporary Chicana Poetry: A Critical Approach to an Emerging Literature*

25. This book tries to explain how minds work. How can intelligence emerge from nonintelligence? To answer that, we'll show that you can build a mind from many little parts, each mindless by itself.

— Marvin Minsky, *The Society of Mind*

26. This is a book about children whom no one heard when they cried. The children at Leake & Watts are in foster care, some at their own request, some at the request

of their families, and some at the insistence of the courts. What they all have in common is a broken and defective family life. Having been abused, neglected, and unloved as young children, they have grown up into adolescents who are angry, unmanageable, and at odds with society.

— Quincy Howe Jr., *Under Running Laughter: Notes from a Renegade Classroom*

27. In 1966 the National Congress of American Indians wanted to give an award to the then director of the Office of Economic Opportunity, R. Sargent Shriver. The NCAI had printed a special form which noted the achievements of the person receiving the award and stated that the award was for meritorious service to the Indian people. At the bottom of the form were several blanks under which the words "President," "Vice-president," and "Secretary" were printed. On the evening on which the award was to be made, the officers of the NCAI were gathered in the organization's offices, filling in the blanks with Shriver's name where it was appropriate. When they came to the blank for the President's name, one of the officers was stopped cold. "Is this our president who is to sign here," he inquired, "or theirs?"

— Vine Deloria Jr., *Behind the Trail of Broken Treaties*

28. The incest taboo is universal in human culture. Though it varies from one culture to another, it is generally considered by anthropologists to be the foundation of all kinship structures. Lévi-Strauss describes it as the basic social contract; Mead says its purpose is the preservation of the human social order. All cultures, including our own, regard violations of the taboo with horror and dread. Death has not been considered too extreme a punishment in many societies. In our laws, some states punish incest by up to twenty years' imprisonment.

— Judith Herman and Lisa Hirschman, "Father-Daughter Incest"

29. This book is about the uses of literacy in the Middle Ages. It concentrates on England in the two and a half centuries from 1066 to 1307 (from the Norman Conquest to the death of Edward I) because these years constitute a distinctive period in the development of literate ways of thinking and of doing business. In the eleventh century literate modes were still unusual, whereas in the thirteenth century they became normal among the rulers. This formative stage in the history of literacy has received less attention from scholars than the invention of printing in the later Middle Ages, although it is no less important. Printing succeeded because a literate public already existed; that public originated in the twelfth and thirteenth centuries. Writing was not new in 1066, of course, either in England or elsewhere. In the royal monasteries of Anglo-Saxon England, as in other parts of Europe, an original literate culture had been created which was distinguished especially by its illuminated manuscripts of parchment. From these royal and monastic roots new uses and forms of writing proliferated in the twelfth and thirteenth centuries and took shapes which would last for generations.

— M. T. Clanchy, *From Memory to Written Record*

A Linguistics Assignment

In the following passage from her book *Getting Computers to Talk Like You and Me,* computer scientist Rachel Reichman uses an excerpt from a lighthearted conversation among friends to raise some fundamental questions about how we can engage in and understand conversation at all. "What kind of knowledge do conversants need to share," she asks, "in order to engage in coherent discourse?" Take a few minutes to read her passage, then turn to the instructions following it.

From *Getting Computers to Talk Like You and Me*

RACHEL REICHMAN

Everyone knows that clear communication requires a speaker to follow certain rules in selecting and ordering the elements of sentences. In English, for instance, we do not demand that someone "Dog the out put" or ask "If dog the came the yet in back"; English grammar does not permit such orderings. Though particular rules vary from language to language, most every language has ordering rules of this kind. Language users are not ordinarily aware of the rules they follow as they speak, but it is in large part the grammatical rules they share that permit mutual understanding.

Beyond the sentence level we do not usually think of our communication as governed by rules. Spontaneous, natural conversations are generally thought to be "rule free," with speakers selecting and ordering their utterances without any constraints. Though as participants in conversations we take for granted this apparent freedom, to the observer it presents a puzzle; indeed, one who looks closely at natural dialogues must often marvel that communication occurs at all. Consider, for instance, the following portion of a spontaneous conversation between three friends, F, C, and R; the excerpt begins as F enters and notices a burn on C's leg:

F: 1. Oh my God, how did that happen?
C: 2. Well, I don't want to go into this again.
F: 3. Tell me briefly.
C: 4. You know I can't tell anything briefly.
F: 5. Wow, right, I have to think about this. All right.
C: 6. Well, starting at the beginning. Ummm. Arthur has
7. a box, it's called a "hot box," okay? It's
8. insulated and you open it up and you put like a
9. tricket, special tricket, in it and you close it.
10. And it's very cold in our room, so Arthur and I
11. sometimes use this in bed, between us when we're
12. snuggling, when we're ready to go to seep. And —

RACHEL REICHMAN specializes in computer science. This excerpt is taken from her work *Getting Computers to Talk Like You and Me* (1985).

R: 13. Don't get too risqué here.

F: 14. Don't get too graphic.

C: 15. You notice the way I use the word "seep"?

F: 16. Huh? "Seep?"

C: 17. "Seep."

R: 18. "Seep?"

C: 19. That's how we say "sleep." "Let's go to seep."

F: 20. Oh, I didn't see that.

C: 21. So that's getting pretty intimate right there, but
22. that's as far as I'll go. And normally —

R: 23. To sleep.

C: 24. Right. And normally it falls out of bed, you know,
25. and I wake up in the morning and I go, "Gee, it's too
26. bad that fell out of bed." Well, the other night it
27. didn't fall out of bed, and I woke up with this burn.

Because we all manage conversations such as this one every day without undue difficulty, we take for granted our ability to follow the point of another person's remarks, and to choose responses that fit coherently into the discussion. A little thoughtful scrutiny reveals, however, that managing even the most ordinary conversational engagement is quite a remarkable feat. The means by which speakers follow each other in spontaneous conversations are far from obvious.

Notice, for instance, that the telling of the story about how C got the burn does not proceed in any simple, straightforward way but is interrupted by several tangential discussions — about whether the story can be told briefly, about whether in the telling the speaker is getting too risqué, and about the speaker's use of a private expression, "to seep" (in fact a metadiscussion about whether her listeners understood the meaning of her language). Though each speaker grasps the other's points and makes her own understood rapidly and easily, such mutual understanding requires a considerable amount of internal interpretation and analysis — clearly much is left unsaid. A most interesting instance occurs in C's next to last utterance, in her statement "And normally it falls out of bed." Given all the interruptions that have gone before, how is it that her conversants understand what "it" means? Earlier in the conversation, understanding at one point gets off track, but even the clarification requires considerable inference ("So that's getting pretty intimate right there") and proceeds with remarkable efficiency. Clearly, in order to follow each other through the twists and turns and jumps of their conversation, the conversants must share a number of implicit assumptions, a common ground, that allows their conversation to flow. But what is the nature of these implicit assumptions, this common ground? What kind of knowledge do conversants need to share in order to engage in coherent discourse?

Reichman's question, "What kind of knowledge do conversants need to share in order to engage in coherent discourse?" reminds us of a similar query raised by cognitive scientists Seymour Papert and Marvin Minsky. They offer a fragment of conversation among children and ask what a child needs to know in order to understand it:

> "That isn't a very good ball you have. Give it to me and I'll give you my lollipop."

To understand this sentence, they observe, a child needs to have knowledge of a number of categories of mental states, activities, and objects. For example, a child needs to know about the category of activities we call *talking,* and the specific activities under that category, like *explaining* (knowing what the sentence "That isn't a very good ball . . ." is doing), *ordering* (knowing what the second sentence, "Give it to me . . ." is doing), *persuading* (the purpose of the two sentences together), and so on. Some other categories of mental states, activities, and objects would be:

Social relations:	Giving. Bargaining. Asking.
Owning:	Belong to. Master of. Captor of.
Eating:	How does one compare the values of foods with the values of toys?
Liking:	Good. Bad. Useful.
Intention:	Want. Plan. Plot. Goal. Cause. Result.
Emotions:	Moods. Dispositions. Conventional expressions.

Following Papert and Minsky's way of thinking about conversation, try to answer Reichman's question by writing an essay in which you discuss the various categories of knowledge her three conversants must share in order to participate in and understand their conversation. (As an alternative, you could write this essay using any short stretch of conversation taped in your class, at a social gathering, at work, off the radio or television.) If you'd like, you could conclude by speculating on this commonplace human phenomenon of talking to each other, or you could address the title of Reichman's book, *Getting Computers to Talk Like You and Me.* What would computers have to be able to do to talk like you and me?

Readings: U.S. Immigration Patterns

The readings in this section offer opportunities to think further about classifying while working with the topic of immigration woven throughout this chapter. If you would like to look back at the earlier readings about immigration, see the tables and charts in the Opening Problem (p. 286), David Cole's "Five Myths About Immigration" (A Professional Application, p. 308), and "The Phases of Culture Shock" by Pamela J. Brink and Judith Saunders, with accompanying readings (A Sociology Assignment, p. 331).

The following readings speak to various aspects of the general issue of immigration. You may read them singly or in combination. Even in combination, however, these readings are not intended to cover thoroughly the issues of immigration to the United States but only to introduce a few strands of that complex topic. In order to contribute to — and to challenge — your work with classifying, we have chosen a range of writing about immigration: Some selections are broad in scope, considering global forces or trends over time, while others focus more particularly on a group, region, or time period. All of the readings offer rich information that will enable you to construct classification schemes that will enhance your understanding of immigration to the United States.

In "The Historical Context of Immigration," Reed Ueda offers an overview of the international and domestic factors that have shaped patterns of immigration to the United States. Ueda's overview is accompanied by a chronology sketching the legislation that has regulated the process of U.S. immigration since the late nineteenth century. In the next piece, Maldwyn Allen Jones focuses on an early phase of that immigration history, the pattern of Irish and German settlement through the first half of the nineteenth century. The Scandinavian migration in the nineteenth century is then examined by Eugene Boe, who emphasizes the economic factors that propelled his own Norwegian ancestors into the American Midwest. Next, Elizabeth Ewen, in an excerpt from *Immigrant Women in the Land of Dollars,* looks at the motives of Italian and Jewish immigrants who came to the cities of the Northeast between 1890 and 1910. Then, in a passage from *Becoming Mexican American,* George J. Sánchez analyzes the social and economic influences upon a period of increased immigration from Mexico, 1900 to 1930. Finally, Alejandro Portes and Rubén G. Rumbaut examine the diverse patterns of recent immigration, challenging stereotypes and offering some political generalizations.

At the end of each reading, you will find Considerations questions intended to help you think about the reading mostly on its own terms but also in relation to the classification strategies stressed in this chapter. At the end of the section, you will also find suggestions for writing about these readings in relation to one another and for pursuing the topic of immigration through research.

In the following passage, historian Reed Ueda provides an overview of trends in U.S. immigration from the late eighteenth century to the present and places those trends in a broader global context. He offers, then, a sense of the economic, political, and social conditions in other countries that set the stage for people to emigrate (those who study immigration tend to call these "push" factors) and the conditions, real or perceived, in the United States that drew people here (often called "pull" factors). In Ueda's analysis, immigration is seen as a dynamic, international phenomenon, one that has virtually defined the United States from its earliest days as a nation.

As an appendix, we attach a chronology, also written by Ueda, of U.S. immigration and naturalization policy — which most often functioned to restrict or select immigration, although, at times, contributed to the "pull" factors that attracted people to the United States.

The Historical Context of Immigration

REED UEDA

The United States became history's first "worldwide" immigration country in the twentieth century. By the 1990s, the flow of newcomers swelled to include people from every region and culture of the globe. Forty million of the sixty million immigrants since the founding of the country — two out of three newcomers — arrived in the twentieth century, making it the greatest era of immigration in national and world history.

The United States had long been distinguished for the continuous and unique role that immigrants played in its population history. From the early nineteenth to the early twentieth century, the United States attracted three-fifths of all the world's immigrants — more than received by all other large immigration-receiving countries in the world combined. Among all the world's immigration countries, the United States accepted by far the greatest variety of nationalities. From the early nineteenth century to World War II, 16 percent of American immigrants came from Germany, 12 percent from Italy, 12 percent from Ireland, 12 percent from the multifarious ethnic enclaves of Austria-Hungary, 11 percent from Great Britain, and 10 percent from Russia. Other English-speaking immigration countries such as Australia and Canada drew their settlers almost wholly from other Anglophone nations. Immigration to Latin American societies also showed a narrow spectrum of national diversity, limited chiefly to Iberian and Italian origins. Ethnic variety in American immigration increased even more in the late twentieth century, especially with the rise of immigration from Asia, the Caribbean, Latin America, the Middle East, and Africa, from which few immigrants had come in the early twentieth century. The U.S. Immigration and Naturalization Service reported admissions in 1990 from thirty Asian countries (including the Middle East), seventeen Central and South American countries, thirteen Caribbean countries, and thirteen African countries.[1]

The United States is the great exception among world nations, most of which — including Germany, Japan, Norway, Scotland, Sweden, and Korea — have no tradition of immigration and little interest in developing one.[2] The German political leader Volker Ruhe expressed the viewpoint of such nations by announcing in 1991, "We [in Germany] are not an immigration country and we will not become one."

Despite the enormous numbers and variety of those who chose to come to Amer-

[1]For cumulative immigration from various countries, see William S. Bernard, ed., *American Immigration Policy* (New York: Harper and Brothers, 1950), Table XIII, p. 311. Bernard reports that 80 percent of immigrants to Australia came from Great Britain, while in Canada 37 percent arrived from Great Britain and another 37 percent from the United States; also he shows that in Argentina, 47 percent of the immigrants came from Italy and 32 percent from Spain; in Brazil, 34 percent came from Italy, 29 percent from Portugal, and 14 percent from Spain. For these breakdowns, see *American Immigration Policy,* Chart 13, p. 204. For historical immigration totals in the United States, see *1990 Statistical Yearbook of the Immigration and Naturalization Service* (Washington, D.C.: U.S. Government Printing Office, 1992), Table 1, p. 47. For countries of origin of immigrants in the late twentieth century, see *1990 Statistical Yearbook,* Table 3, pp. 52–53.

[2]Bernard, *American Immigration Policy,* ch. 10 and Table XVII, p. 314.

REED UEDA (b. 1949) is associate professor of history at Tufts University. Co-editor of the *Journal of Interdisciplinary History,* he has explored the social history of education, urbanization, and immigration in works that include *West End House* (1981), *Avenues to Adulthood* (1987), and *Postwar Immigrant America: A Social History* (1994), excerpted here.

ica, immigrants were a minority among the peoples of the world. It is important to remember that the vast majority of Chinese, Mexicans, Swedes, and Italians chose to remain home. For every Irish immigrant who came to the United States during the potato famine of the 1840s, five people remained in Ireland. There were plenty of reasons to remain home. Leaving meant a painful separation from one's support system. When the immigrants left, they lost everything and everyone familiar. Historian Oscar Handlin has called this uprooting a trauma that left a permanent scar. Nearly all immigrants went through the pain of snapping the ties of extended family life. An immigrant woman arriving at Ellis Island recalled, "We hated to leave. I had a grandfather and grandmother living in Europe and my father was an only child. It was terrible to part with the two of them, but they wouldn't go along. They wanted to die in Europe." The loss of the old moorings filled the immigrants with self-doubt. In Abraham Cahan's early twentieth-century novel *The Rise of David Levinsky,* the protagonist David Levinsky recalls, "Who can depict the feeling of desolation, homesickness, uncertainty, and anxiety with which an emigrant makes his first voyage across the ocean? . . . And echoing through it all were the heart-lashing words: 'Are you crazy? You forget your place, young man!' "[3]

Most people chose to live with familiar oppression and poverty rather than throw everything away to uncertain, unfamiliar promises. The immigrant was a risk taker who had the courage or the recklessness to give up the known, with its limits, for the unknown, with its possibilities. Most immigrants — from Mexican farm laborers to Polish steelworkers — were bold adventurers on voyages of discovery who had to have the resiliency to cope with tremendous social change, pressures, and loss.

Despite the sacrifices and losses, many immigrants persevered to realize a new vision of the individual and society. They found that American conditions of tolerance toward diversity, compared with the rigid boundaries that existed in most other countries, made the forging of new identities and cultural ties inescapable. The immigrant absorbed new ways from neighboring people who were different. The children of Japanese immigrants in Hawaii learned new games, new words, new values, new tastes in food, new styles of dress, and new ways of forming relationships from neighbors, playmates, and classmates who were Hawaiian, Filipino, German, Chinese, and Portuguese. The process of acculturating with unfamiliar surrounding elements had deep roots in the nation's social history. During the American Revolution, the French immigrant Hector St. John de Crèvecoeur described this mixing process in his community: "*He* is an American who, leaving behind him all his ancient prejudices and manners, receives new ones from the new mode of life he has embraced, the new government he obeys, and the new rank he holds."[4]

American immigrants created a new society differing fundamentally from old societies such as those they left in Sweden, Germany, or Japan. These societies took strength from homogeneity. Solidarity came from all people being the same. In the United States,

[3]Oscar Handlin, *The Uprooted,* 2nd ed. (Boston: Little, Brown, 1973), ch. 10; Dale R. Steiner, *Of Thee We Sing: Immigrants and American History* (San Diego: Harcourt Brace Jovanovich, 1987), p. 6. David M. Brownstone, Irene M. Franck, and Douglass L. Brownstone, *Island of Hope, Island of Tears* (New York: Viking Penguin, 1979), p. 24; Abraham Cahan, *The Rise of David Levinsky* (New York: Harper and Brothers, 1917), p. 85.

[4]J. Hector St. John de Crèvecoeur, *Letters from an American Farmer* (1782; New York: Viking Penguin, 1981), p. 70.

the immigrants built a society whose strength came from the immense multiplicity of ethnic groups. Moreover, the society hinged on the existence of conditions that permitted dissimilar groups to act and live together without intrusive government. The resultant mutualism and interdependency helped integrate the nation.

Immigration created the American nation and defined its role in world history. Immigration to America adjusted the balance of human and material resources between nations, creating new international economic and cultural ties that affected the relations between countries. Otto von Bismarck, the "Iron Chancellor" who unified Germany in the 1870s, assessed American immigration as the "decisive fact" of the modern world.[5]

At the heart of American history lay the cycle of national creation and re-creation through immigration. The new nation emerging from the American Revolution grew out of the first immigration consisting of Protestant colonials from the British Isles and northern Europe. After the Civil War, with large numbers of Irish Catholics and newcomers from Germany and Scandinavia, the immigrant nation continued to evolve. By the turn of the century, it received immigrants from southern and eastern Europe, East Asia, Mexico, and the Caribbean. These waves constituted the second immigration. After 1965, the American nation absorbed a great influx of immigrants from around the world in the third immigration.

As an ever-changing society formed out of three historical immigrations, the civic and social foundations of American nationhood shifted accordingly. The historian John Higham has called attention to the need to understand the differences immigration has made for national development. He has pointed out that the first immigration, by bringing diverse population elements before the founding of the country, prepared the way for an eclectic and universalistic form of citizenship. Higham found that the second immigration generated new communal and organizational modes for immigrant adaptation such as machine politics, organized labor, and ethnic associations, as well as cultural modes such as mass entertainment and media. The third immigration has reinforced the developments of the first and second immigrations but is contributing a unique shift: moving the nation toward a transnational, interracial world society and a multicultural politics.[6]. . . .

THE CHANGING WAVES OF IMMIGRATION

An immense tide of European immigration was the cardinal ethnic factor transforming the American nation from the birth of the industrial revolution to the Great Depression. Thirty-five million Europeans uprooted by economic and social distress moved to America in the century after 1830. During this period, the early American nation that grew out of colonization by Great Britain turned into a new immigrant nation of strikingly varied nationalities drawn from the metropolises and far-flung borderlands of the entire European continent.[7]

[5]Nathan Glazer, ed., *Clamor at the Gates: The New American Immigration* (San Francisco: Institute for Contemporary Studies, 1985), p. 3; Bernard Bailyn, *The Peopling of British North America* (New York: Alfred A. Knopf, 1977), p. i.

[6]John Higham, *Send These to Me: Jews and Other Immigrants in Urban America* (New York: Atheneum, 1975), pp. 17–28.

[7]The main outlines of the second immigration are conveyed in Marcus Lee Hansen, *The Atlantic Migration, 1607–1860* (Cambridge: Harvard University Press, 1940); Handlin, *The Uprooted;* Oscar Handlin, *The American People in the Twentieth Century* (Cambridge: Harvard University Press, 1954);

International migration spiraled toward the United States from wider and wider geographic circles. By the Civil War, the chief sources of immigration had spread outside of Great Britain to northern and western Europe. After 1890, the flow of American immigration was fed increasingly by streams originating from southern and eastern Europe, principally from the states of Italy, Austria-Hungary, and Russia. The label "Old Immigrant" was affixed to groups arriving from northern and western Europe, the label "New Immigrant" to groups from southern and eastern Europe. In 1896, immigrants from the latter area for the first time in history composed a majority of newcomers, 57 percent of all immigrants in that year. Their numerical predominance continued into the 1920s.[8]

The largest groups among the New Immigrants from southern and eastern Europe were, in order of their numbers, the Italians, the Slavs, and the Jews. Eighty percent of the Italians came from southern Italy. The Jews came chiefly from the multinational empires of Russia and Austria-Hungary. The Slavs comprised a huge variety of ethnic subgroups such as Poles, Czechs, Russians, Slovakians, Slovenians, Serbians, Bosnians, Montenegrins, Croatians, and Bulgarians, who had come from provincial areas in Germany, Austria-Hungary, and Russia. From 1899 to 1924, 3.8 million Italians, 3.4 million Slavs, and 1.8 million Jews entered the country.[9]

By comparison, in the early twentieth century, immigration from the non-European world was dwarfed in scale and impact. Asian immigration, flowing chiefly to the far western United States, was the first mass migration from outside Europe, coinciding approximately with the rise of southern and eastern European immigration. Chinese, Japanese, and Filipinos composed the bulk of Asian immigrants to America during this time; Koreans and Asian Indians constituted a much smaller influx. The major periods of immigration from the Asian countries ranged in a rough consecutive order. Between 1850 and 1924, 368,000 Chinese immigrants entered the United States. From 1890 to 1924, 270,000 immigrants came from Japan; from 1899 to 1924, 9,200 arrived from Korea and 8,200 from India; and between 1910 and 1930, at least 50,000 to 60,000 came from the Philippines. The American territory of Hawaii was a receiving area of a similarly timed and comparably sized immigration from China, Japan, Korea, and the Philippines.[10]

Maldwyn Allen Jones, *American Immigration* (Chicago: University of Chicago Press, 1960); Philip Taylor, *The Distant Magnet: European Immigration to the U.S.A.* (New York: Harper and Row, 1971); Thomas Archdeacon, *Becoming American: An Ethnic History* (New York: Free Press, 1983); John Bodnar, *The Transplanted: A History of Immigrants in Urban America* (Bloomington: Indiana University Press, 1985); Roger Daniels, *Coming to America: A History of Immigration and Ethnicity in American Life* (New York: HarperPerennial, 1991).

[8]Oscar Handlin, *Race and Nationality in American Life* (Cambridge: Harvard University Press, 1957), pp. 74–77; U.S. Immigration Commission, *Statistical Review of Immigration* (Washington, D.C.: U.S. Government Printing Office, 1911), Table 6, p. 10.

[9]Archdeacon, *Becoming American,* pp. 121–27; Stephan Thernstrom, ed., *Harvard Encyclopedia of American Ethnic Groups* (Cambridge: Harvard University Press, 1980), Appendix I, Table 2, pp. 1036–37.

[10]These figures compiled from U.S. Commissioner-General of Immigration, *Annual Reports;* U.S. Commission on Immigration, *Reports,* vol. 3 (Washington, D.C.: U.S. Government Printing Office, 1911); Bruno Lasker, *Filipino Immigration to Continental United States and to Hawaii* (Chicago: University of Chicago Press, 1931), Appendix A, pp. 348–49. For Asian immigration to Hawaii, see Eleanor C. Nordyke, *The Peopling of Hawai'i,* 2nd ed. (Honolulu: University of Hawaii Press, 1989), ch. 3. For an overview of the successive waves of specific Asian ethnic groups, see Sucheng Chan, *Asian Americans: An Interpretive History* (Boston: Twayne, 1991); Ronald T. Takaki, *Strangers from a Different Shore: A History of Asian Americans* (Boston: Little, Brown, 1989).

Although Asian immigration was relatively small, its pattern of short periodic bursts resembled the New Immigration from southern and eastern Europe. Ninety percent of all immigrants from Italy from the nineteenth century to World War II came in the thirty years from 1890 to 1920. Similarly, 92 percent of all immigrants from Austria-Hungary and Russia in that period arrived between 1890 and 1920. The brief yet intense intervals of immigration from Asia and southern and eastern Europe were circumscribed artificially by the passage of restrictionist laws that reduced the influx from these regions. Limits on admissions were first imposed on Asians at the end of the nineteenth century, but by the 1920s such restrictions affected the New Immigrants from Italy, Austria-Hungary, Russia, and the eastern Mediterranean.

As the supply of Asian laborers in the far west was cut off, agricultural and industrial capitalists began to look toward the reservoir of cheap workers across the border in Mexico. Because of the spread of "peonage," or debt servitude, northern regions of Mexico accumulated surplus labor that began to spill across the U.S. border. In the first decade of the twentieth century, only 31,000 Mexicans arrived, but in the second decade the influx swelled to 185,000. The drain on workers during World War I prodded the U.S. government in 1917 to issue passes to "temporary farmworkers" from Mexico. This was a preliminary experiment in a guest worker system of labor migration that would be expanded in the future.[11]

From 1900 to 1930, more than 100,000 blacks from the West Indies entered the United States. Increasing population and chronic seasonal unemployment in their home islands caused an inter-island migration of laborers. This circulating flow spilled over to Florida and the urban centers of the northeast as new economic, transportation, and communication links between the West Indies and the United States were forged by the spread of the commercial fruit industry.[12]

THE MATRIX OF PUSH AND PULL

Throughout the history of the United States, immigration was generated by an international force field of displacing "push" and attractive "pull" factors. These were byproducts of economic reorganization and political centralization in the transatlantic and transpacific basins. The matrix of push and pull factors covered different regions and changed over time. It created a gigantic demographic watershed that drained off a growing flood of immigration to the United States.[13]

A key push factor was the unprecedented expansion of population in the modern era. In Europe, Asia, and the Western Hemisphere a "demographic transition" — a rise in

[11]Joan W. Moore, *Mexican Americans,* 2nd ed. (Englewood Cliffs: Prentice-Hall, 1976), pp. 38–40; Carlos Cortes, "Mexicans," in Thernstrom, *Harvard Encyclopedia,* p. 699.

[12]Ira deA. Reid, *The Negro Immigrant* (New York: AMS Press, 1939), pp. 61–74, 239–40; Thomas Sowell, *Ethnic America: A History* (New York: Basic Books, 1981), pp. 216–18; Philip Kasinitz, *Caribbean New York: Black Immigrants and the Politics of Race* (Ithaca: Cornell University Press, 1992), pp. 19–25.

[13]Brinley Thomas, *Migration and Economic Growth: A Study of Great Britain and the Atlantic Economy,* 2nd ed. (Cambridge: Cambridge University Press, 1973), chs. 7, 14; Daniels, *Coming to America,* pp. 16–22; Conrad Taeuber and Irene B. Taeuber, *The Changing Population of the United States* (New York: John Wiley and Sons, 1958), pp. 55–58; Richard A. Easterlin, *Population, Labor Force, and Long Swings in Economic Growth: The American Experience* (New York: National Bureau of Economic Research, 1968), p. 30.

the rate of population growth — resulted from improved nutrition and health support systems that lowered death rates. The resulting immense and rapid increase of population redefined economic prospects, eroding available resources for increasing numbers of people. The number of young workers seeking a livelihood grew faster than the number of slots the economy could generate anew or open by attrition. In this fashion, an economic surplus population expanded.[14]

Population increase coincided with regional economic stagnancy to determine the timing of exodus. The demographic transition moved across Europe roughly from west to east, encouraging the progressive "morselizing" or subdividing of land as it moved. Available land also shrank as large landowners accumulated small holdings to increase the output of commercial crops. In the late nineteenth century, the demographic and economic structure of southern and eastern Europe resembled that of western Europe a half-century earlier and became the source of the greatest exodus from Europe after 1890. In specific subregions of East Asia, economic decline and population pressure coincided to produce an impetus for migration that was roughly contemporaneous with that from southern and eastern Europe.[15]

The spread of capitalist manufacturing and marketing introduced new strains into the economic life of the populace. Early industrial capitalism in Europe displaced or marginalized artisans by creating the factory system of production. Peasants lost supplementary income from cottage manufactures when factory goods flooded the local markets. Cottage industries dwindled and eventually disappeared. Also, the emerging capitalist economy grew by boom and bust cycles. As the rural economies of Europe were drawn within an international market, peasants and laborers became more vulnerable to external vicissitudes. Intermittent economic setbacks came to farmers by fluctuating crop prices and to workers by slackening demand.[16]

The differential between the lower demand for labor in Europe, Asia, and Latin America and the higher demand in the United States created a pull factor that combined with push forces to exert pressure to immigrate to America. In contrast to provincial regions in the Eastern Hemisphere and Latin America, the United States was a leading sector of job growth. Commercial farms and plantations in the western states and Hawaii maintained a huge demand for Chinese, Japanese, Filipino, and Mexican laborers. Midwestern and Great Plains states promoted the development of family farms, attracting waves of Scandinavians and Germans. The burgeoning factories of the industrial Midwest and Northeast attracted flocks of southern and eastern European laborers. Both

[14]H. J. Habakkuk and M. Postan, *The Cambridge Economic History of Europe, The Industrial Revolutions and After: Incomes, Population, and Technological Change,* vol. 6 (Cambridge: Cambridge University Press, 1965), ch. 2; Taylor, *The Distant Magnet,* pp. 27–54; Archdeacon, *Becoming American,* pp. 31–32, 120.

[15]Habakkuk and Postan, *Cambridge Economic History,* pp. 60–69; Archdeacon, *Becoming American,* pp. 37–55, 117, 120–27; Bodnar, *The Transplanted,* pp. 23–32, 34–38; Sucheng Chan, "European and Asian Immigration into the United States in Comparative Perspective, 1820s to 1920s," in Virginia Yans-McLaughlin, ed., *Immigration Reconsidered: History, Sociology, and Politics* (New York: Oxford University Press, 1990), pp. 40–47; Lucie Cheng and Edna Bonacich, eds., *Labor Immigration under Capitalism: Asian Workers in the United States before World War II* (Berkeley: University of California Press, 1984), chs. 6–10; Jon Gjerde, *From Peasants to Farmers: The Migration from Balestrand, Norway, to the Upper Middle West* (Cambridge: Cambridge University Press, 1985), chs. 2–5; Walter D. Kamphoefner, *The Westfalians: From Germany to Missouri* (Princeton: Princeton University Press, 1987), ch. 1.

[16]Bodnar, *The Transplanted,* pp. 30–34; Taylor, *The Distant Magnet,* pp. 38–39.

agricultural and industrial labor were more valuable in the United States. Skilled as well as unskilled workers improved their chances for employment there.[17]

The forces of push and pull did not mechanistically determine departure because immigrants were not passive and homogeneous objects. The immigrants emerged with planning and deliberation at specific periods and from middling to lower sectors of homeland societies — not usually the most impoverished. The insecurity caused by the intersection of demographic change and economic transitions in agriculture and manufacturing was not in itself a sufficient cause of emigration. Insecurity prompted immigrants to rethink the shape of their lives and the odds for improvement by staying or moving. Those who were most venturesome and could espy timely opportunity in another country became immigrants. Furthermore, they developed an organized strategy, usually involving family members to help each other gain passage, obtain jobs, and find homes. As a result, most immigrants came to America in a cooperative process of chain migration.[18]

THE EBB AND FLOW OF IMMIGRATION

From 1820 to 1930, yearly arrivals climbed steadily, reaching several hundred thousand by the late nineteenth century. The movement of annual immigration, however, was not linear. It fluctuated in enormous oscillations of fifteen to twenty years, called "long swings." The peak surges in yearly arrivals occurred in three short upward swings from 1882 to 1893, 1903 to 1914, and 1921 to 1927.[19]

Annual immigration rose with economic expansion and declined during recession. A closer analysis of the "time-shape" of immigration, however, discloses a more subtle relationship between immigration and the American economy. It appears that during industrialization in the nineteenth century, immigration both stimulated a rise in economic activity and also responded to rises in economic activity. Before the Civil War, immigration preceded capital investment (particularly in railroads) and thus helped stimulate it. There is evidence that immigration also preceded and stimulated housing construction.

[17]Taylor, *The Distant Magnet,* pp. 182–209; Taeuber and Taeuber, *The Changing Population,* pp. 202–06.

[18]Taylor, *The Distant Magnet,* chs. 2–3; Bodnar, *The Transplanted,* p. 56; Dino Cinel, *From Italy to San Francisco: The Immigrant Experience* (Stanford: Stanford University Press, 1982), pp. 38–70; John S. MacDonald and Leatrice D. MacDonald, "Chain Migration, Ethnic Neighborhood Formation, and Social Networks," in Charles Tilly, ed., *An Urban World* (Boston: Little, Brown, 1974).

[19]The changing annual numbers of immigrants found in historical graphs of immigration have the appearance of mathematical consistency and precision. Yet they are based on varying ways of counting immigrants and thus are not exactly comparable over time. In the nineteenth century, official annual totals included in different periods aliens who arrived but were not admitted, resident aliens returning from a trip abroad, temporary visitors, and travelers passing through the country. From 1894 to 1902, annual immigration totals excluded immigrant aliens traveling as cabin passengers. After 1906, official data for the first time were precise because they were based on a count of admitted aliens seeking permanent residency in the United States whose last permanent residence was a foreign country. Despite the changing rules for counting immigrants, the enumerations were sufficiently comparable to reveal the pattern of annual rise and fall. For a detailed history of the changing enumeration basis for immigration statistics, see U.S. Bureau of the Census, *Historical Statistics of the United States: Colonial Times to 1957* (Washington, D.C.: U.S. Government Printing Office, 1960), ch. C, p. 49. Also see U.S. Commission on Immigration, *Reports,* vol. 3, Table 6, pp. 9–11. Also see Richard A. Easterlin, "Economic and Social Characteristics of Immigration," in Thernstrom, *Harvard Encyclopedia.*

From 1870, however, capital investment preceded changes in immigration. Moreover, throughout the industrializing era from the mid-nineteenth to the early twentieth century, immigration tended to respond to increases in economic productivity in the United States. Whether immigration preceded or responded to economic growth, it consistently had a positive and galvanizing effect on it by increasing the pool of productive workers, savers, entrepreneurs, and consumers.[20]

Annual immigration totals alone do not tell the full story of how immigration affected American society. To gauge the impact of immigration it is necessary to compare the size of yearly admissions with the size of the host society. The resulting ratio is called the rate of immigration. When the rate is charted for the decades since the 1820s, it becomes clear that immigration had a greater impact in the nineteenth century than in the twentieth century. Although the rate of immigration reached its apex in the first decade of the twentieth century, it dropped steeply to the 1920s. It bottomed out from the successive effects of restrictive admissions policies, the severe economic depression of the 1930s, and the disruptions of World War II.[21]

IMMIGRANTS IN THE EARLY TWENTIETH CENTURY

The social history of the twentieth century is impossible to understand without reference to the startling developments in immigration in its first decades. Immigrants flooded into the country with a magnitude and ethnic diversity never before seen. Half of all immigrants who came between the War of 1812 and the Great Depression arrived from 1900 to 1930 alone. The federal Bureau of Immigration classified thirty-nine "races or peoples" among immigrant arrivals in these three decades.[22]

Throughout the era of industrialization, laborers who could perform heavy physical work were in great demand. Thus, most immigrants were young males. In the late nineteenth century, more than two out of three immigrants were between fifteen and forty years old, and male immigrants constituted 60 percent of all arrivals. At the turn of the century, the long-standing majorities of males and of prime-aged newcomers reached historical peaks while the share of females, minors, and the elderly dropped to all-time lows. Over the span of the industrial revolution, the share of industrial and service workers grew progressively larger while the share of agricultural workers fell. Many of the former, however, had engaged in farm labor earlier in their working lives.[23]

The attractive power of the American economy, though exceedingly great, was not absolutely decisive. Many uprooted peasants and laborers decided to resettle in nearby provincial cities or national metropolises where new jobs were available. Such workers circulating within their homelands or neighboring countries outnumbered those who

[20]Harry Jerome, *Migration and Business Cycles* (New York: National Bureau of Economic Research, 1926), p. 208; Thomas, *Migration and Economic Growth,* ch. 7; Simon Kuznets and Ernest Rubin, *Immigration and the Foreign Born,* Occasional Paper 46 (New York: National Bureau of Economic Research, 1954), pp. 4–5; Easterlin, *Population, Labor Force,* pp. 30–32; Thomas Muller, *Immigrants and the American City* (New York: New York University Press, 1992), pp. 69–77.

[21]Archdeacon, *Becoming American,* p. 113.

[22]U.S. Commissioner-General of Immigration, *Annual Reports, 1899–1930* (Washington, D.C.: U.S. Government Printing Office, 1900–31).

[23]Oscar Handlin, *The American People in the Twentieth Century* (Cambridge: Harvard University Press, 1954), p. 8.

moved to America. Moreover, two out of five international migrants from the nineteenth to the early twentieth century chose to settle elsewhere, often in Argentina, Brazil, Canada, South Africa, or Australia. Emigration to America was, first, an alternative to local migrations, and, second, a preference among various possible destination countries.[24]

Capital-intensive manufacturing and labor-intensive agriculture and construction recruited a new form of immigrant labor characterized by transiency and low skill level. The number of immigrants returning to their country of origin rose sharply at the turn of the century. Transient labor migrants were quickly pooled into a work force or let go to leave the country. Their availability grew as increased modernization of international transportation and communications systems allowed them to change residency more easily and at lower cost.[25]

One of the notable changes in immigration patterns in the early twentieth century was the rising number of return immigrants. From 1908 to 1930, four million people departed from the United States permanently. In that period, one left for every three entering. Departures increased both absolutely and in proportion to arrivals in the decade of World War I. From 1911 to 1915, thirty-two people departed for every one hundred who arrived; from 1916 to 1920, fifty-five departed for every one hundred arriving.[26]

Immigrants from a variegated array of ethnic groups returned home. Return migration was an overseas extension of historic patterns of local circular migration. Many southern and eastern Europeans displayed an unusual propensity for temporary migration. From 1911 to 1915, among the Bulgarian-Serbian-Montenegrins, Magyars, and Slovaks, fifty or more immigrants journeyed home for every one hundred arriving in the United States; among the Greeks, Russians, southern Italians, and Croatian-Slovenians forty or more immigrants returned home for every one hundred arrivals. In the next five years surrounding World War I, the return migration rates for these groups multiplied several times. Many who went back were laborers who had come temporarily to the United States to earn income to send home or to take back later. The transient labor migrants from Europe were often called "birds of passage." Immigrants from Asia, such as the Chinese, Koreans, and Asian Indians, who also engaged in heavy return migration, were called "sojourners." Even Old Immigrant groups such as the English, Germans, and Scandinavians showed substantial return rates. Not all groups, however, conformed to the rising pattern of return migration. Most notably, the Welsh, the Jews, and the Armenians showed a strong reluctance to return home. Of course, Russian Jews and Turkish Armenians had little incentive to return to the repressive rule of tsars and pashas. From the 1880s on, the Russian imperial government intensified the ostracism of Jews and supported popular riots against their settlements. In the Ottoman Empire, Turkish potentates subjected the Armenians to similar injustices and brutalities.[27]

[24]Bodnar, *The Transplanted,* pp. 43–45; Taylor, *The Distant Magnet,* pp. 55–56; Cinel, *From Italy to San Francisco,* p. 69.

[25]Michael J. Piore, *Birds of Passage: Migration Labor and Industrial Societies* (Cambridge: Cambridge University Press, 1979), chs. 2, 6; Taeuber and Taeuber, *The Changing Population,* pp. 53–55; Taylor, *The Distant Magnet,* ch. 8; Cheng and Bonacich, *Labor Immigration under Capitalism,* pp. 27–28.

[26]Commissioner-General of Immigration, *Annual Reports, 1926,* Table 78; *Annual Reports, 1930,* Tables 76, 86, 87.

[27]Cinel, *From Italy to San Francisco,* pp. 43–70. An analysis that places return migration from the United States in an international and interregional context is J. D. Gould, "European Inter-

The social characteristics of immigrants varied enormously according to geographic and ethnic origin. Although a distinct differential in industrial and technological development separated northern and western Europe from southern and eastern Europe and other parts of the world, group differences did not follow a simple geographic correlation. Many of the groups with the highest proportions of skilled workers came from outside northern and western Europe. Jews, Bohemians, Moravians, Armenians, Spaniards, Cubans, Pacific Islanders, West Indians, and Africans ranked among those with the highest shares of skilled workers. Also, the groups with the highest proportions of male arrivals were a mix of Old Immigrant and New Immigrant groups. However, in illiteracy a clearer geographic pattern emerged: Old Immigrants were not represented among the groups with the highest percentages of illiteracy. Moreover, the differentials in illiteracy between Old Immigrants and New Immigrants were extremely large. In the first decade of the century, less than 2 percent of the Scandinavians and ethnic groups from Great Britain were illiterate; but more than 50 percent of southern Italians, Portuguese, Ruthenians, Mexicans, Syrians, and Turks and more than 40 percent of several southern Slavic groups were illiterate.[28]

The early twentieth century, however, marked the culmination of the industrial phase of immigration and the beginning of a new stage. New demographic trends started that would continue and grow more pronounced in the middle decades of the century. The proportions of laborers began to shrink, while the share of skilled craftworkers began to grow before 1920. Illiteracy rates began to decline significantly. These changes were decisively consolidated by the creation of restrictive immigration quotas in the early 1920s that favored immigrants from the more industrialized societies of northern and western Europe. In the late 1920s, northern and western European immigrants once more outnumbered immigrants from southern and eastern Europe and Asia. The globalizing immigration trends of the late industrial era that recruited mounting waves of low-skilled labor drew to a close because of revolutionary changes in American immigration policy.

Except for the Alien Act of 1798, which, for the two years of its existence, authorized the president to deport aliens, the United States had until the late nineteenth century no federal legislation restricting admission to or allowing deportation from the country. Although, as Ueda claims, the United States is "the greatest exception among world nations" in the sweep of its traditions of immigration, it also has a troubling history of discrimination in its immigration policies, as you'll see when you survey this chronology.

CHRONOLOGY OF IMMIGRATION AND NATURALIZATION POLICY

1882: Chinese Exclusion Act bars the admission of Chinese laborers and declares Chinese immigrants to be aliens ineligible for naturalized citizenship. Act extended indefinitely by laws passed in 1892, 1902, and 1904.

Continental Emigration. The Road Home: Return Migration from the U.S.A.," *Journal of European Economic History* 9 (Spring 1980): 41–112.

[28]U.S. Commission on Immigration, *Reports,* vol. 3, Tables 15 and 21, pp. 84–85; Handlin, *Race and Nationality,* pp. 89, 96–99.

1891: Congress establishes comprehensive federal control over immigration, establishes the Bureau of Immigration under the Treasury Department to administer immigration laws. Barred persons likely to go on public welfare are those having certain contagious diseases, felons, polygamists, and anyone guilty of "moral turpitude." Federal control extends to deportation of unlawful entries.

1898: In *United States v. Wong Kim Ark,* the U.S. Supreme Court finds that the children of Chinese immigrants are American citizens because they were born in the United States.

1903: U.S. Bureau of Immigration is placed under Department of Commerce and Labor. Congress passes act to recodify existing immigration laws, toughens deportation powers, and bars anarchists and subversives.

1906: Naturalization Act systematizes application for naturalized citizenship and makes knowledge of English a requirement.

1907–1908: Gentlemen's Agreement between the United States and Japanese government, which volunteers to stop emigration of laborers.

1911: The United States Immigration Commission publishes its forty-two-volume report asserting that immigration is damaging the nation and calling for restriction of immigrants from southern and eastern Europe.

1917: Immigration Act requires literacy test for admission and creates an Asiatic Barred Zone from which no immigration is permitted.

1921: First Quota Act limits annual admissions to 3 percent of foreign-born of a nationality in the United States in 1910. An annual ceiling of 355,000 quota admissions is imposed: 55 percent of all admissions to come from northern and western Europe, 45 percent from other countries, nearly all from southern and eastern Europe. Also, new selective measures are installed to permit nonquota or unlimited admissions of immediate relatives of American citizens and immigrants from the Western Hemisphere.

1922: The U.S. Supreme Court finds in *Takao Ozawa v. United States* that Japanese immigrants are aliens ineligible for citizenship.

1922: The Cable Act of 1922 overturns the position expressed by statute and judicial decision that the citizenship of a married woman follows that of her husband. Henceforward, citizenship for married women is established as independent.

1924: The Second Quota Act revises annual admissions quotas to 2 percent of the foreign-born of a nationality in the United States in 1890. This lowers the annual ceiling of total quota admissions to 165,000 while increasing the share of visas for immigrants from northern and western Europe to 86 percent (141,000) and decreasing the share for those from southern and eastern Europe to 12 percent (21,000). Declares immigrants from Asia inadmissible because they are aliens ineligible for citizenship.

1929: The discriminatory National Origins Quota system goes into full effect. Quotas are recalibrated to a complicated statistical breakdown of the American population in 1920 according to different national origin groups that gives 83 percent of annual quota admissions (127,000) to immigrants from northern and western Europe, 15 percent (23,000) to those from southern and eastern Europe, and 2 percent (4,000) to other areas. The annual ceiling of quota admissions drops to 154,000.

1934: Philippines Independence Act restricts immigration from Philippines to fifty admissions a year.

1940: The Smith Act requires registration and fingerprinting of aliens and widens the grounds for deportation. Congress passes a new Immigration and Nationality Act that recodifies existing immigration law and revises naturalization procedures and forms.

1942: Initiation of Mexican foreign laborer program known as the *bracero* program.

1943: Repeal of Chinese Exclusion Act of 1882 provides a small quota for Chinese admissions and makes Chinese immigrants eligible for naturalized citizenship.

1945: President Truman issues executive order permitting entry of 40,000 refugees and displaced persons.

1945: War Brides Act facilitates immigration of foreign-born spouses and children of armed services personnel.

1946: India receives an annual admissions quota and Indian immigrants are permitted to naturalize. Immigrants from the Philippines are also granted eligibility for naturalization.

1948: Congress passes the Displaced Persons Act, the first law expressing the need to admit people fleeing persecution. The law provides for entry of 202,000 refugees uprooted by the war in Europe over the next two years. Refugees are counted against annual quotas in each year and subsequent years (called quota mortgaging).

1950: Internal Security Act expands the grounds for exclusion and deportation of subversives. Membership in the Communist party is made a ground for exclusion or deportation. The law requires aliens to report their address annually. Congress amends the 1948 Displaced Persons Act to increase the number of available visas from 202,000 to 341,000.

1952: McCarran-Walter Act recodifies immigration and naturalization statutes. The discriminatory national origins quota system is retained. A system of occupational preferences is installed. Racial and gender discrimination in naturalization is prohibited.

1953: Refugee Relief Act provides 205,000 nonquota visas and repeals quota mortgaging.

1954: Operation Wetback removes one million Mexican aliens from the Southwest and causes numerous civil liberties violations. United States begins to admit Hungarian refugees.

1959: United States begins to admit refugees from Cuba.

1965: Hart-Celler Act abolishes the restrictive national origins quota system, and creates a worldwide system of equal per country visa limits (20,000 a year). For the first time, annual limits are placed on immigration from the Western Hemisphere. The annual ceiling of limited admissions is raised to 290,000: Eastern Hemisphere nations receive 170,000 admissions, Western Hemisphere nations 120,000. The law establishes an admissions class not subject to limitation that functionally replaces the old nonquota class. A revised occupational and family reunion preference system is to be applied to the Eastern Hemisphere only. The law requires that an admitted alien obtain labor preclearance from the secretary of labor stating that he or she will not displace or harm working conditions of an American worker.

1975: The Indochinese Migration and Refugee Assistance Act establishes an administrative program for resettling refugees from Vietnam and Cambodia.

1976: Congress passes a law to include Laotians in Indochinese resettlement program. Congress passes a law to apply Eastern Hemisphere visa preference system and annual 20,000 per country visa limit to the Western Hemisphere.

1980: The Refugee Act reaffirms cooperation of the president and Congress in setting refugee admissions, and places refugees outside the quota system by removing "refugee" as a preference category. The law correspondingly reduces the worldwide ceiling on annual quota immigration to 270,000 and establishes an administrative program for domestic resettlement of refugees.

1986: Immigration Reform and Control Act (IRCA) establishes amnesty for aliens unlawfully in the country and provides them an opportunity to legalize their status; produces sanctions prohibiting employers from knowingly hiring or recruiting illegal aliens; adjusts to permanent resident alien status Cubans and Haitians who had not been admitted officially and properly; and creates a small quota for aliens from countries underrepresented in annual immigration.

1990: Congress passes a law that revises the entire admissions system and creates an overall flexible cap of 700,000 admissions starting in 1992, to be replaced by a cap of 675,000 in 1995. Congress retreats from exclusion and deportation policies based on ideological and anti-Communist grounds; liberalizes naturalization qualifications and provides for administrative hearings in addition to traditional court hearings for naturalization; and expands the share of "diversity immigrants" from underrepresented countries.

Considerations

1. A number of classification schemes are embedded or implied in Ueda's discussion. Try to make them explicit. State some categories for the kinds of "push" factors that aid in the decision to leave one's home country and that make leaving possible. What are some of the types of "pull" factors? If you worked with the charts and tables at the beginning of this chapter (see the Opening Problem, p. 286), refine and elaborate the scheme you developed to classify types and characteristics of immigration to the United States.
2. Ueda discusses temporary or return migration. What are some of the factors that would contribute to return migration or that would influence an immigrant to establish permanent residence in a new country?
3. One complaint about current immigration is that it strains the economy and drains resources. What light does Ueda's discussion of the "ebb and flow" of immigration shed on this complaint? You might want to refer to David Cole's "Five Myths about Immigration" (p. 308) for more insights on this concern and others.
4. One characteristic often cited about the new wave of immigration — and it is true — is its astounding variability; recent immigrants come from a wide range of countries

with varied languages and cultural practices. This variability is frequently compared in popular media to the more homogeneous nature of previous waves of immigration. What would Ueda say about the purported homogeneity of other immigrant populations in our history?

5. As an aid to making sense of the list of immigration legislation in Ueda's appendix, try creating a scheme to classify the various criteria the United States has established to restrict or encourage immigration; for example, race or nationality, public health, political beliefs, and so on.
6. Immigration has emerged again as a volatile political issue, and the readers of this book undoubtedly have a range of beliefs and opinions about it. What did Ueda's overview help you understand about the role of immigration in U.S. history? How did it reinforce or challenge your previous beliefs?

The following excerpt from Maldwyn Allen Jones's American Immigration *provides an overview of the significant wave of immigration to the United States during the first half of the nineteenth century, focusing on two of the largest migrating populations: the Irish and the Germans. In tracing "patterns of distribution and adjustment," Jones discusses the routes these immigrants took, their places of settlement, and their occupations. He discusses, as well, their effect on the economy, their religious and political beliefs and practices, and the influence of those beliefs and practices on American institutions. And Jones provides a historical perspective on the complex ways these earlier generations of immigrants created both ethnic and American identities, maintaining various political and cultural connections to their homeland while attempting to come to terms with a new society.*

From *American Immigration*

MALDWYN ALLEN JONES

The census of 1860 revealed that out of a total population of almost 31.5 million, the United States had 4,136,000 foreign-born inhabitants. The great bulk lived north of Mason and Dixon's line and east of the Mississippi, the largest numbers being found in New York, Pennsylvania, Ohio, Illinois, Wisconsin, and Massachusetts, in that order. The fifteen slave states had only about half a million foreign-born residents, or 13.4 percent of the total, and of them nearly all lived in the four states of Missouri, Maryland, Louisiana,

---

MALDWYN ALLEN JONES (b. 1922) is Commonwealth Fund Professor of American History Emeritus at University College, University of London. His many works include *American History, 1607–1980* (1984, 2nd ed. 1995), *The Limits of Liberty* (1980), *Destination America* (1976), and *American Immigration* (1960, 2nd ed. 1992), from which this excerpt is taken.

and Texas. In North and South alike the heaviest concentration of immigrants was found in the cities. New York, Chicago, Cincinnati, Milwaukee, Detroit, and San Francisco each had a population of which almost one-half was foreign-born; in New Orleans, Baltimore, and Boston the proportion was well over one-third; and in St. Louis it was more than three-fifths.

Between the different ethnic groups there were significant variations in distribution. Nearly two-thirds of the 1,611,000 Irish were to be found in New York, Pennsylvania, New Jersey, and New England, though there were large numbers in practically every city of any size from San Francisco to Boston, and from New Orleans to Chicago. The 1,301,000 Germans were somewhat more evenly distributed, but there were practically none in New England and more than one-half resided in the upper Mississippi and Ohio valleys, especially in the states of Ohio, Illinois, Wisconsin, and Missouri. The British-born were still more widely dispersed; practically every northern state had a share of the total of the 587,775 people born in England, Scotland, and Wales. Those born in British America, who numbered 249,970, were concentrated in the states immediately south of the St. Lawrence and the Great Lakes; more than one-half were in New York, Michigan, Wisconsin, and Illinois, and most of the remainder were in the six New England states. The smaller immigrant groups were even more highly concentrated. More than half the 43,995 Norwegians had settled in Wisconsin, and virtually all the rest were in Minnesota, Iowa, and Illinois. Likewise, of the 28,281 Dutch nearly two-thirds were in Michigan, New York, Wisconsin, and Iowa.

Analysis of the influences which determined immigrant distribution in the United States may begin with the fact . . . that the overwhelming mass of newcomers came on their own initiative and without assistance. A great many immigrants were completely without resources once they had paid their fares and, on reaching America, were immobilized by their poverty. The authorities in every immigrant port from Boston to New Orleans constantly complained that, while the more prosperous and able-bodied dispersed throughout the country, the more helpless and destitute remained wherever they happened to disembark. The complaint was exaggerated but it had considerable basis in fact.

An equally important circumstance was the tendency for immigrant routes to follow the paths of ocean commerce. The Irish concentration in New England, for example, was largely a product of the New Brunswick timber trade. Those Irish who wanted to reach the United States often found that the cheapest and most convenient method was to take passage first in vessels going out for timber to St. John or St. Andrew's. Here the journey could be cheaply continued in one of the numerous coasting vessels employed in carrying plaster of Paris from the Maritime Provinces to Boston, Providence, and other New England ports. But this was not the only method of entry, for many pioneer Irish men and women made their way from New Brunswick into New England on foot, settling wherever employment could be obtained and acting as nuclei around which Irish settlements could grow. Likewise it was the Le Havre cotton trade which helped give a German coloring to parts of the Mississippi Valley. Most of the Germans seeking passage from Le Havre had perforce to go to New Orleans, but as there were excellent steamboat services up the Mississippi and its tributaries, it was an easy matter to reach St. Louis and Cincinnati, both of which became in consequence strongholds of German culture.

In many cases, immigrants' location was determined by the occupational skill they brought with them from Europe. Skilled industrial workers tended to congregate in the

American centers of their crafts. Thus one found Welsh miners in the anthracite coalfields of eastern Pennsylvania and Cornish miners in the Wisconsin and Illinois lead region as well as in the copper and iron mines of Michigan. For similar reasons Staffordshire potters made almost invariably for East Liverpool, Ohio, or Trenton, New Jersey; Welsh quarrymen settled in slate areas of Vermont, New York, and Pennsylvania; and British textile workers could be found wherever cottons and woolens, silks, hosiery, and carpeting were manufactured in the United States. In the same way the wide dispersal of German Jews in the United States was directly traceable to their menfolk having been predominantly petty tradesmen and professional men.

Agricultural skills, by contrast, could not always be put to use in America. For one thing, not every immigrant farmer possessed the capital needed to embark on American agriculture; for another, the techniques of European farming differed from those required in the New World. Particularly was this so on the frontier, where conditions were unfamiliar to the European and where specialized training in the use of the ax and the rifle was an essential prerequisite of survival, let alone of success. Only rarely, therefore, did immigrants become frontiersmen or pioneer farmers; instead, their role in the westward movement was to take over farms which had already been cleared and whose original owners had moved farther west. . . .

For many immigrants, of course, removal to America was simply one form of participation in that country-to-town movement which was so marked a phenomenon in both Europe and America throughout the nineteenth century. But in no other group was urban concentration so complete as among the Irish. That Irish men and women, though overwhelmingly of rural origin, settled so rarely on the land in the United States was for some contemporaries an inexplicable paradox. One commentator remarked in 1855 on "this strange contradictory result, that a people who hungered and thirsted for land in Ireland should have been content when they reached the New World . . . to sink into the condition of a miserable town tenantry, to whose squalors even European seaports could hardly present a parallel."

Part of the explanation lies in the poverty of the Irish, which practically ruled out the possibility of their becoming independent farmers and which made it imperative for them to obtain immediate employment on arrival. This, of course, was more readily obtainable in the towns than in rural areas. But there were other reasons. Though the Irish were generally country-dwellers, their farming experience was extremely limited, usually consisting only of potato cultivation. Then again, their experiences in Ireland, especially of the events leading to their emigration, had resulted in the land becoming for many the symbol of oppression and insecurity, of unbroken want and misery. And countryfolk though they were, they had been accustomed in Ireland to a gregarious existence and were unsuited by temperament and experience to the loneliness of farm life in America. Moreover, as Catholics, they were reluctant to go to rural regions where churches and priests of their own faith were rarely to be found. A further contributory factor was that women made up so large a proportion of the Irish influx. Even in the 1830s women accounted for 35 percent of immigrants from Ireland, and in the decades after the famine they were unique among foreign-born groups in outnumbering men. Not only were Irish immigrant women generally young and unmarried on arrival, but in America married less frequently — and later — than other groups of immigrants. By emigrating they had opted for a life of paid work, and the vast majority found it. Farming, as a family activity, was largely closed to them, but since they experienced less overt job discrimination than their menfolk, the expanding American urban economy offered them a range of opportunities either as mill workers or, more especially, as domestic servants — an occupation spurned by native-born Americans. It was this concentration in domestic work that largely explained why Irish communities in large Eastern and Middle Western cities housed more women than men.

Numerous attempts were made, especially by members of the Catholic hierarchy, to promote Irish rural colonization in the United States. . . . [T]he strongest advocate of Irish rural colonization was Thomas D'Arcy McGee, who had fled to America in 1848 after the collapse of the Young Ireland movement and who became editor first of the New York *Nation* and then of the *American Celt.* Seeing in rural colonization a method of elevating the moral and material condition of his compatriots and of freeing them from the Know-Nothing[1] hostility they encountered in the eastern cities, McGee organized the Irish Catholic Colonization Convention which met at Buffalo, New York, in February, 1856. The ninety-five delegates, drawn almost equally from the United States and Canada, agreed unanimously on the necessity of removing the Irish from the demoralizing influence of the city to the open spaces of the West but proved unable to do anything to translate their wishes into action. Though the project won the support of some western members of the Catholic hierarchy, it was strongly opposed by the eastern bishops and especially by Archbishop John Hughes of New York, whose influence was so great that his opposition insured the plan's failure. Fearful lest the dispersal of the Irish should lead to a loss of faith, and not unnaturally anxious to keep his flock together, Hughes denounced the whole scheme as one devised for the benefit of western land speculators.

Just as unsuccessful as the colonization projects which aimed at breaking up the urban concentration of immigrants were those whose objective was to preserve the cultural distinctiveness and geographic isolation of particular groups. In the earliest of such schemes the Irish were once again concerned. In 1817 the Irish Emigrant Society of New York petitioned Congress to set aside part of the unsold lands in Illinois Territory for exclusive Irish settlement on extended terms of credit. But Congress saw no reason why an Irishman should be able to acquire land on easier terms than an American and was also strongly opposed to any scheme which, by permitting ethnic enclaves, threatened to slow down the process of Americanization. . . .

It was the Germans who were most prominently associated with attempts to preserve ethnic distinctiveness. Thwarted at home by political reaction, a number of liberals and intellectuals sought to realize the ideals of German nationalism by creating a New Germany within the borders of the American Union. "What would Philadelphia be in forty years if the Germans there were to remain German, and retain their language and customs?" asked one German in 1813. "It would . . . be a German city, just as York and Lancaster are German counties. What would be the result throughout Pennsylvania and Maryland . . . ? An entirely German state where, as formerly in Germantown, the beautiful German language would be used in the legislative halls and the courts of justice."

Such dreams, persisting for more than a generation thereafter, inspired the activities of a number of German colonization societies and other agencies. During the 1830s the

[1]**Know-Nothings:** A mid-nineteenth century political movement in the United States that opposed immigration and blamed immigrants for a range of social and economic problems. (See David Cole's "Five Myths about Immigration" on p. 308.) [Eds.].

Giessener Gesellschaft attempted to mass German immigrants along the Missouri River near St. Louis. Between 1844 and 1847 the *Adelsverein,* a colonization society founded by a group of German princes and noblemen, had similar objectives in sending thousands of German settlers to southwest Texas. In the 1850s it was hoped that by concentrating the stream of German immigration upon Wisconsin, that state might be Germanized.

Although a number of counties in each of these states became predominantly German, hopes of a New Germany in the wider sense were bound to fail. Permanent geographical isolation was out of the question in view of the speed with which the United States was being settled. But what made failure doubly sure was the fact that each venture was made in a region no less attractive and accessible to native-born Americans and non-German immigrants than it was to the Germans themselves. Important, too, was the opposition of German-American leaders to the New Germany idea. Men like Gustav Körner and Carl Schurz realized that German immigrants could hope neither to participate fully in American life nor to be accepted by other Americans if they insisted upon remaining a class apart. . . .

Whether they came individually or in groups . . . immigrants faced the necessity of coming to terms with American life. Having cut themselves loose from the stable, ordered European world into which they had been born, they needed to relocate themselves in the strange new American universe. Their ability to do so was by no means uniform. It varied with the economic status and the cultural background of the newcomers themselves, as well as with the economic and social structure of the regions in which they settled. Even for those whose transplantation was accomplished with a minimum of economic and psychological buffeting, the process of adjustment could be painful and protracted. For many immigrants, immigration was a traumatic experience, resulting in a sense of alienation and isolation. It was often the fate of the first-generation immigrant to remain marginalized, suspended between two cultures but belonging wholly to neither.

Few agencies existed to smooth the path of nineteenth-century newcomers. Until just before the Civil War, immigrants could expect no help on arrival save that thrust upon them by the touts and harpies who infested the landing places. An investigating committee at New York was shocked in 1846 at the amount of outrage and fraud practiced upon newly arrived immigrants; it found "the German preying upon the German — the Irish upon the Irish — the English upon the English." The various ethnic benevolent organizations, like the Irish Emigrant Society of New York and the Deutsche Gesellschaft, did what they could to protect and shelter particular groups, but they lacked the necessary resources and authority.

Only belatedly was the task of immigrant protection assumed by the states. Initially they were concerned only to protect themselves against foreign pauperism. Led by Massachusetts and New York in the 1820s the seaboard states passed laws requiring shipmasters to give bonds for passengers who might become chargeable. But in practice the requirement was nearly always commuted in favor of a fixed rate head tax, the proceeds of which were used to provide immigrant hospitals and other services. The most elaborate reception arrangements were made by New York, which received the bulk of the immigrants. After a state board of immigration had been established in 1847, the Marine Hospital on Staten Island was set aside for infectious cases, hospitals and refuges were built on Ward's Island in the East River, and an employment exchange was opened on Canal Street. Then in 1855 an immigrant depot was instituted at Castle Garden near the Battery, where all immigrants arriving at New York had henceforth to be landed. Here, relatively secure from exploitation, immigrants could change their foreign money, arrange for reliable accommodations, buy railroad tickets, and seek advice about jobs. Only a small percentage of the total immigration received any direct help at Castle Garden, but by the time the institution gave way to Ellis Island in 1892, many thousands of immigrants had been relieved, given temporary shelter, and directed to places where labor was wanted.

The first step in obtaining an American foothold was to find employment. For the fortunate minority with capital or industrial skill this usually presented little difficulty. To be sure, even experienced farmers and skilled artisans often found that they had to adapt their knowledge to American conditions; but within a short time of arrival such men had resumed their familiar activities, their economic adjustment completed. Other immigrants were resourceful enough to turn their European knowledge to new uses. Of the many Jews who in Europe had been traders and petty retailers, a considerable number became in America itinerant peddlers, the more successful of whom in time accumulated sufficient capital to set up retail establishments. But there were some whose previous training could not so readily be turned to account, either because of their inability to speak English or because they came in such numbers as to exceed the American demand. For these reasons many highly qualified German Forty-eighters[2] encountered great difficulties in finding suitable work; often, according to one of the more successful Forty-eighters, "learned professors, writers and artists . . . were forced to support themselves by making cigars, acting as waiters or house-servants, boot-blacks or street-sweepers." Even so, the plight of such men, however pathetic, was hardly to be compared with that of the infinitely more numerous group who came to America with neither skill nor resources — indeed, with no asset at all save brawn and muscle. No immigrant group was without its quota of those whose employment opportunities — and whose mobility, consequently — were thus narrowly restricted. Yet none was so poverty-stricken or so lacking in previous training as the Irish, the great majority of whom therefore became an urban proletariat.

Because of their dependence upon unskilled labor, the Irish introduced a novel element of concentration into the American urban economic pattern. A New York state census in 1855 revealed that one-quarter of New York City's Irish working population consisted of laborers, carters, porters, and waiters, another quarter was made up of domestic servants, and another 10 percent were either tailors or dressmakers. In Boston, where poor transportation facilities immobilized laborers and the absence of large and varied industrial enterprises still further narrowed their opportunities, almost two-thirds of the gainfully employed Irish were either unskilled laborers or domestic servants. This condition had no parallel in other immigrant groups, which tended rather to reflect the dispersion of occupations characterizing the economic organization of American cities. The state census of 1855 showed that no one occupation employed more than a small fraction of the New York Germans. About 15 percent were tailors and 10 percent do-

[2]**Forty-eighters:** Those who left Germany in the wake of the failed revolution of 1848 in which poor German farmers and workers rebelled against the government [Eds.].

mestic servants, but only 5 percent were laborers, waiters, or carters, the rest being distributed among a great variety of occupations.

While the Irish thus came virtually to monopolize unskilled jobs in American cities, they achieved similar prominence in construction work. Finding urban employment sporadic even when it could be obtained at all, Irishmen responded readily to the bait of high wages held out by labor agencies and contractors concerned with canal, railroad, and other construction projects in the West and South. In the construction camps working and living conditions were extremely harsh, and exploitation by unscrupulous contractors frequent; yet despite the warnings of the Irish-American press, Irishmen continued to be drawn to canal- and railroad-building, leaving their families for months at a time in the cities in which they had first settled. Toward the end of the period increasing numbers found employment in industry. During the 1840s Irish immigrants began gradually to replace native farmers' daughters in the New England textile mills, others obtained work in shoe factories, and those who had gained experience of mining during a sojourn in England scattered throughout the Pennsylvania coalfields and the lead mines of Illinois and Wisconsin. Yet even in 1860 the bulk of the Irish were still at the bottom of the occupational ladder.

The effect of immigration upon native labor was a matter of controversy among contemporaries. Some observers maintained that an influx of unskilled labor like that represented by the Irish could serve only to raise the economic status of the rest of the community. "Their inferiority," wrote Edward Everett Hale in 1852, "compels them to go to the bottom; and the consequence is that we are, all of us, the higher lifted because they are here." Though this was true enough in general, the poorer native-born element, such as the free blacks in New York, certainly suffered from Irish competition for unskilled jobs, and not a few artisans were temporarily displaced by the simultaneous introduction to industry of cheap immigrant labor and machinery. Nor did immigrant competition come exclusively from the unskilled; in New York, for example, there were complaints during the 1840s that an influx of German tailors, shoemakers, and cabinetmakers had lowered wage rates and had deprived Americans of work.

Yet in the broad view the economic effects of mass immigration were undeniably beneficial. As well as contributing to the fluidity of the American economy, it hastened the construction of a transportation network and accelerated the growth of industrialism. Neither the factory system nor the great canal and railroad developments of the period could have come into existence so quickly without the reservoir of cheap labor provided by immigration.

The acceleration of the nation's economic development was, however, purchased only at the price of an intensification of its social difficulties. Mass immigration may have augmented America's working force, but it also presented new problems of pauperism, disease, and criminality. Attributed by some Americans to the immigrant's inborn depravity, these evils were really a consequence of social maladjustment to the American environment. The harsh and unfamiliar conditions of life to which many immigrants were condemned by their poverty were bound to have disturbing consequences. Yet the chief sufferer from the immigrant's failure to adjust was not American society but the newcomer.

Obliged to find housing accommodations that were both cheap and within walking distance of their employment, the majority of urban immigrants crowded into old warehouses or dilapidated mansions which had been hastily converted into tenements. Many others lived in flimsy one-room shanties erected out of whatever materials were available or sought shelter in attics and cellars. Darkness, damp, and lack of ventilation were almost universal in such dwellings, in which there was only the most primitive sanitation. These squalid and noisome surroundings proved excellent breeding-grounds for diseases like tuberculosis, smallpox, typhus, and cholera, from all of which immigrants suffered more heavily than the native population. That the immigrant death rate was also higher than that of the native-born population was due not only to unfavorable living conditions in America but to the fact that many immigrants were physically debilitated on arrival owing to long-continued malnutrition and to the hardships of the crossing. . . .

Immigrant poverty was reflected in the fact that, wherever they congregated, the foreign-born constituted a large proportion of those dependent upon state and municipal assistance. Between 1845 and 1860 between one-half and two-thirds of Boston's paupers consisted of immigrants, and in New York City in 1860 no fewer than 86 percent of those on relief were of foreign birth. Crime statistics, too, showed a similar disproportion between foreign-born and native offenders. In 1859, for instance, 55 percent of the persons arrested for crime in New York City were Irish-born, and a further 22 percent had been born in other foreign countries. Yet these statistics are misleading in that few immigrant lawbreakers committed the more serious offenses. In most cases conflict with the law resulted either from petty thievery or, still more commonly, from drunkenness and disorderly conduct.

Demoralization and degradation were not, of course, the invariable accompaniments of immigration. One should guard against painting too black a picture of immigrant life by dwelling excessively upon the misfortunes of the poorest class of newcomers. Even Irish laborers and domestic servants, it should be remembered, were generally able to save enough out of their wages to pay the passage of relatives. Immigrant letters, moreover, were generally animated not by despair but by a sense of accomplishment. Even from the slums, immigrants could write glowing tributes to America, the most eloquent of which was the continued advice to relatives to come and join them.

The persistence of feelings of alienation and isolation could not but stimulate in each ethnic group an awareness of its identity. The strange and often hostile environment in which they found themselves sharpened the nostalgia of immigrants for their homelands, led them to cherish old loyalties, and drove them in upon themselves. The most obvious expression of immigrant yearnings for the familiar was the tendency to congregate in distinct areas. American cities now became agglomerations of separate communities, the ethnic character of which was recognized in such names as Irishtown and Kleindeutschland.[3]

The most striking examples of ethnic concentration were provided by New York City. As early as 1830 the Sixth Ward, especially the insalubrious quarter known as the "Five Points," had taken on a marked Irish coloring. From here during the next generation the area of Irish settlement was successively extended until it covered the whole of the Lower East Side as far north as the Fourteenth Ward and as far east as the Seventh.

But by 1850 a more characteristic ethnic ghetto had developed. Just to the north of

[3]**Kleindeutschland:** "Little Germany" (German) [Eds.].

the Irish district, from the Bowery to the Tenth, Eleventh, and Thirteenth Wards, lay a region known as Kleindeutschland. Until the Civil War it contained about two-thirds of New York's 100,000 Germans. Here, the English language was rarely heard and there was scarcely a business which was not run by Germans. Here also were to be found German churches, schools, restaurants, a *Volkstheater,*[4] and a lending library. But what most attracted the attention of visitors was the number of lager-beer saloons. On Sundays, particularly, these establishments were thronged to overflowing, it being the common practice for people to go from the inn to church and then return to the inn again.

An equally revealing reflection of group consciousness was the banding together of immigrants in autonomous social organizations. This development, which isolated the newcomer far more conclusively than mere geographical segregation, was in most cases due to the exclusive attitudes of the American-born who tended to debar immigrants from participating in existing societies. Most of the numerous Irish militia companies, for example, came into existence only after Irishmen had been refused admission to established companies. Yet it was significant that even British immigrants, whose economic status and cultural background were passports to acceptance, often preferred their own social institutions.

What determined the nature of immigrant groupings was not national feeling, for in Europe immigrants had been hardly aware of their nationality. To most, local and regional affiliations were more important. Immigrants from England usually identified themselves primarily as, for example, Yorkshiremen or Cornishmen, those from Ireland as Dubliners or Kerrymen, and those from Germany as Bavarians or Westphalians. The welding of such groups into national communities, which was the consequence of New World pressures, was a complex and protracted business. In the meantime, linguistic or religious links served as the basis of selection, though the pattern was varied enough to allow for many diverse combinations.

Immigrant associations sometimes represented communal attempts to meet material needs in times of crisis. Thus the numerous mutual aid societies and benevolent associations strove, with varying degrees of success, to provide sickness benefits and to pay funeral expenses. But the real function of these and similar immigrant organizations was to satisfy the desire of their members for companionship and familiar surroundings, and thus to soften the effects of contact with a strange environment. Immigrant militia and fire companies, too, were essentially social clubs; so, also, were the German *Turnvereine,*[5] despite the political activities in which they sometimes engaged.

In addition, each group sought to preserve in America the familiar cultural pattern of the old country. For this purpose the most widely used and most effective formal instruments were the church, the school, and the newspaper. In their religious faith immigrants recognized almost the only pillar of the old life that had not crumbled in the course of the Atlantic crossing. To it, therefore, they clung both as a means of preserving their identity and as a source of security and solace in a bewildering world. Most British immigrants, of course, were fortunate in that neither linguistic nor doctrinal barriers prevented their joining existing American congregations. All other groups, however, had to

[4]***Volkstheater:*** A public theater — literally, a "people's theater" (German) [Eds.].

[5]***Turnvereine,*** or "Turner Clubs," were made up of Forty-eighters (see footnote 2 on p. 376) who were followers of the German leader Turnvater Jahn [Eds.].

rely mainly upon their own efforts if familiar forms of worship were to be re-created; and this aim immigrants were determined to achieve even at the cost of heavy sacrifices.

Some of the difficulty of transplanting an immigrant church resulted from the fact that immigration had often disestablished it. In various parts of Europe the Anglican, Lutheran, Presbyterian, and Reformed churches had been established churches, that is, had been supported by and linked to the state. In America, where church and state were separate and where people were consequently free to join any church or none, the immigrant church had to devise a new basis of membership, reorganize its polity, and recast its attitude toward the civil power.

But equally great difficulties arose when the task of transplantation had already been accomplished by an earlier generation of immigrants. Prolonged controversy and schism were often the result of differences of opinion between newcomers and their Americanized co-religionists. Nineteenth-century German Lutheran immigrants, for example, found many features of the American Lutheran church, which had been founded by Germans in the colonial period, to be strange, distasteful, and eventually unacceptable. It was not merely that English had replaced German as the language of worship but that traditional Lutheran beliefs and practices had been profoundly altered. As a result of the Americanizing influences at work in the half-century after the Revolution, American Lutheranism had lost much of its distinctiveness. . . .

Anxiety to preserve their cultural heritage led both Catholic and Lutheran immigrants to favor the establishment of parochial schools. Yet the motives of the two groups were hardly identical. Organization of a separate Catholic school system resulted from complaints of Protestant proselytizing in the public schools, especially of daily Bible readings from a translation which the Catholic church condemned. But when German, Norwegian, and Swedish Lutherans followed a similar course, it was mainly from the belief that instruction in the mother tongue was essential to the preservation of religious belief. Neither group was wholly successful in its aims, at least in this period, principally because of a lack of funds and trained teachers. Among Scandinavian and German Lutherans, moreover, many parents were unwilling to accept church leadership on the school question and the majority probably sent their children to public schools. The Catholic refusal to accept the common school system, on the other hand, often meant that the children of immigrants received no education at all.

In contrast to the difficulties encountered in attempting to establish autonomous school systems was the comparative ease with which each immigrant group established a newspaper press of its own. Though most immigrants had little previous experience of newspapers, they welcomed the appearance of journals that kept them in touch with happenings in the old country, acquainted them with developments in the immigrant community itself, and interpreted for them a variety of American events and issues. Because of the poverty and illiteracy of many newcomers, a stable immigrant press was slow to develop. Irish-American journalism, particularly, remained a gamble until the great influx of the forties and fifties enlarged the reading public. The leading Irish organs were the New York *Irish American,* founded by Patrick Lynch in 1849, which claimed a circulation of 40,000 in 1861, and the Boston *Pilot,* founded in 1838; but Catholic journals like the New York *Freeman's Journal,* the organ of Archbishop Hughes, had a large Irish readership. The German-language press, which had steadily lost ground during the first quarter of the nineteenth century, began to revive in the 1830s with the founding of such papers as the New York *Staats-Zeitung und Herold,* the St. Louis *Anzeiger des Wes-*

tens, and the Cincinnati *Volksblatt,* all of which had a long existence. But the greatest expansion was to come in the decade or so after 1840. As late as 1843 there was still only one German daily in the United States, but by 1850 there were a score; the total number of German-language papers rose from 40 in 1840 to 133 in 1852, and their general tone and substance were greatly improved by the arrival of a better class of editor. Among smaller immigrant groups, like the Norwegians and the Welsh, newspapers tended generally to be church journals, or at least to be edited by clergymen. These papers, however, served the same function as the immigrant press generally, namely, that of acting as a focus for the immigrant community and of facilitating its Americanization.

For the great mass of newcomers the most difficult, if not the most pressing, problems of adjustment related to their participation in American politics. Since all but a few had been denied the right of suffrage in Europe, previous experience had done little to prepare them for the exercise of political power in the country of their adoption. Whether immigrants were seriously inhibited from political activity by an acceptance of differences in rank may be doubted, for European ideas of status withered quickly in the democratic American atmosphere. Yet it remains true that immigrants were unfamiliar on arrival not only with American political issues but with the democratic process itself. The result was that many newcomers became tools of unscrupulous politicians. While machine politics based on immigrant support was not to reach its apogee until after the Civil War, the urban immigrant tended from an early date to be bound to the machine. Open bribery was not unknown, but the machine's control of the immigrant was a result rather of its continuing attention to his practical needs. Acting through an army of ward heelers, often immigrants themselves, the machine assisted newcomers to find accommodation and employment and afforded them a variety of services and privileges. In return, the mass of newly arrived slum-dwellers were prepared to give their votes, which they otherwise valued little, to those who looked after their welfare.

Nothing could be more misleading, however, than to interpret immigrant political attitudes exclusively in terms of the ignorance and apathy resulting, respectively, from political inexperience and from the necessity of concentrating upon immediate personal problems. All-important though these factors were initially, they exercised less and less influence as immigrants gradually grasped the basic concepts of democracy and, still more, as they came to recognize their personal involvement in the political issues raised during this period. Slavery, expansion, and, above all, nativism were issues of vital concern to the immigrant and proved powerful solvents of political passivity. True, some immigrant groups usually voted in blocs. But this was due largely to a similarity of outlook resulting from a high degree of homogeneity and concentration. If political machines succeeded in retaining the allegiance of immigrants, this was because — in addition to the welfare services they provided — their political attitudes corresponded with immigrant aspirations.

All this becomes clearer, perhaps, when one attempts to explain why it was that, for most of the pre-Civil War period, immigrants gave their support overwhelmingly to the Democratic party. Only in part was this because the Democrats were more systematic and skillful — as well as earlier — than their rivals in attempting to woo the immigrant vote. Equally important was the powerful appeal to the common man of the party of Jefferson and Jackson, the latter of whom especially typified for many immigrants their own yearnings for equality. In addition the Democrats adopted a consistently friendly attitude toward immigrants. In Congress they resolutely opposed any lengthening of the residential qualifications for naturalization, and the national party platform regularly included an enthusiastic endorsement of the asylum concept. The Whigs were in contrast identified by most immigrants as the party of aristocracy, nativism, and temperance. Though the Democratic party became increasingly dominated by slaveholders, this did not at first lessen its appeal to immigrants; the Irish, indeed, because of their hatred of abolitionism, found in this new development a further cause for voting Democratic. Yet . . . the intrusion of the slavery issue into national politics brought to an end the Democratic near-monopoly of foreign-born votes. By the end of the 1850s the Irish were the only immigrant group which still gave the Democrats its undivided support.

Foreign-born devotion to the Democrats was one of the many factors which helped elect Andrew Jackson to the presidency in 1828. In New York, Jackson's majority owed much to a heavy Irish vote, just as in Pennsylvania it was based largely upon solid Scotch-Irish and German support. But it was not until later that immigrant votes began to have a decisive effect upon presidential elections. In 1844 Henry Clay attributed his defeat to the hostility of the foreign-born element toward the Whigs, though in fact the intervention of the Liberty party in New York was just as influential. Franklin Pierce's majority in 1852 was large enough to disprove the claim of his opponents that he had been elected by immigrant votes, but in the much closer contest four years later James Buchanan may well have owed his election to immigrant support, especially in key states like Pennsylvania.

It was in local politics that immigrant influence was most marked. As early as 1820 the Irish had captured control of Tammany Hall, and before the end of the decade were the dominating force in New York City politics. Moving steadily up the political ladder from ward boss to alderman and then to state legislator, the Irish also gained an appreciable number of federal offices during the Democratic administrations. The Germans, though just as consistently Democratic as the Irish — at least until the 1850s — received less political recognition. This was a consequence partly of their language difficulties but also because, in comparison with the Irish, German immigrants were less concentrated and more heterogeneous.

While they thus became increasingly involved in American politics, immigrants continued to agitate European issues. The Irish, especially, retained a lively interest in the politics of their homeland and, wherever they congregated in the United States, formed organizations favoring Irish causes. During the struggle for Catholic emancipation in Ireland during the 1820s, Irish-American associations known as the Friends of Ireland sent money and addresses of encouragement to the Catholic Association in Dublin. . . . The Young Ireland movement, too, aroused tremendous enthusiasm among Irish-Americans, at least until its radicalism incurred the denunciation of the Catholic hierarchy, and the 1850s brought into being a great number of Irish nationalist clubs pledged to work for the independence of Ireland. In similar fashion German and Hungarian Forty-eighters established revolutionary societies in the United States to plan renewed insurrection in their homelands and to agitate for American intervention against the despotic monarchies of Europe. . . .

That the mass of immigrants supported such causes was due partly to sentimental attachment to the homeland, partly to the need to discharge an emotional debt toward her, but most of all to the fact that they afforded a means of group identification and self-assertion. Significantly enough, the groups most inclined to perpetuate Old World interests were those whom American society was most adamant in rejecting.

Considerations

1. Discuss some of the reasons why particular groups of people ended up in the places that they did.
2. Discuss the effect of immigration on the American economy in the mid-nineteenth century.
3. Describe life in the immigrant sections of the major U.S. cities discussed by Jones.
4. Discuss religion and politics in the life of the mid-nineteenth century immigrant.
5. What factors contributed to the development of what Jones calls an "awareness of identity" among particular immigrant ethnic groups?
6. We tend to look back on previous generations of immigrants as "model assimilationists." In what ways does Jones's passage complicate that perception?
7. If you worked on the Sociology Assignment in this chapter (p. 331), you read about some of the motivations, rewards, and challenges surrounding modern immigration to the United States. Have immigrants' motivations and challenges changed since the nineteenth century, or do you see any similarities? Speculate on this question in a brief essay, drawing on insights from Jones and from the readings in the Sociology Assignment.

Beginning in the early nineteenth century, a pattern of immigration began from the Scandinavian countries to the United States. A significant number of these immigrants moved into the territory that would become the Midwest in order to homestead and farm. Writer Eugene Boe's Norwegian forebears followed this pattern, and in the essay below he provides both the historical context for their migration and a narrative sense of what they might have felt and experienced as they found their way in a new land.

From *Pioneers to Eternity: Norwegians on the Prairie*

Eugene Boe

In contrast to the smiling social democracy it is today, Norway in the last century was an overpopulated land of sharp class distinctions. The government, an insular monarchy, allowed only a privileged few any political expression. The clergy were aloof to the blunt realities of poverty and injustice. Nature had yielded her blessings in scant measure, but nothing was done to help or encourage the tens of thousands struggling to survive on little scraps of barren soil. Neighbor had quarreled with neighbor for every square foot of those steep, stony, stumpy upland meadows and the plots staked out were too small to support a family. Indebtedness was inevitable, the grip of creditor on debtor strangulating. Stills on the farms were legal and too many of the luckless could find their only consolation in drink.

In the early decades of the nineteenth century reports began drifting in from across the Atlantic that painted the New World in colors of the Promised Land. A trickle of migrations from Norway to America started in the 1830s. Most of these emigrants set out for the frontiers of Illinois and Wisconsin, where land was available. Their letters home and the eyewitness accounts of visiting missionaries fanned the flames of discontent back in the Old Country and provoked new waves of emigration.

The Indian treaties of 1851 opened up fresh lands for settlement. By the late 1850s Norwegians were swarming into Iowa and the southern counties of Minnesota. When Minnesota shed its territorial status in 1858 for statehood, it early on established an Immigration Department that employed Norwegian-American journalists to prepare pamphlets for circulation in Norway. This literature praised the exhilarating climate, the beauties of prairie and woodland and lakes, and the potential riches of the new state. Verily, the publicists sang, this was the Land of Canaan, a "glorious new Scandinavia."

In 1862 President Lincoln signed the Homestead Act. After January 1, 1863, any person who was twenty-one years old and was either a citizen or had applied for citizenship could file a claim for a quarter section (160 acres) of land and come into ownership of that land after five years' occupation of it. A claimant need have only $14 for the filing fee.

The government land offices and transportation packagers spread the word throughout the Scandinavian countries and the urge to emigrate became epidemic. The Norwegian government and church opposed any exodus of its people. Massive leave-takings were a reproach — and a shout to the world that much was wrong in the little kingdom. They also threatened the country with a kind of self-inflicted genocide, since only the strongest and the youngest of its sons and daughters — the perpetuators of the race — would take up the challenge to escape. The antimigrationists pictured America

---

Author Eugene Boe spent his summers on Swan Lake in Minnesota, near the land that his Norwegian grandfather homesteaded in the late 1860s. Excerpted here is his article "Pioneers to Eternity: Norwegians on the Prairie," from *Immigrant Experience,* edited by Thomas C. Wheeler (1971). Boe authored and co-authored several books, including *Deliverance in Shanghai* (1983), and contributed more than a hundred articles to national magazines.

as a land ridden with poisonous snakes, bloodthirsty animals, and dangerously wild men. . . . Emigration Fever was called "the most dangerous disease of our time, a bleeding of the Fatherland, a Black Death."

Osten and Henrik Boe (Bō) were two young men who caught the fever. With their parents and three sisters they lived on a tiny *gaard* (farm) near the village of Vang. Vang is in the district of Valders, on the southeastern coast of Norway. Behind it the land sweeps upward steeply into a wide, flat sugarloaf of mountains.

The Boes, like their neighbors, subsisted on a little patch of ground that also had to nourish a cow and a few chickens. Finding enough food for mere survival consumed most of the family's energies. The limited rations of milk, eggs, and potatoes were supplemented only by fish taken from a lake nearby.

In the spring of 1864 Osten and Henrik were twenty-five and twenty-one years old, respectively. Since childhood they had heard the tales of a big open country far across the seas. It is doubtful that word of the Homestead Act had reached their hamlet. It was enough for them to be told of a land where bread and meat were plentiful, where neighbor helped neighbor, and there was the chance to breathe and stretch. They had also heard the shocking accounts of the way the red man had slain many of their countrymen in the southern counties of Minnesota. But that uprising had occurred two years earlier and the Indians were peaceful again.

For years the brothers had been saving the trifling sums they were paid for helping local fishermen. Now they had enough put by for the modest fare to take them on their long voyage. A group of Valders folk were setting sail from the port of Drammen and Osten and Henrik would be on that boat.

The brothers were leaving with the blessing of their parents. (Later the daughters were also to go.) The moment of parting must have been painful all around. These farewells were as final as a funeral. Parents and children alike knew they would not lay eyes upon one another again in this world. For the old folks the New World was as fabled and elusive as the lost Atlantis or the Kingdom of Heaven itself. Only the young had any chance of surviving the journey and they would never take that long, long trail back to the Old Country.

One can only imagine that parting. . . .

All morning the parents of emigrating sons have been carrying provisions aboard a sailboat bobbing in the little harbor under a cheerful April sun. Now it is high noon, the boat is loaded, and the captain is eager to set sail. . . .

The sailboat skims across the fjord toward the open sea. It rounds a peninsular cliff and the harbor with the waving parents is lost. Now the old folks must reverse the path back to their village and lonely huts. Fortunately it is spring and the light will hold nearly around the clock until the end of summer. Now, too, is the busiest time, and with fewer hands to help, those left behind will be too burdened to sorrow. The acute sense of loss will not be felt until the long black winter night sets in.

The sailboat hugs the coastline, pitching around those southernmost extremities of land curved like the tip of a tongue. Sweeping off to starboard — fleetingly — is the magnificent fjord-serrated western coast. Then the fjords, the high wooded cliffs, the silvery cascades of waterfall, and finally the long vertebrate of snow-crowned mountains slip away into the mists. The boat becomes a solitary sail on the North Sea.

Later the voyage would bring terror and prayers for God's deliverance. But as

Norway fell back from them irrevocably, the voyagers were filled with the anguish of leaving. . . .

Those who made the crossing by sailboat (steamboats became the usual mode after the late 1860s) spent long wretched weeks on the high seas. Winds were contrary. Storms nearly overturned the vessels time after time and dumped almost enough water inside to sink them. Mold formed on all the rations. The flat bread, or *skriva brod* (a thin-sliced, yellowish-brown bread), dried mutton and ham, *primost* (a brown cheese in cake form made of whey, sugar, and cream), and *gjatost* (goat's cheese) had to be scraped and dried regularly. Seasickness, pneumonia, dysentery, and typhoid fever were common ailments. It was an unusual voyage that didn't have death itself for a fellow traveler. When someone died, the body was wrapped in sails (or a big stone was tied to the feet) and consigned to the ocean. . . .

The boat carrying Osten and Henrik took eight weeks to arrive in Quebec City. To the brothers it was stranger than a dream, this first breath of the New World. They had never been near a real city before. Why, this Quebec with its bustling waterfront must be as big and busy as Kristiania (today's Oslo) or Bergen! So many people, thousands of them, chattering away in a language you couldn't understand. . . .

The two young men slept on the wharves under the open sky for two nights. Then they were herded like swine into a canalboat that took them 150 miles down the St. Lawrence to Montreal. In Montreal they boarded the immigration car — with its steerage accommodations — of a westward-bound train. Crowded and caged, they rattled for days through the Canadian forest and across the breadth of Michigan. At Grand Haven a steamboat took them over Lake Michigan to Milwaukee. Another train, also equipped with an immigrant box car — and then wagons — carried them across Wisconsin to the old French fur-trading town of Prairie du Chien and finally to Decorah, in the northeastern corner of Iowa.

Decorah had been settled a few years earlier by immigrant Norwegians from Voss, Telemark, Sogn, and Valders. New arrivals from those districts always found a welcome there. They joined the households of the earlier immigrants, whose hospitality had no limits. Here the newcomers got their first real indoctrination into the ways and possibilities of America. From their hosts they might pick up a few words of English to help them in any dealings with Yankee tradesmen or civil servants. Visitors shared the labors of the family and able-bodied males could usually earn day's wages working as peripatetic hired hands. It was a marking-time interlude in a kind of staging area that gave the emigrant a chance to get his bearings and to plan his next move.

Osten and Henrik soon became restless in the Decorah settlement. They were too late for it. It was a little too formed, too picked over. Stories of a newer colony of Norwegians had been reaching their ears. These most recent emigrants were settling the village of Northfield, in the new state of Minnesota.

Eager to break fresh ground, the brothers quit Decorah one day in the late spring of 1865 and began the northwesterly trek of 150 miles to Northfield. They traveled the entire distance on foot. For Henrik it would be the end of the journey. For the sixty-odd remaining years of his life, Northfield was home. There he prospered as a hardware merchant. There he married, established a home, and fathered three children who all entered professions. And here, one day in 1876, he was eyewitness to the hair-raising robbery of the Northfield bank by the Jesse James gang.

The charms of the pleasant little Norwegian-American community wore thin on

Osten. Village life lacked something vital. He dreamed of land . . . of a plot of ground he could call his own, of taming it, growing things on it. He listened intently to the tales of homesteading to the north and west, of rich farmland in an open country.

One April day in 1868, when the snow was off the ground at last, he set off on foot for St. Cloud. To reach this little town on the Mississippi River he followed oxcart trails in a north-by-northwesterly direction. It took him nine days to hike the 125 miles of rough terrain. As a prospective homesteader he went to the government land office in St. Cloud, where he was shown maps of surveyed areas. Now he must decide where he wanted to settle and go to inspect the quarter sections in that area that were available for claim. When he came back and paid his filing fee, the land he had chosen would be registered in his name. Six months later he could take possession of his land. If he never left it for five years, he could have a deed to the land.

Osten chose the township of Aastad, Minnesota, because it was the farthest point out of the immigrant thrust in 1868. Only two settlers had filed claims there and no land had been broken beyond it. Aastad lies some 135 miles north and west of St. Cloud. It measures 6 miles square with 36 sections of 640 acres each. Its soil is rich black alluvial loam. The township is a gently rolling prairie punctuated with marshes, creeks, thickets, and thirty clear lakes. Its western edge flattens out and sweeps into the rich valley of the Red River of the North.

The Great Northern and Northern Pacific railroads had not put down their tracks yet. It would be a decade before those caravans of prairie schooners would come creeping like a fleet through the endless sea of green and golden grasses, their canvas tops gleaming brightly in the shimmering light. There was only the old Red River oxcart trail, the St. Paul-Pembina artery of a diminished fur-trading industry. The landscape was a trackless wilderness, immense, beautiful, uncluttered.

Again Osten is on foot. The rucksack and quilt are strapped to his back and he carries an axe to clear the jungle of undergrowth, the snarls of hazel and plum brush and vines. The air is filter-pure and the sky as blue as if it had just been scoured and painted. He passes forests primeval and lakelets and sloughs that hold a mirror to the sky, mounds and relics of prehistoric people, wild roses entwining with the grasses in a thick carpet. As he walks through the deserted land the spirits of antiquity seem to keep him company. His trail takes him closer and closer to the geographical heart of this vast continent, past the point where there is any tree, house, or living creature to break the terrain. The cathedral-like silence deepens as the path bears westward. At night he lies down with the vaulted heavens for a roof overhead. The moon swings above the landscape in solemn grandeur and the North Star is his guiding light. Finally, one sweet morning in May, there is *his* prairie . . . billowing into slopes, rising in low hills, then leveling off to sink into the interminable plain.

This last, roughest segment of his 400-mile hike from Decorah has taken a fortnight of hard pushing. Now Osten is home — at last. But for him the end of the emigrant journey is only the beginning of the immigrant pioneer ordeal.

In the nineteenth century and the early decades of the twentieth century a million Norwegians emigrated to America. Most of them followed in the tracks of Osten and Henrik, pressing westward. (To immigrants, as Archibald MacLeish has remarked, America was "the west and the winds blowing.") When the valley of the Red River of the North was settled, it had the largest concentration of Norwegians outside of Norway. Its great bonanza farms began to harvest millions of bushes of wheat annually and it became known as the Breadbasket of the World.

The wonder is not that so many of these first settlers succumbed, but that so many survived. A partial catalogue of the trials that beset them would show such entries as grasshopper plagues, blizzards, long Arctic winters, stupefyingly hot shadeless summers, prairie fires, earthquakes, cyclones, tornadoes, electrical storms, the devastation of blackbirds and gophers and the chinch bug, hail storms, torrential rains that turned the grain to rot, poor seed and ignorance of good farming practices, oxen running wild, horses and cattle driven insane by mosquitoes, nerve-shattering winds, droughts, crop failures, money panic ("Need brings dogs into bondage," said the bankers), lost or stolen livestock, stem rust in the spring wheat, the constant threat of attack by Indians, killing strikes by pneumonia and influenza and tuberculosis and black diphtheria and typhoid fever, death by freezing, back-breaking labor without end, and the aching loneliness.

For many, the challenge exceeded the limits of human endurance. Perhaps of all the groups who became Americans only our black brothers — those involuntary immigrants who were brought here in chains — were more sorely tested. Many who could not endure the life simply lay down and died. Others took their own lives. (My grandparents and their neighbors could swap horror tales of going into their barns and finding strangers hanging from the hayloft.) Still others found the release of madness.

But those who neither perished, nor committed suicide nor went mad achieved a kind of indestructibility. They lived on and on and on, many of them into their tenth decade and beyond, active, alert, and cheerful. They truly believed it was God's will that had kept them alive so long and that it would have been profane to be idle or to have wished for an earlier grave. . . .

Osten stood on the treeless prairie. The buffalo grasses brushed against the calves of his legs. The plain was so wide that the rim of the heavens cut down on it in a 360-degree circle. He might have wished for some woodlands to remind him of home. But this land was *his* and it would always have a value beyond any riches it might yield. Possession of land made him one with the Norse chieftains. Land had dignity and stability. It stood for the permanence of family and it was something that could be handed down through the centuries.

First he must have a roof over his head. There was only one ripple in the terrain. Into the tough sod he plunged his axe. He hacked out pieces of earth a foot or so wide and began piling these on top of one another to make his dugout in the side of the hillock. It was a one-room sod hut, a home built of dirt, literally a hole in the ground. The walls were dirt, the roof was dirt, and the floor beneath him was dirt. Time brought a few refinements. Tamarack poles supported the roof. Rough windows and doors were cut in the sod walls. Clay steps led to the entrance. The walls, after several years, were boarded up and whitewashed and a floor was put in.

The furnishings were primitive. For sleeping there were mattresses of straw and the used straw was taken out regularly and burned. Benches for eating were made of logs split in half, their legs fastened on with wooden pegs. There was a table and eventually a cupboard with shelves and an open hearth.

Osten lived in this earth house for ten years. Then he built a one-room log house and three years later a large frame house. To the sod hut he brought his bride, the spirited seventeen-year-old girl he had met at Sunday services in a neighbor's granary during his fourth summer on the prairie. Here four of his nine children were born — and died: two in infancy, and two young daughters who, as victims of the dreaded black diphtheria, choked to death in his arms.

In winter blizzards the snow often packed against the door and drifted over the roof, imprisoning the family for days. In the spring, before there were floors, the earth beneath them would give a jar, then another jar, and gophers and garter snakes would surface to share their humble quarters.

When he looked back on that experience, Osten's fondest memories of that first home in the new country were of the winter nights when he lay warm under Caroline's patchwork quilts. A candle burned in the hollowed-out turnip and the hearth ablaze with cow dung gave off the most beautiful colors. Lying there awake he'd gaze out through the wooded slats at the moonlight putting its dazzling shine on the boundless white sea of crusted snow.

Considerations

1. What were the conditions in Norway that led some to emigrate? What were the perceptions of America that contributed to their decision? And what actual events in the United States encouraged immigration?
2. Consider whether your findings in question 1 correspond to the categories of "push" and "pull" factors suggested by Reed Ueda's overview (p. 358). In the case of Osten and Henrik Boe, does one type of factor seem more important, or are "push" and "pull" factors equally important?
3. Using a map of Canada and the United States, trace the path of migration of Eugene Boe's ancestors.
4. The prospect of opportunity and the freedom to shape one's existence are present throughout this account; they are what compel Boe's Norwegian immigrants. But what is it that they bring with them from the old country and in some way retain? Read back through the essay with this question in mind.

Between 1890 and 1924, about 23 million people immigrated to the United States from eastern Europe and southern Italy. Most of them entered the country through New York City, primarily through the depot at Ellis Island. In her book Immigrant Women in the Land of Dollars, *Elizabeth Ewen writes about this vast migration — the largest immigration stream in American history — focusing particularly on the experience of Jewish and Italian women who settled in New York's Lower East Side, one of the most significant immigrant enclaves on the continent. Through a number of small portraits and quotations, Ewen gives us a sense of the human face of this history, as she discusses the conditions in immigrants' home countries that sparked migration, the reactions of those regions to that mass exodus, and the complex responses of the newcomers to America.*

From *Immigrant Women in the Land of Dollars: Life and Culture on the Lower East Side, 1890–1925*

ELIZABETH EWEN

I

By the late nineteenth century, industrialization and urbanization had upset the already precarious economic relationship between peasant agriculture and domestic handicrafts in southern Italy. The unification of Italy under northern control in mid-century had severely affected the ability of the southern Italian peasants to maintain themselves on the land. Increasingly dominated by their landlords by an elaborate system of taxation, mortgage payments, and competition over small landholdings, peasant families found it more and more difficult to maintain themselves. Artisanal activities that had supplemented agricultural production began to disappear. An agricultural depression, caused partially by increased cereal and citrus production in the United States, led to a fall in prices, and many peasants went bankrupt. As the international market economy made serious inroads into traditional life, southern Italians began to migrate in large numbers to the United States and elsewhere.

The Italian peasant, faced with an increasing need for money and an increasing inability to acquire it at home, had three alternatives: "He could either resign himself to his *miseria* [misery], or he could rebel, or he could migrate."[1] Most emigrated, hoping by doing so to maintain the family on the land. The peasants thus saw emigration as an obligation to their own kin — as a way of getting money necessary for the family back home. Emigration was in one sense an act of estrangement, but the motivation was familiar: to maintain the family in its traditional mode of life.

The mass migration of the southern Italian peasantry — over 5 million to the United States between 1890 and 1910 — also functioned to alleviate the growing demographic pressure in the cities and potential revolt in the countryside. Sometimes the act of migration was a kind of revolt. Adolfo Rossi, a well-known journalist and inspector of immigrants, recounted this story:

[1]Silvano M. Tomasi, "The Ethnic Church and the Integration of Italian Immigrants in the United States," in *The Italian Experience in the United States,* ed. Silvano Tomasi and Madeline Engel (New York, 1970), p. 164. Tomasi is paraphrasing a 1911 Italian government report on conditions among the southern peasantry.

ELIZABETH EWEN (b. 1943) is professor of American studies at State University of New York College at Old Westbury. Her work includes *Channels of Desire* (1982), co-authored with Stuart Ewen, and *Immigrant Women in the Land of Dollars: Life and Culture on the Lower East Side, 1890–1925* (1985), from which this excerpt is taken.

> Some time ago, in a Sicilian village, a lot of peasants became dissatisfied with the medieval agricultural methods of the local "feudal lord." These peasants felt that they were neither chattels going with the land, nor serfs. So one fine morning they gathered in front of the lord's house, bunched their shovels in a heap and on top placed the following notice: "Sir, do your farming yourself — we are going to America."[2]

Emigration brought a good deal of money into the southern Italian economy — money that, while it did not change the essential conditions of agriculture, did enable some peasants to buy land, to pay their mortgages and taxes, and to buy donkeys.

The overall structure, however, prevented any basic change. Often returning peasants "found no other opportunity than once again to buy a small piece of property in the same deteriorated rural economy, which they thought, when they left, they had escaped for all time."[3] In 1905 *Il Proletario,* the Italian-American socialist newspaper, noted that "Italians come to America with the sole intention of accumulating money. . . . Their dream . . . is the bundle of money they are painfully increasing, which will give them, after twenty years of deprivation, the possibility of having a mediocre standard of living in their native country."[4] The returning migrant may have come back more prosperous but he returned to the same untenable economic position.

The migrant stream itself revealed a distinct pattern. In the years of peak migration, 1890–1910, approximately 80 percent of the emigrants were male: Adolfo Rossi reported that "excessive emigration is working harm to the nation at large in that it takes from us the flowering of our laboring class . . . 84 percent of Italians coming to the United States are between 18 and 45 years of age. They are . . . producers. This 'human capital' of fresh young men is the contribution of Europe to the new land."[5] Repatriation rates were high: by 1907 seventy-three of every one hundred immigrants were returning each year.[6]

Single women also left but their numbers were fewer. It was far more difficult for a single woman to emigrate by herself: Custom militated against women traveling alone. Those who did thought of themselves as part of the family economy, and left to help their families, to make a better dowry for themselves, or to find a husband. Agnes Santucci, for example, left for the United States at the age of seventeen. Her sister was already there, about to get married: "And so my father says, who wants to go next, to make a living, to help. My father couldn't support us, so he wrote to my uncle that he wanted to send another daughter to his house." In New York two years later Agnes married a man she had known in her hometown.[7]

Occasionally widows or deserted wives emigrated to forget their sorrows and start a new life. Rosina Giuliani, for instance, lived in a small suburb of Bari, where she worked

[2]Quoted in Gino Speranza, "The Effects of Emigration on Italy," *Charities and the Commons* 12 (1904): 470.

[3]Grazie Dore, "Some Social and Historical Aspects of Italian Emigration to America," in *The Italians: Social Backgrounds of an American Group,* ed. Francesco Cordasco and Eugene Buccioni (Clifton, N.J., 1974), p. 31.

[4]Quoted in Tomasi, "The Ethnic Church," p. 164.

[5]Quoted in Speranza, "The Effects of Emigration," p. 468.

[6]Thomas Kessner, *The Golden Door: Italian and Jewish Immigration Mobility in New York City* (New York, 1977), pp. 28–30.

[7]Interview with Agnes Santucci.

as a hat maker and seamstress. She was quite beautiful, and met the son of a wealthy northern family when he passed through town with the army. They married and quickly had a child. He brought his new wife back to his mother's house, but the mother found her unacceptable and threw her out. Rosina went back with her husband to Bari but he soon left, leaving her with two small children. Rather than living out her life in disgrace, and being equipped with a marketable trade, she migrated to the United States at the age of thirty.[8]

But such cases were rare: Most women who migrated went to join their husbands, part of a growing process of establishing families in the United States. The husband, as part of his familial obligation, migrated and saved the money to bring over his wife and small children. After an average of three or four years, the family was reunited in the United States; older parents, however, rarely made the journey. During the separation period, the women generally stayed in their mothers' homes.[9]

Eastern European Jews, on the other hand, although responding to many of the same pressures, represented a different pattern of migration. Industrialization, the May Laws, the overcrowding of cities, and the rampant anti-Semitism created a severe crisis in the already oppressive conditions of Jewish life. Jews moved from the towns to the cities, from artisan to factory labor, and in the process developed a more cosmopolitan and radical perspective. Russia was on the verge of revolution, and repression grew. Many women joined the socialist *Bund,* becoming active in trade union and socialist politics. But it was not easy to subvert the long arm of the czarist police, and many were beaten and jailed. After the failure of the 1905 revolution, pogroms increased and migration became a necessity.[10] Between 1881 and 1914 approximately one-third of all Jews left Eastern Europe.

Jewish migration was primarily a family affair, with an almost even ratio between the sexes — 58 percent male and 42 percent female. This was a distinctive pattern among the "new" immigrants to the United States, as was the fact that repatriation rates were low and that the migration was permanent from the beginning. Moving the entire family was an expensive proposition, however, one that required time and planning. Generally fathers, as well as older sons and daughters, came over first in order to accumulate enough money to send for the rest of the family; economics, fear, and religious preference meant that the grandparents often stayed behind.

Many of the younger women hoped to find men to marry. Bessie Polski was a typical example: She left because there were no Jewish men for the girls to marry.[11] In a story entitled "The Miracle," Anzia Yezierska, a Lower East Side Jewish novelist, told a story that had particular relevance for these women. The heroine was a poor undowered Polish girl whose chances for marriage were slim. Suddenly a letter from America kindled

[8]Interview with Rosina Giuliani's daughters Letitia Feltrinelli and Francesca Campanile (author's file).

[9]Virginia Yans McLaughlin, *Family and Community: Italian Immigrants in Buffalo* (Ithaca, N.Y., 1977), p. 91. For an excellent discussion of this point, see also pp. 96–100, as well as G. E. Di Palma Castiglione, "Italian Immigration into the United States," *American Journal of Sociology* 2 (1905): 185.

[10]Irving Howe, *World of Our Fathers* (New York, 1976); Samuel Joseph, *Jewish Immigration to the United States, 1881–1910* (1914; reprint ed., New York, 1969), pp. 41–44.

[11]Interview with Bessie Polski (tape 139); Carlotte Baum, Paula Hyman, and Sonia Michel, *The Jewish Woman in America* (New York, 1978), pp. 76–89; Sydelle Kramer and Jenny Masur, *Jewish Grandmothers* (Boston, 1976), p. 127.

her dreams: "In America, millionaires fall in love with the poorest girls. Matchmakers are out of style and a girl can get herself married to a man without the worries of a dowry. . . . In America, there is a law called ladies first. . . . The men hold their babies and carry bundles for the women and even help with the dishes." The letter made the rounds of the village. The ticket agents for the steamship companies, seeing how "the letter was working like yeast in the air for America, posted up big signs by all the market fairs: Go to America, The New World, fifty rubles a ticket."[12]

Others married in order to get to America. The young husband would go ahead to earn money for the wife's ticket. But newlywed husbands who sent back divorces instead of tickets were a major problem. Fannie Shapiro recalled: "You got married, [he] took the money, and left you right away to America. Sometimes, he sent for you; sometimes he found somebody else that he liked better, and forgot you. Sent you a divorce."[13]

Some opposed migration, in particular orthodox, middle-class Jewish fathers who had been raised to maintain the religious traditions and practices of Eastern European Jewish life.[14] Many of these fathers considered America *"trayf,"* or not kosher. Mothers, on the other hand, often encouraged migration, feeling it was in the interests of their children — even though this decision was extremely painful. Motherhood, in Eastern European shtetl life, was always more connected to the ways of the world.

But it was, ultimately, pointless to oppose migration. As one memorist put it, "America was in everybody's mouth. Businessmen talked of it over accounts; market women made up their quarrels that they might discuss it from stall to stall; people who had relatives in the famous land went around reading their letters for the enlightenment of less fortunate folks . . . children played at emigrating."[15] But fact and fiction blended into myth; in all the talk, "scarcely anyone knew one true fact about this magic land."[16]. . .

And people acted on their inclinations, despite the resistance represented by the old orthodoxy: "The migration of Eastern European Jews constituted a spontaneous and collective impulse, perhaps even decision, by a people that had come to recognize the need for new modes and possibilities of life."[17]

The promise of America was multiple: The crisis intensified the desire to remake Jewish life in a country that appeared to be a land of milk and honey. While middle-class Jews had a greater stake in staying, the majority of artisans and skilled and semiskilled workers made the decision to migrate.

Anzia Yezierska articulated the magical effect America had in a story entitled "How I Found America" (in her book *Hungry Hearts*). A letter that arrived one day from the husband of one of the townspeople was full of good news: His sun had begun to shine in America because he had become a "businessman": "I have for myself a stand in the most crowded part of America, where people are as thick as flies and every day is like a market day by a fair." At the end of the day he had made a $2 profit: "That means four rubles and before your very eyes . . . I, Gedalyeh Mindel (a water carrier in the old country)

[12]Anzia Yezierska, *Hungry Hearts* (New York, 1920), pp. 115–19, 121, 122–24.

[13]Kramer and Masur, *Jewish Grandmothers,* p. 7.

[14]Howe, *World of Our Fathers,* p. 27.

[15]Ibid.

[16]Ibid.

[17]Ibid. p. 26.

earned four rubles a day, twenty-four rubles a week." He continued with an analysis of his good fortune, reporting that he ate "white bread and meat . . . every day just like the millionaires" and that in America "there were no mud huts where cows and chickens and people live together"; most importantly, "there is no Czar in America."

The letter inflamed the passions of the family, which suddenly erupted into an all-engulfing fantasy. "Sell my red quilted petticoat that grandmother left me for my dowry. Sell the feather beds, sell the samovar. Sure we can sell everything, the goat and all the winter things. It must always be summer in America." That evening the family fetched the pawnbroker and, after much bargaining by the mother, sold all their treasures, which brought them just enough money to buy steamship tickets.[18]

In this story, we see an important exchange: The past is sold off in order to purchase the new. To make the dream come true, the family hocked its old way of life, turning their valued objects into the currency of the New World — cash.

The image of America as the country where money could be made, more money than most people could imagine, was carefully cultivated by a public relations effort mounted by U.S. companies. In both Italy and Eastern Europe this image worked its way into small towns and villages, newly industrialized cities and peasant villages, cultivating a dream that affected everyone. It was specifically aimed at recruiting young men and women of working age and depicted life in America as an unending stream of money. One poster, distributed across Europe by the woolen companies of Lawrence, Massachusetts, depicted a mill on one side of the street, a bank on the other, and workers marching from one side to the other with bags of money under their arms.[19] The poster was designed to reach people who could not read but who could easily understand the image: America was the country of rich workers; money was the means to wealth.

Steamship companies, too, acting as a vanguard of industry, used advertising to recruit immigrants. They sent posters showing prices and sailing dates into even the smallest villages and included editorials and articles from the U.S. newspapers that extolled the prosperity of the United States. Local agents, working on commission, were recruited from "the most varied people who took it upon themselves to convince the future emigrants and to sell them tickets: auditors, priests, pharmacists, and copyists."[20] Selling steerage tickets in fact became a major occupation for large numbers of people in southern and Eastern Europe. Tickets could be paid for in installments, but if the price was $15 in 1890, by 1900 it was between $34 and $37.

In order to present America as a place where the crisis of emigration could be resolved, the posters had to have a strong social aspect: "America was the promised land to the poor, as opposed to the old world where land was denied the peasant."[21] Money and America became synonymous and provided the basis for the realization of long-standing dreams.

This propaganda would not however have met a responsive chord if there had not been personal reports that the United States was the way out. Personal witness, in the form of letters "from persons who have emigrated to friends at home have been the immediate cause of by far the greater part of the remarkable movement from Southern and

[18]Yezierska, *Hungry Hearts,* pp. 254–55, 259.

[19]Elizabeth Gurley Flynn, *Rebel Girl* (New York, 1955), p. 134.

[20]Dore, "Social and Historical Aspects of Italian Emigration," p. 19.

[21]Ibid., p. 19.

Eastern Europe in the last twenty-five years," concluded a report of the Immigration Commission of 1909. The report went on to argue that "recently arrived immigrants are substantially the agencies which keep the American labor market supplied with unskilled laborers from Europe. . . . It is these personal appeals, which, more than all other agencies, promote and regulate the tide of European emigration to America."[22] The immigrant's letters also regulated the flow of migration: Information about wages, depressions, and job possibilities acted as a stimulus or a break. Tickets were often bought in the United States — again on the installment plan — and sent back home.

Returning migrants provided another incentive. In Italy, for instance, returning immigrants were called "americanos," a word meaning "someone who got rich, no one knows how — as if money alone is enough to change people." They became dispensers of "information and inspiration. The money they can show makes a vivid impression."[23]

If the idea of America was a mixture of myths and yearnings, these were necessary to help the potential immigrants make the move to the unknown America. For women the myth contained a transformation to a nonpatriarchal, classless world where millionaires married poor girls, and men took care of children and helped with housework. America represented what was repressed in the old and promised in fantasy. Both Italians and Jews responded to myths of their own making — fostered by American advertising — visions that expressed inner longings denied in a dying and oppressive world.

II

On a sizzling hot day in the summer of 1895 Maria Ganz and her mother walked off the boat onto a New York City pier. They had left their comfortable farmhouse in Galicia to join Lazarus Ganz, who had recently rented a rear tenement apartment in the Lower East Side. For weeks he had been busy preparing their new home; he was flushed with anticipation. Maria's mother walked into her new apartment, looked around slowly, turned to her husband and cried: "So, we have crossed half the world for this?" Maria recreated the scene in her memoirs:

> I can see her now as she stood facing my father, her eyes full of reproach. I am sure it had never occurred to poor, dreamy, impractical Lazarus Ganz that his wife might be disappointed with the new home he had provided for her. The look of pain as he saw the impression the place made on her filled me with pity for him, young as I was. A five-year-old child is not apt to carry many distinct memories from that age of life, but it is a scene I have never forgotten.[24]

On an autumn day in 1896 Leonard Covello, his brothers, and their mother landed in New York, worlds away from their native Avigliano, Italy. They had spent twenty days aboard ship. When the sea became rough, Leonard's mother held her sons close to her heart; the ocean storms mirrored the fear and torment locked inside her body. As Leonard reported later:

[22] Quoted in Isaac Hourwich, *Immigration and Labor* (New York, 1912), p. 94.

[23] Francesco Carase, "Nostalgia or Disenchantment: Considerations on Return Migration," in Tomasi and Engel, *The Italian Experience in the United States,* p. 233; Hourwich, *Immigration and Labor,* p. 96.

[24] Maria Ganz, *Rebels: Into Anarchy and Out Again* (New York, 1920), p. 4.

> And when finally we saw the towering buildings and rode the screeching elevated train and saw the long, unending streets of the metropolis that could easily swallow a thousand Aviglianese towns, she accepted it with the mute resignation as *la volonta di Dio* [the will of God], while her heart longed for the familiar scenes and faces of loved ones and the security of a life she had forever left behind.[25]

A story by novelist Anzia Yezierska captured a mother's lament: *"Oi Veh!* my mother cried in dismay, where is the sunshine in America? She went to her tenement window and looked at the blank wall of the next house. Like a grave so dark. To greenhorns it seemed as if the sunlight had faded from their lives and buildings like mountains took its place."[26] In another mother's story, a question: "Where are the green fields and open spaces in America? A loneliness for the fragrant silence of the woods that lay beyond my mud hut welled up in my heart, a longing for the soft, responsive earth of our village streets. All about me was the harshness of brick and stone, the stinking smell of crowded poverty."[27]

Leonard Covello voiced a similar despair:

> The sunlight and fresh air of our mountain home . . . were replaced by four walls and people over and under and on all sides of us. Silence and sunshine, things of the past, now replaced by a new urban montage. The cobbled streets. The endless monotonous rows of tenement buildings that shut out the sky. The traffic of wagons and carts and carriages, and the clopping of horses' hooves which struck sparks at night. . . . The clanging of bells and the screeching of sirens as a fire broke out somewhere in the neighborhood. Dank hallways. Long flights of wooden stairs and the toilet in the hall.[28]

Nothing prepared people for the immediacy of this experience. America, as myth or image, may have been the Big Rock Candy Mountain, a utopian dream, a piece of heaven, but this heaven turned out to be a concrete prison, a vast wall of steel that blocked out the familiar world of nature, replacing the sunshine with the gray stare of stone and brick and changing silence into an omnipresent screeching tune. Even in Eastern European cities, the woods were a walk away — a place to gather food or sneak away, a space to hide from the pogroms or hold secret revolutionary meetings. New York abolished the forests forever, leaving them retrievable only in memory or in the pictorial reproductions that hung on the walls of tenement apartments as reminders of a world lost but not forgotten.

Not only were the woods lost, but city life seemed to transform the natural rhythms of life, turning night into day. This is how two Italian immigrants put it: "Our first impressions of the brightly lit streets of New York at night time suggested that such excessive illumination was for the prevention of the commission of theft. In Italy, there was no need for street lighting because when it was dark, every good person was supposed to be asleep."[29] For women, the loss of nature also meant a loss of space. An Italian home-

[25] Leonard Covello, *The Heart Is the Teacher* (New York, 1958), p. 19.

[26] Yezierska, *Hungry Hearts,* p. 264.

[27] Ibid., p. 263.

[28] Covello, *The Heart Is the Teacher,* p. 21.

[29] Leonard Covello, *Social Background of the Italo-American School Child* (Totowa, N.J., 1972), p. 94.

worker summed this up when she responded to a question posed by an American social worker in 1911. Did she like America?

> Not much, not much. In my country, people cook out-of-doors, do the wash out-of-doors, tailor out-of-doors, make macaroni out-of-doors. And my people laugh, laugh all the time. In America, it is *sopra, sopra* [up, up, with a gesture of going upstairs]. Many people, one house; work, work all the time. Good money, but no good air.[30]

Anna Kuthan, an immigrant from Czechoslovakia, described her first year in New York in much the same way: "I didn't smile for a long time. Why? Because this was a different country. Everybody was for himself, and there was always money, money, money; rush, rush, rush."[31]

How many first-generation mothers experienced their new environment, with its density of people, filthy crowded streets, and small apartments, as the negation of their previous poor but more natural life? How many times did they compare past and present as they paced the floors of their new homes, thinking, as Yezierska put it: "In America were rooms without sunshine, rooms to sleep in, to eat in, to cook in, but without sunshine." How many asked, "Could I be satisfied with just a place to sleep and a door to shut people out to take the place of sunshine?"[32]

For many, the loss of sunshine was a metaphor that described feelings of alienation and unfamiliarity, an image of mourning for a world left behind, a plaintive moan of entry into the unknown. The abrupt separation from the immediate past was probably hardest on the older generation, whose lives had been shaped in other worlds and different cultures. This separation also spoke to a primary difference between themselves and their children. After all, as Leonard Covello noted, "a child adapts to everything. It was the older people who suffered, those uprooted human beings who faced the shores of an unknown land with quaking hearts."[33]

In the cultures from which these women came, mothers existed within the confines of the home, but that home was the "center of the world, at the heart of the real."[34] For women with small children, pulling up the foundations of a known life was a severe shock, a shock that penetrated to the core of experience and the ways in which experience becomes codified as culture. The loss of the natural, as perceived by the first generation, also meant the loss of familiar social rituals that had given life meaning and value. . . .

The street, however, held a promise. In the spaces of American life carved out for immigrants the only "roses" were other people, family, relatives, friends. Italian and Jewish settlement patterns on the Lower East Side reflected the absolute necessity for family and ethnic cohesion. Italians settled between Pearl and Houston streets, east of the Bowery, while Jewish immigrants inhabited the Tenth Ward, west of the Bowery. Italians moved into the old Irish sections of the Lower East Side; Jews inherited the old German sector. The new immigrants lived and worked huddled together in tenement houses within easy

[30]Quoted in Elizabeth C. Watson, "Home Work in the Tenements," *Survey* 25 (1910): 772.

[31]Interview with Anna Kuthan (tape on file but unnumbered).

[32]Yezierska, *Hungry Hearts,* p. 264.

[33]Covello, *Social Background,* p. 13.

[34]John Berger, "Homegrown," *Village Voice,* 3 July 1984.

reach of the garment district, surrounded by peddler stands and shops where language was not a barrier. If all America allowed its immigrants was a few city blocks, the blocks themselves were transformed to meet the needs of their inhabitants.

Caught in the margins between old and new, the neighborhoods were simultaneously an enclave of old-world custom and new-world adaptation, a curious admixture of tradition and change. For the first generation, a great deal of comfort was derived from this partial reconstruction of the old country: they nestled in communities of common language, bound by ties of custom, ritual, and institutions — a world not lost, but rebuilt.

Considerations

1. What were the conditions in southern Italy that led so many to emigrate? In eastern Europe? In what ways were these conditions similar? How were they different?
2. Discuss some of the motives that, according to Ewen, compelled Italians to set forth, that compelled eastern European Jews. What resistances and uncertainties did they have to wrestle with? Were there differences by gender?
3. What were the images of America that "pulled" these immigrants across the Atlantic? How were these images generated? Do you think they still are in effect today?
4. What were some of the reactions of the immigrants to the Lower East Side?
5. What does Ewen mean when she writes, "Caught in the margins between old and new, the neighborhoods [in the Lower East Side] were simultaneously an enclave of old-world custom and new-world adaptation"? Does her observation apply to immigrant communities you're familiar with today?
6. If you have read, or plan to read, the excerpt from Alejandro Portes and Rubén G. Rumbaut's *Immigrant America: A Portrait* (p. 403), consider the ways in which the wave of immigration between 1890 and 1925 corresponds to and differs from the new wave of immigration described by Portes and Rumbaut.

In this excerpt from the introduction to his book Becoming Mexican American: Ethnicity, Culture, and Identity in Chicano Los Angeles, 1900–1945, *historian George J. Sánchez uses a short case study of an early twentieth-century Mexican immigrant to illustrate some of the "push" and "pull" factors involved in the significant Mexican immigration into Texas, the Southwest, and southern California. As Sánchez follows the case of one immigrant, he discusses the complex and unique cultural history of movement across the Mexican–United States border. Notice, by the way, how Sánchez uses "push" and "pull" factors as a simple classification strategy that helps him organize his discussion. Notice, too, the way he qualifies in the last paragraph a too-simple reliance on that strategy.*

From *Becoming Mexican American: Ethnicity, Culture, and Identity in Chicano Los Angeles, 1900–1945*

GEORGE J. SÁNCHEZ

Carlos Almazán was born into a world on the brink of monumental change. The occasion of his birth around 1890 was undoubtedly celebrated throughout the estate near Zamora, Michoacán, where the Almazán family had resided for as long as anyone could remember. Neighbors congratulated his parents for having another strong boy, one that would, as he grew older, certainly improve the family's economic situation. The Almazáns made their living from the land, and in a late nineteenth-century Mexican community dependent on agriculture, every healthy child proved indispensable to the family's economic subsistence.[1]

Unfortunately, tragedy soon struck — Carlos's father died. Señora Almazán had no choice but to carry on the farm work by herself with young sons. Although she struggled to maintain ownership of the land, the small farm gradually slipped from her hands. Like many others in the region, she became a sharecropper. As Carlos and his brothers grew older, they learned to plant corn and other grains, using old plows that had been passed from generation to generation. Farm work completely occupied their lives. With the help of her sons, who had been propelled by misfortune into early manhood, Señora Almazán gradually managed to stabilize her economic situation after the difficult decade following her husband's death.

But Carlos, now a teenager, grew restless. Tired of the backbreaking work in the fields, he decided to go to Mexico City. Such a decision would have been improbable only a few years before. Zamora and its surrounding communities had been relatively isolated until a newly constructed railroad connected the region to the nation's capital. This transportation network allowed Carlos to leave with high hopes and seek his fortune in the city. It was not long before Carlos made a promising start selling meat and other foods on the streets. He soon married and had children. Yet his prosperity was short-lived. How could he have predicted that Mexico would soon be embroiled in a revolution that would leave him bankrupt? Defeated, Carlos and his family returned to Zamora, but not for long. At the urging of his older brother, Carlos once again made a momentous decision regarding his future: He boarded a train for the north, leaving his homeland for the United States in 1920.

Carlos became part of a massive movement of individuals and families who crossed the Mexican border to the United States in the first three decades of the twentieth century. Approximately one and a half million Mexicans migrated northward between 1900 and 1930, most settling in the Southwest. This process eventually made Mexico one of

[1]Manuel Gamio, *The Life Story of the Mexican Immigrant* (1931; rpt., New York: Dover, 1971), 87–91.

GEORGE J. SÁNCHEZ (b. 1959) is associate professor of history at the University of Michigan, Ann Arbor. This excerpt was taken from his book *Becoming Mexican American: Ethnicity, Culture, and Identity in Chicano Los Angeles, 1900–1945* (1993).

the largest single sources of immigration to the United States. For Mexico, the migration resulted in the loss of about 10 percent of its total population by 1930.[2]

Most scholars who have analyzed this movement north have focused almost exclusively on the socio-economic factors involved in this migration.[3] [I] will review those issues, but will also put into context the larger cultural questions raised by such a massive movement of people between two nations with unique histories. The railroads not only led to economic growth in Mexico and the American Southwest, they also facilitated the transmission of cultural values and practices between the two countries.

By concentrating on cultural transformations occurring in Mexican villages, [I] will also examine the beliefs and traditions that immigrants to the north brought with them. The structure of authority in the village, the rise of Mexican nationalism, and the adaptations in familial customs in this period all played a role in defining the outlook of Mexican immigrants. Finally, [I] will explore the very decision to migrate itself, one which was clearly driven by economic considerations but also culturally conditioned. This examination will stress that the culture Mexican migrants brought with them, rather than being a product of a stagnant "traditional" society, was instead a vibrant, rather complicated amalgamation of rural and urban mores, developed in Mexican villages during half a century of changing cultural practices.

Recent scholarship has made clear that migration to California is not merely a twentieth-century phenomenon. Ever since Mexico had lost its northern territories in the aftermath of the Mexican-American War, there had been movement of Mexicans into the United States. With the discovery of gold in 1848, perhaps as many as 20,000 experienced miners rushed to California from Sonora and Zacatecas, only to be driven out of the mines by the early 1850s. Yet despite the many returnees, this migration probably still signified a larger movement north to California than any other during the entire Spanish (1771–1821) and Mexican (1821–48) eras.

While Mexicans drifted across the border during the remainder of the nineteenth century, most located in the mining towns of southern Arizona or the ranches and farms of south Texas, where they were within easy reach of their homeland. These two states alone accounted for over 80 percent of the 103,393 Mexican-born residents of the United States in 1900. Despite the heavy gold-rush migration to California, the 1900

[2]Ricardo Romo, "The Urbanization of Southwestern Chicanos in Early Twentieth Century," *New Scholar* 6 (1977), 194. Paul S. Taylor explains the difficulties inherent in producing accurate statistical figures for Mexican immigration in this period from American and Mexican government sources in *Mexican Labor in the United States: Migration Statistics,* Univ. of California Publications in Economics, 6, No. 3 (Berkeley: Univ. of California Press, 1930), I, 237–55.

During the 1920s, Mexicans accounted for over 11 percent of the total legal immigration to the United States. Since 1820, Mexico ranks eighth among the nations of origin of legal immigrants to the United States. See Alejandro Portes and Robert L. Bach, *Latin Journey: Cuban and Mexican Immigrants in the United States* (Berkeley: Univ. of California Press, 1985), 79; and Michael C. LeMay, *From Open Door to Dutch Door: An Analysis of U.S. Immigration Policy Since 1820* (New York: Praeger, 1987), 2–3.

[3]For some of the best work from a socio-economic perspective, see Mark Reisler, *By the Sweat of Their Brow: Mexican Immigrant Labor in the United States, 1900–1940* (Westport, Conn.: Greenwood, 1976); Lawrence A. Cardoso, *Mexican Emigration to the United States, 1897–1931: Socio-economic Patterns* (Tucson: Univ. of Arizona Press, 1980). More recent immigration has been analyzed by Portes and Bach, *Latin Journey;* Douglas Massey, Rafael Alarcón, Jorge Durand, and Humberto González, *Return to Aztlán: The Social Process of International Migration from Western Mexico* (Berkeley: Univ. of California Press, 1987).

census reported only 8,086 inhabitants of that state who were born in Mexico. This figure is striking when compared with the approximately eight to ten thousand noted at the time of the signing of the Treaty of Guadalupe Hidalgo in 1848.[4] Although migration had occurred in the last half of the nineteenth century, it paled in comparison to the mass exodus of Mexicans in the first thirty years of the twentieth. This time California, which in particular had received relatively few Mexican immigrants before 1900, experienced a dramatic rise in the proportion of new settlers.

No historian of the period disputes the notion that the American Southwest held strong economic attractions — often characterized as pull factors — for such immigrants. The mining industry in Arizona and New Mexico had encouraged Mexicans to cross the border even in the late nineteenth century. After 1900 the growth of mines in these states, as well as in Colorado and Oklahoma, induced more workers to flock to the area. Mexicans also played a crucial role in the construction and maintenance of southwestern railroad networks. In addition, railroad work provided the transportation by which job seekers moved from site to site throughout the Southwest.

However, it was the expansion of agriculture which created the most pronounced demand for labor, particularly in California. Irrigation revolutionized California farming, allowing arid land to be converted into vast new farms. By 1929, California became the largest producer of fruits and vegetables in the Southwest, a region generating 40 percent of the total United States output. Meanwhile, Mexicans rapidly replaced the Japanese as the major component of the agricultural labor force.

Although certainly paid less than Anglo Americans, a Mexican worker could earn a wage in any of these three industries far above the 12 cents a day paid on several of the rural haciendas of central Mexico. For example, clearing land in Texas paid 50 cents a day, while miners earned well over $2.00 per day. Most railroad and agricultural laborers were paid between $1.00 to $2.00 a day.[5]

The demand for labor created by the expansion of southwestern industry in the early twentieth century was compounded by the curtailment of Asian and European immigration; the Chinese Exclusion Act of 1882, the 1907–08 Gentlemen's Agreement with Japan, and, finally, the Immigration Acts of 1917, 1921, and 1924 all effectively limited other sources of cheap labor.[6] Employers began to look longingly toward Mexico as a source of labor for their steadily increasing needs. Not surprisingly, immigration restrictions directed against Mexicans were at first consistently deferred under pressure by southwestern employers and then, when finally enacted, were mostly ignored by officials at the border. American administrators, in effect, allowed migrants to avoid the head tax or literacy test — instituted in 1917 — by maintaining sparsely monitored checkpoints even after the establishment of the border patrol in 1924.

More characteristic of prevailing American attitudes toward Mexican immigration

[4]Arthur F. Corwin, "Early Mexican Labor Migration: A Frontier Sketch, 1848–1900," in *Immigrants — and Immigrants: Perspectives on Mexican Labor Migration to the United States,* Arthur F. Corwin, ed. (Westport, Conn.: Greenwood, 1979), 25–37; Oscar J. Martinez gives higher estimates of the Mexican population during this period primarily based on an estimated 40 percent margin of error in official statistics. See "On the Size of the Chicano Population: New Estimates, 1850–1900," *Aztlán: International Journal of Chicano Studies Research* 6 (1975), 43–67.

[5]Reisler, *Sweat,* 3–8; Cardoso, *Emigration,* 18–27.

[6]William S. Bernard, "A History of U.S. Immigration Policy," in *Immigration: Dimensions of Ethnicity,* Reed Ueda, ed. (Cambridge, Mass.: Belknap-Harvard Univ. Press, 1982), 87–99.

before the 1930s, however, was the elaborate network of employment agencies and labor recruiters stationed in border towns such as El Paso. These networks provided the workers for the railroads, factories, and farms throughout the West. Although the contract labor provision of American immigration law strictly prohibited the hiring of foreign workers before their emigration, agents often traveled undisturbed to the interior of Mexico and to towns along the border to search out likely candidates.[7]

The pull factors represented by a burgeoning southwestern economy and a federal government willing to allow undocumented migration through a policy of benign neglect were factors which contributed to mass migration across the border during the early years of the twentieth century. But there were complicated "push" factors as well. Changes in the Mexican economy under the thirty-five-year dictatorship of Porfirio Díaz were perhaps even more important than American industrial development in bringing Mexicans to the United States.

The Díaz administration followed a land policy which encouraged the growth of large haciendas at the expense of small farmers and communally owned lands, or *ejidos.* While the more productive haciendas grew significant quantities of sugar and coffee for export, thousands of rural poor were left landless. Previously independent peasants were forced into debt peonage or into joining the growing migratory labor stream. At the same time, the shift to export crops severely decreased the production of maize, the staple food in the Mexican diet. Along with other governmental policies, this decline in production boosted the cost of living. Simultaneously, wages fell because of the labor surplus created by both the land policy and the population boom of the late nineteenth century. By the time of the Revolution of 1910, these factors had combined to bring the rural masses of Mexico to the brink of starvation.

Although the violence and economic disruption brought about by the revolution did not alone cause Mexican emigration to the United States, they certainly played a crucial role in stimulating movement. While *campesinos* crossed the border fleeing for their personal safety, hacienda owners often fled for fear of reprisals from their employees. Warring factions also destroyed farmland and railroads, bringing much of the economy to a halt. Unemployment rose along with inflation, forcing many to leave Mexico simply to survive. For other agricultural workers, revolution severed the bonds of debt peonage, emancipating workers from their haciendas and freeing them to move north.[8]

Migration occurred before, during, and after the revolution, but became practical only after the development of a railroad transportation network in Mexico linking the populous central states with the northern border. Indeed, a clearer understanding of the role of the railroads in creating the exodus reveals that Mexican immigration to the United States cannot be viewed simplistically in push-pull terms. The process was a great deal more complex. The creation of the Mexican railway system was both a product of and had consequences for not just one, but both sides of the border. Accordingly, classifying the factors contributing to emigration into "American" and "Mexican" ones can mask the unique relationship between these two neighbors — a relationship shared by no other country that has contributed masses of immigrants to American society.

[7] Reisler, *Sweat,* 8–13, 24–42.

[8] Ibid., 15–16; Cardoso, *Emigration,* 38–44.

Considerations

1. What broader social and economic trends does the case of Carlos Almazán illustrate?
2. List some of the "push" and "pull" factors involved in the period of Mexican immigration discussed by Sánchez.
3. Why, in Sánchez's analysis, was the development of the Mexican railway system so important?
4. At the end of this excerpt, Sánchez warns against a too-simple classification of forces involved in Mexican immigration to the United States — a too-simple dichotomy of "push" and "pull" factors, or of "Mexican" and "American" ones. Consider why he might want to be cautious about a strict separation of these factors.

In this introduction to their book Immigrant America: A Portrait, *Alejandro Portes and Rubén G. Rumbaut provide an overview of the current wave of immigration to the United States, attempt to dispel some of the misconceptions about this complex and diverse population, and offer a classification scheme to help us understand some of the different reasons people have for migrating to the United States and some of the different paths they may take once they're here.*

From *Immigrant America: A Portrait*

ALEJANDRO PORTES AND RUBÉN G. RUMBAUT

After a lapse of half a century, the United States has again become a country of immigration. In 1990, the foreign-born population reached 19.8 million or 7.9 percent of the total. Although a far cry from the situation eighty years earlier, when immigrants accounted for 14.7 percent of the American population, the impact of contemporary immigration is both significant and growing. Numerous books and articles have called attention to this revival and sought its causes — first in a booming American economy and second in the liberalized provisions of the 1965 immigration act. A common exercise is to compare this "new" immigration with the "old" inflow at the turn of the century.

Sociologist and educator ALEJANDRO PORTES (b. 1944) is a consultant on United States immigration policy. He teaches at Johns Hopkins University. RUBÉN G. RUMBAUT (b. 1948) is a professor of sociology at Michigan State University and a senior research fellow at Michigan State University's Institute for Public Policy and Social Research. This excerpt is from their work *Immigrant America: A Portrait* (1990, revised edition 1996).

Similarities include the predominantly urban destination of most newcomers, their concentration in a few port cities, and their willingness to accept the lowest paid jobs. Differences are more frequently stressed, however, for the "old" immigration was overwhelmingly European and white; but the present inflow is, to a large extent, nonwhite and comes from countries of the Third World.

The public image of contemporary immigration has been colored to a large extent by the Third World origins of most recent arrivals. Because the sending countries are generally poor, many Americans believe that the immigrants themselves are uniformly poor and uneducated. Their move is commonly portrayed as a one-way escape from hunger, want, and persecution and their arrival on U.S. shores as not too different from that of the tired, "huddled masses" that Emma Lazarus immortalized at the base of the Statue of Liberty. The "quality" of the newcomers and their chances for assimilation are sometimes portrayed as worse because of their non-European past and the precarious legal status of many.

The reality is very different. . . . Underneath its apparent uniformity, contemporary immigration features a bewildering variety of origins, return patterns, and modes of adaptation to American society. Never before has the United States received immigrants from so many countries, from such different social and economic backgrounds, and for so many reasons. Although pre–World War I European immigration was by no means homogeneous, the differences between successive waves of Irish, Italians, Jews, Greeks, and Poles often pale by comparison with the current diversity. For the same reason, theories coined in the wake of the Europeans' arrival at the turn of the century have been made obsolete by events during the last decades.

Increasingly implausible, for example, is the view of a uniform assimilation process that different groups undergo in the course of several generations as a precondition for their social and economic advancement. There are today first-generation millionaires who speak broken English, foreign-born mayors of large cities, and top-flight immigrant engineers and scientists in the nation's research centers; there are also those, at the other extreme, who cannot even take the first step toward assimilation because of the insecurity linked to an uncertain legal status. . . .

Many of the countries from which today's immigrants come have one of their largest cities in the United States. Los Angeles' Mexican population is next in size to those of Mexico City, Monterrey, and Guadalajara. Havana is not much larger than Cuban Miami, and Santo Domingo holds a precarious advantage over Dominican New York. This is not the case for all groups; others, such as Asian Indians, Laotians, Argentines, and Brazilians, are more dispersed throughout the country. Reasons for both these differences and other characteristics of contemporary immigrant groups are not well known — in part because of the recency of their arrival and in part because of the common expectation that their assimilation process would conform to the well-known European pattern. But immigrant America is a different place today from the America that emerged out of Ellis Island and grew up in the tenements of New York and Boston.

THE ORIGINS OF IMMIGRATION

Why do they come? A common explanation singles out the 1965 change in American immigration law as the principal factor. According to this view, today's immigrants come because they can, whereas before 1965 legal restrictions prevented them from doing so. Although the 1965 law certainly explains qualitative and quantitative changes in immigration during the last three decades, it is an insufficient explanation. Not everyone in even the major sending countries has immigrated or is planning to do so. Compared to the respective national populations, those who decide to migrate generally represent a minuscule proportion. The question can thus be reversed to ask not why many come, but why so few have decided to undertake the journey, especially with difficult economic and political conditions in many sending countries.

Moving to a foreign country is not easy, even under the most propitious circumstances. It requires elaborate preparations, much expense, giving up personal relations at home, and often learning a new language and culture. Not so long ago, the lure of higher wages in the United States was not sufficient by itself to attract foreign workers and had to be activated through deliberate recruitment. Mexican immigration, for example, was initiated by U.S. growers and railroad companies who sent recruiters into the interior of Mexico to bring needed workers. By 1916, five or six weekly trains full of Mexican workers hired by the agents were being run from Laredo to Los Angeles. According to one author, the competition in El Paso became so fierce that recruiting agencies stationed their employees at the Santa Fe bridge, where they literally pounced on immigrants as they crossed the border.[1]

The question then remains, What are the factors motivating some groups but not others to seek entry into the United States at present? The most common answer is the desperate poverty, squalor, and unemployment of many foreign lands. . . .

These statements are made despite a mounting body of evidence that points in the exact opposite direction. Consider legal immigration. The proportion of professionals and managers among occupationally active immigrants consistently exceeds the average among U.S. workers. During the last two decades, immigrant professionals represented around 33 percent of the total, at a time when professionals and managers ranged between 17 and 27 percent of the American labor force. Although the gap may be somewhat exaggerated by the available immigration data, other sources confirm that recent immigrants are as well represented as the native-American population at the higher educational and occupational levels. For 1990, the census reported the percentage completing four or more years of college as 20.3 percent for natives and 20.4 percent for the foreign born; the number in professional specialty occupations was about the same for both groups: 12 to 14 percent. For this reason, the gap in median household incomes in favor of the native born did not exceed U.S. $2,000 in that year, despite the fact that over 40 percent of the foreign born had been in the United States for ten years or less.[2]

But even if legal immigrants represent a select group from most sending countries, what about the illegals? The evidence here is more tentative because of the difficulty of investigating a surreptitious flow. However, the available studies coincide on two points:

[1]Mario García, *Desert Immigrants: The Mexicans of El Paso, 1880–1920* (New Haven, Conn.: Yale University Press, 1981).

[2]U.S. Bureau of the Census, *The Foreign-Born Population in the United States.* 1990 Census of Population, CP-3-1 (Washington, D.C.: U.S. Department of Commerce, 1993).

The very poor and the unemployed seldom migrate, either legally or illegally; and unauthorized immigrants tend to have above-average levels of education and occupational skills in comparison with their homeland populations. More important, they are positively self-selected in terms of ambition and willingness to work.

Mexico is the source of over 95 percent of unauthorized aliens apprehended in the United States during the last two decades. Although the socioeconomic origins of most immigrants are modest by U.S. standards, they consistently meet or surpass the average for the Mexican population. Illiteracy among Mexican unauthorized immigrants has been estimated at between 3 and 10 percent, at a time when the figure for Mexico as a whole was 22 percent. At the other end, those with at least some secondary education have been estimated by four different studies to hover around 30 percent while only 21 percent had reached similar schooling in the Mexican population.[3] Contrary to the stereotype of Mexican immigrants as overwhelmingly impoverished peasants, up to 48 percent of the unauthorized have been found to originate in cities of twenty thousand or more, in comparison with 35 percent of all Mexicans.

During the 1970s, around 45 percent of Mexican workers made their living from agriculture; a study of apprehended illegals estimated a similar proportion, 49 percent, but another of former illegals who had regularized their situation reduced it to 18 percent. White-collar and urban skilled and semiskilled occupations employed between 35 and 60 percent of unauthorized immigrants prior to their departure from Mexico; these occupations absorbed approximately 30 percent of the Mexican population in comparable years.[4] All studies coincide in that few of these immigrants were unemployed in Mexico, the figure hovering around 5 percent. As one author states, "the findings indicate that it is not the lack of jobs, but of *well-paid* jobs, which fuels migration to the U.S."[5]

Even more conclusive findings come from research in the Dominican Republic, another important source of illegal immigration. Several independent studies conclude that Dominicans who migrate internationally, including those without documents, are more likely to come from the cities, have much higher levels of literacy, be relatively more skilled, and have lower levels of unemployment than the Dominican population as a whole. Among those from rural areas, migrants come predominantly from the sector of medium to large farmers rather than from the landless peasantry.[6]

[3]Frank D. Bean, Harley L. Browning, and W. Parker Frisbie, "What the 1980 U.S. Census Tells Us about the Characteristics of Illegal and Legal Mexican Immigrants" (Austin: Population Research Center, University of Texas, 1985), mimeographed; David S. North and Marion F. Houstoun, "The Characteristics and Role of Illegal Aliens in the U.S. Labor Market" (Washington, D.C.: Linton, 1976), mimeographed; Douglas S. Massey, "Do Undocumented Immigrants Earn Lower Wages than Legal Immigrants? New Evidence from Mexico," *International Migration Review* 21 (Summer 1987): pp. 236–74; see also U.S. Immigration and Naturalization Service (INS), *Report on the Legalized Alien Population* (Washington, D.C.: U.S. Government Printing Office, 1992).

[4]Ibid.

[5]Wayne A. Cornelius, "Illegal Migration to the United States: Recent Research Findings, Policy Implications, and Research Priorities," Discussion Paper C/77-11 (Cambridge, Mass.: MIT Center for International Studies, 1977), mimeographed, p. 4.

[6]David Bray, "Economic Development: The Middle Class and International Migration in the Dominican Republic," *International Migration Review* 18 (Summer 1984): p. 231.

The main reason the poorest of the poor do not migrate across international borders is that they are not able to. In Mexico, "those at the very bottom of the local income distribution are not likely to migrate to the States because they lack even the resources needed to cover the costs of transportation and fees charged by the smugglers."[7] In the Dominican Republic, "There are major legal and financial barriers that prevent the poor from migrating . . . reports suggest that it costs several thousand dollars to be provided with papers and smuggled out of the country."[8] Studies of Haitian unauthorized migration also report that it costs thousands to buy passage aboard barely seaworthy craft bound for south Florida.[9]

But if migrants do not come to escape unemployment or destitution, why do they come? Why, in particular, should middle-class professionals and skilled workers embark on a costly journey, sometimes surreptitiously, and sacrifice work, friends, and family back home? The basic reason is the gap between life aspirations and expectations and the means to fulfill them in the sending countries. Different groups feel this gap with varying intensity, but it clearly becomes a strong motive for action among the most ambitious and resourceful. Because *relative,* not absolute, deprivation lies at the core of most contemporary immigration, its composition tends to be positively selected in terms of both human capital and motivation. The United States and the other industrialized countries play a double role in this process. First, they are the source of much of the modern culture of consumption and of the new expectations diffused worldwide. Second, the same process of global diffusion has taught an increasing number of people about economic opportunities in the developed world that are absent in their own countries.

It is thus not surprising that most of today's immigrants, even the undocumented, have had some education and come from cities, for these are precisely the groups most thoroughly exposed to life-styles and consumption patterns emanating from the advanced world. These are also the groups for whom the gap between aspirations and local realities is most poignant and among whom one finds the individuals most determined to overcome this situation. Educated and skilled workers and small farmers are generally better informed about employment opportunities abroad than the illiterate and the destitute. Those at the bottom of the social structure not only lack the means to migrate, but often the motivation to do so because they are less exposed to the lure of consumption styles in the developed nations and are less aware of the work opportunities in them.

The form that this gap takes varies, of course, across countries and social groups. For skilled workers and small farmers, migration is the means to stabilize family livelihoods and meet long-desired aspirations — a car, a TV set, domestic appliances of all sorts, additional land and implements. For urban professionals, it provides a means of reaching life standards commensurate with their past achievements and to progress in their

[7]Wayne A. Cornelius, "Mexican Migration to the United States: Causes, Consequences, and U.S. Responses," Working Paper (Cambridge, Mass.: MIT Center for International Studies, 1977), p. 7.

[8]Bray, "Economic Development," p. 231.

[9]Jake C. Miller, *The Plight of Haitian Refugees,* chap. 4 (New York: Praeger, 1984); Alex Stepick, "Haitian Refugees in the U.S.," Minority Rights Group Report no. 52 (London: MRG, 1982).

careers.[10] Seen from this perspective, contemporary immigration is a direct consequence of the dominant influence attained by the culture of the advanced West in every corner of the globe. The bewildering number and variety of today's immigrants reflect this worldwide reach and the vision of modern life and individual fulfillment that goes with it.

Back in the nineteenth century, the United States was a growing industrializing country that needed labor; but because its life standards were not a global model and its economic opportunities were not well known, it had to resort to deliberate recruitment. Thus, the vaunted "pull" of U.S. wages had to be actualized by American migration agents sent to Mexico, Ireland, southern Italy, and the Austro-Hungarian empire to apprise people of the "better meals and higher wages" available for work in the eastern canal companies, the western railroads, and later on in industry.[11]

The enormous variety of today's immigrants and the fact that they come spontaneously rather than through deliberate recruitment reflect the attraction of American life-styles and their gradual conversion into a world standard. Immigrants do not come to escape perennial unemployment or destitution in their homeland. Most undertake the journey instead to attain the dream of a new life-style that has reached their countries but that is impossible to fulfill in them. Not surprisingly, the most determined individuals, those who feel the distance between actual reality and life goals most poignantly, often choose migration as the path to resolve this contradiction.

IMMIGRANTS AND THEIR TYPES

Within this general picture, there are significant differences in migration goals and their relative fulfillment. Any typology implies simplification, but it is useful at this point to present a basic classification of contemporary immigrants to organize the upcoming analysis of their process of adaptation. Each basic type is represented by several nationalities; conversely, a national group may include individuals representing different types. These are distinguished by a series of common characteristics of socioeconomic origin and reasons for departure that tend to be associated with different courses of adaptation once in the United States.

Labor Migrants. Manual labor immigration corresponds most closely to popular stereotypes about contemporary immigration. The movement of foreign workers in search of menial and generally low paid jobs has represented the bulk of immigration, both legal and undocumented, in recent years. The Immigration Reform and Control Act (IRCA) of 1986 was aimed primarily at discouraging the surreptitious component of this flow while compensating employers by liberalizing access to legal temporary workers. A decade

[10]See Francisco Alba, "Mexico's International Migration as a Manifestation of Its Development Pattern," *International Migration Review* 12 (Winter 1978): pp. 502–13; Alejandro Portes and Adreain R. Ross, "Modernization for Emigration: The Medical Brain Drain from Argentina," *Journal of Interamerican Studies and World Affairs* 13 (November 1976): pp. 395–422.

[11]Stanley Lebergott, *Manpower in Economic Growth: The American Record since 1800* (New York: McGraw-Hill, 1962), p. 39.

later, Proposition 187, an initiative passed by the California electorate in 1994, sought to discourage undocumented immigration by barring illegal aliens from access to public services. . . . For the moment, it suffices to note the principal ways manual labor immigration has materialized in recent years.

First, migrants can simply cross the border on foot or with the help of a smuggler or overstay a U.S. tourist visa. In official parlance, illegal border crossers have been labeled EWIs (entry without inspection); those who stay longer than permitted are labeled visa abusers. In 1993, the U.S. Immigration and Naturalization Service (INS) located 1.33 million deportable aliens, of which 1.29 million were EWIs. . . .

A second channel of entry is to come legally by using one of the family reunification preferences of the immigration law (left untouched, for the most part, by the 1986 reform and reaffirmed by the Immigration Act of 1990). This avenue is open primarily to immigrants who have first entered the United States without legal papers or for temporary periods and who have subsequently married a U.S. citizen or legal resident. Marriage automatically entitles the immigrant to a legal entry permit; spouses of U.S. citizens are given priority because they are exempt from existing quota limits. . . .

The last avenue is to come as a contract laborer. There was a provision in the 1965 immigration act for the importation of temporary foreign laborers when a supply of "willing and able" domestic workers was not available. This provision was maintained and actually liberalized by the 1986 reform. In both cases, the secretary of labor must certify that a labor shortage exists before Immigration authorizes the entry of foreign workers. Because the procedure is cumbersome, especially in the past, few employers sought labor in this manner. An exception is the sugar industry in Florida, for which "H-2" workers, as they are labeled because of their type of visa, have become the mainstay of its cane-cutting labor force. They come after a selection process in Jamaica and other West Indian countries, live in company barracks during the harvest, and return home immediately after its end. Contract workers are also found in lesser numbers throughout the Eastern Seaboard working in the fruit orchards of Georgia and the Carolinas and in the shade tobacco crop of Connecticut.[12] During the 1970s, 1980s, and early 1990s, approximately twenty thousand H-2 workers per year have been imported, primarily from the West Indies.

The principal magnet drawing foreign manual workers to the United States is undoubtedly the level of U.S. wages relative to those left behind. At $4.25[13] an hour, the U.S. minimum wage is approximately six times the prevailing one in Mexico, which is, in turn, higher than most in Central America. The actual wage many U.S. employers pay their foreign workers exceeds the legal minimum and is significantly higher than that available for skilled and even white-collar work in Mexico and other sending countries.

[12]Terry L. McCoy, "The Political Economy of Caribbean Workers in the Florida Sugar Industry," paper presented at the fifth annual meeting of the Caribbean Studies Association, Willemstad, Curacao, May 1980, mimeographed; Charles H. Wood, "Caribbean Cane Cutters in Florida: A Study of the Relative Cost of Domestic and Foreign Labor," paper presented at the meetings of the American Sociological Association, San Antonio, Texas, August 1984, mimeographed; Josh de Wind, Tom Seidl, and Janet Shenk, "Caribbean Migration: Contract Labor in U.S. Agriculture," *NACLA Report on the Americas* 11 (November–December 1977), pp. 4–37.

[13]The current U.S. minimum wage is $4.75 an hour [Eds.].

This is why relatively well-educated and skilled foreigners are willing to accept these frequently harsh jobs. To them, the trek to the United States and the economic opportunities associated with it often represent the difference between stagnation or impoverishment and attainment of their life's goals.[14]

Whatever their motivation, however, immigrants could not come if there were not a demand for their labor. That demand is strong and growing. Employers value immigrant workers' diligence, reliability, and willingness to work hard for low pay. They argue that American workers are either unavailable or unwilling to perform hard menial jobs. Garment contractors, small electronics firms, and other employers of immigrants have further argued that they would have to close their doors or move abroad if this labor supply were cut off.[15]

This demand is fueled by the favorable position in which employers find themselves. There are no recruitment or other costs in hiring immigrant laborers because they come on their own and bear all the dangers and expenses of the journey. Until recently, there were no legal costs either because the law specifically exempted employers from any liability for hiring illegal aliens. Although the 1986 immigration reform has altered this situation, a number of loopholes still facilitate access to immigrant laborers, regardless of their legal status. In addition, the new law itself has expanded channels for the legal importation of temporary workers.[16]

Under these conditions, it is not surprising that manual labor immigration has continued and grown from year to year. This flow does not represent an "alien invasion," as

[14]Leo R. Chávez, *Shadowed Lives: Undocumented Immigrants in American Society* (San Diego: Harcourt Brace, 1992); Pierrette Hondagneu-Sotelo, *Gendered Transitions: Mexican Experiences of Immigration* (Berkeley: University of California Press, 1994); Wayne A. Cornelius, "Labor Market Impacts of Mexican Immigration: Two Generations of Research," paper presented at the seminar on the urban informal sector in center and periphery, Johns Hopkins University, Baltimore, June 1984; María Patricia Fernández-Kelly and Ana García, "Advanced Technology, Regional Development, and Women's Employment in Southern California," discussion paper (La Jolla: Center for U.S.-Mexico Studies, University of California, San Diego, 1985); Rick Morales and Richard Mines, "San Diego's Full-Service Restaurants: A View from the Back of the House," report (La Jolla: Center for U.S.-Mexican Studies, University of California, San Diego, 1985); NACLA, "Undocumented Immigrant Workers in New York City," *Latin American and Empire Report* 12 (November–December 1979), special issue; Saskia Sassen, "Immigrant and Minority Workers in the Organization of the Labor Process," *Journal of Ethnic Studies* (Spring 1981): pp. 1–34; Fernando Urreu Giraldo, "Life Strategies and the Labor Market: Colombians in New York in the 1970s," report (New York: New York Research Program in Inter-American Affairs, 1982); Roger Waldinger, "Immigration and Industrial Change in the New York City Apparel Industry," in *Hispanics in the U.S. Economy,* ed. George J. Borjas and Marta Tienda (New York: Academic Press, 1985), pp. 323–49; Sherri Grasmuck, "Immigration, Ethnic Stratification, and Ethnic Working-Class Discipline: Comparison of Documented and Undocumented Dominicans," *International Migration Review* 18 (Fall 1984): pp. 692–713; Saskia Sassen, "Changing Composition and Labor Market Location of Hispanic Immigrants in New York City, 1960–1980," in *Hispanics in the U.S. Economy,* ed. George J. Borjas and Marta Tienda (New York: Academic Press, 1985), pp. 299–322.

[15]Wayne A. Cornelius, "Labor Market Impacts of Mexican Immigration: Two Generations of Research," paper presented at the seminar on the urban informal sector in center and periphery, Johns Hopkins University, Baltimore, June 1984; Fernández-Kelly and García, "Advanced Technology"; Sassen, "Changing Composition."

[16]For an analysis of employer-oriented loopholes in the 1986 act, see Alejandro Portes, "Immigration Reform: The Theory and the Realities," *Baltimore Sun,* January 2, 1987, 15A. See also Michael C. LeMay, *Anatomy of a Public Policy: The Reform of Contemporary American Immigration Law* (Westport: Praeger, 1994).

some authors have called it, because an invasion implies moving into someone else's territory against their will. In this instance, the movement is very much welcomed, if not by everyone, at least by an influential group — namely, the urban employers and rural growers who have come to rely on this source of labor. The match between the goals and aspirations of foreign workers and the interests of the firms that hire them is the key factor sustaining the movement from year to year. . . .

Some do stay and attempt to carve a new life in America. Many return, however, because although U.S. wages are higher, the "yield" of these wages in terms of consumption, investments, and social status is often greater back home. Having accumulated enough savings, most immigrants seek to reestablish or gain a position of social respectability, a goal more easily accomplished in their home communities.[17] Manual labor immigration is thus not a one-way flow away from poverty and want, but rather a two-way process fueled by the changing needs and interests of those who come and those who profit from their labor.

Professional Immigrants. . . . This category provides the main entry channel for the second type of immigrants. . . . [T]hese come legally and are not destined to the bottom layers of the American labor market. Labeled "brain drain" in the countries of origin, this flow of immigrants represents a significant gain of highly trained personnel for the United States. In 1993, 109,760 persons classified as professionals and managers arrived as permanent residents; the main contributors included mainland China (13,954), the Philippines (11,164), India (10,210), Great Britain (5,508), and Taiwan (4,708). The overall number and the principal contributors changed little during the 1980s.[18] However, since 1992, under the new provisions of the Immigration Act of 1990, the number of these visas tripled the level that had been the annual norm for the previous twenty-five years.

Foreign professionals and technicians seldom migrate because of unemployment back home. The reason is that they not only come from the higher educational strata, but that they are probably among the best in their respective professions in order to pass difficult entry tests, such as the ECFMG [Educational Council for Foreign Medical Graduates] examination for physicians, or to attract U.S. job offers. The gap that generally makes the difference in their decision is not the invidious income differential between prospective U.S. salaries and those at home. Instead, it is the gap between available salaries and work conditions *in their own countries* and those regarded there as acceptable for people with their education.

[17]Chávez, *Shadowed Lives;* Douglas S. Massey, Rafael Alarcón, Jorge Durand, and Humberto González, *Return to Aztlán: The Social Process of International Migration from Western Mexico* (Berkeley: University of California Press, 1987); Sherri Grasmuck and Patricia Pessar, *Between Two Islands: Dominican International Migration* (Berkeley: University of California Press, 1991); Cornelius, "Mexican Migration"; Ina R. Dinerman, "Patterns of Adaptation Among Households of U.S.-Bound Migrants from Michoacán, Mexico," *International Migration Review* 12 (Winter 1978): pp. 485–501; Patricia Pessar, "The Role of Households in International Migration and the Case of the U.S.-Bound Migration from the Dominican Republic," *International Migration Review* 16 (Summer 1982): pp. 342–64; Douglas S. Massey, "Understanding Mexican Migration to the United States," *American Journal of Sociology* 92 (May 1987): pp. 1372–1403.

[18]U.S. Immigration and Naturalization Service (INS), *1993 Statistical Yearbook* (Washington, D.C.: U.S. Government Printing Office, 1994), Table 21.

Professionals who earn enough at home to sustain a middle-class standard of living and who are reasonably satisfied about their chances for advancement seldom migrate. Those threatened with early obsolescence or who cannot make ends meet start looking for opportunities abroad. A fertile ground for this type of migration are countries in which university students are trained in advanced Western-style professional practices, but then find the prospects and means to implement their training blocked because of poor employment opportunities or lack of equipment.[19]

Because they do not come to escape poverty, but to improve their careers, immigrant professionals seldom accept menial jobs in the United States. However, they tend to enter at the bottom of their respective occupational ladders and to progress from there according to individual merit. This is why, for example, foreign doctors and nurses are so often found in public hospitals throughout the country. But in recent years, a number of foreign professionals — primarily of Asian origin — have had to turn to other pursuits because of new entry barriers to their respective careers in the United States. Common alternatives have been small business or even the unregulated practice of their profession while awaiting better times.[20] Despite these difficulties, these immigrants' economic success has been remarkable. For example, immigration from India during the last two decades has been heavily skewed toward university-educated professionals and technical personnel. In 1990, the median household income of Indian immigrants was $48,320 — $18,000 above the median for the U.S. population and $20,000 above the figure for the foreign born, despite the fact that almost 60 percent of these immigrants had been in the United States ten years or less.[21]

An important feature of this type of immigration is its inconspicuousness. We seldom hear reference to a Filipino or an Indian immigration "problem," although there are over one million Filipinos and over five hundred thousand Indians living in this country. The reason is that professionals and technicians, heavily represented among these nationalities, seldom form tightly knit ethnic communities. . . . Professional immigrants are among the most rapidly assimilated — first because of their occupational success and second because of the absence of strong ethnic networks that reinforce the culture of origin. However, assimilation in this case does not mean severing relations with the home country. On the contrary, because successful immigrants have the means to do so, they attempt to bridge the gap between past and present through periodic visits and cultivating family and friends left behind. During the first generation at least, a typical pattern is the attempt to juggle two different social worlds. Although this is a difficult and expensive task, many foreign professionals actually succeed in it.

Entrepreneurial Immigrants. Near downtown Los Angeles there is an area approximately a mile long where all commercial signs suddenly change from English to strange pictorial characters. Koreatown, as the area is known, contains the predictable number

[19]Portes and Ross, "Modernization for Emigration"; William A. Glaser and Christopher Habers, "The Migration and Return of Professionals," *International Migration Review* 8 (Summer 1974): pp. 227–44.

[20]See Rosemary Stevens, Louis W. Goodman, and Stephen Mick, *The Alien Doctors: Foreign Medical Graduates in American Hospitals* (New York: Wiley, 1978).

[21]U.S. Bureau of the Census, "The Foreign-Born Population" (1993), Tables 1, 5; Rubén G. Rumbaut, "Origins and Destinies: Immigration to the United States since World War II," *Sociological Forum* 9 (1994): pp. 583–621.

of ethnic restaurants and grocery shops; it also contains a number of banks, import-export houses, industries, and real estate offices. Signs of "English spoken here" assure visitors that their links with the outside world have not been totally severed. In Los Angeles, the propensity for self-employment is three times greater among Koreans than among the population as a whole. Grocery stores, restaurants, gas stations, liquor stores, and real estate offices are typical Korean businesses. They also tend to remain within the community because the more successful immigrants sell their earlier businesses to new arrivals.[22]

A similar urban landscape is found near downtown Miami. Little Havana extends in a narrow strip for about five miles, eventually merging with the southwest suburbs of the city. Cuban-owned firms increased from 919 in 1967 to 8,000 in 1976 and approximately 28,000 in 1990. Most are small, averaging 8.1 employees at the latest count, but they also include factories employing hundreds of workers. Cuban firms are found in light and heavy manufacturing, construction, commerce, finance, and insurance. An estimated 60 percent of all residential construction in the metropolitan area is now done by these firms; gross annual receipts of Cuban manufacturing industries increased 1,067 percent during a recent ten-year period.[23]

These areas of concentrated immigrant entrepreneurship are known as ethnic enclaves. Their emergence has depended on three conditions: first, the presence of a number of immigrants with substantial business expertise acquired in their home countries; second, access to sources of capital; third, access to labor. The requisite labor is not too difficult to obtain because it can be initially drawn from family members and then from more recent immigrant arrivals. Sources of capital are often not a major obstacle either, because the sums required initially are small. When immigrants do not bring them from abroad, they can accumulate them through individual savings or obtain them from pooled resources in the community. In some instances, would-be entrepreneurs have access to financial institutions owned or managed by co-nationals. Thus, the first requisite is the critical one. The presence of a number of immigrants skilled in what sociologist Franklin Frazier called "the art of buying and selling" can usually overcome other obstacles to entrepreneurship.[24] Conversely, their absence tends to confine an immigrant group to wage work even when enough savings and labor are available.

Entrepreneurial minorities are the exception in both turn-of-the-century and contemporary immigrations. Their significance is that they create an avenue for economic mobility unavailable to other groups. This avenue is open not only to the original entrepreneurs, but to later arrivals as well. The reason is that relations between immigrant employers and their co-ethnic employees often go beyond a purely contractual bond.

[22]Ivan Light, "Asian Enterprise in America: Chinese, Japanese, and Koreans in Small Business," in *Self-Help in Urban America,* ed. Scott Cummings (New York: Kennikat Press, 1980), pp. 33–57; Edna Bonacich, Ivan Light, and Charles Wong, "Koreans in Small Business," *Society* 14 (September–October 1977): pp. 54–59; Pyong Gap Min, ed., *Asian Americans: Contemporary Trends and Issues* (Thousand Oaks, Calif.: Sage, 1995).

[23]Sergio Díaz-Briquets, "Cuban-Owned Business in the United States," *Cuban Studies* 14 (Summer 1985): pp. 57–64; Alejandro Portes and Alex Stepick, *City on the Edge: The Transformation of Miami* (Berkeley: University of California Press, 1993); Luis J. Botifoll, "How Miami's New Image Was Created," occasional paper 1985-I, Institute of Interamerican Studies, University of Miami, 1985.

[24]E. Franklin Frazier, *The Negro in the United States* (New York: Macmillan, 1949). See also Ivan Light, *Ethnic Enterprise in America: Business and Welfare Among Chinese, Japanese, and Blacks* (Berkeley: University of California Press, 1972).

When immigrant enterprises expand, they tend to hire their own for supervisory positions. Today Koreans hire and promote Koreans in New York and Los Angeles, and Cubans do the same for other Cubans in Miami, just as sixty years ago the Jews of Manhattan's Lower East Side and the Japanese of San Francisco and Los Angeles hired and supported those from their own communities.[25]

A tightly knit ethnic enclave is not, however, the only manifestation of immigrant entrepreneurship. In other cities, where the concentration of these immigrants is less dense, they tend to take over businesses catering to low-income groups, often in the inner cities. In this role as "middleman minorities," entrepreneurial immigrants are less visible because they tend to be dispersed over the area occupied by the populations they serve. Koreatown in Los Angeles is not, for example, the only manifestation of entrepreneurship among this immigrant group. Koreans are also present in significant numbers in New York City, where they have gained increasing control of the produce market, and in cities like Washington, D.C., and Baltimore, where they have progressively replaced Italians and Jews as the principal merchants in low-income inner-city areas.[26] Similarly, roughly two-thirds of Cuban-owned firms are concentrated in Miami, but they are also numerous in other cities such as Los Angeles and Jersey City. The percentage of firms per thousand Cuban population is actually higher in these secondary concentrations than in Miami.[27]

The rise of ethnic enclaves and middleman minorities is generally fortuitous. There are no provisions so far in the U.S. immigration law to encourage foreign businessmen to come here, except as visitors. Congress is currently considering a provision that will grant U.S. residence to a limited number of foreign capitalists who invest in sizable job-creating enterprises. However, no explicit entry preference exists for small immigrant entrepreneurs with little or no capital, and none is likely to be implemented in the future. In general, entrepreneurial minorities come under preference designated for other purposes. Koreans and Chinese, two of the most successful business-oriented groups, have availed themselves of the employment-based preference categories for professionals and skilled workers and, subsequently, of the family reunification provisions of the 1965 and 1990 immigration laws. Cubans came as political refugees and were initially resettled in dispersed localities throughout the country. It took these refugees more than a decade after initial arrival to start regrouping in certain geographic locations and begin the push toward entrepreneurship.

Refugees and Asylees. The Refugee Act of 1980, signed into law by President Carter, aimed at eliminating the former practice of granting asylum only to escapees from

[25]Moses Rischin, *The Promised City: New York Jews, 1870–1914* (Cambridge, Mass.: Harvard University Press, 1962); Irving Howe, *World of Our Fathers* (New York: Harcourt Brace, 1976); Edna Bonacich and John Modell, *The Economic Basis of Ethnic Solidarity: Small Business in the Japanese-American Community* (Berkeley: University of California Press, 1980); William Petersen, *Japanese Americans: Oppression and Success* (New York: Random House, 1971).

[26]Pyong Gap Min, *Middlemen in Contemporary America: Koreans in New York and Los Angeles, 1970–1994* (Berkeley: University of California Press, 1996); Bonacich, Light, and Wong, "Koreans in Small Business"; Illsoo Kim, *New Urban Immigrants: The Korean Community in New York* (Princeton: Princeton University Press, 1981); Alejandro Portes and Robert D. Manning, "The Immigrant Enclave: Theory and Empirical Examples," in *Competitive Ethnic Relations,* ed. Joane Nagel and Susan Olzak (Orlando: Academic Press, 1986), pp. 47–68.

[27]Díaz-Briquets, "Cuban-Owned Business."

Communist-controlled nations. Instead, it sought to bring U.S. policy into line with international practice, which defines as a refugee anyone with a well-founded fear of persecution or physical harm, regardless of the political bent of his or her country's regime. In practice, however, the United States during the Reagan administration continued to grant refugee status to escapees from communism, primarily from Southeast Asia and Eastern Europe, while making it difficult for others fleeing non-Communist regimes such as Guatemala and El Salvador. The granting of asylum has significant advantages over other alternatives. The central difference is that while refugees have legal status, the right to work, and can avail themselves of the welfare provisions of the 1980 act, those denied asylum have none of these privileges and, if they stay, are classified as illegal aliens.[28]

Being a refugee is therefore not a matter of personal choice, but of governmental decision based on a combination of legal guidelines and political expediency. Depending on the relationship between the United States and the country of origin and the international context of the time, a particular flow of people may be classified as a political exodus or as an illegal group of economically motivated immigrants. Given past policy, it is thus not surprising that there are few escapees from rightist regimes living legally in the country. Major refugee groups have arrived, instead, after the Soviet army occupation of Eastern Europe, after the rise to power of Fidel Castro in Cuba, and after the takeover by Communist insurgents of three Southeast Asian countries. Ironically, after the end of the Cold War in 1989 and the collapse of the Soviet Union in 1991, the number of refugees admitted actually grew — once again due to foreign policy interests, and once again largely from the same source countries.

In 1993, a total of 127,343 refugees arrived and were admitted for legal residence in the United States. Of these, 37,604 or 30 percent came from Vietnam, Cambodia, and Laos; Cuba accounted for another 9 percent; the Soviet Union, Poland, and Romania combined represented 39 percent; and Afghanistan and Ethiopia added another 5 percent. Iran and Iraq — the only major non-Communist sources of refugee migration — accounted for 5 percent. Admissions from the Communist or former Communist world still represented about 90 percent of the total in this year.[29]

Major refugee groups living at present in the United States thus tend to share strong anti-Communist feelings, although they are different in many other respects. Their entry into the American labor market, for example, has been heterogeneous, paralleling and even exceeding the diversity among regular immigrants. Political refugees are found today in low-paid menial work, as is the case with many Cambodians, Laotians, Afghans, Ethiopians, and 1980 Mariel Cubans. They are also found at the higher end of the labor market, in prominent and well-paid professional careers, as is often the case with Eastern Europeans and Iranians. Others have veered toward business and self-employment after giving up hopes of returning to their countries. Cubans in south Florida and increasingly the Vietnamese, concentrated in Orange and Los Angeles counties, have followed this route. Finally, there is even the option of remaining out of work, made possible by the

[28]Aristide R. Zolberg, Astri Suhrke, and Sergio Aguayo, "International Factors in the Formation of Refugee Movements," *International Migration Review* 20 (Summer 1986): pp. 151–69; Aristide R. Zolberg, "From Invitation to Interdiction: U.S. Foreign Policy and Immigration since 1945," in *Threatened Peoples, Threatened Borders: World Migration and U.S. Policy,* ed. M. S. Teitelbaum and M. Weiner (New York: W. W. Norton, 1995), pp. 117–59.

[29]INS, *1993 Statistical Yearbook,* Table 35.

welfare provisions of the 1980 refugee act. Asian refugees with little education and work skills are commonly found in this situation.[30]

The official label of refugee conceals differences not only between national groups but within each of them as well. Two categories are generally found in most refugee flows. First, there is an elite of former notables who left because of ideological and political opposition to their countries' regimes. They tend to be among the earlier arrivals and usually have little difficulty validating their claim of political persecution. Second, there is a mass of individuals and families of more modest backgrounds who left at a later date because of the economic exactions and hardships imposed by the same regimes.[31] Depending on the relationship between their home country and the United States, they can be classified as bona fide refugees or as illegal aliens. This diversity in the origins of refugees and the interaction between the earlier elite arrivals and subsequent cohorts goes a long way toward explaining each group's economic and social adaptation.

In 1995, well over a hundred foreign countries and possessions sent immigrants to the United States. . . .

A description of present-day immigration and its diversity would be incomplete if not supplemented by a discussion of what all this means for the host society. Is it good or bad for the United States that so many foreigners from so many different countries are arriving at present? Should the country move decisively to prevent or restrict at least some of these flows? Alternatively, should it continue to maintain, as in the recent past, one of the most liberal immigration policies in the world? Our reply to these questions will be generally optimistic. Overall, immigration has been and will continue to be positive for the country both in terms of filling labor needs at different levels of the economy and, more important, injecting into society the energies, ambitions, and skills of positively selected groups. Qualifications exist, and we discuss them. But in our view, they do not detract from this general assessment.

The political debate about immigration in the United States has always been marked by vigorous calls for restriction. The most ardent advocates of this policy are often children and grandchildren of immigrants who wear their second-generation patriotism outwardly and aggressively. This position forgets that it was the labor and efforts of immigrants — often the parents and grandparents of today's restrictionists — that made

[30]Rubén G. Rumbaut, "Vietnamese, Laotian, and Cambodian Americans," in *Asian Americans: Contemporary Trends and Issues,* ed. Pyong Gap Min (Thousand Oaks, Calif.: Sage, 1995), pp. 232–70; Donald J. Cichon, Elzbieta M. Gozdziak, and Jane G. Grover, "The Economic and Social Adjustment of Non-Southeast Asian Refugees," Report to the Office of Refugee Resettlement, Department of Health and Human Services, Washington, D.C., mimeographed; Rubén G. Rumbaut, "The Structure of Refuge: Southeast Asian Refugees in the United States," *International Review of Comparative Public Policy* 1 (Winter 1989): pp. 97–129; Rubén G. Rumbaut and John R. Weeks, "Fertility and Adaptation: Indochinese Refugees in the United States," *International Migration Review* 20 (Summer 1986): pp. 428–66; Robert L. Bach, Linda W. Gordon, David W. Haines, and David R. Howell, "The Economic Adjustment of Southeast Asian Refugees in the United States," in *World Refugee Survey, 1983* (Geneva: United Nations High Commission for Refugees, 1984), pp. 51–55; Alejandro Portes and Alex Stepick, "Unwelcome Immigrants: The Labor Market Experiences of 1980 (Mariel) Cuban and Haitian Refugees in South Florida," *American Sociological Review* 50 (August 1985): pp. 493–514; James P. Allen and Eugene J. Turner, *We the People: An Atlas of America's Ethnic Diversity* (New York: Macmillan, 1986), pp. 190–96.

[31]Zolberg, Suhrke, and Aguayo, "International Factors"; Cichon, Gozdziak, and Grover, "The Economic and Social Adjustment"; Alejandro Portes and Robert L. Bach, *Latin Journey: Cuban and Mexican Immigrants in the United States* (Berkeley: University of California Press, 1985), chap. 3.

much of the prosperity of the nation possible. Even the fiercest xenophobes have had a hard time arguing that turn-of-the-century groups such as Italian and Polish peasants or the much attacked Chinese and Japanese had a long-term negative effect on the country. Instead, these now successful and settled groups are presented as examples, but exception is taken to the newcomers. There is irony in the spectacle of Americans who bear clear marks of their immigrant origins being among the most vocal adversaries of continuing immigration. Consequences of heeding their advice would be serious, however. Although regulation and control of the inflow from abroad are always necessary, suppressing it would deprive the nation of what has been so far one of its main sources of energy, innovativeness, and growth.

Considerations

1. According to Portes and Rumbaut, what are some of the misconceptions about the current wave of immigration to the United States? What is the reality?
2. What, according to the authors, are the answers to the question, "Why do they come?"
3. With a warning that any typology involves a simplification of complex reality, Portes and Rumbaut offer "a basic classification of contemporary immigrants." Summarize their scheme and provide one or two examples of each type of immigrant group, explaining how each type might follow a somewhat different course of adaptation to life in the United States.
4. Using their own material, or examples and discussion from other readings in this chapter, complicate Portes and Rumbaut's classification scheme. That is, consider ways that the scheme may be incomplete or too rigid or the way distinctions between the categories become fluid, one category blending into another.
5. Portes and Rumbaut conclude their essay by considering the question of whether or not the current influx of immigrants is good for the country. What is their answer and the argument leading to it? What do you think?
6. In their conclusion, Portes and Rumbaut write that "[t]he most ardent advocates of [restrictionist] policy are often children and grandchildren of immigrants." If this is true, why might it be so?

Further Assignments

1. Many of the readings in this chapter explain the conditions, both within the United States and outside of it, that influenced certain foreign citizens to emigrate to America. Develop a scheme for classifying these conditions. (Your scheme could range, for example, from economic conditions in the homeland to means of transportation to kinship and ethnic networks in the United States.) Write an essay that applies the scheme across the readings, making sure to draw on specific examples.

2. One issue that runs throughout the readings in this chapter is the encounter between the values, cultural practices, beliefs, and so on that immigrants bring with them and the values, cultural practices, and so on they encounter in the United States. These encounters are complex and lead to varying combinations of assimilation, negotiation, compromise, or resistance. (Notice that the list we just presented is a simple classification scheme.) Try developing a scheme to help you make sense of some of the general ways people learn to live in a new land. You can consider, for example, the variety of ways immigrants might respond in the economic domain, the political domain, the domain of language, or of cultural beliefs and practices regarding religion, gender, and so on. Use examples from any of the readings and charts on immigration in this chapter. As you work on this assignment, ask yourself whether your emerging classification scheme is doing justice to the complexity of the immigrant experience. You can comment on this issue in your paper.

3. David Cole's essay (p. 308) lists myths about immigration that lead to its opposition. Take up one or more of the myths he describes and flesh out — or oppose — his argument in light of the essays you've read here.

4. Write an essay that compares contemporary immigration trends, as described in the article by Portes and Rumbaut (p. 403), with earlier immigration trends as discussed in the other essays in this chapter. In doing so, try to avoid the simple types of comparisons that Portes and Rumbaut criticize in the early part of their article. To help you get started, you might consider one or more of the following as points of comparison:

- economic factors
- political factors
- opportunities/aspirations
- background of immigrants

5. The charts that open this chapter and the chronology of immigration restrictions on page 367 can all be interpreted as narratives of immigration to the United States. Separately, and as a whole, they provide a story or serial account of immigration. (For a detailed discussion of the serializing strategy, see Chapter 3.) Interpret one or more of these sets of statistics to give a serial account of (1) immigration restrictions, (2) employment or labor trends, or (3) demographic changes.

6. Portes and Rumbaut's article provides a classic example of classifying, as the authors create categories for laborers, professionals, entrepreneurs, and refugees and asylees. In presenting this classification, they also use other strategies discussed in this book: summarizing, serializing, comparing, and analyzing. Analyze Portes and Rumbaut's article in terms of the other strategies used. Does one or more method predominate? Why? How do the methods that the authors employ serve their purposes?

7. In recent years, opposition to immigration and efforts to limit immigrants' access to government benefits and public services have made big news. Research specific measures that are being considered — or that have been enacted — to limit immigration or immigrants' access to benefits and services. Then write a paper describing these measures, the reasons for them, and the reactions to them. If you feel comfortable arguing for or against these restrictions, do so, drawing on the insights from the readings in this chapter and perhaps on some further research.

8. Take one of the immigrant groups discussed in this chapter — Chicanos/Latinos, Asians, Europeans, Scandinavians — or any other immigrant group in which you are interested and do further historical research into one of the following issues involving the group:

- reasons for migrating
- paths or degrees of assimilation
- discrimination toward the group and the group's coping with this discrimination
- settlement patterns in the United States
- trades or professions assumed
- influence on U.S. customs and practices

Write a research paper based on your findings, making sure to draw on illustrations, statistical information, individual immigrants' stories, and any other specific information that will make your paper more compelling.

9. Many of you reading this chapter come from an immigrant background. Interview your parents or grandparents or other family members to find out what you can about your own forebears, the reasons for their immigration, where they settled, what opportunities they found or hardships they faced, and so on. Then write an essay situating what you found out about your own immigrant history in the context of the information provided in the readings.

10. This chapter is about immigration to the United States, which, by definition, deals with people from other countries who move to America. But significant *migration* also occurs within countries, and the United States has a long history of internal migrations of large groups of people: white Midwesterners moving to California, Mexican Americans moving from Texas across the Southwest, African Americans moving — in what is often called the "great migration" — from the South to the industrial Midwest and Northeast. Select one of these migrations, or any other you've read about (or have personal experience with), and research its history: What were the "push" and "pull" factors involved? Who tended to migrate? What did they find in their new home? Keep these, and other, questions in mind. Then, consider the following question: Can you draw parallels between this internal migration and any of the accounts of immigration you've read in this chapter?

5

COMPARING

Assessing Similarities and Differences

COMPARING Across the Curriculum

The first part of this chapter includes a range of readings — most accompanied by assignments — that will get you to think critically about the ways in which comparing is used across the curriculum: in psychology, biology, anthropology, neuroscience, and other fields. In addition to covering various disciplines, we offer various types of writing: autobiography, fiction, poetry, and presentations of research, both for academic and more general audiences. We begin with an Opening Problem that immediately involves you with using — and thinking about — comparing. We then present examples of writers drafting papers on academic topics that involve the strategy (Working Examples, p. 431), followed by a piece showing how a professional writer uses comparing to serve a particular purpose (A Professional Application, p. 444). Next comes a series of cross-curricular assignments intended to deepen and enrich your investigation of the strategy's possibilities and limitations (p. 447).

Woven throughout the first part of this chapter (in the Opening Problem; in the Professional Application; and in the Science Assignment, p. 482) are readings about primate research, a topic that lends itself especially well to the application and investigation of comparing. If this topic interests you and you want to spend more time with it, consider working with Readings: Methods of Inquiry in Primate Research in the second part of this chapter. All of those readings invite basic comparative questions about primate research — questions about language, about social behavior, about medical and evolutionary biology, and about methods of scientific investigation.

Opening Problem: Comparing Two Primatologists

Here is a problem that will involve you in comparing. Read the following two passages from articles by primatologists Francine Patterson and Dian Fossey. Both articles appeared in *National Geographic.* Patterson is a psychologist who studies gorillas — or, more precisely, studies the linguistic capacities of a particular gorilla, Koko, to whom she began to teach American Sign Language in the early 1970s. This report on her work was published in 1978. Dian Fossey became famous studying and protecting African mountain gorillas; her fame grew after her murder and a subsequent movie about her life (*Gorillas in the Mist,* 1988). This early article about her work appeared in 1971.

In a short essay, one that can be rough and experimental, try developing a comparison between these two scientists or their work. Order your comparison in any way that makes sense to you. As you proceed, reflect on the decisions you make. What are those decisions? What happens in writing comparatively?

Here are some cues to help you get going:

- Try to establish a solid basis for comparison. Yes, both writers are women scientists writing about gorillas. What else?
- Can you generalize about how the two scientists approach their research? How do they see their work in relation to the work of others?
- How do the projects of the two scientists differ? How do their working lives? Their environments? Their involvement with their subjects?
- Will you be stressing similarities or differences? Are your comparisons helping you to discover an argument? Do you see an overriding purpose emerging for your essay?

FRANCINE PATTERSON:
CONVERSATIONS WITH A GORILLA

Koko is a seven-year-old "talking" gorilla. She is the focus of my career as a developmental psychologist, and also has become a dear friend.

Through mastery of sign language — the familiar hand speech of the deaf — Koko has made us, her human companions, aware not only that her breed is bright, but also that it shares sensitivities commonly held to be the prerogative of people.

Take Koko's touching empathy toward fellow animals. Seeing a horse with a bit in its mouth, she signed, "Horse sad." When asked why the horse was sad, she signed, "Teeth." Shown a photo of the famous albino gorilla Snowflake struggling against having a bath, Koko, who also hates baths, signed, "Me cry there," while pointing at the picture.

But Koko responds to more complicated motivations too. She loves an argument — and is not averse to trading insults.

At 6:00 on a spring evening last year, I went to the trailer where Koko lives to put her to bed. I was greeted by Cathy Ransom, one of my assistants, who told me that she and Koko had been arguing.

Lest I be alarmed at the thought of an altercation between this slight young woman, who is deaf, and a robust six-year-old female gorilla, Cathy laughingly pointed to the notebook in which Koko's utterances in sign language are logged. The dispute began when Koko was shown a poster of herself that had been used during a fund-raising benefit. Manipulating hands and fingers, Cathy had asked Koko, "What's this?"

"Gorilla," signed Koko.

"Who gorilla?" asked Cathy.

"Bird," responded a bratty Koko, and things went downhill from there.

"You bird?" asked Cathy.

"You," countered Koko.

"Not me, you are bird," rejoined Cathy, mindful that "bird" can be an insult in Koko's lexicon.

"Me gorilla," asserted Koko.

"Who bird?" asked Cathy.

"You nut," replied Koko, resorting to another of her insults. (For Koko, "bird" and "nut" switch from descriptive to pejorative terms by changing the position in which the sign is made.)

"Why me nut?" asked Cathy.

"Nut, nut," signed Koko.

"You nut, not me," Cathy replied.

Finally Koko gave up. Plaintively she signed, "Damn me good," and walked away signing, "Bad."

"When She Is Good . . ." I fully agree with Koko, if she meant that she is good even in a bad situation. I've come to cherish her lies, relish her arguments, and look forward to her insults. While these behaviors demonstrate occasional lapses from sweetness, they also provide reassuring benchmarks in the formal and controlled scientific testing that has monitored Koko's progress since I began to teach her American Sign Language in July 1972.

Of course such subjective behavior as lying is difficult to prove empirically, but when Koko uses language to make a point, to joke, to express her displeasure, or to lie her way out of a jam, then she is exploiting language the way we do as human beings. Certainly that is linguistic, though perhaps not moral, progress.

What makes all this awesome — even for me, after six years of witnessing such incidents — is that Koko, by all accepted concepts of animal and human nature, should not be able to do any of this. Traditionally, such behavior has been considered uniquely human; yet here is a language-using gorilla. (Two years ago she was joined by another of her species, a young male named Michael, who is the subject of similar study and training.)

Enrolling at Stanford in 1970 as a graduate student, I chose nonhuman primates rather than children for my research. In 1971, R. Allen and Beatrix Gardner came to speak. They were by then well-known for their success — it was an area where others had failed — in two-way communication with Washoe, a female chimpanzee.

The Gardners' breakthrough was to perceive that the chimp's difficulty in acquiring language might not be stupidity, but rather an inability to control lips and tongue. So they decided to try to teach Washoe American Sign Language — Ameslan for short — used by an estimated 200,000 deaf Americans. The language consists of gestures, each of which signifies a word or idea.

Washoe endorsed the Gardners' choice by learning thirty-four signs during the first twenty-two months. This was more than eight times the number of spoken words that the chimpanzee Viki, the subject of Keith and Cathy Hayes's six-year effort, learned to utter. After four years of Project Washoe, by 1970, Washoe had acquired 132 signs, and she used these signs in combinations similar to those employed by children during the first stages of learning to talk.

Hearing the Gardners tell their tale persuaded me that attempting to teach chimp sign language would be to pursue the ultimate question with the ultimate animal. At that time I held no brief for gorillas.

Scientist Meets "Fireworks-Child." My initial preoccupation with chimps changed suddenly on the day I accompanied Dr. Karl Pribram, at that time my research adviser, to the San Francisco Zoo to talk with Ronald Reuther, then the director, about using a computer to try to communicate with the zoo's adult gorillas. We walked over to the gorilla grotto.

While Dr. Pribram and the director chatted, my eyes were drawn to a tiny infant clinging tenaciously to her mother. The infant was named Hanabi-Ko, Japanese for Fireworks-Child (she was born on the Fourth of July), but she was nicknamed Koko. Brashly I asked the director if I might try to teach Koko sign language. He said no, and quite rightly, too. Koko was only three months old, and Mr. Reuther did not want to separate her from her mother. Undaunted, I began to learn Ameslan, confident that one day I would have the chance to use it.

Nine months later, on a visit to the zoo, I ran into Martin E. Dias, an ebullient and sympathetic keeper. I asked about Koko. It seemed that Koko's mother had not been producing sufficient milk. As if this were not enough, the gorilla group had been afflicted with an outbreak of dysentery.

Suffering from malnutrition and dehydration, Koko had lost most of her hair, and her tiny body, racked with diarrhea, had become emaciated.

But, moved to the Children's Zoo, Koko had recovered. Perhaps, Marty suggested, the director might now look favorably upon my request to work with and care for Koko. Mr. Reuther immediately acceded. I began to get to know Koko the next day. That was in July 1972.

Gorillas are tragically misunderstood animals. In fact exceedingly shy, placid, and unaggressive, they are conceived to be ferocious, slavering man killers. In a recent poll of British schoolchildren, gorillas ranked with rats, snakes, and spiders among the most hated animals.

On our first meeting, Koko did nothing to advance the cause of gorilla public relations. Quickly sizing me up, the tiny twenty-pound gorilla bit me on the leg. But I was undeterred. People often ask if I am worried about dealing with Koko when she reaches full growth, perhaps 250 pounds. The answer is no, though at 130 pounds she already outweighs me and is astonishingly strong. While many captive chimpanzees become difficult to work with as they mature, gorillas seem to be of quite a different temperament.

Soon after starting work with Koko, I met Carroll Soo-Hoo, the man who had donated Koko's mother to the San Francisco Zoo. Mr. Soo-Hoo brought out photos of himself, a slight man, romping with three 200-pound gorillas. That quelled whatever doubts I may have had about the danger of working with these immensely strong animals. . . .

Are Apes Capable of Language? My colleagues were not very sanguine about teaching Koko sign language. Some questioned the gorilla's dexterity as compared with the chimpanzee's. Others were skeptical about the animal's intellect.

In 1959 Hilda Knobloch and Benjamin Pasamanick had reported: "There is little question that the chimpanzee is capable of conceptualization and abstraction that is beyond the abilities of the gorilla."

My experience has been totally at odds with this assumption. While Koko certainly has been contrary at times, I believe that such brattiness may indicate intelligence rather than its absence.

In 1929 the great primatologists Robert and Ada Yerkes wrote: "It is entirely possible that the gorilla, while being distinctly inferior to the chimpanzee in ability to use and fashion implements and to operate mechanisms, is superior to it in certain other modes of behavioral adaptation and may indeed possess a higher order of intelligence than any other existing anthropoid ape." Now, fifty years later, Koko is bolstering evidence of the gorilla's intellectual primacy.

Initially my work with Koko used many of the techniques of Project Washoe. Experts in the new field of language development in humans — part of the discipline called psycholinguistics — found little agreement about what exactly language was, or when a child could be said to have it. Linguists, however, were virtually unanimous that Washoe did not have language. But by the time I began to publish data on Koko, many early critics of the Gardners had either recanted or softened their criticisms, in part because of the mass of fresh evidence on the language capacities of apes.

At the same time as Project Washoe, Ann and David Premack established two-way communication with Sarah, a female chimpanzee. Sarah spoke and was spoken to through plastic symbols. The Gardners and Premacks were followed by Duane Rumbaugh, who installed yet another female chimp, Lana, at a computer console at the Yerkes Regional Primate Research Center in Atlanta. Lana gradually learned to communicate by typing out statements on an arbitrarily encoded keyboard. The computer was programmed to reject grammatically improper sentences.

The weight of all these experiments helped erode the doubts that an ape could be capable of language. Certainly, the pioneering work of the Gardners, the Premacks, and Dr. Rumbaugh has richly benefited me: I have been able directly to employ methods they discovered by trial and error, and have not had to refight the battle of credibility.

Once I had established that Koko performed at least as well as Washoe — learning the signs for "drink" and "more" within the project's first few weeks — I could probe new areas of the gorilla's potential for language and thought.

DIAN FOSSEY:
MORE YEARS WITH MOUNTAIN GORILLAS

Two black hairy arms circled the tree trunk. A moment later a furry head appeared. Bright eyes peered at me through a lattice of ferns.

I occupied a branch of another tree, slightly downhill from the gorilla who stared at me. We were both in a forest on Mount Visoke in Rwanda, where I have been studying gorillas in the wild.

The face was familiar, not only by its features but by its impish expression; it belonged to Peanuts, one of my favorite gorillas. He is a member of one of the groups I have studied closely, and that have grown used to my presence among them.

Peanuts was wearing an expression I think of as "fun and games"; I have learned to recognize it in gorillas when they want to prolong a contact with me. Slowly, I left the tree and got down into the foliage to make feeding noises to reassure him.

The moments that followed are among the most memorable of my life. They were particularly important to me because this was, in a sense, a farewell visit to the mountain slope. I was shortly to leave Africa for a prolonged stay in Cambridge, England, where I would begin working on a doctoral thesis and other technical reports on gorilla behavior.

Peanuts left his tree for a bit of strutting before he began his approach in my direction. He is a showman. He beat his chest; he threw leaves into the air; he swaggered and slapped the foliage around him, and then suddenly he was at my side. His expression indicated that he had entertained me — now it was my turn. He sat down to watch my "feeding" but didn't seem particularly impressed, so I changed activities; I scratched my scalp noisily to make a sound familiar to gorillas, who do a great deal of scratching.

Almost immediately Peanuts began to scratch. It was not clear who was aping whom. Then I lay back in the foliage to appear as harmless as possible, and slowly extended my hand. I held it palm up at first, as the palms of an ape and a human are more similar than the backs of the hand. When I felt that he recognized this "object," I slowly turned my hand over and let it rest on the foliage.

Peanuts seemed to ponder accepting my hand, a familiar yet strange object extended to him. Finally he came a step closer and, extending his own hand, gently touched his fingers to mine. To the best of my knowledge this is the first time a wild gorilla has ever come so close to "holding hands" with a human being.

Peanuts sat down and looked at my hand for a moment longer. He stood and gave vent to his excitement by a whirling chest beat, then went off to rejoin his group, nonchalantly feeding some eighty feet uphill. I expressed my own happy excitement by crying. This was the most wonderful going-away present I could have had.

Human Pressures Shrink Gorilla's Domain. My farewell handshake with Peanuts came after more than three years of study of the mountain gorilla (*Gorilla gorilla beringei*), largest of the great apes. The animal is already classified by international conservation authorities as "rare." Under constant pressure from man — hunter and farmer — it is being driven into ever-smaller, more-remote mountain areas. Extinction is a real threat.

My studies are conducted from a camp in Rwanda's Parc des Volcans, on the saddle between Mount Visoke and Mount Karisimbi, two of the eight volcanoes in the Virunga range. Camp, which consists of several sheet-metal cabins, stands at 10,000 feet; a rough jeep road starts up the mountain, but the last 2,000 feet must be climbed on foot, a winding, three-mile hike. In addition to the gorillas, local fauna includes duikers and buffalo, and elephants frequently visit a creek in front of my cabin. The nearest store is nineteen miles away.

My work began in 1967 with help from Dr. Louis S. B. Leakey and aid from the Wilkie Brothers Foundation. Shortly thereafter the project gained the support of the National Geographic Society, which has continued to sponsor my research. A report appeared in the *Geographic* of January 1970. Much has happened since, but my job is far from finished.

There had been scientific observations of wild mountain gorillas in the past, notably a research project by Dr. George B. Schaller in 1959–60, a classic in its field. My objective was to take up where these had left off, to form more intimate contacts with gorilla groups and individuals, to observe from close up their behavior, their interactions — and to do this in such a way that my own presence did not affect that behavior. To accomplish this I decided, in a word, to act like a gorilla.

One of the first things I learned about my subjects was that despite their great bulk — 400 pounds or more — and the many tales of ferocious attacks on people, they are in fact among the gentlest of animals, and the shiest. Like most wild creatures they will try to protect themselves when attacked, and to guard their young. But in some 3,000 hours of contact I encountered only a few minutes of aggressive behavior. These incidents were generally initiated by protective adults when their young approached me too closely. In all instances the "charges" proved to be bluff.

A good example of their gentleness and sense of mischief occurred one day when Bravado, a young male, tried to climb past me down a tree trunk where I had settled myself on a limb to observe and take some pictures. Bravado made his way up easily enough, brushing past me as if I were not there. But on the way down he apparently decided I was in the way and should move. Once his head filled my viewfinder, I decided it was time to turn my back to him. Just as I got a good hold on the tree, I felt two hands on my shoulders, pushing down.

I had often seen gorillas do this to one another when they wanted the right-of-way on a narrow trunk. Not wanting to risk a fall, I refused to budge. After another moment of gentle pressure — only a fraction of the mighty shove he could have given me — Bravado moved back. He beat his chest, then jumped out onto a side limb. He hung there by two arms, bouncing deliberately, knowing that his weight would break the branch and thus provide a satisfactorily loud snapping noise. He succeeded; the branch broke with a crash and Bravado landed eight feet below, where he calmly began feeding.

Learning to Sound Like a Gorilla. In my years of study I have watched nine groups of gorillas, but for close-up contacts have concentrated on four. The groups vary in size from five to nineteen members; the average is thirteen. In my field notes I identify groups by numbers, and individuals by names I have chosen, usually trying to match names to the personalities of the animals.

Each group is ruled with unquestioned authority by a dominant male — a silverback, so-called because with age a gorilla's dorsal hair turns silvery gray. Below him may be one or more subordinate silverbacks, then the younger mature males — blackbacks — the females, juveniles, and infants.

During my observations, I have learned much about the animals' feeding habits, their range and movements, their bickering and play. I have watched them build day nests to rest in and night nests to sleep in — crude beds of boughs, leaves, moss, or even loose dirt — sometimes in trees but generally on the ground.

Early in my study I decided that one of the best ways to persuade gorillas to accept my presence was to imitate the sounds they make. In this I had a stroke of luck — though the event itself was most unfortunate. Two young gorillas, captured for a European zoo, had been so mishandled that they were near death, and I volunteered to nurse them back to health. While I cared for them I learned much about gorilla vocalizations.

Popular literature generally describes roars, screams, and *"wraaghs"* as the main components of gorilla vocabulary. I was to learn there is a lot more to the subject than that.

From my two charges, for instance, I learned an infant's version of a sound that I later came to call the "belch vocalization." Their rendition, *"naoom, naoom, naoom,"* was usually associated with eating, and I have since heard this sound many times among wild groups. It does not carry far, and has often been mistaken for a stomach rumble. But in fact it is a distinctive type of gorilla communication, exchanged in situations of maximum contentment.

Typically, one animal expresses his feeling of well-being by giving a belch vocalization. This brings a chain of similar responses from nearby animals. On occasion I have been able to crawl undetected into the midst of a contentedly feeding group and begin a belch vocalization series of my own and have it answered by animals around me.

The belch vocalization is the most common form of intragroup communication. Others include what I call "pig grunts" and "hoot barks." The pig grunt is a harsh staccato sound used in disciplinary situations, as when a silverback settles a squabble or orders his group to move on. Females also use it, in a softer tone, to control their infants.

The hoot bark is more often heard when an animal is curious or alarmed. When given by the dominant silverback, it usually attracts the immediate attention of the group.

Gorilla vocalization has been a particular interest of mine. I have spent many hours recording these sounds, and the tapes have now been taken to Cambridge University for further study. But my prime interest is still the original one: to use the sounds to gain acceptance by the gorillas, and so to study behavior and ranges.

Research Can Help Save Big Apes. Why do gorillas go where they do? Do their routes remain stable or do they vary? How many still survive? What is their present territory? I have compelling reasons for wanting to know. If we are to save the animals from extinction, we must find answers to these vital questions. We must learn the areas of known population concentration before we can provide protection — and thus my interest in both an accurate census of gorilla numbers and a study of gorilla ranges.

Thinking about Thinking

- As you think comparatively about the two pieces, do you find yourself noting miscellaneous similarities and differences, or have you seized upon some central idea that helps you to organize those similarities and differences? If you've found a central idea, what has been gained by focusing on it?
- Having been asked to read the two pieces comparatively, did you find that reading the second one became a more complicated experience than reading the first? Would it have been possible to read the second piece without bringing along something from the first? Did you find yourself reading the second piece as a commentary upon the first? In what ways do our inclinations for comparison shape our reading experience?
- If you go on to work with the topic of primate research woven through this chapter, you will be asked to think about methods of inquiry. In reading comparatively, do you find yourself contrasting the kinds of questions the two scientists ask? What about the means by which they approach their questions? What kinds of methods or techniques do they use to gather their data? What assumptions about primates, about humans, about research seem to underlie what they do?

Comparisons surround us. We naturally compare people, objects, experiences, and circumstances. We compare ourselves with others, compare present situations with past ones, compare our goals with our accomplishments. When confronted with something new, we try to see it in relation to what we already know. We are forever trying to get our bearings by comparing one thing with something else.

Comparisons are so fundamental to academic thinking that entire branches of study bear the word in their titles: comparative literature, comparative religion, comparative anatomy. Even where not so prominently announced, comparison can be a course's central method — the political science course that compares how governments work or the anthropology course that sets out a complex web of comparisons to study which behavior is fundamental to all humans and which varies from culture to culture.

Comparisons also serve as ways to present class material. A history lecture might subdivide the American colonies into three groups and then compare their social and economic characteristics. A philosophy course might begin by setting up Plato and Aristotle as the founders of two distinct philosophical traditions, with the teacher returning to fill in or modify the comparisons as later philosophers are introduced. You'll also notice that many of the chapters and articles you will read in college are organized as comparisons, pieces with titles like "Genetic Engineering: Two Schools of Thought" or "Sea Fiction: A Comparative Study of Jack London and Joseph Conrad."

College teachers use comparison not only to present information but also to elicit it. The comparison/contrast question is one of the standbys of essay examinations: "Compare and contrast the economic theories of Karl Marx and Adam

Smith." "Compare the attitudes toward civil disobedience of Henry David Thoreau and George Wallace." "Contrast the function of pores in humans and stomata in plants." At their best, such questions do not elicit a simple recitation of a comparison already worked out by the instructor; rather, they call up two sets of material that you've learned, and they force you, through comparison, to restructure and reevaluate that material.

The comparison/contrast question is often extended to papers you are asked to write outside of class. In an art history course you might be asked to compare an Egyptian funerary figure with an early Greek statue. In a sociology class you might be asked to write an essay comparing the social impact of state and federal welfare programs. In a cultural geography class you might be asked to assess the comparative role played by climate in the national economies of Venezuela and Argentina. Topics like these usually contain some germ of comparison that has attracted a teacher toward the topic in the first place; once you've inferred or discovered that initial basis of comparison, you have taken your first strong step toward structuring an effective essay. For example, just the knowledge that Francine Patterson and Dian Fossey are both primatologists making claims about gorilla behavior can help you begin to compare their observations.

So far we've been speaking of extensive comparisons, comparisons used to structure whole disciplines, courses, books, lectures, articles, or essays. But this ignores their most frequent and flexible use. They are helpful along the way, in service of some larger purpose. Here is physicist Robert Jastrow turning to a startling comparison — a metaphor — to help us understand what we see when we look at the Milky Way.

> The Galaxy is flattened by its rotating motion into the shape of a disk, whose thickness is roughly one-fiftieth of its diameter. Most of the stars in the Galaxy are in this disk, although some are located outside it. A relatively small, spherical cluster of stars, called the nucleus of the Galaxy, bulges out of the disk at the center. The entire structure resembles a double sombrero with the galactic nucleus as the crown and the disk as the brim. The sun is located in the brim of the sombrero about three-fifths of the way out from the center to the edge. When we look into the sky in the direction of the disk we see so many stars that they are not visible as separate points of light, but blend together into a luminous band stretching across the sky.
>
> — Robert Jastrow, *Red Giants and White Dwarfs*

Comparisons like these provide momentary stopping points, fresh angles of vision, opportunities for clarification: We understand our position in our galaxy better when we can see the galaxy as a sombrero with ourselves on the brim. To work well, however, comparisons need not work so spectacularly. Often they will modestly occupy only a single sentence, or even flash past us in the midst of sentences. Here is a brief quotation from Helena Curtis's textbook *Biology:*

> A fruit is the mature, ripened ovary of an angiosperm and contains the seeds. A great variety of fruits, adapted for many different dispersal mechanisms, have

> evolved in the course of angiosperm history. In most cases, the chief requirement is that the seed be transported some distance from the parent plant, where it is more likely to find open ground and sunlight. Many fruits, like flowers, evolved as a payment to an animal visitor for transportation services.

What is being compared to what in this passage? What new perspective does the comparison provide?

Writers often draw on comparisons in coordination with other writing strategies. Chapter 1 has already stressed how comparisons can help you define. In an economics course you get a surer sense of *fixed supply* when you compare it with *elastic supply.* Similarly, comparing often works in coordination with summarizing: In a political science essay you might find yourself summarizing two writers' views on the conflicts between Israelis and Palestinians in order to compare them. For a biology essay on cell metabolism that is organized sequentially, you might find yourself shaping your account with the familiar comparison of a developing cell and a busy factory. And comparison will play an important role in analysis, for when you analyze you are always asking yourself how well something particular corresponds to something general: Does the short story you've been assigned to write about go along with your English teacher's views about "Hemingway's rigid ideal of masculinity"?

Comparing is perhaps most intimately connected with classifying. In fact, we can say that comparison depends on classification. We're not always aware of the connection, however, because in many academic situations someone else has done the classifying in advance, leaving only the comparing for us. When you are presented with two illustrations, or case studies, or sets of statistics, the instructor presenting them has usually chosen them on the basis of some category they share. Sometimes that basis is obvious, and sometimes it needs to be coaxed out before you can proceed. You'll quickly recognize how to compare two articles on pneumonia or two experts' attitudes on diplomatic relations with China. But you'll have to do some harder searching if you're asked to compare a newspaper account of a press conference with a chapter from a sociology textbook.

It's important to recognize that some things cannot be compared effectively because they cannot be brought into categorical alignment. It's hard to compare two wildly different things — a mushroom, say, and a porcupine. And some comparisons seem logically impossible to make. For instance, an object like a cabinet cannot be compared with a process such as photosynthesis. Why is this so? Take a few moments and invent some pairings of terms that, you feel, cannot be compared. Be ready to explain why not. Are you sure?

Since most things in the universe do have *some* similarity, most things can be brought into some alignment for comparison. The question is always whether the act of comparing helps us understand something more clearly or look at it more freshly. The old saw "You can't compare apples and oranges" may hold for multiplication problems, but it doesn't hold up to inquisitive thinking: If you saw the need, you could compare apples and oranges for citric content, nutritional value, or agricultural yield; you could even compare them as aesthetic objects or as cultural symbols. What matters is the use to which the comparison is put.

Some potential comparisons are unlikely to be of interest if their basis is too broad. The porcupine and the mushroom could, after all, be compared as living things. But what would be the point of the comparison? Would we be likely to learn anything more about either porcupines or mushrooms? If we were to use something we knew about biological classification to help us refine the category further — they're both examples of organisms composed of eukaryotic cells (they are more like each other than they are like bacteria) — we wouldn't be much further along. However, if we refined our perception of the categories in a different way — recognizing, for example, that both organisms have evolved striking mechanisms for self-protection — we'd be on richer ground. We might be able to develop an effective comparison of porcupines and mushrooms as organisms capable of blending into their environmental backgrounds. Or, if we were to restrict the mushroom example to a poisonous type, we could look at the ways that the two organisms have developed adaptive strategies for warding off predators — namely, quills and toxins. Only by prodding a potential comparison inquisitively do we discover what it can yield.

Working Examples

A Working Example from the History of Science

Most comparisons move from similarities toward differences, but sometimes they move in the opposite direction. When the things you are comparing seem startlingly different, your main job often will be to uncover hidden correspondences, basic similarities that don't at first meet the eye. Imagine that your biology instructor has asked you to consider how a human blood cell resembles an office building. At first you may be aware only of differences: The building is vast, the cell microscopic; the building rectangular and vertical, the cell spherical; the building composed of synthetic materials, the cell organic molecules; the building has been built from architectural plans by construction crews, the cell reproduces itself by passing on DNA, its genetic material.

Enumerating these differences may only strengthen the impression that there is no comparison to be made. But consider the ingenious use made of the comparison by Horace F. Judson, a historian of science. Judson describes the state of biological knowledge before the discovery of the genetic importance of DNA. Most molecular biologists felt that a key role must be played by proteins since proteins were present in tremendous variety, carrying on an extraordinary number of cellular functions. Proteins seem as omnipresent in the cell, Judson tells us, as metal in a high-rise under construction:

> Biologists looking into cells were like spectators at a building site, peering through a crack in the board fence at the hole in the ground where a new office tower is going up: so much to see, cranes, shovels . . . scaffolding, pneumatic drills, electric cables, riveters, hoists raising rafts of pipe, a huge steel beam swinging precariously overhead — but yes, everything made of metal, even the folding table in the hut over there with a roll of blue paper spread out on it.
>
> — Horace F. Judson, *The Eighth Day of Creation*

In the same way that a building site appears to an outside observer to consist of metal beams and cables, most of what goes on inside a cell seems, at first glance, to involve proteins. But the key to all the activity is something that initially appears secondary, of minor interest: the strands of nucleic acid at the center of the cell and the roll of blue paper at the construction site. Both are blueprints, the sets of instructions without which none of the other construction could occur.

Comparisons like the one between the cell and the skyscraper are called metaphors when they occur in a single flash, like the comparison we quoted earlier likening the shape of our galaxy to that of a sombrero. When they can be developed in more detail, with several back-and-forth correspondences, they are called analogies. Analogies at their best make something difficult more understandable; metaphors at their best often make something familiar seem refreshingly strange. The emphasis in an analogy is on a set of structural similarities. It would be difficult to find other ways in which the Milky Way resembles a sombrero, but the comparison between a cell and a building, as we've seen, can be developed in some detail:

```
microbiologists . . . spectators
proteins . . . metals
DNA . . . blueprints
microscope . . . crack in the fence
```

Often, we discover that good analogies can be extended even further. If we wanted to extend Judson's analogy, for example, we could compare an office building's headquarters with the cell's nucleus, its air conditioning with the cell's homeostatic mechanisms, its position among other buildings on the street with the position of the cell in relation to other cells in the bloodstream. When you've tapped as rich an analogy as this one, extending it can be fun. But be careful. At some point such analogies may seem only to be showing off; don't lose sight of their clarifying purpose (unless your purpose *is* to show off, as sometimes it may be). Also remember that any comparison has limitations, and it's usually good to show that you're aware of these limitations: Add all the high-rises in North America and you've got only a fraction of the cells in one person's bloodstream; blueprints, unlike DNA, do not reproduce more blueprints; and so on.

A Working Example from American History

The later assignments in this chapter invite some fairly detailed comparisons. As a way of getting your bearings with these potentially complex comparisons, you may want to try some preliminary device, such as a two-column chart arranged like so:

```
                                          A            B

Similarities   1.
               2.
               3.
               etc.
Differences    1.
               2.
               3.
               etc.
```

Or you might make it even simpler by using the two columns to line up your material without committing yourself to where similarities break off into differences or differences blur into similarities. Don't make filling in such a chart an end in itself. Just use it until you feel enough in control of the elements of the comparison that you can begin to write about them.

As an example of working up such a comparison, let's try a variation on an assignment traditionally given in American history classes: the comparison between Alexander Hamilton and Thomas Jefferson. Often this task is presented in a general form, such as "Compare the economic policies of Jefferson and Hamilton." As we noted earlier, such questions are sometimes thinly disguised requests for giving back an already well-organized lecture; but in other situations, the question forces you to synthesize or even rethink what you've learned.

To complicate the task, we ask you to consider two texts, one a set of selections from a biography of Hamilton and the other a set from a book about Jefferson. To keep the task from getting even more complicated, however, we've chosen books by the same scholar. John Chester Miller wrote his biography of Hamilton, *Alexander Hamilton: Portrait in Paradox,* in 1959. In 1977 he wrote *The Wolf by the Ears: Thomas Jefferson and Slavery.* As you read the following excerpts, try taking notes in the rough two-column form we just suggested. As you jot down your notes for the first piece (Miller's more recent book, on Jefferson) which appears below, include not only points where you already sense a potential comparison but points that seem important in their own right. Leave yourself plenty of space for observations that may occur to you later.

JEFFERSON

Late in 1789, after witnessing the opening scenes of the French Revolution, Jefferson returned to Virginia, and in the spring of 1790 he went to New York to assume the post of secretary of state in the cabinet of President Washington. He brought with him to the temporary capital of the United States a retinue of household servants, footmen, and a coachman. Republican simplicity as practiced by Jefferson and other Southerners who came North to serve in Congress or the cabinet never required the renunciation of the services of slaves; and, in Jefferson's case, it did not require the sacrifice of fine furniture, French cooking, exquisite wines, horses, and carriages. On the strength of his appearance — he sported the latest fashions of the French *haut monde* — one would hardly have supposed that a great American democrat had arrived in town or, unless one had read the *Notes on Virginia,* that Jefferson felt the slightest repugnance to slavery. The truth is that he had grown up with slavery and his "people" were essential to his comfort and well being.

Amply as his physical comforts were ministered to, Jefferson found himself involved in some very unsettling diplomatic exchanges with George Hammond, the British minister to the United States who arrived in Philadelphia in 1791 as the first official representative sent by His Britannic Majesty to his former subjects in America. In his negotiations with Hammond, Jefferson distinguished himself as a champion of peculiarly Virginia interests and as a defender of the rights of property, especially that species of property represented by black slaves. In the first clearly defined postrevolutionary confrontation between the rights of black man and the rights of property, Jefferson aligned himself decisively on the side of property. His insistence that slaves be treated as property attributed significantly toward bringing Great Britain and the United States to an impasse from which war seemed the probable outcome.

The treaty of peace of 1783, which brought an end to the war between the United States and Great Britain and established the independence of the United States (a preliminary treaty had been agreed upon as early as November 1782) was ratified by the Continental Congress in January 1784. Among other provisions, the definitive treaty prohibited the British army, when it evacuated the United States, from carrying away "Negroes or other property" belonging to American citizens; it required the United States to desist from interposing any obstacles to the collection of debts owed by Americans to British citizens; and it committed the British to surrender the Northwest Posts (which had been ceded by the treaty of peace) "with all convenient speed" to the United States. In the negotiations conducted by Jefferson with George Hammond in 1791–1793, these three articles were of paramount importance. . . .

Had Jefferson's paramount objective been to gain possession of the Northwest Posts and to make a commercial treaty with Great Britain opening the British West Indies to American ships, he would hardly have adopted the hectoring, abrasive, and unconciliatory tone he used with Hammond. It served no constructive purpose to engage in recriminations, and the question of which nation was guilty of the first infringement of the treaty inevitably degenerated into a mere exercise in mutual vituperation. Manifestly, Jefferson did not give the highest priority to effecting a settlement with Great Britain; he was far more intent upon establishing closer commercial relations with France than with Great Britain, and he was more concerned with vindicating the reputation of the United States than in promoting commercial intercourse with the former mother country — intercourse that he feared might lead to military alliance between the two countries. He still referred to Great Britain as "the enemy," and he had by no means forgotten or forgiven the slights and humiliations he had endured at the hands of high British officials in London in the spring of 1786. Great Britain's governing principles, he had long since decided, were "Conquest, Colonization, Commerce, and Monopoly of the Ocean." Nor could he be persuaded that a nation pursuing such objectives seriously intended to surrender the Northwest Posts or to make a commercial treaty with the United States.

While these negotiations were in progress — if that is the right word to describe this exchange of tirades and outcries of outraged virtue on the part of both men — Alexander Hamilton, as secretary of the treasury, was doing his utmost to undermine Jefferson's position. As early as 1783, Hamilton had taken the position that the United States had no right to demand the return of the slaves. Having been emancipated by British military order, they became, he said, free men, and no compact, however solemn, made between the United States and Great Britain, could alter their status. Under these circumstances, for the United States to demand the surrender of these slaves was, in Hamilton's opinion, "as *odious* and *immoral* a thing as can be conceived." Moreover, Hamilton strongly dissented from Jefferson's view that raising legal obstacles to the collection of debts was a legitimate reprisal for prior British infractions of the treaty. "The debts of private individuals are in no case a proper object of reprisals," he declared; in international law, debts were not subject to confiscation, and public injuries could not discharge private obligations.

With convictions regarding the way American foreign policy ought to be conducted quite as strong as but completely opposite to Jefferson's governing principles, Hamilton took it upon himself to tell Hammond that the American secretary of state was speaking for himself, not for the government of the United States. Without consulting the president, he tried to dissociate Washington and the cabinet from Jefferson's "intemperate violence" and Anglophobia. Jefferson and Madison, he told Hammond, were the victims of "a womanish attachment to France and a womanish resentment against Great Britain.". . .

In his negotiations with George Hammond, Jefferson failed to achieve any of his objectives: The British refused to admit that they were guilty of the first breach of the treaty; they declined to compensate the slaveowners whose "property" they had carried away; and they retained possession of the Northwest Posts. To his government, Hammond described Jefferson as a perfect Frenchman, imbued with all the Frenchman's hatred of "perfidious Albion." This report of Jefferson's Anglophobism had the untoward effect of stiffening the determination of the British government to retain possession of the Northwest Posts. In February 1794, Lord Grenville, the British foreign secretary, declared that because of the refusal of the United States to honor the peace treaty over a period of nine years, Great Britain no longer considered itself obliged to abide by it. Thus, after three years of desultory negotiations, Anglo-American relations were worse than when Jefferson had assumed the office of secretary of state. . . .

During his term of office as secretary of state, and, indeed, during the entire decade of the 1790s, Jefferson was preoccupied with the struggle against Hamiltonian finance and the "monarchism" which seemed to him certain to follow in its train. By the summer of 1790, after a few months' residence in New York, he became convinced that a conspiracy against republicanism, no less formidable than the conspiracy against freedom that Americans had encountered and overcome in the British Empire, existed among highly placed officials in the new federal government and that President Washington was in danger of becoming an unsuspecting abettor of the plot.

In the course of his career, Jefferson was compelled to respond to a succession of threats to freedom and republicanism which demanded his undivided attention. At no time did he permit slavery to take precedence over what he regarded as more immediate threats to the ideals and institutions he cherished. Jefferson viewed the American scene not merely as a philosopher-statesman but, more importantly, as a political activist fighting on many fronts against a legion of enemies hostile to republicanism. Conscious of being beset by dangers on every hand, he was never able to concentrate his attention upon slavery as the paramount, all-encompassing evil of the day.

For this reason, Jefferson appeared during the 1790s to be far more eager to combat Hamiltonian finance and to liquidate the national debt than to eradicate slavery. Since he considered the assumption of state debts (to which he had been persuaded to assent) and the perpetuation of the national debt to be the prime engines of the system of corruption and centralization Hamilton was trying to foist upon the country, Jefferson naturally gave priority to his continuing struggle with the secretary of the treasury. If Hamiltonianism triumphed, the question of slavery would become academic: Farmers and planters, Jefferson predicted, would then be reduced to a more cruel and certainly more exploitative form of slavery to Northern businessmen, bankers, and speculators than the relatively humane servitude experienced by Southern slaves. So fearful was he that these "conspirators against human happiness" would overthrow the republic that in the 1790s he demanded that all holders of government securities and bank stock be prohibited by federal law from sitting in Congress. Since he did not propose a similar morals test for slaveowners, many of whom were members of Congress, Jefferson put himself in the extraordinary position of holding that the ownership of human beings was less reprehensible than the ownership of stocks and bonds.

— John Chester Miller, *The Wolf by the Ears: Thomas Jefferson and Slavery*

Here now are some excerpts from Miller's earlier book on Hamilton. After you've read this second set of passages and taken some notes toward a comparison, try using those notes to develop a plan for an essay. Can you find several contrasts that seem particularly strong or worth noticing? Do you see some way of coordinating these points with one another? Can you think of a controlling idea to keep an essay unified? Take a crack at a plan as soon as you've read this second selection.

HAMILTON

When Hamilton came to the Treasury, the foreign debt of the United States was about $10 million, plus $1,600,000 in arrears of interest. The domestic debt Hamilton estimated to be slightly over $27 million, not including $13 million in accrued interest. The total debt therefore stood at slightly over $50 million. But there was no certainty in these figures: how much debt in the form of certificates had been contracted by the various agencies of the government — the commissary and quartermaster accounts were especially confused — was known, as one congressman observed, only to the Supreme Being. Although commissioners had been appointed by the Continental Congress to settle the accounts of individuals holding claims against the government, their work had not been completed. Nor had the claims of the states against the general government been ascertained: Here was a terra incognita, an impenetrable wasteland of unliquidated debt.

To a less sanguine and resolute man than Hamilton, the national debt might well have appeared more like an albatross hung about the neck of the federal government than a sword with which to vanquish the states. For this mass of paper seemed to lie like a dead weight upon the national economy, stifling governmental credit and diverting into speculation capital which might have been more profitably employed in business enterprise. And, despite all that the government could do, the debt was constantly increasing: Revenue was inadequate to meet even the interest which the government had pledged itself to pay.

Under these circumstances, some Americans were of the opinion that the government ought to repudiate the national debt and start out with a clean financial slate. Why, they asked, should the federal government bankrupt itself in order to repay money that had served its purpose and from which everyone had profited in the form of independence of Great Britain? It seemed to them perfectly proper for the government to inform its creditors that, through no fault of its own, the debt was cancelled. . . .

Displaying an optimism to which nothing in the previous financial experience of the United States gave warrant, Hamilton took the position that the tariff could be made to furnish the government with sufficient revenue to liquidate the national debt and at the same time pay the operating expenses of the government. He admitted of no doubt that the foreign debt must be paid in full, accrued interest and all, but at the same time he declared his determination to stretch every resource of the government in order to do justice to the domestic creditors. Everything he had said and done up to the time of his appointment as secretary of the treasury indicated that he held the satisfaction of these claims to be a prerequisite to the success of the Federal Constitution.

If the domestic creditors were to be paid, the question inevitably arose: Which creditors? For in 1789, the securities of the United States government were for the most part not in the possession of the original holders: They had been transferred — often at a fraction of their nominal value — to purchasers who bought them for speculative or investment purposes. As a result, the evidences of governmental debt had gravitated into the hands of a few, most of whom were residents of the northern states. A class and a section therefore stood to profit from the payment of the debt. . . .

Besides the mass of depreciated securities and paper money issued by the Continental Congress, the people of the United States labored under a heavy load of state debts. Like the national debt, the evidences of state indebtedness had followed the well-worn course from original holders to speculators and investors. Hamilton's constant objective was to bind these men to the national government by the durable ties of "*Ambition* and *Avarice*"; but as matters stood in 1789, ambition and avarice tended to attach the state creditors to the state governments. As long as the states possessed their debts, they were certain to compete with the federal government for the allegiance of the creditor class and for the citizens' tax dollar. The result, Hamilton feared, would be that the states would attempt to pre-empt (as the Constitution, by recognizing concurrent taxation, permitted them to do) the remaining objects of taxation and that the affluent citizens of the United States would be divided against themselves, the state creditors seeking to strengthen the states while the holders of federal securities endeavored to aggrandize the powers and the revenues of the national government.

It can be said of Hamilton that whenever he saw a Gordian knot, he attempted to cut it forthwith. In this instance, he called in his Report on Public Credit for the assumption by the federal government of $25 million of state debts incurred in the prosecution of the War of Independence. Here he acted upon the principle that "if all the public creditors receive their dues from one source, distributed by an equal hand, their interest will be the same. And, having the same interests, they will unite in the support of the fiscal arrangements of the Government." Thus the most valuable members of the community — valuable because they were the most liberally endowed with the goods of this world — would bestow their affections and, Hamilton hoped, their money upon the federal government. With all the creditors, state and national, gathered into the fold of the federal government, Hamilton's vision of a powerful national government, supreme over the states, would begin to assume concrete reality. . . .

Between Hamilton and Jefferson there was as much difference in outward appearance as there was in the cast of their minds. Jefferson — tall, angular, loose-jointed, awkward, ill at ease in company and reserved in his manners — was confronted by a small, well-shaped, meticulously dressed young man who exuded energy, youthfulness, and high spirits. Despite the fact that Jefferson had spent several years in the most polite circles in Europe, his ill-fitting clothes — they always seemed too small for him — his lounging, careless manner — he sprawled rather than sat in a chair — made him appear rather like a frontiersman playing the Virginia gentleman and who still had a long way to go before he mastered the part. Even some of Jefferson's friends felt that he abused a philosopher's privilege of negligence in dress. But Jefferson, the born aristocrat, was sure of himself and of his position in society, whereas Hamilton was a parvenu who could never afford to let down his guard; his family closet contained several skeletons over which he was compelled to mount guard.

Although Hamilton never made the mistake of taking Jefferson to be a kindred spirit, he did not at this time regard him as an enemy. The Virginian's objections to the Constitution had been largely removed by the Bill of Rights; he held *The Federalist* in high esteem; he liked to think of commerce as the handmaiden of agriculture; he was a nationalist who favored making the federal judiciary supreme over the state judges; and he was no friend of an "elected despotism" such as had prevailed in some states during the period of the Articles of Confederation. Most important of all, he had not committed himself formally on the issues raised by Hamilton's report.

And so, when Hamilton encountered Jefferson one day near the president's house, he seized the opportunity of sounding out the secretary of state. . . .

In this memorable conversation in front of the president's house, Hamilton apparently offered Jefferson only the consolation of saving the union: Although Hamilton undoubtedly had in mind some arrangements having to do with the site of the national capital, he did not broach the subject at this time. It was at dinner the next day, attended by Jefferson, Hamilton, and Madison, that the matter was brought up; and it was Madison and Jefferson who set the price for the passage of the funding-assumption bill — the permanent location of the national capital on the banks of the Potomac. And since assumption could not be carried without the support of the

Pennsylvanians, it was agreed that Philadelphia should be made the temporary residence of the government for ten years.

That Hamilton should stoop to bargaining to achieve his objectives struck some of his friends as beneath the dignity of a statesman. Rufus King, who as a United States senator ought to have known better, told Hamilton that "great & good schemes ought to succeed on their own merits and not by intrigue or the establishment of bad measures." But Hamilton was not such a babe in the political woods as to imagine that the purity of his intentions and the rectitude of his measures were a guarantee of success. Putting first things first, he told King, was a policy he had found to yield excellent results: "The funding System, including the assumption is the primary national object; all subordinate points which oppose it must be sacrificed; the project of Philadelphia & Potomack is bad, but it will ensure the funding System and the assumption." To carry that point, Hamilton probably would have been willing to put the national capital in an even hotter spot than the Potomac in mid-August. . . .

By means of the assumption of state debts and the funding of the national debt, Hamilton had succeeded in attaining his first objective — the reestablishment of the credit of the national government. In the Bank of the United States, Hamilton had created an institution designed to concentrate the capital resources of the country in a central bank. Thus the United States was prepared for the capitalistic dispensation, but the answer to the question — to what ends were the new-found wealth of the country to be put? — had not yet been handed down from the Treasury. The answer was forthcoming in the Report on Manufactures Hamilton submitted to Congress in December 1791.

In January 1791, the House of Representatives requested the secretary of the treasury to prepare a plan "for the encouragement and promotion of such manufactures as will tend to render the United States independent of other nations for essentials, particularly for military supplies." As was his settled habit, Hamilton gave the broadest possible interpretation to this directive. In consequence, what Congress received on December 5, 1791, when he submitted his report, was a comprehensive survey of the state of manufacturing in the United States — its extent, variety, the degree of success attained, the obstacles that needed to be overcome, its future prospects, and a disquisition upon the ways and means of promoting manufactures in the Republic. . . .

Other than serving as a guide, benefactor, and partner of business, the government, in Hamilton's philosophy, left individual enterprise to itself. He would tolerate no price-fixing, for example, on the ground that competition was a better regulator of prices than governmental edict. Nor did he envisage governmental interference with business to secure social objectives. Hamilton's ideal was a free economy — free, that is, insofar as curbs upon individual initiative were concerned, but not free in that sense that government abstained from interference of any kind. He insisted only that the interference of government be benevolent and in the interests of the national welfare.

In his inventory of the resources of the United States, Hamilton did not omit the distinctive talents and skills of the American people. He was especially impressed by the inventive genius and the "peculiar aptitude for mechanic improvements" displayed by his countrymen. To turn this aptitude to the account of the state was for Hamilton an essential part of his plan for the encouragement of manufactures; accordingly, he urged Congress "to induce the prosecution and introduction of useful discoveries" by a system of rewards and premiums. To those who introduced machinery into the United States from abroad, even in defiance of the laws of foreign countries prohibiting its exportation, he was prepared to give cash rewards and the temporary grant of exclusive manufacturing privileges.

Nevertheless, no matter how elaborate the system of rewards, Hamilton recognized that few businessmen would be inclined to risk their capital in the establishment of factories in the United States without the assurance of an adequate supply of labor. With western lands acting as a magnet that drew potential factory workers from the eastern states, the problem was not to keep Americans down on the farm but to persuade them to live in cities and work in factories. Nevertheless, Hamilton did not despair of providing American factories with a labor force: There was a plentitude of women, children, and immigrants which might be used to work the machines. The men of the United States would learn their error when they saw the pay checks brought home by their wives and children; plow-jogging was not to be compared with a good steady job in a mill!

In England, little children were leading the factory owners to the promised land of bigger factories and bigger profits. Blessed were these children, for they worked fourteen hours a day, six days a week, and were never known to engage in union activities. Hamilton carried his admiration of British industrialism even to the point of noting with approval that almost half the workers in British cotton factories were women and children, "of whom the greater proportion were children, and many of them of a tender age." That the United States should copy this example seemed to Hamilton highly beneficial not only for the national economy but even for the women and children involved: "In general," he asserted "women and children are rendered more useful, and the latter more early useful, by manufacturing establishments, than they would other wise be."

— John Chester Miller, *Alexander Hamilton: Portrait in Paradox*

Once you've produced your own notes and a plan for an essay, read on. See if the following notes are like the ones you've taken, and evaluate our thinking as we describe the essay possibilities we see emerging.

JEFFERSON	HAMILTON
Secretary of state	Secretary of treasury
His time in France	
His ease with slavery as a way of life	
Slaves as property	
His negotiations with the British minister Hammond about enforcing the treaty of 1783	His efforts to interfere in J's handling of these negotiations
Defender of Virginian interests	Protector of interests of the North, particularly New York

JEFFERSON	HAMILTON
His hostile attitude toward Britain; his friendship with the French	His conciliatory attitude toward Britain; indifference to France?
Despised Hamilton's "monarchism"	Did Hamilton want a king?
Issue of Northwest Posts	
The issue of the return of slaves taken away to England	Slaves in England had become free.
	Tried to dissociate Washington's administration from Jefferson's "womanish" views
Slavery issue subordinate to threats against Republican form of government	
Opposed most of Hamilton's financial proposals:	
Assumption of state debts by national government (though at first he supported this)	Measures for centralizing national power over states and for creating capital with which to encourage industrialization
"Perpetuation of national debt"	
The formation of a national bank? A small group of financial people will have too much control.	National bank further centralized capital and decision making.
Saw interests of northern business opposed to southern agricultural interests	"Report on Manufactures"
Saw main "slavery" issue as exploitation of the South by the North	
His appearance: sloppy but aristocratically at ease	More proper, but nervous
	"Skeletons in the closet"
	Hamilton's anticipated areas of agreement with J: the Constitution, the importance of commerce, admiration for <u>The Federalist</u>, the advantages of more central authority than there had been during the revolution

JEFFERSON	HAMILTON
Accepted new location of nation's capital in return for letting H's financial plan pass.	Made "the Potomac deal" as a way of getting his funding-assumption bill passed
	First to advocate large-scale weapons manufacture
	Valued factory work above farm labor; admired British system of children's and women's labor

How would we go about converting a set of notes like these to a plan for an essay? There's no single best way. We might try to construct the three-part formula demonstrated earlier (Both *A* and *B*. . . ./But *A*. . . ./Whereas *B*. . . .), but judging from the material on our list, we wouldn't find much to develop for the "Both Hamilton and Jefferson . . ." part. Most of the general similarities will sound obvious and silly: "Both Hamilton and Jefferson were important politicians of their day," or "Both Hamilton and Jefferson served in George Washington's administration," or "Both Hamilton and Jefferson were men of strong political opinion." Which, if any, of these general points is worth developing in more detail as a major part of an essay? If we decide that none is, we'll turn away from this strategy.

A second strategy might be to leap to some central contrast, one we think capable of sustaining an entire essay. Often when comparing two passages, we might find, for example, that the perspectives of the authors differ in some fundamental way and that this difference in turn helps explain further differences. In this case, when we are dealing with two passages by the same author, that option will not seem so attractive. Still, after rereading the passages, we might decide that Miller does not approach his two subjects from the same point of view or that he does not maintain the same attitude toward them. In thinking about this possibility, we decided we couldn't detect meaningful differences in approach or tone — he seems equally cool to each. This time the quick leap didn't work.

A third strategy would be to proceed more deliberately, consolidating the list we made, passing over points that seem repetitious or unhelpful or points that simply don't lend themselves to comparison. We would want to be alert to general trends. We might think it odd, for instance, that so many of our notes about Jefferson pertain to the slavery issue; then, remembering the title of Miller's book — *The Wolf by the Ears: Thomas Jefferson and Slavery* — we would recognize that that emphasis is the book's central theme (maybe we've discovered a difference in point of view after all). Perhaps what we notice is important enough to become the controlling point of our essay. Or perhaps it's a point we want to hold onto, waiting to see how it will coordinate with others.

Whatever we do, we're looking for some way to simplify our material so that we can organize a coherent essay. It might help to arrive at some scheme of subtopics, something to suggest how our essay could move along. Here's one example of a plan that might work:

```
The contrasting personalities of Jefferson and Hamilton

The contrast in the regions and interests they represented

Their contrasting political philosophies
```

Here's another:

```
The treaty issue

The slavery issue

Financial issues

The manufacturing issue
```

And another:

```
The contrasting social values of Hamilton and Jefferson

Their contrasting political values

Their economic values

Their moral blind spots
```

We might create an effective essay out of a sequence of subtopics like these. It would depend of course on how well and in what detail we could develop clear comparisons for each subtopic. It would also depend on how well we could link our subtopics as we move from one part of our essay to another. For example, a sentence like this one could link the first and second subtopics in the last plan above: "Just as their social values depended on their upbringings, the political values of Hamilton and Jefferson had much to do with where and how they lived." Without such transitions, we'd risk giving readers the impression that they are reading several separate essays rather than a single sustained one. And even with such transitions readers may be left wondering what the whole has been about.

We're on the strongest ground when we discover a single idea, a thesis, capable of giving coherence to the rest of our points. Good theses can be quite general, and they also can get quite specific. A good thesis needs to be broad enough to cover the comparisons we think are important and focused enough to leave a reader persuaded about something in particular. Here's a short list of possible theses emerging from our notes about Jefferson and Hamilton.

```
     Jefferson and Hamilton illustrate a deep national tension,

one that would lead eventually to the Civil War.

     Politically Jefferson was more revolutionary than Hamilton;

but economically he was more conservative.
```

Although Jefferson is considered the foremost of the "Founding Fathers" after Washington, Alexander Hamilton has had the more lasting influence on American institutions.

John C. Miller treats Hamilton and Jefferson equally; toward both he shows a healthy disrespect.

Jefferson and Hamilton each saw national interests in terms most favorable to his own region of the country.

The dispute between Hamilton and Jefferson was really between two opposing images of aristocracy: one of landed property, the other of monetary power.

Hamilton did not think the United States could be self-sufficient; Jefferson felt that the nation had obtained true independence.

What do you see as some of the strengths and weaknesses of these statements as ideas for structuring an essay? Does any one of them look more promising than the others? You might select one and try planning an essay. Or go back and evaluate your own plan to determine if you would want to modify it in some way. Or wait until you've done some of the other assignments in this chapter and then return for a fresh look at these two important figures in American history. Finally, whether or not you decide to think further about Jefferson and Hamilton, we ask you to take a few moments to think about these two more general questions: What do we gain by acts of comparison? Do we take any risks in thinking comparatively?

A Professional Application

In the following excerpt, Bruce Bower uses the comparing strategy to explore whether monkeys and apes can discern others' feelings and motives based on visual cues. He begins with the example of the children's book character Curious George — who does show an awareness of others' feelings and impulses — to set up a contrast with a conclusion from recent research on the issue: that even the chimp, "our closest evolutionary relative," may be incapable of such complex thought. Bower then goes on to describe the "mirror test," long purported to be a test of primates' self-awareness, as well as more recent research. Notice the different methods researchers use to collect data on the mental lives of primates, and notice, too, the different interpretations researchers sometimes draw from similar data. And, as you read, notice how Bower uses cues to signal comparisons among primates, among studies, and among results. For example:

". . . chimpanzees and orangutans, like human toddlers, . . ."

"Gorillas, on the other hand, . . ."

"In contrast, marked chimps who saw themselves . . ."

"Chimps, however, do show a keen sensitivity to where others look, . . ."

Probing Primate Thoughts

Bruce Bower

In a series of popular children's books, Curious George, a monkey, lets his raging inquisitiveness lead him into all sorts of trouble. George knows when he has erred, though, and always makes amends. The puckish primate also senses that an inner world of thought and emotion pulses around him. For instance, George recognizes that the firemen coming through his door are angry with him for ringing the emergency telephone number, and on another occasion he tries to cheer up a sad-looking girl he meets in a hospital.

Scientists who suspect that real-life apes and monkeys maintain at least a modicum of Georgelike insight into mental lives — their own and others' — have received some setbacks of late. Recent evidence suggests that such mental feats may elude even our closest evolutionary relative, the chimpanzee. What's more, a widely recognized method for studying primate thinking may yield much fuzzier results than its proponents have contended.

The suspicion that nonhuman primates can to some extent discern motives, plans, and strategies behind observed behaviors won a number of converts during the past twenty-five years. Reports that apes could express themselves with simple languages invigorated this view.

In addition, researchers noted that chimpanzees and orangutans, like human toddlers, turn as curious as George when they gaze into a mirror and see themselves in an unexpected light. If an experimenter places dye marks or stickers on their faces and then puts a mirror in front of them, these creatures notice the decorative additions and proceed to use their reflected images to guide their touching of their own faces and then the rest of their own bodies.

Gorillas, on the other hand, tend to pay mirrors no heed. Monkeys react angrily to their own reflections, apparently mistaking them for competitors.

Mirror-wielding investigators generally concluded that self-awareness and a basic appreciation of what others may or may not know arise only in humans, chimps, and orangutans.

Critics now argue that what an ape or monkey does in front of a mirror provides a distorted view of their mental landscape. Some who see merit in the mirror test still doubt that self-awareness and a penchant for mind reading in social situations characterize any species except humans.

"In the last few years, I've become much more open to the possibility that chimps may not develop a mental understanding of themselves and others, at least not to the extent that preschool children do," remarks Daniel J. Povinelli, a psychologist at the University of Southwestern Louisiana in New Iberia. "You can train chimps to use a lan-

---

Bruce Bower (b. 1953) is a behavioral sciences editor at *Science News* in Washington, D.C. "Probing Primate Thoughts" appeared in the January 1996 issue of *Science News.*

guage, but it's unclear whether they understand themselves as mental agents or have a mental disposition toward that language."

The mirror test has served as the gold standard for establishing the presence of self-awareness in primates. Gordon G. Gallup Jr., a psychologist at the State University of New York at Albany, first reported its use in 1970.

Gallup's procedure consisted of applying brightly colored dye marks to the eyebrows and ears of anesthetized chimps that had become accustomed to seeing their mirror reflections. After the numbing medicine wore off, a video camera recorded the chimps' behavior in front of a mirror.

Dye-marked chimps stared at their reflections, touched themselves on the colored patches, and inspected the inside of their mouths and other body areas. In contrast, marked chimps who saw themselves in a mirror for the first time made no effort to inspect dye marks or any other physical features.

Animals that learn to use mirrors to monitor changes in their appearance and to examine their bodies possess knowledge of their own mental experience, Gallup argues. A creature displaying a self-conception of this type can take into account what others may or may not know, he says.

So far, Gallup's mirror procedure has consistently evoked self-inspection only from human children older than eighteen months, chimps, and orangutans. However, there may be less to the mirror test than meets the eye, asserts Marc Hauser, a psychologist at Harvard University.

As expected from prior results, members of one monkey species — cotton-top tamarins — glanced only briefly at their reflections when adorned with the facial dye marks used in previous mirror tests. After the distinctive tufts of white hair on top of their heads were dyed a bright color, however, these monkeys avidly inspected their bodies in mirrors, Hauser and his colleagues report in the Nov. 5, 1995 *Proceedings of the National Academy of Sciences.*

Such behavior may not signify self-awareness. Considerable research, both in the laboratory and in the wild, had already suggested that monkeys conduct their daily affairs without regard for possible motives or other mental states in themselves and others, Hauser notes. Dorothy L. Cheney and Robert M. Seyfarth, both of the University of Pennsylvania in Philadelphia, describe this work in *How Monkeys See the World* (1990, University of Chicago Press).

"The mirror test may address whether members of a species are capable of self-recognition, but it apparently says nothing about self-awareness," Hauser contends.

Gallup rejects this conclusion. In an unpublished follow-up to Hauser's cotton-top tamarin study, he and Povinelli find that marmosets, another monkey species, show no interest in inspecting themselves in mirrors after their white, elongated mustaches have been dyed in attention-getting hues. Gallup now plans to examine videotapes of the mirror-intrigued monkeys in Hauser's experiment. . . .

[H]umans operate in a mental realm that may stay off-limits to apes and other animals, argues Povinelli. By three to five years of age, children conclude that their peers behave according to unseen beliefs, intentions, and other mental states, whereas studies directed by Povinelli now indicate that chimps may not try to decipher others' minds in this way.

In an upcoming Monograph of the Society for Research in Child Development, Povinelli and Southwestern Louisiana colleague Timothy J. Eddy describe fifteen studies they have conducted with preschool children and five- to seven-year-old chimps to explore knowledge about the connection between the mind and the eyes. They have examined more than 100 children and more than 100 chimps.

For instance, chimps apparently fail to grasp that another's eyes provide cues as to where that individual's attention is directed and what knowledge he or she may have gained as a result.

In one investigation, chimps watched as one experimenter left the room and another hid food under one of several cups. Both experimenters later sat in front of the chimp and each pointed to a different cup.

Chimps trying to find the hidden food chose randomly between the experimenters, indicating that they made no connection between seeing and knowing. Three-year-old children also made random choices in comparable studies involving stickers hidden under cups. But four-year-olds routinely opted for the cup indicated by the experimenter who had seen where a sticker was hidden, Povinelli notes.

Chimps, however, do show a keen sensitivity to where others look, he adds. Just as humans do by eighteen months of age, chimps rapidly follow the gaze of a nearby individual. For instance, if an experimenter suddenly looks behind a chimp, the ape turns and looks in the same direction.

Nevertheless, chimps appear not to understand that the eyes can be deployed to signal a mental state of attention, Povinelli says. In further studies, chimps learned to approach a transparent partition and stick an arm through one of two holes to receive food. When an experimenter stood in front of one of the holes, the chimps chose that hole. Next, the chimps could see two experimenters, one positioned in front of each hole.

There was a catch, though — only one experimenter at a time could see the chimps and respond to food requests. In some trials, one experimenter wore a blindfold over his or her eyes and the other wore a blindfold over his or her mouth. Other trials employed one forward-facing and one backward-facing experimenter or one experimenter with open eyes and a partner with closed eyes.

Chimps chose experimenters on a random basis, regardless of whether the potential food givers could see them. In contrast, by two and one-half years of age, children consistently point to the experimenter who can see them.

Chimps older than those in the study might develop an ability to understand seeing more in the way that children do, Povinelli acknowledges. Or perhaps the apes assume a mental state of attention determined by a person's proximity and physical orientation, regardless of sensory cues such as gaze direction.

The possibility also looms that chimps do not reflect on the mental experiences of those they encounter, despite wielding a sophisticated intelligence, Povinelli contends.

Assignments

A Literature Assignment

Both of the following poems are by Gary Soto and were published in a volume titled *Black Hair.* The speaker in each poem is entering adolescence and reacting to important first experiences. Write an essay comparing the speakers' reactions to these experiences: their attitudes toward the events described, the words used, the tones of voice. Here are some questions to get you started:

- Read each poem out loud and try to hear the way each sounds. Do the words in each poem sound the same or different to you: soft, harsh, or what? Circle the words that seem most different. And how about the pace: Do you find yourself reading both at the same speed, with the same rhythm — or not?
- What is the attitude of the speaker in each poem toward key people, toward key events, toward you, the reader?
- Think about the two events described in terms of society's beliefs about adolescence. Do these poems reflect aspects of your own adolescence?
- What is the relation of each of the speakers to the events in the poem: Does he speak from the context of the events, is he reflecting back, etc.?
- Is there any psychological "movement" in the poems? Do the speakers know more about themselves by the end of the poems? Do you know more about them?

Oranges

GARY SOTO

The first time I walked
With a girl, I was twelve,
Cold, and weighted down
With two oranges in my jacket.
December. Frost cracking
Beneath my steps, my breath
Before me, then gone.
As I walked toward
Her house, the one whose
Porch light burned yellow
Night and day, in any weather.
A dog barked at me, until
She came out pulling
At her gloves, face bright
With rouge. I smiled,
Touched her shoulder, and led
Her down the street, across
A used car lot and a line
Of newly planted trees,
Until we were breathing
Before a drugstore. We
Entered, the tiny bell
Bringing a saleslady

GARY SOTO (b. 1952) is the author of twenty-six collections of poetry, essays, fiction, plays, and children's literature. His publications include *Living Up the Street* (1992), *Jesse* (1994), *New and Selected Poems* (1995), and *Black Hair* (1985), in which "Cruel Boys" and "Oranges" appear. He lives in Berkeley, California.

Down a narrow aisle of goods.
I turned to the candies
Tiered like bleachers,
And asked what she wanted —
Light in her eyes, a smile
Starting at the corners
Of her mouth. I fingered
A nickel in my pocket,
And when she lifted a chocolate
That cost a dime,
I didn't say anything.
I took the nickel from
My pocket, then an orange,
And set them quietly on
The counter. When I looked up,
The lady's eyes met mine,
And held them, knowing
Very well what it was all
About.

Outside,
A few cars hissing past,
Fog hanging like old
Coats between the trees.
I took my girl's hand
In mine for two blocks,
Then released it to let
Her unwrap the chocolate.
I peeled my orange
That was so bright against
The gray of December
That, from some distance,
Someone might have thought
I was making a fire in my hands.

Cruel Boys

GARY SOTO

First day. Jackie and I walking in leaves
On our way to becoming 8th graders,
Pencils behind our ears, pee-chee folders
Already scribbled with football players
In dresses, track star in a drooped bra.
We're tough. I'm Mexican
And he's an unkillable Okie with three
Teeth in his pocket, sludge under

His nails from scratching oily pants.
No one's going to break us, not the dean
Or principal, not the cops
Who could arrive in pairs, walkie-talkies
To their mouths, warning:
"Dangerous. They have footballs."
We could bounce them off their heads
And reporters might show up
With shirt sleeves rolled up to their ears,
Asking our age, if we're Catholic.
But this never happens. We go to first
Period, math, then second period, geography,
And in third period, English, the woman
Teacher reads us Frost, something
About a tree, and to set things straight,
How each day will fall like a tree.
Jackie raises his hand, stands up,
And shouts, "You ain't nothing but a hound dog,"
As the spitballs begin to fly.

An Anthropology Assignment

After finding a common basis for thinking about the following passages, write a comparative essay. The first excerpt is a creation myth collected from the Aranda tribe in Australia, and the second is a description of the "big bang" creation theory taken from an astronomy textbook. If you're having a hard time getting started, begin with the obvious. What immediate differences or similarities do you see? Once you've established several obvious similarities or differences, question them, push on them — are they really so obvious? Ask yourself if perhaps there is an interesting difference in what seemed like an obvious similarity, and vice versa. Then you'll be on your way.

In a separate paragraph — one that can be rough and experimental — consider what placing side by side these two very different accounts helped you to see. Consider as well the possibility that comparing the two accounts distorted one or both for you.

An Aranda Creation Story

In the very beginning everything was resting in perpetual darkness: Night oppressed all the earth like an impenetrable thicket. The gurra ancestor — his name was Karora — was lying asleep, in everlasting night, at the very bottom of the soak of Ilbalintja; as yet

This ARANDA creation story appeared in *Aranda Traditions* (first edition, 1947), edited by T. G. H. Strehlow (1908–1978), formerly a professor at Adelaide University in Australia. The Aranda are an aboriginal tribe in Australia.

there was no water in it, but all was dry ground. Over him the soil was red with flowers and overgrown with many grasses; and a great tnatantja[1] was swaying above him. This tnatantja had sprung from the midst of the bed of purple flowers which grew over the soak of Ilbalintja. At its root rested the head of Karora himself: From thence it mounted up toward the sky as though it would strike the very vault of the heavens. It was a living creature, covered with a smooth skin like the skin of a man.

And Karora's head lay at the root of the great tnatantja: He had rested thus ever from the beginning.

And Karora was thinking, and wishes and desires flashed through his mind. Bandicoots[2] began to come out from his navel and from his armpits. They burst through the sod above, and sprang into life.

And now dawn was beginning to break. From all quarters men saw a new light appearing: The sun itself began to rise at Ilbalintja, and flooded everything with its light. Then the gurra ancestor was minded to rise, now that the sun was mounting higher. He burst through the crust that had covered him: And the gaping hole that he left behind became the Ilbalintja Soak, filled with the sweet dark juice of the honeysuckle buds.

[1]**tnatantja:** Decorated pole used in native ceremonies [Eds.]. [2]**bandicoots:** Large ratlike marsupials of Australia [Eds.].

The Big Bang Theory

George O. Abell

Theoreticians have calculated a "standard" model of what the big bang may have been like. In the beginning we imagine a great primeval fireball of matter and radiation. We do not have to imagine any particular mass, or even a finite mass, for the fireball. Its density was very high and it was at a temperature of perhaps 10^{10} °K.

At first the matter consisted only of protons, neutrons, electrons, positrons, and neutrinos, all independent particles. After about 100 seconds, however, the temperature had dropped to 10^9 °K, and the particles began to combine to form some heavier nuclei. This nucleogenesis continued, according to the model, for a few hours until the temperature dropped to about 10^8 °K. During this time, about 20 percent of the mass of the material formed into helium. Some deuterium also formed (deuterium is an isotope of hydrogen with a nucleus containing one proton and one neutron) but only a small amount — probably less than one part in a thousand. The actual amount of deuterium formed depends critically on the density of the fireball; if it was fairly high, most of the deuterium would have been built up into helium. Scarcely any nuclei heavier than those of helium are expected to have survived. So the composition of the fireball when nuclear building ceased is thought to have been mostly hydrogen, about 20 percent helium, and a trace of deuterium.

For the next million years the fireball was like a stellar interior — hot and opaque, with radiation passing from atom to atom. During this time, the temperature gradually

Astronomer George O. Abell (1927–1983) contributed articles to numerous books and journals and wrote *Exploration of the Universe* (1964), *Drama of the Universe* (1978), and *Science and the Paranormal* (1981). Abell was especially interested in the study of galaxies and the large-scale structure of the universe.

dropped to about 3,000 °K, and the density to about 1,000 atoms/cm³. At this point the fireball became transparent. The radiation was no longer absorbed and was able to pass freely throughout the universe. After about 1,000 million years, the model predicts that the matter should have condensed into galaxies and stars.

We emphasize again that the fireball must *not* be thought of as a localized explosion — like an exploding superstar. There were no boundaries and no site of the explosion. It was everywhere. The fireball is still existing, in a sense. It has expanded greatly, but the original matter and radiation are still present and accounted for. The atoms of our bodies came from material in the fireball. We were and are still in the midst of it; it is all around us.

An Education Assignment

Write an essay comparing the following autobiographical accounts by the colonial patriot Benjamin Franklin (1706–1790), and the Black Muslim leader Malcolm X (1925–1965).

Some suggestions: You might want to consider not only the kinds of books these two men read, but their reasons for reading them, and what they finally did with them. Also, you might consider what effects Franklin's and Malcolm X's social and political circumstances had on their reading.

As a variation on the assignment, you might want to reflect on your own history as a reader and work your reflection into your essay. In this case, situate your discussion in the context of Franklin and Malcolm X, using your own experience as a third element in the comparative discussion.

From *Autobiography*

BENJAMIN FRANKLIN

From a child I was fond of reading, and all the little money that came into my hands was ever laid out in books. Pleased with the *Pilgrim's Progress,* my first collection was of John Bunyan's works in separate little volumes. I afterward sold them to enable me to buy R. Burton's *Historical Collections;* they were small chapmen's books, and cheap, forty or fifty in all. My father's little library consisted chiefly of books in polemic divinity, most of which I read, and have since often regretted that, at a time when I had such a thirst for knowledge, more proper books had not fallen in my way, since it was now resolved I should not be a clergyman. Plutarch's *Lives* there was in which I read abundantly, and I still think that time spent to great advantage. There was also a book of Defoe's, called an *Essay on Projects,* and another of Dr. Mather's called *Essays to Do Good,* which perhaps gave me a turn of thinking that had an influence on some of the principal future events of my life.[1]

[1]The books that Franklin mentions range from classical histories to theological tracts to self-improvement books [Eds.].

The *Autobiography* of BENJAMIN FRANKLIN, published in 1791, was first written for his son William in 1771.

This bookish inclination at length determined my father to make me a printer, though he had already one son (James) of that profession. In 1717 my brother James returned from England with a press and letters to set up his business in Boston. I liked it much better than that of my father, but still had a hankering for the sea. To prevent the apprehended effect of such an inclination, my father was impatient to have me bound to my brother. I stood out some time, but at last was persuaded, and signed the indentures[2] when I was yet but twelve years old. I was to serve as an apprentice till I was twenty-one years of age, only I was to be allowed journeyman's wages[3] during the last year. In a little time I made great proficiency in the business, and became a useful hand to my brother. I now had access to better books. An acquaintance with the apprentices of booksellers enabled me sometimes to borrow a small one, which I was careful to return soon and clean. Often I sat up in my room reading the greatest part of the night, when the book was borrowed in the evening and to be returned early in the morning, lest it should be missed or wanted.

And after some time an ingenious tradesman, Mr. Matthew Adams, who had a pretty collection of books, and who frequented our printing-house, took notice of me, invited me to his library, and very kindly lent me such books as I chose to read. I now took a fancy to poetry, and made some little pieces; my brother, thinking it might turn to account, encouraged me, and put me on composing occasional ballads.[4] One was called *The Lighthouse Tragedy,* and contained an account of the drowning of Captain Worthilake, with his two daughters: The other was a sailor's song, on the taking of *Teach* (or Blackbeard) the pirate. They were wretched stuff, in the Grub-street-ballad[5] style; and when they were printed he sent me about the town to sell them. The first sold wonderfully, the event being recent, having made a great noise. This flattered my vanity; but my father discouraged me by ridiculing my performances, and telling me verse-makers were generally beggars. So I escaped being a poet, most probably a very bad one; but as prose writing has been of great use to me in the course of my life, and was a principal means of my advancement, I shall tell you how, in such a situation, I acquired what little ability I have in that way.

There was another bookish lad in the town, John Collins by name, with whom I was intimately acquainted. We sometimes disputed, and very fond we were of argument, and very desirous of confuting one another, which disputatious turn, by the way, is apt to become a very bad habit, making people often extremely disagreeable in company by the contradiction that is necessary to bring it into practice; and thence, besides souring and spoiling the conversation, is productive of disgusts and perhaps enmities where you may have occasion for friendship. I had caught it by reading my father's books of dispute about religion. Persons of good sense, I have since observed, seldom fall into it, except lawyers, university men, and men of all sorts that have been bred at Edinburgh.[6]

[2]**indentures:** Contracts that bound one person to work for another for what was usually a long period of time [Eds.].

[3]**journeyman's wages:** The equivalent of beginning wages (apprentices were not paid) [Eds.].

[4]**occasional ballads:** Ballads written to commemorate a noteworthy event [Eds.].

[5]**Grub street:** The area of London where hack writers worked [Eds.].

[6]**men . . . bred at Edinburgh:** Scotsmen educated at the University of Edinburgh [Eds.].

A question was once, somehow or other, started between Collins and me, of the propriety of educating the female sex in learning, and their abilities for study. He was of opinion that it was improper, and that they were naturally unequal to it. I took the contrary side, perhaps a little for dispute's sake. He was naturally more eloquent, had a ready plenty of words; and sometimes, as I thought, bore me down more by his fluency than by the strength of his reasons. As we parted without settling the point, and were not to see one another again for some time, I sat down to put my arguments in writing, which I copied fair and sent to him. He answered, and I replied. Three or four letters of a side had passed, when my father happened to find my papers and read them. Without entering into the discussion, he took occasion to talk to me about the manner of my writing; observed that, though I had the advantage of my antagonist in correct spelling and pointing (which I owed to the printing-house), I fell far short in elegance of expression, in method and in perspicuity, of which he convinced me by several instances. I saw the justice of his remarks, and thence grew more attentive to the manner in writing, and determined to endeavor at improvement.

About this time I met with an odd volume of the *Spectator*.[7] It was the third. I had never before seen any of them. I bought it, read it over and over, and was much delighted with it. I thought the writing excellent, and wished, if possible to imitate it. With this view I took some of the papers, and, making short hints of the sentiment in each sentence, laid them by a few days, and then, without looking at the book, tried to complete the papers again, by expressing each hinted sentiment at length, and as fully as it had been expressed before, in any suitable words that should come to hand. Then I compared my *Spectator* with the original, discovered some of my faults, and corrected them. But I found I wanted a stock of words, or a readiness in recollecting and using them, which I thought I should have acquired before that time if I had gone on making verses; since the continual occasion for words of the same import, but of different length, to suit the measure, or of different sound for the rhyme, would have laid me under a constant necessity of searching for variety, and also have tended to fix that variety in my mind, and make me master of it. Therefore I took some of the tales and turned them into verse; and, after a time, when I had pretty well forgotten the prose, turned them back again. I also sometimes jumbled my collections of hints into confusion, and after some weeks endeavored to reduce them into the best order, before I began to form the full sentences and complete the paper. This was to teach me method in the arrangement of thoughts. By comparing my work afterward with the original, I discovered many faults and amended them; but I sometimes had the pleasure of fancying that, in certain particulars of small import, I had been lucky enough to improve the method or the language, and this encouraged me to think I might possibly in time come to be a tolerable English writer, of which I was extremely ambitious. My time for these exercises and for reading was at night, after work or before it began in the morning, or on Sundays, when I contrived to be in the printing-house alone, evading as much as I could the common attendance on public worship which my father used to exact on me when I was under his care, and which indeed I still thought a duty, though I could not, as it seemed to me, afford time to practice it.

[7] ***Spectator:*** An English periodical known for its graceful and witty essays [Eds.].

From *The Autobiography of Malcolm X*

MALCOLM X WITH ALEX HALEY

It was because of my letters that I happened to stumble upon starting to acquire some kind of a homemade education.

I became increasingly frustrated at not being able to express what I wanted to convey in letters that I wrote, especially those to Mr. Elijah Muhammad.[1] In the street, I had been the most articulate hustler out there — I had commanded attention when I said something. But now, trying to write simple English, I not only wasn't articulate, I wasn't even functional. How would I sound writing in slang, the way I would *say* it, something such as, "Look, daddy, let me pull your coat about a cat, Elijah Muhammad —"

Many who today hear me somewhere in person, or on television, or those who read something I've said, will think I went to school far beyond the eighth grade. This impression is due entirely to my prison studies.

It had really begun back in the Charlestown Prison, when Bimbi[2] first made me feel envy of his stock of knowledge. Bimbi had always taken charge of any conversations he was in, and I had tried to emulate him. But every book I picked up had few sentences which didn't contain anywhere from one to nearly all of the words that might as well have been in Chinese. When I just skipped those words, of course, I really ended up with little idea of what the book said. So I had come to the Norfolk Prison Colony still going through only book-reading motions. Pretty soon, I would have quit even these motions, unless I had received the motivation that I did.

I saw that the best thing I could do was get hold of a dictionary — to study, to learn some words. I was lucky enough to reason also that I should try to improve my penmanship. It was sad. I couldn't even write in a straight line. It was both ideas together that moved me to request a dictionary along with some tablets and pencils from the Norfolk Prison Colony school.

I spent two days just riffling uncertainly through the dictionary's pages. I'd never realized so many words existed! I didn't know *which* words I needed to learn. Finally, just to start some kind of action, I began copying.

In my slow, painstaking, ragged handwriting, I copied into my tablet everything printed on that first page, down to the punctuation marks.

I believe it took me a day. Then, aloud, I read back, to myself, everything I'd written on the tablet. Over and over, aloud, to myself, I read my own handwriting.

I woke up the next morning, thinking about those words — immensely proud to realize that not only had I written so much at one time, but I'd written words that I never knew were in the world. Moreover, with a little effort, I also could remember what many of these words meant. I reviewed the words whose meanings I didn't remember. Funny thing, from the dictionary first page right now, that "aardvark" springs to my mind. The

[1]**Elijah Muhammad:** U.S. clergyman (1897–1975); leader of the Black Muslims 1934–1975 [Eds.].
[2]**Bimbi:** A fellow inmate [Eds.].

The Autobiography of Malcolm X, co-authored by Alex Haley, was published in 1964, one year before the assassination of MALCOLM X.

dictionary had a picture of it, a long-tailed, long-eared, burrowing African mammal, which lives off termites caught by sticking out its tongue as an anteater does for ants.

I was so fascinated that I went on — I copied the dictionary's next page. And the same experience came when I studied that. With every succeeding page, I also learned of people and places and events from history. Actually the dictionary is like a miniature encyclopedia. Finally the dictionary's *A* section had filled a whole tablet — and I went on into the *B*'s. That was the way I started copying what eventually became the entire dictionary. It went a lot faster after so much practice helped me to pick up handwriting speed. Between what I wrote in my tablet, and writing letters, during the rest of my time in prison I would guess I wrote a million words.

I suppose it was inevitable that as my word-base broadened, I could for the first time pick up a book and read and now begin to understand what the book was saying. Anyone who has read a great deal can imagine the new world that opened. Let me tell you something: From then until I left that prison, in every free moment I had, if I was not reading in the library, I was reading on my bunk. You couldn't have gotten me out of books with a wedge. Between Mr. Muhammad's teachings, my correspondence, my visitors — usually Ella and Reginald[3] — and my reading of books, months passed without my even thinking about being imprisoned. In fact, up to then, I never had been so truly free in my life.

The Norfolk Prison Colony's library was in the school building. A variety of classes was taught there by instructors who came from such places as Harvard and Boston universities. The weekly debates between inmate teams were also held in the school building. You would be astonished to know how worked up convict debaters and audiences would get over subjects like "Should Babies Be Fed Milk?"

Available on the prison library's shelves were books on just about every general subject. Much of the big private collection that Parkhurst had willed to the prison was still in crates and boxes in the back of the library — thousands of old books. Some of them looked ancient: covers faded, old-time parchment-looking binding. Parkhurst . . . seemed to have been principally interested in history and religion. He had the money and the special interest to have a lot of books that you wouldn't have in general circulation. Any college library would have been lucky to get that collection.

As you can imagine, especially in a prison where there was heavy emphasis on rehabilitation, an inmate was smiled upon if he demonstrated an unusually intense interest in books. There was a sizable number of well-read inmates, especially the popular debaters. Some were said by many to be practically walking encyclopedias. They were almost celebrities. No university would ask any student to devour literature as I did when this new world opened to me, of being able to read and *understand.*

I read more in my room than in the library itself. An inmate who was known to read a lot could check out more than the permitted maximum number of books. I preferred reading in the total isolation of my own room.

When I had progressed to really serious reading, every night at about 10:00 PM I would be outraged with the "lights out." It always seemed to catch me right in the middle of something engrossing.

Fortunately, right outside my door was a corridor light that cast a glow into my

[3]**Ella and Reginald:** Two close relatives [Eds.].

room. The glow was enough to read by, once my eyes adjusted to it. So when "lights out" came, I would sit on the floor where I could continue reading in that glow.

At one-hour intervals the night guards paced past every room. Each time I heard the approaching footsteps, I jumped into bed and feigned sleep. And as soon as the guard passed, I got back out of bed onto the floor area of that light-glow, where I would read for another fifty-eight minutes — until the guard approached again. That went on until three or four every morning. Three or four hours of sleep a night was enough for me. Often in the years in the streets I had slept less than that.

The teachings of Mr. Muhammad stressed how history had been "whitened" — when white men had written history books, the black man simply had been left out. Mr. Muhammad couldn't have said anything that would have struck me much harder. I had never forgotten how when my class, me and all of those whites, had studied seventh-grade United States history back in Mason, the history of the Negro had been covered in one paragraph, and the teacher had gotten a big laugh with his joke, "Negroes' feet are so big that when they walk, they leave a hole in the ground."

This is one reason why Mr. Muhammad's teachings spread so swiftly all over the United States, among *all* Negroes, whether or not they became followers of Mr. Muhammad. The teachings ring true — to every Negro. You can hardly show me a black adult in America — or a white one, for that matter — who knows from the history books anything like the truth about the black man's role. In my own case, once I heard of the "glorious history of the black man," I took special pains to hunt in the library for books that would inform me on details about black history.

I can remember accurately the very first set of books that really impressed me. I have since bought that set of books and I have it at home for my children to read as they grow up. It's called *Wonders of the World.* It's full of pictures of archeological finds, statues that depict, usually, non-European people.

I found books like Will Durant's *Story of Civilization.* I read H. G. Wells's *Outline of History. Souls of Black Folk* by W. E. B. Du Bois gave me a glimpse into the black people's history before they came to this country. Carter G. Woodson's *Negro History* opened my eyes about black empires before the black slave was brought to the United States, and the early Negro struggles for freedom.

J. A. Rogers's three volumes of *Sex and Race* told about race-mixing before Christ's time; about Aesop being a black man who told fables; about Egypt's Pharaohs; about the great Coptic Christian Empires; about Ethiopia, the earth's oldest continuous black civilization, as China is the oldest continuous civilization.

Mr. Muhammad's teaching about how the white man had been created led me to *Findings in Genetics* by Gregor Mendel. (The dictionary's *G* section was where I had learned what "genetics" meant.) I really studied this book by the Austrian monk. Reading it over and over, especially certain sections, helped me to understand that if you started with a black man, a white man could be produced; but starting with a white man, you never could produce a black man — because the white chromosome is recessive. And since no one disputes that there was but one Original Man, the conclusion is clear.

During the last year or so, in the *New York Times,* Arnold Toynbee used the word "bleached" in describing the white man. (His words were: "White [i.e., bleached] human beings of North European origin. . . .") Toynbee also referred to the European geographic area as only a peninsula of Asia. He said there is no such thing as Europe. And if you look at the globe, you will see for yourself that America is only an extension of Asia. (But at the same time Toynbee is among those who have helped to bleach history. He has written that Africa was the only continent that produced no history. He won't write that again. Every day now, the truth is coming to light.)

I never will forget how shocked I was when I began reading about slavery's total horror. It made such an impact upon me that it later became one of my favorite subjects when I became a minister of Mr. Muhammad's. The world's most monstrous crime, the sin and the blood on the white man's hands, are almost impossible to believe. Books like the one by Frederick Olmstead opened my eyes to the horrors suffered when the slave was landed in the United States. The European woman, Fanny Kemble, who had married a Southern white slaveowner, described how human beings were degraded. Of course I read *Uncle Tom's Cabin.* In fact, I believe that's the only novel I have ever read since I started serious reading.

Parkhurst's collection also contained some bound pamphlets of the Abolitionist Anti-Slavery Society of New England. I read descriptions of atrocities, saw those illustrations of black slave women tied up and flogged with whips; of black mothers watching their babies being dragged off, never to be seen by their mothers again; of dogs after slaves, and of the fugitive slave catchers, evil white men with whips and clubs and chains and guns. I read about the slave preacher Nat Turner, who put the fear of God into the white slavemaster. Nat Turner wasn't going around preaching pie-in-the-sky and "non-violent" freedom for the black man. There in Virginia one night in 1831, Nat and seven other slaves started out at his master's home and through the night they went from one plantation "big house" to the next, killing, until by the next morning fifty-seven white people were dead and Nat had about seventy slaves following him. White people, terrified for their lives, fled from their homes, locked themselves up in public buildings, hid in the woods, and some even left the state. A small army of soldiers took two months to catch and hang Nat Turner. Somewhere I have read where Nat Turner's example is said to have inspired John Brown to invade Virginia and attack Harpers Ferry nearly thirty years later, with thirteen white men and five Negroes.

I read Herodotus, "the father of History," or, rather, I read about him. And I read the histories of various nations, which opened my eyes gradually, then wider and wider, to how the whole world's white men had indeed acted like devils, pillaging and raping and bleeding and draining the whole world's non-white people. I remember, for instance, books such as Will Durant's *The Story of Oriental Civilization,* and Mahatma Gandhi's accounts of the struggle to drive the British out of India.[4]

Book after book showed me how the white man had brought upon the world's black, brown, red, and yellow peoples every variety of the sufferings of exploitation. I saw how since the sixteenth century, the so-called "Christian trader" white man began to ply the seas in his lust for Asian and African empires, and plunder, and power. I read, I saw, how the white man never has gone among the nonwhite peoples bearing the Cross in the true manner and spirit of Christ's teachings — meek, humble, and Christlike.

I perceived, as I read, how the collective white man had been actually nothing but

[4]The books that Malcolm X mentions are all nonfiction, with an eventual emphasis on books addressing racial issues [Eds.].

a piratical opportunist who used Faustian machinations to make his own Christianity his initial wedge in criminal conquests. First, always "religiously," he branded "heathen" and "pagan" labels upon ancient nonwhite cultures and civilizations. The stage thus set, he then turned upon his nonwhite victims his weapons of war.

I read how, entering India — half a *billion* deeply religious brown people — the British white man, by 1759, through promises, trickery, and manipulations, controlled much of India through Great Britain's East India Company. The parasitical British administration kept tentacling out to half of the subcontinent. In 1857, some of the desperate people of India finally mutinied — and, excepting the African slave trade, nowhere has history recorded any more unnecessary bestial and ruthless human carnage than the British suppression of the nonwhite Indian people.

Over 115 million African blacks — close to the 1930s population of the United States — were murdered or enslaved during the slave trade. And I read how when the slave market was glutted, the cannibalistic white powers of Europe next carved up, as their colonies, the richest areas of the black continent. And Europe's chancelleries for the next century played a chess game of naked exploitation and power from Cape Horn to Cairo.

Ten guards and the warden couldn't have torn me out of those books. Not even Elijah Muhammad could have been more eloquent than those books were in providing indisputable proof that the collective white man had acted like a devil in virtually every contact he had with the world's collective nonwhite man. I listen today to the radio, and watch television, and read the headlines about the collective white man's fear and tension concerning China. When the white man professes ignorance about why the Chinese hate him so, my mind can't help flashing back to what I read, there in prison, about how the blood forebears of this same white man raped China at a time when China was trusting and helpless. Those original white "Christian traders" sent into China millions of pounds of opium. By 1839, so many of the Chinese were addicts that China's desperate government destroyed twenty thousand chests of opium. The first Opium War was promptly declared by the white man. Imagine! Declaring *war* upon someone who objects to being narcotized! The Chinese were severely beaten, with Chinese-invented gunpowder.

The Treaty of Nanking made China pay the British white man for the destroyed opium: forced open China's major ports to British trade; forced China to abandon Hong Kong; fixed China's import tariffs so low that cheap British articles soon flooded in, maiming China's industrial development.

After a second Opium War, the Tientsin Treaties legalized the ravaging opium trade, legalized a British-French-American control of China's customs. China tried delaying that Treaty's ratification; Peking was looted and burned.

"Kill the foreign white devils!" was the 1901 Chinese war cry in the Boxer Rebellion.[5] Losing again, this time the Chinese were driven from Peking's choicest areas. The vicious, arrogant white man put up the famous signs, "Chinese and dogs not allowed."

Red China after World War II closed its doors to the Western white world. Massive Chinese agricultural, scientific, and industrial efforts are described in a book that *Life*

[5]**Boxer Rebellion:** A rebellion by Chinese citizens who opposed the involvement of foreigners in Chinese business and culture [Eds.].

magazine recently published. Some observers inside Red China have reported that the world never has known such a hate-white campaign as is now going on in this nonwhite country where, present birth-rates continuing, in fifty more years Chinese will be half the earth's population. And it seems that some Chinese chickens will soon come home to roost, with China's recent successful nuclear tests.

Let us face reality. We can see in the United Nations a new world order being shaped, along color lines — an alliance among the nonwhite nations. America's U.N. Ambassador Adlai Stevenson complained not long ago that in the United Nations "a skin game" was being played. He was right. He was facing reality. A "skin game" *is* being played. But Ambassador Stevenson sounded like Jesse James accusing the marshal of carrying a gun. Because who in the world's history ever has played a worse "skin game" than the white man?

Mr. Muhammad, to whom I was writing daily, had no idea of what a new world had opened up to me through my efforts to document his teachings in books.

When I discovered philosophy, I tried to touch all the landmarks of philosophical development. Gradually, I read most of the old philosophers, Occidental and Oriental. The Oriental philosophers were the ones I came to prefer; finally, my impression was that most Occidental philosophy had largely been borrowed from the Oriental thinkers. Socrates, for instance, traveled in Egypt. Some sources even say that Socrates was initiated into some of the Egyptian mysteries. Obviously Socrates got some of his wisdom among the East's wise men.

I have often reflected upon the new vistas that reading opened to me. I knew right there in prison that reading had changed forever the course of my life. As I see it today, the ability to read awoke inside me some long dormant craving to be mentally alive. I certainly wasn't seeking any degree, the way a college confers a status symbol upon its students. My homemade education gave me, with every additional book that I read, a little bit more sensitivity to the deafness, dumbness, and blindness that was afflicting the black race in America. Not long ago, an English writer telephoned me from London, asking questions. One was, "What's your alma mater?" I told him, "Books." You will never catch me with a free fifteen minutes in which I'm not studying something I feel might be able to help the black man.

Yesterday I spoke in London, and both ways on the plane across the Atlantic I was studying a document about how the United Nations proposes to insure the human rights of the oppressed minorities of the world. The American black man is the world's most shameful case of minority oppression. What makes the black man think of himself as only an internal United States issue is just a catch-phrase, two words, "civil rights." How is the black man going to get "civil rights" before first he wins his *human* rights? If the American black man will start thinking about his *human* rights, and then start thinking of himself as part of one of the world's great peoples, he will see he has a case for the United Nations.

I can't think of a better case! Four hundred years of black blood and sweat invested here in America, and the white man still has the black man begging for what every immigrant fresh off the ship can take for granted the minute he walks down the gangplank.

But I'm digressing. I told the Englishman that my alma mater was books, a good library. Every time I catch a plane, I have with me a book that I want to read — and that's a lot of books these days. If I weren't out here every day battling the white man, I could spend the rest of my life reading, just satisfying my curiosity — because you can hardly mention anything I'm not curious about. I don't think anybody ever got more out of going to prison than I did. In fact, prison enabled me to study far more intensively than I would have if my life had gone differently and I had attended some college. I imagine that one of the biggest troubles with colleges is there are too many distractions, too much panty-raiding, fraternities, and boola-boola and all of that. Where else but in a prison could I have attacked my ignorance by being able to study intensely sometimes as much as fifteen hours a day?

A History Assignment

Following are two classic overviews of the American Revolution, one written by the American historian Edmund S. Morgan, the other written by British historian G. M. Trevelyan. While the passage by Morgan offers a fairly straightforward account of the events immediately preceding the Revolutionary War, the Trevelyan piece refers to a number of surrounding historical events (like the Stamp Act and the Boston Tea Party) and to British military and political figures (such as British statesman William Pitt, Earl of Chatham — referred to as both Pitt and Chatham by Trevelyan), and it would be easy to get bogged down in these names and events. Keep in mind that the primary source of conflict throughout the first half of Trevelyan's account is Britain's attempt, through various measures, to extract revenue from the colonies without offering participation in the British political process. You needn't be familiar with Trevelyan's many references in order to get a sense of how his concerns as a historian differ from Morgan's.

Write an essay comparing these British and American mid-twentieth century accounts of the American Revolution. Your essay should consider the ways each historian's perspective might shape his rendering of history. The following questions can help you get started:

- On what general kinds of events or issues does each historian focus his discussion: military, economic, social? Do the two historians see the same events as crucial?
- What general attitudes do you find in each piece toward the colonists, the British king and his parliament, the French, and the revolution itself? Do they seem to share the same framework or perspective?
- As you read each account, what images of the colonists develop in your imagination? How do you picture the colonists as Morgan writes about them? As Trevelyan writes about them?

Toward the end of your essay, you might want to speculate on what this assignment suggests about the way history gets written. Another issue to consider is this: As historians writing in the mid-twentieth century, might Morgan and Trevelyan share assumptions not necessarily held by today's historians?

The American Revolution: An American View

Edmund S. Morgan

The men who fixed their signatures to the Declaration of Independence would not have done so without some expectation of success. They knew that they and their countrymen would have to defeat the world's most formidable military and naval power, but in July 1776 this did not look like an impossible task. They had had plenty of evidence in the preceding decade of the corruption and incompetence of British political leaders, and the events of the preceding year seemed to demonstrate that these men would be no better at running a war than they were at running an empire. On April 19, 1775, the uncoordinated militia of the towns of eastern Massachusetts had routed a considerable body of British regulars. Two months later, at Bunker Hill, the same militia met a frontal assault by British troops and punished them terribly. In March 1776, after Washington took command and obtained some heavy guns, he was able to force British troops to evacuate Boston and withdraw to Halifax, Nova Scotia.

Against these facts had to be weighed one notable failure. In the autumn of 1775 the Americans sent an expedition to Canada, hoping to bring that area into the Revolution on their side. By the spring of 1776 it was clear that this expedition had failed. Though the failure was both military and political, Americans reassured one another that no such thing could occur among themselves. If the Canadians lacked the noble urge to be free, if they would not help themselves, then they deserved slavery. Meanwhile American patriots would establish their rights on battlefields closer to home.

The assurance of the Americans was ultimately justified by events: They did win, and their greatest asset was, in fact, their desire to be free. Though this desire did not enable them to maintain in the field a force equal to that of the British, the American armies could always count on popular support. It is true that many Americans took the British side — the best current estimate is that they amounted to a fifth of the population. Many of them shared the view that England had violated colonial rights, but they did not think the violations insufferable, and they turned out in substantial numbers to help the British troops keep the colonies in the empire. Nowhere, however, were they strong enough to enable royal government to survive. At the beginning of the war all the royal governors fled, and only in Georgia, the least populous of the revolting colonies, was British civil government reestablished during the remainder of the war.

A large portion of the population may have been indifferent at the outset, content to stay British if the British won or to go along with independence if the patriots could make it stick. But the war itself sooner or later obliged men to get off the fence on one side or the other. The independent state governments called on their people for military service again and again, for a tour of duty in either the militia or the Continental Army. When the call came, a man had to shoulder a musket in the cause or else abandon home and family and head for the British lines. Most preferred to go along with their country-

---

Historian Edmund S. Morgan (b. 1916) has taught at the University of Chicago, Brown University, and Yale University, from which he has retired as Sterling Professor of History Emeritus. He recently published *Inventing the People: The Rise of Popular Sovereignty in England and America* (1988). *The Birth of the Republic, 1763–1789,* in which this excerpt on the American Revolution appears, was published in 1956.

men; and once they had spent some months in camp, perhaps shooting at the British and being shot at by them, they were likely to return committed to the Revolution.

The Revolution, in other words, became a people's war, and it is doubtful that the British could ever have won more than a stalemate. They might defeat the American forces in the field, as they often did, but victory did not enable them to occupy the country without a much larger force than they ever had. Americans generally owned guns and knew how to use them. A century and a half of defending themselves against French and Indians, the reliance many placed on guns to protect their crops from animals and to provide themselves with meat — these had given them a familiarity with firearms that common people of the Old World lacked. It was this experience that told at Concord and at Bunker Hill. And it would tell again whenever a British army attempted to sweep through the country. Men would gather from the farms, snipe at the troops, ambush them, raid them, until the victory parade turned into a hasty retreat.

This great asset, which made a British victory most unlikely, unfortunately did not ensure an American victory. The local militia were good at harassing the British, but they were the least reliable part of the American forces when it came to pitched battles, and they could never be kept in the field for more than a short time. As soon as a battle was over, sometimes before, they would be on their way home. It took something more than a militia to make the war end in American victory.

How much more it took began to be apparent very soon after Congress took the plunge to independence. On July 2, while the members were adopting their resolution, General William Howe was landing unopposed on Staten Island in New York with several thousand troops. Shortly afterward his brother, Admiral Lord Howe, arrived with a battle fleet, and during the rest of the summer men and supplies poured in until there were more than thirty thousand men in arms on the island. Along with this force the Howes bore a commission enabling them to offer pardon to all Americans, provided they submitted to the authority of King and Parliament. The offer was laughable at this stage, but the force accompanying it was not.

Washington was on hand to oppose the expected attack and had almost as many men available as Howe, but most of them were militia. Washington himself had had a good deal less experience in command than his opponent, and in the ensuing Battle of Long Island (August 26, 1776) he was badly beaten and only saved from losing most of his forces by good luck and by Howe's failure to take full advantage of opportunities. There followed a humiliating series of defeats in which Washington and his army were chased across New Jersey.

There now began to appear, however, two factors which were to weigh heavily in determining the outcome of the war. One was the mediocrity of the commanders England sent to subdue the colonists. It is always difficult to determine in advance whether a field commander will be up to his job — so much depends on chance and on making the right decision at precisely the right moment. There were doubtless men among the British officers in America who might have succeeded in crushing Washington and destroying his army in 1776; but General Howe was a cautious, methodical soldier, not given to taking chances. He pursued war by the rulebook, and though capable of brilliant planning he was not good at seizing unexpected opportunities. After pushing Washington across the Delaware River by December, he called a halt for the winter.

Washington and his subordinates meanwhile were learning about war the hard way. The fact that he and they had the talent to learn was a second factor working toward

American success. In spite of numerous defeats and in spite of the vanishing militia, Washington still had the remnants of an army. When he found that the British were disposed to halt for the winter, he turned and hit them hard. On the famous night of December 25, 1776, he crossed the Delaware and with very little loss to his own men captured 1,000 Hessians under Colonel Rall at Trenton. It was not a battle of great importance in itself, but it showed which commander had the daring and the initiative to win a war, and it restored to the Americans some of the assurance they had begun to lose.

In the following year General Howe along with his subordinate, General Burgoyne, gave the Americans further reason for confidence. With Howe's approval Burgoyne conducted an expedition from Canada down the Hudson Valley to cut off New England from the other colonies. This was the old French strategy, and since the British already held New York, it would have been a simple matter to send a column up from New York to meet the other coming down from Canada. But instead of sending such a column from New York, Howe moved the main body of his troops to Philadelphia. Washington, baffled as he well might be by what Howe was doing, tried to bar the way, but the British troops swept triumphantly into the city. There was probably no city in America that Howe could not have taken with the force at his disposal. Neither did he gain much by his entry — most Americans did not live in Philadelphia.

And while Howe was receiving the encomiums of Pennsylvania loyalists, the farmers of New England and New York were giving Burgoyne a bad time in the Hudson Valley. He had made his march from Canada to the accompaniment of manifestos calling upon the people to come in and be saved from the awful tyranny of the Revolution. They came in, but not to be saved, and Continental troops came in too. On October 17, 1777, at Saratoga, Burgoyne surrendered to them.

He surrendered not only the tattered remains of his forces but also much of the prestige which for Europeans still clung to British arms. Saratoga was a great turning point of the war, because it won for Americans the foreign assistance which was the last element needed for victory. The possibility of such assistance had played an important role in their calculations from the beginning. The Declaration of Independence itself was issued mainly for the purpose of assuring potential allies that Americans were playing for keeps and would not fly into the mother country's arms at the first sign of parental indulgence.

Among possible allies the most likely had always been France. Ever since the peace of 1763 she had been waiting for opportunities of revenge against Britain and observing the alienation of the colonies with growing satisfaction. On May 2, 1776, two months before the Americans declared themselves independent, before they had even asked for aid, Louis XVI, on the advice of his foreign minister Vergennes, made a million livres (about $185,000 or £41,666 sterling) available to them for the purchase of munitions. And Vergennes persuaded Spain to put up an equal amount. The money and supplies which reached America from Europe were of the utmost importance. The money, of which there was much more to come both in gifts and loans, bolstered the credit of the United States and made it possible to finance the war. The munitions were indispensable because America, not yet an industrial country, could scarcely produce what she needed in sufficient quantities.

But money and supplies furnished secretly were different from outright military and naval assistance. France had been ready to give the one before she was asked; the other she was much slower to risk. Congress sent Benjamin Franklin to seek it, and if anyone could have got it by sheer persuasiveness, he could have. The French lionized him, pampered him, quoted him, but Vergennes retired behind his diplomatic fences and waited to see how much staying power the Americans would show. The Frenchman knew what a beating Washington had taken on Long Island, and he did not wish to expose France to a war with Great Britain unless the Americans could carry a real share of the burden. Vergennes was still waiting — and so was Franklin — when news of Saratoga arrived.

It was now Vergennes's turn to move. Saratoga demonstrated that the Americans could force the surrender of a British army. It seemed likely now that with French help they could win. Even England seemed to have reached that conclusion, for a commission under the Earl of Carlisle was directed to offer them everything they had asked for short of independence. Reconciliation was the last thing Vergennes wished to see, and Franklin exploited his fear of it to win the greatest diplomatic victory the United States has ever achieved. In February 1778, France signed two treaties, one of Amity and Commerce in which she recognized the United States and the two countries agreed to help each other commercially, the other of Alliance. This second treaty (on which Vergennes now insisted) gave the Americans all they could have hoped for and exacted almost nothing in return. It was to go into effect in case war should break out between England and France — as it did the following June (1778) — and it stated specifically that its essential purpose was to maintain the "liberty, sovereignty, and independence absolute and unlimited of the United States." France renounced all future possession of the Bermuda Islands and of any part of North America east of the Mississippi. If the United States conquered Canada or the Bermudas in the course of the war, France would recognize them as part of the United States. The two parties agreed to make no separate peace with Great Britain, and neither was to lay down arms until the independence of the United States was assured.

The American Revolution: A British View

G. M. TREVELYAN

The disappearance of the French flag from the North American Continent as a result of the Seven Years' War led to the disruption of the first British Empire. For it relieved the English colonists of the dangers which had made them look for protection to the mother country. At the same time the expenses of the late war and the heavy burden of debt and land-tax with which it had saddled Great Britain, suggested to her statesmen, in an evil hour, that the colonies might be made to contribute something toward the military expenses of the Imperial connection. An attempt to levy contributions toward the future upkeep of royal forces in America was first made through George Grenville's Stamp Duty on legal documents in the colonies. It was passed in 1765, but repealed next year by the Rockingham Whigs on account of the violent opposition which it had aroused beyond the Atlantic. In 1767 indirect taxation on tea and certain other articles was imposed on

---

The books of British historian G. M. TREVELYAN (1876–1962) include *England under the Stuarts* (1904), *The English Revolution, 1688–1689* (1938), and *A Shortened History of England* (1942), in which this account appears.

America by Charles Townshend. Chatham, the strongest English opponent of the policy of taxing the colonies, was then prime minister in name, but in actuality he was far removed from the political scene by gout and melancholia. Of these unpopular taxes the tea duty alone was maintained in a much modified form by George III's henchman Lord North in 1773, for the sake of principle only, as the profits were utterly negligible. Unfortunately, eight years of controversy on the taxation question had so worked upon the average colonial mind, that the overthrow of that principle was regarded as worth almost any disturbance and sacrifice. "No taxation without representation" was the cry, and every farmer and backwoodsman regarded himself as a Hampden, and North as a Strafford.

It was natural that the Americans should object to being taxed, however moderately and justly, by a Parliament where they were not even "virtually" represented. They had always acknowledged an indefinite allegiance to the Crown, though Massachusetts had made very light of it at certain times in the Stuart era, and had even gone to war with France without consulting the Crown in 1643. But Americans had never admitted the supremacy of Parliament, in the sense of conceding that the two Houses sitting at Westminster could vote laws and taxes binding on the Colonies, each of which had its own Assembly. On that issue, as on most issues of constitutional law that have divided the men of our race at great historical crises, there was a good legal case pleadable on either side. But as a matter of political expediency it was most desirable that the colonists should be taxed for imperial purposes by their own representatives rather than by the British Parliament.

Unfortunately they made no move to tax themselves, partly from thrift and partly from indifference to the Imperial connection. When once the French danger had disappeared, the Empire seemed a far-off abstraction to the backwoodsman of the Alleghenies, like the League of Nations to the Middle West today. And even on the sea coast, where the Empire was better known, it was not always better loved: It was represented by Governors, Colonels, and Captains of the British upper class, often as little suited to mix with democratic society as oil with vinegar. Furthermore, the Empire was associated in the mind of the Americans with restrictions on their commerce and their industry, imposed for the benefit of jealous English merchants, or of West Indian sugar and tobacco planters who were then the favorite colonists of a mother country not yet disturbed about the ethics of slavery.

Chatham, or rather that more formidable person, William Pitt, had made the imperial connection popular in America in time of war, and might have made it tolerable even in time of peace. But Chatham had ceased to influence the politics of the Empire, except as a Cassandra prophet warning George III in vain, and being called a "trumpet of sedition" for his pains.

In theory — or at least in the theory that was held in England — the Empire was a single consolidated State. In practice it was a federation of self-governing communities, with the terms of federation undrawn and constantly in dispute. Such a situation was full of danger, the more so as the situation and the danger were alike unrecognized. The defunct Whig oligarchy can hardly be said to have had a colonial policy or any clear ideas about the future of the Empire. Pitt's great Ministry had come and gone. And now, to meet the pressing needs of Imperial finance, George III's ministers had advanced partial and one-sided solutions that proved unacceptable, while the Americans refused to propose any solution at all. A way out could have been found by men of good will summoned to a round-table conference, at which Britain might have offered to give up the trade restrictions, and the Americans to make some contribution of their own to the military expenses incurred by the mother country on their behalf.

But such a conference was outside the range of ideas on either side [of] the Atlantic. England was still in the grip of "mercantile" and protectionist theories of the old type. She still regarded her colonies primarily as markets for her goods, and the trade of the colonials as permissible only so far as it seemed consistent with the economic interest of the mother country. As the historian of our British colonial policy has remarked, "That the measures of 1765 and 1767 precipitated the crisis is obvious enough; but that the crisis must sooner or later have come, unless Great Britain altered her whole way of looking at the colonies, seems equally certain."

As to the hope that America might voluntarily contribute to the Imperial expenses, "America" did not exist. The thirteen colonies were mutually jealous, provincial in thought, divided from one another by vast distances, great physical obstacles, and marked social and economic distinctions. They had failed in 1754 at Albany to combine even for the purpose of fighting the French at dire need, and they were little likely to unite in time of peace for the purpose of negotiating with England on an Imperial question which they denied to be urgent.

And so things drifted on to the catastrophe. On one side was the unbending stubbornness of George III, who dictated policy to Lord North, that easy, good-natured man, so fatally unwilling to disoblige his sovereign. On the other side was the uncompromising zeal of the Radical party among the Americans led by Samuel Adams, to whom separation gradually began to appear as a good in itself.

The general causes rendering it difficult for English and Americans to understand one another were then numerous and profound: Many of them have been removed by the passage of time, while on the other hand the difference of race is much greater today. English society was then still aristocratic, while American society was already democratic. Six or seven weeks of disagreeable ocean tossing divided London from Boston, so that personal intercourse was slight, and the stream of emigration from the mother country had run very dry ever since 1640. In England politics and good society were closed to Puritans, while Puritanism dominated New England and pushed its way thence into all the other colonies; it was Anglicanism that was unfashionable in Massachusetts. English society was old, elaborate, and artificial, while American society was new, simple, and raw. English society was based on great differences of wealth, while in America property was still divided with comparative equality, and every likely lad hoped some day to be as well-off as the leading man in the township. In England political opinion was mainly that of squires, while in America it was derived from farmers, water-side mobs, and frontiersmen of the forest.

In two societies so widely set apart in the circumstances and atmosphere of everyday life, it required people with imaginative faculties like Burke, Chatham, and Fox, to conceive what the issues looked like to ordinary men on the other side of the Atlantic. George III had strength of mind, diligence, and business ability, but he had not imagination.

After the famous outrage on the tea-chests in Boston harbor, the English Government, naturally and deeply provoked, made its fatal mistake. It hurried through Parliament Penal Acts against Massachusetts, closing the port of Boston, canceling the charter of the colony, and ordering political trials of Americans to be conducted in England.

These measures rallied the other colonies to Massachusetts and ranked up behind the Radicals doubtful and conservative forces for whose support the English Government might still have played with success. The Penal Acts meant in fact war with the colonies. They were defensible only as acts of war, and if adopted should have been accompanied by preparations to ensure armed victory. Yet in that very year the British Government reduced the number of seamen in the navy, and took no serious steps to strengthen their forces in America. When the pot boiled over at last, and hostilities broke out of themselves at Lexington, Burgoyne wrote thus from Boston:

> After a fatal procrastination, not only of vigorous measures but of preparations for such, we took a step as decisive as the passage of the Rubicon, and now find ourselves plunged at once in a most serious war without a single requisition, gunpowder excepted, for carrying it on.

During the twelve months preceding Lexington, while the British authorities, having defied New England to the arbitrament of force, contented themselves with the inactive occupation of Boston, the Radical party in the country outside had used the respite to organize revolutionary power and terrorize, or expel, its opponents. Indeed, ever since the original passage of the Stamp Act, the "Sons of Liberty" had employed tarring-and-feathering and other local methods of making opinion unanimous. Even so, the Loyalists in most of the thirteen colonies remained a formidable body. Few, if any, had approved the measures by which the British Government had provoked the war, but they were not prepared to acquiesce in the dismemberment of the Empire, and for social and political reasons of their own they disliked the prospect of Radical rule. Their strength lay among the mercantile and professional men and the large landowners of the coast, and they were stronger in the Middle and Southern Colonies than in New England. Against them were arrayed the humbler folk in most sections, the small farmers and the frontiersmen of the West, organized under leaders of amazing audacity and zeal. The Loyalists were slower to move, more anxious for compromise than war, and they got little leadership either from their own ranks or from the British, who too often treated them very ill and drove them by ill-usage or neglect to join the rebel ranks.

Yet the Radicals would never have overcome the trained soldiers of George III and their own Loyalist fellow-subjects, had they not been led by a statesman of genius who was also a first-class soldier, organizer, and disciplinarian. George Washington belonged by temper and antecedents rather to the Loyalist than the Radical classes. But, although he was first and foremost a gentleman of Virginia, he was also a frontiersman who had seen service against Indians and French beyond the Alleghenies, and who knew the soul of young America as it could only be known in the backwoods. Good Virginian as he was, he was no mere provincial, with feelings and experience limited to his own colony. He had a "continental" mind, and foresaw the nation he created. Some well-informed vision of the astounding future of his country westward, helped to decide George Washington to draw his sword for a cause which was bound, in the stress of war, to become the cause of American Independence. The American militiamen brought to the ranks qualities learnt in their hard struggle with nature — woodcraft and marksmanship, endurance, energy, and courage. But they grievously lacked discipline, save what the Puritan temper supplied to the individual, and what Washington imposed upon the army. His long struggle, as commander-in-chief in the field, with the exasperating ineptitude of the Continental Congress, was a war within the war. Fortunately for him, the British army, in spite of its fine qualities, made mistake after mistake not only in the military but in the political strategy of the contest.

It was a civil war, not a war between two nations, though when the battle smoke at length subsided two nations were standing there erect. Because it was a civil war, and because its issue would decide among other things whether England should in future be ruled by the king acting through Parliament or by Parliament acting through the king, opinion was divided in England no less than in America. Once fighting began, the bulk of the British people supported their government, so long as there was any hope of reconquering the colonies. But they showed so little enthusiasm for the fratricidal contest that recruiting was very difficult, and the government largely employed German mercenaries whose conduct further incensed the colonists. Moreover in England there was always a strong minority, speaking with powers as diversified as those of Chatham, Burke, and young Charles Fox, that denounced the whole policy of the war and called for concession to save the unity of the Empire before it was too late.

Military operations were as ill-conducted by the British as they had been rashly provoked. The troops, as Bunker's Hill showed, were not inferior to the men of Blenheim and Minden. But the military mistakes of Generals Burgoyne and Howe were very serious, and they were rivaled by those of the government at home. Lord George Germain in England planned the Saratoga campaign as Pitt had planned the taking of Quebec, but with very different results. His plan gave the Americans the advantage of acting on the inner lines, for he sent Burgoyne to Canada to march down the Hudson and isolate New England, but without making sure that Howe moved up to meet him from the South. The result was that, while Howe lingered in Philadelphia, Burgoyne and his 5,000 regulars were cut off in the wilderness beside the great river, and surrendered at Saratoga to the American minutemen.

After Saratoga the French despotism felt encouraged to come to the aid of liberty in the New World. This remarkable decision dismembered the British Empire, but it did not thereby achieve its object of restoring the House of Bourbon to world power. For it turned out that the idea of revolution, if once successful in America, could traverse the Atlantic with unexpected ease. And no less unexpectedly, from the broken eggshell of the old British Empire emerged two powers, each destined to rapid growth — a new British Empire that should still bestride the globe, still rule the seas, and still hold up its head against the powers of the continent; and a united American State that should spread from Atlantic to Pacific and number its citizens by scores of millions, in the place of thirteen little, mutually jealous colonies upon the Atlantic coast.

It was well that America was made. It was tragic that the making could only be effected by a war with Britain. The parting was perhaps inevitable at some date and in some form, but the parting in anger, and still more the memory of that moment's anger fondly cherished by America as the starting-point of her history, have had consequences that we rue to this day.

A Literature Assignment

The first reading in this assignment is the opening chapter of *The Big Sleep,* by Raymond Chandler, one of America's most influential writers of detective fiction. Although you might not be familiar with Chandler's novels, you'll recognize the hard-boiled, cynical demeanor of his main character, Philip Marlowe, for Marlowe has been the model for countless movie and television detectives. Read this excerpt and make a list of the characteristics of Chandler's writing: the way in which he describes things; the way he portrays Marlowe, the woman, and their interaction; the mood he creates.

The second reading is from "Murder Is My Business" by Lynette Prucha, and it puts a new slant on the Raymond Chandler tradition of detective fiction. Although Prucha's Angie Marino is similar to Philip Marlowe in many ways, she is a lesbian living in the 1990s. While deliberately imitating Chandler, Prucha offers us the story's events through a very different point of view.

The third reading is a chapter from popular mystery writer Walter Mosley's *Devil in a Blue Dress* (which was made into a movie in 1995), and it offers yet another variation on the Philip Marlowe tradition. The main character in Mosley's mystery novels is Ezekiel "Easy" Rawlins, an African-American man living in post-World War II Los Angeles who, although not a detective, finds himself in the middle of crime and police investigation — this at a time of an uncertain economy, discrimination, and harsh color lines.

Write an essay in which you compare these three examples of detective fiction. You can begin with Chandler, the forerunner and influence, or you can treat all these pieces equally, in any order that makes sense to you. In framing your comparison, consider the ways the writers describe Los Angeles, the mood they create, their dialogue, their characters, their attitudes toward women, the issues that seem to drive their respective stories. If you begin with Chandler, you might also consider the ways the other two writers imitate his writing, make fun of it, or draw on it in some other way to underscore their own perspectives and concerns.

From *The Big Sleep*

Raymond Chandler

It was about eleven o'clock in the morning, mid October, with the sun not shining and a look of hard wet rain in the clearness of the foothills. I was wearing my powder-blue suit, with dark blue shirt, tie and display handkerchief, black brogues, black wool socks with dark blue clocks on them. I was neat, clean, shaved, and sober, and I didn't care who knew it. I was everything the well-dressed private detective ought to be. I was calling on $4 million.

The main hallway of the Sternwood place was two stories high. Over the entrance doors, which would have let in a troop of Indian elephants, there was a broad stained-glass panel showing a knight in dark armor rescuing a lady who was tied to a tree and didn't have any clothes on but some very long and convenient hair. The knight had

Raymond Chandler (1888–1959) was an American detective-story writer who worked creatively within the crime novel formula. His first novel, *The Big Sleep* (1939), whose opening chapter appears here, was made into a film, as were several of his other books.

pushed the vizor of his helmet back to be sociable, and he was fiddling with the knots on the ropes that tied the lady to the tree and not getting anywhere. I stood there and thought that if I lived in the house, I would sooner or later have to climb up there and help him. He didn't seem to be really trying.

There were French doors at the back of the hall, beyond them a wide sweep of emerald grass to a white garage, in front of which a slim dark young chauffeur in shiny black leggings was dusting a maroon Packard convertible. Beyond the garage were some decorative trees trimmed as carefully as poodle dogs. Beyond them a large green house with a domed roof. Then more trees and beyond everything the solid, uneven, comfortable line of the foothills.

On the east side of the hall a free staircase, tile-paved, rose to a gallery with a wrought-iron railing and another piece of stained-glass romance. Large hard chairs with rounded red plush seats were backed into the vacant spaces of the wall round about. They didn't look as if anybody had ever sat in them. In the middle of the west wall there was a big empty fireplace with a brass screen in four hinged panels, and over the fireplace a marble mantel with cupids at the corners. Above the mantel there was a large oil portrait, and above the portrait two bullet-torn or moth-eaten cavalry pennants crossed in a glass frame. The portrait was a stiffly posed job of an officer in full regimentals of about the time of the Mexican war. The officer had a neat black imperial, black mustachios, hot hard coal-black eyes, and the general look of a man it would pay to get along with. I thought this might be General Sternwood's grandfather. It could hardly be the General himself, even though I had heard he was pretty far gone in years to have a couple of daughters still in the dangerous twenties.

I was still staring at the hot black eyes when a door opened far back under the stairs. It wasn't the butler coming back. It was a girl.

She was twenty or so, small and delicately put together, but she looked durable. She wore pale blue slacks and they looked well on her. She walked as if she were floating. Her hair was a fine tawny wave cut much shorter than the current fashion of pageboy tresses curled in at the bottom. Her eyes were slate-gray, and had almost no expression when they looked at me. She came over near me and smiled with her mouth and she had little sharp predatory teeth, as white as fresh orange pith and as shiny as porcelain. They glistened between her thin too taut lips. Her face lacked color and didn't look too healthy.

"Tall, aren't you?" she said.

"I didn't mean to be."

Her eyes rounded. She was puzzled. She was thinking. I could see, even on that short acquaintance, that thinking was always going to be a bother to her.

"Handsome too," she said. "And I bet you know it."

I grunted.

"What's your name?"

"Reilly," I said. "Doghouse Reilly."

"That's a funny name." She bit her lip and turned her head a little and looked at me along her eyes. Then she lowered her lashes until they almost cuddled her cheeks and slowly raised them again, like a theater curtain. I was to get to know that trick. That was supposed to make me roll over on my back with all four paws in the air.

"Are you a prizefighter?" she asked, when I didn't.

"Not exactly. I'm a sleuth."

"A — a —" She tossed her head angrily, and the rich color of it glistened in the rather dim light of the big hall. "You're making fun of me."

"Uh-uh."

"What?"

"Get on with you," I said. "You heard me."

"You didn't say anything. You're just a big tease." She put a thumb up and bit it. It was a curiously shaped thumb, thin and narrow like an extra finger, with no curve in the first joint. She bit it and sucked it slowly, turning it around in her mouth like a baby with a comforter.

"You're awfully tall," she said. Then she giggled with secret merriment. Then she turned her body slowly and lithely, without lifting her feet. Her hands dropped limp at her sides. She tilted herself toward me on her toes. She fell straight back into my arms. I had to catch her or let her crack her head on the tessellated floor. I caught her under her arms and she went rubber-legged on me instantly. I had to hold her close to hold her up. When her head was against my chest she screwed it around and giggled at me.

"You're cute," she giggled. "I'm cute too."

I didn't say anything. So the butler chose that convenient moment to come back through the French doors and see me holding her.

It didn't seem to bother him. He was a tall, thin, silver man, sixty or close to it or a little past it. He had blue eyes as remote as eyes could be. His skin was smooth and bright and he moved like a man with very sound muscles. He walked slowly across the floor toward us and the girl jerked away from me. She flashed across the room to the foot of the stairs and went up them like a deer. She was gone before I could draw a long breath and let it out.

The butler said tonelessly: "The General will see you now, Mr. Marlowe."

I pushed my lower jaw up off my chest and nodded at him. "Who was that?"

"Miss Carmen Sternwood, sir."

"You ought to wean her. She looks old enough."

He looked at me with grave politeness and repeated what he had said.

From *Murder Is My Business*

LYNETTE PRUCHA

Marriage, like death, was big business in downtown Los Angeles. The storefronts along Broadway's Latino thoroughfare proved it. Behind the large window of Bridal City, lace-tiaraed mannequins wearing dusty peach, petal rose, or mint green gowns lined up like snow cones in seasonal shades of popularity.

Sticking out in the midst of all this tacky pomp and circumstance was the Bradbury

---

LYNETTE PRUCHA (b. 1955) is president of Sneak Preview Productions in Hollywood. She co-produced and co-wrote the feature film *Bird of Prey* (1996) starring Richard Chamberlain, Lesley Ann Warren, and Jennifer Tilly, and she's currently working on a film adaptation of her mystery novel *Smokescreen* (1993). Prucha's story "Murder Is My Business" first appeared in *The Womansleuth Anthology* (1990), edited by Irene Zahava.

Building. In that historic edifice, built in 1893 and recently made earthquake-proof, for the bargain price of $1,500 a month in rent, was my one-woman detective agency, MARINO INC.

The INC was stenciled by mistake, but I never bothered to have it removed. It gave the business more authenticity. Business wasn't exactly booming, but I managed to cover my overhead, pay rent on a one-bedroom condo in West Hollywood, eat at City restaurant at least twice a month, and work out with a trainer at a prissy health club on Robertson. Not bad.

My office was done up in what I'd call minimalist chic. Not too much furniture and a view of an adjacent building with a fifty-foot mural of Hidalgo Rodriguez, patron saint of the streets. Actually he was the first capitalist to turn a peso into a million bucks. His image was all the art I needed.

It was a Thursday evening, somewhere between five and six. My part-time intern had gone home for the Christmas holidays, and for two weeks I was winging it on my own. I had reservations for dinner at Engine Company 28 and I was just finishing some paperwork on my last case, when the door to the outer reception area slammed shut.

A meek little voice managed to make itself heard, and I replied by shouting, "In here."

Heels clicked along the tiled floor and I had barely glanced up from an overdue account when my eyes did a ring-around-the-rosy at the looker standing no more than three feet in front of me.

She was younger than thirty, but old enough to know what she was doing. The two-piece lamb's wool suit smelled new and expensive. The glasnost hat had a faux cluster of jewels appliquéd on it. The entire outfit was black, including the silk seamed stockings and the patent leather bag she clutched in her gloved hands.

"Ms. Marino?" she inquired as I pointed for her to have a seat.

"Angie." I pulled out a pack of cigarettes from my top drawer, offered her one, but she declined. I had just inhaled my first puff of the day when she dropped the next line on me.

"My husband murdered me."

I stopped chomping on my cigarette long enough to watch the flicker of melodrama dance in her sea green eyes. For a minute I almost drowned in the turbulence of that ocean.

"You mean tried to murder you?"

"No."

I took another drag of the cigarette to help clear my head. Then I laid the burning stick in a clean ashtray, pushed up the sleeves of my camel jacket, the one I'd purchased in Neiman Marcus two months ago, the one I still owed $314 on. I figured by now I probably owned both sleeves. The rest of the jacket, along with the pockets and snazzy buttons, had a way to go.

She removed her gloves and laid them on my desk. "Let me explain. I don't have much time." She pulled out a handkerchief and clutched the embroidered talisman in her smooth hand. "My husband has been having this affair for three months. I was hoping it would peter out, that Roger would get tired and come back home and behave. We've been married nearly five years. Men are apt to stray sometimes." Her smile contained the thinnest veneer of sarcasm as she crossed her legs and waited for my response.

"Before you go any further, it might help if I knew your name and you understood my fees."

She replied with hesitation. "Ramona Millicent Hunnicut and I'm sure your fees are reasonable."

"Hunnicut Textiles?"

"Yes. I gather you realize I value discretion above all else. If word gets out, it would be quite embarrassing."

"Of course." I was attracted to Ramona Millicent Hunnicut more than I cared to admit. My therapist said I'd moved beyond my damsel-in-distress syndrome. Thank you. No recriminations. Just a healthy dose of curiosity and simple animal attraction operating here. I ground out the tasteless cigarette, thought about my liaison later this evening, and wondered what Mrs. Hunnicut was wearing under the widow's weeds.

"A week ago I did something quite shameful."

I raised an eyebrow and hung on every word. I gestured for her to resume her tale.

"I hired someone to follow Roger. The detective took these pictures." She opened her purse and pulled out two photos. "I have more, but they are in my safe at home."

Roger was a handsome man, tall, with a soft fleece of hair on his muscular chest. The lady-in-waiting kneeling in front of Roger had divine curvature and curly brunette hair that fell on her naked shoulders in frenzied tendrils. The other photo was a little more of the same, only this time, Roger was the supplicant.

"Why did you come to me, Mrs. Hunnicut? Why not Thachter & Associates? I understand they were involved in the Hunnicut investigation about three years ago." I'd suddenly remembered the rumors that had gone around town. Old-monied Hunnicut had been blackmailed by a drug cartel. It appeared Hunnicut refused to use his cargo as a front for laundered dough. The Colombians didn't appreciate his resistance.

Mrs. Hunnicut shifted uncomfortably in her chair. Her lips were creamy smooth, the jaw strong, the nose proud enough.

"My father hired Thachter & Associates. He's dead. I'm in charge now."

"Fine, then why not the dick you hired to take the photos?"

"Mr. Fletcher? I didn't like him. He was beginning to get too familiar."

I started to raise my eyebrows again, but it felt like old hat. I wondered if she meant Ned Fletcher, an operative I'd run into more than once.

"How familiar?" The words spilled out of my mouth.

Mrs. Hunnicut unbuttoned the top of her jacket. "He was a handsome man who tried to take advantage of my shame."

She gave me enough details to convince me she'd done the right thing. I'd had my suspicions about Fletcher, but I never thought he'd go this far. Lousy son of a bitch. He probably figured he'd capitalize on this delicate situation. It had been done before.

"Besides, a friend of mine recommended I work with a woman. At least I know where they stand."

Mrs. Hunnicut leveled a look at me that made my toes curl.

"That's why I came to you. I simply checked the phone book. Before my father died, he tried to buy this building. I saw your name listed, with the Bradbury Building as an address, and I called. Sorry I can't say you came highly recommended, but in my rush to find someone I didn't have the time to make extensive inquiries."

I nodded, waiting for more, but she didn't give it. Her perfume appeared to travel off her body first class and infiltrate my train of thought. I conjured a spring bouquet, the delicacy of thistles blowing in the wind, and a Brazilian rain forest.

"I have no one to turn to. My husband rigged my murder, never suspecting I knew about his infidelities. He had no idea I had gotten into the habit of . . . spying on him."

Nothing like a healthy dose of back-stabbing to spark a marriage, I thought. "That still doesn't explain the fact that you claim to have been murdered. The dead don't often get a chance to talk about it afterward." Somewhere along the line, diplomacy had jumped overboard. Mrs. Hunnicut could be just another nut case looking for attention or drama in her life. But then again she could be telling the truth.

"Let me explain. The day before yesterday, I went sailing with my husband. I gave Roger *Siren's Kiss* as a wedding present. It's a fifty-foot, full-powered Trimaran. Anyway, that night he was in a very good mood. We'd just made love and he was preparing supper for me. Roger's an excellent cook. He insisted I go up on deck and make myself comfortable in this makeshift divan he'd built for my convenience. I often spend hours reading and sunbathing there."

Mrs. Hunnicut's pale face didn't look as though she'd spent too much time exposing herself to the harmful rays of the sun. I could picture her in a 1940s one-piece white bathing suit, though.

"We had been out sailing all day, so I'd imagine we were about two hours from shore. The sky was black and there didn't appear to be a ship in sight."

I opened my desk drawer, stared at the bottle of Rémy, thought better of it, and pulled out a pad instead. "Go ahead," I said, scratching a few notes on the yellow paper.

"Anyway, I felt for the first time in months that perhaps Roger *did* love me, that this affair was just a meaningless diversion. Even on the open sea, I could smell the delicious aroma of the fresh lobster fettucine he was preparing. We both love garlic and herbs."

My stomach did a flip-flop at the mention of food. I had promised myself I wouldn't order an appetizer at dinner, but mentally blew off my good intentions.

"I'd had several glasses of champagne — he'd seen to that. But it must have been something more than champagne because I started to feel as if I was slipping away, like I was becoming one with the sea. The ocean was a bit choppy and I felt the spray of sea salt on my face. I was preparing to get up off the divan when I heard a clicking noise. I opened my eyes and stared into the darkness, but no one was there. Then I heard music coming from down below and Roger's deep baritone voice as he attempted an aria from *Rigoletto.* I was just about to close my eyes again, I suddenly felt so weary, when something snapped underneath me — like a spring — and before I knew it the divan flipped over starboard. I felt my body slap the ice cold ocean." Mrs. Hunnicut shuddered and clutched her handkerchief in her hand.

I urged her to continue. She measured her breathing carefully before commencing.

"I screamed and flailed my arms — I'm a poor swimmer and I was absolutely paralyzed with fear. Fear and an almost crippling relief that it would soon be over."

Her eyes narrowed in pain. Mrs. Hunnicut's voice was chilled with the terror of her recollection. I wasn't quite sure I should believe her story, but something in her straightforward manner told me I'd already bought it.

"I caught sight of the ship receding. I felt myself giving up on it all, Ms. Marino — Angie — and then I succumbed." Mrs. Hunnicut paused, dropped the photos in her bag, and then continued.

"When I came to, I was shivering, my teeth were chattering. In fact the gentlemen who found me thought I was having a seizure. It took several minutes for me to realize I wasn't dead, that I had miraculously been rescued. I had been fished out of the water by two men who were on their way back to shore in a small power boat. They saved my life."

Here Mrs. Hunnicut's voice cracked and she put her handkerchief to her eyes to dab at the tears. Then she coughed.

"What were these men doing out so late at night?"

Mrs. Hunnicut nodded her head. "Needless to say, I really didn't care, but once I had sufficiently calmed down, I was able to observe that they'd gone fishing and probably had a bit too much to eat and drink. I daresay, they didn't expect to fish me out of the Pacific. If it wasn't for the light they had attached to the side of the boat, I wouldn't be here to tell you this story."

I knew a little about boats, enough to know that a floodlight off side would illuminate the dark sea. "Are you sure your husband tried to kill you?"

"Positive. Once Roger returned to the dock, he took his time and thoroughly cleaned down the boat — it's an obsession of his. I borrowed my rescuer's binoculars and watched him from their boat. I could see that he was whistling as he left the dock." Her voice contained an undertone of acidity. She winced slightly and continued. "Then he walked over to his car and drove away."

"But surely the power boat didn't dock at the same time your husband's boat did?"

"No. We made it about a half an hour later. Both boats were motorized, but I'm sure Roger was traveling at a much faster speed."

"He didn't contact the coast guard? No one? Just pretended you disappeared into thin air."

"Yes." Her voice cracked.

Mrs. Hunnicut pulled out a cigarette, tapped it on the desk, and waited for me to light it. I did. I looked at the clock and figured I still had a good forty-five minutes before my dinner engagement. I urged her to go on with her most remarkable tale. "But what about your rescuers? Weren't they suspicious? What did you tell them?"

"Of course they were quite alarmed. I think they thought I was rather mad — you know, off my rocker. I was incoherent for quite some time. They gave me a change of clothes so I'd keep warm and I asked to borrow a hat, so I wouldn't be recognized when I got to shore, just in case. You see, I still didn't know what I was prepared to do."

I leaned back in my chair and listened to the growing stillness outside the window. The process of detailing this confession had a soothing effect on Mrs. Hunnicut. A dead calm.

"You may think this rather strange, but for the past few months Roger's solicitations have been growing in proportion to his infidelity. He'd always been attentive, but lately there didn't seem to be enough he could do for me. Now that he was . . . misbehaving."

Misbehaving? Mrs. Hunnicut had a way with words. I almost expected to hear she'd pulled down his pants and given him a good spanking.

"I think I hate him more for that . . . the false solicitations, the simulated display of his affection, than for what he did to me. He'd stop at nothing to get what he wanted."

"And what *did* he want, Mrs. Hunnicut?" She didn't flutter an eyelash. It never failed to amaze me, this business of murder. How nearly 35 percent of all homicides are caused by family members, a lover, or children. Someone close. Someone trustworthy. Domestic violence is fast becoming the number one crime in the good old U.S. of A.

She looked at me, surprised. "My money of course." Then she took a deep breath. "Before this nightmare happened, I had decided to spend a few days visiting a college friend to clear my mind."

I smiled without knowing it.

"Did I say something funny?"

"No, of course not, Mrs. Hunnicut. Excuse me. But I just got this flash."

"A flash?"

"I know a little about your family, in fact a great deal. You see, it just so happens that we both grew up in northern California and while I didn't go to Stanford, as you did, I attended my fair share of wild sorority parties in my days. I have this hunch that you were one of the Delta Chi's? Class of '80? Am I right?"

Mrs. Hunnicut looked relieved. A blush brushed her face with a tinge of rouge. She smiled broadly and nodded her head. "Please don't remind me of any war stories. I was quite a wild young lady."

There was a twinkle in her eyes, but I couldn't tell if she was laughing with me, or at me. "Please continue, Mrs. Hunnicut."

"Well, I'd only been away for a day when Roger called me. He was telephoning from a phone booth because as he said, he'd been walking down the street, realized that he missed me immensely, and called — just like that — to tell me he loved me. Needless to say, I was delighted, especially when he said he was sending me a surprise. In less than half an hour, a chauffeured limo pulled up in front of my friend's house and I was whisked away. Mary was off at a conference all day so I left her a note and said I'd call and explain everything later."

"So the limo dropped you off at the Marina?"

"Precisely."

"Any witnesses?"

"No. Just the driver."

"Did you get the name of the limo service or the license plate number?"

"Of course not." She dashed out her half-smoked cigarette in the ashtray. "I hardly suspected foul play."

Mrs. Hunnicut got up from her seat and walked to the dusty window. I knew I shouldn't have fired the cleaning crew until I found a suitable replacement. Having a woman like Mrs. Hunnicut in my office suddenly made me realize how drab and undramatic my work space was. I made a mental note to do something about it. Trade in minimalism for a little Italian avant-garde. I fought off the urge to light up another cigarette, my quota being one a day, as I examined Mrs. Hunnicut's long legs. A low whistle involuntarily escaped my lips. She whipped around and looked me in the eye.

"But I was wrong. My husband murdered me. And now I need your help." She moved back over to the desk and leaned as close as decency would allow.

Help her? The entire story smelled as rotten as a bonito left out in the sun. "Why didn't you go to the police?" I asked, pulling away from her. I got up out of my seat.

Mrs. Hunnicut found hers and sat down.

"It seems to me you have a pretty good case," I continued. "Even if it was an accident, your husband never reported you missing. You had the two fishermen as witnesses. And some pretty incriminating proof to support his motive. Why didn't you go to the hospital or your physician if you thought he slipped you a Mickey? We could have used this as evidence in our investigation."

"I don't care to have him arrested." Her lips tightened and puckered slightly. "I want revenge."

I caught a glimpse of myself in the mirror. I didn't look as bad as I should have after twelve hours of work. Pushing back a few stray hairs that had fallen into my wide-opened eyes, I examined Mrs. Hunnicut's determined face. I wasn't in the line of business to avenge murderers. I just helped to put them behind bars, the old-fashioned way. But I was curious, it comes with the territory, and Mrs. Hunnicut looked desperate. The calling of my trade whispered in my ears, You should know better. But the warning was drowned out by a suggestive bellowing in my head: Go ahead, take that occasional walk on the wild side.

"I'll help you," I said. Sure she had a pretty face and a nice pocketbook to match, but I was a sucker for a woman in distress. And more than that, I was intrigued.

Mrs. Hunnicut looked relieved. She smiled. The whites of her perfectly shaped teeth glistened. She wet her lips with her tongue and then smoothed back her hair.

So I hadn't worked out all the kinks in therapy, and when I did, I somehow suspected I might be six feet under.

From *Devil in a Blue Dress*

WALTER MOSLEY

At four in the morning the neighborhoods of Los Angeles are asleep. On Dinker Street there wasn't even a dog out prowling the trash. The dark lawns were quiet, dotted now and then with hushed white flowers that barely shone in the lamplight.

The French girl's address was a one-story duplex; the porch light shone on her half of the porch.[1]

I stayed in my car long enough to light up a cigarette. The house looked peaceful enough. There was a fat palm tree in the front yard. The lawn was surrounded by an ornamental white picket fence. There were no bodies lying around, no hard-looking men with knives on the front porch. I should have taken Odell's advice right then and left California for good.

When I got to the door she was waiting behind it.

"Mr. Rawlins?"

"Easy, call me Easy."

"Oh, yes. That is what Coretta called you. Yes?"

"Yeah."

[1]The main character, Easy Rawlins, had been hired by a white man named DeWitt Albright to find "the French girl," Daphne, for her lover, a wealthy man named Carter. In this excerpt there will also be references to Coretta, a friend of Easy's also known by Daphne, who had recently been murdered, and a reference to John's Place, an illegal Central Avenue jazz bar [Eds.].

WALTER MOSLEY (b. 1952) is a fiction writer known for his series of mystery novels whose hero is Easy Rawlins, an African American working man living in post-World War II Los Angeles. The chapter reprinted here is from *Devil in a Blue Dress* (1990), which was made into a film in 1995. Other novels in the series include *A Red Death* (1991), *White Butterfly* (1992), and *Black Betty* (1994).

"I am Daphne, please to come in."

It was one of those houses that used to be for one family but something happened. Maybe a brother and sister inherited it and couldn't come to a deal so they just walled the place in half and called it a duplex.

She led me into the half living room. It had brown carpets, a brown sofa with a matching chair, and brown walls. There was a bushy potted fern next to the brown curtains that were closed over the entire front wall. Only the coffee table wasn't brown. It was a gilded stand on which lay a clear glass tabletop.

"A drink, Mr. Rawlins?" Her dress was the simple blue kind that the French girls wore when I was a GI in Paris. It was plain and came down to just below her knee. Her only jewelry was a small ceramic pin, worn over her left breast.

"No thanks."

Her face was beautiful. More beautiful than the photograph. Wavy hair so light brown that you might have called it blond from a distance, and eyes that were either green or blue depending on how she held her head. Her cheekbones were high but her face was full enough that it didn't make her seem severe. Her eyes were just a little closer than most women's eyes; it made her seem vulnerable, made me feel that I wanted to put my arms around her — to protect her.

We looked at each other for a few moments before she spoke. "Would you 'ave something to eat?"

"No thanks." I realized that we were whispering and asked, "Is there anybody else here?"

"No," she whispered, moving close enough for me to smell the soap she used, Ivory. "I live alone."

Then she reached out a long delicate hand to touch my face.

"You 'ave been fighting?"

"What?"

"The bruises on your face."

"'Nuthin'."

She didn't move her hand.

"I could clean them for you?"

I put my hand out to touch her face, thinking, This is crazy.

"It's okay," I said. "I brought you $25."

She smiled like a child. Only a child could ever be that happy.

"Thank you," she said. She turned away and seated herself on the brown chair, clasping her hands on her lap. She nodded at the couch and I lowered myself.

"I got the money right here." I went for my pocket but she stopped me with a gesture.

"Couldn't you take me to him? I'm just a girl, you know. You could stay in the car and I would only take a little time. Five minutes maybe."

"Listen, honey, I don't even know you . . ."

"But I need 'elp." She looked down at the knot of hands and said, "You do not want to be bother by the police. I do not either . . ."

I'd heard that line before. "Why don't you just take the taxi?"

"I am afraid."

"But why you gonna trust me?"

"I 'ave no choice. I am a stranger 'ere and my friend is gone. When Coretta tells me that you are looking for me I ask her if you are a bad man and she says no to me. She says that you are a good man and that you are just looking, how you say, innocent."

"I just heard about ya," I said. "That's all. Bouncer at John's said that you were something to see."

She smiled for me. "You will help me, yes?"

The time for me to say no was over. If I was going to say no, it should have been to DeWitt Albright or even to Coretta. But I still had a question to ask.

"How'd you know where to call me?"

Daphne looked down at her hands for maybe three seconds; long enough for the average person to formulate a lie.

"Before I gave Coretta her money I said that I wanted to 'ave it, so I could talk to you. I wanted to know why you look for me."

She was just a girl. Nothing over twenty-two.

"Where you say your friend lives?"

"On a street above Hollywood, Laurel Canyon Road."

"You know how to get there?"

She nodded eagerly and then jumped up saying, "Just let me get one thing."

She ran out of the living room into a darkened doorway and returned in less than a minute. She was carrying an old beaten-up suitcase.

"It is Richard's, my friend's," she smiled shyly.

I drove across town to La Brea then straight north to Hollywood. The canyon road was narrow and winding but there was no traffic at all. We hadn't even seen a police car on the ride and that was fine with me, because the police have white slavery[2] on the brain when it comes to colored men and white women.

At every other curve, near the top of the road, we'd catch a glimpse of nighttime L.A. Even way back then the city was a sea of lights. Bright and shiny and alive. Just to look out on Los Angeles at night gave me a sense of power.

"It is the next one, Easy. The one with the carport."

It was another small house. Compared with some of the mansions we'd seen on the ride it was like a servant's house. A shabby little A-frame with two windows and a gaping front door.

"Your friend always leave his door open like that?" I asked.

"I do not know."

When we parked I got out of the car with her.

"I will only be a moment." She caressed my arm before turning toward the house.

"Maybe I better go with ya."

"No," she said with strength that she hadn't shown before.

"Listen. This is late at night, in a lonely neighborhood, in a big city. That door is open and that means something's wrong. And if something happens to one more person I know, the police are gonna chase me down into the grave."

"Okay," she said. "But only to see if it is alright. Then you go back to the car."

[2]**white slavery:** Coercing or defrauding a girl or woman into becoming a prostitute [Eds.].

I closed the front door before turning on the wall switch. Daphne called out, "Richard!"

It was one of those houses that was designed to be a mountain cabin. The front door opened into a big room that was living room, dining room, and kitchen all in one. The kitchen was separated from the dining area by a long counter. The far left of the room had a wooden couch with a Mexican rug thrown across it and a metal chair with tan cushions for the seat and back. The wall opposite the front door was all glass. You could see the city lights winking inside the mirror image of the room, Daphne, and me.

At the far left wall was a door.

"His bedroom," she said.

The bedroom was also simple. Wood floor, window for a wall, and a king-sized bed with a dead man on it.

He was in the same blue suit. He lay across the bed, his arms out like Jesus Christ — but the fingers were jangled, not composed like they were on my mother's crucifix. He didn't call me "colored brother" but I recognized the drunken white man I'd met in front of John's place.

Daphne gasped. She grabbed my sleeve. "It is Richard."

There was a butcher's knife buried deep in his chest. The smooth brown haft stood out from his body like a cattail from a pond. He'd fallen with his back on a bunch of blankets so that the blood had flown upwards, around his face and neck. There was a lot of blood around his wide-eyed stare. Blue eyes and brown hair and dark blood so thick that you could have dished it up like Jell-O. My tongue grew a full beard and I gagged.

The next thing I knew I was down on one knee but I kept myself from being sick. I kneeled there in front of that dead man like a priest blessing a corpse brought to him by grieving relatives. I didn't know his family name or what he had done, I only knew that he was dead.

All the dead men that I'd ever known came back to me in that instant. Bernard Hooks, Addison Sherry, Alphonso Jones, Marcel Montague. And a thousand Germans named Heinz, and children and women too. Some were mutilated, some burned. I'd killed my share of them and I'd done worse things than that in the heat of war. I'd seen open-eyed corpses like this man Richard and corpses that had no heads at all. Death wasn't new to me and I was to be damned if I'd let one more dead white man break me down.

While I was down there, on my knees, I noticed something. I bent down and smelled it and then I picked it up and wrapped it in my handkerchief.

When I got to my feet I saw that Daphne was gone. I went to the kitchen and rinsed my face in the sink. I figured that Daphne had run to the toilet. But when I was through she hadn't returned. I looked in the bathroom but she wasn't there. I ran outside to look at my car but she was nowhere to be seen.

Then I heard a ruckus from the carport.

Daphne was there pushing the old suitcase into the trunk of a pink Studebaker.

"What's goin' on?" I asked.

"What'a ya think's goin' on! We gotta get out of here and it's best if we split."

I didn't have the time to wonder at her loss of accent. "What happened here?"

"Help me with my bag!"

"What happened?" I asked again.

"How the hell do I know? Richard's dead, Frank's gone too. All I know is that I have to get out of here and you better too, unless you want the police to prove you did it."

"Who did it?" I grabbed her and turned her away from the car.

"I do not know," she said quietly and calmly into my face. Our faces were no more than two inches apart.

"I cain't just leave it like this."

"There's nothing else to do, Easy. I'll take these things so nobody will know that I was ever here and you just go on home. Go to sleep and treat it like a dream."

"What about him?" I yelled, pointing at the house.

"That's a dead man, Mr. Rawlins. He's dead and gone. You just go home and forget what you saw. The police don't know you were here and they won't know unless you shout so loud that someone looks out here and sees your car."

"What you gonna do?"

"Drive his car to a little place I know and leave it there. Get on a bus for somewhere more than a thousand miles from here."

"What about the men lookin' for you?"

"You mean Carter? He doesn't mean any harm. He'll give up when they can't find me." She smiled.

Then she kissed me.

It was a slow, deliberate kiss. At first I tried to pull away but she held on strong. Her tongue moved around under mine and between my gums and lips. The bitter taste in my mouth turned almost sweet from hers. She leaned back and smiled at me for a moment and then she kissed me again. This time it was fierce. She lunged so deep into my throat that once our teeth collided and my canine chipped.

"Too bad we won't have a chance to get to know each other, Easy. Otherwise I'd let you eat this little white girl up."

"You can't just go," I stammered. "That's murder there."

She slammed the trunk shut and went around me to the driver's side of the car. She got in and rolled down the window. "Bye, Easy," she said as she popped the ignition and threw it into reverse.

The engine choked twice but not enough to stall.

I could have grabbed her and pulled her out of the car but what would I have done with her? All I could do was watch the red lights recede down the hill.

Then I got into my car thinking that my luck hadn't turned yet.

A Science Assignment

Primatologists Jane Goodall and Shirley S. Strum are field researchers. Since 1960, Goodall has studied chimpanzees at Tanzania's Gombe Research Center, which she founded. Strum began her long-term study of baboons in Kenya in 1972. In the passages that follow, each researcher offers an overview of her work, placing it in the context of the developing knowledge and controversies of her profession. Goodall's discussion appears in her book *Through a Window: My Thirty Years with the Chimpanzees of Gombe* (1990); the excerpts by Strum are taken from her book *Almost Human: A Journey Into the World of Baboons* (1987).

Write an essay in which you compare some aspect — or perhaps several aspects — of Goodall's and Strum's work. Here are some suggestions. You might consider the two researchers' depictions of their intellectual journeys. With what attitudes did they begin? What influenced their thinking? How did their thinking change? You might also consider their relations to mentors. Strum writes about the influence of anthropologist Stanley Washburn, and Goodall writes about her relationship to her thesis director, ethologist Robert Hinde. Another possibility is to compare the two scientists' research interests: How do chimpanzees and baboons compare as subjects of scientific investigation? For example, what light might either species throw upon issues of human evolution? Or you might consider how Goodall and Strum, as independent thinkers, responded to the methods and models of primate study within which they were expected to work.

If you are interested in the subject of primate research, you may want to do this assignment in coordination with the related material in the Opening Problem (p. 421), the Professional Application (p. 444), and Readings: Methods of Inquiry in Primate Research (p. 506).

The Mind of the Chimpanzee

JANE GOODALL

Often I have gazed into a chimpanzee's eyes and wondered what was going on behind them. I used to look into Flo's, she so old, so wise. What did she remember of her young days? David Greybeard had the most beautiful eyes of them all, large and lustrous, set wide apart. They somehow expressed his whole personality, his serene self-assurance, his inherent dignity — and, from time to time, his utter determination to get his way. For a long time I never liked to look a chimpanzee straight in the eye — I assumed that, as is the case with most primates, this would be interpreted as a threat or at least as a breach of good manners. Not so. As long as one looks with gentleness, without arrogance, a chimpanzee will understand, and may even return the look. And then — or such is my fantasy — it is as though the eyes are windows into the mind. Only the glass is opaque so that the mystery can never be fully revealed.

I shall never forget my meeting with Lucy, an eight-year-old home-raised chimpanzee. She came and sat beside me on the sofa and, with her face very close to mine, searched in my eyes — for what? Perhaps she was looking for signs of mistrust, dislike, or fear, since many people must have been somewhat disconcerted when, for the first time, they came face to face with a grown chimpanzee. Whatever Lucy read in my eyes

---

Best known through her films and articles produced for the National Geographic Society, British ethologist JANE GOODALL (b. 1934) has spent more than three decades in the jungles of Tanzania studying the behavior of chimpanzees in the wild. Her numerous publications include *Grub, the Bush Baby* (1972), *The Chimpanzees of Gombe* (1986), *In the Shadow of Man* (1988), and *Through a Window: My Thirty Years with the Chimpanzees of Gombe* (1991), excerpted here.

clearly satisfied her for she suddenly put one arm round my neck and gave me a generous and very chimp-like kiss, her mouth wide open and laid over mine. I was accepted.

For a long time after that encounter I was profoundly disturbed. I had been at Gombe for about fifteen years then and I was quite familiar with chimpanzees in the wild. But Lucy, having grown up as a human child, was like a changeling, her essential chimpanzeeness overlaid by the various human behaviors she had acquired over the years. No longer purely chimp yet eons away from humanity, she was man-made, some other kind of being. I watched, amazed, as she opened the refrigerator and various cupboards, found bottles and a glass, then poured herself a gin and tonic. She took the drink to the TV, turned the set on, flipped from one channel to another then, as though in disgust, turned it off again. She selected a glossy magazine from the table and, still carrying her drink, settled in a comfortable chair. Occasionally, as she leafed through the magazine she identified something she saw, using the signs of ASL, the American Sign Language used by the deaf. I, of course, did not understand, but my hostess, Jane Temerlin (who was also Lucy's "mother"), translated: "That dog," Lucy commented, pausing at a photo of a small white poodle. She turned the page. "Blue," she declared, pointing then signing as she gazed at a picture of a lady advertising some kind of soap powder and wearing a brilliant blue dress. And finally, after some vague hand movements — perhaps signed mutterings — "This Lucy's, this mine," as she closed the magazine and laid it on her lap. She had just been taught, Jane told me, the use of the possessive pronouns during the thrice weekly ASL lessons she was receiving at the time.

The book written by Lucy's human "father," Maury Temerlin, was entitled *Lucy, Growing Up Human.* And in fact, the chimpanzee is more like us than is any other living creature. There is close resemblance in the physiology of our two species and genetically, in the structure of the DNA, chimpanzees and humans differ by only just over 1 percent. This is why medical research uses chimpanzees as experimental animals when they need substitutes for humans in the testing of some drug or vaccine. Chimpanzees can be infected with just about all known human infectious diseases including those, such as hepatitis B and AIDS, to which other non-human animals (except gorillas, orangutans, and gibbons) are immune. There are equally striking similarities between humans and chimpanzees in the anatomy and wiring of the brain and nervous system, and — although many scientists have been reluctant to admit to this — in social behavior, intellectual ability, and the emotions. The notion of an evolutionary continuity in physical structure from pre-human ape to modern man has long been morally acceptable to most scientists. That the same might hold good for mind was generally considered an absurd hypothesis — particularly by those who used, and often misused, animals in their laboratories. It is, after all, convenient to believe that the creature you are using, while it may react in disturbingly human-like ways, is, in fact, merely a mindless and, above all, unfeeling, "dumb" animal.

When I began my study at Gombe in 1960 it was not permissible — at least not in ethological circles — to talk about an animal's mind. Only humans had minds. Nor was it quite proper to talk about animal personality. Of course everyone knew that they *did* have their own unique characters — everyone who had ever owned a dog or other pet was aware of that. But ethologists, striving to make theirs a "hard" science, shied away from the task of trying to explain such things objectively. One respected ethologist, while acknowledging that there was "variability between individual animals," wrote that it was best that this fact be "swept under the carpet." At that time ethological carpets fairly bulged with all that was hidden beneath them.

How naive I was. As I had not had an undergraduate science education I didn't realize that animals were not supposed to have personalities, or to think, or to feel emotions or pain. I had no idea that it would have been more appropriate to assign each of the chimpanzees a number rather than a name when I got to know him or her. I didn't realize that it was not scientific to discuss behavior in terms of motivation or purpose. And no one had told me that terms such as *childhood* and *adolescence* were uniquely human phases of the life cycle, culturally determined, not to be used when referring to young chimpanzees. Not knowing, I freely made use of all those forbidden terms and concepts in my initial attempt to describe, to the best of my ability, the amazing things I had observed at Gombe.

I shall never forget the response of a group of ethologists to some remarks I made at an erudite seminar. I described how Figan, as an adolescent, had learned to stay behind in camp after senior males had left, so that we could give him a few bananas for himself. On the first occasion he had, upon seeing the fruits, uttered loud, delighted food calls: whereupon a couple of the older males had charged back, chased after Figan, and taken his bananas. And then, coming to the point of the story, I explained how, on the next occasion, Figan had actually suppressed his calls. We could hear little sounds, in his throat, but so quiet that none of the others could have heard them. Other young chimps, to whom we tried to smuggle fruit without the knowledge of their elders, never learned such self-control. With shrieks of glee they would fall to, only to be robbed of their booty when the big males charged back. I had expected my audience to be as fascinated and impressed as I was. I had hoped for an exchange of views about the chimpanzee's undoubted intelligence. Instead there was a chill silence, after which the chairman hastily changed the subject. Needless to say, after being thus snubbed, I was very reluctant to contribute any comments, at any scientific gathering, for a very long time. Looking back, I suspect that everyone was interested, but it was, of course, not permissible to present a mere "anecdote" as evidence for anything.

The editorial comments on the first paper I wrote for publication demanded that every *he* or *she* be replaced with *it,* and every *who* be replaced with *which.* Incensed, I, in my turn, crossed out the *its* and *whichs* and scrawled back the original pronouns. As I had no desire to carve a niche for myself in the world of science, but simply wanted to go on living among and learning about chimpanzees, the possible reaction of the editor of the learned journal did not trouble me. In fact I won that round: The paper when finally published did confer upon the chimpanzees the dignity of their appropriate genders and properly upgraded them from the status of mere "things" to essential Being-ness.

However, despite my somewhat truculent attitude, I did want to learn, and I was sensible of my incredible good fortune in being admitted to Cambridge. I wanted to get my PhD, if only for the sake of Louis Leakey[1] and the other people who had written letters in support of my admission. And how lucky I was to have, as my supervisor, Robert Hinde. Not only because I thereby benefited from his brilliant mind and clear thinking,

[1]**Louis Leakey** is the famed Kenyan anthropologist who first conceived and later supported the research of both Goodall and Dian Fossey (p. 425) [Eds.].

but also because I doubt that I could have found a teacher more suited to my particular needs and personality. Gradually he was able to cloak me with at least some of the trappings of a scientist. Thus although I continued to hold to most of my convictions — that animals had personalities; that they could feel happy or sad or fearful; that they could feel pain; that they could strive toward planned goals and achieve greater success if they were highly motivated — I soon realized that these personal convictions were, indeed, difficult to prove. It was best to be circumspect — at least until I had gained some credentials and credibility. And Robert gave me wonderful advice on how best to tie up some of my more rebellious ideas with scientific ribbon. "You can't *know* that Fifi was jealous," he admonished on one occasion. We argued a little. And then: "Why don't you just say *If Fifi were a human child we would say she was jealous.*" I did.

It is not easy to study emotions even when the subjects are human. I know how I feel if I am sad or happy or angry, and if a friend tells me that he is feeling sad, happy, or angry, I assume that his feelings are similar to mine. But of course I cannot know. As we try to come to grips with the emotions of beings progressively more different from ourselves the task, obviously, becomes increasingly difficult. If we ascribe human emotions to non-human animals we are accused of being anthropomorphic — a cardinal sin in ethology. But is it so terrible? If we test the effect of drugs on chimpanzees because they are biologically so similar to ourselves, if we accept that there are dramatic similarities in chimpanzee and human brain and nervous systems, is it not logical to assume that there will be similarities also in at least the more basic feelings, emotions, moods of the two species?

In fact, all those who have worked long and closely with chimpanzees have no hesitation in asserting that chimps experience emotions similar to those which in ourselves we label pleasure, joy, sorrow, anger, boredom, and so on. Some of the emotional states of the chimpanzee are so obviously similar to ours that even an inexperienced observer can understand what is going on. An infant who hurls himself screaming to the ground, face contorted, hitting out with his arms at any nearby object, banging his head, is clearly having a tantrum. Another youngster, who gambols around his mother, turning somersaults, pirouetting and, every so often, rushing up to her and tumbling into her lap, patting her or pulling her hand toward him in a request for tickling, is obviously filled with *joie de vivre.*[2] There are few observers who would not unhesitatingly ascribe his behavior to a happy, carefree state of well-being. And one cannot watch chimpanzee infants for long without realizing that they have the same emotional need for affection and reassurance as human children. An adult male, reclining in the shade after a good meal, reaching benignly to play with an infant or idly groom an adult female, is clearly in a good mood. When he sits with bristling hair, glaring at his subordinates and threatening them, with irritated gestures, if they come too close, he is clearly feeling cross and grumpy. We make these judgments because the similarity of so much of a chimpanzee's behavior to our own permits us to empathize.

It is hard to empathize with emotions we have not experienced. I can imagine, to some extent, the pleasure of a female chimpanzee during the act of procreation. The feelings of her male partner are beyond my knowledge — as are those of the human male in the same context. I have spent countless hours watching mother chimpanzees

[2]***joie de vivre:*** "The joy of life" (French) [Eds.].

interacting with their infants. But not until I had an infant of my own did I begin to understand the basic, powerful instinct of mother-love. If someone accidentally did something to frighten Grub, or threaten his well-being in any way, I felt a surge of quite irrational anger. How much more easily could I then understand the feelings of the chimpanzee mother who furiously waves her arm and barks in threat at an individual who approaches her infant too closely, or at a playmate who inadvertently hurts her child. And it was not until I knew the numbing grief that gripped me after the death of my second husband that I could even begin to appreciate the despair and sense of loss that can cause young chimps to pine away and die when they lose their mothers.

Empathy and intuition can be of tremendous value as we attempt to understand certain complex behavioral interactions, provided that the behavior, as it occurs, is recorded precisely and objectively. Fortunately I have seldom found it difficult to record facts in an orderly manner even during times of powerful emotional involvement. And "knowing" intuitively how a chimpanzee is feeling — after an attack, for example — may help one to understand what happens next. We should not be afraid at least to try to make use of our close evolutionary relationship with the chimpanzees in our attempts to interpret complex behavior.

Today, as in Darwin's time, it is once again fashionable to speak of and study the animal mind. This change came about gradually, and was, at least in part, due to the information collected during careful studies of animal societies in the field. As these observations became widely known, it was impossible to brush aside the complexities of social behavior that were revealed in species after species. The untidy clutter under the ethological carpets was brought out and examined, piece by piece. Gradually it was realized that parsimonious explanations of apparently intelligent behaviors were often misleading. This led to a succession of experiments that, taken together, clearly prove that many intellectual abilities that had been thought unique to humans were actually present, though in a less highly developed form, in other, non-human beings. Particularly, of course, in the non-human primates and especially in chimpanzees.

When first I began to read about human evolution, I learned that one of the hallmarks of our own species was that we, and only we, were capable of making tools. *Man the Toolmaker* was an oft-cited definition — and this despite the careful and exhaustive research of Wolfgang Kohler and Robert Yerkes on the tool-using and tool-making abilities of chimpanzees. Those studies, carried out independently in the early twenties, were received with skepticism. Yet both Kohler and Yerkes were respected scientists, and both had a profound understanding of chimpanzee behavior. Indeed, Kohler's descriptions of the personalities and behavior of the various individuals in his colony, published in his book *The Mentality of Apes,* remain some of the most vivid and colorful ever written. And his experiments, showing how chimpanzees could stack boxes, then climb the unstable constructions to reach fruit suspended from the ceiling, or join two short sticks to make a pole long enough to rake in fruit otherwise out of reach, have become classic, appearing in almost all textbooks dealing with intelligent behavior in non-human animals.

By the time systematic observations of tool-using came from Gombe those pioneering studies had been largely forgotten. Moreover, it was one thing to know that humanized chimpanzees in the lab could use implements: It was quite another to find that this was a naturally occurring skill in the wild. I well remember writing to Louis about my first observations, describing how David Greybeard not only used bits of straw to fish for termites but actually stripped leaves from a stem and thus *made* a tool. And I remember too receiving the now oft-quoted telegram he sent in response to my letter: "Now we must redefine *tool,* redefine *Man,* or accept chimpanzees as humans."

There were, initially, a few scientists who attempted to write off the termiting observations, even suggesting that I had taught the chimps! By and large, though, people were fascinated by the information and by the subsequent observations of the other contexts in which the Gombe chimpanzees used objects as tools. And there were only a few anthropologists who objected when I suggested that the chimpanzees probably passed their tool-using traditions from one generation to the next, through observations, imitation, and practice, so that each population might be expected to have its own unique tool-using culture. Which, incidentally, turns out to be quite true. And when I described how one chimpanzee, Mike, spontaneously solved a new problem by using a tool (he broke off a stick to knock a banana to the ground when he was too nervous to actually take it from my hand) I don't believe there were any raised eyebrows in the scientific community. Certainly I was not attacked viciously, as were Kohler and Yerkes, for suggesting that humans were not the only beings capable of reasoning and insight.

The mid-sixties saw the start of a project that, along with other similar research, was to teach us a great deal about the chimpanzee mind. This was Project Washoe, conceived by Trixie and Allen Gardner. They purchased an infant chimpanzee and began to teach her the signs of ASL, the American Sign Language used by the deaf. Twenty years earlier another husband and wife team, Richard and Cathy Hayes, had tried, with an almost total lack of success, to teach a young chimp, Viki, to talk. The Hayes's undertaking taught us a lot about the chimpanzee mind, but Viki, although she did well in IQ tests, and was clearly an intelligent youngster, could not learn human speech. The Gardners, however, achieved spectacular success with their pupil, Washoe. Not only did she learn signs easily, but she quickly began to string them together in meaningful ways. It was clear that each sign evoked, in her mind, a mental image of the object it represented. If, for example, she was asked, in sign language, to fetch an apple, she would go and locate an apple that was out of sight in another room.

Other chimps entered the project, some starting their lives in deaf signing families before joining Washoe. And finally Washoe adopted an infant, Loulis. He came from a lab where no thought of teaching signs had ever penetrated. When he was with Washoe he was given no lessons in language acquisition — not by humans, anyway. Yet by the time he was eight years old he had made fifty-eight signs in their correct contexts. How did he learn them? Mostly, it seems, by imitating the behavior of Washoe and the other three signing chimps, Dar, Moja, and Tatu. Sometimes, though, he received tuition from Washoe herself. One day, for example, she began to swagger about bipedally, hair bristling, signing *food! food! food!* in great excitement. She had seen a human approaching with a bar of chocolate. Loulis, only eighteen months old, watched passively. Suddenly Washoe stopped her swaggering, went over to him, took his hand, and molded the sign for *food* (fingers pointing toward mouth). Another time, in a similar context, she made the sign for *chewing gum* — but with *her* hand on *his* body. On a third occasion Washoe, apropos of nothing, picked up a small chair, took it over to Loulis, set it down in front of him, and very distinctly made the *chair* sign three times, watching him closely as she did so. The two food signs became incorporated into Loulis's vocabulary but the sign for chair did not. Obviously the priorities of a young chimp were similar to those of a human child!

When news of Washoe's accomplishments first hit the scientific community it immediately provoked a storm of bitter protest. It implied that chimpanzees were capable of mastering a human language, and this, in turn, indicated mental powers of generalization, abstraction, and concept-formation as well as an ability to understand and use abstract symbols. And these intellectual skills were surely the prerogatives of *Homo sapiens*. Although there were many who were fascinated and excited by the Gardners' findings, there were many more who denounced the whole project, holding that the data [were] suspect, the methodology sloppy, and the conclusions not only misleading, but quite preposterous. The controversy inspired all sorts of other language projects. And, whether the investigators were skeptical to start with and hoped to disprove the Gardners' work, or whether they were attempting to demonstrate the same thing in a new way, their research provided additional information about the chimpanzee's mind.

And so, with new incentive, psychologists began to test the mental abilities of chimpanzees in a variety of different ways; again and again the results confirmed that their minds were uncannily like our own. It had long been held that only humans were capable of what is called "cross-modal transfer of information" — in other words, if you shut your eyes and someone allows you to feel a strangely shaped potato, you will subsequently be able to pick it out from other differently shaped potatoes simply by looking at them. And vice versa. It turned out that chimpanzees can "know" with their eyes what they "feel" with their fingers in just the same way. In fact, we now know that some other non-human primates can do the same thing. I expect all kinds of creatures have the same ability.

Then it was proved, experimentally and beyond doubt, that chimpanzees could recognize themselves in mirrors — that they had, therefore, some kind of self-concept. In fact, Washoe, some years previously, had already demonstrated the ability when she spontaneously identified herself in the mirror, staring at her image and making her name sign. But that observation was merely anecdotal. The proof came when chimpanzees who had been allowed to play with mirrors were, while anesthetized, dabbed with spots of odorless paint in places, such as the ears or the top of the head, that they could see only in the mirror. When they woke they were not only fascinated by their spotted images, but immediately investigated, with their fingers, the dabs of paint.

The fact that chimpanzees have excellent memories surprised no one. Everyone, after all, has been brought up to believe that "an elephant never forgets" so why should a chimpanzee be any different? The fact that Washoe spontaneously gave the name-sign of Beatrice Gardner, her surrogate mother, when she saw her after a separation of eleven years was no greater an accomplishment than the amazing memory shown by dogs who recognize their owners after separations of almost as long — and the chimpanzee has a much longer life span than a dog. Chimpanzees can plan ahead, too, at least as regards the immediate future. This, in fact, is well illustrated at Gombe, during the termiting season: Often an individual prepares a tool for use on a termite mound that is several hundred yards away and absolutely out of sight.

This is not the place to describe in detail the other cognitive abilities that have been studied in laboratory chimpanzees. Among other accomplishments chimpanzees possess pre-mathematical skills: They can, for example, readily differentiate between *more* and *less*. They can classify things into specific categories according to a given criterion — thus they have no difficulty in separating a pile of food into *fruits* and *vegetables* on one occasion, and, on another, dividing the same pile of food into *large* versus *small* items, even though this requires putting some vegetables with some fruits. Chimpanzees who have been taught a language can combine signs creatively in order to describe objects for which they have no symbol. Washoe, for example, puzzled her caretakers by asking, repeatedly, for a *rock berry.* Eventually it transpired that she was referring to Brazil nuts which she had encountered for the first time a while before. Another language-trained chimp described a cucumber as a *green banana,* and another referred to an Alka-Seltzer as a *listen drink.* They can even invent signs. Lucy, as she got older, had to be put on a leash for her outings. One day, eager to set off but having no sign for *leash,* she signaled her wishes by holding a crooked index finger to the ring on her collar. This sign became part of her vocabulary. Some chimpanzees love to draw, and especially to paint. Those who have learned sign language sometimes spontaneously label their works, "This [is] apple" — or bird, or sweet corn, or whatever. The fact that the paintings often look, to our eyes, remarkably unlike the objects depicted by the artists either means that the chimpanzees are poor draftsmen or that we have much to learn regarding ape-style representational art!

People sometimes ask why chimpanzees have evolved such complex intellectual powers when their lives in the wild are so simple. They answer is, of course, that their lives in the wild are not so simple! They use — and need — all their mental skills during normal day-to-day life in their complex society. They are always having to make choices — where to go, or with whom to travel. They need highly developed social skills — particularly those males who are ambitious to attain high positions in the dominance hierarchy. Low-ranking chimpanzees must learn deception — to conceal their intentions or to do things in secret — if they are to get their way in the presence of their superiors. Indeed, the study of chimpanzees in the wild suggests that their intellectual abilities evolved, over the millennia, to help them cope with daily life. And now, the solid core of data concerning chimpanzee intellect collected so carefully in the lab setting provides a background against which to evaluate the many examples of intelligent, rational behavior that we see in the wild.

It is easier to study intellectual prowess in the lab where, through carefully devised tests and judicious use of rewards, the chimpanzees can be encouraged to exert themselves, to stretch their minds to the limit. It is more meaningful to study the subject in the wild, but much harder. It is more meaningful because we can better understand the environmental pressures that led to the evolution of intellectual skills in chimpanzee societies. It is harder because, in the wild, almost all behaviors are confounded by countless variables; years of observing, recording, and analyzing take the place of contrived testing; sample size can often be counted on the fingers of one hand; the only experiments are nature's own, and only time — eventually — may replicate them.

In the wild a single observation may prove of utmost significance, providing a clue to some hitherto puzzling aspect of behavior, a key to the understanding of, for example, a changed relationship. Obviously it is crucial to see as many incidents of this sort as possible. During the early years of my study at Gombe it became apparent that one person alone could never learn more than a fraction of what was going on in a chimpanzee community at any given time. And so, from 1964 onwards, I gradually built up a research team to help in the gathering of information about the behavior of our closest living relatives.

From *Almost Human: A Journey into the World of Baboons*

Shirley S. Strum

It was not until I reached Berkeley as an undergraduate in September 1965 that I finally found my niche. As I lived through the Free Speech movement and the Vietnam War protests, I found myself confronting, over and over again, questions about human nature, about what was innate and impossible to modify, and what was flexible and worth changing.

For a while I toyed with abnormal psychology, then sociology. But it was my first cultural anthropology class that finally convinced me: Here was the right approach. The course looked at human behavior from a cross-cultural perspective. One class led to another: I decided to major in anthropology.

Then the other shoe dropped. I sat with a thousand other students, mesmerized, as Sherwood Washburn traced the human inheritance back further and further, to the earliest prosimians, those least progressive primates of sixty millions years ago. As Washburn held the fossil of a tiny prosimian in his hand for the class to see, I marveled that this minute creature had experienced the world, when it was alive, more the way I did than my own dear cat, Crazy. Like me, it perceived its surroundings in depth and in color. Its delicate primate hands already had finger pads and nails, and its brain had changed and grown to control them. I felt linked not only to a few thousand years of art or culture, but to millions of generations, to something bigger than I had ever imagined existed.

Sherwood Washburn was a soft-spoken, small man. His salt-and-pepper hair went perfectly with the modest glasses and Ivy League dress that reflected his East Coast upbringing and Harvard education. All other stereotypes stopped there. When he spoke about the essentials of evolutionary principles or about human evolution, he cast a spell. He was no showman, doing tricks to entertain and amuse; he simply knew his subject — he created much of the field during his lifetime — and enjoyed it with a fervor and intensity that was contagious. Until I attended his introductory class on human evolution, I knew little and cared less about the subject. Suddenly it seemed the most important way to understand human behavior. His version of the evolutionary perspective offered me exactly the answers I was seeking — a rich approach to the topic of why we are the way we are.

It would probably embarrass Washburn to know the extent to which he became my guru, but I was not alone. A long string of undergraduates and graduates, before and after me, reacted in the same way. For several decades, Washburn contributed more students to the profession than anyone else, and I joined them, going to every seminar, every lecture that was available.

But I had a problem. Although those fossilized remains told the basic story, I found the bones rather boring. It was the *behavior* they implied that interested me. I couldn't

---

Shirley S. Strum (b. 1947) is a professor of anthropology at the University of California, San Diego. She is a student of primate behavior and is the author of *Almost Human: A Journey into the World of Baboons* (1987), excerpted here.

see myself dissecting rotting cadavers and becoming an expert on bone shafts, or sitting in the blazing sun painstakingly excavating small bits of fossilized bone with a toothbrush.

My salvation came when I discovered how useful the behavior of living primates can be in reconstructing the evolution of human behavior. It was a new field, and only a few universities offered graduate training programs in it. I entered Berkeley's graduate school in September 1969, so that I could stay close to Washburn and his remarkable insights. . . .

The study of primate behavior is a relatively new phenomenon; a few field studies had been done before World War II, most notably by C. R. Carpenter, a psychologist who worked on gibbons, howler monkeys, and spider monkeys in the 1930s. The 1950s saw a spate of studies, primarily on monkeys in Africa and Asia. George Schaller worked with gorillas, one of the great apes of Africa, and a variety of abortive studies on Asian apes were undertaken. The Japanese were studying the monkeys native to their own country and were sending their scientists to investigate primates in other parts of the world. But Sherwood Washburn and his students were the first to become actively engaged in these field projects with a view to understanding human evolution.

Expectations in those early days were very different from what they came to be later. A season's work seemed reasonable, although one year's coverage was a desirable goal. Most of what was known about wild primates before then was simply anecdotal. In the new studies, the choice of species to investigate was dictated as much by opportunity and convenience as by any set of priorities, since it was felt that a great deal could be learned from *any* species. True, some species seemed more relevant to questions of human evolution than others. Our unique human adaptation developed when our ancestors came out of the forest and began living on the African savannah. This has happened only a few times during primate evolution: Aside from the hominids — our immediate ancestors — baboons and patas monkeys are the only primate inhabitants of the open veld. Vervets can be found in the narrow strips of riverine forest that penetrate the bushland and open savannah, but they don't actually live in the open away from trees. Baboons are particularly interesting because they forage out in large groups, facing the dangers of savannah life through group action, much as we imagined our ancestors did, unlike patas monkeys, who live in small groups and survive by stealth.

Although baboons are biologically more distant from humans than chimpanzees, their lifestyle and their ecological setting, thought to be of critical importance in determining behavior, made baboon models central to reconstructions of the earliest stage in human evolution. Several baboon studies combined the expertise of observers trained in anthropology, psychology, and zoology. During this formative period in the development of behavioral reconstructions of human evolution, baboons were *the* model, as well as the most studied nonhuman primate.

Between the 1950s and early 1960s and the time I set out for Kenya, important changes occurred in our view of nonhuman primates, including baboons. The more we learned about wild primates, the more variation there seemed to be, not just *between* species but *within* species. It became increasingly difficult to trust all the grand generalizing.

When Washburn and his student [Irven] DeVore wrote their early papers on baboons and human evolution, they were confident that studying baboons told them something important and specific about human evolution. As more and more variations were documented, it became harder than ever to feel justified in making such comparisons. If the behavior of baboons in one place didn't accurately predict the behavior of baboons living somewhere else, how would we be able to use such behavior patterns as models for comparatively distantly related humans? A number of first-class scientists deserted the field, deciding to study humans rather than animals in an effort to understand human behavior.

At the same time, the chimpanzees' star was rising. Anatomically, chimps and humans share a number of characteristics distinct from monkeys or prosimians, which can be seen in the organization of the shoulders, ribs, pelvis and, to some degree, the hands and feet. And chimpanzee brains, while small by human standards, are nonetheless several degrees above monkey brains in both size and organization.

Jane Goodall's study of wild chimpanzees at the Gombe Stream in Tanzania, begun in 1960, revealed many new behaviors closely resembling those of humans. Although primarily fruit eaters, chimpanzees did occasionally hunt and eat prey. They used tools and even shared food, two characteristics previously thought to be uniquely human. In addition, genetic studies, especially sequencing DNA, demonstrated an even closer biological affinity between chimpanzees and humans. Some scientists estimated that chimps and people shared 96 percent of their genetic material, while other scientists raised the percentage to a startling 99 percent. Had this been true of any other pair of animals, the two would have been classified as sibling species, but humans like their uniqueness. The old hierarchy of beings evident in the Bible, in Greek science and even in the Renaissance is alive and well in modern science. The Supreme Being comes first, then humans, then the nonhuman animals, ordered by virtue of their ability to act like humans.

Chimps definitely posed a problem. Each time chimpanzees demonstrated a humanlike ability, the definition of what was human changed. Man the hunter became man the toolmaker became man the food sharer became man the user of language. Even this last definition is under attack now that a variety of apes can converse with their human observers in American Sign Language, or by symbols on a computer or board.

Although chimpanzees replaced baboons as the model for reconstructing the evolution of human behavior, baboon studies and the baboon model have had a surprisingly lasting influence. I often wondered why this was so, and only later gained some insight.

Baboons are ubiquitous in Africa, from the arid regions of Ethiopia all the way down to the tip of the continent. If numbers and distribution count, they are second only to humans in their success as a primate.[1]

It seemed that baboons could adapt their behavior to many different kinds of environment without having to change much of their basic anatomy. They are definitely a

[1]True, Asia has its baboon equivalent — the macaques, sometimes called the baboons of the East. Although they live in the same variety of environments and climates, there are thirteen different species containing more than forty-five subspecies, each uniquely adapted to its own particular environment. This compares to only two, three, or five baboon species, depending on which taxonomist you listen to: savannah baboons (including olive, yellow, and chacma), hamadryas — and the Guinea baboons. There are three other monkeys — mandrills, drills, and geladas — which closely resemble baboons in many respects.

primate success story. By comparison, chimpanzees are on the verge of extinction, so where has all their near humanness gotten them?

In the heyday of the baboon model, ideas about primates reflected baboon studies to a disproportionate extent. When you read about "the primate male," "the primate female" or "the primate group," you were for the most part reading about baboons and about savannah baboon society. Other nonhuman primates were known to live in a variety of styles, such as mated pairs (like some prosimians and even the advanced lesser apes) or single male groups, where several females shared the same male as mate and protector, but it was the multi-male group as represented by baboons that was taken as the norm of primate social organization. Several unrelated adult males lived with many more females and their young in a cohesive and well-organized group. It traveled as a unit, feeding, resting, moving, sleeping together. The group was a primate's greatest asset, a resource for assistance in all aspects of life: foraging, socialization, protection. Baboons illustrated just how this would work.

But the lasting appeal of baboons has more to it than that. The books that continued to pay homage to baboons had a message: Our human origins hark back to a male-dominated society with a clear division of labor, one in which males hold all the power and females acquire status only through their association with a "dominant" male. In this society, males vie with one another, using force to attain dominance and claim their rightful spoils. What expectations should we have of modern humans if a killer ape (actually a killer baboon) still lurked within us, as Robert Ardrey has suggested? What if only primate males have political prowess? Could there ever be a woman president; should we even allow it? What if females are evolutionarily so constructed as to be able to do nothing except rear babies? These ideas influenced an entire generation in the fifties and sixties.

The original baboon studies by Washburn, DeVore, and an English psychologist, Ronald Hall, created a neatly constructed picture of baboon society. Yet even in 1972, when I was starting out, the fact that this idea should still be considered of such importance, especially in the face of all the new primate evidence, distressed me. As I traced the history of ideas about baboons, I found that the picture changed and became simplified the more often it was retold by the scientific and lay community. There was no mistaking its compelling message: Males were the building blocks and the cement of the group. They were the focus and the power. They were the structure and the stability, the essence and the most valuable part.

Male baboon bodies were fighting machines, with powerful muscles, thick mantles of hair, and razor-sharp canines. With such equipment, males competed with one another for whatever good things there were: food, females, a place to sit. Although the most effective way to compete was through aggression, males did not seem to fight *all* the time. In fact, once they *had* fought, they achieved a certain rank; thereafter, lower-ranking males gave way without protest, while those of higher rank confidently strode up to their rewards. This male-dominance hierarchy, arrived at as a result of aggressive contests and maintained through threat and bluff, was what gave the group its social structure.

What were the females supposed to be doing? Their lives were meant to revolve around babies: bearing them, nurturing them, socializing them into proper adults. There seemed to be a certain number of rather subtle relationships among the females, but they were always subordinate to the males. A temporary sexual liaison with a male could be useful, for his company could result in greater protection or more or better food, but this rise in status was short-lived.

All eyes were focused on the males. Females and youngsters jockeyed for positions near a dominant male and vied for the right to groom him. It was to their advantage to do so: The males watched out both for external dangers and internal strife; they were the guardians and the protectors.

This social order and the differences in sex roles were constantly visible, the early studies noted, in the way the group moved in its environment. A baboon troop on the move resembled a series of concentric circles: In the center were the dominant males and the females with young babies; surrounding them were the rest of the females, older youngsters, and lower-ranking males; finally, on the periphery, were the least important young and adolescent males. Should a predator surprise the troop, it would certainly snatch up one of these peripheral and clearly expendable members, while if the danger was detected early enough, as few as three full-grown males, canines flashing, bodies nearly doubled in size by their erect mantles of hair, presented a sight formidable enough to chase away any intruder.

A few other studies painted a different picture. Thelma Rowell had observed the same species of baboons as Washburn and DeVore, but hers lived in a forest. In such an environment, males were the first to flee from danger to the safety of the trees, leaving the females and youngsters to fend for themselves. Dominance between males seemed less clear-cut, less powerful and pervasive.

Tim Ransom's study of baboons at the Gombe Stream Reserve exposed a wealth of complexity in baboon social relationships, including observations that interactions between females were not as subtle as they had first seemed to be. His research supported the conclusion of studies on the free-ranging macaques of Cayo Santiago and the Japanese macaques, both of which demonstrated that females had dominance hierarchies.

What about baboons? The transformation of baboons in the early baboon studies to the simple picture of male dominion, and the tenacity of that picture, whether conscious or unconscious, dovetailed nicely with ideas in Western culture of how the world should be. Modern society should contain a "natural" division of male and female roles, a division into male political power and female domesticity, the interpretations seemed to say.

I had my doubts about this picture of baboon society from the beginning. I knew about Rowell's study, and about the macaques, about Tim's findings. "Go out and watch baboons," Washburn had told me. I was doing just that, and the more I watched the Pumphouse Gang,[2] the less my observations jibed with the baboon "model." At first I had assumed the discrepancies were due to my inexperience and general ineptitude, but time gave me both experience and confidence. These baboons were not playing by the rules.

First of all, it was apparent that males were only temporary members, transients, integral parts of their society for just a brief period. There are no all-male bands outside the group, nor are males particularly friendly with one another once they reside together in the same troop.

Since males come and go, they couldn't be expected to provide the stable core of

[2]**Pumphouse Gang:** Nickname for the group of baboons Strum observed, named after an essay and 1968 book by Tom Wolfe. (In Wolfe's essay the Pumphouse Gang is a group of surfers.) [Eds.].

the group. Upon closer examination, it was clear that Pumphouse males certainly didn't. They couldn't. Much of their time was spent in working out their own relationships and trying to achieve some degree of stability among themselves. This did not appear to be easy.

Furthermore, I tried hard to see the neat dominance hierarchy that males were supposed to have, but it was almost impossible to line up the males or to say which male in any pair was really the dominant one. Ray and Big Sam were a good example. One day Ray would come out ahead; the next, sometimes even within the hour, Big Sam would be the winner. Undaunted, Ray would try again until he won. Stubbornly, Big Sam would refuse to let the issue drop.

True, the situation between all the males in the troop was not always chaotic. Carl and Sumner seemed to have everything worked out between themselves fairly well, but as relationships between the other males changed, the balance of the entire troop would be upset. Even if Carl and Sumner didn't reverse their ranks each day, when Ray decided to harass Sumner instead of Big Sam, Carl felt the effects.

It was all very confusing. I could detect no stable dominance relationships among males, and certainly no linear dominance hierarchy. As if that wasn't bad enough, what ranking I could find predicted little or nothing of importance. One of the main keys to an understanding of the whole male-dominance argument has been that males fight for rank because once they achieve it they are thought to have a better chance at getting important resources. In fact, high-ranking males were believed to monopolize *the* most important resource — sexually receptive females. To my surprise, although certain aggressive males might have the advantage in Pumphouse at times, it seemed to be the loser who got the important rewards like receptive females, specially prized food, the majority of the grooming.

The first time I saw it happen with an estrous female, I couldn't believe my eyes. Ubiquitous Ray was harassing Big Sam for all he was worth. This was nothing unusual, except that this time Big Sam was in consort, following and monopolizing a receptive female. I had mastered the description of the scene, using my ethogram of behaviors to record the sequence, the give-and-take of aggressive signals between males. I had told myself smugly that *I* knew what was going to happen next: Ray was winning, and would claim his rightful prize, the female.

He did win, but when Big Sam rushed off to avoid any further confrontation, Ray followed, tailing close behind him for the next hour and leaving the female to her own devices. Before I knew what was happening, Rad, who had been sitting on the sidelines keeping track of all this with what appeared to be calm disinterest, raced up and claimed the female, beginning a new consortship. There were no objections.

Why fight and not take the prize? Why fight at all? I was sure I must have missed some vital aspect of the exchange between Ray and Big Sam, and that what I thought had happened, hadn't. But the pattern recurred: Males acted aggressive around some prized resource, and then both winner and loser walked off. Further, I couldn't identify the dominant male in the troop, and no male acted the part. So what was the good of dominance? Why would a male fight and risk severe injury for something that seemed to benefit him so little? And there was a complication within the complication: Although the males were aggressive toward one another, they were less aggressive than I had expected. There was no linear or stable dominance among the males; they were much less aggressive than they were supposed to be, and — most confusing of all — aggression between them didn't seem related to who got the rewards they prized. The males were consistent in just one thing: They were not doing what they were supposed to be doing.

That was the bad news. The good news was that the females were much easier to understand, and their role made a lot more sense than before. They and their offspring were the stable core of the group. They had to be; they were the only permanent members. Peggy lived with the Pumphouse Gang the entire thirty-odd years of her life; any son of Peggy's stayed with the troop until he was adolescent, then wandered off to another group. Once there, his stay might be as short as a month or, as I was to find later, for as long as ten years. But ten years was less than a third of Peggy's entire life. No matter how you viewed it, males were only temporary members of a group. The females were permanent.

Moreover, females were predictable. Their first allegiance was to their family. Families themselves had ranking principles; Peggy's family was a good example of this. Mother was on top, the children below in reverse order of age. All the adult females had their own dominance rank vis-à-vis one another. The linear hierarchy I had found to be missing among the males was alive and well among the females, who originally had been assumed to have only "subtle" relationships. Of course there were many "subtleties" that I was still to discover, but knowing a female's rank and her family helped me to predict how she would behave in the vast majority of interactions she had with other families.

The female hierarchy seemed very stable. When a female was in consort with an adult male she might gain some extra immunity from attack by higher-ranking females, but her own rank did not really change: It was more like having a brief vacation from the normal daily routine, nothing permanent or serious. Female roles were more than simply that of baby makers. Matriarchs were not only the protectors of their children, warding off bullies from within the troop and dangers from outside it; they were also the policers, maintaining peace and order within the family and between families. They were the primary focus of family attention, and directly and indirectly wielded a great deal of influence.

Males were not exactly irrelevant, but they certainly were not the prime movers described in the earlier reports. Their sheer size and strength made them dominant to all the females and youngsters, but their sphere of influence was actually much narrower than one would have predicted.

Who, then, was the "leader," the dominant individual who determined where the troop went and played the main role in its defense and order keeping? No one, male or female, fitted this description. Males and females were not equals; they played complementary roles, one no better than the other. Because females spend their entire life in the same troop, they know their home range intimately, while, as Thelma Rowell has suggested, males know areas outside it that might contain resources critical to survival during difficult periods such as severe droughts. The males benefit from the females' knowledge and leadership on some occasions; on others, they take the lead.

The Pumphouse Gang certainly fitted this description. Ray learned the basics — where to go for food, drink, and sleeping sites — by first observing the troop from outside, and then by becoming one of its members. He was never in the lead in troop progressions, except perhaps when he tried to get in front of the group *after* it had made up its mind to shift locations. Yet many months later, when dry-season shortages were making themselves felt and he had made a few female friends, Ray tried hard to influence the females and their children to follow him beyond the edge of their familiar world. He moved out determinedly, glancing back at Naomi and the others, signaling to them to follow. And follow they did, at least until they reached the boundary of the Pumphouse Gang's home range, where they seemed to be held back by some kind of invisible fence. Ray managed to walk through it, but seeing his army lagging behind, he stopped and indicated that they should continue. They refused, and it took him five minutes of come-hither looks, grunts, and glances, not to mention several false starts, before he managed to move them beyond the imaginary barrier. Once they got going, they stayed close to Ray as he marched them to a food-rich grove of acacias. Hence Pumphouse's home range was enlarged, at least during this period.

I was not finding a simple reversal of roles in Pumphouse; females were not politically powerful and central while males were powerless and peripheral. The picture was much more complicated and interesting. Females did not rely on males to protect their infants, but those babies were given extra protection *because* there were males in the troop. Most internal disputes were taken care of within the framework of the female hierarchy and family system; if a gross injustice seemed about to occur, or when disputes threatened to drag on unresolved, a male would permit himself to become involved, particularly if he was a friend of one of the protagonists. Both males and females had power, and both sexes exercised it. Both males and females were involved in caretaking, since males frequently became almost surrogate mothers to their infant friends. Both sexes were political, and both sexes were socializing forces. Which was the most important role? Which sex or individual was the most important within the group? These seemed impossible questions to answer, and might not even be appropriate ones to ask of the baboon society I was observing.

The major differences between males and females were equally fascinating. Described in straightforward terms, they seemed simple: Types of relationships and sequences of interactions were different. But what it boiled down to was something more ephemeral, both psychologically and emotionally. Males and females, even within the same troop, seemed to live in different worlds. Males were part of a dynamic system, challenging, testing, and trying to resolve what appeared to be unresolvable relationships with one another. Among the males, nothing stayed the same for very long; stability was a goal that all seemed intent upon but none ever captured. The only predictable characteristic in male relationships appeared to be their unpredictability.

By comparison, females were dull. Their lives were well ordered and predictable; dominance rank, family, and friendships governed the outcome of female interactions. I wondered why the females bothered putting up a fight, since they knew the outcome even before a dispute started. This was the most interesting aspect of female behavior; although everything seemed predetermined, females still tried to maneuver.

At their core, males and females were opposites: Males were dynamic, females were stable; the outcome of interactions between males was unpredictable, between females extremely predictable. Males were willing to take risks; females were conservative. Both systems, dynamic and conservative, coexisted within the troop, but they also intersected during sexual encounters and in friendships, where a kind of compromise was reached. Friendships between males and females were much stronger and longer lasting than male–male relationships, but they were much shorter and more ephemeral than female friendships.

It was a remarkable set of findings. No male dominance. The reduced effectiveness of aggression to obtain what one wanted. Complementarity of roles within the troop for both males and females, yet a wide divergence in psychological and emotional propensities. Females certainly had an elevated place in Pumphouse when compared with the early descriptions of baboons that had had such an impact on anthropological thinking. The new picture was anything but simple. Much as dogmatic feminists might relish evidence of a primeval matriarchy where female triumphs over male, the baboons pointed in another direction: complementary equality. Just how complementary and how equal I had yet to discover, but the basic outline was obvious.

I suspected that no one would be happy with my findings — neither the feminist anthropologists now spotlighted by the media nor their adversaries, the original interpreters of baboon society. There was no guarantee that I would even be believed. If my initial findings were accurate, the implications would extend beyond baboons to interpretations of the evolution of our own human behavior. If we believe the old position — which took baboons to be the best model of a savannah primate/hominid — or the newer argument that there were principles to be discovered about how any primate could possibly live on the savannah, the same conclusion was inevitable after observing the Pumphouse baboons: Aggression, male dominance, and male monopoly of the political arena are not necessary aspects of the lifestyle of the earliest humans. If, on the other hand, we sincerely believe that life, for humans, is based on aggressive competition, male hierarchical relations and male domination, then we may have to come up with new theories and new answers for why this should be so. We can no longer simply say that it is "the natural order of social life.". . .

When I looked at the baboon world through "baboon spectacles," I saw a complicated landscape, characterized by sophistication and social intelligence, populated by animals with long memories who, relying on social reciprocity, were of necessity "nice" to one another. In this world, males and females shared a complementary importance in the life of the group. When I looked at the baboon world through my own academic lenses, I saw what I had been taught to see, which was something quite different. Many issues, including aggression, dominance, and sexual roles, went out of focus as I changed from one pair of glasses to the other.

It was now becoming obvious that the clear, sturdy, unambiguous framework I had brought with me from Berkeley, simply buttressed and functionally elegant, had become transmogrified. In its place had risen a heretical, complex, slightly threatening structure, parts of which were totally unexpected despite being well grounded in the day-to-day realities of baboon lives. This structure grew as my discoveries grew, continually open to new findings. The foundations of my inherited framework — the concepts of aggression and dominance — had simultaneously become less important and more interesting when placed within the new view I was constructing.

Up until the 1930s, scientists thought of aggression as both abnormal and dysfunctional, since, to them, it appeared disruptive to the basic fabric of social life. The pioneering ethologists, including Konrad Lorenz, famous for his popular as well as scientific books, fundamentally changed this position. They began to look at animals from a new evolutionary perspective, one that inevitably turned aggression into an adaptive behavior. It became normal rather than abnormal, central rather than perverse; aggression was the way in which animals solved the critical problems of competition and defense.

As such, aggression came to be known as an important evolutionary feature of animal society. It soon also became vital in another way: Aggression frequently resulted in dominance hierarchies which controlled and organized the interaction between individuals and, through those individuals, the group itself. Assuming, as most biologists did, that all essential resources were limited, an individual depended upon aggression and dominance for both survival and success. Thus, competition, reproduction, defense, aggression, and dominance became inextricably linked in models of both animal and human societies.

Anthropologists such as Washburn contributed another dimension to the developing perspective on aggression: the importance of functional anatomy and a knowledge of primate evolution. Many physical differences between male and female monkeys and apes seemed to result directly from their different aggressive behavior. The conclusion was obvious: Primates have the biological basis for aggression, use this equipment frequently, and are highly rewarded when successful.

With this perspective in mind, Washburn turned his attention to humans, attempting to chart the development and possible transformation of aggression during evolution. First, it was obvious that humans lacked the nonhuman primate anatomy of aggression. Since aggression was an important means of communication about competition and defense, Washburn inferred that another factor must have been used instead. Human language was his prime candidate. If hominids could talk about issues of competition and defense, they might no longer need the special physical means to convey aggressive intentions, threats, and displays. If so, language could have opened the way for a social system in which aggressive behavior was not constantly rewarded, as it appeared to be in nonhuman primate groups.

It seemed to Washburn that in the course of human evolution, language made possible a new and complex social life, a life that in itself modified the human body, emotions, and brain. In fact, the specific part of the brain that makes language possible could really be considered the "social brain," to use Washburn's terminology, functioning as a mediator of social pressures and helping to produce appropriate social actions. Washburn and countless others, scientists and laymen alike, felt that aggression was deeply rooted in primate anatomy and physiology; it had had a long and important evolutionary history. But Washburn went further; he argued that during primate evolution, unique human events significantly altered both the biology of aggression and its role in the lives of individuals.

It was here that I began to depart from Washburn's ideas. What if aggression turned out to be neither so inevitable nor so central, not just among humans but perhaps among all the higher primates? What if the earlier position on aggression that marked a major advance in the study of animal behavior inadvertently and unconsciously *overemphasized* the role of aggression in the daily lives of many animals?

Even without my baboon evidence it would seem reasonable to expect that alternatives to aggression must exist. Any act of aggression held high risks: serious injury, even death. Wouldn't animals seek safer ways of achieving their goals? Even the strong and powerful might find themselves temporarily incapacitated. How would they behave then? What about the small and weak? Wouldn't they still have the same problems to solve? How could they do so without any aggressive advantage?

I was reminded of the relationship between predators and prey — the better the predators' strategies, the more pressure was put on the prey to find ways to avoid being caught. Shouldn't the same evolutionary processes that developed aggressive capabilities also have developed alternatives to aggression, as potential losers sought a way to not always be a loser?

The conclusion seems apparent. If aggression existed, then alternatives should also exist. Yet not all species might be capable of finding such alternatives. Social strategies among the baboons required that individuals assess complex situations, then modify what they might have done, based on past and present experience. This needs a special type of intelligence, an extremely retentive memory and enough brainpower to integrate many different pieces of information. Could ants employ social strategies? I had my doubts.

Viewed this way, it seemed obvious that primates are among the prime candidates capable of finding and using alternatives to aggression. Their brains and learning skills form part of the basic primate adaptation.

Where did this leave us?

Watching the baboons convinced me to take a new stance on the place and importance of aggression in the lives of animals. Aggression might be just *one* option instead of the *only* option that an individual could choose when he needed to defend himself or to compete with others. Furthermore, with alternatives possible, aggression suddenly would become less inevitable. Individuals should have acquired flexibility in their responses, being prepared for the possibility of aggression but not necessarily locked into reacting in an aggressive way.

Also, it seemed logical that the potency of aggression would decline once alternatives existed. Baboon social strategies would allow aggression to be circumvented, reversed, or redressed. Was this why aggressive solutions apparently had been displaced from the lives of the Pumphouse Gang? What does an aggressive winner do when the loser gets around him without using aggression? In the end he is forced into a type of chess game, with checkmate achieved only when he counters with his own social options. When a male baboon grabbed an infant as a buffer against his aggressive opponent, the opponent had few choices. He had to grab another infant or a female, or else leave. Those who had no infant to use set themselves the task of making friends with females and infants, ensuring that they would have social alternatives in the future.

I was not suggesting that aggression was evolutionarily insignificant for baboons, for nonhuman primates, or even for humans. Among monkeys and apes it was undeniable; many aspects of anatomy were linked to their aggressive behavior. Many differences between male and female bodies, where they existed, reflected their varying aggressive proclivities: the male's big canines, greater male muscle mass, shoulder mantles of hair, and other bodily features used in aggressive displays. Yet no matter how ancient aggression might be, the social alternatives we observe in humans today — the ones that Washburn credited to the advent of human language — most certainly predate the hominids.

If we recognize that social tactics and individual flexibility in aggressive responses began much earlier in primate evolution than originally was believed (the thrust of my baboon argument), then it becomes more difficult to claim, as many had, that aggression is inevitable, not merely among humans, but among all the higher primates. For that matter, the argument extends to any other animal capable of creating social strategies.

What if inside us humans lurked the legacy not of a killer ape, but of a polite and sophisticated baboon? Would sports be a necessary safety valve for our aggressive *instincts*? Would armies be the inevitable result of an inability to contain our deeply rooted human aggressiveness, as some have claimed? If anything, as Washburn suggested, language would certainly improve social communication and increase social options for humans, further undercutting the necessity for aggression in daily life.

Without the central cornerstone of aggression in animal society, could dominance still play its crucial evolutionary role in structuring individual lives and animal groups? Certainly the evidence from the Pumphouse Gang suggested that dominance played a minor role among males and an as yet enigmatic but pervasive role in the lives of females and their families. Yet families and friendships were at least as important as hierarchy in providing organization and stability to the female core of the troop. Neither the baboon evidence nor my new argument could be stretched in any way that would produce the male dominated, male hierarchically organized society of the old baboon and baboon-based human models. How important was dominance and hierarchy to society, whether baboon or human? I would have to search further for the answer to that question, but I knew that the old answers were no longer satisfactory.

The original views of aggression and dominance also carried with them suggestions about the evolution of differences between males and females and the "natural" division of roles between the sexes in human society.

A society based on aggression and male dominance (the baboon model) was augmented further along those lines when early hominids took up a hunting way of life, this evolutionary argument claimed. Women now stayed at home, caring for children and gathering nearby plant foods while men went out to hunt. Women were unable to hunt because of several handicaps: They were always encumbered with children and couldn't run as well as men because of changes in human anatomy. The trend to a larger brain during human evolution (culminating in a brain that is more than triple the size of ape brains) came into direct conflict with another anatomical trend. In order to walk efficiently on two legs — bipedalism is a hallmark of human adaptation — the pelvic diameter had to be as small as possible. Larger-brained babies needed exactly the opposite, a large pelvis for safe passage through the birth canal. Human females were saddled with a compromise: Their pelvises were larger than those of the males, giving critically needed space to babies during birth but making them less bipedally efficient, particularly when running.

These handicaps were compounded by a change in the condition of human newborns. As brain size continued its remarkable expansion, it was also likely that human infants born at a more premature point, by monkey and ape standards, survived the hazardous birthing process better than full-term babies. The more immature human newborns became, the more dependent on maternal care they were. They lost even the most rudimentary monkey and ape abilities, such as being able to cling to their mothers at birth or being able to move around on their own shortly thereafter.

Arguments about the "natural" division of roles between males and females in hominid groups were based on this scenario. Females were inevitably confined close to home by domestic responsibilities, while males were forced to meet the new challenges of hunting. Taking such risks also held advantages; hunting activities conferred a special status and power on males. The division of labor and roles was completed by an exchange of goods between men and women: meat for vegetables, and perhaps, as some suggested, sex for meat when males bought favors from females or females used sex as a special resource to barter for food and protection critical to their survival and that of their family. Because hunting was a way of life for humans for more than 90 percent of human evolutionary history, the hunting society, its roles, underlying emotions and psychology were deeply embedded in human biology and difficult to erase from later human behavior.

In the last ten years, a groundswell among the feminists has tried to change what is viewed as a "sexist" model for the evolution of human society. The debate rages on, as proponents of female rights and female power try to demonstrate that gathering was more important than hunting to our ancestors, and that consequently women were more important than men in hominid hunter-gatherer communities.

What I had observed among the Pumphouse baboons strongly challenged some of the traditional arguments about human sex roles and their evolutionary origins. Unfortunately for the feminist position, the baboon evidence did not support the reversal of roles they sought. Instead, the baboons suggested that there was an array of sex differences in behavior, emotions, and psychology in the primate pattern that predated the innovations of hunting. Yet there was equally strong evidence for a complementary equality of male and female in most social domains, including politics and caretaking. More provocative still was the discovery of social reciprocity among individuals. This meant that even without bipedalism, without the invention of tools, without hunting and gathering, without the development of the large human brain, with its capacity for language and culture, and without extremely dependent infants to restrict female movement, male and female baboons are involved in a complicated exchange of favors.

Such baboon insights are both provocative and complex. Male and female psychologies are already very different among baboons. There is no doubting that females are conservative in trying new behaviors like hunting or in breaking out of old patterns like family rankings; they are unwilling to take risks or strike out on their own. They prefer the safety and reassurance of being with the group and staying close to family and friends. Stability is a goal that they achieve a remarkable amount of the time, sometimes in the face of formidable odds. Males are just the opposite: Dynamic risk takers, they seize as many opportunities as they can. If stability and a status quo are indeed their goals, these are elusive, at least in male relationships with other males.

To me the baboon facts suggested that the division of roles others credit to the new hunting lifestyle of the hominids was already present among the Pumphouse baboons. Their relatively minor predatory adventures illustrated but did not create the differences between male and female proclivities. Having meat to share, as among hominid hunters, might increase the variety of exchanges between males and females, but neither reciprocity nor sexual politics originated with hunting and gathering. Although baboons shared only meat and no other foods, male and female friends bartered social and sexual favors in a complicated tit for tat that formed the foundation of their friendship. Males also bartered favors with their infant friends, and to a much lesser degree, with their male allies.

The final point that the baboons made is perhaps the most striking: There is nothing inherently powerless or impotent in female roles, no matter how involved these are with raising young and being the stable core of the group. The old arguments assumed that these were the only roles and functions females had: But among female baboons, they formed the basis for a variety of other political and leadership positions. When knowledge and social influence create power, as they do among baboons (and among humans), females are socially powerful because they have both. More important still, whenever alternatives to aggression exist, even giants find themselves needing the smaller or weaker members of their society in order to create effective social options for their own survival. Experience, social skill, and social manipulations were important to individual baboon survival and success. Real power resided with those who were "wise" rather than those who were "strong," those who could mobilize allies rather than those who try to push through with brute force.

Underneath all the cultural posturings and institutional edifices, I don't think that modern humans are any different from baboons in this regard. Those who believe that we are different will have to find new evolutionary explanations for how humans changed.

It seemed to me that the study of baboons and other monkeys and apes was even more important in reconstructing human evolution than the earlier simple models implied. Baboons could help to provide not just examples but important principles. As we better understand how evolutionary changes occur in complex primate groups, we also come to understand what is possible for primates. This is the best way to set the starting point for the scenario of human evolution. We are left to discover what was probable for the early hominids by placing what is possible within the context of hominid biology, anatomy, and ecology. In the future, evolutionary reconstructions will thrive only if they focus on processes and governing principles in primate societies rather than on single species, no matter how similar we think those species are to us humans.

Although I was committed to this new kind of approach, and did not want to reinstate a baboon model of human evolution, I was constantly struck by how much more like humans the baboons now seemed. They learned through insight and observation, passing new behaviors from one to another both within a single lifetime and across many lifetimes. This is social tradition, the beginnings of what eventually became "culture." Their social maneuvers and social sophistication raised them to new heights. The cumulative effect of my years of watching, analyzing, and interpreting baboon behavior was that I felt more and more at ease in applying human terms and concepts to the baboons.

I had no stake in human uniqueness: Each species is unique. But the similarities intrigued me. It was the similarities that made it possible to imagine how behaviors could evolve through time. How would hominid innovations occur? It was hard to believe in sudden large leaps into thin air without some preexisting material to work from. Evolutionary reconstructions of human behavior become more believable the greater the continuum between human and nonhuman primate behavior. The baboons managed to add many new stepping-stones to that route.

Talking about baboons in more human terms left me open to criticism — that I was projecting human behaviors onto these nonhuman creatures which they did not, in fact, possess. And I wanted to go further still: If human terms were appropriate to monkey *behavior,* wasn't it possible that baboons might be considerably more humanlike emotionally, psychologically, intellectually? My university training had profoundly impressed on me the dangers of anthropomorphism. Yet it was the baboons themselves who were responsible for my change of heart. I was a reluctant voyager; I had resisted them at every step, yet now, having traversed the entire road, many of the old distinctions between baboons and humans blurred.

I turned to history to see if I could find any support for this change in my position, and as I reviewed the development of ideas about animals during the last few centuries I found some surprising but reassuring answers.

The same animals could be saints or demons, stupid brutes or sentient beings, depending on the culture and the era. A remarkable change in thinking was brought about as a result of Darwin's ideas. Westerners, who at that time believed that nonhuman animals — monkeys and apes in particular — were considerably lower than the angels, were now faced with a conundrum. If humans were truly related to these creatures, then either we were baser than we thought, or else — and this was much more appealing — *they* must be nicer, brighter, and more humanlike than we had first painted them.

The post-Darwin period saw animals take on a sentimental appeal; animal abilities were elevated to a degree that we, as humans, could be proud of. The *animals* hadn't changed; it was *human* expectations and interpretations that had turned around. This was why the ethologists of the 1930s became so adamant against attributing human qualities and abilities to animals. They recognized how inappropriately it had been done, and instead wanted to be able to understand animals in their own terms.

But just as the pendulum had swung one way with the Victorians and post-Victorians, the early ethological approach made it swing equally drastically the other way. The ethologists urged that complex behaviors be reduced to the smallest possible unit and later reassembled into meaningful clusters. They recognized the importance of having rigorous methods and hard facts with which to back up statements and conclusions which, otherwise, could be fraught with biases and projections. The problem came in choosing just what to study. Important areas of animal behavior were difficult to study in this rigorous fashion. Emotions, psychology, and the mind all fell by the wayside as the modern investigators began with what was easiest to tackle well.

Initially, scientists felt we would someday learn just how to study these important but difficult areas. Soon what had been omitted for the sake of convenience began to appear irrelevant. The position that it was hard to study these issues subtly shifted to the position that these were unimportant aspects of behavior, that we could explain what an animal was doing simply by referring to its outward behavior. Researchers who talked about what animals might "feel," "think," and "decide" were being unscientific and sentimental. The efforts of dedicated scientists had inadvertently robbed nonhuman animals of many of their important abilities.

The line between unwarranted anthropomorphism and what I came more and more to see as simply giving back to the animals abilities that they had lost to historical circumstances was a narrow and difficult one to walk. I was still uneasy with the idea that the longest-term resident males decided to leave Pumphouse because they *understood* that if they stayed they might enter into unsuitable matings with their own daughters. At the same time I could accept the idea that Peggy knew exactly what she was doing when she groomed Dr. Bob into a stupor and then stole the tommy carcass from him. I was convinced that she and Olive both acted premeditatively and manipulatively when Peggy attacked Dr. Bob's friend in the escalating competition over the meat he possessed, and when Olive screamed at Toby later during the day on which he had first dominated her.

I had many male examples as well. Males used sophisticated tactics around consorts, convincing others that they weren't interested while arranging to be at the right place at the right moment to claim the female. Males incited the aggression of other followers, ducking out just when the going got rough, only to appear again at the critical moment. Males harassed an unsuspecting infant on its way to be groomed by its mother and then whisked the female away from her confused consort in the pandemonium that ensued.

Were Pumphouse baboons conscious of what they were doing? It now seemed to me that they were no less — and perhaps much more — aware of their actions than most humans.

Was it anthropomorphic to believe that baboons were intelligent manipulators of their social world; to think that they weighed alternatives and made decisions; to think that even without language they had mental symbols that allowed them to think first and act later, that allowed them to create remarkable unwritten contracts of social reciprocity? Upon reflection it seemed peculiarly human, particularly anthropo*centric,* to *deny* them these abilities. As I searched further, I found that a few other investigators of animal behavior were reaching similar conclusions.

Readings: Methods of Inquiry in Primate Research

The readings in this section offer further opportunities to think and write comparatively while working with the topic woven through this chapter: primate research. If you would like to look back at some of the readings about primates earlier in the chapter, see "Conversations with a Gorilla" by Francine Patterson and "More Years with Mountain Gorillas" by Dian Fossey (Opening Problem, p. 421); "Probing Primate Thoughts" by Bruce Bower (A Professional Application, p. 444); and "The Mind of the Chimpanzee" by Jane Goodall and excerpts from *Almost Human: A Journey into the World of Baboons* by Shirley S. Strum (Science Assignment, p. 482).

First, a note on the term *primates.* As a biological classification, *primates* refers to the order of animals that includes all species of monkeys, baboons, lemurs, the great apes, and human beings. In practice, however, the term is applied to the nonhuman species. Among these, the great apes — gorillas, orangutans, and especially chimpanzees (including bonobo, or pygmy, chimpanzees) — have attracted much of the research attention, mostly because of their behavioral and biological resemblance to humans: Chimpanzees are said to share over 98 percent of their genetic makeup with human beings. For ethical and economic reasons, however, the great apes are seldom the subjects of medical research. That role is played by various species of monkeys, most notably vervets and macaques.

Primate research, perhaps because it does touch upon so many basic human issues, provides revealing glimpses of scientists at work — and of scientists in disagreement. Scientists who study primates disagree about *methods,* how to design studies that produce meaningful data. They also disagree about the underlying assumptions and expectations that frame their research and about whether nonhuman primates can serve as models of humans in research. The researchers who work with primates come from various fields, including medicine, psychology, anthropology, biology, and ethology (the study of animal behavior). Each of these disciplines brings its own kinds of questions to the study of primates, but all of them share as background an overarching philosophical question: What can studying primates tell us about ourselves? Primate studies also offer compelling testimony of how scientists develop research interests and, often, of how those interests turn to passions.

The following readings offer glimpses into three areas of primate research: investigations of the language capacities of chimpanzees and gorillas, medical research conducted on primates in laboratories, and field research on the behavior of primate species in their natural habitats. Each of these research areas, as you will see, is dominated by its own methods of inquiry. Behavioral experiments, medical investigations, and field observations follow very different procedures, provoked by quite different kinds of questions. In this section you are offered a pair of readings in each of these three categories and thus have the opportunity to make comparisons both within and across categories. This coverage of primate research is not intended to be comprehensive but only to indicate some of the range and variety of scientific inquiry about primates.

We begin with a pair of readings addressing the issue of whether the great apes have the capacity for language. "How Nim Chimpsky Changed My Mind" by Herbert Terrace is an influential firsthand account by a psychologist disillusioned with his own experiments with the linguistic capacity of primates and skeptical of the work of other language researchers. Roger Lewin's article, "Look Who's Talking Now," reports on the work of primatologist Sue Savage-Rumbaugh and the startling accomplishments of a bonobo chimpanzee. Next comes a pair of readings from *The Monkey Wars,* Deborah Blum's investigation of the uses of primates for medical research. In "The Black Box" Blum describes the experiments of the neurosurgeon Stuart Zola-Morgan. In "Not a Nice Death," Blum describes the research of veterinarian Roy Henrickson and considers the implications of "the monkey model" for investigating AIDS. The last pair of readings represents recent field research on apes in their natural environments. In an excerpt from *How Monkeys See the World,* Dorothy L. Cheney and Robert M. Seyfarth interpret the data they have collected on the vocal behavior of vervet monkeys. In "Ethological Studies of Chimpanzee Vocal Behavior," John C. Mitani develops a series of hypotheses about the vocal behavior — specifically the "pant hoots" — of chimpanzees.

At the end of each reading you will find Considerations questions intended to help you think about the reading mostly on its own terms but also in relation to the strategies of comparison stressed in this chapter. At the end of the section, you will also find suggestions for writing about these readings in relation to one another and for pursuing the topic of primate research through research of your own.

In the following article psychologist Herbert Terrace describes his language research with a chimp named Nim. Terrace's project began as an attempt to replicate and refine the experiments of other researchers (those noted in his third paragraph) who succeeded in training apes to use some of the gestures of American Sign Language. Although his initial findings supported those of other researchers, Terrace eventually became skeptical not only of his own research results but also of the methodology of the earlier experiments. What are his criticisms, and on what basis does he conclude that the apes had not achieved "grammatical competence" as language users? What does "grammatical competence" mean, and why should that be the crucial issue?

How Nim Chimpsky Changed My Mind

HERBERT TERRACE

> . . . there was no attraction for me in imitating human beings; I imitated them because I needed a way out, and for no other reason. . . . And so I learned things, gentlemen. Ah, one learns when he has to; one learns when one needs a way out; one learns at all costs.
>
> — Franz Kafka, "A Report to an Academy"

In Kafka's short story, a chimpanzee explains how the gift of language made him feel human. For the past decade, a number of psychologists have been presenting evidence that real apes have acquired this gift. According to their reports, more than a dozen chimps, two gorillas, and an orangutan have learned extensive vocabularies in one or another visual language. Even more intriguing are claims that the apes have mastered a fundamental aspect of human language: the ability to create sentences.

How persuasive is the evidence for such claims? The researchers themselves have

HERBERT TERRACE (b. 1936) is a psychology professor at Columbia University. He has published many articles and several books, including the 1979 study *Nim.* "How Nim Chimpsky Changed My Mind" appeared in *Psychology Today* in 1979.

been clearly positive about their conclusions, which have been the focus of much discussion both in scientific journals and in the popular press.

According to Beatrix and R. Allen Gardner, who trained a female chimp named Washoe in American Sign Language (ASL), "The results of Project Washoe presented the first serious challenge to the traditional doctrine that only human beings have language." David Premack, who trained a juvenile female chimp, Sarah, to use a series of plastic chips representing words, has reported that "Sarah comprehended (and in a few cases produced) sentences formed by a process more demanding than that of combining phrases." And Duane Rumbaugh, who taught another female chimp, Lana, to communicate with symbols displayed on a computer terminal and called lexigrams ("Yerkish"), has argued: "Apes spontaneously string word units (signs, lexigrams) together. Additionally, they learned prescribed grammatical rules for ordering strings, thereby demonstrating at least elementary syntactical ability."

If these claims are valid, I might agree with Penny Patterson of Stanford University, whose experience in teaching sign language to a gorilla named Koko led her to declare that "Language is no longer the exclusive domain of man." After a five-year research project of my own, however, I am skeptical about such pronouncements. When I began my study with a male chimp called Nim Chimpsky, I hoped to demonstrate that apes can, indeed, form sentences. I wanted to go beyond the anecdotal evidence reported by other studies and show that grammatical rules are needed to describe many of an ape's utterances.

Initially, the regularities I observed in thousands of Nim's communications in sign language suggested that he was, in fact, using a grammar. However, after analyzing videotapes of his "conversations" with his teachers, I discovered that the sequences of words that looked like sentences were subtle imitations of the teacher's sequences. I could find no evidence confirming an ape's grammatical competence, either in my own data or those of others, that could not be explained by simpler processes.

The sentence and the word are the two basic features of human language that separate it from other forms of animal communication. In contrast to the fixed character of most animal sounds, the word is flexible in meaning. Many species of birds, for instance, sing one song when in distress, another when courting a mate, and still another when asserting territorial rights. It does not appear possible to teach birds to produce different songs in these situations.

But human language is most distinctive because of its use of the sentence. A sentence expresses a particular meaning with a set of words and phrases that stand in a particular grammatical relationship to one another. Unlike words, whose meaning can be learned one by one, most sentences are not learned individually. Instead, children master grammatical rules that allow new meanings to be created by arranging or inflecting a set of words, or by substituting one word for another. Having mastered a few subject-verb-object sequences, such as *John hit Bill,* a child readily produces other subject-verb-object sequences without explicit training, such as *Bill hit John, John ate the apple, Bill chased the cat,* and so on. Psychologists, psycholinguists, and linguists agree that knowing a human language entails knowing a grammar. How else can one account for a child's ultimate ability to create an indeterminate number of meaningful sentences from a finite number of words?

In their first efforts to determine whether chimpanzees have similar capabilities, researchers quickly discovered that the chimps could not reproduce spoken language. These failures might be explained by anatomical limitations of the chimpanzee's vocal tract: It is incapable of producing the broad range of sounds that constitute spoken human language. That is one reason why experimenters attempted to teach them visual languages such as Yerkish and ASL.[1]

Washoe, Sarah, and Lana each acquired vocabularies of more than 100 words in their respective languages. Their trainers interpreted these words as they would corresponding words in human languages: names of people, objects, actions, attributes, and various relationships. In more recent studies, other apes have acquired similar vocabularies. Penny Patterson recently reported that Koko has acquired a vocabulary of more than 400 signs of ASL.

The words learned by each of these apes were symbolically arbitrary, in the sense that it was not generally possible to infer their meanings from their form. In Sarah's language, for example, the word *apple* is a triangular piece of blue plastic. In Yerkish, the word *apple* is a nonsense geometric form on a red background. In ASL, *apple* is made by pressing the knuckle of the index finger into the cheek and twisting forward.

Apes can undoubtedly master larger vocabularies and learn them at a faster rate than, say, dogs. However, a dog who learns some arbitrary posture in order to beg, or responds to his master's command to sit, also demonstrates that it can understand arbitrary words. There is virtually no evidence, though, that domestic animals can produce sequences of the "words" they have been taught, at least not in any systematic manner.

Given that apes have been observed to produce sequences such as *Washoe more eat, water bird, May gave Sarah apple, please machine give Lana apple,* it is natural to ask whether such sequences were generated by a grammar. It is difficult to answer this question, if for no other reason than that linguists have yet to devise a decisive test of whether a sequence of words constitutes a sentence. Even if an animal produced such a sequence, we could not conclude that it was a sentence. A well-known hypothetical experiment shows why.

Imagine a monkey who has not been taught anything about language pressing the keys of a typewriter in a random manner. Some small fraction of what it types might make sense to an English-speaking reader. In theory, the monkey's typing could even include a phrase or a sentence written by Shakespeare. It is gratuitous to attribute grammatical competence to a monkey because of a few chance responses on its typewriter. When viewed in the larger perspective of the monkey's total output, meaningful sequence is seen as a chance utterance.

Another way to perform this experiment is to train the monkey to produce specific sequences in order to obtain a reward. Monkeys, pigeons, and chimpanzees can readily learn such tasks. So can human beings, as when they learn to dial a phone number.

What is important to recognize about variations of the monkey-at-the-typewriter experiment is that neither the symbols nor the relationships between the symbols have

[1]It is estimated that ASL is used by more than 500,000 deaf and hearing people in the United States alone. This makes ASL the fourth most frequently used language in the country (after English, Spanish, and Italian). Recent research on sign language shows that it can express any concept or idea that can be expressed in spoken language. Other distinct sign languages exist in many countries: England, France, Israel, China, and Japan, to name a few.

specific meanings. Although the words and word order may be meaningful to an English speaker, they may be meaningless to the animal producing them.

This is not to say that Sarah and Lana did not understand how to use certain symbols in order to obtain a piece of apple. That they clearly could do. What is at issue is whether the chimps related the symbols to their nonverbal understanding of why they were given the food. In sentences like *Mary give Sarah banana* or *machine give Lana Coke,* that understanding does not appear to be based on a perception of the symbols *Mary* and *machine* as subjects, of *give* as a verb, and of *Sarah* and *Lana* as indirect objects. The only symbols that Sarah and Lana varied systematically were the names of the rewards they sought to obtain: *Coke, banana, movie,* and so on. If Sarah and Lana did not know the meanings of the first three symbols of the sequences they produced, it is erroneous to suppose that they understood the relationship between the symbols. Yet it is just that type of knowledge that would allow one to regard Sarah's and Lana's sequences as sentences rather than as a sequence of three nonsense symbols *A, B,* and *C,* and one meaningful symbol *X.*

Washoe combined many of her signs without being trained specifically to do so, producing sequences such as *more drink* and *open hurry.* When shown a swan for the first time by Roger Fouts, her main trainer, Washoe signed *water bird.* Since such combinations were not learned by rote training and Washoe was not required to make any of them, Fouts and the Gardners interpreted them as elementary sentences.

That conclusion seems premature, for a number of reasons. One is a flaw in the Gardners' system of recording data. With one minor exception, they recorded Washoe's combinations in only one order: In most cases, this was the order that would be followed in English. But that was not necessarily the order in which she signed. Thus, the combinations *more drink* and *drink more* were both recorded as instances of *more drink.* Since Washoe learned that either *more* or *drink* would be rewarded, it is not surprising that both signs occurred in the same utterance. But *more* and *drink* may not be related grammatically.

Typically, Washoe had to be drilled about the names and attributes of things in her environment. Her response to *what that?* was usually a name; to the question *color that?*, she would respond with an attribute. For answering correctly, the chimp was rewarded with tidbits of food, hugs, brief bouts of tickling, and signed praise. From the account of the occasion when Washoe signed *water bird,* there is no way of knowing why she made these signs. When asked *what that?* in the presence of a swan, she may have first responded *water.* If that was not what the trainer had in mind, it is reasonable to expect that, as a result of previous vocabulary drills, she would then have signed *bird,* which was also appropriate to the situation.

Even if Washoe's signs were not evoked by questions, one cannot conclude that she created a new meaning by combining the signs *water* and *bird* in a novel manner. Before doing so, it would be necessary to know if she combined other adjectives and nouns in the same way; for example, *red* and *crayon,* or *big* and *doll.* Without such information, there is no way of knowing whether *water* and *bird* are unrelated signs, each appropriate to its context, or a "true" (adjective plus noun) construction.

To decide whether a signing ape can create a sentence, it is necessary to have a record of *all* its utterances during a study. The investigator must look for evidence that a grammatical rule, such as sign order, was used to communicate different meanings. For example, how frequently did *more* precede the names of a variety of objects and actions when the chimp seemed to want more? How frequently did adjectives precede or follow nouns? Without a thorough record, we are left with only anecdotal examples of an ape's ability to create sentences — which may not have much more credibility than a passage from Shakespeare typed by a monkey.

The goal of Project Nim, which I started in 1973, was to collect and analyze a large corpus of a chimpanzee's sign combinations. The subject of the study was an infant male chimpanzee who was born at the Oklahoma Institute for Primate Studies. I chose the name Nim Chimpsky in honor of the well-known linguist who has argued that language is innate and unique to the human species. (Of course, I also had in mind the irony that would result if Nim could, indeed, create sentences.)

Nim was one week old when he was flown to New York in December 1973. He lived initially in a researcher's home in Manhattan, and later with three of his teachers in a university-owned mansion in the Riverdale section of the Bronx. Nim became the sole student in a small classroom I designed for him in the psychology department at Columbia University. The classroom allowed his teachers to focus his attention more easily than they could in his home. It also provided good opportunities to introduce him to many activities conducive to signing, such as looking at pictures, drawing, and sorting objects.

At home, Nim was treated like a young child. He slept on a loft bed in his own room and was toilet trained by the age of two and a half. My purpose was not to make Nim into a middle-class chimpanzee, but rather to provide him with as many opportunities to sign as possible. Situations in which Nim liked to behave as his teachers did — by dressing, helping to prepare meals, or cleaning up the house — provided natural opportunities for learning signs.

Nim formed particularly close attachments to certain members of the project. I maintained a strong and continuous bond with him throughout the project. During the first eighteen months, Stephanie LaFarge, the experienced chimp mother with whom he lived, was the central person in his life. Following his move to Riverdale, he became closely attached to Laura Petitto, an outstanding teacher who supervised his care at home and in the Columbia classroom. After Laura left, when Nim was thirty-four months old, he became closely attached to two other resident teachers, Bill Tynan and Joyce Butler.

During the four years he lived in New York, Nim was taught by more than sixty volunteer teachers, as we were unable to pay enough to keep a small group of skilled, permanent caretakers. At least six people were needed to work with Nim, since it was hard for any one of them to sustain the energy needed to focus his attention and anticipate his reactions for more than five or six hours a day; also, every hour spent with Nim required at least an hour of preparation and recordkeeping. Because of Nim's emotional reactions to the many changes in personnel, it became increasingly difficult to command his attention.

Both at home and in the classroom, Nim's teachers kept careful chronological records of what he signed. During each session, the teacher dictated into a cassette recorder as much information as possible about Nim's signing and the context of that signing. A one-way window in a wall of the classroom and a concealed opening below that window allowed the project members to observe and videotape Nim and his teachers without being seen. The videotapes proved to be invaluable, enabling us to reevaluate Nim's performance and to look at details that took too long for teachers to describe during the limited time they had available for dictating.

Nim learned to express 125 signs during the forty-four months of the project. Two of the most interesting ones were the signs for *angry* and *bite,* which he often displayed to a person he was about to attack while exhibiting a clear warning of aggression — his lips drawn back to expose his teeth, his hands raised over his head, and his hair standing on end. Having signed *angry* or *bite* in these situations, however, the physical expressions of Nim's anger subsided. If this observation can be confirmed with other chimpanzees, an important use of human language will have been duplicated by apes: expressing an emotion through symbols rather than physical acts.

Nim learned to sign *dirty* when he needed to use the toilet. He also learned that this sign had a reliable effect on his teachers' behavior: The teacher interrupted whatever he or she was doing and took him to the bathroom. On many occasions, Nim signed *dirty* right after he had been taken to the bathroom. At other times, he signed it and then showed no interest in using the toilet. The misuse of *dirty* was often accompanied by a slight grin and an avoidance of eye contact. Typically, it occurred when Nim did not want to cooperate with his teacher or was given a new teacher. Like a child saying, "I need to go to the bathroom" when he or she doesn't have to go, Nim used the sign *dirty* to manipulate his teachers' behavior.

Other apes have also learned to use the sign *dirty* to express a need to use the toilet. Indeed, it is claimed that both Washoe and Koko have signed *dirty* as an expletive. Washoe signed *dirty* in the presence of a macaque monkey she did not like, and *dirty Roger* when Roger Fouts refused to take her for a walk. Koko signed *you dirty bad toilet* when she was unjustly accused of having damaged a doll.

Fouts and Penny Patterson have interpreted this use of the word as evidence that apes are capable of cursing. However, a simpler explanation suffices: Notice that each presumed use of *dirty* as an expletive occurred in trying situations and that the sign *dirty* was a reliable way, actually the most reliable way, to get the teacher to remove the ape from those situations.

During a two-year period, Nim's teachers recorded more than 20,000 of his utterances that consisted of two or more signs. Almost half were two-sign combinations, of which 1,378 were different from one another.

One characteristic of Nim's two-sign combinations led me to believe they were primitive sentences. In many cases, Nim used particular signs in either the first or the second position, no matter what other sign he combined it with. For example, *more* occurred in the first position in 85 percent of the two-sign utterances in which *more* appeared (such as *more banana, more drink, more hug,* and *more tickle*). Of the 348 two-sign combinations containing *give,* 78 percent had it in the first position. There were 946 instances in which a transitive verb (such as *hug, tickle, give*) was combined with *me* and *Nim,* and in 83 percent of them, the transitive verb occurred in the first position.

These and other regularities in Nim's two-sign utterances were the first demonstrations of a reliable use of sign order by a chimpanzee. By themselves, however, they do not justify the conclusion that they were created according to grammatical rules. Nim could have simply imitated what his teachers were signing, although at first such an explanation seemed doubtful — for a number of reasons. Nim's teachers had no reason to sign many of the combinations Nim had produced. Nim asked to be tickled long before he showed any interest in tickling his teacher; thus, there was no reason for the teacher to sign *tickle me* to Nim. Likewise, Nim requested various objects by signing *give* + *x* (*x* being whatever he wanted) long before he began to offer objects to his teachers. More generally, all of Nim's teachers had the clear impression that his utterances typically contained signs that we had never used with him.

Other explanations of the regularities of Nim's two-sign combinations were possible. But the statistical analyses showed that they did not result from Nim's preferences for using particular signs in the first or second positions of two-sign combinations. And the sheer number of Nim's combinations — and the regularities in them — makes implausible the hypothesis that Nim, like a monkey at a typewriter, was combining signs at random.

The more I analyzed Nim's combinations, the more certain I felt that I was on solid ground in concluding that they were grammatical and that they were comparable to the first sentences of a child. It was not until Nim was returned to Oklahoma Institute for Primate Studies (when our funds ran out) that I became skeptical of that conclusion. Ironically, it was my newly found freedom from data-collecting and from teaching and looking after the chimp that allowed me and other members of the project to examine Nim's use of sign language more thoroughly.

What emerged from our new analyses was a number of important differences between Nim's and a child's use of language. One of the first facts that troubled me was the absence of any increase in the length of Nim's utterances. During the last two years that Nim was in New York, the average length of his utterances fluctuated between 1.1 and 1.6 signs. That performance is like what children do when they *begin* combining words.

As children get older, the average length of their utterances increases steadily. This is true both of children with normal hearing and of deaf children who sign. After learning to make utterances relating a verb and an object (*eats breakfast*), the child learns to link them into longer utterances relating the subject, verb, and object (*Daddy eats breakfast*). Later, the child learns to elaborate these utterances into statements such as *Daddy didn't eat breakfast,* or, *When will Daddy eat breakfast*?

Despite the steady increase in the size of Nim's vocabulary, the mean length of his utterances did not increase. Although some of his utterances were very long, they were not, as a rule, very informative. Consider, for example, his longest, which contained sixteen signs: *give orange me give eat orange me eat orange give me eat orange give me you.* While a child's longer utterances expand upon the meanings of shorter utterances, this one does not. Furthermore, the maximum length of a child's utterances is related very reliably to their average length. Nim's showed no such relationship.

The most dramatic difference between Nim's and a child's use of language was revealed in a painstaking analysis of videotapes of Nim's and his teacher's signing. A doctoral dissertation written by Richard J. Sanders, one of his teachers, showed that Nim's signing with his teachers bore only a superficial resemblance to a child's conversations with his or her parents. What is more, only 12 percent of Nim's utterances were spontaneous — that is, 88 percent were preceded by a teacher's utterance. A significantly larger proportion of a child's utterances is spontaneous. But even if there were no differences in spontaneity, there were differences in creativity.

As a child gets older, the proportion of utterances that are full or partial imitations of his or her parent's language decreases from less than 20 percent at twenty-one months to almost zero by the time the child is three years old. When Nim was twenty-six months old, 38 percent of his utterances were full or partial imitations of his teacher's. By the time he was forty-four months old, the proportion had risen to 54 percent.

As children imitate fewer of their parents' utterances, they begin to expand upon what they hear their parents say. At twenty-one months, 22 percent of a child's utterances add at least one word to the parent's prior utterance; at thirty-six months, 42 percent are expansions of the parent's prior utterance. Fewer than 10 percent of Nim's utterances recorded during twenty-two months of videotaping (the last twenty-two months of the project) were expansions. Like the mean length of his utterances, this value remained fairly constant.

The videotapes showed another distinctive feature of Nim's conversations that we had been unaware of. He was as likely to interrupt his teacher's signing as not. In contrast, children interrupt their parents so rarely that interruptions are all but ignored in studies of their language development. A child learns readily what one takes for granted in a two-way conversation: Each speaker adds information to the preceding utterance and each speaker takes turns in holding the floor. Nim rarely added information and showed no evidence of turn-taking.

None of the features of Nim's discourse — his lack of spontaneity, his partial imitation of his teacher's signing, his tendency to interrupt — had been noticed by any of his teachers or by the many expert observers who had watched Nim sign. Once I was sure that Nim wasn't imitating what I signed *precisely,* I had felt that it was less important to record the teachers' signs than it was to capture as much as I could about his signing: the context and specific physical movements, what hand he signed with, the order of his signs, and their appropriateness.

We found in our photographs examples of situations in which the teacher's signs had prompted Nim's signs. . . . [For example,] our discourse analysis revealed that Nim's teacher was signing *you* while Nim was signing *me;* she was signing *who* while he was signing *cat.* Because these were the only four photographs taken of this discourse, we cannot specify just when the teacher began her signs. It is not clear, for example, whether the teacher signed *you* simultaneously or immediately prior to Nim's *me.* It is, however, unlikely that the teacher signed *who*? after Nim signed *cat.*

I have reason to believe that prompting by the teacher also influenced Washoe's signing. Indeed, the only two films about the Gardners' work with Washoe support the idea that prompting has played a much greater role in "conversations" with chimpanzees than previously recognized. In a *Nova*-produced film, *The First Signs of Washoe,* Beatrix Gardner signs *what time now*? and Washoe interrupts to sign *time eat, time eat.* A longer version of the same exchange, shown in the second film, *Teaching Sign Language to the Chimpanzee Washoe,* began with Gardner signing *eat me, more me,* after which Washoe gave her something to eat. Then she signed *thank you* — and only then asked *what time now*? Washoe's response *time eat, time eat* can hardly be considered spontaneous, since Gardner had just used the same signs and Washoe was offering a direct answer to her question.

The potential for misinterpreting an ape's signing because of inadequate reporting is made plain by another example in both films. Washoe is conversing with her teacher, Susan Nichols, who shows the chimp a tiny doll in a cup. Nichols points to the cup and signs *that;* Washoe signs *baby.* Nichols brings the cup and doll closer to Washoe, allowing her to touch them, slowly pulls them away, and then signs *that* while pointing to the cup. Washoe signs *in* and looks away. Nichols brings the cup with the doll closer to Washoe again, who looks at the two objects once more, and signs *baby.* Then, as she brings the cup still closer, Washoe signs *in. That,* signs Nichols, and points to the cup; *my drink,* signs Washoe.

Given these facts, there is no basis to refer to Washoe's utterance — *baby in baby in my drink* — as either a spontaneous or a creative use of "in" as a preposition joining two objects. It is actually a "run on" sequence with very little relationship between its parts. Only the last two signs were uttered without prompting from the teacher. Moreover, the sequence of the prompts (pointing to the doll, and then pointing to the cup) follows the order called for in constructing an English prepositional phrase. In short, discourse analysis makes a chimpanzee's linguistic achievement less remarkable than it might seem at first.

In his discussion of communicating with an animal, the philosopher Ludwig Wittgenstein cautions that apparent instances of an animal using human language may prove to be a "game" that is played by simpler rules. Nim's and Washoe's use of signs suggests a type of interaction between chimp and trainer that has little to do with human language. Nim's and Washoe's signing appears to have the sole function of requesting various rewards that can be obtained only by signing.

First, the teacher tries to interest the chimp in some activity such as looking at a picture book, drawing, or playing catch. Typically, the chimp tries to engage in such activities without signing. The teacher then tries to initiate signing by asking questions such as *what that*?, *what you want*?, *who's book*?, and *ball red or blue*?

The more rapidly the chimpanzee signs, the more rapidly it can obtain what it wants. It is therefore not surprising that the chimp frequently interrupts the teacher. From the chimpanzee's point of view, the teacher's signs provide an excellent model of the signs it is expected to make. By simply imitating a few of them, often in the same order used by the teacher, and by adding a few "wild cards" — general purpose signs such as *give, me, Nim,* or *more* — the chimpanzee may well produce utterances that appear to follow grammatical rules. What seems like conversation from a human point of view is actually an attempt to communicate a demand (a nonconversational message) as quickly as possible.

It might be argued that Nim and Washoe had the potential to create sentences but did not do so because of motivational rather than intellectual limitations. Perhaps Nim and Washoe would have been more motivated to communicate in sign language if they had been raised by smaller and more consistent groups of teachers, thus sparing them emotional upheavals. Quite possibly a new project, administered by a permanent group of teachers who are fluent in sign language and have the skills necessary for such experiments, would prove successful in getting apes to create sentences.

The personnel in the new project would have to be on guard against the subtle and complex imitation that was demonstrated in Project Nim. Requiring proof that an ape is not just mirroring the signs of its teachers is not unreasonable; indeed, it is essential for any researcher who seeks to determine, once and for all, whether apes can, like humans, create sentences. Nor is it unreasonable to expect that in any such experiment, ape "language" must be measured against a child's sophisticated ability. That ability still stands as an important definition of the human species. Much as I would have preferred otherwise, a chimpanzee's "Report to an Academy" remains a work of fiction.

Considerations

1. What are the claims that have been made by previous researchers about apes' language capacities, and what does Terrace find inaccurate about these claims?
2. What do language researchers seem to mean by "grammar," and how does it differ from our more usual use of that term? Why does grammar matter in language work with apes?
3. Describe the role played by Terrace's own research experience in criticizing the work of others. Do you think it biases him or makes him more objective?
4. How does Terrace make use of research on children's language learning? What do comparisons with children enable him to argue about apes?
5. Terrace makes several references to the research of Francine Patterson. Look back at the piece by Patterson in the Opening Problem at the beginning of this chapter (p. 421). Does that piece seem vulnerable to his criticisms?

In the following piece Roger Lewin reports on recent language research at the Yerkes Primate Center in Atlanta by primatologist Sue Savage-Rumbaugh. As you read, you'll want to consider how Savage-Rumbaugh's research differs from that of other researchers. Notice that Lewin provides a short summary of earlier research and also summarizes the criticisms raised by Herbert Terrace (see the previous article). For Lewin, the disagreements among scientists are based in disagreements about language. How, according to Lewin, does Savage-Rumbaugh's "more naturalistic approach"— her method of inquiry — depart from the "either/or" framework that has dominated the discussion until recently?

Look Who's Talking Now

Roger Lewin

A little over a decade ago, studies of ape language seemed to have been discredited in respectable intellectual circles. Half-a-dozen projects, in which individual chimpanzees had been taught various forms of sign language, were summarily dismissed by some scholars as irrelevant to their ultimate goal — an understanding of the evolution of human language.

For instance, in March 1980, Herbert Terrace, a psychologist at Columbia University,

An associate of the Peabody Museum at Harvard University, Roger Lewin (b. 1944) has written several books on anthropology and human evolution, including *Origins Reconsidered* (1992, with Richard Leakey), *Complexity: Life at the Edge of Chaos* (1993), *The Origin of Modern Humans* (1993), *The Sixth Extinction* (1995, with Richard Leakey), and *Patterns in Evolution* (1996).

New York, stated in a landmark paper in *Science* that the apes were doing little more than mimicking their instructors, a skill that, in different ways, rats and pigeons acquire with ease. The apes displayed no sense of grammatical structure in their use of symbols, he said. Later the same year, Thomas Sebeok, a linguist at Indiana University, went so far as to suggest at a major conference in New York that ape-language researchers were, at best, victims of self-delusion or, at worst, perpetrators of outright fraud. As a result of these assaults, funding for ape-language studies virtually dried up. Many journals, including *Science,* subsequently refused to publish what little research was being written up.

In one of those nice accidents of history, 1980 also saw the birth of a pygmy chimpanzee called Kanzi, whose activities were destined to force a reevaluation of language abilities in apes and challenge the new Terrace/Sebeok position. Kanzi lives with Panzee and Panbanisha at the Language Research Center in Atlanta, part of Georgia State University. Not only is he said to approach some of the key criteria of grammatical rules in his use of "words" on a lexigram, but he is also able to comprehend complex spoken sentences, a first in ape-language studies. Sue Savage-Rumbaugh, Kanzi's guardian at the Language Research Center, last summer described her charge's accomplishments at a Wenner-Gren Foundation meeting in Portugal. Participants were impressed. "There was a consensus that the new data on chimpanzees . . . go even further than previous ape studies in making us question the nature of human uniqueness," says Iain Davidson of the University of New England, Australia.

There has long been an interest in the origin of human language. Scottish kings and Egyptian pharaohs are said to have kept infants locked up in isolation, with the expectation that their untutored tongues would give a clue to the nature of the first language humans ever uttered. The origin of language eventually emerged as a subject for respectable academic study. But a dichotomy of views has had an important influence on the conduct and perception of ape-language studies. On one hand, there is the continuity school, which views human language as part of a cognitive continuum, rooted in our apelike ancestors. Opposing this view is the discontinuity school, for which language is a uniquely human trait with no direct evolutionary connection to ape brains.

Ape-language studies, which began in earnest in the 1960s, were anchored in the first of these two schools. By seeking to demonstrate in apes the existence of some of the elements of human language, such as the use of various kinds of symbols within a grammatical structure, researchers hoped to reveal the "cognitive substrate" of human language in our close relatives. To those in the discontinuity school, the most prominent of whom was Noam Chomsky, ape-language researchers were searching for something that did not exist. If language is a uniquely human trait, then no semblance of it could be discovered in apes, because none is present, they argued. Claims to have demonstrated any kind of continuity therefore must be illusory.

Sebeok was — and still is — firmly in the discontinuity school, and was by far the most outspoken of the critics. "Ape-language research is replete with personalities who believe themselves to be acting according to the most exalted motivations and sophisticated manners, but in reality have involved themselves in the most rudimentary circuslike performances," Sebeok proclaimed at the 1980 New York gathering. The mention of "circuslike performances" was a less than subtle reference to a famous vaudeville horse, Clever Hans, which, according to his trainer, could solve arithmetical problems and communicate the answers by tapping his hoof on the ground the appropriate number of times. In fact, the trainer was signaling to the horse, by almost imperceptible and completely unconscious movements of his body when Clever Hans reached the right solution. Not surprisingly, the ape-language researchers objected strongly to Sebeok's characterization of their work. "Vituperative criticism," was Savage-Rumbaugh's riposte.

These florid criticisms aside, many ape-language researchers had indeed strayed into sticky territory, largely of their own making. Many of the experimental approaches used were not rigorous enough to demonstrate unequivocally what was being claimed; self-delusion through an inability to separate mere mimicry from creative symbol production was therefore a real possibility.

ALL OR NOTHING TO SAY

More fundamental, however, was the way the experimental task was framed: Namely, apes would either have elements of grammar that would parallel human language, or they would not. There was no middle ground. This uncompromising position had effectively been imposed on the field by the philosophy of the discontinuity school. Although ape-language researchers, by definition, were not of this school, its tradition — that human language was something special, and that anything less than the real thing was irrelevant — permeated linguistics.

Savage-Rumbaugh has been involved with ape-language studies since the early 1970s, first at the University of Oklahoma, where Roger Fouts had been training a chimp called Washoe, and later at Georgia State University and the Yerkes Primate Center, with Lana and others. With a background in developmental psychology of children, she enthusiastically switched her attention to chimpanzees once her graduate work was completed. "I thought chimps were extremely intelligent and had a lot to tell us about ourselves, including language origins," she says. Her early experience with Washoe and others was, however, discouraging. "I fairly quickly became disillusioned with the work," she recalls. "It wasn't that I thought the chimps didn't know anything, and that it was all imitation. But I did think that the results were being overinterpreted, that exaggerated claims were being made. This often happens in a new area of science."

With concerns over the validity of ape-language work similar to those voiced by Herbert Terrace, Savage-Rumbaugh therefore moved to Yerkes, where she eventually developed an important new approach. While Terrace was at Columbia University, testing chimpanzees' language abilities by looking for production of grammatical structure under strict laboratory conditions, Savage-Rumbaugh began to shift emphasis, both in technique and questions asked. Instead of putting the chimpanzees through rote learning of symbols, gradually building up the vocabulary a symbol at a time, she decided to take a more naturalistic approach. She set out to employ a large vocabulary of symbols from the beginning, using them as language is used around human children. This way, the chimpanzees might pick up language as children do. "The traditional approach assumes limited ability, and in effect imposes that on the animals," she explains.

The shift in questions asked was away from an emphasis on grammatical structure, at least in the beginning, and toward comprehension. "I had been concerned that comprehension had never been considered an issue at all, just whether the chimp could produce a symbol on cue and could produce combinations of symbols," she says. "It seemed reasonable to me — obvious even — that comprehension was an important element of language, that language is first acquired through comprehension, and that production flows from that."

The Language Research Center team applied this approach to some extent in its work with Austin and Sherman, two young common chimpanzees. But Savage-Rumbaugh's initial motivation for going to the primate center had been to work with pygmy chimps, also known as bonobos. Slightly smaller than common chimpanzees, and with darker coloration, bonobos are something of an enigma in the primate world. They live in Zaire in dense forest which makes field study extremely difficult. Their range is rapidly being destroyed, so they may soon be extinct under natural conditions. Much of what is known about these animals has come from research at primate centers such as Yerkes. Largely from anecdotal accounts, it was said that bonobos were more vocal than common chimpanzees, and communicated a wider range of information through facial expression and gestures. Initially, Savage-Rumbaugh had been studying this non-verbal communication, but she decided to embark on a language project too. If nothing else, it would provide an interesting comparison between the two species.

Matata, a mature bonobo female, was the first subject chosen for the project, which began in 1981. But Matata did not come alone. Six months earlier she had kidnapped a newborn infant and kept it as her own. This was Kanzi. While Savage-Rumbaugh and her colleagues were working with Matata, Kanzi ran around, getting into mischief and generally performing playfully, as young chimpanzees are wont to do. "Kanzi often interrupted his mother's training sessions by leaping on her head, her hand, or the keys, just as she was about to select a symbol," the Language Research Center team reported. "He would also leap on her hand just as she was reaching for a piece of food, grab it away, and run off. . . . During this period, Kanzi did not engage in any behaviors that suggested he knew that specific symbols were associated with specific foods."

Some ape-language programs have employed American Sign Language, in which the trainers teach the appropriate signs by repeatedly "molding" the animals' hands and fingers to the correct shape. Savage-Rumbaugh believes that this laborious process interferes with communication. Instead, the Language Research Center system employs an extensive "lexigram," a matrix of 256 geometrical shapes on a board. Instructors touch the symbols, which represent verbs and nouns, to create simple requests or commands. At the same time, the sentence is spoken verbally, with the objective of testing comprehension of spoken English.

Although she was clearly intelligent in many ways, Matata was a poor learner, and never appeared to pick up the use of more than half-a-dozen symbols. "At that stage, a year into the project, I was very disappointed," says Savage-Rumbaugh. "But then someone said they thought that Kanzi understood something of what was being said around him." There had been no effort to teach Kanzi anything, merely to tolerate his presence. Nevertheless, once the suggestion had been made that he might understand some of the spoken language, careful testing showed it to be true. "He had picked up the half-dozen symbols we had been trying to teach Matata, but he had done it with no instruction, just naturally as human children do." From this point onward, an even greater effort was made to place language learning in a naturalistic context.

Georgia State University's Language Research Center incorporates a twenty-three-hectare forest where, during the warmer months, food is supplied at seventeen named locations. When Kanzi was young, most of his days were spent in the forest, where much of the communication concerned going to specific locations for specific food items. A young ape's life focuses very much on food and play, but here these activities were elevated to elements of communication. Kanzi was joined by a sister, Mulika, born to

Matata when he was two and a half. The two siblings grew up together, both immersed in the language-learning milieu. They therefore provided a direct comparison with Austin and Sherman, the two common chimpanzees that Savage-Rumbaugh had worked with earlier.

DOUBLE STANDARDS

Language acquisition in humans is a relatively slow process, spread out over some half-dozen years. Over a similar period Kanzi's language abilities changed too, becoming more sophisticated in both comprehension and structure. Savage-Rumbaugh suggests that this similar, albeit slower and more limited, developmental process in bonobos indicates the presence of a cognitive substrate of language in apes. She accuses critics who charge that what Kanzi does is not language of applying a double standard. "Because we know that children eventually will develop language, their abilities at an early age are given more significance than similar abilities in apes," she says. "When children make up novel words it is called lexical innovation, but when chimpanzees do the same thing it is called ambiguous. Grammatical structure in young children is often ill-formed, but we don't say that they don't have language. We need better methodologies, which can be applied to humans and apes, without regard to the end point of language development."

How far did Kanzi go in his language development? "Impressively far," says Savage-Rumbaugh, "certainly further than any common chimpanzee." Now ten years old, Kanzi has a vocabulary of some 200 words. But it is not the size of his vocabulary that is impressive, it is what the words apparently mean to him that catches the attention. Experimental psychologists are familiar with the prodigious feats of association that even the most humble animal may perform. Chimpanzees, being very clever, are therefore likely to be able to behave in complex ways that might mimic language abilities, but are founded on mere association — the linking of sounds and symbols with objects in the absence of true understanding. Savage-Rumbaugh believes that what Kanzi does goes beyond this, and is firmly in the territory of the rudiments of language.

Recently, the Language Research Center team conducted tests on Kanzi's comprehension. This involved giving him a series of sentences — requests to do things — delivered by someone out of his sight. Karen Brakke and other team members in the room with Kanzi wore earphones; they could not hear the instructions and so could not cue Kanzi, even unconsciously. None of the sentences was practiced, and every one was different.

"The first ones were relatively simple, like 'Can you put the raisins in the bowl,' and 'Can you give the cereal to Karen,'" explains Savage-Rumbaugh. "He did those kind of things very easily, so we made it more difficult, like 'Can you go to the colony room and get the telephone.' There were four or five things in the colony room, things that normally weren't there, so it had to be a specific response, a specific understanding on Kanzi's part."

Already, these kinds of abilities were beyond what Austin and Sherman had been able to do. For one thing, the common chimpanzees had been unable to learn and comprehend spoken English, and instructions had to be via the lexigram. Even so, they seemed unable to hold details of the instruction long enough in their mind to complete a task composed of several components.

Going one step further in complexity, Savage-Rumbaugh and her colleagues discovered an interesting discrimination that Kanzi made with the structure of certain instructions. Because the instruction "Go to the colony room and get the orange" might be thought simply to be linking the colony room and the orange that he finds there, they added a complication. With an orange in front of Kanzi, the instruction was repeated. About 90 percent of the time Kanzi seemed uncertain, fumbled with the orange in front of him, and then went to the colony and fetched the orange from there. But, if the instruction was phrased "Get the orange that's in the colony room," Kanzi had no hesitation. The element of the phrase, ". . . that's in the . . ." is the key. "This suggests to me that the syntactically more complex phrase is producing better comprehension than the simple one," says Savage-Rumbaugh. "I had not predicted that." Kanzi displayed this level of comprehension when he was nine years old, but not when he was younger than six years old.

Kanzi's word production also increased with age, again indicating some kind of developmental process at work. In collaboration with Patricia Marks Greenfield, a psychologist at the University of California, Los Angeles, Savage-Rumbaugh showed that in producing word combinations, Kanzi was able not only to learn simple grammatical rules, but also to invent his own rules. The rule he learned, which he picked up from his keepers, was that in two-word utterances, action precedes object. During the first month Kanzi employed no specific order for action and object symbols, but during the last four months he did so to a statistically significant degree. "This developmental trend from random ordering to an ordering preference was also found for human children at the two-word stage," the researchers note.

One rule that Kanzi invented himself involved the combination of symbol and gesture, as in "chase" followed by pointing to someone. Marks Greenfield and Savage-Rumbaugh observe that Kanzi's rule, "place lexigram first," had considerable generality as well as originality. "Most important, in none of the relations was there a human model for the rule. This is strong evidence for creative productivity."

A second rule Kanzi invented involved the combination of several action symbols, such as chase, tickle, hide, slap, bite, hug, and so on. Of such components is a pygmy chimpanzee's life composed. And, interestingly enough, the way in which Kanzi combines these words reflects the structure of his life. Certain of these symbols, such as chase and tickle, appeared first to a highly statistically significant degree in two-symbol utterances. Others, such as hide, slap and bite, appeared second in such utterances, also to a statistically significant degree. Kanzi's rationale, it seems, is that lexigrams that appear first represent an invitation to play, while those in second place represent the content of the play. "In effect, Kanzi's rule of syntactic order corresponded to Kanzi's own rules of behavioral order and, indeed, to those of pygmy chimps in general in the wild," say the researchers.

These and other observations persuade Marks Greenfield and Savage-Rumbaugh that they are witnessing real evidence of the cognitive substrate that underlies human language. "The capacity for grammatical rules (including arbitrary ones) in Kanzi's semiotic productions shows grammar as an area of evolutionary continuity," they say. "We might prefer to speak of 'protogrammar' rather than grammar. However . . . the comparative data are such that if we speak of bonobo rules as protogrammar, we should apply the same term to the two-year-old child." No double standards.

Many psychologists are extremely impressed with Kanzi and the implications of the observations. For instance, Emil Menzel, of the State University of New York at Stony Brook, says: "I've seen the tapes, and they are very convincing; there's no cueing here." He believes, however, that many people will not accept the observations for what they really imply. Specifically, he is referring to the supporters of the discontinuity theory, which states that human language is rooted in cognitive processes for building mental models of the world, and is not solely a means of communication. No rudiment of this uniquely human capacity can therefore be expected to exist in apes. "If you take the Sebeok view, nothing will convince you," he laments.

Menzel is right. "Facts do not convince me," says Sebeok. "Theories do. Ape-language research is bereft of theories." Savage-Rumbaugh responds with a challenge: "The singular fact that an ape can learn simple language when given exposure that is similar to that of a child reveals the inadequacy of both the continuity and discontinuity theories, for neither of them addresses the role of the communicative partner." She also accuses Sebeok of being uninformed about Kanzi's abilities. "I would have to conclude that he has not read any of the work from this project for some time," she says. "Ape language is helping us formulate new theories of language acquisition that have an evolutionary basis."

Although Terrace acknowledges that the Kanzi project is important, "because he didn't have to be drilled to learn symbols," he does not accept Kanzi's behavior as evidence of rudiments of language. "Kanzi still uses the symbols to get things, to ask for things," he complains. "He is not using them to share his perception of the world. I'd like to see reliable evidence of referential response, like 'I've experienced X,' rather than the simple statements you get."

"We are simply dealing with a matter of degree," responds Savage-Rumbaugh. "Yes, Kanzi uses his symbols to get things, and to ask for things; but so do young children. In fact, the predominant symbol use of normal children is 'requesting.' Kanzi's percentage is higher, but he can reliably tell you some things, such as when he is going to be 'good' or 'bad,' what he has just eaten or where he is headed while traveling. Terrace has consistently refused to acknowledge this."

To demand that language usage in apes must conform exactly to the human pattern in order to be accepted as a "cognitive substrate" of language is not only unreasonable, it is irrelevant, says Savage-Rumbaugh. "With a brain one-third the size of our own, Kanzi is likely to fall down somewhere, and the more we understand what he cannot do, the more we can pinpoint the specific kinds of skills that must have evolved in early hominids."

Meanwhile, Kanzi is apparently on the verge of a new simian world. His capacity for comprehension far outstrips his capacity to produce language using the lexigram. "He gets extremely frustrated," says Savage-Rumbaugh. He often gets very vocal at these times, a kind of high-pitched squeaking. Is he trying to imitate speech? "It may be a long shot, but all these other things I've tried have been surprises," she says. "He tries very hard. He looks right at you and makes these sounds. When you talk back to him he vocalizes more and more." The Georgia State University researchers are working with the idea of analyzing Kanzi's sound spectrum, to see if there is sufficient breadth to develop into rudimentary speech.

And if Kanzi were to talk what would he say? Maybe the first thing he'd say is that he is fed up with Terrace claiming that apes don't have language.

Considerations

1. Does Savage-Rumbaugh's work with Kanzi differ in important ways from previous language experiments with other apes? What comparisons can be made?
2. In offering his overview of the language research with apes, Lewin divides the experts into two camps: those who believe in a "cognitive continuum" and those of the "discontinuity school." Explain the differences in point of view.
3. Why study apes and language? What motives, do you think, drive the researchers, and do they vary from researcher to researcher?
4. Early in his article Lewin refers to the work of Herbert Terrace (see the previous reading). According to Lewin, what has been his influence upon subsequent research? Has he had an influence, do you think, upon the work of the primatologist, profiled in this article, Sue Savage-Rumbaugh? If you read Terrace's piece, do you find either Terrace's or Savage-Rumbaugh's stance more convincing? Why?

In the following excerpt from her book The Monkey Wars, *science writer Deborah Blum profiles the neurosurgeon Stuart Zola-Morgan, whose research on memory is conducted on macaque monkeys. If you've read the previous pieces about language researchers, you may want to compare their interests and approaches with those of Zola-Morgan: How do Zola-Morgan's research interests, methods, and assumptions differ from those of the language researchers? As you read about Zola-Morgan, you'll also want to consider Blum's treatment of him. Does she want us to view him and his research sympathetically? How can you tell?*

The Black Box

DEBORAH BLUM

The most direct way to explore the head of a monkey is with a power drill and a scalpel. Open the skull. Burrow into the brain.

If you're interested in the machinery of the brain, you go straight in like that. A scientist like Duane Rumbaugh,[1] chasing intelligent behavior, has no need to pry open the skull. He wants to watch the monkey in action.

It's different, though, for a researcher interested not in the monkey as a whole animal, but in one crucial part — the brain itself. The body protects the brain well, buffer-

[1]**Duane Rumbaugh** is a primatologist at the Yerkes Research Center and is husband of Sue Savage-Rumbaugh, whose work is described in the previous reading (p. 517) [Eds.].

DEBORAH BLUM (b. 1954) is a journalist for the *Sacramento Bee.* "The Black Box" and "Not a Nice Death" (see p. 529) are excerpts from her Pulitzer Prize–winning work, *The Monkey Wars* (1994).

ing it with layers of armor, concealing it. A neuroscientist, an investigator seeking the inner workings of the brain, must go inside it to understand it. No technology yet available, no imager, no powerful combination of magnets and computers, can yet see the live brain in all its intricate and everchanging detail. If you really want to know, then you make a path through blood and bone. Otherwise, if you are too squeamish, you walk away from the secrets within the skull.

People complain that there is no unexplored, unmapped territory left in the world. A neuroscientist knows that's not true, that the most mysterious territory left on earth lies within the skull. In the operating room, you begin to understand how mysterious. It takes tedious hours to get to the brain; a mind-numbing repetition of cut and snip. Yet still, every time, there's this moment when the barriers are cut away — the skin, the muscle, the skull, the thick, gray membrane that lies beneath the bone. The folds of the brain show through. They are gleaming, wet, shell-pink, coiled into fine loops. In that moment, a monkey brain shines as brightly, offers as much challenge as a human brain.

Neuroscientists have been chasing that challenge forever. Or so it seems sometimes to Stuart Zola-Morgan, a man who has given his career to coaxing secrets out of the unknown territory. Zola-Morgan is a research scientist in psychiatry, a neurosurgeon at the University of California, San Diego. He also holds an appointment at the Veterans Affairs Medical Center, at the UC-San Diego campus. He chairs the animal research committee of the national Society for Neuroscience, a group dedicated to defending animal research. He's a lover of good jokes, magic tricks, old movies, and the brain. His operating room is a long way from Rumbaugh's Georgia laboratory, in miles and in approach. It's a long way from Roger Fouts's laboratory too. This is not research that puts the animal first at all costs. The brain is the holy grail here, and the monkeys are among the tools needed — vital and valuable — on the quest.

When Zola-Morgan explains the magic of the brain to his students, he calls it "the black box." His hands shape the box in the air — not so big, grapefruit-like. He makes a simple curve, revealing nothing of the webbed complexity inside. "I tell graduates that it's as if whoever runs the show says, 'Look, here's this black box. There's lots of complications in how it works. And if you spend endless days, and nights and years, I may reveal to you just a little about how it works. I may let you have a tickle.' So then I look out at the students and I say, 'Do you still want to do this?'" He starts to grin. "It weeds them out." He thinks about it a minute himself, graying brown hair crammed under blue surgical cap, brown eyes thoughtful behind steel-rimmed glasses, gloves peeled off for a break, hands freshly scrubbed — and steady. He's been chasing the mystery for decades and his interest hasn't flagged. "Even the tickle is so amazing."

It is because monkeys are so like us — their intelligence so tantalizingly similar to our own — that they have become such a good model of the human brain. Zola-Morgan uses monkeys because he can't answer his questions without them. He uses them because they give good answers, because in trying to decipher the mysteries of their brains, he gets closer to understanding ours. He believes without question that the pursuit is worthwhile, that the use of monkeys in his research pays off. It does more than feed a fascination; it promises knowledge that can be used to help people with brain damage, afflictions such as Alzheimer's disease, and crippling strokes.

If you follow his work through even a single surgery, the tradeoff as he sees it becomes clear: There is a price to be paid for knowledge. In this case, the price is in the lives of another species.

Surgery days begin early for Stuart Zola-Morgan. On a cool January morning, the mist still wraps silently through the dripping palms, fig and orange trees, callas and bleeding heart ferns that tangle around his home in south San Diego. Inside, the scene is anything but quiet. Rhett, the Yorkshire terrier, and Lizzie, a mutt, bounce off the door, begging to go out. Zola-Morgan's wife, Susan, a veterinarian at UC-San Diego, brews coffee, easing into the day. Coco, the cat, snoozes on the floor.

Zola-Morgan is too edgy to sit still. He stands by the window, looking out into the garden, but the wet leaves just blur away. In his mind, he sees the operating room. He knows that at the campus they're already prepping the monkey for surgery. Sitting for breakfast seems intolerable. He grabs a cup of coffee, snatches a package of Pepperidge Farm Mint Milano cookies, climbs into his red Toyota, and sends the car plunging through the mist, down the steep hill of his driveway.

It's like being a fish on the hook. On mornings like this, Zola-Morgan's work reels him in, the tug of an invisible line between his operating room and his bed. His current series of experiments focus on some of the brain's smallest, most elusive structures. They seem to demand the inner buzz, maybe even the jolt of coffee and cookies. He can guarantee himself a minimum of eight hours in the operating room, below ground, in the basement of the UC-San Diego Medical School. Gowned in blue scrubs, ringed by white-tiled walls, shiny with disinfectant, his gloved hands smudged with blood, he will slowly, carefully, cut his way down to the monkey's brain.

Getting there it is always a lengthy procedure, at once tedious and grisly. On these mornings, Zola-Morgan arrives at his campus operating room at 8:30. He must wash up, don his scrubs, hat, booties, two pairs of sterile gloves, before he even approaches the waiting monkey.

He uses crab-eating macaques, a close relation of the rhesus. The monkeys are less scrappy than rhesus macaques, less hardy. This day's monkey had come, months before, from the Philippines. It would be already motionless on the steel operating table, eyes closed, deep in an anesthetic-induced sleep when the doctor gets there. As youngsters, crab-eating macaques sport tufts of hair that poke from the tops of their heads; they look like monkeys with Mohawk haircuts. For surgery, the macaque's head is shaved clean.

Zola-Morgan's first job is to brace the head. There is no wiggle room in brain surgery. He opens the monkey's mouth and inserts a metal T-bar, the top of the tee catching behind the sharp canine teeth. Two metal prongs, blunt-ended, grip the area just outside the edge of the animal's eye sockets. With teeth and eyes anchored, the monkey's head is held rigidly still, awaiting the first cut. Holding a scalpel, Zola-Morgan traces a T-cut onto the top of the head, a line behind the brow-bone, a perpendicular cut down the back of the head. Where the knife touches, blood glimmers bright red, showing through the skin like the pulp of a fruit. He rolls the severed skin away from the muscle.

He has learned to risk a little extra blood. Ten years of operating on monkeys prejudiced him against cauterizing the tissue to control bleeding. The brief burn of electric current rapidly clots blood, but it cooks cells as well, slowing the healing in the muscle. He prefers anesthesia that lowers blood pressure, slowing the flow, indirectly reducing bleeding. He learned the trick from neurosurgeons who operate on people. He asked them for ways to make the surgery less traumatic.

But the dense tissue over the monkey's skull — the powerful muscle that give its jaws such strength — is about ten times thicker than the comparable muscle in a human head. It is crammed with blood vessels. The cut muscle inevitably runs red. As the surgery progresses, gauze pads, soaked with blood and saline, pile up around the scientist's feet.

And the tough muscle holds hard and tight to the skull, resisting his efforts to pull it away. It is a good hour until he can see the left cheekbone, the pinkish-white curve of the zygomatic arch. Still, he has to free it further, hitching a square of gauze behind the bone, dragging it up and down until the muscle is polished off and the arch stands clear. Then, using a drill that fills the room with the whine of metal on bone, he breaks out the arch. He cuts on, opening a path through the muscle to the skull. Then more drilling, making a walnut-sized hole in the skull itself. Then, carefully, he chips away the bony skull to expose the tissue that covers the brain, the thin, gray rubbery-looking sheet of the dura. And then the whole process must be repeated on the other side of the head.

The surgeries have been known to tick away for so long that Zola-Morgan's graduate students, working with him and his colleagues in the operating room, despair of ever getting a meal. Sometimes they sneak out, holding their sterile gloved hands in the air, opening their mouths like young birds while their friends stuff in chocolate or pretzels.

And all of that is mere preparation, what must come before starting on the main task of the surgery — playing with the brain's internal switches.

Now, the approach becomes not unlike that of a new homeowner exploring his circuit-breaker box, trying to figure out what controls what. Flip this switch and the kitchen lights cut out. Flip that one and there goes the living room, the garage, the bedrooms. What Zola-Morgan tries to do is to turn off parts of the monkey's brain and then see what happens to its memory.

The research team knows from experience that you can train macaques to pick up objects in a certain order: first the green block, then the red. It's a simple task of memory. The question is, will a monkey remember that order if Zola-Morgan has removed part of his brain? What part? Will the monkey remember that green came before red if you flip off this switch? That one?

What if you probe into the brain, down into the temporal lobe, just in front of the ears, to the place where Alzheimer's disease begins its ruinous journey through memory? What if you probe right to the hippocampus, a gray ridge of cells curled deep into the lobe? Named for its distinctive, seahorse shape — "hippos" is Greek for horse, "kampos" for sea monster — the coil of cells floating in a sea of neurons has been thought to be the gatekeeper of memory. It has been suspected of being the thing that chooses, that says "Save this thought. Let this one go."

So if you carve it out, what then? What if you chiseled away the brain tissue on either side of it, leaving gaps, dark spaces in the brain? What would be lost? What would stand?

Driving from his home, crammed amid the morning rush of Southern Californians on Interstate 5, Zola-Morgan anticipates the surgery, hoping he will get to ask those questions. He knows, as it has happened before, that the operation could fail on the table. It takes a good four hours just to open up the brain, bracing the monkey on its stomach as scalpel and drill bite deeper and deeper. Even unconscious, the monkeys' bodies are vulnerable to the shock of invasion, so much so that sometimes just turning the animal over will cause its heart to stutter to a stop.

The researchers try to prevent it, using only the healthiest, toughest animals, running blood tests before the surgery, checking against signs of illness. The monkeys can fool them. The animals are born to hide illness. A crab-eating macaque, its instincts tuned to the rainforests of Asia, has good reason to suffer in silence. In the wild, an obviously ill animal is a target. A cry of pain is a siren call for predators. The crab-eaters grow up learning to hide their vulnerabilities, including those that make them a bad risk for surgery. Ketamine, the popular drug used to immobilize animals before surgery, will overwhelm a diseased liver. Zola-Morgan has lost animals for just that reason. The monkey never showed a symptom until the drug was administered.

Out of the seventy monkeys used in his experiments during the past decade, a half-dozen died in surgery. He has become religious about doing blood tests before surgery, checking the function of the liver. He guards, as best he can, against the loss of an animal.

He knows too well that even if the operation succeeds, the brain will not suddenly open up, unfolding like a flower in spring. The brain is unforceable; it will be understood sliver by sliver, if at all. He has resigned himself to that. He hopes to live a long time. He doubts it will be long enough to answer his questions. The unyielding intricacy appeals, in a curious way, to the clockmaker traits in him, the part that likes to go hands-on with gears, cogs, and wheels. "My mother says I was always doing this when I was small, taking things apart."

He'd started out, at the University of Massachusetts in Amherst, planning to study human brains directly. But the clockmaker in him didn't like the kind of experiments you could do with people. They were too unpredictable, too blurry with emotional response, too messy. "I started to become a little disenchanted," Zola-Morgan says. "There was a lack of rigor. I don't mean that in a negative way, I just wasn't as comfortable with it as others were." He was pondering his future when Harvard University ran a want ad in the local paper. "It said something like, 'Interested in monkey business? Call this number if you'd like to study primates.'" Curious and restless, he called. The Harvard group was studying high-fat diets, taking baby monkeys by caesarean section and hand-rearing them on a formula diet. The little monkeys were unexpectedly showing signs of stress, rocking themselves, sucking their toes constantly. "It took someone with basic Psychology 101 to know they needed interaction with other monkeys, they were too isolated," Zola-Morgan said. But from that start, he became interested in monkey behavior, and then interested in the physical processes that drove the behavior.

"I just fell in love with the brain. This organ that was so complicated and so mysterious and so responsible for our behavior. And what really interested me was memory. That seemed to be at the core of who we are. The funny thing is that, back then, we thought memory, at least, was simple. It was very straightforward. And I've spent my career making it more complicated, finding that there's more than one memory system, that they operate by different processes, that they're housed in different structures. The harder you look, the more remarkable a mechanism the brain is."

Neuroscientists have dubbed the 1990s the Decade of the Brain, the era when new technology and new insight will finally allow humans to understand the machinery inside their heads. Sometimes, they are sure that will happen. Sometimes, they think even astronomers have an easier job. Astronomers analyze stars just a few hundred billion miles away; they merely pick apart the composition of some distant blur of light. Researchers such as Zola-Morgan are trying in a sense to turn themselves inside out, to use their brains to understand their brains. It seems, sometimes, like the last test of human intellect — to understand itself.

Considerations

1. Consider Blum's use of comparison in this profile of Zola-Morgan. To what use or uses does she put her comparisons?
2. Monkeys' intelligence is "tantalizingly" similar to that of humans, says Blum (p. 525), thus the appeal of monkeys in brain research. Using a definition of "tantalizing" as a jumping-off point, consider how Blum uses the theme of tantalization throughout this reading.
3. One of Blum's concerns in *The Monkey Wars,* the book from which this excerpt is taken, is to present the heated disagreement between researchers who work with animal subjects and animal rights activists who oppose this research. In what ways does this excerpt show the influence of this issue, and do you get any sense of where Blum herself stands in the debate?
4. What are the similarities and differences between the research concerns of neuroscientists like Zola-Morgan and those of language researchers like Terrace and Savage-Rumbaugh in the previous readings? Where do you suppose Zola-Morgan would stand in the disagreement between the "continuity" and "discontinuity" schools described by Lewin in the previous reading?

Here is a second piece by Deborah Blum, the journalist who profiled the neurosurgeon Stuart Zola-Morgan in the previous reading. This excerpt, like the previous one, comes from her book The Monkey Wars, *in which Blum offers a complex overview of the controversies surrounding the laboratory treatment of primates. Here she describes the work of veterinarian Roy Henrickson, whose discovery of an AIDS-type virus in macaque monkeys has given momentum to a promising but problematic line of investigation in AIDS research. Notice the attention that Blum gives in this piece to "the monkey model" of medical research: What are its strengths and weaknesses?*

Not a Nice Death

DEBORAH BLUM

Roy Henrickson knew all about watching monkeys die.

They died all the time when he first came to the California Regional Primate Research Center. It was almost routine. Monkeys bled to death from fight injuries. Monkeys wasted away from incurable diarrheas. Before Henrickson arrived, almost 500 monkeys

DEBORAH BLUM (b. 1954) is a journalist for the *Sacramento Bee.* Like the previous piece, "Not a Nice Death" is excerpted from Blum's the *Monkey Wars* (1994).

had been killed by Simian Hemorrhagic Fever, a racing infection that ripped blood cells apart, causing the animals to drown in their own fluid. The center's death rate was 18 to 25 percent in the early 1970s. Losses were so dismal that the federal government threatened to close the place down.

Henrickson came on as chief vet in 1972. His predecessor had quit, burned out. That might have worried another veterinarian. It struck Roy Henrickson as a challenge. He was Hawaiian-born, a big man with blue eyes, dark hair, and such a passionate love of travel that he plastered maps across every available wall of every office. As a primate vet, he'd traveled to India and Malaysia, to study and understand the animals in their native homes. Earlier, Henrickson had lived in the Chilean Andes, working in a Trappist monastery, caring for the monks' animals. He'd tried private practice; it bored him, and so did the dogs and cats. He'd considered zoos but thought they were too political. The primate center, with its chattering monkeys and desperate need of help, intrigued him.

The setup at the center was primitive, Henrickson remembers. Cages were concrete slabs, rimmed with iron bars. No one thought about monkeys liking to perch or climb. Old tomato boxes had been tossed in for shelter. It was seat-of-the-pants veterinary medicine at first. Henrickson packed his instruments and supplies into a suitcase and lugged them from cage to cage. He also set up a regular clinic. He isolated ailing monkeys from the well ones. He left healthy colonies alone, refusing to shift them around. He fussed over diet, reading nutrition labels on monkey chow bags, adding in fresh fruit. Within a few months, the accidental death rate had fallen below 5 percent.

He was still feeling smug about it when the monkeys started dying again.

It was different this time, a wild, lethal slide out of control. It was early fall in 1976, the days still cooking with the heat that lingers past a Central Valley summer. The center had a colony of stumptail macaques then, cousins of the rhesus macaques. The stumptails were sweet animals, Henrickson says, more trusting than rhesus and by far more gentle. In the crisping heat of summer, the baby stumptails would sunburn, their small faces brightening to deep pink. Henrickson would painstakingly smear sunscreen and ointment on them and they would cling, looking up while he rubbed the cream in. "They were beautiful animals," he says. "I really liked them." They were suddenly dying away and whatever it was, it was a terrible death, a cascade of infections, cramming one on top of each other, wearing the little monkeys out.

"I'd been thinking, 'Well, you're pretty good, Roy. Sort of a hero.' The disease had really just fallen off because we'd quit moving the monkeys around so much, mixing them and their infections together. It was the equivalent of closing down the gay baths in San Francisco. And [then] this hit the stumptails. I was pulling my hair out. I thought it must be something in the soil. I was out there with a shovel digging up dirt, sending it off to be tested. And the stumptails, they were just babies and we couldn't save them. I can't tell you how much you mind something like that. It was enormously stressful."

The stumptail epidemic passed without ever being diagnosed. Henrickson, angry and frustrated, saved blood samples and slices of tissue from the lost monkeys, stored them in the center's supercooled freezers, ice solid at 70 degrees below zero Fahrenheit. Then in the early 1980s, monkeys suddenly started dying again. This time it was rhesus macaques. This time, Henrickson was determined not to let the disease, whatever it was, get away from him. He assigned a postdoctoral assistant full time to do nothing but clinical workups on each animal, looking for the common pattern.

When the pattern emerged, it would mean more, much more, than the deaths of a group of monkeys in Northern California. It would weave itself into a much bigger picture, a frightening one. At the New England Regional Primate Research Center, near Boston, a similar epidemic was also destroying macaques. And this time, there was something similar spreading into the human population. A troubling illness was emerging, a disease that caused a lethal collapse of the immune system, crippling the body's ability to fight off infection. The human disease was AIDS, Acquired Immune Deficiency Syndrome.

The New England scientists realized, and then the California researchers, that the monkey disease was almost a mirror of the human one. Like AIDS, it was a virus that eventually crumbled the immune system into unworkable bits. All the infections — in the stumptails, the rhesus, the humans — sprang from the same family of retroviruses. Retroviruses can seem both primitive and sophisticated. They are too basic to contain DNA; they rely on the genetic structure of their host. They can whip the human genes around, though, like a ringmaster at a circus. If a retrovirus wants to make copies of itself in human cells, or monkey cells, then it gets the copies made. The human virus is best known now as Human Immunodeficiency Virus (HIV). The monkey virus, the mirror, is Simian Immunodeficiency Virus (SIV).

When Henrickson and his colleagues in Davis went back and analyzed the frozen blood of the lost stumptails, it was SIV they found locked into the cells. No one is sure where, exactly, HIV moved out of the dark and into the human population. But in macaques, there's no doubt. Their version of the disease began at the hands of humans. SIV in macaques is a disease born in captivity. It was carried by African monkeys who were packed into research centers with Asian macaques. Most probably, researchers think, it was transferred by the casual handling of animals, such as reusing needles. The most clear-cut case occurred at the Tulane Regional Primate Research Center. Scientists there tried to infect rhesus macaques with leprosy by injecting the tissue from sooty mangabeys that carried leprosy bacterium. They didn't realize at the time that mangabeys were silent carriers for SIV. The macaques became much sicker than anyone had expected.

At the California center, the evidence is purely circumstantial: Back in the 1970s, there were sooty mangabeys at the Davis site; their frozen blood samples also reveal the knotted presence of SIV. Nobody had known anything was wrong with them. Again, the mangabeys exhibited no symptoms. Scientists now believe the African monkeys were exposed to the immunodeficiency viruses thousands of years ago; they have learned to live with them. Like humans, the macaques are newcomers in retrovirus country, hopelessly vulnerable.

The monkey model for AIDS, then, was created by mistake. It was there, undiagnosed, before the human disease became suddenly visible. It was there when Roy Henrickson was frantically digging up the dirt on the laboratory grounds. Without the human disease, this would have been considered a mistake in monkey management — the loss of valuable monkeys to a stray virus. But with AIDS at large, things were different. When they realized what they had, researchers regarded it as a gift. What incredible timing. Just as the human disease spiked up, so did the monkey ailment. Exactly when they needed it. They seemed to have the perfect model.

In the beginning, scientists thought they had the virus trapped; some virologists were predicting a vaccine by the mid-1980s. Now, there is doubt a vaccine will be developed before the year 2000, or even until the next century. Perhaps the monkey model for AIDS was oversold and perhaps it never was a perfect model. The story, though, also illustrates the limits of animal models, the tradeoffs of using animals to solve human problems. After the splashy successes — the vaccines for polio, measles, mumps — perhaps we were too sure of conquering all. The AIDS virus, if nothing else, has proved the limits of the tools at hand.

The progress slowed to the point that Henrickson himself, ever restless, left Davis for UC-Berkeley in 1985. He wanted a new challenge. "It was tremendously exciting in the early days of AIDS research," he says. "But after a while, I realized I'd ridden the high." He's still at Berkeley, and it's fair to say that the big, Bay Area university, surrounded by militant animal activists, has provided Henrickson with endless challenge. He plans, though, to take early retirement by 1995, and spend his time consulting and traveling. He already has invitations to a primate colony off the coast of Java and to a research station in Kenya.

The struggle to overcome — or even understand — the AIDS virus has been left to those with patience. Or stubbornness. Or both. Back in Davis, virologist Nick Lerche (pronounced LAIR-key) has been working with the primate virus ten years now. Lerche heads the California primate center's Simian Retrovirus Laboratory. He remains a believer that the basic design of an anti-AIDS vaccine will come in macaques. But when? "I go up and down," Lerche says. "I think we were naive in the beginning. We didn't understand the complexity of the immune system or the biological systems we were working with. I think we'll find it in the monkey model, but it's going to be slow. . . . Originally, everyone wanted to hit the home run and we thought we could. The funding agencies thought so, too. It just hasn't happened. The easy stuff has all been done. Now we're having to step back."

Lerche thinks they don't really even have the model yet. Not the one that will unlock the disease. How can they? They don't fully understand the virus or its family; they can't completely explain the body's response to it. Not the monkey response, not the human response either. After ten years, they're still trying to figure out what the model should be. When pushed, Lerche searches carefully for a word to describe where they are. "Evolving," he chooses finally. "The model is still evolving."

Any animal model in medical research is imperfect. A monkey is not a boy; a cat is not a girl. The animal is being experimented on for ethical reasons, as an acceptable substitute for the human being. If you want to study the effect of drugs on the lungs of infants, you don't slice up the lungs of human babies. You use the lungs of baby macaques instead. Heart transplants were developed in dogs. Vision studies are done in cats, peeling open the brain to study visual nerve development. Tests for poisons, checks for carcinogens, these are routinely done in rats and mice, not in people.

If you can't get the human result, you get as close as you can, edging across the species, beginning in rats, working up to primates. You hope that your animal will be a good "model" of what happens in humans. Sometimes hope isn't enough. . . .

If you accept animals as the ethical substitute for humans — and that can be a big if — then maybe you just prepare to wait out the monkey model of AIDS.

And maybe not. Maybe you wonder why the disease continues to run out of control, even as the federal primate centers spend a third of their $40 million-plus annual budget on AIDS research. Maybe, as animal advocates do, you start thinking ethics isn't even the fundamental issue. Maybe it is that animals are a lousy model for this disease, that they tell us much about how monkeys get sick, and nothing about how retroviruses chew their way through the human immune system. The work may have told scientists a lot about retroviruses in rhesus macaques, or crab-eaters, or pigtail macaques, or even chimpanzees. Has it told them anything about the people dying alone on the wards of urban hospitals?

Activists think not. They see two things going to waste: money and lives. Their attitude can be summed up in the title of a short essay in the quarterly magazine of the *New England Anti-Vivisection Society:* "Experimenters Fiddle While AIDS Rages."

In other words, primate research on AIDS is a vulnerable target. In their early certainty, researchers helped make it one. Virologist Robert Gallo, of the National Cancer Institute, once announced that if he just had 500 chimpanzees, that's all it would take to guarantee a vaccine against AIDS. Obviously, it's not that easy. Chimpanzees now often seem a dubious model for the disease. They are also rare, so their use is politically sensitive. Researchers such as Roger Fouts have publicly denounced putting a dwindling chimpanzee species into further jeopardy in order to make almost no progress against the disease. Chimpanzees in AIDS research perhaps serve best as a haunting example of the biological tradeoffs of being almost human.

From the beginning, researchers thought the perfect model for AIDS would require the human virus — putting it into another animal, such as a monkey. There are actually two variants of the human AIDS virus, christened HIV-1 and HIV-2. The second is still grounded in Africa, slower to move, milder in its course. HIV-1 is the killer and the invader, moving from country to country in a way that reminds people how little political boundaries are worth. When the studies first began, scientists tried to infect rhesus macaques with HIV-1. Nothing. The monkeys blew the virus off as if it didn't exist. Virologists took samples of spleen, lymph node, bone marrow, brain, and plasma from AIDS patients and injected them into other primates — crab-eating macaques, stumptail macaques, capuchins, squirrel monkeys. They got nothing.

The only nonhuman primate that could be induced to respond to HIV-1 was the chimpanzee. Inject the human virus into chimpanzees and they promptly booted up an immune response. You could track the antibodies, swarming against the AIDS virus, in their blood. They didn't get sick, though. At first, scientists thought perhaps it was just that HIV had a long latency in chimpanzees, as it does in humans. Now, there are some seventy chimpanzees plugged into AIDS research programs. Some of them have been HIV-positive for eight years. None of them have shown even a quiver of actual illness. No one understands it. Why don't primates so nearly human become sick like humans do?

Considerations

1. How does Blum characterize Roy Henrickson's work and his temperament as a scientist?
2. Briefly compare macaques and chimpanzees as models for humans in AIDS research. What are the advantages and disadvantages of medical research with these species?
3. Robert Gallo, perhaps one of the best known AIDS researchers, comes under criticism in this piece. Why?
4. Explain how the same sequence of events can be seen as "a mistake in monkey management" and a research "gift" (p. 531).

5. Having read two pieces by Deborah Blum, can you characterize her perspective? Do you detect any differences, for example, in her discussion of Stuart Zola-Morgan and Roy Henrickson? Do you get any sense of the "monkey wars" alluded to in the title of her book?

Unlike the laboratory studies of the language researchers and medical researchers, the research of primatologists Dorothy L. Cheney and Robert M. Seyfarth is conducted in the natural habitats of the animals they study — in this case, that of vervet monkeys. Thus their field studies share some of the basic conditions of the research by primatologists such as Dian Fossey, Jane Goodall, and Shirley S. Strum (see earlier readings, pp. 425, 483, and 491). As you will see, however, the perspective and techniques of Cheney and Seyfarth differ in important ways from those of these other field primatologists. One difference is in Cheney and Seyfarth's attitude toward experimentation. They are not content only to observe the monkeys over long periods as they go about their lives; they also manipulate the monkeys' environments in ways that yield data focused upon particular hypotheses.

The excerpts below are taken from Seyfarth and Cheney's book How Monkeys See the World: Inside the Mind of Another Species. *We have included an opening section sketching their general method and two later sections on vervet communication. As they describe their work in testing their hypotheses about "alarms" and "grunts," you'll notice that Cheney and Seyfarth's own language presents some difficulties. It's not simply that they employ a sophisticated vocabulary; it's also that they employ words of caution, exactitude, and understatement — they rightly show a reluctance to say more than their data can support. This cautious language can cloak the significance of Cheney and Seyfarth's own results. As you read, try highlighting those results. What conclusions do their experiments allow Cheney and Seyfarth to draw? What other generalizations might their results support?*

From *How Monkeys See the World: Inside the Mind of Another Species*

Dorothy L. Cheney and Robert M. Seyfarth

THE MONKEYS AND THEIR HABITAT

We conducted our research in Amboseli National Park, which lies at the foot of Kilimanjaro in southern Kenya. Between 1977 and 1989 we monitored demographic changes in eleven social groups of vervet monkeys living at the western end of the park. We studied

---

Dorothy L. Cheney (b. 1950) and Robert M. Seyfarth (b. 1948) are professors at the University of Pennsylvania, Cheney in biology and Seyfarth in psychology. Their current research focuses on free-ranging baboons in the Okavango Delta in Botswana. They have co-authored several articles and books, including *How Monkeys See the World: Inside the Mind of Another Species* (1990), excerpted here.

three of these groups intensively and continuously for the entire eleven-year period and an additional three groups for a five-year period between 1983 and 1988. The behavioral data discussed in this book are drawn from research we conducted from 1977 to 1978 (sixteen months), 1980 (nine months),1983 (nine months), 1985 to 1986 (nine months), and 1988 (three months). When we were not in the field, our colleagues Sandy Andelman, Marc Hauser, Lynne Isbell, Phyllis Lee, Shari Milgroom, and Richard Wrangham and our research assistant Bernard Musyoka Nzuma continuously observed the primary study groups. Our debt to each of these scientists is enormous, since without this teamwork and cooperation, collection of the long-term data on vervet behavior would not have been possible. Special acknowledgment is due also to Tom Struhsaker, who first studied vervets in Amboseli, and to David Klein, who initiated a study of group A in 1975 and generously provided us with information on their demography when we began our research in 1977. . . .

On average, a vervet group is comprised of between one and seven adult males, between two and ten adult females, and their offspring. Females become sexually mature between four and five years of age, whereas males reach full adult size at around six years. Although mortality rates are high, two females are known to have lived until they were at least seventeen years old.

The social structure of vervet monkeys is similar to that found in other Old World monkeys, particularly baboons (*Paplo cynocephalus*) and the various species of macaques (genus *Macaca*). Adult females typically remain throughout their lives in the groups in which they were born, maintaining close bonds with their maternal kin even as adults. As a result, the stable core of any vervet group consists of several families of closely related adult females (mothers, sisters, and their adult daughters) and their dependent offspring.

Unlike females, vervet males migrate from their natal groups at around sexual maturity and transfer to a neighboring group. Migration in Amboseli is risky, and during adolescence the mortality rate among males is higher than that among females. Some males simply disappear, others are known to have been taken by predators, and still others are the targets of considerable aggression from adult males and females in their new groups. Perhaps to minimize the cost of transfer, many males, particularly those transferring for the first time, transfer to neighboring groups in the company of age mates or maternal brothers. Often the group they join is one that has received migrants from the males' natal group in years past. Transfer to a neighboring group minimizes the distance traveled and increases the probability that a male will have allies in his new group.

Males transfer two, three, or more times during their lives. Fully adult males are more likely to transfer alone and to travel far, crossing a number of vervet territories before joining a new group (Cheney and Seyfarth 1983). As far as we know, no male ever returns to his natal group. These characteristics of male transfer are not unique to vervets but have been documented in other Old World monkeys with similar social organizations (reviewed in Pusey and Packer 1987). . . .

METHODS OF OBSERVATION AND ANALYSIS

It is no accident that the most detailed behavioral studies of nonhuman primates have been conducted on ground-dwelling species like baboons, macaques, vervets, chimpanzees, and gorillas. In marked contrast to the unfortunate investigator whose job it is to follow an arboreal species that ranges high in the canopy of a dense rain forest, those of us who study semiterrestrial species of monkeys and apes have been spoiled by our ability to observe subjects at close range on the ground. After a two- to three-month period of habituation, all of our vervet groups became accustomed to observers on foot, and we were able to follow the animals at distances of as close as two to three [meters]. We did not mark or capture the animals in any way but instead identified individuals by fur color, nicks and breaks in tails and ears and, most important, their facial features. . . .

To collect systematic data on the social behavior of vervet monkeys we used a method of observational sampling originally described by Jeanne Altmann (1974; see also Hinde 1973; Dunbar 1976; and Cheney et al. 1987 for a more complete description of sampling procedures). On a typical day we would select a group for study and drive to its sleeping trees, arriving between 7:00 and 7:30 in the morning. There, from a previously prepared list of the individuals in that group, each of us would select one animal and follow it for ten minutes, recording all social interactions, the identities of the individuals involved and the duration of grooming bouts. These *focal animal samples* were supplemented by ad libitum data[1] gathered on behaviors of particular interest, such as alliances (when two animals join together and direct aggression against a third) or encounters between neighboring groups. In addition, we tape recorded as many vocalizations as possible, noting the time of the call, the animals involved, and the behavior immediately preceding and following each vocalization. Observations continued until all individuals in the group had been sampled at least once. We then moved on to another group.

The advantages of focal animal sampling are that it preserves information about sequences of interactions and permits direct calculation of rates of behavior. Moreover, by keeping the length of our focal samples relatively short (ten minutes as opposed to thirty minutes or an hour, for example) we decreased the probability that a subject would go out of sight during the sample period and minimized the length of time between samples. During a typical month we sampled each individual in every group twice every three days, providing a fairly uninterrupted record of behavioral changes over time. Observation sessions with each group were scheduled so that by the end of each month an equal amount of data had been collected on all individuals and the data from each group had been drawn from a similar distribution of time periods. Ideally, such a sampling regime yielded, for every group, a representative cross section of vervet behavior throughout the day.

Our analysis owes much to the work of Robert Hinde (1976a, 1976b, 1983a, 1983b, 1987), who not only pointed out the limits of purely descriptive work but also introduced a theoretical framework for studying what he called the "deep structure" of nonhuman primate groups. The goals and methods of this approach are now well documented, widely used, and form the basis for much of this chapter. . . .

ALARM CALLS

In 1967, Tom Struhsaker reported that vervet monkeys in Amboseli give different-sounding alarm calls in response to at least three different predators: leopards, eagles, and snakes. Each alarm call elicits a different, apparently adaptive escape response from other vervets nearby. A loud, barking alarm call is given to leopards (*Panthera pardus*) and other cat

[1]**ad libitum data:** Data gathered "at one's leisure" (Latin) [Eds.].

species like caracals (*Felis caracal*) and servals (*Felis serval*). Hereafter we refer to this call as the vervets' *leopard alarm.* When vervets on the ground hear a leopard alarm, they run into trees. Leopards in Amboseli typically hunt vervets by concealing themselves in bushes and pouncing on a monkey as it walks by (Altmann and Altmann 1970; pers. obs.). Apparently, vervets are safe from leopards when they are in trees because the vervets' small size and agility make them difficult to catch.

In contrast, vervets give an acoustically different alarm call — a short, double-syllable cough called an *eagle alarm* — in response to the two large species of eagle that prey on them — the martial eagle (*Polemaetus bellicosus*) and the crowned eagle (*Stephanoaetus coronatus*). Both species can take vervets of all age-sex classes. They hunt monkeys from the air, attacking from a long stoop at great speed (Brown 1966; Brown and Amadon 1968). Both raptor species seem skilled at taking monkeys in trees and on the ground (Brown and Amadon 1968; pers. obs.). Vervets on the ground respond to eagle alarms by looking up in the air or running into bushes. Vervets in trees respond to eagle alarms by looking up, and occasionally running down, out of the tree, and into a bush.

Finally, when vervets encounter pythons (*Python sebae*) or poisonous snakes like mambas (*Dendroaspis* spp.) and cobras (*Naja* spp.), they give a third, acoustically distinct alarm call, onomatopoetically termed a *chutter.* We refer to this as the vervets' *snake alarm.* Pythons hunt vervet monkeys primarily on the ground, by hiding in tall grass. The monkeys' best defense against a python is to be constantly aware of where the snake is. Upon hearing a snake alarm, vervet monkeys on the ground stand bipedally and peer into the grass around them. Once they see the snake, the monkeys often approach and mob it, repeatedly giving snake alarms from a safe distance.

Based on Struhsaker's (1967a) description, vervet monkeys certainly seemed to be using calls to denote different external referents (e.g., Altmann 1967; Marler 1977a, 1978), an interpretation that directly contradicted views of primate vocalizations held at the time. Nevertheless, legitimate doubts about this interpretation were raised. W. John Smith, for example, described vervet alarms as "referring to different escape tactics" and with "no referents external to the communicators" (1977: 181), while the psycholinguist John Marshall claimed, "Even the alarm calls of the vervet monkey which seem, superficially, to be 'naming' the type of predator are more plausibly regarded as expressing no more than the relative intensity of the fearful and aggressive emotions aroused by the various predators" (1970: 234). Given the information available at the time, Smith and Marshall were appropriately conservative in their interpretation of the mechanisms underlying vervet alarms. Each distinguished between calls that provide information only about the signaler's emotional state or subsequent behavior (a relatively simple, straightforward explanation) and calls that denote a specific external referent (an explanation that implied more complex cognitive processes). There seemed no need to attribute sophisticated mental processes to the vervet monkeys when simpler mechanisms could adequately account for their behavior. Not discussed was the possibility that calls might *both* denote external referents and signal other sorts of information.

In 1977, working in collaboration with Peter Marler, we began a study of vervet monkey alarm calls with the goal of testing these different hypotheses. Our research was conducted in the same area where Tom Struhsaker had carried out his original study. We began by tape recording alarm calls and observing the behavior of vervet monkeys in actual encounters with leopards, eagles, and pythons. We then analyzed our recordings by playing them into a sonograph, a machine that filters (or, in recent years, digitizes) the incoming signal and then displays this signal on a sound spectrogram. Spectrograms show, for each instant in time, the amount of energy present at different frequencies.

As Struhsaker had originally reported, we found that leopard, eagle, and snake alarm calls are easily distinguished by ear and easy to tell apart when displayed as sound spectrograms. Each type of alarm call also exhibits consistent acoustic features from one individual to the next (Seyfarth, Cheney, and Marler 1980b). In some cases there are sex differences in the vocalizations of adults; in others there are not. Adult males and adult females give acoustically similar eagle alarms and acoustically similar snake alarms; however, the leopard alarms given by adult males and adult females are acoustically quite distinct. Male leopard alarm calls consist of a repeated series of barks, whereas female leopard alarms consist of only a single, high-pitched chirp. Like Struhsaker, we found that each alarm call type elicits different escape responses.

Although our observations were consistent with Struhsaker's suggestion that the monkeys' different alarm calls denote different classes of predators, there were, as noted earlier, alternative explanations. For example, each call might have been a general "alerting" signal that caused animals to look all around them. Then, once the monkeys had spotted the predator, they could have responded on the basis of what they had seen. If this were the case, acoustic differences among alarm call types would be largely irrelevant. Alternatively, as Marshall (1970) had suggested, different alarm calls might simply reflect different levels of fear or excitement in the presence of different predators. Supporting this view, we found that leopard alarm calls (particularly those given by adult males) are generally louder and longer than eagle alarm calls, which are louder (but not longer) than snake alarm calls (Seyfarth, Cheney, and Marler 1980b).

Playback experiments allowed us to test these alternative explanations because they provided us with a means of examining separately how variation in a call's acoustic features and variation in other contextual events affected the monkeys' responses to a particular vocalization. When conducting an experiment, we first waited until no predator was in the area and a number of individual vervets were visible on the ground or in a tree. We then began filming our subjects' behavior. After ten seconds we played, from a concealed loudspeaker, a leopard, eagle, or snake alarm call that we had previously recorded from an individual in the subjects' own group.

If vervet alarm calls were simply general alerting signals, the monkeys should have responded in similar ways to all of the acoustically different calls. If call meaning was determined primarily by context, then the response to each alarm should have varied depending on the context in which it was presented. By contrast, if each call's meaning was determined largely by its acoustic features, a given call type (leopard, eagle, or snake alarm) should have elicited a functionally consistent set of responses regardless of the context in which it was presented. Finally, if calls conveyed information primarily about the emotional state of the caller and only secondarily about the type of predator that had been seen, it should have been possible to blur the distinction among responses to the different call types by varying acoustic features associated with a signaler's level of excitement.

Alarm call playbacks produced two sorts of responses. In response to all three types of alarm, subjects looked toward the speaker and scanned the surrounding area. They behaved as if they were searching for additional cues, both from the source of the alarm call and elsewhere. More important, however, each type of alarm call also elicited a distinct set of responses. When subjects were on the ground, leopard alarms caused a significant number to run into trees. Eagle alarms caused a significant number of subjects to look up in the air or run into bushes, and snake alarms caused them to stand bipedally, looking down at the ground around them. When subjects were in trees, eagle alarms caused them to look up, and, in some cases, to run down, out of the tree and into a bush. Snake alarms caused monkeys to look down (Seyfarth, Cheney, and Marler 1980a, 1980b).

These qualitatively different responses demonstrated that the different alarm calls alone, even in the absence of a predator, provide the monkeys with sufficient information to make distinct and apparently adaptive responses. We also found that varying the length and amplitude of alarms — two features that would presumably mirror a signaler's level of fear or excitement — had no effect on the responses alarm calls evoked. Variation in the acoustic structure of different call types was the only feature both necessary and sufficient to explain differences in response (Seyfarth, Cheney, and Marler 1980b).

This is not to suggest that there is no emotional, or affective, component to the vervets' alarm calls. Encounters between vervet monkeys and their predators are often emotionally charged events, and monkeys responding to an alarm call almost certainly attend to such features as loudness, length, rate of delivery, and the number of individuals alarm calling in order to assess how close a predator is and whether it poses an immediate danger. Over the years we have noticed that if a predator is actually attacking, more animals give alarm calls, alarm calls are louder, and (to our ears at least) calls sound more "urgent" and the signalers seem more "distressed" than when a predator is not engaged in an attack. . . .

On another occasion we played a snake alarm call to three individuals foraging in tall grass. Two subjects, the juveniles Leslie and Sedaka, responded by standing on their hind legs and peering at the ground around them, but a third subject, adult female Borgia, did nothing. Disappointed, we completed the experiment, put away the camera, and began collecting data on social behavior. A few hours later, one of us was following Borgia as she foraged toward the area where our experiment had been conducted. Entering the area, Borgia stood on her hind legs and scanned the ground around her. Clearly, our experiment had conveyed quite specific information to Borgia even though she had not chosen to act on it at the time.

Here again, we do not mean to argue that alarm calls provide information *exclusively* about external referents; a referential function by no means rules out the possibility that calls also convey information about the caller's subsequent behavior or about the conditional probability that a caller will act in certain ways given certain other events (e.g., Smith 1977; Hinde 1981). Obviously, the fact that different predators evoke both acoustically distinct alarm calls and different escape responses means that in many cases there will be a close link between alarm call type and behavior. Even in human language, where the referential function of signals is not in doubt, it is often difficult if not impossible to distinguish whether someone's use of a particular word refers to a specific object or to the likelihood that she will, at some time in the future, behave in a certain way (e.g., Marler 1961). Our experiments, then, are not meant to disprove the notion that calls provide information about subsequent behavior. Instead, we suggest that information about the caller's subsequent behavior is not the only information transmitted by the vervets' alarms, nor is it invariably the most important; vocalizations may also denote objects and events in the external world. . . .

Further evidence of the monkeys' ability to classify alarm calls into types independent of other cues comes from research on captive vervets by Michael Owren (Owren and Bernacki 1988; Owren 1990a, 1990b). Using alarm calls that we had tape recorded in Amboseli, Owren trained two vervet monkeys to distinguish between the eagle and snake alarms given by one adult female, Alaska Pipeline. One vervet subject had been born in the wild and captured at approximately age two; the other had been raised in a captive group. During the experiments, each female was seated in a restraining chair, wearing headphones. When she heard an eagle alarm she was rewarded for pushing a lever to the right; when she heard a snake alarm she was rewarded for pushing the lever to the left. Both vervets learned to distinguish between Alaska Pipeline's alarms. This was perhaps not surprising, since all calls came from the same individual, and variation other than between alarm call type was minimal. Once the animals had completed training, however, they were tested with 48 eagle and snake alarms that had been recorded from 17 different animals, including adult males, adult females, and juveniles. These calls exhibited considerable acoustic variation due to individual differences, the caller's age, sex, level of excitement, and the quality of our recordings. Despite such variation, the subjects immediately classified these novel stimuli with an accuracy that was significantly above chance. In the face of considerable idiosyncratic variation from one vocalization to the next, the monkeys still sorted calls into the same acoustic classes that were functionally important to vervets in the wild.

Given these results from both field and laboratory, we suggest that "semantic" and indexical information are combined in vervet alarm calls, much as they are combined in human speech. Each type of alarm refers to, or denotes, a particular type of predator. Different types of alarm are distinguished by their different acoustic properties and convey a meaning that is relatively independent of the context in which they are given. Supplementing and enriching this semantic information are indexical features that provide information about, for example, a caller's identity, her level of fear and anxiety, or the probability that she is likely to flee. Semantic information is of primary importance, but it is by no means the only sort of information conveyed. . . .

VERVET MONKEY GRUNTS

Like the players at Wimbledon, vervet monkeys frequently grunt to each other during normal social interactions. The vervets' grunts are harsh, raspy signals that sound like a human clearing his throat with his mouth open. As Struhsaker (1967a) originally noted, grunts are given in at least four distinct social circumstances. First, a monkey may grunt as she approaches a more dominant individual; second, a monkey may grunt as she approaches a subordinate. Third, monkeys often grunt as they watch another animal, or as they themselves, initiate a group movement across an open plain. Fourth, grunts may be given when a monkey has apparently just spotted the members of another group. Even to an experienced human listener, there are no immediately obvious audible differences among grunts, either from one context to another or across individuals. When grunts are displayed on sound spectrograms, there are also no consistent differences in acoustic structure from one context to the next. Although grunts are occasionally answered by other group members, in most cases grunts evoke no salient behavioral responses.

Changes in the direction of gaze, which are difficult to measure in the wild, seem the only obvious response when one individual grunts to another.

Vervet monkey grunts, therefore, are strikingly different from alarm calls. While alarm calls given in response to different predators are easily distinguished acoustically, grunts given in different social contexts sound very much alike. Unlike alarm calls, grunts occur in quiet, relatively relaxed circumstances and evoke no obvious response from those nearby. From an observer's perspective, watching monkeys grunt to each other is very much like watching humans engaged in conversation without being able to hear what they are saying: the creatures *seem* to be exchanging some sort of information, but we have no idea what it is. . . . If one relies solely on observation, the only way to measure a call's meaning is through the responses it evokes in others. And since these responses are hardly discernible, we seem to be faced with an intractable problem.

Grunts also recall the Wimbledon referees' dilemma. Like tennis referees, we cannot through observation alone distinguish between calls that provide information exclusively about the caller's behavior or emotional state and calls that also function to denote objects or events in the environment.

Given these methodological dilemmas, the most obvious starting place is to adopt Smith's (1977) influential view that the meaning of an animal's vocalization (that is, the information it conveys to others) is a function of its message (in this case, its acoustic properties) and of the context in which it is given. Animals, Smith argues, have relatively small repertoires of signals, each of which conveys a broad, general message. A small repertoire of general signals can nevertheless elicit a variety of responses because of variation in the contexts in which calls are given. Applied to vervet grunts, this hypothesis would predict that vervets are using a single vocalization in a variety of circumstances. The grunt itself is a manifestation of a particular level of arousal and provides general information about the vocalizer's identity, location, or subsequent behavior. Variation in the responses evoked by different grunts is accounted for by variation that the receiver perceives in the context in which they are given.

In contrast, consideration of the vervets' alarm calls suggests an alternative explanation: namely, that what seems to a human listener to be one grunt is in fact a number of different grunts. Each grunt type conveys specific information that depends more on a call's acoustic properties than on the context in which it is given.

To test between these hypotheses, we designed the following set of experiments. First, grunts from the same individual were tape recorded in each of the four social contexts described above. Then, over a number of months, we played each grunt to subjects from a concealed loudspeaker and filmed their responses. For example, we might play Bokassa's *grunt to a dominant* to Duvalier on one day and then, three or more days later, play Bokassa's *grunt to another group.* Throughout these trials we allowed social context to vary freely. Tests were conducted, for instance, when there were dominant or subordinate animals nearby, when the group was foraging or resting, or when animals were at the center or the edge of their range. We reasoned that if the grunts were really one vocalization whose meaning was largely determined by context, subjects should show no consistent differences when responding to different calls. Instead, responses should be a function of the variable contexts in which calls were presented. On the other hand, if each of the grunts was different, and if each carried specific information that was relatively independent of context, we should find consistent differences in responses to each grunt type, regardless of the varying circumstances in which it was played.

Our overall method thus parallels that adopted by Quine's[2] imaginary linguist, who, unable to determine what his subjects' words mean, poses hundreds of yes-no questions in an attempt to clarify one word's meaning relative to that of another. In our case, unable to determine what the vervets' grunts mean through observation, we asked subjects, "Is grunt A different from grunt B? If so, is grunt A different from grunt C? Do grunts B and C differ?" and so on.

As an example of the results we obtained, consider the comparison between grunts that had originally been given to a dominant and grunts that had originally been given to another group. Here we used as stimuli one grunt of each type from three different individuals. Eighteen subjects heard first one call and then, a few days later, the other. Subjects responded in many ways, but two responses appeared consistently and were consistently different across the two grunt types. Grunts to a dominant caused subjects to look toward the loudspeaker, whereas grunts to another group caused subjects to look out, toward the horizon, in the direction the loudspeaker was pointed (Cheney and Seyfarth 1982a). Grunts to another group therefore directed the listener's attention away from the speaker and in the direction toward which, under normal conditions, the vocalizer would have been facing.

Consistent differences in responses to different grunt types appeared in many, but not all, of our paired comparisons. Grunts to a subordinate, grunts to a dominant, grunts to an animal moving into an open area, and grunts to another group all elicited responses that were consistently different from each other. There was, however, no difference between the responses elicited by grunts to a dominant male and grunts to a dominant female (Cheney and Seyfarth 1982a).

By their behavior, then, the monkeys seemed to be saying that although their grunts sound more or less the same to us, to *them* each grunt transmits a specific sort of information. In many cases, this information can include events external to the signaling individual, such as the approach of another group or the movement of animals into an open area. Although the vervets' grunts are, in many ways, different from their alarm calls, the two sorts of vocalizations function in a similar manner.

Since monkeys responded in consistently different ways to different grunt types despite variation in social context, we conclude that the information conveyed by grunts — like the information contained in human words — depends as much, or more, on a particular call's acoustic properties than on the circumstances in which it is given. Of course, this does not mean that contextual variables are irrelevant. Common sense suggests that context must be important for vervets, just as contextual cues can enrich and modify the meaning of words for humans. Results suggest, however, that in many cases monkeys make less use of contextual cues than they do of acoustic features when interpreting the meaning of a particular call. . . .

Finally, a brief comment on the apparent function of vervet grunts. Reviewing the results of our experiments, together with data on naturally occurring grunts, we find that the different calls are often associated with different beneficial social consequences. When subordinate animals grunt to a dominant, or dominant animals grunt to a subordinate, grunts decrease the probability that the subordinate will move away from the

[2]**Philosopher W. V. O. Quine**, who published *Word and Object* (1960), in which the "imaginary linguist" is discussed [Eds.].

dominant. Grunts increase the likelihood that subordinate and dominant individuals will forage, feed, or sit together (unpublished data). Grunts to a subordinate, therefore, allow dominant animals to interact with those of lower rank when they choose without frightening them away, whereas grunts to a dominant give subordinate animals the opportunity to interact with those of higher rank. The grunt given by animals as they themselves move into an open area or as they watch other animals do so directs listeners' attention both toward the caller and outward, in the direction the caller is facing. By so doing, these particular grunts may decrease the risk of predation by increasing the number of vigilant animals. Finally, grunts to another group also direct attention outward, in the direction the caller is facing, and therefore serve as the initial warning that another group is nearby.

There are, then, ample reasons why vervets need more than one grunt and why natural selection may have favored individuals who can use at least four acoustically different grunts in these four different circumstances. This post hoc explanation, however, begs an important question: Why stop at four? Having watched vervets for many years, and having seen them die at high rates, we can think of many situations in which the monkeys could make good use of a vocalization but have not apparently developed one. Vervet mothers, for example, have no call that conveys the information *follow me.* Mothers often leave their infants in what seem to be vulnerable positions, and they make no apparent attempt to let the infants know that they are moving off or where they are going. On one occasion, for example, a mother walked away, leaving her infant in a tree just as a group of baboons was approaching. When the infant suddenly became aware that her mother was gone she vocalized loudly, attracting both the mother's and the baboons' attention. The mother looked toward her infant but made no sound; she apparently had no way to signal that the infant should simply follow her.

It has been suggested that a crucial evolutionary transition occurs whenever a species begins to divide a graded stream of acoustic sounds into discrete categories (Marler 1976a). Implicitly, such arguments assume that once categorical signaling has been achieved *in principle,* the most difficult problem has been surmounted and individuals will be free to develop a large number of discrete, highly specific signs. Data from vervets, however, suggest that other constraints are at work. Vervets may be able to divide a graded series of sounds into discrete categories, but their repertoire of calls, compared with human language, is still not very large. In terms of evolutionary function, we can easily explain why the vervets have so many grunts, but we cannot explain why they have so few.

WORKS CITED

Altmann, J. "Observational Study of Behaviour: Sampling Methods." *Behaviour* 49(1974): 227–65.

Altmann, S. A. "The Structure of Primate Social Communication." *Social Communication Among Primates.* Ed. S. A. Altmann. Chicago: University of Chicago Press, 1967.

Altmann, S. A., and J. Altmann. *Baboon Ecology.* Chicago: University of Chicago Press, 1970.

Brown, L. "Observations on Some Kenya Eagles." *Ibis* 102(1966): 285–97.

Brown, L. H., and D. Amadon. *Eagles, Hawks, and Falcons of the World.* New York: McGraw-Hill, 1968.

Cheney, D. L. "Interactions and Relationships Between Groups." *Primate Societies.* Ed. B. B. Smuts, D. L. Cheney, R. M. Seyfarth, R. W. Wrangham, and T. T. Struhsaker. Chicago: University of Chicago Press, 1987.

Cheney, D. L., and R. M. Seyfarth. "How Vervet Monkeys Perceive Their Grunts: Field Playback Experiments." *Anim. Behav.* 30(1982a):739–51.

———. "Non-Random Dispersal in Free-Ranging Vervet Monkeys: Social and Genetic Consequences." *Am. Nat.* 122(1983):392–412.

Dunbar, R. I. M. "Some Aspects of Research Design and Their Implications in the Observational Study of Behaviour." *Behaviour* 58(1976):79–98.

Hinde, R. A. "On the Design of Check-Sheets." *Primates* 14(1973):393–406.

———. "Interactions, Relationships and Social Structure." *Man* 11(1976a):1–17.

———. "On Describing Relationships." *J. Child Psychol. Psychiatr.* 17(1976b):1–19.

———. "Animal Signals: Ethological and Games-Theory Approaches are Not Incompatible." *Anim. Behav.* 29(1981):535–42.

———. "A Conceptual Framework." *Primate Social Relationships: An Integrated Approach.* Ed. R. A. Hinde. Oxford: Blackwell Scientific, 1983a.

———. "General Issues in Describing Social Behavior." *Primate Social Relationships: An Integrated Approach.* Ed. R. A. Hinde. Oxford: Blackwell Scientific, 1983b.

———. *Individuals, Relationships, and Cultures.* Cambridge: Cambridge University Press, 1987.

Marler, P. "The Logical Analysis of Animal Communication." *J. Theor. Biol.* 1(1961):295–317.

———. "An Ethological Theory of the Origin of Vocal Learning." *Ann. N.Y. Acad. Sci.* 280(1976a):708–17.

———. "Primate Vocalizations: Affective or Symbolic?" *Progress in Ape Research.* Ed. G. H. Bourne. New York: Academic Press, 1977a.

———. "Affective and Symbolic Meaning: Some Zoosemiotic Speculations." *Sight, Sound and Sense.* Ed. T. A. Sebeok. Bloomington, Ind.: Indiana University Press, 1978.

Marshall, J. C. "The Biology of Communication in Man and Animals." *New Horizons in Linguistics.* Ed. J. Lyons. Harmondsworth, England: Penguin, 1970.

Owren, M. J. "Acoustic Classification of Alarm Calls by Vervet Monkeys (*Cercopithecus aethiops*) and Humans. I. Natural Calls." *J. Comp. Psychol.* 104(1990a):20–28.

———. "Acoustic Classification of Alarm Calls by Vervet Monkeys (*Cercopithecus aethiops*) and Humans. II. Synthetic Calls." *J. Comp. Psychol.* 104(1990b):29–40.

Owren, M. J., and R. H. Bernacki. "The Acoustic Features of Vervet Monkey Alarm Calls." *J. Acoust. Soc. Am.* 83(1988): 1927–35.

Pusey, A. E., and C. Packer. "Dispersal and Philopatry." *Primate Societies.* Ed. B. B. Smuts, D. L. Cheney, R. M. Seyfarth, et al. Chicago: University of Chicago Press, 1987.

Quine, W. V. O. *Word and Object.* Cambridge, Mass.: MIT Press, 1960.

Seyfarth, R. M., D. L. Cheney, and P. Marler. "Monkey Responses to Three Different Alarm Calls: Evidence for Predator Classification and Semantic Communication." *Science* 210(1980a):801–3.

———. "Vervet Monkey Alarm Calls: Semantic Communication in a Free-Ranging Primate." *Anim. Behav.* 28(1980b):1070–94.

Smith, W. J. *The Behavior of Communicating: An Ethological Approach.* Cambridge, Mass.: Harvard University Press, 1977.

Struhsaker, T. T. "Auditory Communication Among Vervet Monkeys (*Cercopithecus aethiops*)." *Social Communication Among Primates.* Ed. S. A. Altmann. Chicago: University of Chicago Press, 1967a.

Considerations

1. Cheney and Seyfarth say they employ a method of "observational sampling" (p. 535). What does this method entail, and what seem to be its strengths and weaknesses?
2. Who is Tom Struhsaker, and how does Cheney and Seyfarth's work connect to his?

3. As subjects of investigation, how do grunts differ from alarm calls?
4. At several places in their discussion, the authors acknowledge the importance of *context* in analyzing the sounds made by monkeys. Explain why context is important. Explain also why the authors nevertheless seek to *deemphasize* context.
5. Explain the evolutionary issue raised by Cheney and Seyfarth in their final paragraphs.
6. On the whole, the authors argue that monkey communication is more complex than it appears. Do you think that they would be receptive to the view that monkeys are capable of language? Why or why not?
7. Dian Fossey, in her piece included in the Opening Problem (p. 425), seems to have some strong assumptions about the vocalizations of gorillas and what they mean. How do Cheney and Seyfarth's attitudes and findings compare with hers?

Here follows another piece about field research on primate vocalization, in this case the "pant-hoots" of chimpanzees. You will want to note some of the ways in which Mitani's observations of chimpanzee vocalizations resemble and differ from Cheney and Seyfarth's observations about vervet monkeys in the previous piece. Also keep in mind that the communication behavior of chimpanzees in the field may be pertinent to the language issues raised in the chapter's earlier readings. One striking feature of Mitani's piece, however, is its avoidance *of the larger evolutionary issues, including claims about grammar and language, in favor of more specific, functional questions about communication. As in the previous piece by Cheney and Seyfarth, you will note the frequent recurrence of the term* hypothesis *in reference both to studies that were conducted and studies that might be conducted. Notice how Mitani uses this term in creating the image of himself as a thoughtful researcher operating within a disciplined scientific tradition. What else contributes to this impression?*

From "Ethological Studies of Chimpanzee Vocal Behavior"

John C. Mitani

Recent field and laboratory studies of chimpanzees and bonobos have revealed behavioral and ecological diversity heretofore unsuspected among members of the genus *Pan.* Despite new data regarding virtually all aspects of the behavior and ecology of

---

John C. Mitani (b. 1954) is associate professor of anthropology at the University of Michigan, Ann Arbor. His current research focuses on the vocal behavior of African apes. "Ethological Studies of Chimpanzee Vocal Behavior" appeared in *Chimpanzee Cultures* (1994).

chimpanzees and bonobos, we currently lack detailed information regarding their vocal behavior in the wild. Pioneering field investigations of Peter Marler (Marler and Hobbett 1975; Marler and Tenaza 1977) over twenty-five years ago at the Gombe National Park have been followed by only a few systematic investigations of the vocalizations of chimpanzees (Clark and Wrangham 1993).

In an attempt to fill this gap in knowledge, I initiated a series of field investigations into the vocal behavior of the great apes. Here I summarize some results of my studies of wild chimpanzees by focusing on two traditional ethological questions; namely, the functional significance and the development of calls. As a first step in an ongoing and long-term project, I ask these questions with respect to the chimpanzee's species-typical, long distance call: the *pant-hoot.*

. . . My research relies on the comparative method to generate and to test hypotheses. By framing explicit questions and addressing them with comparative field data, the ethological approach adopted here serves to highlight behavioral diversity within and between individuals (Tinbergen 1963; Goodall 1986).

AN ETHOLOGICAL FRAMEWORK

I begin by assuming that an understanding of chimpanzee vocal behavior is impossible without detailed information regarding their social systems and behavior. An ethological framework that stresses the importance of interpreting behavior within the natural social and environmental settings of chimpanzees is, therefore, a fundamental first step in the analysis of the chimpanzee vocal communication system. Chimpanzees are unusual among diurnal anthropoid primates given that they do not live in stable groups. Instead, individuals form loosely organized unit-groups, or communities whose members associate in temporary parties that vary in size and composition (Goodall 1986; Nishida 1990). A tendency for males to aggregate contributes to the variable structure of chimpanzee parties. Mature males are more social than mature females; males are often found together and frequently engage in reciprocal grooming. In addition, males form alliances in which they direct aggression jointly toward conspecifics.[1] Patterns of associations, grooming, and alliance formations are nonrandom, with specific individuals forming preferential relationships with others.

THE CALL

Within the unusually fluid, fission-fusion chimpanzee society, individuals emit a loud call known as the pant-hoot. Both males and females utter this call in a variety of situations, including in response to another calling individual, during travel, upon arrival at a particularly rich food source, and in response to strange conspecifics (Goodall 1986). Pant-hoots given by male chimpanzees can be divided acoustically into four distinct parts. Pant-hoots may begin with an introductory series of low-frequency tonal elements. These grade into a buildup phase, consisting of a series of shorter elements, delivered at faster rates and uttered both on inhalation and exhalation. Buildups are followed by a climax portion, including one or more high-frequency, high-amplitude elements whose acoustic properties resemble those of screams. Calls end with a brief letdown; letdown elements do not appear to differ significantly from those of the buildup.

[1]**conspecifics:** Other males of relatively equal social standing [Eds.].

CALL FUNCTION

Previous fieldwork conducted at multiple study sites provides an important set of comparative observations from which to generate hypotheses regarding the functional significance of pant-hooting. The relative instability of chimpanzee parties has led some researchers to suggest that individuals use pant-hoots primarily to establish and maintain contact with spatially separated conspecifics (Reynolds and Reynolds 1965; Goodall 1968; Wrangham 1977; Ghiglieri 1984). Two lines of evidence, one social, the other ecological, have been cited to support this hypothesis. First, early field observations suggested that chimpanzees pant-hooted more often when they were in large parties and, presumably, spread out more than when they were in cohesive, smaller parties (Reynolds and Reynolds 1965). Second, fieldwork by Wrangham (1977) at Gombe and Ghiglieri (1984) in the Kibale Forest indicated that males who arrived at food trees and gave pant-hoots were joined more often by others than males who did not call. Recent fieldwork has failed to replicate either finding: observations of chimpanzees in the Mahale Mountains revealed no relationships between calling frequencies and party size variables (Mitani and Nishida 1993), and field research at the Kibale Forest indicated that males who called were no more likely to be joined than were noncallers (Clark and Wrangham 1993).

These conflicting observations led Toshisada Nishida and me to reopen an investigation into the functional significance of the male chimpanzee's pant-hooting behavior. As noted above, it is difficult to evaluate the function of nonhuman animal calls without information regarding the social behavior of individuals. Accordingly, I begin by examining social relationships between our male chimpanzee study subjects, and I follow this by presenting data regarding the behavioral contexts in which males pant-hoot. . . .

Nishida and I conducted observations of the M group chimpanzees at the Mahale Mountains National Park in western Tanzania. Mahale has been the site of long-term observations of chimpanzees during the past twenty-seven years and, as a result of this fieldwork, the demographic and social histories of all study subjects were relatively well known (Nishida 1990). Seven of the ten adult males of M group were included in this study. Due to the fission-fusion nature of chimpanzee society, it was not possible to find and follow the three remaining males on a systematic and regular basis, and insufficient observations led to their exclusion from the following analyses. For this study, our field protocol included observing individuals during one-hour sampling periods in which we recorded, either notationally or on audio tape, all calling activity by focal males as well as details of social interactions that occurred.

Our behavioral observations accord with results from previous studies at Mahale by indicating that the seven focal males can be ranked in a linear hierarchy (Hayaki et al. 1989). In addition, further analyses revealed that males formed nonrandom patterns of alliance, association, and grooming. With these observations regarding male social relationships as a background, I proceed to explore the hypothesized spacing function of pant-hooting by examining the situations in which calls are given.

Figure 1 shows the observed and expected behaviors of two high-ranking males immediately preceding and following calling. Expected behaviors were computed by assuming that males would call in proportion to the amount of time they spent in each activity. Both males traveled significantly more before and after calls than expected. Although sample sizes for the other five focal males did not permit statistical analysis,

FIGURE 1. Contexts of Pant-Hoot Production for Two High-Ranking Males. (A) Activities before calling. (B) Activities after calling. Observed and expected percentages of pant-hooting are shown. Expected percentages were calculated by assuming that males called in proportion to the time they spent in each activity. Traveling preceded and followed calling more often than expected, and feeding followed pant-hooting more frequently than expected (χ^2 tests using call frequencies, df = 2, 2-tailed $p < .001$ for all comparisons). See text for further explanation.

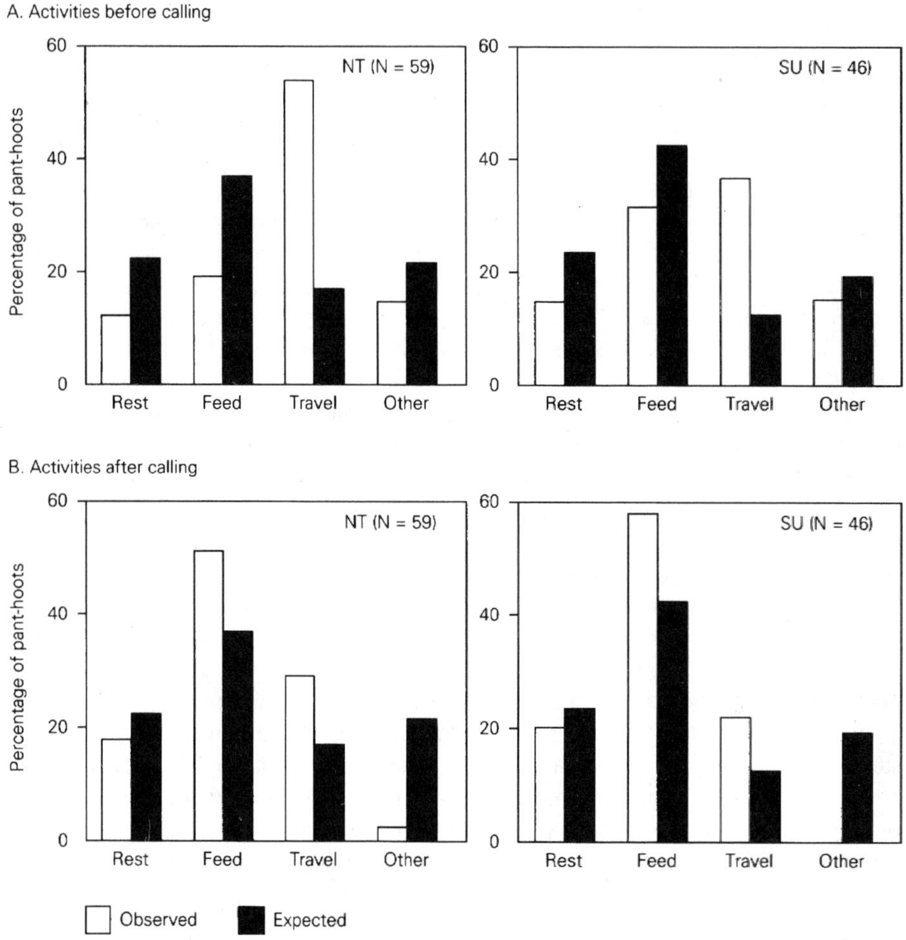

similar trends were evident for them as well. Both males for whom sufficient data are available fed more often after calling than expected on the basis of chance. A similar tendency to feed after calling was not apparent for the other five focal subjects, however. These data regarding the behavioral activities associated with pant-hooting are consistent with the hypothesis that male chimpanzees call to maintain contact with conspecifics. By pant-hooting, males appear to signal a change in their locations to others (Boesch 1991).

If males call simply to maintain contact with all members in their group, one might expect all males to call equally often and to call more when spread out, as they are in large parties, compared with when they are moving in a more tightly clustered manner in smaller parties (Reynolds and Reynolds 1965). Additional observations did not support either prediction. First, males did not call equally often. We found a significant relationship between calling activity and rank: High-ranking males gave significantly more calls than low-ranking males (Mitani and Nishida 1993). Second, our attempts to correlate party size variables with calling activity did not reveal any relationships (Mitani and Nishida 1993).

This last result was particularly puzzling given prior suggestions, based largely on qualitative impressions, that calling frequency and party size are positively related. Our unexpected finding led us to entertain a new hypothesis, namely that instead of calling to indicate their spatial location to members in the unit-group, males pant-hoot only to maintain contact with particular individuals. Specifically, we propose that male chimpanzees may gain by maintaining contact with selected individuals — allies, frequent associates, grooming partners, and estrous females — from whom they receive fitness benefits.

To investigate this hypothesis, we examined the frequencies with which a male called in each of three situations: when all the focal male's preferred alliance, association, or grooming partner(s) were with him; when all the partner(s) or estrous[2] female(s) were presumably nearby and within earshot; and when all the partner(s) or female(s) were presumed absent. For the first situation, we scored allies, frequent associates, and grooming partners as being with the focal male if they were within his sight during an entire one-hour sample period. Given the fission-fusion nature of chimpanzee society, this condition was rarely met, and a sufficient sample existed only for preferred associates. For the second situation, we assumed male partners or estrous females were nearby even if they were not within sight of the focal male during an entire sample period but were observed with the subject or heard during either the hour immediately preceding or the hours following the sample. For the third situation, we considered individuals absent if they were not observed during the day the sampling took place.

Results of these comparisons indicated that a male called significantly more often when his alliance partners were nearby compared with when the were absent. Control comparisons involving randomly selected males who were not favored partners showed no differences in calling frequencies between the two conditions. Similarly, a subject male called significantly more when his association partners were nearby compared with when they were either absent or with the focal individuals. In contrast, controls involving males other than favored associates showed no differences among the three situations. While these data indicate that males may call to attract potential allies or associates, grooming relationships did not appear to influence calling patterns: A male called equally often when his favored grooming partners were nearby compared with when they were absent. Moreover, observations did not support the hypothesis that pant-hooting performs an intersexual function: Calling by a male was not affected by the presence or absence of estrous females.

I interpret these results within the ethological framework provided by our current

[2]**estrous:** Sexually receptive [Eds.].

understanding of the social lives of chimpanzees. Association and grooming patterns indicate the strong bonds that exist between male chimpanzees. These bonds are further strengthened by the cooperative relationships in which males engage while forming alliances. Males form selective coalitions that have significant reproductive consequences. Male rank is often determined by coalitionary behavior and, at the Mahale study site, rank is positively related to mating success (Nishida 1983). These observations lead one to consider how males maintain their cooperative relationships within a very fluid society where animals are often spatially separated. Given that communication processes mediate social interactions, the vocal behavior of chimpanzees may provide an effective means to maintain these important relationships. Field observations indicated that males may call to enlist the company and support of allies and frequent associates; males called more often when their preferred associates and allies were nearby compared with when they were absent. Note that a logical extension of the selective recruitment hypothesis is that males should show decreased levels of calling when they are with frequent associates and allies. Our data set did not permit a complete test of this prediction, but it did show that males decreased their calling rates when they were with associates compared with when those associates were nearby.

CALL DEVELOPMENT AND VOCAL LEARNING

Our current understanding of vocal learning processes in animals derives largely from ethological studies of male songbirds (Marler 1991). Laboratory and field evidence reveals that learning plays a major role in the development of the production of bird songs. In the laboratory, young birds raised in acoustic isolation from conspecific sounds typically develop abnormal song; in the field, neighboring male birds frequently share local song dialects.

Perhaps somewhat surprisingly, there is little evidence that the calls of nonhuman primates undergo significant acoustic modification during development (Snowdon and Elowson 1992). For example, in the case of nonhuman primates, both social isolates raised in the absence of any auditory feedback and cross-fostered infants grow up to produce species-typical sounds. In addition, conditioning has been shown to have only limited effects on altering the acoustic morphology of sounds produced by primates, and hybrid individuals give calls that do not resemble either of their parents.

The conclusion that the acoustic morphology of nonhuman primate calls is not subject to developmental modification is unexpected and puzzling given their long maturation periods. During these prolonged developmental periods, learning plays an important role in shaping the many behaviors that will contribute to growth, maintenance, and reproduction in later life. These considerations provided the impetus for a reexamination of the question of vocal learning by chimpanzees. One correlate of the process of vocal learning in humans and songbirds is the formation of local dialects and, as a first step in this investigation, I along with colleagues from Japan, Great Britain, and the United States have examined microgeographic variation in the calls of chimpanzees living in two neighboring populations (Mitani et al. 1992).

For this comparison we chose to analyze the pant-hoots of males from the two well-studied chimpanzee populations of the Mahale National Park and Gombe National Park. These populations are separated by approximately 150 kilometers along the eastern shore of Lake Tanganyika and belong to the same subspecies, *Pan troglodytes schweinfurthii.* As the result of the spread of human habitation, these populations are now isolated, although genetic continuity presumably existed between them until recently. Tape recordings of pant-hoots from Gombe were provided by Peter Marler, who in 1967 conducted a preliminary study of chimpanzee vocal behavior around the banana provisioning station (Marler and Hobbett 1975; Marler and Tenaza 1977). Calls from Mahale were tape recorded by a team of researchers associated with Nishida's long-term field research at the Kasoje Research Station (Richard Byrne 1984, Toshikazu Hasegawa 1988, and John Mitani 1989–90).

Our initial visual inspection of audio spectrograms and aural monitoring of pant-hoots indicated that calls of males from the two populations did not differ qualitatively. Closer examination of these calls, however, revealed differences in subtle features of the buildup and climax portions. Specifically, males at Mahale gave significantly shorter buildup elements at faster rates than males from Gombe. In addition, the Mahale males uttered higher-frequency climax elements that spanned greater frequency ranges than those produced by the Gombe males. . . . A subsequent analysis using recently recorded calls from Mahale confirmed that males from the two populations produce acoustically distinguishable calls (Mitani and Brandt in press).

While the results of our acoustic analyses suggest that the Mahale and Gombe chimpanzees utter their pant-hoots in subtly different ways, the causal factors underlying these differences are open to further empirical investigation. Two hypotheses subject to immediate test are that anatomical and habitat differences account for the vocal variability between the two populations. Chimpanzees at Mahale are significantly larger than those at Gombe (Uehara and Nishida 1987), and this variation in body size would lead one to predict that the larger Mahale chimpanzees would have deeper voices than the smaller Gombe males (Gouzoules and Gouzoules 1990). A similar prediction derives from consideration of the habitats occupied by the two study groups and the theory of signal detection. The Mahale study group inhabits a more densely forested area than the Gombe community (Collins and McGrew 1988) and, in these forested habitats, reflections and scattering off of multiple surfaces tend to degrade signals and hinder the efficient transfer of information (Wiley and Richards 1978). Under such circumstances, natural selection should favor individuals who produce low-frequency sounds, which degrade relatively less than higher frequency signals. Contrary to both expectations is the finding that the Mahale males utter climax elements with higher frequencies than those of the Gombe males.

If anatomical and habitat differences do not underlie the vocal differences between the Mahale and Gombe males, three additional hypotheses may provide alternative explanations. First, vocal differences commonly exist between and within species of nonhuman primates (Snowdon 1986): and genetic variability may account for the differences in pant-hoots between the Mahale and Gombe males. The degree of genetic differentiation between the Mahale and Gombe populations remains an unanswered empirical question, whose resolution is currently being addressed using recently developed DNA amplification techniques (Takasaki and Takenaka 1991).

Second, one significant finding of recent research into the vocal behavior of nonhuman primates is that these animals vary the acoustic structure of their calls in subtle and semantically significant ways in different behavioral contexts (Cheney and Seyfarth 1990). In a similar fashion, Goodall (1986) has suggested that pant-hoots delivered in different behavioral situations vary acoustically. While our sample of calls from Gombe was recorded primarily around the provisioning station and the majority of pant-hoots from Mahale were taped in the chimpanzees' natural habitat, the observed vocal differences between Mahale and Gombe males may be due to variations in call usage. Our current, limited sample of tape recordings does not preclude this possibility, although preliminary analysis indicates that Mahale males do not alter the acoustic structure of their calls in different situations (Mitani unpublished data). More recordings will be needed to test whether variations in call usage contribute to the vocal differences found here.

If anatomical, habitat, genetic, and contextual differences do not adequately account for the observed variability in pant-hoots between populations, then a third hypothesis is that these acoustic variations are dialectal. Dialectal differences are of special interest since they bear on the issue of vocal learning. Learning combined with limited dispersal after vocal acquisition has taken place commonly leads to dialects, and vocal learning in animals is frequently inferred from the existence of dialects (Kroodsma 1982). However, intraspecific population differences in vocalizations have been shown only rarely among primates (Green 1975), and the absence of dialects is consistent with the paucity of evidence for vocal learning in these animals.

WORKS CITED

Boesch, C. "Symbolic Communication in Wild Chimpanzees?" *J. Human Evol.* 6(1991):81–90.

Clark, A. and R. Wrangham. "Chimpanzee Arrival Pant-Hoots: Do They Signify Food or Status?" *Internat. J. Primatol.* (In press).

Cheney, D., and R. Seyfarth. *How Monkeys See the World.* Chicago, Ill.: Univ. of Chicago Press, 1990.

Collins, D. A., and W. McGrew. "Habitats of Three Groups of Chimpanzees (*Pan troglodytes*) in Western Tanzania Compared." *J. Human Evol.* 17(1988):553–74.

Ghiglieri, M. *The Chimpanzees of the Kibale Forest.* New York: Columbia Univ. Press, 1984.

Goodall, J. "The Behaviour of Free Living Chimpanzees in the Gombe Stream Area." *Anim. Behav. Monogr.* 1(1968):161–311.

———. *The Chimpanzees of Gombe.* Cambridge, Mass.: Belknap Press, 1986.

Gouzoules, H., and S. Gouzoules. "Body Size Effects on the Acoustic Structure of Pigtail Macaque (*Macaca nemestrina*) Screams." *Ethology* 85(1990):324–34.

Green, S. "Dialects in Japanese Monkeys: Vocal Learning and Cultural Transmission of Locale Specific Behavior?" *Z. Tierpsychol.* 38(1975):304–14.

Hayaki, H., M. Huffman, and T. Nishida. "Dominance Among Male Chimpanzees in the Mahale Mountains National Park, Tanzania." *Primates* 30(1989):187–97.

Kroodsma, D. "Learning and the Ontogeny of Sound Signals in Birds." *Acoustic Communication in Birds,* Vol. 1. Ed. D. Kroodsma and E. Miller. New York: Academic Press, 1982: 1–23.

Marler, P. "Song Learning Behavior: The Interface with Neuroethology." *T. Neurosci.* 14(1991): 199–205.

Marler, P., and L. Hobbett. "Individuality in a Long Range Vocalization of Wild Chimpanzees." *Z. Tierpsychol.* 38(1975):97–109.

Marler, P., and R. Tenaza. "Signaling Behavior of Apes with Special Reference to Vocalization." *How Animals Communicate.* Ed. T. Sebeok. Bloomington: Indiana Univ. Press, 1977: 965–1003.

Mitani, J., and K. Brandt. "Social Factors Influence the Acoustic Variability in the Long Distance Calls of Male Chimpanzees". *Ethology.* (In press).

Mitani, J., T. Hasegawa, J. Gros Louis, P. Marler, and R. Byrne. "Dialects in Wild Chimpanzees?" *Am. J. Primatol.* 27(1992):233–43.

Mitani, J., and T. Nishida. "Contexts and Social Correlates of Long Distance Calling by Male Chimpanzees." *Anim. Behav.* 45(1993):735–46.

Nishida, T. "Alpha Status and Agonistic Alliance in Chimpanzees." *Primates* 24(1983):318–36.

———. *The Chimpanzees of the Mahale Mountains.* Tokyo: Univ. of Tokyo Press, 1990.

Reynolds, V., and F. Reynolds. "Chimpanzees of the Budongo Forest." *Primate Behavior.* Ed. I. DeVore. New York: Holt, Rinehart, Winston, 1965: 368–424.

Snowdon, C. "Vocal Communication." *Comp. Primate Biol.* Ed. G. Mitchell and J. Erwin. New York: A. Liss, 1986: 495–530.

Snowdon, C., and M. Elowson. "Ontogeny of Primate Vocal Communication." *Topics in Primatology,* Vol. 1, *Human Origins.* Ed. T. Nishida, W. McGrew, P. Marler, et al. Tokyo: Univ. of Tokyo Press, 1992: 279–92.

Takasaki, H., and O. Takenaka. "Paternity Testing in Chimpanzees with DNA Amplification from Hairs and Buccal Cells in Wadges: A Preliminary Note." *Primatology Today.* Ed. A. Ehara, T. Kimura, O. Takenaka, and M. Iwamoto. New York: Elsevier, 1991: 613–6.

Tinbergen, N. "On the Aims and Methods of Ethology." *Z. Tierpsychol.* 20(1963):410–33.

Uehara, S., and T. Nishida. "Body Weights of Wild Chimpanzees (*Pan troglodytes*) of the Mahale Mountains National Park, Tanzania." *Am. J. Phys. Anthro.* 72(1987):315–21.

Wiley, R.H., and D. Richards. "Physical Constraints on Acoustic Communication in the Atmosphere: Implications for the Evolution of Animal Vocalizations." *Behav. Ecol. Sociobiol.* 3(1978):69–94.

Wrangham, R. "Feeding Behaviour of Chimpanzees in Gombe National Park, Tanzania." *Primate Ecology.* Ed. T. Clutton Brock. London: Academic Press, 1977: 503–38.

Considerations

1. Mitani says his research "relies on the comparative method." What sorts of comparisons does his research involve? Try identifying as many comparisons as you can, being specific about what is being compared to what.

2. The term *hypothesis* appears frequently in this article. What are hypotheses, and do they precede or follow observations? Explain with reference to the article.

3. Mitani says that he has taken "an ethological approach." What does that seem to mean? How might an ethological approach differ from other forms of research?

4. From Mitani's perspective, what conclusions can and cannot be drawn about the functions of pant-hooting in chimpanzee society?

5. Explain the language term *dialect* and why it may be relevant to the study of chimpanzee vocalization. Does Mitani seem to think that chimpanzees have dialects?

6. Notice that on page 551 Mitani refers to the work of Cheney and Seyfarth, the authors of the previous piece. How does this study compare to theirs? Can you draw any comparisons between the pant-hoots of chimpanzees and the alarm calls or grunts of vervet monkeys?

Further Assignments

1. Write an essay comparing the methods of laboratory and field researchers. You may draw on any of the readings in this chapter, including those in the Opening Problem (p. 421), the Professional Application (p. 444), and the Science Assignment (p. 482).

2. Anthropologist Shirley S. Strum (p. 491) writes about the way she came to challenge the "baboon model" of social aggression that had been widely accepted by primatologists. Research results are usually interpreted in relation to some prevailing model, but sometimes important research results challenge a prevailing model, throwing its explanatory power into question. Refer back to pages 13–16 in Chapter 1 (Defining) to get a sense of how the term *model* is used in a number of contexts. You can also refer to a scientific dictionary or a research methods textbook. Then write an essay that compares the influence of research models upon the work of two or more scientists encountered in this chapter.

3. Why are issues of primates and *communication* so different from issues of primates and *language*? Write an essay that establishes common ground between the two terms while clearly differentiating them.

4. Scientists function within communities of other scientists. Drawing on the evidence you find in this chapter, how do community influences help to shape and sustain the research of individual scientists? How do scientists attempt to differentiate themselves without alienating their communities? Are there scientists who are uncomfortable in their scientific communities, and if so, what do they do about that discomfort?

5. Some of the writers in this chapter are writing for general audiences (Goodall, for example, or Blum), others for scientific audiences (Mitani, for example, or Cheney and Seyfarth). What are some of the differences between the popular and scientific styles, and what accounts for these differences?

6. Many of the scientists represented in this chapter employ a comparative method. Can you generalize about the ways in which primatologists employ comparisons and comparative perspectives? Do some comparisons seem more fundamental or more effective than others?

7. What is ethology? Define the term and then illustrate your definition with examples drawn from this chapter. You might want to consider the criticisms of ethology made by Goodall (p. 483) and Strum (p. 491), and you might want to consider excerpts from Mitani or Cheney and Seyfarth as examples of contempo-

rary ethology at work. What seems to distinguish ethology from other ways of studying animals?

8. Most of the readings in this chapter touch upon issues of evolution. Read over the chapter's selections, collecting as many references to evolution as you can, and group these references into categories. From the various perspectives you've encountered, what seem to be the important evolutionary questions attached to primate research? Do different kinds of researchers — for example, psychologists, ethologists, medical researchers — ask different kinds of evolutionary questions? Write an essay illustrating and explaining your classification scheme.

9. The readings in this chapter touch upon the following primate species: gorillas, chimpanzees, baboons, macaque monkeys, and vervet monkeys. Using these species and any others you might know about (for example, orangutans, lemurs, rhesus monkeys), write an essay that classifies these species according to the interest or value that they have for humans. Base your essay at least in part upon the chapter's readings. But you can also draw upon further research or upon the role that primates play in popular culture. As a postscript, you might want to consider whether the human-centered classification that you've described ignores or takes into account the critical perspective of animal rights activists.

10. Investigations of apes and language sometimes make comparative references to the development of language in children. For instance, the gorilla Koko might be said to possess the working vocabulary of a three-year-old child. Beginning with a college textbook on child development, investigate the issue of language acquisition in children. Based on your reading, do comparisons between the learning of children and of apes discourage or encourage the view that apes are capable of language?

11. Deborah Blum's book *The Monkey Wars,* from which we have excerpted two selections, is primarily about the disagreements between animal rights groups and the medical research community. After consulting Blum's book and following up on a few of her citations, write an essay in which you explain the ethical conflicts between the two points of view.

12. Most scientific fields are still dominated by men. But primatology, especially field research, is a field in which women scientists have played especially prominent roles. Why might this be so? Two books you might consult in addressing this question are *Walking with the Great Apes* by Sy Montgomery, which profiles Jane Goodall, Dian Fossey, and Birute Galdikas, and *Primate Visions* by Donna Haraway, which offers an ambitious survey of primatology through the lenses of gender, race, and class.

6

ANALYZING

Perspectives for Interpretation

ANALYZING Across the Curriculum

The first part of this chapter includes a range of readings — most accompanied by assignments — that will get you to think critically about the ways in which analyzing is used across the curriculum: in literature, biology, political science, history, and other fields. In addition to covering various disciplines, we offer various types of writing: short stories, a news account, personal reflection, and presentations of research, both for academic and more general audiences. We begin with an Opening Problem that immediately involves you with using — and thinking about — analyzing. We then present examples of writers drafting papers on academic topics that involve the strategy (Working Examples, p. 567), followed by a piece showing how a professional writer uses analyzing to serve a particular purpose (A Professional Application, p. 580). Next comes a series of cross-curricular assignments intended to deepen and enrich your investigation of the strategy's possibilities and limitations (p. 583).

Woven throughout the first part of this chapter (in the Opening Problem; in the Professional Application; and in the Economics Assignment, p. 589) are readings in Caribbean culture and literature, which lend themselves especially well to the application and investigation of analyzing. If this topic interests you and you want to spend more time with it, consider working with the readings in the second part of this chapter. Specifically, these readings encourage you to consider the "cultural politics" of the Caribbean — the way that even the most commonplace behaviors and interactions are influenced by larger social forces. (For a more detailed discussion of this term, see p. 623.) You may find that investigating the cultural politics of the Caribbean prompts you to examine the social forces that affect your everyday behavior and values.

Opening Problem: Analyzing a Short Story

Here is a problem — interpreting a short story — that will involve you in writing analytically. Begin by reading the following story, "The Two Grandmothers," by the Jamaican writer Olive Senior. When you've read it, jot down a few notes and observations and then try drafting a few rough paragraphs about the story.

> Mummy, you know what? Grandma Del has baby chickens. Yellow and white ones. She makes me hold them. And I help her gather eggs but I don't like to go out the back alone because the turkey gobbler goes gobble! gobble! gobble! after my legs, he scares me and Mr. SonSon next door has baby pigs I don't like the mother pig though. Grandma lives in this pretty little house with white lace curtains at all the windows, Mummy you must come with me and Daddy next time and you can peek through the louvers Grandma calls them jalousies isn't that funny and you can see the people passing by. But they can't see you. Mummy why can't we have lace curtains like Grandma Del so we can peek though nobody ever goes by our house except the gardeners and the maids and people begging and Rastas selling brooms. Many many people go by Grandma Del's house and they all call out to her and Grandma Del knows everyone. My special friend is Miss Princess the postmistress who plays the organ in church she wears tight shiny dresses and her hair piled *so* on her head and she walks *very slow* and everybody says she is sweet on Mr. Blake who is the new teacher and he takes the service in church when Parson doesn't come and Miss Princess gets so nervous she mixes up all the hymns. Mr. Mack came to fix Grandma's roof and Grandma said "poorman poorman" all the time. Mr. Mack's daughters Eulalie and Ermandine are big girls at high school in town though Eulalie fell and they don't know what is to be done. Mummy, why are they so worried that Eulalie fell? She didn't break her leg or anything like that for she is walking up and down past the house all day long and looks perfectly fine to me.
>
> Mummy, I really like Grandma Del's house it's nice and cosy and dark and cool inside with these big lovely oval picture frames of her family and Daddy as a baby and Daddy as a little boy and Daddy on the high school football team, they won Manning Cup that year Grandma says did you know that Mummy? And Daddy at University and a wedding picture of Daddy and you and me as a baby and all the pictures you send Grandma every year but those are the small pictures on the side table with the lovely white lace tablecloth in the picture frame on the wall is Great-grandpapa Del with a long beard and whiskers he makes me giggle and he is sitting down in a chair and Great-grandmama is standing behind him and then there is a picture of Grandma herself as a young lady with her hair piled high like Miss Princess and her legs crossed at the ankles she looks so lovely. But you know what, Mummy, I didn't see a picture of Daddy's father and when I asked Grandma she got mad and shooed me away. She gets even madder when I asked her to show me her wedding picture. I only want to see it.

Mummy do you know that Grandma sends me to Sunday School? And then we stay over for big church and then I walk home with her and all the people it's so nice and only Parson comes to church in a car. Mummy did you go to Sunday School? I go with Joycie a big girl next door and Grandma made me three dresses to wear. She says she cannot imagine how a girl-child (that's me) can leave her home with nothing but blue-jeans and T-shirts and shorts and not a single church dress. She has this funny sewing machine, not like Aunt Thelma's, she has to use her feet to make it go just like the organ in church Miss Princess pumps away with her feet to make it give out this lovely sound she works so hard you should see her and the first time I went to Grandma's church I was so scared of the bats! The church is full of bats but usually they stay high up in the roof but as soon as the organ starts playing on Sunday the bats start swooping lower and lower and one swooped so low I nearly died of fright and clutched Grandma Del so tight my hat flew off.

Did I tell you Grandma made me a hat to go to church with her own two hands? She pulled apart one of her old straw hats, leghorn she said, and made me a little hat that fits just so on my head with a bunch of tiny pink flowers. Grandma didn't send it with me though or my Sunday dresses she says she will keep them till I return for she knows that I am growing heathenish in town. When Grandma dresses me up for church I feel so beautiful in my dresses she made with lace and bows and little tucks so beautiful and my hat, I feel so special that my own Grandma made these for me with her own two hands and didn't buy them in a store. Grandma loves to comb my hair she says it's so long and thick and she rubs it with castor oil every night. I hate the smell of castor oil but she says it's the best thing for hair to make it thick and soft and after a time I even like the smell. Grandma Del says my skin is beautiful like honey and all in all I am a fine brown lady and must make sure to grow as beautiful inside as I am outside but Mummy how do I go about doing that?

Nights at Grandma's are very funny. Mummy can you imagine there's no TV? And it's very, very dark. No street lights or any lights and we go to bed so early and every night Grandma lights the oil lamps and then we blow them out when we are going to bed, you have to take a deep breath and every morning Grandma checks the oil in the lamps and cleans the shades. They have "Home Sweet Home" written all around them. So beautiful. She cleans the shades with newspapers. She says when I come next year I'll be old enough to clean the shades all by myself. Grandma knows such lovely stories; she tells me stories every night not stories from a book you know, Mummy, the way you read to me, but stories straight from her head. Really! I am going to learn stories from Grandma so when I am a grown lady I will remember all these stories to tell my children. Mummy, do you think I will?

II

Mummy you know Grandma Elaine is so funny she says I'm not to call her Grandma any more, I'm to call her Towser like everybody else for I'm growing so fast nobody would believe that she could have such a big young lady for a granddaughter. I think it's funny I'm practicing calling her Towser though she is still my grandmother. I say, "Grandmother, I mean Towser." Grandma Del introduces me to everyone as her Granddaughter she calls me her "little gran" and Grandma Elaine says, "Darling, the way your Grandmother Del looks and conducts herself she couldn't be anything but a Grandmother and honey she and I are of entirely different generations."

Grandma Elaine says such funny things sometimes. Like she was dressing to go out last night and she was putting on make-up and I said "Grandma"— she was still Grandma then — I said, "Grandma, you shouldn't paint your face like that you know, it is written in the Bible that it's a sin. Grandma Del says so and I will never paint my face." And she said, "Darling, with all due respect to your paternal Grandmother, she's a lovely lady or was when I met her the one and only time at the wedding, and she has done one absolutely fantastic thing in her life which is to produce one son, your esteemed father, one hunk of a guy, but honey, other than that your Grandmother Del is a country bumpkin of the deepest waters and don't quote her goddamn sayings to me." Mummy, you know Grandma Elaine *swears* like that all the time? I said, "Grandma you mustn't swear and take the name of the Lord in vain." And she said, "Honeychile with all due respect to the gray hairs of your old grandmother and the first-class brainwashing your daddy is allowing her to give you, I wish my granddaughter would get off my back and leave me to go to Hell in peace." Can you imagine she said that?

She's really mad that you allow me to spend time with Grandma Del. She says, "Honey, I really don't know what your mother thinks she is doing making you spend so much time down there in the deepest darkest country. I really must take you in hand. It's embarrassing to hear some of the things you come out with sometimes. Your mother would be better advised to send you to Charm School next summer you are never too young to start. Melody-Ann next door went last year and it's done wonders for her, turned her from a tomboy into a real little lady." (Though Mummy, I really can't stand Melody-Ann any more, you know) "And your mother had better start to do something about your hair from now it's almost as tough as your father's and I warned your mother about it from the very start I said 'Honey, love's alright but what about the children's hair?' If you were my child I would cut it right off to get some of the kinks out. Mummy, you won't cut off my hair, will you? Daddy and Grandma Del like it just the way it is and what does Grandma Elaine mean when she says my hair is tough, Mummy?

Anyway, Mummy, can I tell you a secret? Gran, I mean Towser, told me and says it's a secret but I guess since you are her daughter she won't mind if I tell you. Do you know that Towser has a new boyfriend? He came to pick her up on Saturday night, remember I told you Joyce was staying up with me and we watched TV together while Towser went out? That's the time she was painting her face and she put on her fabulous silver evening dress, you know the strapless one and her diamonds with it, the ones her husband after Grandpapa gave her, and I was so proud she was my grandmama she looked wonderful like a million dollars and when I told her so she let me spray some of her perfume on myself before Mr. Kincaid came. He is a tall white man and he kissed Towser's hand and then he kissed my hand and he had a drink with Towser and was very nice and they drove off in this big white car like what Uncle Frank drives Mummy, a Benz, and Towser was looking so pleased the whole time and before Mr. Kincaid came she whispered and said her new boyfriend was coming to take her to dinner and he was so nice and handsome and rich. Towser was looking as pleased as Eulalie did when the mail van driver was touching her when they thought nobody was looking but I was peeking through the louvres at Grandma Del's and I saw them.

But Mummy, I don't know why Towser wants me to spend more time with her for she is never there when I go; always rushing off to the gym and the pool and dinners and cocktails or else she is on the phone. I love Towser so much though, she hugs me a lot and she says things that make me laugh and she gives me wonderful presents. Do you know she made Joyce bake a chocolate cake for me? And my new bracelet is so lovely. It's my birthstone you know, Mummy. You know what, Grandma Elaine, I mean Towser says she is going to talk to you about taking me to see my cousins Jason and Maureen in Clearwater when she goes to do her Christmas shopping in Miami. Oh Mummy, can I go? You know all the girls in my class have been to Miami and you've never taken me. Mum, can we go to Disneyworld soon? I'm so ashamed everyone in school has been to Disneyworld and I haven't gone yet. When Towser goes out Joyce and I sit in the den and watch TV the whole time except I usually fall asleep during the late show but Joyce watches everything until TV signs off, and next morning when she is making me breakfast she tells me all the parts that I missed. Mummy, can't we get a video? Everyone in my class has a video at home except me. You know Towser is getting a video she says she is getting Mr. Kincaid to give her one as a present. Towser is so much fun. Except Mummy, what does she have against my hair? And my skin? She always seems angry about it and Joyce says Grandma is sorry I came out dark because she is almost a white lady and I am really dark. But Mummy what is wrong with that? When I hold my hand next to Joyce my skin is not as dark as hers or Grandma Del's or Daddy's even. Is dark really bad, Mummy?

III

Mummy, did you know that a whistling woman and a crowing hen are an abomination to the Lord? That's what Grandma Del told me and Pearlie when Pearlie was teaching me to whistle. Don't tell Grandma but I *can* whistle. Want to hear me? -! -! -! Ha ha. Mummy, can you whistle? Pearlie is my best friend in the country she lives near to Grandma in this tiny house so many of them and all the children sleep together in one room on the floor and Mummy, you know what? Pearlie has only one pair of shoes and one good dress and her school uniform though she hardly goes to school and some old things she wears around the house that have holes in them. Can you imagine? And you should see her little brothers! Half the time they are wearing no clothes at all. Mummy can you send Pearlie some of my dresses and some of my toys but not my Barbie doll? She doesn't have any toys at all, not a single one.

And Pearlie is just a little older than me and she has to look after her little brothers when her Mummy goes out to work. She had to feed them and bathe them and change them and while she is changing the baby's nappies her little brothers get into so much trouble. And when they break things when her mother comes home she beats Pearlie. Poor Pearlie! She can balance a pan of water on her head no hands you know. I wish I could do that. She goes to the standpipe for water and carries the pan on her head without spilling a drop. Sometimes I go with her; I borrow a pan and though it's smaller than Pearlie's I always end up spilling the water all over me and the pan gets heavier and heavier till I can hardly bear it before we get to Pearlie's house. Pearlie can wash clothes too. I mean real clothes, not dolly clothes.

Really. Her baby brother's nappies and things and she cooks dinner for them but the way they eat is really funny. They don't have a real kitchen or anything she has three big rocks in the fireplace and she catches up a fire when she is ready and she has to fan it and fan it with an old basket top and there is a lot of smoke. It makes me sneeze. Then when the fire is going she puts on a big pot of water and when it is boiling she peels things and throws them in the water to cook — yams and cocos and green bananas and that's what they eat, no meat or rice or salad or anything. Pearlie uses a sharp knife just like a big person and she peels the bananas ever so fast, she makes three cuts and goes zip! zip! with her fingers and the banana is out of its skin and into the pot. She says you must never put bananas and yams to boil in cold water for they will get drunk and never cook. Did you know that?

Once I helped her to rub up the flour dumplings but my dumplings came out so soft Pearlie said they were like fla-fla and she won't let me help her make dumplings again. Pearlie has to do all these things and we only get to play in the evenings when her mother comes home and can you imagine, Mummy, Pearlie has never seen TV? And she has never been to the movies. Never. Mummy do you think Pearlie could come and live with us? I could take her to the movies though I don't know who would look after her baby brothers when her mother goes to work. You know Pearlie doesn't have a father? She doesn't know where he is. I'd die without my Daddy. Grandma Del says I'm to be careful and not spend so much time with Pearlie for Pearlie is beginning to back-chat and is getting very force-ripe. Mummy, what is force-ripe?

Sometimes I play with Eulalie's baby. His name is Oral and he is fat and happy and I help to change his nappy. He likes me a lot and claps his hands when he sees me and he has two teeth already. He likes to grab hold of my hair and we have a hard time getting him to let go. Mummy why can't I have a baby brother to play with all the time? Eulalie and Ermandine love to comb my hair and play with it they say I am lucky to have tall hair but Grandma Del doesn't like Eulalie and Ermandine any more. She says they are a disgraceful Jezebel-lot and dry-eye and bring down shame on their father and mother who try so hard with them. Sometimes my Grandma talks like that and I really don't understand and when I ask her to explain she says, "Cockroach nuh bizniz inna fowl roos" and she acts real mad as if I did something wrong and I don't know why she is so vexed sometimes and quarrels with everyone even me. She scares me when she is vexed.

You know when Grandma Del is really happy? When she is baking cakes and making pimento liquor and orange marmalade and guava jelly. On, she sings and she gets Emmanuel to make up a big fire out in the yard and she gets out this big big pot and we peel and we peel guava — hundreds of them. When we make stewed guava she gives me a little spoon so I can help to scoop out the seeds and I have to be real careful to do it properly and not break the shells. Mummy, right here you have this little glass jar full of stewed guavas from Grandma Del that I helped to make. Grandma gets so happy to see her kitchen full of these lovely glass jars full of marmalade and guava jelly. But you know what? Grandma just makes it and then she gives it all away. Isn't that funny? And one time she baked a wedding cake and decorated it too — three cakes in different sizes she made and then she put them one on top of the other. Grandma is so clever. She allowed me to help her stir the cake mix in the bowl but it was so heavy I could barely move the spoon. When it was all finished she let me use my fingers to lick out all the mixing bowls. Yum Yum. Why don't you bake cakes so I can lick out the bowls, Mummy?

And this time I found that I had grown so much I couldn't get into the church dresses Grandma made for me last time and Grandma made me some new dresses and she says she will give the old dresses to Pearlie. Mummy can you believe that everyone in church remembered me? And they said: "WAT-A-WAY-YU-GROW" and "HOW-IS-YU-DAADIE?" and "HOW-IS-YU-MAAMIE?" till I was tired. Mummy that is the way they talk, you know, just like Richie and the gardener next door. "WAT-A-WAY-YU-GROW." They don't speak properly the way we do, you know. Mummy, Eulalie and Ermandine don't go to church or school any more and Ermandine says when I come back next year she will have a little baby for me to play with too and Eulalie says *she* will have a new little baby.

IV

Mummy, you know what the girls in school say? They say I am the prettiest girl in school and I can be Miss Jamaica. When I'm big I'll go to the gym like you so I can keep my figure and I must take care of my skin for even though I have excellent skin, Towser says, I must always care for it. Towser spends hours before the mirror every morning caring for her skin and her new boyfriend Mr. Samuels is always telling her how beautiful she looks. Towser really loves that. Mr. Samuels is taking her to Mexico for the long Easter weekend and Towser is going to Miami to buy a whole new wardrobe for the trip. She says she is going to bring me all the new movies for the video. Mummy, when I am old like Grandma will men tell me I'm beautiful too? Can I have my hair relaxed as soon as I am twelve as you promised? Will you allow me to enter Miss Jamaica when I am old enough? You know Jason likes me a lot but he's my cousin so he doesn't count. Mom, am I going to Clearwater again this Christmas to spend time with Jason and Maureen? Maureen is always fighting with me you know but Jason says she's jealous because she isn't pretty like me, she's fat and has to wear braces on her teeth. Will I ever have to wear braces? Mom, when I go to Miami can I get a training bra. All the girls in my class are wearing them and a make-up starter kit? Mom, when are we going to get a Dish?

V

Mom, do I have to go to Grandma Del's again? It's so boring. There's nothing to do and nobody to talk to and I'm ashamed when my friends ask me where I'm going for the holidays and I have to tell them only to my old grandmother in the country. You know Gina is going to Europe and Melody-Ann is spending all of her holidays in California and Jean-Ann is going to her Aunt in Trinidad? Mom, even though Grandma Del has electricity now she has only a small black and white TV set and I end up missing *everything* for she doesn't want me to watch the late show even on weekends, and Grandma's house is so small and crowded and dark and she goes around turning off the lights and at nights Grandma smells because she is always rubbing herself with liniment for her arthritis she says and it's true Grandma is in terrible pain sometimes. Mummy what is going to happen to Grandma when she is real old? She's all alone there.

She got mad at me when I told her I didn't want her to rub castor oil in my hair any more because I was having it conditioned and the castor oil smells so awful. And on Sundays Grandma still wants me to go to church with her. It's so boring. We have to *walk* to church and back. It's *miles* in the hot sun. I can't walk on the gravel road in my heels. If a parent passed and saw me there among all the country bumpkins I would die and Grandma says I am far too young to be wearing heels even little ones and I tell Grandma I'm not young any more. I'll be entering high school next term and everybody is wearing heels. She criticizes everything I do as if I am still a baby and she doesn't like me wearing lip gloss or blusher though I tell her you allow me to wear them. And Grandma still wants me to come and greet all her friends, it's so boring as soon as somebody comes to the house she calls me and I have to drop whatever I am doing, even watching TV, and I have to say hello to all these stupid people. It's so boring Mom you wouldn't believe it, there's nobody but black people where Grandma lives and they don't know anything, they ask such silly questions. And they are dirty. You know this girl Pearlie I used to play with when I was little she is so awful-looking, going on the road with her clothes all torn up and you should see her little brothers always dirty and in rags with their noses running. I can't stand to have them around me and Pearlie and everybody is always begging me clothes and things and I can't stand it so I don't even bother to go outside the house half the time. When anybody comes I can see them through the louvres and I just pretend I am not there or I am sleeping. And everybody is just having babies without being married like Pearlie's mother and they are not ashamed. The worst ones are those two sisters Eulalie and Ermandine, you can't imagine how many babies they have between them a new one every year and Grandma says not a man to mind them.

But Mummy, something terrible happened. That Eulalie and I got into an argument. She's so ignorant and I told her that it was a disgrace to have babies without being married and she said, "Who says?" and I said, "Everybody. My Mummy and Grandma Elaine and Grandma Del for a start." And she said, "Grandma Del? Yes? You ever hear that she that is without sin must cast the first stone?" And I said, "What do you mean?" And she said, "Ask your Grannie Del Miss High-And-Mighty since her son turn big-shot and all. Ask her who his father? And why she never turn teacher? And why her daddy almost turn her out of the house and never speak to her for five years? And why they take so long to let her into Mothers' Union?" And Eulalie wouldn't tell me any more and they were so awful to me they started singing "Before A married an' go hug up mango tree, A wi' live so. Me one," You know that song, Mummy? I went home to ask Grandma Del what Eulalie meant, but Mummy, when I got home it was just weird I got so scared that I got this terrible pain in my tummy, my tummy hurt so much I couldn't ask Grandma Del anything and then when I felt better, I couldn't bring myself to say anything for I'm scared Grandma Del will get mad. But Mummy, do you think Grandma Del had Daddy without getting married? Is that what Eulalie meant? Mummy, wouldn't that make Daddy a bastard?

VI

Mummy, please don't send me back to stay with Auntie Rita in Clearwater again. Ever. Nothing, Mummy . . . It's that Maureen. She doesn't like me.

Mummy, am I really a nigger? That's what Maureen said when we were playing one day and she got mad at me and she said, "You're only a goddamn nigger you don't know any better. Auntie Evie married a big black man and you're his child and you're not fit to play with me." Mummy, I gave her such a box that she fell and I didn't care. I cried and cried and cried and though Auntie Rita spanked Maureen afterward and sent her to bed without any supper I couldn't eat my supper for I had this pain in my tummy such a terrible pain and Uncle Rob came into the bedroom and held my hand and said that Maureen was a naughty girl and he was ashamed of her and *he* thought I was a very beautiful, lovely girl. . . .

But Mummy, how can I be beautiful? My skin is so dark, darker than yours and Maureen's and Jason's and Auntie Rita's. And my hair is so coarse not like yours or Maureen's but then Maureen's father is white. Is that why Maureen called me a nigger? I hate Maureen. She is fat and ugly and still wearing braces. . . .

Mummy, why can't I have straight hair like Maureen? I'm so ashamed of my hair. I simply can't go back to Clearwater.

VII

Mom, I don't care what Dad says I can't go to stay with Grandma Del this summer because the Charm Course is for three weeks and then remember Towser is taking me to Ochi for three weeks in her new cottage. Do you think Towser is going to marry Mr. Blake? Then I am going with you to Atlanta. You promised. So I really don't have any time to spend with Grandma this summer. And next holidays remember, you said I can go to Venezuela on the school trip? I don't know what Dad is going on about because if he feels so strongly why doesn't he go and spend time with his mother? Only that's a laugh because Daddy doesn't have time for anybody any more, I mean, is there a time nowadays when he is ever at home? I know Grandma Del is getting old and she is all alone but she won't miss me, she quarrels with me all the time I am there. Mom, I just can't fit her in and that is that.

OK. You know what? I have an idea. Why don't we just take a quick run down to see Grandma this Sunday and then we wouldn't have to worry about her again till next year. Daddy can take us and we can leave here real early in the morning though I don't know how I am going to get up early after Melody-Ann's birthday party Saturday night, but we don't have to stay long with Grandma Del. We can leave there right after lunch so we will be back in time to watch *Dallas.* Eh, Mom?

— Olive Senior, "The Two Grandmothers"

When you've had a chance to draft the paragraphs offering some of your responses to "The Two Grandmothers," take a few minutes to read this excerpt by Merle Hodge of Trinidad from an article about the cultural politics of the Caribbean.

We live, very comfortably, in certain arrangements that perform all the functions of family — the socialization of the young, the provision of the material and emotional needs of all family members, the regulation of sexuality. Again, these arrangements do not fit the storybook prescription: In our family systems the head of the family can be female or male; legal marriage is not mandatory; the family spills beyond one household to include cousins, aunts and uncles, grandparents, and even godparents as functional members of a family.

These arrangements have survived for generations, despite official disrespect and attempts to force us all into the storybook family mold. And again there is ambivalence, a contradiction between our daily experience and the norms to which we subscribe, for we firmly believe that a "real" family consists of husband, wife, and children, with the husband as head, and that any variation on this model is an anomaly — even if it is an anomaly which we live.

In religion there is the same contradiction between "standard" religion — that is, Christianity — and a certain interpretation of the supernatural and styles of worship inherited from our African past which hold a strong attraction for us but which we are very careful to disown.

The culture of the Caribbean, then, has never gained validity in the eyes of Caribbean people. In the colonial era, Culture with a capital "C" was the culture of the colonizing country. Whatever we were practicing was not "real" culture. The colonial era came to an end and we moved into independence. Theoretically, we could now begin to build up a sense of our cultural identity. But we immediately found ourselves in a new and more vicious era of cultural penetration. Television, which is basically American television, came to Trinidad and Tobago in 1962, the year the British flag was pulled down. The same pattern can be seen all over the Caribbean — withdrawing the most obvious trappings of colonial domination and installing a Trojan horse[1] instead.

— Merle Hodge, *Challenges of the Struggle for Sovereignty: Changing the World Versus Writing Short Stories*

Hodge was not writing about Senior's story when she made these comments. But in prompting our own thinking about the characters in Senior's story, it's fair to ask what Hodge might say about them. Using her generalizations as a frame of reference, try writing about the story again, considering it in light of what Hodge says about Caribbean life.

Thinking about Thinking

When you have finished writing about the story, consider the following questions:

- How did your eventual essay differ from your initial responses to the story?
- When you were asked to consider Senior's story from a perspective provided by Hodge, did you find Hodge's perspective compatible? Did you begin to look at the story differently? Did different details emerge as important?
- In what ways did Hodge's perspective help to focus what you wrote about the story? In what ways did it distort or restrict what you might have said otherwise?
- How does writing about this story analytically differ from other kinds of writing you've done about literature?

This chapter, like the analytical problem you have already attempted, asks you to look at particular texts from particular theoretical frameworks or points of view. Now, in a sense, if you've been doing assignments in the earlier chapters of this book, you already have been writing analytically. Analysis occurs whenever you look at something closely and selectively, interpreting what you see. So you have written analytically if you've defined a word by examining some of the ways in which it is used;

[1]**Trojan horse:** An apparent gift that turns out to have destructive consequences (named for the hollow wooden horse in which Greeks hid and gained entrance to Troy) [Eds.].

you've analyzed a poem by thinking about its images one by one, serially; you've analyzed a group of visual images by sorting them into meaningful categories; you've analyzed two researchers' approaches by comparing them; in the act of summarizing a reading, you've begun to analyze it. In this chapter, however, we take this general sense of analysis a little further, sharpening it to meet some of the biggest challenges of academic writing. For in most academic situations, analysis is seldom simply a matter of looking and selecting. What we see depends on how we look.

Imagine yourself standing on a local hill staring up at the night sky — cloudless and clear, dominated by clusters of stars, some brighter or denser than others. The view is exhilarating. Now imagine yourself having to write about that sky for an early assignment in your astronomy class, coming to some conclusions about the relationships of stars. Where would you begin? Which of your first impressions would you put to use? What words would you choose? What else would you like to know? Without understanding something about the assumptions, methods, and terminology of astronomers, you would not get very far in your analysis — at least not far enough to please an astronomer. But if you approached the job equipped with some astronomical learning, you'd be on surer footing. Your analysis would still depend on what you could see and what you chose to look at carefully, but those choices would be better informed. If, after looking at the sky some more, you decided to let your analysis be guided by some single hypothesis or point of view — for example, the idea that the densest band of stars is likely to belong to the galaxy we ourselves inhabit — you'd be on your way to writing an effective analysis. To do more, you'd need to know more — about light, about telescopes, about atomic theory, about the movement of the earth, about the means of stellar measurement, about what you couldn't see as well as what you could.

Keep in mind that writing assignments calling for analysis may give you little or no guidance. Consider this question from a take-home exam in a U.S. history course:

> Analyze the trends in U.S. foreign policy since 1945.

Not only does this assignment suggest no particular perspective, it provides only the vaguest of analytical objects. Sometimes, despite the word *analyze* in the question, such assignments are calling for summary: "Tell me what I've told you about U.S. foreign policy." But when calling for genuine analysis, such questions are worded so broadly as to leave the crucial decisions to the students. And the choices can be bewildering. Which of the myriad events and relations are you to choose, and from which perspectives should you consider them? How do you define the term *foreign policy* anyway? Does it include only what has happened or also what has not? What do you write about, and how?

Of course, in practice, the question is not so frightening. In fact, if forced, most of us could write a response in a few minutes (as an experiment you might want to try doing this; then compare your response to someone else's). Besides, the question does imply some framework. The phrasing "since 1945" suggests that that year should be treated as pivotal, a time when something important began or shifted (you could start your essay "When World War II ended . . ." or "Foreign policy in the nuclear age . . ."). More important, in the context of the history course you would not really face a limitless number of possibilities — you'd have read or heard about events and issues that, by consensus, have been treated as crucial in U.S. foreign policy, and you'd have been exposed to several perspectives, including your teacher's, for interpreting them. In fact, these perspectives will have done much to determine which issues and events you see as important.

The difference between this question in theory and in practice helps us make a further point about analysis. Objects of analysis seldom come to us neutrally, as something dispassionately to be examined from whatever perspectives we choose. They invariably come to us already shaped by those who have found them worth our attention. Knowing that should keep us restless. The best informed and most thoughtful analyses will recognize and negotiate this limitation, using a perspective both to help us see and to provoke us to see more.

In a book like this we cannot hope to ground your analytical thinking in the sorts of experience you'll get within specific disciplines. But even without these fuller frameworks, we can offer assignments that ask you to look at particular texts from particular points of view. We think that such assignments help to demonstrate — as you may have seen when you tried applying Hodge's comments to Senior's story — the power of such perspectives for shaping, or reshaping, what you see. We hope that this recognition, in turn, will encourage you to think critically about the perspectives sometimes imposed on you. Good analytical writing comes as frequently from resisting an offered point of view as from embracing it.

Working Examples

A Working Example from Psychology

Let us illustrate what analytical writing involves by imagining a classroom situation. For a class in the psychology of human relations, your instructor presents you with the following short reading passage and tells you that it is an excerpt from a novel called *The Collector* written by the British novelist John Fowles. You're asked to write a short analytical commentary on the interaction between the two characters. After reading the passage, try analyzing it.

> I picked up my knitting and put it away. When I looked round he was standing there with his mouth open, trying to say something. And I knew I'd hurt him, I know he deserves to be hurt, but there it is. I've hurt him. He looked *so* glum. And I remembered he'd let me go out in the garden. I felt mean.
>
> I went to him and said I was sorry and held out my hand, but he wouldn't take it. It was queer, he really had a sort of dignity, he was really hurt (perhaps that was it) and showing it. So I took his arm and made him sit down again, and I said, I'm going to tell you a fairy story.
>
> Once upon a time (I said, and he stared bitterly bitterly at the floor) there was a very ugly monster who captured a princess and put her in a dungeon in his castle. Every evening he made her sit with him and ordered her to say to him, "You are very

handsome, my lord," and every evening she said, "You are very ugly, you monster." And then the monster looked very hurt and sad and stared at the floor. So one evening the princess said, "If you do this thing and that thing you might be handsome," but the monster said, "I can't, I can't." The princess said, "Try, try." But the monster said, "I can't, I can't." Every evening it was the same. He asked her to lie, and she wouldn't. So the princess began to think that he really enjoyed being a monster and very ugly. Then one day she saw he was crying when she'd told him, for the fiftieth time, that he was ugly. So she said, "You can become very handsome if you do just one thing. Will you do it?" Yes, he said, at last, he would try to do it. So she said, then set me free. And he set her free. And suddenly, he wasn't ugly any more, he was a prince who had been bewitched. And he followed the princess out of the castle. And they both lived happily ever afterwards.

I knew it was silly as I was saying it. Fey. He didn't speak, he kept staring down.

I said, now it's your turn to tell a fairy story.

He just said, I love you.

And yes, he had more dignity than I did then and I felt small, mean. Always sneering at him, jabbing him, hating him and showing it. It was funny, we sat in silence facing each other and I had a feeling I've had once or twice before, of the most peculiar closeness to him — *not* love or attraction or sympathy in any way. But linked destiny. Like being shipwrecked on an island — a raft — together. In *every* way not wanting to be together. But together.

I feel the sadness of his life, too, terribly. And of those of his miserable aunt and his cousin and their relatives in Australia. The great dull hopeless weight of it.

— John Fowles, *The Collector*

What did you decide was going on between the two people? If you responded as most readers do, you may have said something like this:

> It's a young woman and her boyfriend. She's breaking up with him, and he seems to be pretty immature about it. She feels sympathy for him and wants to let him down gently, but she's also determined to get out of the relationship.

If pressed to provide evidence to support these conclusions, you could provide plenty:

> "I've hurt him. . . . I felt mean."
>
> "I went to him and said I was sorry. . . . he was really hurt . . . and showing it."
>
> "So I took his arm. . . ."
>
> "He just said, I love you."
>
> "I feel the sadness of his life, too, terribly. . . . The great dull hopeless weight of it."

There's also the fairy story. Some readers have pointed out that the story the woman tells seems designed to equate her with the princess and him with the monster. The story thus pushes him away while also holding out a vague hope for a future together.

If you've analyzed the passage along these general lines, you may also feel some misgivings. Stop for a moment now. Can you think of any ways this general analysis falls short? On the one hand, it seems a plausible explanation. But do you find any moments that seem puzzling? Make a short list of such moments.

If you have read John Fowles's novel, you probably have been reading this discussion impatiently. The story, you know, is not about a typical romantic falling-out. It's about a hostage-taking. As one student has put it,

> He holds the woman captive because he's in love with her. He isn't violent, and he doesn't go after her sexually, but he also doesn't want to let her go. She does her best to talk him out of keeping her prisoner, hinting with the fairy tale that if he'll release her, they can be friends later. She knows he probably won't fall for this, but she's desperate.

Disappointed? Knowing what happens in the novel seems, in effect, to put an end to the analytical effort. If you were asked now to write about the passage, what would you find to say? There seems little to do but to summarize the story as the student we just quoted has done. In an odd way, what we know about the facts of the case seems to flatten out and deaden the analysis.

But consider what can happen when we approach the passage from a fresh perspective. Read the following paragraph about the Stockholm theory and then try writing about *The Collector* excerpt from the point of view suggested by the expert quoted here, Dr. Frank Ochberg.

> Most hostages suffer some degree of psychological damage, a mix of helplessness, fear, rage, and a sense of abandonment. . . . One sign of stress is known as the "Stockholm syndrome." . . . The syndrome is a kind of bonding between captors and captives, and is named for a Stockholm bank robbery in 1973 in which the hostages came to idolize their captors and ultimately refused to testify against them. In some cases, hostages have reportedly fallen in love with their jailers of the opposite sex, and the captors have become protective of their hostages. "When someone captures you, he places you in an infantile position," says Dr. Frank Ochberg, director of the Michigan Department of Mental Health. "It sets the stage for love as a response to infantile terror — he could kill you but he doesn't, and you are grateful."
>
> — *Time,* December 24, 1979

The Stockholm theory suddenly provides a powerful lens through which to view what happens between the two characters in Fowles's story. Or, to put it another way, the idea can become a kind of analytical searchlight: As we reread the passage, it throws some features into sudden prominence, illuminating details we hadn't noticed or didn't know how to interpret. For instance, some of the same phrases that at first kept us from recognizing the situation as a hostage-taking now take on a new meaning: "I've hurt him. . . . I felt mean"; "I had a feeling . . . of the most peculiar closeness to him"; "I felt the sadness of his life." Here is how one student analyzed the passage in light of the Stockholm theory:

In this passage from The Collector, we see a classic example of someone caught up in the "Stockholm syndrome." As Dr. Frank Ochberg has described it, the Stockholm syndrome occurs when victims of a hostage-taking form attachments to their captors. Captives, Ochberg says, usually feel "a mix of helplessness, fear, rage, and a sense of abandonment." In such situations captives may be impressed by the seriousness of their captors, while they themselves begin to feel small and dependent. Captives become grateful for small favors. "He could kill you," says Ochberg, "but he doesn't, and you are grateful." In this way a strong bond can develop between captor and captive--they are living through a stressful situation together.

This helps to explain why the captive in The Collector can feel guilty about hurting the feelings of the person she should hate. She displays the mixture of feelings that Ochberg describes when she says, "I know he deserves to be hurt, but there it is. I've hurt him. . . . I felt mean." She feels petty and "small" when she tries to trick him with the fairy story, and she sees him, by contrast, as a person of "dignity." She feels great sympathy for him: "I felt the sadness of his life, too, terribly." Above all, she feels the power of the bond that has developed between them. Even though this is a situation that he has created, it now feels as though they both are captive to it:

> It was funny, we sat in silence facing each other and I had a feeling I've had once or twice before, of the most peculiar closeness to him--not love or attraction or sympathy in any way. But linked destiny. Like being shipwrecked on an island--a raft--together.

In her own confusion and stress, she's formed an enormous attachment to the person who has made her vulnerable.

This is a persuasive piece of analysis, isn't it? Notice how the writer has made skillful use of the theoretical material about the Stockholm syndrome, using it to introduce the discussion of the passage itself in the second paragraph. Also notice the skillful blend of short quotations and paraphrasings throughout both paragraphs. The energy of the analysis seems to build with the gathering evidence. Where once there seemed only "the facts" of the kidnapping, there now seems a strong point of view to be applied, a case to be made.

Yet it's also possible to feel dissatisfied with the analysis. Did you? Sometimes a powerful point of view can block out other ways of looking; and clear, coherent explanations can smother potential disagreements and objections. For that reason, it's a good intellectual habit to practice a little resistance. With some skeptical prodding — asking yourself: What if it isn't so? — you'll sometimes find opportunities to show your independence. Here, for example, is how another student resisted the Stockholm explanation, organizing her objections into an effective essay:

> The relationship we see in <u>The Collector</u> does not conform to the Stockholm syndrome. According to the theory described by Dr. Frank Ochberg, victims of hostage-takings develop strong feelings of affection for their captors, coming to idolize them, sometimes even falling in love with them. Fearing for their lives, they become infantilized, and they feel love "as a response to infantile terror."
>
> The young woman in <u>The Collector</u> doesn't seem to fit this description at all. In the first place, she feels no terror. She begins by leisurely putting down her knitting, and she proceeds calmly to tell her captor a belittling story. Second, she isn't infantilized. In fact, it's the other way around--the captor is infantilized, becoming in effect a big baby. She sits him down to tell her fairy tale, and he sulks in response. Third, there's clearly no idolization involved. She admits he has some dignity, but basically she regards him with pity: "I feel the sadness of his life." Pity involves looking down--and that's the opposite of idolization. Finally, she does not love him. She explicitly says this twice. She admits she was "always sneering at him, jabbing him, hating him and showing it." And even when she admits to feeling as if she has been shipwrecked with him, she is careful to say that the feeling is "<u>not</u> love or attraction" but simply a feeling of "linked destiny."
>
> The Stockholm syndrome may occur in some captor/captive

relationships, but this isn't one of them. Perhaps the theory applies only to true hostage-takings, when the captor has some ulterior ambition. Here the kidnapper has what he wants and seems helpless about what to do next. We should be reluctant to slap an abstract theory onto a case as strange as this one.

Do you find this analysis persuasive too? More or less so than the first essay? What are some of the decisions that this writer has made in developing her counteranalysis? Notice that in this essay the theoretical passage about the Stockholm syndrome has become as much the subject of attention as the passage from *The Collector.* Notice also that in helping the writer think about the relation between the two characters, the theory proves useful even in rejection.

Of course it isn't always necessary to either accept or reject the application of a theory in its entirety. Thus, one legitimate approach to the question of whether the passage from *The Collector* conforms to the Stockholm theory is to argue both sides. But here you need to be careful. Few readers respond favorably to an analysis that seems to say, "Maybe it is, but then again maybe it isn't." If well handled, however, a two-sided approach allows you to balance one set of evidence against another, while coming to a complex but emphatic judgment. Here is the opening paragraph of one such essay:

At first sight, the passage from The Collector seems to lend itself well to the Stockholm theory. The Stockholm syndrome offers a way of understanding the mixture of anger and tenderness we see in the victim. But on more careful reading, the narrator's feelings toward her abductor cannot be explained so neatly.

Notice how this paragraph forecasts an analytical structure: First we'll see how the theory *might* be applied, and then we'll see the ways in which it doesn't work. By contrast, here's another opening that reverses these emphases, promising first to show what makes the theory and the case an ill fit and then to show an underlying similarity more important than the differences:

The relationship in The Collector is far from a classic illustration of the Stockholm syndrome. There are half a dozen ways in which the relationship between the young woman and her captor does not resemble that of the Stockholm bank robbers and their hostages. Yet the Stockholm theory does apply in one fundamental and crucial way--the formation of a strong emotional bond.

Both of these opening paragraphs promise interesting analyses. Both writers will use the perspective offered by the Stockholm theory to arrive at their own interpretations of the passage from *The Collector.*

Most of the assignments in this chapter take the form we have been demonstrating: One text serves as an object of analysis and another offers a perspective from which to analyze it. Sometimes we offer the objects first, sometimes the perspectives. As you approach the assignments, we urge you to try out strategies like those we've just described. Don't simply clamp one text on the other. See what you can say about the two texts independently; then see what you can say about one from the perspective offered by the other; then see what you can say in resistance to that view. When you've thought about your choices and tried out a few sentences, decide how you want to approach your analysis and proceed with a general plan. The key is to stay flexible in your thinking — observe, respond, question, evaluate, reconsider. Write when you're ready, but keep in mind that the act of writing will itself lead to more thinking, perhaps even to a new plan.

A Working Example from Biology

As mentioned earlier (see p. 566), you will sometimes be asked to analyze without being offered a perspective. Apparently in such cases you are free to write from whatever point of view you choose. But this apparent freedom is sometimes deceiving. Analytical assignments never come entirely free of context, and usually they are meant to draw on something specific that a class has provided. Consider the following analytical assignment from a biology exam. You are given Table 1 along with the terse instruction "Analyze the following data."

How do we find a perspective for interpreting these data, and how free are we to choose? We can tell that the experiment concerns fertilization in a species of sea urchin at various times and temperatures, but what about it? We could begin by consulting what we've learned in the course about marine animals in general or about sea urchins in particular. For example, we might know that sea urchins range widely along both coasts of North America, that they consume kelp, and that they have relatively few predators. We would also have learned that, like other marine

TABLE 1. Fertilization of Sea Urchin Eggs (*Strongylocentrotus purpuratus*) at 17°C by Sperm at Various Temperatures.

Sperm Temperature (°C)	Percent Fertilization at Elapsed Time				
	0–2 min.	2–5 min.	30 min.	60 min.	24 hr.
3	2	22	10	4	0
10	95	85	65	25	0
17	100	98	64	31	9
24	61	70	50	28	0
31	0	2	0	0	0

animals, they fertilize externally (eggs are fertilized outside the female's body). Information like this seems to go partway toward establishing a perspective, at least by orienting us to the animal under investigation. But when we look back at the table, we may see that generalizations about sea urchin behavior won't really be of much help in establishing a perspective for interpreting these particular data.

More useful will be what we've learned about how to read tables and about how experiments are designed. We would have learned, for instance, that the data presented in this table must be the results of a specific experiment designed to ask and tentatively answer a single question — a hypothesis. In looking closely at the table we will not be so much choosing *our* perspective as trying to deduce the hypothesis expressing the perspective of the experimenter. What question guided this experiment? We may not be able to tell for certain, but as we look at how the data are presented, we can close in on a few possibilities: a question about fertilization success over time, a question about fertilization success across a range of temperatures, a question about the interaction of time and temperature on fertilization success.

If we look a little more closely at how the table is set up, we can gather something more about the experiment's assumptions and expectations. Look at the row corresponding to each sperm temperature. What do you notice about 17°C? At 17°C sea urchin fertilization was more successful than at the other temperatures. Do you notice anything else? We can see that the 17°C readings occupy the central position in the rows, with two equally spaced readings above and below. Notice also from the title on the table that 17°C was the temperature at which the eggs were maintained. What do these two details imply about what the experimenter expected? Take a moment and write out what you think. What can you conclude about how we should approach the data?

Here's how one student decided to go about answering the question:

The hypothesis here seems to be that sea urchin sperm are most successful in fertilizing at 17°C; and the results seem to confirm that hypothesis. The results also suggest that as the temperature moves away from 17°C, fertilization percents decline, but not equally. Sperm colder than 17°C do better than sperm warmer than 17°C. At 10°C the youngest sperm attained 95% fertilization, whereas at 24°C the freshest sperm achieved only 61% fertilization.

Another interesting result was that the sperm in the experiment seemed to rapidly lose their fertilizing ability. Even at 17°C, only 31% of the eggs were fertilized by sperm after 60 minutes. But some fertilizing ability was retained even after 24 hours, suggesting that at the optimal temperature, fertilization is at least possible one day after sea urchins have released their sperm and eggs.

There are also some oddities in the results. One would expect the maximum fertilization to occur, across all temperatures, with the freshest sperm. But for two of the temperatures, 3°C and 24°C, the percent of fertilization is actually greater in the 2-5 minute range than in the 0-2 minute range. And at 3°C the sperm at 30 minutes were more successful (10%) than those at 0-2 minutes (2%). Does this suggest that sperm at more extreme temperatures go through some sort of "adjustment period" that lasts at least a few minutes? Even at the extremely warm 31°C, some fertilization occurred, but not instantaneously.

Overall the results confirm that sea urchin fertilization is most successful at 17°C. But the results also indicate that there isn't a narrow band of temperature within which sea urchins must fertilize. Even at extremes of temperature, some fertilization occurs--at least if sperm get to eggs fairly quickly.

This analysis succeeds not by establishing an independent perspective but by deducing the perspective from which the experiment itself was conducted. The expectation about 17°C becomes a kind of interpretive backbone for the rest of the discussion. In relation to that central observation, other trends become observable. There is plenty of freedom for the inventive observation of details once the main experimental point of view has been established. But this freedom becomes meaningful only after recognizing the basic perspective built into the table.

The success of the preceding analysis does not mean, however, that more critical approaches aren't available. One student did find a way to show some further independence. After analyzing the experiment's main results in a fashion similar to the first student, this writer moves on to look at what the data *don't* tell us. Notice how she maintains a productive skepticism by thinking about gaps in the data, odd bits of evidence, and features that might have biased the results.

These results leave me unconvinced about several points. First, there is the presumption that 17°C is the optimal temperature for sea urchin fertilization. Yet the table can't establish whether 17°C is really any better than 14°C, or even 19°C. We would have to test other temperatures between 10°C and

24°C to be confident that we were testing the optimal temperature.

Another problem is that maintaining the eggs at 17°C may have biased the results. It's possible that sperm kept at 17°C are simply more efficient in fertilizing eggs at the same temperature, without having to adjust to a temperature change. Sperm in the ocean might have to function at various temperatures, but how often would they have to adjust to a 7°C or more shift in temperature between the time they leave the male and the time they reach the eggs? This is further evidence that 17°C may not necessarily be the optimal temperature for fertilization. I suspect that sperm might be able to do equally well, or better, at lower temperatures. In fact, if we look at the data, we can see that, for several time spans, there aren't great differences between the percent fertilization at 10°C and at 17°C. In fact, at 30 minutes, the fertilization success at 10°C is even slightly higher.

Finally, what does this experiment reveal about sea urchin fertilization in nature? It's impossible to tell from this table alone how the sperm and egg were brought together, but probably the fertilization took place in laboratory glassware, not in the more chaotic ocean environment. But even under such controlled conditions, if sperm quickly lose their ability to fertilize eggs, what does that imply about the efficiency of fertilization of sea urchins in their natural habitat? Wouldn't successful fertilization be much less likely than these readings suggest? How would sea urchins even arrive at the fertilized stage in significant enough numbers to survive all the rest that will happen to them before getting the chance to mature? On the other hand, these long odds against success may explain why there is not more of a population explosion among sea urchins.

These additional paragraphs add something rare and welcome. The writer thoughtfully examines both the evidence and its limitations and also looks for ways to place the experimental results in a larger context — the sea urchins' natural environment. The writing is inventively skeptical, but also speculative and curious.

A Working Example from Political Science

Just as there are times when the object of analysis seems to get more attention than the perspective from which it is analyzed — as with the table of results in the biology experiment — there are also times when the analytical perspectives get more attention than objects of analysis. Consider the following term paper assignment from a course in political theory:

> You have been asked to read the article "Conceptual Models and the Cuban Missile Crisis" by Graham T. Allison. Write a paper that critically examines and tests the three models he describes. Which model, in your view, offers the most useful means for understanding the process of political decision making in times of crisis?

Clearly, the assignment will call for some defining, some summarizing, and some comparing. What are the three models described by Allison, and how do they differ? On what basis would we be able to declare a preference for one over the others? One possibility, of course, is that Allison himself has a preference and that we can be persuaded to demonstrate our understanding by echoing his preference. Perhaps there will be helpful clues in his article. Let's take a quick look at the three models with this question in mind: Where do Allison's own preferences lie? Here is how he describes the first, most familiar perspective.

> RATIONAL POLICY MODEL
>
> Most analysts explain (and predict) the behavior of national governments in terms of various forms of one basic conceptual model, here entitled the Rational Policy Model (Model I).
>
> In terms of this conceptual model, analysts attempt to understand happenings as the more or less purposive acts of unified national governments. For these analysts, the point of an explanation is to show how the nation or government could have chosen the action in question, given the strategic problem that it faced. For example, in confronting the problem posed by Soviet installation of missiles in Cuba, rational policy model analysts attempt to show how this was a reasonable act from the point of view of the Soviet Union, given Soviet strategic objectives. . . .
>
> What is striking about . . . the literature of foreign policy and international relations are the similarities among analysts of various styles when they are called upon to produce explanations. Each assumes that what must be explained is an action, i.e., the realization of some purpose or intention. Each assumes that the actor is the national government. Each assumes that the action is chosen as a calculated response to a strategic problem. For each, explanation consists of showing what goal the government was pursuing in committing the act and how this action was a reasonable choice, given the nation's objectives. This set of assumptions characterizes the rational policy model. . . .

Notice the hints in this description that Allison is dissatisfied with this conventional way of looking at political decision making. The opening phrasing "Most analysts explain . . ." suggests that other analysts have other, better explanations. Then in the next sentence (see the phrasing "analysts attempt to understand . . .") the word "attempt" underscores the potential inadequacy of this model, as does the insistent repetition of the word "assumes" in subsequent sentences.

How does Allison seem to feel about the second model he describes?

ORGANIZATIONAL PROCESS MODEL

A "government" consists of a conglomerate of semifeudal, loosely allied organizations, each with a substantial life of its own. Government leaders do sit formally, and to some extent in fact, on top of this conglomerate. But governments perceive problems through organizational sensors. Governments define alternatives and estimate consequences as organizations process information. Governments act as these organizations enact routines. Government behavior can therefore be understood according to a second conceptual model, less as deliberate choices of leaders and more as *outputs* of large organizations functioning according to standard patterns of behavior.

To be responsive to a broad spectrum of problems, governments consist of large organizations among which primary responsibility for particular areas is divided. Each organization attends to a special set of problems and acts in quasi-independence on these problems. But few important problems fall exclusively within the domain of a single organization. Thus government behavior relevant to any important problem reflects the independent output of several organizations, partially coordinated by government leaders. Government leaders can substantially disturb, but not substantially control, the behavior of these organizations.

To perform complex routines, the behavior of large numbers of individuals must be coordinated. Coordination requires standard operating procedures: rules according to which things are done. Assured capability for reliable performance of action that depends upon the behavior of hundreds of persons requires established "programs." Indeed, if the eleven members of a football team are to perform adequately on any particular down, each player must not "do what he thinks needs to be done" or "do what the quarterback tells him to do." Rather, each player must perform the maneuvers specified by a previously established play which the quarterback has simply called in this situation.

At any given time, a government consists of *existing* organizations, each with a *fixed* set of standard operating procedures and programs. The behavior of these organizations — and consequently of the government — relevant to an issue in any particular instance is, therefore, determined primarily by routines established in these organizations prior to that instance. But organizations do change. Learning occurs gradually, over time. Dramatic organizational change occurs in response to major crises. Both learning and change are influenced by existing organizational capabilities. . . .

Compared with the first perspective, this one seems startling, doesn't it? The "government" involved in the decision making seems to resemble some vast machine. (Which phrases contribute to this impression?) Notice that in describing this model, Allison does not use such phrases as "many analysts assume. . . ." Evidently this idea is less familiar, one he would like us to consider before exercising our skepticism. Nevertheless, in his final sentences, he seems to be calling attention to something brittle and inflexible about the way this model accounts for things: "the behavior of these organizations . . . is . . . determined primarily by routines," but political crises often call for new solutions to problems. Allison wants us to entertain this fresh perspective without submitting to it completely.

Allison then goes on to offer a third perspective.

> BUREAUCRATIC POLITICS MODEL
>
> The leaders who sit on top of organizations are not a monolithic group. Rather, each is, in his own right, a player in a central, competitive game. The name of the game is bureaucratic politics: bargaining along regularized channels among players positioned hierarchically within the government. Government behavior can thus be understood according to a third conceptual model not as organizational outputs, but as outcomes of bargaining games. In contrast with Model I, the bureaucratic politics model sees no unitary actor but rather many actors as players, who focus not on a single strategic issue but on many diverse intranational problems as well, in terms of no consistent set of strategic objectives, but rather according to various conceptions of national, organizational, and personal goals, making government decisions not by rational choice but by the pulling and hauling that is politics.
>
> The apparatus of each national government constitutes a complex arena for the intranational game. Political leaders at the top of this apparatus plus the men who occupy positions on top of the critical organizations form the circle of central players. Ascendancy to this circle assures some independent standing. The necessary decentralization of decisions required for action on the broad range of foreign policy problems guarantees that each player has considerable discretion. Thus power is shared.
>
> The nature of problems of foreign policy permits fundamental disagreement among reasonable men concerning what ought to be done. Analyses yield conflicting recommendations. Separate responsibilities laid on the shoulders of individual personalities encourage differences in perceptions and priorities. But the issues are of first order importance. What the nation does really matters. A wrong choice could mean irreparable damage. Thus responsible men are obliged to fight for what they are convinced is right.
>
> Men share power. Men differ concerning what must be done. The differences matter. This milieu necessitates that policy be resolved by politics. What the nation does is sometimes the result of the triumph of one group over others. More often, however, different groups pulling in different directions yield a resultant distinct from what anyone intended. What moves the chess pieces is not simply the reasons which support a course of action, nor the routines of organizations which enact an alternative, but the power and skill of proponents and opponents of the action in question.

Notice how Allison's final sentence is designed to reorient us toward the three models. The "not . . . nor . . . but . . ." structure conveys Allison's theoretical preferences: "What moves the chess pieces is not simply the reasons which support a course of action [Rational Policy Model], nor the routines of organizations which enact an alternative [Organizational Process Model] but the power and skill of proponents and opponents of the action in question [Bureaucratic Politics Model]." This third model, then, is the one to which Allison wants to give most stress. It's not that the first two perspectives lack explanatory power; it's that this last model can explain more.

Having worked through Allison's text in this way, we are better equipped to see where the theoretical differences lie — and where Allison himself stands. We might also judge from the title of his article that he has undertaken this three-part discussion in order to then argue for the importance of his Bureaucratic Politics Model in understanding the Cuban Missile Crisis of 1963.

But where does this leave us in *our* assignment? Will it be enough simply to paraphrase the three models, demonstrating that we understand the differences among them, and then go on to rehash what Allison demonstrates about bureaucratic politics during the Cuban Missile Crisis? No, it won't. The full analytical request lies embedded back in the wording of the assignment: "Write a paper that critically examines and *tests* . . ." How do we test a model? It won't be enough merely to summarize Allison's findings about the Cuban Missile Crisis. Evidently, we are being asked to locate some other political crisis, one we can research, and to decide if one or another of the three models best fits. The work we've done in sorting through the three models helps, but we're just getting started. The success of the paper — and we're now beginning to see why it was called a *term* paper — will depend on our locating a crisis that we can read about in enough detail to evaluate how well the models seem to work in a case other than the Cuban Missile Crisis. We have been given the responsibility of choosing a crisis to analyze — and of discovering one that leads us back to "critically examine" the usefulness of the three models. If you actually had to do this assignment, how would you proceed to find a crisis to analyze (The Gulf War? The Bosnian crisis? The intervention in Haiti?), and how would you decide whether you have the basis for writing about it analytically?

A Professional Application

In the following passage, writer and researcher Catherine A. Sunshine discusses the ways in which Caribbean culture expresses both "synthesis and resistance."

By "synthesis" she means that Caribbean cultural forms — such as language, family, religion, music — show the combined influences of the many groups that have populated the Caribbean: African, Indian, European, Asian, North American. By "resistance" she means that Caribbean cultures have also found ways to prevent the colonial and postcolonial powers that have dominated the region politically and economically (chiefly Europe and the United States) from also dominating those cultural forms. In this stretch of analysis Sunshine looks at how this double pattern of synthesis and resistance can be found in the festival of Carnival and in calypso. As you read this passage, notice how Sunshine works to keep the two parts of her analytical framework in sight. Note the repetition, for instance, of the term "synthesis" along with many related words: "merged," "combines," "absorbed," "blending," "incorporated," "unifying." Then note the many "resistance" words: "undercurrent," "fought back," "subversive," "social protest," "rebelliousness." Notice, too, how her well-chosen quotations support and vitalize her analysis.

From *The Caribbean: Survival, Struggle, and Sovereignty*

CATHERINE A. SUNSHINE

SYNTHESIS AND RESISTANCE

[One] theme which marks Caribbean cultures is synthesis: the blending of diverse cultural elements into new, original forms. The merger of Africa and Europe is at the root of Caribbean cultures. Other strong influences include India, Latin America, and the United States.

Carnival provides a rich example of this process. In colonial Trinidad, the French Catholic elite celebrated the pre-Lenten season with masked balls and parades. Black Trinidadians had their own "Canboulay" celebrations commemorating emancipation from slavery. Eventually these traditions merged into the Carnival of today.

> From its opening moment of *jour ouvert* and the "ole mas" costume bands to its finale, forty-eight hours later, in the dusk of Mardi Carnival, the Trinidadian populace gives itself up to the "jump up," the tempestuous abandon of Carnival. . . . Port of Spain becomes a panic of mob art: the Sailor Bands, sometimes of 5,000 or more . . . the Seabees groups, mocking their original United States Navy inspiration with their exaggerated high-ranking officer titles and overblown campaign ribbons . . . impertinent personifications of, variously, Texas Rangers, French Foreign Legionnaires, British Palace Guards, and Nazi High Command officers . . .[1]

And underneath it all runs "a powerful undercurrent of Shango, bamboo-tamboo, canboulay[2]— the African traditions in Caribbean culture."[3]

The West Indian music known as calypso provides another example of creative synthesis. Originating in Trinidad in the 1800s, calypso has roots in the African oral tradition. Early lyrics were in French Creole, then shifted to English toward the end of the century. Musical influences on calypso included French and Spanish music, East Indian drumming, and black Revivalist spirituals. During World War II, with hundreds of U.S. troops in Trinidad, calypso absorbed influences from rhythm and blues, swing and bebop, along with an increasing degree of commercialism.

The same blending process underlies the Afro-Latin cultures. The *merengue* of the Dominican Republic was originated by the peasantry using drums and other African instruments. Middle and upper class Dominicans scorned the merengue, preferring to

[1]Gordon K. Lewis, *The Growth of the Modern West Indies* (New York: Monthly Review Press, 1968), pp. 30–31.

[2]**Shango:** A cult in which Yoruban gods (especially Shango, a god of thunder) are worshipped and called upon to help individuals, families, or communities; *bamboo-tamboo:* the knocking together of joints of bamboo in celebration of Carnival (from the French *tambour bambou,* or "bamboo drum," the predecessor of the steel drum now used by calypso bands); *canboulay:* the carrying of lighted torches and beating of drums to celebrate the emancipation of slaves. Eventually the canboulay celebrations for Emancipation Day (August 1) were transferred to mark the opening of Carnival [Eds.].

[3]Gordon K. Lewis, *The Growth of the Modern West Indies,* pp. 31–32.

CATHERINE A. SUNSHINE (b. 1953) is a U.S.-born writer and researcher with a special interest in the Caribbean. She is editor of *Caribbean Connections,* a series of anthologies for secondary schools, and is working on a forthcoming volume in a series about Caribbean migration to the United States. This excerpt is taken from her book *The Caribbean: Survival, Struggle, and Sovereignty* (1985, revised 1988).

dance the waltz. But gradually, a change occurred: Spanish instruments such as the *tres* and *cuatro,* the accordion and the *bandoneón* were incorporated into merengue alongside the drums. This Europeanized merengue was called *merengue de salón* — parlor merengue — and was popular with town-dwellers. Merengue is now a national passion spanning all classes in the Dominican Republic.

Closely connected to the theme of synthesis is the theme of culture as resistance which runs through Caribbean history. By borrowing elements of culture and transforming them, Caribbean people fought back against cultural domination. This often is expressed in satire, as in the ribald parodies of Carnival. The Jonkonuu parade which once flourished in Jamaica, Belize, and the Bahamas combines African elements such as the horsehead, cowhead, and devil costumes with grotesque masked caricatures of British royalty. Such irreverent humor has its roots in the slavery era, when one form of slave resistance was subtle mockery of the ruling class.

In West Indian cultural resistance, the drum has always held pride of place. Drums were used in Africa for long-distance communication, and slaves on the plantations continued this practice. Fearful of slave revolts, the planters outlawed the drum. After emancipation, the planters and missionaries banned drumming as subversive and an obstacle to the assimilation of the blacks. But they could never totally suppress it. In 1884 riots broke out in Port of Spain when the colonial authorities banned the use of drums for Carnival.

The ban on drumming gave rise to a substitute known as *bamboo-tamboo,* the practice of beating out rhythms on the ground with cured sticks. In the late 1930s, young men in the urban slums of Trinidad turned to using metal biscuit tins and old oil drums, and the modern steelband — "pan" — was born. . . .

CALYPSO: VOICE OF THE SMALL MAN

In the eyes of the outside world, two cultural phenomena have come to represent the Caribbean and symbolize the vibrancy of its culture. Both have their origins in the West Indian working class: reggae / Rastafarianism, originating in Jamaica, and carnival / calypso, originating in Trinidad. Although strongest in their countries of origin, both of these cultural "complexes" have spread throughout the Caribbean and are claimed by West Indians as the region's original creations.

Calypso is one of the earliest authentic West Indian art forms. It is rooted in the African oral tradition, in which songs of praise or derision were sung as a form of pointed social comment. In the modern Caribbean, calypso serves as the "voice of the small man," who enjoys a vicarious social protest through the scathing commentary of the calypsonian. The dominant characteristics of calypso are wit (preferably spicy), colorful language, and opinionated reference to social or political events of the day. For instance, a calypso composed in the 1930s commented on the abdication of Edward VIII from the British throne.

Believe me, friends, if I were King
I'd marry any woman and give her a ring
I wouldn't give a damn what the people say
So long as she can wash, cook, and dingolay.

Many calypsos were banned by the colonial authorities in the 1930s for being "profane." Although sex was a popular topic, what the authorities actually objected to was the boldness of calypsonians in mocking and embarrassing the ruling class. A 1950 calypso by the Growling Tiger, for example, broke social taboos by denouncing the misdeeds of a British expatriate official in Trinidad.

The Assistant Director of Education
He found himself in confusion
Drunk and driving his motor car
Dangerous to the public, what behavior!
He is a disgrace to my native land
So the public should demand his resignation.

Calypso's unifying power comes from its effectiveness as a means of mass communication. The most popular numbers receive air play all over the region, informing people in other territories of current issues in the country where the song originates. While the official version of events is contained in the news media, the average person's interpretation (which may be quite different) is publicized through the calypso.

Calypso is closely linked to Carnival, the festival held in the days leading up to Lent. Carnival is biggest in Trinidad, but also is traditional in Grenada, St. Vincent, Antigua, Aruba, and Brazil. The Carnival season begins in January with the opening of the calypso tents. Here the public gets to hear the season's new crop of calypsos and size up contenders for the title of Calypso Monarch. In the "pan yards," steel bands rehearse for their competition, which in Trinidad's past often took the form of a violent clash. The climax comes on the two days before Ash Wednesday. Sunday night is "Dimanche Gras,"[4] when the Calypso King and Queen are chosen. In the dawn hours of Monday morning begins J'Ouvert (*jour ouvert,* or open day), when costumed masqueraders converge on Port of Spain for two days of unbroken revelry.

> Up on the Hill Carnival Monday morning breaks upon the backs of these tin shacks with no cock's crow, and before the mist clears, little boys, costumed in old dresses, their heads tied, holding brooms made from the ribs of coconut palm leaves, blowing whistles and beating kerosene tins for drums, move across the face of the awakening Hill, sweeping yards in a ritual, heralding the masqueraders' coming, that goes back centuries for its beginnings, back across the Middle Passage, back to Mali and Guinea and Dahomey and Congo, back to Africa where Maskers were sacred and revered. . . .
>
> The music burst forth from the steelband; shouts went up, and the steelband and the masqueraders . . . the robbers and the Indians and the clowns — the whole Hill began moving down upon Port of Spain. . . .
>
> — From *The Dragon Can't Dance* by Earl Lovelace
> (Essex: Longman Group Ltd., 1969)

Carnival has become more commercialized since the 1960s, losing some of its original spirit of rebelliousness and mock violence. In becoming a major tourist attraction, however, it also has become a Caribbean unifier, as people from the other islands and from Caribbean communities abroad flock to Trinidad for the yearly event.

[4]**Dimanche Gras:** Fat Sunday [Eds.].

Assignments

A Psychology Assignment

Read the following newspaper story, and as you do, ask yourself about the gunman's possible motivations. What could drive someone to take a hostage and then to take one's own life? Then read the passage by Martin E. P. Seligman, a psychologist who is interested in conditions that can lead to feelings of helplessness and depression.

This excerpt is not easy to understand, but you'll find it helpful to read it once and then to go back and ask yourself what connections Seligman establishes among *traumatic event, fear, helplessness, depression,* and *competence.* You might want to jot these connections on paper. You might also want to try to apply Seligman's theory to your own experience: Can you think of events in your own life, and your own reactions to them, that could support or qualify his theory?

Write a short essay in which you consider to what extent the incident reported in the article "Gunman Kills Himself After Hostage Drama" can (or cannot) be understood in terms of Seligman's theory of helplessness.

Gunman Kills Himself After Hostage Drama

CHARLES P. WALLACE AND TIM WATERS

A night-long siege and hostage drama in a Hollywood hotel room ended early Saturday when a twenty-six-year-old gunman killed himself. He apparently was depressed over having multiple sclerosis.

No one else was injured by the gunman, whose seventeen-year-old hostage was grabbed by police officers and pulled to safety minutes before he committed suicide.

The tense drama was played out in a twenty-second floor room of Holiday Inn in the heart of Hollywood, forcing the evacuation of guests from three floors and from a busy nightclub in the building.

The gunman, armed with a rifle, was identified by police as Robert B. Rose of Leucadia, a town about thirty miles north of San Diego. The hostage was not identified.

Rose's mother, Mary, said after the incident that her son had been under intensive psychiatric care for a number of years. She said he learned in January that he had multiple sclerosis, a disease of the central nervous system.

"I think this was sort of the last straw as far as he was concerned," she said.

Police said Rose checked into the hotel late Saturday night, went out, returned with the seventeen-year-old girl, and went to his room.

There, a police department statement said, he pointed the rifle at the girl, threatened her life, warned that he would commit suicide, and ordered her to take off her clothes. When she did, he threw the clothing out the window.

Shots were fired from the window at about 11:15 PM. By coincidence, amateur radio operators from a group known as EARS were on the roof of the building at the time as part of a new program to help the police keep watch in high-crime areas of Hollywood.

They reported the shooting to the police, who closed off the top of the hotel, evacuated the other guests, and summoned the Special Weapons and Tactics team.

Guests waited out the confrontations in the lobby, many wearing pajamas and wrapped in blankets.

CHARLES P. WALLACE (b. 1950) is a journalist living in Washington, D.C., and TIM WATERS (b. 1952) currently works in public affairs for the Washington Department of Wildlife. This article appeared in the *Los Angeles Times* on May 10, 1981.

Most appeared to be foreign tourists. They were startled by the sudden arrival of scores of police officers, some carrying automatic rifles, and house detectives from the hotel.

"It's just like that television program, SWAT," said John Edwards, a tourist from Perth, Australia.

During telephone negotiations between the police and the girl, Rose reportedly asked to see a Roman Catholic priest and have food brought to the room.

A pizza was left outside the barricaded room. Rose, according to police, forced the girl, then wearing only a towel, to pick it up. When the girl stepped outside, she was grabbed by officer Donnelley D. Mowry and pulled to safety.

Police said Rose pointed his rifle at other officers in the corridor. The police fired one shot and Rose retreated, closed the door, and fired four times. The police returned fire and one shot apparently grazed Rose's chest.

At 2:00 AM, police heard a gunshot in the room. Three hours later, after using tear gas, police stormed the room and found Rose dead. They said he shot himself in the mouth.

Rose's mother said she last talked to her son on Monday. He told her that he was living with a friend in Los Angeles and driving a taxi.

Rose, the youngest of five children, was a "very brilliant young man and a very depressed man," she said.

His mother, who learned of the incident when a friend told her husband about hearing a news account on the radio, said she is thankful that no one else was injured.

PERSPECTIVE

On Learned Helplessness

MARTIN E. P. SELIGMAN

When a traumatic event first occurs, it causes a heightened state of emotionality that can loosely be called fear. This state continues until one of two things happens: If the subject learns that he can control the trauma, fear is reduced and may disappear altogether; or if the subject finally learns he cannot control the trauma, fear will decrease and be replaced with depression.

For example, when a rat, a dog, or a man experiences inescapable trauma he first struggles frantically. Fear, I believe, is the dominant emotion accompanying this state. If he learns to control the trauma, frenetic activity gives way to an efficient and nonchalant response. If the trauma is uncontrollable, however, struggling eventually gives way to the helpless state I have described. The emotion that accompanies this state is, I believe, depression. Similarly, when an infant monkey is separated from its mother, great distress is produced by the traumatic experience. The monkey runs around frantically, making distress calls. Two things can happen: If the mother returns, the infant can now control her again, and distress will cease; or if the mother does not return, the infant eventually

---

Psychologist MARTIN E. P. SELIGMAN (b. 1942) has studied the conditions that can lead to feelings of helplessness and depression. He is the author of *Learned Optimism* (1991), *What You Can Change & What You Can't* (1993), and *The Optimistic Child* (1995). His *Helplessness: On Depression, Development, and Death,* excerpted here, was published in 1975.

learns that it cannot bring mother back, and depression ensues, displacing the fear. The infant curls up in a ball and whines. Such a sequence is in fact what happens in all primate species that have been observed. . . .

Many theorists have talked about the need or drive to master events in the environment. In a classic exposition, R. W. White proposed the concept of *competence.* He argued that the basic drive for control had been overlooked by learning theorists and psychoanalytic thinkers alike. The need to master could be more pervasive than sex, hunger, and thirst in the lives of animals and men. Play in young children, for example, is motivated not by "biological" drives, but by a competence drive. . . .

A drive for competence . . . is, from my point of view, a drive to avoid helplessness. The existence of such a drive follows directly from the emotional premise of our theory. Since being helpless arouses fear and depression, activity that avoids helplessness thereby avoids these aversive emotional states. Competence may be a drive to avoid the fear and depression induced by helplessness.

An Education Assignment

The following passage comes from a historical study by Harvey J. Graff; in it he suggests that literacy instruction in school had purposes other than simply developing the ability to read and write. The passage is somewhat difficult, so don't be surprised if you have to read it more than once. When you reread it, you might find it helpful to ask yourself the following questions:

- Graff's passage contains several quotations; what sort of position in society would you think is held by the speaker of those lines?
- Graff seems to agree that literacy might make a worker "more skilled, more knowledgeable about his work," but then adds "but only partly so." Why does he qualify what seems like a good thing?
- In what ways might instruction in literacy have more than one purpose?

PERSPECTIVE

The Moral Basis of Literacy Instruction

HARVEY J. GRAFF

Literacy's benefits were primarily social and integrating, and only rarely connected with job pursuits. Nonetheless, literacy could be essential, for the promise of the school had to be conveyed: "Every man, unless he wishes to starve outright, must read and write, and cast accounts, and speak his native tongue well enough to attend to his own partic-

Professor of history and humanities at the University of Texas at Dallas, HARVEY J. GRAFF (b. 1949) has written and edited numerous books on literacy and its history, including *The Literacy Myth: Literacy and Social Structure in the Nineteenth Century City* (1979), *The Labyrinths of Literacy* (1987), and *The Legacies of Literacy* (1987), which won a Critics Choice Award from the American Educational Studies Association. The two lessons come from nineteenth-century schoolbooks.

ular business." These were ominous tones, but the implications of these needs were nowhere elaborated: Did the individual benefits from the everyday uses of literacy make the worker more skilled, more knowledgeable about his work? Yes, but only partly so; educated labor, it was claimed, was more productive than uneducated labor. The educated mechanic was not disruptive; he was superior because he was orderly, punctual, and content.

These moral functions of schooling intersected with work in another way, too. Schooling had the additional important task of assuring that manual workers did not aspire to rise above their station in life. Farmers or agricultural workers, for example, must be educated *not* to view their activities as narrow or regard them with contempt and disgust; they were not to be schooled so that they would want to leave their work, "in order to attain to a position of importance and influence." Education meant the cultivation of the workers (that is, if properly conducted) not the alienation of them from their positions.

Now move on to Figures 1 and 2: a vocabulary lesson and a penmanship lesson, both from nineteenth-century schoolbooks. Take a moment and look at them. One has a set of nine words, all of which are then used in the sentences immediately below them; the other has words and lines that the student has to copy. As you look at these lessons, quickly jot down any thoughts or impressions that

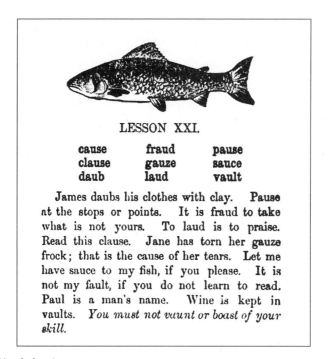

LESSON XXI.

cause	**fraud**	**pause**
clause	**gauze**	**sauce**
daub	**laud**	**vault**

James daubs his clothes with clay. Pause at the stops or points. It is fraud to take what is not yours. To laud is to praise. Read this clause. Jane has torn her gauze frock; that is the cause of her tears. Let me have sauce to my fish, if you please. It is not my fault, if you do not learn to read. Paul is a man's name. Wine is kept in vaults. *You must not vaunt or boast of your skill.*

FIGURE 1. A Vocabulary Lesson.

Source: First Book of Lessons, for the Use of Schools, authorized by the Council of Public Instruction for Upper Canada. Series of National Books, Montreal and Toronto: James Campbell and Sons, 1867, pp. 28–29. [Records and Archives Centre, Toronto Board of Education]

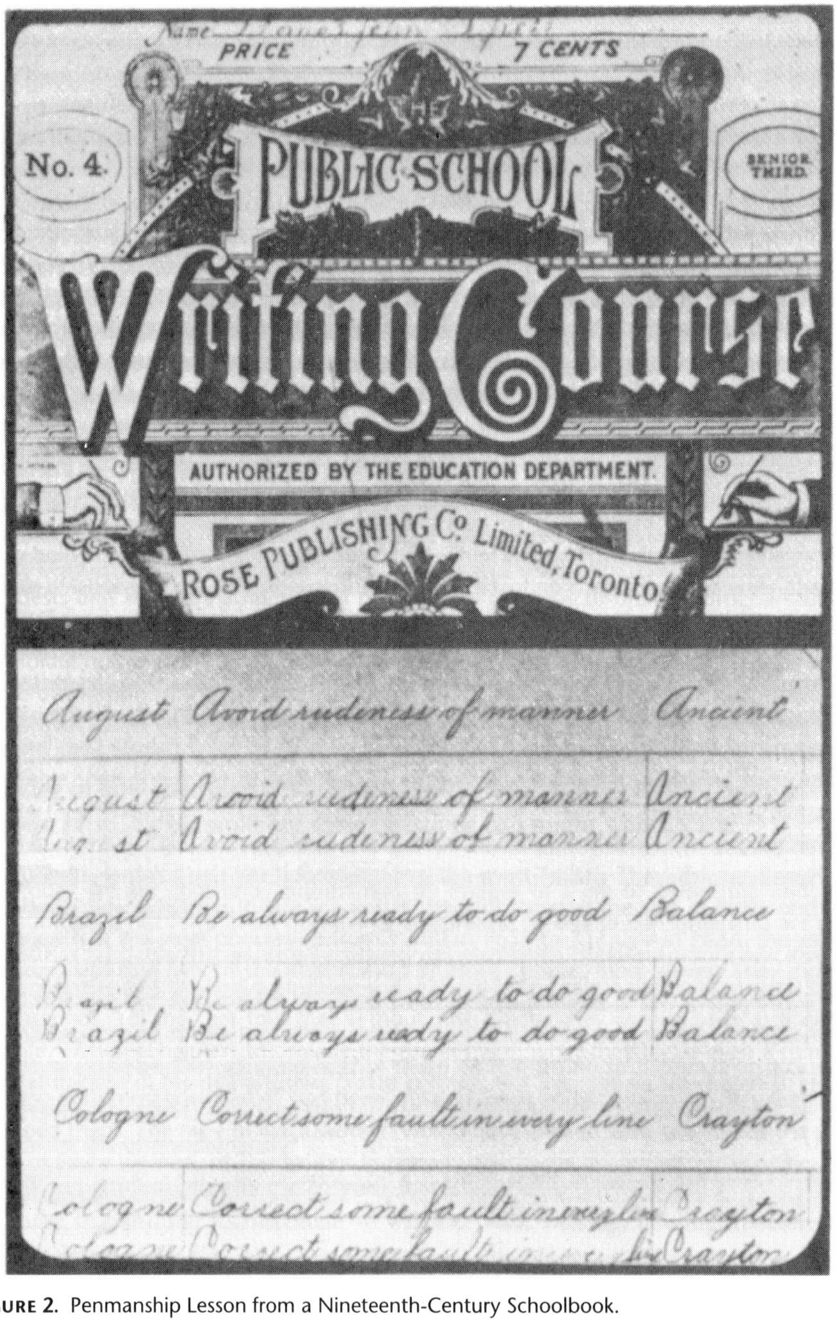

FIGURE 2. Penmanship Lesson from a Nineteenth-Century Schoolbook.

come to mind — anything at all. Then in a short essay, apply the perspective on literacy instruction provided by Harvey J. Graff to these examples drawn from a literacy curriculum. What does his perspective help you understand about the lessons?

An Economics Assignment

In the following excerpt, economist Trevor M. A. Farrell theorizes about decolonization, the process by which a former colony arrives at political and economic autonomy. Farrell wants to distinguish between genuine decolonization, whereby a nation and its people achieve a true measure of self-determination, and decolonization in name only, wherein a former colony and its people, despite appearances, remain subservient to foreign interests. Notice that Farrell begins his discussion of decolonization by quoting a classic definition of colonialism. After reading his observations, you will be asked to use them as an analytical frame for a description of the tourist economy in the Caribbean.

PERSPECTIVE

Decolonization in the English-Speaking Caribbean

TREVOR M. A. FARRELL

In the nineteenth century, John Stuart Mill enunciated what is still one of the best, frankest, and most succinct descriptions of what a colonial relationship is about, a definition which permits one to see the essence of the colonial condition. In his *Principles of Political Economy,* Mill declared: "If Manchester, instead of being where it is, were on a rock in the North Sea . . . it would still be but a town of England, not a country trading with England: It would be merely, as now, the place where England finds it convenient to carry on her cotton manufactures. The West Indies, in like manner, are the place where England finds it convenient to carry on the production of sugar, coffee, and a few other tropical commodities. All the capital employed is English capital; almost all the industry is carried on for English uses; there is little production of anything except the staple commodities, and these are sent to England, not to be exchanged for things exported to the colony and consumed by its inhabitants, but to be sold in England for the benefit of the proprietors there."

The essence of the colonial condition is twofold. First, the organization of the resources of the colonized is effected in the interests of the alien, colonizing power, rather than in the interests of the colonized. . . .

Second, colonialism fundamentally implies the lack of control over the dynamic of

---

TREVOR M. A. FARRELL is a professor of economics at the University of the West Indies in Trinidad and Tobago. Excerpted here is his article "Decolonization in the English-Speaking Caribbean," which appeared in *The Newer Caribbean: Decolonization, Democracy, and Development* (1983).

one's own movement or development (whether political, economic, or cultural). Herein lies an essential difference between dependence and interdependence or even ordinary, relative weakness vis-à-vis another country. The classic colony is unable to make its own decisions, to choose how to adjust to a given configuration on the international scene. Its response is dictated or tightly circumscribed by the dominating power.

At a technical minimum in assessing decolonization one has therefore to focus on two fundamental issues: In whose interests, preponderantly, are a country's resources organized, and to what extent is a country in control of its own dynamic.

Now that you've read Farrell's generalizations about decolonization, consider the following description of the tourist economy of the Caribbean, where the various island nations are former European colonies. The excerpts below are from *Last Resorts: The Cost of Tourism in the Caribbean* by journalist Polly Pattullo. Pattullo first describes the influence of three "key players" in the tourist industry: airlines, tour operators, and hotels. She then goes on to describe the employment opportunities generated by tourism.

When you have reread these excerpts from Pattullo and looked back at the discussion of decolonization by Farrell, write an essay on whether tourism in the Caribbean, as presented by Pattullo, illustrates decolonization. Keep in mind that you don't have enough information to answer this question in a definitive way, but you can make a judgment about how the information presented by Pattullo would be regarded from a perspective like Farrell's.

If you are interested in the subject of cultural politics in the Caribbean, you may want to do this assignment in coordination with the related material in the Opening Problem (p. 557), the Professional Application (p. 580), and Readings: Caribbean Literature and Cultural Politics (p. 623).

From *Last Resorts: The Cost of Tourism in the Caribbean*

POLLY PATTULLO

THE AIRLINES

It was the introduction of the long-haul jet aeroplane in the early 1960s which transformed the Caribbean, bringing it within reach, both technologically and financially, of the ordinary holiday-maker. Every day of the year, airport departure boards in Miami, New York, London, Paris, Toronto, and Amsterdam flash up Caribbean destinations — Montego Bay, Nassau, Antigua, Fort de France, and so on.

Yet for the most part it is not Caribbean-owned airlines which shuttle to the sun. In

---

POLLY PATTULLO (b. 1946) writes for the *Guardian* newspaper in London and for *Caribbean Insight,* a political and economic monthly. She also works for Co-operation for Development, a British development agency. Her publications include *Women and Work* (with Lindsay Mackie, 1977), *Power and Prejudice* (with Anna Coote, 1990), and *Last Resorts: The Cost of Tourism in the Caribbean* (1996), from which this excerpt is taken.

1992, foreign airlines controlled nearly three-quarters of the seats to the region, with American Airlines alone picking up more than half of those seats. American Airlines, KLM, British Airways, Air France (the last three reflecting old colonial links), and foreign-owned charter companies dominate the Caribbean skies. In contrast, regional airlines get a tiny slice of the schedules. In 1991, nine regional airways (Air Aruba, ALM, Air Jamaica, Bahamasair, BWIA, Cayman Airways, Guyana Airways, LIAT, and Surinam Airways) scrambled around for just 29 percent of seats from the United States, 19 percent of seats from Canada, and 15 percent from Europe. These small, under-equipped, state-owned regional airlines are not only outclassed by the international carriers, but, in their struggle to survive, they lose phenomenal amounts of money. In 1992, for example, Air Jamaica's operating deficit totaled U.S. $5 million.

The effect was, as the Economist Intelligence Unit report pointed out in 1993, that the regional airlines were "at the mercy of the major airline blocks of North America and Europe." In addition, said the Unit, the collapse of PanAm, TWA, and Eastern Airlines meant that the Caribbean was dangerously dependent on American Airlines, a situation which was causing "great concern."

This vulnerability means that the big suppliers cannot only elbow out smaller airlines but, through their market power, can also decide route strategies (developing "hubs" such as Puerto Rico was a favorite device in the 1980s), schedules, and fares, and control reservation systems. For example, it was a blow to Trinidad when British Airways announced its withdrawal of direct flights to Port of Spain in 1994; and in 1995 St. Lucia suffered when American Airlines decided to drop two of its weekend flights out of New York.

British Airways has traditionally played tough in its routing strategy. In 1985, in a secret deal with the Antiguan government, it paid U.S. $280,000 for exclusive rights to the London–Antigua route, thereby denying landing rights to BWIA, the region's only locally owned airline flying to Europe. This arrangement ended in 1992, and by then BWIA had managed to expand into continental Europe, gaining a foothold in Zurich and Frankfurt. Yet those routes remained vulnerable, never more so than in late 1994, when rumors spread that BWIA's new private-sector American owners were planning to axe the European routes. In the event, reassurances were given that the routes were safe, to the relief of St. Lucia and Grenada especially, both heavily dependent on a growing European trade.

Plans for the Caribbean region to pool resources and amalgamate their own airlines "to make use of economies of scale instead of being burdened by them" and to counter the giant international carriers have not been successful. In 1993, a modest proposal by the CTO[1] for regional airlines to collaborate in a number of areas to save U.S. $64 million a year was barely discussed by a Caricom[2] heads of state meeting. Plans to merge BWIA and Air Jamaica, with British Airways as the "strategic partner" management interest, failed in 1994, and before the year was out both airlines had been privatized. Only Air Jamaica remained solely in Caribbean hands, bought by Butch Stewart of Sandals Resorts. . . .

Foreign interests have continued to proliferate in the air despite the warning of the

[1]**CTO:** Caribbean Tourism Organization [Eds.].

[2]**Caricom:** Caribbean Community, a thirteen-member organization representing the English-speaking countries [Eds.].

West Indian Commission's *Time for Action.* As the report put it in its understated style, the "provision of those services must not become wholly a matter of chance, depending on calculations and decisions made elsewhere in response to considerations far removed from the goals and objectives of West Indian integration."

THE TOUR OPERATORS

If foreign airlines decide the routes, the schedules, and the prices (flights have never been cheap), the tour operators and wholesalers play another crucial role. Like the airlines, the tour operators are largely foreign-owned. Based in the cities of North America and Europe, they put together the component parts which make up a holiday. They select the flights, choose the hotels, organize ground transportation and day trips. Sometimes these services are sold by travel agents broken into small sectors; more usually they come as one giant prepacked, beribboned offering.

Tour operators deal in volume, negotiating with the airline for "allocations," seats by the planeload, organizing charter flights and booking "block off" hotel rooms by the floor. They get good prices for large volume sales and drive a hard bargain for the best deals. Their control over the package holiday means that independent travelers to the Caribbean often find it hard to get an airline seat (the tour operators buy "allocations" and until they release them, flights register as full).

The mass market tour operators concentrate on the larger hotels, linking them into on-line reservations systems. In the 1990/91 season, for example, more than 200 of the Caribbean's largest hotels tapped into the U.S. wholesalers' tour programs, of which thirty-three were in Jamaica, twenty-seven in the Bahamas, and twenty-three in Barbados. Indeed, in such a competitive climate, the smaller hotels have found it difficult to work outside this network, and only in 1995 did the CTO introduce a scheme to link them into a booking system with tour operators.

Tour operators are tough negotiators and put pressure on hotels to increase their discounts, especially in lean years and in the off-season. This is especially true for the smallest hotels, the majority of which tend to be locally owned and can least afford to have their profit margins reduced. Winnie Charles turned her family home into the Golden Beach Hotel on the south coast of Barbados in 1980. Her experience with her twenty-six–room business is typical of small hoteliers. "Tour operators beat you down. They say they can get their price at another hotel so you have to reduce your rates. Some of them are greedy. We feel the small hotels should all agree to a rate and stick to it but it doesn't happen." . . .

Like the airlines, the power of the tour operators lies in their ability to direct the flow of the tourist trade. At the same time, they have the power to withdraw it. "This is an important chain," says the acting Airtours manager in Barbados, Helen Williams. "We are in a very powerful position. It's a strong hotelier who turns us down. My job is to make sure that the hoteliers don't go elsewhere." Airtours, on the other hand, is free to go where it likes. The company, which has a tougher reputation than most other British tour operators, started a program in the Dominican Republic in 1989, but stopped for what it described as "purely commercial" reasons. It also expanded to Cuba in 1994, but did not repeat its program there the next year, again for "commercial reasons."

Airtours' first foray into the Caribbean was to Barbados in 1987 when it provided a Caribbean holiday (£299 for fourteen nights, room only) for economy-conscious English tourists. Peter Odle, president of the Barbados Hotel Association, had been responsible for first inviting Airtours to Barbados to help boost the summer occupancy rate. "I cut the first deal with them. We had no summer business." According to Mr. Odle, "Airtours promised to increase its rates after the first season when it offered dog-cheap rates of U.S. $22–25. Then in the second season, it played one hotel off against another and didn't give an increase. They have no loyalty to anyone."

While tour operators spread their business into new islands, packaging ever more varied holidays, the financial deals take place in the metropolitan cities. As was pointed out in *The Other Side of Paradise* [by Tom Barry, Beth Wood, and Deb Preusch]: "Owing to the transnational nature of the business, payments for services actually delivered in the Caribbean go directly to the New York headquarters of Sheraton or Hertz, never even passing through agency offices in Jamaica or the Dominican Republic."

Yet, as a small Caribbean-based travel agent explains: "Tour operators contract directly with hotels, with airlines, and with ground operators. We couldn't do without them. They are the most important people in the business." And a hotel owner in St. Lucia concedes: "Tour operators are tough. You can't make it without the tour operators because they control the airline seats. You have to court them."

THE HOTELS

So if Caribbean hotels depend on foreign-owned airlines and tour operators, who owns the hotels themselves?

In 1989 around 63 percent of the region's rooms were owned by foreigners. In some countries, the percentage was even higher: St. Maarten, Anguilla, and the Caymans (82 percent); Antigua (87 percent); and Aruba (88 percent). There has, however, been an indigenizing process in countries like Jamaica and Barbados where there is a high rate of local ownership. This is also true, for very different reasons, in some smaller destinations such as Dominica and St. Kitts. At one point in the 1980s, Caribbean governments also owned hotels, but they have since disposed of most of them.

Eight of the world's fifteen largest hotel chains and all four of the most gigantic (Holiday Corporation, Sheraton Corporation, Ramada Inns, Marriott Corporation) operated in the Caribbean at the beginning of the 1990s. These companies do not own charming hillside inns; they run large, modern, formatted, and computerized citadels. Indeed, despite periods in the 1970s when multinationals took flight, a 1982 study found that the Caribbean region had a larger concentration of multinational-affiliated hotels than any other region in the world.

The story of Paradise Island, off Nassau in the Bahamas, reflects one pattern of hotel ownership: from rich men's retreat to transnational investment. The originally named Hog Island had become a favorite picnicking spot for the Nassau smart set by the time Axel Wenner-Gren, a Swedish industrialist said to be the world's richest man, bought a slice of it in 1939. He dredged a pond to make a lake, cut canals, and christened his estate Shangri-La. In 1961 he sold it for more than £3,600,000 to Huntingdon Hartford, the New York railway tycoon, who began a major building expansion by investing U.S. $10 million into Paradise Island.

Twenty years later, there were some 3,000 hotel rooms on Paradise Island. Almost 90 percent of these were managed and/or owned by five foreign companies. These were Holiday Inn, Club Med, Sheraton, and Loews, and, above all, Resorts International, the former Mary Carter Paint Company, which had bought most of the island from Hartford in 1966 and came to control 42 percent of its hotel rooms. By 1985 Resorts International owned four hotels on Paradise Island, the Paradise Island bridge, the Paradise Island airport, and Paradise Airlines. At one point, it also owned more than 25 percent of hotel rooms in the whole of the Bahamas.

This was not the end of the story, for in 1989 Resorts International filed for bankruptcy with debts of U.S. $913 million. Four years later, Sun International of South Africa acquired 60 percent of the equity for U.S. $75 million. And in December 1994, Chairman Sol Korzner, whose company also owns Sun City in the former homeland of Bophuthatswana and 31 hotels and casino resorts in southern Africa, France, and the Indian Ocean, announced the opening of Paradise Island's renamed U.S. $250 million Atlantis Resort with 1,150 rooms, 12 restaurants, a casino, and the world's largest outdoor aquarium and lagoon. Mega-investment at a global level had taken place over many years.

The sanitized luxury of Paradise Island is one aspect of hotel ownership in the Caribbean. At the other end of the spectrum is the small, locally owned hotel. Yet as the industry expands, the larger hotels arrive, traditionally foreign-owned and foreign-managed. In some cases, the independent, local hotelier finds it difficult to retain a foothold. Occasionally, locals feed off mass tourism, picking up business generated by the big boys, but often the local owner has neither the contacts, the money, nor the means to be part of computer tourism.

Local ownership, however, has increased and continues to do so. In 1995, for example, Barbadians owned one quarter of Barbados' luxury hotels, two thirds of the "A" class hotels, and all the apartments and guesthouses on the island.

In Jamaica, with its larger population and more diversified and sophisticated economy, a further process of local ownership has occurred. Local ownership now dominates, at around 90 percent of the island's 12,000 or so hotel rooms. Leading the way, at an international level, are two Jamaican companies. These have broken the First World's hegemony in mass-market tourism with the successful introduction of the all-inclusive holiday. Butch Stewart of Sandals and John Issa of Super Clubs have spearheaded the development of what has been described as "the most important innovation in the Caribbean hotel sector during the last decade."

It is worth looking at Sandals because, like Super Clubs, it is a home-grown marketing success and has been copied all over the region. "All hoteliers are now calling themselves all-inclusive. When we saw that all-inclusives would grow out of trees, we rolled the dice and said we're going to be at the top of the tree," says Stewart. Success for Sandals, he claims, comes from value for money. "We have the biggest watersports business and fitness centers, brand-new restaurants, great entertainment. You have quality choices and with all that you end up with value for money you can't get anywhere else in the world."

Stewart, originally a businessman with a car parts distribution company, started Sandals in 1981 when he revamped an old hotel in Montego Bay as an all-inclusive couples-only resort. By 1994, the Sandals chain owned and operated six hotels in Jamaica, two in St. Lucia, and one in Antigua. Sandals Royal Bahamian and Sandals Barbados were due to open in 1995. By then Sandals had more than 2,600 rooms throughout the Caribbean and in 1994 had been named the world's number one "independent resort group" by the *Travel Trade Gazette,* an international trade paper.

Stewart's crucial role in Jamaica was highlighted in April 1992 when, at a crisis point for Jamaica's exchange rate, he deposited U.S. $1 million per week into the island's commercial banks at a rate four Jamaican dollars below the prevailing rate. It was a move designed to help prevent the Jamaican dollar's collapse. As a result, other Jamaicans moved their U.S. dollars back into local banks and the currency stabilized. Sandals, according to its own press release, provides Jamaica with 10 percent of its hard currency.

The enclave culture of Sandals and Super Clubs (and those other all-inclusives, such as Jalousie, which have jumped on the bandwagon of the pioneers) has introduced a new ingredient into the Caribbean tourist cocktail. Not everyone is enjoying the taste, but the tourist establishment has welcomed the likes of Sandals with open arms. As Allen Chastenet, a former director of tourism in St. Lucia, puts it: "All-inclusives have brought security to tour operators and airlines. At the same time, they can also provide an umbrella for small, local developers. Sandals has a U.S. $15 million a year advertising budget. It can help put St. Lucia on the map."

The success of Stewart and Issa has not, until recently, prompted the rest of the Caribbean business community to move into the hotel business. However, Stewart thinks that this will change. "Traditionally they saw it as for those already established in the trade. They see it as a risk and have been timid, but the younger people are moving into the business," he says. . . .

EMPLOYMENT

For every new hotel room in the Caribbean, roughly one more new job is created. In a region beset by chronically high unemployment, any job, even though low paid, seasonal, unskilled, and with few prospects, might seem welcome. For as Jean Holder, Secretary-General of the Caribbean Tourism Organization, states, employment in tourism is "the difference between social order and social chaos." Tourism provides not just direct employment in hotels, casinos, restaurants, shops, and transport, but also indirect employment in the services and industries spawned by the industry. It also fuels a peripheral "informal" economic belt where the poor and unskilled strive to earn an income from selling or providing services to tourists on a casual basis.

Whether tourism is an efficient generator of jobs is a matter of debate, but what is significant is that the Caribbean relies on a strategy that equates jobs with tourism. On the tiny island of Aruba, for instance, the pursuit of tourism brought unemployment down from 40 percent in 1985 to virtually zero a decade later. The assumption that tourism will provide, reflects the region's dependency on tourism; at the same time it highlights the lack of alternative forms of employment, especially in the smaller islands.

This view finds telling expression at the formal opening of a new hotel. The gala occasion where government bigwigs, local celebrities, airline executives, hotel owners, public relations officers, and tourist board officials rub shoulders for cocktails and long speeches is not only used as a demonstration of faith by the investors in the stability and well-being of the country, but also provides an opportunity for local politicians to celebrate the biggest job creation scheme since, quite possibly, the opening of the last hotel.

When the Rex Grenadian Hotel opened in December 1993 in appropriate style, the then Prime Minister Nicholas Brathwaite was there to savor the moment; his speech revealed the extent to which Grenada has come to rely on tourism. Pointing out that some 150 people were to be employed at the 212-room hotel — the island's largest — he indicated that "workers must regard themselves as stake-holders with everything to lose if the venture fails." The Rex, owned and managed by Marketing and Reservations International, had instantly become one of the island's biggest employers. The local newspaper *Grenada Today* pointed out that more than 75 percent of the hotel's staff had been previously unemployed and had no experience of hotel work.

In one generation, the coming of tourism has changed the pattern of employment and the structure of communities forever. Peasant economies have been molded into service sectors where cane-cutters become bellhops and fishermen are turned into "watersport officers." Where statistics exist, the slide away from agriculture into the service sector in the last thirty years (and in some islands in the last fifteen years) looks dramatic. Rural communities, first dislocated by migration, now find that the young move to the tourist, coastal areas looking for casual work in the way that in other parts of the world they drift to the cities. Traditional life-patterns are altered as women become wage-earners, often for the first time, in the hotel sector where the demand for domestic work is high. Economic interests become more stratified with the higher-class locals identifying with the tourist interests and better able to exploit the opportunities offered by foreign capital and personnel than the unskilled majority.

Throughout the Caribbean, up to one in six workers finds direct employment in tourism, more than in any other region of the world according to the World Travel and Tourism Council. Accurate figures are hard to come by, but the Caribbean Tourism Organization estimates that in 1994 tourism provided direct employment for 216,000 people in the region, with some 580,000 gaining indirect employment from the industry.

In general, it is the countries with the most "mature" tourist industry, the biggest hotels, and the least diversified economies which are most dependent on tourism employment. The mass tourism of the Bahamas, for instance, supports 45,000 jobs, representing 35 percent of formally employed labor. In more diversified economies, such as the Dominican Republic, Barbados, and Jamaica, the figures are lower despite the importance of tourism to the economy as a whole. For example, 71,710 Jamaicans were employed full-time by the tourism industry in 1992, which amounted to some 8 percent of the total workforce. In contrast, work generated by tourism in countries such as Trinidad and Guyana has made, to date, little impact on employment figures.

In the hotel sector, Caribbean nationals are largely concentrated in unskilled jobs. Until very recently, they tended not to be in the top jobs. Middle management posts are now often held by Caribbean nationals, while white-collar jobs in the front-office and sports sections of hotels are sought after by the school-leaving children of the local middle class. Most hotel work, however, is relatively low grade: the security officers at the gate, bellboys in the foyer, "room attendants" servicing the bedrooms, gardeners sprucing up the foliage, cooks, barmen, waitresses in the restaurants and bars, watersport "officers," and deckchair attendants. Many of these workers remain unskilled and untrained. . . .

Tourism still offers, as Gordon Lewis wrote almost thirty years ago, opportunities "at once more comfortable, more exciting, and more socially prestigious than work in the agricultural sector." In larger hotels with high occupancy rates, a (rare) all-year-round clientele, and trade union representation, employees may be reasonably well paid; a "room attendant" with good tips can make more in the peak season than a shop assistant or a clerical worker.

A long-standing trade union movement within the hotel sector has helped to improve wages and conditions, especially in the more mainstream resorts. Indeed, one reason given for the reluctance of investors to buy into the Caribbean is what they consider to be high labor rates. According to the Economist Intelligence Unit, total payroll and related costs were 13 percent of room revenue in the Caribbean in 1990, compared to 6.1 percent in Africa and 9.2 percent in Latin America. Only Europe and North America had higher costs.

However, for most hotel employees, especially in the smaller establishments, both the perception and the reality of the industry entail seasonal work, low wages, poor conditions, and scant security. Yet for both men and women, any sort of paid employment offers a certain status, an opportunity for a guaranteed income, however small, which is not subject to the sun, rain, or a fickle market. For women, hotel work is regarded as suitable employment since it takes place in "respectable surroundings" and is an extension of traditional domestic skills. Indeed, women switch to hotel work from domestic service as "helpers" because of higher pay, regular hours, and better conditions despite the disruptions to family life caused by shift work.

For similar reasons men see employment in the tourist trade as preferable to traditional work in fishing or agriculture. A young man from Bequia explained: "Man, when I working in de hotel in de harbour last year, even though I getting paid really bad wage I at least know dat each week I gonna get dollar for pay for food and thing. An when I finish work I know I ain't hafi think about going fishing or nutting."

Indeed, one of the few surveys into worker attitudes in Caribbean hotels found a high "worker satisfaction" rating. Of 654 hotel employees interviewed in 1990 at twelve of the larger hotels (including six all-inclusives) in Jamaica's main resort areas of Montego Bay, Ocho Rios, and Negril, almost every worker felt "very positive" about being part of the tourist industry. "The hotel workers in these larger hotels have a strong tourism self-image and feel a sense of pride in being part of a vital industry," commented the survey done by the Jamaican pollster, the late Carl Stone.

Most of the interviewees also enjoyed their work: They liked working with people, dealing with foreigners, learning about foreign countries, learning useful skills, getting basic training and experience. The job satisfaction was far higher than that for the Jamaican labor force as a whole: 87 percent compared to 61 percent (in the 1982 national work attitudes survey). Of those who did not like their work, most complained of unfair accusations of stealing guests' property, management harassment, and poor relations with other workers.

In contrast to the high rate of job satisfaction, there was general dissatisfaction in relation to other criteria. Except for employees at the all-inclusive Sandals resort, workers complained of "relatively low wages and meager benefits" and did not believe that "they were getting a fair share of the benefits." At Sandals only 35 percent felt that they did not receive fair shares, but 73 percent of other hotel workers said wages and benefits were low. The resentment of these workers was fueled by the belief that the hotels were making hefty profits. Grassroots opinion supported the view of workers: Asked whether they thought hotel workers got full benefits from tourism, between 70 and 78 percent of respondents outside the industry said they thought wages and benefits were very low.

It is the small resorts with the smallest hotels, often locally owned and staffed, which for the most part pay the least and offer the least job security. The bottom end of the market is also less efficient in creating jobs. On Bequia, for example, where there are only small hotels and guesthouses, in some establishments in the early 1980s not only was pay very poor (a day's wage for a waitress was only twice as much as the price of a beer), but sackings were common. Local employers would dismiss staff for "being too familiar wid tourists," "not showing respeck and manners," and for "taking nah pride in dey job," knowing that there was a ready supply of labor available.

A Science Assignment

Anna Brito is a medical researcher who made important discoveries in the 1960s about the workings of the body's immune system. Brito made her early discoveries in a London research lab — headed by an established English biologist — and at first had great difficulty persuading her superior of their importance. This frustrating period in Brito's life is described by science writer June Goodfield in her book *An Imagined World: A Story of Scientific Discovery.*

As a possible perspective for thinking about Brito's experience, we offer first a passage by Evelyn Fox Keller. In this passage, Keller, a historian and philosopher of science, is interested in the ways that scientists communicate — or fail to communicate — their findings to other members of the scientific community. Read the passage a few times, then try to list some of the factors that Keller claims determine or affect scientific communication.

After reading and thinking about the comments by Keller, go on to read about Anna Brito. Then write an analytical essay about the problems encountered by Brito. Does Keller's theory about scientific language account for Brito's initial difficulties, or would you explain those difficulties in some other way?

PERSPECTIVE

The Language of Science

EVELYN FOX KELLER

Scientists and philosophers of science tend to speak as if "scientific language" were intrinsically precise, as if those who use it must understand one another's meaning, even if they disagree. But, in fact, scientific language is not as different from ordinary language as is commonly believed; it, too, is subject to imprecision and ambiguity and hence to imperfect understanding. Moreover, new theories (or arguments) are rarely, if ever, constructed by way of clear-cut steps of induction, deduction, and verification (or falsification). Neither are they defended, rejected, or accepted in so straightforward a manner. In practice, scientists combine the rules of scientific methodology with a generous admixture of intuition, aesthetics, and philosophical commitment. The importance of what

EVELYN FOX KELLER (b. 1936) is a professor of history and philosophy of science at the Massachusetts Institute of Technology. She is the author of *Reflections on Gender and Science* (1985), *Secrets of Life, Secrets of Death: Essays on Language, Gender and Science* (1992), and *Refiguring Life: Metaphors of Twentieth Century Biology* (1995). Her book *A Feeling for the Organism: The Life and Work of Barbara McClintock,* from which this passage is excerpted, was published in 1983.

are sometimes called extrarational or extralogical components of thought in the *discovery* of a new principle or law is generally acknowledged. (We may recall Einstein's description: "To these elementary laws there leads no logical path, but only intuition, supported by being sympathetically in touch with experience.") But the role of these extralogical components in persuasion and acceptance (in making an argument convincing) is less frequently discussed, partly because they are less visible. The ways in which the credibility or effectiveness of an argument depends on a realm of common experiences, on extensive practice in communicating those experiences in a common language, are hard to see precisely because such commonalities are taken for granted. Only when we step out of such a "consensual domain" — when we can stand out on the periphery of a community with a common language — do we begin to become aware of the unarticulated premises, mutual understandings, and assumed practices of the group.

Even in those subjects that lend themselves most readily to quantification, discourse depends heavily on conventions and interpretation — conventions that are acquired over years of practice and participation in a community.

Biologist Anna Brito: The Making of a Scientist

June Goodfield

[Anna Brito] arrived in London toward the end of that remarkable decade 1956–66, when the tide of research on the lymphoid system[1] was in full flood. The landmark discovery of the indispensable role played by the thymus gland in the regulation of the immune system was linked to a crucial observation: Removing the thymus from adult animals had no effect whatever. Removing it immediately after birth, however, resulted in a deficient immune response, which was shown when the animals thus treated then accepted foreign skin grafts. Ultimately the animal died — from gross immune deficiency, we know now, for half its immune system was missing.

During the years 1960 to 1964, similar evidence and similar discoveries about the thymus were being reported in a variety of publications by scientists who had been working with different animals. The advance in immunological understanding took place on a very broad front, and many factors, from luck to habit, influenced the order in which such reports were published and thus the priority in claiming credit. Scientific publications have different lead times and different lag times. A letter can sometimes be published in *Nature* very quickly, as happened when Watson and Crick reported the structure of DNA. On the other hand, the *Proceedings of the Royal Society of Medicine* and other similar journals can sometimes take upward of two years to print an article they

[1]**lymphoid system:** All organs involved in deploying white blood cells (lymphocytes) to remove bacteria and other foreign particles from the body [Eds.].

British writer and educator June Goodfield (b. 1927) is president of International Health and Biomedicine, Ltd. in England. She has written numerous books on science and the history of science, including *The Siege of Cancer* (1975), *Playing God: Genetic Engineering and the Manipulation of Life* (1977), *An Imagined World* (1981), and *A Chance to Live* (1991).

have accepted. At any rate, in a three- to four-year span, many studies of the thymus function were published: on the rabbit, mouse, and chicken (Dr. Robert A. Good in the United States); on the rat (Dr. Byron Waksman in the United States); on the mouse (Dr. Jacques Miller, working in England, and Dr. Delphine Parrott, also in England). Everyone was looking at the thymus, and all were correctly concluding that it was crucial to the development of immunity and the production of lymphocytes. But they were not certain whether there was one population of lymphocytes, or two, or even more; and if there was more than one population, was the thymus gland responsible for them all?

With questions like these in mind, the head of the laboratory Anna was to join had made a collection of microscope slides. The slides were the sectioned organs of mice, some of which had had their thymus glands removed — the thymectomized ones — and some of which were normal. A few of the thymectomized mice had died "naturally," but most animals — experiments and controls — had been deliberately sacrificed at various stages, from the newborn right through to the adult. The slides were arranged in a chronological order which roughly corresponded to the time the animals had had their thymuses removed, the lengths of time they had lived, and the stage at which they had been killed. Thinking that the sectioned organs might indeed reveal something — though she would not guess what — Dr. Vera had sent them to two of the finest pathologists in London. Each separately assured her that there was nothing of significance to be seen apart from some hyperactivity of the plasma cells, those cells whose function is to produce antibodies. This apart, it certainly wasn't worth anyone's spending much time with the material.

In the matter of the visiting scientist, Dr. Vera had no choice. One day the director of the Imperial Cancer Research Fund (ICRF) informed her that a Portuguese woman was coming to the institute to train with them. She was somewhere in her late thirties, had a lot of scientific experience that included a great deal of animal pathology and cancer research, and, of course, was fluent in English. Dr. Vera had also met one of the directors of the new institute in Portugal, to which Anna would eventually return when her training was complete, and from him, too, she was given to understand that the visitor was terribly bright, terribly experienced, in fact, "terribly everything."

Everybody, it turned out, had been thoroughly misled, including Anna herself. Her prospective boss in Lisbon actually wished her to train as a virologist and had said this to the director of ICRF. It was not until many years later that Anna learned that his real intention had been to have her learn those aspects of virology and immunology which would be relevant to his own future work. Therefore, all the virologists at Mill Hill had been asked if they would train the visitor, and the answer had been no.

Anna arrived on a weekend, just as Dr. Vera was going off to a scientific meeting in Holland. She phoned Anna at the Gulbenkian Foundation, welcomed her warmly but briefly, and added, "Don't come to the lab until we are back." But Anna *did* go to the lab, and when Dr. Vera returned from Holland, there she was, already installed. Dr. Vera's first view of the new arrival was of a short, round-faced, dumpy Portuguese wearing a lab coat much too large for her, which made her look even dumpier and shorter. She was far too young and wore an expression of great amiability combined with what looked like total incomprehension, even stupidity.

It was quite clear to Dr. Vera that the new arrival was not going to be welcome in the laboratory at that particular time. So the very first morning she kept Anna alongside her while she did some routine operational techniques on mice — taking out their thymuses — and, while she worked, tried to find out just what the foreigner knew, or could do, or could even *say.* She swears now that Anna had never *seen* a mouse in her life. . . . Indeed, her only experience in pathology had been strictly limited to human material.

Thus the first move was to place her where she could be supervised but not put off by an unwelcoming atmosphere; the second was to try to think up something she could *do.* She was installed in a building named the Hut, which had a pleasant view of grazing horses, and she was lent a microscope until such time as one would be purchased for her. Finally, Dr. Vera handed her the whole slide collection of mouse sections and told her to sit quietly and look at them, "just for fun." Then she was to report on what she could see. Anna is short and the laboratory stool was low. The bench, on the other hand, was high. If she put the microscope on the bench and sat on the stool, she couldn't see down the eyepiece. So she opened a drawer halfway down the bench, popped the microscope into the drawer, and looked down the microscope from a more convenient height. She reconstructs Dr. Vera's actions in these terms:

> She must have thought: Here is this nit from Portugal, and the only thing she can do is look down a microscope. So we might as well give her something to look at, and so as not to frighten her, we might as well tell her that it doesn't matter if she doesn't find anything. That is why she said, "Look just for fun." This is a crucial joke now. Everything I have ever done since then has been just for fun. That was really very good.

From time to time, Dr. Vera would come in and see how she was getting on. Anna didn't say very much; in fact she *couldn't* say very much, because at that time her English was quite limited. Whenever she wished to communicate with Dr. Vera, she would turn around, pin some paper on the wall, and draw what she wanted to say. Thus the conversation, though friendly, was somewhat restricted, limited to the drawings on the wall and to the cells down the microscope. And though Dr. Vera made it clear that she was available if help was needed, none was ever asked for, except once when Anna needed a translator to help negotiate the rent for a bed-sitting room.

The most prosaic of circumstances and the most unlikely of situations can nevertheless be the source of intensely exhilarating creative experiences. Anna consistently refers to those that derive from creativity or discovery as imparting the conviction of "belonging." Even though what is discovered has always been there, the scientist seeing it for the first time has the sense of calling it into being, and thus of belonging not only to the moment of discovery but also to the fact discovered and even to the scientists who will study it next. This is why she maintains that making a discovery is not so very different from being in love or making love. You can be in an enormous desert in respect to your personality and emotions; then you see someone, love them, and you belong. In the same way one is in an enormous desert of space and nature; then you see something new, understand it, and again you belong.

The first moment of illuminating observation may have been intensely exhilarating, but from then on it was all struggle, lasting nearly a year. She had arrived in London on February 29, and by the end of March she knew that she really had discovered something. Day after day she had sat in her little corner, looking down the microscope, but scientists don't think too highly of other people who only look down microscopes. She didn't do any experiments; she hadn't really done any experiments in her life. In any case, she thought that sitting in her little corner, being "as quiet as the mice," was what she was supposed to do, and that is what she did. Periodically she tried to tell Dr. Vera just what it was she was seeing, but at first Dr. Vera didn't understand and, when she finally did, she didn't believe it.

Four months after Anna arrived, on June 20, 1964, Dr. Vera went to Anna's room and said that since she didn't seem to be doing very much, or seem to be very interested in the work, "perhaps she would like to go home." This was a very English way of putting it. The Gulbenkian Fellowship still had months to run.

Dr. Vera now says she was being grossly unfair, but to be fair to her in turn, one must remember that she was being pressured to get rid of the "nuisance" who was occupying space and tying up a microscope. And she did think Anna's progress was a little slow. She had expected to see some light dawning — even though she believed there was nothing significant on the slides — or hear some intelligent comment about something. Anna was absolutely furious but altogether silent. "I was bloody angry. I thought she was incredibly unfair, because I knew by then that I had seen something new." But after four months she had already acquired some of the mannerisms and manners of the English, and she knew that in public one pretended not to have emotions.

But what *had* she seen that she thought was really fundamental? In simple terms, this: She had noticed a fact that others had missed — that there were great empty spaces in the center of the spleens and lymph nodes of those mice that had lost their thymus glands.

The spleen in any animal consists of two parts: an outer red pulp and an inner white pulp, which contains a lymph node called the *Malpighian body.* Lymph nodes anywhere are all structurally similar, with an outside layer and a central core packed with lymphocytes, but in animals that have lost their thymus there is, within twenty-two to fifty days, a depletion of the lymphocytes from the central core of the spleen and the lymph nodes. This depletion shows up on microscope sections of these organs as a blank white space in the white pulp.

Why this empty space? Anna had worked out the reason: There is an empty space because the T-lymphocytes, those lymphocytes that need the thymus gland to mature, are missing, and there is nothing to fill the space until, after some fifty days, other cell types gradually drift into the blank areas. *But no lymphocytes do.* Thus she realized not only that there are two distinct populations of lymphocytes but also that these populations remain distinct. In the adult animal the T-lymphocytes always occupy the central or "thymic-dependent" area of the spleen and the lymph nodes, while the second population occupies the "thymic-independent" area surrounding the central core. Why each lymphocyte population occupies its own separate and specific zone is a question she is still trying to answer.

Dr. Robert A. Good, one of the pioneers in thymus work, assesses Anna's discovery in these terms:

> Her work was, I think, *the* crucial work in that regard. I was very much impressed with what she had done. You can talk about the fact that the field was ripe, and it was. There was no question about that, because Dr. Turk was coming at it from another point of view also, and maybe all of us would have come to the same place. But before we ever got around to the mouse, she came up with this entire definition of separate lymphocyte

> populations: that in the adult organs there were thymic-dependent areas. And she discovered this on the basis of her studies, and her careful analysis of the histopathology of the mouse lymph nodes in the spleen. All sorts of people had been looking at the material and had not seen — simply not seen — the sharpness of the disassociation. As a novice coming into the field she just cracked it, just like that. It was her work that gave us the picture.

Why did a novice coming into the field manage to crack the problem whereas other, far more experienced people had not?[1]

Dr. Vera says that, first, it was because the novice had a "clean" mind, a mind not cluttered with any preconceptions, either of what lymphoid tissue ought to look like or with previous knowledge of the material under the microscope. She was not only able and willing to look at the material under the microscope with unprejudiced eyes; she was bound to do so. But secondly, she was tantalized and wanted to find the reason why some of the thymectomized mice had died "naturally." (No immune response!) Other people had blithely assumed that these mice had died because they just suddenly took sick. But Anna did not make that assumption, and so she was painstaking and willing to look and look and look again; to go back and forward with the slides; to look systematically at the sequences of age, time of thymectomy, and death; to be utterly patient; to spend literally hours at the microscope rather than pick up one or two slides at random and give a snap judgment. That is what the two pathologists had done and what most pathologists regularly do at postmortems; they pick up two or three sections of material, look at them, and say, "The patient died of X."

Anna may remember her willingness to spend hours at the bench but does not now consciously remember all her questions. She does remember feeling that Dr. Vera must surely have had some point in giving her the slides, and therefore they had to be studied carefully. When I asked her why she thought others had not seen — let alone appreciated — the disassociation referred to by Dr. Good, she replied, "Somehow they seem not to have been able to for various reasons. For one reason they tended to look only at the slides of the later stages, and by then it was too late — both in the sequence of sections and the age of the animal. The crucial changes had occurred earlier, and there was nothing after that to follow up. The fact that Dr. Vera had mice of all sorts and of all ages enabled me to start at the very earliest stages and pick up a gradual progression in the story of the missing lymphocytes. So I consistently asked for the various age groups until I could trace the development through time. Also I did have a very good training in pathology, and I was a good observer."

She may have been furiously angry when at the end of June Dr. Vera suggested that she might like to go home, but she says now that it was the best thing that ever happened to the "nice little Portuguese girl." Eventually it did filter through to Dr. Vera that her visitor was very angry indeed, and finally they decided to leave things as they were while Dr. Vera went on holiday. By the time she came back Anna had recovered her poise and was able to thank Dr. Vera for "the shake," which so far as she was concerned had done two things: First, it had shown her that she could, and must, plan experiments and

[1]Dr. Byron Waksman had also seen the phenomenon of localized lymphocyte depletion in the rat and guessed its significance. But he did not tie in this observation to the circulation of lymphocytes or do any experiments on this point.

do them, and second, that she really did have genuine scientific questions — that she hadn't just been sitting there like a dummy. This realization in itself proved a source of confidence. The episode also showed that she had to look after herself, and, if she intended to carve out a scientific career, she had better start right there and then.

"So I became much less sloppy and much more defiant. Also I became an experimentalist. Before this I was an observer, a creative observer possibly. But then I went to work with two women who were first-class experimentalists. So I became a scientist."

As for Anna's observation of the mouse sections, of course, Dr. Vera still couldn't believe it. She didn't in fact believe it until almost a year later when an experiment proved it. She herself had anticipated some depletion of lymphocytes in the thymectomized animals, and was not surprised about that, and she herself had earlier observed the areas of depletion even to the extent of seeing that parts of the lymph nodes were apparently empty, without a lymphocyte in sight. What did surprise her to the point of incredulity was the specificity, the selectivity of the depletion Anna pointed out — not only that there were empty areas but that they were so clearly defined that later scientists were able to say, "Normally the T-lymphocytes would be right here, and the others there." But basically Dr. Vera was an experimentalist and thus extremely skeptical of all pathologists, and because she respected those people who did things with their hands at the bench she would not draw a conclusion on observation alone. The pathologists were "the dead meat people," who could only explain away somebody else's genuine scientific questions.

But there was one observation which was really sophisticated, subtle enough to make her stick with Anna's claim and not reject her finding out of hand. Lymphocyte destruction naturally occurs in all animals that have had a viral or other infection. In such cases one *expects* to see empty areas in the lymph nodes. But Anna had been sharp enough to spot similar empty areas in the tissues of *healthy* thymectomized mice, where gross cell destruction would not be expected to have occurred. This was a puzzling clue — to something, an impressive observation that cried out for explanation, a fact suggesting that Anna was on to something important.

But it is all very well being in a "desert" and seeing something you think no one else has seen. It is all very well to take an existing situation and try to refract a different light through it, to make another picture for other scientists to see. The problem is to persuade the world — or the community of your colleagues — to see things the way you now see them — i.e., differently. Albert Szent-Gyorgyi was once in a group with other Nobel Prize winners and was being plagued by the press with questions like "What did you feel when you made your discovery?" And Szent-Gyorgyi said, "I felt bloody angry. Because there it was, *the thing,* and I was the first one to see it. But then I had to go and tell all these other people." You can have your moment of illumination, and it can be a mystical experience, an exhilarating experience, but unless it comes alive for other people it remains just what it was before — a stone in an empty desert.

It took a full year to persuade Dr. Vera of the fact of Anna's finding, and then of the significance of the finding, and then of the truth of the finding. But it did become a little more likely when a few months later a paper was published by some famous scientists, and in the photographs illustrating their paper the depleted areas were clearly visible. The authors themselves neither saw that fact nor its implication, but Dr. Vera could see that their photographs matched what Anna said she saw on the slides and had drawn in her diagrams. Nonetheless Dr. Vera's continuing cautious reluctance reflected the natural and proper skepticism of the scientist and the fact that, as an experimentalist, she really was unable to perceive the fact *without* the experiment. One may have a good microscope eye, one may see something that is genuinely there and make a valid discovery, but in the absence of a demonstrable specific function, established by experiment, immunologists are not going to be impressed. For them a thing exists only when the function has been demonstrated.

The months between June and September 1964 were the first months in the making of a scientist. "The design of my first experiments was awful," Anna recalls. "Dr. Vera called them diabolical. This is always so with scientific beginnings." By then Dr. Vera had no intention of making Anna a highly skilled technician who could learn a couple of techniques and then go back to Portugal and practice them for the rest of her life. She may have been skeptical of her findings, and would never accept them without careful proof, but she had sensed Anna's potential and was going to make her a scientist. And that is precisely what she did. Anna says, "I learned so much from that woman — it is unbelievable. It is like sculpture. The scientist I am today has been carved down from the person I was. Cut, cut, cut; all the extraneous mess cut right away."

Early that autumn Anna had brought Dr. Vera her first carefully drawn diagrams of the mouse slides showing the clearly defined empty areas on the lymph nodes and the spleen. She pointed to the zone in the middle of the spleen and said, "This is the thymus-dependent area," and, pointing to the area surrounding the inner zone, said, "This is the thymus-independent area." When Dr. Vera protested that she couldn't call it a "thymus-dependent" area because she didn't know whether it had been inhabited by T-lymphocytes, Anna had replied that she could see it had been. But she was informed that she still couldn't say so until it had been proved — until she had shown, in fact, that if there are holes in tissues because of missing cells, you can fill the holes in by injecting the right cells.

All that Dr. Vera was prepared to admit at that time was the *possibility* of a prediction. If they labeled the T-lymphocytes with radioactive isotopes and injected them, and if Anna was right, the lymphocytes should turn up in those thymus-dependent areas where Anna predicted they would. Recalling this time, Anna remembers being horribly nervous. If the cells behaved as she believed they would, "I'd be in luck." Indeed she was. The experiment was done; radioactively labeled thymus-lymphocytes were injected into some mice which had had their thymus glands removed and into the controls which had not. By autoradiography — that is, by sectioning the organs and taking photographs of the radioactively labeled cells — their route through the arteries and the capillaries could be followed and their arrival into precise areas in the spleen and lymph nodes established. When Dr. Vera saw the clinching evidence of the autoradiographs, showing the cells in their predicted places, she said, "I think I begin to understand." Anna was moved to tears: "It was an unforgettable moment."

A Literature Assignment

The following story, "The Management of Grief" by Bharati Mukherjee, is about the aftermath of a devastating airplane crash. Write an analytical essay about Mukherjee's story. For an analytical perspective, consider the theory offered by one of the story's characters, the social worker Judith Templeton. On page 613, Templeton outlines "the stages of grief" through which people who are mourning loved ones must pass — at least according to her textbook explanation. Summarize Templeton's theory, then consider whether the various characters in the story, including Mrs. Bhave, are somewhere in the stages of grief. Does Templeton's theory enhance or limit your insight into the characters?

The Management of Grief

BHARATI MUKHERJEE

A woman I don't know is boiling tea the Indian way in my kitchen. There are a lot of women I don't know in my kitchen, whispering, and moving tactfully. They open doors, rummage through the pantry, and try not to ask me where things are kept. They remind me of when my sons were small, on Mother's Day or when Vikram and I were tired, and they would make big, sloppy omelets. I would lie in bed pretending I didn't hear them.

Dr. Sharma, the treasurer of the Indo-Canada Society, pulls me into the hallway. He wants to know if I am worried about money. His wife, who has just come up from the basement with a tray of empty cups and glasses, scolds him. "Don't bother Mrs. Bhave with mundane details." She looks so monstrously pregnant her baby must be days overdue. I tell her she shouldn't be carrying heavy things. "Shaila," she says, smiling, "this is the fifth." Then she grabs a teenager by his shirttails. He slips his Walkman off his head. He has to be one of her four children, they have the same domed and dented foreheads. "What's the official word now?" she demands. The boy slips the headphones back on. "They're acting evasive, Ma. They're saying it could be an accident or a terrorist bomb."

All morning, the boys have been muttering, Sikh Bomb, Sikh Bomb. The men, not using the word, bow their heads in agreement. Mrs. Sharma touches her forehead at such a word. At least they've stopped talking about space debris and Russian lasers.

Two radios are going in the dining room. They are tuned to different stations. Someone must have brought the radios down from my boys' bedrooms. I haven't gone into their rooms since Kusum came running across the front lawn in her bathrobe. She looked so funny, I was laughing when I opened the door.

The big TV in the den is being whizzed through American networks and cable channels.

"Damn!" some man swears bitterly. "How can these preachers carry on like nothing's happened?" I want to tell him we're not that important. You look at the audience, and at the preacher in his blue robe with his beautiful white hair, the potted palm trees under a blue sky, and you know they care about nothing.

The phone rings and rings. Dr. Sharma's taken charge. "We're with her," he keeps

---

BHARATI MUKHERJEE (b. 1940) was born in Calcutta, India, and immigrated to the United States in 1961. A professor of English at the University of California at Berkeley, her works include the novels *The Tiger's Daughter* (1975), *Jasmine* (1989), *Holder of the World* (1993), and *Leave It to Me* (1997), and the short story collections *Darkness* (1985) and *The Middleman and Other Stories* (1988), in which "The Management of Grief" appears.

saying. "Yes, yes, the doctor has given calming pills. Yes, yes, pills are having necessary effect." I wonder if pills alone explain this calm. Not peace, just a deadening quiet. I was always controlled, but never repressed. Sound can reach me, but my body is tensed, ready to scream. I hear their voices all around me. I hear my boys and Vikram cry, "Mommy, Shaila!" and their screams insulate me, like headphones.

The woman boiling water tells her story again and again. "I got the news first. My cousin called from Halifax before six AM, can you imagine? He'd gotten up for prayers and his son was studying for medical exams and he heard on a rock channel that something had happened to a plane. They said first it had disappeared from the radar, like a giant eraser just reached out. His father called me, so I said to him, what do you mean, 'something bad'? You mean a hijacking? And he said, *behn,* there is no confirmation of anything yet, but check with your neighbors because a lot of them must be on that plane. So I called poor Kusum straightaway. I knew Kusum's husband and daughter were booked to go yesterday."

Kusum lives across the street from me. She and Satish had moved in less than a month ago. They said they needed a bigger place. All these people, the Sharmas and friends from the Indo-Canada Society had been there for the housewarming. Satish and Kusum made homemade tandoori on their big gas grill and even the white neighbors piled their plates high with that luridly red, charred, juicy chicken. Their younger daughter had danced, and even our boys had broken away from the Stanley Cup telecast to put in a reluctant appearance. Everyone took pictures for their albums and for the community newspapers — another of our families had made it big in Toronto — and now I wonder how many of those happy faces are gone. "Why does God give us so much if all along He intends to take it away?" Kusum asks me.

I nod. We sit on carpeted stairs, holding hands like children. "I never once told him that I loved him," I say. I was too much the well brought up woman. I was so well brought up I never felt comfortable calling my husband by his first name.

"It's all right," Kusum says. "He knew. My husband knew. They felt it. Modern young girls have to say it because what they feel is fake."

Kusum's daughter, Pam, runs in with an overnight case. Pam's in her McDonald's uniform. "Mummy! You have to get dressed!" Panic makes her cranky. "A reporter's on his way here."

"Why?"

"You want to talk to him in your bathrobe?" She starts to brush her mother's long hair. She's the daughter who's always in trouble. She dates Canadian boys and hangs out in the mall, shopping for tight sweaters. The younger one, the goody-goody one according to Pam, the one with a voice so sweet that when she sang *bhajans* for Ethiopian relief even a frugal man like my husband wrote out a hundred dollar check, *she* was on that plane. *She* was going to spend July and August with grandparents because Pam wouldn't go. Pam said she'd rather waitress at McDonald's. "If it's a choice between Bombay and Wonderland, I'm picking Wonderland," she'd said.

"Leave me alone," Kusum yells. "You know what I want to do? If I didn't have to look after you now, I'd hang myself."

Pam's young face goes blotchy with pain. "Thanks," she says, "don't let me stop you."

"Hush," pregnant Mrs. Sharma scolds Pam. "Leave your mother alone. Mr. Sharma will tackle the reporters and fill out the forms. He'll say what has to be said."

Pam stands her ground. "You think I don't know what Mummy's thinking? *Why her*? that's what. That's sick! Mummy wishes my little sister were alive and I were dead."

Kusum's hand in mine is trembly hot. We continue to sit on the stairs.

She calls before she arrives, wondering if there's anything I need. Her name is Judith Templeton and she's an appointee of the provincial government. "Multiculturalism?" I ask, and she says, "partially," but that her mandate is bigger. "I've been told you knew many of the people on the flight," she says. "Perhaps if you'd agree to help us reach the others . . . ?"

She gives me time at least to put on tea water and pick up the mess in the front room. I have a few *samosas* from Kusum's housewarming that I could fry up, but then I think, why prolong this visit?

Judith Templeton is much younger than she sounded. She wears a blue suit with a white blouse and a polka dot tie. Her blond hair is cut short, her only jewelry is pearl drop earrings. Her briefcase is new and expensive looking, a gleaming cordovan leather. She sits with it across her lap. When she looks out the front windows onto the street, her contact lenses seem to float in front of her light blue eyes.

"What sort of help do you want from me?" I ask. She has refused the tea, out of politeness, but I insist, along with some slightly stale biscuits.

"I have no experience," she admits. "That is, I have an MSW and I've worked in liaison with accident victims, but I mean I have no experience with a tragedy of this scale — "

"Who could?" I ask.

" — and with the complications of culture, language, and customs. Someone mentioned that Mrs. Bhave is a pillar — because you've taken it more calmly."

At this, perhaps, I frown, for she reaches forward, almost to take my hand. "I hope you understand my meaning, Mrs. Bhave. There are hundreds of people in Metro directly affected, like you, and some of them speak no English. There are some widows who've never handled money or gone on a bus, and there are old parents who still haven't eaten or gone outside their bedrooms. Some houses and apartments have been looted. Some wives are still hysterical. Some husbands are in shock and profound depression. We want to help, but our hands are tied in so many ways. We have to distribute money to some people, and there are legal documents — these things can be done. We have interpreters, but we don't always have the human touch, or maybe the right human touch. We don't want to make mistakes, Mrs. Bhave, and that's why we'd like to ask you to help us."

"More mistakes, you mean," I say.

"Police matters are not in my hands," she answers.

"Nothing I can do will make any difference," I say. "We must all grieve in our own way."

"But you are coping very well. All the people said, Mrs. Bhave is the strongest person of all. Perhaps if the others could see you, talk with you, it would help them."

"By the standards of the people you call hysterical, I am behaving very oddly and very badly, Miss Templeton." I want to say to her, *I wish I could scream, starve, walk into Lake Ontario, jump from a bridge.* "They would not see me as a model. I do not see myself as a model."

I am a freak. No one who has ever known me would think of me reacting this way. This terrible calm will not go away.

She asks me if she may call again, after I get back from a long trip that we all must make. "Of course," I say. "Feel free to call, anytime."

Four days later, I find Kusum squatting on a rock overlooking a bay in Ireland. It isn't a big rock, but it juts sharply out over water. This is as close as we'll ever get to them. June breezes balloon out her sari and unpin her knee-length hair. She has the bewildered look of a sea creature whom the tides have stranded.

It's been one hundred hours since Kusum came stumbling and screaming across my lawn. Waiting around the hospital, we've heard many stories. The police, the diplomats, they tell us things thinking that we're strong, that knowledge is helpful to the grieving, and maybe it is. Some, I know, prefer ignorance, or their own versions. The plane broke into two, they say. Unconsciousness was instantaneous. No one suffered. My boys must have just finished their breakfasts. They loved eating on planes, they loved the smallness of plates, knives, and forks. Last year they saved the airline salt and pepper shakers. Half an hour more and they would have made it to Heathrow.

Kusum says that we can't escape our fate. She says that all those people — our husbands, my boys, her girl with the nightingale voice, all those Hindus, Christians, Sikhs, Muslims, Parsis, and atheists on that plane — were fated to die together off this beautiful bay. She learned this from a swami in Toronto.

I have my Valium.

Six of us "relatives" — two widows and four widowers — choose to spend the day today by the waters instead of sitting in a hospital room and scanning photographs of the dead. That's what they call us now: relatives. I've looked through twenty-seven photos in two days. They're very kind to us, the Irish are very understanding. Sometimes understanding means freeing a tourist bus for this trip to the bay, so we can pretend to spy our loved ones through the glassiness of waves or in sun-speckled cloud shapes.

I could die here, too, and be content.

"What is that, out there?" She's standing and flapping her hands and for a moment I see a head shape bobbing in the waves. She's standing in the water, I, on the boulder. The tide is low, and a round, black, head-sized rock has just risen from the waves. She returns, her sari end dripping and ruined and her face is a twisted remnant of hope, the way mine was a hundred hours ago, still laughing but inwardly knowing that nothing but the ultimate tragedy could bring two women together at six o'clock on a Sunday morning. I watch her face sag into blankness.

"That water felt warm, Shaila," she says at length.

"You can't," I say. "We have to wait for our turn to come."

I haven't eaten in four days, haven't brushed my teeth.

"I know," she says. "I tell myself I have no right to grieve. They are in a better place than we are. My swami says I should be thrilled for them. My swami says depression is a sign of our selfishness."

Maybe I'm selfish. Selfishly I break away from Kusum and run, sandals slapping against stones, to the water's edge. What if my boys aren't lying pinned under the debris? What if they aren't stuck a mile below that innocent blue chop? What if, given the strong currents. . . .

Now I've ruined my sari, one of my best. Kusum has joined me, knee-deep in water that feels to me like a swimming pool. I could settle in the water, and my husband would take my hand and the boys would slap water in my face just to see me scream.

"Do you remember what good swimmers my boys were, Kusum?"

"I saw the medals," she says.

One of the widowers, Dr. Ranganathan from Montreal, walks out to us, carrying his shoes in one hand. He's an electrical engineer. Someone at the hotel mentioned his work is famous around the world, something about the place where physics and electricity come together. He has lost a huge family, something indescribable. "With some luck," Dr. Ranganathan suggests to me, "a good swimmer could make it safely to some island. It is quite possible that there may be many, many microscopic islets scattered around."

"You're not just saying that?" I tell Dr. Ranganathan about Vinod, my elder son. Last year he took diving as well.

"It's a parent's duty to hope," he says. "It is foolish to rule out possibilities that have not been tested. I myself have not surrendered hope."

Kusum is sobbing once again. "Dear lady," he says, laying his free hand on her arm, and she calms down.

"Vinod is how old?" he asks me. He's very careful, as we all are. *Is,* not was.

"Fourteen. Yesterday he was fourteen. His father and uncle were going to take him down to the Taj and give him a big birthday party. I couldn't go with them because I couldn't get two weeks off from my stupid job in June." I process bills for a travel agent. June is a big travel month.

Dr. Ranganathan whips the pockets of his suit jacket inside out. Squashed roses, in darkening shades of pink, float on the water. He tore the roses off creepers in somebody's garden. He didn't ask anyone if he could pluck the roses, but now there's been an article about it in the local papers. When you see an Indian person, it says, please give him or her flowers.

"A strong youth of fourteen," he says, "can very likely pull to safety a younger one."

My sons, though four years apart, were very close. Vinod wouldn't let Mithun drown. *Electrical engineering,* I think, foolishly perhaps: This man knows important secrets of the universe, things closed to me. Relief spins me lightheaded. No wonder my boys' photographs haven't turned up in the gallery of photos of the recovered dead. "Such pretty roses," I say.

"My wife loved pink roses. Every Friday I had to bring a bunch home. I used to say, why? After twenty odd years of marriage you're still needing proof positive of my love?" He has identified his wife and three of his children. Then others from Montreal, the lucky ones, intact families with no survivors. He chuckles as he wades back to shore. Then he swings around to ask me a question. "Mrs. Bhave, you are wanting to throw in some roses for your loved ones? I have two big ones left."

But I have other things to float: Vinod's pocket calculator; a half-painted model B-52 for my Mithun. They'd want them on their island. And for my husband? For him I let fall into the calm, glassy waters a poem I wrote in the hospital yesterday. Finally he'll know my feelings for him.

"Don't tumble, the rocks are slippery," Dr. Ranganathan cautions. He holds out a hand for me to grab.

Then it's time to get back on the bus, time to rush back to our waiting posts on hospital benches.

Kusum is one of the lucky ones. The lucky ones flew here, identified in multiplicate their loved ones, then will fly to India with the bodies for proper ceremonies. Satish is one of the few males who surfaced. The photos of faces we saw on the walls in an office at Heathrow and here in the hospital are mostly of women. Women have more body fat, a nun said to me matter-of-factly. They float better.

Today I was stopped by a young sailor on the street. He had loaded bodies, he'd gone into the water when — he checks my face for signs of strength — when the sharks were first spotted. I don't blush, and he breaks down. "It's all right," I say. "Thank you." I had heard about the sharks from Dr. Ranganathan. In his orderly mind, science brings understanding, it holds no terror. It is the shark's duty. For every deer there is a hunter, for every fish a fisherman.

The Irish are not shy; they rush to me and give me hugs and some are crying. I cannot imagine reactions like that on the streets of Toronto. Just strangers, and I am touched. Some carry flowers with them and give them to any Indian they see.

After lunch, a policeman I have gotten to know quite well catches hold of me. He says he thinks he has a match for Vinod. I explain what a good swimmer Vinod is.

"You want me with you when you look at photos?" Dr. Ranganathan walks ahead of me into the picture gallery. In these matters, he is a scientist, and I am grateful. It is a new perspective. "They have performed miracles," he says. "We are indebted to them."

The first day or two the policemen showed us relatives only one picture at a time; now they're in a hurry, they're eager to lay out the possibles, and even the probables.

The face on the photo is of a boy much like Vinod; the same intelligent eyes, the same thick brows dipping into a V. But this boy's features, even his cheeks, are puffier, wider, mushier.

"No." My gaze is pulled by other pictures. There are five other boys who look like Vinod.

The nun assigned to console me rubs the first picture with a fingertip. "When they've been in the water for a while, love, they look a little heavier." The bones under the skin are broken, they said on the first day — try to adjust your memories. It's important.

"It's not him. I'm his mother. I'd know."

"I know this one!" Dr. Ranganathan cries out suddenly from the back of the gallery. "And this one!" I think he senses that I don't want to find my boys. "They are the Kutty brothers. They were also from Montreal." I don't mean to be crying. On the contrary, I am ecstatic. My suitcase in the hotel is packed heavy with dry clothes for my boys.

The policeman starts to cry. "I am so sorry, I am so sorry, ma'am. I really thought we had a match."

With the nun ahead of us and the policeman behind, we, the unlucky ones without our children's bodies, file out of the makeshift gallery.

From Ireland most of us go on to India. Kusum and I take the same direct flight to Bombay, so I can help her clear customs quickly. But we have to argue with a man in uniform. He has large boils on his face. The boils swell and glow with sweat as we argue with him. He wants Kusum to wait in line and he refuses to take authority because his boss is on a tea break. But Kusum won't let her coffins out of sight, and I shan't desert her though I know that my parents, elderly and diabetic, must be waiting in a stuffy car in a scorching lot.

"You bastard!" I scream at the man with the popping boils. Other passengers press closer. "You think we're smuggling contraband in those coffins!"

Once upon a time we were well brought up women; we were dutiful wives who kept our heads veiled, our voices shy and sweet.

In India, I become, once again, an only child of rich, ailing parents. Old friends of the family come to pay their respects. Some are Sikh, and inwardly, involuntarily, I cringe. My parents are progressive people; they do not blame communities for a few individuals.

In Canada it is a different story now.

"Stay longer," my mother pleads. "Canada is a cold place. Why would you want to be all by yourself?" I stay.

Three months pass. Then another.

"Vikram wouldn't have wanted you to give up things!" they protest. They call my husband by the name he was born with. In Toronto he'd changed to Vik so the men he worked with at his office would find his name as easy as Rod or Chris. "You know, the dead aren't cut off from us!"

My grandmother, the spoiled daughter of a rich *zamindar,* shaved her head with rusty razor blades when she was widowed at sixteen. My grandfather died of childhood diabetes when he was nineteen, and she saw herself as the harbinger of bad luck. My mother grew up without parents, raised indifferently by an uncle, while her true mother slept in a hut behind the main estate house and took her food with the servants. She grew up a rationalist. My parents abhor mindless mortification.

The zamindar's daughter kept stubborn faith in Vedic rituals; my parents rebelled. I am trapped between two modes of knowledge. At thirty-six, I am too old to start over and too young to give up. Like my husband's spirit, I flutter between worlds.

Courting aphasia, we travel. We travel with our phalanx of servants and poor relatives. To hill stations and to beach resorts. We play contract bridge in dusty gymkhana clubs. We ride stubby ponies up crumbly mountain trails. At tea dances, we let ourselves be twirled twice round the ballroom. We hit the holy spots we hadn't made time for before. In Varanasi, Kalighat, Rishikesh, Hardwar, astrologers and palmists seek me out and for a fee offer me cosmic consolations.

Already the widowers among us are being shown new bride candidates. They cannot resist the call of custom, the authority of their parents and older brothers. They must marry; it is the duty of a man to look after a wife. The new wives will be young widows with children, destitute but of good family. They will make loving wives, but the men will shun them. I've had calls from the men over crackling Indian telephone lines. "Save me," they say, these substantial, educated, successful men of forty. "My parents are arranging a marriage for me." In a month they will have buried one family and returned to Canada with a new bride and partial family.

I am comparatively lucky. No one here thinks of arranging a husband for an unlucky widow.

Then, on the third day of the sixth month into this odyssey, in an abandoned temple in a tiny Himalayan village, as I make my offering of flowers and sweetmeats to the god of a tribe of animists, my husband descends to me. He is squatting next to a scrawny *sadhu* in moth-eaten robes. Vikram wears the vanilla suit he wore the last time I hugged him. The *sadhu* tosses petals on a butter-fed flame, reciting Sanskrit mantras and sweeps his face of flies. My husband takes my hands in his.

You're beautiful, he starts. Then, *What are you doing here*?

Shall I stay? I ask. He only smiles, but already the image is fading. *You must finish alone what we started together.* No seaweed wreathes his mouth. He speaks too fast just as he used to when we were an envied family in our pink split-level. He is gone.

In the windowless altar room, smoky with joss sticks and clarified butter lamps, a sweaty hand gropes for my blouse. I do not shriek. The *sadhu* arranges his robe. The lamps hiss and sputter out.

When we come out of the temple, my mother says, "Did you feel something weird in there?"

My mother has no patience with ghosts, prophetic dreams, holy men, and cults.

"No," I lie. "Nothing."

But she knows that she's lost me. She knows that in days I shall be leaving.

Kusum's put her house up for sale. She wants to live in an ashram in Hardwar. Moving to Hardwar was her swami's idea. Her swami runs two ashrams, the one in Hardwar and another here in Toronto.

"Don't run away," I tell her.

"I'm not running away," she says. "I'm pursuing inner peace. You think you or that Ranganathan fellow are better off?"

Pam's left for California. She wants to do some modelling, she says. She says when she comes into her share of the insurance money she'll open a yoga-cum-aerobics studio in Hollywood. She sends me postcards so naughty I daren't leave them on the coffee table. Her mother has withdrawn from her and the world.

The rest of us don't lose touch, that's the point. Talk is all we have, says Dr. Ranganathan, who has also resisted his relatives and returned to Montreal and to his job, alone. He says, whom better to talk with than other relatives? We've been melted down and recast as a new tribe.

He calls me twice a week from Montreal. Every Wednesday night and every Saturday afternoon. He is changing jobs, going to Ottawa. But Ottawa is over a hundred miles away, and he is forced to drive two hundred and twenty miles a day. He can't bring himself to sell his house. The house is a temple, he says; the king-sized bed in the master bedroom is a shrine. He sleeps on a folding cot. A devotee.

There are still some hysterical relatives. Judith Templeton's list of those needing help and those who've "accepted" is in nearly perfect balance. Acceptance means you speak of your family in the past tense and you make active plans for moving ahead with your life. There are courses at Seneca and Ryerson we could be taking. Her gleaming leather briefcase is full of college catalogues and lists of cultural societies that need our help. She has done impressive work, I tell her.

"In the textbooks on grief management," she replies — I am her confidante, I realize, one of the few whose grief has not sprung bizarre obsessions — "there are stages to pass through: rejection, depression, acceptance, reconstruction." She has compiled a chart and finds that six months after the tragedy, none of us still reject reality, but only a handful are reconstructing. "Depressed Acceptance" is the plateau we've reached. Remarriage is a major step in reconstruction (though she's a little surprised, even shocked, over *how* quickly some of the men have taken on new families). Selling one's house and changing jobs and cities is healthy.

How do I tell Judith Templeton that my family surrounds me, and that like creatures in epics, they've changed shapes? She sees me as calm and accepting but worries that I have no job, no career. My closest friends are worse off than I. I cannot tell her my days, even my nights, are thrilling.

She asks me to help with families she can't reach at all. An elderly couple in Agincourt whose sons were killed just weeks after they had brought their parents over from a village in Punjab. From their names, I know they are Sikh. Judith Templeton and a translator have visited them twice with offers of money for air fare to Ireland, with bank forms, power-of-attorney forms, but they have refused to sign, or to leave their tiny apartment. Their sons' money is frozen in the bank. Their sons' investment apartments have been trashed by tenants, the furnishings sold off. The parents fear that anything they sign or any money they receive will end the company's or the country's obligations to them. They fear they are selling their sons for two airline tickets to a place they've never seen.

The high-rise apartment is a tower of Indians and West Indians, with a sprinkling of Orientals. The nearest bus stop kiosk is lined with women in saris. Boys practice cricket in the parking lot. Inside the building, even I wince a bit from the ferocity of onion fumes, the distinctive and immediate Indianness of frying *ghee,*[1] but Judith Templeton maintains a steady flow of information. These poor old people are in imminent danger of losing their place and all their services.

I say to her, "They are Sikh. They will not open up to a Hindu woman." And what I want to add is, as much as I try not to, I stiffen now at the sight of beards and turbans. I remember a time when we all trusted each other in this new country, it was only the new country we worried about.

The two rooms are dark and stuffy. The lights are off, and an oil lamp sputters on the coffee table. The bent old lady has let us in, and her husband is wrapping a white turban over his oiled, hip-length hair. She immediately goes to the kitchen, and I hear the most familiar sound of an Indian home, tap water hitting and filling a teapot.

They have not paid their utility bills, out of fear and the inability to write a check. The telephone is gone; electricity and gas and water are soon to follow. They have told Judith their sons will provide. They are good boys, and they have always earned and looked after their parents.

We converse a bit in Hindi. They do not ask about the crash and I wonder if I should bring it up. If they think I am here merely as a translator, then they may feel insulted. There are thousands of Punjabi-speakers, Sikhs, in Toronto to do a better job. And so I say to the old lady, "I too have lost my sons, and my husband, in the crash."

Her eyes immediately fill with tears. The man mutters a few words which sound like a blessing. "God provides and God takes away," he says.

I want to say, but only men destroy and give back nothing. "My boys and my husband are not coming back," I say. "We have to understand that."

Now the old woman responds. "But who is to say? Man alone does not decide these things." To this her husband adds his agreement.

Judith asks about the bank papers, the release forms. With a stroke of the pen, they will have a provincial trustee to pay their bills, invest their money, send them a monthly pension.

"Do you know this woman?" I ask them.

[1]***ghee:*** Clarified butter [Eds.].

The man raises his hand from the table, turns it over and seems to regard each finger separately before he answers. "This young lady is always coming here, we make tea for her and she leaves papers for us to sign." His eyes scan a pile of papers in the corner of the room. "Soon we will be out of tea, then will she go away?"

The old lady adds, "I have asked my neighbors and no one else gets *angrezi* visitors. What have we done?"

"It's her job," I try to explain. "The government is worried. Soon you will have no place to stay, no lights, no gas, no water."

"Government will get its money. Tell her not to worry, we are honorable people."

I try to explain the government wishes to give money, not take. He raises his hand. "Let them take," he says. "We are accustomed to that. That is no problem."

"We are strong people," says the wife. "Tell her that."

"Who needs all this machinery?" demands the husband. "It is unhealthy, the bright lights, the cold air on a hot day, the cold food, the four gas rings. God will provide, not government."

"When our boys return," the mother says. Her husband sucks his teeth. "Enough talk," he says.

Judith breaks in. "Have you convinced them?" The snaps on her cordovan briefcase go off like firecrackers in that quiet apartment. She lays the sheaf of legal papers on the coffee table. "If they can't write their names, an X will do — I've told them that."

Now the old lady has shuffled to the kitchen and soon emerges with a pot of tea and two cups. "I think my bladder will go first on a job like this," Judith says to me, smiling. "If only there was some way of reaching them. Please thank her for the tea. Tell her she's very kind."

I nod in Judith's direction and tell them in Hindi, "She thanks you for the tea. She thinks you are being very hospitable but she doesn't have the slightest idea what it means."

I want to say, humor her. I want to say, my boys and my husband are with me too, more than ever. I look in the old man's eyes and I can read his stubborn, peasant's message: *I have protected this woman as best I can. She is the only person I have left. Give to me or take from me what you will, but I will not sign for it. I will not pretend that I accept.*

In the car, Judith says, "You see what I'm up against? I'm sure they're lovely people, but their stubbornness and ignorance are driving me crazy. They think signing a paper is signing their sons' death warrants, don't they?"

I am looking out the window. I want to say, *In our culture, it is a parent's duty to hope.*

"Now Shaila, this next woman is a real mess. She cries day and night, and she refuses all medical help. We may have to —"

"— Let me out at the subway," I say.

"I beg your pardon?" I can feel those blue eyes staring at me.

It would not be like her to disobey. She merely disapproves, and slows at a corner to let me out. Her voice is plaintive. "Is there anything I said? Anything I did?"

I could answer her suddenly in a dozen ways, but I choose not to. "Shaila? Let's talk about it," I hear, then slam the door.

A wife and mother begins her new life in a new country, and that life is cut short. Yet her husband tells her: Complete what we have started. We, who stayed out of politics and came halfway around the world to avoid religious and political feuding have been the first in the New World to die from it. I no longer know what we started, nor how to complete it. I write letters to the editors of local papers and to members of Parliament. Now at least they admit it was a bomb. One MP answers back, with sympathy, but with a challenge. You want to make a difference? Work on a campaign. Work on mine. Politicize the Indian voter.

My husband's old lawyer helps me set up a trust. Vikram was a saver and a careful investor. He had saved the boys' boarding school and college fees. I sell the pink house at four times what we paid for it and take a small apartment downtown. I am looking for a charity to support.

We are deep in the Toronto winter, gray skies, icy pavements. I stay indoors, watching television. I have tried to assess my situation, how best to live my life, to complete what we began so many years ago. Kusum has written me from Hardwar that her life is now serene. She has seen Satish and has heard her daughter sing again. Kusum was on a pilgrimage, passing through a village when she heard a young girl's voice, singing one of her daughter's favorite *bhajans.* She followed the music through the squalor of a Himalayan village, to a hut where a young girl, an exact replica of her daughter, was fanning coals under the kitchen fire. When she appeared, the girl cried out, "Ma!" and ran away. What did I think of that?

I think I can only envy her.

Pam didn't make it to California, but writes me from Vancouver. She works in a department store, giving make-up hints to Indian and Oriental girls. Dr. Ranganathan has given up his commute, given up his house and job, and accepted an academic position in Texas where no one knows his story and he has vowed not to tell it. He calls me now once a week.

I wait, I listen, and I pray, but Vikram has not returned to me. The voices and the shapes and the nights filled with visions ended abruptly several weeks ago.

I take it as a sign.

One rare, beautiful, sunny day last week, returning from a small errand on Yonge Street, I was walking through the park from the subway to my apartment. I live equidistant from the Ontario Houses of Parliament and the University of Toronto. The day was not cold, but something in the bare trees caught my attention. I looked up from the gravel, into the branches and the clear blue sky beyond. I thought I heard the rustling of larger forms, and I waited a moment for voices. Nothing.

"What?" I asked.

Then as I stood in the path looking north to Queen's Park and west to the university, I heard the voices of my family one last time. *Your time has come,* they said. *Go, be brave.*

I do not know where this voyage I have begun will end. I do not know which direction I will take. I dropped the package on a park bench and started walking.

A Sociology Assignment

The first account here, by Paul Tough, describes "moshing," the practice at some rock concerts and clubs of hurling oneself into others or of "crowd surfing." Following that reading are excerpts from the works of a number of social theorists. After thinking about their perspectives, write an essay analyzing moshing with the aid of any three of the theorists.

Some of the excerpts are written in a fairly difficult style. It might be helpful to summarize each in a simple sentence or two, then begin working with the perspectives you understand best. If the number of perspectives seems overwhelming, just be methodical and begin with one. How would the author account for the behavior described in Tough's article? Then move on to a second perspective. As you consider additional perspectives, note what each perspective reveals to you. Are you finding similarities and differences? These similarities and differences in perspective might offer one way to begin your analysis of moshing. Although you need use the perspectives of only three of the theorists in your essay, you might find it useful at this early stage of your work to consider all of them.

Into the Pit

PAUL TOUGH

From the outside, it looks like a riot, a street fight, a battle in a war we didn't even know was going on. Several hundred scruffy teenagers, dressed in a weird hybrid of Pacific Coast Lumberjack and Early Heroin Addict, are crushed together in a fleshy, roiling mass in front of a stage. They are attending a concert; they are also, it seems, trying to kill one another. Granted, they're doing it gracefully, without Uzis or broken bottles. It's strictly skin on skin: torsos slam into one another, chests collide, heads recoil, noses bleed; clothing is ripped off, trampled underfoot, forgotten; bodies fall and disappear, sucked into the sweaty undertow. Occasionally a warrior is tossed above the crush and passed along from hand to hand. It's unspeakably hot, often painful, certainly claustrophobic — all in all, just another night in the mosh pit.

I'm not exactly the kind of person you'd expect to find in the pit; I'm more one of those mid-20's, *New York Review of Books*–subscribing, relationship-discussing, National Public Radio–listening guys. You know the type. Concert-going for my generation was an exercise in bigness, all flash pots and laser shows and speakers the size of apartment buildings. We were told that these events were about community — that as we stood in Row 478 and sang along to "Born in the U.S.A.," we were somehow spiritually joined to the 50,000 others by our sides, each holding a lighter aloft, squinting at our far-off icons.

Yet even as we stood there dumbly, an alternative was taking form. In tiny, sweaty clubs, punk-inspired bands like Gang Green and the Dead Kennedys cranked out songs of unrelieved cacophony, while at their feet angry youngsters in leather jackets and mohawks hurled themselves into one another, punching and kicking. Although those bands never got within spitting distance of the Billboard charts, their musical descendants, led by Nirvana, are going multiplatinum. And in the wake of that success, the small cluster of enraged, drunk, slam-dancing punks has given way to vast seas of teenagers pounding into one another exuberantly, heaving each other into the air, climbing on stage to join their antiheroes and then propelling themselves back into the waiting crowd.

For some time now, the pit has drawn me. Not as a sociological experiment or any-

PAUL TOUGH is a senior editor at *Harper's Magazine.* "Into the Pit," excerpted here, first appeared in the *New York Times Magazine* on November 7, 1993.

thing; it just looked like fun. So on this brisk night, I've decided to enter the mosh pit for the first time, to see, from the inside, what I've been missing. I've chosen a concert by a local hard-core quartet called Helmet, at the venerable Roseland Ballroom in mid-Manhattan. From what I've heard of Helmet, they're a couple of steps removed from the mainstream, the kind of 4/4 band whose music makes you want to hop up and down and throw yourself into walls.

As the crowd drifts in from 52d Street, I survey them nervously, hoping no one points. Teenagers are, after all, the great ostracizers, and I am about as outside as I can get: fantastically aged, incorrectly attired, vastly ignorant, way uncool. Everyone else definitely belongs: the wardrobe choices lean heavily toward torn flannel shirts, baggy shorts, black concert T-shirts, high-top sneakers or Doc Martens, baseball caps worn backward, and dyed hair. Body language favors the slouch, the hunch, the hands jammed in the pockets.

Near the stage, I run into Adam, a 20-year-old college student from New Jersey. He's a big guy, with a linebacker's body and intelligent, if somewhat addled, eyes. I tell him I'm worried that my aging body will suffer permanent damage in the chaos of the pit. "Oh yeah," he says eagerly. "People get hurt. But if you're gonna play you gotta pay, right? You don't go out there to purposefully hurt anybody. . . ."

He stops himself, considering.

"Well, actually, some people do." He breaks into a grin. "But, hey, pain goes away."

At a few minutes after 9:00, Helmet wanders out and unleashes its assault. Down below, on the floor, the crowd does the same. My distance from the stage quickly dissolves into just a few yards as we all surge forward, crushing the spaces between us. A girl next to me, her face nervous and flushed, yells to her boyfriend: "I'm getting out of here. I can't take this," and for a second — my lungs trying to suck in oxygen, a tingle of panic rising in my spine — I consider joining her.

But almost immediately I realize I'm part of a mob; I'm going to do whatever they — *we* — decide to do. We start by pushing, and soon our pushes are met with others — from the front moving back, from the sides moving in, a thousand people all pushing and grinding and leaning. Our motion is slow, almost sensual, and we ebb and flow, lazily clutching one another for support. I'm swept from the front row to the pit's ragged border, from the left side to the right side — one minute in a crowd full of pretty high-school girls, the next surrounded by sweaty guys in baggy jeans and no shirts, their skinny chests slippery, bouncing and sliding off one another. Already I'm drenched with sweat. I'm hoping it's all my own, but a lot of it, I realize, is not. My hair is pasted to my head; my shirt, soaked, has darkened from a sky blue to a deep purple; my jeans are so clammy I can hardly bend my legs.

The music hammers away, those of us with earplugs — the majority, it appears — experiencing the sound more in our chests than in our ears. No one's watching the band; they've become background, providing incidental music for the real show, which is us, riding the tides and swells like surfers.

I'm turned around, my back to the stage, and a guy wearing oversize green shorts and a T-shirt that says "Primus" on it is standing in front of me, trying to get my attention amid the din. He keeps miming something — cupping his hands together in front of him, pointing up in the air — until finally I get it: He wants a lift.

I crouch down and lace my fingers together. He steps on my hands, puts one hand on my shoulder, and with the other grabs the top of my head. I grunt and throw him back over my shoulder, then twist and watch as he goes airborne, spreading his arms out into wings and landing with solid force, many foot-pounds of pressure, on a dozen unsuspecting people. The crowd sags momentarily, but then he's lifted up and sent on his way, bobbing along a stream of upstretched hands.

Suddenly my body starts moving faster than my feet, and I pitch backward. A second later I'm sprawled on the floor, thinking that it's probably a bad place to be, and then someone's on top of me, his sweaty back pressed against my face, and then down comes someone else on top of him, and all I can see is boots, lots of boots. I'm pretty sure that this is it, that I'm about to be trampled — remember those eleven kids at that Who concert in Cincinnati? — when a couple of hands grab my shirt and pull me up, a bit too fast, flinging me in the air slightly, and people are thumping me on the back and grinning, a look in their eyes like, "Man wasn't that *great*?"

I'm starting to think that things are out of control, that whatever sense of order and civility this crowd might have had has evaporated, when a young man to my right suddenly yells, "Sneaker!" and throws his arms open wide. Magically, the crowd around him parts, and he kneels down, undisturbed. Some riot: We are a relentless force, we cannot be stopped . . . until some guy needs to tie his shoe. He finishes and nods to the crowd, and we swarm back into the gap we'd cleared.

As Helmet continues to fire off sonic volleys, I see to my left another guy, shaved head, wild grin, swimming over the crowd toward the band. The strap of his canvas satchel is wrapped around his neck a couple of times; the bag drags behind him as he gropes his way, arduously, to the front. At last, he reaches his destination, and the masses hoist him up onto the stage, next to the band. He pays no attention to the musicians he's inches away from, and they ignore him, too, concentrating on their own role: pounding and shrieking and ferociously feeding back. The crowd is ecstatic. Together we have struck the last blow to the border between us and the band.

Here are the theoretical perspectives on violence and aggression. They range from theories that locate the impulse toward violence deep in our very nature to those that claim that violence emerges in various social situations and contexts. There is also a range of opinion on the purpose and function of violence and distinctions made between kinds of violence.

The bit of truth behind all this — one so eagerly denied — is that men are not gentle, friendly creatures wishing for love, who simply defend themselves if they

---

The founder of psychoanalysis, SIGMUND FREUD (1856–1939), wrote *Civilization and Its Discontents* in 1930. K. E. MOYER (b. 1919) is the author of nearly a dozen books on aggression and hostility, including *Violence and Aggression* (1987). BRUNO BETTELHEIM (1903–1990) was a highly influential developmental psychologist who published prolifically from the 1950s until his death on subjects such as the legacy of Freud, the complex relationships between children and parents, and the psychology of fairy tales. ELDON E. SNYDER and ELMER SPREITZER, professors emeritus of sociology at Bowling Green State University, have co-authored many writings on the sociology of sport, including the book *Social Aspects of Sport* (3rd ed., 1989). RENÉ GIRARD (b. 1923), a professor of French language, literature, and civilization at Stanford University, published *Violence and the Sacred* in 1977. This book elucidates ritual violence against the backdrop of a wide range of allusions to history, myth, language, psychology, and religion. DAVID D. GILMORE (b. 1943), in his study *Aggression and Community: Paradoxes of Andalusian Culture* (1987), explores the cultural paradoxes of Andalusia, a region of southern Spain.

are attacked, but that a powerful measure of desire for aggression has to be reckoned as part of their instinctual endowment. The result is that their neighbor is to them not only a possible helper or sexual object, but also a temptation to them to gratify their aggressiveness on him, to exploit his capacity for work without recompense, to use him sexually without his consent, to seize his possessions, to humiliate him, to cause him pain, to torture and to kill him. *Homo homini lupus*[1]; who has the courage to dispute it in the face of all the evidence in his own life and in history? This aggressive cruelty usually lies in wait for some provocation, or else it steps into the service of some other purpose, the aim of which might as well have been achieved by milder measures. In circumstances that favor it, when those forces in the mind which ordinarily inhibit it cease to operate, it also manifests itself spontaneously and reveals men as savage beasts to whom the thought of sparing their own kind is alien.

— Sigmund Freud, *Civilization and Its Discontents*

There are individuals who are physiologically prone to violent behavior. Frank Ervin estimates that there are at least half a million persons known to have brain disorders which result in intense feelings of anger and recurring physical assault on others without reasonable provocation, although this estimate may be high. He also suggests that there are a number of people with this type of brain disorder who have not been diagnosed. As the population grows, there will be an increase in the absolute number of these biologically violence-prone individuals, and because of the crowding and increase in contact, the number of available victims and innocent provocateurs will also increase. The result will be a significant rise in the number of incidents of senseless mass murder and irrational attack.

— K. E. Moyer, *Violence and Aggression: A Psychological Perspective*

Today we are constantly bombarded by images of a life of ownership and consumption, but for a great number of people the means to consumership are slim. This is particularly true of many young people before they find a sure place in our economic system, and even more so for those from marginal or submarginal backgrounds. Yet they are told that without such things they cannot have a satisfying life. They feel helpless to provide themselves with what they feel is even a minimal satisfaction of the demands we create in them. But they see no alternative to reaching their goals except through violence, while the pressures of frustration only tempt them more to use it.

— Bruno Bettelheim, *Violence: A Neglected Mode of Behavior*

Athletic competition draws together participants and crowds of spectators under conditions where the usual rules, norms, and division of labor may easily be disturbed and thus lead to aggressive and violent confrontations. In sociology, the

[1]***Homo homini lupus:*** From the Latin, "man's inhumanity to man"; literally, "man is a wolf to man." [Eds.].

term *collective behavior* designates such relatively unstructured situations. Collective behavior includes such phenomena as crowds, panics, riots, mass hysteria, revivals, fads, fashions, rumors, and social movements. These forms of behavior include the breakdown of socially structured behavior, transitory norms, and a relative absence of traditional social control mechanisms. . . .

The Contagion Theory of Collective Violence. According to this theory, crowds initially show their volatility by "milling," where individuals become increasingly tense, restless, uneasy, and excited. With increased excitement, emotion, and reciprocal stimulation, people are more likely to act together when influenced by a common impulse or mood than they are to act separately. If this process escalates in intensity, there is a *social contagion* stage that refers to a rapid and nonrational dissemination of a mood or form of conduct. This social contagion often induces spectators to become active participants. . . .

The Convergence Theory of Collective Violence. While the notion of contagion is helpful in examining crowd behavior, it does not explain why this feeling or emotion usually does not spread to all members of an audience at a contest. Are some people more or less susceptible to the spread of contagion than others? *Convergence theory* has tried to explain this aspect of crowd behavior. Whereas contagion suggests that individuals are transformed into unruly crowd participants after being "infected" by social contagion, "convergence theory argues that the crowd consists of a highly unrepresentative grouping of people drawn together *because* they share common qualities." For example, a high school athletic contest may bring together a large number of young spectators who are more likely to engage in volatile and lawless behavior. Moreover, such an aggregation of spectators may include an unusually large number of males who are inclined to express their machismo through attacks on the players or spectators of the opposing team.

The Emergent Theory of Collective Violence. Both the contagion and convergence theories of crowd behavior contend that there is a "oneness" between individuals in the crowd. This unanimity is a result of the common impulse of excitement or the uniformity of background characteristics of the crowd members. On the other hand, [Ralph] Turner and [Lewis] Killian have proposed that the motives, attitudes, and behavior of individuals in a crowd are not uniform. Rather, through interaction between participants, common standards or norms emerge that provide guidelines for behavior. A "consensus on appropriate conduct is established in the crowd, and crowd members as well as observers refer to this norm" . . . . The emergent theory emphasizes that collective behavior, like patterned forms of behavior, develops through social norms, interaction, and consensus that specifically apply to the situation at hand. . . .

It assumes that norms evolve through social interaction, and different norms may emerge according to the time and place.

— Eldon E. Snyder and Elmer Spreitzer,
Social Aspects of Sport

> In his study *Violence and the Sacred,* René Girard speaks of "the dual nature of violence" which most people find "incomprehensible." According to Girard, violence as part of ritual is necessary in order to control violence and to prevent it from running rampant in society: "Violence is not to be denied, but it can be diverted to another object, something it can sink its teeth into." Girard traces motifs in Greek drama and observes ritual sacrifice in primitive societies in order to illustrate how ritual sacrifice can promote "an act of violence without risk of vengeance." The function of this act "is to quell violence within the community and to prevent conflicts from erupting." He argues that we must learn to accept this other side of violence in the form of ritual if our society is to remain healthy. He concludes that "Beneficial violence must be carefully distinguished from harmful violence, and the former continually promoted at the expense of the latter. Ritual is nothing more than the regular exercise of 'good' violence."
>
> — Quotations from René Girard, *Violence and the Sacred*

The following perspective needs a few sentences of context. Andalusia is a region of southern Spain, and in the book *Aggression and Community: Paradoxes of Andalusian Culture,* anthropologist David Gilmore examines symbolic expressions of Andalusian culture — from gossip and nicknames to the "carnaval" festival — to unearth what seem to be contradictory impulses within this society. The description below offers a complex explanation for festival activities that could be perceived as violent and antisocial.

> The festivities consist of masquerades, promenades, and music. The local people and some visitors parade through the streets, drinking, accosting others, singing, making merry. With normal repressions relaxed, the atmosphere is tinged with a hysterical, almost explosive excitement. But the happiness, the pleasure, and the release consist not only of good fellowship (as outsiders would conceive of that term), but also of myriad acts of interpersonal violence and verbal aggression. During the four days of freedom, the celebrants enthusiastically flail each other with bamboo poles. When they tire of that they screech obscenities at rivals, bombard one another with choice bits of embarrassing gossip, pass on stories, revile comrades, divulge secrets, betray confidences. All this mockery is expressed in song, verse, and the most eloquent prose people can muster. The streets echo not only with good cheer, but also with spiteful epithets, luscious insults, treachery. Scores are settled as men and women pound each other with ribald tirades composed lovingly weeks beforehand.
>
> Meanwhile, as the world goes happily mad, there is organized entertainment. Local minstrels parade through the streets belting out biting lyrics that pillory selected nonconformists. Bystanders take up the chorus once they catch the drift, while the hapless targets slink miserably away to lick their wounds in private. "It is the festival of gossip," celebrants scream lustily. "It is the only time of the year when we are truly *juntados* (joined together)," people say.
>
> Joined together, yes, united in space and in spirit. People are indeed brought together by the festival of punishment and pleasure. But by what social magic is a longing for sociability intensified rather than reduced by mutual repulsion and by released violence? From a sociological point of view, how do we explain this to-

getherness arising from bellicosity, this happy union of scrappy combatants? But we cannot do better than to take them at their word: The people unite to fight. Their aggression brings them together in search of foes; they need their enemies for the pleasure of berating them. So we have another conundrum: Group unity comes from personal discord. Love for the community, for the group, is expressed as a friendly animosity toward other people.

— David D. Gilmore, *Aggression and Community: Paradoxes of Andalusian Culture*

Readings: Caribbean Literature and Cultural Politics

The readings in this section offer opportunities to think further about analyzing in the context of Caribbean culture and literature, the topic woven through this chapter. If you would like to look back at the chapter's earlier readings treating this topic, see the story "The Two Grandmothers" by Olive Senior and the accompanying paragraphs by Merle Hodge (Opening Problem, p. 557), the passage from Catherine A. Sunshine's *The Caribbean: Survival, Struggle, and Sovereignty* (A Professional Application, p. 580), and the Economics Assignment (p. 589).

The following readings explore issues of cultural politics in the Caribbean and its literature. *Cultural politics* refers not to the actions of political leaders but to the negotiations of everyday life, including the ways even our most commonplace behavior is influenced by larger social forces — how power is distributed, how the economy operates, how history continues to shape our lives. How we relate to one another, what we do at school or work, the language we use, the rituals in which we participate, the values that we give to one kind of music or art over another — these are all expressions of cultural politics. Although this chapter concentrates on cultural politics in the Caribbean, you may find that it prompts you to think about your own life too. How do even the most personal aspects of your life — your family relationships, your choice of friends, your decisions about how to spend your time, the way you talk — show the influence of cultural politics?

By way of context for these readings about the English-speaking Caribbean, let us offer some historical background. Many of you know the Caribbean only through the distorting lens of tourism, or really only through tourist advertisements: Come swim, snorkel, fish, golf, dine, play, and take the sun in the Caribbean. People from the Caribbean, of course, have a different view. Or rather they have many different views, since no two islands have the same history and since each island is culturally diverse. If you yourself come from a Caribbean country, you will be a kind of authority. You may be called upon to help to educate your classmates, and your instructor too, about your part of the region.

Despite the diversity, we can offer as background a few generalizations that hold true across the Caribbean. One is that each Caribbean island is deeply influenced by its history of colonization and slavery. Columbus was the first European colonizer, establishing a Spanish settlement in 1493 on the island he named Hispaniola (which now comprises two countries, Haiti and the Dominican Republic — see the map on the next page). In the sixteenth and seventeenth centuries, a host of European interests contended for power and territory. In doing so, they drove off or eliminated the Carib and Arawak Indians who had occupied the islands. By the late seventeenth century, the colonial pattern had assumed more or less the shape that would last well into the nineteenth century — and which remains embedded in the islands' institutions and in their languages, for example in the Spanish of Cuba, the French of Martinique, the Dutch of Curaçao, and the English of Jamaica.

The people who seized the Caribbean were Europeans, but the people who slaved there were Africans. The Spanish were the first to import African slaves to the Caribbean, but with the astonishingly rapid growth of the sugar industry in the mid-seventeenth century, the demand for slave labor grew correspondingly, a demand met ruthlessly by all the colonizing countries. Ships that would eventually return to Europe laden with sugar would first travel to Africa, where they would take on, for the notorious "middle passage," their human cargo. Some of the slaves who survived the transatlantic trip would eventually be destined for the cotton plantations of North America; but more disembarked at places like Port Royal, Jamaica, or St. Pierre, Martinique, or Bridgetown, Barbados.

On no Caribbean island did the African population submit without resistance to their European overseers. But there were often many cultural differences among the slaves themselves, for they were apt to come from various regions of Africa, speaking different languages. Moreover, when slaves did succeed in banding together in active resistance, they were violently suppressed. Only in Haiti, under the leadership of Toussaint L'Ouverture, did slaves succeed in establishing an independent nation (in 1804) through armed rebellion. Many islands — Jamaica is one example, Barbados another — have bitter histories of thwarted or partially successful uprisings.

During the early colonial period the population of most Caribbean islands became 80 to 90 percent African, 5 to 10 percent European, together with a gradually increasing mixed-race population, a result of the extramarital behavior of the planter class. On most of the islands the people of mixed race often received special powers and privileges, sometimes attaining a kind of middle-class status, so that among people of African descent there often grew up an intense awareness of social differences attached to gradations of difference in skin color.

Partly because of discontent on the islands, partly because of shifts in the economics of sugar, and partly from abolitionist pressures in Europe, slavery was abandoned throughout the Caribbean by the middle of the nineteenth century. Emancipation came to slaves in the British colonies in 1834, more than a

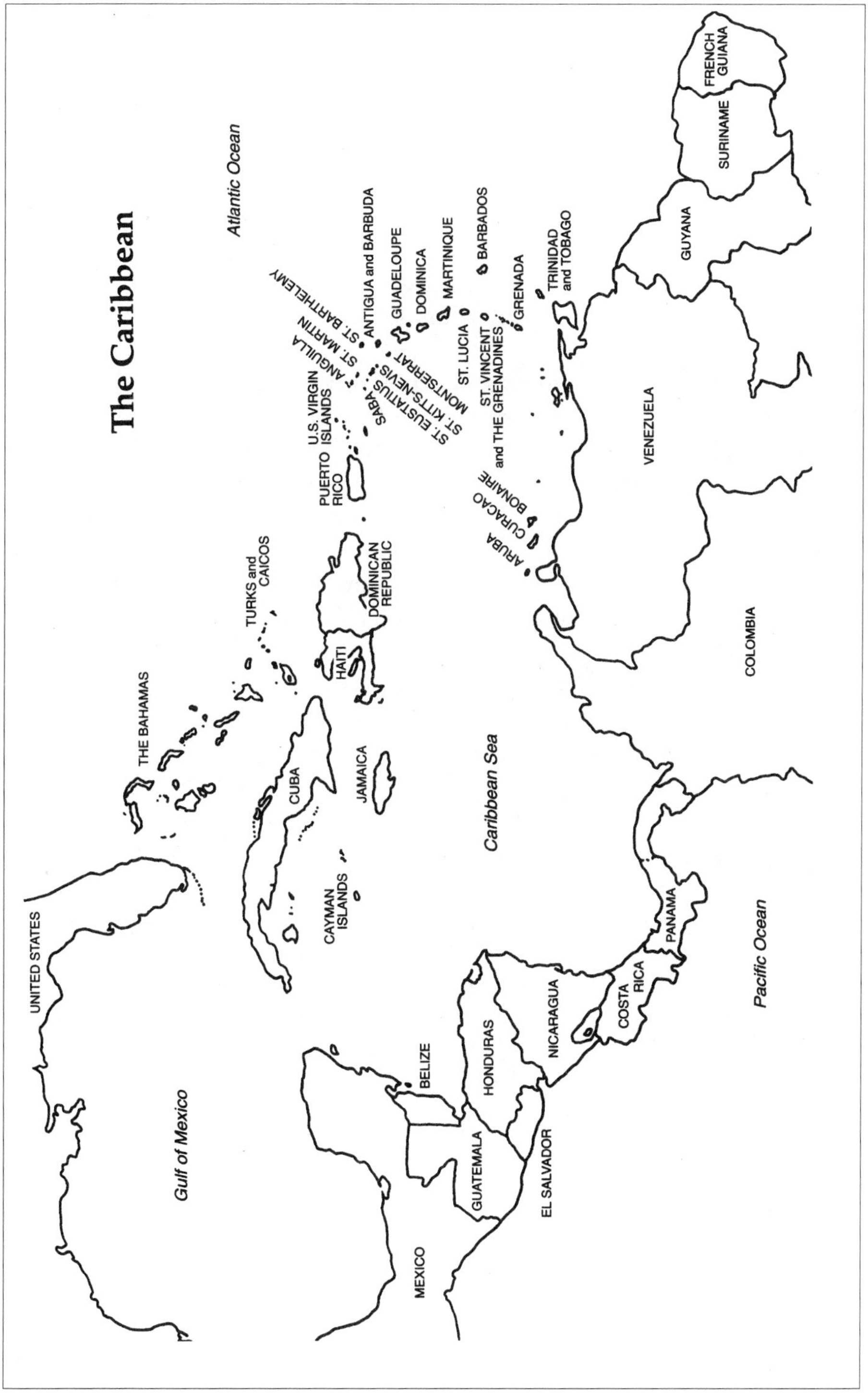
The Caribbean
Atlantic Ocean
Gulf of Mexico
Caribbean Sea
Pacific Ocean
UNITED STATES
MEXICO
BELIZE
GUATEMALA
EL SALVADOR
HONDURAS
NICARAGUA
COSTA RICA
PANAMA
COLOMBIA
VENEZUELA
GUYANA
SURINAME
FRENCH GUIANA
THE BAHAMAS
CUBA
CAYMAN ISLANDS
JAMAICA
HAITI
DOMINICAN REPUBLIC
TURKS and CAICOS
PUERTO RICO
U.S. VIRGIN ISLANDS
ANGUILLA
ST. MARTIN
ST. BARTHELEMY
SABA
ST. EUSTATIUS
ST. KITTS-NEVIS
MONTSERRAT
ANTIGUA and BARBUDA
GUADELOUPE
DOMINICA
MARTINIQUE
ST. LUCIA
BARBADOS
ST. VINCENT and THE GRENADINES
GRENADA
TRINIDAD and TOBAGO
ARUBA
CURAÇAO
BONAIRE

generation before the American Civil War. However, emancipation did not bring much economic freedom. For the most part, the economic and political structures that controlled the islands remained in place after the visible apparatus of slavery was removed. In many colonies, when exslaves refused to work for low wages on plantations, the planters turned aggressively toward importing indentured laborers from East India. In fact, during the latter nineteenth and early twentieth centuries, two great population shifts occurred. Large numbers of Asian immigrants, especially Indians, were brought to the Caribbean; and large numbers of people from the Caribbean began to emigrate, seeking economic opportunities elsewhere. Today many people from Caribbean countries live in cities like London, Toronto, Miami, and New York.

During the latter part of the twentieth century, as the direct influence of Europe upon the Caribbean has declined (most of the British colonies did not gain official independence until the 1960s), the U.S. influence has increased. Sometimes that influence has taken the form of military intervention — as in the 1983 invasion of Grenada. But much of it has been cultural — the kind of influence conveyed by U.S. radio and U.S. movies. And much of it has been economic. The U.S. economic domination in the Caribbean, including the development of a pervasive tourist industry, has provided a contemporary variation on the familiar theme of economic exploitation.

The six readings that follow alternate between nonfiction and fiction. We've arranged the sequence so that each of the nonfiction pieces can be used to provide an analytical perspective for the story that follows it. But you may want to write about the pieces singly, or in other combinations, or perhaps from a perspective of your own. In combination, the readings touch upon cultural politics in a number of English-speaking Caribbean islands: Jamaica, Trinidad, Antigua, Barbados. Even in combination, however, these readings are not intended to address more than a few strands of the complex subject of cultural politics in the Caribbean.

In the first reading, poet and scholar Edward Kamau Brathwaite looks at how standard English, as imported and imposed by the colonial educational system, has nervously coexisted with a homegrown, creolized English, a "nation language." Then, in an excerpt from Merle Hodge's novel *Crick Crack Monkey,* we witness a girl in her first encounters with the educational system of Trinidad. Next comes a second excerpt from Catherine A. Sunshine's *The Caribbean: Survival, Struggle, and Sovereignty* (another excerpt from this book appears in the Professional Application, p. 580), in which Sunshine describes some culturally important aspects of religious differences in the Caribbean, focusing on how several versions of Christianity express class distinctions and serve social needs. Then, in the opening sections of a novel set in Jamaica, Michelle Cliff takes her central character through a series of experiences that characterize the uneasy relationship between Jamaicans and their historical legacies. The last two readings deal with tourism in the Caribbean. In an excerpt from *A Small Place,* Jamaica Kincaid, formerly of Antigua, offers a scathing view of Caribbean tourism and of the tourist mentality. Finally, in the story "Visiting," Roger McTair dramatizes social tensions among visitors to a tourist bar in Barbados.

At the end of each reading, you will find Considerations questions intended to help you think about the reading both on its own terms and in relation to the analyzing strategies stressed in this chapter. At the end of the section, you will also find suggestions for writing about these readings in relation to one another and for pursuing the topic of cultural politics in the Caribbean through research of your own.

In the following passage, Edward Kamau Brathwaite of Barbados describes the relation between standard English as imposed by the schools and creolized English ("nation language") as used in people's home and working lives. The excerpt is taken from a book about Caribbean poetry, History of the Voice *(1984), and you'll note that Brathwaite respects "nation language" both for its cultural independence and its poetic power, a submerged power that he associates with "the African aspect" of Caribbean experience. Notice how in his own prose Brathwaite is able to maintain a tone both of scholarly authority and of barely subdued anger as he traces the history of colonialism in the Caribbean and its influence on language.*

Nation Language

EDWARD KAMAU BRATHWAITE

The Caribbean is a set of islands stretching out . . . on an arc of some 2,000 miles from Florida through the Atlantic to the South American coast, and they were originally inhabited by Amerindian people: Taino, Siboney, Carib, Arawak. In 1492 Columbus "discovered" (as it is said) the Caribbean, and with that discovery came the intrusion of European culture and peoples and a fragmentation of the original Amerindian culture. We had Europe "nationalizing" itself into Spanish, French, English, and Dutch so that people had to start speaking (and thinking) four metropolitan languages rather than possibly a single native language. Then with the destruction of the Amerindians, which took place within thirty years of Columbus's discovery (one million dead a year) it was necessary for the Europeans to import new labor bodies into the area. And the most convenient form of labor was the labor on the edge of the *slave* trade winds, the labor on the edge of the hurricane, the labor on the edge of Africa. And so Ashanti, Congo, Yoruba, all that mighty coast of western Africa was imported into the Caribbean. And we had the arrival in our area of a new language structure. It consisted of many languages but basically they had a common semantic and stylistic form. What these languages had

Writer, poet, playwright, and editor EDWARD KAMAU BRATHWAITE (b. 1930) was born in Barbados and is generally regarded as one of the West Indies' most prolific and talented authors. He currently teaches comparative literature at New York University. Brathwaite's works include *Sappho Sakyi's Meditations* (1992), *Middle Passages* (1992), *Shar* (1990), and the poetry collections *X/Self* (1987), *Third World Poems* (1983), and *Sun Poem* (1982). "Nation Language" appeared in *History of the Voice: The Development of Nation Language in Anglophone Caribbean Poetry* (1984).

to do, however, was to submerge themselves, because officially the conquering peoples — the Spaniards, the English, the French, and the Dutch — insisted that the language of public discourse and conversation, of obedience, command, and conception should be English, French, Spanish, or Dutch. They did not wish to hear people speaking Ashanti or any of the Congolese languages. So there was a submergence of this imported language. Its status became one of inferiority. Similarly, its speakers were slaves. They were conceived of as inferiors — non-human, in fact. But this very submergence served an interesting interculturative purpose, because although people continued to speak English as it was spoken in Elizabethan times and on through the Romantic and Victorian ages, that English was, nonetheless, still being influenced by the underground language, the submerged language that the slaves had brought. And that underground language was itself constantly transforming itself into new forms. It was moving from a purely African form to a form which was African but which was adapted to the new environment and adapted to the cultural imperative of the European languages. And it was influencing the way in which the English, French, Dutch, and Spaniards spoke their own language. So there was a very complex process taking place, which is now beginning to surface in our literature.

Now, as in South Africa (and any area of cultural imperialism for that matter), the educational system of the Caribbean did not recognize the presence of these various languages. What our educational system did was to recognize and maintain the language of the conquistador, the language of the planter, the language of the official, the language of the anglican preacher. It insisted that not only would English be spoken in the anglophone Caribbean, but that the educational system would carry the contours of an English heritage. Hence . . . Shakespeare, George Eliot, Jane Austen — British literature and literary forms, the models which had very little to do, really, with the environment and the reality of non-Europe — were dominant in the Caribbean educational system. It was a very surprising situation. People were forced to learn things which had no relevance to themselves. Paradoxically, in the Caribbean (as in many other "cultural disaster" areas), the people educated in this system came to know more, even today, about English kings and queens than they do about our own national heroes, our own slave rebels, the people who helped to build and to destroy our society. . . .

I think, however, that language does really have a role to play here — certainly in the Caribbean. But it is an English which is not the standard, imported, educated English, but that of the submerged, surrealist experience and sensibility, which has always been there and which is now increasingly coming to the surface and influencing the perception of contemporary Caribbean people. It is what I call, as I say, *nation language.* I use the term in contrast to *dialect.* The word "dialect" has been bandied about for a long time, and it carries very pejorative overtones. Dialect is thought of as "bad English." Dialect is "inferior English." Dialect is the language used when you want to make fun of someone. Caricature speaks in dialect. Dialect has a long history coming from the plantation where people's dignity is distorted through their language and the descriptions which the dialect gave to them. Nation language, on the other hand, is the submerged area of that dialect which is much more closely allied to the African aspect of experience in the Caribbean. It may be in English: but often it is in an English which is like a howl, or a shout or a machine-gun or the wind or a wave. It is also like the blues. And sometimes it is English and African at the same time.

Considerations

1. What does Brathwaite find "paradoxical" about the English that is taught in Caribbean schools?
2. How does Brathwaite define "nation language," and how did it develop? How is it related to standard English?
3. Brathwaite speaks of "an English which is not the standard, imported, educated English, but that of the submerged, surrealist experience and sensibility." Look up the word *surrealist* in an unabridged dictionary, or, if you can, a dictionary of art history. Why has Brathwaite found this particular word appropriate?
4. Use Brathwaite's comments on the educational system of the Caribbean as a perspective for writing about the experience of Merle Hodge's narrator in the following excerpt from *Crick Crack Monkey.*

Merle Hodge's novel Crick Crack Monkey *(1970) is set in Trinidad during the 1950s, when the island had not yet become independent of Britain. The novel is about the childhood of a girl, Tee, who after the death of her mother, moves between the households of two rival aunts. In the episode presented here, one of the aunts, Tantie, reluctantly enrolls Tee in "Coriaca EC." See whether you can figure out the source of Tantie's hostility toward the Hinds family that runs the school, and see whether you can deduce the author's view of her character's first educational experience. Also, notice the author's use of what Edward Kamau Brathwaite, in the previous reading, calls "nation language." What purposes does it serve?*

From *Crick Crack Monkey*

MERLE HODGE

I looked forward to school. I looked forward to the day when I could pass my hand swiftly from side to side on a blank piece of paper leaving meaningful marks in its wake; to staring nonchalantly into a book until I turned over the page, a gesture pregnant with importance for it indicated that one had not merely been staring, but that that most esoteric of processes had been taking place whereby the paper had yielded up something or other as a result of having been stared at.

At the next reopening Tantie took me to school so early in the morning it was still a

MERLE HODGE lives in Trinidad, where she teaches at the University of the West Indies. She has a graduate degree in French literature from the University of London. Her novel *Crick Crack Monkey* was first published in 1970. Her most recent novel is *For the Life of Laetitia* (1993).

little dark. But when we got to the school there was already a restless army of women outside the closed gate with children squashed among them, children beginning to send up a peevish protest. The women seemed to be directing a great deal of temper at an unconcerned man sitting on a box inside the schoolyard reading a newspaper. Never once did he throw a glance in our direction, for all the abuse and gesticulation of the women; he sat immobile, and every time he made the slightest movement the crowd surged forward irresistibly, arriving no farther than crushing each other's feet and grinding tempers thinner.

After an age, with the sun's heat and the crowd growing, a voice called to the watchman from inside the building; he nodded, folded up his newspaper with exaggerated thoroughness, laid it aside, and set out toward the gate at a resentful pace.

At the gate he faced the women and delivered a brief, sullen speech: "Mind how allyu come-in this gate. If allyu push, ah closin it back."

"Mr. Oliver, shut yu face an' open the damn gate," was one of the replies he received.

We charged. Or the women charged and we children tumbled in among them. We were making for a door.

Suddenly there was no further progress to be made — we were being flattened into each other's backs and standing on the same spot; for those at the very front had filled up the office and the greater part of the throng was still outside.

So we stood for another age, with people minus their charges squeezing their way back out through the tightly pressed company who were not altogether inclined to assist them by giving way. As more and more people left we were edging closer and closer to the door — until the rumor made its way out to us that there was no more room in ABC class.[1] Immediately people with older children began to struggle forward, to the irritation of those with ABC candidates, who remarked loudly at their lack of manners in pushing and jostling.

When that movement was complete there still remained a sizable crowd of people who apparently had no intention of giving ground. The watchman appeared from nowhere ostensibly transporting a bucket of something from one point to another, but looking as though this were a moment he had waited for with keen relish. As he slouched past us he muttered: "Why allyu do' go-home, yu can't understan' or what, no room is no room!" and was instructed by a pugnacious voice to go an' scratch his arse.

Then Mr. Thomas made his way with difficulty through the crowd adamantly installed inside his office and who seemed to think he was attempting escape; he stood in our midst, closely hemmed in, and pleaded with us distraughtly to go away. When nobody budged he rubbed his temples and threw up his hands in frustration:

"Look, what allyu want me to do, put allyu children to siddong on one-another head? I tell yu I ain' have no more room in ABC — try the RC[2] school, put them by Mis' Hinds, send them up Coriaca school, I do' care what allyu do, jus' carry them 'way and yu could bring them back when they pass ABC!"

When a few people at the edge of the crowd began to move off rather precipitately

[1]**ABC class:** Primary school [Eds.].

[2]**RC:** Private Roman Catholic school [Eds.].

we needed no further persuasion. With one accord we surged out of the schoolyard, and soon we were but the hairsbreadth of civilization away from pushing each other over and running over the fallen. It was nevertheless a race, if a slightly shamefaced race, down the road and across the Savannah to the RC school. Many of Tantie's cronies were in the hustling company — none acknowledged the other.

Then we were before the gate of the RC school. But the gate was shut and there was a piece of cardboard with letters on it that must have conveyed the fact that there was no more room. Behind the gate there was a plump nun with red cheeks and glasses, her hands together as if she was praying, her head cocked on one side and a regretful smile on her face; I thought too that her eyes were shut, only it might have been her glasses. And she was swaying diagonally, presumably also with regret.

The race slackened, the women relaxed into cronies again, thrown back in a heap together, their rivalry abruptly amputated. They gathered in a chattering knot which dwindled after a while as they went off with their children, still delivering their piece o' mind in loud tones. The nun swayed on and smiled regretfully, as if she had been wound up and placed at the gate to do so.

So Tantie had to take me down to Mrs. Hinds, a horrible capitulation, for she'd always sworn she'd never send a dog of hers there, that woman was a mauvais'-langue[3] horse-face maco with nothing to do but mind people business. We marched down to Mrs. Hinds, Tantie muttering all the way her disapproval and disgust blasted government wouldn' build school for the chirren what the blasted government there for but to build school for the chirren now look my cross I have to put the chile by these shitters all they know is to run behind the Reveren' arse an' he wife an' smell every fart they blow when it was black-arse Reverend Joseph God res' he soul they used to find their arse to Hell up in Coriaca Church on a Sunday morning me I would shit on all o' them jus' you remember you going there to learn *book* do' let them put no blasted shit in yu head.

As we walked up the concrete steps a disorderly chanting straggled out to us from behind a half-open door.

Mrs. Hinds was sitting with a piece of embroidery. The children were placed around two tables, the boys at one and the girls at the other. Tantie and Mrs. Hinds had a brief discussion, Mrs. Hinds turgid with dignity, Tantie akimbo and insolent.

I was given a place among the chanting which went on and on and became more and more disorderly as more and more voices either dropped out, chanted at half a second's interval after the confident voices or simply became a drone keeping in time with the rhythm. Mrs. Hinds embroidered. After some time, at around the seven-times table it must have been, there were only about four tenuous voices articulating anything, the rest were a rhythmic drone. Then even the drone slackened; and Mrs. Hinds looked up from her embroidery with an inquisitive expression on her face, whereupon the drone immediately quickened again. When the noise came to a complete halt Mrs. Hinds said "All right, recess," and I nearly fell off my end of the bench as all my colleagues rose abruptly. Everybody pushed toward the door in a horrible noise and confusion; a sharp interjection from Mrs. Hinds and they stood stock still: "Orderly, orderly, file out orderly!"

I remained in my place. "Recess, darling, you don't want to go out and play?" Go

[3]**mauvais'-langue:** Slanderous bad-mouthing (from the French) [Eds.].

out and play indeed, when I had come to this place to read and write and all the other mysteries one performed at school! Go out and play I would indeed not. This whole enterprise known as school was proving a trifle unexpected in more than one of its aspects.

Mrs. Hinds went out and after a while a bell rang and the children tumbled in again. Mr. Hinds came in through another door and stood at the head of the boys' table wagging a ruler and looking stern, waiting for them to settle down. He had a graying twirly moustache and wore a brown suit on the jacket of which there was some kind of a badge in the shape of a shield, and a tie that had gold and blue stripes; he frequently flapped his jacket and mopped his head, but however hot it became never did it seem to occur to Mr. Hinds to remove his jacket.

Everyone knew that Mr. Hinds had been up in England in his young-days, that was why he talked in that way, that he had fought in the war and that he had nearly got to be a lawyer but instead he had come back to be the Headmaster of Coriaca EC.

High on the wall behind Mr. Hinds hung a large framed portrait of Churchill. It was Mr. Hinds's daily endeavor to bring the boys to a state of reverence toward this portrait; when they became rowdy he would still them into shame at their unworthy behavior in the very sight of the greatest Englishman who ever lived etc., or he would still them into incomprehension because in his angry rhetorical transports he soared into a vocabulary that fell like gibberish on the ear. But all his own outraged respect, all his resounding tales of the war and the glorious victories for some reason never did infect us with the required awe — for us the personage on the wall was and remained simply Crapaud-Face.[4]

To Mrs. Hinds's noble bottom I have already referred. When she stood she always had her arm resting on top of it or brushing swiftly over it as if to see whether it was still there, or perhaps to smooth it out of existence.

But Mrs. Hinds didn't do too much standing. She sat in her chair with a piece of embroidery or other sewing and from time to time addressed someone without raising her head in a slow, commanding voice that grated effortlessly over the bedlam. Often her mother came tottering and groping into the room and arranged herself laboriously onto a chair. She had a cloth around her head with gray plaits sticking out all around from under it, and she was known to us as The Ol'-Lady. Conversation between Mrs. Hinds and The Ol'-Lady was a slow business, for Mrs. Hinds had to repeat every other word as The Ol'-Lady's hearing wasn't too good, and her voice was like a foreign radio station, fading out and in and cracking, and all the *s*'s fizzing out through the spaces between what teeth she had.

On my first day at school Mrs. Hinds called to me to come to her with my slate. Across the top of it she made a row of identical creatures and handed slate and pencil back to me saying: "Here, make A for Apple," and took up her embroidery again. I went back to my place and after a few moments of bewilderment followed my neighbor's example in filling up the whole slate with things of the approximate shape of those made by Mrs. Hinds.

Everybody else was scraping away at their slates, and occasionally someone effaced their hieroglyphics with a liberal wash of water (or spit) and then waved their slate about in the air singing:

[4]**Crapaud-Face:** Toad-Face (from the French) [Eds.].

Jumbie Jumbie[5] *dry mih slate*
I'll give yu a penny toba-cco

and often slates tended to be waved smack into neighbors' faces, which tended to generate loud strife. Everybody seemed to know what they were about, everybody seemed to be in the middle of something.

My reading career also began with A for Apple, the exotic fruit that made its brief and stingy appearance at Christmastime, and pursued through my Caribbean Reader Primer One the fortunes and circumstances of two English children known as Jim and Jill, or it might have been Tim and Mary.

At about twelve o'clock we sang grace, "Hands together, eyes shut!" and anyone caught with so much as one eye half-open receiving a sound slap. Then we scampered out, with admonitions from Mrs. Hinds to "Go straight home, don't dilly-dally on the way!"

On afternoons the tempo was slow. Lunch was still heavy in our bellies, the sun which had battered down at us on the way back to school was still outside besieging the walls, cooking the air inside the schoolroom, and everyone felt most like sleeping. So we stood and counted in unison to a hundred, or recited nursery rhymes about Little Boy Blue (what, in all creation, was a "haystack"?) and about Little Miss Muffet who for some unaccountable reason sat eating her curls away.

Or under Mrs. Hinds's direction we would recite Children of the Empire Ye Are Brothers All, or sing God Save the King and Land of Hope and Glory.[6] This with many angry interruptions, Mr. Hinds stamping and shouting and making us begin all over again and threatening to make us go and stand in the sun and sing even as in the depths of adversity his regiment had stood in biting cold and sung songs of patriotism and the snow had rung with the strains of God save the King, because we were slouching and not standing properly at attention — "Not an eyelid must bat not a finger must twitch when we honor the Mother Country." Mr. Hinds was inordinately pleased with this morsel of his own composing which to his mind must have been worthy of "Not a drum was heard, not a funeral note / As his corpse to the rampart we hurried. . . ."

After recess we would settle down to another session of scraping, chattering among ourselves while some unfortunate stood unenviably close to Mr. Hinds and stuttered out his reading-lesson about Tim and Jim who did a jig on the mat for a fig. Mrs. Hinds sat with her needlework and if her mother was there chatting with her. They discussed the state of affairs in the household of such and such a child whose family was doomed to destruction because the father drank and the mother never sent the children to church. They discussed the pernicious "Save-soul" Sunday-school to which so many Santa Clara children went — those people the way they carry on inside that place sometimes passing you would think they were singing calypsoes all the Reverend can warn these ignorant people not to send their children there for it's just like sending them to Baptist or Shango.[7]

[5]**Jumbie:** Ghost, spirit [Eds.].

[6]**Children of the Empire . . . Land of Hope and Glory:** Mrs. Hinds is steeped in British hymns and military lore [Eds.].

[7]**Baptist or Shango:** See Catherine A. Sunshine's discussion of African religions on page 636 [Eds.].

Every Sunday afternoon Tantie dressed Toddan and me and sent us to the Pentecost Sunday-school in preference to that of the Anglican church. Tantie never went near any kind of church herself, but there was no discussion as to our attendance, we went and that was that. It was just as though grownups sent us to see whether we could make better sense of it than they had been able to themselves.

Mrs. Hinds naturally did what she could toward our redemption. For the day began and ended with the intoning of the sounds which we could perform without a fault while our thoughts drifted elsewhere behind our tightly shut eyes:

Our father (which was plain enough)
witchartin
heavn
HALLE
owèdbethyname
THY
kingdumkum
THY
willbedunnunnert
azitizinevn. . . .

When we had got to the end of that there was still the long and rather more path of Ibelieveingoderfathalmitie. Then we sang either

We are but little children weak
Nor born in any high estate —

which was of course The Estate — but who would want to be born up in there? Or else the other sweet and opaque one:

Gen Terjesus me kan mile
Loo kupon thy little chile
Pi teemy simpliss City
Suh fumee to come to thee

From the conversation of Mrs. Hinds and The Ol'-Lady I gathered to my puzzlement that Toddan and I (glances in my direction fraught with concern) were being "dragged-up," and — how desirable a fate (glances of envious awe and admiration) — that our Daddy was "Up-There" and was surely going to send for us. So one day I asked Tantie what they meant.

My puzzlement remained because the next thing I knew Tantie was battling and struggling to get past Mikey, who was barring the front door and saying do' bother Nennen do' bother with the ol'-bitch and Tantie was shouting and out of breath and shouting that she was going down and spit on that bitch so help mih Gord and Mikey said do' bother Nen yu will only get the child putout man wait till she leave there then you an'me will go and spit on the bitch and Tantie was panting and shouting get outa mih way boy. In the end Mikey had to help her back into the house and put her into a chair where she sat fanning herself while he went to fetch a cup of water. On his way to the kitchen he hissed at me fiercely under his breath: "Now yu will know to keep yu tail shut an' do' come-home with everything yu hear them two dotish ol'-witch say!"

* * *

One indolent afternoon we were sitting scraping on our slates and chattering and Mrs. Hinds was sewing and raising her voice in order to penetrate to The Ol'-Lady; Mr. Hinds was taking up the reading lesson of an individual known as Duncey-Joseph. It was Duncey-Joseph who had one day stalled for five minutes at g-r-a-p-e-s until, instructed in a roar from Mr. Hinds to "Look at the picture and say what you see!" had looked at the picture, lit up with sudden triumph and announced: "G-r-a-p-e-s — chennette!"

Duncey-Joseph was stalling and stuttering and Mr. Hinds was bellowing, now at him (right into his ear so that Duncey seemed to start several inches upward) now at the rest of us: "Silence! You nincompoops!" at which a kind of frightened hush would ensue, pregnant however with suppressed giggling, for Mr. Hinds's word "nincompoops" which we never heard elsewhere always seemed to us the height of incongruity, issuing as it did from the mouth of one who, we were certain, never committed the lapse of etiquette known to us by its onomatopoeic final syllable.

After the hush the bedlam would reinstate itself and swell to its former volume, with scraping and chattering and Jumbie Jumbie dry mih slate and Mrs. Hinds shouting a word to her mother. And Duncey-Joseph stalled and stuttered and Mr. Hinds bellowed and wiped his forehead and flapped his jacket. There were two sugar-bees trapped in the room, now zooming about our heads, now bashing themselves against a windowpane, their buzzing becoming more and more enraged.

Suddenly there was a sharp crack and Duncey-Joseph's high-pitched wail. Our din stopped abruptly. Alarm seized us, for Mr. Hinds's ruler was rarely satisfied with one victim at a time.

"Damn you! Damn you! You confounded nincompoop!" He flung Duncey's book across the room to where it hit the wall and fell in an undignified heap on the floor. No one had the faintest inclination to giggle at Mr. Hinds's terminology. "You nincompoops!" thundered Mr. Hinds, his ire spreading over us all as we fully expected it would. "Go home all of you, go home and never come back here! You'll never get anywhere, you'll never better yourselves, you'll never be anything but —" Mr. Hinds choked with anger — "*piccaninnies!* Here I stand, trying to teach you to read and write the English language, trying to teach confounded *piccaninnies* to read and write, I —" his voice rose and rose and he leaned further and further over the table so that the boys nearest him were paralyzed into an uncomfortable slanting position — "I who have sat on the benches of the Inns of Court!" He was banging his ruler on the table. "I who have marched to glory side by side with His Majesty's bravest men — I don't have to stand here and busy myself with — with —" his thundering became a mighty hiss: "with *little black nincompoops!*" He flung the ruler down and hurried out, vehemently mopping his forehead and flapping his jacket.

A thick stillness remained. The Ol'-Lady sat tense, frowning with incomprehension, still straining forward as if an explanation was yet to come which would clear up her perplexity. When only the silence continued, growing taut with our sense of something horribly amiss having taken place, quite beyond the ordinary run of Mr. Hinds's rampages, she groped after Mrs. Hinds: "Elda! Elda! What happen? What happen?" Mrs. Hinds looked stricken; she was staring out of the door through which her husband had precipitated himself, and the voice of The Ol'-Lady seemed to jerk her back into a place where she would much rather not be. She dismissed us, hurriedly and with her composure in a state of disarray that we never saw before and never since.

* * *

Various kindly and elderly folk had long since assured me that my mother had gone to Glory. And now at school I had come to learn that Glory and The Mother Country and Up-There and Over-There had all one and the same geographical location. It made perfect sense that the place where my mother had gone, Glory, should also be known as The Mother Country. And then there was "Land of Hope and Glory/Mother of the Free. . . ."

Every Sunday at Sunday-school we were given a little card with a picture and a Bible verse — pictures of children with yellow hair standing around Jesus in fields of sickly flowers, and with yellow rays emanating stiffly from all these personages, or the children with yellow hair kneeling with their hands clasped and their faces upturned toward some kind of sun that had one fat ray coming down at them. Thus it was that I had a pretty good idea of what kind of a place Glory must be, and of what happened to you there; for also at Sunday-school we sang:

Till I cross the wide, wide water, Lord
My black sin washèd from me,
Till I come to Glory Glory, Lord
And cleansèd stand beside Thee,
White and shining stand beside Thee, Lord,
Among Thy blessèd children. . . .

Considerations

1. Summarize how Tee came to enroll in the school operated by Mr. and Mrs. Hinds. Why does her aunt view this as "a horrible capitulation"?
2. Tee and her schoolmates seem to mishear or misinterpret much of the prayers and hymns that they are asked to learn. What are some examples, and what purposes do these misinterpretations serve in Hodge's narrative?
3. Examine Mr. Hinds's outburst (p. 635). What is the source of his frustration, and how do you think we are meant to regard him? What role does his use of English play in his characterization?
4. What are the racial overtones of the English hymn quoted in the last lines? Why does Hodge choose to end this episode of her novel with these lines?
5. Analyze this story from a perspective suggested by Edward Kamau Brathwaite in the previous piece, "Nation Language."

Catherine A. Sunshine's discussion of Carnival and calypso is excerpted in the Professional Application (p. 580). In the following passage, Sunshine turns to the topic of religion, analyzing the historical role played by the Christian church in the subjugation of slaves. She goes on to look at how in more recent times the various versions of Christianity have continued to express social divisions and how some versions of Christianity have been modified or transformed by spiritual traditions originally brought from Africa. In making her points about the links between Christianity and racism, notice how Sunshine is able to enlist historical quotations for dramatic support of her claims.

From *The Caribbean: Survival, Struggle, and Sovereignty*

CATHERINE A. SUNSHINE

In the case of the British colonies, where Anglicanism and Protestantism were dominant, the Church's role focused on subduing and assimilating the Africans. Originally, there was little interest in Christianizing the slaves, and the few early missionary efforts which did reach out to blacks were marked by racism and elitism. Count Zinzendorf, a Moravian leader, said in 1739:

> God punished the first Negroes by making them slaves, and your conversion will make you free, not from control of your masters, but simply from your wicked habits and thoughts, and all that makes you dissatisfied with your lot.[1]

This led to an ironic situation in which those blacks who became Christians often prayed for their white oppressors, saying in one case: "Father, forgive them, for they know not what they do. . . . Buckra (the master) left him God in England, and the devil in Jamaica stir him up to do all this wickedness. Poor thing! Him eye blind, and him heart hard."[2]

In fact, the impact of this early Christian teaching remained superficial, since African religious beliefs and practices continued to dominate the plantation until the 1830s. In the slave world people turned to African religions such as Shango and Kumina, or to *obeah* (sorcery) for spiritual and practical help. Through the dances and drumming, masks and rituals, the slaves realized a link to their ancestral home. At the same time, these practices were used to provide protection against the planters. The obeah-man or woman could give the slave a charm to be worn to protect him against the cruelty of the overseer. Charms and potions could also be used to take revenge on fellow slaves who collaborated with the Europeans. The planters' fear of obeah magic was one reason they finally allowed the slaves to be Christianized:

> In short, I know not what I can do with him, except to make a Christian of him! This might induce the negroes to believe that he [the obeah-man] has lost his infernal power by the superior virtue of the holy water. . . .[3]

[1]Idris Hamid, *Troubling of the Waters* (Trinidad: Rahaman Printery, 1973), p. 63.

[2]James M. Phillippo, *Jamaica: Its Past and Present State* (London: Unwin Brothers, 1843), p. 158.

[3]M. G. Lewis, *Journal of a West Indian Proprietor* (New York: Houghton Mifflin, 1929), p. 124.

CATHERINE A. SUNSHINE (b. 1953) is a U.S.-born writer and researcher with a special interest in the Caribbean. She is editor of *Caribbean Connections,* a series of anthologies for secondary schools, and is working on a forthcoming volume in a series about Caribbean migration to the United States. This excerpt was taken from her book *The Caribbean: Survival, Struggle, and Sovereignty* (1985, revised 1988).

In contrast to obeah, an individual practice, most Afro-Caribbean religions were strongly rooted in and reinforced a sense of community. An example is myalism, which originated in Jamaica in the 1760s as a "pan-African" religious society drawing on elements from various African religions. Myalism was based on the idea that misfortunes were the result of sorcery, and that certain rituals could protect against harm. It apparently served as a catalyst for unity and cooperation among slaves of different African ethnic groups.

Following the American Revolution, many loyalists from the southern United States fled to the Caribbean. They brought with them their African-American slaves and servants, who introduced the Baptist religion to Jamaica. As a result, myalism incorporated two important Baptist practices: possession by the Holy Spirit — similar to the African belief in ancestor possession — and baptism by immersion in water.

This marriage between myalism and the Baptist religion, known as the Native Baptist movement, attracted members rapidly. When missionaries arriving in the 1830s tried to convert Jamaicans to mainline Christianity, they had to compete with the powerful and entrenched myalist / Native Baptist complex.

When it became clear that emancipation was inevitable, the colonial authorities encouraged the churches to help assimilate the blacks. The Anglican, Dutch Protestant, and French Catholic churches were favored for this role over the nonconformist Moravian, (English) Baptist, and Methodist churches.[4] By 1830–31, the churches were allowing blacks into their worship and had begun to open up parochial schools to teach them to read and write. The goal of this education was not enlightenment toward social freedom, however, but preparation for servile roles in the colonial church and planter-dominated society. The ruling class . . .

> demanded and obtained [an agreement] that the school would not be used to affect adversely the supply of manual labor on the plantation, nor to encourage the coloured people to wish to rise too quickly up the social ladder.[5]

The Baptists, Methodists, and Moravians played a more positive role, forming an alliance with the freed slaves to help them become independent from the planters. In Jamaica, where a majority of the exslaves left the plantations and moved to the hills, the nonconformist churches provided thousands of acres of land bought with church money. As a result, these denominations were initially seen as "liberators." The Methodist Church in Jamaica doubled its membership between 1831 and 1841, while the Baptists tripled from 10,000 to 34,000 during the same period.[6]

Even among these churches, however, the white leadership made clear that its task was not to arbitrate between master and former slave. The Church was forbidden to meddle in "social and poiitical questions," its task being to pacify the rebel spirit in the

[4]Called "nonconformist" because they refused to conform to the rules and practices of the Church of England (Anglican Church).

[5]Keith D. Hunte, "The Church in Caribbean Development," in David I. Mitchell, *With Eyes Wide Open* (Barbados: CADEC, 1973), p. 143.

[6]Philip D. Curtin, *Two Jamaicas: The Role of Ideas in a Tropical Colony 1830–1865* (New York: Atheneum, 1970), p. 162.

blacks through education and Christian teaching.[7] Thus just a few years after emancipation, missionaries reported with pride that:

> cunning, craft, and suspicion — those dark passions and savage disposition before described as characteristic of the Negro — are now giving place to a noble, manly, and independent, yet patient and submissive spirit.[8]

RISE OF THE AFRO-CHRISTIAN CULTS

Such "success" blinded the missionaries to the real process taking place: black disenchantment with the white churches and the steady growth of Afro-Christian syncretic religions. Mistaking church attendance for assimilation, the missionaries failed to realize that the blacks were merely allowing the practice of Christianity to coexist and blend with their African religious beliefs.

The racial, class, and color bias of colonial society was scarcely affected by emancipation. The failure of the mission churches to challenge these social attitudes drove many blacks away within a decade after emancipation. For one thing, the churches discouraged the baptism of illegitimate children, which meant that at least 70 percent of the population was barred from full privileges of membership in the Church. Governed by a Victorian, white European morality, the missionaries regarded the reluctance of the blacks to marry as evidence of "deep cultural defects which would take a long time to remove."[9]

Also disturbing to many blacks who converted to Christianity was that the training of black leaders — primarily in the nonconformist churches — did not mean oversight of a congregation, much less denominational leadership. Rather, blacks became deacons (servants), teachers, and preachers *within* the congregation. These new positions had a social impact in terms of providing jobs, but they were confined to service roles in support of the white missionaries. The training of native leaders and lay agents within these churches facilitated the entry of blacks into service occupations in the larger society, such as clerks, subordinate estate managers, and school teachers.

This gradual social integration was not accompanied by a lessening of racist attitudes, but by their intensification, as blacks moved closer to whites in the social spectrum. As in the postreconstruction period in the United States, it became common in the Caribbean to hear blacks referred to as "niggers." As late as 1870 the West Indian Anglican Church was publicly asserting that blacks had the right to "spiritual equality" with whites, but not cultural equality.[10]

As a result of these attitudes and practices, between 1842 and 1865 the mission churches in Jamaica lost up to half the members they had gained since 1831. Black children dropped out of the church schools. Many blacks trained as native ministers (especially Baptists) left to pastor their own African and Afro-Christian churches.

[7]Noel Leo Erskine, *Decolonizing Theology: A Caribbean Perspective* (Maryknoll, N.Y.: Orbis Books, 1981), p. 74.

[8]Phillippo, p. 253.

[9]Lilith M. Haynes, *Fambli* (Guyana: CADEC, 1971), p. 40.

[10]Haynes, p. 36.

While the European churches preached deference to the system, the essence of the black religions was resistance. Native Baptists figured prominently in the Montego Bay revolt just before emancipation, and afterward, the myalist / Native Baptist movement became the core of resistance to the hardship of the postemancipation years. In 1841–42, the connection of the cult to plantation work stoppages led the planters to outlaw myalism, and the movement went underground.

As with other elements of West Indian mass culture, however, the attempt to suppress myalism only led to its resurgence in a stronger, if altered form. In the early 1860s, the mission churches in Jamaica launched a united assault on black religion, aimed at a sweeping conversion to "pure" Christianity. But their attempt to stir up a Christian religious frenzy in Jamaica produced unexpected results: The revival turned African in form, with oral confessions, trances, dreams, prophecies, spirit seizures, and wild dancing. This marriage of myalism and Christianity came to be called Revivalism — the strongest of the Jamaican native religions until the emergence of Rastafarianism in the 1930s. . . .

Religion is . . . closely linked to class. Jamaican author Leonard Barrett tells of the division in his own family between his mother's relatives, who belong to the brown middle class, and his father's family, black Jamaicans from the peasantry. The former are Christian churchgoers, while the latter follow the Afro-Christian Pocomania cult.[11] As people move up the social ladder, they tend to leave the African syncretic religions in favor of mainline denominations such as the English Baptists, Methodists, and Presbyterians. Each country also has its high-status denominations historically associated with the colonial ruling class: Anglicanism in territories colonized by Britain, Catholicism in those colonized by the French and in the Dominican Republic, U.S. Protestantism in Puerto Rico, and Dutch Protestantism in the Netherlands Antilles.

[11]Leonard Barrett, *The Sun and the Drum: African Roots in Jamaican Folk Tradition* (Jamaica: Sangster's Book Stores Ltd., 1976), pp. 11–12.

Considerations

1. Explain how, in Sunshine's view, the Christian church historically has been a major political force in the Caribbean.
2. Before and after the emancipation of slaves, the various denominations of Christianity were not culturally equal. According to Sunshine, what were some of the key differences among them?
3. What is "myalism," and how did it co-exist with the forms of Christianity imported to the British colonies?
4. If you've read the previous excerpt by Merle Hodge, use insights provided by Sunshine to analyze the religious tensions dramatized in Tantie's conflict with Mr. and Mrs. Hinds.

5. Apply some portion of Sunshine's commentary as a framework for analyzing the religious behavior and social relationships in the opening pages of Michelle Cliff's *Abeng*, which follows.

The following selection comprises the first three chapters of Michelle Cliff's novel Abeng, *set in Jamaica (*abeng, *Cliff tells us, is an African word for conch shell and refers to the instruments used both by planters to call slaves to work and by rebellious slaves to communicate with one another).* Abeng *is an unusual novel, composed, as you'll see, of short, interspliced sections, some of which are about Cliff's central character Clare Savage, but others of which range widely over Jamaican history and modern Jamaican society. One of her historical emphases is upon the Maroons, the slave group that successfully revolted in the early eighteenth century, forced a treaty in 1739, and maintained autonomous control of a portion of Jamaica for fifty years thereafter. You'll find that the modern emphasis of Cliff's main story line, set in 1958, is upon contrasts in religion. As you read, you might want to jot down some of the differences you notice: How many distinguishable religious groups does she show us, and in what ways do their differences matter?*

From *Abeng*

MICHELLE CLIFF

CHAPTER ONE

The island rose and sank. Twice. During periods in which history was recorded by indentations on rock and shell.

This is a book about the time which followed on that time. As the island became a place where people lived. Indians. Africans. Europeans.

It was a Sunday morning at the height of the height of the mango season. High July — and hot. No rain probably until October — at least no rain of any consequence.

There was a splendid profusion of fruit. The slender cylinders of St. Juliennes hung from a grafted branch of a common mango tree in a backyard in town. Round and pink Bombays seemed to be everywhere — brimming calabashes in the middle of dining tables, pouring out of crates and tumbling onto sidewalks. Small and orange number

---

MICHELLE CLIFF (b. 1946) was born in Kingston, Jamaica, and was educated in New York City and London. Her works include the short story collection *Bodies of Water* (1990) and the novels *Free Enterprise* (1993), *No Telephone to Heaven* (1987), and *Abeng* (1984), excerpted here. Cliff is Allan K. Smith Professor of English language and literature at Trinity College in Connecticut.

elevens filled the market baskets at Crossroads, the baskets carried on the heads of women traveling to town from country. Green and spotted Black mangoes dotted the ground at bus stops, schoolyards, country stores — these were only to be gathered, not sold. The fruit was all over and each variety was unto itself — with its own taste, its own distinction of shade and highlight, its own occasion and use. In the yards around town and on the hills in the country, spots of yellow, pink, red, orange, black, and green appeared between the almost-blue elongated leaves of the fat and laden trees — and created a confusion underneath.

The Savages — father, mother, and two daughters — were getting ready for church, the first service of the day. "This is the day the Lord has made. Let us rejoice and be glad in it." Mr. Savage chanted as he shaved. The girls were bickering over something or other in the room they shared, and at the same time filling their small plastic purses with a shilling for collection, clean handkerchief with SUNDAY embroidered in the corner, and a ripe number eleven.

It seemed to many people that all the children on the island were carrying pieces of the fruit with them. Khaki pockets bulged out of shape with roundness and in defiance — just one slip on the pavement could release juice or sap, and there would be hell to pay. Mouths everywhere burned from the sap and tingled from the juice; teeth caught the hairs from the seed and tightened around the yellow and gold fibers — even though there was bounty, it was important to reach every last bit of flesh — to complete the mango, and move on to the next.

It was as if the island was host to some ripe sweet plague. Because of the visitation, peppermint and chocolate sales had dropped off, so had paradise plums, bullah cakes — and the Fudgie men who peddled popsicles from wooden boxes on the backs of their bicycles noticed fewer responses to their cry of FUDGEEEE. The new-to-the-island soft custard stand on the Halfway Tree Road reported that they were not doing very well, but expected sales to pick up in the heat of August, when the mangoes would be finished and the avocado would be in season.

Mangotime was not usually such a business, but this was 1958 and the biggest crop in recent memory — as the *Daily Gleaner* itself reported. The paper ran an editorial which spoke of God's Gift to Jamaica, and concluded by telling all inhabitants to be hospitable to the tourists.

Some of the mystery and wonder of mangotime may have been in the fact that this was a wild fruit. Jamaicans did not cultivate it for export to America or England — like citrus, cane, bananas. So much was this so, that when walking through Harlem or Notting Hill Gate, Brooklyn or Ladbroke Grove, island people were genuinely shocked to see a Bombay, half-ripe usually ("Picked much too young"), nesting in a bed of green excelsior, showing through a display window, priced out of reach ("Lord, have mercy, we use them to stone dogs back home"), and they wondered where the mango had come from. Someone somewhere else must be exporting the fruit. For them, the mango was to be kept an island secret.

They did not cultivate the mango, but they made occasional efforts to change the course of its development. These efforts were usually few and far between and carried out with care and discretion. A branch was sliced from a common mango tree and replaced with a branch from a St. Julienne — the former could withstand all manner of disease or weather; the latter was fragile. But the Jamaican taste was growing for the St.

Julienne, which was judged to be consistently full and deep in its sweetness, while the common mango was termed unpredictable, with a sweetness that could be thin and might leave an aftertaste. That was as far as cultivation went in 1958, though — a few grafts here and there — they did not tamper further.

There were other wild fruit on the island — the bush of Jamaica had long been written about as one of the most naturally fruitful places on earth — but the mango was supreme among all other growing things — the paragon: "Mother Sugar herself."

It was a surprising fruit — sometimes remaining hidden for years behind vines and underbrush — saving its sweetness for wild pigs and wild birds.

In 1958 Jamaica had two rulers: a white queen and a white governor. Independence-in-practically-name-only was four years away. The portrait of the white queen hung in banks, department stores, grocery stores, schools, government buildings, and homes — from countryside shanties to the split-levels on the hills above Kingston Harbor. A rather plain little white woman decked in medals and other regalia — wearing, of course, a crown. Our-lady-of-the-colonies. The whitest woman in the world. Elizabeth II, great-granddaughter of Victoria, for whom the downtown crafts market — where women came from the countryside to sell their baskets and Rastafarians[1] sold their brooms and old Black men sold their wood-carvings to the passengers of cruise ships and Pan-American Clippers — was named.

The monetary system of the island was based on the pounds/shillings/pence of the "mother" country. The coins and notes were similar to those struck and printed for Great Britain itself. The coins came from the Royal Mint and the notes from the Bank of England, popularly called the Old Lady of Threadneedle Street. There were two basic differences: Jamaican money bore the word JAMAICA, and the sovereign crest of the island — an Arawak Indian and a white conqueror: Only one of these existed in 1958.

The population of the island was primarily Black ("overwhelmingly," some sources said), with gradations of shading reaching into the top strata of the society. Africans were mixed with Sephardic Jews, Chinese, Syrians, Lebanese, East Indians — but the large working class, and class of poor people, was Black.

It was the Sunday custom of the Savages to attend their first church service at the John Knox Memorial Church at Constant Spring. Of light brown stucco, the long low building had mahogany louvers running the length of the two far aisles — the louvers were turned down against the sun. The pews were also mahogany, and were divided down the middle by one single center aisle. The church was spare and clean in its design — the only decoration, if that is what it could be called, was a large cross behind the pulpit, carved of Godwood — the original tree — the tree of Eden. Commonly known as the birch gum.

There was no church choir at John Knox; a Scottish schoolteacher played Presbyterian hymns at a harpsichord, which had been shipped to Jamaica in a box and was reassembled by the minister. The instrument had never adjusted to the climate. The

[1]**Rastafarians:** Members of a Jamaican political-religious movement who worship former Ethiopian emperor Haile Selassie and believe blacks will soon be redeemed after longtime subjection to the white race [Eds.].

schoolteacher explained to the congregation that a harpsichord had to be tuned each time it was to be played; even so, tuning upon tuning never made the instrument sound quite right. There was a gravelly tinkle in its voice, far more than a harpsichord is supposed to have, and it was easily drowned out by the passing traffic, the voices of the congregation, the pair of croaking lizards who lived behind the cross of Godwood, sounding a double bass in the wrong tempo, as the schoolteacher tinkled out the prelude, when the congregation entered, and the postlude, when they left the church. Although they were not able to say so, most of the congregation felt that the harpsichord had been a mistake — not meant even in the most perfect of climatic conditions to accompany a hundred voices. It seemed that English people must sing softer — or not at all — and that the climate of that place — damp and dreary — surpassed the clear light and deep warmth of Jamaica. They had always thought their island climate a gift; the harpsichord told them different. The schoolteacher advised the congregation to tone down their singing, to consider the nuances of harmony and quiet — but this didn't work.

The minister of the church was a red-faced Englishman, who preached plainly and briefly, and had been a major in the King's Household Cavalry during the last war. He had emigrated to Jamaica in 1949, and since then had spent his afternoons at the bar of the South Camp Hotel, where he drank beer and played skittles with English soldiers and merchant seamen. On special days he led the congregation in "God Save the Queen" — during the Suez Crisis of 1956[2] they had stood and sung it every Sunday for a month. On other, more ordinary Sundays, they sang the standards — "Onward Christian Soldiers, Marching as to War"; "Faith of Our Fathers, Living Still, in Spite of Dungeon, Fire and Sword"; "Fairest Lord Jesus, Ruler of All Nature"; "Fling Out the Banner, Let It Float, Skyward and Seaward, High and Wide" — in which the banner of righteousness carried by the Christian soldiers mingled with the Union Jack.

The congregation at John Knox was Black and white — Jamaican and English and American. Mostly of the middle class. The church was Mr. Savage's choice for worship.

In 1958, and for some time before, the two most socially prestigious churches in Kingston were Holy Cross, the cathedral at Halfway Tree, and the Kingston Parish Church, downtown on King Street, near King's Parade, founded in 1692.

Holy Cross Cathedral was the church of the island's wealthy Catholics — most of them Lebanese and Syrian and Chinese, some Spanish. These were the same people who sent their daughters to the Convent of the Immaculate Conception, a group of pink-stucco Spanish-tiled-roof villas, set back on green lawns next to a golf course. The Protestants sent their daughters to St. Catherine's, a red-brick girls' school, which was less grand but more severe than Immaculate Conception.

The Parish Church was High Anglican — it was the church of attendance of the white governor, and members of the royal family stopped there when the queen's yacht, *H. M. S. Britannia,* docked in Kingston Harbor. A very large stone edifice, it was foursquare and had been built to last. A rood screen had been imported from a church in Canterbury; a choir loft had been carved by a team of local craftsmen — in 1820, before the slaves were freed.

[2]**Suez Crisis of 1956**: When Egyptian President Gamal Abdel Nasser threatened to limit Western access to the Suez Canal, England and France briefly invaded Egypt, and hostilities began to broaden before a cease-fire was declared in late 1956 [Eds.].

In 1958, while digging near the churchyard during some renovations to the building, workers uncovered a coffin of heavy metal — a coffin of huge proportions. Not the shape of a coffin at all — shaped like a monstrous packing case, made of lead and welded shut. A brass plate which had been affixed to the coffin and etched with an inscription informed the vicar that the coffin contained the remains of a hundred plague victims, part of a shipload of slaves from the Gold Coast, who had contracted the plague from the rats on the vessel which brought them to Jamaica. Others, many others, would have died onboard and their bodies dropped in the sea along the Middle Passage — the route across the Atlantic from Africa — or the Windward Passage — the route from the Atlantic to the islands of the Caribbean Sea. The people in the coffin had died in a *barracoon* in Kingston — a holding pen — a stockade.

The coffin should be opened on no account, the plaque said, as the plague might still be viable. The vicar commissioned an American navy warship in port to take the coffin twenty miles out and sink it in the sea.

After the morning service, the Savages left Constant Spring and drove to their house on Dunbarton Crescent, where Dorothy, the Black woman who worked for them, prepared Sunday dinner. When the family had eaten, and she had cleaned up, she caught the bus to Trench Town, where her three-year-old daughter lived with Dorothy's mother. The Savages left also, for their weekly seabath at Tumbleover, a rocky and wild beach, unsheltered by cove or harbor, opposite the mangrove swamps on the Palisadoes Road, between Kingston Airport and the Gypsum factory at Rock Fort — a fort built by the Spanish, with the cannon still in place.

There was a wicked undertow at Tumbleover, and huge waves unbroken by a reef. Underneath the water was smooth rock covered with slippery sealife, and no foothold to be had. Once in the waves, a swimmer had to relax and ride the breakers — far out and then in. The beach was usually deserted, with only the water's force as background noise, and occasional planes circling to land at Palisadoes.

A Sunday afternoon not long before this Sunday afternoon, Clare, the elder Savage daughter, who was twelve years old, found a trilobite fossil embedded in the rocks under the water, and Mr. Savage had explained in great detail how old the world was, and how insignificant was man.

"Clare, if you took a broomstick; or if you took an obelisk from ancient Egypt, like Cleopatra's Needle, and made a pinprick at the tip — that would represent the history of mankind; the rest all came before us. Think about it. Consider it."

Clare's relationship with her father took the form of what she imagined a son would have, if there had been a son. Mr. Savage took his daughter to a mountaintop to prove to her that the island had exploded from the sea. True to his theory — she was his daughter; she assumed the idea belonged to him — there were fragments of seashells and pieces of coral on top. He explained to her how the entire chain of the West Indies had once been underwater. He spoke of mountain-folding, the process by which flat rock becomes peaks and slopes. While this process usually took thousands of years, Mr. Savage preferred to believe that Jamaican mountains had been created in cataclysm. All of a sudden.

Perhaps, he said to his daughter, the islands of the West Indies — particularly the

Greater Antilles,[3] which were said once to have been joined — were the remains of Atlantis, the floating continent Plato had written about in the *Timaeus,* that sank under the sea. It had been an ideal place, too good for this world. "But then there was a great and powerful earthquake, and the continent came back up again — and was first joined in a chain and then was split apart into islands." He stopped; then thought further. "Or maybe the islands were an undersea mountain range, and emerged when Atlantis went under the Mediterranean. When the volcano erupted in Crete." He paused again.

"Some say that Crete and Atlantis were one," still trying to forge some connection between the pieces of knowledge he possessed, and how he wanted things to be.

Mr. Savage was fascinated by myth and natural disaster. He collected books on Stonehenge, the Pyramids, the Great Wall of China — he knew the details of each ancient structure and was convinced that all were connected to some magical source — some "divine plan," he said. Nothing, to him, was ever what it seemed to be. Nothing was an achievement of human labor. Devising arch and circle; creating brick from straw and mud and hauling stones to the site of construction. Mr. Savage was a believer in extraterrestrial life — in a mythic piece of machinery found in a bed of coal: part of a spaceship, he concluded; proof that we had been visited by beings from another planet, who might be observing us even now. Most people thought him focused out, most of the time, while they were focused in, or down. "Down to earth," was what they called his wife — sometimes his complement, sometimes his opposite. To pass the time until his deliverance, he went to the racetrack, courted women on the sly, drank rum and water, and moved from job to job, while his wife kept her faith, saved her own money from her job in a downtown hotel, spoke sometimes with her relatives, and prayed for a better day.

Clare's father was no commonplace dreamer, one whose visions were only slightly distorted by rum; he didn't have dreams anywhere near the realm of accomplishment. His visions — which included the second coming, the end of the world, Armageddon — would be achieved only by waiting; only through intervention from the outside — when God judged the time was right. In the meanwhile he tried to pass these ideals on to his elder daughter — calling her an Aztec princess, golden in the sun. "Clare, you would have certainly been a choice for sacrifice — you know the Aztecs slaughtered their most beautiful virgins and drank their blood." It did not occur to Clare to question her father's reading of history — a worldview in which she would have been chosen for divine slaughter.

Most often, she became his defender. When he talked about his notions of space and time and magic to her mother's family, they only laughed at him. Telling him the planets were but dust. Illusions created by God to speak of his glory. Dust and shadow was the rest of the universe. Earth was the one concrete reality. And this life, life on Earth, just a gateway to the life everlasting. Which was the one true realm of existence. Many of them only waited to pass into that realm.

This particular afternoon, Mr. Savage had just stepped into the water, when he came running and screaming out again — "Shark! Shark!" He was howling and shaking

[3]**Greater Antilles:** Caribbean islands including Cuba, Haiti, the Dominican Republic, Jamaica, and Puerto Rico [Eds.].

and pale. He claimed a shark had swum up right beside his thigh and touched him. Mrs. Savage went into the water to prove it was safe now, and the girls, Clare and Jennie, who was seven, followed her. But it was no use. "As God is my judge," Mr. Savage vowed, "I am never going into the sea again — never."

In later weeks, the family moved from Tumbleover to Cable Hut, a beach sheltered by reef and cove, but Mr. Savage only disappeared into the shed where they sold rum, and reappeared when one of the girls was sent to get him, and they were ready to leave for home.

CHAPTER TWO

The afternoon of the shark scare the Savages returned home and changed again into church clothes, for the evening service at the Tabernacle of the Almighty on Mountainview Road. Mrs. Savage's place of worship.

The Tabernacle was a small cement-block building separated from the road by a gravel parking lot. Most of the congregation came on foot — the parking lot belonged to the grocery store next door, and the land for the Tabernacle was leased from the shopkeeper, Mr. Chin. The church had aluminum louvers, open to the sounds of cars and the lights of the street, but the building had been baking all day under a zinc roof, and the louvers also let in a breeze from the harbor. At the back of the church the dark outlines of the foothills of the Blue Mountains were shadowed.

As the car drove toward the Tabernacle, Clare could see the congregation moving along the road. All the women seemed to wear the same white plastic-straw hat, and white shoes; their dresses were pastel shades — lime-green, pale blue, light pink. The men were dressed in dark suits, some with a fine gray stripe, light wool or gabardine, and dark shoes and socks. The boy children wore the khaki most Jamaican boys wore, with their school insignia showing in the colors of the epaulets on their shoulders. The girl children were small replicas of the women. Everyone on the road carried a Bible or hymnal in their hands.

The service at the Tabernacle began with Sister Icilda and Sister Girlie singing a duet to the Lord Jesus with their hands folded in on each other in front of their bosoms. Their bottom lips trembled as they strained for the high notes. Secretly — never to their faces — the congregation called them Miss Titty and Miss Tatty, so prim and alike were they. All dressed in white — virginal and deadly serious — they needed no vicar to temper their relationship with the Almighty. This apparent purity seemed to invite ridicule — of which the sisters were entirely oblivious.

After their duet, Brother Emmanuel began as he usually began. Each week pointing a sharply nailed and polished finger at a random communicant (man, woman, or child), and booming: "You . . . You . . . Brother or Sister . . . are on a slip-pery sli-ide to HELL!" It was the brother's standard preface to a sermon in which all in the room were condemned — "unto your children and your children's children" — for the sin and wretched hopelessness of their lives.

When Brother Emmanuel rested, sitting back in his overstuffed chair and taking a breath, Sister Shirley pumped the old pump organ and the congregation rose to her call, led by the choir, to sing hymns like "Blessed Assurance! Jesus is mine/Oh what a foretaste of glory divine!/Heir of salvation, purchase of God/Born of His spirit, washed in His blood." Or "Rock of ages, cleft for me/Let me hide myself in Thee/Let the water and the blood, from Thy wounded side which flowed/Be of sin the double cure, cleanse me from its guilt and power."

The hymns at John Knox seemed to suggest a historical and almost equal relationship with the idea of God — that this God would support the travel of the Word to faraway "climes" and distant "heathen" by almost any means necessary — "marching as to war." The hymns sung by the people in the Tabernacle suggested something else. The necessity of deliverance. A belief in their eventual redemption. In the balm of Gilead.

During the service — every Sunday evening — someone would be seized with the spirit, and jump up and fall down moaning, or sway faster and faster back and forth, calling on God to hear her, asking his forgiveness. Those so possessed were almost always women. When a sister got the spirit, two white-gowned sisters came forward to make sure that the jumping or swaying or fainting communicant would not do damage to herself. At the start of a full-fledged seizure, Brother Emmanuel would signal Sisters Icilda and Girlie to start a hymn — and again all would rise, and Sister Shirley would pump, and the church would rock back and forth with the vibration of voices, organ, and possession.

There were more women than men in the church tonight, Clare thought. There were always more women than men. And the women became possessed. And the women sang louder. At times, it occurred to her, the church seemed only women — as Brother Emmanuel's body, and his authority, melted into the purple satin of his chair.

The congregation of John Knox was for the most part families — brown and Black and red and white mothers and fathers and children. The Tabernacle consisted for the most part of Black women — sitting and singing in groups and pairs and alone.

When Clare visited her grandmother — her mother's mother — in St. Elizabeth, a parish in the deep country — she sometimes helped her prepare the house for Sunday meeting. The two began on Saturday — cleaning the floors, then waxing them, using half a coconut husk for a brush to bring out the shine on the broad mahogany planks. They dusted and waxed the furniture, and dry-mopped and wet-mopped the painted concrete floor of the porch. On Sunday morning they began by cutting flowers — blossoms of mimosa or mountain pride, blooms of hibiscus or bougainvillea — and putting them into the cut-glass pitcher which Clare's great-grandmother had taken with her when she left her family to run off with one of their servants. This woman, Judith, never saw the family of her mother and father again, but she made her own. She raised five children in a two-room house in the country, with her husband, Mas Samuel, keeping chickens and planting and tending a slope of coffee to keep them going. "Granny," she was called, and Clare had never known her; she had only heard that Granny had become a "bitter old woman," while Mas Samuel became beloved by all around. He outlived his wife by fifteen years, and Clare had known him when she was a baby, but couldn't recollect his face. "Such a sweet brown man. So sweet." That was what people said.

The cut-glass pitcher, carved on its sides with diamond shapes, was all that now remained from Granny's first life. It was prismatic, and split the light in the parlor, casting stripes of color which reflected on the polished floor.

From Judith's second life, there remained the spine of Clare's grandmother's house, two rooms to which two more had been added, one on either side. And Granny's grave, a concrete rectangle at the side of the house next to the flower garden. There was an open book at Granny's head, inscribed with her name and the dates of her life, the names of her dead and living children, and the name of her husband, whose own grave was a yard away.

The pitcher filled with flowers and rainbows sat in the center of the long-legged parlor table on a lace cloth, the family Bible beside it. The old wooden louvers around the room were opened wide to let in the sunlight, because Clare's grandmother, Miss Mattie, did not want to use the kerosene lamps. In the light, spots of dust floated around the room, and Clare, who had been taught about ashes to ashes, dust to dust, liked to think they were bits of the mysterious Granny, whose life and death fascinated her. What she knew of them.

Once the parlor was ready, they went into the yard. Miss Mattie carried her penknife and Clare gathered short sticks, which her grandmother sharpened with the knife — these they put by the front steps, for the members to scrape the red mud from their shoe soles before entering the house. The red mud was clay, heavy and difficult to get off once it dried.

Finally the two — the sorceress and her apprentice, but she wasn't a sorceress, just a woman who led Sunday services — went into the dining room to prepare the communion tray. Slices of a fresh loaf of hard-dough bread were cut into small squares (this is my body, which is broken for you), and Miss Mattie opened her ceremonial bottle of red South African wine and poured some into small glasses which were put on the tray next to the bread (this is my blood, which is shed for you). Clare's grandmother sang softly as she made this ritual, and would not allow her granddaughter to speak or to join in. She closed her eyes briefly over the tray, and then carried it into the parlor, where she placed it on the lower shelf of the long-legged table (this do in remembrance of me). And it caught one of Granny's rainbows. The blood-wine making a mirror in which Clare could detect her own reflection.

Clare was no longer needed. Her grandmother closed all the doors to the parlor and went into her room to dress for the service, and to see that her husband was also dressed. Clare went to the river to meet her friend Zoe, and to swim — she would return only when she knew her grandmother's church was over and the congregation had left.

In 1733, Nanny, the sorceress, the *obeah*-woman, was killed by a *quashee* — a slave faithful to the white planters — at the height of the War of the Maroons.

Nanny, who could catch a bullet between her buttocks and render the bullet harmless, was from the empire of the Ashanti, and carried the secrets of her magic into slavery. She prepared amulets and oaths for her armies. Her Nanny Town, hidden in the crevices of the Blue Mountains, was the headquarters of the Windward Maroons — who held out against the forces of the white men longer than any rebel troops. They waged war from 1655–1740. Nanny was the magician of this revolution — she used her skill to unite her people and to consecrate their battles.

There is absolutely no doubt that she actually existed. And the ruins of her Nanny Town remain difficult to reach.

The Tabernacle was alive with voices and movement.

"Um-hmm."

"Oh, yes, Lord. Oh, yes."

"Amen, Brother."

These words were being spoken in ones or twos — together or distinct — as

Brother Emmanuel got into the substance of his sermon. It was the usual message he gave his congregation every week. Brother Emmanuel was not a man of any rare gifts of imagination — he just plied his trade as a man of God, Sunday after Sunday, striving to be a respected somebody on his own account, as well as trying to save the souls of his flock from damnation. He was not inspired in his delivery of the word — for instance, no one could remember him telling a joke to illustrate one of his sermons. Perhaps preachers were not meant to tell jokes. He had said something funny once, but the joke was not meant to be. Brother Emmanuel had begun a sentence with "brethren," then glanced across the congregation and his eyes met with those of Sisters Icilda and Girlie. His mind reckoned with the presence of so many women in his congregation, and he matched brethren with "sistern" — which the congregation of course heard as "cistern." Some smiled — Brother Emmanuel coughed, then continued.

Now, he was in full swing —

"No dancing, children . . . No dancing, no movies . . . No dancing, children, no movies, and no liquor. These t'ings are the work of the devil. These t'ings serve us not, except to weaken us — in spirit *and* in body."

"Yes, Brother. Yes. Lord."

"We mus' not smoke the weed, mus' not smoke tobacco, nor ganja, my children. For with these t'ings, we become as lotos eaters, and we accomplish no-t'ing in our days."

"Mm-hmm. Yes, Brother. Wunna speak true."

"And let there be no carousing among my flock, no contention between mother and child, husband and wife, sister and brother, woman and man. Contention will mek us weak. Contention will tun us 'gainst one another. Contention will tun us from the Lord Almighty, the maker of heaven and of earth, in whom all t'ings are possible."

"Yes, Brother. Yes, Lord."

"We mus' bide our time. We mus' be patient. We will wait on the Lord. This is the way, children. This is the way to the life everlasting. In which we will all meet over yonder. In the sweet by-and-by. When the trumpet of the Lord shall sound, and the world shall be no more. When the saints of earth have gathered over on the other shore, and the roll is called up yonder I'll be there. When the roll, when the roll is called up yonder, I'll be there."

With that, Sister Shirley pumped the organ and the congregation rose.

In front of the Tabernacle, next to the grocery store which carried dried saltfish and soft drinks and cooking oil and rice and sundries, was a rum shop, where men with criss-crossed red eyeballs swung in and out all hours of the day and all days of the year. Down the road was a moviehouse, the Rialto, which showed triple features of American gangster movies and B-grade westerns and jungle serials starring Johnny Sheffield. There was a shop next to the moviehouse which sold raffle tickets. And another close by which was an offtrack betting parlor, selling wagers on the Epsom Derby and the Grand National at Aintree, as well as the races at home. Number one South Windward Road was known to be a badhouse, where women, gambling, rum, ganja, and all manner of *sint'ing*[4] could be had.

The men who were in the Tabernacle were being sorely tempted. As were their brothers outside. And there was little that Brother Emmanuel could do to alleviate the

[4]***sint'ing:*** "Something"; something sinful [Eds.].

temptation. To relieve them. The space the temptation entered could not be filled by hymn-singing or sermons, no matter how terrifying. The space had been carved so long ago, carried so long within, it was a historic fact. "Every dog have him day, every puss their four o'clock," was something people said — but saying this was not enough.

The white Jesus, with his chestnut hair, brown eyes, and soft mustache, was handsomer than the white queen, and seemed kinder, but the danger to these men was beyond him. The men — when they worked — were servants to light-skinned or white families; waiters at South Camp, Myrtle Bank, or Courtleigh Manor; porters at Palisadoes Airport. They pumped gas at Texaco or Esso stations. They swept sidewalks. They carried garbage. They cut grass and trimmed hedges. Killed rats. Fed dogs. They balanced trays of Red Stripe beer or Appleton Estate rum on their upturned palms. They were paid with a small brown envelope of cash. They lived from week to week.

The women in the Tabernacle had their spaces of need also — but for most of them, the space had been reduced over time, so that the filling of it became a matter for family. Their anguish in this life became for them identifiable in the faces of the people they were part of. Their pain was unto themselves. As the men's relief was unto themselves. But to the women fell the responsibility for kin — sisters, mothers, children.

The women also served. Cleaned. Mopped. Cooked. Cared for babies lighter than their own. Did other people's laundry. Bought other people's goods in the markets at Crossroads and Constant Spring. They too received some cash each week. To their mothers and sisters and their aunts they gave some toward the care of their children. They saw these children perhaps once a week, if the children were kept in town. Less often if they were not. Many of these women had never been married, but they kept their children and gave them names and supervised their rearing as best they could. Some had been married, but their husbands had left them for America to pick fruit. Or for the north of England to work in factories. Others had husbands employed in households or hotels in different parts of Kingston — these men lived-in, as did their wives — and over the years these people lost touch. So much was ranged against the upkeep of these connections. At times they felt the cause of their losses lay in themselves — their people's *wuthlessness.*

"Like one of the family" was a reality they lived with — taking Christmas with their employers and saving Boxing Day[5] for their own. "Like one of the family" meant staying in a small room with one light and a table and a bed — listening to a sound system which piped in Radio Jamaica. They waited for tea-time and prepared lap trays dressed with starched and ironed linen cloths. They asked missis for the key to the larder so they could remove caddies of Earl Grey or Lapsang Souchong leaves, tins of sardines, English biscuits, Cross and Blackwell or Tiptree preserves — gooseberry or greengage plum.

Sometimes this other family became more familiar to them than the people they were closest to. The people they were part of.

An hour a week with Jesus and Brother Emmanuel, backed up by Sisters Icilda and Girlie and the choir, Sister Shirley and her pump organ, eased them somewhat. It was a steady easing — they too lived from week to week. They could count on the ease and there was no one who could take it away from them. They were "washed in the blood of the Lamb."

* * *

[5]**Boxing Day:** A holiday, similar to American Labor Day, celebrated the day after Christmas [Eds.].

In the beginning there had been two sisters — Nanny and Sekesu. Nanny fled slavery. Sekesu remained a slave. Some said this was the difference between the sisters.

It was believed that all island children were descended from one or the other. All island people were first cousins.

CHAPTER THREE

> Do-fe-do mek guinea nigger come a Jamaica.[6]
>
> — proverb

The people in the Tabernacle could trace their bloodlines back to a past of slavery. But this was not something they talked about much, or knew much about. In school they were told that their ancestors had been pagan. That there had been slaves in Africa, where Black people had put each other in chains. They were given the impression that the whites who brought them here from the Gold Coast and the Slave Coast were only copying a West African custom. As though the whites had not named the Slave Coast themselves.

The congregation did not know that African slaves in Africa had been primarily household servants. They were not seasoned. They were not worked in canefields. The system of labor was not industrialized. There was in fact no comparison between the two states of servitude: that practiced by the tribal societies of West Africa and that organized by the Royal African Company of London, chartered by the Crown. These people did not know that one of the reasons the English Parliament and the Crown finally put an end to the slave trade was that because of the Victorian mania for cleanliness, manufacturers needed West African palm oil to make soap — soon the trade in palm oil became more profitable than the trade in men and women and the merchants shifted their investments.

No one had told the people in the Tabernacle that of all the slave societies in the New World, Jamaica was considered among the most brutal. They did not know that the death rate of Africans in Jamaica under slavery exceeded the rate of birth, and that the growth of the slave population from 1,500 in 1655 to 311,070 in 1834, the year of freedom, was due *only* to the importation of more people, more slaves. They did not know that some slaves worked with their faces locked in masks of tin, so they would not eat the sugar cane as they cut. Or that there were few white women on the island during slavery, and so the grandmothers of these people sitting in a church on a Sunday evening during mango season, had been violated again and again by the very men who whipped them. The rape of Black women would have existed with or without the presence of white women, of course, but in Jamaica there was no pretense of civility — all was in the open.

Now her head is tied. Now braided. Strung with beads and cowrie shells. Now she is disguised as a *chasseur.*[7] Now wrapped in a cloth shot through with gold. Now she stalks the Red Coats as they march toward her cave, where she spins her Akan chants into spells which stun her enemies. Calls on the goddesses of the Ashanti forests. Remembers the battle formations of the Dahomey Amazons. She turns her attention to the

[6]**Translation:** Fighting among themselves brought West African slaves to Jamaica.

[7]***chasseur:*** Hunter [Eds.].

hunt. To the cultivation of cassava and yam and plantain — hiding the places for use in case of flight.

The forests of the island are wild and remind her of Africa. In places the mountains are no more than cliff-faces. The precipices of these mountains often hold caves she can use for headquarters or to conceal the weapons of her army. She mixes dyes from roots and teaches others to cast images on the walls. She collects bark from the trunk and limbs of the birch gum to touch to the skin of her enemies while they sweat — and instructs her followers in the natural ways of death. She moves on her elbows and knees across narrow rock ledges. Through corridors created by stone.

The entryways are covered in some places with vines — in others with cascades of water. She teaches her troops to be surefooted and to guard the points of access. They hunt with bow and arrow. Spears. Warclubs. They fill the muskets stolen from plantations with pebbles, buttons, coins. She teaches them to become bulletproof. To catch a bullet in their left hand and fire it back at their attackers. Only she can catch a bullet between her buttocks — that is a secret she keeps for herself.

She teaches them if they are caught to commit suicide by eating dirt.

The capture of the island from the Spanish had been an afterthought. The British fleet, under the command of Penn and Venables, following the orders of the Lord Protector Oliver Cromwell, was unable to take Santo Domingo, and so moved on Jamaica. This took place in 1655. Over the course of the next 180 years, until freedom was obtained in 1834, there was armed, sustained guerrilla warfare against the forces of enslavement. A complex intelligence system between the rebels and the plantation slaves. A network of towns and farms and camps independent from the white planters. An army of thousands — literally thousands — called the Maroons. And this army had moved over the mountains now shadowed at the back of the Tabernacle.

Their name came from *cimarrón:* unruly, runaway. A word first given to cattle which had taken to the hills. Beyond its exact meaning, the word connoted fierce, wild, unbroken.

Through the open louvers came the light from the rumshop and the voices of drinkers staggering home. The smell of the sea and the smell of mangoes mixed with each other.

The people in the Tabernacle did not know that their ancestors had been paid to inform on one another: given their freedom for becoming the *blackshots* of the white man. The *blackshot* troops were the most skilled at searching out and destroying the rebels — but they also had a high desertion rate and had been known to turn against their white commanders in battle.

The people in the Tabernacle did not know that Kishee, one of Nanny's commanders, had been killed by Scipio, a Black slave — but of course they did not know who Kishee had been.

They did not know about the Kingdom of the Ashanti or the Kingdom of Dahomey, where most of their ancestors had come from. They did not imagine that Black Africans had commanded thousands of warriors. Built universities. Created systems of law. Devised language. Wrote history. Poetry. Were traders. Artists. Diplomats.

They did not know that their name for papaya — *pawpaw* — was the name of one of the languages of Dahomey. Or that the *cotta,* the circle of cloth women wound tightly to make a cushion to balance baskets on their heads, was an African device, an African word. That Brer Anancy, the spider who inspired tricks and tales, was a West African invention. Or that Cuffee was the name of a Maroon commander — the word had come down to them as *cuffy,* and meant upstart, social climber.

Some of them were called Nanny, because they cared for the children of other women, but they did not know who Nanny had been.

When the English troops advanced on Nanny Town the second time, she decided to move her army across the Blue Mountains — so when the Red Coats arrived the village would be abandoned and the enemy would be confused. At night she and her army set out to find Cudjoe, the leader of the Maroons across the island, and to join with him in a final attack to defeat the whites and take control of the island for the Africans. Her warriors marched in front and behind. In the center of the single file were the women and children, the old people, the young men and women who carried provisions. They had planted all along the route, and Nanny had marked the places where they could take shelter for a day and a night, while the warriors hunted for wild pig, and the others built fires to roast the meat. They marched in this way for over a hundred miles, and finally reached Accompong Town, where Cudjoe and his men were.

A settlement in the Cockpit Country, the land of endless funnels in the earth, the land of look behind. At the heart of the limestone plateau which forms the center of the island. A place of seemingly purposeless crevasses — created when the island sank during the Pliocene Period and the limestone layers dissolved in places — the dissolution stopping where the limestone met with insoluble rock. Swallow-holes. Cockpits. Places to hide. Difficult to reach. Not barren but deep and magnificent indentations populated by bush and growth and wild orchids — collectors of water — natural goblets.

Nanny moved forward to the small dark man with the hump on his back. Cudjoe wore knee-length breeches, an old ragged coat, and a hat with no brim. On his right side he carried a cow's horn of gunpowder and a bag of shots for his musket. From his left shoulder a sheathed cutlass dangled from a strap. His Black skin was reddened from the bauxite in the earth. His followers — those who now surrounded him — were also reddened men. His eyes met with those of Nanny — the small and old Black woman whose only decoration was a necklace fashioned from the teeth of white men. She did not speak, but instructed Kishee to begin the negotiations with Cudjoe. Kishee told him of their plan to join with Cudjoe and his men — the Leeward Maroons — against the Red Coats. He told Cudjoe about the band of Miskito Indians brought to the island to fight against them. The Miskitos — almost every one — had come over to the Maroon side. Through the Miskitos the Windward Maroons had contacted the Spanish on Cuba; and the Spanish governor agreed to respect the freedom of all the Africans on the island, if the rebels won the colony back for Spain.

Cudjoe refused this offer of alliance. He only gave the Windwards temporary refuge before their journey home. They stayed a short time in his camp, then walked back across the plateau and the mountains, through the rainforests, to their own territory.

Not long after, Nanny was murdered, and Cudjoe signed a separate peace with the British governor, in which he was permitted freedom and promised to hunt down other rebels for the Crown. He and his followers became known as the King's Negroes.

Some said he had tired of fighting. Others that he wanted to consolidate his power.

* * *

The service was over and the congregation was wishing a "good evening" to Brother Emmanuel. The Savages left with the others and drove home through the by-now-cool night, in which the scent of ripe mangoes was present and heavy. As Mr. Savage drove along the Halfway Tree Road his headlights flashed on the side of Holy Cross — CASTRO SÍ, BATISTA NO. In black paint. In large letters against the cathedral.

Considerations

1. Analyze Cliff's characterization of Clare's father. What do you think we're supposed to make of him? Support your view with evidence. How do you decide on a perspective from which to view him?
2. Who are Nanny and the Maroons, and why do you think Cliff has placed them so prominently in her novel?
3. What are the effects of so many disruptions in the narrative about Clare? Why do you think Cliff chooses not to tell Clare's story straightforwardly?
4. What conclusions can you draw about the congregation of the Tabernacle? Does Cliff present the members sympathetically or condescendingly?
5. Classify the religious behaviors that we encounter in these pages. What significant differences can you notice from one group to the next?
6. Analyze this excerpt from *Abeng* from a perspective suggested by Catherine A. Sunshine in the previous piece.

Jamaica Kincaid is mainly a writer of fiction. But in A Small Place *(1988), she has turned to nonfiction in offering an analysis of the cultural politics of her native Antigua. Much of that book is an effort to understand the forms of corruption among Antiguans, but she begins her book with an examination of the tourist industry or, more specifically, the motives of tourists, whom she addresses as "you," her reader. As you read, consider the effects of this "you."*

From *A Small Place*

JAMAICA KINCAID

You disembark from your plane. You go through customs. Since you are a tourist, a North American or European — to be frank, white — and not an Antiguan black returning to Antigua from Europe or North America with cardboard boxes of much needed cheap clothes and food for relatives, you move through customs swiftly, you move through customs with ease. Your bags are not searched. You emerge from customs into the hot, clean air: Immediately you feel cleansed, immediately you feel blessed (which is to say special); you feel free. You see a man, a taxi driver; you ask him to take you to your destination; he quotes you a price. You immediately think that the price is in the local currency, for you are a tourist and you are familiar with these things (rates of exchange) and you feel even more free, for things seem so cheap, but then your driver ends by saying, "In U.S. currency." You may say, "Hmmmm, do you have a formal sheet that lists official prices and destinations?" Your driver obeys the law and shows you the sheet, and he apologizes for the incredible mistake he has made in quoting you a price off the top of his head which is so vastly different (favoring him) from the one listed. You are driven to your hotel by this taxi driver in his taxi, a brand-new Japanese-made vehicle. The road on which you are traveling is a very bad road, very much in need of repair. You are feeling wonderful, so you say, "Oh, what a marvelous change these bad roads are from the splendid highways I am used to in North America." (Or, worse, Europe.) Your driver is reckless; he is a dangerous man who drives in the middle of the road when he thinks no other cars are coming in the opposite direction, passes other cars on blind curves that run uphill, drives at sixty miles an hour on narrow, curving roads when the road sign, a rusting, beat-up thing left over from colonial days, says 40 MPH. This might frighten you (you are on your holiday; you are a tourist); this might excite you (you are on your holiday; you are a tourist), though if you are from New York and take taxis you are used to this style of driving: Most of the taxi drivers in New York are from places in the world like this. You are looking out the window (because you want to get your money's worth); you notice that all the cars you see are brand-new, or almost brand-new, and that they are all Japanese-made. There are no American cars in Antigua — no new ones, at any rate; none that were manufactured in the last ten years. You continue to look at the cars and you say to yourself, Why, they look brand new, but they have an awful sound, like an old car — a very old, dilapidated car. How to account for that? Well, possibly it's because they use leaded gasoline in these brand-new cars whose engines were built to use nonleaded gasoline, but you musn't ask the person driving the car if this is so, because he or she has never heard of unleaded gasoline. You look closely at the car; you see that it's a model of a Japanese car that you might hesitate to buy; it's a model that's very expensive; it's a model that's quite impractical for a person who has to work as hard as you do and who watches every penny you earn so that you can afford this holiday you are

---

JAMAICA KINCAID (born Elaine Richardson in 1949) grew up in Antigua and now resides in Vermont. A frequent contributor to *The New Yorker,* Kincaid is also the author of the story collection *At the Bottom of the River* (1983), the novels *Annie John* (1985) and *Lucy* (1990), *Autobiography of My Mother* (1996), and a commentary on life in Antigua, *A Small Place* (1988), which is excerpted here.

on. How do they afford such a car? And do they live in a luxurious house to match such a car? Well, no. You will be surprised, then, to see that most likely the person driving this brand-new car filled with the wrong gas lives in a house that, in comparison, is far beneath the status of the car; and if you were to ask why you would be told that the banks are encouraged by the government to make loans available for cars, but loans for houses not so easily available; and if you ask again why, you will be told that the two main car dealerships in Antigua are owned in part or outright by ministers in government. Oh, but you are on holiday and the sight of these brand-new cars driven by people who may or may not have really passed their driving test (there was once a scandal about driving licenses for sale) would not really stir up these thoughts in you. You pass a building sitting in a sea of dust and you think, It's some latrines for people just passing by, but when you look again you see the building has written on it PIGOTT'S SCHOOL. You pass the hospital, the Holberton Hospital, and how wrong you are not to think about this, for though you are a tourist on your holiday, what if your heart should miss a few beats? What if a blood vessel in your neck should break? What if one of those people driving those brand-new cars filled with the wrong gas fails to pass safely while going uphill on a curve and you are in the car going in the opposite direction? Will you be comforted to know that the hospital is staffed with doctors that no actual Antiguan trusts; that Antiguans always say about the doctors, "I don't want them near me"; that Antiguans refer to them not as doctors but as "the three men" (there are three of them); that when the Minister of Health himself doesn't feel well he takes the first plane to New York to see a real doctor; that if any one of the ministers in government needs medical care he flies to New York to get it? . . .

Oh, but by now you are tired of all this looking, and you want to reach your destination — your hotel, your room. You long to refresh yourself; you long to eat some nice lobster, some nice local food. You take a bath, you brush your teeth. You get dressed again; as you get dressed, you look out the window. That water — have you ever seen anything like it? Far out, to the horizon, the color of the water is navy-blue; nearer, the water is the color of the North American sky. From there to the shore, the water is pale, silvery, clear, so clear that you can see its pinkish-white sand bottom. Oh, what beauty! Oh, what beauty! You have never seen anything like this. You are so excited. You breathe shallow. You breathe deep. You see a beautiful boy skimming the water, godlike, on a Windsurfer. You see an incredibly unattractive, fat, pastrylike-fleshed woman enjoying a walk on the beautiful sand, with a man, an incredibly unattractive, fat, pastrylike-fleshed man; you see the pleasure they're taking in their surroundings. Still standing, looking out the window, you see yourself lying on the beach, enjoying the amazing sun (a sun so powerful and yet so beautiful, the way it is always overhead as if on permanent guard, ready to stamp out any cloud that dares to darken and so empty rain on you and ruin your holiday; a sun that is your personal friend). You see yourself taking a walk on that beach, you see yourself meeting new people (only they are new in a very limited way, for they are people just like you). You see yourself eating some delicious, locally grown food. You see yourself, you see yourself. . . . You must not wonder what exactly happened to the contents of your lavatory when you flushed it. You must not wonder where your bathwater went when you pulled out the stopper. You must not wonder what happened when you brushed your teeth. Oh, it might all end up in the water you are thinking of taking a swim in; the contents of your lavatory might, just might, graze gently against your ankle as you wade carefree in the water, for you see, in Antigua, there is no proper sewage-disposal system. But the Caribbean Sea is very big and the Atlantic Ocean is even bigger; it would amaze even you to know the number of black slaves this ocean has swallowed up. When you sit down to eat your delicious meal, it's better that you don't know that most of what you are eating came off a plane from Miami. And before it got on a plane in Miami, who knows where it came from? A good guess is that it came from a place like Antigua first, where it was grown dirt-cheap, went to Miami, and came back. There is a world of something in this, but I can't go into it right now.

The thing you have always suspected about yourself the minute you become a tourist is true: A tourist is an ugly human being. You are not an ugly person all the time; you are not an ugly person ordinarily; you are not an ugly person day to day. From day to day, you are a nice person. From day to day, all the people who are supposed to love you on the whole do. From day to day, as you walk down a busy street in the large and modern and prosperous city in which you work and live, dismayed, puzzled (a cliché, but only a cliché can explain you) at how alone you feel in this crowd, how awful it is to go unnoticed, how awful it is to go unloved, even as you are surrounded by more people than you could possibly get to know in a lifetime that lasted for millennia, and then out of the corner of your eye you see someone looking at you and absolute pleasure is written all over that person's face, and then you realize that you are not as revolting a presence as you think you are (for that look just told you so). And so, ordinarily, you are a nice person, an attractive person, a person capable of drawing to yourself the affection of other people (people just like you), a person at home in your own skin (sort of; I mean, in a way; I mean, your dismay and puzzlement are natural to you, because people like you just seem to be like that, and so many of the things people like you find admirable about yourselves — the things you think about, the things you think really define you — seem rooted in these feelings): a person at home in your own house (and all its nice house things), with its nice back yard (and its nice back-yard things), at home on your street, your church, in community activities, your job, at home with your family, your relatives, your friends — you are a whole person. But one day, when you are sitting somewhere, alone in that crowd, and that awful feeling of displacedness comes over you, and really, as an ordinary person you are not well equipped to look too far inward and set yourself aright, because being ordinary is already so taxing, and being ordinary takes all you have out of you, and though the words "I must get away" do not actually pass across your lips, you make a leap from being that nice blob just sitting like a boob in your amniotic sac of the modern experience to being a person visiting heaps of death and ruin and feeling alive and inspired at the sight of it; to being a person lying on some faraway beach, your stilled body stinking and glistening in the sand, looking like something first forgotten, then remembered, then not important enough to go back for; to being a person marveling at the harmony (ordinarily, what you would say is the backwardness) and the union these other people (and they are other people) have with nature. And you look at the things they can do with a piece of ordinary cloth, the things they fashion out of cheap, vulgarly colored (to you) twine, the way they squat down over a hole they have made in the ground, the hole itself is something to marvel at, and since you are being an ugly person this ugly but joyful thought will swell inside you: Their ancestors were not clever in the way yours were and not ruthless in the way yours were, for then would it not be you who would be in harmony with nature and backward in that charming way? An ugly thing, that is what you are when you become a tourist, an ugly, empty thing, a stupid thing, a piece of rubbish pausing here and there to gaze at this and taste that, and it will never occur to you that the people who inhabit the place in which you have just paused cannot stand you, that behind their closed doors they laugh at your strangeness (you do not look the way they look); the physical sight of you does not please them; you have bad manners (it is their custom to eat their food with their hands; you try eating their way, you look silly; you try eating the way you always eat, you look silly); they do not like the way you speak (you have an accent); they collapse helpless from laughter, mimicking the way they imagine you must look as you carry out some everyday bodily function. They do not like you. *They do not like me!* That thought never actually occurs to you. Still, you feel a little uneasy. Still, you feel a little foolish. Still, you feel a little out of place. But the banality of your own life is very real to you; it drove you to this extreme, spending your days and your nights in the company of people who despise you, people you do not like really, people you would not want to have as your actual neighbor. And so you must devote yourself to puzzling out how much of what you are told is really, really true (Is ground-up bottle glass in peanut sauce really a delicacy around here, or will it do just what you think ground-up bottle glass will do? Is this rare, multicolored, snout-mouthed fish really an aphrodisiac, or will it cause you to fall asleep permanently?). Oh, the hard work all of this is, and is it any wonder, then, that on your return home you feel the need of a long rest, so that you can recover from your life as a tourist?

That the native does not like the tourist is not hard to explain. For every native of every place is a potential tourist, and every tourist is a native of somewhere. Every native everywhere lives a life of overwhelming and crushing banality and boredom and desperation and depression, and every deed, good and bad, is an attempt to forget this. Every native would like to find a way out, every native would like a rest, every native would like a tour. But some natives — most natives in the world — cannot go anywhere. They are too poor. They are too poor to go anywhere. They are too poor to escape the reality of their lives; and they are too poor to live properly in the place where they live, which is the very place you, the tourist, want to go — so when the natives see you, the tourist, they envy you, they envy your ability to leave your own banality and boredom, they envy your ability to turn their own banality and boredom into a source of pleasure for yourself.

Considerations

1. What would you judge to be Kincaid's purpose in this opening chapter of her book? Try writing it out in a sentence. How would you support your claim?
2. Analyze the "you" that Kincaid creates as a kind of character in this passage. What are some of "your" characteristics? Are "you" a stereotype? How does Kincaid's characterization of "you" contribute to her argument?
3. This excerpt may be read as a savage indictment of outsiders who exploit the Caribbean for their own ends. What are the indications that Kincaid's critique is more complex? To whom else does she attribute blame?

4. If you've read the Economics Assignment (p. 589), compare Kincaid's view of tourism with that offered by Pattullo. Would Kincaid agree with the analytical perspective offered by Farrell?
5. How might some of what Kincaid says here be applied in interpreting the short story that follows, "Visiting" by Roger McTair?

In the following story, a vacationer from Trinidad suddenly finds himself part of an incident in a hotel bar in Barbados. The various interactions of this story's characters provide a nuanced image of a culture (or maybe just a subculture?) that is dominated by the tourist business. As you read the story, note McTair's skill with dialogue, how the voice of each character implies something distinct about his or her social position.

Visiting

ROGER MCTAIR

"There should be bridges between islands," Solomon said, looking over the bay. Clapham wiped the bar's counter thoughtfully, and said, "Yes, sir."

"Hey! Cut out the 'sir' business," Solomon said, "all my friends call me Sol, or Sol-oh; get it, sol-oh. I'm just a Trinidadian from over the sea; one hour by plane. If we had a bridge between Bridgetown and Port of Spain you could drive in eight hours."

"Can't drive," Clapham replied. "All I have is an old Raleigh bicycle." He wiped the already spotless bar again and again.

A light, warm breeze agitated the palm trees and well-cut decorative shrubs and the hot scent of flowers mixed with the salt tang of the sea. The music from the hotel stopped and the sound of the rolling sea took its place. Clapham stopped wiping the counter and waited, attentively.

A small group of men and women walked down the gravel path that led from the hotel grounds and parking lot. They sat on the other side of the circular outdoor bar, exchanging jokes, laughing and talking. Solomon turned on his stool to contemplate the bay. This was the last day of his vacation and he felt a little melancholy. He wished there was a moon over the bay. He whistled some bars from "Mood Indigo." There were lights twinkling out to sea. Must be an ocean liner touring the islands, Solomon thought.

"That's Ellington, isn't it?" Clapham asked under his breath.

"Yes," Solomon said. "The Duke himself."

Clapham moved smoothly and quietly in his limited space. His voice was soft and

---

ROGER MCTAIR (b. 1943) grew up in Trinidad and now works as a freelance writer and filmmaker in Toronto. "Visiting" appears in *The Faber Book of Contemporary Caribbean Short Stories* (1991), edited by Mervyn Morris.

soothing as he served the laughing tourists. The three men and four women joked loudly with the old barman. He just smiled. There was a whining, nasal twang to their voices. Solomon could not decide if the accents were midwestern or southern. Not that he was an expert on American accents, he told himself. He kept his back to the thatched bar and watched the waves rush on the sand. He tried to block out their voices. It was his first visit to another island. The damn place felt like home; somewhat. This bay could be Salybia, or Point Cumana, but it wasn't, it was in another island, 200 miles away, Clapham's soft accent reminded him.

A white-haired white man, immaculate in evening wear, leaning on the arm of a middle-aged black man walked slowly down the gravel path. He sat on a bench under a palm tree some yards from the bar. He wore a red carnation in his lapel. His manservant was dressed in a black chauffeur's tunic from a thirties English movie. The old man settled himself on the bench and leaned his hands on his cane. He stared out to sea. His manservant stood impassive and erect a little distance behind the bench.

Ah, the Antilles, Solomon thought, sipping his rum and closing his eyes. He had intended to go to New York for this vacation, until Beckles had asked him if he had ever been to Grenada. No, he had said. You ever been to Barbados? You ever been to Jamaica? No! Beckles smiled. You ever been to Toronto? Yes, he had said. Montreal? Yes! Brooklyn? Yes! Beckles smiled again.

Solomon booked for three weeks in Barbados.

He was about to whistle the Ellington tune when someone sat next to him. He opened his eyes; it was an attractive blonde woman. She smiled at him. Solomon smiled back. She had very good teeth and looked thirtyish. Solomon caught a pleasant whiff of cologne. She was tastefully dressed in a light summer dress that moved lightly when she moved. Her hair was cut short and looked as if it had just been styled. She kept putting her hand to her head as if she had more hair to feel. Then she would gingerly touch the short cropped cut. Clapham came over and took her order. Solomon nursed his drink.

She made small-talk with Clapham, Solomon watched the dark expanse of sea.

"Do you work around here?" she said, looking at Solomon. Solomon swung around very slowly on the stool. Clapham wiped the formica counter again with clean precise motions. Solomon thought he saw a hint of a smile on his face.

"This is my third visit here. You do have a very lovely island."

Solomon said nothing.

"Sometimes, in winter? In Ottawa; I'm from Ottawa," she paused, looking intently into Solomon's face, "In Canada. . . ?" Solomon nodded.

"Sometimes in winter, in Ottawa . . ."

"In Canada . . ." Solomon said helpfully.

". . . yes, in Canada! I see these people eh! Immigrants? You know, not only like Negroes eh? Black? But East Indians, Latin Americans, even Portuguese, like they are from a warm climate eh. And they look so miserable in the cold and snow, and I always wondered . . ."

Solomon smiled. He knew the old barman was smiling behind his straight face and lowered eyes.

". . . how they could leave their lovely warm countries . . ." She seemed relieved to have spilled it out. Solomon was relieved too. He had heard the sentiment many times before.

Three more people joined the Americans, a thin man in a white safari outfit and two women in evening dress. "We've been doing the limbo," the thin man said. There was another exchange of banter, and laughter. One of the party ordered more drinks. The newcomers stood in a knot behind the seated group. They laughed loudly at any remark one of their number made.

The old man in evening dress looked over reprovingly. His manservant's face was blank.

Clapham served their new drinks. The men made a great fuss about getting the check. "Noisy, aren't they," the woman from Ottawa said to Solomon. The band from the hotel began playing again. A calypsonian sang along with the band. The calypso was the hit of the season. The Americans began singing too:

She say she don't like bamboo
but she don't mind meh cane
She say cane juice real sweet
It does reach to she brain.
The cane getting soft
the juice pulping out
sweet cane juice dripping
all over she mouth.
We jump in a taxi
She get on the plane
She say next year she coming
ForCane again and again.

One of the Americans did not sing. He just danced on his stool. His hair fell in his face as he moved to the music. He waved his hands a lot. His hands and his forearms were really big. His friends thought he was very funny.

The thin man in the safari suit began doing a limbo on the sand. The others followed in a twisting line, laughing, dancing around the bar, kicking up sand, singing loudly:

She say next year she coming
ForCane again and again.

Clapham impassively washed glasses. Occasionally he glanced at the revellers. He moved in the cage of the enclosed bar like a gray-haired ghost.

The old man in the evening dress whispered something to his manservant. The manservant walked briskly down the gravel path toward the hotel. The old man leaned forward on his walking stick, frowning. The Americans did not notice.

"This is really disgusting," the woman from Ottawa said, "do you want to go to the hotel bar?"

"No," Solomon said, "I'm OK here. I'm talking with Clapham."

"I came with some people," she said. "They are all in there dancing to that."

"You'd better get accustomed," Solomon said. "You'll be hearing it every day until you leave."

She pulled her mouth down in a little gesture of distaste. Solomon smiled a little to himself.

The Americans danced down the beach and to the edge of the surf. They formed a conga line, high stepping and laughing. They were breathing heavily when they returned.

"I don't know your name," the woman from Ottawa said.

"Solomon," he said. "Eric Solomon."

"Mine's Margaret, Margaret Robinson. I'm staying at the Hilton. Do you live around here? Are you, ah, connected with the hotel?"

"I suppose," Solomon said, "I'll have to be nice and let you know that I'm a visitor, just like our happy friends over there, just like yourself." She didn't say anything for a while. Solomon spun on his stool and watched the sea. The twinkling lights had gone. The hotel band played "Big Bamboo," "Dick the Handyman," "Benwood Dick," "My Pussin'," "Miss Tourist," "No Money No Love." Then they played "Sweet Cane Juice" again.

"I've made a fool of myself, haven't I?" she said.

"Why . . ."

"You come to Barbados, and I guess you expect . . ."

"And I'm black, male, sitting here . . ." He thought he might as well bring it into the open.

The band swung into "Big Bamboo."

"No! No!" she said. "It wasn't that." She looked embarrassed. "I'm sorry."

"Don't be sorry," Solomon replied. "It's an easy mistake. It happens often in these islands."

She shook her head in dismay as if she thought Solomon had misunderstood.

A young man and woman walked down the path to the bar. The woman slowed as the couple reached the edge of the path. The man had already stepped toward the bar. She stopped and whispered urgently to her companion. He nodded his head, urging her forward. She followed him reluctantly. They sat next to Margaret and Solomon, leaving empty stools between them and the Americans. The woman was dressed up as if she had just left a wedding reception. The man wore a dark gray suit, the jacket cut high and open at the neck in the appropriate tropical formal style. Margaret ordered another drink. The Americans waved Clapham over just as the couple sat. Clapham began mixing and serving them drinks. He turned toward the newcomers. As the man opened his mouth to order, Clapham reached under the counter searching for a bottle of something.

The young man raised his voice, "Like you ignoring me. I've been waiting here for service and you ignoring me."

Clapham turned to him and said, "I'll be with you in a minute, sir, I am serving these people."

"Don't give me that, mahn, I've been here five minutes and you ain't piss on me, mahn. You ain't even look at me, mahn. You serving all these blasted white people and have we here hole-up waiting." He looked significantly at his companion. She looked straight across the bar into the shadows. Solomon noticed her fingers were locked tightly together.

The Americans got very quiet and very serious. They stared at the young man. They stared at Margaret and Solomon. They looked at each other.

"This is my blasted country," the young man shouted.

One of the Americans vaulted into the bar and said, "I'll serve you . . ." One of the women laughed; a nervous laugh. "It's OK," the American said to Clapham, moving him out of the way, "I'll serve him."

He spread his hands wide and leaned over the counter. Clapham looked horrified and dumbfounded. The young man was taken aback, groping for words.

"Whaddya want," the American said quietly. "I'll serve ya." He was big. Eric thought he had the biggest neck he had ever seen. It was like a tree trunk. "Well, what do you want? Whaddaya drinking?" the American said again; he was leaning, huge hands on the counter, "Tom Collins, Martini, on the rocks, rum and water, planter's punch, bourbon and water, daiquiri, Black Russian."

"You hear that, you hear that," the young man said to his girl, "I don't have to stay here in my own country and take these insults, mahn."

Just as he got up to leave, three uniformed policemen came crunching down the gravel path. The uniformed manservant was with them trying to keep up. The couple looked up, the woman uncomfortable, the man defiant. Two of the policemen headed straight for them. The other strode around the bar and took up a position behind Solomon. Solomon noticed he was big too, not as massive as the American but certainly not inconsequential. He held a baton in his hands, slapping it occasionally in his palm: thwack. thwack. thwack. thwack. Solomon kept a watch on him out of the corner of his eye.

"What's the matter here?" the senior policeman asked.

"This is my country. They can't come here and insult me in my own country." There was a hint of pleading under the defiance in the young man's voice.

The American still leaned over the bar. "He said he wanted a drink, I offered him a drink, I was going to serve him. It's his country." His face was very blank; his eyes were cold, hard, and gray.

The senior policeman said to the angry man, "We don't want any trouble, why don't you find a nice local place to drink and leave these people alone?"

"They don't have to go, officer," the American said. "I'll serve 'em. I'll serve 'em whatever they want."

The policeman looked betrayed. The man and woman began moving away.

"Isn't this a local place?" Margaret from Ottawa whispered to Solomon.

"I'll explain later," Solomon replied.

"Hey," the big American called, "you too good to drink with us, fella? We're not good enough for you? C'mon, I'll buy you a drink. You don't have to go. I'll drink with you. I'll drink with anybody."

The senior policeman looked nonplussed. The manservant moved to take up his position behind the old man in evening wear. The young couple quickly walked down the path, the man striding, head held high, the woman scurrying, chased by the sound of the sea.

They disappeared into the dark. The policeman turned from their wake to look at Solomon sitting suspiciously silent at the bar. Solomon stared back. He was very aware of the third policeman somewhere at his backside. The thick-necked American turned and looked directly at him. His eyes are battle-dress green, Solomon thought.

"I'll serve you too if you want."

Solomon smiled. He kept his gaze on the two policemen in front, thinking the island uniforms are different, but the faces are just the same. He wished he could see the big policeman at his back. He had moved behind Solomon's stool. Solomon's head and neck felt very tense and exposed.

Margaret from Ottawa got very angry. "Why don't you stop making a fool of yourself." She glared at the American, then at the policemen. "He's not a beachboy. He's a visitor. A tourist, just like me, just like you."

The policemen looked very dubious. Solomon could hear the one at his back breathing and slapping the baton; thwack. thwack. thwack. thwack.

The other Americans looked on bemused. They seemed to be waiting to see what would happen next. A gust of wind shook the palm trees. Solomon felt an urge to pucker his lips and whistle "Mood Indigo." He pressed them together instead.

"That's right," Clapham said. "He's staying at the hotel, he's a visitor. He's been here more than a week."

"Well, as long as he doesn't give any trouble," the senior policeman said, looking imperious.

"Gor blimey," Clapham said, his eyes on fire. "He's been sitting here talking to me for two hours. What you mean coming now talking about trouble, what trouble? He don't have anything to do with this."

"Easy old man, easy," the American said, holding up his hands in mock terror. Clapham turned on him and said, "Can you leave my bar now please." The American said "Yes sir, if you want, sir. It's your country." He vaulted one hand over the counter. His friends laughed heartily.

The policemen marched away, heels crunching into the gravel path. Just as they left the one behind him stared Solomon over from head to toe. His forehead was furrowed in a hard, fleshy knot. He kept slapping the baton in his palm as he walked away. Solomon felt a cold bead of perspiration roll down his armpit and settle in his shirt.

The old man and his manservant got up slowly and walked past the bar. "Good night, Major," Clapham said. The old man tipped his forehead.

"Can you believe it?" Margaret said. "Black Russian indeed."

Solomon just tried to quiet his breathing.

Clapham emptied and washed the glasses the Americans had left. It was nearly midnight. The band had stopped.

The woman from Ottawa said, "I've never been down south alone. I've always come with my husband. We've had a lovely time. We got divorced two months ago, just like that."

"Sorry," Solomon said.

"I'm sorry about tonight too."

"Don't be sorry."

"Could we do something tomorrow? Sightseeing? Touring? I've never seen much of the island."

"I'm leaving tomorrow morning at eight," he said, "and there's nothing much to see. Plantation house, plantation mansion, rum distillery, sugar mill, sugar windmill."

"There must be more," she said.

"Well, it isn't all Carnival and Crop-over,[1] but they won't show you the slave-breeding stations in the countryside. None of them advertise that."

[1]**Carnival and Crop-over:** For a discussion of Carnival, see Catherine A. Sunshine's excerpt in A Professional Application (p. 581). Crop-over began as a celebration of the end of the sugar-cane harvest but is now a general celebration featuring decorated carts, calypso, and other attractions [Eds.].

"Don't say that," she said. "I'm so sorry."

"No need to be," Solomon said, draining his drink. "It has nothing to do with you. You're just visiting."

She reached out and touched him on his arm. Her hand lingered. He looked at her and she made a funny little face. They looked at each other, her hand still resting on his arm.

"You should go," he said, nodding past the lighted pathway to the hotel. "Isn't it past your bedtime?"

Clapham said nothing for about five minutes after she left. He closed the counters, measured the bottles, washed the sink, and rang up the register. Solomon sat watching him work.

"I remember when they wouldn't allow colored people to come to these bars," he said at last, "no colored people at all."

"Black people," Solomon corrected him.

"Gor blimey, I been saying colored people all my life. I can't change; too old, Sol-oh man, too old. Too kiss meh rass old," he laughed.

"You know," Solomon said, "I know a beach just like this in Trinidad."

"Coming back next year?" Clapham asked.

"I dunno. We need a bridge. My mother never been to Barbados and she's nearly sixty; been to England though; twice."

Clapham laughed a little louder. "Damn it, mahn, I been to England and New York."

"Never been to Trinidad, eh?"

"No man, I got children and grandchildren in Brooklyn, Queens, Leeds, Manchester, and London. Big children, big grandchildren. Don't know a soul in Trinidad, though."

"You know me, man."

"Some time nuh, I going to check out Trinidad . . . check out your big-able island."

"Well, I have to pack," Solomon said.

They shook hands. Solomon walked along the beach to the hotel. There was a new security guard on duty. He took a precautionary step toward Solomon. "Visitor," Solomon said. "Room 1009," making himself very clear. The guard let him pass. He looked confused and anxious.

Across the hotel lobby Solomon saw the Americans waiting for an elevator. They were still happy. He walked to the front desk. There were no messages. He wasn't expecting any.

He had the elevator to himself.

A light, warm wind blew the sea-smell into his room. From his balcony he could hear the sea. That and the sound of insects were the only sounds. Everything was asleep. The sky was overcast and heavy, light spilled halfheartedly from the hotel gardens to the beach. There was an outline of beach and surf, silhouetted trees, and a dark, dense mass he knew to be water.

Goddam Antilles, he thought, leaning over the balcony. The fear and anger he had felt at the outdoor bar exploded in his temples. He wondered if there was any escape. Goddam Antilles. Maybe he should go live in Canada. Then he thought of Margaret, divorced, excursion fare from Ottawa. Not unattractive either.

It was an hour's flight to Trinidad; he slept all the way. Waiting, it seemed forever, for his luggage at Piarco Airport he thought he should have made Clapham a firm invitation to visit Trinidad.

". . . If there was a bridge . . ." He whistled a bit of "Mood Indigo" under his breath.

Someone waiting for luggage began humming "Sweet Cane Juice." Two or three others picked up the melody. Solomon got his bags. There was a lineup. It seemed the whole line was humming "Sweet Cane Juice."

It took two hours to clear customs and immigration.

Considerations

1. What happens to Solomon in this story? Try describing it in two ways: a brief summary of events and a longer summary of his psychological reactions.
2. Using the lens of tourism, describe the interrelationships of the various characters in this story. How do their roles in the tourist economy help account for their actions?
3. To whom does the title of the story refer? Is there more than one possibility? In the context of the story, what are the connotations of "visiting"?
4. This story is set in the contemporary Caribbean, long after Barbados's independence from England. But there are indications in the story that Barbados is not free of the colonial influence. What are some of these indications?
5. As an analytical perspective for writing about "Visiting," consider the preceding piece by Jamaica Kincaid or one of the selections in the Economics Assignment, page 589.

FURTHER ASSIGNMENTS

1. Locate a tourist guidebook to the Caribbean. Analyze its approach and contents in light of the issues raised in this chapter. Keep an open mind since some guidebooks are quite informative about Caribbean cultures and offer reliable accounts of Caribbean history.

2. In various ways the stories in this chapter by Olive Senior (p. 557), Merle Hodge (p. 629), Michelle Cliff (p. 641), and Roger McTair (p. 660) testify to the lasting British influence upon Britain's former colonies. Write an essay in which you analyze the extent of British influence. In the contemporary Caribbean, does that influence seem to be yielding to other influences?

3. After rereading Edward Kamau Brathwaite's comments about standard English and "nation language" (p. 627), go back to the stories in this chapter to ex-

amine their language. Write an analytical essay about the use of language in one or more of these stories.

4. Consider what Merle Hodge says about family life in the Caribbean (p. 564) and apply her perspective to one or more of the pieces of fiction in this chapter, including possibly her own.

5. Consider the economic overview offered by Trevor M. A. Farrell (see the Economics Assignment, p. 589). Then analyze one or more of the stories in this chapter from an economic perspective.

6. In a section of her book not excerpted in this chapter, Catherine A. Sunshine has said:

> Racial perceptions in the Caribbean differ somewhat from those in Europe, and, especially, the United States. In U.S. society persons are generally defined as either "white" or "black," unless they are Hispanic or Asian. The slightest trace of African ancestry usually qualifies even a light-skinned person as "black." In the Caribbean, by contrast, skin color is seen as part of a continuum in which small variations become socially important. Brown-skinned persons are distinguished from those who are black; indeed there has traditionally been a world of social distance between them.
>
> These color/class divisions carry with them cultural implications. At the top of the pyramid, the white elite waves the banner of its European origins, the English mores of Jamaica's upper class, or the Frenchness of Martinique's native white *bekes*. This sets the standard for the society, becoming the goal toward which the brown and black middle class aspires. Historically, Caribbean societies have idealized the culture of the colonizer and looked down upon the culture of the mass. Yet ironically, it is from the original and vibrant mass cultures — not the imitative culture of the elite — that a Caribbean identity has emerged.

Using this passage to establish your framework, write an essay analyzing issues of color and class in one or more of this chapter's fictional works.

7. Create your own definition of *cultural politics* (you may want to consult the discussion on p. 623). Then demonstrate the complexity of the idea by analyzing the ways in which cultural politics influence people's everyday experiences in one or more of the chapter's readings. As an alternative assignment, write an essay that considers the cultural politics of your own everyday behavior. For example, do you see ways in which larger social, historical, or economic forces have shaped your tastes in music, the language you use with friends, how you choose to spend your time, and so on?

8. In trying to interpret stories, readers often focus upon central conflicts. The conflicts might be between two characters, among several characters, between

a character and an entire environment, or between clashing value systems. Sometimes the conflict occurs within the mind of a single character.

Either by sketching an outline or by drafting a set of short descriptive paragraphs, try to classify the types of conflict you find in the stories you've read. As you review your categories, do some seem more important, or more central, than others?

9. Research the intimate relationship between the development of the sugar industry and the Atlantic slave trade. Two books with which you might start are *The Making of the West Indies* by F. R. Augier et al. (1978) and *Stand the Storm* by Edward Reynolds (1985).

10. Roger McTair's "Visiting" (p. 660) includes an example of a calypso song. After considering this song and its relation to the themes of McTair's story, research the subject of calypso. What are its traditions? Is the calypso in "Visiting" typical or unusual? (You might want to use Catherine A. Sunshine's observations about calypso on p. 583 as a starting point.) Speculate upon the role of calypso in the cultural politics of the Caribbean.

11. Although this chapter has stressed a number of contemporary authors from the English-speaking Caribbean, we have, of course, omitted many others, including many writers whose fame is well established. Choose one of the writers from the following list and report on that writer's work in relation to issues raised in this chapter: George Lamming, Earl Lovelace, V. S. Naipaul, C. L. R. James, Jean Rhys, Samuel Selvon, and Derek Walcott.

12. Locate a contemporary writer from a part of the Caribbean not represented in this chapter — for example, Cuba, Haiti, or Puerto Rico. Report on the writer's work, taking into account how issues of "cultural sovereignty" (Merle Hodge's term) have influenced it. How does the cultural situation of the writer you have chosen compare with that of writers working in the aftermath of British colonialism? And what role does that situation play in the writing? Although you will want to offer an overview of your writer's career, you may want to focus most of your analysis upon one or two representative works.

APPENDIX

Assignments for Field Study

The four assignments in this appendix move you out of the writing classroom and onto the campus, into the lecture hall and the library, your home or workplace, the street and neighborhood. We ask you to use the strategies you've mastered so far to think about, organize, and present various kinds of data you'll collect by observing, recording, and exploring one or more of four topics: the ways students on your campus greet each other, the uses of literacy, humor, and the various kinds of language that comprise work in your major. These topics are embedded within assignments that are arranged by level of difficulty. The first assignment is fairly easy to undertake: It requires an hour or two to collect data and can be completed in a few days. Each of the subsequent assignments requires more involvement and time, with the final assignment — an exploration of the language of your major — potentially requiring several weeks or more to do successfully.

- In Assignment 1, "Greeting Behavior of College Students," we ask you to observe, as an anthropologist might, the things people say and do on your campus when they meet each other and then to come to some conclusions about the ways people carry out this commonplace behavior.
- In Assignment 2, "Defining Literacy," we ask you to gather information on the ways written language is used in some domain of your life and, from that information, to attempt a definition of literacy.
- In Assignment 3, "What's Funny?," you are encouraged to collect or record everyday examples of the comic — jokes, cartoons, sitcoms — and, through them, to come to some conclusions about how humor works and what makes something funny.

- In Assignment 4, "Exploring the Discourse of Your Major," the most challenging of these field study assignments, we ask you to investigate your major — or, if you're undecided, a major you're curious about — by investigating the language that constitutes it: from descriptions of the major in the college catalog, to the things students say about it, to the ways faculty conduct research within it. This assignment is accompanied by a set of brief optional readings that you can use to further develop your investigation of the language of your major.

Depending on your schedule, you and your instructor can decide to select several assignments in sequence or to concentrate on one of the four alone.

Assignment 1: Greeting Behavior of College Students

This exercise asks you to work directly from your own observations. Put yourself in the position of an anthropologist trying to gather data, as objectively as possible, about a culture he or she has set out to observe. In this case, the culture is that of a college campus. The behavior you have set out to observe is greeting behavior, that is, what people do verbally and physically when they encounter someone they know. After talking over this term with your friends and classmates, set aside some times and places for observing varieties of greeting behavior detectable on campus. You might situate yourself at a single spot on campus and take notes of what you observe. But beware: The selection of a single spot may limit the sorts of behavior to which you have access. Such a strategy might focus your observations, however, and you can let that focus be apparent in your title, for example, "Greeting Behavior Among Students En Route to Class."

When you are satisfied that your observations have led you to some interesting distinctions and a good range of behavior, write an essay classifying the greeting behavior you have observed. Are there any comparisons you can make based on the way you classified your data? What conclusions do classifying, and comparing, help you to draw about greeting behavior on your campus? You might want to include discussion of any problems you had developing your classification scheme and how you resolved them. Of special interest would be problems arising from the very nature of your data: the behaviors you had to observe and label. If you have done any of the assignments in the classifying chapter, you might consider the difference between working with material already provided to you versus data you have to collect.

Assignment 2: Defining Literacy

Pick a setting — your home, the place where you work, your place of worship, a store, a gym, a video arcade, a movie theater — and make a list of every use of written language you see, no matter how trivial it may seem. In your home, for example, you might find newspapers and books but also grocery lists, print on packages, labels on clothes or appliances, and so on. In a movie theater, you might find announcements on the marquee, print on a ticket, exit signs, signs for the men's and women's restrooms, and the menu at the refreshment stand. Make note of characteristics of what you observe: Is there more than one language? Is the written language you see in print or script, is it small or large, does it stand by itself or is it combined with symbols, pictures, or charts? Is the spelling standard or nonstandard (for example, "quik" for "quick")? Also make note, as best you can, of what the writing's purpose seems to be (for example, to inform, entertain, warn) and how people seem to use it, or talk about it, or ignore it. In what circumstances do people in the setting you chose generate written language themselves? (For example, in a restaurant, an employee may be writing down orders, a customer may be working a crossword puzzle, and so on.)

Do you hear of or otherwise find out about written materials that are not present but that influence people's behavior (for example, an advertisement that brought them to the gym or restaurant, or documents like contracts and procedural manuals that affect how people conduct their work)? What, to the best of your ability, do you make of this "unseen" written material?

On the basis of your observations, write a paper in which you attempt to define literacy as it is used in the setting you chose. That is, what is the literacy of the restaurant? The gym? The movie theater? The college classroom? Use specific examples from your notes. Consider the way this context-specific literacy, this literacy of a particular place as you have defined it, may be similar to or different from the definition you find in the dictionary. What do you make of the similarities or differences?

As a next step in this assignment, you might consider this comparative move: Pair up with someone who selected a site different from the one you chose and together write a paper — or present an oral report — comparing the literacy of the two sites. For example, how is the literacy of the gym you selected similar to or different from that of the restaurant another student observed, and what do you make of the similarities or differences? That is, what does the comparison add to your understanding of the definition and the uses of literacy?

Assignment 3: What's Funny?

The subject of humor is notoriously difficult to grasp. How do we define what we are talking about when we discuss humor? Certainly, jokes, as deliberate efforts to elicit laughter, are part of the territory. So are comedy acts, comic movies and plays, TV situation comedies, the columns of humorists like Paula Poundstone and Dave Barry, and the many comic strips that pack the pages of most daily newspapers. Comedy in most of these forms has become a kind of commodity in our society. Even if we do not quite know what it is, we know where to find it and can expect it to be delivered on demand. But comedy is also interwoven more subtly as part of our day-to-day and face-to-face experience. And it can erupt at times and in places where we least expect it — like a not quite unexpected visitor to whom the door is always open.

This assignment will send you out of the classroom to explore the comic and to come to some conclusions about how it works and why. The assignment begins with some guidelines for conducting field research on the comic, broken down into six units to help you zero in on particular comic materials and events: Jokes, Pictures, Performance, Comedy Shows and Comic Movies, Comedy in Drama, and The Comedy of the Everyday.

Once you have collected your information on the comic, you can move to a set of questions that will guide you in thinking critically about what you've found. You should choose three or four of the units, including the last one, "The Comedy of the Everyday." Each unit requires you to collect, describe, or record comic material or events. You won't need much to begin: a keen ear and eye, a notepad (one small enough to fit easily into a pocket or a purse), possibly an audiotape recorder, and your sense of humor.

Jokes

Jokes surround us. We hear them on radio and television; we read them in the newspapers and in magazines; friends ask us if we've "heard the one about . . ." We use jokes to connect with others, to lighten a situation, to share in a laugh, but also to blunt the effect of bad news or a disastrous event, to express anger and resentment, to assert superiority, even to hurt others.

Pick a two-day period and write down every joke you hear or read, whether or not the jokes strike you as funny or objectionable or trivial. Begin to think about how you might classify them, how you might sort out what you have into sensible categories.

Pictures

The daily newspaper — and especially the Sunday paper — has pages of comic strips (or "funny papers" or "funny pages") and at least one political cartoon.

Magazines often carry cartoons, some of them political. There are comic books, of course, and just walk through a card shop noticing how many of the cards rely on humor. A lot of advertisements — in the newspaper, in magazines, on billboards — try to raise a smile too.

Select a dozen or so examples of printed humor — political cartoons or comic strips or greeting cards — and ask yourself what it is about the *visual* nature of the material that contributes to the comic: the way a piece is drawn, the layout, the way print is combined with illustration.

Performance

A stand-up comic shakes her shoulders, raises her voice, looks skyward, and fires the punchline; an uncle tells a funny story about your parents, and you still like to hear it, and enjoy watching him tell it, though you've heard it before; you have a friend who tells the best jokes. Their performances are central to the laughter.

Telling a joke or comic story effectively involves a number of skills: timing, gesture, modulation of the voice. Watch a stand-up comic (either at a comedy club or on a television show or on videotape), or a person telling a joke, or a relative or friend telling a funny story. You'll want to capture the routine or joke or story in your notes (or, if permissible, on audiotape), but pay special attention to the *delivery,* the way the person performs the material. Pay attention to:

pacing and timing,

facial expressions and gestures,

body movements,

any changes in voice, shifts in pitch, assuming of other voices, and so on.

Comedy Shows and Comic Movies

Prime-time television is built around situation comedy, or sitcom, and a new comic film is released once a week. In fact, a cable network, Comedy Central, is devoted entirely to comedy. This kind of humor is a multimillion-dollar business and is shared by more Americans than almost any other form of entertainment. But what makes it work?

Select a sitcom or a comic cartoon or movie and study it with the following questions in mind:

What are the characters like? Are they sympathetic, believable, exaggerated? Are they male or are they female? What socioeconomic class do they come from, what region or race or ethnic background? Are any of these factors central to the comedy?

How does the humor emerge? Is it through jokes and one-liners? Through the relationships between characters? Through situations the characters find themselves in? Is it helped along by laugh tracks or by other cues?

How is the humor situated in the plot? Is it in clearly defined segments or woven throughout the story? Is the whole story comic, or are there other elements: a romance, a conflict?

If you have the time and interest, you might study both a sitcom and a comic cartoon or movie and use the preceding questions to help you think about the differences between the two forms. A variation would be to study a skit or two on a comic-satiric variety show like *Saturday Night Live* and compare it to a situation comedy. How are the characters different? The ways the pieces are structured? The pacing? Do the different forms seem to have different purposes?

Comedy in Drama

One of the interesting things about humor is the way it can be used in serious settings: in drama, for example, or in romances, action-adventure films, or soap operas. Writers and directors might use comedy in such settings to offer momentary relief from tension, or to make a character sympathetic, or to signal to the audience a shift in the development of the story, or to set the audience up for an unexpected twist in the story.

Select a television show or movie that is *not* billed as a comedy — anything from soap operas to action-adventure — or a play, anything from a Shakespearean tragedy to a contemporary urban drama, and study it with the following questions in mind:

Exactly where in the plot do the comic moments come?

What purpose or purposes do they seem to serve?

What effect did they have on you?

The Comedy of the Everyday

There is, of course, something a little contrived about the way we've set up the previous units: We ask you to seek out occasions of the comic. But one of the intriguing things about the comic is the way it simply surfaces in our lives. We don't set out, day by day, to find laughs; rather we stumble across humor — laughter emerges, and in all kinds of settings.

For one day, make note of everything you see or hear that strikes you as funny: people's behavior, advertisements or television commercials, jokes, stories, what you see on the way to school, at work, at dinner, your dog's or cat's antics, things babies do, events that are supposed to be solemn, and so on. Record, as best you can given the circumstances, what happens as well as what immediately precedes and follows the funny moment. Jot down, as well, any thoughts you have: associations, memories, whatever you can to help explain why what you heard or saw struck you as funny.

What do these moments suggest to you about your own sense of the comic, your personal definition of what's funny?

Suggestions for Writing

1. You have just collected information on a range of comic material. As a first step in defining the comic, do *one* of the following:

Pick one category for which you have a lot of material (for instance, jokes or cartoons or greeting cards) and develop a classification scheme for them.

Pick two items within a category (for instance, two cartoons) or two items from different categories (like a sitcom and a comedian's stand-up routine) that strike you as very different and compare the two.

Pick a comic event (a funny story, a joke, a scene within a sitcom, movie, or play) and carefully examine what led up to it or how its elements build on one another. How does the sequencing of these elements contribute to the humor?

What does your classification scheme or comparison or serial examination suggest about the comic? Try using what you did to write out a definition of the comic. It can be tentative and informal.

2. As a next move, you might want to consider your tentative definition in light of your study of what *you* found funny as you moved through a typical day in your own life. What did you think was funny and why? How does the definition of the comic that is implied in your self-study compare with the tentative definition you developed out of question 1?

3. As a final move, you might try to bring your definitions together. Feel free to go back and reconsider information you collected, but didn't use in responding to question 1. At this point, how would you define the comic?

Assignment 4: Exploring the Discourse of Your Major

One of the most important things you'll do during your first years in college is to declare a major — or, as many people do, change your mind and change your major. This assignment sends you out onto the campus to explore your major and the academic discipline that supports it (chemical engineering, for example, is a major, but engineering is its discipline). For research, we'll ask you to look at college catalogs, skim textbooks, attend a class, talk with students, look at student writing and exams, and investigate the kinds of work done by professors in the field you've chosen. If you haven't yet decided on a major, you can select one you're curious about; perhaps the research you do will help you to decide whether or not to pursue it.

In learning about a major, you will also be learning about the specialized language, the discourse, associated with it. *Discourse* is a particularly useful word for this specialized language. It refers both to written and to spoken language, and it suggests language that is public and somewhat formal. Discourse also suggests communication among people who already share a number of assumptions and values. The term implies a kind of general agreement within a discipline about which concepts are central, which approaches are likely to be fruitful, which topics are of mutual interest and open to disagreement. For example, among biologists the concept of evolution is deeply woven into the background of all work within the discipline — it's not an idea open to debate. On the other hand, the pace and patterns of evolutionary developments are subject to aggressive inquiry and argument among biologists. Both the assumptions and the arguments are part of the discourse of biology.

By stressing matters of academic discourse, we are asking you to pay attention to those features of language that impose barriers to new students. The research you do in this assignment, by making that discourse less mysterious, should help you to begin to move more comfortably in the language of your major and make that language your own.

The next section, Perspectives for Exploring the Discourse of Your Major, contains suggestions for conducting field research. We offer a large number of possible research activities from which to choose a smaller number that you find manageable and interesting. The section titled Optional Readings: Complicating the Issues presents readings that ask you to move out of your disciplinary research to face broader questions about American higher education. You and your instructor can decide if you will incorporate the readings into your work.

Perspectives for Exploring the Discourse of Your Major

We present three units to guide your field study of your major:

Views from outside the discipline

Views from inside the discipline

Views from further inside the discipline

During the opening phase of your research, we ask you to formulate some first impressions, gather some general knowledge, and get a sense of how your major is viewed by people at a distance from it. During the second phase, we ask you to look at the major from the point of view of undergraduates taking courses — what can you glean about their experiences? Finally, we ask you to venture further, researching the activities and concerns of people professionally immersed in the discipline of your major.

How much research you do and how much time you spend on each phase are matters of negotiation between you and your instructor. In each unit below, we have provided more possibilities than any one person would want to pursue. We suggest you use these as prompts to stimulate your research, not as a checklist of research activities. You ought to do at least one item from each of the three units, but obviously your research will be richer if you are able to do several from each. You'll need one or two hours for each of the activities you decide to attempt, but try not to put more than two hours into any one activity, or that activity may become a research project in its own right.

The units are flexible enough for you to shape your research according to your preferences, but we do strongly recommend that you try at least one interview. At the end of each of the three units, we've made suggestions about interviews you might conduct, but you might be able to think of other possibilities. Also keep in mind these interviewing suggestions: If possible, bring a tape recorder and ask the person you're interviewing for permission to tape your conversation. Prepare questions ahead of time and make them real questions, ones that the interviewee will find interesting to think about. Don't ask for information you could easily obtain elsewhere, and don't ask questions that can essentially be answered with yes or no responses. Before interviewing someone, wait until you have enough background information to engage the other person in a serious and probing conversation. Allow for the possibility that the conversation might not move in exactly the sequence you foresee.

Though you can work exclusively with Perspectives for Exploring the Discourse of Your Major, you might also want to look to the excerpts in Optional Readings: Complicating the Issues. Let these observations and opinions percolate a bit, adding some energy to what you're doing. As you skim your college catalog, do you see signs of what David S. Russell calls "tightly knit, turf-conscious disciplines and departments"? Is Elizabeth Chiseri-Strater accurate in claiming that styles of classroom discourse differ sharply between male and female students? Do you see indications in a journal article that its author is writing, as the graduate student quoted by sociologist Howard Becker says, "in a shorthand that only members of the profession can decipher"? As you gather information, look ahead to the purposes you may ask that information to serve. Here, then, is the list of research activities from which to choose.

Views from Outside the Discipline

The following suggestions are appropriate to the initial phase of your research, as you begin to define your major from the perspective of an interested outsider. Attempt at least one.

Self-Survey. As a prelude to your research, take a few minutes to reflect, in writing, upon your choice of a major. If you feel you've already decided on a major, write about how you arrived at that decision. What has attracted you? If you haven't yet decided upon a major but intend simply to research one of the fields that interests you, write about making that choice. Which majors attract you? Why?

Then take a few more minutes to write out your initial impressions of the major you've decided to research. You probably know more about this field than you think you do, though it's also possible that you have some misconceptions. You might try jotting down your impressions as items on a list, but in no particular order. You also might try to do this by freewriting: Simply put pen to paper and write whatever comes to mind; don't censor yourself, and don't stop until you've accumulated several pages of impressions. Later you may want to come back to what you've written to see in what ways your initial impressions have been confirmed and in what ways they've been complicated or overturned.

Folk Wisdom. Do an informal survey among students on your campus who are not majors in the field you're studying. What do they think about the discipline? What have they heard about particular courses and teachers? What are the students like who do major in the field? What seems to distinguish the people who do well in this major from the ones who don't do so well? What do students in this major go on to do? Find out something about the department's reputation. Is there a consensus among students, or does it depend on whom you talk to? If it feels like you're only listening to gossip, don't worry. Collecting gossip can be research.

The College Catalog. The college catalog is an official document, designed primarily to give an overview of your college to people interested in attending it. It may be interesting to compare this official view to the more informal kinds of information you've begun to assemble. It will also be instructive to see something of how the discipline is structured on your campus. See if you can find any categories of specialization within your major (for example, some schools subdivide political science into political theory, American politics, comparative politics, and international politics). What does the catalog say about the sequence of courses? Do you get a sense of what varying routes students might take as they progress through prerequisite courses to more specialized ones? How possible is it to specialize *within* a specialization? Are courses differentiated only by content, or do there also seem to be differences in approach or method? What questions about the discipline in general or the department in particular does the catalog leave unanswered? Finally, jot down a few notes on the language of the course descriptions. Is it hard or easy reading, intimidating or inviting? Is the language specialized? Does it get more so as you read about advanced courses?

A Session with an Adviser. In most colleges, students meet at least once a semester with an adviser. Until you've declared a major, your adviser is unlikely to be someone from the discipline you're most interested in. But an adviser is prepared to answer many of your questions about various departments and course offerings. If you find yourself with an advising session while doing your research, think about how to help it contribute to your work. If you have no advisement session scheduled, you might like to schedule one. See if you can get the adviser to set aside a little more time than customary. What can this person tell you about your potential major? Do you have some questions your adviser can't answer?

A Newspaper or Magazine Article. Locate a newspaper or magazine article in which an expert from your discipline is interviewed or quoted as an authority. How does the writer of the article portray this expert? What aspects of the article make this expert's work a subject of interest for general readers? Does the article imply a view of what this expert's field of study is like? Does it imply a public value for the discipline?

An Interview. See if you can locate someone who has majored in your field in the past but who is not now in academics. Did the person put the major to professional use? Did he or she benefit from it in other ways? Does the person have any regrets about his or her choice of a major? Has he or she kept in touch with the field? How would this person define or describe the discipline? If the department you're interested in has a Web site, you might be able to post a questionnaire for students there.

Views from Inside the Discipline

The following suggestions are appropriate to the second phase of your research, as you begin to learn more about your major by looking at courses and speaking with other students who have chosen the major. You should do at least two from this group.

A Classroom Lecture. Attend a lecture in one of the introductory courses of your major (it can be a course you're taking, but it needn't be). With the permission of the professor, tape record this lecture while also taking notes. Later, with the help of your notes and the tape recording, summarize the lecture and look for a perspective from which to analyze it. Besides the actual content of the lecture, what else could you notice? Did you notice anything about the language of the lecture or the values of the lecturer? Did certain terms recur? Were there assumptions that everyone in the classroom seemed to share? Did the lecture depend entirely upon words, or did the presentation also depend upon visual elements such as charts, slides, objects, and physical demonstrations? How would you describe the lecturer's style of presentation? Did he or she involve the student audience in the presentation? Did student participation seem integral or only peripheral?

If you feel you learned something of value by attending the lecture of an introductory class, try attending an advanced class. Again, taping the lecture while taking notes is a great advantage for later reflection. If you find that the lecture in the advanced class is over your head, keep making observations anyway. What is it in the speaker's language that is giving you difficulty? What would you need to know to put you on solid ground? Can you formulate some questions that would help you to clear up what you've heard?

An Introductory Textbook. Locate an introductory textbook and scan its contents. How is its material organized? What seems to receive major emphasis? Which points about the discipline seem to be most basic? What are some of the key terms and concepts that you notice recurring? Do the explanations depend upon words only, or do illustrations also play a major role? What about statistics, tables, and graphs? Overall, what sort of reader does the textbook seem to call for?

If you've learned something valuable about the discipline by browsing an introductory textbook, try working a little with a more advanced textbook. What common features do you notice in the two books? Is the language similar? Considering the introductory textbook in light of the more advanced one, which terms and concepts in the introductory text seem most important in giving continuity to the discipline?

The Discussion Group, Quiz Section, or Lab Presentation. Attend one of these more participatory classes. How does the language of this meeting differ from that of a lecture? How do you account for the differences? What constants carry over from a lecture to these smaller classes? If you are able to get a printout of an electronic class "discussion," analyze the language. How is it like and unlike traditional, spoken discussion? What else do you notice?

The Conference or Tutoring Session. This can be a session of your own or one you observe — though you may meet some reluctance here, since tutorial sessions tend to be private. If you do get to record such a session, you'll want to reflect on what differences you notice between the language of this session and other forms of academic discourse you've looked at, differences in language, in tone, in the behavior of the participants.

Student Writing. See if you can locate examples of writing — either papers or exams — produced by students in your major. If you get a rich sample of student writing, you may want to develop some comparisons. What is expected of student writers in this major? What distinguishes a good performance from a not so good one? How are papers organized? What do they set out to accomplish? What role is played by features other than language, such as figures, graphs, and charts? How do instructors respond to student papers? What can you notice either about the language of student writers or the language in which teachers respond to student writers?

Some departments, and some undergraduates, keep copies of old exams and essay assignments on file. If you get a sampling of these exams and assignments, try analyzing them: Do certain types of questions recur? What can you notice about the language of the questions? Do certain themes emerge? Are some methods emphasized over others? What writing skills seem required? Which of the critical strategies from this book would prove most useful?

A Club Meeting. At many colleges there are clubs or associations that bring together students with similar interests. Often these groups are quite small, and sometimes they are accused of being cliquish. But they may offer another interesting angle on a major. Attend a meeting. Do the people at the meeting seem to share a certain perspective? Are diverse views represented? Are any faculty present? Does the meeting have a dominant tone? What can participants tell you of the club's history? How would you characterize the discourse of the meeting? Is it different from the language you've encountered in books and classes? If so, how?

A Student Interview. Interview a student who is majoring in the field. Use what you have learned thus far to create meaningful questions. Ask questions not only about courses and teachers but about the language and central concepts of the discipline. Is the person you interview aware of any disagreements within the field? What does he or she know about how the professors in this field spend their research time? What does he or she think about some of the questions raised in the readings we attach to this assignment? Is the field interdisciplinary? Is it changing? What do people who major in this field tend to do with their lives? Who are considered some of the leaders in the discipline? Use your interview to build on what you already know, to fill in gaps, and to stimulate the thinking that will enable you to write about your discipline in a way that does more than simply rehash information.

A Web Site. If the department you're interested in has a Web site, you may be able to get a lot of information there: course descriptions, syllabi, notices about meetings and conferences, and departmental contacts. How would you characterize the language and presentation of the site? Formal? Informal? Some combination?

Views from Further Inside the Discipline

The following suggestions are appropriate to the final phase of your research, as you look at activities of professionals within the discipline, including the research interests of campus faculty. You should do at least two from this group.

Journal Articles. One of the primary ways academics record and convey their work is through articles in specialized journals. (Some examples are *American Psychologist, Nature, Journal of Black Studies, Research in the Teaching of English,* and *Econometrica.*) Go to the library, and with the help of a reference librarian, locate titles of representative journals in your field. (You may also find that some relevant journals are available on the Internet.) Select a sample of volumes of these journals and scan the titles of articles. If the articles begin with abstracts, try reading an abstract or two. Do the titles, abstracts, and articles seem accessible to you, or are they distanced by specialized language? Do you notice any words or kinds of words that seem more prominent than others? With the reference librarian's help, locate some journal articles by faculty on your campus. Can you make any connections between articles you find and the classes taught on your campus?

Scholarly Books and Monographs. Academics often share their work through scholarly books and monographs (a monograph is a short book usually focused on a specialized issue). The audience for these books is usually quite small, consisting of other scholars sharing the author's specialization within the discipline. With the help of a reference librarian, go to the area in your library where books in your discipline are located. Browse awhile, stopping to look through any books that catch your interest. Skim prefaces, introductions, opening and concluding chapters. Can you form any conclusions? What observations can you make about the language of the books you examine?

Conferences. Much professional activity occurs at conferences. See if you can discover which are the most prominent annual conferences of your discipline. Or you might learn about a specially convened conference, a one-time gathering, organized to address issues of special interest. Often the proceedings of such conferences, or a portion of them, are published. Usually there is a program of activities printed for participants. If you can locate one of these documents, skim it. What do the various presentations have in common? How do they differ? What can you notice about their language? What else, besides formal presentations, seems to go on at these conferences? What seem to be the hottest or most controversial subjects of discussion? Do certain names seem especially prominent? Which terms recur most frequently?

Public Lectures. A public lecture by a scholar in your discipline is often, though not always, an effort to cross disciplinary boundaries. The audience at such lectures usually consists of people who are interested nonspecialists. The speaker is forced to present what he or she has to say in a way that is comprehensible to people interested but not necessarily well versed in the discipline. If you attend this sort of public lecture, record it and take notes. Does the language seem to differ from the language of textbooks, or journal articles, or conferences?

Electronic Discussion Groups. Increasingly, academics are using the Internet and e-mail to share information about their fields. Usually, electronic discussions (which you can take part in by subscribing to an Internet mailing list or posting to a newsgroup) are informal — more like a conversation than, say, a presentation of research in a journal or monograph. Nevertheless, electronic forums can give you valuable insight into how academics present and debate issues and what types of questions are important to them. What type of language do they use? How is the language different from — and similar to — that of journals, books, lectures, and so on? How do people present themselves and their comments? What else do you notice?

Descriptions of Graduate School. If you are attending a university that has a graduate program in your discipline, another level of investigation is open to you. If your college does not have a graduate program, you can still learn something about such programs from your college library, or possibly from faculty in your discipline. A percentage of the students who major in your discipline will eventually choose to go to graduate school, and all of the teachers in your college's department will have attended graduate school. The best way to find out more about graduate school is through conversations and interviews, but if you can't arrange these, you can also learn a good deal from graduate catalogs. Locate a few, and flip through them. How do graduate course offerings differ from undergraduate ones? What are graduate students expected to do? Another interesting, though sometimes daunting, source of information is dissertation abstracts. With the help of a reference librarian, locate an index of dissertation abstracts in your discipline. This reference book will contain brief summary accounts of the dissertations that graduate students have written as the final stage in obtaining their degrees. If you locate some dissertation abstracts, look at six or eight of them, seeing what conclusions you can draw, both from the language of the abstracts and from the titles themselves.

Interview of a Graduate Student or a Professor. Following the advice we've given for conducting interviews, do an interview with an academic insider from your discipline. Let your previous research inform the questions you ask. You might want to look ahead to the topics raised by the readings at the end of this assignment. Be thinking of how your interview can help you in writing a paper about your investigations. Here, for example, are some questions you might want to ask:

> What are the discipline's fundamental assumptions or driving questions? Are they fairly stable now or in a state of change?
>
> What are the discipline's fundamental methods of inquiry? What are the strengths and limitations of those methods?
>
> What are the most important forms of discourse in your field? How does the most important work get done?
>
> How important is writing in your discipline, and where would one go to find examples of good writing?
>
> When students first come to your discipline, what difficulties are they apt to have in handling its discourse — whether with writing, reading, listening, or speaking?

Suggestions for Writing

1. Bring together all the information you've gathered. Do you notice any patterns? Can you create any categories to organize or simplify what you have? Have you discovered interesting similarities and differences? Do certain concepts or terms recur? Certain methods? Which ideas are fundamental? What sorts of data

seem most important? After thinking about the information you've gathered in light of these questions, try writing some generalizations about the discipline.

2. As you look back at your own first impressions of the major, which, if any, of those impressions do you find inaccurate? Reflect on where these misimpressions may have come from. What has a closer look at this field contributed to your way of thinking about it? As you investigated your field, did your sense of the field widen or contract? Is its focus wider or narrower than you first thought? Does work in this field connect with work in other fields, or does it seem self-contained? Having thought about the information you collected in light of the questions here and in question 1, try to write a definition of your major that would be helpful to other students.

3. Employing the definition that you've drafted in question 2, write a short essay about the discourse of your major. Try to develop or enhance your definition by getting specific about the language you've encountered in your research. Have you discovered concepts, terms, formats, forums that seem especially important to communication within the major? What most interests students who've selected this major, and do these interests seem to differ from those of professionals in the discipline? How different is the discourse between students and faculty from the discourse of faculty with other professionals?

Optional Readings: Complicating the Issues

In assembling your research materials so far, you've been encouraged to proceed as if entering a disciplinary tunnel, seldom looking for a fuller, wider view. Now, with the following readings, we offer you the opportunity to step back and think about your potential major in the larger context provided by critical questions about American colleges, about undergraduate experience, and about the nature of education in general.

The section begins with three pieces about students, written by teachers interested in understanding students' academic lives and choices. As a participant-observer in dormitory culture at Rutgers University, anthropologist Michael Moffatt reports on the economic, vocational, and social motives for how students choose their majors. Writing from an ethnographic and feminist point of view, composition specialist Elizabeth Chiseri-Strater reports on the discourse styles of two students, one male and one female, whose academic lives she closely studied at the University of New Hampshire. And sociologist Howard S. Becker writes about an encounter with a graduate student troublingly immersed in the disciplinary language of sociology.

The chapter continues with five pieces that seek to establish a wider context for thinking about majors and disciplines. In a historical overview, David R. Russell describes how the modern university has evolved sharply away from a nineteenth-century model that provided a single curriculum for a single class of students. Next,

Lynne V. Cheney, in a report written in her capacity as chair of the National Endowment for the Humanities, looks critically at the relation between research and teaching in American colleges and universities. In another report based on a national study, Ernest Boyer lays out the ongoing debate between the proponents of specialized and general education, and he goes on to propose "the enriched major" as an antidote to intellectual narrowness. Then, college administrator Raymond J. Rodrigues writes about how the distinct "cultures" of academic disciplines can blind faculty to deeper cultural issues and prospects for curricular change. Finally, Lisa Guernsey raises questions about academic authority and the use of new electronic media. The chapter closes with further writing assignments.

Although each of the readings has its own distinct concerns, these readings are also linked by the intertwined themes of community and language. What does it mean to belong to an academic community or to speak academic language? Or are there no such things, only disciplinary communities and disciplinary languages? Or are those ideas of disciplinary community and language also misleading as frames applied to academic work? These are complex questions about which your own research and experience will have prepared you to think and write.

As an anthropologist studying a community of students, Michael Moffatt deals not with education in general but with the perceptions, beliefs, and behavior of the students he observed and interviewed, undergraduates living in dormitories at Rutgers University during the 1980s. He found that the students he observed did think actively about their majors, though seldom in terms of intellectual interest. Rather, the deciding influences in choosing a major had to do with occupational prospects, level of difficulty, and status. Moffatt, who refers to himself as "the anthropologist," was evidently successful in making himself an inconspicuous part of the community he was observing.

Vocationalism and the Curriculum

MICHAEL MOFFATT

On paper, the curriculum of a large liberal-arts-based college such as Rutgers is a pluralistic universe of knowledge, a cornucopia of possible learning for the intellectually adventuresome student. Rutgers College students could study with about 950 faculty members in the wider university in the mid-1980s, organized into fifty-two different departments and programs whose majors were accepted by the college. All this choice might not be altogether a good thing, educational authorities sometimes worried. What

MICHAEL MOFFATT (b. 1944) is a professor of anthropology at Rutgers University in New Brunswick, New Jersey. Besides *Coming of Age in New Jersey* (1989), from which this excerpt is taken, he is author of *An Untouchable Community in South India* (1978).

guided the students through it? What general or unifying principles were they likely to discover in their college educations?

THE HIERARCHY OF THE MAJORS

For most of the students, however, the curriculum was organized in a very simple way. There were useful subjects, subjects that presumably led to good careers, and there were useless ones. Some of the useless subjects were "interesting," the students conceded. You might study one or two of them on the side in college, or if you could not stand any of the useful majors, you might actually major in something more eccentric:

> *Dorm Resident* (Hasbrouck Fourth lounge, September 1984): What did you say your name was again?
>
> *Anthropologist:* Mike.
>
> *Student:* Someone told me you're in anthropology?
>
> *Anthropologist:* Yup.
>
> *Student:* That seems like kind of a strange thing to be majoring in. I mean, what will you ever *do* with anthropology?
>
> *Anthropologist:* I'm not majoring in it. I *am* an anthropologist. And what I'm doing with it right now is studying *you.*
>
> *Student:* Oh, *you're* the guy . . . I've got to stop sitting around out here without my glasses on.

Oddballs aside, however, your bread-and-butter choice, your main field of study, ought to be something "practical," most of the students agreed.

Thus, in one recent year, almost three-quarters of the upperclassmen at Rutgers College were majoring in just ten departments while the remaining forty-two departments and programs divided up the other 28 percent of the undergraduates among themselves, in much smaller numbers. As most undergraduates understood them, eight of the ten top majors were sensible vocational choices. Economics presumably led to business, psychology to psychotherapy or to counseling, political science to law school, biological sciences to medical school, communication to work in the media, and mathematics to the sciences or to teaching. Accounting and computer science require no explanation. Only English and history were apparently pure liberal arts choices. But many of the students majoring in English had in fact double majors, and their other choice was usually a more useful one. Moreover, it was widely believed, the ability to write well made a difference in the business and professional world after college.

These top ten majors and all the rest then fell into a gradient of status in general student opinion, one that was based on three criteria. First, how good was the occupation to which a given subject presumably led? Second, and closely related, how difficult was that subject at Rutgers? And third, much less important, how much social good did the occupation or profession in question accomplish? By all three measures, biological sciences was number one. What real world profession, after all, was more prestigious than doctor? Doctors also made a lot of money and, conveniently, helped people. Premed was a very difficult major as well, the students agreed, known for its early "weeding courses," for its difficult prerequisites such as organic chemistry, believed by the students to be expressly designed to weed out underqualified undergraduates. Some of the other hard sciences were almost equally tough in undergraduate opinion, though they were taken far less often, perhaps because their target occupations were not as well known. And then came two very popular, respected choices: engineering and computer science.

Majors in the social and behavioral sciences ranked below most of those in the hard sciences. These subjects were definitely easier, the students believed, but they did still point you toward known professions or semiprofessions. And they were often about relevant, human things as well: psychology and psychotherapy, sociology and social work, and so on. Economics had a special position in the social sciences. Like the rest of them, it was considered to be only moderately difficult. This meant that many students could handle it, however; Bio-sci was simply too tough for the average undergraduate. And, though the students did not see business as a socially beneficial occupation, they did see it as one of the surer routes to personal benefit, to a middle-class or an upper-middle-class income. Economics was thus the most popular single choice by a factor of three over the next favorite major at Rutgers in the 1980s, and it had the same popularity nationwide in the 1980s.

Finally, bringing up the rear, behind the hard sciences and the bigger and the better-connected of the social and behavioral sciences, came the poor old humanities. The students often equated the humanities with all of the liberal arts; and every one of them, the students usually agreed, was a "gut"[1] major that prepared you for nothing at all in life. Sometimes capable, hardworking students did choose to major in these subjects out of pure interest in them. But to do so, they had to swim upstream against student opinion; they had to be forever excusing themselves to their friends for their peculiar choice. "He's a throat personality[2] in a gut major," an acquaintance of one such misplaced student joked about him in 1978.

What made most students think that some majors were more difficult than others? First of all, like many of their elders, the students firmly believed that mathematical and scientific knowledge was intrinsically harder to attain, more cumulative, and more precise than the knowledge typical of the social sciences and the humanities. You could not fake a knowledge of mathematics, they believed, whereas reading and writing, the cognitive skills that counted most outside the sciences, were much more "subjective." Reading as most students thought of it was actually entirely unproblematic; who, after all, could not read by the time they got to college? Writing, on the other hand, could be difficult. Writing was obviously not a talent everyone possessed. There was some difference of opinion among the students as to whether it could be learned or not. But if you could write, then you could "bullshit" your way through almost any course in the humanities or the social sciences, the students believed. For who could say why one paper received an A and another a B?

> Most engineers [believe] that their discipline is far more demanding in terms of time, brainpower, and competition than any others, except Pharmacy or the other sciences. . . . Non-engineering majors . . . have the easiest life in college. To study their material requires only reading whereas engineering requires reading, comprehension, and

[1]**gut:** Easy, undemanding [Eds.].

[2]**throat personality:** In Moffatt's words, "a hard-working, aggressive student," as in "cutthroat" [Eds.].

problem-solving. . . . However, I do respect [nonengineers] for the amount of papers they must write.

— Senior male, engineering major

Nonscience majors sometimes tried to argue back against these collective put-downs of their chosen fields, but they also often accepted them as well:

Sociology, sometimes known as the "articulation of the obvious," is an example of a discipline lacking esteem. People . . . more readily accept mathematical science because [it] represents concrete knowledge. Whereas Human Communication, Philosophy, Anthropology, and Sociology, some of the many liberal arts, are based more on abstract thinking and abstract principles.

— Sociology major, undergraduate paper

The most serious and intellectual of all students seem to be those in engineering and premedicine. . . . Unfortunately psychology majors are not seen as very intellectual or challenged academically. When a person is a psychologist, it is respectable, but before they get there they are seen as having a gut major and an easy course load. . . . For some it is a major to take when you don't know what else to major in.

— Junior male, psychology major

The students had another, even more convincing reason for ranking the majors according to difficulty, however: their own correct sense that the various academic departments and programs in the college gave widely differing grades for widely differing amounts of required work. And the difficulty of a given subject did tend to correlate with its perceived vocational desirability, for a very simple reason. Administratively, the college and the larger university had been set up to operate as an academic marketplace. Under guidelines from the state of New Jersey, the resources the academic deans gave to the various departments — faculty positions, secretaries, budgets — were partially "enrollment driven." The more students your department taught, the more resources you could demand and the larger and more influential your department could potentially become within the university. The fewer, the smaller you were likely to shrink.

Therefore, professors in student-poor departments were often encouraged by their chairmen to "up their enrollments" by making their classes more attractive. Better teaching was one way to do so. Easier grading was another obvious technique. Faculty members in the student-rich departments, on the other hand, often felt overburdened. The deans never increased their resources fast enough, they complained, and therefore they had too many distracting undergraduates around: How would they ever get their research done? They could thus afford to be much tougher in their grading. They could afford to "maintain standards." They could afford to "resist grade inflation." They could even institute weeding courses!

The degree to which this economy of supply and demand actually determined grading and the perceived difficulty of different majors was indicated by a list that the dean's office of the Faculty of Arts and Sciences, the biggest faculty unit serving Rutgers College, quietly circulated to all its departments once a year, probably in an effort to shame its easier departments into shaping up. In these lists, the departments and programs were ranked according to the percentage of A's, B pluses, and B's that each one had given across all its undergraduate courses during the previous year. The 1986 list (Table 1) had the easiest departments at the top, the most difficult at the bottom. The

Table 1. Departments and Programs, Easiest to Toughest Grading (Faculty of Arts and Sciences Departments and Programs at Rutgers College). Capital letters represent those in the ten most popular majors.

1. American Studies	17. Religion
2. Italian	18. Sociology
3. German	19. Philosophy
4. Hebraic Studies	20. ENGLISH
5. Spanish and Portuguese	21. Geology
6. Chinese, Comparative Literature, and Slavic Languages and Literature	22. HISTORY
7. Women's Studies	23. Art History
8. Linguistics	24. Statistics
9. Puerto Rican Studies	25. PSYCHOLOGY
10. Labor Studies	26. Physics and Astronomy
11. African Studies	27. BIOLOGICAL SCIENCES
12. Classics and Archaeology	28. COMPUTER SCIENCE
13. POLITICAL SCIENCE	29. Medieval Studies
14. French	30. ECONOMICS
15. Biochemistry	31. Chemistry
16. Anthropology	32. Interdisciplinary Studies
	33. MATHEMATICS

range was striking, as were the distributions. The department at the top was over two times easier than the department at the bottom. It had given 72 percent A's, B pluses, and B's, while the department at the bottom had given 30 percent. Also note the degree to which the humanities really were easiest according to this evidence, the social sciences somewhat harder, and the hard sciences hardest. Finally, note the generally direct correlation between the majors in highest demand and some of the tougher subjects (in capitals) in Table 1.

Most students did not know about the existence of this list, but they did have a working sense of what it reported. At the easier end of the scale, for instance:

> I've made the dangerous discovery that I can do a various amount and even quality of work and maintain good grades. Thus it has become a matter of how little work I can get away with and keep my [B average] or better. The nature of my major (English) aids in maintaining my lax study habits. Since exams are totally subjective and paper topics are chosen by the students, one doesn't need to read all of the books and attend all of the lectures. This year I have become amazed at just how little work is necessary.
>
> — Junior female

Considerations

1. Moffatt says that the students he studied in the mid-1980s often saw majors in terms of relative status. Has that been your experience in researching your major? Did you get a sense of its relative status among undergraduates at your college?
2. Did you find evidence of the three criteria through which, according to Moffatt, students evaluate majors? Do you agree with his assessment of their comparative importance? Did you find other criteria?
3. Explain what Moffatt means by saying that grades within a major are determined by an "economy of supply and demand." Did you find that grades — and perceptions about

difficulty — significantly influenced which students, and how many, select the major you've studied?

4. The students Moffatt studied don't seem very interested in the "discourse" of their major, at least not in most of the ways we've encouraged you to research discourse. Do you see this as a limitation in Moffatt's study or an accurate reflection of the real absence of such concerns in students' lives? Or are the students concerned with a different kind of academic discourse?

In the passage below, from an ethnographic study conducted among juniors and seniors at the University of New Hampshire, Elizabeth Chiseri-Strater writes about two contrasting styles of classroom discourse, one of which she associates with men and the other with women. The male style involves the mastery of isolated course material and functions most comfortably either in a traditional lecture or debate format. The female style is more collaborative and open-ended, more likely to circle back through material seeking connections outside the course; it's a style more compatible with discussion formats.

In conducting her research Chiseri-Strater selected a small number of students to serve as subjects of case studies; then she attended their classes, noted their behavior, looked closely at their writing, and interviewed them frequently. Nick and Anna are two of the students she observed most closely and in whom she found the sharpest contrast. The courses that Chiseri-Strater refers to are an art history lecture course taken by Anna, a political science seminar taken by Nick, and an English course, Prose Writing, taken by both students. As you read this excerpt, you'll want to reflect upon your own research: Did you also find significant contrasts in the styles of classroom discourse, and did those contrasts fall along gender lines?

Gender, Language, and Pedagogy

ELIZABETH CHISERI-STRATER

When gender issues emerged as central to this study, I was not surprised since I had made a conscious effort to include both female and male college students. As a researcher, though, I discovered the importance of gender-related issues through the eyes of my informants, by watching subtle behaviors like Nick's dominating and Anna's

---

ELIZABETH CHISERI-STRATER (b. 1943) is an associate professor of English at the University of North Carolina, Greensboro. She contributed chapters to *Portfolio Portraits* (1992) and to *Nuts and Bolts* (1993) and is the author of the forthcoming text *Fieldworking: Reading and Writing Research.* Her book *Academic Literacies,* from which this excerpt is taken, was published in 1990.

muted speech patterns. After choosing to work with Anna, I originally speculated that she would be the student who would suffer most from the mastery model of teaching that is most often endorsed in higher education. But Anna proved me wrong by working against the dominant discourse style and creating her own mode of learning. One clue to her transformation of mastery learning is mirrored in a quotation she used in a paper for art history. The quote, taken from a feminist critique of women's values, attacks the pyramid model of life where men are placed at the top under god, with nature at the bottom: "This vertical view of reality is a lie, a construct created to justify patriarchal subordination and control. We live in a circle, not along a line" (Cheatam and Powell 1986, 160). While Anna uses this quotation in her art history paper to discuss the kind of caring for the land that ecofeminism[1] endorses, it also describes the recursive and circular pattern of learning that women students often bring to educational settings. In the end, Anna becomes a successful learner, not because she adapts to the mastery model but because she makes a conscious effort to "connect" her coursework, an approach documented by feminist scholars looking at the different learning styles of women students. Nick, however, remains the separate knower within the academic setting, compartmentalizing and isolating his coursework.

Although it is easy to accept that male and female students might display different learning styles, it is less comfortable to admit that the university as an institution primarily rewards mastery or what Nick calls "abbreviated learning." "Mastery" was the preferred pedagogical model rewarded in both political science and art history, as exhibited in the presentational styles of the lecture and the debate.

The lecture/recitation format, represented by Anna's art history course, Walter Ong (1978) suggests, derives from the man-made university system without contributions from the discursive, epistemic,[2] and intellectual traditions of women. Lecturing involves the student in a passive style of learning and encourages what Gilligan (1982) and her colleague Nona Lyons (1983) have called "separate knowing," an epistemology that rests upon impersonal authority and rule systems for establishing truth — William Perry's "dualistic" stage of thinking (1970). What seems potentially abusive about the lecture format is the exclusion of how the knowledge within the discipline comes to be; knowledge is invisibly constructed and presented as absolute. Listening to the mega-scholar's mind at work is like being part of an appreciative but nonparticipatory audience.

Certainly the lecture format serves some useful pedagogical purposes in higher education, but we might question its privileged position in so many university courses. When Mary Hall, the "reflective practitioner" (Schön 1983), turned her classroom over to her students, engaging them as novice art-critics, they joined her as exploring, involved learners, forging their understanding of works of art together, even taking risks in their responses. After this class discussion, one student in the class told me, "Getting through all this material is her agenda, not ours."[3] Rather, the student's agenda is to learn how to "do" this mental activity called critiquing art. If we accept learning as a

[1]**ecofeminism:** Environmental movement holding that the Western conquest of nature is linked to patriarchal efforts to dominate women [Eds.].

[2]**epistemic/epistemology:** Related to ways of knowing or theories of obtaining knowledge [Eds.].

[3]We should point out that the student is referring to the teacher's typical practice of lecturing on a large body of material without encouraging a lot of student interaction and discussion [Eds.].

"process" and not mere transmission, a class discussion — aside from involving students as learners — prepares for the critical thinking they will later use in writing for the discipline and presumably in all their courses.

Classroom discourse style revealed itself as the most gender-sensitive feature of the settings under consideration in this study. Linguist James Gee suggests that discourse can be thought of as a kind of "identity kit," which comes "complete with the appropriate costume and instructions on how to act and talk so as to take on a particular role that others will recognize" (1987, 1). The way that talk in particular was used in courses corresponded to the pedagogical model for learning encouraged there. Considerable feminist scholarship suggests that it is through oral language use as well as written discourse conventions that patriarchal institutions such as the university have sustained their powers. Many women academics themselves have expressed their discomfort over the combative and argumentative model that pervades the profession, wherein women are expected to be publicly assertive authorities who challenge the intellectual views of others in their fields.

Nick's Seminar in Political Thought demonstrates another primarily male discourse style — the combative model of the debate. Even though the class is billed as a seminar, in which discussions should ostensibly take place, all of the verbal interactions flowed through the professor, as each student worked alone to "master" the material under consideration. The only access to the political meanings of the texts in this great book's curriculum is through the professor, who serves as censor for all alternative interpretations. The seminar emphasizes a hierarchical and unbalanced power structure, wherein the professor and his graduate students both control and interrupt the stream of talk. Rather than building on individual student contributions, each student engages in separate "bilateral" exchanges with the professor. Although students learn to be verbally aggressive, the class members do not become intellectually aggressive and language serves as a weapon rather than a tool for constructing understandings. This kind of seminar model may be, in fact, more deceptive than the strict lecture format because it masquerades as an egalitarian forum in which each voice counts.

It has clearly seemed easier for educators to understand and accept the language differences found among other cultures, such as native American Indians (Philips 1972), Hawaiians (Au 1980), urban blacks (Baugh 1983), and rural blacks (Heath 1983), than to acknowledge the differences in how men and women use language within that microcosm of society we call academic life. The continued exploration in the ways classroom discourse encourages — or, in the case of gender issues, perhaps discourages — learning offers one of the most exciting research areas available, one that has been better mined at the early childhood and elementary level (Barnes 1976; Wells 1986; Cazden 1980; Bruner 1983), but that needs further research in higher education. The growing number of scholarly articles and books devoted to gender differences in language use . . . point to one critical issue: that we need to provide opportunities for students, male and female, in our classrooms to have experiences shaping ideas through collaborative talk, rather than monologic discourse. The more collaborative style of Prose Writing courses encouraged a shared discursive floor as well as listening to others, a way of knowing often attributed to and valued by women. This discourse style needs to play to a larger audience in our college classrooms, beginning with professors listening to the wide range of voices of our students, rather than only to themselves talking. Male students need to listen and hear what their female classmates have to say rather than interrupt and dominate discussions. Women students need to hear their own voices raising questions and confronting issues. And women's silences need not always be interpreted as unarticulated knowing but as thoughtful reflection and productive meditation. Language should be used to transform experiences rather than simply to transmit knowledge.

Ironically, while Anna succeeds within the male-dominated university setting, Nick is left unsatisfied in spite of his familiarity with mastery learning. Ultimately, I think, Nick will remain adversarial, distanced, and possibly alienated from his learning if he is not invited to participate in more conversations and fewer debates. A feminist pedagogy is required in higher education, not just for women, who need their learning style reaffirmed, but for male students as well, whose educations will be shortchanged if they are channeled through coursework without being asked to reflect on, revise, rethink, and personally construct what they are learning in one course and connect it to other courses and finally to themselves.

Educational practices should not be adjusted to make the classroom climate a warmer place for women so that they can then adopt the traditional, accepted, and patriarchal modes of discourse. Instead, feminist teaching practices can also empower the male student who is too often allowed to march through his coursework without exposure to alternative ways of learning and knowing. Constructed knowing, as it has been renamed by feminist thinkers, benefits both males and females in the academy by switching the emphasis away from agonistic[4] discourse toward dialogue, exploration, and sharing.

[4]**agonistic:** Characterized by competitiveness; the desire to win in debate [Eds.].

WORKS CITED

Au, K. H. "Participation Structures in a Reading Lesson with Hawaiian Children: Analysis of a Culturally Appropriate Instructional Event." *Anthropology and Education Quarterly 11* (1980): 91–115.

Barnes, D. *From Communication to Curriculum.* Harmondsworth, England: Penguin, 1976.

Baugh, J. *Black Street Talk.* Texas: University of Texas Press, 1983.

Bruner, J. *Actual Minds, Possible Worlds.* Cambridge: Harvard University Press, 1986.

Cazden, C. *Classroom Discourse: The Language of Teaching and Learning.* Portsmouth, N.H.: Heinemann, 1980.

Cheatam, A., and M. Powell. *This Way Daybreak Comes: Women's Values and the Future.* Philadelphia: New Society Publishers, 1986.

Gee, J. "What is Literacy?" Paper presented at the Mailman Conference on Families and Literacy. Harvard Graduate School of Education, Cambridge, Mass., 1987.

Gilligan, C. *In a Different Voice: Psychological Theory and Women's Development.* Cambridge, Mass.: Harvard University Press, 1982.

Heath, S. B. *Ways with Words: Language, Life, and Work in Communities and Classrooms.* New York: Cambridge University Press, 1983.

Ong, W. "Literacy and Orality in Our Times." *ADE Bulletin* 58(1978): 1–7.

Perry, W. G. Jr. *Forms of Intellectual and Ethical Development in the College Years: A Scheme.* New York: Holt, Rinehart and Winston, 1970.

Phillips, S. "Participant Structures and Communicative Competence: Warm Springs Children in Community and Classroom." *Functions of Language in the Classroom.* Ed. C. B. Cazden et al. New York: Teachers College Press, 1972.
Schön, D. *The Reflective Practitioner: How Professionals Think in Action.* New York: Basic Books, 1983.
Thorne, B., C. Kramarae, and N. Henley, eds. *Language, Gender and Society.* Rowley, Mass.: Newbury House, 1983.

Considerations

1. Describe the basic contrast in discourse styles claimed by Chiseri-Strater. Does your own research support her claims?
2. The topic of classroom discourse styles might be separated from issues of gender. Do you think it should be, or are the two inextricably woven together?
3. If you also read the piece by David R. Russell (p. 698) about the history of American universities, consider how that history might be brought to bear on what Chiseri-Strater says about discourse styles and gender.
4. What does Chiseri-Strater mean, in her last sentence, by "agonistic discourse," and how is that connected with a feminist critique of traditional university pedagogy?

In working with graduate students on their dissertations, Howard S. Becker reports often being confused by ponderous and inefficient language. Here Becker tells the story of his conversation with one such student whose attitude toward sociological language he began to question. The story dramatizes the role of specialized language in entering an academic discipline while underscoring the limitations of that language.

If You Want to Be a Scholar

HOWARD S. BECKER

Rosanna Hertz, now a colleague but then a very advanced student, came into my office one day and said she'd like to talk to me about a chapter of her thesis-in-progress, which I had edited for her. She said, in a careful tone which I supposed hid a certain amount of irritation, that she agreed that the writing was improved — shorter, clearer, on the

---

HOWARD S. BECKER (b. 1928) is a professor of sociology at the University of Washington in Seattle. His many books include *Outsiders* (1963), *Art Worlds* (1982), and the forthcoming *Tricks of the Trade.* This excerpt is taken from *Writing for Social Scientists* (1986).

whole much better. But, she said, she didn't quite understand the principles that governed what I had done. Could I go over the document with her and explain them? I told her that I wasn't sure what principles governed my editorial judgment, that I really edited by ear. . . . But I agreed to do my best. I wondered whether I actually did follow any general principles of editing and thought that, if I did, I might discover them by trying to explain them to her.

Rosanna brought her chapter in a few days later. I had rewritten it extensively, cutting a lot of words but, I hoped, not losing any of her thought. It was a very good piece of work — rich data, imaginatively analyzed, well-organized — but it was very wordy and academic. I had removed as much of the redundancy and academic flourish as I thought she would stand for. We went over it, a page at a time, and she quizzed me on each point. None of my changes involved technical sociological terms. Where she wrote "unified stance" I substituted "agreement," because it was shorter. I replaced "confronted the issue" with "talked about," because it was less pretentious. A longer example: Where she wrote "This chapter will examine the impact of money or, more specifically, independent incomes on relations between husbands and wives with particular regard to the realm of financial affairs," I substituted "This chapter will show that independent incomes change the way husbands and wives handle financial affairs," for similar reasons. I removed meaningless qualifications ("tends to"), combined sentences that repeated long phrases, and when she said the same thing in two ways in successive sentences, took out the less effective version, explaining what I was doing and why as I went along.

She agreed with each of my ad hoc explanations, but we weren't discovering any general principles. I asked her to take over and work on a page of text I hadn't done anything to. We went over a few lines and then came to a sentence which said that the people she was studying "could afford not to have to be concerned with" certain things. I asked how she thought she could change that. She looked and looked at the sentence and finally said that she couldn't see any way to improve that phrasing. I finally asked if she could just say that they "needn't worry" about those things.

She thought about it, set her jaw, and decided that this was the place to make her stand. "Well, yes, that is shorter, and it certainly is clearer. . . ." The thought hung unfinished as blatantly as if she had spoken the four dots aloud. After a prolonged and momentous silence, I said, "But *what*?" "Well," she said, "the other way is *classier.*"

My intuition told me the word was important. I said that she could repay all the favors she owed me by writing five pages explaining exactly what she meant when she said "classier." She looked embarrassed — it's obvious now that I was taking unfair advantage both of friendship and professorial authority — and said she would. I couldn't blame her for making me wait a couple of months for those pages. She told me later that it was the hardest thing she had ever had to write because she knew she had to tell the truth.

I am going to quote from her letter at length. But this is not just a matter of one author's character and language. "Classier" was an important clue precisely because Rosanna was saying out loud what many students and professionals in the scholarly disciplines believed and felt but, less courageous, were less willing to admit. They had hinted at what she finally wrote and the hints convinced me her attitude was widespread.

The letter I got was four double-spaced pages, and I won't quote all of it or quote it in sequence because Rosanna was thinking out loud when she wrote it and the order is not crucial. She began by remarking,

> Somewhere along the line, probably in college, I picked up on the fact that articulate people used big words, which impressed me. I remember taking two classes from a philosophy professor simply because I figured he must be really smart since I didn't know the meaning of the words he used in class. My notes from these classes are almost nonexistent. I spent class time writing down the words he used that I didn't know, going home, and looking them up. He sounded so smart to me simply because I didn't understand him. . . . The way someone writes — the more difficult the writing style — the more intellectual they sound.

It is no accident, as they say, that she learned to think this way in college. The excerpt expresses the perspective of a subordinate in a highly stratified organization. Colleges and universities, pretending to be communities of intellectuals who discuss matters of common interest freely and disinterestedly, are no such thing. Professors know more, have the degrees to prove it, test students and grade their papers, and in every imaginable way sit on top of the heap while students stand at the bottom. Some resent the inequality, but intelligent students who hope to be intellectuals themselves accept it wholeheartedly. They believe, like Rosanna, that the professors who teach them know more and should be imitated, whether what they do makes sense or not. The principle of hierarchy assures them that they are wrong and the teacher right. They grant the same privileges to authors:

> When I read something and I don't know immediately what it means, I always give the author the benefit of the doubt. I assume this is a smart person and the problem with my not understanding the ideas is that I'm not as smart. I don't assume either that the emperor has no clothes or that the author is not clear because of their own confusion about what they have to say. I always assume that it is my inability to understand or that there is something more going on than I'm capable of understanding. . . . I assume if it got into the *AJS* [American Journal of Sociology], for example, chances are it's good and it's important and if I don't understand it that's my problem since the journal has already legitimated it.

She makes a further point, which other people mentioned as well. (Sociologists will recognize it as a specific instance of the general problem of socialization into professional worlds.) . . . Graduate students learning to be academics know that they are not real intellectuals yet — just as medical students know they are not yet real doctors — and search eagerly for signs of progress. The arcane vocabulary and syntax of stereotypical academic prose clearly distinguish lay people from professional intellectuals, just as the ability of professional ballet dancers to stand on their toes distinguishes them from ordinary folks. Learning to write like an academic moves students toward membership in that elite:

> While I personally find scholarly writing boring and prefer to spend my time reading novels, academic elitism is a part of every graduate student's socialization. I mean that academic writing is not English but written in a shorthand that only members of the profession can decipher. . . . I think it is a way to . . . maintain group boundaries of elitism. . . . Ideas are supposed to be written in such a fashion that they are difficult for

untrained people to understand. This is scholarly writing. And if you want to be a scholar you need to learn to reproduce this way of writing.

Considerations

1. Summarize Rosanna's attitudes about writing sociology. Did you find similar attitudes in conducting your own research?
2. Rosanna is a graduate student, but can you relate to any of what she is trying to do with her writing? Do you recognize any of your motives in the motives she reveals?
3. Does "scholarly language" necessarily involve "academic elitism"? Why, or why not?
4. As a graduate student, Rosanna is presumably part of a "discourse community" of sociologists. To what extent does she seem to feel part of such a community? Does Rosanna's case confirm or argue against the idea that such communities exist?

David R. Russell is interested in the development of the modern research university from the small American college. In this passage, he discusses the differences between the American college of 100 years ago — which admitted a tiny percentage of the population and provided, in effect, a single curriculum — and the modern university, which offers a far wider range of study to far more people.

Academic Discourse: Community or Communities?

DAVID R. RUSSELL

Before the advent of the modern university in the 1870s, academia was indeed a single discourse community. Institutions of higher learning built an intellectual and social community by selecting students primarily on the basis of social class (less than 1 percent of the population was admitted), which guaranteed linguistic homogeneity, and by initiating them intellectually through a series of highly language-dependent methods — the traditional recitation, disputation, debate, and oral examination of the old liberal curriculum. Equally important, most students shared common values (Christian, often sec-

DAVID R. RUSSELL (b. 1951) is an associate professor of English at Iowa State University, where he teaches in the Ph.D. program in Rhetoric and Professional Communication. He co-edited *Landmarks in Writing Across the Curriculum* (1994). These excerpts appear in Russell's book *Writing in the Academic Disciplines, 1870–1990: A Curricular History* (1991).

tarian) with their teachers (primarily ministers). They pursued a uniform course of study and were then duly welcomed as full members of the nation's governing elite.[1]

The modern university changed all that. It provided the specialized knowledge that drove the new urban-industrial economy and a new class of specialized *professionals* (the term came into use during the period) who managed that economy, with its secular rationale and complex bureaucratic organization — what Burton J. Bledstein has aptly called "the culture of professionalism."[2] Beginning with the land-grant colleges of the late nineteenth century and continuing with the rise of the modern university on the German model, the academic discourse community became fragmented. Numbers swelled, with enrollments tripling as a percentage of the population between 1900 and 1925 alone. Students from previously excluded social groups were admitted, destroying linguistic homogeneity. The new elective curriculum was introduced to prepare students for a host of emerging professional careers in the new industrial society. The elective curriculum compartmentalized knowledge and broke one relatively stable academic discourse community into many fluctuating ones. And the active, personal, language-dependent instructional methods of the old curriculum were replaced by passive, rather impersonal methods borrowed from Germany or, later, from scientific management: lecture, objective testing, and the like. Ultimately, the professional faculty who replaced the gentlemen scholars and divines of the old curriculum came to see secondary and undergraduate education as only one of several competing responsibilities (along with graduate teaching, research, and professional service). And the teaching of writing — initiating the neophytes into a discourse community — suffered accordingly.

Because it is tempting to recall academia's very different past and hope for a very different future, the term *academic community* has powerful spiritual and political connotations, but today academia is a *discourse* community only in a context so broad as to have little meaning in terms of shared linguistic forms, either for the advancement of knowledge (which now goes on in disciplinary communities and subcommunities) or for the initiation of new members (who are initiated into a specific community's discourse). Thus, to speak of the academic community as if its members shared a single set of linguistic conventions and traditions of inquiry is to make a categorical mistake. In the aggregate of all the tightly knit, turf-conscious disciplines and departments, each of its own discourse community, the modern university consists. Many have wished it otherwise.

Despite these profound changes, American educators have continued to think of the academic community as holding out a single compositional norm, which would speak intelligently about the multiform new knowledge to a "general reader." . . . Though academia held onto a generalized ideal of an academic community sharing a single advanced literacy, there was never any consensus in the modern university about the nature of that community or its language. Academic discourse, like academia itself, continued its drive toward increasing specialization. The university became an aggregate of competing discourse communities; it was not a single community. But the myth of a single academic discourse community — and a golden age of student writing — endured.

[1]See S. Michael Halloran, "Rhetoric in the American College Curriculum: The Decline of Public Discourse," *Pre/Text* 3 (1982): 246–256.

[2]Burton J. Bledstein, *The Culture of Professionalism: The Middle Class and the Development of Higher Education in America.* New York: Norton, 1976.

American academia today (and for the last hundred years or so) is a community primarily in a broad institutional sense, a collection of people going about a vast enterprise, in much the same way that we speak of the "business community" as a sector of national life. The academic disciplines are in one sense united through their common missions: teaching, research, and service. But disciplines have been so diverse, so independent, and so bound up with professional communities outside academia that they require no common language or even shared values and methods within the university in order to pursue those missions. Those genres and conventions of writing that are shared by all academic disciplines are also shared by professional communities outside academia. And within academia, the conventions (and beyond them the assumptions and methodologies) of the various disciplines are characterized more by their differences than by their similarities. . . . Indeed, an academic is likely to have more linguistic common ground with a fellow professional in the corporate sector than with another academic in an unrelated field, except in regard to purely institutional matters (governance, academic freedom, teaching loads, etc.). As a leading sociologist of higher education, Burton Clark, puts it, academia is made up of "small worlds, different worlds."[3]

[3]Burton R. Clark, *The Academic Life: Small Worlds, Different Worlds* (Princeton: Carnegie Foundation for the Advancement of Teaching, 1987).

Considerations

1. How, according to Russell, do contemporary American colleges and universities differ from their predecessors?
2. What does Russell mean by saying that modern colleges and universities no longer have "linguistic homogeneity"? What factors account for its loss? Did you find evidence of this loss in your own research?
3. What does Russell think is misleading about the term "academic community," and why does he prefer to speak of "discourse communities"? In your research did you find evidence of such community in the discipline you investigated?
4. Have you found evidence that modern academic disciplines are "small worlds, different worlds"?

In Tyrannical Machines *(1990) Lynne V. Cheney, former chair of the National Endowment for the Humanities, offers a "Report on Educational Practices Gone Wrong and Our Best Hopes for Setting Them Right." In her chapter on colleges and universities, she writes about the tension in the American system between research and teaching.*

Tyrannical Machines

LYNNE V. CHENEY

For decades critics have been saying that institutions of higher education do not do enough to encourage good teaching. Classicist William Arrowsmith made this point in 1967, observing that "at present, the universities are as uncongenial to teaching as the Mojave Desert to a clutch of Druid priests."[1] Almost a quarter century later, historian Page Smith asserts that faculties "are in full flight from teaching. . . . In many universities, faculty members make no bones about the fact that students are the enemy. It is students who threaten to take up precious time that might otherwise be devoted to research."[2]

This situation has not come about because faculty members necessarily prefer research. In a recent survey, 71 percent reported that their interests either leaned toward or lay primarily in teaching.[3] But the road to success — or even to survival — in the academic world is through publishing. Anthropologist Bradd Shore notes, "If you fail at the teaching and fail at the service but still do terrific scholarship, you are likely to get tenure," but not the other way around.[4] A senior literature professor, who himself publishes actively, reports that "the way one prospers is by finding time away from teaching to get one's own work done."[5] Philosopher Thomas Flynn relates the advice he received as a young assistant professor trying to get tenure: "Beware of the students. They will destroy you."[6]

The most dramatic examples of how research is valued over teaching occur when faculty members who have won campuswide awards for teaching suddenly find themselves without jobs. A 1988 article in the *Chronicle of Higher Education* even raised the possibility that teaching awards, by implying that a faculty member is not as serious about research as he or she should be, are "the kiss of death" as far as achieving tenure is concerned.[7] Economist Thomas Sowell reports, "I personally know three different professors at three different institutions who have gotten the Teacher of the Year Award and were then told that their contracts would not be renewed."[8]

[1]William Arrowsmith, "The Future of Teaching," *The Public Interest* (Winter 1967), 55.

[2]Page Smith, *Killing the Spirit: Higher Education in America* (New York: Viking, 1990), 6.

[3]*The Condition of the Professoriate: Attitudes and Trends,* 1989 (Princeton, N.J.: The Carnegie Foundation for the Advancement of Teaching, 1989), Table 30.

[4]Bradd Shore in "The Nature of Teaching," *Emory Magazine* (March 1990), 15.

[5]Quoted in Louis F. Brakeman and Katherine M. Loring, *What One Has Within, What the Context Provides: Sources of Faculty Professional Vitality in the Great Lakes Colleges Association* (Ann Arbor, Mich.: Great Lakes Colleges Association, 1988), 50.

[6]Thomas R. Flynn in "The Nature of Teaching," *Emory Magazine* (March 1990), 13.

[7]Scott Heller, "Teaching Awards: Aid to Tenure or Kiss of Death?" *The Chronicle of Higher Education,* 16 March 1988, A14.

[8]Thomas Sowell, "On the Higher Learning in America: Some Comments," *The Public Interest* (Spring 1990), 69.

Administrator, scholar, and writer LYNNE V. CHENEY (b. 1941) was chair of the National Endowment for the Humanities for two terms and is currently the W. H. Brady Jr. Distinguished Fellow at The American Enterprise Institute. In addition to *Tyrannical Machines* (1990), from which this excerpt was taken, she has authored four other reports on issues in the humanities and education.

The emphasis on research is greatest at research universities where 64 percent of the faculty report spending five hours or less per week on formal classroom instruction and 86 percent report spending six or more hours per week on research. At liberal arts colleges, by contrast, only 16 percent of the faculty report less than five hours a week in the classroom; and 48 percent report spending six or more hours on research.[9] Even at liberal arts colleges, however, the emphasis on research is growing. Fifty liberal arts schools have banded together under the lead of Oberlin College and are considering calling themselves "research colleges." Schools such as Colorado College, Grinnell, and Wellesley have reduced the number of hours faculty teach so that they have more time to do research. A recent survey of twelve liberal arts colleges reported that faculty frequently distinguish between teaching and "what they often call, significantly, *'my own work,'*" or research.[10]

Faculty members often blame administrators for the emphasis placed on research, but administrators are responding to powerful external forces. The money that flows to their institutions and the prestige their schools enjoy will be largely dictated by the research those institutions do. Thomas Sowell points out that hundreds of millions of federal dollars flow into research at universities. "Money talks in academia as elsewhere," Sowell notes, "and what money says on most campuses is 'do research.'"[11] Emory University's Frank Manley observes that academic reputation is established through the public act of publishing, not through the more private act of teaching. "The people who have status outside the University, who are writing and publishing, are the ones who are going to get the status inside the University," says Manley. "They are the ones who are looked upon with most favor by the administrators because they are the ones who have the marquee value for the University."[12]

The model that increasingly drives all of higher education — the tyrannical machine that reigns — was first established in the United States at the end of the nineteenth century. Derived from German universities, this model emphasized the production of knowledge rather than its diffusion. Both Daniel Coit Gilman and G. Stanley Hall, influential spokesmen for the new university ideal, thought that the scholar's proper role lay in producing "bricks" for the rising temple of knowledge.[13] William James was among the first to note that such a single-minded view threatened a system in which there were many paths to excellence. It was in a 1903 essay on the Ph.D. — the degree associated with the new, research-oriented university — that James coined the phrase "tyrannical machine."

Across the country are thousands of faculty members whose professional lives run counter to [this] prevailing culture of academia. At a liberal arts college in the Midwest

[9]1989 *National Survey of Faculty,* conducted for the Carnegie Foundation for the Advancement of Teaching (Princeton, N.J.: The Wirthlin Group, 1989), Questions 9A, 9D.

[10]Brakeman and Loring, *What One Has Within,* 48.

[11]Sowell, "On the Higher Learning in America," 68.

[12]Frank Manley in "The Nature of Teaching," *Emory Magazine* (March 1990), 14.

[13]Alexandra Oleson and John Voss, *The Organization of Knowledge in Modern America,* 1860–1920 (Baltimore: The Johns Hopkins University Press, 1979), 287–295; Abraham Flexner, *Daniel Coit Gilman: Creator of the American Type of University* (New York: Harcourt, Brace and Company, 1946), 50–56; G. Stanley Hall, *Life and Confessions of a Psychologist* (New York: D. Appleton and Company, 1923), 248–249.

where a new emphasis on publication has led to a cutback in course offerings, a literature professor teaches as many courses as he possibly can to try to make up the shortfall. "I am permitted to teach on an unlimited basis," he says, "and I do. If I did not do this many students would not be able to take a literature course."[14] All too often, however, a decision to emphasize teaching exacts a price. At the University of Maryland, associate professor Maynard Mack Jr. notes that his own focus on teaching "is not a fast track to that promotion. I should minimize my campus responsibilities and produce a second book."[15]

Nowhere is the countertrend to academia's current culture stronger than in community colleges. The mission of these institutions is clear. "We are a practical teaching college," in the words of one professor.[16] But in a system of higher education that does not place high value on teaching, community colleges rank low in prestige. Having less status than four-year colleges, they command fewer resources. Their faculty members earn less even though they teach more. The overwhelming majority of community college faculty spend more than eleven hours a week in the classroom; 10 percent spend more than twenty hours a week.[17] Many find year-round employment a necessity. "If you don't teach," says Evelyn Edson of Piedmont Virginia Community College, "you work at Shoney's [a fast-food restaurant] in the summer. You get some kind of job."[18] The result can be too little time to undertake the reading and reflection that make for better teaching, too little time to exchange ideas with other faculty members about issues in one's field or ways to improve courses and curricula.

[14]Quoted in Brakeman and Loring, *What One Has Within,* 41.

[15]Quoted in Carol Innerst, "University of Maryland Professor Infects Students with Passion for the Bard," *Washington Times,* 4 April 1990, A10.

[16]Quoted in Burton R. Clark, *The Academic Life: Small Worlds, Different Worlds* (Princeton, N.J.: The Carnegie Foundation for the Advancement of Teaching, 1987), 118.

[17]1989 *National Survey of Faculty,* Question 9A.

[18]Evelyn Edson, conversation with the author, 30 April 1990.

Considerations

1. Explain what Cheney means by the "tyrannical machine" of her title.
2. "Money talks in academia as elsewhere," Cheney quotes economist Thomas Sowell as noting. In investigating your major did you see the influence of money upon the substance and quality of the discourse? If so, explain. If not, speculate upon how that influence might be invisibly present.
3. In terms of Cheney's critique, we might say that in contemporary universities, one form of discourse — communication with students — is sacrificed to another: discourse among colleagues. In your own research, did you find any indications of this discrepancy?
4. If you've also read the piece by David R. Russell (p. 698), compare the two writers' views of "discourse communities" in the American education system.

Ernest Boyer was the primary author of a study about higher education in the United States, conducted by the Carnegie Foundation for the Advancement of Teaching. Boyer surveyed students, teachers, and administrators across the country before synthesizing his findings and offering his recommendations. In the chapter from which these excerpts are taken, Boyer turns to the issue of general education versus specialized education.

The Enriched Major

ERNEST BOYER

"What's your major?"

If there were a contest for the most popular question on the American campus, that would be the winner. The latest edition of the *College Blue Book* lists more than six thousand different majors and the number is rapidly expanding. From Sun Belt colleges to universities in the Ivy League, careerism dominates the campus.

At most colleges in our study, we found the baccalaureate degree sharply divided between general and specialized education. Students overwhelmingly have come to view general education as an irritating interruption — an annoying detour on their way to their degree. They all too often do not see how such requirements will help them get a job or live a life.

This unhealthy separation between the liberal and the useful arts, which the curriculum and the faculty too often reinforce, tends to leave students poorly served and the college a weak and divided institution. We take the position that if the undergraduate experience is to be renewed, general and specialized education must be viewed as contributing to common, not competing, ends.

Most students agree that pursuing a special field of study, one that leads to a career, is the main reason for going to college — and for staying, too. Over a third of the undergraduates at public institutions and slightly fewer of those at private ones say that if college did not increase their prospects for employment they would drop out.[1]

The push toward career-related education has come to dominate most campuses and, during the past fifteen years, it has dramatically increased. At almost all colleges in our study, new vocational majors have been added and old ones have been split up into smaller pieces. One East Coast university had just one major in forestry in 1965. By 1975, forestry had become a separate college offering four different majors. By 1985, when we visited the institution, the college had seven majors in this division, including three spe-

[1]The Carnegie Foundation for the Advancement of Teaching, National Survey of Undergraduates, 1984.

ERNEST BOYER (1928–1995) was U.S. Commissioner of Education and president of the Carnegie Foundation for the Advancement of Teaching. He authored several studies about education, including *The Basic School* (1995) and *College: The Undergraduate Experience in America* (1987), excerpted here, which is the companion to *High School: A Report on Secondary Education in America* (1983).

cialties in horticulture alone: fruit and vegetable horticulture, ornamental horticulture, and turf-grass horticulture. . . .[2]

In our national survey of faculty we found attitudes about specialized and general education split almost down the middle. On one hand, 45 percent of the faculty reported that they would prefer teaching courses that focused on "limited specialties," rather than those that covered a wide variety of material. On the other hand, about half the faculty said that undergraduate education in America would be improved if there were *less* emphasis on specialized training and more on liberal education. About 40 percent agreed that the typical undergraduate curriculum has suffered from the specialization of faculty members. Then again, about half the faculty said they prefer teaching students who have a clear idea of the career they will be taking. . . .

This ambivalence reflects, we suspect, a deeper conflict among faculty over goals. We found, for example, that on some campuses, faculty opposed new career-related majors because they were considered "too novel" or "too new." Overlooked in such debates was the fact that most disciplines that now have status within the academy — modern languages, laboratory sciences, for example — were themselves once considered too novel for the academy to embrace. Professor Frederick Rudolph reminds us that at the turn of the century, "At [the University of] Chicago chemists fought zoologists over disputed scientific territory, and economists fought sociologists as both laid claim to statistics. History and classics fought for control of ancient history at Harvard."[3] We conclude that the "newness" of a proposed field of study is not a sufficient reason for its rejection, nor should tradition alone be used to justify holding to an existing major.

We also found a resistance to new majors not just because of newness, but because the graduates would work in less prestigious fields. We heard it argued, for example, that it is all right to prepare students to be doctors, but not nurses. To educate future college teachers is applauded, but to prepare students to teach in elementary school is considered a less worthy task. To dig ruins of the past as an archaeologist is considered a respectable career objective, but to work with ruined lives in an urban jungle as a social worker is a less well-regarded field of study. Lost in these debates was the recognition that college graduates, instead of being demeaned by all but the prestigious professions, can, in fact, lift up a job and give it meaning.

But the most heated curriculum debates we encountered focused not on the newness or the status of a major, but on whether the proposed program was too "job-related." Here the battle lines were most sharply drawn. Many faculty members, especially those at liberal arts colleges, voiced the opinion that it is inappropriate for colleges to offer majors that are primarily "vocational." At one faculty meeting we attended, a science professor declared that the college would be "demeaned" if it offered programs that lead directly to a job. At a small college in the Northwest, the faculty recently voted down a proposed major in computer science. "It doesn't belong in the curriculum in the liberal arts. It's tied too closely to a job," we were told.[4]

[2]The Carnegie Foundation for the Advancement of Teaching, College Visits, 1984–85.

[3]Frederick Rudolph, *Curriculum: A History of the American Undergraduate Course of Study Since 1636* (San Francisco: Jossey-Bass, 1977), p. 178.

[4]The Carnegie Foundation for the Advancement of Teaching, College Visits, 1984–85.

Again, what we found missing in these discussions was the recognition that a university education has always been considered "useful." Samuel Eliot Morison reminds us that the first formal universities were "distinctly purposeful."[5] There was a utility to learning and students enrolled to prepare themselves for what was considered worthy work. The University of Salerno[6] was a medical school and the universities that followed in its wake — Bologna, Paris, Oxford, Cambridge — offered only four courses of study — law, medicine, theology, and the arts. The first three were explicitly vocational, and law was the most popular of all the medieval studies.[7]

The practical nature of the medieval university was portrayed vividly by C. P. Snow in a short narrative history of Cambridge University. Students, he wrote, studied a curriculum that would seem to us "arid, valueless, just word chopping." They attended classes in "cold, comfortless, straw-strewn rooms," some "in bitter poverty and half starved." They did this for one motive; "if they could get their degree, jobs lay ahead. Jobs in the royal administration, the courts, the church; jobs teaching in the schools — the fees were not light, and the teachers made a good living. The training was in fact vocational, and jobs lay at the end."[8]

The point is that all students, regardless of their major, are preparing for productive work. As with engineering and business and computer science, a student who majors in English or biology or history will, it is assumed, someday become employed and use what he or she has learned for some useful end. Even the most traditional colleges expect their graduates to move on to careers. And a great embarrassment for a department occurs when its graduates "cannot get placed."

This is not to suggest that colleges become vocational schools; nor does it mean that every kind of career preparation is appropriate for the baccalaureate degree. In response to marketplace demands, many institutions are offering narrow technical training and providing credentialing for occupations, devoid of rich intellectual content. Therefore, in judging the merits of a major, the issue is not the newness, or status, or even the utility of the program. Rather, the basic test of a proposed major is this: Does the field of study have a legitimate intellectual content of its own and does it have the capacity to enlarge, rather than narrow, the vision of the student?

We conclude that career preparation in the undergraduate experience means more than a job. At its best, such an education will help students not only to be technically prepared but also to discover the personal and social significance of work. Thomas F. Green puts the challenge this way:

> . . . if we are to understand the relationship between education and work we need to make a *sharp distinction between work and job.* There is an enormous difference between the person who understands his career as a succession of jobs and a person who under-

[5]Samuel Eliot Morison, *The Founding of Harvard College* (Cambridge, Massachusetts: Harvard University Press, 1935), p. 7.

[6]**University of Salerno:** A medieval university in Salerno, Italy, dedicated to medical research [Eds.].

[7]Arthur Levine, *Handbook on Undergraduate Curriculum* (San Francisco: Jossey-Bass, 1978), pp. 496–98.

[8]C. P. Snow, *The Masters* (New York: Charles Scribner, 1951), pp. 363–64.

> stands the succession of jobs he has held as all contributing to the accomplishment of some work. . . . Work is basically the way that people seek to redeem their lives from futility. It, therefore, requires the kind of world in which hope is possible, which is to say, the kind of world that yields to human effort.[9]

The challenge then is to enlarge lives by bringing meaning to the world of work. And the special task of the undergraduate college is to relate the values of liberal learning to vocation. Therefore, what we propose, as a centerpiece of the undergraduate experience, is the *enriched major.* By an *enriched major* we mean encouraging students not only to explore a field in depth, but also to help them put their field of special study in perspective. The major, as it is enriched, will respond to three essential questions: What is the history and tradition of the field to be examined? What are the social and economic implications to be understood? What are the ethical and moral issues to be confronted?

[9]Speech by Thomas F. Green, based upon his book *Work, Leisure, and the American Schools* (New York: Random House, 1968).

Considerations

1. What is the fundamental academic tension with which Boyer is concerned?
2. If you've read the excerpts from Lynne V. Cheney's report (p. 701), compare the view of American universities offered by Boyer with that offered by Cheney.
3. If you've read the passage by Michael Moffatt (p. 686), compare the attitudes toward vocation that he found among the students he studied with the idea of vocation as advocated by Boyer.
4. What is your opinion about Boyer's discussion of the undergraduate experience and work and of the way he (with Thomas F. Green) defines work?
5. In researching your major, did you find any evidence of the three features Boyer identifies with an "enriched major": a sense of the discipline's history, a sense of its social and economic implications, or a sense of the moral issues attached to it?

As a university administrator, Raymond J. Rodrigues is concerned with the overall quality of undergraduate education and with issues that bridge the disciplines. In the following excerpt, he sees contemporary efforts to produce a multicultural curriculum against the backdrop of academic disciplines that are already multicultural in a different sense.

Rethinking the Cultures of Disciplines

RAYMOND J. RODRIGUES

The increasing ethnic and racial diversity of our colleges and universities is forcing many faculty members to reexamine their curricula. How should the influx of culturally diverse students affect our courses? Should we abandon the European cultural heritage that has served us so well? Should engineering courses on irrigation, for example, include an investigation of the social role of the *acequia* system in Hispanic or Native American cultures — or should that material remain just in anthropology courses?

Faculty members' questions reveal not only uneasiness with the political implications of change, but also a genuine inability to grasp the rationale behind some suggestions for curricular reform.

Too often, academics cannot see the profound intellectual or "cultural" values inherent in their particular disciplines. We rarely recognize that "multicultural" tensions can be found not only in matters of ethnicity and race, but also between and among our disciplines. If we could recognize how culture-bound our disciplines have made us, and if we could appreciate the enhanced perspectives that interdisciplinary connections allow, perhaps integrating multicultural content into our curricula might make more sense to us.

In reviewing the tenure and promotion files of faculty members from all departments at my university and in directing periodic reviews of departments, I have been struck by how utterly distinct the worldviews of faculty members from different disciplines can be. Writing a textbook is judged to be scholarship in one department but pedagogy in the next. Advising the city council on how to manage traffic patterns is rewarded as commendable service in Department X but discounted in Department Y since such service takes time from department activities.

In one humanities department, helping students to apply ideas and thus induce broad concepts for themselves is considered to be the best teaching. But in a neighboring social-science department, lecturing about the conceptual taxonomies of the discipline is considered to be the best teaching, and application is seen as watering down course content. These different ways of valuing professional behavior are not mere fancies of the moment, but are grounded in generations of disciplinary evolution.

My realization is not new. Thirty years ago in *The Two Cultures and the Scientific Revolution,* C. P. Snow described faculty members in the two "cultures" of science and literature as "comparable in intelligence, identical in race, not grossly different in social origin, earning about the same incomes, who had almost ceased to communicate at all, who in intellectual, moral, and psychological climate had so little in common."

As undergraduates, we are recruited into a specific intellectual culture by virtue of

---

RAYMOND J. RODRIGUES (b. 1938) is vice president for academic affairs at University of Texas, Brownsville, and his special interests include teaching writing with computers and multicultural education. He co-authored *Teaching Writing with a Word Processor* (1985) and *The Computer Writing Book* (1989) with Dawn Rodrigues. The article from which these excerpts were taken appeared in the *Chronicle of Higher Education* in April 1992.

our having shown skill and interest in a particular discipline. Once admitted to graduate school, we are gradually socialized into the accepted ways of thinking and behaving within the discipline. As untenured faculty members, we are rewarded for emulating our colleagues. For example, we learn at which national conference a literature professor should present a paper to receive the most acclaim. We find out whether a junior faculty member will be respected for teaching a 100-level course or whether such a task is a burden to be avoided. We learn whether we should prefer to conduct environmental research in the field or in the laboratory with an electronic-imaging device.

Whatever the preferable behavior, those who are successfully socialized into the culture of their disciplines are rewarded. The result is that in their internal communications and policy-making, faculty members assert the cultures of their disciplines: particular ways of knowing their world and communicating that knowledge to their peers.

That insight helps to explain why so many faculty members on institutionwide committees are unable to comprehend the assumptions and conceptual frameworks of colleagues in other fields, although in their own disciplines they can analyze and synthesize the most complex of concepts. Thus, what is new on college and university campuses today is not cultural diversity, which has always existed among disciplines, but the fact that diversity is now defined in terms of ethnicity and race.

Can we capitalize on the different worldviews among disciplines, using them to help faculty members understand not only colleagues from diverse disciplines but also colleagues and students from diverse ethnic cultures? We know that a kind of multicultural communication does occur in interdisciplinary teaching and research projects, which bring together faculty members with common goals and related interests. For example, a writing-across-the-curriculum project developed by a team of engineering and composition professors enables the engineering professors to understand writing as more than mere syntactic correctness. It also helps the composition specialists to understand that effective writing for an engineer is not the same as it is for a literary critic.

The more faculty members from different disciplines work together on curricula, the more respect they begin to develop for each other's cultures. Thus, the biology professor gains new insights into molecular and cellular behaviors through the lens provided by the specialist in human pathology. A sociologist comprehends more fully the current class distinctions on a Caribbean island when a historian introduces the sociologist to the 130-year-old travel writings of Anthony Trollope.

New ways of viewing and conceptualizing their worlds enable scholars to make intellectual leaps that transcend their disciplinary cultures. The more we find ways to bring faculty members from diverse disciplines together to solve common intellectual problems, the more they will begin to appreciate how the cultures of other disciplines influence their colleagues' thinking. In turn, they may become more aware of the cultural roots of their own intellectual worldviews and thus become more willing to incorporate content from diverse racial and ethnic experiences into their research and teaching.

I am not so naive as to suggest that it is easy to leap from understanding our discipline-based cultures to accepting ethnic and racial diversity in the content of our courses. But if we are ever to succeed in the latter goal, we gradually must lead our colleagues from their own culture-bound disciplines into other intellectual frameworks and, eventually, beyond those to the cultures of other ethnic and racial groups. Diversity is more than just a game of numbers or political expediency. In a world as diverse as ours, we need the intellectual breadth and depth throughout the university that other cultures can provide.

Considerations

1. From Rodrigues's point of view as a college administrator, what is his major criticism of college faculty?
2. Rodrigues is concerned with two different kinds of cultural limitations. What are they, and what relation does he see between them?
3. Can you rephrase Rodrigues's concerns in terms of discourse? That is, in what ways does the disciplinary and departmental structure of the college and university affect the ways faculty use language?
4. If you read the piece by Howard S. Becker (p. 695), ask yourself what Becker and Rodrigues might have to say to each other.
5. David R. Russell (p. 698) offers a historical view of changes in the socioeconomic class of students attending institutions of higher education; Elizabeth Chiseri-Strater (p. 691) raises the issue of gender; and Rodrigues notes the increasing racial and ethnic diversity in the college population. As you did your research, did you find any effects of this diversity on curriculum, on teaching, or on the language disciplines use to describe themselves and their work?

Does the anonymity allowed by on-line communication foster more open, democratic or more hostile, cowardly academic discourse? Does anonymity undermine the notion that scholars should put their names — and titles — behind what they say, or is requiring such attribution unnecessary and exclusionary? In the following article, writer Lisa Guernsey poses such questions to a number of academics.

Scholars Debate the Pros and Cons of Anonymity in Internet Discussions

LISA GUERNSEY

The use of on-line pseudonyms and other methods of shielding one's identity appears to be catching on around the world. Scholars are no exception. . . .

Hiding one's identity is not difficult. Many e-mail programs make it possible for people to be known only by the jumble of letters and numbers that make up their addresses. Other programs automatically attach a name to mail as it is sent but make it possible for users to decide whether they will be known by name, a set of initials, or an alias.

Most people on scholarly mailing lists allow their names to be attached to their messages, but many enjoy some measure of anonymity by not disclosing their academic rank or disciplines. This allows a professor, a graduate student, or even an undergraduate to raise a controversial issue or ask an embarrassing question without anyone's knowing his or her full identity.

For many scholars, discussions unencumbered by lengthy titles, departments, or institutional names represent the Internet at its best. The exchanges demonstrate the openness and, as many call it, the "democratic" quality of the Internet. People interested in a topic can converse and share ideas, they say, without having to expose themselves as "merely" graduate students, community-college instructors, or assistant professors.

But several scholars, including some who engage in these types of discussions themselves, are wary of identity-free communication's going too far. And some are appalled that anonymous or pseudonymous communication has any place in academic life at all. Scholars must be willing to put their real names behind their words, they say, especially in academe, where ideas and the words used to represent them are the profession's only product.

People who study anonymous communications point out that the Internet is not the first medium to trigger these issues. People have hidden their identities ever since their words could be separated from their physical presence, says Edgar A. Whitley, an information-systems professor at the London School of Economics and Political Science who has explored the notion of on-line anonymity.

"The role of the body is clearly important in face-to-face communication, and removing the body from the interaction can help change the basis of the interaction," he writes in a paper on identity and cyberspace, "but haven't other technologies, like the letter and the telephone, done similar things?"

Letters and telephone conversations, however, have never been major media for

---

LISA GUERNSEY (b. 1971) is assistant editor of electronic projects at *The Chronicle of Higher Education,* where she writes regularly for the Information Technology section, in which this article was featured on October 4, 1996.

scholarly discussion. Before the days of the Internet, print journals and face-to-face conferences were the primary forums for in-depth, specialized discussions among researchers at different universities. Both of those arenas required signatures and nametags. Anonymous journal articles were, and are, printed very rarely, if ever.

But in the speeded-up world of the 1990s, the exchange of scholarly ideas has become common on mailing lists, World Wide Web sites, and MOOS (Multiple-user Object-Oriented domains) on the Internet and in chat rooms on services such as America Online and CompuServe.

Many say being able to talk with other scholars on-line — without anyone's knowing their race, their sex, or their credentials — helps them to feel more confident about their ideas. "For me, it's a matter of evading prejudgment," wrote a man who identified himself as "Ross" on a mailing list dedicated to discussing the psychology of the Internet. . . .

Some people also choose to leave their names off e-mail messages so that they can experiment with an idea. "I think there's a real strength obtained at times by testing out ideas, particularly contentious ones, from the safe haven of anonymity," says Heather Fraser, a graduate student in social work at Monash University, in Australia, who is doing research on the use of newsgroups.

Paula Davidson, a computer-science instructor at the University of North Carolina at Asheville and at Warren Wilson College, plans to hold a nameless chat session for her students this fall. "Anonymity might allow my students to ask me questions more freely," she says. "They'd be free of the worry that they should already know or understand something."

But Ms. Davidson, who spends much of her own on-line time in MOOS and chat rooms, is not ready to fully embrace the idea of anonymous interchanges. "I find myself uncomfortable with the concept of anonymity," she says. The identity she dons in the MOOS, she says, is like an "an extension of myself, not something hidden or secretive."

Many share her ambivalence. The thought of floating controversial ideas without worrying about the backlash is appealing. But people hesitate when they imagine conversations getting out of hand. The freedom to post messages anonymously can lead a writer to be careless or even hostile, some say. And those who choose not to put their name behind their words are sometimes eyed with suspicion.

Some mailing lists prohibit anonymous postings altogether. H-Net, a collection of more than 75 moderated mailing lists for scholars in the humanities, does not post any message that is not signed, and participants are required to subscribe to the lists under their real names.

"H-Net lists are similar to academic conferences, where the discussions after papers, during roundtables, and informally in the lobby are of great importance to scholars," says Richard Jensen, a professor of history at the University of Illinois at Chicago and executive director of H-Net. "We don't want anyone without a nametag — or with a paper bag over the head." . . .

Others say the drawbacks of exposing one's name and title are minor compared to the benefits of getting one's name out there. "In my opinion, it's against people's interest to stay anonymous in academia," David Ducheyne wrote on a mailing list this summer.

What's more, says Mr. Ducheyne, a researcher at the University of Ghent, in Belgium, being anonymous for research purposes or to provoke reactions is simply "unethical."

What about leaving out one's title? Is that, too, unethical? Participants on some mailing lists have debated whether graduate students who sign their names with their departments — without mentioning that they are not members of the faculty — are purposely misleading people to avoid the "graduate student" label.

But there are instances in which people's identities are disguised for good reason, some argue. The identity of those who submit articles to peer-reviewed journals has customarily been hidden from reviewers, notes Clare Davies, a research fellow at De Montfort University in Milton Keynes, England. On-line communication may facilitate that tradition, she says.

Women historically have escaped the effects of prejudice by writing books and articles under pseudonyms or with only a first initial. Some who study on-line communications say there is evidence that women now are doing the same thing on the Internet.

In a study at an unnamed Midwestern university, J. Michael Jaffee and his colleagues observed the pseudonyms that women selected for an electronic conference. More women than men chose names that reflected neutral gender or one other than their own, reported Dr. Jaffe, a communications professor at the University of Haifa, in Israel. This suggests that women may feel less susceptible to stereotypes — and possibly more comfortable communicating with others — when they can mask their gender, he says.

Considerations

1. Have you used the Internet or e-mail? What is your opinion about the issues raised in this article?
2. What does this article suggest to you about the way authority is granted in academic life? Why does anonymity become such an issue?
3. Can you relate to this desire to remain anonymous in an academic setting? Why or why not?
4. Guernsey notes that some scholars find it helpful to communicate with others without revealing their gender or race. Did you find evidence in your research of gender or race discrimination that might be addressed, or in some way lessened, by anonymous communication? If you read the essays by Elizabeth Chiseri-Strater (p. 691) or Raymond J. Rodrigues (p. 708), try to bring their insights to bear here. For example, do you think that anonymous electronic communication could make college classrooms "a warmer place for women," as Chiseri-Strater advocates, or does it ultimately do women — and men — a disservice? Do you think that anonymous discussions could further, or inhibit, efforts to incorporate diverse concerns into the curriculum? To the degree possible, ground your discussion in your research findings.
5. This article describes one effect of new electronic media on language use within the academy. In your research, did you find evidence of other effects of electronic media on academic scholarship and communication?

Further Assignments for Exploring the Discourse of Your Major

1. English professor David Bartholomae has written, "Every time a student sits down to write for us," that student "has to learn to speak our language, to speak as we do, to try on the peculiar ways of knowing, selecting, evaluating, reporting, concluding, and arguing that define the discourse of a community." Based on your investigations, agree or disagree with his claim as it pertains to your field of study.

2. Academic discourse is often assumed to be written language, consisting of textbooks, reports, articles, and scholarly monographs. But it can be argued that as much or more of the most influential academic discourse is actually oral. If you've found this to be so, write an essay that makes the case. Keep in mind that you can define academic discourse quite broadly.

3. Imagine that someone — a friend, a counselor, a parent — is trying to talk you out of the major you're considering. Use the information you have gathered to argue in favor of your choice.

Alternatively, imagine that you want to talk a friend out of the major you've been researching. Use the information you have gathered to argue against this choice.

4. Academic writing is sometimes characterized as a solitary act and sometimes as a conversation — that is, an ongoing, active social process. Which position best matches your data? Write an essay arguing for one position or the other.

5. Several of the writers in this appendix speak of a tension or disparity between the role of teacher and the role of researcher. Discuss any evidence of this tension among faculty of the discipline you studied.

6. You've researched a major at your school as it is currently offered. Yet each department, like your school itself, also has an institutional history. Over a period of time academic departments shift in response to outside pressures, internal politics, and the academic interests of faculty and students. Such histories are difficult to trace, but they can be revealing. It can be interesting to know, for example, how the course offerings of a department have changed over five or ten years, and whether the size and offerings of a department have fluctuated in relation to student demand or other factors. In your research you may have come across some signs of your discipline's institutional history at your college. If so, you might want to pursue this history through a new series of interviews. Write an essay detailing your findings.

7. Did you discover any unresolved issues animating discussion among professionals in your discipline? These could be about key concepts, about differences

in research methods, or about basic assumptions as to what a field should be and do. What role do these issues play, if any, in the education of undergraduates? Of graduate students? In the working lives of faculty?

8. If you've had the opportunity to compare findings with a student in your class who has investigated a discipline other than yours, consider writing a collaborative essay comparing the discourse of the two disciplines.

9. Some critics of the American college system say that the most distorting influences upon undergraduate education have been economic. What evidence of economic influence do you find in the readings of this appendix or in your own research? Do you agree that the economic influences upon contemporary college education have been profound and negative?

10. Write an essay about the concept of "discourse community." Is it stretching the term *community* to claim communities can be found in academic disciplines? Did you discover a discourse community in your research?

11. The effects of computers on college communication and even course content are striking and pervasive. Investigate and write about the effect of e-mail, Internet access, and other computer technology on a major you are interested in. As you do so, consider the following questions: How has the technology changed the way courses are taught now from, say, ten years ago? (To gain a sense of history here, look at old catalogs, department newsletters, and reports, and talk to graduate students or faculty.) Does the technology seem to be entirely beneficial, or do you see drawbacks as well? How, and how well, is your college — and, in particular, courses in your major of interest — training students in the uses of the new technology?

12. Most of the authors of the Optional Readings take a negative view of immersion in the discourse of a single discipline. But is there a case to be made for that immersion? Are there rewards beyond the vocational one? If you think so, write an essay explaining the benefits. You'll want to draw on your own research to make your case.

13. Since the 1980s, many colleges have tried to make courses — and college life in general — more representative of the interests and concerns of a diverse group of students — for instance, concerns of various ethnic and racial groups, and of women. What efforts has your college made to incorporate diverse concerns into course offerings, student activities, and other aspects of student life? On the basis of interviews with students and faculty, information drawn from your campus newspaper, any relevant college reports you can obtain, and, of course, your own experiences, investigate these efforts and their effectiveness. Do you think the efforts have enhanced or hindered education at your college and, specifically, in a major you're interested in?

Acknowledgments *(continued from page iv)*

Graham T. Allison. "The Cuban Missile Crisis." Excerpted from "Conceptual Models and the Cuban Missile Crisis," *The American Political Science Review*, vol. 63, no. 3 (September 1969). Reprinted by permission of the American Political Science Association and the author.

Rita L. Atkinson, Richard C. Atkinson, and Ernest R. Hilgard. "Alcoholism and Drug Dependence" in *Introduction to Psychology*, Eighth Edition, by Rita L. Atkinson, Richard C. Atkinson, and Ernest R. Hilgard. Copyright © 1983 by Harcourt Brace and Company, reprinted by permission of the publisher.

"Aranda Creation Story," from *Aranda Traditions* by T.G.H. Strehlow (Melbourne University Press, 1947). Reprinted by permission of the author's literary estate.

Howard S. Becker. "If You Want to Be a Scholar." From *Writing for Social Scientists* by Howard S. Becker. Copyright © 1986 by The University of Chicago. Reprinted by permission of the University of Chicago Press.

Helen Benedict. From *Virgin or Vamp: How the Press Covers Sex Crimes* by Helen Benedict. Copyright © 1992 by Helen Benedict. Used by permission of Oxford University Press, Inc. Excerpts from articles by Cynthia Gorney. Copyright © 1978, *The Washington Post.* Reprinted with permission.

W. Lance Bennett and Martha S. Feldman. From *Reconstructing Reality in the Courtroom: Justice and Judgement in American Culture.* Copyright © 1981 by Rutgers, The State University. Reprinted by permission of Rutgers University Press.

Thomas Bentz. Excerpt reprinted by permission of the publisher from *New Immigrants: Portraits in Passage* by Thomas Bentz. Copyright © 1981, The Pilgrim Press, New York, New York.

Carl Bernstein and Bob Woodward. Reprinted with the permission of Simon & Schuster from *All the President's Men* by Carl Bernstein and Bob Woodward. Copyright © 1974 by Carl Bernstein and Bob Woodward.

Deborah Blum. "The Black Box" and "Not a Nice Death." From *The Monkey Wars* by Deborah Blum. Copyright © 1994 by Deborah Blum. Used by permission of Oxford University Press, Inc.

Eugene Boe. Excerpts from "Pioneers to Eternity: Norwegians on the Prairie." From *The Immigrant Experience* by Thomas C. Wheeler. Copyright © 1971 by Doubleday, a division of Bantam Doubleday Dell Publishing Group, Inc. Used by permission of Doubleday, a division of Bantam Doubleday Dell Publishing Group, Inc.

Bruce Bower. From "Probing Primate Thoughts," *Science News*, January 20, 1996. Reprinted with permission from *Science News*, the weekly newsmagazine of science. Copyright © 1996 by Science Service.

Ernest Boyer. "The Enriched Major" from *College: The Undergraduate Experience in America*. Copyright © 1987, The Carnegie Foundation for the Advancement of Teaching. Reprinted with permission.

Edward Kamau Brathwaite. From *History of the Voice: The Development of Nation Language in Anglophone Caribbean Poetry*, published by New Beacon Books Ltd. in 1984. Reprinted by permission of the publisher.

Pamela Brink and Judith Saunders. "The Phases of Culture Shock." Reprinted by permission of Waveland Press, Inc. from Pamela Brink, ed., *Transcultural Nursing: A Book of Readings* (Prospect Heights, IL: Waveland Press, Inc., 1976 [reissued 1990]). All rights reserved.

Jane E. Brody. "What Sodium Does." From *Jane Brody's Nutrition Book* by Jane Brody. Copyright © 1981 by Jane E. Brody. Reprinted by permission of W. W. Norton & Company, Inc.

Raymond Chandler. Excerpt from *The Big Sleep* by Raymond Chandler. Copyright © 1939 by Raymond Chandler and renewed 1967 by Helga Greene, Executrix of the Estate of Raymond Chandler. Reprinted by permission of Alfred A. Knopf, Inc.

Alston Chase. From "How to Save Our National Parks." Copyright © 1987 by Alston Chase. Reprinted by permission of the author. Originally appeared in *The Atlantic Monthly.*

Dorothy M. Cheney and Robert M. Seyfarth. From *How Monkeys See the World.* Copyright © 1990 by the University of Chicago. Reprinted by permission of the University of Chicago Press.

Lynne V. Cheney. "Tyrannical Machines." From *Tyrannical Machines: A Report on Educational Practices Gone Wrong and Our Best Hopes for Setting Them Right* (Washington, DC: National Endowment for the Humanities, 1990).

Elizabeth Chiseri-Strater. "Gender, Language, and Pedagogy." Reprinted by permission from Elizabeth Chiseri-Strater, *Academic Literacies: The Public and Private Discourse of University Students* (Boynton/Cook Publishers, A Subsidiary of Reed Elsevier Inc., Portsmouth, NH, 1991).

Michelle Cliff. From *Abeng.* Copyright © 1984 by Michelle Cliff. Excerpt from *Abeng* was reprinted with the permission of Michelle Cliff.

David Cole. "Five Myths About Immigration." Reprinted with permission from the October 17, 1994, issue of *The Nation.*

Collier's Encyclopedia. Table on Immigration to the United States, 1831–1970. From "Immigration," by Oscar Handlin, *Collier's Encyclopedia,* Volume 12, pp. 522–539. Copyright © 1992 by Collier Newfield, Inc. Reprinted by permission of the publisher.

Bernard Cooper. "English as a Second Language." Copyright © 1989 by Bernard Cooper. Reprinted by permission of the author. "This is Just to Say" by William Carlos Williams, from *Collected Poems: 1909–1939, Volume I.* Copyright © 1938 by New Directions Publishing Corp. Reprinted by permission of New Directions Publishing Corp.

Len Cooper. "The Damned," *The Washington Post,* June 16, 1996. Copyright © 1996 by Len Cooper. Reprinted by permission of the author.

Jim Daniels. "Digger Goes on Vacation." From *Places/Everyone* by Jim Daniels. Winner of the 1985 Brittingham Prize in Poetry. Copyright © 1985. (Madison: The University of Wisconsin Press.) Reprinted by permission of The University of Wisconsin Press.

Elizabeth Ewen. Excerpted selection from *Immigrant Women in the Land of Dollars: Life and Culture on the Lower East Side, 1890–1925.* Copyright © 1985 by Elizabeth Ewen. Reprinted by permission of Monthly Review Foundation.

Jim Fisher. Selection from Jim Fisher, *The Lindbergh Case.* Copyright © 1987 by Jim Fisher. Reprinted by permission of Rutgers University Press.

Dian Fossey. From "More Years with Mountain Gorillas." *National Geographic,* October 1971. Reprinted by permission of The Diget Fund.

John Fowles. From *The Collector* by John Fowles. Copyright © 1963 by John Fowles Ltd. By permission of Little, Brown and Company.

Benjamin Franklin. From *Autobiography and Other Pieces* by Benjamin Franklin, edited by Dennis Welland, 1970, by permission of Oxford University Press.

Deborah Franklin. Excerpted from "The Shape of Life." *Discover*, December 1991. Deborah Franklin/© 1991 The Walt Disney Co. Reprinted with permission of *Discover* Magazine.

Howard Gardner. Excerpt from *Frames of Mind: The Theory of Multiple Intelligences* by Howard Gardner. Copyright © 1983 by Howard Gardner. Reprinted by permission of Basic Books, a division of HarperCollins Publishers, Inc.

David D. Gilmore. From *Aggression and Community* by David D. Gilmore. Copyright © 1987 by Yale University. Reprinted by permission of Yale University Press.

Daniel Goleman. From *Emotional Intelligence* by Daniel Goleman. Copyright © 1995 by Daniel Goleman. Used by permission of Bantam Books, a division of Bantam Doubleday Dell Publishing Group, Inc.

Jane Goodall. "The Mind of a Chimpanzee." Excerpt from *Through a Window* by Jane Goodall. Copyright © 1990 by Soko Publications Ltd. Reprinted by permission of Houghton Mifflin Co. All rights reserved.

June Goodfield. "Biologist Anna Brito" from *An Imagined World* by June Goodfield. Copyright © 1981 by June Goodfield. Reprinted by permission of Georges Borchardt, Inc.

Harvey J. Graff. "The Moral Basis of Literary Instruction." From *The Literary Myth: Literary and Social Structure in the Nineteenth-Century City* (Academic Press, 1979). Reprinted by permission of the author.

The Brothers Grimm. "The Singing Bone." From *Complete Brothers Grimm Fairy Tales* edited by Lily Owens. Copyright © 1981 by Crown Publishers. Reprinted by permission of Crown Publishers, Inc.

Nora Ellen Groce. "They Were Just Like Everyone Else," pp. 1–3, 3–5 from *Everyone Here Spoke Sign Language: Hereditary Deafness on Martha's Vineyard* by Nora Ellen Groce. Cambridge, MA: Harvard University Press. Copyright © 1985 by Nora Ellen Groce. Reprinted by permission of the publisher.

Lisa Guernsey. From "Scholars Debate the Pros and Cons of Anonymity in Internet Discussions." *The Chronicle of Higher Education*, October 4, 1996. Copyright © 1996, The Chronicle of Higher Education. Excerpted with permission.

Douglas Harper. From *Working Knowledge: Skill and Community in a Small Shop* (University of Chicago Press). Copyright © 1987 by Douglas Harper. Reprinted by permission of the author.

John Haugeland. From *Artificial Intelligence: The Very Idea*. Copyright © 1985 by The Massachusetts Institute of Technology. Reprinted by permission of The MIT Press.

Merle Hodge. Excerpt from *Crick Crack Monkey* by Merle Hodge. Copyright © 1970 by Merle Hodge. Reprinted by permission of Andre Deutsch Ltd. Excerpt from "Challenges of the Struggle for Sovereignty: Changing the World versus Writing Stories" by Merle Hodge from Selwyn Cudjoe, ed., *Caribbean Women Writers: Essays from the First International Conference* (Wellesley, MA: Calaloux Publications, 1990). Reprinted by permission.

Garrett Kaoru Hongo. "And Your Soul Shall Dance" from *Yellow Light*. Copyright © 1982 by Garrett Kaoru Hongo, Wesleyan University Press, by permission of University Press of New England.

Ted Howard and Jeremy Rifkin. "Eugenics in America." From *Who Should Play God?* by Ted Howard and Jeremy Rifkin. Copyright © 1977 by Center for Urban Education.

Used by permission of Delacorte Press, a division of Bantam Doubleday Dell Publishing Group, Inc.

Edwin Hutchins. Excerpt from "The Social Organization of Distributed Cognition" from Resnick, Levine and Teasley, eds., *Perspectives on Socially Shared Cognition*. Copyright © 1991 by the American Psychological Association. Reprinted by permission.

Albert Jacquard. "Sexual Reproduction." From *In Praise of Difference* by Alfred Jacquard. Copyright © 1984 by Columbia University Press. Reprinted with permission of the publisher.

Maldwyn Allen Jones. From *American Immigration*. Copyright © 1960 by The University of Chicago. Reprinted by permission of the University of Chicago Press.

Horace Freeland Judson. From *The Eighth Day of Creation*, expanded edition, by Horace Freeland Judson. Copyright © 1996 by Cold Spring Harbor Laboratory Press. Reprinted by permission of the publisher.

Michael B. Katz. Excerpt from *In the Shadow of the Poorhouse: A Social History of Welfare in America* by Michael B. Katz. Copyright © 1986 by Basic Books, Inc. Reprinted by permission of Basic Books, a division of HarperCollins Publishers, Inc.

Evelyn Fox Keller. "The Language of Science." From *A Feeling for the Organism: The Life and Work of Barbara McClintock* by Evelyn Fox Keller. Copyright © 1983 by W.H. Freeman and Company. Used with permission.

Thomas Kessner and Betty Boyd Caroli. From *Today's Immigrants*. Copyright © 1982 by Thomas Kessner and Betty Boyd Caroli. Reprinted by permission of Oxford University Press.

Jamaica Kincaid. From *A Small Place* by Jamaica Kincaid. Copyright © 1988 by Jamaica Kincaid. Reprinted by permission of Farrar, Straus & Giroux, Inc.

Conrad Phillip Kottak. "Rites of Passage" from *Cultural Anthropology*, 3rd ed. Copyright © 1982. Reproduced with permission of The McGraw-Hill Companies.

Roger Lewin. "Look Who's Talking Now," *New Scientist*, 27 April 1991. Copyright © 1991 by *New Scientist*. Reprinted by permission of the publisher.

Duncan Lindsey. From *The Welfare of Children* by Duncan Lindsey. Copyright © 1994 by Oxford University Press, Inc. Used by permission of Oxford University Press, Inc.

Renee Loth. From "Woburn, Science, and the Law," *The Boston Globe Magazine*, February 9, 1986. Reprinted courtesy of *The Boston Globe*.

Frederick K. Lutgens and Edward J. Tarbuck. "Earthquakes" from *Essentials of Geology*, 5/e by Frederick K. Lutgens and Edward J. Tarbuck. Copyright © 1995. Reprinted by permission of Prentice-Hall, Inc., Upper Saddle River, NJ.

McGraw Hill Dictionary of Scientific and Technical Terms, 3rd ed., edited by Sybyl P. Parker. Copyright © 1984. Disease definitions reproduced with permission of The McGraw-Hill Companies.

Michael L. McKinney. From *Evolution of Life: Processes, Patterns, and Prospects*. Copyright © 1993. Adapted by permission of Prentice-Hall, Inc., Upper Saddle River, NJ. Figures 2-19 and 2-21 from Reed Wicander and James S. Monroe, *Historical Geology* (West Publishing, © 1989). Reprinted by permission of Wadsworth Publishing Co. Figure from *Biology* by Barrett/Abramoff/Kumaran/Millington, © 1986. Reprinted by permission of Prentice-Hall, Inc., Upper Saddle River, NJ.

Reginald McKnight. "The Kind of Light That Shines on Texas." From *The Kind of Light That Shines on Texas* by Reginald McKnight. Copyright © 1992 by Reginald McKnight.

First appeared in the *Kenyon Review*. Reprinted by permission of Christina Ward Literary Agency.

Roger McTair. "Visiting." Copyright © 1990 by Roger McTair. Reprinted by permission of the author. Originally published in *The Faber Book of Contemporary Caribbean Short Stories*.

Nancy Mairs. "On Being a Cripple" from *Plaintext* by Nancy Mairs. Copyright © 1986 The Arizona Board of Regents. Reprinted by permission of the University of Arizona Press.

Malcolm X. From *The Autobiography of Malcolm X* by Malcolm X with the assistance of Alex Haley. Copyright © 1964 by Alex Haley and Malcolm X. Copyright © 1965 by Alex Haley and Betty Shabazz. Reprinted by permission of Random House, Inc.

William M. Marsh and Jeff Dozier. "The Hydrologic Cycle" from *Landscape: An Introduction to Physical Geography*. Copyright © 1981 by William M. Marsh and Jeff Dozier. Reprinted by permission of the authors.

Jonathan Marshall. "Childhood Poverty is Abundant," *San Francisco Chronicle*, October 7, 1996. Copyright © *San Francisco Chronicle* 1976. Reprinted by permission.

John Chester Miller. Excerpts from *The Wolf by the Ears: Thomas Jefferson and Slavery*. Copyright © 1977, 1991. Reprinted by permission of the University Press of Virginia. Excerpt from *Alexander Hamilton: Portrait in Paradox* by John C. Miller. Copyright © 1959 by John C. Miller. Reprinted by permission of HarperCollins Publishers, Inc.

Quentin Miller. "Reconstructing a Crime." Copyright © 1997 by D. Quentin Miller. Reprinted by permission of the author.

John C. Mitani. From "Ethological Studies of Chimpanzee Social Behavior." Reprinted by permission of the publisher from *Chimpanzee Cultures*, edited by Richard W. Wrangham, W. C. McGrew, Frans B. M. de Waal, and Paul G. Heltne. Cambridge, MA: Harvard University Press. Copyright © 1994 by the Chicago Academy of Sciences.

Michael Moffatt. "Vocationalism and the Curriculum." From *Coming of Age in New Jersey: College and American Culture*. Copyright © 1989 by Rutgers, The State University. Reprinted by permission of Rutgers University Press.

Edmund S. Morgan. "The American Revolution: An American View." From *The Birth of the Republic, 1763–1789*, rev. ed., © 1956, 1977 by the University of Chicago. Reprinted by permission of the University of Chicago Press.

Stephen S. Morse. "Stirring Up Trouble." This article is reprinted by permission of *The Sciences* and is from the September/October 1990 issue. Individual subscriptions are $21 per year in the U.S. Write to The Sciences, 2 East 63rd Street, New York, NY 10021.

Walter Mosley. From *Devil in a Blue Dress* by Walter Mosley. Copyright © 1990 by Walter Mosely. Reprinted by permission of W. W. Norton & Company, Inc.

Bharati Mukherjee. "The Management of Grief." From *The Middleman and Other Stories* by Bharati Mukherjee. Copyright © 1988 by Bharati Mukherjee. Used by permission of Grove/Atlantic, Inc. and Penguin Books Canada Ltd.

Oxford English Dictionary. Definitions of "intelligence," "career," and "technology" from the *Oxford English Dictionary*, 2nd edition, 1989, by permission of Oxford University Press.

Talcott Parsons. "Social Systems." Reprinted with the permission of The Free Press, a Division of Simon & Schuster, from *Structure and Process in Modern Societies* by Talcott Parsons. Copyright © 1960 by The Free Press. Copyright renewed 1988.

Francine Patterson. From "Conversations with a Gorilla" by Francine Patterson, Ph.D., *National Geographic*, Vol. 154, No. 4, October 1978. Reprinted by permission of The Gorilla Foundation, Woodside, CA 94062.

Polly Pattullo. From *Last Resorts: The Cost of Tourism in the Caribbean.* Reprinted by permission of Latin America Bureau, London.

Kevin Phillips. "The Downside of the American Dream." From *The Politics of Rich and Poor* by Kevin Phillips. Copyright © 1990 by Kevin Phillips. Reprinted by permission of Random House, Inc.

Lynette Prucha. From "Murder Is My Business" by Lynette Prucha in Irene Zahava, ed., *The Womansleuth Anthology*. Copyright © 1990 by Lynette Prucha. Reprinted by permission of the author.

Alejandro Portes and Rubén Rumbaut. From *Immigrant America: A Portrait*, 2nd ed. Copyright © 1996 The Regents of the University of California. Reprinted by permission of the Regents of the University of California and the University of California Press.

Robert Redfield. "Little Communities." From *The Little Community.* Copyright © 1955 by the University of Chicago. Reprinted by permission of the University of Chicago Press.

Rachel Reichman. From *Getting Computers to Talk Like You and Me.* Copyright © 1985 by The Massachusetts Institute of Technology. Reprinted by permission of The MIT Press.

Raymond J. Rodrigues. "Rethinking the Cultures of Discipline." Copyright © 1992 by Raymond J. Rodrigues. Excerpted from *Chronicle of Higher Education*, April 1992. Reprinted by permission of the author.

Mike Rose. Excerpt from *Possible Lives: The Promise of Public Education in America.* Copyright © 1995 by Mike Rose. Reprinted by permission of Houghton Mifflin Company. All rights reserved.

Ellen Israel Rosen. From *Bitter Choices: Blue-Collar Women in and out of Work* by Ellen Israel Rosen. Copyright © 1987 by The University of Chicago. Reprinted by permission of the University of Chicago Press.

David R. Russell. "Academic Discourse." From *Writing in the Academic Disciplines* (University of Southern Illinois Press, 1991). Reprinted by permission of the publisher.

George J. Sánchez. From *Becoming Mexican American: Ethnicity, Culture, and Identity in Chicano Los Angeles, 1900–1945* by George J. Sánchez. Copyright © 1995 by George J. Sánchez. Reprinted by permission of Oxford University Press, Inc.

Esmeralda Santiago. *When I Was Puerto Rican* (pp. 213–218, 220, 221, 225–230). Copyright © 1993 by Esmeralda Santiago. Reprinted by permission of Addison-Wesley Longman Inc.

Melanie Scheller. "On the Meaning of Plumbing and Poverty" from *Utne Reader*, March/April 1991. Reprinted with permission of Melanie Scheller and the *North Carolina Independent Weekly.*

Lisbeth B. Schorr. From *Within Our Reach* by Lisbeth B. Schorr with Daniel Schorr. Copyright © 1988 by Lisbeth Bamberger Schorr. Used by permission of Doubleday, a division of Bantam Doubleday Dell Publishing Group, Inc.

Martin E. P. Seligman. "On Learned Helplessness." From *Helplessness: On Depression, Development, and Death* by Martin E. P. Seligman. Copyright © 1975 by Martin E. P. Seligman. Reprinted by permission of W. H. Freeman & Company.

Olive Senior. "The Two Grandmothers" from *Arrival of the Snake-Woman and Other Stories* by Olive Senior (1989). Reprinted by permission of Addison Wesley Longman Ltd.

Arloc Sherman. Excerpt from *Wasting America's Future* by Children's Defense Fund. Copyright © 1994 by Children's Defense Fund. Used by permission of Beacon Press, Boston.

Mark Singer. "Profile of Filmmaker Errol Morris." Excerpted from *The New Yorker,* February 6, 1989. Reprinted by permission.

Nancy Sommers. "Revision Strategies of Student Writers and Experienced Adult Writers," *College Composition and Communication,* December 1980. Copyright © 1980 by the National Council of Teachers of English. Reprinted with permission.

Gary Soto. Lines from "Cruel Boys" from *Black Hair* by Gary Soto. "Cruel Boys" is copyright © 1985 by Gary Soto. Used by permission of the author. "Oranges" from *New and Collected Poems* by Gary Soto. Copyright © 1995 by Gary Soto, published by Chronicle Books, San Francisco. Reprinted by permission of the publisher.

Ulli Steltzer. Haroutioun Yeretzian interview. Excerpted from *The New Americans: Immigrant Life in Southern California* by Ulli Steltzer. Copyright © 1988 by NewSage Press. Reprinted by permission of the publisher.

Shirley Strum. From *Almost Human: A Journey into the World of Baboons* by Shirley Strum. Copyright © 1987 by Shirley C. Strum. Reprinted by permission of Random House, Inc.

Catherine A. Sunshine. "Unifying Themes in Caribbean Cultures" from *The Caribbean: Survival, Struggle, and Sovereignty* by Catherine A. Sunshine. Copyright © 1988, reprinted by permission of EPICA. Excerpt from *The Dragon Can't Dance* by Earl Lovelace. Copyright © 1979 by Earl Lovelace. Reprinted by permission of Simpson Fox Associates Ltd.

Gresham M. Sykes. From *The Society of Captives: A Study of a Maximum Security Prison.* Copyright © 1958 by Princeton University Press. Reprinted by permission of Princeton University Press.

Studs Terkel. "Roberto Acuña" from *Working* by Studs Terkel. Reprinted by permission of Donadio & Ashworth, Inc. Copyright © 1972, 1974 Studs Terkel.

Herbert Terrace. "How Nim Chimpsky Changed My Mind." Reprinted with permission from *Psychology Today* Magazine. Copyright © 1979 (Sussex Publishers, Inc.).

Jeanette A. Thomas. "The Sounds of Seal Society." With permission from *Natural History,* March 1991. Copyright © the American Museum of Natural History 1991.

Barbara Tomlinson. Compilation of brief quotations from *The Buried Life of the Mind: Writers' Metaphors for Their Writing Processes.* Used by permission of Barbara Tomlinson.

Paul Tough. From "Into the Pit," *The New York Times Magazine,* November 7, 1993. Copyright © 1993 by Paul Tough. Reprinted by permission of the author.

James S. Trefil. "How the Universe Will End." From *Smithsonian,* June 1983. Copyright © 1983 by James S. Trefil. Reprinted by permission of the author.

G. M. Trevelyan. "The American Revolution: A British View." From *A Shortened History of England.* Copyright © 1942 by G. M. Trevelyan. Reprinted by permission of Addison Wesley Longman Ltd.

Reed Ueda. "The Historical Context of Immigration" from *Postwar Immigrant America: A Social History,* by Reed Ueda. Copyright © 1994 by Bedford Books of St. Martin's Press. Reprinted by permission of the publisher.

Charles P. Wallace and Tim Waters. "Gunman Kills Himself After Hostage Drama," *Los Angeles Times*, May 10, 1981. Copyright © 1981, *Los Angeles Times.* Reprinted by permission.

Patricia J. Williams. Pages 136–138 from *The Alchemy of Race and Rights* by Patricia J. Williams. Cambridge, MA: Harvard University Press. Copyright © 1991 by the President and Fellows of Harvard College. Reprinted by permission of the publisher. Excerpt from "A Court Fails, An Old Woman Dies, and the Police Stand Trial" by Margaret Taylor, *The New York Times*, March 19, 1987. Copyright © 1987 by The New York Times Co. Reprinted by Permission.

INDEX OF AUTHORS AND TITLES

Selections are indexed both by author and title. Following each entry, the academic discipline represented appears in brackets.

READINGS BY DISCIPLINE